Black Shirt and Smoking Beagles

The Biography of Wilfred Risdon: an unconventional Campaigner

by J L Risdon

Black Shirt and Smoking Beagles

The Biography of Wilfred Risdon: an unconventional Campaigner

First Edition November 2013

ISBN 978-0-9927431-0-9

Black Shirt and Smoking Beagles is an imprint of Wilfred Books
www.wilfredbooks.co.uk

Cover design by the author from an original design by Nigel Ward.

Typeset by the author, using predominantly the Baskerville font, at various point sizes as required to suit the context.

Printed and bound by McRay Press, Scarborough, North Yorkshire.

For Hannah and Ellie:
"If you put your mind to it, you can accomplish anything."

My sincerest gratitude & appreciation for their assistance with this seemingly never-ending project are due to:

Robert Edwards, Hilda Kean, Matthew Worley and the Friends of Oswald Mosley [FOM] for background reference material; the late John Warburton for his personal recollections; family members: Len, Des and Gary Risdon for their personal recollections and permission to use them; the lovely ladies of the National Anti-Vivisection Society at Millbank Tower, London, for their charming hospitality and endless patience: Research Director - Jessamy Korotoga; Senior Researcher - Christina Dodkin; and Executive Assistant - Angie Greenaway; Phil Tomaselli for his photography skills; Jeff Wallder for his excellent inside information, facilitating photographic prints and personal reminiscences and, together with my great friend Nigel Ward, for their consistent encouragement and constructive suggestions; Mike Springall at the McRay Press in Scarborough and finally, to many other people, too numerous to mention, who have helped with references, sources, or general encouragement, without which this would have been so much harder, if not impossible, to achieve. I thank you all.

FOREWORD

It might seem slightly odd for the author to be writing his own foreword, and that much is conceded, but the reason for it, prior to the initial print run, is pure expediency: I am endeavouring to secure the contribution of suitably laudatory text from an appropriate personage, but to prevent its absence from delaying with said print run, thereby facilitating the earliest possible availability of the completed work, please do not be offended by this 'placeholder text', which will be replaced as soon as the 'real' text becomes available. Perhaps it is a fair question why a foreword should be considered necessary at all, but an impartial, and possibly also dispassionate reader can generally be relied upon to provide an assessment of the work that might never have occurred to the author; having said that, I would consider it an honour if someone with a position of some eminence in the world of politics and/or animal welfare were able to write a foreword for this work which, notwithstanding my obvious partiality, I have no hesitation in heartily commending to readers of biographies and, in addition to that, anyone who enjoys a cracking good yarn! Thank you.

Jon Risdon, October 2013

Black Shirt and Smoking Beagles

INTENTIONALLY BLANK

Black Shirt and Smoking Beagles

CONTENTS

APPENDICES

Photograph credits

A1 The author's collection.
2 The author's family.
3 Leonard Risdon.

B1 ***Echo and Weymouth Dispatch***, 17/10/1924, courtesy of Maureen Attwool.
2 Courtesy of the Friends of Mosley Archive.
3 Charles Wilfred [Bill] Risdon: Wilfred's nephew.
4 Private archive.
5 Private archive.

C1 Courtesy of Robert Edwards.
2 Private archive.
3 Private archive.

D1 Private archive.
2 Private archive.

E1 Private archive.
2 Private archive.

F1 Private archive.
2 Leonard Risdon.

G1 © Copyright The National Anti-Vivisection Society.

H1 Leonard Risdon.
2 Courtesy of the Friends of Mosley Archive.
3 Courtesy of Tim Rose at photobucket.com.
4 Leonard Risdon.

1.Wilfred's birthplace, no. 13 Clarence Place, Lower Weston, Bath: left of centre with beige detailing. In 1898, Wilfred's father was able to afford to rent the larger house next door [facing], no. 12, for a further seven years, to accommodate the seven children still at home.

2.Wilfred's father, Edward George Fouracres Risdon 1855-1931. This *carte de visite* style portrait was probably taken around 1885.

3.Wilfred's handbook on electoral practice, in its original binding, published by the British Union of Fascists & National Socialists in 1936.

1. Labour candidate in 1924

3. Older brother Charles and sister & surrogate mother Jessie in the garden of father EGF's Bournemouth home

2. A fresh-faced Director of Propaganda in 1933

4. An official portrait as Assistant Director General (E)

5. A rare smile for the official publicity photo as "Director of Propaganda who organised the Albert Hall meeting" in June, 1934

1. This crop from the original image, which was obviously posed, has a modern 'filmic' look [*à la Reservoir Dogs*] about it; the date was September 29, 1933, but the location is unknown; Alexander Raven Thomson, British Union's economic expert, is on Wilfred's left.

2. Here Wilfred, on the left of Mosley in his German-style leather coat, anxiously scans the crowd for signs of trouble before a meeting at Sheffield City Hall on the 28th of June, 1934.

3. Although Wilfred did occasionally wear his service medals for official occasions, like meeting a delegation of Italian *Fascisti* in London in 1933, he did not wear military ribbons on his tunic like some of his colleagues here did, in this 1935 shot with the informative caption.

Discussing the Tour. From left to right, Raven Thomson, Clement Bruning, Wegg Prosser, Bill Risdon, and Mick Clarke.

1. One of "the Big Men of National Socialism" in 1937, embarking on a "Country-wide BU Platform Campaign", after the banning of political uniforms under the Public Order Act of 1936.

2. Still looking remarkably youthful in 1937, Wilfred is seen here hugely enjoying the joke at his expense, on his given name, in ***Selsey Bilge*** at the Selsey Blackshirt Summer Camp in August.

1. A lovely atmospheric study, probably taken in his office at NHQ in 1938, by which time he was Chief Agent for British Union. The size of the office reflects his status in the Movement.

2. Wilfred's last speech for British Union, as guest of honour at the annual dinner of Kingston upon Thames Branch 14 March 1939, by which time his plans for leaving BU and joining the London and Provincial Anti-Vivisection Society were starting to take shape, although that didn't preclude him from praising Mosley's economic policies as the only practicable alternative for Britain, according to the subsequent report of the event in ***Action***: "We will attain the ideal of the early Socialists who were not concerned with internationalism…" Wilfred can be seen sitting at the table in front of the central window, and the person next but one to his left, grinning to himself but studiously avoiding the camera, is British Union's resident MI5 'mole' and Wilfred's colleague in Industrial matters, 'Captain' James McGuirk Hughes, *alias* P G Taylor.

1. Wilfred, here 5th from right, is in 'mufti' in his capacity as Deputy Director of Political Organisation, at *Black House* in Chelsea, to instruct aspirant Speakers for the Movement on a course in 1934; William Joyce, left of centre, next to Raven Thomson, seems unconcerned by the camera; a young recruit, Robert Saunders, to whom Wilfred wrote on several occasions, is between Joyce & Thomson; the BUF lawyer, Captain Lewis, is at the front on Wilfred's left.

2. Wilfred and his Lurcher in the garden of his rented house in Ruislip: the date is unknown, but it was possibly August 1940, perhaps just after his release from '18B' in Brixton Prison.

One of the few photographs of Wilfred during his time with the National Anti-Vivisection Society, at least not in an 'official' capacity, such as giving a speech at a public meeting, or as a member of a delegation presenting a petition, or lobbying for a cessation of vivisection. This picture was taken in late 1963 or early 1964, around the time of the illness that hospitalised him for a spell, and kept him away from work at Harley Street for a couple of months or more. Here he is seen looking tired but relaxed, indicated by his pose, perhaps sharing a joke with an onlooker, while a Chauffeur respectfully holds open the limousine door for Executive Committee member, Diana Hamilton-Andrews, who is holding the lead of her presumed pet Corgi [perhaps in emulation of a more widely-known and revered royal owner of Corgis?], whose name is "Topaz Regina of Teifi (popularly 'Dum Dum')! This photograph appeared alongside an article by Wilfred in February of the latter year, in the monthly magazine of the National Anti-Vivisection Society, which periodical went under different names at various times, but then was called simply ***Animals' Defender***; the Article was called ***Why This Needless Cruelty***: see note 85 of Chapter 14 for an extract from the article.

2. One of his many public meetings.

1. The last known photo of Wilfred in his beloved garden.

3. The Brassard worn at BU NHQ.

4. Possibly one of the last photos of Nellie, working in a Reading Bookshop, date unknown.

INTRODUCTION

It is highly unlikely that more than a relatively small number of people - perhaps a couple of dozen, give or take - will have heard of Wilfred Risdon, before reading this book, much less know anything about him or his work; I would like to think that by the time they have finished reading it, most, if not all of its readers, will be prepared to accept, as I truly believe, that he played an important part in the weaving of what became the tapestry of twentieth century history. In saying this, I do not wish to overstate this importance or aggrandise him as a personality [and I feel sure that he would be the first to refute this, were he still here], but his working life, both inside and outside his immediate circle, was conducted on the periphery of wider recognition and, notwithstanding the value of his work, which is the essential *raison d'être* for this biography, one of the inevitable tragedies associated with it is that virtually nobody who knew him, either in a personal, or professional capacity, or both, is still alive to offer any sort of contribution, apart from the few that I have been lucky enough to garner here during the course of my research.

The path to the production and completion of this book has been a somewhat convoluted one; perhaps no more than most, but still worth recounting briefly [and I hope readers will forgive my use of the first person in this introduction]. Because I never encountered this relative while he was alive, even though that eventuality was possible; I was twelve years old when he died in 1967; I had no knowledge of him [and the reasons for this will be partially explained by the narrative] until I was well into my middle years: unfortunately, my father's family line was not very good at 'staying in touch' with far-flung relatives, for a variety of reasons, and Wilfred's 'black sheep' reputation, no matter how inaccurate or undeserved, did not help! It is worth mentioning here, at the outset, that for the sake of consistency, I have referred to my subject as Wilfred throughout: I do not claim any sort of proprietorial ownership, but not only was he a direct relative, he was also a human being, and it is his humanity, with all its faults, but also the potential to strive for perfection, which I wanted to emphasise in this work, hence my favoured use of his given name; also, it would have felt incongruous for me to use his family name, Risdon, when that is also mine; finally, I make no apology for my writing style, however eccentric it might be considered, and I use the style of the original copy in the reference notes, where possible.

This leads me to a statement about the content of the biography, and the way in which it has been constructed. The fact that I am a first-time biographer will possibly be evident very quickly to experienced readers and writers of biographers, but I did not feel the need to conform to a particular style of writing [as in construction of the work], not having read more than a relative handful of biographies as informal preparation, other than recognising that it was essential to accompany the admittedly incomplete historical narrative with as much supporting reference material as I deemed necessary; and certainly a much larger proportion than in a few biographies I have read, for whatever reason. I was very lucky that there is almost a plethora of material from the middle period of Wilfred's life and, whilst I have not included every single reference to him, or every piece he might have written, in full, during this period, I have not skimped. My reservations about this were allayed by the introduction to an excellent and highly-regarded biography of George Orwell by Bernard Crick [from a 1992 paperback edition], in which this obviously very capable biographer describes very similar concerns to mine; from the longer section which I quote in the note [**1**], there are three extracts I will give here, which are particularly apposite:

> "None of us can enter into another person's mind; to believe so is fiction. We can only know actual persons by observing their behaviour in a variety of different situations and through different perspectives";
>
> "Orwell's ambitions as a writer were modest and what he valued was publication"; and
>
> "the texture of this biography is necessarily lumpy and uneven, both because I quote so much, to let Orwell and his contemporaries tell their own tales as far as possible, and because the sources are so uneven and bear no relationship to the relative importance of events in his life."

The first quote should be self-evident; the third one is not included simply as an apology [and I sincerely hope that this work is not "lumpy and uneven"!] but I think that there is a parallel; and although the second one might seem somewhat oblique, what I mean by its inclusion is that, for lack of any personal memoirs or letters, etc., I have had to let Wilfred's writing speak for him, but this necessarily and inevitably presents a less than true picture of him as a complete person, so I have had to indulge in a certain, minimal, amount of the 'surmise' which Crick eschews, and it has been virtually impossible to "repress proud inclinations to 'recreate a life' or to imagine too often what someone 'really felt' on some crucial occasion", although it has only been done when there was no alternative. It is only fair that I should point out that this is not intended to be either an *apologia* for, or conversely by the same degree, a condemnation of the two main strands of Wilfred's working life, namely his politics and his anti-vivisection work: consequently, there is very little examination of opposing views, other than where they were strictly relevant to the circumstances being described; I have tried to be as objective as possible, despite my own variance on several of the main themes from Wilfred's views but, inevitably, it is impossible not to comment occasionally, especially where there is a current resonance with contemporary events, although generally these are to underline how incisive certain analyses of situations were, and how lamentable it is that changes in societal attitudes were not made nearly 100 years ago, which could have had such far-reaching positive effects in the twenty-first century. Also, without wishing to broach here in great depth one of the inevitably most contentious areas of Wilfred's political [and, in a broader sense, personal] life, because it will be dealt with in the course of the narrative, and analytically in the conclusion, I do want to elucidate that although the term 'anti-Semitism' is used frequently in a generic sense, it is nevertheless used with some reservation.

I first encountered Wilfred as a result of my family history research, which [the latter] is a common enough occurrence in middle years, made all the easier now thanks to the prevalence of online archives and websites geared to family history research, although even twenty years has made a big difference! In my usual methodical fashion, I canvassed a mailing list of potential relatives garnered from a family name directory sold by one of a number of enterprising companies set up to capitalise on this burgeoning market, and one of the many replies on my template enquiry form was from a gentleman by the name of Leonard [Len] Risdon; after exchanging a couple of letters [which seems unconscionably slow by today's standards] it transpired that we were, indeed, directly related; Len's father, Bert, was my grandfather Charlie's younger brother, immediately preceding Wilfred by four years [a Christmas Day baby, no less]; but Len also told me of a potentially very interesting relative called Wilfred Risdon, who had been involved in politics in his early life, but had then gone on to work in animal welfare [there was more detail than that, but to relate it here would be to pre-empt the book]. The name of Oswald Mosley, which was mentioned in connection with Wilfred, did not mean a huge amount to me at the time, even though I was aware that he had been very active in politics, and controversially so, in the first half of the twentieth century.

My research was given something of a 'kickstart' in 1999, when I saw an advert in a family history magazine, to which I subscribed at the time, asking for people who thought they had 'interesting' relatives to write in, as the advertisers were putting together a series of programmes on a theme of 'blood ties' to celebrate 'the millenium' [a usage I never liked] the following year. The possibility of appearing on television was a small part of the attraction of the project, to tell the truth, given that I had recently begun working as a background artist [aka 'extra', which has always struck me as demeaning] for film & television, but more significant was the possibility that the production company would find stuff out to which I might not easily have access; which indeed proved to be the case. I sent in details of two relatives: Wilfred, and my great great grandfather, Edward, who had been a jeweller, very possibly moving in elevated and wealthy circles in the 1850s, but had also evidently been an inveterate gambler, and committed suicide at the tragically early age of 31, although [luckily for me!] not before siring my great grandfather, Edward George Fouracres Risdon, who was Wilfred's father. The production company replied very quickly, and it was Wilfred in whom they were interested, naturally enough because of the Mosley connection. By the time we came to shoot our pieces, they had been able to build up a reasonable profile, although it was very clear to me, almost from the outset, that they were trying to emphasise the anti-semitism aspect of Mosley's political ethos, and they wanted me to be aware of Wilfred's willing participation; I preferred to be circumspect. Having said the foregoing, it was a very enjoyable experience, and I was very well looked after and courteously entertained; in addition, I was able to keep all the information they had found, including the names of contributors who had been very useful, and continued to be so to me, for which I am eternally grateful. I was promised a copy of the finished piece, although I wasn't sure in advance if it would be the main theme of the programme [which were half an hour in length, if I recall correctly] or a shorter 'insert'. The first series arrived, but without the appearance of my piece; there never seemed to be any doubt that a second series would follow, notwithstanding the reduced relevance if it was not shown during the 'millenium' year, but that was of no great significance to me; it then transpired that there would not be a second series, because the presenter of the first series, Martha Kearney, had decided to leave, which meant [by some unfathomable logic of production] that all of the pieces which had already been shot, including mine, could not be used, if a different presenter was fronting the programme, and it would have cost too much to reshoot them, so my contribution was left on the proverbial cutting room floor [story of my life!] In fairness, I did receive a videotape of a 'rough cut' of my piece, so I can't complain unduly.

Subsequent to this, my life went through a fairly significant change, which meant that family history was not a top priority, but I couldn't forget about Wilfred, and over a period of time, I read books on and around the subject of his work, and amassed quite a collection of reference material, especially as a result of correspondence with people who knew of him reasonably well. I always knew that I wanted to produce something which detailed his life and work, but it was only a couple of years ago, after many discussions with a close and very dear friend, who had great respect for what Wilfred had tried to achieve, while acknowledging the difficulty of overcoming the uninformed prejudice of a significant proportion of the population of Britain [sponsored and encouraged, in no small part, by vested interests in the mass media and government], that I finally decided to concentrate on a biography; I knew it would not be a small or quick task, but I also knew I had to do it thoroughly and although, inevitably, it has taken a lot longer than I first anticipated, it has been a very rewarding process, so I hope that as many readers as possible, especially those who are not tempted by 'celebrity' status, or disconcerted by the lack thereof, will enjoy reading this life story, and come away with a greater understanding of humanity [and ideally, a greater tolerance], as much as I have enjoyed producing it. In conclusion, I would respectfully request that it should be read with an open mind, conscious of the fact that just because an orthodoxy is widespread or commonly accepted does not make it right [or wrong, for that matter]; and, reprehensible clichés though they might be: truth is the first casualty of war, and history is written by the victors.

Thank you.

NOTES

1 The subject of this biography was hugely influential, so the introspection was appropriate:

> "What kind of biography, then, have I tried to write about a man with this kind of achievement? I began with the naïve idea that the main task would be to know the character of Orwell as well as humanly possible, while all the time working away at the facts, so that by knowing him, understanding his inwardness, entering into his mind, I could supply his motivations, perhaps even correcting his own later accounts of them, and make sensitive suppositions (i.e., guess) at what was happening when documentation was lacking. But simultaneously reading a lot of 'good biography' and beginning to grapple with the evidence for this book, not in any rational order (as I had hoped) but simply as it came, dictated by ease of access to papers and the proximity of age of certain witnesses, I grew to be sceptical of much of the fine writing, balanced appraisal and psychological insight that is the hallmark of the English tradition of biography. It may be pleasant to read, but readers should realize that often they are being led by the nose, or that the biographer is fooling himself by an affable pretence of being able to enter into another person's mind. All too often the literary virtues of the English biographical tradition give rise to characteristic vices: smoothing out or silently resolving contradictions in the evidence and bridging gaps by empathy and intuition (our famous English 'good judgement of character' which, compared to the French stress on formal criteria, lets us down so often); and this all done so elegantly that neither contradictions nor gaps in the evidence are apparent to any but scholarly eyes carefully reading the footnotes or cynically noting their lack. None of us can enter into another person's mind; to believe so is fiction. We can only know actual persons by observing their behaviour in a variety of different situations and through different perspectives. Hence the great emphasis I found myself placing on reporting the views of his contemporaries at unusual length and in their own words, neither synthesizing nor always sensitively resolving them when they conflicted. Wyndham Lewis once remarked that good biographies are like novels. He did not intend to let the cat out of the bag.
>
> Some good bad biographies appear to be, epistemologically speaking [Epistemology is the investigation of what distinguishes justified belief from opinion], novels indeed. That is the extreme of the empathetic fallacy. A contrary extreme is a purely empiricist presentation of the evidence, such as one can find in biographies written by professional historians. But they too deceive themselves if they think to avoid selectivity simply by offering a commentary on extracts from original archives. Rather than produce a symbolic distillation called 'basic character', they throw a cloud of dust - called facts - in our eyes. Common sense suggests that one can and must characterize Henry VIII, Wallenstein, Shaftesbury, Woodrow Wilson or Lloyd George, indeed offer rival contemporary characterizations too, but without abandoning the evidence and the chronicle of events for the seductive short-cuts and pseudo-certainties even of 'empathy', still less of literary psychoanalysis.

INTRODUCTION

One has only the evidence that one can find. Which papers survive and which do not is largely accidental; there is no neat proportionality between the records and periods of Orwell's life. His letters to his agent, for instance, survive and are a continuous series from 1930 to 1949, but his agent's letters to him, which would add much to the tale, were foolishly destroyed. Orwell was not the kind of man to keep intimate diaries or to write long personal letters. For most of his career he was too strapped for cash, too hard pressed earning a living by book-reviewing and column journalism to have done so, even had he wished; and to say that he was careless about preserving copies of letters he did write would be to imply that he should have seen some point in doing so. Orwell's ambitions as a writer were modest and what he valued was publication. He was not born to the literary purple of the Bloomsbury group, whose every scribbled note to 'come to tea on Tuesday' seem to contain phrases of wit, malice or insight or insight written in the knowledge or hope that one day they would be published or be useful to some relative writing a biography. Which is the more valuable record of a state of mind, or interesting human document: a file of self-conscious literary letters carefully preserved by the sender, or a few hasty but argumentative letters sent without copies to a friend who happens to destroy them? Gaps in the evidence are inevitable and should not be disguised either by expanding with surmise what we do not have, or by contracting, for the sake of balanced chapter lengths, what we do have.

Thus the texture of this biography is necessarily lumpy and uneven, both because I quote so much, to let Orwell and his contemporaries tell their own tales as far as possible, and because the sources are so uneven and bear no relationship to the relative importance of events in his life. Of course one tries to fill gaps, or to find other sources of evidence. Any scholar will know the ghastly disproportion of time one spends searching for people or papers that one is relatively unlikely to find compared to the speed and economy with which one assimilates an important section of a large and well-ordered correspondence in an archive. But when one does have to speculate, when a gap in the evidence seems crucial to the coherence of other parts of the record, one should simply say so clearly. I use words like 'probably' and 'possibly' and 'might' as little as possible, but do so when coherence dictates. A biographer has a duty to show how he reaches his conclusions, not to pretend to omniscience; and he should share things that are moot, problematic and uncertain with the reader.

The need to present conflicts in evidence rather than to resolve them all neatly is particularly acute because there is so much good writing about Orwell by famous men of letters who either only knew him in the last years of his fame, or did not in fact pay much attention to him before. They are eye-witnesses of a few years but can only speculate about and offer hearsay evidence for the long formative years when he was struggling to succeed as a writer. As poets and novelists, they do not always make the distinction clear, so I have always sought and, when I could find it, preferred the direct evidence of people who knew him at the relevant times. A good memory has nothing to do with literary abilities. Indeed sometimes when people have published their memories of someone, their writings act as a block to any further memories, and, when interviewed, they simply repeat and defend, consciously or unconsciously, their published position.

...

I realize that the externality of my method runs the risk that I appear unsympathetic to Orwell, putting him in the box, as it were, under oath and treating his testimony critically. I would rather run this risk, however (liking him very much, but admitting, not surprisingly, that the works are greater than the man), than pontificate about character and states of mind. Sympathy must be present in a biographer - otherwise one would grow sour living for so long with someone one disliked; but sympathy is not, once again, a reliable short cut to establishing, so far as is possible, what actually happened at the time. An honest biographer must be more dull than he could be, must repress proud inclinations to 'recreate a life' or to imagine too often what someone 'really felt' on some crucial occasion."

George Orwell: A Life; Penguin, 1992, by Bernard Crick

1: EARLY LIFE

Wilfred Risdon was born on January 28th, 1896, in a modest, but respectable, working class district of the city of Bath, Somerset, the last of 12 children [2 of whom died in infancy] to Edward George Fouracres Risdon, a bespoke boot and shoe maker, and Louisa who, as well as raising all these children was, at various times, a boot & shoe machinist. She was 4 or 5 years older than Edward and born in Exeter, where they married and it is very likely that they met; Edward, whose mother's maiden name was Fouracres [a prosperous Exeter metalworking family, specialising in cutlery] hence the third forename, was born in Devonport, but as a result of the itinerant nature of his father's trade, journeyman jeweller [and, very likely, an inability to settle anywhere too long], his parents moved around quite a lot, so it is altogether possible that Edward spent his formative years in and around Exeter.

There is an anecdotal story that Edward attended a Bluecoat School, but the details are confusing, and it has so far been impossible to corroborate this; suffice to say that Edward's father Edward [with no other known forenames] committed suicide at the age of 31 [the end of another fascinating, although ultimately tragic, life story], which must have been a devastating blow for the seven year old EGF, and no doubt influenced his later personality. Again anecdotally, it has been suggested that EGF was an adherent of the Plymouth Brethren, which group possibly provided solace for his distraught mother; he is known to have been strict, but not domineering, as a parent [not unusual in the Victorian era]; indeed, not incapable of wry or sardonic humour, but little is known of his specific religious leanings, outside the umbrella rubric of Christianity. That notwithstanding, Wilfred is known to have been something of a religious zealot in his youth, something which wouldn't have been unduly frowned upon at the beginning of the twentieth century, or regarded as evidence of a precocious need to impose his will upon predominantly older people; probably readily humoured and accommodated.

Wilfred had two uncles, Ralph Alexander and Charles R., who also worked in the shoe industry; Ralph was born in Plymouth, maybe two years after EGF, and died in Bath; Charles was born in Bath so, even though the family might have moved back to Devon at some stage, the connection with Bath was well established before EGF moved there some time between 1886 and 1889, where his last four children were born. Given all this association with the boot & shoe industry, it would have been entirely consistent if this had been how Wilfred started his working career, but the census of 1911 shows Wilfred, at the age of 15 [presumably having finished school at the age of 13 or, if he was lucky, 14] working in bookbinding: the reason for this is a matter for pure speculation [aside from the tenuous leather connection].

The next, documented, event in his life was inevitably a momentous one, when he volunteered for the armed services in August 1914, on the outbreak of a horrendous war, which went under a variety of names down the years; for some inexplicable reason, later in life, Wilfred reckoned that he had been underage when he joined up, about which he had had to lie to be accepted, but in fact he was only a few months short of the lower age limit of 19 [if he is, indeed, correct in this later assertion], and not the "actually just short of my seventeenth birthday" that he claimed in an appeal hearing [**1**] which he must have known would be closely documented and scrutinised. The reason for this is most probably quite prosaic; it is unlikely that he would have attempted to be mendacious, had he even wanted to be, which doesn't seem to fit the general pattern: the more likely explanation is either that his numeracy skills were somewhat lacking [although stretching credibility somewhat], or that his age had not been a matter for regular discussion at home, and he had somehow become genuinely confused. This is consistent with a discrepancy of two years on his marriage licence, in 1935, when his age is shown as 37.

It is not yet known for certain where, and for which regiment Wilfred volunteered in August 1914, but it is a documented fact that he came through the war relatively unscathed, suffering some level of injury and shellshock, leaving the service with the permanent rank of Sergeant in the Royal Army Medical Corps [**2**] [RAMC]. Wilfred later stated [1940] that from November 1914, he served in France and Belgium throughout the war, spending "a good deal of the war" as a stretcher bearer with No. 1 Field Ambulance attached to the First Black Watch, and went through with the Army of Occupation in Germany, and stayed there until his Division, the First Division, "came back to England in cadre strength" and later, possibly early 1919, he was demobilised [although it is more than likely that he would have remained on the Reserve List for another couple of years, hence the later reported duration of his war service as being 6 years].

There is an anecdotal story in the family, from a relative who knew Wilfred quite well, that he was asked at the end of his war service if he would be willing to sign up for the 'Black and Tans' in Ireland, but he refused; it is difficult to know how this could be corroborated, so it will have to remain an unknown quantity, but in my view, it is entirely consistent with Wilfred's character that he would have seen the conflict in Ireland, and the perceived need for a heavy-handed security force as a situation in which he wanted no part, so I am content to believe the story, even without evidence. Charles Loch Mowat [***Britain Between the Wars, 1918-1940***] referred to "Such a reign of terror [as] not easy to condone." and "the greatest blot on the record of the Coalition and perhaps upon Britain's name in the twentieth century ...".

Hereafter, some specific speculation is necessary, with regard to the beginning of his working career proper, and the point of its commencement, because it is known that he worked as a miner, a radical departure from bookbinding, and spent time in South Wales, not unusual for West Country miners, where he came into contact with Aneurin Bevan and, almost inevitably, the South Wales Miners' Federation [SWMF], which would have represented his induction into [and, inescapably also, indoctrination in] Socialist politics. The reason for the speculation is that Bevan was awarded a scholarship by the SWMF to the Central Labour College [**3**] in 1919, and several sources have confirmed [presumably what he told them] that Wilfred was in competition with Bevan for the scholarship, losing out of course, as history records, but it stretches credibility somewhat to believe that Wilfred can have been demobbed, gone to Tredegar, engaged in a course of study in addition to his everyday colliery work, applied for the scholarship and been rejected, all in a matter of a few short months?

My feeling, which I have yet to corroborate, is that Wilfred decided, some time after 1911, on a change of direction and became a miner, a very brave choice [**4**], probably starting in the local coalfield in and around Radstock, then discovering the potential in South Wales, and moving there some time before August 1914, giving him long enough to find a way into union work and socialist politics, meeting Bevan [who became the youngest person to chair a union lodge, in Tredegar in 1916, so obviously precociously ambitious **5**] in the process, and very possibly corresponded with him during the war, when Bevan could have kept him apprised of developments at home, including the projected scholarship, which Bevan possibly encouraged Wilfred to compete for [or maybe *vice versa*?].

Of course, it is entirely possible that this career move was meticulously planned, even by someone so young, if the object for Wilfred was to find a way into a parliamentary sphere of influence, which is not illogical for someone with his evident proselytising zeal; it must have been clear to Wilfred, even as a teenager [a term not in use then], possibly influenced by his father's Christian socialistic leanings, that the background of material substance necessary for qualification in Tory and Liberal circles [although there was some Liberal-Labour association in the early days, for strategic reasons] was not available to him, neither was the ideology of either palatable for him, so an apprenticeship, both literal and metaphorical, in union-based working class politics was the only means by which he could enter the hallowed echelons of parliamentary government, at that time still considered to be relevant and effective.

The next actual record we have of Wilfred's location is in 1923; the early 1920s, especially in South Wales, were a period of regular industrial strife, including strikes and lockouts, but it is more than possible that the disappointment he felt at the loss of an ostensibly golden opportunity in London [although very possibly, certain members of the SWMF felt that to be rid of the volatile Bevan for a couple of years [**6**], was a good enough reason for awarding him the prize] spurred Wilfred on to seek 'pastures new' and fresh stimulation, where he could put his education and talents to good use. He will, no doubt, have been involved in union work to some extent, and had some contact with socialist politicians, especially as a Labour presence in Parliament had been established [**7**]; Bevan had realised early on that, although grass roots work at local union level was important, to some extent that could be minimised or even obviated if political reforms via the legislature could restructure society along more socialistic, class-levelling lines, hence his desire for a Labour 'apprenticeship', and Wilfred would undoubtedly have been of like mind on that, so given the setback of the missed opportunity in London, his first thought appears to have been to roll up his sleeves, and make himself useful at ground level in the Labour Party.

For all it was a hotbed of socialist fervour, Tredegar was probably too well served for Wilfred to make any headway, so it made a lot of sense for him to return to his roots, at least regionally, and he probably looked for a position as a canvasser or organiser somewhere in the south west of England, not too far from home, although he was well used to living independently by this time. Labour had been making steady gains in parliamentary representation, and to a large extent, this was a result of the spread of constituency parties, rising from 73 in 1906 to 179 by 1914 [**8**]; if not exponentially, the number of Labour MPs certainly grew significantly: 1918 [the "coupon" election], 63; 1922, 142; 1924, 191. There was also funding available, for elections, in addition to what local organisations were able to pay [**9**], so it made sense for Wilfred to acquaint himself with the arcana and technicalities of electoral law, some of which he would have been familiar with from his groundings in Tredegar, a study which stood him in very good stead, not only just after the war, when a salary would have been a distinct advantage, but also later, as international relationships deteriorated towards another disastrous war. ***The Representation of the People Act*** of 1918 had also opened up the franchise to more working class men [and some women], so there was a 'ready market', as it were, for what Labour was selling.

By 1924, Wilfred was living in Weymouth with his brother Charles who, being twelve years older than Wilfred, probably would have seemed more like an uncle than a brother to him, especially as Charles had also been quite independent, working as a dairyman and marrying for the first time in 1907 when Wilfred was only 11 and, unfortunately, Charles was evidently not the most gregarious of men. In late 1921 or early 1922 however [**10**], he suffered a tragedy: his wife, Ellen Ann, whose father John Sheppard, from Radstock, had been a railway porter, died from tuberculosis. According to newspaper reports concerning the election of October 1924, in which Wilfred was a candidate, Wilfred had already been living in Weymouth for three years, so it is altogether possible that it was this event which brought Wilfred to Weymouth in the first place: the 1922 Voters' List for Weymouth shows Charles Henry and his wife Ellen Ann at the same address, 10, Bradford Road [at that time, part of a relatively new local authority housing development, commenced in 1916, off Chickerell Road, not far from town **11**], but these directories normally took some time to compile, print & distribute, so inevitably they were somewhat out of date when they first appeared. The Spring, 1923 list shows Charles Henry and Wilfred living at the same address, so it entirely plausible that Wilfred went to Weymouth to console his brother, and at the same time gaining a base from which to develop a constituency for Labour, in what was [and remained, as it transpired] a staunchly conservative area [**12**].

In the election of December, 1923 [**13**], although the Conservatives were still the largest party in Parliament by virtue of actual seats won, they could not command an overall majority, with the Liberals having 158 seats, and Labour 191; Herbert Asquith, the Liberal leader, [because he stood for 'Free Trade'] refused to put Stanley Baldwin back into office so, on the 18th of January, 1924, Ramsay MacDonald [as he was generally known] became the first Labour Prime Minister, as a consequence of which, some 2 months later one Oswald Mosley, "like most upper-class recruits" [**14**] of whom more later, joined the Independent Labour Party, "one of the affiliated organisations, to the left of the main party" [**15**]. Metaphorically, the task which lay ahead for Labour was like drinking from a poisoned chalice and, after a stormy and, frankly, ineffectual [some would call it disastrous] ten months in office, Ramsay MacDonald's minority government was voted out of office when the Conservatives and Liberals formed a temporary alliance, after scandal and mismanagement had wrecked Labour's reputation, notwithstanding its public perception to a large extent as a hitherto unknown quantity, as a party of government [**16**].

It is more than possible that Wilfred was envisaging another campaign of solid, reliable work for Labour in this forthcoming election, as he had done less than twelve months previously, despite the disconcerting odds given Labour's public perception [**17**], in his current capacity as an election Agent, and it is not known if he had hitherto harboured any aspirations to candidacy, but the matter was decided by a paucity of suitable candidates [**18**] for one of the region's parliamentary Divisions, Dorset South, which included the town of Weymouth, so Wilfred accepted the nomination [**19**]. He appears to have had no problem acquiring support from 72 people to either propose or second him [none of whom, incidentally, was his brother and housemate, Charles **20**], as opposed to the 70-odd [including, in addition to proposer and seconder, on the first paper, "assentors"] for the Conservative candidate, Robert Daniel Thwaites Yerburgh, 34, Brevet Major, of Cadogan Square, London S.W., including F. Cavendish Bentinck of Corfe Castle [**21**] and the gloriously named Fetherstonhaugh Henry Rupert Frampton, of Moreton, Dorset.

If the result, outside the circles of those supporters who would think of themselves as passionately committed, was variously [and with reasonable justification, it has to be said] predicted to be a foregone conclusion, Wilfred nevertheless threw himself into a hectic and demanding schedule of public meetings to espouse the cause, in the face of local scepticism and occasional hostility, of the Socialist message. ***The Echo and Weymouth Dispatch*** of Friday, October 17th, 1924, helpfully carried a photograph of a very serious, but youthful looking MR. WILFRED RISDON, (South Dorset), along with a photo of another of the Dorset Labour candidates, MRS. LOUIE SIMPSON, (West Dorset), looking equally serious, but bedecked in a huge, feather-trimmed hat. Support for Wilfred was urged upon the audience by Mrs. Bruce Glasier [**22**], and given a ringing endorsement by Miss D. Francombe, the Chairman of a meeting at the Sidney Hall, Weymouth on Tuesday night, October 14th, 1924, at which Wilfred opened his campaign [**23**]. According to one local newspaper, Wilfred "was well received, [and] said there were people with whom he disagreed, but he would not like to think they were his enemies. For his own part he had no desire to be at enmity with any fellow being on the face of the earth. … Now the fight had been brought on them they were going to fight hard and to fight clean." [**24**], a metaphor to which he would return later, somewhat ruefully but undaunted.

Admirable British politeness and respect were in evidence when the candidates met for the first time during the campaign, when they visited the offices of the Deputy Returning Officer, Mr. W. T. Wilkinson [**25**]. The campaign trail was a punishing schedule, with Wilfred covering, on one occasion, Moreton, Winfrith, Wareham and Wool in the same evening [**26**]; on another, he addressed meetings at Owermoigne, Osmington, Preston and The Triangle, Weymouth [**27**]. Occasionally, there were minor incidents which, in retrospect [especially in our technologically sophisticated modern times] can seem comical, but Wilfred accepted them with characteristic good humour [**28**]; some events were touchingly sweet [**29**]; but generally, it was a question of 'doing the rounds', and being as positive and 'upbeat' as possible [**30**]: at least Wilfred didn't, by all accounts, have to endure the sort of rowdy, and often belligerent, interruptions to his meetings which were to become such an unwelcome & unnecessary feature of his later political career. Interestingly, given the not entirely unexpected aristocratic support for his Conservative incumbent rival mentioned above, a meeting of the Swanage Labour Party, at which Wilfred's candidacy was confirmed, was chaired by a Mrs. Cavendish Bentinck [**31**], so this would be either evidence of even-handed local patronage, or realistically more likely, evidence of interfamilial political differences - aristocratic converts to Socialism were by no means unusual. At this point, it would be pertinent to give a brief exposition of the manifesto which Wilfred was delivering at these meetings.

Most people have a general perception of what Socialists stood for in the early days, but the difficulty they [i.e., Labour] had to work with as an integral part of the overall socialist movement was that it was exactly that: a movement, a relatively loose association of groups which, ostensibly, all supported the same cause, but in fact, both the theory and the practice of all these groups varied quite widely, making it difficult for the proponents such as Wilfred, let alone the general public, to view a cohesive picture of policy crystallised from all the disparate ideology. This inevitably created a perception that the majority of policy was somewhat reactive, made up 'on the run', and there is some basis to this accusation, but it is not entirely fair [all political parties exhibit this tendency to a greater or lesser extent, vacillating between a grudging acceptance that they have to give their supporters, the voters, some power to determine the policies, as an elemental implementation of 'democracy', and conversely, the belief that they alone should determine policy, because they hold the reins and 'they know best'], and Labour was still reeling from its first, bruising encounter with the reality of the parliamentary rough-house: the repercussions of the travails of the parliamentary Labour Party were rippling out and trickling down into the local, divisional parties, Wilfred's current domain. Wilfred was clearly not the sort to parrot the party line automaton-like: he had plenty of experience of hard, grinding physical work and the less physically demanding but equally important union organisation which was essential to prevent abuses and bit by bit improve the lot of the working man and woman, to truly believe that what he was saying and selling to a predominantly supportive, but occasionally [and, in all fairness, quite rightly] sceptical audience was unquestionably necessary and right.

Inevitably, the first point Wilfred had to dispense with as quickly and painlessly as possible was the reason for the election in the first place. This has already been alluded to [see note 16], and although the Campbell case could perhaps be seen as the catalyst, by far the most important issue, although it was not specifically a policy matter, was the public perception of Labour as a party of government: "The issue and the immediate reasons for the fight were perhaps somewhat cloudy to some people. The point re. the vote of censure was a legal point, but the real issue was that the Labour Party, which had been held up for years past as unfit to govern, had made tremendous strides and headway in the affairs of the State in the short period of eight months and it had become necessary for their political opponents if they desired to retain party prestige to get rid of the Labour Government as speedily as possible." [**32**] The proposed Russian loan, to which Wilfred did not allude anywhere near as fulsomely as Mrs. Bruce Glasier, had been most unfairly criticised, and generally misunderstood, as far as the Socialists were concerned [**33**]: "The idea of their political opponents if that [the unfairly weighted committee of investigation] had been carried out successfully was to damage the status of Labour so that when the division on the Russian Treaty was taken Labour would have been accounted for and removed" [**34**] - as indeed they were!

After the ground had been cleared, so to speak, Wilfred could then proceed to first lay out an illustration of where Labour had succeeded, as one commentator noted: "There was something in the past achievements of the Government that was worthy of support" [**35**]. "Turning to the record of the Government, Mr. Risdon said that about twelve months ago their candidates promised relief from food taxation and that promise was nobly fulfilled in the reduction of thirty millions in food taxes in the first Labour Budget." [**36**] Next, Wilfred could speak about a subject of which he had personal experience: "Other promises made had been fulfilled in connection with ex-Service men and the recipients of Old Age Pensions. It was the first act of the Labour Pensions Minister, Mr. F. O. Roberts, to remove the stigma of pauperisation from men who lost their reason when serving their country and were placed in mental institutions. (applause)" [**37**]

Following that was a subject which perhaps did not have such immediate impact at that time, although its significance was growing: education. He conceded that the Government's success had been limited, but progress had been made, and he advocated smaller class sizes and [presumably free] meals for schoolchildren; also, they had given more free places in the secondary schools, and he couldn't resist a jibe at the opposition in connection with what is today still a very contentious subject: university - they wanted to see increased opportunities. [**38**]

Next to a subject of obvious importance: housing. Here, he went on the offensive: "… to those who said that they [Labour] were not building houses, he would say, What have you done to give effect to Mr. Wheatley's Bill in your locality?" [**39**] "Mr. Wheatley's was the only scheme that offered a possibility of over-coming the housing shortage." [**40**] Unemployment could not be avoided, of course: although he refrained from making a specific attribution, there were, contrary to the common perception, which incorporated "an untruth", less unemployed than during the corresponding period the year before under the previous administration, and the numbers registered as available for work had increased [**41**] - not apparently a contradiction in terms? On the subject of peace, given that the spectre of war was still relatively fresh in people's minds, Wilfred gave almost sole responsibility for its preservation to the Prime Minister, Ramsay MacDonald. [**42**] Next on the agenda was agriculture: very pertinent for a town like Weymouth, with a large rural catchment area. More success here: although the wages boards which had been reinstated by Labour in fulfilment of "another pledge" hadn't yet achieved their full potential, there was nevertheless cause for agricultural workers to believe that their lot was improving [**43**].

These were the main topics which were reported by the local newspapers [and most meetings were shorter than the one reported above, purely as a logistical necessity, so the range and/or depth of the topics covered would have had to be reduced], although it is very likely that Wilfred already had the skill to read an audience and tailor the presentation to suit the probable reception; he was not averse to gentle humour [**44**], but neither was he afraid to use colourful, albeit 'clean' language if the situation demanded it [**45**]. Although "leave 'em laughing when you go" was probably not one of Wilfred's mottoes, and it would not have always been appropriate, given the seriousness of most of the topics being discussed, Wilfred nevertheless endeavoured to close a meeting in a positive, 'upbeat' mood which would instil confidence in his audience, and he appears to have genuinely believed that Labour could not only win this true-blue Conservative seat, but be returned to power at Westminster.

At the meeting which was most comprehensively reported on, at the Sidney Hall in Weymouth, he said that "Personally he had no doubt that the Labour Government would get returned. (applause) He believed that within the past eight months Labour had given sufficiently convincing proof of its capacity to govern. He had every faith in the electorate of this country on this occasion to see that the Labour Party's programme was not interrupted by a different party being returned. (applause)" [**46**] At another meeting, at Preston, he said on entering the room [another schoolroom]: "We are going to win all along the line." [**47**] Unfortunately, this confidence [or realistically, in retrospect, overconfidence] was not to be vindicated by the result. On polling day, the weather was atrocious [which appears to have been country-wide **48**], which will, no doubt, have discouraged many people, especially those with no transport of their own, or access to the conveyances which the more affluent Conservative party machine had at its disposal, from turning out to vote; this, and the backing predominantly given to the Conservatives by the Liberals in Wilfred's constituency, with no candidate of their own, contributed to a convincing defeat for Labour in South Dorset [**49**], and in the country as a whole [**50**].

One major issue which must have had an influence upon the result for Wilfred, even if only peripherally, but also helped to persuade many Liberals to switch their allegiance to the Conservatives, was the Zinoviev Letter "bombshell": on October 25th, i.e., four days before the election, the Foreign Office published a letter purporting to originate from Zinoviev of the Communist International to British Communist Leaders, urging them to infiltrate the Labour Party and the army; the instinctive, and almost certainly accurate defence that the letter was a forgery [in which, according to Robert Skidelsky, the Conservative party machine was "heavily implicated"] was fatally undermined by the apparent authorisation by the Foreign Secretary, Ramsay MacDonald, of an official protest to Russia against this interference in British affairs [**51**].

True to form, Wilfred was gracious in defeat [**52**], but once the dust had settled [arguably more quickly for Wilfred than it would have done for the victorious Major Yerburgh], he had to decide the way forward. It is most likely that he went back to his previous activities of political organiser and, when required, election agent. At his 18B Appeal hearing in 1940 [**Appendix D**], he volunteered that he was "organising the South West counties of England" before his "years in the Midlands" of 1928 and '29, but he must already have been developing, or possibly even cultivating, an association with Birmingham, as evidenced by his statement about a residential college for 'working men', in Birmingham, that he "used to go there a lot" in that earlier period, so why set his sights further north from Weymouth?

By 1920, Labour had already appointed 112 full time election agents, in addition to a further 24 appointed by affiliated organisations [**53**], so there was a reasonably good, established national network; although they looked to London for their policy direction, the local organisers enjoyed a high degree of autonomy [**54**], so Wilfred would have carried quite a weight of responsibility for one so relatively young but, as with so many other young men in that new dawn, the carnage they had recently experienced forged a whole new ethos and preparedness for the struggles that lay ahead. It is not unduly surprising that Wilfred was expected to carry out what, in reality, amounted to the duties of two people, mainly because of the cost element, which would have been a heavy burden on party finances [**55**], so Wilfred's organisational talents would have been stretched to the limit, an indispensable training nonetheless.

Although, admittedly, given the nature of the area [**56**], it probably wouldn't have helped him a great deal in his election fight, but Wilfred hadn't been sponsored by a union [**57**], so he was, pretty much, 'on his own'. Although Wilfred wasn't one, by all appearances, to give up easily, it is altogether possible that he might have become frustrated with the torpor, or unthinking acceptance of Conservative paternalism, of the local working populace, and his concomitant lack of success in whipping them up to a socialistic fervour: the area was not renowned for its radical embrace of left wing ideals [**58**]; notwithstanding that, it would take a few more years before disillusionment with the Labour message would really set in. At this great distance, it is easy to overlook how relatively lucky Wilfred was in his position: Matthew Worley [**59**] tells us that "For most of the period after 1922, there were never more than two paid agents among the whole of the region's divisional Labour Parties", so it is more than likely that Wilfred had his feet in both camps, i.e., the Labour Party and the Independent Labour Party.

It is altogether possible that, under the existing regional structure in the south west of England, Wilfred received, if not the requisite instruction [which he might also have given himself while still in Tredegar], then the first experience of work as an election agent [**60**]. 'Political organiser' was a somewhat nebulous nomenclature, which probably covered any work he did which wasn't specifically that of an election agent; Wilfred's next career phase probably started with a development that took place around the time when he was feeling at his lowest, and which determined the direction in which he was going to move: Birmingham. In 1924, the incumbent south west regional organiser, Edwards, was replaced by one Clem Jones, latterly the divisional Labour Party agent in Smethwick [**61**].

NOTES

1 This was the hearing of Wilfred's appeal against detention under Defence Regulation 18B(1A) in May, 1940; ***HO 45/23670.*** See ***Appendix D***

2 There was already an honourable pattern of conscientious objection to participation in armed conflicts within the labour movement, and mining in particular [although this was by no means universal in South Wales: once the war was well under way, miners' agents became voluntary recruiting agents, a pattern of reversal to be demonstrated by socialists in the subsequent war], notwithstanding deliberate selection of the RAMC as an option for reasons of humanistic altruism; whether the following was a positive influence upon Wilfred's decision about what contribution to make to the war effort is unknown, but it has to remain a possibility; on the 1st of August, 1914, the Board of the Admiralty made an application to the executive of the South Wales Miners' Federation [SWMF], asking that the members should forego two Bank Holiday days, but the executive passed a resolution which included the following:

> "We do not consider it necessary for defensive purposes to ask the miners to work on these two days and we decline to encourage, or in any way countenance the policy of active intervention by this country in the present European conflict, and we are also strongly of the opinion that there is no necessity for Great Britain, in any degree, to become involved in the war between Austria and Serbia, and we call upon the Government to continue its position of neutrality, and to use all its influence in the attempt to limit the area of the present conflict, and to bring it to a speedy termination."

Nevertheless, the country embarked upon a disastrous war, and Wilfred obviously felt impelled by his Christian principles to make a positive contribution, rather than abstain [and thereby, as a pragmatic assessment, remain impotent], so without any known specialist medical knowledge, he joined the RAMC, whose members were specifically non-combatants. Wilfred might have known of Charles Gibbons, a Londoner who became a collier in the Rhondda Valley, gaining a 2-year scholarship to the CLC in 1912, and served as a Sergeant in the RAMC in Egypt and Palestine.

History of the South Wales Miners' Federation, vol 1, by Ness Edwards, 1938

3 The Central Labour College, in London, was a breakaway from Ruskin College Oxford; the SWMF [itself the agglomerative result of many years of local and often factional union activism] saw the Central Labour College as an obvious conduit through which socialist ideology could be brought to the working classes nationally, the idea being that students would return to their own areas after graduation and spread the good word, teaching Marxian economics and industrial history. There had already existed local Labour Colleges and the requisite supporting framework in Wales [for example, the South West Labour College League in Monmouthshire], but to support such a national operation, financing would be required, so a Plebs League [of which there were many, from 1909 onward] was formed, and when the Central Labour College broke away from Ruskin, miners' councils started charging an extra levy on their members; the Western Valleys (Monmouthshire) Miners' Council was the first, with a penny levy.

Ruskin College had been established at Oxford University in 1896, by two Americans, Walter Vrooman and Charles Beard, with an ex-curate in the Church of England, Dennis Hird [who had been given an ultimatum because of his preaching of socialism within the church, by the Bishop of London, Dr. Frederick Temple, whose view, interestingly, was that socialism would destroy the liberty of the individual] as Principal 3 years later, but by August 1909, presumably as a result of ideological differences, the Central Labour College had been set up as a separate entity in two houses in Bradmore Road, Oxford, and district units of the SWMF had already decided to withdraw their scholarships and transfer them to the CLC; by an overwhelming majority, the Amalgamated Society of Railway Servants had decided to do likewise, causing existing students to secede to the new College.

The Ruskin authorities convened a conference at Oxford on October 30th, 1909, to propose a new constitution, but the fatal blow, as far as the secessionists were concerned, was the defeat of a motion, by 27 votes to 4, to add the Labour Party to the other, non-party-affiliated organisations on the new Governing Council. In September 1911, the breakaway College moved to London, but it wasn't until 14th of November, 1911, that the desired permanent home at 11 & 13 Penywern Road, Earls Court, the purchase of which had been facilitated by an overdraft made possible by the deposit of securities with a bank by George Davison, high in the European management of Kodak, and a "philosophical anarchist", was formally opened with a public reception.

History of the South Wales Miners' Federation, op. cit.
The Central Labour College, 1909-29, by W.W. Craik, 1964

4 Mark Starr, a champion of workers' education in Britain and America over a period of more than seventy years, had a very similar early life to Wilfred's: he grew up in Somerset, and considered himself "lucky to stay at school until 13" - his father "never went to school and started work at seven scaring crows in the wheat field"; he went underground at 14, after a false start in the building industry, carrying powder at night to miners who were blasting a roadway; soon he was promoted to carting boy, who were used to go where it was inaccessible for horses, pulling a sled or wagon, often drenched in water, with a chain around his neck - "the harness they gave to young fellows made me a socialist", he said; like a brother before him, he left the West Country for South Wales, the Rhondda Number One District, where his written work and good record on the pit shop committee earned him a scholarship to the CLC. He chose to be a CO [Conscientious

Objector] in the war, trying to avoid prison by convincing the judge of his knowledge and the relevance of historical materialism; unfortunately, the judge wasn't swayed, sentencing Starr to one year in Wormwood Scrubs, although fortuitously for him, his relative fame as a writer earned him the option of civilian work outside the gaol during his sentence.

"A Pioneer in Workers' Education: Mark Starr and Workers' Education in Great Britain", ***Ronda Hauben, Llafur, IV, 2, 1985, pp. 96-100, 102.***

5 Much has been written about Bevan already, but as a contemporary it is attractive to consider that he might have been something of a soulmate for Wilfred, given his uniquely Welsh flavour of chapel religious observance, albeit with a very pronounced rebellious streak, and his interest in what was known at the time as social science, especially the physical wellbeing of his workmates; before the war he would have been closely involved with the Tredegar Working Men's Medical Aid Society [TWMMAS], especially given the disparate and often ruinously expensive nature of medical services at that time: although he is credited by at least one source [David Llewellyn, ***Nye: The Beloved Patrician***] as having founded that organisation, in fact, it "was developed from the existing Doctor and School Fund, mostly through the work of its secretary, Walter Conway (d.1933) during the 1890s.

The Society provided medical treatment for workmen in exchange for a weekly donation from their wages" [Gwent Record Office, [TWMMAS] (1873-1995), Records: http://www.archiveswales.org.uk/] and Bevan was "inspired by the egalitarian principles on which the [TWMMAS] had been based, applied socialist zeal and Welsh determination to create the National Health Service in 1948, the most far-reaching piece of social legislation in British history" [***Milestones in Welsh Medicine:*** http://www.caerdydd.ac.uk/]. This was long after the known association of the two men had ceased, but during the rubbing of the shoulders, as it were, in the early days, they must have exchanged ideas, at the very least, including, among others, an abhorrence for the forthcoming war, although that manifested itself in different ways. Michael Foot, in the first volume of his biography of Bevan, ***Aneurin Bevan, I, 1897-1945***, offers an interesting example of this, together with a tantalising possibility of a mention of Wilfred:

> "During 1918 and the early months of 1919 he first became a well-known figure in Tredegar. He had always chosen to associate himself with men older than himself and now the younger men began to look to him as a leader, easily forgetting that he was as young as themselves. Owing to his opposition to the war, he was a marked man among many of the returning soldiers who attempted through the Servicemen's organisations to build up a counter-force against the 'Left' elements which had stayed at home and come to the fore while they were in France. An I.L.P. meeting on the Tredegar Recreation Ground where Aneurin was the chief speaker nearly led to a rough house; the place was invaded by a mob which had sworn to throw him into the nearby pond. He and Bill Hopkins and *another friend* [my emphasis] left the town for a

few days and went for a holiday to Llandrindod Wells where they renewed their vows to purge their local Jerusalem which stoned its prophets."

Perhaps this was a taste of things to come for Wilfred?

6 Bevan is referred to as a "problem child", in connection with his time at the CLC, having "already been very much 'in the wars' with the pit management, as well as with some of the 'diehards' on the pit lodge and pit committees, and with the old leaders in the Federation." He was by no means the only contentious [and, at times, downright belligerent] miner in South Wales; another CLC alumnus, Noah Ablett, although slightly older than Wilfred and Bevan, was instrumental in the formation of the Industrial Democracy League, from which "the famous ***Miners' Next Step*** emerged [1912], which brought down upon the heads of its authors all the deep damnation that the South Wales coalowners were able to get their literary hacks to articulate. Although the IDL did not succeed in getting their ambitious programme of reform implemented, they did succeed in greatly clarifying the subjective mood of the mineworkers and in converting, to a certain extent, the SWMF into a more centralised industrial union."

The Central Labour College, op. cit.

7 The first socialist Member of Parliament was Robert Cunninghame Graham, who stood for North-West Lanarkshire in 1886, albeit on a Liberal ticket. The Independent Labour Party [ILP] was established in 1893 in Bradford, West Yorkshire, with James Keir Hardie, MP for West Ham, as its first leader and arguably, the first Labour Member of Parliament. The Labour Representation Committee [LRC] was formed in 1900, with James Ramsay MacDonald [also of the ILP] as its first Secretary, to support working class candidates in elections. Initially, the socialist parliamentary candidates had, to some extent, 'piggybacked' on an association with Liberal politicians, if not using the Liberal ticket, as above, given the overall acceptance of the Liberal Party within the British political establishment, although it was a relationship which was inevitably not destined to last; nevertheless, even as late as 1915, "new tendencies" in the Liberal Party were almost invariably ILP members.

In 1903, the LRC agreed with the Liberal Party that only one candidate from the two parties should contest a seat with the Conservative at the following election. In 1906, 29 LRC-sponsored candidates won seats in the election and thereupon set up a separate party in Parliament, calling itself the Labour Party; one Labour MP, John Burns, was invited by the Liberal Government to join the Cabinet, thereby becoming the first Labour Minister. The ILP was by no means the only socialist propaganda group in existence at the time, the Fabian Society and the Social Democratic Federation, which was described by Mark Starr [***op. cit.***] as having "dogmatically advocated the Marxist doctrine and the class struggle", being two notables, but the ILP had the highest profile. From the very beginning, there was overlap, but also tension between the two, the radical and often unorthodox ideas originating in the ILP, and the Labour Party being the home of more aspirationally respectable, Fabian policies, espousing "the inevitability of gradualness" in the day to day tedium of parliamentary progress.

John Simkin: http://educationforum.ipbhost.com/
http://www.bbc.co.uk/

Cairns King Smith; unpublished PhD dissertation, University of Chicago, 1936: A Comparison of the Philosophy and Tactics of the Independent Labour Party with those of the Labour Party of England 1924-31

The years immediately following the war were surprisingly turbulent:

"Industrial strife, councils of action, mass demonstrations and unemployed organisation would all become characteristic of 1919-21, before the recession began to stifle such activity and eat into Trade Union funds & membership. With the economic recovery apparently floundering, Labour positioned itself as the voice of those who suffered in its wake, offering an alternative to the economic insecurity & unemployment that had emerged in many places by the early 1920s."

Labour's advance in South Wales was steady and noticeable:

"In South Wales, Labour took control of Monmouthshire County Council and Glamorgan County Council in 1919, winning the latter by securing 51 out of a possible 78 council seats. Thirteen Welsh Urban District Councils were also won for Labour in the same year, many of which - Abertillary, Bedwas and Machen, Brynmawr, Maesteg and Rhondda among them - would be Labour controlled throughout the interwar period (and beyond)."

Labour Inside the Gate: A History of the British Labour Party between the Wars, by Matthew Worley

8 http://www.telfordlabourparty.org.uk/site/history.htm

9 This website explains the derivation of the name:

"The 'Coupon' election was so called in reference to the signed letter of endorsement that selected Coalition candidates received from Lloyd George and the Conservative leader, Bonar Law. Historians have since argued that the coupon essentially sealed the fate of those Liberals who were not fortunate enough to be amongst the 159 Liberals who did receive the Coalition's backing. Those Liberals whom Lloyd George chose to abandon were left defenceless against Coalition candidates, who had a full claim on the spirit of national unity and patriotism that characterised Britain's war-weary mood following the end of hostilities."

http://www.liberalhistory.org.uk

The Trade Unions had been an integral part of the LRC from the outset, and they were allowed to finance Labour candidates and, thereby, election campaigns after 1913. Also, MPs were granted a salary in 1911, ending the previous domination of the independently wealthy [Conservative] or self-made men [Liberal].

http://www.bbc.co.uk/schools/

There were fees available to peripatetic activists to be had for speaking to local Labour parties, although it would have been a rather precarious sort of existence trying to survive on these alone, as evidenced by

Francis Beckett, in his biography of his father, John, with whom Wilfred came into contact before too long:

> "The notoriety attached to a rebel left-wing Hackney councillor ensured that John lost his job. ... He became one of the small army of full-time ILP speakers who toured the country, from one draughty meeting hall to another, selling the socialist message. He lived by taking modest fees from the local parties whose meetings he addressed. He loved the hard work, the comradeship, the discovery that he had the ability to lift an audience."

The Rebel who lost his Cause: The Tragedy of John Beckett, MP, by Francis Beckett

Jim Simmons, a native of Birmingham, who also came to Socialism through a strong religious conviction, was, similarly to Wilfred, an agent & organiser for the Birmingham ILP Federation, and in 1918, his weekly wage for this activity was £3 10s., a very respectable amount for the time, but to lessen the financial burden, it was suggested that he take speaking engagements, as Beckett did, for 2 weeks every month, although Simmons was exhorted to give the proceeds of his earnings to the Federation 'kitty', rather than keep them for himself, as Beckett did, presumably because he lacked the security of a regular wage.

Soap-Box Evangelist, by Jim Simmons

10 Ellen's death is registered in the first quarter of 1922, so it could could have occurred in late 1921.

11 ***Information courtesy of Maureen Attwool***

12 Although there were, according to Matthew Worley, "localised centres of union strength" with which Wilfred and his family might have had a connection, namely "both the Somerset Miners' Association (SMA, affiliated to the Miners' Federation of Great Britain) and the National Union of Boot and Shoe Operatives (NUBSO) [which] had a significant presence in the Frome constituency", the conservative ethic [and Conservative umbrella of care & control] was still strong: "... after 1918 'gentry, clergy and farmers' provided in many rural areas a 'dynamic leadership' which 'skilfully exploited the possibilities offered by new village institutions - ploughing matches, Women's Institutes, village halls and those connected with the war - to reinforce paternalism and discourage radical political action.'"; the latter point being one which Worley considers [among others] blocked Labour's advance: "a patriotic and imperialist Conservatism, which, in the aftermath of the bloodiest war in Britain's history and, given the region's extensive military and, still more, naval connections, was a formidable obstacle."

Labour's Grass Roots: Essays on the Activities of Local Labour Parties and Members, 1918-45, ed. Matthew Worley.

There was still, just, a Liberal presence in the town, although the obviously Conservative-oriented ***Southern Times and Dorset County Herald***, of October 25th, 1924, rather pompously gave a generally bleak assessment [with a hint of alarm at Labour's advance mixed in with the scorn]:

"The nominations in this county on Saturday were, generally speaking, 'according to plan'. There were none of the last-minute surprises, in South Dorset [Wilfred's Division] especially, that had been spoken of as possible. It is no secret that the Liberal Party in that division have made desperate endeavour to get a candidate who might worthily maintain their high tradition. But in South Dorset, as in the West, the Liberal organisation has of late suffered such decay that there is little effective force left. The debacle of the Liberal Party has been coincident, practically speaking, with the rising of the new Labour-Socialist movement. This, it would be idle to deny, has developed with extraordinary rapidity, to the utter emasculation of South Dorset Liberalism, to which a small but very courageous remnant still cling. The Unionist party regard this as by no means a healthy condition of party politics. Liberalism was a far better enemy to fight than Socialism, as understood to-day. The only satisfaction that can be found in the present political election in South Dorset is that the Liberal party are perforce driven to range themselves on the side of their traditional opponents."

Courtesy of Maureen Attwool

13 No less than today, unemployment was a matter of grave concern, linked inevitably with the country's ability to trade and, although this was by no means a new idea, the Prime Minister, Stanley Baldwin, was convinced that the use of trade tariffs, known popularly as Protection, was the way to stimulate the economy and, thereby, alleviate unemployment; the opposition parties, not entirely unpredictably, took a different view, so Baldwin went to the country to seek a mandate for his policy. The proponents of free trade won the day, and Baldwin's gamble failed. Interestingly, in terms of Wilfred's later career, a victory rally was held by the Labour Party on the 8th of January, 1924, at the Albert Hall, which also served to confirm & celebrate the decision of the labour movement leadership, taken four weeks earlier, to support Ramsay MacDonald's premiership even in a minority administration, if that was how events should transpire.

Labour … Wars, op. cit.

14 ***Oswald Mosley, by Robert Skidelsky***

15 Interestingly, especially in view of his post-second war Europeanism, and his earlier opposition to 'internationalism', Mosley's speech to the ILP annual Conference [at which the normal prerequisite of a year's membership to qualify for parliamentary candidature was waived, in his case] in April, 1924, which was well-received, included support for an amendment to a motion calling for "an amalgamation or federation of all the European countries", calling for no less than world federation, which he described as revealing "a more thorough-going international spirit, beyond the rather narrow conception of the European confederation".

Ibid.

16 The Attorney General, Sir Patrick Hastings, had decided to prosecute the Communist, J.R. Campbell, for an article in the ***Daily Worker*** in which he urged soldiers not to fire on fellow workers [in the course of civil unrest]; this was held to be an incitement to sedition. Notwithstanding the withdrawal of the prosecution because of left wing pressure, Ramsay MacDonald's replies in the House to questions on the case were deemed to be evasive, and the Conservatives saw this as their opportunity to exploit the "Red Bogey" and force Labour out of office, which they did very successfully.

Ibid.

17 The estimable ***Southern Times and Dorset County Herald, 18/10/24*** fulminated thus:

"In brief, the country will have now to decide upon its attitude to Socialism. ... Is the country, in effect, prepared to give the Socialists the opportunity of changing the existing social order, or will it express firmly and decisively its adherence to the present system and its development on the lines upon which we have reached our present stage of progress and civilisation? ... The Socialist Government, broken and humiliated, has issued a strident manifesto of its record and its aims, claiming that it has continuously striven to promote peace as the supreme need of the country and the restoration of industry and commerce. ... The record of the work done towards the transformation of the existing economic and industrial havoc has been barren, and the country to-day is in infinitely worse plight than it was when the members of the Government put their 'prentice hands to the work."

Courtesy of Maureen Attwool.

18 ***Southern ... Herald, ibid.; Courtesy of Maureen Attwool:***

"Labour has cast its net far and wide, and dolorous appeals have gone up to headquarters to avert the humiliation of allowing the seat to go by default. Apparently the Labour caucus is indisposed to waste its resources on forlorn hopes, and *faute de mieux* the South Dorset Labour organisation has desperately decided to put up their agent, Mr. Wilfred Risdon, to wage what surely should be the most hopeless encounter in the whole history of local politics."

19 Although, at the adoption meeting, there were three other candidates:

"SOUTH DORSET CONTEST. MR. W. RISDON ADOPTED BY LABOUR. Mr. Wilfred Risdon, of Weymouth, has been chosen as the Labour candidate for South Dorset. The choice was made at a meeting of the Divisional Council of the South Dorset Labour Party, held at the Sidney Hall, Weymouth, on Saturday night. There were four candidates to choose from. Mr. Risdon is well-known in the Division as agent and organiser for the Labour Party. While he is candidate, the duties of agent and organiser will be undertaken by Mr. C.J. Dashfield, of Swanage. Mr. Risdon, who is a native of Bath, took up his residence in Weymouth three years ago, and during his stay in Weymouth has been closely associated with Labour activities. From 1914 to 1920, Mr. Risdon was in the Army, most of the time with the RAMC. Mr. Risdon is to be formally adopted at a meeting to be held at the Sidney Hall Weymouth, on Tuesday, preceding a meeting of the ILP, at which the principal speaker will be Mrs. Bruce Glasier, B.A. Mr. Risdon has been invited to attend the ILP meeting."

Unknown newspaper, 13/10/24. Courtesy of Maureen Attwool. It is possible that two of the other three candidates could have been as detailed here [under the headline "SOUTH DORSET POLITICAL PARTIES BUSY"]:

> "Labour is spoiling for a fight again, and the names of several probable candidates have been mentioned. The activities of the Independent Labour Party will have been noted with a good deal of interest in the last few months, one of the leading workers being Miss Gertrude Tennant, who has written several books of local "colour". Mr. E.J. Johnson, of Derby, a former Liberal and actively associated with the Western Temperance League, who has spoken several times in Weymouth and the district, has since gone over to the Labour party, and his name is being mentioned as a possible candidate."

Southern Times, 11/10/24. Courtesy of Maureen Attwool.

20 It is more than possible that political ideology, perhaps its very existence and the necessity which Wilfred felt for it, as well as its substance, was a bone of contention between Wilfred and Charles [and, very probably, the wider family, both then, and down through the succeeding generations, especially in the light of Wilfred's later political affiliations], given that Charles became Steward of a Liberal Club in Winchester, in a few years' time: this might have been a purely expedient move, of course, given that in 1928, Charles had transplanted himself with his recently acquired young second wife, Mary Elizabeth [May] Smyth and their two children [the first, a daughter, Gwendoline, having died in infancy] Kathleen Marguerite [Rita] and Charles Wilfred [Bill], possibly to escape the opprobrium accrued as a result of marrying a domestic servant of apparently [according to the mores of the time] questionable propriety, and the position at the Liberal Club gave him chance to establish a base while assessing the potential of re-establishing himself in his former vocation of dairyman, which he did with some reasonable success.

There were three children from the first marriage: Henry Charles [Harry], born 1908, went to live in Sheppey and became a Co-op shoe shop manager, giving sterling service as a Section Leader in the National Fire Service during the second war, and producing and performing in a variety show [described as 'the irrepressible "Rissy"'] presented by C Division, NFS, at the Sheerness Pavilion, in aid of the NFS Benevolent Fund: "three hours' entertainment which was a sure-fire hit from start to finish." [courtesy of Brian Risdon of Sheerness, Harry's son]; Doreen Nellie, born 1910, and Florence Hilda [Floss], born 1913. These three children were all born in Bath, but the two girls stayed in Weymouth, setting up homes for themselves there, providing a loving family environment for later children of a fractured family.

21 This was very probably a close relation of Lord Henry Cavendish Bentinck, "descendant of the famous Lord George Bentinck of 'Young England' fame, [who] came from a tradition of Tory rebels". According to Robert Skidelsky, Bentinck was one of "such attractive Tory rebels" who were drawn with the aforementioned Oswald Mosley "into the Cecil orbit":

"Lord Robert Cecil was Mosley's first - and only - living political hero. Of him Mosley later wrote: 'He was nearly a great man and he was certainly a good man; possibly as great a man as so good a man can be'. Cecil was 'one of those genuinely high-minded Tory aristocrats who have done so much through the centuries to preserve England from revolution ... his passionate, non-doctrinaire idealism was perfectly attuned to the mood of an aristocratic ex-officer, radicalised by the war. Moreover, Lord Robert was a man with a cause. His cause was the League of Nations. ... To that cause he devoted his life ... For some years Mosley made Cecil's cause his own, vigorously championing the League at public meetings up and down the country and serving on the Executive of the League of Nations Union ... Nevertheless, there was a vital difference between the Mosley and Cecil approach to the League. For Mosley the League meant a concentration of power and willingness to use power to settle international problems; it was akin to [George Bernard] Shaw's vision of a union of Higher Powers to keep the unruly lower ones under control.'"

Oswald Mosley, op. cit.

22 Mrs. Bruce Glasier was "one of the pioneers of the Socialist movement. [she] had been a friend of Keir Hardie and William Morris, and also of the Prime Minister, Ramsay MacDonald." She was "a speaker who possesses a powerful voice, which easily filled the wide hall, [and] frequently stirred her hearers to enthusiastic applause." She "said that it was splendid to see a young banner bearer of the cause in Weymouth. 'See you send him to Parliament with a great majority' she added, amidst renewed applause."

Dorset Daily Echo and Weymouth Dispatch, 15/10/24. Courtesy of Maureen Attwool

23 ***Ibid.***

"Miss Francombe said that Mr. Risdon was well known. They needed experience in the party, but also they needed young men and women of physical strength and mental moral enthusiasm. She felt sure that they had made a wise choice in Mr. Risdon. (Applause) He had made a close study of world politics. While he was serving in the war he resolved that he would do all in his power to bring about world peace and to resolve those evils that existed in the present capitalistic system which placed profits before human life and human happiness."

24 ***Ibid.***

25 ***Dorset ... Dispatch, 18/10/24. Courtesy of Maureen Attwool:***

"They advanced and shook hands cordially; Mr. Risdon remarking 'I am pleased to see you looking so fit' and the Major returning the compliment. The group, which included Mr. David Cook (Conservative Agent), Mr. Dashfield (Labour Agent), Mr. Vere L. Oliver and Mr. H.A.G. Stevens, stood chatting cordially, while the nomination notices were being prepared."

26 ***Ibid.***

27 ***Ibid.:***

"The former and latter meetings were held in the open air. Permission to use the schoolroom at Owermoigne was refused, but Mr. Risdon was cordially received by a large crowd on the village green, and given an attentive hearing."

28 ***Dorset ... Dispatch, 17/10/24. Courtesy of Maureen Attwool:***

"Mr. Wilfred Risdon, the Labour candidate, visited Upwey and Broadwey last night. There was a fair number of electors at Upwey to hear his views. His arrival was delayed, and he at once plunged into his subject and held the attention of his hearers while he expounded the Labour policy. The Broadwey meeting was arranged to be held in the Schoolroom, but the gates and room were found to be locked. It appears that there is no caretaker for the purpose and therefore when the room is engaged the keys have to be obtained from the schoolmaster's house, and those who hire the 'rooms have to prepare it for a meeting and attend to the oil lamps and sometimes provide the oil! When the situation was explained to Mr. Risdon, he accepted it, but some of his hearers made strong comments on the incident. The meeting was held in the road leading to Upwey Station and opposite the school."

29 ***Southern Times, 18/10/24. Courtesy of Maureen Attwool:***

"WYKE REGIS.; LABOUR MEETING—On Wednesday evening Mr. G. Bellingham presided over a meeting of the supporters of Mr. W. Risdon in the Assembly-rooms. Addresses were given by Mr. W. Risdon, the candidate, and Mr. Dashfield. The candidate was presented with a black cat as a mascot." [it is not known what happened to the cat!]

30 ***Southern Times, 25/10/24. Courtesy of Maureen Attwool:***

"OPTIMISTIC LABOUR CANDIDATE; Speaking at one of his meetings at Weymouth on Wednesday evening, Mr. Wilfred Risdon, the Labour candidate, said that it was a happy augury of the times, when the Labour Party could hold a meeting in one of the schools with a woman as chairman (Miss Francombe) and the candidate one of the working class, when they could utilise the democratic institutions of the country to return him to represent them in the House of Commons. Judging by the reception he had had throughout the constituency, there was every possibility that that was going to happen, that South Dorset was coming into line with other constituencies, and that there was going to be a landslide that would astonish the people who had combined to keep Labour out."

31 ***Southern Times, 18/10/24. Courtesy of Maureen Attwool***

32 ***Southern Times, op. cit. Courtesy of Maureen Attwool***

"Labour was asked to accept the findings of a committee of investigation, consisting of seven members who had gone into the division lobbies condemning the Labour Government in advance, and another three were to be drawn from Labour ranks, it being stipulated that they were not to be ministers or front-rank men. That did not sound to him [Wilfred] to be a fair deal. Ramsay MacDonald also did not think it a satisfactory arrangement."

Dorset ... Dispatch, 15/10/24. Courtesy of Maureen Attwool

33 Mrs. Bruce Glasier was one of the small, but significant number of women who were not seen merely as appendages of their husbands in political matters, but were educated and self-possessed enough to forge a

political career of their own; she was born Katharine St. John Conway, and by 1924, she had been a widow for four years, but continued working for both arms of Labour until her death in 1950. Before she married her husband, John Bruce Glasier, she turned down a proposal from George Bernard Shaw; Glasier was illegitimately born John Bruce, but his mother [née McNicholl] took the name Glasier when the family moved to Glasgow. Glasier was one of the earliest members and leading lights of the ILP.

http://www.spartacus.schoolnet.co.uk/Wglasier.htm

http://www.spartacus.schoolnet.co.uk/TUglasier.htm

"A more usual I.L.P. attitude [in 1920] was that of Mrs. Bruce Glasier who, as editor of Labour Leader [an official ILP newspaper], quite specifically dissociated theI.L.P. from an attack by [Philip] Snowden on the Bolsheviks. [ref. ***Forward***, a Labour paper, 25/11/20] She argued that whatever were the excesses of the Bolsheviks, they were forced to them by the exigencies of Intervention and Blockade. With this argument the bulk of I.L.P.-ers agreed;"

"The Independent Labour Party and Foreign Politics 1918-1923", *Dowse, R.E., Bulletin of the Institute of Historical Research, 1962*

"Russia, which suffered as no other nation had suffered, more decimated than any other nation, was a nation at war with every capitalist government and the Liberals and Tories who were going to destroy the Labour movement for daring to think of organising peace with the people of Russia and organising a productive loan to be spent in this country, these people — (applause) Thank God the people knew the truth before she began to tell it. They reckoned the people were a lot of fools, but even in the south they knew a bit (laughter). … Turning to the present position, Mrs. Glasier said that Ramsay MacDonald understood that industries on this side of Western Europe could not live without the vast raw material from that larger half of Europe which was Russia. Cutting off Russia meant the dear loaf and gave them the wheat and timber trusts and led to the idleness of the textile trade in England. The power of Russia to buy had been destroyed. In a stirring final appeal Mrs. Glasier asked them all to make human brotherhood the law of life."

Dorset … Dispatch, 15/10/24. Courtesy of Maureen Attwool

34 ***Ibid.***

35 ***Ibid.***

36 ***Ibid.***

37 ***Ibid.***

38 ***Ibid.:***

"The public schools were, originally, built for the working classes of the country and not for those classes by whom they had been appropriated and to whose use they were devoted. They would come into their heritage and children of capacity to benefit by education would be able to go from the elementary to the secondary schools and thence to the colleges and the Universities."

39 John Wheatley was one of the "Clydesiders", a group of strongly left-wing Glasgow socialists whose views were so radical and, oftentimes, rebellious, ["the shock troops of the left"] that they were almost indistinguishable from the Communists with whom they regularly associated; he was the Minister responsible for housing during the ill-fated first Labour Government, and the only left-winger in that Cabinet: "the Government's only real success". He instituted a large programme of local authority [originally known as "council housing"] house-building, but through a combination of circumstances, it did not come to fruition during the time Labour was in office. According to his son, Francis, John Beckett was the only person to whom Wheatley:

> "confided his real view of his friend [James] Maxton, as a good and brave man who could not lead an effective political movement. John persuaded Wheatley that what was needed was a new political party - an organised party, not a loose association. Wheatley took the message back to a sceptical Maxton, and with some difficulty persuaded him. This strange triangle - Wheatley and John Beckett in London, Wheatley and Jimmy Maxton in Glasgow - decided that the ILP was to be transformed into a new political party, to do all the things they had dreamed of, and to replace the Labour Party. In 1929 John believed firmly that Wheatley, with himself at his side, was going to lead Britain into the new Jerusalem. The exciting times of 1920 had come again. … As part of the plan, Wheatley stood for the National Administrative Council (NAC) of the ILP - its ruling body - at the ILP Easter conference. He had left the NAC some years before. During the conference he was taken ill, but returned to London the next week, and dined with John on Tuesday evening. … Wheatley died on 12 May, 1930 [i.e., three weeks after the end of the conference]."
>
> ***The Rebel… etc., op. cit.***

40 ***Dorset … Dispatch, 15/10/24. Courtesy of Maureen Attwool:***

> "Instead of appealing to the builders only, Mr. Wheatley called both sides together to see if they could work together efficiently, amicably and swiftly. They must have houses where people could live in a state of human decency, and not as at present, often in conditions not fit for animals to live in, conditions that must breed much of the crime, insanity, and horrors paraded in the police court. Mr. Wheatley's was the only scheme that offered a possibility of over-coming the housing shortage."

41 ***Ibid.:***

> "They were told that there was more unemployment than under Conservative administration. The people who said that were telling an untruth; they were juggling with figures. Instead of unemployment increasing it had decreased, and they were able to say that during eight months of Labour administration that there had been an average of a hundred thousand less unemployed than during the corresponding period of last year under a Conservative Government. And thousands were put on the 'live register' at the Employment Bureaux, who were not there during the Conservative administration."

42 ***Ibid.:***

> "Dealing with the work for peace of the Labour Government, Mr. Risdon claimed that the contribution of Ramsay MacDonald for world peace was greater perhaps than that of any other single individual in the whole world (applause)."

43 ***Ibid.:***

"On the question of agriculture which was a question which would have to be faced in this constituency they found that another pledge had been fulfilled by Labour who had set up the County Wages Committees and the National Wages Board. They were in an attenuated form as compared with previously, but they would give the agricultural worker some sort of a regulation of his wages which would, they hoped, stop him from going down to the degrading conditions which had prevailed during the last few years."

44 ***Dorset ... Dispatch, 18/10/24. Courtesy of Maureen Attwool:***

"At an enthusiastic meeting at Owermoigne, Mr. Risdon said the Labour Party were a harmless set of people, and he wished to remind his hearers that for the last eight months their affairs had been in the care of the Labour Party. (hear hear) Yet nothing terrible had happened. Not only in this country, but in other countries, a Labour Government had been returned. (hear hear)."

45 ***Ibid.:***

"Questions were invited, and a gentleman asked: What has Labour done for the working man? Mr. Risdon replied that the Labour Government had removed a burden of 30 millions from the table of the working man (applause).

The questioner: I am talking about the farm labourer who gets 30s. per week. Was it not promised that the cost of living should be reduced?

Mr. Risdon: the tax was taken off, but you have to thank the blood-sucking combines.

Mr. Risdon said he would support drastic action against the profiteers, who were committing a worse crime than murder."

46 ***Dorset ... Dispatch, 15/10/24. Courtesy of Maureen Attwool***

47 ***Dorset ... Dispatch, 18/10/24. Courtesy of Maureen Attwool***

48 According to Oswald Mosley, who was "bitterly disappointed at having failed to pull off what would have been a spectacular upset against the national trend", "a downpour of rain washed the lifeless body of the last of the Chamberlains back to Westminster." [***Oswald Mosley, op. cit.***]

"Polling began very quietly at eight a.m., and the wretched weather did not improve matters very much afterwards. Here were some of the morning reports at the polling stations:—

GUILDHALL— 'Very few polled in the morning; not 200 up to 12 o'clock.'

HOLY TRINITY SCHOOLS— 'Quietest election ever known; rain keeping back many voters.'

MELCOMBE REGIS SCHOOLS— 'Very quiet all the morning, but improvement later on.'

ST. JOHN'S SCHOOL— 'Better than we expected, considering the appalling weather.'

CROMWELL-ROAD SCHOOLS— 'Little doing in the morning and afternoon, but great rush in the evening.'

The Conservatives had a fleet of cars at their disposal, which brought hundreds to the polling booths who otherwise would probably not have stirred out of doors. … A large number of cars were on active service at Swanage during the day, and, as heavy rain fell during the whole of the afternoon and evening, the cars proved invaluable in bringing voters to the poll. So many cars were offered that it was found possible to send some to Wareham and Corfe to lend assistance there.

In the St. John's, Weymouth, district, hundreds abstained from voting, though many lived within less than 100 yards of the polling station."

Southern Times, 01/11/24. Courtesy of Maureen Attwool

49 The final voting figures were: Yerburgh (Con): 13,900; Risdon (Lab): 5,821. Majority: 8,079, on a turnout of 19,721 [out of a total electorate of 28,810]. At the previous election, on a turnout of 20,632, the Conservative majority had been 5,084, so much smaller, but the Labour vote had been only 3,602, so Wilfred had theoretically gained approximately 2,220 of the previous Liberal vote of 5,973, rather than all of them going to the Conservatives, in the face of exhortations to the contrary:

"Three-cornered elections which offered clear tactical advantages to the Socialists have been officially discouraged on both sides, and, rather than lend a hand to the enemies of the Constitution, party organisers have been enjoined to withdraw their candidates and leave a clear field in which to engage the Socialists. The appeal of the Liberals in South and West Dorset was, therefore, foredoomed. Both divisions were typical cases in which the seat could not possibly be won by an Asquithian candidate, and the only effect of such a nomination would be to give a valuable strategic lift to the real enemy. Mr. Buckpitt [in West Dorset] has come out boldly as a Liberal who finds it consistent with his principles to stand side by side with Major Colfox in his struggle with the by no means inconsiderable element of Socialism which has grown up in this division.

We suggest to the Liberals of South Dorset that Mr. Buckpitt's example is one that they may usefully follow in such a crisis as this. Major Yerburgh is frankly in no danger whatever against such a candidate as the Labour Party have chosen as their champion. But it is important, in view of the vital issues involved, that there should be no doubt about the poll to be cast in this election. All who are not Socialists are appealed to to close their ranks, whatever their party labels may be, and even, if necessary, to endure the temporary hardship of a political negation in order to win a decisive victory in this class war, and to keep the Constitution together.

In all parts of the country Unionists and Liberals alike are accommodating themselves to the present exigencies. In this we see the best hope of the complete discomfiture of the Socialism which is masquerading as Labour in so many divisions. In constituencies where the Socialist is opposed only by a Liberal the Unionists will find ample justification for giving their votes to the Liberal, and by the same tactical plan the Liberals will not fail to give their support to the Unionist candidates where there is a straight fight between a Conservative and a Socialist. The issue in those cases is clear, and Mr. Buckpitt has given a courageous lead to his political friends how to escape being impaled on the horns of a dilemma."

Southern Times, 25/10/24. Courtesy of Maureen Attwool

50 The Labour Party lost 50 seats overall, enabling Baldwin to form his second Conservative Government. Unsurprisingly, this caused a rally in "the markets":

"The results of the General Election have exceeded the most optimistic forecasts of the Unionist leaders. ... The victory of the Conservative party at the election caused a general advance in prices, particularly of British funds, home railway securities, and the shares of big industrial concerns. The effect on the exchanges was even more marked, the pound appreciating in terms of virtually every foreign currency."

Southern Times, 01/11/24. Courtesy of Maureen Attwool

51 ***Oswald Mosley, op. cit.***

Jim Simmons also offered a depiction of the hysteria whipped up by the Conservatives:

"The spirit of victory was in the air - until the last few days when I felt an undercurrent - the 'Red Bogey' was having its effect; the Tories had played it up for all they were worth; Lady Steel-Maitland [the wife of the Birmingham, Erdington, candidate, Sir Arthur Steel-Maitland, Simmons's opponent], addressing a meeting of women, held up a poster, embellished with a skull and crossbones that screamed under the caption 'SOCIALISM!!', Blasphemy, Revolution, Bloodshed, Sedition, Bolshevism, etc., etc.; in her peroration she said: 'In Russia they are atheists, the Labour candidate supports Russia; the Soviet Government has nationalised women - the Labour candidate supports the Soviet Government. Ladies, you cannot vote for a man who would destroy our religion, homes and morality.' [Syllogism of the worst kind: Simmons's wife, Beatrice was at the meeting and challenged these assertions, and was ejected.]

Soap Box Evangelist, op. cit.

52 ***Southern Times, 01/11/24. Courtesy of Maureen Attwool:***

"Mr. RISDON, who seconded the vote of thanks, said he wished to associate himself with the expressions made by Major Yerburgh on the help that had been so cheerfully afforded by all the officials. He also particularly wished to thank those voters who had turned out in the downfall to vote for him. He realised how difficult it was for many of the voters to get to the poll, and he had for them the greatest admiration in the enthusiasm they had shown. Although he had lost the election they were not defeated, and they never would be defeated. (cries of hear, hear)

The crowd here broke out into singing 'Three cheers for the Red, White and Blue.'

Mr. RISDON, concluding, said there had been some straight hitting, hard hitting, and frequent hitting, and he thought they had both enjoyed it thoroughly. (hear, hear)"

53 ***Labour ... Wars, op. cit.***

54 Matthew Worley explains the organisational setup:

"Both the organisers and the regions remained firmly under the remit of the party centre; the organisers were paid from London, had no regional offices, and functioned as co-ordinators rather than political decision makers. Subsequently, they served to take many of the day-to-day administrative responsibilities away from Head Office; acting as a point of contact between centre & locality, while more generally undertaking the management of election campaigns and ensuring the maintenance of the regional party apparatus in-between times. The regional organisers solved local problems, helped with appointments, and advised local agents & officers. In short, they sustained the party apparatus below the realm of Head Office.

As a keen centraliser and close ally to [Arthur] Henderson, [national agent Egerton] Wake directed the extension of the party across the country, orchestrating a series of regional & local conferences to consolidate party organisation and disseminate central party policy. These would seek to rally local support via the appearance of a known party leader - often Arthur Henderson - and simultaneously allow Head Office to circulate (and ensure the adoption of) a broadly uniform political perspective. From his position as secretary to the NEC [National Executive Committee] sub-committee on organisation, Wake endorsed and recommended Labour candidates, reported on the party's by-election preparations, and helped in the selection of local party agents."

Ibid.

Arthur Henderson, "in a real sense", was "the creator of the modern Labour Party". As a result of writing the party's constitution and setting up its organisation after the war, he ensured that the Labour Party could enrol individual members. John Beckett was only a member by virtue of his membership of the ILP, which goes some way to explain the rather ill-defined, and often fractious relationship between the two parties. Beckett took pride in the fact that he never actually joined the Labour Party, for which he had no respect or liking at all, and "which he considered a dreary and uninspired machine." [***The Rebel..., op. cit.***] In 1921, the ILP affiliated to the Labour Party, bringing some 35,000 members, although this fell to 30,000 by 1925. [***Labour ... Wars, op. cit.***]

This is contradicted somewhat by another source, Arthur Marwick; "The Independent Labour Party in the Nineteen Twenties", in ***Bulletin of the Institute of Historical Research, vol. XXXV, 1962, pp. 62-74:*** "... for the two great post-war membership booms of 1918-20 [ref.: Total membership rose from 30,000 to 45,000. ILP, ***Report of the Annual Conference, 1918, p. 26;*** ILP, ***Rept. of the Ann. Conf., 1920, p. 18***, and statistics in FJP {Statistical material relating to party finances, etc., in the possession of former ILP general secretary, Mr. Francis Johnson (FJP)}] and 1923-5. [ref.: When total membership rose to around 56,000. ILP, ***Rept. of the Ann. Conf., 1925, p. 97.***]"

55 ***Labour ... Wars, op. cit.:***

"... the cost of appointing just one agent could prove problematic; ... More often, part-time agents were appointed for the duration of an election contest, while many parties relied on the centrally appointed regional organiser to help co-ordinate and manage their affairs."

56 ***Labour's Grass Roots, op. cit.:***

"... it was exceptional for candidates to receive official union sponsorship, and indeed, became more so after the early '20s."

57 ***Ibid.:***

"Under the 1918 Labour Party constitution, divisional Labour Parties comprised, essentially, two elements: affiliated organisations (chiefly Trade Union branches) and individual members. Divisional Labour Parties in the south west were often weak in both respects in this period. This helps to explain the nature of Labour politics in the region."

58 ***Ibid.:***

"What, if any, were the chief common characteristics of Labour grass root politics in south west England in this period? First, the party in the south west was not particularly left wing; moderation tended to be the dominant trend. South west divisional Labour Parties were not, at least before the Popular Front agitation of the later 1930s, much affected by left wing campaigns; nor were they notably critical of Labour's efforts in government in 1924 & 1929-'30. Fred Gould might have been 'caught up in ideas of "Workers' Control" in industry' while secretary of the small NUBSO branch in Midsomer Norton during the Great War, but he showed no signs of radical leanings as Labour candidate and MP in the 1920s …"

59 ***Ibid.***

60 ***Ibid.:***

"The region was not left totally to its own devices. In 1920, the national party machine was reorganised and a new regional structure was created. Under this scheme, Great Britain was divided into 9 areas. Area 6 (later 'F'), 'South-Western', comprised the 4 counties [Cornwall, Devon, Dorset & Somerset] plus Wiltshire & Bristol. Like all the other areas, it had a district (later regional) organiser and a woman organiser. Their job was to work under the direction of party headquarters to advise divisional Labour Parties, develop organisation where it existed and to establish it where it did not, to assist in the training of agents, and 'generally to co-operate in the organisation work of the Party as required by the Head Office'. The first regional organisers were J.H. Edwards & Annie Townley."

61 ***Ibid.***

2: FROM NEW HORIZONS TO NEW PARTY

Wilfred Risdon could have been forgiven for thinking that he was not cut out to be a Member of Parliament, at least for the foreseeable future: notwithstanding the overwhelming circumstances, alluded to in the previous chapter, which militated against his success, it would have been perfectly natural for him to feel somewhat despondent with the result, and that, perhaps, he should concentrate on what he knew and, demonstrably, did best, which was political organising and electoral support work. Although it is difficult to pinpoint a precise moment when his association with Birmingham began, it is entirely logical to suppose that Clem Jones, the erstwhile divisional Labour Party agent in Smethwick, who had replaced the incumbent south west regional organiser, J. H. Edwards, during that election year, will no doubt have given Bill much support and encouragement, and very probably regaled him with details of the glorious fight currently taking place in Birmingham, where Oswald Mosley [**1**], a recent convert to socialism [**2**], had tried, and only very narrowly failed [**3**], to dislodge one of the highest profile members of the "Birmingham Caucus", Neville Chamberlain [**4**]. Unfortunately, specific documentary references to a timescale to encompass Wilfred's graduation from a West Country to a Birmingham sphere of activity are very hard to come by. Several commentators, who either knew and worked with Wilfred in later years [**5**], or who interviewed him for publications about Mosley's fascist period [**6**] say that Wilfred established a working relationship with Mosley quite early on in Birmingham but, frustratingly, they do not specify a start point. It must therefore be accepted as a realistic possibility that Wilfred might have had 'feet in both camps', as it were, for two or three years after his election defeat, but it perhaps made sense to take up residence in Birmingham in 1925, so that he could develop his associations with the city while still also serving the interests of existing and potential Labour voters in the West Country, which is effectively 'next door' geographically. In his 1940 Defence Regulation 18B appeal hearing [**Appendix D**] Wilfred makes specific reference to Fircroft College [**7**], which still exists, and is situated between the Bournville and Selly Oak areas in Birmingham, south west of the city centre [**8**]. Originally, Fircroft was "a residential College for working men", in the words of Wilfred's chief inquisitor, Mr. Norman Birkett, KC [**9**], who had experience of it dating back to 1911, which was only 2 years after its foundation by George Cadbury junior [who was still running it in Wilfred's time] in his former family home, "a beautiful Edwardian building set in six acres of gardens" [**10**]. Wilfred states that, prior to 1928, "I used to go there [Fircroft] a lot when I was organising the South West counties of England.", so it seems more logical that he would have struck up a working relationship with an establishment in Birmingham while he was living there, while still travelling south & west, as the situation demanded. He might well have been taking classes in political education for working men, something he was very familiar with; this 'roving brief' also probably meant that he was becoming more involved with the Independent Labour Party, for a variety of reasons.

Wilfred was a staunch trade unionist, in support of which he never wavered for the next fifteen years, and the Labour Party effectively grew out of the political organisation of the unions, but he was still, at heart, an evangelist for socialism, and the ILP was the vehicle with which he felt its ethos of societal change could be achieved; also, although it is virtually impossible to get any sense of how much this might have been perceived at the time by those involved, the force for change which was the ILP was already steadily declining [**11**] so perhaps Wilfred heeded a call to rally to the cause and support the radical alternative. However, and whenever, the rapport with Mosley began, and whatever Wilfred's position, if any, within Mosley's electoral organisation was in those first months, the reality was that Mosley took himself off with his wife, Cimmie, after the Ladywood disappointment, to travel and study in India [**12**], returning in time for the 1925 ILP Easter Conference at Gloucester, so perhaps this was when he and Wilfred met for the first time? There is no reason to suppose that Wilfred did not attend such an important event in the calendar for a Socialist, and he was certainly no rank & file ground level member. Before his departure, Mosley had revealed an ambitious plan to his Ladywood supporters [**13**], so when he returned, his plans, which might have been Wilfred's first experience of him and his vision, were fully formed [**14**], although, according to Mosley [**15**], they were "discussed during debates" in April, then "stated in detail in a speech at the I.L.P. Summer School in August".

Although somewhat overshadowed by the subsequent decade and its momentous events, the decade comprising the 1920s was nonetheless full of political, economic and social upheaval. Almost inevitably, the exigencies forced upon the country by the arguably avoidable spending of the war had produced a slump, with its concomitant unemployment, protested in demonstrations [**16**] and there were "demands for the classic remedies of economy and deflation" [**17**]. One of the latter-day pioneers of the socialist movement, George Lansbury, was jailed on the first of September, 1921, along with 29 other councillors, for refusing to pay to London County Council its 'precept' [contributions for common expenses of the county] as long as Poplar Council's burden of poor relief was so heavy: "embarrassing prisoners as they were", they were held for nearly six weeks [**18**]. The contracting economy produced by the slump revived enthusiasm for protective trade tariffs, used quite widely during the war [and not entirely withdrawn thereafter] and which precipitated the election at the end of 1923. Labour specifically, and socialism in general, had an uphill struggle still, but despite that, the forces of the Establishment didn't have it all their own way: there was disharmony abroad, though they were generally united in their opposition to the alternative: "Bolshevism, the triumph of the Socialists" [**19**]. The revolutions in Russia had both excited and frightened the British socialist movement; could democracy be achieved without dictatorship, could socialism be achieved by constitutional, democratic means? Grasping the nettle, the ILP entered into negotiations to achieve 'Socialist Unity', and a common front against allied intervention in Russia, early in 1919, with forerunners of the British Communist Party, the British Socialist Party and the Socialist Labour Party; they were unsuccessful, however, "partly over differences of opinion on the use of parliamentary action." [**20**]

The academic argument which was embodied in the philosophical and ideological differences between the political parties, namely the belief of the Conservatives [and, to some extent, the Liberals], that commerce and its champions should be supported because it is good for society as a whole; as against the argument of the socialists [and the more socialistically-minded Liberals], that society should be supported because it is good for commerce, might not have been defined in those terms in this decade, but it was certainly relevant: the problem was the speed of progress. Now that socialism and its protagonists had entered the field of debate, the conservative establishment, for all it might have achieved some societal improvement in a slightly condescending, patrician way hitherto, could not rely on its preference for 'business as usual' going unchallenged: unfortunately, that only served to bog progress down in a mire of very often unnecessarily fractious debate. Socialism [or, at least, the British version of it] was always postulated on the premise of a good life for all members of society, but those who were at the bottom of the heap, as it were, needed the most help; the crucial issue was how this was to be achieved: direct action, or parliamentary democracy? Certain enlightened industrialists, such as Robert Owen [**21**], had taken the view that, apart from it being his Christian duty, it made sense pragmatically that well fed and comfortably housed workers would be more productive; his ethos was championed, very probably not for the first time, and definitely not the last time, by the 1923 chairman of the ILP, Sidney Webb, in that he "preached not 'class war', but the ancient doctrine of human brotherhood", as reported in ***The Times*** of 27th of June, 1923 [**22**]. The problem was that all this garnering of support for socialist parliamentary action with its "inevitability of gradualness" took time, and Mosley, notwithstanding his growing dislike of party politics, was painfully aware of this. While there was no immediate prospect of returning to Parliament in 1925, apart from building up his support base in Birmingham, a process in which Wilfred's knowledge and methodical approach will have proved invaluable, Mosley concentrated his attention on the economic debate in general, and that ironic scourge of the working man specifically, unemployment. Contrary to the later general perception of him, outside the circle of his followers, as an arrogant and distant megalomaniac, in Skidelsky's opinion he was, at this time, "moved by strong humanitarian feelings" [**23**]. The ***Birmingham Proposals***, or as they came to be known, ***Revolution by Reason***, were not solely Mosley's work, as he later readily acknowledged in his autobiography, ***My Life*** [**24**]. He had read, and obviously understood, the work of Keynes [**25**], whose concepts Mosley "and others" considered "basic economics", but "it was necessary to do more" [**26**].

Mosley considered that his own "chief contributions" to the ***Proposals*** were three, all of which concerned banking and the control of the money supply and credit [**27**]; however, according to Robert Skidelsky, Mosley's plan was more Keynesian than the theories of three of the ILP's leading economic thinkers, J. A. Hobson, E. F. Wise and H. N. Brailsford, which were known as "underconsumptionist": "it concentrated in the first instance on increasing total demand, not in redistributing demand from one section of the community to another." [**28**] Ladywood and other Birmingham branches of the Labour organisation were called upon to support a composite resolution which Mosley moved at the 1925 ILP Easter Conference, calling for the nationalisation of the banking system, a strategy which Skidelsky says was implicit in the Leninist analysis: "Lenin had stressed the primacy of banking in the capitalist system. Banks controlled industry because they provided the credit necessary for it to carry on. If the Government controlled the banks, it would control industry without the need for wholesale nationalisation." [**29**] Industrial relations, already frequently on a knife-edge, were deteriorating; two weeks after Mosley's speech in April 1925, Winston Churchill returned the economy of the country to the gold standard. Keynes foresaw disaster [**30**]; a general strike threatened in protest at the coal-owners' intention to reduce miners' wages, at the end of June, was only averted when the Government promised on the 31st of July to pay the industry a subsidy pending the report of a royal commission of inquiry: in a bitter speech at Southport, Mosley argued that, even if wages came down, it would not save the mining industry [**31**]. One commentator pointed out a few years later that, had the unions, at that time, felt strong enough to dictate terms, the government would have been powerless to resist [**32**]. The General Strike materialised less than a year later, again precipitated by unrest in the coal industry. That national upheaval is too large a subject for the scope of this work, but its implementation was very strongly felt in Birmingham. It is not known if Wilfred took an active rôle in its organisation in Birmingham, where "most of the strike committee were rounded up on charges of stirring up disaffection" [**33**], but the miners stayed out on strike well into the autumn; this allowed Mosley, who had been ambivalent about the General Strike, to throw himself wholeheartedly into support for the miners, a cause which would have been close to Wilfred's heart, and brought him into contact with Arthur Cook, "the fiery miners' secretary" [**34**], with whom Wilfred would have had an instant rapport, due to the similarity of their backgrounds [**35**].

The year 1926 also saw Mosley's return to Parliament, in which Wilfred will undoubtedly have been involved. Mosley had only just managed to escape from being dragooned into candidacy for the Forest of Dean constituency with his honour intact the previous June [**36**], but he didn't particularly relish kicking his heels until another chance to skirmish with Chamberlain in 1929 either; he did want to remain loyal to Birmingham however, and in November 1926, the sitting Labour MP for Smethwick [just 'over the border'; therefore, outside the city boundary, an emotive move], John Davison, an official of the Ironfounders' Society [**37**], duly obliged by retiring on grounds of ill-health. After the technicalities were ironed out, Mosley was adopted [**38**] and, despite the inevitable 'dirty tricks', was returned at the by-election with a thumping majority [**39**]. Nearly a year before this, Mosley and his wife had spent time in America [**40**], a visit which was to affect profoundly his economic thinking, and as soon as he was back 'in harness', he began promoting credit expansion and "managed capitalism", which helped to set the stage for future union unrest [**41**]: given that Wilfred was a professed syndicalist [**42**], it is not hard to understand why he will have been fairly easily won over to an ethos of direct action, even if it did entail state interference in union affairs, an idea which was not necessarily anathema to socialists, however.

During 1927, the disjunction between the Labour Party and the ILP continued and, if anything, increased; Wilfred will have used all his knowledge and charm to stimulate debate and galvanise enthusiasm in both camps, while at the same time mitigating such acrimony as might arise between them. As Matthew Worley tells us, there was still continual overlap and cross-pollination [**43**], but it looked rather like the Labour Party was beginning to gain the upper hand, in spite of its hitherto shaky parliamentary performance; the main factor was the increase in size and consequent influence of the divisional parties, and a growing perception that the ILP was the home of unrealistic ideologues: perhaps even anarchists, given the flirtation with communism, notwithstanding the actual reluctance of the ILP collectively to commit to such a thing. Wilfred understood Marxian thinking, but he was no Communist, and he used his elevated sphere of influence within the ILP to best effect.

The main event of 1928 for the Socialists was the ***Cook-Maxton Manifesto***. The description given by Skidelsky is sketchy, to say the least [**44**], but Paul Davies is rather more fulsome, in his biography of Cook [**45**]. At the end of 1927, the Government had set up a series of consultations, with the aim of investigating and mitigating the current industrial unrest [no doubt in the Government's favour, if at all possible], and the two main participants were founder of Imperial Chemical Industries [ICI] and head of Amalgamated Anthracite Collieries in South Wales, Sir Alfred Mond, and TUC president Ben Turner, hence they came to be known as the 'Mond-

Turner Talks'. Cook peremptorily dismissed Mond's invitation to the Miners' Federation of Great Britain [MFGB] in November, to participate in the discussions, but on December 20th, he was overruled by the TUC General Council [**46**]. However, at the end of March 1928, the ILP 'Clydesiders' and William Gallacher of the recently constituted Communist Party of Great Britain [CPGB] determined to take a stand in support of Cook, and after a meeting at the House of Commons between Cook and the Scottish radicals, it was decided to issue a manifesto bearing the names of ILP chairman James Maxton and Arthur Cook [**47**]; apparently, Maxton had not consulted his Executive over this [**48**]. He said that the campaign to publicise the manifesto [and his supporting pamphlet called ***Mond's Manacles***] should be "conducted rather in the manner of a religious revival" [**49**].

Ultimately, the Mond-Turner initiative was a failure; for all the willingness which the TUC had shown towards conciliation, the employers' organisations rejected both invitations to participate in discussions, and the joint report produced by the group, and it was seen as a defeat for Arthur Cook's industrial policy [**50**]. By now, according to Wilfred's own definitive assertion, he had entered his "years in the Midlands", although he was based in Birmingham; in 1930, he gave his address as Acock's Green, and there is every reason to suppose that he was there at least a year before that [**51**]. The first known documentary confirmation of Wilfred's arrival in the top echelons of the ILP hierarchy is found in the minute book for the West Bromwich branch of the ILP, a record of an Executive Committee [EC] meeting held on June 28th 1929, when he is referred to as "the new organising Secretary for M.D.C." [the Midlands Divisional Council **52**]. Unfortunately, records from ILP branches are rather patchy, so it is difficult to get an exact picture of Wilfred's involvement at this time, but there are several entries in the minute book for this branch that mention Wilfred, over the course of 18 months [see **Appendix B** for details], at the end of which time Wilfred still had feet in two camps, but this time the camps were rather further apart than the Labour Party and the ILP.

Although the ILP had come into existence before the Labour Party [and its precursor, the Labour Representation Committee or LRC], it is harder to discern the exact structure & formation of the ILP at any given time; according to Matthew Worley [**53**], after the reorganisation of the Labour Party by Arthur Henderson in 1918, which arguably set it on course for electoral success in fairly short order, "the loose but federal structure of the ILP, in which local sections varied considerably in terms of the political & social character, meant a coherent ILP policy and strategy were both difficult to discern and implement." [**54**] As always, terminology could be confusing: Wilfred was Midlands Organiser for the Midlands Divisional Council, but to the Labour Party, a division was not the same thing; it was analogous with a parliamentary constituency, which in itself comprised several or many local organisations. The ILP divisions were analogous to Labour regions or districts, and in 1925, according to a website called "hayes peoples history" [sic] **[55]**, the divisions, which had selected delegates for the 1925 National Labour Party Women's Conference in Birmingham, comprised: Yorkshire, Midlands, East Anglia, London & South, Wales and Lancashire; quite why Scotland was excluded is a mystery, and it begs the question of whether the south west had also been excluded, for unknown reasons, or if it meant that there was no south west division, and thus the requisite responsibilities were apportioned between London & South and the Midlands, which would give Wilfred a huge area to cover. Another commentator **[56]** tells us definitively that there were nine ILP divisions, but without specifying them, so it is still a matter for conjecture whether the south west had its own division.

Nonetheless, this would have meant that he was occupied with ILP work on a full time basis, which wouldn't have left much slack to accommodate Oswald Mosley's needs, as & when they arose, but as it happened, Mosley was very busy at Westminster with business of his own; it wasn't until 1930 that he was planning to make a decisive break with the past and take a leap into the political wilderness. Just because he was again a Member of Parliament however, he didn't neglect his constituency **[57]**, so it is very likely that he will have renewed his political association and, to some extent, social friendship with Wilfred: at this time, the Mosleys held annual 'get-togethers' at their country property in Denham, Buckinghamshire, and although they were primarily for Mosley's Smethwick supporters, party faithful such as Wilfred were included as well **[58]**. There were also ILP Summer Schools, which were a very well-established tradition, and it was at one of these that Wilfred met the woman who was to become his wife, some years hence, but of that, more later, as it deserves its own chapter.

Relations between the two significant arms of the labour movement were still somewhat difficult, akin to the ILP driving, with its foot on the accelerator [but not steering], and the Labour Party trying to minimise progress which was in danger of becoming too rapid, with its foot on the brake. Around the time of the General Strike, the ILP published ***Socialism in our Time*** **[59]** and ***The Living Wage***, which was described by Arthur Marwick **[60]** as "one of the socialist classics of the inter-war years". It goes without saying that none but the most radical and potentially revolutionary socialists expected ideas such as those propounded in these publications to be implemented any way other than piecemeal or without a fight. A new Labour Party programme, partly the result of ILP encouragement [or, alternatively, goading!] was approved in principle at the 1928 Labour Party Conference at Birmingham, and the programme, guaranteed to ruffle feathers by declaring the party to be a socialist party, was called ***Labour and the Nation*** **[61]**.

The election which had been expected for 1929 duly took place, and this time, just for a change, it was held in late spring, instead of the customary autumn with its foul weather, so Labour, still hampered by limited resources and the consequent lack of transport for election day, hoped for fine weather. Outside the hothouse of Birmingham, "[u]nemployment and policies for world peace dominated the campaign. Lloyd George's pledge to conquer unemployment gave the Liberals great confidence. Labour, however, simply annexed Lloyd George's programme, claiming that it would carry it out better than he. The Conservatives were left rather short-winded.…Yet it was a dull campaign. Stunts and alarms were lacking." [**62**] Mosley would, no doubt, have taken issue with any suggestion of hijacking of other parties' programmes! In Birmingham [and the surrounding areas], Wilfred will have been very busy; Mosley was aiming for nine Labour seats, out of the twelve available, instead of the lamentable one gained in 1924. Mosley used his own resources to finance the campaign and candidates; he also made it possible for the Labour Party to produce a series of four-page election sheets throughout the city all through the campaign [**63**].

One of the highlights of the campaign was Mosley's debate with the Conservative MP for Handsworth, Commander Oliver Locker-Lampson, at a venue well acquainted with rowdy political meetings, the Rag Market, a huge hangar of a multi-purpose industrial building in the heart of Birmingham, now long gone, as a regrettable consequence of well-intentioned 1960s urban redevelopment. Locker-Lampson's speech was both silly [claiming that the General Strike was manufactured in Moscow] and insulting, calling Mosley "'Comrade' Mosley because of his Communistic leanings', leading to "repeated booings from Labour supporters, with Mosley repeatedly appealing to the audience to give Locker-Lampson a fair hearing. In his own speech, Mosley made mincemeat of his opponent." [**64**] Mosley increased his majority at Smethwick to 7,340, but he was somewhat chagrined that the fear which he had publicly [but humorously] expressed to his local supporters, of his wife beating his majority at Stoke on Trent, proved to be well-founded: Cimmie's majority was 7,580. That apart, there was reason to celebrate: six of the nine seats were secured, and the biggest upset was the defeat of Baldwin's Minister of Labour, Sir Arthur Steel-Maitland, at Erdington, by Jim Simmons: Mosley was ecstatic [**65**]. For the first time, Labour was the largest party in Parliament with 287 seats, and took office for the second time, although not all Labour MPs came back with high hopes about "the potential for Labour-sponsored socialist change"; James Maxton, Member for Glasgow Bridgeton, for example [**66**].

While Wilfred was dealing with a never-ending round of quotidian procedural matters for the ILP in Birmingham & the Midlands [**Appendix B**] Mosley was inhabiting somewhat more lofty echelons in hallowed halls. According to Skidelsky, "Mosley … expected office and got it." [**67**]

However, it was, in a manner of speaking, 'lose some; win some'; Ramsay MacDonald had considered Mosley for the plum post he would have relished, Foreign Secretary, but the Prime Minister was also aware of how many other senior men he had to satisfy, so he appointed party manager Arthur Henderson; although Mosley's quasi-ministerial post of Chancellor of the Duchy of Lancaster was outside the Cabinet, it did have the compensation of enabling him to fulfil some sort of unspoken promise, tackling the ever-worsening problem of unemployment, "a job for which he felt himself uniquely qualified." [**68**] It would be extremely easy to devote a large section of this chapter to this arguably pivotal period but, without wishing to oversimplify the events and their repercussions, I would prefer to only sketch them in lightly, as Wilfred's involvement in them was negligible, but their effect upon him at their culmination was very significant. Both Skidelsky [***Oswald Mosley, op. cit.***] and Cross [***The Fascists in Britain, op. cit.***] deal with this period in some detail [although Cross is somewhat more concise].

Mosley brought in two of Wilfred's erstwhile Birmingham colleagues Allan Young [**69**] and John Strachey [**70**]; Young as his private secretary, and Strachey as his parliamentary private secretary: there is every reason to believe that this was strategic as much as tactical, if not more so, given their previous ideological contributions and administrative prowess. Mosley was eager for action, but the new Lord Privy Seal, J. H. ["Jimmy"] Thomas [**71**], as his nominal superior, exemplified the caution operated by the previous Labour administration. Predictably, the point of contention was how reversal of the upward trend of unemployment and the desired economic recovery was going to be financed: Thomas appeared to be at something of a loss to see how this could be achieved domestically [**72**], so he pinned his hopes on a recovery some time in the near future of the export trade, especially with one of our traditionally loyal imperial trading partners, Canada [**73**]. Mosley wasn't satisfied with pipe dreams however; he wanted immediate action which, of course, didn't materialise. The main problem, in Mosley's mind, which would be another aspect of his later political ethos, was that he could only persuade local authorities to carry out plans for local works schemes providing much-needed employment, recommended by central government, not order them to [**74**]. Not all of his colleagues were convinced of the efficacy of his solution [**75**]; but he did earn praise, both as a team player, [**76**] and for supporting a traditional socialist ideal [**77**] during this period.

By the end of 1929, it was becoming clear to Mosley that he needed to take a firm hand on the tiller himself, and steer events in a more propitious direction [**78**], but this unilateral and, arguably, autocratic action was almost guaranteed to ensure overly critical examination of his suggestions, and very likely to cause internecine unpleasantness [**79**]. Inevitably, news of what had become known as the ***Mosley Memorandum*** leaked out to the Press, which ratcheted up the impetus for a definite resolution of the issue, one way or another [**80**]. It took over two months for the Cabinet to begin considering the document, although there was already a damning assessment on the table weighing against it, and the final rejection did not emanate from the Cabinet until the middle of May: it literally gathered dust on a shelf [**81**]. There was widespread support for Mosley and condemnation of Thomas from Labour's left wing [**82**] but to Mosley, the situation either seemed hopeless, or he determined that the only effective course of action was to resign, [or perhaps both **83**] which he did, on the 20th of May 1930, and this gave him the opportunity to set out his case in public, on his own terms, first to the Parliamentary Labour Party [PLP] and then in the House, in his resignation speech [**84**]. The crucial question, [although a strategy had already been quite comprehensively considered and was significantly well-formed] was: what to do next, now that he was a free agent, independent again, albeit still nominally a socialist?

While all of this was going on 150 miles away, Wilfred was by no means idle. Birmingham was frequently home to large and important political gatherings, and 1930 was no exception. Easter was traditionally when the annual ILP Conference took place, and Birmingham was the venue for the 1930 gathering; the responsibility of organising this significant event fell to Wilfred, and he acquitted himself with customary success. This wasn't the only party event around this time for which Wilfred was responsible; the Midlands Divisional Conference took place at Leicester on January the 25th & 26th, 1930, for which delegates were requested from the local party organisations by him [**Appendix B**]. A 60-page souvenir booklet was produced for the Easter conference, with acknowledgments in the introduction including "the debt of gratitude to our comrade Joseph Southall, for preparing the very effective cover design." This cover incorporated a sketched head & shoulders portrait of James Maxton in pride of place at the top, and a small line drawing of Birmingham Town Hall at the bottom, supported by a rock-hammer on one side, and an artist's palette, complete with brushes, on the other! The overall effect is a pastiche of William Morris, a socialist hero.

There was also an article [see **Appendix C** for the full text], full of fraternal exhortation, under the heading "GREETINGS FROM M.D.C." and a photograph of what one presumes was the full complement of the council, including only one woman, sitting next to George Butler, the Chairman, whose importance warranted a separate cameo-style portrait [looking probably twenty years older than his actual age of maybe 25!] which, in true democratic fashion, was larger than Wilfred's passport-style head & shoulders portrait denoting his position as Midlands Organiser. Curiously, Wilfred's name is spelled "Wilfrid" whenever it is written in full [including the photograph caption], which, given his normal lack of obvious ostentation, seems like an aberrant affectation. In the group photograph, he certainly does appear very relaxed in his pose, louche even, compared to his twelve comrades, leaning back on a bench with his hands in his pockets and his legs crossed, an easy smile on his face. His 'official' portrait is, understandably, somewhat more formal, but the overall effect is almost androgynous, with his luxuriant wavy hair and full lips. The contents of the booklet include, in addition to the conference programme, a wide selection of articles both educational and informative [see **Appendix C** for the full list], such as a ***Brief History of Birmingham***, and reports on three different socialist schools. The conference, which encompassed three full days, included three separate gatherings of the main executive responsible for the running of the party, the National Administrative Council [NAC].

Without access to the official ***Report of the Annual Conference***, it is only possible to glean a few indications of what transpired there, but they are all significant. The resolution with perhaps the most beneficial and far-reaching consequences was that for a National Health Service [**85**], although this had certainly been mooted before 1930, and with an ironic "inevitability of gradualness" took another 18 years to see implementation; a six-year war economy did nothing to help of course. Rumblings about disaffiliation from the Labour Party, on the grounds of differences of ideology and the policies necessary to implement it, had been evident within the ILP for some time, although there is no specific reference to it in connection with Wilfred in the documentary sample of his dealings with the West Bromwich party [**Appendix B**]; the measure which had the most significant [and, eventually, arguably disastrous] consequences for the ILP was Maxton's seemingly authoritarian [or, at the very least, doctrinaire] resolution that the ILP group in Parliament, which comprised 140 Members, should be reconstructed on the basis of ILP policy: a form of continuous whipping, in a parliamentary sense. The resolution passed, but only a small minority of the parliamentary group acceded [86], and served to hasten the terminal decline of the cohesion of the party which, in truth, had been set in train well before this.

It is interesting to speculate as to what Wilfred's attitude towards Maxton's resolution would have been; he appears to have been very loyal, not only to individuals, but also to ideals, so it is very likely that, also bearing in mind his military background [albeit of non-combatant status] he would not have been averse to the idea of some level of authoritarianism in party affiliation: however, I think he also acknowledged that sometimes the greater good has to take precedence and, seeing the evidence of incipient impotence being openly displayed by the party which had for some years claimed his loyalty, he was very probably ready for a change of affiliation which was to suggest itself almost immediately. Although Mosley's faithful lieutenant, John Strachey, was in evidence at Birmingham, and demonstrated his loyalty to Maxton by supporting his resolution, no mention was made of Mosley who, as alluded to above, did not 'have his troubles to seek' in the spring of 1930, no doubt garnering support for his bold initiative. When support, from the Cabinet at the summit of the hierarchy, was not forthcoming, Mosley resigned his post and became a 'back bench' MP. Although it might have been the case that he did not set out with the intention of becoming the figurehead of a new political group which might eventually bring down the Government, he was unquestionably the catalyst for this very dénouement.

The small parliamentary group of ILP MPs loyal to Maxton was already expressing discontent, not, as exemplified at the Easter Conference, with & within itself, but with the wider Labour group in Government and was, according to Cross, "already in a state of semi-independence" [**87**]. Ostensibly, and ostensively, during the summer of 1930 Mosley was "canvassing support for his proposals among MPs." [**88**] He was aiming to state his case at the event which seemingly had supplanted the ILP Easter Conference in importance, namely the Labour Party Conference, which that year was being held at Llandudno in October, so in the meantime, he had to use all his guile and wiles where necessary to win over the waverers. In a speech at Leicester on the 20th of July, he went beyond his criticism of the Government to broach ideas which had started crystallising in his mind; reform of the parliamentary process [**89**]. Not that he was a lone maverick in this; Winston Churchill had made a good "case for structural reform in his widely-discussed Romanes Lecture at Oxford on the 19th of June" [**90**], which in retrospect, appears to encompass nascent ideas for a corporate state. There was another group, known as the "intelligentzia", comprising Members who were less radical than the ILP leftwingers, but nevertheless deplored the poor performance of the Government and the somewhat lumpen, unquestioning support "of the solid mass of trade-union MPs" [**91**].

In the autumn of 1930, the "intelligentzia" had coalesced into what quickly became known as the "Mosley Group", with another erstwhile colleague of Wilfred, W. J. Brown, MP for Wolverhampton West, acting as secretary and, if anything, providing rather than inspiring the initial impetus to form a new movement within the ILP [**92**]; another member of the "inner core of the Mosley group", and well known to Wilfred, was another 1929 first-time parliamentarian, Aneurin Bevan. Although he "was receptive to Mosley's bright new ideas", and "found the fare and company at the Mosleys' Smith Square [London] house to his liking", on an emotional level he couldn't break the ties of loyalty to the miners of Ebbw Vale, making it "difficult to follow the leadership of an ex-Tory baronet." [**93**] Mosley had one last try with party orthodoxy; his speech at Llandudno, according to Fenner Brockway, "got the greatest ovation he had ever heard at a party conference." [**94**] However, a motion that the National Executive Committee [NEC] should examine fully his proposals and report on them was defeated, albeit narrowly; undaunted, he was buoyed by the applause, which seemed to justify his intentions [**95**]. Mosley reconstituted the ***Memorandum*** into a ***Manifesto***, but at his instigation, Strachey, with contributions from Bevan & Brown, redrafted it with a leftward slant to make it more palatable in "the attempt to acquire a definite following." [**96**]

The ***Manifesto*** was published on the 13th of December 1930, and was presented as "an immediate plan to meet an emergency situation"; in a restating of the theme of Mosley's very first election address as a gallant war hero in 1918, he exhorted that "The State should constitute a public utility organisation to turn out houses & building materials as we turned out munitions during the war", and in eliciting support, it invited "any in our party or the nation who agree with [it] to state their agreement" [**97**]. Somewhat rashly perhaps, but no doubt spurred on by the palpable groundswell of support from all sides [**98**] Mosley started putting in place all of the elements essential to the creation and administration of his new political party, including premises [an office at number one, Great George Street, Westminster], and the same month, January 1931, the proposals presented in the two documents, the ***Memorandum*** and the ***Manifesto***, were published by Macmillan's as a 61-page pamphlet entitled "***A National Policy***", with the authors given as Aneurin Bevan, W. J. Brown, John Strachey and Allan Young [**99**]: the game was afoot!

NOTES

1 Please see **Appendix A** for a brief biographical synopsis of Mosley.

2 According to Robert Skidelsky [***Oswald Mosley***]:

> "When he joined the Labour Party, Mosley made it clear that he would not want to fight Harrow [his current constituency] again: he could hardly have failed to notice that the further left he moved the smaller his majority became. Besides, he wanted to win his spurs in the Labour Party by a dashing act. Offers of seats poured in from all over the country."

Colin Cross [***The Fascists in Britain***] tells us that

> "Within six months of his joining the Party he received some fifty enquiries from constituencies looking for Parliamentary candidates."

Mosley [***My Life***] himself actually trumps this:

> "Invitations poured in from all over the country to address mass meetings, and very soon I was invited to stand for Parliament by more than seventy local Labour constituency organisations."

Skidelsky [***Oswald Mosley, op. cit.***] takes up the story:

> "In July [1924] Mosley made his choice. Dr. Dunstan, the Labour candidate for Ladywood, Birmingham, had just been expelled from the party in line with its decision to exclude individual Communists from membership. Mosley was invited to address the Ladywood party. The bait was Neville Chamberlain, the sitting Conservative member. Mosley had fought Chamberlain's Rent Act, [which had the effect of] removing wartime rent controls, clause by clause through Parliament the previous year. The great Chamberlain dynasty was still unbroken in power in Birmingham. What more spectacular feat could there be than to defeat a Chamberlain in his own fortress? And so Mosley came to Birmingham. 'It was a large and enthusiastic meeting which met at Clark Street Council Schools on Monday evening last for the purpose of adopting a Labour candidate for the Ladywood Parliamentary Division.' began the report in Birmingham's Labour weekly, the Town Crier. 'Mosley's speech', concluded the ***TC***, 'roused the audience to great enthusiasm, and was greeted by volley after volley of applause. … The Chairman then moved a resolution proposing the adoption of Mr. Mosley as Labour candidate for the Ladywood Division, which was carried with complete unanimity.' [Birmingham ***Town Crier, 25/07/24***]"

Skidelsky [***ibid.***] throws us another intriguing little titbit about the Rent Act:

> "Mosley campaigned on the full ILP programme of nationalising railways, mines and banks. The strongly pro-Tory Birmingham press gossiped about the Mosleys sunning themselves at Biarritz. For years this was to be the standard line of attack on the 'rich Socialist'. Stung by this charge, Mosley dubbed Chamberlain the 'landlord's hireling' - a reference to [his] rent act. Chamberlain took him literally. He indignantly denied that he was in anyone's pay and called upon Mosley 'as a gentleman' to withdraw. Mosley withdrew nothing: he never did [sic]."

3 Both Skidelsky [***ibid.***] and Cross [***The Fascists in Britain, op. cit.***] give

useful information but, as usual, the former is more detailed:

"... on the actual polling day itself many Birmingham Labour supporters, without transport, were kept indoors by a massive thunderstorm. Even so, the voting was desperately close. When the first count was completed Mosley was the victor with a majority of 2. Chamberlain immediately asked for a recount, in which 60 votes shown for Mosley on the first count 'disappeared' leaving Chamberlain with a majority of 77. 'All the Labour officials' wrote the Town Crier, 'believe that the final figures given do not agree with the total votes cast.'"

Mosley himself gives a tantalising, although probably advisedly circumspect, extra detail:

"The count was a drama: there were two re-counts. First Chamberlain was in by seven, then I was in by two, and finally he was in by seventy-seven. It was alleged by some of our people that votes had disappeared, and uproar broke out with men fighting in the crowded public gallery and people pointing to the floor as they bellowed—'That one's got 'em in his pocket'. It appeared from our enquiry that their allegations could not be sustained."

My Life, op. cit.

4 Inevitably, politics was inextricably bound up with business in Birmingham, and the Chamberlain family was virtually paramount:

"Joseph Chamberlain's critics had bitterly complained that Victorian Birmingham was run in the interests of businessmen, particularly those of the Chamberlain family and its associates. After 1918, when Joseph Chamberlain's Birmingham political empire was directed by his sons, the Chamberlains not only continued their close association with local industry but extended their connections to many of the new national combines. With few exceptions, the Birmingham Unionist M.P.s returned with their leaders to Parliament between 1918 and 1939, were also closely connected with local or national industry and finance. Many held key positions in British government or in leading employers' organisations. In well under a century, therefore, Birmingham had changed from a city of essentially small workshops and employers to a centre of large-scale industry whose industrialists were among the most powerful citizens in the land."

The Birmingham Labour Movement, 1918-1945, by R.P. Hastings.

Personal loyalties very easily overrode political affiliations [***ibid.***]:

"Continued Unionist political success in Britain's largest industrial city was based upon a variety of factors. Not least of these was a strong personal loyalty to the Chamberlains. By 1876, at the close of Joseph Chamberlain's famous mayoralty, the family had become the dominant municipal and political influence in the city. The change-over in 1886 from Liberalism to Liberal Unionism by both Birmingham's M.P.s and her electorate, without damage to existing majorities, suggests that personal loyalty was an important factor in Birmingham elections. From 1886-1945, the Chamberlain tradition remained unbroken in the person of the political master and his sons. Even in the Liberal landslide of 1906, and at the election of the first Labour government in 1923, Birmingham stayed undividedly loyal to Unionism. In this context, the early radicalism of both Joseph and Neville Chamberlain undoubtedly helped.

Joseph Chamberlain rose to local popularity upon a programme of municipal socialism and inspired such loyalty among Birmingham artisans that they were prepared to riot for him. When he died in 1914 this devotion lived on and as late as November 1935 a visiting journalist could still report:

'Joe Chamberlain's spirit is not dead. Indeed it is still a potent political force. One of the most remarkable facts about Birmingham is that the Unionist Party is often extraordinarily strong in the very worst slums of the city ... Labour canvassers are still told 'My father voted for Joe Chamberlain and what was good enough for him is good enough for me.' It is as if Joe were still alive.'"

The Caucus was effectively an imported concept, from the United States, and the dictionary definition, according to the ***New Oxford American Dictionary***, is:

1 a meeting of the members of a legislative body who are members of a particular political party, to select candidates or decide policy.

• the members of such a body.

2 a group of people with shared concerns within a political party or larger organization.

• a meeting of such a group.

Ostensibly, this seems completely innocuous, but it is quite clear that in Birmingham at least, where this system operated, it was quite overtly used as a means of manipulating the electorate although, in fairness, it can be argued that all political parties manipulate the electorate to a greater or lesser extent, and thereby all operate a Caucus. Trygve R. Tholfsen, of Louisiana State University, offers this perspective:

"In 1868 the Birmingham Liberal Association won the first of a series of dazzling victories in parliamentary and municipal elections. Contemporaries immediately recognized the presence of a new phenomenon in English [sic] politics: disciplined control of a mass electorate by a tightly organized party apparatus. At first glance the Liberal machine seemed un-English, and the Tories gleefully imported an American epithet to describe it. The traditional interpretation of the caucus, as set forth by Ostrogorski [M. Ostrogorski, Democracy and the Organization of Political Parties, New York, 1902], followed contemporary opinion in emphasizing the novelty of the institution. In his view, 'the organization of the electoral masses' by the Liberal Association represented a sharp break with the past. He traced its origin to the minority clause of the Reform Act of 1867, which gave each Birmingham elector two votes to divide among the candidates for three seats, thus challenging the Liberals to develop an organization capable of circumventing the Act. After their success in the 'vote as you are told' election of 1868, the Liberal politicians, according to Ostrogorski, continued to use the caucus as a contrivance for manipulating an electorate that might otherwise have exercised independent judgment. This interpretation remains of considerable value, particularly in its treatment of the oligarchic implications of modern democracy."

"The Origins of the Birmingham Caucus", by Trygve R. Tholfsen,

Louisiana State University, New Orleans; The Historical Journal, II, 2 (1959), page 161.

Asa Briggs shows how the challenge faced by Labour in Birmingham was, if not unique, certainly very different:

"The young Labour Party in Birmingham grew up in a different sort of environment from Labour parties in most other parts of England. While facing powerful established party organisations, it received frequent encouragement & help from outside. The result was that during the First World War Neville Chamberlain's best ally in pushing forward his scheme for a municipal bank, in itself an adventurous proposal, was a Labour councillor, Eldred Hallas. Chamberlain recognised the link. After welcoming the Trades Union Congress to Birmingham in 1916, he wrote, concerning labour relations in England as a whole, that the Midlands 'were the most likely part of the country for experiments to start in, and the moment may come when there will be work for me to do in smoothing the way.' The local distinctness of Birmingham and its politics was to remain of great importance in national politics & economics throughout the interwar years."

History of Birmingham vol. II: Borough & City 1865-1938 by Asa Briggs

5 John Charnley, from Hull:

"I recall some of the other fine men and women who played prominent parts in our national movement. Bill Risdon, for example, an industrial specialist and former member of the Independent Labour Party … A retiring personality, very likeable, he was a competent speaker who gave a cool, logical exposition of economic policy."

Blackshirts and Roses, an Autobiography, by John Charnley

"… Wilfred Risdon, an old friend and associate of my I.L.P. days … I account Risdon one of the most quietly capable organisers I have yet met in political life."

The Streets are still: Mosley in Motley, by Alexander Miles. Unpublished typescript in University of Warwick Modern Records Centre Trades Union Congress files; MSS 292/743.11/2

6 Skidelsky [***Oswald Mosley, op. cit.***] is almost peremptorily brief [and very possibly wrong]:

"Bill [a later commonly used nickname for Wilfred] Risdon, who had *joined* Mosley [my emphasis] in the ILP, saw him as the heir to Robert Owen."

Colin Cross [***The Fascists in Britain***, ***op. cit.***] is slightly more forthcoming:

"With two of the ILP organizers in Birmingham Mosley established close relations. They were Allen [sic] Young, a Cydesider and an acute economist, and Bill Risdon, a miner from South Wales [sic] whose early political career had been in association with Aneurin Bevan. Young and Risdon were both to follow Mosley out of the Labour Party but meanwhile they buttressed his unofficial primacy in Birmingham and West Midland politics."

7 At the time of writing, the archive of Fircroft College is being catalogued at Birmingham City library, with the guidance of the city library archivist, by an erstwhile employee of the college, prompted by a lucky escape [of the archive, not the employee!] in a serious fire at the college in 2008.

According to George Barnsby, in his copious history of Birmingham & Black Country socialism, Fircroft was one of the main locations, under the auspices of the King's Norton branch, of classes run by the Workers' Education Association [WEA], which was seen by many as a competitor, of slightly dubious provenance, to the organisation based on the Central Labour College in London. Barnsby explains:

> "We can now turn to the activities of the local Workers' Education Association. Hostility between them and the Plebs began before the war. Silvester* tells us that it was 1913 when he, together with William Paul, both members of the SLP [Socialist Labour Party], formed the Birmingham Social Science Class. Paul was the main tutor, until he was called up in 1917. Warfare with the WEA was thus declared in 1913. Silvester puts the core of the dispute in the Plebs Magazine of January 1918 thus:
>
> 'The bone of contention between the reactionaries who support the WEA and the revolutionaries who support the Central Labour College is - Can education in Social Science be non-partisan and impartial?'
>
> Much space in the Plebs has been devoted to showing that this question can only be answered in the negative. The circumstances that led to the founding of the Plebs League and ... establishment of the CLC were derived from the ideas in the heads of Oxford dons who, in the interests of their class - the Capitalist Class - desired to 'dope' the education given to working class students at Ruskin College. Their partisan efforts to impose bourgeois economics on the students met with a vigorous resistance. Since that time Ruskin college has been the central home of that emasculated teaching of sociology described as non-partisan and impartial of which the various branches of the WEA are the provincial depots."

So from this we can see that, assuming Wilfred was aware of the differences in interpretation of socialist ideology and thus its implementation in education for the working people, given his previous experience, albeit preparatory, of the CLC organisation, it shows at the very least a willingness to accommodate such differences as existed for the sake of the greater good, the liberation of the workers from the shackles of ignorance. Barnsby gives us some specific details about Fircroft:

> "The 1924/25 WEA annual report gave a history of the midland district. The first Birmingham branch had been formed in 1905, two years after the foundation of the WEA, and a midland district was formed the same year. A full time officer had been in place since 1907. The organisation had been particularly fortunate in their chairmen 'who had rendered invaluable services to the cause of education and to the development of our Association', the report went on. These chairmen were Dr. Charles Gore (1906-12), Sir Oliver Lodge (1912-19) and Prof. J.H. Muirhead (from 1919). All of these were closely connected with Birmingham University.
>
> The 1922/23 report shows WEA classes in Birmingham centred on a King's Norton branch and taking place at Fircroft College. There was one Tutorial Class on Social Psychology, tutor A. Barrett Brown (soon to become principal of Ruskin College). There were also Preparatory Classes on the Growth of the Nation, Law, and Economic Geography. In addition there

were Study Circles at Stirchley where Tom Hackett lectured on Modern Problems and Selly Oak where there was a class on Banking & International Finance.

Three years later Birmingham WEA activity was still centred on the King's Norton branch. Classes were now classified as either Tutorial or One Year. There were two Tutorial Classes - on Social History and Economics. There were five One Year Classes - three at Fircroft (Regional Geography, Literature, and Modern European History), Tom Hackett was still at Stirchley Institute but now lecturing on the Evolution of Society, and there was an Economics class at Northfield Institute.

It does not appear, therefore, that the WEA made great headway in this period. It was, and remains, an important source of working class education, relatively well funded with University and thus government money. But it can never escape the suspicion that such funds are available to divert the Labour movement from Marxist educational rivals and that those educated in WEA classes are drawn from middle class rather than working class students. As far as commitment and sacrifice for working class aims are concerned the Labour Colleges were valiant but disadvantaged competitors. None showed more commitment or made such sacrifices in Birmingham as Fred Silvester and T.D. Smith."

*Fred Silvester and T.D. Smith, known as "T.D." were both committed to Communism and workers' education, and worked tirelessly to further these causes in & around Birmingham.

Socialism in Birmingham and the Black Country 1850-1939, by George J. Barnsby

Fircroft was located in what was previously a large private house:

"Next to the leader, the building was the most essential requisite for such an experiment. And it happened that just below Clare Cottage in Oak Tree Lane, Bournville, where Tom Bryan lived, a large house, "The Dell", had become vacant. In their early plans Tom Bryan and George Cadbury, Junior, had looked to make a beginning in a cottage. But they were quick to see the possibilities of "The Dell". The building was not in every way suitable, but it would accommodate about twenty men, and it had a considerable garden attached to it. The situation was also convenient. Not only was Tom Bryan living next door to "The Dell", but Birmingham had given birth to the Adult School Movement, and it was fitting that the new development should centre in Birmingham. The "The Dell" was sufficiently close to Woodbrooke to enable residents to take advantage of all the facilities offered at Woodbrooke under the guidance of Dr. Rendel Harris, who warmly encouraged this forward step, and at the same time Woodbrooke was sufficiently far off to ensure that the new settlement would have a character of its own. Largely through the initiative and financial backing of George Cadbury, Junior, plans for altering and furnishing the house were put in hand. The place was renamed, and became "Fircroft". The first term began on January 12, 1909, when twelve young men went into residence."

Tom Bryan: First Warden of Fircroft, by H.G. Wood & Arthur E. Ball

Similarly to Wilfred, Tom Bryan [1865-1917] was the son of a devout and evangelical Christian, so it is no great surprise that he also became one, and recognising the potential of "the organised Labour Movement", he joined the new new Independent Labour Party at its inception in 1893, when he was studying at the Bradford Theological College. Not long after moving to Bournville in 1903 to take up a position at the Friends' Settlement at Woodbrooke, and he & his wife became Quakers:

"Woodbrooke was opened in September 1903. It had its origin in the Summer School movement in the Society of Friends. It was to be a kind of permanent Summer School. The main subjects of study were the Bible and modern social conditions. At Woodbrooke Friends and others were to get the benefit of the light that modern historical and literary study has thrown upon the Bible, and also guidance in understanding the intricate problems which the citizen of to-day has to solve. Those who promoted the experiment of Woodbrooke felt that if the work of the society of Friends was to be effective, they must enable the younger generation of Friends both to understand the modern world and to rediscover the Bible and the Quaker message. Tom Bryan sympathised with these aims. He had been drawing nearer to Friends, consciously or unconsciously, for some years. The Fellowship of Followers which he established at Browning Hall, in its freedom from creed-tests and its emphasis on practical brotherliness, in many ways embodied the ideal of the Society of Friends. Soon after settling in Bournville Mr. and Mrs. Bryan joined Friends, and were among the original members of Bournville Village Meeting when it was opened in 1906. … The special aims of Woodbrooke also appealed to him. In his study of the Bible he had long been intensely humanist."

Ibid.

Bryan's association with the Adult School movement, in a teaching capacity, had begun in 1895, when one was opened at Browning Hall, Walworth, south London. The Adult School movement, as a separate entity [as opposed to general notions of provision of educational facilities subsequent to the meagre schooling for children available in the 18th century] grew out of the Christian Sunday Schools, although this source contradicts the above claim of Birmingham as the founding city:

"Meanwhile, an adult school movement emerged, closely allied to Sunday Schools but devoted exclusively to the education of adults rather than treating them as something of an afterthought to children's education.

In 1798 William Singleton and Samuel Fox, a Methodist and a Quaker, opened the first adult school in Nottingham, to teach bible reading, writing and arithmetic to young women employed in the lace and hosiery factories. A few years later, in 1811, the Rev. Thomas Charles opened a Sunday School exclusively for adults in North Wales. But it was really the founding of an Institution for instructing Adult Persons to read the Holy Scriptures in Bristol the following year that launched the adult school movement. From Bristol, adult schools spread rapidly through the south of England and the Midlands and South Wales and to a lesser extent into northern England."

A History of Adult Education in Great Britain, by T. Kelly, and Final Report of the Adult Education Committee, HMSO [1919], cited in A History of Modern British Adult Education, by Roger Fieldhouse and Associates

8 http://www.fircroft.ac.uk/locationmap.pdf

Fircroft's 'mission statement' has broadened out somewhat from its early days, and it now "committed to providing a quality learning experience to all of its students", who include both genders.

> "One hundred years on from the birth of the College, its mission of 'social justice' is more relevant than ever. The College runs a number of short courses throughout the year, many of which are aimed at students with no or few prior formal qualifications, helping them to improve their skills and confidence, achieve personal and career goals and to reach their true potential. There is also a full time Access to Higher Education programme for students who wish to go on to University.
>
> Fircroft has a wealth of expertise in working closely with voluntary sector organisations to fulfil their purpose and mission. The College runs a number of courses and programmes tailored toward this sector, and is also able to design and deliver customised training."

http://www.fircroft.ac.uk/About_Fircroft_College.htm

9 Mr. Birkett's career will be more fully examined later, but Brian Simpson tells us that "for two short periods [he had been] a Liberal MP".

In the Highest Degree Odious: Detention Without Trial in Wartime Britain, by Alfred William Brian Simpson

10 http://www.fircroft.ac.uk/About_Fircroft_College.htm

11 According to Matthew Worley:

> "Given that Labour was largely founded on the trade union movement, those parties established in industrial areas tended to be dominated by the relevant trade union branches. This was particularly so in mining constituencies, but those members affiliated via their trade union also made up the bulk of Labour's divisional organisation in most towns, cities & industrial localities. Of course, an affiliated member was not necessarily an active member. Nor was trade union domination necessarily conducive to Labour's electoral advance. The party's association with a particular trade union (or unions) could deter as well as attract potential support; inter-union rivalry was sometimes evident; and overt union influence could shape a party's priorities in a way that failed to complement the wider constituency. Elsewhere, in areas where the trade union presence was less concentrated or well-established, as in Scotland, London, parts of Yorkshire and cities such as Norwich, the influence of the socialist ILP on Labour activity continued to be important during the 1920s. Yet, the very formation of divisional parties challenged the ILP's place within the wider Labour Party, allowing non-union members to join Labour directly and assume the propaganda & social activities previously associated with the ILP. Accordingly, the ILP suffered a steady decline in both membership & influence from the early 1920s, leading eventually to its disaffiliation in 1932."

Labour's Grass Roots: Essays on the Activities of Local Labour Parties and Members, 1918-1945, Ed. Matthew Worley. He also says:

> "… the complex interaction of loyalties felt by ILP members cannot be easily discounted. Many in the ILP continued to believe that their party had a special role to play within the wider Labour Party as the keeper of the socialist flame and the distributor of socialist wisdom."

Labour Inside The Gate, by Matthew Worley

12 Mosley himself is somewhat uncharacteristically sparing in his description of this period [***My Life*, *op. cit.***]:

> "The interval between 1924 and my return to Parliament in 1926 was valuable to the development of my political thinking. … I was free for intensive reading and reflection for the first time since my period in hospital and of quiet administrative work at the end of the war, and also able to travel through India and America and gain further valuable experience.
>
> The background of my economic thinking was first developed by a study of Keynes—more in conversation with him than in reading his early writings, for he did not write General Theory until the thirties—and later by my American journey, which brought me in contact not only with the brilliant economists of the Federal Reserve Board but also with the American technocrats, very practical people who were paid the enormous sums which the United States even then accorded to its most valuable technicians."

Skidelsky [***Oswald Mosley, op. cit.***] gives a bit more detail:

> "The two years following Mosley's defeat for Ladywood formed the first of the creative periods of his life. Politicians, he [said], should have time for reflection, learning and recuperation. He and Cimmie travelled to India at the end of 1924: at Port Said he picked up a copy of George Bernard Shaw's ***The Perfect Wagnerite***: did he already see himself as the revolutionary hero Siegfried?"

13 ***Ibid.*:**

> "Before his departure … he had revealed an ambitious plan to his Ladywood supporters. Birmingham was the home of 'unauthorised programmes' [footnote: this is a reference to Joseph Chamberlain's 'unauthorised programme' of 1885. A more apposite reference might have been to Thomas Attwood, the Birmingham banker and ironmaster who opposed Peel's return to the gold standard in 1819 and put forward proposals for cheap money to revive industry at a time when one fifth of Birmingham was on relief following the Napoleonic wars. He later joined up with the Chartists]. It was time to have another. 'Birmingham must be to the Labour Movement what Manchester has been to Liberalism' he declared. This was the origin of the ***Birmingham Proposals***, the first of Mosley's great plans for realising his dream of a land fit for heroes. Mosley's decision to apply himself to the economic problems shaped the course of his life."

Given the previous, and still relatively recent strength of Liberalism in Birmingham, I would say that Mosley's comment, certainly if not disingenuous, is somewhat unfair, but perhaps it suited his argument to undervalue Birmingham's latterday Liberalism.

14 "By March 1925 the ***Birmingham Proposals*** were fully hatched."
Oswald Mosley, ibid.

Mosley [***My Life, op. cit.***] says that he had named his 'study of the subject at the I.L.P. Summer School in August 1925' ***Revolution by Reason***, very probably a deliberately provocative title, and his 'chief assistant in working out the ***Birmingham Proposals***', John Strachey, who had 'one of the best analytical and critical intelligences I have ever known', produced an 'excellent book on the ***Birmingham Proposals*** … a lucid and admirable exposition', with the same name.

15 ***Ibid.***

16 Mowat tells us:

"The first big demonstration occurred in October 1920, when crowds of unemployed men, converging on Whitehall to support a deputation of Labour mayors seeking to see Lloyd George, were charged upon by the police, mounted and on foot, and beaten about by police batons - the first of many such attacks in the annals of the unemployed, resulting in broken heads and loss of blood though not life. In the winter of 1920-'21 there were many demonstrations in London in favour of 'work or full maintenance', particularly before the offices of boards of Poor Law Guardians. During 1921 there were two big demonstrations in London (July 11th and October 4th), the latter ending in a battle in Trafalgar Square. There were similar demonstrations in Sheffield, Dundee, Bristol, Leicester, Cardiff, Glasgow and several towns in Lancashire. In Liverpool, there was a riot on the 13th of September when a crowd of about 5,000, refused a hall for a meeting, invaded the Walker Art Gallery. In 1922 the first of the hunger marches of unemployed men took place: delegates, one coming from as far as Glasgow, converged on London on the 17th of November."

Britain Between the Wars 1918-1940, by Charles Loch Mowat

17 ***Ibid.***

18 The financing of unemployment was an unresolved mess [***ibid.***]:

"As always, the Poor Law stood as the residuary legatee for cases of distress. Families not covered by the unemployment insurance scheme or insufficiently aided by it, or stranded during the 'gaps' between periods of unemployment benefit (often about a month) all resorted to the Guardians and received outdoor relief. … Many Guardians refused outdoor relief altogether; others paid at scales varying from 15s. per week for a man and wife and 5s. for each child to Poplar's more generous rate of 33s., plus 10s. for rent (the origin of a new bogey, 'Poplarism'): the Ministry of Health's scale for London was 25s. for man and wife. The burden was, naturally, heaviest on industrial and working class towns least able to bear it. The Ministry of Health tried to keep the Local Authorities' expenditures within bounds, and could, under the Local Authorities (Financial Provisions) Act of 1921, refuse permission for increased borrowing. … a Bill was subsequently passed [after the 'celebrated protest of the Poplar Council'] spreading a greater part of the costs of relief over London as a whole."

19 ***Ibid.:***

"On his side, however, Lloyd George had strong support for continuance of the Coalition either in its present form or under the *aegis* of some new party. Among the Liberals its chief defender was Churchill, among the Conservatives all the leaders of front rank: Austen Chamberlain, Birkenhead, Balfour, Salvidge, and for a long time, Bonar Law, Curzon, Lord Derby and Walter Long. Their arguments were simple: the alternative was Bolshevism, the triumph of the Socialists, perhaps with a minority of the votes in an election fought between three or four parties."

This prediction was to be proved correct at the end of 1923.

20 *Ibid.*

21 One of many good references for Robert Owen is this: http://www.robert-owen.com/

22 ***Britain … Wars, op. cit.:***

"Next year [1923] the chairman [of the ILP] was Sidney Webb, representative of the Fabian and intellectual, middle class side of the party. Speaking at the annual conference, in the Queen's Hall, London, he declared that 'from the rising curve of Labour votes it might be computed that the party would obtain a clear majority … somewhere about 1926. … Socialism was rooted in political democracy and every step towards their goal was dependent on getting the support of at least a numerical majority of the whole people.' No one need fear that the British electorate would ever go too fast … The founder of British socialism, he reminded the party, was not Marx, but Robert Owen …"

23 ***Oswald Mosley, op. cit.:***

"If any single thing converted him to socialism it was the impact of the slums of Britain's great industrial cities with their stunted, undernourished, ragged, disease-ridden, vermin-infested inhabitants. They were the unbearable negation of everything the modern world was about - the negation of science, of intelligence, of community; an insult to the sacrifice of the war generation. They epitomised the helpless or selfish acceptance of disgraceful industrial conditions. The slums started a train of thought which led directly to the Birmingham Proposals: they were the product of poverty. Yet for the first time in history the economic system was capable of eliminating poverty. Together the machines and men were available to produce the goods and services the people needed; but they were standing idle. In May 1924 a journalist had taken Mosley round the Liverpool slums. 'This is damnable', Mosley said. 'The rehousing of the working classes ought in itself to find work for the whole of the unemployed for the next ten years.' This was an exceedingly acute and perceptive remark. It brought together two things sundered in orthodox socialist economic thought: unemployment and poverty."

24 ***My Life, op. cit.:***

"At that time I was surrounded by a brilliant group of young men, among whom I best remember John Strachey, Allan Young and Sydney Barnet Potter, who were all with me at Birmingham. I have already noted that the part of this constructive thinking which was not of my own creation—notably the Import Control Board system—was the work of E. F. Wise and E. M. H. Lloyd, who were close associates but not in the Birmingham group. John Strachey was with me as candidate for the Aston Division of Birmingham, which he won at the 1929 election: I had met him just before the 1924 election and suggested his adoption. He was my chief assistant in working out the ***Birmingham Proposals***, and had one of the best analytical and critical intelligences I have ever known; … At every stage of this thinking I discussed its development with him—both in England and in journeys to France and Italy—and far more than any other of my companions he aided the slow evolution of the complete idea with the clear and acute understanding of his first-rate mind."

25 John Maynard Keynes, 1883-1946:

"So influential was John Maynard Keynes in the middle third of the twentieth century that an entire school of modern thought bears his name. Many of his ideas were revolutionary; almost all were controversial. Keynesian economics serves as a sort of yardstick that can define virtually all economists who came after him."

http://www.econlib.org/library/Enc/bios/Keynes.html

26 ***My Life, op. cit.:***

"The present epoch has already seen the doctrine of Keynes fully implemented, and before long we shall see the decision between these two opinions in the coming economic situation. The difference between us in the sphere of monetary policy at that time was stated in my speech on the ***Birmingham Proposals*** ..."

27 ***Ibid.:***

"(1) The requirement of consumer credits in addition to producer credits and their combination with national planning.

(2) The recognition that banking and credit were the key points of the economy and that their command was essential to any effective planning by Government.

(3) The possibility of maintaining an expanding island economy by monetary manipulation behind a floating exchange rate."

28 ***Oswald Mosley, op. cit.:***

"Where the Hobsonian influence is felt is in his proposal that the new demand should be directed towards satisfying working class necessities rather than capitalist luxuries. This, as well as the general emphasis on planning, gives his proposals their socialist form."

29 ***Ibid.:***

"On the 3rd of May, 1925, Mosley introduced his 'unauthorised programme' to Birmingham. Over 5,000 people queued for seats in the Birmingham Town Hall which seated only half that number. 'Send the money to the necessitous areas.' Mosley cried. 'Give it to the poor whose demand is for the things which matter to this country and will stimulate employment in the great staple industries; do away with the Poor Law and the "dole".' On the 11th of June Mosley and Strachey laid their plan before the delegate meeting of the Birmingham Labour Party. The President, A. E. Ager, explained that if the proposals were approved they would be embodied in a resolution for the Labour Party Conference in the name of the Birmingham Labour Party. Strachey explained that it was necessary by vigorous state action to break the vicious circle of destitution. ... A vigorous discussion followed. ... 'There were no short cuts to Socialism' was the view of Fred Sharkey, one of Birmingham's "cryptos". ... Rejecting the policy of a mere redistribution of wealth, Mosley said that the fundamental problem was 'the need to create new wealth by drawing upon all the latent power of production in the country.' Three weeks later when the debate was resumed, Mosley's resolution calling for the nationalisation of the banks and the use of the national credit to break 'the vicious circle of poverty and unemployment' was carried by 65 votes to 14 and so became the ***Birmingham Proposals***. [***Town Crier***, ***10/07/25***] The campaign of persuasion continued. On the 11th of August Mosley presented his plan in a paper read to the ILP Summer

School at Easton Lodge: it was later published under the title ***Revolution by Reason***."

Easton Lodge, near Dunmow, Essex, was the home of Frances 'Daisy' Maynard, who became the Countess of Warwick after her husband, Lord Brooke, inherited the earldom; she also, famously, had a nine-year liaison with Edward, Prince of Wales. However, she became something of a social pariah, after espousing the cause of socialism, and making her home available for socialist gatherings such as summer schools, possibly to assuage her guilt:

"However, alongside her life within this grand social scene, the Countess continued to play an increasingly active role in the welfare of the local community, with particular emphasis on educational reform, and especially for women.

Even though the Countess of Warwick is inextricably associated with high society and immense wealth, in fact she had, by the end of the 19th century, given her life over to Socialism and was deep in debt. The transformation to Socialism had taken place after stinging criticism from and lengthy discussions with Robert Blatchford, the then editor of the left-wing paper, ***The Clarion***. The attack on her lifestyle followed a particularly extravagant social event at Warwick Castle in 1895, the *Bal Poudre*.

It was her enthusiasm for the Socialist cause and pacifism that ultimately severed Daisy's links with royalty and The Establishment."

http://www.eastonlodge.co.uk/content/'daisy'-years-1865-1938

30 ***My Life, op. cit.:***

"In his celebrated attack, ***The Economic Consequences of Mr. Churchill*** [1925], Keynes argued that the British currency had been overhauled by 10%. This meant 10% on the prices of British exports which could only be met by further wage reductions and more unemployment. Keynes's prophecy was almost immediately fulfilled. ... Mosley's comment was: "'All the workers of this country have got to face a reduction of wages." murmurs Mr. Baldwin between a sermon and a subsidy.'"

31 ***Ibid.***

32 Professor Harold Laski had this to say:

"Legislation protecting the interests of the miners and the railwaymen has always been a function of their strength of their unions; and nothing is surely more significant than the admission by high authority that the subsidy was granted to the coal-owners in 1925 (to make possible the maintenance of the existing level of wages) not because it was desirable, but because the state was not, at the moment, adequately prepared to fight organised labour."

Democracy in Crisis, by Harold J. Laski, Professor of Political Science at the University of London, 1933

33 ***Oswald Mosley, op. cit.***; although Mowat [***Britain Between the Wars etc., op. cit.***] tells us that "at Birmingham the entire strike committee was arrested"!

34 ***Ibid.***

35 Arthur James Cook was born in Wookey, Somerset on November 22nd, 1883:

"A deeply religious woman, [Cook's mother] Selina led her family out of the Church of England and into Baptist nonconformity; furthermore, she was involved in the nascent Salvation Army. Such convictions were passed on to all her children, and were likely to instil in Arthur Cook a sensitivity towards injustice and a desire for social reform & improvement. The roots of his later socialism were grounded in the humanitarianism to which he was exposed as a child. Although eventually he rejected the chapel, he remained a Christian all his life. …

Arthur became a boy preacher of local notoriety, touring the chapels delivering his own sermons to Sunday Schools and adult congregations. It seems evident that Cook, like many other trade union leaders, gained his first experience as an orator in the chapel pulpit. When Arthur was 17 he was offered a place at a Baptist college to train for the ministry. According to Cook's sister Louise, this would have pleased their mother, but Cook had already decided to leave Somerset and travel to South Wales to work in the coal mines. The reason for Cook's decision seems to have been overwhelmingly pecuniary. … Cook was set to join a mass migration from the agricultural fringes of south-western England into the booming South Wales coalfield. From Somerset alone in the 1890s an average of 1,000 boys a year were sucked into Glamorgan by the attraction of pit work & higher earnings. With £5 saved up and his box full of sermons, Arthur left with some friends for the Rhondda valleys. The year was 1901 and he was 17 years old; [he] was to spend the next 20 years of his working life underground. …

When Cook began work at the Trefor colliery he joined the South Wales Miners' Federation which had been founded in 1898. … Arthur, a young man with an intense interest in the wellbeing of his fellows, became deeply affected by the social & economic developments within the coalfield. … The circumstances surrounding Cook's leap out of nonconformity into socialism are unclear. It is likely that his first formal move towards political activity occurred in 1906. An ILP branch had been established in Porth the previous December, and Cook apparently later came into contact with William Trainer, an ILP propagandist sent into the Rhondda on a recruiting mission. According to John Strachey, who knew Cook quite well, Cook joined the ILP soon afterwards and, as he 'did nothing by halves', immediately became an active and outspoken member of his branch. … At the age of 40 and only 4 years since leaving the coalface, [at the end of March, 1924] Cook became Secretary of the largest and most powerful union in Britain, responsible for nearly 800,000 members."

A.J. Cook, by Paul Davies

36 ***Oswald Mosley, op. cit.:***

"In June 1925 the Birmingham Labour Movement had brought heavy pressure on him to withdraw from a by-election at the Forest of Dean [even though he had been endorsed by the NEC {National Executive Council}: ref. ***NEC minutes, 24/06/25*** & ***Minutes of the Birmingham Borough Labour Party, 23/06/25*** for opposition]. There seemed nothing for it but to fight Chamberlain again in 1929; but in July 1926 Chamberlain, seeing the writing on the wall, had shifted his own candidature to Edgbaston, Birmingham's Belgravia. Having thus accomplished his primary aim of driving Chamberlain out, Mosley felt free to leave Ladywood. An opportunity to contest neighbouring Smethwick arose at the end of the year and Mosley decided to take it."

37 Although Cross [***The Fascists in Britain, op. cit.***] calls him "a railwayman".

38 ***Ibid.:***

"Initially, Mosley's trouble came more from his own party than from the Opposition. His wealth, arrogance, and radicalism had made him anathema to a powerful section of the bourgeois leadership. Thus when John Davison, an official of the Ironfounders' Society and the sitting Labour Member for Smethwick, announced his resignation on 22 November 1926 on grounds of ill-health, and Mosley was hurriedly selected in his place, the NEC refused to endorse him because of a 'technical irregularity'. After much trundling of Labour politicians to and from London this little local difficulty was sorted out and Mosley was officially adopted on 4th November 1926 [footnote: the NEC considered it had been 'steamrollered' by the Smethwick Executive and demanded a new conference where the claims of other candidates {Aldermen Willetts & Betts} could be considered; notwithstanding, Mosley was elected *nem con*: ref. ***Town Crier & New Leader 03/12/26***] .... The real objections to Mosley were revealed when at the height of the by-election Philip Snowden warned the Labour Party not to 'degenerate into an instrument for the ambitions of wealthy men' and referred to candidates being 'put up at auction to the highest bidder'."

39 ***Ibid.:***

"... [T]he ***Birmingham Post*** charged Mosley with being 'devoid of any sporting instinct, of any regard for the ordinary conventions of political controversy, of any desire to "play the game"'. Mosley's reply was characteristic: 'This is not a kissing match, but a stand up fight.'... In a last-minute effort to turn the tide [of public expectation of a Labour victory], the Rothermere & Beaverbrook press discovered a "Red plot" when the Communists Gallagher [sic] and McManus turned up at Smethwick urging the workers to support Mosley and a mysterious Chinaman, studying elections, appeared in his entourage. Mosley's majority of 6,582 on an 80% poll surprised even his most optimistic supporters. To a crowd of 8,000 outside the Town Hall he said: 'This is not a by-election, it is history. The result of this election sends out a message to every worker in the land. You have met and beaten the Press of reaction ... Tonight all Britain looks to you and thanks you. My wonderful friends of Smethwick, by your heroic battle against a whole world in arms, I believe you have introduced a new era for British democracy.'"

40 ***Ibid.:***

"Early in 1926 he and his wife sailed for America to study labour conditions, in true Fabian fashion. Perhaps like the Webbs in Russia 8 years later, they went in search of a new civilisation .... the fundamental lesson of America was that high wages could go hand in hand with private enterprise. Ford had produced 'the cheapest article and paid the highest wages in the world.' From 1926 the idea of a 'managed capitalism' began to take root in his mind. He was not the only left wing politician to see America rather than Russia as a model for the working class. 'If this is capitalism,' wrote

Brailsford, the leading ILP theoretician of the 1920s, 'it is a variety which has discarded the fundamental principle on which Marx based his prediction. The case against it is no longer that it makes poverty by its very success; the case against it is rather that it is an unchecked autocracy.' … In terms of structure, the ILP's policy of the Living Wage was very similar to Mosley's. It even provided for the nationalisation of the banks and the use of credit policy to keep up the price level: an indication that Brailsford, like Mosley & Strachey, had been reading his Keynes …"

41 ***Ibid.:***

"The attitude of the Trade Union leaders was also ambiguous. The Mond-Turner conversations between leading unionists and employers in 1928 suggested that the union leaders too realised that a national effort had to be made to overcome the economic problem. These conversations in fact marked the first industrial approach to a producers' policy. Soon afterwards, Ernest Bevin, the powerful general secretary of the TGWU, was to become a convert to the Keynesian approach; but what the unions were utterly opposed to was state interference in collective bargaining. As Henry Pelling has pointed out, workers tended to regard the State 'as an organisation run by and for the benefit of the wealthy'. So the unions fell back on an attitude that has been well described as 'collective laissez-faire'. National planning of production, including the planning of prices & incomes, meant state interference with wage bargaining; and the unions were not prepared to have anything to do with it."

42 ***New Oxford American Dictionary:***

syn•di•cal•ism |ˈsɪndɪk(ə)lɪz(ə)m|

noun historical

a movement for transferring the ownership and control of the means of production and distribution to workers' unions. Influenced by Proudhon and by the French social philosopher Georges Sorel (1847–1922), syndicalism developed in French labour unions during the late 19th century and was at its most vigorous between 1900 and 1914, particularly in France, Italy, Spain, and the U.S.

DERIVATIVES

syn•di•cal•ist |ˈsɪndəkələst| noun & adjective

43 ***Labour inside the Gate, op. cit.:***

"Following Maxton's election to the ILP chair in April 1926, the leftward drift was set in place, coinciding with a continued decline in ILP membership and the further limiting of ILP influence within the Labour Party. By the end of the decade, Labour's divisional parties had more firmly established themselves, while new and younger Labour members could and did enter straight into the constituency party rather than via the ILP, particularly outside Scotland. Very crudely, something of a 'catch-22' began to develop for the ILP in such circumstances: as ILP members began to merge into the Labour Party, so the existing ILP organisation was utilised increasingly by the more active left wing; as the left wing became more active, so many ILP members began to merge into the Labour Party. As this suggests, ILP perspectives were not uniform. … the complex interaction of loyalties felt by ILP members cannot be easily discounted. Many in the ILP continued to believe that their party had a special role to play within the wider Labour Party as the keeper of the socialist flame and the distributor of socialist wisdom."

44 ***Oswald Mosley, op. cit.:***

"By the late 1920s there was a strong grassroots movement in the ILP in favour of disaffiliation from the Labour Party. Mosley would have none of this: the Party must stay united, he insisted, to win a majority at the next general election. This view placed him on the 'sensible' wing of the NAC [National Administrative Council], together with ["Manny"] Shinwell & P.J. Dollan. The crisis came in June 1928 with the publication of the Cook-Maxton Manifesto. Ostensibly a protest against industrial collaboration, it was intended by Wheatley & Gallacher to be a sounding-board for a new political party. Ironically, in the light of his later views, Mosley moved to heal the breach."

45 ***A.J. Cook, op. cit.***

46 ***Ibid.:***

"Cook's opposition to the 'Mond-Turner Talks' has been dismissed as emotional rather than reasoned. Certainly [he] objected bitterly to the hypocrisy and futility which he believed underlay the discussions. He was disgusted by talk of peace [with employers] when thousands of miners and their families suffered. He also laid the blame for the MFGB's defeat in 1926 at the door of the same cabal of union leaders which was flirting with the Mond group. However, Cook had reasoned and understandable objections. To him the whole principle of collaboration was contrary to the true function of trade unionism; at a time when capitalism appeared to be entering a period of crisis, he objected to the TUC's efforts to co-operate in its survival. Not surprisingly, given his explicitly Marxist viewpoint, Cook found himself in a tiny minority within the General Council. On December 20th, the General Council decided by 24 votes to 3 to accept the invitation from the Mond group of employers."

47 ***Ibid.:***

"It seems that Cook's role at this stage was purely titular, although the ***Manifesto*** that was issued in June, addressed to 'the workers of Britain', expressed the humanitarian and sentimental socialism so typical of [him]. The ***Cook-Maxton Manifesto*** criticised existing Trade Union and Labour Party leaders for abandoning the principles of the early pioneers of the movement. The left wingers announced plans for a series of public meetings throughout the country to gauge support for their stance against capitalism: 'Conditions have not changed. Wealth & luxury still flaunt themselves in the face of poverty-stricken workers who produce them. We ask you to join the fight against the system which makes these conditions possible.'"

48 Arthur Marwick tells us that:

"In all this the N.A.C. as such was not consulted. Maxton had quite deliberately gone behind the back if the I.L.P. to appeal directly to the working class. Of the vigorous Marxist-orientated ***Manifesto***, Mr. [Archibald Fenner] Brockway, followed word for word by Mr. McNair, has said that it was a popular and condensed statement of the existing I.L.P. '***Socialism in***

Our Time' policy [footnote reference: ***Brockway, Inside the Left***]. It was, of course, nothing of the sort."

Fenner Brockway, as he was commonly known, was ILP general secretary in 1928. Interestingly, Marwick tells us that, in amongst the disharmony caused by Maxton's action, as reported by the Birmingham ***Town Crier***, on 29/06/28, as well as Labour's own ***New Leader*** [13/07/28], "a number of branches refused co-operation", but he does not specify which.

"The Independent Labour Party in the Nineteen Twenties"*, by Arthur Marwick; Bulletin of the Institute of Historical Research, Vol. XXXV, pp. 62-74, 1962.*

49 ***A.J. Cook, op. cit..***

50 ***Ibid.:***

"Ultimately … Cook's scepticism proved justified. … Some employers refused to recognise Trade Unions or forfeit their right to 'dismiss troublemakers'; many employers did not wish to encourage a revival in union membership, and 'many disliked taking action which could restore the prestige of the TUC after the 1926 débâcle'. Arthur Cook was not surprised … for Cook the central message of ***The Miners' Next Step*** was as valid as ever. Ultimately, the Mond-Turner talks petered out. But in 1928 Cook's policy had been defeated decisively."

51 The ***Birmingham Souvenir***, produced for the ILP 1930 Easter Conference [**Appendix C**], was compiled & edited by Wilfred, and on page 26 of at least 59, it featured an advert for a "Summer School Holiday" and interested parties were invited to "Send a postcard for particulars to:–

W. Risdon.

136 Stockfield Road,

Acocks Green,

Birmingham."

Given that the conference was held in April, allowing time for preparation of the booklet it's very likely that Wilfred will have been well ensconced at this address before then. The house no longer exists, although the buildings on the present site appear to be quite recent, so it might have been redeveloped more than once.

52 "Minutes of E.C. Meeting Held June 28th [1929] - Com. J. Holland presided.

3 …

Letter read from Mr. W. Risdon the new organising Secretary for M.D.C. asking for a date in which to visit the Branch. Sec. reported that he had fixed up July 3rd for his visit.

Circular read read from M.D.C. calling our attend-tion [sic] to the new resolutions drawn up by that body. The chairman read each clause seperate [sic] and it was decided to recommend the question of Subs be brought forward to the General Meeting." [full details in **Appendix B**]

53 ***Labour Inside The Gate, by Matthew Worley***

54 ***Ibid.***

55 http://ourhistory-hayes.blogspot.com/

56 Ian Bullock, reviewing [04/01/2010] Gidon Cohen's ***The Failure of a Dream***: http://www.independentlabour.org.uk/

57 ***Oswald Mosley, op. cit.:***

"To a small circle of friends in the Birmingham Labour Party he was a hero. They included John Strachey, Dick Plummer (manager of the ILP's ***New Leader***), Allan Young & Sydney Potter, ILP candidate for Sparkbrook until 1928: Mosley was best man at his wedding that year to Ursula Spicer ... Mosley was the key figure in Labour's advance in Birmingham and the Midlands. He took an impoverished, sluggish party by the scruff of the neck, infused it with his own dynamism (and money) and used it to break the hold of the Chamberlain dynasty."

58 ***Ibid.:***

"Once a year hundreds of Smethwick Labour supporters (and Cimmie's followers at Stoke [her parliamentary constituency]) would depart by charabanc for Denham, there to have their socialist faith fortified by luncheon in the hay barn, impromptu sports, funfairs, singing, dancing, not to mention a speech from Ramsay MacDonald on the theme that socialism is not just a matter of wages but of soul. 'Beauty spots like Denham', said the party leader, 'must be available to the whole people'; but to cynics the excursions to Denham looked less like practical experiments in socialism than lavish exercises in feudal patronage."

59 ***Britain ... Wars, op. cit.:***

"On the suggestion of Clifford Allen, its chairman, the ILP appointed 7 commissions to work out the details of socialist policy for a future Labour government. These commissions published reports elaborating socialist policies for agriculture, finance, the Empire, India, the Trade Unions and industrial policy, the reform of Parliament. The report which attracted most attention was that on ***Socialism in our Time***, written by J.A. Hobson, H.N. Brailsford, E.F. Wise & Arthur Creech Jones and signed by F.W. Jowett as acting chairman of the ILP. Its main author was Wise, an ex-civil servant of brilliant mind; ... at its Easter conference in 1926, just a month before the General Strike, the ILP enthusiastically endorsed the ***Socialism in our Time*** report (although previously denounced by Ramsay MacDonald)."

60 ***The Independent ... Twenties, Marwick, op. cit.***

The same authors of ***Socialism in our Time*** also produced ***The Living Wage.***

61 ***Britain ... Wars, op. cit.:***

"In 1927 the Labour Party began to draft a new programme, partly spurred to this by the ILP. The result, however, only caused dissension, not only with the ILP, but among the party leaders. ***Labour and the Nation*** was the final product. It was drafted by R.H. Tawney, and approved in principle at the Labour Party Conference at Birmingham in 1928. This was a revised, longer and more imprecise version of ***Labour and the New Social Order***. It declared the party to be a socialist party. Its aim was the 'organisation of industry…in the interest…of all who bring their contribution of useful service to the common stock.'"

62 ***Ibid.***

63 ***Oswald Mosley, op. cit.***

64 ***Ibid.***

65 ***Ibid.:***

"Mosley was overjoyed. Simmons's election agent recalled 'Mosley running across Victoria Square, easily outstripping the crowd at his heels, with his huge strides, throwing his hat in the air and nearly breaking the back of our little 4-seater car … as he jumped upon it to congratulate us.' [ref. ***Labour Magazine, 01/04/31***]"

66 ***Labour Inside The Gate, op. cit.***

67 ***Oswald Mosley, op. cit.***

68 ***Ibid.***

69 According to his own brief CV in ***The Political Problem of Transition***, Allan Young was [up to 1931]: 'born August 18th, 1895. Member of the National Amalgamated Furnishing Trades Association before the War. 1921-24, Constituency Agent for the Labour Party in the Farnham Division of Surrey, Chippenham Division of Wiltshire, and Wrekin Division of Shropshire. 1924-27, Borough Organizer for Birmingham. 1927-31, Political Secretary to Sir Oswald Mosley;'. He omits to say that he was born in Glasgow. Matthew Worley [***Labour … Wars, op. cit.***] somewhat muddies the waters of Young's own account by saying that Mosley 'paid for Allan Young to become party organiser', and Skidelsky fills in some gaps [while omitting Young's earlier political experience]:

"Mosley relied heavily on efficient research assistance. From 1924 this role in his entourage was increasingly filled by Allan Young whom he had met in Birmingham. The son of a "bookish" railway clerk from Glasgow, Young had served in the war and knocked about the Far East before coming to Birmingham as agent for the borough Labour Party in April 1924. Young was a brilliant constituency organiser. He soon fell under Mosley's spell and in 1927 resigned his job to become Mosley's full-time political secretary [footnote: Mosley's personal secretary for many years was George Sutton]."

Oswald Mosley, op. cit.

70 Strachey has already been mentioned in the notes, but Skidelsky gives a good brief biographical reference:

"Evelyn John Strachey, son of St Loe Strachey, editor of the ***Spectator*** and a nephew of Lytton Strachey … Born in 1901, Strachey was educated at Eton & Oxford … He read history, but did not take a degree, joining his father on the ***Spectator*** in 1922. When Mosley met him 2 years later - probably at the Webbs' - he had already joined the Labour Party and started working for the ILP. Mosley helped him get a constituency at Aston, Birmingham, for the general election of 1924 … Both men were, as Hugh Thomas writes, 'refugees from the upper class' in a largely proletarian or lower-middle-class world. Both had a very similar cast of mind: cold, logical, rational."

Ibid.

71 Thomas was seen very much as a conservative element in the Labour ranks in the crisis years of 1930 and '31, although in the first Labour Government, some people 'twisted a passage from an old book by J.H. Thomas to argue that the people's savings would be in danger of confiscation.' [***Ibid.***]

Two good sites with full biographies are the following:
http://en.wikipedia.org/wiki/James_Henry_Thomas and
http://www.spartacus.schoolnet.co.uk/TUthomas.htm

According to one source, 'The Lord Privy Seal or Lord Keeper of the Privy Seal is one of the traditional sinecure offices in the British Cabinet.'
http://www.tudorplace.com.ar/Documents/lord_privy_seal.htm

However, the 'official' site is rather more respectful [notwithstanding the grammatical error!]:

> "The Lord Privy Seal is one of the great officers of state along with posts such as the Lord Chancellor and the Lord Great Chamberlain. The full title is Lord Keeper of the Privy Seal and originally the post holder had responsibility for the monarchs [sic] personal (privy) seal. Today the post of Lord Privy Seal is an office within the Cabinet and has recently been linked to the post of Leader of the House of Commons."

http://www.parliament.uk/site-information/glossary/lord-privy-seal/

72 ***Oswald Mosley, op. cit.:***

> "Most of [Thomas's] early activity was talk, but there was just enough hint of action to suggest more in the future. A £37.5m 5-year road building programme was announced. A 'Home Development Bill' was introduced on 15th of July 1929, making it easier for railway companies to borrow money (Thomas was secretary of the NUR)."

73 ***Ibid.:***

> "£1m was allocated for colonial development. In August Thomas set off for Canada in pursuit of a great scheme for expanding imperial trade. Certainly there was nothing lethargic about him in these early months."

74 ***The Fascists in Britain, op. cit.:***

> "At first his main work outside Parliament, beyond attending the fruitless meetings of the Unemployment Committee, was to persuade local authorities to run works schemes to help their unemployed. Local-authority deputations found Mosley blazing with enthusiasm and returned to their towns with a high opinion of the young minister. Mosley was less satisfied. He was irritated that he, a minister of the central government, had to persuade rather than order the local authorities to carry out national plans. In his later, Fascist, policy Mosley insisted that the central government should have complete power of command over local authorities. The existing system, he said, was as unworkable as a business organisation would be if it allowed local authorities to disobey head office."

75 ***Oswald Mosley, op. cit.:***

> "No one at Whitehall believed that such 'relief works', as they were contemptuously called, could make any major contribution to the unemployment problem, which was an 'export' problem … Mosley, Lansbury and Johnston were not invited to attend the interdepartmental Committee of

Civil Servants until the third meeting on 27th of June [1929]. By then all the key decisions had been taken. At the first meeting on 11th of June Thomas, true to his bargain with Snowden, had announced that it 'was no part of the Government's Unemployment policy to undertake schemes of relief work pure and simple.'"

76 ***Ibid.:***

"Put in charge of piloting the Colonial Development Bill through the House, [Mosley] positively purred through the committee stages taken on 18th and 19th of July, under considerable provocation from the Conservatives. 'His skill, tact, good temper & grasp of detail' earned general praise, according to the ***Sunday Express*** of 21/07/29. Fenner Brockway of the ILP expressed particular appreciation when Mosley accepted a left wing amendment guaranteeing conditions of native labour. 'His name will live as the Minister responsible for the first Act laying down these important principles to protect native labour from exploitation.' commented the ***New Leader*** of 23/07/29."

77 ***Ibid.:***

"Labour's one distinctive 'cure' for unemployment was removing the old from industry by giving them better pensions. This would create vacancies for large numbers of unemployed. It was brought into Labour's programme at the insistence of the miners; and this made Mosley its warm advocate."

78 ***Ibid.:***

"Ever since 1925 Mosley had been arguing that what was needed was a home-market unemployment policy. To his horror he realised that the Government had not the slightest intention of trying anything of the kind … It was with these experiences [mainly acrimony in the interdepartmental Committee] behind him that Mosley decided to write yet another Memorandum, this time not to urge some particular measure but, much more ambitiously, to advance an alternative unemployment policy. He told Ramsay MacDonald about the plan on the 13th of December - one of the rare opportunities of renewing his previously intimate relationship with his party leader. Whether RMD listened to what Mosley was saying is doubtful. What seems clear is that he encouraged Mosley to go ahead … Mosley, for his part, interpreted these vague murmurs of approval as promises of support when his document came before the Cabinet. Nor was Arthur Henderson entirely discouraging … [Mosley] worked furiously on it over the Christmas recess."

79 ***Ibid.:***

"Early in January [1930] Thomas announced that the Bank of England and the City of London were ready to 'give financial advice and backing' to the rationalisation (or modernisation) of the basic industries. This whole strategy was directly opposed to everything that Mosley and the left wing of the Labour Party stood for. … Thomas certainly knew what was afoot. Early in January Mosley 'casually' told him that he 'had jotted down a number of new proposals on "our special problem"' and added: 'Some of these ideas you will agree with and some you'll probably turn down; but in any case Jim, I'd like you to see them.' Whether Mosley told him on this occasion that he definitely intended to appeal over Thomas's head to the Cabinet is not clear. He was determined that his new proposals should not be stalled in Thomas's department as all his previous ones had been. … John Strachey & Allan Young no doubt helped more actively with its preparation; but the style alone suggests that Mosley was the sole author. The Memorandum was initialled on the 16th of January 1930. Mosley immediately sent a copy to Keynes: 'The enclosed document' he wrote, 'is of course very confidential but I should greatly value your opinion on it….'"

80 ***The Fascists in Britain, op. cit.:***

"News that Mosley had submitted a memorandum leaked quickly to the Press, appearing first in the ***London Letter*** of the ***Manchester Guardian***. There followed weeks of newspaper speculation and by the time the Cabinet finally rejected it, in March [sic] 1930, Mosley's public reputation was at stake."

81 ***Oswald Mosley, op. cit.:***

"The Cabinet Committee to consider the ***Memorandum*** met for the first time on the 14th of March 1930. Before it was a draft report submitted by Sir Frederick Leith-Ross rejecting every single proposal which Mosley made … It took … until the first of May to produce a final report, almost identical with the one considered on the 14th of March. This came before the Cabinet on the 8th of May. Another Cabinet Committee, this time headed by RMD, was formed to discuss the report with the advisory ministers…."

82 ***Ibid.:***

"The [Labour] Party itself was growing restive. At party meetings on the 19th of February, the 12th & 19th of March and the 9th of April, 80 Labour backbenchers demanded a discussion on the ***Memorandum***. They were told that the Cabinet was considering it. From two Labour journalists came slashing attacks on Government unemployment policy. Thomas's reliance on the City, the Bank of England and the traditional export industries was 'perilously mistaken', wrote H N Brailsford of the ILP's ***New Leader*** on 14/02/30. It was to the home market that the Government should look. 'For our part, we believe that … the main emphasis ought to be put on the provision of work' rather than the doles, wrote the ***New Statesman*** the next day. 'Let Mr. Thomas be left to get on with rationalisation and other long-run measures for industrial revival; but let us have also another department, under a Minister of its own, with the sole mission of working out a big scheme for employing the unemployed at useful work. If this is the outcome of the ***Lansbury-Mosley Memorandum***, both the Labour Party and the country will have good cause for satisfaction.'"

83 ***Ibid.:***

"The only course of action that seemed to hold out any prospect of success [for Mosley] was to resign from the Government and appeal directly to the Labour Party. What advice the Webbs gave on this critical occasion [when he dined with them on the 19th of May] is not recorded. Beatrice found the Mosleys 'sincere and assiduous in their public aims', which from her was high praise indeed. At any rate, the decision to resign was taken some time that evening … Mosley handed in his letter of resignation to RMD at lunchtime the following day. Ministers made a last effort to get him to change his mind. Mosley was adamant … [his] resignation was an important political event, but it did not become overwhelmingly so until his parliamentary speech of the 28th of May 1930."

84 ***Ibid.:***

"On the 22nd of May 1930 Mosley appealed to the PLP against the Cabinet's verdict ... Mosley's eloquence was largely offset by Arthur Henderson's shrewdness ... When Henderson produced his compromise formula Mosley 'turned to his satellite moon (whom some would hold to have been his evil genius) John Strachey ... to consult him about acceptance. Strachey's counsel was to refuse. "What the people want is Action."' So Mosley declined to withdraw: 29 MPs supported him; 210 supported the Government. ... Rarely can a parliamentary speech have been greeted with such unanimous critical acclaim. 'Has RMD found his superseder in Oswald Mosley?' asked Beatrice Webb. Even the unfriendly ***Times*** agreed that it had made a 'profound impression'....The remainder of the press was even more fulsome [footnote: ***Morning Post, Daily Mail, Daily Express, Daily Herald, Evening Standard, Daily Telegraph, Daily News, Spectator 31/05/30, Nation 07/06/30, Observer 01/06/30***]."

85 ***The Independent ... Twenties, Marwick, op. cit.***

86 ***Britain ... Wars, Mowat, op. cit.:***

"There were 140 MPs who belonged to the ILP, but only 37 of these had been elected with the financial support of the ILP. At the ILP Conference at Birmingham at Easter 1930, Maxton obtained passage of a resolution that the ILP group in Parliament should be reconstructed on the basis of acceptance of ILP policy. This was done, but only 18 of the 140 accepted membership on these terms. Between this smaller group [footnote: including Maxton, Jowett, Brockway, W.J. Brown, Strachey, E.F. Wise, R.C. Wallhead, Kirkwood, J. McGovern, Campbell Stephen and Jennie Lee, a miner's daughter who had been elected for North Lanark in 1928 at the age of 24] and the rest of the Labour Party differences became strained and personal."

87 ***The Fascists in Britain, op. cit.:***

"Disappointment with the Government's record had brought the [Parliamentary Labour] party to a highly fissile state. The 17 members of the Parliamentary Group of the ILP were already in a state of semi-independence, with James Maxton as their leader, and John Beckett, MP for Peckham, as their whip."

88 John Beckett had a dispassionate viewpoint on this:

"John on his own account stayed aloof, sharing Maxton's distrust both of Mosley himself and of the proposals. John was certainly not among Mosley's supporters, although on the first of August 1930 [Hugh] Dalton wrote in his dairy, rather bewilderingly: 'Beckett - Sandham - Mosley. The Posing Peacocks and the Booby. But against the Tired Timidity of Leaders, not a quite unnatural foreground.'"

The Rebel who lost his Cause: The Tragedy of John Beckett, MP, by Francis Beckett

89 ***Oswald Mosley, op. cit.:***

"Mosley called for a new parliamentary 'machine' to replace the 19th century one. Parliament, he said, must become a workshop not a talkshop."

90 ***Ibid.:***

"Parliament, he asserted, was supreme in handling "political questions" which had dominated the 19th century. It was much less successful in handling economic issues which had come to dominate the 20th century. These should be handled by an economic sub-parliament 'free altogether from party exigencies, and composed of persons possessing special qualifications in economic matters'."

91 ***The Fascists in Britain, op. cit.***

92 ***Oswald Mosley, op. cit.:***

"Brown, the son of a Battersea plumber, had entered Parliament for Wolverhampton West in 1929, aged 34. Founder of the Civil Service Clerical Association, he had soon become a stern critic of Snowden's deflationary policy. An able, fiery man, burning with indignation, he wanted Mosley to leave the Labour Party and start a new movement within the ILP."

93 ***The Fascists in Britain, op. cit.***

94 ***Oswald Mosley, op. cit.:***

"From his seat on the floor of the hall to which [Mosley] had returned he had to get up to acknowledge the cheering which refused to die away. 'There were many to say that here was the Moses to lead them out of the wilderness' wrote the ***Morning Post*** the next day. One delegate, with more contemporary parallels in mind, was heard to shout 'The English Hitler' ..."

95 ***Britain ... Wars, op. cit.:***

"Mosley ought to have noticed, not the ovation his speech received, but the cheers which greeted the Prime Minister's two speeches - the first drawing on the grief which all felt at the death 2 days before (05/10/30) of Lord Thomson, the Air Secretary and 48 of the 54 persons on the airship ***R101*** when it burst into flames and was wrecked near Beauvais, in northern France, while on a test flight to India. Instead, Mosley believed, as Lord Randolph Churchill had done over 40 years earlier, that he had a real party following, and prepared to lead it."

96 ***Oswald Mosley, op. cit.:***

"In its final form, it was a collective enterprise in the truest sense of the word - a tribute to Mosley's capacity to subordinate his own ideas to ideas of others. Indeed, judged by Mosley's own evolution since his resignation the most striking thing about the ***Manifesto*** was its dropping of the imperialist theme."

97 ***Ibid.***

98 ***Ibid.:***

"There was expected and unexpected support. Walter Elliot, Bob Boothby, Moore-Brabazon & Harold Macmillan fired off letters of generous praise to the national papers. Harold Nicolson applauded in a BBC broadcast on the 12th of December. Garvin in the ***Observer*** lauded Mosley for his 'brilliant fearlessness'. The ***Manifesto*** had a surprisingly good press from religious journals. ... Soon after his resignation from the Government [Mosley] had been introduced to Sir William Morris (later Lord Nuffield) by Colonel Wyndham Portal, a soldier turned businessman. The motor-car manufacturer knew little about politics, but was convinced the country was in a mess and that something needed to be done about it. In September he called for a 'strong Government ... a real leader.' Mosley, he decided, was the leader the country needed. In December he praised the ***Manifesto*** as a 'ray of hope', seeing it as the nucleus of an 'industrial party' to bring the country out of its 'slough of despond'."

99 ***The Fascists in Britain, op. cit.***

3: GOING IT ALONE

Creating a completely new political party, not just realigning a disparate collection of disgruntled Members [realistically, an ever-present feature of British politics] and allowing them to coalesce into a noisy group [but as yet ineffective, as had generally been the case hitherto] of like mind, was a radical step, and sent shockwaves emanating through the British Establishment; there had been previous attempts at similar undertakings [and some contemporary efforts, which almost threatened to mask the fledgling New Party **1**], but none with so charismatic and well-placed a figurehead as was Mosley, and the changes of allegiance of a significant number of sitting Members shook all the major parties quite severely. In truth, Mosley wasn't the sole instigator of the New Party; as alluded to in Chapter 2, W. J. Brown, the sitting Labour MP for Wolverhampton West, had provided significant impetus for this departure and, according to John Beckett, Mosley had actually prevaricated somewhat before deciding to take the plunge, which could just as easily be interpreted as evidence of political maturity in wanting to weigh up the possible ramifications, as it could be evidence of indecision [**2**].

Nevertheless, Mosley was prepared to provide the public face for this new venture, no doubt fuelling the public perception by some of his need for attention; Beatrice Webb, who had previously been impressed by Mosley's socialist fervour, and whose husband Sidney was in the Cabinet, did not see any future in this move, comparing him unfavourably with Hitler, who had yet to show his true colours internationally [**3**]. The core of this group was based in Birmingham, putting Wilfred, notwithstanding his personal connection with Mosley, at the heart of events as they unfolded; prior to the formation of the New Party, what had already become known as "Mosleyism" had been described as "Birminghamism rampant", and there was also significant support from the mining community, another area where interests coincided with Wilfred's [**4**].

As can be seen in **Appendix B**, Wilfred was still active within the ILP, in his capacity of Midlands Divisional Organiser, right up to early February 1931, even though plans for the official inception of the New Party, which actually took place on the first of March [although Mosley had the previous day, perhaps against medical advice, appealed for volunteers and funds at head office, despite the pneumonia racking him, and with hindsight rashly promising to run 400 candidates at the next election], must have been well advanced; no doubt there will have been many reasons for this, not the least of which will have been loyalty, although according to Skidelsky, "the New Party's open bid for ILP support [was] facilitated by the initial willingness of many ILP Branches to tolerate membership of both organisations" [**5**]. Birmingham Borough Labour Party however, as personified by its president,

Jim Johnson, was not impressed, appearing to be more disappointed than aggrieved, acknowledging [as he could hardly avoid] the help Mosley had given the Party machine specifically, and the Socialist Movement generally, in Birmingham and the West Midlands; in a contemporary article in ***Labour Magazine***, he said, somewhat sniffily, that "The New Party will appeal to the people with catch phrases and quack remedies in a definite attempt to smash the Labour Party and to discredit its leaders for ever. The centre of their attack in the Midlands is to be Birmingham." [**6**] This suggestion of violence from the New Party, either verbal or physical, or both, was unwarranted, and appears to have been made in the spirit of 'offence being the best form of defence', and was an obvious attempt to cast the party and its proponents in a bad light from the outset; aggressive criticism of the opposition, although generally falling short of actual violence, was a common feature of British adversarial party politics, but there was actually a concerted campaign, including "violent opposition", ironically instigated by the socialists, in a precursor of the later Communist "class against class" policy, to prevent this new movement gaining any credence in the public view [**7**].

During the planning period, Mosley was doing his best to sever his connection with existing Birmingham affiliations: "the painful task of disengaging himself from Smethwick", according to Skidelsky [**8**]; however, he didn't want to reveal the details of his plans until the very last moment [**9**]. Unfortunately, Mosley's health, whose unreliability had already been noted by the likes of Beatrice Webb, broke down again, right at the very moment when his galvanising vigour was most needed, and it was left to the rank & file members, no doubt including Wilfred, and the few 'celebrity' [as they would now be referred to] figures, to take the yoke, although Mosley did just manage to find the strength to try and persuade W. J. Brown to override the wishes of his union and remain within the New Party but, alas, to no avail [**10**]. Wilfred was undoubtedly one of the earliest members of the Party, and his talents were very quickly put to use, initially in a general organising and, crucially, a recruiting capacity in Birmingham [**11**]. Here one has to read between the lines, as there are no specific references to be had to Wilfred's day-to-day activities over the next few weeks, before the first major challenge [other than the metaphorical and physical struggles of public meetings] arose for the party. The meetings commenced with no delay, despite Mosley's incapacity, in the month of March 1931, and there is no reason to suppose that Wilfred did not have a hand in organising at least some of these [**12**]; the first was, understandably, in London, at the Memorial Hall, Faringdon Street; then the campaign hit the provinces. Disruption occurred at that first meeting and, according to Skidelsky, "pursued the New Party team through the country", although the rabble only succeeded in actually breaking up two of the meetings: Dundee on the 19th, and Hull on the 23rd [**13**].

The aforementioned challenge, which arose in April 1931, was the by-election in Ashton-under-Lyne, near Manchester, "[a] Lancashire cotton conglomerate of unrelieved drabness" [**14**], as a result of the death of the incumbent Labour MP. According to Cross, Mosley had been "[b]rooding on his own", "convalescing at Monaco" after his illness, and he decided to hit back at Labour "in the place where it would hurt most". [**15**] Ashton was regarded as a marginal seat, having been gained in 1929 with a majority of 'only' 3,407, and Wilfred was given the significantly important task of election Agent for the high-profile candidate with the appropriate working class background, Allan Young: this fact is not mentioned generally, rather curiously given the nature of the job; Cross is a notable exception [perhaps because he was able to interview Wilfred personally for his book], and Skidelsky unfortunately confuses the issue by giving the impression that Dan Davies, Strachey's Agent at Aston [Birmingham], was also Agent here [**16**]. Young was the personal choice of Mosley, according to Cross, but his reasons for the fight, which went beyond traditional party loyalties, and the risk he was prepared to take, did not go down well with the committee of the Manchester New Party branch, which promptly resigned in protest [**17**]. As Young's electoral Agent, Wilfred will have been at the heart of the planning of the campaign; he probably wouldn't have had a problem with the local volunteers for the campaign, as reported by the ***Evening Standard***; indeed, he might well have had a hand in recruiting them; however, what he thought of what Skidelsky presumed to be Harold Nicolson's [**18**] contribution to the campaign, "fourteen strapping young men wearing plus-fours", was another matter! [**19**]

There is a slight variance between Skidelsky's and Mosley's own reports of the meetings in this campaign; the former tells us [***Oswald Mosley***] that, on his return "from his sickbed", six days before the poll, Mosley held two big meetings, at the Palais de Danse, and the Drill Hall; whereas Mosley himself [***My Life***] maintains that he held three meetings at the Drill Hall, "which held nearly four thousand", but omits to mention that, prior to his arrival, the "New Party team" had braved the inclement elements to speak outdoors [**20**]. In any event, it was, of necessity, a somewhat rushed campaign, the prosecution of which Wilfred had neither the time, nor the resources [unusually for Mosley although, given his absence through illness and tendency to autocratic leadership, understandable] to exploit fully, and it is to the credit of both Young and Mosley that neither reportedly held the virtually inevitable result against him. Labour was beaten into second place by the Conservative candidate [**21**], and the New Party candidate achieved the "creditable showing" of 16% of the votes cast, 4,472 [**22**], just saving his deposit [**23**], no doubt also a face-saving result, at the very least. The Labour supporters, predictably, did not take the result well; a crowd, described as "hundreds" by Skidelsky, of "howling Labour militants" made its presence felt, even before the New Party contingent appeared on the steps of the Town Hall [having already, on police advice, arranged "for the ladies of the party" to leave surreptitiously by a side exit] and it was immediately obvious at whom the venom was directed: Mosley [**24**]. He later played down this turn of events in his autobiography, blaming Communist orchestration, as well as the oft-quoted remark, made to John Strachey, that "That is the crowd that has prevented anyone doing anything in England since the war." [**25**], and Strachey's revelation "that this was the moment when fascism was born" [**26**]: even contemporaneously, that was somewhat melodramatic, notwithstanding the difficulty in agreeing upon a consensual definition of 'fascism', because Mosley had been toying with the idea of fascism for some time before this, both inwardly and in private discussions; he already thought of the New Party as a "modern movement" [**27**], with its inevitably fascistic connotations.

What is generally not noted as occurring when Mosley characteristically faced down the angry mob and metaphorically parted the Red Sea, to leave the scene with dignity intact, is that he turned to Wilfred and said "We saw worse than this in the war, Bill": Cross, again, is a notable exception [**28**]. Mosley himself is minimal in his summation of the remaining period of the New Party's existence: apart from mentioning a few high-profile defections [described here below], he merely says that "The days of the New Party were now numbered. We had to develop a different character to meet an entirely new situation." [**29**] That is true in retrospect, but the everyday reality, of which Wilfred was an integral part, was that the New Party would struggle on for another year before Mosley bowed to the inevitable, in one sense, but also anchored himself as an independent force to be reckoned with, in another. The public meetings continued, but at a less frenetic pace, and after Ashton the main focus of attention, internally, was upon security, and protection of personnel at these regularly rowdy meetings. Deliberate disruption of political meetings was by no means new, but it is a fact that there was a publicly stated policy by the opposition to crush this fledgling movement, and the embodiment of that invariably involved more than mere heckling [something Mosley positively relished]; there was a concerted and undeniably communist-sponsored campaign of aggression at New Party meetings [although a future collaborator for Wilfred, John Beckett, also felt the sting of this campaign **30**]; politics at this time was becoming, to a greater or lesser extent, factionally defended with paramilitary support [**31**]. What Wilfred thought about this is unknown; his adoption of noncombatant status during the war, whether this was a conscious decision or not, albeit fifteen years previously, since when plenty had happened in his life, is fairly clear evidence of his dislike of the military solution and its trappings, including uniforms; however, he must also have been aware that one of the most precious attributes of the British way of life, freedom of speech, was under threat, so it is most likely that he would have been in favour of Mosley's preferred and publicly-stated [and genuine; not purely expedient] option: "the good old English fist" [**32**].

Mosley, with his constantly evolving political ethos was already becoming *persona non grata* within the Establishment and its voice, the national media [**33**], so a 'secret' conclave [so secret that it was immediately reported in the Press] was urgently convened for the New Party hierarchy on the 14th of May. Mosley, Strachey, Young and "Bill" Allen were among the leaders who attended. There was no argument that New Party speakers should be ensured a fair hearing, but notwithstanding general agreement that the youthful element should be the focus of the recruitment and training, Strachey and Young were beginning to feel uneasy about the anti-left wing thrust of the 'protection' being proposed [**34**]. This conclave was followed within a couple of weeks or so by an all-encompassing 'Congress' at the Mosleys' modest country retreat at Denham. This wet weekend in June, "a mixture of country-house party and ILP summer school", according to Skidelsky, was an occasion when all opinions and, no doubt, grievances, could be aired. Mosley was prepared to support the regional organisers, of whom Wilfred was now one, in building up the regional structures first, in preference to the contesting of further by-elections, for the time being, as favoured by the "active young men based on London" [**35**]. Events of only a few months later would force them to reappraise this policy. This was possibly the first meeting between Wilfred and the newly appointed New Party Chief Agent, F M Box [**36**], a former Conservative Party agent.

It is clear that some time in the middle of 1931, Wilfred was despatched to the north east of England, to develop a regional organisation, and thereby build membership and loyalty. Here Wilfred was in a somewhat invidious position; he was on a salary, and it was important for the Party to broaden its appeal beyond the relatively politically sophisticated confines of London, which he undoubtedly worked very hard to achieve, but this tends to highlight Mosley's so far ill-defined objectives: he knew what he didn't want, but apart from the generalities of social reform and being poised to spring into action "to fight communism in a revolutionary situation" [**37**], he wasn't sure about how to achieve what he did want [**38**]. That said, local branches did undoubtedly make a contribution [**39**]. Wilfred became one of the six regional organisers, and by the beginning of October, he had created branches in Hull [stretching the 'north-east' appellation somewhat], Newcastle & Gateshead, with the latter, mentioned in the ***Evening Chronicle*** of the 10th of October 1931, comprising "a relatively large party of some fifty members" [**40**]. Wilfred was just getting into his stride, so to speak, in the north east, when the previous understanding was overturned by events at Westminster. With the economic situation deteriorating dangerously during the summer of that year [prior to which Mosley saw no reason not to go off to the Continent for his customary summer holiday], on the 24th of August

Ramsay MacDonald and four members of the Labour Cabinet had joined forces with the Conservatives in a National Government to save the pound [naturally enough, a higher priority than providing work for the huge numbers of unemployed], thereby causing Mosley to cut short his holiday, returning on the 26th, and forcing a reappraisal by him of the likelihood of success in appealing to Labour to support the New Party's avowed aim of assisting the working classes, given that Labour had "transformed the crisis into a class conflict" [**41**]. Mosley, with Nicolson's support, toyed with the idea of joining the National Coalition, but wisely [although not in everybody's opinion, inevitably] he demurred, preferring to keep his Party untainted by what he conjectured the inevitable failure of this reconstituted Government, saying with no intentional irony "The movement is more important than the Party" [**42**].

At the same time as bringing forward both the publication date for the new weekly Party periodical, ***Action***, and the dates for the autumn speaking campaign, Mosley initiated a plan for an "active force" of stewards, supplied in part by a nationwide network of athletic clubs which was aimed at British youth; this was overseen by a former world welterweight boxing champion, Gershom Mendeloff, aka Ted "Kid" Lewis. Wilfred had to include this into his remit in the north east, as well as "the whole Boy Scout paraphernalia of uniforms, badges, saluting, flags, etc. into the Youth Movement", which "Glyn Williams was busily introducing" [**43**]. Unsurprisingly, this created internal tensions almost immediately; as early as July, before the latest national crisis became apparent, the intellectuals [generally less inclined to physical 'action'] began to resent the "fascist overtones" of the more aggressive party members, which had Mosley's apparently tacit approval [**44**], but Wilfred was evidently prepared to assimilate the two sides [even though he would not have considered himself an intellectual, notwithstanding his socialist convictions] to move the programme forward.

Towards the end of July, three of the most significant founder members of the party left. According to Skidelsky, Mosley had asked John Strachey to submit a memo defining the New Party's attitude towards Russia, and what Mosley described as Strachey's "strange memorandum" no doubt used the cover of trying to "force the question of the New Party's place in the political spectrum" [**45**] as a way of clarifying once and for all if Mosley was for the workers or against them; later Mosley would apparently ignore the subtext, describing it as "contradicting directly the whole basis of the policy we had long agreed together", claiming charitably that "John Strachey and others like him were taken in by a front of plaster concealing an ugly visage, which happily is not yet in charge of England and certainly does not represent the mass of the British people." [**46**] The memo was rejected by a majority of 3 votes in the New Party Executive, so on the 24th of July, the only two supporters of the memo, Strachey and Allan Young, resigned from the party; one of the party's leading intellectuals, Cyril Joad, left two days later, ostensibly in a huff over Mosley's rejection of his request for more influence in shaping New Party policy, but also fearing "the 'cloven hoof' of fascism" [**47**].

These defections didn't affect Wilfred personally, notwithstanding his previous close association with Allan Young, a similarly instinctive socialist, but he would have been painfully aware of the damage it would do to the credentials of the party in the eyes of the workers he was trying to woo, aside from his new quest of the youth who would have known little about Young and probably cared less. Matthew Worley goes so far as to associate Wilfred with "Bill" Allen and Box, ex-Conservatives, as "looking for something far more hard-headed and militant" [**48**]; that might or might not be true, but it is very probably the case that by then, Wilfred will have had his fair share of consensual committee politics. Just before the aforementioned schism, the Executive had decided to disband any local organisation outside the 50 constituencies that were going to be contested at the next election, which also served to alienate grass roots organising members; whether any of the 26 seats which didn't 'make the cut' were in Wilfred's region, when the election finally materialised, is not clear, but of the 24 which did, only one, Gateshead, was, so the net result would have been Wilfred doing more street-level work, something with which he was well familiar, and less liaison. It would appear that he was having to make the proverbial 'silk purse from a sow's ear', accruing a poor share of the Party's resources, which must have been one of several tests of his loyalty along the way, and it is hardly surprising that the main party branch for which he was responsible, Gateshead, didn't have a smooth passage to the general election [**49**].

Since the National Government had been formed in late August, following Ramsay MacDonald's resignation on the back of the austerity measures recommended by the May Committee [**50**], it considered that it was in a strong enough position to go off the gold standard on the 21st of September, leaving the way clear for an election to be called on the 8th of October [the date, with a mixture of planning and happy happenstance, of publication of the first issue of ***Action***], as Mosley had recognised in his final House of Commons speech; once again, he dallied with the Tories, but only to try to ensure a clear run against Labour candidates in a few seats; he certainly wasn't about to turn his back on his personal project to rejoin any of the old parties. Wilfred's main focus in Gateshead was supporting the candidacy of his old friend from Birmingham, James Stuart Barr; seemingly, Barr's main opponent was the general secretary and one of the founder members of the Transport and General Workers' Union [TGWU], Ernest Bevin [**51**]. Here, Wilfred encountered strong opposition; not from local Labour supporters, but from within the Party itself: as reported in the ***Evening Chronicle*** of October 3rd and 10th, 1931, following Wilfred's appeal to prepare the way for Barr's candidature [very possibly in preference to a more popular local candidate], several members resigned "on the grounds that the organisation is a Fascist dictatorship not acceptable to working-class members", and one of the branch's Executive members, J. Swanston, summed up his feelings thus: "[T]he policy of getting up a mobile force to act as a bodyguard to satisfy persons who are looking for limelight in the political world does not appeal to me." [**52**]

The hustings meetings in the campaign generally passed off relatively peacefully, apart from when Mosley himself was speaking, seeming to bring out the best of enthusiasm and the worst of truculence in audiences; some, apparently, "attracted hardly any response at all". Despite Wilfred's best efforts, as reported by the ***Evening Chronicle*** of October 23rd, Barr "turned up at an election meeting in Gateshead to find just six people in attendance" [**53**]; fat chance of a disturbance there! Wilfred might have allowed himself a wry smile when reading reports of a veritable riot at the meeting at Birmingham's Rag Market just before this; had he been there, no doubt he would have defended himself and, by extension, freedom of speech, but he was probably not sorry to have escaped the inevitable injury, however minor. The election manifesto comprised a 5-point programme of reform of Parliament; scientific protection; national planning; imperial co-operation; and a General Powers Bill for government, enabling it to rule by Orders in Council, instead of the current situation, seemingly endless debates in the House with minimal results, and it was this apparently fascist manoeuvre which concerned socialists the most. "A certain surrender of political liberty as now understood may be an essential corollary of such a movement and such an achievement", Mosley had written a year before, when his "contemplated movement" was still taking shape [**54**].

The election was a humiliating rout for the New Party, with not one candidate elected, thereby confirming Nicolson's prediction in a document dated 25th of September 1931, entitled ***Notes on the Future of the New Party***, that the party would fall between the two stools of a National Coalition which would "'take from us' slogans of unification, patriotism, insulation and planning"; and an "openly socialist" Labour Party, which would "eclipse the New Party's anti-capitalist position and, similarly, base its programme on an economic plan". Barr's defeat at Gateshead did have the effect of splitting the vote sufficiently to deny Bevin a seat, gifting the seat to the surprising [and, no doubt, surprised!] winner, the "Liberal National" candidate, Thomas Magnay [**55**]. Mosley was the first to concede that something had to change, if his concept of a New Movement was to bear fruit. The first response, hardly surprisingly, was to economise and take stock; the already limited national apparatus of the party was to be further reduced by the closure of regional offices, and the dismissal of all paid staff except Box, Dr. Forgan and Peter Howard; the central office in Great George Street was also now surplus to requirements, meaning that the New

Party virtually ceased to exist as a political party. The flag would now be carried by the embryonic Youth Club organisation, known as NUPA [a slightly American sounding mnemonic for NuParty], which had been started in September, to embody Mosley's assertion that a youth organisation was vital for a virile modern movement such as his. Naturally, this left Wilfred with a problem; he was as committed to the movement as ever, and Mosley would have been keen to retain his services to develop the youth movement in the north east, but he had severed his connections with his previous base in Birmingham, and he needed an income to survive.

His solution, somewhat unexpectedly given his background of manual labour, was to open an advertising agency, which he would later describe as being [in the September of the following year] "small and struggling" [**56**], which is hardly surprising, considering the economic climate prevailing at the time. Cynically, one might take the view that the intervening years between his mine work and his current impecunious state had made him soft, and he was still relatively young, but it could also be construed as pragmatism; Mosley would have made it abundantly clear to him that for all the party was no longer viable, the movement most certainly was, and he needed to be in a position where he could make himself available to cultivate and encourage the youth side of the movement, notwithstanding the precarious state of the mining industry in the north east. It is interesting to speculate whether Wilfred's acquaintance with a former ILP high flyer, John Beckett, who ten years or so earlier had relinquished "a promising career in advertising to become a full-time politician" [**57**] influenced his decision. Coincidentally, Beckett was also MP for Gateshead from 1924 to 1929, so Wilfred might well have called upon him for local knowledge.

No doubt for a variety of reasons, Wilfred's budding north east section of the New Party dwindled to a rump of committed supporters, essentially because of withdrawal of what had hitherto been, admittedly, limited resources, and the new year started with an instruction from headquarters to forgo any pretensions to local autonomy, for the sake of the limited but powerful target of youth [**58**], although Wilfred did receive some physical assistance [**59**]. During its limited 13-issue print run, ***Action***, finally deemed a ruinously expensive luxury, while skirting around the subject increasingly on people's lips, Fascism, did fulminate on two subjects at the core of New Party ideology, the Corporate State and, something in Wilfred's remit latterly, the youth movement, although the messages transmitted seemed mixed [**60**]. One thing was for certain: the organisational and operational styles of the New Party were increasingly displaying military characteristics [**61**]; as mentioned above, the youngsters were wearing uniforms, and the drilled and trained stewards, who came to be known as "biff boys", also had a uniform of sorts, grey flannel trousers and shirts, as suggested by Harold Nicolson, "in one last effort to preserve English middle-class respectability" [although few of the stewards, if any, would have been in a hurry to wear the official Party "colours" favoured by Nicolson, the orange of the marigold flower]. The London organisation was stripped down to the bare minimum [**62**], and the existence of a political party was formally terminated in April 1932 [**63**]. Notwithstanding the coyness of ***Action***, discreet moves had been going on in the background, as early as the fallout from the election débâcle [**64**], to consider the application of Mosley's interpretation of the creed of Fascism to the New Party, or what it was to become; for Mosley, the allure of military discipline in a civilian political setting was almost irresistible [**65**].

In January 1932, Mosley went to Rome, accompanied by Nicolson, W.E.D. ["Bill"] Allen [**66**] and Christopher Hobhouse [**67**], to study the Italian version of Fascism at close quarters. Mussolini advised Mosley against trying "the military stunt" in England, although calling himself a Fascist made sense [**68**]; the *Duce's* counsel on the first point was well-meant, but unnecessary. No doubt confident in the knowledge that his loyal and industrious acolytes were doing their utmost in trying circumstances to further his cause, Mosley was uninhibited in his pursuit of both leisure and sport during 1932; the Villa d'Este in Como [admittedly allowing Cimmie to convalesce after Michael's birth at the end of April] and the Venice Lido were locations of the leisure [**69**]; fencing and "the new craze of all-in wrestling" represented the sport [**70**]. In between all this apparent hedonism, Mosley did find time to apply himself to a reconciliation of the currently existing disparate fascist groups, using Dr. Forgan as an intermediary, with a view to uniting them, now that he saw this as the way forward, naturally under the assured guiding hands of his leadership. Even though he was critical of the two main fascist groups in Britain [**71**], he did chair a meeting on the 27th of April, when two exponents of what was becoming Mosley's new creed fulminated to NUPA on "The Blindness of British Politics under the Jew Money-Power". During May and June, Mosley worked on "his exposition of the policy and philosophy of the new movement" [**72**], ***The Greater Britain***. A former member of the British Fascist Grand Council, Neil Francis-Hawkins, whose proposal for a merger had been rejected by the leader of the British Fascists, provided Mosley with a membership and subscription list, to which, in addition to his own members, he sent a circular letter announcing the formation of a new political movement [**73**].

Wilfred was evidently gratified by this demonstration of positive action, and he was one of the privileged few to receive an advance copy of Mosley's book, a month ahead of the publication date; he sprang into action, creating one of the very first branches in the country of the platform for Mosley's new crusade: the British Union of Fascists [**74**]. The name was significant: in the face of doubts, if not actual dissension, Mosley felt the adoption of the label Fascist was important, and not automatically redolent of foreign influence; as was the movement's emblem, and the origin of its name, the Fasces [**75**]. Wilfred was later to assert [**Appendix D**] that he did not much care for the use of the Fasces, essentially because of what he saw as its foreign origin, but this objection was not "so rooted" because it was pointed out to him that it was used not only as a political symbol, but also in most of the civil institutions of the country. Even though the organisation was effectively 'up and running' before this, courtesy of stalwarts like Wilfred, the official launch was set for Saturday, October the first; thirty-two founder members, most of whom wore black shirts, attended a solemn inaugural ceremony at the former New Party office at Great George Street, and Mosley read out a message to his fellow travellers in an upper room [**76**]: the next stage of the journey was under way.

A conclusion to this chapter is in order, because it is the end of the first phase of Wilfred's life, the search for a meaning to all of his hitherto well-intentioned but generic socialism, when he was prepared, albeit latterly with increasing disenchantment, to trust the established leaders of the left to do just that, lead: sadly, he was disappointed. Now he had a creed, espoused by a leader he revered, that he believed would bring the change which was so sorely needed in Britain. In retrospect, it is unfortunate, for obvious reasons, that this creed was Fascism, but at the time, it was either poorly enough known, or understood, or both, notwithstanding its apparently foreign origins, for its adherents to be able to see beyond the crude attempts at derogation by its opponents; add to that the obvious fact that, initially, Wilfred was not unduly concerned with its name: more relevant and, indeed significant, was the fact of its leader, and its intent.

What is clear is that the New Party was the embodiment of the break from party politics which Mosley had been striving for, and the moulding of a vehicle which its proponents would hold up as a shining example of a way of cutting through the debate and dealing with issues, rather than adhering to a party line, whereas its detractors would decry it as a glaring example of the cult of personality which Mosley was building up around himself. By 1930, Wilfred had seen enough of party politics to know that a party line was very often a physical obstacle to progress, and he was prepared to trust Mosley as a leader, which means that he must have agreed sufficiently with Mosley's analysis of the problems, and the action required, to risk leaving behind his relatively comfortable existence as a career Socialist and throw his hat in the ring with this group of evident outcasts. The final word can, quite rightly, be left to Wilfred himself to sum up this juncture, as he was to write nearly five years later [**77**]:

> "We who set out to do this in the New Party in 1931 had to exclude from our minds all prejudices and start from the existing evil to find a remedy for that evil. We gradually built up an economic policy (and that policy incidentally has never yet been seriously criticised by any of our present-day economists) which fitted the needs of the moment.

In that policy we found three vital factors, all of which were essential to success, all of which constitutes fundamental differences from Socialism. We found that Nationalism was essential as opposed to Internationalism. We found that class collaboration was essential on a national basis, as opposed to class antagonism on an international basis. We found that the preservation of the rights of private property, carrying with it certain new obligations for the owners of private property, was essential, as opposed to the abolition of private property rights. (Please remember those three points – they will crop up again later.)

We also decided that the interests of thc State as a whole comprised the interests of every section within the State. That just as in the human body every limb and every organ is attuned to serve the whole of the body, so in society every sectional interest must be subordinated to the general interest of the State as a whole. This is the corporate conception of society, and this was where we arrived definitely at what is called Fascism or National Socialism."

NOTES

1 According to Robert Skidelsky:

"Unfortunately for him, starting new parties appeared to be the height of fashion just then. Beaverbrook was running a candidate against Baldwin at the St George's by-election; Churchill had just left the opposition front bench over India; Sir John Simon had removed a dozen or so Liberals from the Lloyd George fold; the ILP was hovering tremulously on the brink of leaving the Labour Party. The tiny New Party got somewhat lost among all these splinters."

Oswald Mosley, by Robert Skidelsky

There had also been much earlier attempts:

"The Fabian rejection of class war in favour of a collectivist-anticollectivist alignment also favoured a new grouping. In 1901 Sidney Webb called for a Party of National Efficiency displaying 'virility in government', involving the 'close co-operation of a group of men of diverse temperaments and varied talents, imbued with a common faith and a common purpose', dedicated to removing the slums, destroying the sweated trades & eliminating inefficiency in government and education. A year later he formed a dining club, the Coefficients, intended as the 'General Staff' of a new Social-Imperial Party. Its galaxy of talent included Viscount Milner, who dreamed of 'a nobler socialism which will take the place of socialism based on class warfare', and Carlyon Bellairs who later supported the BUF. Here we find much of the political ancestry of the inter-war projects with which Oswald Mosley was involved - the Centre Party idea of 1920, the New Party, the BUF."

Ibid.

2 ***The Rebel who lost his Cause: The Tragedy of John Beckett, MP, by Francis Beckett:***

"There are several versions of the manner in which the débâcle happened. The truth is that Mosley, after sitting on the fence for some weeks, declared at a small private gathering his willingness to proceed."

3 ***The Fascists in Britain, by Colin Cross:***

"[Beatrice Webb] compared Mosley with Hitler, not yet in power, and observed that the British electorate would not stand a Hitler. 'Mosley has bad health, a slight intelligence and an unstable character - I doubt whether he has the tenacity of a Hitler. He also lacks a genuine fanaticism. Deep down in his heart he is a cynic. He will be beaten and retire.'"

4 ***Oswald Mosley, op. cit.:***

"Eight of the 17 [Labour MPs who signed the ***Mosley Manifesto***] came from the Black Country complex, thus justifying Frank Owen's description of Mosleyism as 'Birminghamism rampant'. Six sat for mining constituencies: three - Batey, Bevan & Cove - were former miners; McShane's father was a miner on the Clyde. The mining connection was of course emphasised by [Arthur] Cook's signature [the only non-MP]. Mosleyism in the Labour Party therefore drew its strength from two sources - the Black Country and the coalmines."

5 As evidenced by the minutes of the Birmingham ILP Branch, 09/04/31

Ibid.

6 The plans for the New Party had evidently not escaped Mr. Johnson's attention:

"... it appears that for many months now, long before any public pronouncements were made, thoughts of a New Party occupied the minds of some half-a-dozen people. The taking-over of the offices at St. George Street [sic] and the gatherings that have taken place there were not lost sight of, and one can say definitely that the formation of the New Party was being proceeded with at the same time as the parties concerned were supposed to still be loyal, if disappointed members of the Labour Party."

Birmingham Labour and the New Party*; J. Johnson, Labour Magazine, Vol. 9, 1931, pp. 534-6*

7 ***The Fascists in Britain, op. cit.:***

"The Labour National Executive immediately expelled them all [Dr. Robert Forgan, Cynthia Mosley & John Strachey] - a redundant step since all had resigned - and declared the New Party a proscribed organisation. Henderson, the Party Secretary, regretted the loss of Mosley, to whom in biblical terms he was wont to refer as 'the rich young man', but he would not tolerate any attempt to split the Labour Movement. Under Henderson's guidance Transport House prepared plans to crush the New Party at birth. Everywhere the New Party speakers met violent opposition, being treated as upper-class traitors to the workers' movement."

8 ***Oswald Mosley, op. cit.***

9 ***Ibid.:***

"As late as mid-February he had given his constituency executive 'emphatic denials' that he was planning to break with Labour. A meeting had been arranged with the Smethwick Trades & Labour Council for Wednesday the 25th. However, on [the] Tuesday, following the press leaks, Mosley asked Lawrence, the Council's president, and Stonier, its secretary, to come to see him in London. Lawrence asked Mosley whether the press reports of his activities were true. Mosley said they were, but that the publicity had not been of his own seeking. He told them that he intended to form a new political party and expected that other groups in the Labour Party, including the ILP, would later join him. Lawrence begged him to reconsider. As long as he stayed in the Labour Party, Smethwick would loyally support him in his quarrel with the Government. Mosley replied that the Labour Party was going to 'rack & ruin' and that he had to try to organise an alternative to chaos. Lawrence responded that as long as the ship was afloat it was everyone's duty to keep it so. Stonier, on their way out, told Allan Young that he was 'a bloody fool' to have anything to do with Mosley's plan. They both agreed, however, to take no action till Mosley had had a chance to come down and explain himself."

10 ***The Fascists in Britain, op. cit.:***

"From the start, misfortune dogged the New Party's footsteps. The early confusions about who was and who was not a member were followed immediately by Mosley catching influenza which turned first to pneumonia and then to pleurisy, putting him out of action for the first six weeks. The work of launching the Party fell on Forgan, Cynthia Mosley and Strachey, who travelled the country to carry out a speaking programme which had been planned for double their number."

Beckett gives details of the Brown *farrago*:

"Brown said that he could not take part because of the attitude of his union and his inability to forfeit their financial support. Mosley guaranteed him against financial loss, and went with Strachey to interview the union executive, who gave permission for Brown to participate. Brown then went to bed, ill. Mosley and Strachey rushed to Highgate to see him, but he was not well enough to be interviewed at any length. Mosley then broke down, and the new movement was ushered in with little welcome from its leaders and inspirers. Mosley retired to bed in Smith Square the day after Brown retired to his bed in Highgate."

The Rebel who lost his Cause: op. cit.

Mosley himself provides added colour:

"The New Party was launched on March 1, 1931. ... On the eve of the opening meeting I fell ill with pleurisy and pneumonia, quite a serious matter before the discovery of antibiotics. I could scarcely lift my head from the pillow. It was too late to postpone the party's inauguration, for the placards were out all over the country. I was advertised to speak at the opening meeting and was to have been seconded by W. J. Brown, M.P., who was experienced and effective both in the House and on the platform. It was decided that the meeting should continue with Brown as the main speaker, assisted by Cimmie and John Strachey. But a message came that Brown could not attend, and he was not available on the telephone.

I ordered an ambulance to take me to his house in the suburbs, where I found him at home. After being carried into his living-room on a stretcher, I asked his reasons for not attending the opening meeting. Then something occurred which I had only seen rarely before; his face seemed to be pulled down on one side like a man suffering a stroke and he burst into tears. He said he would lose his trade union job and his family would be ruined. His fears appeared to me exaggerated because he knew I had already obtained a guarantee from Lord Nuffield to cover his salary for several years. He had never previously voiced these apprehensions, and had always posed as a man of decision, of iron will and resolution.

The very few men in whom previously I had observed this phenomenon had likewise usually rather emphasised their determination and courage before they found themselves averse to getting out of a trench when the time came. W. J. Brown was evidently experiencing the same sensations. I had myself carried back to the ambulance."

My Life, by Oswald Mosley

11 Jim Johnson alludes to it generally in injured tones:

"... when a Socialist with any knowledge of the use they are attempting to put their money to thinks the matter over, he finds it difficult to keep calm. I repeat that one's blood boils at the attempts to buy candidates, organisers, and propagandists, now loyal members of our Movement, by offers of good jobs. I understand that Allan Young has denied the truth of this statement as far as Birmingham is concerned, stating that only Mr. Dan Davies was offered a position. This is, in any case, a mere quibble, for I did not write in my ***Town***

Crier article that the offers were made to people in Birmingham. But here again he is wrong for I know of at least one other case in Birmingham where correspondence will prove that an offer was turned down. The point that matters is that offers have been made, and in what part of the country matters nothing. The whole business is beneath contempt."

Birmingham Labour etc., op. cit. R.P. Hastings is no more specific:

"Since it was essentially a midland movement, Mosley's withdrawal to form his New Party in February 1931 was, perhaps, even more damaging locally than the MacDonald defection. To man his new organisation he took with him John Strachey, M.P. for Aston, Allen [sic] Young, former Borough Labour Party organiser and candidate for Sparkbrook, who became the secretary of the New Party, and a number of other key Birmingham figures."

The Birmingham Labour Movement, 1918-1945, by R.P. Hastings

12 Matthew Worley has the details:

"… the New Party's early forays into the public arena attracted significant interest, if not always of the kind expected. For all the overspill meetings and packed halls recorded in local newspaper reports, the popular response to the New Party was mainly a mix of curiosity and, from the left, resentment at the split in Labour's ranks. As the party was quick to realise, big crowds did not necessarily provide the basis for ready support. [footnote] Some newspaper estimates of the crowds attending the New Party's early meetings include: 3,500 in Stoke, ***Evening Sentinel***, 9 March 1931; 2,500 in Liverpool, ***Liverpool Post and Mercury***, 13 March 1931; 10,000 in Glasgow, ***Glasgow Evening News***, 19 March 1931; 4,000 in Cardiff, ***Western Mail*** and ***South Wales News***, 23 March 1931."

Oswald Mosley and the New Party, by Matthew Worley

13 ***Oswald Mosley, op. cit.:***

"The disrupters were always a small minority and in only two cases - at Dundee (19/03) & at Hull (23/03) - did they succeed in breaking up meetings. If the country was not 'demanding' action, as Mosley thought, it seemed very curious to meet those who were: 3,000 at Aston, Stoke & Liverpool, 2,000 at Leeds, two consecutive meetings of 2,000 at Glasgow. From the first then, there emerged a pattern which hardly varied throughout the 1930s: vast audiences of the curious come to hear the prophet, groups of angry Labour militants & communists determined to prevent him from being heard. The 'case' stated by the New Party's earliest orators was the ***National Policy*** written by Allan Young, John Strachey, W.J. Brown & Aneurin Bevan and published at the end of February."

14 ***Ibid.***

15 ***Ibid.***

16 ***Ibid.:***

"Despite [the] difficulties [of having virtually no time to inform the local electorate] Allan Young & Dan Davies, Strachey's agent at Aston, did succeed in creating a scratch organisation in an astonishingly short space of time."

17 ***The Fascists in Britain, op. cit.:***

"Mosley decided to fight the election even at the risk of splitting the left-wing vote and handing the seat to the Conservatives. The Manchester committee of the New Party resigned in protest, but Mosley, insisting that the modern movement would appeal to right as well as left, pressed ahead and chose Young as the New Party candidate. With Risdon, late of the Birmingham ILP, as agent, Mosley and Strachey moved into Ashton to conduct a vigorous campaign. Conservatives and Labour retaliated by concentrating their Lancashire resources on Ashton."

18 Harold Nicolson was one of the undoubtedly intellectual early converts to Mosley's cause, partly because he occupied Mosley's social *milieu*, being "of course, friends of long standing", but he also brought with him, as well as a traditional confidence in established constitutional politics, a bigotry far worse than that perceived in Mosley. Nicolson came from a career in journalism, latterly, and edited the New Party weekly, ***Action***, for a short, but disastrous [in terms of sales because of the highbrow nature] period from October 1931. Norman Rose sums him up:

"Harold Nicolson [born in November, 1886] was a homosexual who lived with a wife [Victoria 'Vita' Sackville-West, a lesbian, whom he married on the 1st of October 1913] some of the time at Sissinghurst Castle in Kent, and they had two sons, Nigel and Ben. He entered the Diplomatic Service in August 1909 when he passed his exam with distinction, second in his year. He was obviously conventionally racist [describing two Haitian delegates at Edward VII's funeral in 1910 as 'beastly niggers'] and mildly anti-semitic: he watched a play early in his career which concerned 'a Catholic who has a loathing for Jews … the Catholic challenges a Jew to a duel only to discover that the Jew is his father. I must say I sympathise with the Catholic and not a bit with the Jew father … I don't think Jews will be able satisfactorily to write about their own race because they do not see the funny side of it. I think when I grow up I shall try to write a pro-semitic piece.' He never did. … Nicolson was at the Foreign Office during the first world war, under Lord Curzon [Cynthia Mosley's father] and Lord Grey."

Harold Nicolson, by Norman Rose

19 ***Oswald Mosley, op. cit.:***

"Five days after Young's arrival the ***Evening Standard*** reported 'young men with fine foreheads and an expression of faith' dashing from room to room at the New Party offices, brandishing proofsheets and manifestos. … These local volunteers were soon supplemented by 'fourteen strapping young men wearing plus-fours' - presumably Harold Nicolson's contribution to the campaign."

20 ***Ibid.:***

"The New Party team of Young, Cynthia Mosley, Strachey, Cyril Joad & Captain Eckersley (formerly chief engineer at the BBC) all spoke valiantly in the pouring rain: Cimmie, in particular, drew big audiences of wide-eyed girls, perhaps attracted more by her clothes than her politics. Since there were not enough cars, helpers or days to organise a proper canvass, New Party loudspeakers blared out dance music to attract attention.".

21 ***Ibid.:***

"The New Party intervention did not hand the seat to the Tories: with average by-election swings to the Right throughout 1930 & '31 of 8.4%, Ashton would have gone comfortably Tory in any case. If anything, the New

Party reduced the Conservative majority, by capturing a sizeable proportion of the Liberal vote which over the country as a whole was swinging heavily to the Conservatives."

22 ***My Life, op. cit.:***

"just about the number who attended these meetings [at the Drill Hall]."

23 ***Oswald Mosley, op. cit.:***

"Had the exits from the halls led straight to the polling booths, Alan [sic] Young might have swept in to Westminster on the strength of Mosley's oratory alone; but the New Party's attraction seemed much less potent the morning after, when old faiths and habits reasserted themselves. ... 'It was more than was expected when the election opened but not as good as was hoped after the success of the meetings' was Harold Nicolson's verdict."

24 ***Ibid.:***

"Shouts of 'Traitor', 'Dirty Dog', 'Judas', 'You let the Tories in' were hurled at the New Party group. [Labour candidate] Gordon's son ran up the steps of the Town Hall and denounced Mosley for wrecking his father's chances."

25 ***My Life, op. cit.:***

"This is true, but it is clear that I did not mean they were averse to change. What I meant then and mean now is that the long-experienced and entirely dedicated agents and warriors of communism always play on the anarchy inherent in the Left of Labour to secure confusion, disillusion and ultimately the violence which is essential to their long-term plan. In a crisis they will prevent any major reform or ordered progress through the medium of the Labour Party."

26 ***Oswald Mosley, op. cit.:***

"At that moment of passion and of some personal danger, Mosley found himself almost symbolically aligned against the workers. He had realised in action that his programme could only be carried out after the crushing of the workers and their organisation."

27 ***Ibid.:***

"Instead of being born in an appropriate Futurist structure of glass, steel & ferro-concrete, the 'modern movement' first saw the light of day in a beautiful old Georgian house overlooking St James's Square. Here ILP workers, Oxford hearties and delicate intellectuals mixed uneasily in Cimmie's tastefully furnished rooms."

28 This is "Risdon's recollection" from a 1961 interview for his book. ***The Fascists in Britain, op. cit.***

29 ***My Life, op. cit.***

30 ***The Rebel who lost his Cause: op. cit.:***

"To add to John's troubles [lack of funds to fight Peckham in the 1931 election], the communists decided to devote all their considerable energies in London to ensuring that he was not returned. His views were closer to theirs than those of any other London Labour candidate, and that was why they opposed him so fiercely. The Communist Party in 1931 believed that its first duty was to destroy other people and parties of the left, because they competed with it for the allegiance of the working class. It is an absurd and self-defeating way to behave, but it is the way in which several left-wing groups, such as the Socialist Workers' Party 50 years later, buried and destroyed the ideals for which they fought.

Their main tactic was to destroy John's meetings. They would turn up *en masse* where he was due to speak, and sing and chant to prevent him from doing so. For John this was another staging post on the road to fascism. His response was to organise a defence force and to put in charge of it a well-known local boxer. It was the first sight in British politics of the type of bodyguards for which, within three years, Sir Oswald Mosley was to become notorious."

This final observation is debatable.

31 ***Oswald Mosley, op. cit.:***

"***The Daily Worker*** was at this time advocating a Workers' Defence Corps against Fascism, 29/05/31. The Communists and Social Democrats in Germany both had paramilitary units."

32 ***Ibid.:***

"Rumours that he was recruiting 'storm-troopers' to attack the workers forced Mosley into hurried denials. 'We are simply organising an active force of our young men supporters to act as stewards', he explained to reporters. He tried to undo the damage of the comparison with Mussolini and Hitler. 'The only methods we shall employ will be English ones. We shall rely on the good old English fist.'"

33 ***Ibid.:***

"The importance of the public meeting was heightened by the Press boycott of which John Strachey complained so bitterly at the beginning of June [footnote: 'Indeed, I have definite evidence of a boycott; explicit instructions have been issued in certain quarters that no mention must be made of the Mosley Party. We're on the political correspondents' blacklist.' said Strachey in an interview for ***World's Press News***, 04/06/31. Earlier in the year a scheduled BBC discussion on the future of Parliament between Mosley and Lord Eustace Percy had been 'postponed' at the last minute; it never took place, reference ***Sunday News***, 15/02/31]."

34 ***Ibid.:***

"They all agreed that meetings must be protected from organised disruption and that young recruits should be enlisted, trained (through judo and boxing) and disciplined specifically for this purpose. (Mosley was particularly keen on the Party being 'fit' and 'in training': he himself had just taken up fencing again after a lapse of many years.) This led on to the question of whether the Party should formally develop a youth movement. Strangely enough the strongest support for this came from the left-wingers who were anxious to recruit 'young workers' to counteract what they considered the pernicious influence of the strapping Oxford hearties in their plus-fours and sports cars. ... Strachey himself did not object to the organisation of force; but he wanted it to be exerted on the workers' side. ... To Strachey and Young these plans for a 'physical force' to deal with left wing interrupters marked a significant stage in the development of the New Party's anti-worker alignment."

35 ***Ibid.***

36 ***Ibid.:***

"He was 'for nearly a quarter of a century ... one of the most popular of the highly-placed Liberal-Unionist officials' with considerable experience of organising industrial constituencies, reference the ***Daily Herald***, 05/05/31."

Frank M. Box was living in the Roundhay area of Leeds when he joined the Conservative Party as an agent in November, 1904; he was 32 years old, and his commencing salary was £350, excluding bonus, which was a considerable sum for those days. By October 1924, his salary, excluding bonus, was £1,000 per annum; at some stage, he moved to Ealing, in London. He resigned on the 31st of January 1929, and immediately qualified for a yearly pension of £500; there is a note in the Conservative Central Office staff register which states, cryptically, "Invited to join Superannuation Fund but declined to do so". It is not known if he started working for Mosley before the creation of the New Party, but it is a reasonable assumption.

Courtesy of Jeremy McIlwaine, Conservative Party Archivist, Department of Special Collections & Western Manuscripts, Bodleian Library, Oxford.

Alexander Miles, who considered Wilfred "an old friend and associate from my I.L.P. days", and would go on to work with him in the post-New Party organisation, of which more later, considered that Box "buried the New Party".

The Streets are still/Mosley in Motley, typescript memoir, undated [c.1937] by Alexander Miles, MSS 292/743.11/2, University of Warwick Modern Records Centre

37 ***Oswald Mosley, op. cit.***

38 ***Oswald Mosley and the New Party, op. cit.:***

"... the cultivation of a mass party membership organised in constituency branches and designed to form an electoral machine was never a priority. Indeed, the party put relatively little effort into developing its apparatus outside of London; though money and printed material were sent, the centre soon appeared to view its scattered local bases as costly sites of irritation. In the new political world envisaged by Mosley, there was little space for the formal niceties of most existing mainstream party organisations. Nor did the New Party appear to have much time for the whist drives and party socials so beloved of rank-and-file members in the Labour, Liberal and Conservative parties."

39 ***Ibid.:***

"... local New Party branches did form and did endeavour to play some role in the pursuit of Mosley's ambition."

40 ***Ibid.***

41 ***Oswald Mosley, op. cit.***

42 ***Ibid.***

43 ***Ibid.***

44 ***Oswald Mosley and the New Party, op. cit.:***

"By July, two competing tendencies could be discerned within the youth movement. On the one hand, there existed a group gathered around

Winkworth that comprised 'not an actual fighting force, but something in the form of cohorts, on a quasi-Hitlerist model, of young men (mostly from the well-to-do classes, including a number of Oxford and Cambridge undergraduates)'. ... On the other, a more cerebral section of erstwhile ILPers continued to mistrust both the fascist overtones of Winkworth's group and the Oxonian presence of Howard."

Peter Howard was introduced to Mosley by Harold Nicolson, and was captain of the Oxford, and later England, rugby team, and was responsible for a lot of the "heartier type of Undergraduate" who found their way into the Party.

45 ***Oswald Mosley, op. cit.***

46 ***My Life, op. cit.***

47 ***Oswald Mosley, op. cit.***

48 ***Oswald Mosley and the New Party, op. cit.:***

"Their moral code began to clash with that put forward by Nicolson and his fellow party intellectuals. They understood their inherent 'Britishness' to have deeper roots, drawing both from the *esprit de corps* of the wartime trenches and, later, the feudal surround of an Elizabethan England."

Worley also describes Wilfred as being one of three members who had been "vocal ILP critics of the Labour Party".

49 ***Ibid.:***

"There was, from the outset, only limited interaction between the party centre and the local branches outside of London; the regional offices proved too thinly spread and too ill-equipped to properly maintain a national party organisation. Not surprisingly, this tended to breed either resentment or blind obedience. In Gateshead, the aforementioned party branch splintered in the prelude to the 1931 general election."

50 ***Oswald Mosley, op. cit.***

The May Committee was chaired by the retiring chairman of the Prudential Insurance Company and this

"provided the Chancellor with the worst possible scenario for the future and proposed cutting national expenditure by £96m of which £66.5m was to be found by cutting 20% from unemployment benefit. The ploy misfired. What had been a manageable crisis became an unmanageable one as the financial world was led to believe that Britain was on the brink of bankruptcy. £50m of borrowings swiftly drained away as foreign owned sterling was withdrawn. The New York Federal Reserve Bank would only lend a further £80m if the main proposals of the May Report were implemented. MacDonald knew there was no chance of persuading Labour MPs to accept such measures, especially as many were discussing the alternative of going off the Gold Standard. In August, with Parliament in recess, MacDonald resigned, leaving his colleagues to assume that this would result in a Tory or Tory/Liberal Coalition government. Instead he formed a 'National' Government of Tories and Liberals with himself as Prime Minister and Snowden still Chancellor of the Exchequer."

Socialism in Birmingham and the Black Country 1850-1939, by G.J. Barnsby

51 James Stuart Barr was an ILP member and Labour College organiser in Birmingham, who was first appointed 'Division 6' organiser, in October 1925, in place of one of the pioneers of workers' education in the Midlands, T. D. Smith, whose new rôle was to 'assist' in Division 12, which covered Northampton and Mansfield; something of a tall order, for someone based in West Bromwich. Division 6, which had been formed in January, 1922, with Smith as its secretary, had branches in Smethwick, West Bromwich, Wolverhampton and Stourbridge. Barr is described as a "new broom [who] swept very vigorously", reinvigorating the hitherto flagging movement in Birmingham & the Black Country.

Ibid.

Wilfred shared some commonality of background with Bevin, although the latter was some fifteen years older; the hustings were probably good-natured.

http://en.wikipedia.org/wiki/Ernest_Bevin

52 ***Oswald Mosley and the New Party, op. cit.***

53 ***Ibid.***

54 ***Ibid.***

55 ***Ibid.***

http://en.wikipedia.org/wiki/Thomas_Magnay

56 **BACK TO THE FIRST YEAR:** ***Early Days Of British Union Recalled; By W. Risdon. ACTION, No. 86, Oct. 9, 1937; page 7***

57 ***The Rebel who lost his Cause etc., op. cit.***

58 ***Oswald Mosley and the New Party, op. cit.:***

> "... in the autumn of 1931, the proposed dissolution of the regional offices promised to further strip down the party's limited apparatus. From 1 January 1932, following a letter from Mosley dated 23 November, party branches were made directly subordinate to the central executive; their brief was to carry out propaganda work and facilitate the formation of a disciplined youth movement."

59 W.J. Leaper, another erstwhile colleague, was sent to help: Leaper was a journalist and ex-ILP member from Bradford who moved to Newcastle, taking up a position on the ***Evening Chronicle***, as detailed later:

> "WILLIAM JOSEPH LEAPER. A journalist. Started as 'printer's devil' at the age of twelve and served apprenticeship as a compositor. In France, 1916 to 1919. Has been reporter, descriptive writer, sub-editor, and art editor. Formerly member of the Independent Labour Party, and of the Labour Party. Honorary Secretary of the Yorkshire Independent Labour Party Wool Textile Commission. Joined the New Party immediately on its formation by Sir Oswald Mosley, resigning from the ***Yorkshire Post***, so as to be free for political work. Contested the Shipley Division of Yorkshire for the New Party at the 1931 General Election. Joined the British Union of Fascists and helped to found the Newcastle branch in September, 1932. Resigned from the ***Newcastle Evening Chronicle*** to join the ***Fascist Week*** in November last."

MEN IN FASCISM: ***William Joseph Leaper; Fascist Week, No. 18, Mar 9-15, 1934; page 5***

60 ***Oswald Mosley, op. cit.:***

"The last issue of ***Action***, no. 13, came out on 31/12/31. ... Less distinguished, but unfortunately equally characteristic of the New Party, were effusions from Peter Cheyney urging 'the establishment of a country-wide system of Nupa-Shock Propaganda Controls by June 1933, and the completely organised Political-Shock-Youth Movement by June 1935.' On the central issue of Fascism, ***Action***, like the New Party, refused to commit itself. Harold Nicolson was convinced that the 'Corporate State' was the answer to the impending 'proletarian revolution' (no. 1); but did this make the New Party fascist? Certainly not, Harold Nicolson replied, horrified: 'We do not believe in formulas ... We shall take from all ...'' (no. 11). To prove his point he published articles praising Communism and Soviet planning. Mosley gave a somewhat different answer: the New Party was fascist in theory, but not in method; but this was then further qualified when he said that the New Party's theory came from the commodity boards worked out by him and his friends in the Labour Party (no. 12). With these [apparently] unsatisfactory prevarications, the New Party followers had to be content for the time being."

61 ***Oswald Mosley and the New Party, op. cit.:***

"This New Movement essentially mirrored the youth movement apparatus ..., with local branches reconstituted into 'groups' comprising ten members and a 'group leader'. Once more than ten members had enrolled, then the group would sub-divide into two groups and form a 'control', with the erstwhile group leader becoming a 'control leader' overseeing two newly-selected group leaders. The process would then be repeated in accord with further growth, providing a 'division' and a 'divisional leader' responsible for each control. Above all this, the maintenance and direction of the movement was to be overseen by a 'director' and 'assistant director' appointed to each designated area by Mosley. In particular, the local branches were to provide 'self-supporting' clubs committed to a range of political, social and sporting activity, including lectures, athletics, sporting events and regular 'club nights'. Subscription to the New Movement was set at 3d per week (1d for the unemployed)."

62 ***Ibid.:***

"... the party's London branches experimented with a new type of organisation modelled along paramilitary lines and extended across the national party in June 1932. ... little evidence remains as to the extent of the party's local organisation in 1932. We know that the London party continued to function through its two Nupa clubs ... . By the summer of 1932, Great George Street had likewise been adapted to serve as a hostel for unemployed members."

63 ***Oswald Mosley, op. cit.:***

"At a Party meeting on the 5th of May, 1932 Mosley announced his decision to close down the New Party, but to keep on with NUPA on a reduced scale [footnote: finance for the NUPA clubs was apparently coming from the 'Cousins Group', a commercial firm with sporting connections, ref. ***HN MS, 05/01 & 01/02/32***]. Harold Nicolson welcomed the former decision, as freeing Mosley to stand for Parliament as an independent, but strongly objected to the latter."

64 ***Ibid.:***

"Lord Rothermere…definitely encouraged [Mosley, in the aftermath of the election defeat] to go forward with Fascism, promising to put the ***Daily Mail*** behind it…. Mosley himself inclined to the … possibility [that the economic crisis would intensify… and 'Communism's inevitable and historic opponent will arise to take the place of a flabby conservatism']. If some form of Fascism was inevitable, he would argue to his friends, it was better for him to get in on the ground floor and make sure that the movement took a reputable English, rather than a more violent continental form. No one in Mosley's immediate circle shared his belief in the coming crisis."

65 ***Ibid.:***

"Something in him was irresistibly drawn not so much to Fascism as to the idea of a politics half-civilian, half-military, a 'mobilisation of ex-servicemen for the achievements of peace', as he put it in a speech in November. Harold Nicolson and Forgan were becoming alarmed by the extent to which he was starting to share the fantasies of Cheyney & Bingham. 'They really are the devil', wrote Harold Nicolson on the 16th of November, blaming Mosley's increasing involvement with Fascism on their pernicious influence."

66 Allen was one of the few original Conservative members of the New Party; he was also a rich Ulster Unionist, and John Beckett considered him a friend. He was an early recruit, and crossed the floor of the House, to sit with his new colleagues on the Labour back benches.

67 Christopher Hobhouse was a practising barrister and an author; he was commissioned by John Betjeman in 1935 to write a study of Derbyshire for the ***Shell Guides***, for which he was editor, and he was to participate in the Kinder Scout mass trespass in 1932.

http://www.independent.co.uk/travel/uk/the-guides-green-and-pleasant-lanes-2221671.html

68 ***Oswald Mosley, op. cit.***

69 ***Ibid.:***

"… in reaction against socialism and the tensions of the previous years, he had started to indulge to the full his taste for the gay life, and the playboy once more seemed to overshadow the politician. His continental journey to study 'the modern movement' in January 1932 was typical …."

70 ***Ibid.:***

"Nor was life in London devoted to unremitting political toil. Strachey and Young had complained that it was impossible to get Mosley to transact important New Party business because he was so busy fencing … It … took up a formidable amount of time. Throughout 1932 he was fencing all over England. Fencing was not the only sport that claimed him. Early in 1932 he became a fan of the new craze of all-in wrestling, and a snap at this time shows him, in the somewhat incongruous company of Lady Margot Asquith, intently watching one *Norman the Butcher* performing at David Tennant's Gargoyle Club."

71 ***Ibid.:***

"There were two fascist groups already in existence. The first was the British Fascists, jocularly known as the 'BFs' by Mosley's Birmingham friends in the 1920s. Started in 1923 by Miss Rotha Lintorn-Orman, 'a forthright spinster of 37 with a taste for mannish clothes' [ref. Colin Cross], it was an extreme right wing group with a disproportionate number of generals and admirals and dedicated to unrelenting struggle against the powers of evil represented by Bolshevism. ... The Imperial Fascist League had been founded by a retired veterinary surgeon and specialist in camel diseases, Arnold Spencer Leese, in 1928. 'One of those crank little societies ... mad about the Jews', Mosley not unfairly dubbed it. ... For his part, Leese refused all co-operation with Mosley, believing him to be in the pay of the Jews. This rejection of his overtures did not discourage Mosley too much."

72 ***Ibid.***

73 ***The Fascists in Britain, op. cit.:***

"Dear Sir,

You have, no doubt, read in the papers of the recent formation of the British Union of Fascists and I am enclosing herewith a short manifesto and membership form in the belief that they will be of interest to you.

A fuller statement of policy explaining the need for such an organization will be found in my new book, ***The Greater Britain***, which can be obtained from your local bookseller or direct from these Headquarters.

The Movement is indeed a 'Union of Fascists' and many members and officials drawn from all existing Fascists' organizations are now in the ranks of the British Union of Fascists.

Recent events more than confirm the necessity for Fascist organization. Our object is no less than the winning of power for Fascism, which we believe is the only salvation for our country. We appeal for the co-operation of those who have long believed in Fascism, but have been disappointed with the lack of progress and want of constructive policy in former Fascist organizations. We are now organizing active measures to advance the Fascist cause, including constant propaganda meetings and route marches through our great cities. We need your help. Will you give it?

Yours faithfully,
Oswald Mosley."

74 He was to write, a few years later:

"In September of 1932 I received my advance copy of ***The Greater Britain***. How eagerly I read it. It was the goods. Date of publication was a month ahead. Before a week had passed two hundred circulars had been sent out to people all over the north of England (I was in Newcastle at the time), warning them of the forthcoming publication and of the intention to signalise the advent of the book by the formation of a branch of the British Union in Newcastle.

The day arrived, and ten or a dozen people met together in the office from which I was directing a small and struggling advertising agency. Most of us had been associated in the work of the New Party, which had gone down with colours flying at the beginning of the same year. There were in the group a postal worker, a journalist, a commercial traveller, a printer, a student from Armstrong college, a doctor, two typists and a married woman; fairly representative for so small a group. The plunge was taken, and the Newcastle branch was started on its adventurous career."

BACK TO THE FIRST YEAR*: Early Days Of British Union Recalled; By W. Risdon. ACTION, No. 86, Oct. 9, 1937; page 7*

75 ***Oswald Mosley, op. cit.:***

"Forgan and Allen strongly advised against [using the term 'Fascist' in the name] arguing that nothing 'foreign' would ever succeed in Britain. The NUPA militants urged him to adopt the name as well as the idea. Mosley hesitated, but in the end decided to call his movement the British Union of Fascists, 'union' standing for that rallying together of the best elements in the British nation which had always been his dream, 'fascist' for the creed which would animate them. For its emblem he adopted the fasces carried by the lictors of ancient Rome, the bundle of sticks symbolising unity, the axe the power of the state."

76 ***The Fascists in Britain, op. cit.:***

"Mosley unlocked the door, pausing for photographs, and unfurled a black banner emblazoned with the fasces emblem in silver. In later years the ceremony was to be held in mystic remembrance, the gathering of the founders 'in an upper room' being recalled on every anniversary. Quietly Mosley spoke of the need for utter dedication to the Fascist cause. 'We ask those who join us', he said, 'to march with us in a great and hazardous adventure. We ask them to be prepared to sacrifice all, but to do so for no small and unworthy ends. We ask them to dedicate their lives to building in this country a movement of the modern age … Those who march with us will certainly face abuse, misunderstanding, bitter animosity and possibly the ferocity of struggle and danger. In return we can only offer to them the deep belief that they are fighting that a great land may live …'"

77 ***ACTION, No. 60, Apr. 10, 1937; Page 11***

4: ALL IS POTENTIAL

Although the British Union of Fascists commenced its operations at the beginning of October, 1932, with headquarters at Great George Street in an area of London with the appropriate portent, Westminster, the branch in Newcastle, which Wilfred had set up the previous month, required his personal attention and presence for a little while longer, so it wasn't until February 1933 that he was able to leave it in the hands of colleagues, albeit within a semi-military command structure, and migrate south to take up the significant and demanding post for which Mosley needed him: Director of Propaganda. Two observations are germane here: it begs the question as to whether this function was not hitherto considered necessary, which seems unlikely; and it is appropriate to discount a commonly-held misapprehension, namely that propaganda is a term used solely to define misinformation. Definitions are inherently mutable, and a wide-ranging discussion here of the variations in meaning of the term would be spurious: the meaning as it applied to Wilfred will be easily apparent in the succeeding paragraphs.

The primary means which Mosley used to propagate his message was public meetings, whose organisation was Wilfred's responsibility [although ***Fascist Week***, in one of its earliest editions in December 1933, described Wilfred's "Chief job" in a biographical profile as "the training and organisation of speakers throughout the country." **1**]. His position was sufficiently prestigious and demanding to warrant an assistant, one Carlyle Elliot whom, according to Miles, Wilfred had encountered "in the North East" [**2**]. Wilfred reported in 1937, looking "BACK TO THE FIRST YEAR", that when he joined "the tiny band of enthusiasts working at Great George Street ... There were meetings every night" [and it is clear that he relished the camaraderie, despite the risk of injury **3**], although Skidelsky contradicts this when he tells us that there were few meetings "in the early months of fascism", by which perhaps he meant only high-profile, indoor meetings, not the open-air, close-quarters meetings which Wilfred enjoyed.

There was an uncontroversial opening rally in Trafalgar Square on the 15th of October, to announce the arrival of the Movement, quite possibly organised by Mosley himself [**4**]. This first phase of the Movement was later referred to as "respectable Fascism", and what Skidelsky regards as its highlight was the encounter between Mosley and one of Wilfred's erstwhile heroes, James Maxton, "under the benign chairmanship of Lloyd George", at the Friends' Meeting House, Euston Road, on the 24th of February, 1933, so very probably Wilfred's first administrative undertaking in his new post [**5**]. Apparently, the ILP had recently "adopted the Red Shirt" [**6**], so their stewards wore them for this occasion to distinguish them from the BUF's stewards in their black shirts: there was no trouble.

It will be illustrative at this juncture to highlight another feature of the propaganda function which was regarded as highly desirable and effective: education. This was one of Wilfred's abiding passions, politically speaking, alongside trade unionism, and there was inevitably a connection between the two; using the medium of the Movement's periodicals, he wrote a series of articles elucidating very cogently how members could make themselves useful by disseminating the ethos of British Union [an abbreviation which Wilfred favoured, having suggested it to Mosley], beginning with the most basic of participatory activities: arranging a meeting [**7**]. Later on in his career with Mosley, he would write articles emphasising the importance to workers of knowing how the electoral system worked, so that they could exploit it to its best advantage, as well as exposing the flaws and failings of communistic Socialism.

The first big public meeting Wilfred arranged was at the Free Trade Hall in Manchester, on March 12th; this was, in fact, according to a list published in ***The Blackshirt***, one of 35 London & provincial meetings scheduled for that month [**8**]; another one was to be held at Wilfred's old 'stamping ground', Birmingham Town Hall, on the 26th. There was also listed a "B.B.C. BROADCAST by SIR OSWALD MOSLEY", on the 15th: one of the last to be granted to him by the national voice. Realistically, the Manchester meeting would have been reported upon by the BUF's periodical anyway, but the circumstances dictated a broadside from The Leader: there had been trouble. Disruption was fomented both in advance and during the meeting by Communists, via the medium of a manifesto entitled "Unity Against Fascist Reaction", as explained in a separate column in ***The Blackshirt***, headed "WHO IS TO BLAME? Violent Red Manifesto", alongside Sir Oswald's tirade which was entitled "POLICE USED TO PROTECT RED FLAG / OLD GANG ALARMED BY RAPID FASCIST ADVANCE / The Truth About the Manchester Meeting".

Whilst the manifesto [or at least, the strident section quoted] was not, examined objectively, the "direct incitement to attack the Fascist meeting" it was labelled as [**9**], it did mendaciously and fallaciously connect Mosley's Movement with Hitler's Fascists, using lurid language such as "Mosley is Hitlerism in Great Britain. Like Hitler he intends to mislead the workers … Fascism means death to the British working class—it means Fascist murder gangs stalking the streets of Britain.", and the message implicit in "the mightiest fighting front of the working class must be displayed against Fascist terror" was not difficult to comprehend. Mosley's principal complaint, even though "a very good order, with only slight interruption, was maintained throughout my speech, which was very well received" and "No one was molested by any member of the Fascist Defence Force until after questions had begun", was that the removal of a man "after repeated requests to refrain from shouting in a manner which prevented others from hearing the answers to questions" and "addressing to a steward the filthiest observation which one man can address to another ("lousy bastard")", which "was resisted by his supporters, and this began the fight", necessitated the police, "who had ordered the Blackshirts to withdraw", taking control of the meeting, which would not have been countermanded by Mosley, given that "I gave orders not to fight against the forces of the Crown in accordance with the policy declared in advance in my book on our policy, and subsequently maintained in every order issued to the Fascist Defence Force."

This had the effect of protecting the Communists [even though "[t]he fight was practically at an end when the police entered the meeting"], who "used razors, bludgeons and chairs in their attacks upon the Fascist Defence Force", and this "protection of the police, and that alone, enabled the Communists to break up the meeting", "the only meeting of the British Union of Fascists which has ever ended in disorder." [**10**]. Wilfred's own thoughts on the matter weren't published until four years later when, in addition to revealing that "[t]he first meeting I addressed in Stephenson Square [Manchester] … yielded the usual 'spot of bother'", he regaled his readers with a breezy, almost flippant anecdote containing reminiscences of his personal acquaintances [**11**] at the Free Trade Hall meeting. Neither he, nor his employer and mentor, were evidently deterred by this "bother".

The following month, Wilfred was one of a party of fourteen from the BUF who visited Rome for Mussolini's International Fascist Exhibition, at which representatives of all the European 'modern movements' attended, including a certain Hermann Göring, who led the German group [**12**]. Sir Oswald and his wife were accorded the honour of sharing the saluting platform with the *Duce* for a march-past on the 21st of April; the ***Evening Standard*** of four days previously was more concerned with the contrast between Mosley's sartorial elegance and "the violence of the Fascist salute" [**13**]. Although they had appeared together with Mussolini on the balcony of the Palazzo Venezia prior to the parade, on the day Mussolini took the salute on a covered balcony a quarter of a mile away, leaving the Mosleys alone on the saluting platform, and the Blackshirt contingent thereunder for two hours in the streaming rain, acknowledging the salutes of the entire parade [**14**]. Three months later, at the beginning of August, a party of Italian *Fascisti* made a reciprocal visit, and as contemporary photographs show, Wilfred made a point of wearing his service medals for the occasion: the handshakes and formal greetings, including an exchange of regalia, were polite but businesslike.

A short while after returning from Rome, Cynthia Mosley became ill with appendicitis; she had had to recuperate in Como after a difficult pregnancy and birth of their son Michael only a year earlier, but had evidently recovered sufficiently to assist her husband with the birth of his new baby, notwithstanding her previous scepticism of Fascism in general.

The operation in the London Clinic was successful, but within two days peritonitis set in, and the doctors were powerless to prevent her death. For all his barely concealed and cavalier philandering during his marriage, Mosley was genuinely grief-stricken, no doubt including a large helping of remorse, which must have had a palpable effect on the new Movement and its personnel, despite its somewhat macho militaristic swagger, but executive officers such as Wilfred will have been able to contribute very little consolation in a personally empathetic way. Mosley's "response was to hurl himself furiously into his movement. Henceforth he would live only for his faith" [**15**].

At the beginning of April, the Movement felt sufficiently confident to make the first of several moves, "[o]wing to the very rapid increase in our membership", to "temporary offices at No. 12, Lower Grosvenor Place, S.W. 1." [**16**]; temporary it was indeed: they were there for four months. On the weekend of the 5th & 6th of August, the BUF "moved to the truly enormous Whitelands College, now known as 'Fascist Headquarters', Kings Road, Sloane Square" [**17**]. It had previously been rumoured that Mosley was interested in buying Wellington Barracks from the War Office, but the premises next door, which he officially renamed "Black House" [and his detractors called, not inaccurately, the "Fascist Fort" or the "Fascist Barracks"] suited his purposes very well, given that it included lecture rooms, dormitories, a gymnasium and a parade ground [**18**]. Although many of the central London-based Blackshirts would have regarded Black House as their home, the organisation's top officials, who, according to Cross, numbered between 20 and 30, treated the place as an office and only slept there if they were kept late at work [**19**]. No doubt Wilfred will have been away quite a lot, having to travel in connection with his speaking commitments, but kept rooms there anyway.

As a measure of his importance within the hierarchy of the BUF, Wilfred's salary was second only to Robert Forgan's, as Director of Organisation; it is difficult to be precise here: Cross [who interviewed many contributors personally] tells us that Forgan's [but irritatingly, not Wilfred's] was, during the first two years, £600, rising to £700 when he was promoted to Deputy Leader [**20**]. However, another authority [**21**] quotes contemporary Home Office information, supplied courtesy of one "P. G. Taylor" [of whom more later] which explained that in 1934, Dr. Forgan was on £10/week [so £520/year], followed by Wilfred Risdon, on £7/week [so £364/year]: something of a discrepancy, although easily explained if Cross's annual figure was rounded up. It is also possible that Taylor was playing a double game here, being disingenuous with the figures, an idea which is not without foundation, given the murky world of deception this character inhabited, but his reasons for doing this, if such is indeed what he did, have to be a matter for speculation.

By way of comparison, as early as 1922, when he became general secretary of the newly-formed Transport & General Workers' Union, with a membership of 300,000, Ernest Bevin received a salary of £650 per annum, so there seems no reason to doubt Wilfred's assertion in 1940 [**Appendix D**] that his salary was somewhat less than he had enjoyed hitherto from the ILP. Interestingly, Wilfred said during his 18B appeal hearing that "during most of these years [meaning, presumably, in the context of the issue under discussion, 1933-37] I was on a salary, nothing like the salary I was on in the Labour Party, and the reason given for that was that the Movement was too hard up to pay me any more." It is unclear why he would have given the impression that he was not permanently salaried with Mosley, and this, along with discussion of the final point, will be dealt with in the appropriate chapter. Perspective can also be gained from the weekly pay of a "typical seaman" at the end of 1931; 25s. 1d. [£1.25], down from 31s. 6d. [£1.57½] as a result of government austerity measures, which sparked the Invergordon "mutiny" [**22**]. A "typical working man's non-parlour house" had fallen from £350 in 1931 to under £300 in 1933, mainly due to a combination of economies in the building trade and more favourable terms available from the building societies; council house rents varied between 7s. and anything up to 15s. a week [**23**].

In March of 1933, a new member joined the staff of the BUF; one who was to have a profound effect upon Wilfred's standing within the Movement, and his personal relationship with Sir Oswald Mosley. Wilfred was surely pragmatic enough to know that he could never, even if he should want to, aspire to the sort of open and easy-going friendship with "Tom" Mosley [as his intimates called him] such as was, in a sense, very much taken for granted by the likes of Bob Boothby and Harold Nicolson, coming as they did from Mosley's social stratum; but Mosley was clever enough [and this was something very probably genuinely meant, not a cynical device to curry favour and win converts] to know that a camaraderie engendered by a shared experience, such as the baptism of fire of the recent war, and the subsequent striving to prevent a recurrence by means of a more just society which was fairer to all, was guaranteed to accrue contemporaries who shared this vision [**24**]: Wilfred was one such. He probably didn't idolise Mosley, but he would have been well aware of Mosley's force of personality and potential as a world-changing politician, so he would very likely have been perfectly happy with being regarded as a trusted and faithful lieutenant, rather than as a bosom friend who could be discarded for emotional reasons.

William Joyce was a small man; small in stature, and very conscious of it, which probably went some way to explaining his vanity, but that would be too simplistic on its own. He was highly intelligent, which he no doubt enjoyed flaunting, given that some people who were aware of their own limited abilities found this threatening, and the alarmingly large scar on his face [certainly the result of an attack, although the circumstances of its occurrence were a matter for debate] would, no doubt, have given people not disposed to belligerence a reason to be careful. He could also be very likeable, it has to be said, when he chose, but he tended to be very sparing with this indulgence. He was, however, highly ambitious, and this, coupled with his fierce, proud Britishness [ironic, given that he was the son of a naturalised American, born in Brooklyn, New York, and raised in Ireland] and extreme anti-semitism, eventually helped to dislodge Wilfred from his position of authority and, to some extent, respect, from Mosley's new Movement which was gaining new members perhaps too quickly, especially members of a more reactionary bent, who were able by virtue of their status to influence Mosley directly, and set in train a certain confusion with regard to policy and direction, [not that Mosley would have been in a hurry to acknowledge that at the time] leading to some decisions which could later very easily be pinpointed as the obvious causes of the Movement's demise, not the least of which was a dilution of the early pure socialist ethos.

Wilfred was anti-semitic, in the popularly-understood sense; that much must, at the very least, be conceded: but in mitigation [which will be expanded upon in the book's conclusion] it is fair to say that in the first quarter of the twentieth century, anti-semitism [or, more accurately, anti-Jewish sentiment] was fairly evenly distributed across all shades of the societal and political spectrum in Britain, as described by such eminent authorities as Professor Colin Holmes; which is not an attempt to excuse it, merely the statement of a fact. Of course, it could take many forms, from a general xenophobia, through an undercurrent of a vaguely targeted but instinctive dislike, to a vehement and irrational [but always well-defined] hatred. All the evidence points to Wilfred's falling somewhere in the middle: its origin was undoubtedly religious, coming as he did from a zealous, almost [as we would say today] fundamental Christian background; but it undoubtedly developed in a more political direction, given Wilfred's socialist education and experience in his formative years. These should not have been guaranteed to make Wilfred more anti-semitic than he might already have been, but his understanding of economic theory brought him to the conclusion that Marxist materialism, with its Jewish ancestry [as he saw it], along with the potential surrendering of national control to foreign [and easily corrupted] figureheads, with "un-British" agendas, as required by the Russian brand of Communism, was not the answer.

So for Wilfred, a programme of political education through his propaganda, moving towards political control gained through constitutional democratic means for the good of the country and the Empire, was the right way to go; therefore, his position as Director of Propaganda in the BUF suited him very well. There is no doubt that anti-semitism was present in the ethos of many members right from the very beginning of the BUF but, to a large extent, it was a personal matter, certainly not a specific policy matter, as it later became: of course, it would be both foolish and spurious to assume that this did not have a low-level effect on the Movement's propaganda, not only Wilfred's, given that propaganda was very much the *modus operandi* of the Movement as a whole, but incitement to violence was not an option openly manifested. In fact, to the contrary, it was officially prohibited [**25**]: the British Jewish lobby was generally supportive in the early days [**26**] and Mosley's nominal deputy, Dr. Robert Forgan, found the evident turning of the tide distasteful, and tried, ostensibly at Mosley's behest, to negotiate "a *modus vivendi* between Fascists and and Jews" in talks at the Savoy Hotel, but to no avail [**27**].

When he first became a member [February 1933, when Wilfred took up his directorship], Joyce was a volunteer, retaining his paid position as "a very successful tutor at a correspondence school" [**28**], which he had held for six years after graduating with a first class honours degree at Birkbeck College, London University [**29**]. His prowess as a public speaker, which very quickly earned him a status second only to Mosley himself in popularity [**30**], combined with his obvious administrative capabilities, convinced him that he had a very useful future with the BUF as a salaried employee, something which Wilfred tried to advise him against [**31**]: subjunctive hypothesising is futile of course, but it is interesting to speculate whether Wilfred saw Joyce as a threat from the very outset; a young nephew was given a private intimation of Wilfred's assessment of Joyce only a year later: "You have just met one of the most dangerous men in Great Britain" [**32**]. He also commenced his written output in earnest [although not immediately under his own name]: the first identifiable evidence is an article in ***The Blackshirt*** no. 27, Oct. 28-Nov. 3, 1933, on page 1, bylined "W. J." and entitled "WHOSE BLOOD? WHY?", fulminating on the hypocrisy of pacifists who had begun clamouring for war against Germany, with its apparently anti-democratic and belligerent Fascist Government.

For the time being, Wilfred had little option but to tolerate Joyce for the good, at least in the short term, of the Movement; it was lacking reliable, effective speakers and, with the best will in the world, Wilfred could only devote a limited amount of time to speaking himself; also, he must undoubtedly have been a good enough judge of character to know that, sooner or later, Joyce's vanity would overcome his willingness to rein in his naked ambition, which would become exposed when he overreached himself. The question, of course, was how much damage he might do to the Movement and, synchronously, to Wilfred himself. Time would tell. According to Cross, Joyce was very soon [i.e., by "the end of 1933"] put "in charge of the relatively small Propaganda Department", so theoretically answering to Wilfred, and his annual salary was £300, "which was less than he thought he deserved" [**33**]. Cross says that by the end of its first year of existence, the scale of the spending of "the youthful BUF" on propaganda was higher than any other mainstream political party, possibly even including "the wealthy Conservative Central Office" [**34**], so a huge responsibility for

Wilfred, given the fluctuation in the Movement's funds.

This was also the period when the 'left-wing', socialistic origins of the Movement were inexorably being converted to a more conservative, even reactionary, 'right-wing' outlook, to a large extent as a result of the influx of a disparate cadre of ex-military types, with the inevitable emphasis on discipline as an end in itself, rather than an element which contributed to producing the ordered, rational-thinking "thought-deed man—the man capable of both thought and action" originally desired by Mosley [**35**]. A now little-known aspect of the BUF at this time was the Fascist Union of British Workers [FUBW] which, although short-lived, was relatively effective. Wilfred did not have a documented connection with it, and although he would have agreed with the association of Fascism [even though he was not entirely comfortable with the term] and trade unionism, he would very possibly have been aware that, for all he supported the ethos of Fascism in its British implementation, many currently ununionised working class people might have been deterred [thanks to adverse, condemnatory propaganda focusing on perceived central European outrages] from joining an all-encompassing, overtly fascist trade union [**36**], when the goal, in his view, was the total unionisation of British workers within their separate skill-sectors and trades, under the banner of the Fascist Movement. A fine distinction perhaps, but one that would have been an essential element of Wilfred's conception of a British fascist Government headed by Mosley, the Corporate State.

Originally created as a local initiative by a former local leader of the National Unemployed Workers' Movement [NUWM], J.P.D. Paton, and Michael Goulding, at the BUF's Battersea branch [previously, as trumpeted by ***The Blackshirt***, the constituency and "one of the staunchest strongholds of the Moscow men" [**37**], Saklatvala], it was integrated into the national movement in April 1933, under the leadership of Charles Bradford, a Welsh ex-Communist steel erector, moving to Black House in August of that year. Although the FUBW was strongest in London, it had branches in towns and cities around the country, including Wilfred's former areas of influence, Newcastle and Birmingham [**38**]. Alongside criticism of the Labour Party, there was also derogation of trades union officials, an area where Wilfred's advice and experience could have been sought, as would that of his erstwhile colleague Alexander Miles, previously secretary of the Gateshead branch of the NUWM, and well-versed experientially in local trade union machinations. Although this is, of necessity, only a brief synopsis of the lifespan of this section, it was only peripherally associated with Wilfred's career progression in the BUF. The FUBW was wound up in June 1934, and incorporated into the Industrial Section of the Propaganda Department, notionally under Wilfred's jurisdiction [**39**] although, as ever in the BUF, there was overlap with other departments.

The beginning of 1934 saw a definite boost for the BUF with a campaign of support from Lord Rothermere in his national daily newspaper, the ***Daily Mail***. While the New Party was still struggling to find its feet, being assailed from all sides in the aftermath of the general election farrago, Lord Rothermere explicitly encouraged Mosley to actively consider Fascism as a way forward, promising to put the ***Daily Mail*** behind it, although it took over two years for this to happen. Harold Harmsworth, and his brother Alfred, first produced the ***Daily Mail*** in 1896, and it was modelled on American newspapers. Both were obviously patriotic, although Harold appeared to be the more committed of the two, supporting the first world war in the ***Mail*** and their other mass-circulation tabloid, the ***Daily Mirror***, after Alfred, now Lord Northcliffe, sold his shares in it to Harold. For all Rothermere's professed patriotism, he must have given Wilfred and his socialist compatriots cause for concern when he published the Zinoviev Letter four days before the 1924 general election.

Mosley inclined to the view that Fascism was essential because of the inability of "a flabby conservatism" to combat Communism in the unavoidable economic crisis, thereby necessitating the rise of its "inevitable and historic opponent … If some form of Fascism was inevitable, he would argue to his friends, it was better for him to get in on the ground floor and make sure that the movement took a reputable English, rather than a more violent continental form" [**40**]. One of Rothermere's competitors, Lord Beaverbrook [born William Maxwell Aitken in Canada] argued, along with Keynes and many of Mosley's friends that he was exaggerating the scale of the forthcoming 'crisis', but these arguments seemed to have precisely the opposite effect upon Mosley [**41**], so Rothermere's support must have been very gratifying for him [although that did not prevent ***The Blackshirt*** from publishing an occasional criticism of the ***Daily Mail*** [**42**].

The headline of Rothermere's ***Daily Mail*** of Monday, January the 15th, 1934, "Hurrah for the Blackshirts", has subsequently achieved iconic status, and as a rallying cry, it was instantly successful, providing Wilfred with the national boost to his propaganda that he really needed at that point; it was also, arguably, the catalyst for the eventual conversion of the Movement from a socialist-oriented revolutionary party to a militaristically oriented reactionary party, a place where Wilfred would feel increasingly uncomfortable. That was some time in the future though, and it was a gradual process. The ***Daily Mail*** was an ideal platform from which to publicise the BUF's already large public meetings, which were growing inexorably. A week into Rothermere's campaign, the ***Observer*** was also able to note that "the Left wing is considerably stronger than the Right", and professing some surprise that, on Sunday the 21st of January 1934, "[Mosley] should be holding a mass meeting in the Birmingham Bingley Hall, which holds 15,000 people." [**43**].

Either the ***Observer*** had overestimated the size of Bingley Hall, or it had only been just over half full, but despite that, there was no serious trouble [although hardly surprising in the event, as "[t]he meeting ... was stewarded by between two and three thousand Blackshirts, most of whom were local members"], which could have had a bearing on space available for the audience, which was not deterred by ticket prices "from 7/6 to 1/-, ... all places being quickly filled" [**44**]; naturally enough, it was reported as "THE TRIUMPH OF BIRMINGHAM" [**45**] and "BIRMINGHAM ENTHUSIASM" [**46**]. Some idea of the cost of organising an operation like this can be gained from the information that some two thousand Blackshirts were fed a meal of cold beef and ham at teatime in the Hall before the meeting began, and a hot meal was provided at the Birmingham Headquarters for local members afterwards [**47**]. Coincidentally, on the same page where this information can be found in ***The Blackshirt*** is a column written by "BILL RISDON / Director of Propaganda" entitled "ARRANGING A MEETING".

In a very real way these earlier meetings can be regarded as steps along the way to the first big test, a meeting at the Albert Hall. Prior to that, near the end of February Wilfred was able to find the time in a meeting arranged by The Women Clerks and Secretaries Association at the Kingsway Hall, to debate a proposal by Ellen Wilkinson [**48**], one of the female stalwarts of the labour movement, that "Fascism means the enslavement of Women". Wilfred "with his usual lucidity, gave a brilliant exposition of Fascist aims", and despite explaining "how much more effective would be the voice of women in the Corporate State than it is under the present Parliamentary system", the vote was lost, mainly because "the majority, however, had come strongly encased in their prejudices, and these were supported by several gangs of hooligans who made it extremely difficult for Mr. Risdon to state his case, subjecting him to a continuous barrage of interruptions. Miss Wilkinson, it should be noted, was not interrupted once, despite the presence of many Fascists in the hall." [**49**].

Wilfred's 'rank' at this time was A/A/O, Area Administrative Officer, and the fact that William Joyce was also assigned the same rank as his [albeit with a smaller geographical remit, West London] when he became a staff officer must have irked him more than somewhat, despite Joyce's obvious abilities. The Movement was clearly and overtly non-democratic, and its officers were not elected but appointed, by the Leader; one generally neutral and only occasionally negative commentator, F. L. Carsten, maintains that officers wielded absolute authority within their spheres [**50**]; clearly this was not the case with Wilfred: he could see that it was only a matter of time before Joyce, with his equal status, would look for, and seize any opportunity to best his more moderate and easy-going colleague [aka 'rival']. The nomenclature applied to the executive officers could vary according to the context, and therefore present a source of confusion, certainly for outsiders; to the uninformed, the title "Director of Propaganda" would suggest that Wilfred was in overall control of the Movement's propaganda output, but this would appear not to have been the case [to which he also alluded somewhat uncharacteristically irritably in his 18B appeal hearing, **Appendix D**; this could have been cleverly done for effect, of course, to engender sympathy among his interlocutors]: a letter was published in ***Fascist Week*** the week prior to the The Albert Hall meeting, giving the lie to a recent story in the ***Daily Herald*** that there had been an exodus of disgruntled NHQ officers.

The letter [**51**] was signed by ten officers, the first of whom was R. A. Plathen, National Propaganda Officer, followed by P. M. Moir, Propaganda Officer, followed by Wilfred [curiously acquiring an extra middle initial, 'R'] as Area Administrative Officer. Perhaps this was because there was sufficient overlap between the BUF's definition of the terms propaganda and administration and, realistically, propaganda [as mentioned above] was present in every aspect of the Movement; 'Dick' Plathen, who was also described as "National Political Officer" [**52**], presumably oversaw the written propaganda output, at that time, ostensibly under Wilfred's control, but it is hardly surprising that confusion might have crept in, especially if it was stage-managed by Joyce; organisation was another area of responsibility where boundaries were somewhat ill-defined. Joyce's name was not appended to the letter to the ***Daily Herald***, because he did not qualify for inclusion by virtue of joining after the founding of the BUF.

An attempt at clarification of the remit of Wilfred's department was made in ***The Blackshirt*** at the beginning of April, but there does not appear to be any artifice in the timing. Again his title A/A/O is used, which seems odd, but perhaps because this is an official, internal, quasi-military designation, rather than the all-encompassing Director of Propaganda, which was only intended for laymen? Despite being regarded as a "house organ", ***The Blackshirt*** was sold to the public before the advent of the revitalised ***Action*** two years later, so the phraseology used was no doubt reasonably well considered for both purposes. Although no doubt seen as a weakness by some, Wilfred was obviously well-liked; "The Propaganda Department at N.H.Q. is under the leadership of ever-smiling and imperturbable A/A/O Risdon, who is ably backed by his aide-de-camp, D/A/O Carlyle-Elliott. [sic]" The sub-departments were detailed, the second one an area in which Wilfred would play an increasingly active part, in years to come; London meetings, constituency canvassing, and provincial meetings. It would be relevant to quote the rest of the article in full:

> "Propaganda work is manifold. The London Meetings Department arranges all details for meetings in the Greater London Area, of which over 500 are held weekly. New ground is broken, stewards, and speakers are detailed to take along sufficient propaganda literature.
>
> N.H.Q. speakers are trained in the tutorial classes held each week by A/A/O Joyce. Details of policy, and the technique of speaking, in which a very high standard is set, are part of the training the speaker must acquire before being passed out as competent. He is then sent to branch meetings where the ground has been broken. During the winter months most meetings have been

> held indoors, but even during the worst weather there has been no absolute cessation of outdoor propaganda activity.
>
> Perhaps the most important phase of the department's work is the arranging of the Leader's meetings. Careful organisation and infinite attention to detail is absolutely necessary to ensure the success of these meetings. Hitherto, every meeting at which the Leader has spoken has been an unqualified success. Packed halls has been the rule, and already hundreds of thousands of people have listened to the Leader.
>
> The crowning success of Propaganda's efforts is expected to be the huge gathering at the Royal Albert Hall on April 22, when the Leader will address over 10,000 people. Careful plans have been made, and tickets at prices ranging from 7/6 to 11/- are now available. Early application is necessary to ensure a seat." [**53**]

It obviously made sense to mention the Albert Hall meeting at the end of this piece, but its position straddling the centrefold belies anything other than general information, given that this event had been in the planning for some time already. In the same issue, there was an exhortation from the Leader to learn "at once the Fascist Songs which have been written and accepted as official songs of the Movement." It was not an order as such [but why should any member want to refuse?]; "It is the Leader's desire"; and "It is also the Leader's wish that these songs should be sung by all Fascists present at the meeting in the Royal Albert Hall on Sunday, April 22. As it will be impossible to publish these songs with the music in time for this meeting, Community Singing meetings will be held thrice weekly prior to the Royal Albert Hall meeting, in the Club Room, N.H.Q." [**54**] The aforementioned Carsten remarked, before a neutral assessment of the Albert Hall meeting, that "The meetings, like the Hitler meetings, were superbly staged." [**55**] Although the Albert Hall was not much bigger in terms of audience numbers than some of its predecessors, the venue did lend itself to a new departure for the Movement: public spectacle as a propaganda tool. It would be naïve to suppose that, as well as having experienced Italian Fascist events personally, Wilfred was not aware of recent German National Socialist rallies, such as those held at Nürnberg, and captured not only in publicity stills, but by Hitler's favourite film-maker, Leni Riefenstahl [**56**], and although inevitably, there was an element of 'stage-management' in the meetings [**57**], the aspiration was always to do this in an 'English' way, wherever possible. Of course, the rally was reported and lauded in the two Fascist periodicals [although respectfully omitting any mention of the Leader's limp however], but Cross gives a concise report [**58**]:

> "[Mosley's] speaking technique was not fully developed at the time of the first Albert Hall rally, but the Fascist pageantry was already mature. The great silver fasces hung over the organ. While waiting for the meeting to begin the audience sang the BUF songs, 'Britain Awake!' and 'Mosley'. Punctually at eight o'clock there was a fanfare of trumpets. Through the door in double file came a procession of Blackshirts carrying Union Jacks and Fascist standards.

> They marched through the hall and positioned themselves round the rostrum. Then, after an electrically tense pause, Mosley appeared - alone. From head to foot he was in black, the only relief being a silver fasces shining in the buckle of his belt. The 10,000 audience stood up, many of them raising their right arm in the Roman salute. Through a tunnel of arms Mosley limped across the length of the hall to the rostrum; his chin was high and his face, deathly pale, wore a relaxed, confident expression. He spoke for an hour and forty minutes, outlining the basis of the BUF creed."

Two points are worth mentioning: the first is that what Cross calls the "Roman salute" [and what quickly came to be known as the "Nazi" salute] was always, Mosley maintained, an ancient British, 'open-hand' form of respectful salutation; also, his speech was made, as always, without the benefit of notes so, although not specifically *extempore*, it did however give him the option of improvising, should the opportunity or necessity arise. On the night, the meticulous planning paid off; this didn't mean that Wilfred was able to concentrate on it to the exclusion of all else, of course: in the run-up to the event, Wilfred spoke at his own public meetings as far afield as Bath, Welwyn, Stockport and Sheffield. Despite that, the meeting went off without a hitch, and was generally reckoned to be very successful. ***Fascist Week*** printed a photograph of Wilfred in pride of place on the front page, top left, captioned "W. RISDON, *Director of propaganda, who organised the Albert Hall meeting*", to accompany its review of the event [**59**].

A week before the Albert Hall meeting, Mosley opened the new Manchester branch premises in Northumberland Street, Higher Broughton, which was to play a pivotal rôle in Wilfred's career in the BUF before very long; however, in the afterglow of the Albert Hall, there was an even bigger meeting to plan: Olympia. It was obvious that there was an appetite in the capital for meetings or rallies which could cater for hitherto unheard of numbers of people, in this country anyway, so because "thousands of disappointed people were turned away" from "[t]he tremendous success of the Albert Hall meeting … [the] Organisation [was] taking the bold step of engaging Olympia, for a colossal meeting to be held on Thursday, June 7, the day after Derby Day." [**60**] By the end of May, nearly 10,000 seats had already been sold, "and each day shoals of letters with demands for seats are being received by the Propaganda Department." [**61**] It would appear that Wilfred had no speaking engagements for the interim, understandable in view of the tremendous responsibility on his shoulders.

Wilfred's "aide-de-camp", Deputy Administrative Officer [D/A/O] Carlyle Elliot (N.H.Q.) was quietly promoted to be Officer-in-Charge of National Meetings in the middle of May and, in view of the lack of any statement of retrospective seniority [this was very often to be seen in the "Official Gazette and Bulletin" section in ***The Blackshirt***, after individual announcements] presumably it was effective immediately [**62**]; this was not automatically any sort of criticism: Wilfred's deputy had, very probably, been fulfilling this function for some time and, given the rigidly hierarchical nature of the Movement, this appointment was probably just the mere acknowledgement and confirmation of that fact and, in any case, Wilfred was probably glad to be free of the responsibility, given the burgeoning number of national meetings at which the Leader did not speak, leaving Wilfred free to concentrate on the smooth organisation of Mosley's meetings alone. The opposition must have realised that they had let pass a valuable opportunity to blacken the reputation of the BUF at the Albert Hall, so they geared up for a decisive demonstration next time. It is not clear if the cryptic notice, in the same edition of ***The Blackshirt*** as the one in which Carlyle Elliot's promotion was announced, that "We have received information which proves that the Communist Party are attempting to form storm sections, so in future we must look for greater organised opposition." [**63**] was a specific reference to the forthcoming Olympia meeting, but it was no great secret that trouble, with its concomitant adverse publicity for the BUF, was prepared for by the opposition. ***The Daily Worker*** printed a major article [24/04/34] justifying violence; on the 15th of May, it published a statement by a prominent Communist urging workers "to use force … it is no use talking about constitutional methods", and two days later, it published the first of many calls for a "counter-demonstration" at Olympia to meet Mosley's "challenge to the working-class" [**64**].

Special Branch, very likely with the aid of 'moles' and informers, had nothing of interest to report about the BUF's preparations; the Communists, however, warranted several mentions in reports. The CPGB was providing members with black shirts, for obvious reasons [28/05/34]; many stated their intention to carry missiles at the counter-demonstration [04/06/34]; and they had been "especially active among the Jewish elements in the East End, from whom they hope to obtain a large number of demonstrators" [07/06/34] [**65**]. There were roughly 2,000 Blackshirts at Olympia, of whom 1,000 were stewards; that might sound like a lot, but out of a total audience of between 12,000 and 15,000 [reports vary, inevitably], not including the stewards, odds of 6:1 could have been overwhelming if a large section of the crowd had turned violent, but the opposition was clever enough not to concentrate its forces in one area, as a rule. As expected and, indeed, desired by the opposition, there was trouble outside the exhibition hall before the event had even begun; Dundas had requested that the BUF should have dispensation to keep order outside as well as inside Olympia, but in retrospect, the refusal has to be seen as the right decision [**66**]; as it was, the 760 foot and mounted police struggled to keep order, in the face of about 10,000 protesters who jeered & jostled not only the Fascists, but also the audience arriving for the event [**67**]. This could have been a serious 'public relations' gaffe on the part of the anti-Fascists, given the nature of the audience; this meeting had come to be seen as something of a social event, partly as a result of Rothermere's supportive publicity, and it attracted a mix of "MPs, peers, diplomats, big-business men and leading journalists" [**68**], who were "curious to see the new phenomenon" [**69**]. On this occasion, the audience was not expected to loyally sing along to Fascist songs: "It was entertained by a band playing popular tunes, in the manner of big public meetings at the time." [**70**] The decoration of the hall was minimal, no doubt on the basis that overtly fascist regalia could intimidate and possibly deter influential potential converts; the emphasis was on the message, not the medium. Cost was no doubt also a factor; a large portion of the BUF's income was provided by these public meetings, and although some free seats were always allotted [there were 2,000 at Olympia] the majority were paid for. The meeting started forty minutes after the advertised time and, five minutes later, when Mosley began speaking, he only managed to utter one [albeit fairly long] sentence, before shouting started. The protesters were warned by Mosley to desist, but they were not given a second chance and ejected when they started again. No sooner had Mosley returned to his speech than a different part of the hall provided the disturbance, and this pattern continued for an hour, until two protesters decided to raise the stakes and climb precariously out on the overhead girders, where they proceeded to shout slogans and throw down leaflets [**71**].

It is only in ***The Blackshirt*** that the information that "the men who undertook this perilous mission on the rafters [to persuade the protesters to desist] were not rank-and-file Blackshirts, but very senior officers—Mr. E. R. Piercy, the commander of the Defence Force, and Mr. Francis-Hawkins, who commands the London Area, being chief among them." can be found, and this was very probably in the spirit of reinforcing the notion of the duty of hierarchical discipline prevalent in the Movement. A length of rope, with which the vocal protester lashed out at his opponent, only narrowly missed, thereby avoiding what could have been a fatality, had the Blackshirt fallen [**72**]. Mosley's speech finally lasted three quarters of an hour longer than the originally scheduled one and a quarter hours, as a result of all these interruptions. One of the less emotive elements of the controversy surrounding the unfortunate outcome of this event was the use of searchlights, allegedly to pick out troublemakers in the crowd and intimidate them; it is true that the loudspeaker cables were cut, a very common ploy by the opposition, and the "arc lamps" mentioned by a few press reports the day after were used by newsreel companies there to film the event: naturally, they would want to illuminate any disturbances so that they could be captured on film for the credulous cinema audiences. The ***Manchester Guardian*** of June the 8th reported that Mosley went on speaking through the disturbances, even though there was a period when his voice could not be heard [**73**].

The biggest mistake made by the BUF at this event was not the speech; the opposition to Jewish influence, in and of itself, in British society was not yet a strategic doctrinal element [the speech dealt mainly with economic issues with which the diverse audience would readily identify]; it was the lapse in the heretofore reliable discipline of the stewards, or inefficient screening and training of new recruits, or both, which meant that some of them used apparently excessive force to restrain and remove protesters, and this was understandably seized upon by anti-Fascists in the post mortem. Small comfort perhaps, but there were no deaths, on either side; only about 50 people were ejected, Fascists injured by a fearsome array of weapons displayed by Mosley after the event were included in the injured treated at the nearby hospital, and the only person detained in hospital for any length of time, a Sheffield University student named Jacob Miller, who claimed he had been "bludgeoned with a formidable weapon over the head until half dead", was able to interrupt Mosley from the floor three weeks later at a meeting in Sheffield, with no hint of any previous injury [**74**]. The opposition appeared well pleased rather than outraged; the tone of the report in the ***Daily Worker*** was that of a good fight well fought: the Communists were beginning to realise the value of the liberal conscience as an ally and a propaganda tool. Skidelsky's assessment is both sanguine and balanced; Mosley was let down by his stewards who, after all, were doing what was essential for him: protecting his freedom of speech, which the opposition was desperate to prevent at almost any cost, but in the context of events unfolding on mainland Europe, they very quickly came to be seen as the thuggish weapon of a putative dictator in waiting [**75**].

Wilfred's own take on the spotlight situation, alluded to some years later in his 18B appeal hearing [**Appendix D**] could, of course, have been cleverly weighted to support his notion of gradual and corrosive disenchantment, but it is unlikely to have been entirely disingenuous, despite an element of ambiguity in the wording; he said that "the people who arranged the spotlight were people who did so contrary to my advice": he must have made his feelings about this known to the Leader, and "because I was opposed to that sort of thing I was given a different job." The final meeting in the Leader's 'summer campaign' was to have been held at the White City arena, London, scheduled for August 5th, and the day had been nominated "Blackshirt Sunday". Although this venue only held "little over 5,000", it must be assumed that the organisation was Wilfred's responsibility. Arrangements were going ahead, and provincial branches exhorted by ***The Blackshirt***, in the usual trumpeting style, to select and organise the financing of transport for the most worthy members [because the branches could not expect handouts from national headquarters; they had to be self-supporting] when, in the middle of July, the event was quietly cancelled. Although the article in ***The Blackshirt*** [**76**] began with the reason, the headline shouted the fact that there would be a "GREAT BLACKSHIRT RALLY IN HYDE PARK ON SEPTEMBER 9th", and "NEWCASTLE TOWN MOOR MEETING FIXED FOR JULY 29". The Sunday of the White City event was right in the middle of the Empire Games, and the venue's managing director,

Brigadier General Critchley, MP "indicated that the arrangements … cannot proceed without serious danger of damage to the running tracks, etc., … and that an appeal had been made to him on behalf of Imperial Sports to cancel this date." Despite what should have been obvious questions about the late realisation by the management of this apparent potential for damage, the Movement respected it, especially given its espousal of all things associated with the British Empire, and immediately announced "an even greater rally … in Hyde Park, which … is in many ways a more suitable place for a great Blackshirt rally than the White City." [**77**]

The Newcastle meeting would also be a good addition, having been postponed earlier after the intervention of the Home Secretary, because of local fears for the safety of the women & children who would be present on the Town Moor on June 24th, the day originally scheduled, which coincided with a fête popular with families. There were smaller provincial meetings for the Leader to be organised [3,000 at both Sheffield and Swansea] and Wilfred was also still speaking at his own public meetings; at the beginning of July, he addressed "a large meeting at Folkestone Town Hall … [which] was the first indoor meeting organised by the local branch, and it was obvious that a large number of people attending were definitely sceptical of Blackshirt policy. But before the meeting finished the audience openly expressed its appreciation with bursts of applause and cheering." [**78**] William Joyce was doing his best to convince everyone that he was the authority on public speaking, with many articles published in ***The Blackshirt***. By the beginning of 1934, in addition to his high rank of A/A/O he was already a Director of Research at NHQ, yet his chief job was "holding meetings in all parts of the country, and assisting in the promulgation of Fascist policy", so he was obviously champing at the bit for some career advancement, at Wilfred's expense if necessary.

In July 1934, Mosley's brief endorsement by Lord Rothermere came to an end. They had known each other socially for some years, and as the troubled 'twenties became the volatile 'thirties, Rothermere had been looking for a politician to support who stood for the same 'patriotic', pro-Empire line that he did, so he was very much in agreement with Mosley's political direction as he moved into Fascism, having given earlier encouragement, as mentioned above. Mosley describes him as being a somewhat impulsive, mercurial character, and it is clear from his autobiography that he found Rothermere's public support slightly embarrassing, as well as useful [**79**], so his withdrawal of this support, although on the one hand it cast the mark of Cain on him, on the other hand it allowed Mosley, and by extension his members, to be free of any dichotomy of purpose: according to Skidelsky, "the real significance of Olympia was to reveal the incompatibility between 'blackshirt man' and 'Rothermere man'." [**80**] Rothermere made no bones about the reason for his *volte-face*: his Jewish advertisers had threatened to take their business elsewhere [**81**]; the termination of this relationship also had another unfortunate consequence: the loss of a potentially lucrative business opportunity. Although Mosley was indisputably a rich man, he was sensible enough to realise that it would be foolhardy in the extreme to bankrupt himself in the quest for his version of Utopia; he freely admitted that "[f]rom first to last I gave about £100,000 of my own money to our movement in the thirties." [**82**]: a fortune by anybody's standards, but a political organisation such as his was disastrously expensive, even without supporting the national network of branches [indeed, they had to be self-supporting and pay a "tax" of a percentage of their "takings" **83**] and rich patrons without their own agendas were virtually non-existent [**84**].

The missed business opportunity was a joint venture with Rothermere to manufacture and distribute cigarettes: "I warmly welcomed his proposal, for a straightforward business deal seemed to me the best and cleanest way to raise large funds, and I was sure our people would co-operate with enthusiasm in a proposition offering such benefit to the party." [**85**] In his usual precipitate fashion, Rothermere purchased "£70,000 worth of machinery" and engaged a capable expert "of the combine on the production side" on a fat salary; all was going full steam ahead when Mosley received a message that Rothermere could not proceed "and had decided to sell all the machinery for what it would fetch." Mosley "reacted strongly" and played the Northcliffe card: his brother would not have allowed himself to be coerced in this fashion. However, on this occasion, Mosley did not prevail: Rothermere was adamant, and the association was at an end [**86**]. In his autobiography, Mosley also alludes mysteriously to "a business opening in his locality" suggested to him by a "young member of the movement", which turned into "a great enterprise", but demurs from revealing details of its success [**87**].

It has to remain a matter for speculation as to whether Wilfred requested reassignment in September 1934, as a response, in part, to Joyce's ambitious manoeuvring, and Wilfred's perception of the diminution of his authority which, despite his pragmatic acceptance of military discipline in such an organisation of which he was a leading light, was essential if the unquestioning observance of the chain of command was to be preserved; or whether Mosley considered that Wilfred had, in a year and a half, successfully established an efficient and highly effective department, which could reliably be left in the capable hands of others, leaving Wilfred free to use his indisputable talents in a different, although inevitably related [given the all-pervading nature of propaganda in the BUF], area of the Movement. Whichever of those was, in fact, the case, in the autumn of 1934 Wilfred left the relative security of National Headquarters, on a mission to Manchester.

NOTES

1 He was also described as an "Authority on politics and economics, expert in election law. Wrote for the Labour Party a treatise on Parliamentary election practice." The same edition reports that he was a guest at the wedding of "Fascist Chief of Staff" Ian Hope Dundas to Miss Pamela Ernestine Dorman, sister of another BUF member, Geoffrey Dorman, and niece & god-daughter of the late Sir Ernest Shackleton.

Fascist Week, no. 7, Dec. 22-28, 1933, p3 & p5

Dundas was a very young, but able recruit, according to Cross:

> "On the organizational side the most important acquisition was Ian Hope Dundas who, at the age of 24, became Mosley's Chief of Staff. Dundas, who had recently resigned a commission in the Royal Navy, had an impeccable social background, his father having been 28th Chief of Dundas and an admiral. … In so far as he reduced to order the chaotic affairs of a rapidly growing movement, Dundas was a success, but his methods created a faintly Ruritanian atmosphere."

The Fascists in Britain, by Colin Cross

2 ***The Streets are still/Mosley in Motley, typescript memoir, undated [c. 1937] by Alexander Miles, MSS 292/743.11/2, University of Warwick Modern Records Centre***

Wilfred's acquaintance with Carlyle Elliot was confirmed by ***The Blackshirt*** a year after Wilfred's move, in another fairly detailed retrospective on the Newcastle branch:

> "The Newcastle Branch of the British Union of Fascists was one of the earliest to be formed in the country. Mr. W. Risdon had been supplied with an advance copy of "The Greater Britain", and in September 1932 he called together a few friends to discuss it. At this first meeting were present in addition to himself, Mr. and Mrs. Leaper, and Mr. Carlyle Elliot. It is a significant fact that Risdon, Leaper and Elliot are now prominent officers on the National Headquarters Staff. The result of this meeting was a decision to form a branch of the BUF and Mr. Risdon was unanimously requested to act as Organiser. Membership increased slowly until February 1933, but by that time the efforts of the members were beginning to bear fruit. During that month Mr. Risdon was transferred to London to become Propaganda Officer. At this time the branch numbered about forty members.
>
> Leaper and Elliot commenced a series of open-air meetings in County Durham starting at Crook. Contact was also established with Michael McCartan who had joined the Movement in October 1932, and who ranks as one of its earliest members. At Sunderland an attempt was made to hold a meeting outside of the Boilermakers Hall by Leaper and Michael Jordan, who was also an active Fascist worker. This first attempt to bring Fascism to Sunderland ended in disorder. The meeting was broken up with violence from the 'Red' section of the crowd. How vastly different was the meeting which Mr. Risdon addressed in Sunderland three weeks ago. Then the Defence Force enabled the speaker to put over our policy for the first time in

Sunderland without one murmur from the opposition."

From All Quarters; Newcastle Branch; Early Adventures: *The Blackshirt, No. 43, Feb.16-22, 1934*

3 Wilfred's enthusiasm and lust for life are very evident here:

"Shortly after the establishment of the Newcastle group I left for London. There I joined the tiny band of enthusiasts working at Great George Street for the establishment of a truly national organisation. What memories are evoked when looking back on those days. What comradeship is recalled by a remembering of the personnel of those days. Most of them are still with us, either marching in our ranks or keeping step with us in spirit. Those were marvellous days, fraught with happy associations, and will always be remembered as among the happiest, as well as the most eventful, in my whole life.

There were meetings every night, with an open Morris van ("Old Bill") to take us to the more distant of them. There were songs and parodies sung on the outward and return journies – and what songs and parodies they were. Often there were cuts and bruises on the return trip which had not been there on the outward journey. But how we did LIVE.

The Blackshirt was on sale in those early days – and how they did sell. Twelve dozen was quite an average for one member in one night. I admit that it often meant keeping at it from six in the evening until two the next morning, starting on the homeward bound workers at Victoria, Waterloo, Charing Cross and the other stations, then on to the theatre and cinema crowds, then on to the supper crowds and the general night life of the West End and Soho. Santini's for a coffee in the small hours and at last back to hand in the cash – sold **out**!"

BACK TO THE FIRST YEAR / Early Days Of British Union Recalled / *By W. Risdon: Action, no. 86, Oct. 9, 1937, p.7*

4 ***Oswald Mosley, by Robert Skidelsky:***

"[it was not possible] in the early days to take fascism entirely seriously as a revolutionary force. Indeed, the opening fascist rally at Trafalgar Square on the 15th of October had a positively festive air about it: Cim turned up with the children, Brendan Bracken and [Winston's son] Randolph Churchill looked in."

5 ***Ibid.:***

"… according to Lloyd George it was by Mosley a 'brilliant debate … the swordsmanship was superb …'"

A socialist publication, ***The New Clarion***, was not uncomplimentary:

"For the first twenty minutes Mosley talked Socialism, except that he referred to a corporate state instead of the co-operative commonwealth."

The New Clarion, 04/03/33, in* "Left Wing Fascism in Theory and Practice: The Case of the British Union of Fascists", *by Philip M. Coupland, University of Glasgow; Twentieth Century British History, Vol. 13, No. 1, 2002, pp. 38-61

The 'competition' was scathing, in an early parallel of internecine socialist squabbling, and no guesses necessary as to who was among the targets:

"A supporter of another fascist organization, the British Fascists, dismissed 'the propaganda of the British Union of Fascists' as 'merely a Socialistic attack on capitalism under the name of Fascism'. Mosley had 'practically staffed the BUF' with ex-socialists who had 'brought their ILP propaganda with them'."

British Fascism, Special Summer Propaganda Number, undated; c. 1933, 11, in Ibid.

6 The sardonic edge to the assignation of 'colours' was never far away:

"The entertaining information has been published that the I.L.P. has adopted the Red Shirt. Apart from the amusing spectacle of the old sheep in the Russian Wolf's clothing, it is interesting to note the imitation of Fascist tactics.

When the British Union of Fascists first popularised the Grey Shirt and the Black Shirt we were told that these methods were un-English and would never go down in this country. So successful, however, have they proved that some three months after our start the forty-year-old I.L.P. has been driven to copy us.

Soon the still older Parties will be following suit; members of the Carlton Club will be seen wearing a blue blouse beneath a well-polished top hat. But this adoption of appropriate clothing must not go too far, or the present Cabinet will exchange trousers for skirts."

SHOT AND SHELL: *The Blackshirt, No. 1, February 1933*

7 **ARRANGING A MEETING By BILL RISDON Director of Propaganda: *The Blackshirt, No. 40, Jan. 26-Feb. 01, 1934:***

"What does the term 'Propaganda' convey to the average mind? Meetings? Speeches? Yes. These are forms of propaganda, and it should be said, very useful propaganda, but there are others and it is desirable that each and every form of propaganda should be fully utilised for Fascism.

The printed word as well as the spoken word should be used for Fascist Propaganda and both the printed word and the spoken word fail to attain their objective until they have made contact with those who do not yet understand our aims and aspirations. The street-corner meeting attended by a handful of people who are already supporters of Fascism is not a 'propaganda meeting'.

Fascist literature read by Fascists is not 'propaganda'. Only when you have passed your literature to those who don't know, and delivered your speech to those who have not yet been convinced of the objects and purport of Fascism do your efforts become 'propaganda'. I propose therefore, to take advantage of the offer of space in the ***Blackshirt*** to give a few suggestions, indicating means whereby propaganda activities may be made more effective."

8 **THE FASCIST DIARY: *The Blackshirt, No. 2, March 1933, p. 4***

9 It made sense to print the opposition's belligerent propaganda:

"The manifesto was a direct incitement to attack the Fascist meeting, couched in the most violent language. We have yet to learn that the Manchester police have arrested any Communists for this incitement.

The manifesto is headed "Unity Against Fascist Reaction". It is described as a manifesto of the Manchester Local of the Communist Party of Great Britain, and is addressed to the members of the Labour Party, I.L.P., Trade Unions, Co-ops. It contains the following passage:—

> Comrades,
>
> To-day Mosley has come to Manchester in an attempt to draw under the black banner of Fascism the tremendously powerful forces of the Industrial workers of Manchester.
>
> In view of the terrific onslaught of Hitler's Fascists against the German working class, and the development of Fascism and war throughout the world, the Communist manifesto has called for *Unity of the Workers, Communists and Labour Organisations, in every country in the world.*
>
> **WHAT IS MOSLEYISM?**
>
> Mosley is Hitlerism in Great Britain. Like Hitler he intends to mislead the workers ... Fascism means death to the British working class—it means Fascist murder gangs stalking the streets of Britain. Workers of the Labour Party, I.L.P., and Co-op. Guilds, the mightiest fighting front of the working class must be displayed against Fascist terror.
>
> *Long live the heroic German working class. Long live the Unity of the Workers against Fascist terror and reaction.*
>
> Secretariat, M/C Local C.P.G.B.

Can anyone deny that this manifesto was a direct incitement to attack our Fascist meeting? Can anyone point to any action taken by the police against its authors?"

The Blackshirt, No. 3, March 18th, 1933, p. 1

10 ***Ibid.***

11 Wilfred obviously enjoyed the *esprit de corps* of the Movement:

"One of my early jobs in the first year of the Movement was the organisation of the first Free Trade Hall, Manchester, meeting. This was the first big meeting in the provinces, and what a meeting! It was here that I first met Charlie and Joe Dickenson, Miss Cordery, 'Pop' Reynolds and his two 'big boys' Dan and Jimmy, and many others, who I have been proud to number among my friends and comrades from that day on.

The first meeting I addressed in Stephenson Square brought in recruits and yielded the usual 'spot of bother'. Eventually came the Free Trade Hall meeting with 'Mosley Speaking' as its advance cry. The great hall crowded to capacity and thousands in queues outside unable to gain admittance. Piercy, Brindley, Lou Bellott, and a whole bunch of the boys from London had come up by excursion for this first provincial meeting. Again there was the usual 'spot of bother', and it is talked about to this day wherever 'Mancunians' gather together."

BACK TO THE FIRST YEAR / Early Days Of British Union Recalled / By W. Risdon: *Action, no. 86, Oct. 9, 1937, p.7*

12 ***The Fascists in Britain, op. cit.***

13 ***Oswald Mosley, op. cit.:***

"Pictures from Rome show Mosley's black shirt incongruously swathed in a double-breasted waistcoat. The beautiful cut of his coat is ill-attuned to the violence of the Fascist salute. And I do not wonder that the Italians who welcomed him to Rome averted their eyes from Sir Oswald's trousers, which were in elegant but startling contrast to their own breeches and leggings."

14 ***The Fascists in Britain, op. cit.***

15 ***Oswald Mosley, op. cit.:***

"'He now regards his movement as a memorial to Cimmie and is prepared willingly to die for it.' [Harold Nicolson] … an appeal for a Cynthia Mosley Memorial Fund to build a children's nursery in the poorest part of Westminster went out over the signatures of Ramsay MacDonald, Stanley Baldwin, George Lansbury and Lloyd George. Robert Boothby and Brendan Bracken were the joint treasurers. It was built and stands today in Lambeth."

http://www.walcotfoundation.org.uk/MosleyCMMF.html

16 ***The Blackshirt, No. 5, April 17, 1933, page 1***

17 ***The Blackshirt No. 16, Aug. 12-18, 1933, page 2:***

"Membership has grown to such an extent during the last few months that the move was indispensable. The new building is big enough for all our present requirements, and forms an ideal headquarters."

18 ***The Fascists in Britain, op. cit.:***

"In an emergency, the BUF declared, 5,000 Blackshirts could live there as a self-contained unit."

19 ***Ibid.***

20 ***Ibid.***

21 ***Major P.G. Taylor, Agent Provocateur, by Bryan Clough, author of State Secrets: The Kent-Wolkoff Affair***

http://www.oswaldmosley.com/p-g-taylor.htm

22 ***Britain Between the Wars 1918-1940, by Charles Loch Mowat, Ch. 7, S. 10***

23 ***Ibid.***

24 Alexander Miles was aware of this on his first experience of the BUF:

"The national headquarters of the British Union of Fascists was then located at no. 12, Lower Grosvenor Place, near Victoria Station and, incidentally, near Buckingham Palace. I arrived there in the early part of July 1933, and I must confess that I was favourably impressed of what I found there. Older members of the Socialist Movement, having experienced the fervour of the pioneer days, and others who remember the spirit of the Socialist and Labour Party membership in the years immediately after the war, may find it difficult to believe that in the Fascist Movement in 1933 there was a spirit of comradeship or brotherhood, equal to the best of the early days of the Socialist Crusades youth and early maturity. [sic]"

The Streets are still/Mosley in Motley, op. cit.

Mosley commented on this atmosphere as well, in his autobiography:

"In practice, there was far more consultation with members before policy was published or decisions taken than in any other party. Not only did I always consult my colleagues at headquarters, but in my constant journeys throughout the country I consulted all members. This was done both in regular conferences and in the assembly of blackshirts after every meeting, when I not only addressed them but also moved among them talking to individual members. I felt deeply that we owed each other this friendship, and their companionship was one of the joys I have known in life. It was also an essential method for obtaining the vital information which produced efficiency, because it was difficult in these conditions for anything important to be kept from me."

My Life, by Oswald Mosley

25 ***Oswald Mosley, op. cit.:***

"The BUF ... got under way without an anti-Jewish policy but with a number of anti-Semites in its ranks - William Joyce was the most notable recruit in this category. Its intensely nationalist 'Britain for the British' line gained it further support among a group of people who were disposed to dislike foreign immigrants, of whom the Jewish community at that time formed the largest number, and to associate them with unsavoury crimes and antisocial practices ... Even before it had started, a couple of anti-Jewish incidents were reported in the press. 'The facts are', said a New Party statement issued on behalf of the leader in Antibes, 'that anti-Jewish propaganda is neither authorised nor approved by Sir Oswald.' ... A further statement issued by the BUF in October said Jews had nothing to fear from Fascism unless - significantly - they were associated with its 2 enemies, Communism & International Finance. In December 1932 Mosley was assuring Lord Melchett that 'anti-Semitism forms no part of the policy of this Organisation, and anti-Semitic propaganda is forbidden'. A.K. Chesterton confirms that 'speakers who put over their personal views on the Jewish question were barred from the rostrum; some were expelled'. Some Jews even joined: the party line had been settled and there it was to remain officially for almost two years. ... From the earliest days, according to Chesterton, a Jewish body calling itself the British Union of Democrats 'sent round van-loads of Jews all over the country to break up Blackshirt meetings.'"

26 ***The Fascists in Britain, op. cit.:***

"The early BUF battles were on two fronts, against the minority Fascist groups on one side and against the militant anti-Fascists on the other. The dissident Fascists received much attention, their existence being regarded as a slight on the authority of Mosley's leadership. Arnold Leese's Imperial Fascists were easily the most dangerous; they wore uniforms similar to those of the BUF and the public found it hard to distinguish the one organization from the other. The Mosley Fascists tended to get the blame for Leese's violent outbursts and for the anti-Jewish slogans and swastikas which Leese's men painted on synagogues. The ***Jewish Chronicle*** was at some pains to distinguish between Mosley and Leese, declaring in March 1933: 'The Mosley Fascists themselves are our best supporters in the fight against the Imperial Fascist League.' Leese caused intense irritation among the Mosley Fascists by calling them the 'Kosher Fascists' and by hammering away at the allegation that Cynthia Mosley, through her grandfather Levi Leiter, was half Jewish [which was untrue]. ***Blackshirt*** retaliated by calling Leese a 'little tyke'."

27 ***Ibid.*** Dr. Forgan was also trying to recruit John Beckett to the BUF:

"In 1933 and 1934 he took the lead in persuading John to join the British Union of Fascists. John could not have known - no one knew until, 60 years later, Professor Geoffrey Alderman examined some Jewish records in New York and published his findings - that by the early summer of 1934 Forgan was more or less offering his services to the Board of Jewish Deputies as a spy in the Mosley camp.

He was supposed to be acting as Mosley's emissary, negotiating a *modus vivendi* between fascists and Jews. In fact, he told Board Chairman Dr. Laski that he found it impossible to work with Mosley, that despite protestations to the contrary Mosley was deeply anti-Semitic, and that he intended to leave. But Mosley was paying him £700 a year, he had a wife and children, and he had to earn a living. Also, though he did not mention it to Laski at the time, he had serious personal problems. His wife had attempted suicide, and he had sent his daughter to stay for several months with another fascist leader, William Joyce, and his wife. ... Laski told him rather sharply that the Board of Deputies did not buy opponents."

The Rebel who lost his Cause: The Tragedy of John Beckett, MP, by Francis Beckett

28 ***The Fascists in Britain, op. cit.***

29 ***Haw-Haw: The Tragedy of William and Margaret Joyce, by Nigel Farndale:***

"Macnab [one of his Black House colleagues] called him a polymath: his special subject at Birkbeck was German philology, which included Icelandic, Old Norse and Gothic; he was also fluent in German, French and Latin and had a reasonable command of Italian."

30 Descriptions of his style are legion, but to quote a few:

"In the BUF he quickly developed a brilliant talent as a public speaker, within months ranking second only to Mosley in popularity."

The Fascists in Britain, op. cit.

"His usual account of the moment at which he became an active fascist is, naturally, rather more elevated. It happened, he said, when he went to a meeting at Paddington Baths. Mosley was ill, and the meeting was taken by a young man called William Joyce, of whom John had never before heard. He described the effect three years later, in a pamphlet called ***National Socialism Now***: "Within ten minutes of this 28 year old youngster taking the platform I knew that here was one of the dozen finest orators in the country. Snowden's close reasoning and unerring instinct for words were allied with Maxton's humour and Churchill's daring."

The Rebel who lost his Cause: etc., MP, op. cit.

"I have recalled William Joyce's platform performance at Liverpool Stadium in November 1933. What a vitriolic tongue! But personality? You could almost feel the vibrations of his personality coming over the loudspeakers."

Blackshirts and Roses, an Autobiography, by John Charnley

31 ***The Fascists in Britain, op. cit.:***

"Against Risdon's advice, he abandoned his teaching career to take a salaried BUF post, first as Area Administrative Officer for West London and later as Propaganda Officer at National Headquarters, where his classes for speakers were a big attraction."

His original designation was D/A/O [Deputy Administrative Officer]. By the end of January 1934, he had already been promoted to A/A/O, and he was a Director of Research at National Headquarters, although the reality beyond the grand titles, initially at least, was that his chief job was "holding meetings in all parts of the country, and assisting in the promulgation of Fascist policy."

Fascist Week, no. 12, Jan. 26th-Feb. 1st, 1934, p5

32 Courtesy of Leonard Risdon, who would have been 10 years old at the time.

Certainly, Joyce's appearance could be intimidating, despite his height:

> "Joyce I found a brilliant little fellow in many ways, whose admirers dignified him with the title of "professor", a distinction to which he certainly was not entitled. A story was current in the movement as to how he acquired the scar which disfigured his face, no doubt at the time rendering him more interesting to the ladies, who raptly admired him at policy classes. The story was that at a Trafalgar Square meeting in the B.U.F. early days, Joyce was a Steward and was attacked by a Jewish Communist who slashed him with a razor. I believed there is some truth in the story but that it really relates not to his membership of the B.U.F. but to an earlier Fascist body. At all events, Joyce never contradicted the story and pleasured in describing himself as a more implacable enemy of the Jews than Mosley could ever be."

The Streets are still/Mosley in Motley, op. cit.

According to Farndale's chronology, the injury was inflicted on the 22nd of October 1924, and Joyce was returning home from stewarding a speech by a Conservative candidate at Lambeth Baths hall, so not quite as glorious maybe?

Haw-Haw: The Tragedy of William and Margaret Joyce, op. cit.

33 ***The Fascists in Britain, op. cit.***

34 ***Ibid.***

35 ***My Life, op. cit.***

36 Philip Coupland tells us that

> "An internal BUF document suggested that the FUBW's rôle might be 'compared to that of the TUC in relation to the Labour Party'. In, no doubt to some, a chilling parallel with Germany, a 'Brownshirt Corps' came into being: 'Although it recruited from amongst existing members of the BUF it was also possible to join the FUBW exclusively. It was presumably those who were solely members of the latter body who wore the brown shirt that was its official uniform.'"

Left Wing Fascism in Theory and Practice etc., op. cit.

37 ***The Blackshirt, No. 1, February 1933, page 4***

38 ***Left Wing Fascism in Theory and Practice etc., op. cit. & The Blackshirt passim, 1934***

39 Miles was, understandably, aggrieved, recording Mosley's explanation that

> "'he did not propose to countenance anything in the way of a Trade Union rivalling the existing Trade Union machine' and forbade him from 'setting up Fascist Trade Unions'. Miles's belief was that 'the real explanation' was that Mosley 'feared the growth of the Fascist Union of British Workers and was determined to put a stop to its progress'."

Mosley also put his foot down to stop a workers' insurance scheme for the membership, to be administered by its director, J. Barney, a clerical union official, who had been recruited by Robert Forgan; despite a preparatory notice in ***The Blackshirt*** in April 1934 of "an announcement [which] will shortly be made regarding the British Union Approved Society", nothing more was heard of it, and Miles believes that the scheme was "'wet-blanketed' by the administrative officers." Barney resigned in disgust not long after the closure of the FUBW.

Left Wing Fascism in Theory and Practice etc., op. cit.

40 ***Oswald Mosley, op. cit.:***

"Something in him was irresistibly drawn not so much to Fascism as to the idea of a politics half-civilian, half-military, a 'mobilisation of ex-servicemen for the achievements of peace', as he put it in a speech in November [1931]."

41 ***Ibid.***

42 The moral point of the story was slightly confused:

"'DAILY MAIL' SURPRISE.

KILLJOY ATTITUDE TO DOG RACING "TOTES"

We are surprised that ***The Daily Mail*** should have suggested that if "Totes" are permitted on greyhound tracks they should be required to make a "substantial contribution" to the Exchequer or *to charity*.

If "Totes" are morally right why should they, as Sunday cinemas are, but should not, be required to contribute to *charity*? If they are not right they should not be permitted at all. The suggestion is typical of the hypocritical killjoy; hence our surprise at seeing it in ***The Daily Mail***."

The Blackshirt, No. 1, February 1933, page 4

43 ***Left Wing Fascism in Theory and Practice etc., op. cit.***

44 ***The Blackshirt, No. 40, January 26th-February 1st, 1934, page 1***

45 ***Fascist Week, No. 12, Jan. 26th-Feb. 1st, 1934, page 1***

46 ***The Blackshirt, No. 40, January 26th-February 1st, 1934, page 1***

47 ***Ibid.***

48 Ellen Wilkinson was born five years before Wilfred in Manchester, and stayed very much to the left of the Socialist Movement, helping to found the Communist Party of Great Britain [CPGB], after being a pacifist and becoming the first female organiser at the National Union of Distributive and Allied Workers [NUDAW] during the first world war. She might also have crossed paths with Wilfred when she was Labour MP for Middlesbrough East until losing her seat at the 1931 general election.

http://womenshistorynetwork.org/blog/?p=694

The Kingsway Hall

"was [originally] the Kingsway Hall Methodist Church, erected in 1912 as the worshipping centre of the West London Mission.

Built for Evangelical purposes, it was considered to have the finest acoustics in London for recording orchestral and choral repertory. Kingsway Hall soon became the most sought after recording venue for orchestral music in England, due to its central location and excellent acoustics. ... The last final [sic] recording was made with Deutsche Grammophon: Giacomo Puccini's Manon Lescaut, which finished taping on January 5th 1984.

In 1998 Cola Holdings acquired Kingsway Hall and launched

a multi-million pound refurbishment to build the 4* Deluxe Kingsway Hall Hotel. The façade of the building is the original and the inside was completely renovated. Our reception desk is in the approximate location where orchestra members once recorded."

http://www.kingswayhall.co.uk/history.html

49 ***The Blackshirt, No. 45, March 2nd-8th, 1934, page 4***

50 ***The Rise of Fascism, by F. L. Carsten***

51 "**FASCISTS' LETTER TO 'DAILY HERALD'** / Affirming Loyalty

Following statements in the ***Daily Herald*** *alleging that the majority of the original office holders in the British Union of Fascists had left, a number of officers who have been in the Movement since its inception wrote to that paper denying the allegation and affirming their loyalty to the Leader. So far the* ***Daily Herald*** *has not published the letter. The* ***Fascist Week*** *prints it below.*

It is to be regretted that your paper claiming, as it does, to tell the truth, does not conduct some semblance of investigation into the authenticity of statements or claims made to you by alleged "ex-Fascists".

To-day's issue publishes an amusing diversion in the statement that 'the majority of the original Mosleyite office-holders have already left, and the others are leaving at the rate of dozens a week.'

In answer to the first, we, the undersigned, have been members and officers from varying periods *prior* to, or immediately upon, the formation of the B.U.F.

Our devotion to our Leader and our Cause is unswerving, our Leader is always amongst us – despite his fully occupied day, he always finds time to talk and laugh with the 'boys'.

Members *do* leave us: we do not need all the men who claim ostensibly to be Fascists. Neither does Fascism permit the survival of the 'Bluffer' and the 'Grumbler'. There is room in our ranks only for men who know sacrifice and service – not self-gain and individual advancement.

The article in question refers to very few members nearly all of whom have not *left* – but have been *expelled* from this organisation for reasons not always connected with Fascism.

We, undersigned, have been active members and officers (of the B.U.F.), of not less than 18 months' service.

R.A.Plathen (National Propaganda Officer)
P.M.Moir (Propaganda Officer)
W.R.Risdon (Area Administrative Officer)
A.F.T.Scotton (Deputy Administrative Officer)
L.Kershaw (Deputy Administrative Officer)
J.C.Elliott (Deputy Administrative Officer)
A.E.Mills (Company Officer)
A.E.Sproston (Branch Officer)
W.Lyall (Branch Officer)
N. Francis-Hawkins (O.C. London)"

Fascist Week, No. 23, Apr. 13-19, 1934, page 8

52 It is hard to be sure how much overlap there was in these positions:

"**MEN IN FASCISM** / Richard Plathen

RICHARD PLATHEN Age 33. Was an active member of the New Party, and at one time was Assistant Director of Organisation to the NUPA. Joined the British Union of Fascists in its early stages and quickly earned promotion. Is a fluent and convincing speaker, and in the course of his work as a National Political Officer has held meetings in practically all the important centres of Britain. Was the leader of the Blackshirts arrested in connection with tithe war activities at Wortham, Suffolk."

Fascist Week, No. 22, Apr. 6-12, 1934, page 5

53 ***The Blackshirt, No. 50, April 6th-April 12th, 1934, page 2-3***

54 ***Ibid.***

55 ***The Rise of Fascism, op. cit.***

56 http://www.historylearningsite.co.uk/leni_riefenstahl.htm

"In 1933, Riefenstahl made a short film about the Nazi Party's rally of that year. She was asked to make a much grander film of the 1934 event. This led to probably her most famous film - "Triumph of the Will". The film won awards in both Nazi Germany and Fascist Italy but also, ironically, in 1937, it won the *Grand Prix* in Paris. The film used camera angles rarely seen before and frequently used shadowy images as opposed to images that were visually clear. The cameramen also did some of their work on roller skates."

http://www.leni-riefenstahl.de/

57 Blackshirts were expected to hail their Leader when he entered, as well as being exhorted to be on their best behaviour:

"... when the eyes of all England, and even of the whole world are upon the Albert Hall, it behoves every Fascist present to provide a fine example to those strangers who are also present. They must put Fascist discipline and Fascist orderliness into practice.

...

One bad example alone may ruin the meeting in the eyes of the world for it will surely be exaggerated by the hostile press.

Everybody, therefore, must do his utmost and keep constantly in mind that sacred trust which the training of the Blackshirt entails.

...

On the stroke of eight, to a thunderous roar of 'MOSLEY', the Leader will enter. Those who have heard him before will know that he reaches his greatest heights on the most important occasions and that this will be no exception."

The Blackshirt, No. 52, April 20th-April 26th, 1934, page 2-3

58 ***The Fascists in Britain, op. cit.***

59 ***Fascist Week, No. 25, April 28th-May 3rd, 1934, page 1***

60 ***The Blackshirt, No. 55, May 11th-May 17th, 1934, page 4***

61 ***The Blackshirt, No. 57, May 25th-May 31st, 1934, page 3***

62 ***The Blackshirt, No. 56, May 18th-May 24th, 1934, page 4***

63 ***Ibid.***

64 ***Oswald Mosley, op. cit.***

65 ***Ibid.***

66 ***The Fascists in Britain, op. cit.***

67 ***Ibid.***
68 ***Ibid.***
69 ***Oswald Mosley, op. cit.***
70 ***Ibid.***
71 ***Ibid.***
72 ***The Blackshirt, No. 60, June 15th, 1934, page 3***
73 ***Oswald Mosley, op. cit.***
74 ***Ibid.***
75 ***Ibid.***
76 ***The Blackshirt, No. 64, July 13th, 1934, page 1***
77 ***Ibid.***
78 ***The Blackshirt, No. 63, July 6th, 1934, page 11***
79 There was obviously a genuine friendship, despite the misunderstanding:

> "He began our overt companionship in his abrupt, impulsive way. A genuine patriot, he was concerned with the way things were going and had over the years discussed the situation with Lloyd George, Churchill, myself and others. He was a great business executive, dynamic in all his dealings, and he passionately wanted to get something done for England. He observed with ever growing interest the progress of the blackshirt movement, and finally his action was characteristic. I had not seen him for some time, and he was at Monte Carlo when he suddenly sent me a telegram affirming his support. Then the headlines came pelting like a thunder-storm: 'Hurrah for the Blackshirts' was the theme. He returned, and the pace began to quicken; a new aeroplane was built on his initiative and given the name of one of our slogans: Britain First. Nothing was too large or too small for use in Lord Rothermere's drive to support our movement. The ***Daily Mail*** organised a beauty competition for women blackshirts. He was staggered not to receive a single entry, and I was embarrassed to explain that these were serious young women dedicated to the cause of their country rather than aspirants to the Gaiety Theatre chorus."
>
> ***My Life, op. cit.***

80 ***Oswald Mosley, op. cit.:***

> "In a formal exchange of letters with Rothermere, ending their association, Mosley insisted he was leading a revolutionary, not a conservative movement … As one of Mosley's followers [Richard] Reynell Bellamy put it, 'Those who were worthy of the cause stuck it out, and found that the almost universal hostility put more iron into their souls …'"

81 ***My Life, op. cit.:***

> "For instance, when Lord Rothermere was supporting me, they took him out at the point of the economic gun. He was quite frank in explaining that he pulled out on account of his advertisers, and the firms in question were under Jewish influence. This was confirmed in recent years by Randolph Churchill: 'I have seen the ***Daily Mail*** abandon the support of Sir Oswald Mosley in the thirties under the pressure of Jewish advertisers' (***Spectator***, December 27, 1963). Lord Rothermere withdrew from our support in July 1934, and later letters were published between us on the 20th of that month."

82 ***Ibid.:***

"This was to me a heavy burden because I was never as rich as I was supposed to be, but I have always retained sufficient of my inheritance to render me entirely independent. Too many tears should not be shed for this sacrifice of £100,000 as, with relative leisure for a short time after the war and opportunity to make money, I soon got most of it back again in transactions so normal, indeed banal, that they are not worth recounting. Others in the thirties made comparable sacrifices and things were always kept going; sometimes with much difficulty and with many ups and downs."

83 ***Ibid.:***

"Some branches were relatively rich, with local businessmen forming clubs and circles for their support. Industrialists and merchants of more moderate stature than the Nuffields, Rothermeres and Houstons used also to support our headquarters. Large luncheons were organised at restaurants like the Criterion for this purpose, at which I used to speak. A club entirely independent of us was also formed, at which I met similar gatherings, sometimes with felicitous and lucrative results. My experiences at that time were diverse."

84 ***Ibid.:***

"The Rothermere experience had two effects on me; the first to suggest that despite all my preoccupations, money might be made for politics in business, and the second to make me more than ever reluctant to be dependent for political finance on the caprices of the rich."

85 ***Ibid.***

86 ***Ibid.:***

"The long struggle fluctuated, but I lost. He felt that I was asking him to risk too much, not only for himself, but for others who depended on him. He was a patriot and an outstanding personality, but without the exceptional character necessary to take a strong line towards the end of a successful life, which might have led to a political dog-fight. In my view, the matter could have been quite reasonably settled if he had stood firm."

87 ***Ibid.:***

"We started simply as two individuals, without any connection with the party; though I intended, of course, to use the proceeds entirely for the movement. From this relatively limited base I built in a few years a large concern which was only frustrated by the arrival of war. After the war others did in different ways what I had been doing, but all doors of that kind were then closed to me for a long period. It was a great enterprise and I shall always be proud of my part in an attempt without precedent. Some day far hence the full story may possibly be told; but not at present, or by me, for this would infringe my rule of never mentioning names and persons who were not known to have any dealings with me. They were Englishmen engaged in legitimate business and it would be wrong now to tell the story. In addition to speaking at least four times a week all the year round, except for one month's holiday, and also organising our movement, I was engaged for several years in the building of a big business."

5: SAVING KING COTTON

Whatever the reasons for Wilfred Risdon's transplantation from National Headquarters in London to the Northern Command Headquarters in the autumn of 1934 might have been, with hindsight it seems fairly clear that, had he not made the move when he did, not only might his time with Mosley have been shorter than it actually was, if, in tandem with the feelings of doubt growing within him, he had allowed himself to become embroiled in the events unfolding around him [which would have been virtually unavoidable at NHQ]; but also his career might have been arguably less successful than it turned out to be; however, these considerations are purely academic, and therefore ultimately futile. The Propaganda Department he had headed since February 1933 had grown significantly, despite the confusing overlap with other departments [with the inevitable budgetary repercussions which Mosley was either not aware of, or unwilling to resolve **1**], but the internecine jockeying must have begun to weigh heavily on Wilfred's shoulders, so, although the move to Manchester did not absolve him completely of responsibility for the propaganda function of the organisation, quite the reverse in fact, the clear air between the two physical locations must have been a tonic for him, at the very least.

One of the lesser-known aspects of British Union propaganda, in addition to that disseminated by Wilfred's department, was the use of film to spread the message; film as a medium had been around for more than a generation, but the relative complexity of the processing and generally high cost meant that, even by the 1930s, only a small number of 'ordinary' people could envisage any active participation of their own, although there was a rapacious market amongst the 'general public' for the output of the established studios. British Union was critical [**2**] of the "debased standard of the cinema world" [and, by extension, the British film industry], both on the production and the distribution sides, [later because of the perceived Jewish domination, although as yet this was not explicitly stated] so it was recognised that Fascists should take the initiative and produce their own propaganda films: "Old world film companies will not help us: so we start our own films. We prophesy that very soon our own film section will be as powerful in propaganda effect as is now the Fascist Press." [**3**] This wasn't the first foray into the medium of celluloid to spread the message of Mosley's economic thinking; three years previously, the New Party had made a film entitled [in the mood of national urgency then prevalent] ***Crisis***, more as a response to the press boycott which was pretty obviously being enforced, than as a creative endeavour for its own sake, but it had been banned by the film censor, for the unpardonable sin of daring to depict MPs snoring in their seats in the Mother of Parliaments [and, thereby, bringing British politics and democracy into disrepute: unpardonable!], and which was categorised by Robert Skidelsky as "one of the very rare examples in England this [sic] century of political (as opposed to moral) censorship." [**4**]

On Tuesday, May 8th, 1934, "the first all-Fascist film [was] shown at headquarters" and was described as being "of historic beginning.": "Fascism must look for its growth from its members: it cannot look for assistance from the old world, with its old world ideas." [**5**] The claim that the film was, as well as being directed and photographed by, also acted by Fascists, was rather stretching the definition of the term acting, but it is nonetheless understandable that they would want to celebrate their competence in producing a relatively complex article with no outside assistance. At least one member of the BUF's Milan branch was involved in making the film so, unsurprisingly, it included "Some good shots of Milan Branch … These showed members of the Branch marching to the local cenotaph." [**6**] Other than that, the film was a mixture of scenes both before and during the recent Albert Hall meeting which had been orchestrated by Wilfred, the Stoke-on-Trent meeting, and scenes of activity at headquarters, with appearances by Mosley himself, as one would expect, and Dr. Forgan, among other senior officers at work in their respective departments, but not, apparently, Wilfred [a deliberate decision perhaps, not only because of professional detachment, but also with an eye to the future?], who is not mentioned in either of the BUF periodicals which carried reports on the event, which was more than just a worthy showing of a potential propaganda device; an 'in-house' orchestra played selections prior to the showing of the film, "and at the special request of the Leader, 'A Marching Song' was played after the performance. 'Up Fascists' and the National Anthem brought the evening to a close." [**7**]

Contrary to what was possibly the general perception at the time, outside the movement, and what has undoubtedly gained wide acceptance in the intervening period, the movement was ready, and apparently willing, to publicise its failings in certain areas, and that of fascist film making was no exception: on the night, the apparatus which was intended to synchronise the sound with film failed to operate [but the record of the Leader's speech was played on the radiogram, by way of compensation] and the shortcomings in production standards were acknowledged, but an expectation of an improvement in these standards appears to have been taken for granted, given that this necessity was not included in the rationale behind the appeal for funds, to allow the work to continue, which was made by Wilfred on the night [**8**]. This was not the first film showing which was incorporated into BUF branch activities; Bromley branch pre-empted National Headquarters by a couple of months, but the film shown on that first occasion, ***Metropolis***, was a suitably appropriate professional example, and there was no hint of any moral uplift to be gained from the showing, in the subsequent report in ***The Blackshirt*** [**9**]. This was a private initiative, of course, given the autonomy of branches which was expected, economically speaking, under the guiding banner of BUF principles. Admission was free, but a collection was made to defray the cost of films and to assist the club funds. There is no obvious connection between the BUF's film-making activities, such as they were, and Milan branch, the opening of whose larger premises, at *Piazza Missori*, was reported upon in the same issue of ***The Blackshirt*** as was Bromley's innovation, other than Milan being the base for at least one of the cameramen for the first 'all-Fascist' film; the Organiser, John Celli, was also aware of the advantages of a familiarity with media techniques, in that "Frequent radio broadcasts are [sic] given to Britons in Italy" by him [**10**].

Another example of a member, who was not named, taking an interest in film making for the benefit of the Movement at this time was to be found in Leeds, where "This northern branch has now moved into its permanent quarters at 27, Cavendish Road. … One Member, interested in cinematography is making a film of the branch progress." [**11**] Overall though, it would appear that cinematography within the Movement was relegated to a subordinate position, compared to the other manifestations of propaganda, and it is unlikely that Wilfred will have had the time, or the budget, to take an active involvement in the medium after the end of 1934. The emphasis of his work was still very much the organisation of public meetings [**12**], and the confusion caused by the overlap between departments which had a responsibility for propaganda output appears never to have been resolved; given that the importance of, and the necessity for propaganda was an integral part of a movement for political change which was the BUF, it is perhaps telling that the Propaganda Department only rated fifth in significance, behind the Organisation, Foreign Relations, Publications ["Busiest Department at N.H.Q." **13**] and Research ["Facts and figures"] Departments in the "Work of N.H.Q. Departments" series which ***The Blackshirt*** helpfully ran in the spring of 1934.'

Arguably the heaviest burden of responsibility within the movement fell upon the shoulders of Doctor Robert Forgan, the undisputed deputy to Mosley himself: "It is difficult to say where the work begins and ends. With the exception of Defence Force Control and Publications, *almost every other Department* comes under the direct control of Dr. Forgan." [my emphasis; **14**] so it is somewhat ambiguous as to whether that included Propaganda or not; he was allegedly not in the best of health and his resignation, first reported in ***The Blackshirt*** of the 12th of October, was ostensibly for this reason, and the report in the following week's edition did not deviate from that line, although it was somewhat more effusive in its praise, in a very short article. The first article mentions that his duties at National Headquarters had been rearranged in the spring, by which hopefully palliative measure "the strain [would be] relieved to some extent", but "[t]hat expectation has, unfortunately, not been realised." [**15**] What both of these articles fail to mention is that, in June of that year, Forgan had been sent to inspect the Scottish branches "in order to get him away from headquarters" [essentially because Mosley was concerned that he was not stringent enough with fiscal controls on the Movement, which was his primary function], which elevated the ex-Conservative F. M. Box as "the virtual deputy for Sir Oswald Mosley". Also, among other charges against Dr. Forgan, according to a Special Branch report dated 10 October, 1934, it was asserted that "he had shown bad judgement in his choice of subordinate officers" [**16**]; it is very likely that this was a thinly veiled assault on the usefulness, and perhaps even trustworthiness of working class Socialists like Alexander Miles, whose recruitment by Wilfred was validated by Dr. Forgan, so it would be hardly surprising that with this development, Wilfred saw that his position within the movement had suffered a significant setback.

During this first phase of Wilfred's career as an ostensibly loyal but, as it later transpired, a somewhat tentative Fascist, Doctor Robert Forgan had undoubtedly been one of his mentors and ideological colleagues, whose devotion to his duty, combined with an easy-going yet incisively astute personality, had been a shining example which Wilfred had willingly followed. The doctor was almost universally well liked and, in addition to his medical knowledge, the basis for a career in itself, his knowledge and understanding of politics was indisputably wide, hence Mosley's lack of reservation in making Forgan his deputy; he had also collaborated with Wilfred in New Party days on a 'street-block' system for electoral canvass, upon which Wilfred was to capitalise to great effect in years to come. However much anyone could be said to be, Forgan was not an instinctive Fascist, and he had become increasingly disenchanted with the direction in which the organisation was moving, with its emphasis on military discipline and the inexorable slide towards doctrinal anti-semitism, urged on by the likes of Joyce, Beckett and Chesterton. His efforts at conciliation towards an equitable co-existence with the Jews in Britain had come to naught, and by mid-1934 he was seen by the reactionary side of the movement as an unfortunate [and finally, expendable] hangover from earlier, dangerously social-democratic days.

After the initial flush of enthusiasm and tolerable co-operation enjoyed by the movement in 1933, 1934 was the first year of the internecine jockeying which was to characterise the remaining years of the BUF's existence, in part as a result of "the influx of all these ex-officers and titled people" [**17**] which Lord Rothermere's patronage stimulated, who readily and ideologically identified with the original rump of British fascists who transferred their allegiances at the inception of the BUF, and together they worked [although not specifically in deliberate unison] to increase the power of the administration over the revolutionary tendencies of the *politicos*. The first example of the grass roots, rank and file side of the membership being knocked back was the suppression of the FUBW [see Chapter 4], although it was characterised officially as a reorganisation, whereby this separate body, albeit with a definite fascist flavour, was seen as acquiring too distinct an identity, which could, admittedly, have caused some confusion and proved to be a distraction for the wavering workers, so it was absorbed into the Industrial Section of the Propaganda Department, which was not automatically an outcome to gratify Wilfred a great deal. Perhaps he rationalised it by directing his gaze to the hopefully not-too-distant future, when all workers would be unionised and obviously better provided for all round, under the all-encompassing protection of the Corporate State in the Government of British Union.

The summer of 1934 was not noticeably different for Wilfred in terms of the number of disparate locations he visited in the course of his work of organising meetings for the Leader, but two factors operating at this time were significant: William Joyce's influence within what was still nominally Wilfred's department and domain was growing, and Wilfred seemingly encountered a certain amount of unconcealed disquiet amongst the rank and file in the north of the country. As detailed in earlier chapters, Joyce was never going to be happy just being an anonymous functionary: he was committed, passionate, and not unduly sentimental about what is now termed 'collateral damage' caused in the furtherance of his career. He was obviously and undeniably [even to Wilfred, notwithstanding any personal animosity] a highly valued member of the movement, whose most visible asset was his ability to galvanise an audience, and inspire other members to aspire to his level of competence as a speaker, but it must nevertheless have caused Wilfred some disquiet when Joyce's leading articles on public speaking, over which Wilfred still had notional control, were published in ***The Blackshirt*** in the summer. Wilfred was very likely enough of a pragmatist to accept that his duties required him to spread his energies in many different directions at once, so some sharing of the workload could have been welcome, but it is a matter for conjecture whether he would have seen it as delegation by default or the beginning of a gradual process of reduction in status and value, perhaps even amounting to sidelining.

If his testimony to the 18B Appeal Committee [**Appendix D**] is to be believed, the doubts about Wilfred's place within the movement, and his long term prospects, had started to become apparent after the Olympia rally in June; unfortunately, he doesn't give any details of his actions, but when asked by the chairman of the Appeals Board, Mr. Norman Birkett, KC, for his reaction to the apparent display of vanity by Mosley on the platform "in a spotlight", Wilfred responds by saying "Yes, I think it was possibly for that reason I ceased just after that meeting to be active in propaganda, because the people who arranged the spotlight were people who did so contrary to my advice, and because I was opposed to that sort of thing I was given a different job." This is actually an answer with many layers of complexity, so although it is very possible that Wilfred would have been expecting just such a question to be asked, it seems unlikely that he would have learnt it like a script, which makes it very clever, in my view. Taking the first part of his answer for example, it is quite possible that he was being free with his definition of the word "active"; he was obviously still involved with the dissemination of propaganda for and on behalf of the movement after Olympia, but perhaps his statement of the effect before the cause was significant? Notwithstanding their previous personal regard, it is unlikely that he would have capriciously provoked Mosley, however resentful Wilfred might have felt [although that appears to be out of character], especially given the prevailing employment conditions, but it is a measure of Wilfred's strength of character that he was prepared to express his disapproval, when "The only people he [Mosley] valued were those who gave him absolute and uncritical admiration ..." [**18**]. Rather a sweeping statement, in truth coming from the son of a former member who felt he had good cause to be aggrieved with the Leader, and opinions vary on this point of course, but Mosley's leadership style was becoming undeniably more autocratic, something he no doubt saw as positive.

Alexander Miles, later to be another disgruntled ex-member [who subsequently brazenly asked Mosley if he could be re-admitted to the Movement!] gives an insight into this period of turmoil, which appears to have lasted some little while, although in truth, the process could have commenced before Olympia; apparently, Wilfred's Propaganda Officers were continually being recalled and "carpeted by [Forgan's successor] Mr. Box for 'Indiscipline' - the favourite charge. Risdon was kept busy defending his departmental Officers from charges of this nature, and consequently hampered in the efficient running of the Propaganda machine." [**19**] According to Miles, thanks to arguments cooked up by the "officer caste", all meetings should come under the control of Administrative Officers [of whom Wilfred was himself one] "to secure efficiency ... and the Department of Propaganda should be limited to the securing, equipping and training of speakers, who should then be placed at the disposal of the Administrative side." [**20**] That might or might not have been true, and very probably "calculated to have the effect of stripping Risdon of power", given his socialist background, but Joyce was also complicit in this, in an entirely self-aggrandising way, building on his success in the area of public speaking: "Their success in this direction ultimately led to the position in which William Joyce later found himself, as Propaganda Chief with power to make speakers, but having made them, no power to control them, whereby he reverted to the position in which he was before he became a Blackshirt, namely, a mere 'Usher' or perhaps we should say 'Tutor'." [**21**] Not an atmosphere conducive to mutual co-operation and fraternal progress, one might think.

It is difficult to be specific about the dissatisfaction with the state of affairs which Wilfred encountered in the north of the country, particularly in

Lancashire, given the Movement's understandable reticence to let any information about cracks in the façade of solidarity escape to the outside world; notwithstanding the propensity of MI5 & Special Branch to indulge in a certain amount of embroidery or over-zealousness, or both, in their monitoring of the movement [of which Mosley was well aware] in their crusade to keep the establishment powers informed about the potential revolutionaries who were slightly less distasteful than the Communists, they are often the only source of information which doesn't require the interested party to have to 'read between the lines' of the official BUF output: a Special Branch report of the 17th of January 1935 [**22**] claimed, somewhat nebulously, that Wilfred was "'organising some subversive plot' and 'nursing a grievance because some of the people who joined the movement after he did have been given prominent positions', and he was accused of plotting with other disenchanted Blackshirts to present 'an ultimatum to Sir Oswald Mosley, demanding ... the dismissal of certain officials at King's Road.' For whatever reason, nothing came of this and, with Forgan's departure, the national leadership had fundamentally shifted from left to right." [**23**]

Although there might be an element of truth here, perhaps as a result of an inadvertently incautious comment which came to the notice of an informant, it seems much more likely that, unless Mosley had already made himself unapproachable [which I don't think is the case] Wilfred would have preferred to confront his Leader privately, if at all possible, with his concerns, given their history of working together over a period of ten years: a not inconsiderable length of time; also, looking at the apparently peremptory manner in which two of Mosley's erstwhile valued contributors, Beckett and Joyce, were despatched a couple of years later, on which their propensity for a somewhat juvenile habit of ridiculing Mosley and his officers in private might have had no small bearing, it is unlikely that Mosley would have tolerated such open rebellion from one of his stalwarts. Although the modern concept of 'job satisfaction', over & above the gratification to be gained from the knowledge of a job well done, was not relevant here [and, at the same time, the militaristic aspect of the movement, with its concentration on 'duty', must not be overlooked], Wilfred will nevertheless, even though it was not specifically part of his brief, have wanted [with no conscious irony associated with the element of altruism] to do what he could to help his comrades who were genuinely committed to the movement and its principles; also, a malicious informant with his own agenda must be another possibility for this speculation.

As 1934 ended, and 1935 began, Wilfred was probably very glad to be able to escape to the relative calm of Manchester, allowing him to concentrate on developing the membership in the cotton-producing areas of the north west of England, which were under such pressure from abroad for the available markets. This was not just a cynical grab for numbers to boost the image of the movement in the national consciousness either: although

Wilfred was well aware of the significance of such an achievement, he was doing what he felt that his previous work in left-leaning socialist politics had qualified him for; to achieve the best possible standard of living for his fellow working man and his dependants, which was being rapidly eroded as a result of the reduction in manufacturing capacity, and the consequent loss of employment. The main target of the movement's ire at that time was the President of the Board of Trade, Walter Runciman, who was accused of dereliction of duty and not working hard enough to encourage constructive export trade, by halting the export of jobs and trade to countries like India [albeit part of the British Empire] and Japan.

Although the travails being faced in Manchester and the north west of England as a whole were only one aspect of a general dismantling of the country's manufacturing capability which had been proceeding insidiously over a period of years, the cotton trade had been suffering no less hard than coal and shipping, to name only two other high-profile examples in different regions. In January 1934, following the recent signing of a trade agreement between India & Japan, which was, apparently, "to pave the way for the talks that are to take place between Britain and India on one hand, and Britain and Japan on the other. ... the rank and file members of the Manchester Chamber of Commerce ... compelled their leaders to call a meeting for Monday next (January 22)." In advance of that meeting, ***The Fascist Week*** commented that "Well might indignant firms in Manchester declare that 'the time has now arrived for the initiation of a common policy of a more publicly active character'." [**24**] This policy was laid out by ***The Blackshirt*** in articles by one of the Movement's economic experts, Alexander Raven Thomson, under the thinly-veiled *nom de plume* Alexander Raven: "TEXTILE TRADES WILL BENEFIT FROM FASCISM / Corporations Will Control Industry / EXTENDED AND PROTECTED HOME MARKET" [**25**].

A so-called 'Blackshirt Cotton Campaign' began in Lancashire during the summer of 1934, apparently under the leadership of a Commander Tillotson, whose branch designation and/or affiliation was not explained, and the direction of "[h]is chief Propaganda Officer, Captain Wright, of Preston" [**26**], and a well-appointed new regional headquarters [later to acquire the sobriquet 'Northern Command Headquarters'] had already been opened in Manchester in April, in Higher Broughton. No direct mention is made of Wilfred in connection with this campaign in either of the movement's periodicals at this time, but from the number of high-profile meetings and public events which he attended in the north west, it looks like he was being 'eased in' to overall control [possibly contingent with the truculence he displayed following the Olympia meeting, as mentioned above], with an especial object in mind of boosting the membership in that strategic region; what is certain is that a large rally being planned for Hyde Park [London] on Sunday, September 9th, was being organised by "Blackshirt Officers" [**27**], effectively under the direction of William Joyce, so it looks at this point very much like the end of Wilfred's rôle of organising the large national meetings. This meeting, according to Colin Cross, was "[t]he last big rally before the Movement became anti-Semitic" [**28**], which is a rather ill-defined statement, because the Movement had exhibited plenty of actions with perceived anti-semitic tendencies before this, but what he meant was that from this point on, all of Mosley's speeches made reference to 'Aliens' generally or Jews specifically in connection with control of finance and banking in Great Britain [and the world].

Cross goes so far as to say "It was largely on this Jewish question that Forgan resigned from the BUF in October 1934."; again, there has to be an element of truth in that, but more likely is that this was one of many factors involved in the Doctor's decision. There was no equivocation in Mosley's speech at the Manchester Belle Vue stadium on September 30th however: "The mention of the Empire makes the alien mob yell louder than ever. It will take something more than the yelping of a Yiddish mob to destroy the British Empire." This line of rhetoric was not necessarily intended as the main thrust of his speech, which was the BUF's support for, and policy to assist the Lancashire textile industry, but it was an inevitable consequence of the vocal opposition which was raised from the outset [**29**]. It is not known if Wilfred organised this meeting, although it is very likely that he did, given its location; naturally, it would be a spurious and misleading connection to make with this, and the fact that, apart from the noisy interruptions to Mosley's speech, there was no trouble at this meeting; but a week later, at the Millbank Drill Hall Plymouth, a meeting which was confirmed with the booking of the hall only 24 hours earlier, the disruption almost escalated to the point where the three policemen who had entered the hall would have had no choice but to terminate the meeting, but Mosley himself jumped down from the platform and intervened, and serious trouble was averted when "[t]he ringleaders were ejected along with many of their hooligans who rushed uninvited outside." [**30**]

Cross takes the view that Mosley could still have held back from the overtly and publicly anti-semitic policy, but he was persuaded to pursue it, after some hesitation, because "wherever he turned for advice within the Movement the officials he most trusted were urging him to attack the Jews, who, they explained, were attacking Fascism." [**31**] We are left to make up our own minds as to who these "most trusted" officials were, and it appears likely that Wilfred will not have numbered among those so honoured, if the reports of his potentially disloyal behaviour are to be believed but, that notwithstanding, he evidently had no difficulty accommodating the Movement's publicly-stated change of tack. Around that time, although still nominally Director of Propaganda, Wilfred was now becoming thought of more for his expertise in industrial matters [although in fairness, this was not merely a recently acquired speciality], rather than for his acknowledged accomplishments in the field of propaganda, and he took up residence in Manchester to direct operations in the north west; Cross is of the opinion that Wilfred was successful enough with his recruitment campaign to present a threat to the Labour Party although, unfortunately, his success was short-lived, through no fault of his own [**32**].

In the middle of this hectic whirl of activity, as well as a change of semi-permanent location, Wilfred altered his personal status in a very unequivocal way. From the foregoing, it will be obvious that Wilfred was unattached and, in many ways, that will be no great surprise, because to him, the work was more than just a vocation; it was a way of life, demanding long hours of dedication to no doubt often tedious, but necessary, and exhausting, travel, meetings and interminable paperwork; many members were married, and the contribution of both women members and unaffiliated partners should by no means be underestimated, but the demands of high office were not conducive to successful and long-term marriages, so, notwithstanding the reticence of the Movement generally to let private matters intrude into official business [apart from the occasional publicly announced wedding and christening], it might come as some surprise that Wilfred had had some sort of relationship with the same woman for a few years, and in 1935, while he was busy [although, in truth, probably no busier than usual] with his Lancashire campaign, he decided to make the relationship official, but only from a legal point of view: for whatever reason, a desire for privacy being a prime candidate, there was no announcement in the Fascist press, which one might otherwise have expected from such a high-profile Officer in the Movement. In view of the history of his future wife, and the fact that, outside his immediate circle of friends and trusted associates, Mrs. Risdon was effectively invisible to the Movement, it seems appropriate that this relationship should be examined in detail in the next chapter.

NOTES

1 ***Fascist Week, no. 14, Feb. 9th-15th, 1934, p7:***

"One of the busiest departments at National Headquarters, Chelsea, is the Propaganda Department … [which] is responsible for the organisation of all the big Blackshirt meetings in Great Britain. Plans are being made this year to double the number of meetings held last year. Meanwhile, the Propaganda Department has outgrown its offices and larger accommodation has had to be provided in another part of the building."

2 ***Fascist Week, no. 24, April 20th-26th, 1934, p4:***

"What do our present film magnates produce for public consumption? Outside of an occasional masterpiece, a Walt Disney, or a Nature Study, little but a series of sentimental trash, sexual aphrodisiacs or criminal heroics."

3 ***Fascist Week, no. 27, May 11th-17th, 1934, p4***

4 ***Oswald Mosley, by Robert Skidelsky***

5 ***Fascist Week, no. 27, May 11th-17th, 1934, p4***

6 ***Ibid.***

7 ***The Blackshirt, no. 55, May 11th-17th, 1934, p1***

8 ***Ibid.:***

"While, of course, the standard of production was not quite up to professional level the performance was very creditable indeed and every encouragement should be given to those concerned in producing Fascist Films.

A/A/O Risdon made an appeal for funds which are vitally necessary if the work is to go on. Arrangements can be made for the film to be shown to branches."

9 ***The Blackshirt, No. 52, April 20th-April 26th, 1934, p. 4:***

"The debut of the first B.U.F. Cinema Show was an unqualified success. It took place in the Bromley Branch premises on Sunday, April 8. The film "Metropolis" was shown, and as this is a rather long film there was no time for more. Future presentations include "The White Hell of Pitz Palu", "The Wrecker" and "Faust". By arrangement with Fascist Parker, branches can give cinema shows in their own premises. Costs are small, and no alterations to premises are necessary."

10 ***Ibid.***

11 The premises were very spacious and probably quite impressive:

"The building is a large eighteen-roomed house standing in its own grounds. Ample accommodation is available for the resident staff, and in addition there are two club-rooms. There is a dry canteen and the whole building is decorated in the B.U.F. colours, black and grey. The Women's Section have their own offices and club in the building."

Branch News: *The Blackshirt, No. 51, April 13th-April 19th, 1934, p. 3*

12 ***The Blackshirt, No. 67, August 3rd-August 9th, 1934, p. 10:***

"'Bill' Risdon, Director of Propaganda, ought to know something about words. Not long ago he told me his propaganda officers were holding more than a thousand street-corner meetings a week. They each speak for an hour at the rate of 120 words a minute, and answer questions for another hour."

13 *The Blackshirt, No. 48, March 23rd-March 29th, 1934, p. 4*

14 *The Blackshirt, No. 43, February 9th-February 15th, 1934, p. 4*

15 *The Blackshirt, No. 77, October 12th, 1934, p. 7*

16 *PRO, HO144/20140/243, cited in* **Left Wing Fascism in Theory and Practice: The Case of the British Union of Fascists** *by Philip Coupland, Twentieth Century British History, Vol. 13, No. 1, 2002, pp. 38-61*

It is also interesting to speculate as to whom Forgan's confidential assertion, that he was "having doubts about his leader's sanity", which somehow found its way into MI5 and Special Branch reports in early October, after returning to London "without Mosley's knowledge" in early September, was made, most incautiously as it transpired; Mosley was certainly aware, if not at the outset, then certainly before too long, that he had at least 2 MI5 'moles' in his organisation: P. G. Taylor [*aka* James McGuirk Hughes] and W. E. D. ["Bill"] Allen [*aka* James Drennan], and although plausible, it nevertheless seems highly unlikely that Forgan would not also have known this, so if it was not one of these characters, then to whom was this highly contentious snippet of information confided?

BLACKSHIRTS TORN: INSIDE THE BRITISH UNION OF FASCISTS, 1932-1940, ***by Thomas Norman Keeley, MA Degree submission, Simon Fraser University, Canada, 1998***

It is also possible that William Joyce could have 'ratted' on Dr. Forgan: it is not clear whether Mosley knew that Joyce had been recruited by Maxwell Knight of MI5 in 1932, to report on political extremism, on both the 'left' and the 'right', but there can have been little doubt, at the end of 1934, about Joyce's commitment to the BUF, even though in private he was known to refer to Mosley as "The Bleeder". Knight evidently asked Joyce, when he was DofP, if he was willing to "go to Germany, work his way into National Socialist circles there and send back inside information." For whatever reason [probably because he was then very well set up, he would have had to leave the BUF to enable him to be a member of the NSDAP, and very likely didn't want the risk such an undertaking would involve] he declined, although that notwithstanding, his MI5 contacts would prove useful a few years later.

Haw-Haw: The Tragedy of William and Margaret Joyce, by Nigel Farndale

Blackshirts and Roses, an Autobiography, by John Charnley

The privilege of having the last word on Dr. Forgan should arguably be awarded to Mosley himself:

> "Dr. Forgan was distinguished more for his agreeable manners and pleasing personality than for platform performance; he was neither a speaker nor an administrator, but excellent in public relations."

My Life, by Oswald Mosley

As mentioned in Chapter 4, Taylor's story will be related later, as he only has a relatively peripheral association with Wilfred at this point. Allen was probably one of Mosley's earlier associates from a similar social stratum, an old Etonian, Ulsterman and ex-Unionist MP [although he is also frequently described as "an ex-Tory buccaneer", whatever that means!], who joined the New Party in 1931 and the BUF on its formation; he didn't appear to have any specific function within the Movement until he became chairman of the board of ***Action***, which recommenced publication in February 1936; before then he wrote for the Movement [Skidelsky called him "a propagandist writer of great flair"], including the *Letters of Lucifer*, for the early ***Blackshirt***, and his book ["his most notable work": Keeley], written under the *Nom de Plume* James Drennan, ***BUF, Oswald Mosley and British Fascism*** [1934].

17 ***MRC, MSS292/743/11/2, unnamed typescipt memoir [attributed to Kay Fredericks] cited in Left Wing Fascism etc., op. cit.***

Kay Fredericks was, for a while, an official photographer for the BUF.

18 ***The Rebel who lost his Cause: The Tragedy of John Beckett, MP, by Francis Beckett***

19 ***The Streets are still: Mosley in Motley, by A. Miles, MRC, MSS292/743.11/2***

20 ***Ibid.***

21 ***Ibid.***

22 ***PRO, HO144/20140/243, cited in Left Wing Fascism ..., op. cit.***

23 ***Ibid.***

24 ***Fascist Week, no. 11, January 19th-25th, 1934, p6***

25 ***The Blackshirt, No. 68, August 10th, 1934, p. 4***

26 ***The Blackshirt, No. 70, August 24th, 1934, p. 7***

27 ***The Blackshirt, No. 69, August 17th, 1934, p. 1***

28 ***The Fascists in Britain, by Colin Cross***

29 ***The Blackshirt, No. 76, October 5th, 1934, p. 2***

30 ***The Blackshirt, No. 77, October 12th, 1934, p. 2***

31 ***The Fascists in Britain, op. cit.***

The ***Fascist Week*** attempted to clarify the attitude towards Jews in May 1934:

> "In response to many inquiries, the Fascist Week restates the attitude of the British Union of Fascists towards Jews.
>
> There will be no racial or religious persecution under Fascism in Britain, but Jews will be required to put the interests of Britain before the interests of Jewry.
>
> This principle applies equally to every section of the population and is embodied in the Fascist principle of Britain first.
>
> Our reasons for excluding Jews from membership of the British Union of Fascists are:–
>
> 1. Jews and the Jewish Press in this country have bitterly opposed Fascism.
>
> 2. The great majority of Jews have shown themselves to be international in outlook and have placed the interests of their own race before the interests of the country in which they reside.
>
> The British Union of Fascists seeks to bring about a national renaissance

and cannot afford to have in its ranks members whose outlook is not 'Britain First'."

Attitude to the Jews: ***Fascist Week, no. 26, May 4th-10th, 1934, p4***

32 Wilfred's recruiting techniques were obviously very successful:

"During 1935 there was an energetic campaign in Lancashire to enlist cotton workers for Fascism on the promise that a Mosley Government would close competing cotton mills in India, exclude Japanese cotton goods from Empire markets and deal with the 'Jewish' capitalists of the City who produced cheap cotton with sweated labour abroad instead of investing their money in Lancashire mills. The BUF opened about a score of propaganda centres in the cotton towns which, under Risdon's direction, enrolled new members by the thousand and were so successful as seriously to worry the Labour Party. The campaign had no lasting effect; when the propaganda eased off in 1936, probably through lack of funds, Fascist support melted away entirely …."

The Fascists in Britain, op. cit.

6: MARRIAGE

Wilfred Risdon married Nellie [not her given name, as detailed below] Geen, formerly James, at Leeds North Register Office on Wednesday, March 20th 1935: the location is something of a surprise, but quite easily explained; however, the timing is more difficult to fathom. Wilfred's address was given on the marriage certificate as 17, Northumberland Street, Broughton [Manchester, although it is not specified], the address of Northern Command Headquarters, as he was deep into his Cotton Campaign for the British Union of Fascists at this time; Nellie's address was in Henconner Avenue, Leeds, so it is being assumed that she was working in that city [**1**], in her capacity as Hospital Nurse, as stated in the "Rank or Profession" column of the certificate. Nellie was trained as a Midwife, but the description given on their marriage certificate doesn't automatically mean that she was not working in her specific field of expertise; perhaps just that maternity nurses were not always seen as specialists [and she had only fairly recently qualified]: no doubt they could very easily cover for general nurses as necessary, but not vice versa. The address is a semi-detached house, probably with three bedrooms, in a very pleasant looking, quite densely wooded part of Leeds, referred to as Potternewton, which appears to be situated between Chapel Allerton [north], Chapeltown [east], Scott Hall [south] and Miles Hill [west]; overall, towards the northern border of greater Leeds. To the south of the house, a subsequently-constructed apartment block now rather spoils the view, but this would not have been a concern for Nellie and her family [assuming her children were with her].

The houses in this section of Henconner Avenue were apparently built in the second half of 1933; according to a conveyance dated February the 6th, 1934, number 17 was bought, for the princely sum of "Five hundred and Twenty five pounds" by a Mabel Nora Clark, described as a Certified Midwife, and who just happens to have been one of the witnesses at Wilfred and Nellie's wedding the following year, so the most likely explanation seems to be that either: a) Wilfred knew the builder of the house [**2**], through his business connections, and Nellie was able to persuade her colleague Mabel Clark to buy the house [Nellie presumably living in 'digs' or Nurses' hospital quarters hitherto] and take on Nellie as a tenant; or b) Mabel Clark was financially comfortable enough to be able to at least find the deposit for the house at the appropriate juncture [although no mortgage is mentioned on the conveyance], and Nellie was lucky enough to be asked to become a tenant, in the process also helping financially, perhaps. A significant question here has to be, as alluded to above, whether Nellie had her two children with her at this point: if she did, a three-bedroomed house would have been the absolute minimum practicable, given that they were one of each gender, Sheila being eleven and Brian nine years old at the time, but unless it was seen as a safe option to allow both children in the same bedroom, at a time when children arguably developed more slowly than they do now, it would have necessitated Nellie sharing her bedroom with her daughter; undoubtedly there would have been many families at that time, in the poorer areas of Leeds certainly, who would not have had such a luxury as separate bedrooms, which is now very much taken for granted. Before expanding on Nellie's family though, it is perhaps as well to return to the beginning of her story, for it is somewhat convoluted...........

According to the GRO, Nellie was born Margaret Ellen James on March the 10th 1895, thereby giving the lie [literally!] to her age of 37 years, as stated on the marriage certificate, exactly as did Wilfred; this is not the first time that this age discrepancy has been remarked upon [see **Appendix D**], but perhaps the first recorded instance [for Nellie anyway]? Notwithstanding the illegality, from an official point of view, this sort of inaccuracy was probably very common, although in this case, seemingly inconsequential. Also very common is the adoption of a pseudonym, usually closely related to one's given name[s], possibly the result of the bestowing of a nickname by friends or relatives. Nellie was born in Cardiff, then in the county of Glamorganshire; little is known of her very early life but, according to her son Brian [**3**], her father, David James, was a railwayman. Brian states that his mother married "at a very young age to Alfred Geen, a Miller by trade." [**4**] Perhaps the first part of that statement is what his mother told him; she married the first time in 1925, when she would have been at least 28 years of age, which is stretching the credibility of the definition "very young" more than somewhat: although perhaps, this was a convenient cover-story by Nellie [to her children] to account for at least one of her children being born 'out of wedlock'? Brian Risdon also imparts the information that "[a]fter Sheila and I were born Mother decided to get a divorce (unheard of in those days)." [**5**] That is not entirely true; for a woman to divorce her husband in those days might have been unusual, and very possibly made difficult as a result of the mores of contemporary society, but certainly not unheard of; and this is where the story starts to become rather interesting.

Unfortunately, documentary evidence of divorce is not so easy to come by as is evidence of the other three aspects of 'legal' registration: births, deaths & marriages. It was not possible to find any evidence of a divorce between Margaret Ellen [aka Nellie] Geen [petitioner] and Alfred Geen [respondent], which does not automatically mean that the process did not take place; however, there was a paper trail for a divorce proceedings of Helena Lillian *orše* [otherwise] Lily Lena Geen versus Alfred Geen. At first sight, and not knowing the foregoing, this might seem like the right case, perhaps with Nellie adopting a different pseudonym, and the date of filing of the Petition, 18th of July 1923, could be plausible; but on further reading, it becomes clear that this is definitely a different case: same husband, but another wife! Alfred Geen was indeed a flour miller by trade; or more correctly, "Labourer at Flour Mills", according to his first marriage certificate; on the 16th of April, 1906, the 22-year old Alfred Geen, Bachelor, married Helena Lilian Preece, Spinster, also 22, at the Bible Christian Church, Cowbridge Road, Cardiff; Alfred was living at Ystynia Avenue, Pontcanna Street, Cardiff, and his spouse was living at 150, Pembroke Road, Cardiff; Alfred's father John was a blacksmith, and Helena's father Luke, now deceased, had been a farm labourer. The marriage was witnessed by Mary Geen [mother?] and George Preece [brother?]. So far, so good. After the wedding, the happy couple lived in the same street as Helena's mother for a while, before moving on, as was very common in those days; in the course of the next few years Alfred William [07/01/07], Albert John [29/03/10] and Trevor [09/10/12] were born. Lily appears not to have had a trade or occupation, other than mother [and probably housekeeper for her widowed mother, before her marriage], and by July of 1923, she had to register the petition in the High Court of Justice, Probate Divorce and Admiralty Division (Divorce) as a "Poor Person" [although she'd had to start the proceedings eight months earlier, to be sure that her impoverished status would be legally recognised]. At the time of entering the petition, Lily was living at number 31, Albert Street, Canton, Cardiff; however, for unexplained reasons, she was stated to be domiciled in England, at an undisclosed address. Her erstwhile husband was living at number 67, Hartledon Road, Harborne, Birmingham, and appropriately enough, was also domiciled in England. The first stated ground for the petition is that "the said ALFRED GEEN has left your Petitioner and kept away from her without cause for two years and upwards." [**6**] The cause is made abundantly clear in the next item: "That the said ALFRED GEEN has frequently committed adultery with NELLIE JAMES." [**7**] Over a period of just under two years, between November 1921 [by which time he was already keeping away from Lily] and July 1923, "the said" Alfred "lived in adultery with the said" Nellie at two different addresses in Birmingham, although curiously, the second address was a sort of interlude of around 3 months away from the first address, after which they went back to the first address. Perhaps the first address needed refurbishment during their tenure?

Unsurprisingly, Lily was asking "[t]hat her marriage with the said ALFRED GEEN may be dissolved; That she may have the custody of the children of the marriage; [and] That she may have such further and other relief as may be just." [**8**] At first, things seemed to go Lily's way: a Decree Nisi was granted on the 21st of November, 1923; however, on the 21st of May, 1924, the King's Proctor made his presence and recent activity in the process known, presumably at the Royal Courts of Justice, Strand, in the County of Middlesex [the hearing for the granting of the Decree Nisi had been allowed at Cardiff or Swansea, presumably so that the Petitioner could appear in person]. Somehow, Alfred's counsel must have been made aware that, allegedly, Lily was not as innocent a party as she was claiming to be, and invoked the office of the King's Proctor, who was empowered to make enquiries in connection with possible inconsistencies or untruths in a Petitioner's case [**9**]. There is no record, in the file of the case, of what transpired at the King's Proctor's first appearance; perhaps it was to be briefed on the case, or given official sanction by the Judge to make his investigations, but six days later, he filed a "Plea of the King's Proctor" with the court which effectively scuppered Lily's case completely. It stated that Lily had, herself, committed adultery around May 1923 [in other words, after committing herself to beginning the divorce process] with an unnamed [and, at the time, unknown] third party, as a consequence of which, a stillborn baby was born in December, 1923, in Cardiff [**10**]. This begs the question of whether Lily appeared in person at the proceedings for the granting of the Decree Nisi the previous month; her 'delicate condition' would have been very noticeable, and must have raised eyebrows?

The third party could have been one Richard Fred Golsworthy: although this is not specified, his affidavit was sworn on the 30th of June, 1924, and this, along with the Statement and Notice of Motion with the same date, filed on behalf of the King's Proctor, was read at the Court proceedings at the High Court of Justice [Strand] on the 7th of July, 1924, with the result that "the Decree Nisi in this Cause … be rescinded, the Petition dismissed, and the Petitioner condemned in the Costs of the King's Proctor." [**11**] Lily can hardly have been unaware of the circumstances which thus came to light; nevertheless, it must have come as a tremendous shock to her that, whatever might have been her original reasons for wanting to be free of her husband, her later perfidy had been her undoing. What became of her, and the children, subsequent to these proceedings is unknown, but the financial repercussions must have been a huge burden; it would appear that Alfred was unencumbered in his concurrent *affaire*; but it also raises doubts over his marital status with regard to Nellie and, indeed, what their marital status was ***as*** a couple.

The circumstances of Alfred and Nellie's meeting are unknown; they were both from Cardiff, although Alfred was 14 years older than Nellie: a substantial age difference, although this generally matters more to society at large than it does to the partners concerned. This means that Nellie would have been 10 years old when Alfred married Lily; without wishing to impute any pædophile inference upon that, it is perhaps possible that Alfred knew Nellie as a child and could have engineered the circumstances whereby they formed a relationship, however consensual? It is odd that they 'consummated' their partnership in Birmingham; there is a lot to be said for keeping an extra-marital affair well away from one's home area, but there must have been good reason for choosing Birmingham as a base instead of, say, Bristol or Gloucester, which were easily accessible from Cardiff, but far enough away to avoid casual gossip. Alfred's work is one distinct possibility; also, if Nellie wanted to work and train in any capacity as a Nurse, Birmingham should certainly have presented very good potential. In 1921, she was 25 years of age, so easily old enough to take on the responsibilities of nursing; that being the case, why did it take her until 12 years later to qualify as a Midwife? Her own children could provide an answer to this question. Sheila's birth was registered in King's Norton, then in the county of Worcestershire, in 1923, right in the middle of Alfred's divorce proceedings, so they clearly were not married at this point; the aforementioned Brian's birth was registered in West Bromwich, then in the county of Staffordshire, in 1925.

As mentioned above, it has not been possible to date to find any evidence of a divorce of Alfred Geen from his wife Lily, following the failure of her petition on the grounds of Alfred's adultery, but this doesn't mean that there wasn't one; that notwithstanding, Alfred and Nellie were married at Birmingham South, then in the county of Warwickshire, in 1925, which left less than 18 months for Alfred to terminate his legal connection with Lily: it is not improbable that Lily's mendacity would have induced a judge, if indeed the process went as far as a court room, to look favourably upon Alfred's suit, despite his own proven adultery. A rather convoluted case, but no doubt not particularly unusual. Brian Risdon does not say how long it was, after he and his sister were born, before his mother divorced their presumed father, to take up her nursing studies. This is unfortunate, but not necessarily a result of disingenuousness on Brian's part; unless he took it upon himself, at some point, to check and corroborate the details, he only had his mother's version of events to go on. He says that he and his sister "were placed in foster homes while Mother studied Nursing in Birmingham." [**12**]; this rather gives the impression that Birmingham was not their home town, but it could also just be imprecise phraseology; it might be possible to obtain fostering records, but archives are patchy. He continues: "She [his mother] was very successful and became a State Certified Midwife. Of course all the work and study and measly pay left Mother little time to visit Sheila and I [sic]." [**13**] The first part is true: Nellie Geen was enrolled as a midwife under the authority of the Central Midwives Board, following an examination, but not until May 27, 1933. [**14**] Assuming that Nellie did not commence her training before Brian was born, and even if he is correct that Nellie divorced Alfred soon after he was born, it means that the two children could have been in foster care for up to eight years, which is a long time [notwithstanding the somewhat questionable rationale for the children being fostered just so that Nellie could further her career].

The other curious aspect of Nellie's qualification is her address in May 1933, according to the CMB registration: why would she choose to say she was living back in Cardiff [4, Burnaby Street, Splott]? Could this have been connected with the fostering? Her recent activity certainly seems to have been either in Birmingham, or centred around it, and it looks like the most likely location for the event which brings her into this story: her meeting with Wilfred. She might not have been actively seeking a new personal relationship, but if Brian is correct in his assertion [no doubt the result of hearing his mother's version of history related whenever appropriate] that Nellie divorced Alfred at the earliest possible opportunity, it seems fairly obvious that their relationship was little more than a passionate fling, not destined to last, although it lasted long enough to produce two children, the legitimisation of whom seems to be the only sensible reason for the marriage. There is also the not insignificant matter of the grounds for the divorce, but without documentary evidence, that has to remain open to speculation.

It is very likely that Wilfred's arrival in Birmingham coincided approximately with Brian's arrival into the world, but there is no way of knowing if Wilfred could have thereby either suggested or facilitated Nellie's decision to divorce her then husband at a later date. No information has been found, to date, to corroborate Brian's assertion that his mother became active in socialist politics in Birmingham, but neither is there any specific reason to discount it; participatory events were a perfectly respectable aspect of political involvement, and very good for galvanising the rank & file to spread the good word enthusiastically; the presence of a well-known and liked public figure, such as George Bernard Shaw [as mentioned by name by Brian **15**] didn't go amiss either. Summer schools would undoubtedly have been a favourite opportunity for Socialists to get together and compare notes in a relaxed and convivial setting, and Wilfred will very probably have been heavily involved with these from the beginning of his tenure in Birmingham, given his status in the Labour Party, and his responsibilities as an organiser. Nellie must have been at the very least passably intelligent and articulate, to enable her to satisfy the requirements of her studies, and they had a common experience in south Wales to share, despite the disparity of nationality. Socialist summer schools, under the auspices of the Labour Party and ILP, were a well established, regular event; they were a very important, but also popular, aspect of the socialist ideal of adult education; according to the Maxton Papers, "[James] Maxton was the inspiration behind the establishment of the ILP summer schools, which were held at Letchworth in England during the 1920s, '30s and '40s." [**16**] The Summer School was originally an American idea, which was subsequently pioneered in Scotland and thereafter emulated in the rest of Britain, not least by the Fabians. [**17**] As previously elucidated, Letchworth was not the only venue for socialist summer schools; another venue was Easton Lodge, in Essex [see Chapter 2, note 29, for background information], and closer to home for Nellie, hence the strong likelihood that this could have been the place where she met Wilfred, was Wood Norton [**18**], which is mentioned in the full-page promotion ["Have you tried a Summer School Holiday?"], including photographs, in the ***Birmingham Souvenir*** [**Appendix C**] which Wilfred produced for the 1930 Independent Labour Party Easter Conference. Although it might have been possible for Nellie to stay at a residential summer school outside her home area, assuming that it was not practicably possible for her to take the children, who were still of [normal] school age in the early '30s, it would have been much more useful to attend a school which was within only a couple of hours' travelling time from home.

Unfortunately, nothing is known of the development of Wilfred and Nellie's relationship, subsequent to their initial meeting, because no official sources make any references to it; as a result of the somewhat itinerant nature of Wilfred's work, it must have been very difficult to engage in what might be coyly described as a 'courtship', but perhaps this suited both parties well enough, given Nellie's marital status. Discounting the irrational attraction known as 'chemistry', which might well have been a factor in their compatibility, in addition to a shared political ideology, they also had south Wales in common; although Wilfred's area of activity at Tredegar was some little distance from Cardiff, it was nevertheless close enough to count. The Welsh language is unlikely to have been a shared element, neither is mining, but an inherent love of a native land, or an adopted land in Wilfred's case, and an appreciation of the culture in general, will no doubt have been very important as talking points for them. Taking on a ready-made family might have required some adjustment for Wilfred, but there is nothing to suggest that he didn't love his step-children, which, regrettably, is not always the case; Nellie's younger child, Brian, had nothing but praise for him [**19**], and both children took his name, presumably after the wedding.

Having gained her all-important qualification in 1933, with its concomitant elevation in earning potential, Nellie would understandably have wanted to reclaim her children at the earliest possible opportunity, to set up a happy home, and there is no reason not to think that Wilfred would have wanted to contribute in the most effective of ways - financially. Without specific documentary evidence, the reason for choosing Leeds as a base must again be left to pure speculation; not too hard to find plausible reasons though: good work opportunities; far away from her home area and possible repercussions; and a relatively anonymous location, as far as Wilfred was concerned, to obviate the possibility of malicious gossip within the Movement. After they were married, of course, that would be different; he could afford to be open about his new wife and family, but not, so it would seem, to the extent of publicising it as some of his colleagues did. In 1933, Wilfred was based in London, but the whole of England [in fact, arguably, the whole of the British mainland] was his domain, operationally speaking, so he could, very easily, have passed through Leeds, given its central location in the north, on many occasions in the course of travelling to and/or from professional engagements. Late in 1934, as detailed in the previous chapter, Wilfred took up residence in Manchester, not much more than a couple of hours' distance from Leeds, even back then. There can have been no question in Wilfred's mind and, no doubt, not in Nellie's either, that having realised that they were compatible, there was every reason to put the fledgling relationship on a respectable and legal footing to establish permanence [not least for the sake of the children] and there was only one course open to them which satisfied those requirements: marriage. The timing was probably determined by Wilfred's busy schedule, and there is nothing in any of the known sources to suggest that there was a honeymoon, in the sense of a holiday away; rather awkward, with two young children [12 & 10] in tow, if one wanted to avoid straying from the truth.

As previously stated, the wedding was at Leeds North register office; without question, this will have been the nearest one to Nellie's home address, and will have facilitated a ceremony with the minimum of fuss and logistical requirements. The witnesses, as required by law, were the afore-mentioned M. N. Clark, and T. Quintin Dunlop, about the latter of whom nothing whatever is known; no mention of a member of the Leeds branch of British Union with this name has been found but, as alluded to above, Wilfred was probably very happy to avoid any recognition of his personal affairs so close to home, so the chances are that the other witness might also have been one of Nellie's work colleagues. Another oddity about the certificate is that the rank or profession of Nellie's father is omitted; he was most likely deceased, as was Wilfred's [albeit only fairly recently, in 1931], but Wilfred's father's rank or profession was stated, "Surgical Boot Maker", so why not David James's?

Unfortunately, Brian does not throw any light on the trajectory of Wilfred and Nellie's marriage and, by extension, their home life, as opposed to Wilfred's professional career, from then on; from information supplied by the Land Registry [20], as a result of extrapolation from an address in Wilfred's arrest details [see **Appendix D**] at the end of February 1936 [so almost exactly a year after their wedding] Wilfred bought a house in a leafy suburb of north-west London, 70 Torrington Road, Ruislip Manor, which is undoubtedly large enough to have been a family home for him, Nellie and the children, and was indeed intended to be so; what is clear, however, is that Wilfred and Nellie stayed together and ostensively happy until Wilfred's relatively early death. Brian emigrated to Canada, which will be enlarged upon on in note 1 to **Appendix E**, and Sheila spent some time in Oklahoma City, USA, possibly necessitated by her husband's employment, but she returned to England, according to Brian, some time after her mother's death, which will be explained in Chapter 14; both had children of their own. Both Brian and Sheila, as previously stated, took on Wilfred's name after their mother's remarriage, which must later have been a matter of preference, because although they were still under the age of majority in

1935, they must presumably have had the option to relinquish it upon reaching majority, so it was a distinct vote of confidence in their stepfather. Nellie [registered as Margaret Helen Risdon] died in 1981, at Henley on Thames, in Oxfordshire; prior to her death, she had been working in a bookshop, at Reading, Berkshire. There is no evidence that she involved herself in any political activities, other than supporting Wilfred in all he did.

NOTES

1 No evidence of employment in Leeds has yet been found.

2 The Land Registry is a veritable mine of information here; it appears that the land on which Mabel's house was built was part of a larger parcel of land

> "containing Ten thousand Five hundred and Forty-five square yards or thereabouts conveyed to the vendors by a Deed of Conveyance dated the Seventeenth day of July One thousand Nine hundred and Thirty-three and made between James Dearden Longley of the one part and the Vendors of the other part)";

Longley was, presumably, the previous owner of the land [and what appears to be a relative, Percy Longley, was listed as "now or recently" owning a property to the south of number 17 Henconner Avenue] which was conveyed to the builders of number 17, George Monkman and George Hedley Monkman, "both of Nowell Lane Works Harehills in the City of Leeds Builders and Contractors carrying on business together in co-partnership under the name or style of "Geo. Monkman & Son" (hereinafter called "the Vendors")"; number 15, to the east of number 17, was still the property of the builders, presumably awaiting a buyer, and number 19 to the west was described as being contracted by the builder owners to a James Alfred Hunt.

Courtesy of Graham Cole and the Land Registry offices at Durham and Nottingham

3 ***Letter from Brian Risdon, dated February 9th, 1998, in the author's possession***

Brian Risdon died in 2003, but his life from 1943 will be expanded upon in Chapter 13 and **Appendix E.**

4 ***Ibid.***

5 ***Ibid.***

6 ***The National Archives, J77/2001 - C423659***

7 ***Ibid.***

8 ***Ibid.***

9 http://dictionary.reference.com/cite.html?qh=king%5C%27s+proctor&ia=luna

> "A British judiciary officer who may intervene in probate, nullity, or divorce actions when collusion, suppression of evidence, or other irregularities are alleged."

10 ***The National Archives, J77/2001 - C423659: Plea of the King's Proctor:***

> "<u>In the High Court of Justice</u> / <u>Probate Divorce and Admiralty Division</u> / (<u>Divorce</u>) / <u>B E T W E E N</u> / HELENA LILIAN (otherwise Lily Lena) Geen Petitioner / and / ALFRED GEEN Respondent / THE KING'S PROCTOR SHOWING CAUSE / PLEA OF THE KING'S PROCTOR
>
> The King's Proctor showing cause why this decree <u>nisi</u> pronounced in this suit on the 21st day of November 1923 should not be made absolute says :-

1. That divers material facts respecting the conduct of Helena Lilian Geen, the above named Petitioner, have not been brought to the notice of this Honourable Court as hereinafter set forth.

2. That in or about the month of May 1923 at a place at present unknown to the King's Proctor, the said Helena Lilian Geen committed adultery with a man whose name is at present unknown to the King's Proctor, in consequence whereof she was on the 5th day of December 1923 at the City Lodge Hospital, Cardiff, in the County of Glamorgan, delivered of a seven months' still born male child of which child the above named Respondent was not the father.

THE KING'S PROCTOR THEREFORE prays that your Lordship will rescind the decree nisi pronounced in this suit and dismiss the Petition and will make such further and other order as may be just.

Dated the 27th day of May 1924.

W. H. Chapman
for the King's Proctor."

11 ***Ibid.: Rescinding Decree - King's Proctor***

12 Letter from Brian Risdon, ***op. cit.***

13 ***Ibid.***

14 ***The Midwives Roll, 1935, roll no. 86731; Central Midwives Board*** Published by Burgess and Son, Abingdon, 1935. Courtesy of Katherine Szentgyorgyi, The Nursing and Midwifery Council.

15 Letter from Brian Risdon, ***op. cit.***

16 No doubt another reason why Wilfred respected Maxton:

"Being the son of a headmaster and by profession a teacher, it was perhaps inevitable that throughout his life James Maxton would take a keen interest in the provision of working-class education, both for children and adults. His views on education were a product of his strong socialist beliefs. He argued that under the existing system of industrial capitalism, the education system would always favour the middle classes at the expense of the working classes and that the education system itself, because of this, would remain largely unchanged.

Maxton also helped to organise and run classes for adults. In partnership with John Maclean he held classes in 'citizenship' at Pollokshaws Academy in 1910, and in 1915 he assisted Maclean with the teaching of Marxist economics at the Labour College in Glasgow.

Maxton believed that an annual gathering in congenial surroundings of the party's most able activists, alongside the party's political leadership, would be the perfect setting to discuss and debate the party's future strategies. Many prominent labour politicians and supporters gave guest lectures at Letchworth over the years, including George Orwell, Clement Attlee and Aneurin Bevan [perhaps presenting Wilfred with an opportunity to catch up with his old friend].

The ILP summer school was more than just a socialist debating society; it was at this event that Maxton and the party's main thinkers attempted to combine theory with practice. Letchworth was the place where many of the ILP's main political campaigns were discussed and planned. The 'socialism in our time' campaign and the ILP's decision to disaffiliate from the Labour Party were both decided upon at ILP summer schools."

http://gdl.cdlr.strath.ac.uk/maxton/maxton035.htm

Letchworth was "a new model town favoured by progressive intellectuals":

"Everywhere there are people of good will who quite honestly believe that they are working for the overthrow of class-distinctions. The middle-class Socialist enthuses over the proletariat and runs 'summer schools' where the proletarian and the repentant bourgeois are supposed to fall upon one another's necks and be brothers for ever; and the bourgeois visitors come away saying how wonderful and inspiring it has all been (the proletarian ones come away saying something different)."

Bernard Crick: Orwell as a comic writer;

http://theorwellprize.co.uk/george-orwell/about-orwell/bernard-crick-orwell-as-a-comic-writer/

By 1937, Orwell was scathing about Socialists no less than Fascists:

"'One day this summer,' Orwell writes in The Road to Wigan Pier, 'I was riding through Letchworth when the bus stopped and two dreadful-looking old men got onto it. They were both about sixty, both very short, pink and chubby, and both hatless. ... They were dressed in pistachio-coloured shirts and khaki-shorts into which their huge bottoms were crammed so tightly that you could study every dimple. Their appearance created a mild stir of horror on top of the bus. The man next to me ... murmured "Socialists."' 'He was probably right,' the passage continues. 'The Independent Labour Party were holding their summer school in the town.' (Orwell neglects to say that he was attending it.)"

This same article mentions the location for the Schools:

"Annie Besant, a theosophist and campaigner for birth control, opened* the St. Christopher School—where the Independent Labour Party gathering was held—and which today still offers only vegetarian food (its pupils admit to nipping out to McDonald's)."

http://kendrive.blog.co.uk/2007/10/13/more_about_letchworth~3128181/

*This is not strictly true: the initial sponsorship for the school came from the Theosophical Society, for which one of its conditions was the adherence to "an entirely vegetarian diet for both boarders and day pupils"; the founder and first Head Master [now Head Teacher] was Dr. Armstrong Smith, from 1915 to 1918.

http://en.wikipedia.org/wiki/St_Christopher_School,_Letchworth

17 The original article was published in the ***New Statesman*** in 1913:

"It is just forty years since an American Methodist bishop conceived the idea for the Chautauqua Institution - the first, still the largest, and by far the most astonishing summer school in the world. ... Its original inspiration was evangelical: it was designed by its founder as a summer educational retreat for Sunday-school teachers; and its puritan strictness has been maintained throughout, despite its astounding growth and success.

The pioneer of summer schools in these islands is, beyond question, Professor Patrick Geddes. His school, on Castle Hill, Edinburgh, was the first successful experiment in Britain. Today the schools are so numerous that to frame a complete list would be a practical impossibility. They take every kind of colour - social, philosophical, literary, political and religious. Needless to say, it is the small minorities, the little eager cults, the groups of idealists, who have seen most clearly and exploited most cleverly the possibilities of the summer school as an agency of propaganda.

But the Social Question is the real and avowed basis of those schools which may claim to be most nearly related to the vital interests of the time. Here, we have the Fabian Summer School, fortunate beyond almost all others in its superb situation on Derwentwater as also in the concreteness of its programme and the surprisingly varied interests represented by the men and women whom it attracts.

Out of the two months of its regular session, one week will be given up to discussions connected with the Control of Industry, and another to a joint conference between the Executives of the Fabian Society and the Independent Labour Party on the forthcoming autumn and winter campaign. For the rest of the time, until the middle of September, the Fabians will roam at large among modern problems of all sorts. They will consider, with Mrs Sidney Webb, the Spheres of Science and Religion in Social Reconstruction, and with Sir Sydney Olivier the momentous interaction of White Capital and Coloured Labour; they will seek to thread the appalling maze of Casual Labour, and turn their holiday experiences to account in piling up the case for the Nationalisation of Railways.

There may be some who suspect that Fabians' celebrated expertness of organisation is applied not only to the debates in the fine room of Barrow House, but to mountain excursions, to bathing parties, and even fancy-dress balls. The truth is that the school affords a happy illustration of the real democracy - the comradeship of public servant and factory operative, tradesman and journalist, university professor, employer, and trade union official, in an atmosphere far removed from the absurd and deadening snobbery of the professional world."

"This article, [was] written anonymously for the New Statesman (but possibly by S K Ratcliffe) during the first year of the magazine's life. The Chautauqua Institution in New York State described was founded in 1874, and still holds nine weeks of educational and cultural activities every summer. Selected by Robert Taylor"

http://www.newstatesman.com/education/2008/07/summer-school-chautauqua

18 The Hall, which is now a Grade II listed building, dates back [according to the BBC website, link below] to mediæval times; during the Victorian period it was a stately home, and owners include the king of England [unsubstantiated], Edward Holland, the local Liberal MP [1806-1876] who was sometime president of the Royal Agricultural Society and a second cousin of Charles Darwin; it was also the last home in England of Philippe, Duc d'Aumale, of the Bourbon-Orléans family [1869-1926], the last pretender to the throne of France; it has had a somewhat chequered history, but at the time when it was used, albeit briefly, for Summer Schools, it was otherwise a normal [private] school. During the second world war, the BBC bought it to use as a safe provincial broadcasting centre, away from the dangers of London; temporary buildings, including a dozen studios, were erected; it became "for a while" a monitoring station, and pursuant to the BBC's designation of it as an engineering training centre, a certain amount of local controversy was caused by the construction of a 10-storey deep "fully functioning nuclear bunker" "[b]uried … into the hillside". The Hall itself was latterly a luxury hotel and conference facility, but appears not to have been financially viable; at the end of 2011 it underwent refurbishment to reopen as the same in 2012 [or possibly a retirement home; see the first link below].

http://www.independent.co.uk/news/media/tv-radio/the-bbc-bunker-they-dont-want-you-to-know-about-2121187.html

http://www.subbrit.org.uk/rsg/sites/w/woodnorton/ http://www.bbc.co.uk/historyofthebbc/collections/buildings/wood_norton.shtml

http://en.wikipedia.org/wiki/Wood_Norton,_Worcestershire

19 Letter from Brian Risdon, ***op. cit.:***

"… a wonderful man … Bill was also a Book Critic, an accomplished Carpenter and a Garden lover to say nothing of the animals that he enjoyed and loved. Both Margaret and he loved literature and were avid readers."

20 ***Courtesy of Emma Sturdy at the Land Registry***

The vendor of the house was a company, George Ball (Ruislip) Ltd., and the transfer was dated 28 February 1936. The property was first registered at the Land Registry on the 28th of August 1930, and according to the Local Studies section at the London Borough of Hillingdon Archives, the house would have been very recently built, so the likelihood is that the individual plots were first registered as soon as they had been allocated, and before building had commenced, hence the time-lag between the first registration in 1930 and the purchase in 1936. The house was part of a large estate:

"George Ball is very well known locally as a builder who developed a huge part of Ruislip Manor, including Torrington Road. As you note, the properties were developed before World War Two and covered the area south of the tube line and Ruislip Manor station. The estate was known as Manor Homes and the houses are two or three variations on a theme of terraced or semi detached homes in a 1930s style.

My guess is that your relative bought the house new in 1936. He would have been one of several thousand buying a Manor Home in the few years before the war, so there would not necessarily have been any connection with George Ball. Even if there was a personal connection, its unlikely that this would be mentioned in the sale documents.

Manor Homes were widely advertised as being the latest style with all mod cons. Many families who bought them worked in London and the advertising for the houses emphasised that the husband could commute easily to and from the city and be back home in his 'rural' home quickly. George Ball advertised the estate with a huge sign specifically aimed at people using the tube into London.

I suppose they would typically be office workers - perhaps lower management, that sort of thing. Each had a small front and back garden and often a few fruit trees in the back. The streets had grass verges and were lined with cherry trees, so were attractive and at the time it was a desirable place to live.

The Manor Estate covered a huge area. The transition from farm land in rural Middlesex to a housing estate swallowed up by the London suburbs happened very quickly indeed. John Betjeman's poem 'Middlesex' tells you what he thought of this sudden change - when Elaine gets off at Ruislip Gardens she is probably going home to a George Ball house, as this is the station at the other end of the housing estate. Betjeman was writing twenty years later of course and he is being rather ascerbic. [sic]"

Courtesy of Samantha, Local Studies, London Borough of Hillingdon, Central Library, High Street, Uxbridge

John Betjeman's poem can be found by following this link:
http://www.johnbetjeman.com/middlesex.html

7: MANCHESTER

In many ways, given its historical importance in the period of the industrial revolution, and aside from its [for Mosley] fortuitous connection with the latterly struggling textile industry, Manchester should be considered second only to London in importance as a trade centre that was not also a port [such as Liverpool], so it is fitting that it was chosen to spearhead an expansion of membership of the BUF in 1934/5. There is no reason to suppose that Wilfred Risdon felt any more or less at home there than he did anywhere else in England, or Wales, for that matter; he was used to moving around, as the demands of his vocation and employment dictated. It should come as no surprise that there was a desperate need for improvements to the conditions suffered by workers in Manchester, and the privations of Birmingham's workers would still have been relatively fresh in Wilfred's mind. As well as the Free Trade Hall meetings, as previously detailed, some of Mosley's earliest meetings for the new British Union of Fascists were at Hyndman Hall [**1**], "a large three storey building in Liverpool Street taken over by South Salford Branch of the Social Democratic Federation [**2**; a groundbreaking socialist group which later, almost inevitably, split and whose more radical left-wing members formed the Communist Party of Great Britain] in 1906."

The building had been the focus of many secular socialist activities for workers in Manchester, not only political, but also artistic [**3**], with a special interest in films for the workers [**4**] so, although Mosley's early meetings might have been welcomed, given his recently socialist background, his later perceived antagonism towards the Socialists means that references to his use of this building appear to be somewhat grudging, from which a certain embarrassment can be inferred [**5**]. Only a couple of years before Mosley used it to propagate his message, the Hall had been the rallying point for a march by the National Unemployed Workers' Movement [NUWM] to Salford Town Hall, to protest against the Government's unjust targeting of the workers in a bid to save money [a misguided policy which seems to be repeating itself in the twenty-first century] and which culminated in what became known as "The Battle of Bexley Square" [**6**], thanks to the violence of the Police, sparking uncomfortable memories of the "Peterloo Massacre" [**7**].

Outdoor meetings were also necessary and, in some ways, more useful, as audience numbers were sometimes larger [although the downside was that they were often more rowdy]; Stevenson [often misspelled as 'Stephenson', including by Wilfred] Square in central Manchester [see Chapter 4] was one venue; Queen's Park, Harpurhey [**8**], was another, and was only 'a stone's throw' away [no irony intended!] from the future Northern Command Headquarters in Higher Broughton. Number 17, Northumberland

Street was not alone among local or regional headquarters in being almost palatial, but it was among the largest, although this was a luxury which the organisation would not be able to afford for much longer. Given that Wilfred would be spending a great deal of his time in that locality in 1935, it made perfect sense for him to make it his base for the foreseeable future, and hence it was his address when he married Nellie [see Chapter 6] in April that year; he was to have another address, albeit briefly, before he finally left Manchester: see note 68 below.

The house, although it should more appropriately be referred to as "a ... substantial villa", had a name, *Thornleigh*, and according to Dr. Wise [**9**] it was built for a local merchant in the late 1870s; it was also a substantial plot, according to the 1939 conveyance, of 3,649 square yards. Prior to the property's purchase in 1934, by the BUF Trust Ltd., it had been owned by a "Managing Director" by the name of Cyril Dodd [**10**]. As reported in the BUF periodicals [**11**], the new premises were opened by Oswald Mosley [although there seemed to be some ambivalence as to which of the appellations "Branch Premises", or "headquarters" was more appropriate, as both terms were used in the same diary entry in one of the papers]. Strangely, they do not report, as does Dr. Wise [**12**], that the opening ceremony was performed by Mosley "flanked by two columns of his Blackshirts in full uniform", although perhaps the BUF publications always assumed that their readers would have expected such a procedure anyway. Apparently the response of the onlookers was entirely positive, and Mosley addressed 150 Blackshirts "[o]n the lawn, at the back of the building ... drawn up to welcome him" [**13**] after the opening; a photograph, captioned "A PROUD MOMENT", was printed in the first combined edition of ***The Blackshirt and Fascist Week***, showing "[a] section of Manchester Blackshirts", some of whom were probationers wearing grey trousers, instead of the black trousers they were allowed to wear when they were considered worthy of the uniform. The Leader, striding purposefully towards the camera, is wearing a light-coloured lounge suit; it is interesting to speculate as to why he was sometimes in uniform, and sometimes in 'mufti': presumably dictated by the occasion. The officer matching Mosley's step behind him is also out of uniform, although his lounge suit is dark in colour. Wilfred is nowhere to be seen [**14**].

Perhaps it was not essential for Wilfred to be present on this occasion; it was before the commencement of the Cotton Campaign, albeit only a few months; although the Leader did speak at Preston the day before the opening, and Wilfred spoke at Stockport Town Hall the previous Monday, so it would have made good sense logistically for him to stay in the area; perhaps there was a photograph showing Wilfred which could not be used as a result of lack of space in the papers [although it seems like a fair assumption that he did not go out of his way to court publicity himself]. Manchester was always going to be a very important centre for BUF activity, and given the pre-existing Communist presence which was inherently anti-fascist, and relatively large Jewish population in the city and its environs, it was inevitable that there would be trouble from the very beginning; as recalled by Wilfred himself, the first big public meeting for the Leader which he organised was in Manchester, at the Free Trade Hall, on March 12th, 1933, and the Communists determined to disrupt it at all costs [for details, see Chapters 4, especially notes 9, 10 & 11, and Chapter 5]. Dr. Wise [**15**] mentions the FTH meeting, but he is careful not to specify the allegiances of the opposition: his version of events is also different, in that he alleges that the Police had to be called, whereas Mosley maintains that the Police were already there, and took control of the meeting to prevent the trouble escalating, to which Mosley dutifully acceded [see Chapter 4, page 106]; the subsequent report in ***The Blackshirt*** makes no mention of Jewish involvement; it is purely Communist [**16**].

The Cotton Campaign 'kicked off' in earnest in August 1934 and the first big local meeting for the Leader, aside from a multitude of smaller meetings [**17**] arranged either by or for the local propaganda officers, was a rally at Belle Vue Park in Manchester on September 29th. The headline of the BUF newspaper the following week faced up foursquare to the racially indeterminate interrupters: "BLACKSHIRT CHALLENGE TO ALIEN OPPOSITION"; and was, naturally, positive: "Impressive Scenes At Manchester", although the magnitude of the audience was unspecified [apart from being described as "vast"], perhaps for a good reason - poor turnout [1,000 Blackshirts were reported to be in attendance; **18**]. The substance of the rally, at which a searchlight was used, "making it abundantly clear that the overwhelming majority were listening in intense earnestness to the Fascist argument", was a challenge to "The International Capitalists", but the Jewish component of this vexatious group was not left to the imagination. The contrast between the alien basis of the money-men, and how it would directly affect 'local people' was a useful point to emphasise [**19**], as was the value of the local workforce, which was being cruelly exploited [**20**]. The vocal attempts at interruption by the opposition were the only hints of trouble on that occasion, and the evening was rounded off by a firework display, but before this, Mosley made reference to a matter which was evidently an abiding concern, and which was to acquire more urgent relevance in the succeeding years: the need to prevent another horrific war [**21**], most definitely not to aid & abet alien financiers.

Dr. Wise does not make specific reference to the Belle Vue rally, or any trouble emanating from it; but he does quote the ***Manchester Guardian***'s mentions of fighting when the BUF marched "through the Jewish areas of the city" [**22**] in November 1934, as if they were somehow 'no-go' areas, and "[a] local Jewish member of the Young Communist League who lived on Waterloo Road, Hightown [Cheetham Hill] and was later to fight in Spain, Maurice Levine" who accused the BUF of being provocative, leading to "scuffles with the inhabitants of Strangeways, who were very sensitive to the menace of fascism in their midst." [**23**] There is no reason to suppose that Wilfred was involved in this 'provocation', or that this was even his intention, although a general public presence was a good way to keep the Movement and its adherents uppermost in the minds of the local inhabitants. He 'inherited' a ready-made network of local branches [eight in Greater Manchester and ten in the surrounding towns were opened between 1932 and 1934 - a measure of the Movement's popularity at that time **24**], and as well as being very good bases for Wilfred's recruitment drive, the towns or suburbs in which they were situated provided locations for Mosley's meetings early in 1935 [**25**].

Dr. Wise seems to think that "the focus of recruitment shifted to the North West", "[w]ith rapid decline of the BUF in Southern England after 1934 when Lord Rothermere and his ***Daily Mail*** group withdrew their support" [**26**]; certainly, there appears to have been a change of focus within the BUF, and whether or not Wilfred was the reason for this, or the vehicle by which it could be achieved, he was demonstrably successful: according to Dr. Wise, citing Richard Thurlow, another authority on British Fascism, "for a time, Mosley seriously contemplated moving his headquarters [from the 'Black House' in Chelsea] to Northumberland Street." [**27**] That might or might nor be true, but Thurlow appears to be in a minority here, although perhaps he has reached this conclusion from the reports compiled by MI5 'spies', not always without their own agenda, as referred to by John Beckett's son Francis, which relate that "[t]he year 1935 saw unrelenting trench warfare in BUF headquarters, chronicled in detail by MI5 … The detail of the MI5 notes show [sic] that their spies must have served them very well, and it seems likely that they had other spies in addition. There was hardly a meeting or discussion of the smallest importance which they did not record …" [**28**]

Robert Skidelsky tells us that after the *imbroglio* of the Olympia rally, as well as "[t]he rôle of Jews at Olympia also [bringing] the anti-Jewish forces to the fore in the Fascist party …", contrary to the public pronouncements, it also caused Mosley to reassess his expectations of early success: "Mosley began to talk privately of a struggle lasting 30 years." [**29**] This was very much the view, albeit less pessimistic, which had been held by the more traditionally socialist hands in the Movement, not the least of whom was Wilfred, but also including Alex Miles, and Wilfred's erstwhile mentor, Robert Forgan: "Forgan's viewpoint was that held by Risdon, myself and others experienced in political life - the viewpoint expressed in the phrase 'Ten to fifteen years of hard work before we can think of power.'" [**30**] Miles was convinced that Mosley was always playing off the tensions prevalent in the country, whether accurately perceived, contrived, or otherwise, eschewing the conventional ballot, and waiting for the call from the desperate politicians, probably Conservative, who had exhausted their stock of orthodox political solutions, and would see Mosley as their 'Knight in Shining Armour' [**31**]; that was probably essentially true [although it is debatable that he 'eschew[ed] the conventional ballot', as a means to power, at any rate], but by 1935, the pendulum was swinging back.

During that year, Mosley changed the emphasis of the Movement away from a quasi-military organisation, towards a more conventional [but still very much maverick] political movement, and although economic prudence was a priority, he still managed to increase staff numbers at NHQ! [**32**] The emphasis on the political side should have pleased Wilfred, but the 'fly in the ointment' would soon be the new Director General, Neil Francis-Hawkins, who could not have been much more different from the previous incumbent, Dr. Forgan, who had himself been briefly superseded by the ex-Conservative F. M. Box. Francis-Hawkins was not much liked within the Movement [**33**], certainly not by those members attuned to the ever changing nature and the cut & thrust of politics, but was regarded as being efficient, not least by Mosley himself. When his biographical profile was published in ***Fascist Week*** in March 1934 [**34**], he was still below his highest position in the Movement, but he had a history of inclination to Fascism before joining the New Party, and "[h]is ability in this direction [planning the organisation of the Movement] brought him rapid promotion", so he was marked for success from the beginning; unfortunately, he was a single-minded martinet, so it was virtually guaranteed that he would polarise the officers with whom he had to deal.

No doubt in an endeavour to make the most effective use of his position as "In Charge in Lancashire", with a staff of 20 people [**35**], Wilfred put in as many personal appearances as was practicable, as reported in ***The Blackshirt***, including high-profile visits to Southport, only one month before his wedding [**36**], Burnley [**37**] and Liverpool [**38**]. Before his stint at Manchester had even started, Wilfred had had to accommodate being deposed as Director of Propaganda by William Joyce; no doubt Wilfred's potentially heretical independence of mind after Olympia [see **Appendix D**] had a bearing on this but, mindful of Wilfred's value in the field of propaganda, especially how it related to the unconverted workers, and to the Movement as a whole, Mosley perhaps presented Manchester as a 'sideways move' which would still allow Wilfred to contribute to the Movement's propaganda output, and oversee it in a background capacity.

Wilfred's last published reference as DofP was at the beginning of August 1934 [so he had lasted barely 18 months in the job, but such brevity of tenure was not unusual in the BUF] in a short, and slightly frothy piece in ***The Blackshirt***, giving no indication whatsoever of what was to come [**39**]; there was no mention at all of Wilfred during the rest of the month, but Joyce, with no rank stated, just his name as author of the piece, published an article towards the end of August lauding Hitler's "triumph" in the election for Reich President "[b]y the will of 90 per cent of the German electorate"

[**40**]; his "very successful meeting in Oldham" was also reported [**41**]; and by the last ***Blackshirt*** of August, Joyce's elevated status was confirmed on the front page, in an article trumpeting his success in gaining summonses against the Editor of the ***Daily Worker***, "in respect of articles and advertisements appearing ... in connection with the Blackshirt rally to take place [in Hyde Park] on September 9." [**42**] There was also, in the same issue, a notice informing speakers that they must submit to registration, if they wish to "be allowed to speak on behalf of the Movement" [**43**], thereby stamping Joyce's authority on that aspect of his propaganda work [and perhaps also incidentally reflecting unfavourably upon Wilfred's stewardship of this function?]. Although it might be entirely coincidental, given Mosley's ultimate authority in most matters, not least those of high-level promotion, Joyce's elevation, with the associated increase in incidences of almost fawning editorial reports about his activity, seems to occur at the same time as a change in the editorship of ***The Blackshirt***; the previous editor, Rex Tremlett, appears to have been impartial, as far as personalities were concerned, but he was evidently not able to take the pressure which the work entailed, and resigned through ill-health in the middle of May 1934 [**44**]. The first of Joyce's front page articles in ***The Blackshirt*** was at the beginning of May [**45**], when the assistant editor [who, given Tremlett's precarious state of health, in reality probably was already in overall control] was poised to succeed Tremlett officially, and this was Wilfred's erstwhile colleague and founder member from Newcastle, W. J. Leaper.

It is difficult to be precise about personal allegiances and animosities within the BUF at any given period, and no doubt these will have shifted to one side or the other as the years progressed: Wilfred's former colleague and early recruit into the Movement, Alex Miles, notwithstanding his ambivalence about Mosley himself, is quite specific that Leaper was one of a triumvirate with John Beckett and Raven Thomson who "worked together hand in glove to build up their own importance and to down Joyce, Risdon, Elliott and others, including myself." [**46**] Miles's association of Wilfred with Joyce is interesting, given the circumstances, but perhaps Joyce's naked ambition was seen as simply that within the Movement, rather than any personal slight towards Wilfred; certainly Mosley was, for the most part, meritocratic in his attitude and his appointments [**47**]; on the other hand, Beckett, who isn't quoted by his son as mentioning either Wilfred or Leaper, in connection with his time at the BUF, is derogatory about Raven Thomson [**48**], and includes Chesterton with Joyce as "the two men who, after Forgan's departure, John liked best" [**49**].

During his 1940 Defence Regulation 18B Appeal Hearing [see **Appendix D**], Wilfred avoided specifying any particular regular or long-term associations within NHQ ["... I found myself associated with first one person and then another who appeared to be getting annoyed with the same things I was. There was no idea of forming a group to campaign or anything like that ..."], and apart from one passing reference to William Joyce [concerning his conduct when he was no longer with the BUF], the only remarks directed at another officer which might be considered derogatory concerned Francis-Hawkins: "... he had no political knowledge whatever. He was a man who had been put into a high position without a real political background that would enable him to do justice in that position, and the fact that one after the other people whom I believed to be decent clean and loyal were pushed out of their positions and eventually out of the Movement." Although Wilfred considered it "rather invidious to quote cases", he was charitable about Chesterton, albeit with a qualification: "He was a man with a brilliant background and had a really good Army record, but he was always in trouble because these people did not just like him. He had a weakness upon which they played. He was a vain man, but one would expect vanity in a member of the Chesterton family: but he was a brilliant and honest man." Almost inevitably, Joyce is regarded quite widely as being more able than Wilfred as a Director of Propaganda, but the most likely reason for this is that Joyce rode the virtually unstoppable tide of anti-Semitism which came to dominate the Movement, pretty much from the time he took over [**50**], but which he himself was instrumental in initiating, and which, also inevitably, caused friction and violence at public gatherings, which was guaranteed not only to keep the Movement in the public eye, for all the wrong reasons, but also thereby to alienate the vast majority of potential working class converts who could not see beyond the 'logic' of Joyce's bigotry to the well-reasoned financial arguments which Mosley had started out with, and which Wilfred supported [**51**].

Unfortunately for the BUF at this time, the contemporary economic climate and outlook were steadily improving, which was more as a result of trading conditions in the world as a whole, rather than anything which could be directly attributed to specific policies on the part of the National Government [**52**]; this meant that one of the main planks of Mosley's economic argument, underconsumption, was no longer such a vital factor, certainly with the middle classes [**53**], whom Mosley was loath to overlook, even though he saw the largest rump of potential members among the working classes: it just meant that he and his Movement were going to have to work a lot harder to keep his numbers high [and, perhaps more significantly, avoid the damaging desertions]. Another factor which Mosley had to take into account, and which he ignored at his peril [even if the substance of the propaganda was far more likely to be understood only by the better educated echelons of British society] was that he was not the only economic reformer in the country: John Maynard Keynes was one, whose economic theories had come, by the mid-thirties, to be widely acknowledged, including by Mosley himself, even if not 'taken on board' wholeheartedly by the British Government. Another was one of a small group who, while sharing Mosley's realisation that capitalism was badly, if not actually fatally flawed, had arrived at a rather different manifestation of a solution: the National Dividend ["a Logical Successor to the Wage" **54**]. He was Major Clifford Hugh Douglas, and his scheme was generally known as Social Credit [**55**]; this is a complex subject [**56**], which will be dealt with in more detail in a later chapter, because the BUF reached something of an accommodation with the Greenshirts [as the movement came to be known, although this is actually a distraction from the core economic policies] after initial suspicion [which applied to all other groups, indicative of the "if you're not with us, you're agin' us" mindset] and occasional hostility; the Social Crediters were partly responsible for that, even if inadvertently, as they tended to get lumped into the generic 'anti-Fascist' groupings [although they did occasionally actively participate in anti-Fascist marches: this was probably indicative of inconsistency in both the pronouncements and the practice of official policy, something not unique to the BUF]. There was a certain bond between both Movements however, even if not officially sanctioned by Mosley, in being proponents of economic theories which were far enough outside orthodoxy as to be considered fantastical, unworkable and even dangerous, notwithstanding their similarities [support was always qualified, however]. Greenshirts regularly attended BUF meetings in 1935, evidently without any trouble.

At the beginning of 1935, Wilfred's 'sideways move', although still in force for the time being, was somewhat downgraded when he was appointed, alongside T. L. Butler, as a deputy to Miles's nemesis, F. M. Box [see Chapter 3, note 36], by now a senior figure, who was made head of Political Organisation [**57**]. Wilfred was undoubtedly capable of doing Box's job, but perhaps it was felt that it would have been too much to ask for him to combine his efforts in Lancashire to boost recruitment with what would clearly have been a very demanding job [although not so demanding with the aid of 2 capable deputies?]; or else it was an expedient appointment for Box, given his length of service with Mosley [a good few years less than Wilfred's] and, perhaps the clincher, his previous position as Conservative Chief Agent before he joined Mosley [**58**]. As mentioned earlier, Eric Piercy was appointed Chief Inspector of Branches, an itinerant position, whereas there were also area inspectors, based at NHQ, who would keep track of regional developments; presumably, Wilfred was outside this loop as his recruitment project required him to be based in Manchester. This was one side of the coin, as it were: the other side was the Blackshirt side. The Defence Force was effectively disbanded and henceforth, the Blackshirts would constitute the paramilitary side of the party and be responsible for stewarding meetings. The head of this new amalgamated wing was Dundas, with Francis-Hawkins as his deputy, and as with the Organisation side, there would be NHQ-based visiting inspectors. John Beckett, who "effectively took control of strategy and propaganda" [even though Joyce was officially Director of Propaganda] when Italy invaded Abyssinia, because "Mosley spent much of 1935 in Italy" [**59**], was put in charge of national canvassing; Raven Thomson was made head of Policy.

Wilfred certainly had a difficult task on his hands: although he was indisputably successful in his recruitment strategy, once the new members had joined, the responsibility for them passed into the hands of others; also, the bulk of new recruits were non-unionised working class, which was awkward, because although the BUF held out the prospect of full unionisation in the Corporate State, it also regularly criticised the current union setup, which meant that there was no great incentive for these workers to join existing unions in the interim, and there was no particular cohesion or long-term loyalty in this group of non-unionised workers, such as there was with union members. According to one later commentator, "the working class recruit was typically one who had not been educated into trade union or Labour Party membership" [**60**], and this also had the unfortunate effect of setting in motion a vicious circle: the middle class members who were somewhat more affluent, and would have contributed more in the way of capital into the branches, were discouraged, in a very class-based way, from joining, hence the provincial branches tended to be in the poorer, run-down areas, which also discouraged more affluent potential members.

Some good work had been done by Wilfred's friend and colleague, Alex Miles, in Manchester before Wilfred's arrival, aiming to recruit workers into the FUBW [see Chapter 4], which would have circumvented the problems associated with the mainstream unions, but Mosley eventually decided that he could not tolerate this: he "did not propose to countenance anything in the way of a Trade Union rivalling the existing Trade Union machine", the real explanation for this [according to Miles] being that Mosley "feared the growth of the Fascist Union of British Workers and was determined to put a stop to its progress" [**61**]. The local membership of the FUBW had been recruited from the "Municipal Lodging House, and the Labour Exchange queues" [**62**], and Miles published 2 propaganda newssheets, one of which, the ***Siren***, was still extant, according to a July 1935 Special Branch report, after Miles had moved on [**63**]. At the end of February 1935, Manchester "was the only [BUF] area holding its ground", with a membership of 1,500, undoubtedly the result of a combination of Wilfred's recruitment and propaganda work, and Mosley's inspiring speeches [**64**].

Spring 1935 was a struggle for the Movement as a whole: "By May, the movement was barely keeping its head above water [and] Lancashire appeared to be the only active area" [**65**], so Wilfred was obviously doing something right, in very trying circumstances. By the summer, Mosley decided that the Movement could no longer sustain such an expensive national headquarters setup as embodied in Black House in Chelsea [the reasons for which were various, including a significant reduction in funding from Mussolini, but this will be dealt with in more detail later; declining membership overall was very significant, however], and the recent reorganisation had discarded the military-style Central Defence Force, so he moved into smaller premises, albeit on three floors, in Sanctuary Buildings, Great Smith Street, Westminster, overlooking the House of Commons; apparently, the new premises were jocularly known within the Movement as the "gas works" [**66**]. The move was announced in ***The Blackshirt*** in the third week of June, and it might just be a coincidence that the Movement was able to hang onto its impressive location just long enough to be able to salute the royal couple on the route of "the last of their Jubilee Drives", which passed the almost immodestly decorated buildings, outside and opposite which "[s]everal hundred Blackshirts, eager to show their loyalty and devotion to their Majesties ... crowded the pavement and when their Majesties arrived the salute was given and there was a burst of cheering." [**67**]

Wilfred's whereabouts during that summer and autumn appear to be something of a mystery: there are no mentions whatsoever of his activities in ***The Blackshirt*** between June and November, and yet appearances and speeches by the other three main personalities of the Movement, Mosley, Joyce and Beckett are reported with almost monotonous regularity. It is quite possible that he and Nellie 'escaped' for some sort of honeymoon; this is pure speculation, of course. What is clear, however, is that Wilfred appears to have vacated his accommodation at the Higher Broughton headquarters following his marriage, for fairly obvious reasons, and occupied a small terraced house [**68**] within easy walking distance, less than half a mile away, but he was only there for around a year because, as alluded to briefly at the end of Chapter 6, at the end of February 1936, he bought a house in Ruislip Gardens, north west London, so that he was once again 'close to the action'. According to Francis Beckett, as soon as the organisation was set up in the new premises at Westminster, Mosley instituted a Central Council [perhaps a small-scale emulation of Mussolini's Fascist Grand Council?] which included John Beckett, Joyce and Chesterton, and the newly arrived Major General Fuller, and "'[w]e understood', wrote John, 'that this council would discuss the whole work of the movement, and although there were also a number of bureaucrats on the council, they were not gifted men, and we felt confident, once we were sure of being consulted, of our ability to sway Mosley by the force and sincerity of our arguments.' I am quite sure that John wrote this rubbish entirely seriously." [**69**].

It is strange that Beckett doesn't mention Wilfred in this connection, although there are no direct references to Wilfred at all in his son's book, so this does not automatically mean that Wilfred was excluded from the Central Council; he would naturally have been quite justified in feeling aggrieved had he actually been excluded, despite his currently itinerant brief, and his Manchester base. Beckett was scathing, subsequently, about this arrangement in 1935, the aforementioned year of "unrelenting trench warfare at BUF headquarters" and [notwithstanding a personal interest on the part of this author] it is difficult to recognise Wilfred in this description: "The Central Council, in which John had foolishly placed his hopes, turned out to be a weekly waste of time. Apart from General Fuller, himself, Joyce and Chesterton, 'the other members sat silent and stupid, occasionally starting up with fury when it occurred to them, that someone was arguing with the Leader. After three months General Fuller declared he had no more time to waste, and attended no more.'" [**70**]

The Central Council might or might not have had the same members as the Policy Committee, of which Wilfred definitely was one, which Cross mentions in connection with an incident the following year [**71**], but its name suggests that it had a subsidiary function to that of directing the Movement from the top, as it were, so perhaps this is indicative of the beginning of Wilfred's gradual slide down the 'league table' of personalities at the top of the BUF. The main world event of 1935, that did not appear to have required Wilfred's involvement, officially at least, was Italy's invasion and annexation of Abyssinia [now Ethiopia]; Mosley happened to be in Italy when the invasion took place, and he saw it as a good opportunity to both campaign against war with Italy by concentrating on Great Britain's interests at home, and currying favour with his main benefactor, Mussolini, in so doing. John Beckett is generally credited with coming up with the slogan "Mind Britain's Business", which caused much confusion when it suddenly appeared overnight in multifarious locations, generally chalked or painted on any likely wall or bridge, accompanied by the symbol of the lightning flash within a circle [similarity to the German SS symbol not disdained], which had been created by a member and became the replacement for the Fasces symbol, although it quickly came to be referred to as the "flash in the pan", not least by some high-ranking officers in the Movement.

Beckett and Joyce appear to have consolidated their positions within the Movement in this year, and even though it seems hard to believe that there was a personal motive for any detriment which Wilfred suffered to his career within the BUF in 1935, especially given their mutual history of political activism as opposed to a concentration on dispassionate organisational efficiency [as in the case of deskbound officers of the ilk of Francis-Hawkins], they were nevertheless content to ride the crest of the wave of popularity, even if it was at Wilfred's expense; Joyce was not immune from criticism from the Leader, however: according to a Special Branch report of the 6th of June, 1935, Joyce was defended against censure from Mosley for not holding sufficient meetings [because he "was apparently worried about the expenses incurred by the move, and by the party's outstanding debts"] by the 'Treasury' [the department that had been created by Dundas just over a year earlier, comprising originally himself, Dr.

Forgan and Major Tabor], of which the two principal members were currently messrs. Box and Francis-Hawkins! As well as having a guiding hand and authoritative voice in the Movement's propaganda output that year, Beckett was also involved in directing a national canvass, which had been instigated twelve months previously [**72**]; there was some overlap with propaganda in these activities, but however much Wilfred might have wanted to be part of that operation in 1935, he would have been pragmatic enough to concede that he could not accommodate that with his regular duties [even though his qualification of having actually been an election agent probably trumped Beckett's of being an elected MP, notwithstanding Beckett's 'hands-on' approach to his election campaign at Gateshead in 1924].

By late 1935 Wilfred reappears, at least to the extent of having material published by the Movement, and he was starting to concentrate on a subject dear to his heart, which was to assume ever greater significance over the next 4 years: the central and fundamental position of the Trades Unions within the Corporate State [although Beckett, styled as "ex M.P. For Gateshead", had been involved here as well, back in August 1934, giving "FASCIST FACTS FOR TRADE UNIONISTS; CORRUPT AND COWARDLY LEADERS FEAR THE BLACKSHIRTS" **73**]. Wilfred regarded himself as "a life-long Trade Unionist" and "always insisted that Trade Unions as such, as an organised force, should be a responsible section of the Government of a country" [see **Appendix D**] so he would no doubt have been discomfited by the alleged inclusion of a large number of Trades Union officials in the demonstrations at the Belle Vue meeting on the 29th of the previous September [**74**]. At the beginning of November, the same issue of ***The Blackshirt*** in which the future and ill-fated Edward VIII, while still the Prince of Wales, courted controversy by saying publicly that slums "must be abolished", had a half-page article by Wilfred printed that incorporated a phrase which was going to assume increasing resonance in the next two years: "POWER ACTION OF FASCISM; MEMBERS STAND BY THEIR UNIONS" [**75**]. It looked very much like he was back on track again, having been able to lay claim to a goal worthy of his mettle.

NOTES

1 This was a relatively unprepossessing brick building, although the top floor was a fairly unusual shape; it was named after H.M. Hyndman [see note 2 below]; photograph:

http://www.flickr.com/photos/salfordandmanchester/2410414050/sizes/l/in/photostream/

> "The large club room on the ground floor had a fireplace with a surround on which Jack Williams had painted WORKERS OF THE WORLD, UNITE. YOU HAVE NOTHING TO LOSE BUT YOUR CHAINS. YOU HAVE A WORLD TO WIN. In 1930, at the initiative of Larry Finley, the Workers' Arts Club was established in the hall with the aim of promoting working class activity in all fields of sport and culture."

The battle of Bexley Square: Salford unemployed workers' demonstration - 1st October, 1931;

http://libcom.org/history/battle-bexley-square-salford-unemployed-workers-demonstration-1st-october-1931

> "Next to [the Workers' Arts Club] was a cinder croft, and behind that the main gasworks for Salford. ... it was a three-storey building, with rat-infested cellars. The top floor was a boxing gym - where later a number of boxers were to be recruited into the Communist Party and the YCL. ... On the floor underneath the gym there was a room that was kept for meetings, and on Saturday political groups would organize dances or socials there. The floor wasn't really fit for dancing - it was absolutely torn to ribbons by people's boots! It wasn't a very big room anyway. But there would be a little band - three or four instruments and people would dance. Downstairs, on the ground floor, there was a bar and a snooker table. There'd always be people playing snooker, and that's where the debates were held, in that room, to the click of snooker balls."

Ewan MacColl: The early years;

http://www.wcml.org.uk/contents/activists/ewan-maccoll/life-and-times/the-formative-years/

2 The Democratic Federation, credited as Britain's first socialist party, was formed in 1880 [or 1881*], "consisting of an alliance of radical grouplets and individuals", by H.M. [Henry Mayers] Hyndman, and later transformed into the Social Democratic Federation in 1883 [or 1884*], "when the group adopted an explicitly socialist platform." Hyndman was a controversial figure, not dissimilar to Mosley in his reversal of political affiliation and dominant, authoritarian control of his party; for a convert to socialism, he also held decidedly 'right-wing' imperialist and nationalist views, supporting the Boers in the second Boer War, while criticising those advocating home rule in Ireland and expressing hostility to the experiments in democracy which were taking place in the United States. After discovering Marx from a biography of Ferdinand Lassalle, Hyndman was converted to socialism by Marx's analysis of capitalism, even though he had doubts about some of Marx's ideas.

Although his tenure as leader had not been untroubled, the fractures started when the SDF left the Labour Representation Committee [LRC] over ideological differences, and when the SDF merged with the ILP in 1911, he set up the British Socialist Party; Hyndman's support for Britain's involvement in the war in 1914 caused another split, and he set up the National Socialist Party two years later; there seems to be some uncertainty as to whether he remained leader of this party until his death in November 1921, or if he reverted it to the SDF in 1919: the balance of opinion appears to favour the latter. "[T]he group gradually dissolved into the Labour Party" after Hyndman's death, and "[i]t finally disbanded in 1941."

Peter Barberis, John McHugh and Mike Tyldesley, Encyclopedia of British and Irish Political Organizations

It is interesting to speculate whether Mosley knew of Hyndman and his politics before using the Hall for meetings. The Wikipedia National Socialist Party page is at pains to point out how it was nothing to do with 'Nazism', with its weary, virtually universally accepted 'right-wing' associations:

> "It should not be confused with the German **NSDAP**, which was created three years after the British **NSP**. At the time when the **NSP** was established, the term 'national socialism' carried none of its present-day right-wing connotations. The British **NSP** was firmly on the left-wing of politics and was in no way associated with the doctrine of Nazism (in fact, the **NSP** was dissolved by the time German Nazism began to emerge)."

http://en.wikipedia.org/wiki/National_Socialist_Party_(UK)#cite_note-1

*There is a minor discrepancy in dates between Hyndman's own Wikipedia page and that for the SDF;

http://en.wikipedia.org/wiki/Henry_M._Hyndman

http://en.wikipedia.org/wiki/Social_Democratic_Federation

3 One of the many frequenters of the establishment was the father of James Miller, later to take the stage name Ewan MacColl:

> "Ewan MacColl was born in Salford and named James by his parents, Betsy and William Miller. William was an iron-moulder, militant trade-unionist and a communist from Stirlingshire. Betsy Hendry was from Auchterarder, in Perthshire. When William was unemployed she supported the family, cleaning houses and offices, and taking in washing. ... William and Betsy, as well as being active socialists, were accomplished singers and storytellers, and these aspects of their lives were to become deeply ingrained in their son's development. ...
>
> 'Occasionally, when my father was unemployed for long periods, he'd spend time in the Workers' Arts Club. The Workers' Arts Club was in Hyndman Hall, [69] Liverpool Street, Salford. I wrote a song inspired by that scene when I worked in Theatre Workshop. It was called 'Dirty Old Town'. ... The Workers' Arts Club was an extraordinary institution. I don't know how it got the name 'Arts Club', because there was very little in the way of arts;'"

Ewan MacColl: The early years; op. cit.

Ewan went on to father an offspring who, using his assumed name, was to achieve fame and a measure of success in her own right, before her early death in a tragic swimming accident in Mexico in 2000; Kirsty MacColl:

"Kirsty MacColl was the daughter of folk singer Ewan MacColl and dancer Jean Newlove. She and her brother, Hamish MacColl, grew up with their mother in Croydon, where she attended Park Hill Primary School and Monks Hill High School, making appearances in school plays. At the time of MacColl's birth, her father had been in a relationship with folksinger, multi-instrumentalist and songwriter Peggy Seeger since 1956 (a relationship that would continue until his death in 1989), and already had a son with her."

http://en.wikipedia.org/wiki/Kirsty_MacColl

4 The building was the headquarters of, although not the only venue for, a workers' film society:

"The Salford Social Democratic Land and Building Society was the owner of Hyndman Hall, the Social-Democratic Federation's headquarters. In 1930 at a special meeting they agreed to add to their Objects a commitment to building or buying a venue 'for the exhibition of cinematograph films, plays, dramatic and musical performances, particularly those of interest to the Working Class, or may hire a building for any such purposes...' ... Out of this decision came the Manchester and Salford Workers' Film Society, with the first screening in November 1930."

Manchester and Salford Workers' Film Society; Origins;

http://www.wcml.org.uk/contents/creativity-and-culture/leisure/workers-film-society/

5 Dr. Yaakov Wise, something of an authority on Fascism in Manchester, makes a terse, unreferenced mention of it:

"On Saturday October 1st 1932 Mosley founded the British Union of Fascists to implement his policies. His early meetings were held at Hyndman Hall in Liverpool Street, Salford."

FASCISM IN MANCHESTER; compiled and edited by Z. Yaakov Wise, MA, PGCE;

http://www.art.man.ac.uk/RELTHEOL/JEWISH/fascism.htm

6 One of many battles with Police at this time:

"Edmund and Ruth Frow's account of the National Unemployed Workers Movement's activities in Salford, its demonstration in 1931 against cuts in the dole, the subsequent battle with the police and aftermath.

'Some of the unemployed were members of Salford NUWM which met weekly at the Workers' Arts Club in Hyndman Hall, Liverpool Street. There were usually at least a hundred present each paying a penny subscription. ... Although the main issue was unemployment, wider topics of economic and political interest were aired in discussion.'"

The battle of Bexley Square; op. cit.

7 On 16 August 1819 armed cavalrymen and soldiers attacked a large peaceful crowd in Manchester:

"Local radicals had called the meeting as part of a campaign for the political reform of parliament, a campaign given renewed vigour by the distressed economic conditions since the end of the Napoleonic Wars. The campaign was particularly strong in the new northern towns such as Manchester where handloom weavers found themselves pauperized as wages fell. By 1 p.m. tens of thousands of men, women and children had gathered on St Peter's Field, many having risen at dawn and marched in procession from outlying towns. The town authorities feared an uprising and had made extensive preparations.

They gathered in a house overlooking the field and the meeting had scarcely begun before they ordered the arrest of the main speaker, Henry Hunt, and sent in the Manchester Yeomanry who had been drinking heavily. The horsemen attacked the closely pressed crowd with their newly sharpened sabres. The authorities then sent in the regular army who swept the crowd from the field. Some Yeomanry pursued the fleeing people through the streets. There was rioting later in the evening in the New Cross area, where the army opened fire.

At least 18 died either on the field or later from their injuries, whilst many hundreds were injured. This unprecedented massacre was dubbed 'Peterloo' by the radical press, contrasting this shameful episode with the Allied victory at Waterloo some four years earlier. Attempts to hold the town authorities and military to account, however, were unsuccessful as they were vigorously supported by the Tory government.

When the poet Shelley heard about Peterloo he wrote an angry poem The Masque of Anarchy, although it was not published until 1832. In later years it became a popular recitation at radical and socialist meetings."

Peterloo Massacre, 1819;

http://www.wcml.org.uk/wcml/en/contents/protests-politics-and-campaigning-for-change/peterloo/

8 Queen's Park was a very useful open-air location for public meetings:

"Queen's Park was one of Britain's first municipal parks created in 1846; designed and laid out by Joshua Major in 1845. The park was originally arranged around Hendham Hall, home of the Houghton family; however this was demolished in 1884. The park incorporated a labyrinth, sheds and greenhouses; however by 1930, these had been removed from the park."

http://en.wikipedia.org/wiki/Harpurhey

Interestingly:

"In 1914, a shelter on the Rochdale Road boundary of the park is reported as having been 'tacitly reserved for a local "Parliament", consisting in the main of retired elders of the district who met daily during the summer to discuss and criticise the affairs of the city and nation.' In the winter, the members held their meetings in the ground floor of the Museum which served as a refreshment room."

http://www.manchester.gov.uk/info/200073/parks_and_open_spaces/1832/queens_park/4

Unfortunately, even here there could be trouble, with meetings broken up:

"**Free Speech in Manchester**

A meeting of a working men's debating society in Manchester, known as the Queen's Park Parliament, was addressed by Mr. Alan Chorlton, M.P., on the "Water grid" last Friday night, and it ended in disorder, broken up by a small party of interrupters and an unpleasant incident in which the chairman, Mr. W. D. Ball, had a glass of water thrown in his face.

Mr. Chorlton managed to give the paper which was to have opened the debate, but he was constantly interrupted with totally irrelevant cries of "What about the Unemployment Bill?" or "What about two shillings a head for children?" A few members managed to make brief speeches in the debate, but the chairman had frequently to appeal for order, and, eventually, he named a woman as an interrupter. The woman came to the platform, speaking volubly, and she was followed by a man, who picked up a glass of water and threw it in the chairman's face. To avoid further trouble the meeting was closed, and the police interposed to prevent any real disorder developing."

The Fascist Week, no. 21, March 30th-April 5th, 1934, page 3

9 ***FASCISM IN MANCHESTER: op. cit.***

10 ***Slater's Directories of Manchester and Salford, cited in ibid.***

11 ***The Blackshirt, no. 51, April 13th-April 19th, 1934, page 3***

The Fascist Week, no. 23, April 13th-April 19th, 1934, page 5

12 Hilda Cohen's family lived 35 Northumberland Street, and she was an eye-witness to the opening ceremony.

Bagels with Babushka, Hilda Cohen, cited in FASCISM IN MANCHESTER op. cit.

13 ***The Blackshirt, no. 51, op. cit.:***

"In a short speech the Leader said, 'The progress of our Movement is not only a surprise to the old parties, it is even a surprise to ourselves."

14 There is also a photograph in the same edition which does show Wilfred in a group of Blackshirts surrounding "the Leader on the steps of the Gloucestershire Area Headquarters", but no date is given; even though a few of the Blackshirts on the periphery of the group are saluting [not all in the same direction!], most appear quite relaxed [although not slouching!], but Wilfred looks equally as determined as Mosley, gazing resolutely ahead.

The Blackshirt incorporating The Fascist Week, no. 58; June 1st, 1934, page 5

It had been decided to combine the two BUF weekly newspapers because "[i]t has been considered for some time that in many respects the news contents of the '***Fascist Week***' and the member organ '***The Blackshirt***' overlap", so "[f]rom the 1st June, therefore, the only official paper of the B.U.F. will be '***The Blackshirt***'."

The Blackshirt, no. 51, May 18th-May 24th, 1934, page 1

15 ***FASCISM IN MANCHESTER op. cit.:***

"In 1933 one of his meetings at the Free Trade Hall was the scene of rioting, and police had to be called to separate various factions."

16 ***The Blackshirt, No. 3, March 18th, 1933, p. 1***

17 Predictably, although entirely understandably, ***The Blackshirt*** was upbeat:

"The propaganda campaign which is being carried out by the British Union of Fascists in Lancashire has aroused intense interest among the cotton operatives, and large numbers of recruits are being enrolled.

Meetings which are held twice a day in all important centres are drawing huge crowds, and very little opposition is in evidence. The Blackshirt cotton policy is everywhere receiving the approval of the people most concerned with this trade."

The Blackshirt, no. 69, August 17th, 1934, page 7

18 ***The Blackshirt, No. 76, October 5th, 1934, p. 1***

Audience number was specified by one later author, citing an MI5 report, as 2,500, of which, allegedly, "one-quarter were protesting communists" and "[t]he 800 Blackshirts in attendance were enclosed by wooden barriers in a police cordon, and the benches which the BUF supplied for the public were empty for the most part."

MI5 Report, 8 October, 1934. PRO HO144/20142/224, cited in **BLACKSHIRTS TORN: INSIDE THE BRITISH UNION OF FASCISTS, 1932-1940,** ***by Thomas Norman Keeley, MA Degree submission, Simon Fraser University, Canada, 1998***

19 ***Ibid., page 2:***

"This evening's entertainment, provided by this little crowd brought here by Jewish money, is likely to cost the citizens of Manchester £1,000."

20 ***Ibid.:***

"Here in Lancashire you have the finest workmen in the world; but when the competition in the production of cotton goods is against slave-labour, they cannot hope to compete."

21 ***Ibid.:***

"Not till Fascism is supreme, as it will be supreme, can you carry through these great measures of reform. Fascism is a policy of the whole nation, and we shall not tolerate those who sabotage the nation. Nor will we permit them in their alien quarrels to involve us in war with the world. We fought Germany once in a British quarrel—we will not fight her again in a Jewish quarrel."

22 ***Manchester Guardian, 05 & 26/11/34, cited in*** **Anti-Semitism and the BUF,** ***W. Mandle, cited in FASCISM IN MANCHESTER op. cit.***

This could also be a reference to Mosley's November 25th meeting at the Free Trade Hall, where

"[t]housands of people, anxious to gain admission, had to be turned away, and inside, a large majority of the audience was enthusiastically in favour of Fascist policy. ... The anti-Fascists, as usual, did their best to create disorder, first in the meeting, and later in the streets, when large numbers cowardly attacked small batches of Blackshirt stewards as they emerged from the Hall. ... The Leader left the Free Trade Hall in a motor car, which the Reds rushed when it was turning the corner near the Central Library. They were, however, beaten off and the Leader journeyed to the area headquarters without further incident. Isolated groups of Blackshirts were attacked en route to their headquarters, particularly in Bury New Road, a Jewish quarter. Several Blackshirts received minor injuries."

The Blackshirt, No. 84, November 30th, 1934, p. 1

The Free Trade Hall had an illustrious and appropriate history, for a campaigning movement, but a sadly predictably less lustrous future in store:

"The Free Trade Hall, Peter Street, Manchester, was a public hall constructed in 1853–6 on St Peter's Fields, the site of the Peterloo Massacre and is now [2011] a hotel. The hall was built to commemorate the repeal of the Corn Laws in 1846. The architect was Edward Walters. The hall subsequently was owned by Manchester Corporation, was bombed in the Manchester Blitz and rebuilt. It was Manchester's premier concert venue until the construction of the Bridgewater Hall in 1996. It was designated a Grade II* listed building on 18 December 1963."

http://en.wikipedia.org/wiki/Free_Trade_Hall

23 **From Cheetham to Cordova: A Manchester man of the thirties*, by M. Levine, cited in FASCISM IN MANCHESTER op. cit.:***

"The BUF had its headquarters in Northumberland Street in Higher Broughton. A favourite café of theirs was Walter's on Great Ducie Street near Victoria Station, and they would walk through Strangeways along Bury New Road to Northumberland Street to provoke the Jewish population ..."

24 **Illusions of Grandeur: Mosley, Fascism and British Society 1931-1981*, by D. Lewis, p.64, cited in ibid.***

"Between October 1933 and June 1934 branches were opened in Platting, Stretford and Altrincham as well as in surrounding Lancashire towns including Bolton, Bury, Blackpool, Rochdale, Accrington and Preston. Branches existed in Ashton-under-Lyne, Hulme, Rusholme, Withington, Blackley, Salford, Oldham, Southport and Fylde by July 1934. These were all controlled from 17 Northumberland Street where a full-time Northern regional organiser and nine other staff were based."

Ibid.

25 ***Oswald Mosley, by Robert Skidelsky:***

"Early in 1935 Mosley himself spoke to packed meetings in Blackburn, Accrington, Darwen, Oldham, Earlstown, Ormskirk, Ashton, Preston and many other cotton centres, explaining how the BUF policy of excluding Japanese goods from India, removing the Indian tariff against British cotton goods, and excluding foreign textiles from the Crown Colonies would give employment to 65,000 Lancashire workers."

26 ***FASCISM IN MANCHESTER op. cit.***

This supposition is also supported by another author, who cites security service files, even going so far as to name specific towns:

"By August and September, 1934, the BUF had lost momentum, especially in the counties of Yorkshire and Devonshire, the cities of Birmingham and London, and the towns of Bournemouth and Bedford. It had ceased to make progress anywhere or with any segment of the population."

MI5 Report, HO144/20142/215, 08/10/34, cited in BLACKSHIRTS TORN:, op. cit.

27 ***Ibid.***

28 ***The Rebel who lost his Cause: The Tragedy of John Beckett, MP, by Francis Beckett***

The beginning of that year, 1935, was also the time when Wilfred was supposed to have been organising some sort of plot in Lancashire, ostensibly because he was "[a]ngry over having been passed over for promotion in favour of people who had more recently arrived to the party, [and] he was apparently providing Mosley with deceptive, overly optimistic reports on the movement's progress in Lancashire. He was ... planning to enlist the help of leading Lancashire fascists to disrupt the movement there unless Mosley dismissed certain officers at National Headquarters." There is every chance that Box is one of these "certain officers", although the military expert, Fuller, who came to be as equally disliked as Box, could have been another. Beckett had allegedly also organised a delegation to demand that the Leader dismiss Box, but if true, it was not carried through.

Box fell out with Mosley himself, for unknown reasons, over Mosley's appointment of the ex-Suffragette Mary Richardson to take charge of part of Wilfred's area in Lancashire, and he was sufficiently annoyed about it to tender his resignation, although it was either retracted, or not accepted; Lady Maud Mosley also contemplated leaving the Movement over the matter, even though she was not an ally of Box, because his section had "severely angered the women's section", and she also complained that Box's close associate, Cleghorn, had "insulted members in the north, causing many resignations, and a consequential closure of branches". According to Special Branch, Mosley took Wilfred's "threat" sufficiently seriously to send Richardson "to the north", but whether this was to monitor or to assist is unspecified. Box's own resignation threat could have indicated some loyalty to his immediate subordinate, Wilfred, but it could also just as easily have been the result of pique that Mosley was undermining his authority by casting aspersions on the capabilities of his staff.

Special Branch Report, HO 144/20144/182, 18/01/35, cited in BLACKSHIRTS TORN:, op. cit.

Whether Richardson achieved anything significant in "the north" is academic, because by the end of 1935 she was sufficiently disenchanted about the disparity in treatment between male and female members, giving the lie to "the 'feminist' pronouncements of the BUF" and the obvious privilege shown in the appointment of either aristocratic or upper-class leaders of the Women's Section, that she presented, with other women, her own "demands to the great Mosley", and was promptly expelled. Miles considered "that her expulsion was due to her 'refusal to accept the theory of the women as "permanent junior partner"'."

Cited in Left-Wing Fascism, op. cit.:
MRC, MSS127/NU/GS/3/5D, Richardson to Marchbank, 01/11/35;
Some Problems of Constructing and Reconstructing a Suffragette's Life, Hilda Kean;
Women and Fascism, Martin Durham

29 ***Oswald Mosley, op. cit.***

Although he does not specify a time period for this observation, Skidelsky also quotes another intellectual fascist sympathiser, Douglas Jerrold, who had noticed the same frame of mind in Mosley:

> "Interestingly, Jerrold [founder & editor of the ***English Review***] reported that Mosley 'does not believe that he will succeed in his own chosen fashion. He does believe that it is somebody's duty to keep alive in times of tolerable prosperity an active distrust of the political machines, so that when adversity comes, the people may not find themselves without hope.'"

Georgian Adventure, by Douglas Jerrold, cited in ibid.

30 ***The Streets are still: Mosley in Motley, by A. Miles***

31 ***Ibid.:***

> "Mosley had become [sic] the view point of the 'coup d'état', the strictly law abiding one, of course, where Conservatives, forced with the choice between 'Mosley or Moscow' would ask Mosley

> to take over. The lines of development upon which Mosley wrested [sic], showed this view clearly enough. On one occasion when I was arguing for a 'mass basis' for the Movement was obtainable only if we outrivalled the Labour machine in its day by day service to the people - Mosley reflected - 'I cannot and will not wait while we build a service machine better that that of the Labour Movement. We must find a better method.' Forgan, I am convinced, saw the smallness of this 'quieter [sic] method' and probably said so and resigned."

Dr. Wise also quotes a Home Office report on the BUF, which emphasises Mosley's apparent 'gadfly' approach to politics, but which had a direct relevance to Wilfred and his move to Manchester:

> "It is worth noting that in late 1934 and early 1935, Mosley had, as was his wont, attached himself to the issues of the moment. He had taken up the issue of India 'in hope of attracting the well known Conservative leaders opposed to the [home rule] Bill to join the BUF', and had strategically moved part of his headquarters staff to Manchester in order to 'take advantage of developments.'"

HO 144/20144/237, cited in FASCISM IN MANCHESTER, op. cit.

32 Skidelsky has the details, quoting Colin Cross [***The Fascists in Britain***]:

> "'During 1935, Mosley carried through an extensive reorganisation, centralising control of branches through a system of headquarters inspectors, inaugurating strict financial controls and turning the bias of the Movement away from semi-military training, designed to suppress a Communist revolution, towards a more conventional plan for winning power at a general election.' National Headquarters was gradually built up to a staff of 140 officials, headed by a director-general. For the first time, the two central principles of fascist organisation - leadership and team spirit - were fully applied."

Oswald Mosley. op. cit.

The military influence was not completely eradicated however: the predominant elements of the reorganisation were recommended by a military expert, Major General J.F.C. ["Boney"] Fuller,

> "a recent convert to the BUF. Fuller had been Chief of Staff to the British Tank Corps in 1917; he had then been Chief Instructor at the Camberley Staff College, and Military Assistant to the Chief of the Imperial General Staff. He had retired from the army in 1933 in order to devote himself to writing. ... [Mosley] asked Fuller to carry out research [after Fuller wrote to Mosley in the summer of 1934] and to produce a report on the way in which he considered the BUF should be reorganised. Fuller produced his report on the 8th of October, some 3 weeks before the [second] Albert Hall meeting.:
>
> > 'After two months' close study at NHQ I am of the opinion that the Movement cannot fail to succeed if certain radical changes are made in its organisation & discipline. ...'"

Fuller identifies the direction the Movement should be pursuing, which Wilfred will have wholeheartedly endorsed:

> "As the ultimate object of the Movement is to establish constitutionally a new form of government the immediate object is to win a number of seats in the next general elections. Consequently all means should be directed towards this end."

He was also rather critical of the Movement's propaganda, calling it "somewhat crude", but this was probably not a direct criticism of Wilfred and his recent work: to be fair, his focus had been more on the logistics of Mosley's high profile meetings, and his actual 'hands on' influence on the propaganda output which would have been seen by the general public, especially since the ascendancy of Joyce, certainly for the whole of that year, if not longer, must have been minimal, probably frustratingly so.

Fuller also recommended that Mosley should endeavour to make his position "less solitary & unapproachable", but Mosley wasn't quite ready to implement that at the end of 1934, although he did accept the need for change:

> "Eventually early in 1935 Mosley announced his decisions about reform in an article in ***Blackshirt*** entitled '*The Next Stage in Fascism*'. Discipline, especially at NHQ, was to be tightened up: the atmosphere of headquarters would be 'that of a workshop rather than of a clubhouse or playground'. The organisation of the Movement would be even more specifically on army lines. Every Blackshirt was to be a member of a unit of 5 or 6; units were to be part of Sections; Sections were to be part of Companies; and so on in a hierarchical structure up to the single Leader at the top."

Beyond the Pale, Sir Oswald Mosley 1933-1980, by Nicholas Mosley

33 At the end of June 1934, Special Branch was reporting that Box was "now Director of Organisation, British Union of Fascists", and between then and the beginning of October that year "Dr. Forgan's position has been a nominal one only and T.M. Box [sic] has been the virtual deputy for Sir Oswald Mosley."

HO 144/20141/84, 27/06/34 & HO 144/20142/243, 10/10/34, cited in BLACKSHIRTS TORN:, op. cit.

There was no shortage of assessments of Francis-Hawkins by other members:

> "It became necessary to find other means of stopping the strike-breakers and to do so, I called upon practically the whole of the available headquarters staff. Eric Piercy, National Staff Officer, in Command of the Defence Force, came up with some of his 'boys', Risdon, too, appeared, and, of all people, Neil Francis-Hawkins, then Officer in Charge of London Command whose last experience of a strike had been as a member of the strike-breaking Organisation for the Maintenance of Supplies, in 1926 [the National Strike]."

The Streets are still, op. cit.

> "The dispute was between those who saw the BUF's future in terms of a military organisation appealing to law and order, and emphasised a style of disciplined marches and demonstrations, and those who saw a need to expound propaganda and convert the masses to fascist ideology. The first faction was led … by … Neil Francis-Hawkins (the chief administrator) and Ian Dundas, the latter group by William Joyce, John Beckett and A.K. Chesterton." [curious that Wilfred is not included?]

Fascism in Britain 1918-1935, Richard Thurlow

"Beckett is very bitter about the conduct of the campaign. He stated quite bluntly that he considered Francis-Hawkins and [his deputy] Donovan to be utter fools and that if Sir Oswald Mosley was not as great a fool as they are, he is certainly far too complacent; that perhaps the shock … will induce Mosley to place less credence on the counsels of Francis-Hawkins and his friends …"

"The security services", cited in The Rebel who lost his Cause, op. cit.

"Power within the Movement fell into the hands of those most willing to believe in the dream-world that Mosley created. Neil Francis-Hawkins achieved rapid promotion, until by 1936 he was Director-General, ranking second only to Mosley. Tactically this was a mistake. A politician of Mosley's stamp needed a strong man at his elbow, capable of questioning decisions and acting as devil's advocate - the rôle which Strachey had once filled. In matters of organization Francis-Hawkins was competent though bureaucratic, but he had no ambition to influence the Movement's basic policy; he seemed to regard Mosley as infallible. Mosley himself had self-conscious ideas of how he should behave as Leader. He believed in a clear-cut delegation of responsibility and reserved for himself as Leader *absolute control of policy and propaganda* [my emphasis], a staggering burden for a movement so active as the BUF. Equally clearly, he believed it was no part of the Leader's function to worry about day-to-day administrative details and in Francis-Hawkins he found a competent man to look after them. The mistake was that on the day-to-day details depended the morale of the Movement, and there was irritation at the absolute authority held by so non-political a man as Francis-Hawkins. The 'political' leaders - men like Beckett, Chesterton and Joyce - were irritated at having to beg Francis-Hawkins's permission for petty items of expenditure, and quarrelled with Francis-Hawkins's selection of men for junior posts. As Francis-Hawkins gathered his own aides - B.D.E. Donovan, a schoolmaster, and U.A. Hick, a retired army officer - a state of near civil war broke out at National Headquarters. Within the Movement there were rumours of favouritism and even of promotion based on homosexual friendships; for the latter there is no evidence, but the fact that such rumours could spread was indicative of low morale if not of morals. … The secret of Francis-Hawkins's influence must have been his unquestioning loyalty, a quality to which Mosley attached high value when so many were leaving him."

The Fascists in Britain, op. cit.

"The chief organisation men were Neil Francis-Hawkins, the Director-General from 1935 onwards, and Bryan Donovan, his assistant. Francis-Hawkins, a fat surgical instrument salesman, with a British Fascist background in the 1920s, was a first class administrator and brought much-needed order to British Union's affairs, following the Forgan régime. He drove himself unceasingly, working 12 hours a day, expected others to do so and thereby caused much wife-trouble at NHQ. His loyalty to Mosley was a byword. … Between the politicals and the bureaucrats a perpetual battle raged in the Policy Directorate, a group of senior officials appointed by Mosley to thrash out major policy questions. The central issue was whether the energies & resources of the movement should best go to building up the organisation or to mounting a more radical propaganda. For Joyce, Beckett and Chesterton, Mosley was far too cautious. They disliked the BUF's half-hearted anti-Semitism and wanted to make it a central issue. They also intensely disliked its military aspects, the uniforms and saluting, which they saw as emanations of Francis-Hawkins's tidy, bureaucratic mind, as well as Mosley's megalomania. Mosley tried to hold the balance, but he tended to come down on Francis-Hawkins's side. In return, he was rewarded with unswerving loyalty; and it is true to say that he kept the allegiance of the bureaucrats far better than that of the political individualists for whom the BUF in the end provided an inadequate vehicle for their ideas & ambitions."

Oswald Mosley, op. cit.

With regard to the suggestions of homosexuality, Nigel Farndale is unequivocal in his biography of Joyce and his first wife:

"[Maxwell] Knight [head of MI5] secretly applauded the anti-Semitism of Joyce and Mosley and often made anti-Semitic jokes, regardless of the company. He was possibly also attracted by another aspect of Blackshirt life: Black House was a haven for gay men: Neil Francis-Hawkins, Director General of the BUF was an active homosexual. It may also have been that conservative-minded gays and lesbians felt socially excluded to some degree so as a compensation they exaggerated their conservatism in order to feel included."

Haw-Haw: The Tragedy etc., op. cit.

34 **MEN IN FASCISM;** ***The Fascist Week, no. 17, Mar 2-8, 1934; page 5:***

"**NEIL FRANCIS-HAWKINS**. Has been a Fascist by conviction for many years. Joined the New Party early in 1931, and was one of the first members of the British Union of Fascists. Starting in the ranks he was among the nucleus of foundation members responsible for planning the organisation of the Movement. His ability in this direction brought him rapid promotion and he is now an Area Administrative Officer. Was for some time Adjutant of the National Defence Force, taking complete charge in Mr. Piercy's absence. Is now Officer-in-Charge of Organisation of the London Area."

35 Courtesy of Jeffrey Wallder:

HO 144/20144

This is somewhat at variance with Dr. Wise's assessment [although to be fair, not all of Wilfred's staff were necessarily based at Northumberland Street]:

"These [local branches] were all controlled from 17 Northumberland Street where a full-time Northern regional organiser and nine other staff were based. The BUF North West Office was re-organised on 1st January 1936. The staff then expanded to five senior BUF officers each with their own personal secretary; two to three accounts clerks; one press officer; two to three mail and register clerks; one van driver and four orderlies and messengers.†

Two of the senior staff were William [sic] Risdon and A Findlay. Another was Dick Bellamy. … He returned to Britain in the early 1930s and was shocked by the poverty and conditions he found. Within a few months of its foundation Bellamy joined the BUF and eventually became Senior Staff Officer in charge of Northern Headquarters in Northumberland Street."

†Fascism and Fascists in Britain in the 1930s: a Case Study of Fascism in the North of England in a Period of Economic and Political Change, *S. Rawnsley, [unpublished PhD thesis, University of Bradford], cited in FASCISM IN MANCHESTER, op. cit.*

36 ***The Blackshirt, no. 96, February 22nd, 1935, page 12:***

"THE LEADER IN SOUTHPORT FENCING BOUT

Branch's First Annual Dance; LARGE NUMBER OF VISITORS

Held at the Palace Hotel, Birkdale, the first annual dance of the Southport branch was a great success, a feature being the number of non-members who attended to see the Leader give a fencing display. …

Shortly after ten o'clock the Palace Blue Rhythm Band, under Don Bowden, struck up 'Onward, Blackshirts' and the Leader appeared, clad in regulation white fencing kit. …

Later in the evening he made a short speech, stressing the progress which the Movement is making. Amongst the large number of visitors present were A.A.O. Risdon, Commandant Findlay, A.A.O. Plathen, P.O. Broad, A.O. Wright and Mrs. Wright, D.A.O. Collins, and many officers and members from other branches, with their friends. A pleasing feature was the subsequent signing of a number of new members, both Lady Mosley and the Leader having several conversations with interested people during the evening."

37 ***The Blackshirt, no. 110, May 31st, 1935, page 8:***

"BLACKSHIRT NEWS

The Following are Extracts from Local Reports

Burnley The eagerly awaited visit of Maud Lady Mosley to Burnley took place on Saturday, May 18. She was met by a guard of honour, headed by the group organiser and unit leader. A.A.O. Risdon, A.O. Wright, and P.O.s Rimington and Lyall were also present.

In a few well-chosen words Lady Mosley expressed her thanks and appreciation for the beautiful bouquet and address of welcome, presented to her by members of the branch. In their speeches Lady Mosley and Mr. Risdon emphasised the necessity for more canvassing, and the members are doing their utmost to carry out the wishes of the Leader."

38 ***The Blackshirt, no. 113, June 21st, 1935, page 8:***

"BLACKSHIRT NEWS

The Following are Extracts from Local Reports

Liverpool On the evening of Wednesday, June 5, the Liverpool branch and its membership were honoured by a visit from the Leader. Sir Oswald, who was accompanied by A.A.O. Francis-Hawkins, Director of Blackshirt Organisation, A.A.O. Risdon, and Commandant Findlay arrived at 9 p.m., and was greeted by a storm of applause from enthusiastic Liverpool Blackshirts. Addressing first the entire membership, the Leader drove home the necessity for organising in wards. He afterwards discussed local conditions with the Liverpool officers."

39 ***The Blackshirt, no. 67, August 3rd, 1934, page 10:***

"Heard At Headquarters, By Blackshirt; SOMETHING ABOUT WORDS

Words are the weapons, as well as the plaything, of the gossip writer, so if at times I seem a little harsh with some of you people let it be for the good of your souls.

'Bill' Risdon, Director of Propaganda, ought to know something about words. Not long ago he told me his propaganda officers were holding more than a thousand street-corner meetings a week. They each speak for an hour at the rate of 120 words a minute, and answer questions for another hour."

40 ***The Blackshirt*, *no. 70, August 24th, 1934, page 6***

41 ***Ibid., page 7***

42 ***The Blackshirt, no. 71, August 31st, 1934, page 1:***

"Two summonses against the Editor of the ***Daily Worker*** were issued at Old Street Police Court on Friday last on the application of Mr. William Joyce, Director of Propaganda of the British Union of Fascists, who made allegations against the editors [sic] of incitement to violence and a breach of the Public Meetings Act of 1908."

"The last big rally before the Movement became anti-Semitic was in September 1934 at Hyde Park ... William Joyce was in charge of the arrangements and three days before the rally he unsuccessfully prosecuted the Daily Worker at Bow Street for 'incitement to violence' in urging anti-Fascists to counter-demonstrate ..."

The Fascists in Britain, op. cit.

43 ***Ibid., page 10***

44 Both periodicals carried exactly the same article:

"Dr. Forgan has sent us the following statement for publication:

Mr. Rex Tremlett, Deputy-Director of Publications, Editor of the ***Fascist Week*** and the ***Blackshirt***, has resigned these positions for reasons of health.

Mr. Tremlett had a severe breakdown at the end of last year, consequent on the strain of overwork on behalf of the movement during the summer and autumn months. He returned to his duties in January, but latterly has been in indifferent health and feels the necessity of a prolonged holiday and rest.

The Leader, therefore, has reluctantly accepted his resignation.

Mr. Tremlett joined the movement in the spring of last year and threw himself wholeheartedly into the varied activities of the organisation. He was appointed Assistant Editor of the ***Blackshirt***.

In November last he founded the ***Fascist Week***, and in the last few months he has been Editor of both journals. In addition, he has had full responsibility for the whole of the Publications Department and has performed most of the Press publicity work of the movement.

On his recovery he hopes to be able to resume his work for the movement in other directions, and he will carry with him the best wishes of all for a speedy recovery to his normal state of health."

The Blackshirt, no. 56, May 18-24th, 1934, page 2

The Fascist Week, no. 28, May 18-24th, 1934, page 3 [with photo]

Keeley, with a perhaps incautious reliance upon Special Branch and MI5 reports as his main source of material, quotes Tremlett as saying that he resigned his post because he refused to work with "cads, thieves and swine" any longer, and that he had been one of the "[m]ore promising ones [who] were improperly utilized and often left in disgust."

Special Branch Report, HO/20142/240 [undated], cited in BLACKSHIRTS TORN:, op. cit.

45 This was a rather highbrow piece, entitled "If you want to be a speaker", including classical references and the comical lines "male speakers will derive some advantage from a decent haircut and the avoidance of exotic hirsute appendages.", and "Monocles should not be worn."!

The Blackshirt, no. 54, May 4th-10th, 1934, page 1

46 He continues:

"One of their methods was to attack all officers of the Departments presided over by Joyce and Risdon. One of these officers was A. K. Chesterton whose vitriolic pen was often stimulated by liquor. I do not suggest Chesterton got drunk, but merely that he liked his liquor good and often. In this respect I plead guilty myself, but perhaps I am a little more capacious in that respect: longer experience perhaps. At the time of which I speak, Beckett and Leaper were - 'as thick as thieves'."

The Streets are still, op. cit.

Miles is being somewhat disingenuous here [as opposed to Wilfred's loyal avoidance of the issue, see **Appendix D**], because Chesterton was sent to the Royal Bethlem Hospital in early April 1935, "chronically inebriated" [if the Special Branch report is to be believed], and yet "Mosley would not entertain the suggestion of dismissing or demoting the man he regarded as his ablest propagandist."

Special Branch Report, HO 20144/74, 11/04/35, cited in BLACKSHIRTS TORN:, op. cit.

Joyce also had troubles of a more personal nature: at the end of 1934, Joyce's wife Hazel had an affair with Eric Piercy, the head of I Squad, the élite section of the Defence Force and effectively Mosley's personal bodyguard; Hazel became pregnant, which obviously would have caused unwelcome gossip at headquarters and distinct embarrassment beyond, so to remove the protagonist from the situation, Mosley took Piercy out of Black House by appointing him Chief Inspector of Branches. Unfortunately, in the circumstances, Joyce already had a daughter, Heather. After Joyce and Hazel separated, Joyce moved in with a colleague, Angus Macnab; their paths had crossed when they had been put jointly in charge of the public speaking classes at NHQ. Macnab was a gifted translator of Latin & Greek poetry, and the two men amused themselves by conversing in Latin.

Haw-Haw: The Tragedy of William and Margaret Joyce, by Nigel Farndale

47 According to Robert Skidelsky, Mosley put it very simply:

"Give a man a job to do; sack him if he fails."

Oswald Mosley, op. cit.

48 It is unclear whether this is a quote from John Beckett, but it could be:

"Raven Thomson [the BUF ideologue and philosopher] is a dangerous idiot who frothed about the Jews and boasted that he would soon be elected and giving orders … Beckett … confided [to whom?] that he felt so exasperated at the incompetence and lack of realism …"

"The security services", cited in The Rebel who lost his Cause, op. cit.

49 ***The Rebel who lost his Cause, op. cit.***

50 Robert Skidelsky tells us that:

"From the end of 1934, the BUF switched its propaganda line to the Jew as the power behind the throne. The main theme which was worked into all Mosley's 'bread and butter' speeches is that at the root of all the proximate sources of distress lurks 'international Jewish finance ..."

Oswald Mosley, op. cit.

51 ***Ibid.:***

"The BUF ... got under way without an anti-Jewish policy but with a number of anti-Semites in its ranks - William Joyce was the most notable recruit in this category. Its intensely nationalist 'Britain for the British' line gained it further support among a group of people who were disposed to dislike foreign immigrants, of whom the Jewish community at that time formed the largest number, and to associate them with unsavoury crimes and antisocial practices ..."

The Rebel who lost his Cause, op. cit.

One author seems to think that Joyce "accrued increasing power" within the organisation partly as a result of some affinity between him and Mosley, describing him as "Mosley's closest friend in the BUF", and that "Mosley's new anti-Semitic line also doubtless reflected the influence of radical anti-Semites – the likes of Chesterton, Joyce, and Beckett – at the party's inner core." It is very probably true that Joyce was talked about, although most likely in private, as a possible successor to Mosley, given the latter's intermittent poor health, but real friendship [in my opinion] played very little part in this: Mosley was undoubtedly gregarious, especially with like-minded individuals in a work context, but he saw no conflict between his intellectual analysis of problems and his impetus for action, whereas Joyce was avowedly anti-intellectual, ironically so given his lofty prose which was littered with classical references, and Mosley instinctively felt more comfortable socialising with other members of his social *milieu*, such as Bob Boothby and his future brother-in-law 'Fruity' Metcalfe, notwithstanding their divergent political views, although he did have great respect for Raven Thomson: "Intellectually Raven Thomson towered above the men I had known in the Labour Cabinet of 1929, and in firmness of character he seemed in an altogether different category to most of the contemporary politicians." [***My Life, op. cit.***].

Beyond the Pale, op. cit., cited in BLACKSHIRTS TORN:, op. cit.

The same author also cites a Special Branch report of 27th June 1934 as the source for Joyce having "his sights set on Ian Hope Dundas' [sic] position as chief of staff", so perhaps Wilfred's deposition was an unfortunate consequence of Joyce's expediently enforced gradated rise in the Movement?

Special Branch Report, 27/06/34; HO 144/20141/84, cited in ibid.

This perception that Joyce was more self-serving than dutiful in his aspirations was also seeping out into the wider Movement: a respected Branch Officer, G. S. Gerault, submitted a report to Mosley, "in the aftermath of Olympia", perhaps to alleviate Mosley's barely concealed depression, expressing distinct reservations about Joyce and his obvious preference for Hitler over Mussolini:

"'It should be realised that the country is 95% against Hitler. ... There is an undoubted feeling throughout the Movement that the Leader is being jockeyed either knowingly or unknowingly into an impossible position by Assistant Administrative Officer Joyce; and there are those who say that he is now, to all intents & purposes, the Movement. This feeling is intensified when members see pamphlet after pamphlet on policy appearing over this officer's signature; when they should either be anonymous or signed by the Leader.'

Confronted by this, Mosley could hardly continue to claim that he was too busy to be able to know what was going on. ... When Joyce was informed of the criticisms of him and his pamphlet [on India; published at the end of July 1934] he reacted in a way which seems to have become increasingly typical of those with influence at headquarters; he went to the Deputy Leader [Dr. Forgan] and complained that there was a 'plot' against him. ... Announcements were made about reforms and the strengthening of discipline; but what the public saw was mainly the style of Joyce taking over."

Beyond the Pale, op. cit.

52 ***Britain between the Wars 1918-1940, by Charles Loch Mowat:***

"One such policy, devaluation [thereby aiding the attempt to regulate trade in the interests of recovery], had little lasting effect. Sudden fluctuations in exchange rates were prevented by the Exchange Equalisation Fund, opened in July 1932; but the attempt to use it also to buy gold and keep the Pound down in value was countered by the new government in the United States, under president F. D. Roosevelt, which revalued the gold reserve and devalued the Dollar in 1933. The fund was later used against the Franc, until France went off gold in September 1936 and joined a tripartite agreement with Great Britain and the US to use equalisation funds to maintain stability. Actually, the Pound, which fell from $4.85 to $3.37 after devaluation, rose to $5.13 and settled down to around $4.99 by the end of 1933. ..."

53 ***Ibid.:***

"Two things stand out in the recovery of the 1930s: increasing consumption and the development of the home market, and the consumer and service industries. These were the tendencies of the 1920s. The Depression made remarkably little difference and any setback had been more than made good by 1934. The cost of living fell heavily in the 1930s, thanks to the fall in world commodity prices, but wage rates fell very little; consumption by the working classes fell only slightly and by 1934 had recovered to the level of 1929. In spite of the low incomes of the unemployed and of workers on short time the real income of the working classes was on the increase. For the middle classes the increase in spendable income between 1929 and 1932 was greater than for the working classes, but their consumption was not greatly affected."

54 http://douglassocialcredit.com/resources/resources/major_douglas'_proposals_for_a_national_dividend.pdf

55 Douglas had been working on his theories for restructuring of the national economy since the first world war:

> "It is hardly necessary to draw attention to the insistence with which we are told that in order to pay for the war we must produce more manufactured goods than ever before ..."

The Delusion of Super-Production; C. H. Douglas, The English Review, December 1918;

http://douglassocialcredit.com/douglas.php#writings

> "When two opposing forces of sufficient magnitude push transversely at either end of a plank – or problem – it revolves: there is Revolution ..."

What is Capitalism?; C.H. Douglas, The English Review, XXIV (1919): pp. 166-69;

http://douglassocialcredit.com/douglas.php#writings

56 The Social Credit movement still exists and offers practicable solutions:

http://douglassocialcredit.com/index.php

57 ***BLACKSHIRTS TORN:, op. cit.***

58 Box had joined the New Party after the rift in July 1931, when Allan Young and John Strachey left [see Chapter 3], and he immediately became a member of the Executive, combining his rôle of Chief Agent with Young's former rôle as National Secretary.

Oswald Mosley and the New Party, by Matthew Worley

59 ***The Rebel who lost his Cause, op. cit.***

60 **Fascism and Fascists in Britain in the 1930s: A Case Study of Fascism in the North of England in a Period of Economic and Political Change*; Stuart J. Rawnsley, University of Bradford, PhD Thesis, cited in BLACKSHIRTS TORN:, op. cit.***

61 ***The Streets are still, op. cit., cited in Left Wing Fascism in Theory, 20th Century British History, vol. 13, pt. 1, pp. 38-61, 2002, Oxford University Press***

62 ***Ibid.***

63 ***Special Branch Report, HO 144/20145/236, 03/07/35, cited in Left Wing Fascism, op. cit.***

64 ***BLACKSHIRTS TORN:, op. cit.***

65 ***Special Branch Report, HO 144/20144/46-8, 09/05/35, cited in ibid.***

The BUF was also up against many alternatives that were available around the country for unemployed workers, which were mostly voluntary [although attendance was sometimes "encouraged"], and which varied in their appeal, so Wilfred definitely had his work cut out for him; Charles Loch Mowat details these quite comprehensively in chapter 9 [*The Secret People and the Social Conscience: the Condition of Britain in the 1930s*] of his work ***Britain Between the Wars 1918-1940 [op. cit.].***

66 ***Oswald Mosley, op. cit.***

67 ***The Blackshirt, no. 112, June 14th, 1935, page 1***

68 Howe Street is the other side, the western side, of Bury New Road to

Northumberland Street and, in fact, it is debatable whether both of these addresses should more accurately be described as being in Kersal Dale, instead of Higher Broughton; number 31 Howe Street is the penultimate house in a terrace of charming, if unprepossessing modest size houses with decent sized front gardens [it is interesting that a recent photograph, available on Google Streetview, shows this garden as having significantly more vegetation than any of its near neighbours: this is not obviously or easily attributable to Wilfred, of course], bay windows and single dormers in the roof. It seems most likely, extrapolating from information available from the Land Registry, that Wilfred rented this house: there is no record in the file for this property of a transfer in Wilfred's name. This information came to light on the transfer deed for the sale of 70, Torrington Road, which will be enlarged upon in Chapter 13; it seems odd that his address of seven years prior to this one should have been a necessary inclusion, although perhaps that was a 'legal' requirement.

Courtesy of Graham Cole at the Land Registry, Durham office.

69 ***The Rebel who lost his Cause, op. cit.***

70 ***Ibid.***

71 ***The Fascists in Britain, op. cit.***

72 **"Branch Officers should cut this out and retain it for reference":**

"**BUILDING THE BLACKSHIRT VOTE**
Arrangements For Intensive Campaign
By JOHN BECKETT

...

Like all the bunkum of the old parties, the difficulties of electoral work are greatly exaggerated. With a few simple rules any enthusiastic Fascist, guided by commonsense and a gift of leadership, can beat the old, paid party hacks at their own game. See that your branch begin now to build the machine which will bring power to British Fascism."

The Blackshirt, no. 62, July 6th, 1934, page 5

73 ***The Blackshirt, no. 67, August 3rd, 1934, page 4***

74 Individuals, who were not acting under the official banner of the Manchester Labour Party and Trades Council, but who demonstrated against the meeting, "according to an anti-Fascist handbill that was distributed in the vicinity of Belle Vue", were officials of the NUR, T & GW Altogether Builders, ETU, Amalgamated Union of Upholsterers, Tailors' and Garment Workers' Union, Ashphalters' [sic] Union, Amalgamated Machine Grinders and Glaziers, GMW[U] and the Bleachers' and Dyers, Foremen's Guild'.

The Blackshirt, no. 76, October 5th, 1934, page 6

75 The article is too long to quote in full, and will be dealt with in context in the next chapter; the theme was enlarged upon over the following year, and finally released as a pamphlet under Wilfred's name, which is reproduced in **Appendix G**, but an excerpt from the original article is appropriate here:

"POWER ACTION OF FASCISM - MEMBERS STAND BY THEIR UNIONS

By W. Risdon

The history of Trade Unions presents to us a picture of the constant swinging of a pendulum – Industrial Action – Political Action – Industrial Action – Political Action – the two phases replacing one another with monotonous regularity, and, what is more to the point, both in turn failing with the same monotonous regularity.

Industrial action works out in practice to be strike action. It is my contention, and it has always been my contention, that strikes are futile. The only time when a strike could be successful would be a time when a 'boom' is in being and markets rising. At such a period concessions are granted in response to the **threat** of a strike without that threat being put into effect.

In modern times, however, the great majority of trade disputes are fights in defence of existing standards when, during periods of depression, those standards are threatened with reductions. In such circumstances a strike is able to achieve little or nothing which will be of benefit to the workers concerned."

The Blackshirt, no. 132, November 1st, 1935, page 2

8: POWER ACTION AND ACTION PRESS

In many respects, the Abyssinian crisis of mid-1935 was a godsend for Mosley: the British Union of Fascists was created from the *débâcle* of the New Party for the same reason the earlier organisation was brought into existence; namely, to present a solution to the economic crisis currently gripping Great Britain, but with a more specific focus on the political methods which appeared to be achieving some measure of success in Italy and Germany; so the combination of inevitable lack of consensus and ironically oxymoronic war-mongering by the 'pacifists' in the ineffectual League of Nations gave Mosley the opportunity to beat the drum [literally] for peace at home, with a policy which was a combination of non-intervention, and societal improvements that were possible by concentrating on British interests alone. A campaign was launched in ***The Blackshirt*** at the end of August 1935, highlighting the two-pronged approach of the campaign; it was headlined "MIND BRITAIN'S BUSINESS", but with a sub-heading "The Leader's Campaign of Peace Meetings" [**1**]. It also introduced the new 'corporate logo', the Circle and Flash, although somewhat embarrassingly, it was printed upside down, with the lightning appearing to emanate from the ground up!

All of the top echelon BUF speakers were out doing the rounds that summer, spreading the message of peace, with the notable exception of Wilfred; perhaps he was working intensively on his Trade Union criticisms, as mentioned at the end of the previous chapter, but as seems common for all the senior BUF officers, he was no doubt also involved in other relevant activities, not least propaganda, despite the crossover into spheres of influence of his colleagues; he was also working on an electoral agent's training course: see below. He must surely have arranged the Leader's meeting at the Manchester Free Trade Hall on September 1st, but the administrative situation in Manchester was becoming somewhat confused: a reference was made to "Propaganda Headquarters, Manchester", with no other indications as to its location, in ***The Blackshirt*** in early October [**2**], but within 3 months, there was a mention of a "Northern Headquarters" in Corporation Street, Manchester, which was the result of the country being divided up into northern and southern "zones" [**3**].

Restructuring of a Movement such as this was not unusual or unexpected, but this latest change was also perhaps an unintentional result of the internal strife which characterised most of 1935 within the BUF; virtually none of the top echelon officers escaped criticism or censure from the Leader, so whether by happenstance or by design, Wilfred did well to 'keep his head down' as much as possible during this somewhat acrimonious phase of the Movement's existence, including, for which Wilfred can surely not have been held in any way responsible, "the recent breakdown of the propaganda department" [4]; perhaps also, he was pragmatic enough to realise that staying in Mosley's 'good books', especially after his recent alleged episode of rebellion, made very good sense, if this should be possible without having to compromise his principles to any extent. As mentioned previously [see Chapter 7, note 72], there was a major canvass under way by the Movement, as there was a general election expected later that year, but as it drew near, conscious of the Movement's unpreparedness in that area, Mosley decided, probably very wisely, that the Movement would not contest any seats at all [although there was some speculation about Mosley himself contesting either Ormskirk in Lancashire or Evesham, Worcestershire **5**], adopting the slogan "Fascism Next Time", which first saw the light of day at the end of October [**6**].

Wilfred's polemic on the ineffectuality of the current Trades Union setup and the Labour politicians whom it sponsored, no doubt influenced to a very high degree by his recent experience in recruiting new members for the BUF in Lancashire, not many of whom will have been union members, appeared the very next week. It was not an exhortation for workers to join Trades Unions so that they could change them from within; rather it was a brief illustration of how support for the BUF would confer upon them the "'Power Action' of Fascism" which would "be applied by the workers themselves through the Corporate machinery of the Organised State". Although it was Wilfred's contention that strikes were "futile", if "strike action is called for, (failing a better weapon) to defend the status of members of their own industry", by "[t]hose of our members who are trade unionists [and] are loyal trade unionists", "they will stand by their fellows in their own industry, not because they think the strike to be the ideal weapon but because they know that when up against it the least they can do is to fight, and until better weapons are placed in their hands they will fight loyally with such weapons as they have." These "better weapons" would be found in the "'Power Action' of Fascism" [**7**]. If it should come to a 'general strike', as it had in 1926, the members of the BUF, Wilfred reliably informed them, would be "dead against it"; the second, but more doctrinal reason against it being that it "ceases to be industrial and becomes political. The attack of a 'general strike' is an attack upon the State, not an attack upon the employers of a given industry. Fascism is always prepared to defend the State, and could not in any circumstances lend itself to an attack on the fabric of the State as a whole." [**8**] If workers were prepared to accommodate that circumscription, then their future under the coming Corporate State would be assured. In a shorter article in the same issue of ***The Blackshirt***, headlined "Fascist Industrial Policy", the Leader was quoted as also making reference to the term "Power Action", which was used as a sub-heading to the article [**9**]. This does allow an inference that he did not originate the expression, but that he was prepared to embrace it, and propagate it, for the greater good of the Movement.

It is difficult to be certain when Wilfred's tenure at Manchester came to an official end; as the autumn of 1935 moved towards winter, he was more visible, in terms of public appearances, and most, but not all, were in the north of England: he spoke at Lancaster on November 8th [at an indoor meeting where the audience was described as "small but appreciative"], Ripon on the 10th, and Darlington ["prolonged applause"] on the 12th [**10**]. Exceptions to this continuity were the meeting Wilfred had at the Kennard Hall, Cardiff: this is most likely to have been on Sunday, November 3rd; and the Pump Room, Tunbridge Wells, on Monday, November 4th [**11**], so perhaps he was getting back to his earlier, countrywide, roving brief. There was also another meeting to organise for Mosley at the Free Trade Hall on the 6th of November, which was "another triumph. ... Hundreds failed to gain admission." [**12**]. The Leader was engaged in another frenetic round of speaking, at locations as diverse as Newcastle upon Tyne, Stoke on Trent, and Shoreditch, but it obviously made sense for Wilfred to arrange the Free Trade Hall meetings, given his experience and the fact that he was 'on hand'.

In the November 29th edition of ***The Blackshirt***, Wilfred reasserted his position in the top echelon by broadening out the Trades Union discussion, saying that: "Since writing my recent article on 'Power Action' I have been asked for something in greater detail showing how Power Action is built up and how it functions.", in an article entitled "WHICH WILL YOU HAVE - The "Power Action" of FASCISM or the Farce of Present Day politics? W. RISDON outlines the FASCIST SYSTEM". This headline was perhaps an overstatement [the final sentence of which he was not personally responsible for], and somewhat misleading; although he was, ostensibly, a loyal member of British Union, he did not think of himself, first and foremost, as a Fascist, but British Union was, by definition, a fascist organisation, so that is what he had to be, and be seen to be; also, the article was not dealing with the fascist system as a whole [a multi-faceted philosophy], but the aspect of it which was most relevant to working people, whether Trades Union members or not, and that was the Corporate State. This strategic subject was usually the speciality of the BUF's chief ideologist, Alexander Raven Thomson, when the Leader himself was not dealing with it, so for Wilfred to be able to make official pronouncements about it, while not necessarily a privilege, was not an opportunity which was generally open to rank & file members, who nonetheless had to be informed about the details of it for their speeches and the inevitably consequent questions.

At the end of that year, a photograph was published on the front page of ***The Blackshirt***, albeit down in the bottom right hand corner, which had the look of an annual class or company record; the epitome of fascist utilitarianism was that there was no caption, other than a helpful listing of the names of those thus depicted, and all of the participants had resolute, if not grimly fixed expressions: no easy smiles in evidence. Perhaps reassuringly for

Wilfred, he was situated on the front row, on Mosley's left [biblical connotations notwithstanding!], between the Director General, Neil Francis-Hawkins, and William Joyce who, ironically, was on the far left [although, as ever, it is a matter of viewpoint: from the reader's point of view, Joyce was on the far right], although it is entirely possible that there was a similarly utilitarian reason for this placement. The ordering of the back row is obviously a matter of physical stature, so John Beckett, being a tall man, was immediately to the left of the tallest man, noticeably so, Robert Gordon-Canning, and William Leaper, currently editor of ***The Blackshirt***, but who was soon to lose his position to Beckett [**13**], was on the far left, behind Joyce. The photograph certainly seems to confirm Wilfred's status in the BUF, but as much as at any other time in the history of the Movement, changes were still taking place; it was continuing to evolve.

The first major development of 1936 was the confirmation of Francis-Hawkins as Director General, effectively of the whole organisation, but with the qualification "of Organisation", the body which actually controlled the Movement, thus marking the zenith of his arguably meteoric rise within British Fascism [**14**]; as previously mentioned, for "administrative purposes" the country was divided into two zones, "Northern and Southern, the Northern to be controlled from Northern Headquarters, 26, Corporation Street, Manchester." [**15**] There was no mention of number 17, Northumberland Street, which presumably remained as a local headquarters for the central Manchester BUF, as part of the stable of properties owned by the BUF Trust Ltd. Wilfred's next speech, just over a week before the next publicly momentous event for the organisation, the reappearance of a name from the past, ***Action***, was 'in-house', as it were, for the Westminster (Abbey) branch, and it was on a subject dear to his heart, politically, to which he would return with increasing regularity: electoral organisation [**16**].

There was another minor glitch in Wilfred's career at this time however, which, although it might have seemed relatively trivial in itself at the time, possibly lost him a few more 'Brownie points' in Mosley's eyes, in as much as it could be construed as an expression of individuality, not something that was encouraged in Fascism. As mentioned above, the Movement had undergone some restructuring in an attempt to make it more streamlined and efficient: the previous year, Mosley's well-intentioned bifurcation of the Movement into Political Organisation and the Blackshirts had not gone smoothly, in that the PO had failed to establish itself at the local level; consequently, within only a few months [arguably too soon, but 'action' was always the byword] he decided that the entire district organisation would operate under the control of the Blackshirt Organisation, and that Political Organisation would operate solely in an advisory capacity, providing District Officers with specific instruction on political matters [**17**]. However, no differentiation was to be allowed between

Blackshirts and political members [including Executive Officers]: all were expected to undertake political work [**18**].

It was also decided that a real incentive was needed for the membership, to encourage active participation and reward them accordingly, the main manifestation of that being initially a more visible and accessible career path within the Movement. The rank & file membership was divided into three sections: division one comprised members who gave five nights' service per week; division two was those giving two nights every week; and division three was composed of non-active recruits: "a mass of members of people [sic] supporting but not necessarily active in the movement." [**19**] This was sufficiently galvanising to produce doubled sales of ***The Blackshirt*** by the end of June 1935, and that no doubt encouraged the Publications Department to press ahead with plans for a second newspaper, which also embodied [again] a separation to some extent of the internal and external profiles of the BUF. The short-lived New Party had only had one publication, the even shorter-lived ***Action***, and for over half of the life of the BUF, up until the end of June 1935, it had managed with one newspaper, ***The Blackshirt***; ***Fascist Week***, which had a run of 19 months, had been intended predominantly for the members, but it nevertheless had to be presentable enough for the public at large, as its first editorial made clear [**20**]; however, by May 1934, the cost of producing two papers, albeit of different size but with overlapping content, had become unsustainable, so it was decided to merge them [**21**]. Only a year later, this position was reversed, despite the cost implications.

The new publication was introduced with a sense of pragmatism: "Reports that we have received from Fleet Street have confirmed our belief that the paper is going to be good. Experts who have seen the "dummy" like it. They are expecting that we will spoil its sale, and therefore its existence, by converting it into a propaganda paper. They know, as everybody experienced in political journalism knows, that propaganda sheets are not the slightest bit of use for converting the multitudes. People buy papers to read, not to be instructed in politics." [**22**] There was even a certain humility: "You can help us with criticism. We welcome the critic who has something to say or something to suggest. The task of making ***Action*** a success does not rest with us alone. It is an effort for the whole Movement." [**23**] Another incentive which wasn't publicised in print, but which was nevertheless effectively communicated to the membership, was the privilege of wearing a new uniform [which had to be purchased: it was not provided *gratis*] cut in the style of the Brigade of Guards, the qualification for which was ostensibly the sale of a minimum [and, ideally, increasing] number of newspapers through street sales; since the publishing arm of the Movement now had the name Action Press Limited, the outfit quickly acquired the sobriquet "Action Press Uniform" [although there were others, less polite]. Somewhat confusingly, ***The Blackshirt*** continued to be published by Sanctuary Press Ltd., the name deriving from the Movement's address, Sanctuary Buildings, in Great Smith Street, Westminster.

Notwithstanding the public perception of a mass of members clad all in arguably ominous black, the wearing of uniform within the Movement had always been something of a bone of contention; Wilfred had happily worn the black shirt or fencing-style tunic [**24**], depending upon the occasion, on which the only permissible ostentation was the Movement's iconic symbol of the Fasces, and later, flash & circle badge, because he was aware of the benefit of a certain level of military discipline from his war service in the RAMC, and the distinctive shirt or tunic definitely would have been an asset at public meetings, as an aid to identification as & when trouble occurred; also, he undoubtedly enjoyed a shared sense of pride in belonging to a Movement which was actively seeking to catalyse a better society. However, quite early on, the élite section of the Fascist Defence Force, I Squad, had adopted breeches and riding boots with the fencing style tunic, which could only give a paramilitary appearance. Whether he accepted the argument that the black shirt facilitated a classless aspect of the Movement is another matter, as he must inevitably have been aware of the better cut and material used by more affluent members, which created some friction, as perceived by Wilfred's colleague Alex Miles, among others [**25**]. After the 1935 reorganisation, it became accepted for members of the 'political' wing, who would have included Wilfred, to wear plain clothes [also known colloquially in military circles as 'mufti'], presumably a lounge suit, at work, "although it was allowed that they might wear the undress shirt" [**26**], which would have been a plain black shirt with a conventional collar, and tie. This was to be supplemented when on BUF premises by the wearing of an "Executive Officer Brassard"; "a red armband with gold fasces with the words 'Executive Officer' to be worn on duty", which was introduced in BUF Standing Orders dated 20th December 1934 [**27**].

For Wilfred, however, the new uniform was a line he was not prepared to cross; despite its official description as a "police style uniform … its introduction led to more disputes within the Policy Committee. Beckett, Risdon and others argued that the simple black shirt had been in use long enough to be generally recognized [sic] and accepted. The new uniform would arouse unnecessary hostility." [**28**] In 1940 [see **Appendix D**] Wilfred assured the Appeals Committee that he "did strenuously object, and I refused ever to wear it because that struck me as being the introduction of militarism at least in form." When the chairman, Mr. Norman Birkett, KC, asked him if the uniform included the 'armlet', Wilfred reiterated: "Yes. I never wore that uniform, I refused ever to don it." [for a picture of the epaulette Wilfred would have been entitled to on his uniform tunic, as an Executive Staff Officer, follow the link from note 27] The armlet was scarlet, with a white flash in a blue circle on a white background, with a blue border, patriotically British colours; however, "from a distance it looked like the swastika armband of the Nazis." [**29**]; the biggest potential problem of the cumulative effect of riding boots [*aka* 'jackboots'], riding breeches, military tunic with "the chromium highlights of [a] belt-buckle" [**30**] and peaked cap [with more highlights of Fasces surmounted by flash-and-circle], all in black, but supplemented by the scarlet armlet, was that this would send out all the wrong signals.

Mosley was later somewhat coy about his own involvement with this perceived sinister development, and it depends upon one's viewpoint as to whether that should be construed as disingenuous, or not: "I accepted the invitation to wear it myself, in order to encourage others." In retrospect, he was either contrite or pragmatic, again debatable, admitting that it had been a "mistake … an error and a dereliction of duty" which combined with other circumstances to distance the Movement from the mass of the people he was trying to win over [**31**]. There was one area where the tactic didn't entirely miss, where the Movement had arguably its best mass support, and that was the East End of London, but the uniform did provoke significant disorder and violence from the opposition; nothing new, of course, but it was sufficient to precipitate a proscription which removed the mainstay of the Movement's identity. Before that though, there was a brief period of relative success. Mosley wore the new uniform for a meeting at Victoria Park, Bethnal Green, on Sunday June 7th, and spoke to "[a]n audience of over 100,000" [**32**]. There was no trouble, despite a somewhat half-hearted counter-demonstration, either at the meeting, or during the marches to and from it. There was, however, no mention in either of the Movement's papers immediately after a meeting two weeks previously, at the Carfax Assembly Rooms, Oxford, of when steel chairs were ripped up and thrown at the Blackshirt stewards, and a "notable indoor battle" was fought [**33**].

In fact, pretty much everywhere apart from the East End of London, there was trouble at British Union meetings that summer and autumn, predominantly the outdoor meetings and marches; Hull, on the 12th of July was particularly violent ["6 Blackshirts were knocked unconscious by iron bars while defending Mosley as he tried to address a huge crowd at the Corporation Field" **34**], and although it was more likely an over-reaction in the heat of the moment, rather than a genuine assassination attempt, the offside rear window of Mosley's car was penetrated by some sort of bullet in a side street [**35**]. The Movement had already apparently dropped any pretence of wanting to do anything other than emulate the 'Nazis' in Germany [**36**] when it changed its name from The British Union of Fascists to The British Union of Fascists and National Socialists, or British Union for short, which was confirmed in the Movement's constitution; this was actually more to Wilfred's liking: not the full name, but the shortened form, as he related to the 18B Appeal Hearing in 1940 [**Appendix D**]: "… it is interesting to note that the title "British Union" which is now the title of the Movement was the one I suggested as a better title at that time." However, it was the uniform which caused the politicians the most anger.

The Government had disliked the Blackshirt uniform from the very beginning: the BUF was certainly not the only political group to wear a coloured shirt at this time, but the black outfit, with its [to some] threatening appearance, notwithstanding the similarity to a police uniform, did give rise to suggestions of a 'private army': "[uniforms] definitely raised MPs' hackles" [**37**]. The Government decided that something must be done: current legislation was clearly not sufficiently effective; the catalyst was a march planned for the 4th of October, to support British Union's bid for electoral success in the East End [**38**], in the next year's municipal elections, and the march would stop in each ward putting up a candidate, to enable Mosley to give a speech. The "Battle of Cable Street" has passed down into folklore as a defeat for Mosley, but the name is a misnomer, as far as British Union was concerned. In the months preceding the march, British Union's relentless meetings and rallies 'provoked' the Jews and Communists, working together, into violent protests; on the day of the march, around 100,000 protesters [**39**], whose motto was "They shall not pass", would provide a warm 'welcome' for 3,000 Fascists [**40**]. Despite the windscreen of his Bentley being smashed, and being struck in the face by a stone, Mosley inspected the massed Blackshirts: 6,000 police were on hand to keep the peace [**41**].

The 'battle' ensued after Police Commissioner Sir Philip Game, with Home Secretary Sir John Simon's permission [**42**], decided that it would be far too dangerous for all concerned if the march proceeded beyond the Royal Mint, where the Fascists were currently assembled; Mosley dutifully acceded to Game's order to stand down; the protesters were not going to disperse so readily however, and violently resisted the police's efforts to dismantle the barricade which had been erected across Cable Street. One hundred people, including police, were injured, although fortunately, there was not a single death; eighty-three protesters were arrested [**43**]; the following day, Mosley travelled to Berlin for his marriage on the 6th to Diana Guinness [née Mitford], at the home of Joseph & Magda Goebbels, and at which Adolf Hitler was an honoured guest. Even though British Union was not directly responsible for the violence at Cable street, the Government was nervous enough to take a decisive step: a Public Order Bill was introduced into the House of Commons on the 10th of November; the following month it was added to the statute book as the Public Order Act. Skidelsky is in no doubt that "its critical provisions were directed specifically at fascist activities … as such it was a value judgement against fascism and in favour of its opponents" [**44**]; neither was there any doubt in Parliament: for example, the MP Lovat Fraser was quoted as saying "I hope that the action that we take tonight may crush Sir Oswald Mosley's movement." [**45**] It did not, but it was a definite setback; on the issue of uniforms, Wilfred had been proved right, but sadly, the banning of the uniform did not prevent further violent opposition: "in fact, the most violent outdoor clash in the 1930s took place after the banning of the uniform, on the route of Mosley's procession through Bermondsey … on the 4th of October, 1937 [the first anniversary of 'Cable Street'] … The one occasion when Mosley was injured at a political meeting [was] in November 1937 when his head was gashed open by a brick - also occurred after the passage of the Public Order Act" [**46**]. The last point is slightly contentious, because in truth, Mosley had been very lucky to escape serious injury before POA was enacted.

The priority now, for the Movement as a whole, but for Wilfred in particular, was the development of the electoral machine: since the spring of 1936, Wilfred had been Chief Agent for British Union; "a position of great responsibility, only to be held by a man of outstanding qualities." [**47**] ***The Blackshirt*** of the 4th of April declared that declared that a correspondence course for the training of election agents had been prepared: "The Leader has expressed the wish that all Fascist Agents will be found from within the ranks of the Movement, and the active co-operation of the Members in this training scheme will provide the Organisation with an adequate corps of skilled Agents for the tremendous task which lies ahead of us in our progress to power." [**48**] Wilfred was also corresponding personally with prospective trainees, signing himself as Chief Agent [**49**]. This didactic element, which suffused all of the Movement's work, notwithstanding the fascist ideology, about which Wilfred had cause for ambivalence, must have given him great satisfaction, and it also harked back to his socialist days, when worker education was seen as crucial: according to the ***Fascist Week*** of 22-28 December, 1933, he was an "Authority on politics and economics, expert in election law. Wrote for the Labour Party a treatise on Parliamentary election practice." [**50**], so understandably, he was very keen to put all that experience to good use.

By the end of 1936, Mosley had seen fit to consolidate the restructuring of the Movement with the introduction of a top level of Executive Officer, only 2 steps removed from the Leader himself: Assistant Director General, and Wilfred's position was sufficiently secure for him to be appointed Assistant Director General of Organisation, Electoral; a glowing tribute, accompanied by a photograph of him looking distinctly middle-aged, in the relatively new ***Action*** in January 1937, very possibly penned by the editor, John Beckett [who, otherwise, seemed strangely tight-lipped about him], stated that "'Bill' Risdon presents a strong challenge to this generalisation; [that i]t is often said that no man is indispensable in any organisation." [**51**] One of his subordinates was a Captain Erskine Atherley, who was "entrusted with the task of building a canvass organisation in all districts and providing training for potential canvassers. This is the real foundation of election machinery." [**52**] He was possibly one of the influx of ex-officers who were so resented by the rank & file socialists such as Alex Miles, but his provenance was quite similar to that of the contentious Box, so he should have been an able deputy for Wilfred. By this time, Wilfred's erstwhile colleague Miles was no longer in the organisation, but had requested readmittance late in 1936, even though inbetweentimes he had been fomenting anti-Fascist protests! [**53**]

Whilst electoral matters were naturally at the forefront of his efforts before the test of the municipal elections, albeit a localised test, Wilfred did not ignore his other favourite concern, union affairs, and in September, 1936, he wrote a long article in ***The Blackshirt*** about a dispute in an industry in an area which were both very familiar to him: coal mining in South Wales. The article, which, strangely, went under the byline of William Risdon [and bizarrely, this mistake was repeated several times], was entitled "The Fight Between The Rival Unions Is Causing A STORM OVER BEDWAS; Why Not One Big Union?" [**54**] It concerned the spurious dispute, as he saw it, between the Communist-controlled South Wales Miners' Federation [SWMF] and the "Company" union at the Bedwas pit that was owned by Sir Samuel Instone, who therefore personified "international finance", because he was Jewish, having changed his name in December, 1914, from Einstein; the crucial recourse for the miners, he argued, was to acknowledge and accept the "Power Action" of Fascism, which when "wielded by the miners themselves [would] solve the accumulated problems of 100 years of mis-management in the mines of Britain."

There was also a very real and persistent concern about a recurrence of international war, which, while not created by the Abyssinia conflict, had nonetheless been exacerbated by it [at the end of the previous May, ***The Blackshirt*** had very informatively printed a "Summary of [the] Abyssinian Dispute" **55**]; from time to time this concern was editorialised in British Union's publications, for example in February, 1937: the front page of ***Action*** displayed a photomontage below the banner headline "WHO WANTS WAR?" [**56**], and this policy would continue until the Movement's fears proved to be all too well founded. However, Wilfred's sights were set on elections; prior to his announcement about the decision to contest the municipal elections in east London, Mosley had made it clear, because of funding strictures, that any member wanting to stand as a Fascist candidate in a municipal contest would have to do so of his or her own volition, as an Independent, and that was the situation on November 2nd 1936, "Municipal election night", when Wilfred spoke at Winchester, apparently not in support of a local candidate. This was an outdoor meeting, quite probably because all of the appropriate halls would have been required for use as polling stations, but the "[a]udience [was] deeply interested in policy." [**57**] Evidently, a few Fascist candidates were successful, but it was kept very low-key, probably to avoid distracting from the official project [**58**].

During this period, Wilfred collated all of his experience in electoral matters in a small book, published by the Movement, called "***A Guide to***

Constituency Organisation" [**59**]; no doubt, the aforementioned treatise on Parliamentary election practice, written nearly ten years previously when he was still a card-carrying Socialist, would have formed the basis of this, albeit updated to reflect his current ideology and appropriate alterations to the relevant legislation. The book might have been small, but in broader terms, the subject of electoral correctness was vitally important to the Movement: in fact, one upon which Mosley was prepared for his whole future to depend, as the leader of a Movement sworn to uphold the British constitution, and to achieve power by legal and constitutional means, so not one in which any chances of legal ramifications, as a result of inaccuracy caused by ineptitude could be afforded, and the fact that it was entrusted to Wilfred, above anyone else in the Movement, was a ringing endorsement and recognition of his value to British Union, a direct consequence of his knowledge and experience.

The focus of the official project was the date of March 4th, 1937, and the campaign commenced in earnest on February 3rd, when Mosley spoke at Shoreditch, one of the three wards being contested [the other two being Limehouse and Bethnal Green], although each ward was allotted two British Union candidates. The Leader was not one of the candidates, but naturally he would have thrown his whole weight of personality and presence behind the campaign, especially with it being 'so close to home'. Before this, however, Wilfred was already busy with the crucial strategic background work, and on January 3rd, the first batch of prospective election agents sat their exam at national headquarters: out of those sitting, a total of nine candidates, including two women, were awarded a second class certificate as a result of achieving the requisite minimum of more than 75 out of a possible 100 points [**60**]; the next general election was not expected until 1939 at the earliest, or more likely 1940, so in theory it would allow for a well staged programme of agent education and appointment. A list of prospective parliamentary candidates was already being printed, with 'passport style' photographs in most cases, week by week in the British Union papers; however, the choices of candidates proved to be contentious, given the customary autocratic methods that were used [**61**].

There was always going to be antagonism between British Union supporters in the East End and the local Jewish population [although Skidelsky maintains that "most east Londoners were non-Jewish" **62**], but the thrust of the British Union campaign was not specifically, or even overtly anti-Semitic, although individual candidates might have ignored Mosley's exhortation of the previous October "to refrain from attacking the Jews at public meetings" [**63**]; according to ***Action*** of February 13th 1937, "THE BRITISH UNION ELECTION SLOGAN IN EAST LONDON" was "VOTE BRITISH", and the page of election information was accompanied by a photograph of Mosley in suitably pugnacious pose ["in fighting Mood"] leaning forward on a speaking platform with fist outstretched [**64**].

The candidates were: Limehouse, Charles Wegg Prosser and Mrs. Anne Brock Griggs; Bethnal Green North East, 'Mick' Clarke and Alexander Raven Thomson; and Shoreditch, William Joyce and Jim Bailey [**65**]. It would appear that Wilfred did not speak during this campaign: hardly surprising really, given how busy he must have been. Mosley's own speeches, which "drew thousands" [**66**], were devoted mainly to attacking the Labour Party for its inability to solve the housing problem, particularly acute in the East End; attacking the Communist slogan "Vote Labour and Save Madrid" [a reference to the Spanish civil war, which had broken out the previous July] with his own undeniably patriotic slogan "Vote British and Save London" [**67**].

The campaign was intense and lively, but notwithstanding the Jewish section of the population, it was hampered somewhat by the "unfavourable" composition of the municipal register: "it was confined to householders, which excluded not just [Mosley's] teenage supporters but young men & women in their early twenties who still lived with their parents, a not uncommon situation in a hugely overcrowded area." [**68**] Interpretations of the result vary, understandably, according to the affiliations of the commentator: according to John Beckett, who was "very bitter about the conduct of the campaign" [**69**], "[r]ight up to the count, Mosley, against all the evidence, was certain of victory, telling John the canvass results proved it." [**70**] Conversely, he wrote an article in ***Action***, published two days after polling day, entitled "A SUMMARY OF A GREAT BATTLE"! [**71**] As the ***Observer*** remarked [**72**], "True, none of their candidates was returned, but the size of their vote was a surprise even to those in touch with the East End." The results were: Bethnal Green, Raven Thomson 3,028 and Clarke 3,022 [23%]; Shoreditch, Joyce 2,564 and Bailey 2,492 [14.8%]; and Limehouse, Griggs and Wegg Prosser 2,086 each [16.3%], so not a landslide, but neither was it, as Francis Beckett characterised it, "an utter humiliation" [**73**].

As would be expected, Mosley put a brave face on the results: "Destiny has enabled the British Union in our first election fight to secure by far the best result yet recorded in any first fight of a Fascist and National Socialist Movement in any great country." [**74**] It would have been odd if Wilfred had not been given the opportunity to comment, although he had to suffer the indignity of another variant of his name ["William Risden, Chief Agent of the British Union"], but he was nevertheless engagingly buoyant, without being unrealistic: "What the [electoral] machine has done (in the recent L.C.C. elections) was eminently satisfactory. This was a real test, which was survived with flying colours."; and "Our machine is now an established fact. It has stood its first strain. Our workers have gained their first experience of elections." [**75**] Shortly [**76**] after this, at best, partial success, Mosley decided that the organisation could not sustain such a high number of salaried headquarters staff [although Cross gives the impression that they were not all based at NHQ 77]: this might seem counter-intuitive if he was, indeed, trying to build up a national electoral machine, even if, admittedly, a certain amount of organisational work could be carried out regionally; staff numbers were being slashed, by over one hundred [**78**], to be effective immediately. "The dismissed officers were to call at the office the next day to collect their outstanding wages." [**79**]

Mosley assumed, either naïvely, or blithely [or both], that most, if not all, of the redundants would take him up on his request to continue to work for the Movement on a voluntary basis; most did, according to Mosley himself [including his most capable ideologue, Raven Thomson **80**, who was at that time Director of Policy; a very senior position], but there were some, including a few very highly placed Executive Officers, who didn't. Wilfred was safe, for the time being at least: his function was currently crucial to the Movement's plans; his knowledge and experience, which combined with his oft-remarked accommodating personality [although not significant in allegedly meritocratic and utilitarian fascist ideology] ensured that he was currently effectively indispensable. Some interpreted Mosley's decision in very personal terms [**81**]: Joyce and Beckett, unsurprisingly, took it quite badly. Cross is rather hyperbolic about them in his assessment of this affair, but he is one of many commentators who interpret this action as tactical, not merely forced upon Mosley by economic constraints, which will be enlarged upon in the next chapter [**82**]. Although either one or both of them retained their membership, briefly [**83**], Joyce's departure was not widely opposed, however much he might have thought he had a loyal following: it is undoubtedly true that he was seen previously by some as a possible successor to Mosley as Leader and, again, opinions vary as to whether Joyce had considered usurping Mosley prior to his enforced redundancy [**84**]; but consequent to it, he tried to foment some sort of revolt within the Movement, which was unsuccessful [85]. He and Beckett then formed their own party, the National Socialist League, which was never a serious competitor for British Union, and Joyce transferred his allegiance and idolatry to Hitler [**86**].

As well as the redundancies, some of the premises were also dispensed with: Cross says that "[t]he Northern Command headquarters at Manchester was to be closed altogether." [**87**], but it is not clear whether he means the Corporation Street headquarters, which might have been rented, or Northumberland Street, Wilfred's previous base; according to Dr. Wise [**88**], number 17 Northumberland Street was sold in 1937 [or possibly early 1938] to a Jewish "furniture importer and wholesaler" on behalf of "the strictly orthodox Jewish community", somewhat ironic in the circumstances. Notwithstanding the alleged economic imperative, in retrospect Mosley's action ["this act of decentralisation as it was euphemistically described", as Skidelsky puts it **89**] would seem to be counterproductive, if not actually fallacious, if the regions didn't have the command structure or the premises to support it. However, thankfully, that was not Wilfred's concern. He was able to concentrate on his specialist areas, in a reasonably safe salaried post; nevertheless, he could hardly have been unaware of the ominous clouds which were gathering over international horizons, and in the coming months, he would have to play, undoubtedly quite willingly, a strongly supporting rôle in the increasingly urgent campaign to convince a lumpen public that another world war would be the inevitable outcome of their hesitation or, worse than that, their refusal to endorse Mosley's assessment of the auguries: had they done so, this would have, according to him, given him the authoritative voice, in the international arena, that could prevent the coming holocaust.

NOTES

1 ***The Blackshirt no. 123, August 30th, 1935, page 1***

2 ***The Blackshirt no. 129, October 11th, 1935, page 6:***

"**Manchester (East).**—A successful formation meeting was held at Propaganda Headquarters, Manchester, when Messrs. Simmonds and Jack explained to members of the East Manchester District the campaign plans for the extension of Fascism in the district.

Members volunteered for sales and propaganda work. The meeting can record a great stride forward in the creation of an important district in Manchester.

The district welcomes all unattached members who live East of Manchester (Ardwick and Gorton). They should communicate with East Manchester District, c.o. 17, Parkfield-street, Rusholme, Manchester."

3 ***The Blackshirt no. 142, January 10th, 1936, page 5:***

"... For administrative purposes the country is divided into two zones, Northern and Southern, the Northern to be controlled from Northern Headquarters, 26, Corporation Street, Manchester."

4 Again, the majority of this information comes from informers to the security services, so it must be treated with some circumspection, but it will probably be predominantly accurate:

"By the middle of July, conflict and dissent within the party's ranks was occurring with increased frequency, and Mosley had had enough of it. A minor complaint by the loose cannon, Budd, was the final straw. Mosley set up a court of inquiry, comprised of [sic] Major Lucas, Taylor, and Captain Reaveley to examine interparty [sic] strife. Written statements would be taken from witnesses and submitted to the leader.

The knives which some members had long been sharpening were now put to use. Not surprisingly, F. M. Box was the popular target. A.K. Chesterton blamed him as well as his deputy, Cleghorn, for impeding the movement and for provoking the ire of several officers, including Joyce, Beckett, Leaper, Donovan and Piercy. Joyce placed the blame for the recent breakdown of the propaganda department squarely on the shoulders of Box. Beckett criticized him for the improper working of the treasury, and Leaper accused Box of trying to make him look bad in Mosley's eyes.

The leader interviewed each of these men separately, and made it clear to them that Box had only been appointed as director-general in light of Robert Forgan's failure to keep the party on a sound financial footing. Now that Box had managed to get the party through a financially difficult period by instituting a rather unpopular retrenchment program, he and his deputy, Cleghorn, were mere political advisers on electoral issues. Mosley thus discredited the efforts of, and demoted his ablest political mind in order to keep the peace in his leadership cadre.

William Joyce must have been pleased with the outcome of the inquest, though he did not escape entirely unscathed. Once again the leader censured him for not holding enough meetings. It was noted that he should have held 300 national meetings between November 1934 and May 1935, but only held 70. Naturally, Joyce tried to pin the blame for this on Box, but Mosley was not convinced. Others were also scolded. In a July 11th meeting with his senior officers, Mosley reprimanded the treasury for meddling in political matters. John Thompson was upbraided for not heeding complaints about the department's dilatoriness. Cleghorn was also censured for his lack of tact. Mosley also criticized Raven Thomson, Beckett, and Leaper for their clandestine discussions concerning party matters, and for not coming forward with their complaints in 'a fascist and manly spirit'. To prevent a similar buildup of resentment, Mosley announced that in future, officers with grievances were to discuss them openly at weekly meetings, which would replace the old research department. The treasury would also be abolished. John Thompson, now the sole financial officer, would field questions concerning the party's fiscal matters. More serious issues were to be dealt with by the policy propaganda directory, comprising Box, Raven Thomson, Joyce, Beckett, Leaper, and Thompson; and the organizing department, consisting of Cleghorn, Dundas, Fuller, and Francis-Hawkins."

Special Branch Report, 16 July, 1935. PRO HO144/20145/222-5, cited in BLACKSHIRTS TORN: INSIDE THE BRITISH UNION OF FASCISTS, 1932-1940, by Thomas Norman Keeley, MA Degree submission, Simon Fraser University, Canada, 1998

5 ***Special Branch Report, 26 June, 1935. PRO HO144/20145/245, cited in BLACKSHIRTS TORN: etc.; op. cit.***

6 ***The Blackshirt no. 131, October 25th, 1935, page 1:***

"**FASCISM NEXT TIME**

INTENSIVE CAMPAIGN BY BLACKSHIRTS; BUILDING UP A COMPLETE MACHINE FOR THE NEXT ELECTION; TO OVERTHROW THE POWER OF MONEY; By OSWALD MOSLEY

... Therefore I summon the Movement which has never failed me to a great campaign, which shall be remembered as a decisive advance-guard action. Three weeks of the most intensive propaganda we have yet attempted will be followed by redoubled efforts to complete our election machine.

... A complete machine means sufficient trained agents to fight enough seats to win a Parliamentary majority and sufficient trained candidates. It is a sufficient number of trained agents that we chiefly lack, and without them the election machine cannot be created. ... Trustworthy Fascists must go through that highly technical training, and already we have made a substantial beginning by the training of agents in selected constituencies. ...

Straight dealing with the public will pay in the long run and will bring its reward in the decisive struggle.

For that reason I have always said "We will fight when our machine is ready and not before." By that decision I stand, and it follows that we shall not contest this election. ..."

7 ***The Blackshirt no. 132, November 1st, 1935, page 2***

8 ***Ibid.***

9 ***Ibid., page 5:***

"**The leader Condemns Strikes and Lock-Outs**

... The Labour leaders, too, support democratic Government by talk which is incapable of action. **The working-class has tried industrial and political action. Both have failed. Fascism gives them the opportunity of Power Action. ...**"

10 ***The Blackshirt no. 135, November 22nd, 1935, page 2:***

"**DARLINGTON HALL PACKED TO HEAR FASCIST SPEAKER**
Mr. W. Risdon Applauded

When Mr. W. Risdon addressed a public meeting in the Temperance Hall at Darlington on Tuesday, November 12, the hall was packed to the doors well before the advertised time of the meeting, and over 200 people had to be turned away.

Mr. Risdon explained the principles of Corporate Organisation. He delivered a powerful attack on the democratic system of to-day and contrasted the advantages of Fascist government with the inadequacies of our present Parliamentary procedure.

At the end of his speech there was prolonged applause and Mr. Risdon dealt with a large number of questions.

The meeting finished with an enthusiastic gathering singing the National Anthem."

The Lancaster meeting was reported in the ***Blackshirt News*** section on page 8.

11 There is some confusion over the date, because the text gives the impression that the meeting was held on the Sunday prior to the publication date of the issue in which it was printed, but that can't have been possible, because it had already been publicised that Wilfred was speaking at Ripon on Sunday 10th of November, so even if he was speaking in the morning at Cardiff, which was unusual [especially for a Sunday, when observance of religious services was expected] he would not have been able to get to Ripon that evening, with any degree of certainty; it is more likely that these reports from local areas were compiled 'a week in hand', so it would have been referring to Sunday November 3rd.

"**Cardiff** The weekly meeting in Albany Road is attracting larger crowds than ever. On Saturday Mr. O'Neill addressed a gathering of about 300.

On Sunday Mr. Risdon was given a splendid reception at the Kennard Hall."

BLACKSHIRT NEWS: *The Blackshirt no. 134, November 15th, 1935, page 8*

The report for the Tunbridge Wells meeting was more specific:

"**Tunbridge Wells** Mr. Risdon addressed a meeting at the Pump Room, Tunbridge Wells, on Monday, November 4. The majority of the audience appeared very much impressed by the statements made."

BLACKSHIRT NEWS: *The Blackshirt no. 135, November 22nd, 1935, page 8*

12 ***The Blackshirt no. 134, November 15th, 1935, page 5***

13 This was to take place when ***Action*** was initiated, and both that and ***The Blackshirt*** were published under the corporate banner of Action Press Ltd. Beckett took over as editor of both publications; little is heard of Leaper in the BUF after this. He was allegedly [although probably clandestinely, if not unknowingly] part-Jewish, as was Beckett, in fact. At some stage [unless this is an amazing coincidence], he qualified as a barrister, and after the war, he appears to have published several books on different aspects of the law, including advertising:

> "The first guide to advertising law I remember was published in 1961 by W. J. Leaper. It was, in its day, the seminal work on the subject. Not that in 1961 there was much law on the subject. The Advertising Standards Authority (ASA) had not come into existence nor the plethora of home-grown and EU-inspired law that has developed since. ... When W. J. Leaper was writing in 1961, advertising law was not a recognised legal specialism. Today it is, ..."

Business Law Review, May 2011

http://www.bloomsburyprofessional.com/Article/224/Book-Review--Advertising-Law-and-Regulation-2nd-Edition.html

Also copyright and performing rights:

> "For legal aspects of the industry, see W.J. LEAPER, *Copyright and Performing Rights* (1957), an early history of copyright in England and the implications of the Berne Convention and the Universal Copyright Convention;"

Publishing; bibliography:

Copyright © 1995 Encyclopaedia Britannica, Inc. All Rights Reserved;

http://www.uv.es/EBRIT/macro/macro_5005_38_74.html

Another review gives somewhat more detail [the professional qualification might be incorrectly OCRed]:

> "Copyright and Performing Rights, by W. J. Leaper, Li.B., Barrister-at-Law. Stevens & Sons Ltd., 1957. 219 pp., 25s.
>
> This handbook, says the preface, is intended to serve as a practical guide on the complicated subjects of copyright and performing rights. It is a law book, but written as much for the layman—be he writer, composer, publisher or gramophile —as for the lawyer.
>
> The writer of a legal textbook can go about his task in either of two ways. He can set out the actual text of the relevant Acts of Parliament, with appropriate comments and references to decided cases after each section, and usually a general introduction; this is the method adopted by Mr. D. H. Mervyn Davies in his ***The Copyright Act***, 1956 (Sweet and Maxwell, 21s.) Or he can rewrite the whole subject in his own way and with his own classification and order of topics, introducing references to the Acts and cases where necessary this is the method used by Mr. Leaper. The really voluminous tome sometimes combines both methods: thus the old editions of the standard work by Copinger on ***The Law of Copyright*** (a new edition is in preparation) set out the law in several hundred pages according to the writer's own system, and included the texts of the Acts in an appendix.
>
> For the layman who is not accustomed to finding his way about Acts of Parliament the second method is probably the better one. In a subject like copyright, however, which (since the 1956 Act came into operation) is based so much on the words of Parliament, it is inevitable that even this method will result in most of the words of the Act being incorporated into the book, though in a different order. Mr. Leaper's book, therefore, is not easy reading, but requires close attention to detail if the right answer to the reader's particular problem is to be found."

http://www.gramophone.net/Issue/Page/August%201957/35/855911/

Leaper's 'jewishness appears to have been no secret, although perhaps not at the time, and for some, there are no degrees, just 'all or nothing':

"Notable Jewish members of British Union included John Beckett (BU Director of Publications and Editor of ***Action***), Bill Leaper - Editor of the ***Blackshirt***, and Harold Soref - a BU Standard Bearer at the Olympia meeting who later became Tory M.P for Ormskirk."

http://www.oswaldmosley.com/british-union.htm

14 **BLACKSHIRT APPOINTMENTS:** ***The Blackshirt no. 142, January 10th, 1936, page 5:***

"**Mr. Neil Francis-Hawkins, formerly Director of Blackshirt Organisation, has been appointed Director-General of Organisation of the British Union of Fascists.**

The department formerly known as Blackshirt Organisation is now merged into the new department known as the Department of Organisation, which is responsible for the political and administrative machinery of the Movement throughout the country."

15 ***Ibid.***

16 **BLACKSHIRT NEWS:** ***The Blackshirt no. 148, February 21nd, 1936, page 7:***

"**Westminster (Abbey)** Mr. Risdon, on Feb. 12, spoke on electoral organisation, and outlined methods of canvassing and the work of election agents. He also stressed the importance of getting the electoral machine ready as soon as possible in order to overcome difficulties which might arise, if there should be an unexpected election at any time."

This appears to have been part of an organised programme of speeches on this subject at this time: NHQ wrote to the Acting District Officer in Dorchester, Robert Saunders, in early February, "to the following effect:–

'Risdon is to address a meeting of DOs and ADOs (Canvass) at Exeter on March 12th. No other engagement is to prevent you from attending this very important meeting.'

As you are likely to be appointed ADO (Canvass) will you please keep this day free?"

Copy in author's possession of letter dated 18/02/36 to E. A. Burch, Esq.; original in the University of Sheffield, Special Collections Archives: courtesy of Lawrence Aspden.

17 ***BLACKSHIRTS TORN: etc.; op. cit.***

18 ***Special Branch Report, 20 June, 1935. PRO HO144/20145/269, cited in ibid.***

19 ***Ibid.***

20 ***Fascist Week no. 1, November 10th-16th, 1933, page 4:***

"**The Newly Born**

Our initial circulation will comprise largely of [sic] members of the British Union of Fascists, because they are all expected to buy a copy – those who can afford it, anyway.

But the general public too, will buy several thousand copies because they are interested in Fascism – even if they hate it – and this is the first Fascist paper in Great Britain to be placed through the normal newsagents channels.

Our sister paper 'The Blackshirt' has done very well indeed and so have the individual Fascists who have sold it on the streets. But now a bigger paper is necessary and so 'The Fascist Week' has been produced to reach a wider public."

21 *The Blackshirt no. 56, May 10th-24th, 1934, page 1:*

"**'Blackshirt' and 'Fascist Week' to Merge**

PAGE OF NEW PAPER TO BE KEPT FOR BRANCH NEWS

It has been considered for some time that in many respects the news contents of the 'Fascist Week' and the member organ 'The Blackshirt' overlap, and as a result it has now been decided to amalgamate these two papers. This amalgamation will come into effect with the issue of the 1st June, and the new paper will be called 'The Blackshirt, incorporating the Fascist Week'. The price of the paper will be 2d. The size of the new paper will be the same as the present 'Fascist Week'."

22 *The Blackshirt no. 147, February 14th, 1936, page 5:*

"It is no exaggeration to say that in spite of the thousands of meetings held in all parts of the country, the tens of thousands of copies of 'The Blackshirt' that have been printed, and the millions of pamphlets and leaflets that have been distributed, the majority of the inhabitants of these islands have either a vague or a distorted idea of our aims and our methods.

We have to teach those men and women in a manner acceptable to them. We rely upon them to vote for us at election times, and therefore our propaganda must be put to them in a manner that will interest them and convince them all."

23 *Ibid.*

24 Mosley was touched by the original gesture embodied in the adoption of the fencing-style shirt:

"We began well—I still think that at the time and in the conditions we faced it was right, and certainly necessary—with the simple black shirt, which anyone could buy or have made at home for a few shillings; private enterprise produced them in bulk. Soon our men developed the habit of cutting the shirt in the shape of a fencing-jacket, a kindly little tribute to my love of the sport; also this form had the practical advantage that it gave the opponent nothing to grasp, in particular no tie which he was wont to pull adroitly for purpose of strangulation."

My Life, by Oswald Mosley

25 Robert Forgan was credited with the idea of the 'Mixed Canteen' at Black House, which was supposed to allow all classes and ranks of men to mix together easily in a relaxed atmosphere, but Alex Miles wrote that Forgan "would probably now count it as one of his mistakes":

"Let it suffice to say that the 'Mixed Canteen' was a concession to the wealthy or socially distinguished members, or visitors to N.H.Q."

The Streets are still: Mosley in Motley, by A. Miles

Mosley himself alluded to the subtle difference without defining it:

"Another essential was to get a barracks where men could be concentrated and trained. This was provided by Whitelands College near to the Chelsea Barracks; ... There were large sleeping-quarters and a drill or sports ground at the back for training. A *mess* and *canteen* were established, so that men could both live and sleep there." [my emphasis]

My Life, op. cit.

Kay Fredericks, "one-time BUF photographer", ascribed the persistence of the class system in the BUF to "the influx of all these ex-officers and titled people", as a result of "Lord Rothermere's patronage":

"Thus, whereas Mosley and others later spoke of the BUF as 'classless', at the time a state mole reported 'considerable unrest among the rank-and-file …, which takes the form of grumbling about food, class-conscious officers, discipline, and the hours of work'. Fredericks's account detailed the pervasive class culture amid the putative 'brotherhood of fascism'. In the Black House the 'men's canteen' catered for the rank and file, while the so-called 'Mixed-canteen' was known as the 'boss-class canteen'. Fredericks wrote that 'if a Blackshirt who was employed as a cleaner at H.Q. went into the mixed canteen, he would not be turned out, but would certainly be made to feel uncomfortable and ill at ease'. Those with money wore superior uniform shirts, which 'immediately became known as "boss-class" shirts'.".

Kay Fredericks's typescript memoir, MRC, MSS292/743/11/2; and Special Branch Report, HO144/20142/81 18/07/34, cited in Left Wing Fascism in Theory, 20th Century British History, vol. 13, pt. 1, pp. 38-61, 2002, Oxford University Press

26 **The Black Shirt in Britain: The Meanings and Functions of Political Uniform,** ***by Philip M. Coupland, in The Culture of Fascism: Visions of the Far Right in Britain [eds] Julie V. Gottlieb, Thomas P. Linehan***

27 Courtesy of Tim Rose. For a photograph of a pristine replica, go to http://gwargamesp.18.forumer.com/index.php?s=e73b63f6d1c2da4c7296a5a02c46e04b&showtopic=6273&st=15&hl=

28 ***The Fascists in Britain, by Colin Cross***

29 ***Ibid.***

30 ***The Black Shirt in Britain:, etc., op. cit.***

31 ***My Life, op. cit.:***

"My mistake was in allowing the development of a full military uniform for certain men who qualified to wear it. Technically, the matter had nothing to do with me, for I was divorced by our Constitution from the management of the financial side of the movement, and this was in origin a purely commercial matter. The company producing our supporting newspaper, ***Action***, supplied the military uniform to any man who gave five nights' service a week to the party and sold a certain number of copies of the paper. I think even these men wearing the special uniform had to pay for it; but they were allowed to wear it on certificate of the party that they gave five nights' service, and of the journal that they sold the requisite number of papers. It was called the **Action Press Uniform**.

I was not therefore responsible for the uniform, but undoubtedly I could have used my influence to stop it and I did not; on the contrary, I accepted the invitation to wear it myself, in order to encourage others. The reason was that the men were desperately keen to wear it as a mark of distinction, a party honour. They were soldiers, good soldiers, and soldiers like a smart uniform. With my background I simply had not the heart to stop them, and so much to disappoint them. It was an error and a dereliction of duty, for I should have known that while we could have got away with the simple black shirt, the uniform made us much too military in appearance and would create prejudice. The old soldier in me got the better of the politician."

32 *The Blackshirt, June 13, 1936, page 1*

33 *Oswald Mosley, op. cit.*

34 *Ibid.*

35 From the report, it's not entirely clear why the car was in such a vulnerable location, but it must have been obvious that Mosley was not on board, and it is most likely that someone in the crowd besieging the car discharged a firearm to deter the driver:

> "**SHOTS AT THE LEADER'S CAR**
>
> The Leader's car and driver were cut off in a side street by a mob of Reds, and were only able to get away by driving straight at the mob. The driver said that as some of the mob were trying to wrench off the doors and drag him out, he heard a loud report and there was a splintering of glass from the rear off-side window. A neat round hole appeared in the window, and as the glass was made of Triplex, it could hardly have been anything but a gun or pistol of some sort."

The Blackshirt, no. 169, July 18th, 1936, page 8

Unless the photograph printed a year later in ***Action*** has been inexplicably reversed [perhaps for 'technical reasons'?], the driver's report is inaccurate, as the photograph clearly shows that it is the nearside rear window which is holed.

Action, no. 90, November 6th, 1937, page 1

36 Mosley also appears to have, unfortunately [whether inadvertently or not], adopted Hitler's style of acknowledging the adulation with a crooked arm salute, with the palm laid back; photograph, captioned *The Leader in Victoria Park.*

The Blackshirt, no. 169, July 18th, 1936, page 5

37 *Oswald Mosley, op. cit.:*

> "… the key to Mosley's defeat in this area of politics was uniforms. No-one, except the odd right wing eccentric (for example, Sir Robert Turton) was prepared to support Mosley's right to parade about in uniforms. … 'A uniform in politics symbolises force, to be used either now or in the future.' (from a House of Commons debate)"

38 *The Blackshirt, no. 169, July 18th, 1936, page 4:*

> "**Important Statement by The Leader**
>
> In view of the nature of the following pronouncement we have pleasure in ceding our usual editorial space to the Leader of the British Union.
>
> **The British Union will contest East London seats at the L.C.C. elections on March 4 next. That is my answer to the lies told in Parliament on July 10 last by the Parties who now conspire to prevent us putting our case to the people. The charges against the British Union relate in particular to East London. So we shall take the opportunity of the L.C.C. elections to ask the verdict of the people of East London. They know our work in their midst, and others only read about it from the Press and Parliamentary speeches of our opponents. The people of East London are in a position to judge the truth, and unless these attacks on our members cease we shall ask them for a verdict which will enlighten others who cannot judge for themselves. We shall ask East London to say that our fight for Britain for the British is justified until the whole nation has opportunity to vote for our case and our cause. East London will be asked to choose between us and the Parties of Jewry. The people will be asked by their vote to give the Parties of Jewry 'notice to quit'.**

Local elections are not generally our concern, because we believe the corruption of local government cannot be cleansed until we have a Fascist and National Socialist Government for the whole armed by the people, at a General Election, with power to act in their name.

The present tactics of our opponents compel us to fight this election on a national issue, which is the conspiracy of the old Parties to prevent us exposing the real Government of Britain by their masters of Jewish finance which goes on behind the sham of Party warfare at Westminster. To prevent that exposure no lie is too gross and no abuse of their authority too base. We shall, therefore, appeal to the people to answer them with their votes.

Whether at a Local or General Election we shall present our full policy of 'Britain First'. The task is to persuade and convince the people of the justice of our case, and all Fascists must not only refrain from violence in action or speech, which is contrary to our orders and discipline, but must be on their guard in action and speech not even to give our enemies a chance to 'frame them up' and thus damage the cause. The issue is now with the people, and to them we appeal for the right to expose the enemies and serve the interests of our native land.

OSWALD MOSLEY"

39 ***BLACKSHIRTS TORN: etc.; op. cit.***

40 The Communists and ILP apparently viewed the march in the context of the Spanish civil war, and planned to prevent it by force.

Oswald Mosley, op. cit.

41 ***BLACKSHIRTS TORN: etc.; op. cit.***

42 ***Ibid.***

43 ***Ibid.***

44 ***Oswald Mosley, op. cit.***

45 ***Ibid.***

Members did continue to wear the Blackshirt uniform at "purely private" functions, presumably for sentimental reasons:

"**DUFF COOPER'S OPPONENT**

[photograph]

Major-General J. F. C. Fuller addressing members of the Westminster (St. Georges) Division at a meeting held last Friday. He is the prospective British Union candidate for that seat, which is held at present by Mr. A. Duff Cooper (Minister for War). Being a purely private function, members are seen wearing the now illegal Blackshirt uniform!"

The Blackshirt, no. 205, March 27th, 1937, page 4

46 ***Ibid.***

The meeting was in Liverpool, as related by Mosley in ***My Life, op. cit., p 261***

47 ***Action, no. 49, January 23rd, 1937; page 8:***

This biographical profile [also see below] lamented that:

"It is unfortunate that his duties leave him little time to speak, for he is a brilliant speaker."

The Blackshirt, no. 154, April 4th, 1936, page 6:

"**TRAINING OF ELECTION AGENTS**

Correspondence Course Prepared

A Correspondence course of training for Election Agents has been prepared by the Department of Organisation (Electoral Instruction), and will be available in the course of the next fortnight.

The course of training is open to any member of the BUF who desires to undergo such training.

Those who wish to avail themselves of this opportunity should make immediate application to their District Officer for enrolment.

Question papers will be submitted to students with each part of the course, and the answers will be returned before the next part of the course is despatched. At a later date arrangements will be made for the examination of students for intermediate and final certificates.

The Leader has expressed the wish that all Fascist Agents will be found from within the ranks of the Movement, and the active co-operation of the Members in this training scheme will provide the Organisation with an adequate corps of skilled Agents for the tremendous task which lies ahead of us in our progress to power.

Show him your response that adequate personnel is available to carry out the slogan of 'Fascism Next Time.'"

49 ***Copy in author's possession of letter dated 04/04/36 to R. Saunders, Acting District Officer; original in the University of Sheffield, Special Collections Archives: courtesy of Lawrence Aspden.***

50 ***Fascist Week, 22-28 December, 1933, page 5***

51 Wilfred's 'bio' was about as glowing as it was possible to be:

"**BRITISH UNION PERSONALITIES**

No. 12 – W. RISDON

(Assistant Director-General of Organisation, Electoral)

It is often said that no man is indispensable in any organisation. 'Bill' Risdon presents a strong challenge to this generalisation. He has a fine record of successful service, and his unique qualifications, combined with an extraordinary patience, have enabled him to build up the political organisation, without which we could not hope to tackle the old parties who excel at political machinery, though at nothing else.

'Bill' Risdon has always been a true Socialist. After fighting for his country through the whole of the War, he – with many other idealists – set about making victory real and permanent for the working masses of the people. As a miner in South Wales he joined the I.L.P. In 1924 he contested the South Dorset Division. Later he went to Birmingham as organiser for the whole of the Midlands. It was there that he formed his association with Sir Oswald Mosley. He played an important part in the creation of the brilliant organisation which drove the Chamberlain's [sic] from their family constituency at Sir Oswald's challenge.

When Mosley broke with the Labour Party over unemployment Risdon resigned his job with the I.L.P. and became one of the founders of the New Party, acting as agent at Gateshead in the 1931 Election. He later founded the Newcastle branch of the B.U. in the face of great difficulties. In April, 1933, he was called to London as Director of Propaganda. During that time he organised the first great Albert Hall rally, confounding the critics, who thought it impossible for a new Movement to fill that great hall. Then, as Deputy Director of Political Organisation, he took charge of Manchester, working there for over a year.

Now, he is Chief Agent at National Headquarters, a position of great responsibility, only to be held by a man of outstanding qualities. It is unfortunate that his duties leave him little time to speak, for he is a brilliant speaker.

His is the highest type of popularity, for it has grown throughout the Movement, from comradeship tested in tight corners, and that West Country-bred courtesy which treats all men alike, from the humblest servant."

Action, no. 49, January 23, 1937, page 8

52 It is unusual to see a Blackshirt described as "too unostentatious":

"**BRITISH UNION PERSONALITIES**
No. 15–CAPT. ERSKINE ATHERLEY

Administrator (Electoral)

Captain Atherley has been entrusted with the task of building a canvass organisation in all districts and providing training for potential canvassers. This is the real foundation of election machinery. What manner of man is he to whom this responsibility has fallen?

He has the technical qualifications, for he is a fully qualified election agent, trained in the Conservative Party, whose agent's certificate he holds, and for whom he has acted as agent in two General Elections and one by-election. He came to us in January, 1934, thoroughly disgusted with the Conservative betrayal of our interests in India and has been a keen and enthusiastic supporter since that date.

Atherley's early training and experience were interesting. He was educated at Bedford School, was commissioned in 1912 to the Manchester Regiment, served through the Great War, was given a Staff appointment with the R.A.F. in India from 1919 to 1923, hence he might claim some personal interest in the Indian betrayal which so incensed him.

In the British Union he has earned his spurs, working in his own district (Richmond) both before and since his appointment to the staff at N.H.Q., but his contribution is always made without ostentation. In fact, there are many who know him well who insist that he is too unostentatious.

He does his own job of work, meticulously but unobtrusively, and he is fortunate in having a post for which he is well fitted and which he thoroughly understands.

The Movement owes much to this quiet worker for his past services, but who would dare to compute the value of his present activity if he succeeds in building up the canvass organisation which is required for the electoral machine on which the future of the British Union so largely depends."

Action, no. 53, February 20, 1937, page 8

53 According to Philip Coupland:

"Miles claimed that he resigned on 24 February 1936, the BUF that he was sacked on 24 March 1936, and then requested to be readmitted to the movement in a letter dated 2 November 1936. … John Charnley wrote in his autobiography [***Blackshirts and Roses, op. cit.***] that dismissal followed his report to Hector McKechnie that Miles was insincere.

George Chester, General Secretary of the National Union of Boot and Shoe Operatives (NUBSO), recalled a conversation with someone who had recently left the BUF and was now 'organising meetings in opposition to Fascism'. … This person was … described as organising anti-fascist meetings, as Miles did in Hyde Park. Around the same time Special Branch also recorded that Miles was working part-time in London for NUBSO, in which his uncle held 'a good position' (PRO, HO144/20147/142, Special Branch Report, 21 May 1936)."

Left Wing Fascism etc., op. cit.

On this subject, Miles himself was taciturn, confining himself to stating that "Fascism is a betrayal of Youth's glowing idealism!", and ending with a rambling, virtually incomprehensible paragraph:

"To all of us, who live somewhat of peace [sic], in a little of liberty, by the sacrifices of the past generations, I say from my painfully gathered knowledge of Fascism, save for those who are to follow us, the possibilities of human freedom, realisable by the democratic path, faulty and halting though our progress on it be, and destroyed, not for ever - that cannot be - but for a very long period, if, through Mosley or another, the falsities of Fascism are fastened upon this people!"

The Streets are still: etc., op. cit.

54 ***The Blackshirt, no. 178, September 19th, 1936, page 5***

55 ***The Blackshirt, no. 162, May 30th, 1936, page 2***

56 ***Action, no. 51, February 6, 1937, page 1***

57 **ON THE MARCH:** ***The Blackshirt, no. 186, November 14th, 1936, page 6***

58 One member, Vincent Keens, had an arguably contentious letter published in ***The Blackshirt*** requesting information on successful Independent Fascist candidates:

"**OUR READERS' OPINIONS**

BLACKSHIRTS IN MUNICIPAL ELECTIONS

In the Municipal elections of November 2, many Independent Candidates were returned. I wonder how many of these were Fascists. One Independent Fascist Candidate who was returned was Lieut.-Col. D. Smith, J.P., O.B.E., who is D.O. of the Torquay District. Although quite a newcomer in the Borough of Dartmouth, for which he was returned, he was [illegible] in the order of the five Independent Candidates and only missed being in the second place by eight votes.

It will be interesting to know how many members of the British Union were successful.

Yours in Fascism, VINCENT KEENS"

Ibid., page 4

59 The book was conveniently pocket-size, and was very simply, but not unattractively presented, in the customary utilitarian style, with the name spread over three lines and a large Fasces at the bottom, for easy identification; hard-backed in an orange cloth [page A]; it was relatively expensive at one shilling, but it was clearly comprehensive:

"This handbook on the work of a Constituency Agent has been prepared by Mr. W. Risdon, who has had long and varied experience in different parts of the country, experience which is shown by the judgement exercised in covering the various points in both branches of an agent's work in as few words as possible while omitting nothing that is necessary in the early stages.

Meant primarily for the use of Political Officers or Agents in charge of Constituencies, this guide deals with the two main questions with which Agents will always be concerned, namely, Registration and Election Law."

60 ***The Blackshirt, no. 194, January 9th, 1937, page 6:***

"Those who were unsuccessful at this attempt will have an opportunity to sit again at the next examination. These exams will be held at three-monthly intervals.

W. RISDON, Chief Agent."

61 Colin Cross gives details of one member who was known to Wilfred, because of his background, but Cross is critical of the electoral machine, which technically was Wilfred's overall responsibility, and he would certainly have taken issue with the comment:

"Between 1936 and 1938 Mosley selected 80 candidates for 79 constituencies. ... The choice of candidates was made entirely from National Headquarters and caused further dissensions and jealousies in the Movement. In a high proportion of the seats the candidates were imposed by National Headquarters simply as a means of spurring local organizations into greater activity. Nowhere outside East London did British Union have anything approaching an effective electioneering organization.

In a few instances the candidates were chosen more for their names than for their services to the Movement. ... Nevertheless a high proportion of candidates were full-time officials. Candidates of social standing included ... Ralph Gladwyn Jebb of Downton Manor, near Salisbury, who was candidate for Dorset West. Jebb was a friend of Mosley, worked actively for British Union and was the only person to receive the Movement's highest badge of honour, the 'Gold Distinction'."

The Fascists in Britain, op. cit.

This last fact is contradicted by a report in ***The Blackshirt*** at the beginning of October, 1937, in which 9 Gold Distinctions are announced, none of which is Jebb; 34 Bronze Distinctions are announced, of which Jebb is the final one:

"We have very much pleasure in announcing, on this Fifth Birthday Anniversary, the names of members whose magnificent services to the Movement have led to the bestowal upon them of the higher British Union honours. These will be presented to them by the Leader at the forthcoming area conferences.

It should be noted that the list is not complete, owing to the late arrival of recommendations from many districts."

The Blackshirt, no. 231, October 2nd, 1937, page 7

In fact, Jebb was upgraded to Gold, the only member on this occasion to receive the top distinction, in October 1938; there were 24 recipients of the Bronze Distinction:

"The following is a list of awards gained by British Union members for conspicuous service to the Movement. This is the second list of gold and bronze awards which has been published and would have appeared on Oct. 1

the birthday of British Union but was postponed owing to the crisis."

Action, no. 140, October 22nd, 1938, page 13

Wilfred wrote to Jebb assuming that he was a complete novice, so his letter extended over three pages, but he took care not to be condescending:

"I am writing at the request of the D.G., to offer you technical advice in connection with your prospective candidature.

We realise that in most cases our prospective candidates are without previous experience and that they feel somewhat diffident in consequence thereof. I have jotted down a number of points and suggestions, hereunder, which you might find useful in these circumstances, and I shall be pleased to give any further advice which you may need if you will write to me briefly outlining your particular difficulties.

...

In the event of friction arising in your constituency between two groups of members keep clear of any such dispute, if it is humanly possible to do so. It is not the business of the candidate to take sides in a dispute. Your only justification of intervention in matters of this description will arise if you find it possible to reconcile the two groups and bring them together to work in a spirit of amity without taking sides with one party or the other. ..."

Copy in author's possession of undated letter to R. Jebb, Esq., the Manor House, Downton, Wilts.; original in the University of Sheffield, Special Collections Archives: courtesy of Lawrence Aspden.

There is a very short biographical profile of Jebb in Action in November, 1936, to support his parliamentary candidacy:

"Author of four best sellers, a book on ships, and another on Fascism, Mr. Jebb also found time to do mining in Cyprus and Nigeria before the War, and, during the War, which he served through, he was gassed at Ypres and Mentioned in Despatches.

Has been a member of the British Union for over three years and is a speaker of great power and knowledge."

Action, no. 41, November 28, 1936, page 7

62 ***Oswald Mosley, op. cit.:***

"... what happened is that gentile east Londoners sought out the BUF in order to make it a vehicle for their local grievances. Mosley went to where his 'natural' support lay. He sympathised with the east Londoners' grievances: Britain for the British was a theme going back to 1918. He established a strong emotional rapport with east London audiences. ... Many at the time have since alleged that Mosley marched and campaigned in Jewish areas to provoke violence and gain publicity as though east London were somehow a Jewish preserve. In fact most east Londoners were non-Jewish and the bulk of fascist campaigning was done in non-Jewish areas where its support lay."

63 ***Ibid., citing PRO, MEPOL2/3043, among others:***

"... in July 1936 Mosley insisted that the law [as it then stood] be obeyed, which aroused great opposition from militant British Union anti-Semites like Joyce & Beckett, who were urging a policy of courting arrests & imprisonment to 'intensify antagonism towards Jews'. In an article in ***The Blackshirt*** of October 3rd 1936 [***no. 180***] Mosley wrote: 'Mere abuse we forbid. … [It] is bad propaganda, and alienates public sympathy.' Sir Philip Game's report to the Home Office submitted at the beginning of October 1936, together with the Special Branch report for the same month, gives the following account of the dissension within British Union at this time:

'The British Union of Fascists (Sir Oswald Mosley) has given a definite warning to its speakers to refrain from attacking the Jews at public meetings, it being emphasised that arrests of its members for Jew baiting is likely to do the Fascist movement in this country more harm than good.

… an influential section of the BUF's leading officials strongly deprecates any suggestion that the party should modify its policy … and is urging the necessity for showing the country that fascists are not afraid of facing imprisonment for speaking what they believe to be the truth about the Jews. On the 15th of September William JOYCE (Director of Propaganda) called together the principal Party speakers and delivered to them what amounted to a tirade against Jews and the attitude taken up by the Government on anti-Semitism. While he advised them to refrain from indulging in personal abuse of Jews (expressions such as 'filthy swine', etc.) he exhorted them not to retreat in the face of Police persecution and declared that, if necessary, all Fascist speakers should be prepared to face imprisonment rather than comply with the dictum of the authorities that they were not to attack Jewry. Large scale arrests would, in his opinion, inevitably tend to intensify antagonism towards Jews.'"

64 ***Action, no. 52, February 13th, 1937, page 7***

65 Skidelsky, in an unattributed quote, calls Bailey "a cockney … [with] a large personal following", and that, like most East End Mosleyites, he was in the furniture trade.

Oswald Mosley, op. cit.

66 ***Ibid.***

67 ***Ibid.***

68 ***Ibid.***

69 ***The Rebel who lost his Cause: etc., op. cit., citing "The security services":***

"Beckett is very bitter about the conduct of the campaign. He stated quite bluntly that he considered Francis-Hawkins and Donovan to be utter fools and that if Sir Oswald Mosley was not as great a fool as they are, he is certainly far too complacent; that perhaps the shock … will induce Mosley to place less credence on the counsels of Francis-Hawkins and his friends. … The headquarters staff who went to east London … were worse than useless … Raven Thomson [the BUF ideologue and philosopher] is a dangerous idiot who frothed about the Jews and boasted that he would soon be elected and giving orders. … Beckett … confided that he felt so exasperated at the incompetence and lack of realism … on the night of the election that he had very nearly resigned from the movement. … Headquarters officials who were sent down to work did nothing but sit around the fire in the election agent's room … and order or bully the voluntary workers."

70 ***Ibid.:***

"John said his reading of the results was that they could not possibly win. Mosley was furious, and later severely reprimanded the man who had showed John the canvass returns. William Joyce picked up, and passed to John, an authoritative rumour that Mosley wanted to be rid of both of them."

71 ***Action, no. 55, March 6th, 1937, page 9:***

"I have never seen such a campaign as the one that closes to-day [March 4] in East London."

72 ***Undated, cited in Action, no. 56, March 13th, 1937, page 7***

73 ***The Rebel who lost his Cause: etc., op. cit.***

74 ***Action, no. 55, March 6th, 1937, page 9***

75 ***Action, no. 57, March 20th, 1937, page 7:***

"Minor adjustments to the machine will be required for further fights. Extended training will be required by our members who will have to operate the machine. These are mere details; the central outstanding facts are that the machine is good, the workers magnificent. Hence the future is ours.

Borough Council elections and Parliamentary elections are yet to come; but when they do come along, may they be tackled with the spirit that wins – not over-confidence, but a determination to collect and poll every available vote for the British Union."

76 On this particular issue, there seems quite a surprising variance in the details from different sources: Beckett says "Five days later" [***The Rebel who lost his Cause: etc., op. cit.***]; Cross [***The Fascists in Britain, op. cit.***] says "A fortnight after the LCC election"; Farndale, in his biography of Joyce [***Haw-Haw: The Tragedy of William and Margaret Joyce***], says "April 1937", so more than a fortnight later; and Mosley himself [and Keeley {***BLACKSHIRTS TORN: etc., op. cit.***} who, for a change, uses Mosley as the source, instead of MI5 or Special Branch] is the furthest removed, writing "In May 1937"! [***My Life, op. cit.***] Interestingly [from the point of view of impartiality], British Union's own publication confirms Beckett as being correct: a brief statement was printed in the ***Action*** of March 20th, and it was also confirmed that "John Beckett has relinquished the editorial chair." The subsequent sentence, however, seems hopeful, if not actually disingenuous: "We are happy to be able to announce, however, that he has arranged to continue to write articles for ***Action*** regularly." The official statement was as follows:

"The following statement was issued to the Press on March 11, 1937, by the British Union: "A reduction and consolidation of H.Q. staff has been made in order to place the finances of the British Union on such a stable and durable foundation that the Movement is assured of staying power [sic] whether the struggle be long or short."

Sir Oswald Mosley will write on the rearrangement of the organisation in the next issue of *The Blackshirt*.

On sale next Saturday."

Action, no. 57, March 20, 1937, page 9

77 ***The Fascists in Britain, op. cit.:***

"A fortnight after the LCC election Mosley summoned over a hundred of his salaried speakers and officials to National Headquarters. As he entered the room they snapped stiffly to attention and saluted."

The more detailed article mentioned in the previous note confirmed that it "involved a reduction and consolidation of our Headquarters Staff." Generally, it was long on aspiration and short on detail, but Mosley was careful to stress that "It is true that I am not responsible under our Constitution for the finances of the Movement and that I have no participation in B.U.F. Trust or other companies which employ our permanent staff." There was some specific detail:

"**We have been able to preserve the two essentials: (1) Two papers which spread our propaganda; (2) Sufficient Staff at H.Q. and in the country to conduct an effective organisation without which propaganda has neither direction nor purpose.**

We have been obliged to eliminate all personnel and expenditure which were not essential to these two purposes and to the building of our electoral machinery. Our main propagandists are now in the position of those of other Movements and of the great number of voluntary speakers in our own Movement, namely they have to maintain themselves in ordinary occupations and will be free only to give voluntary service.

...

I have been obliged to part with at least the daily companionship of old friends and fellow fighters in National Socialist struggle. The great way in which they have taken it has made it an even deeper and more moving experience. Nearly all of them have written me or informed me that every moment of their spare time is available in a voluntary capacity and many have seen me and said to me in a dark hour things I shall never forget my whole life long."

The Blackshirt, no. 204, March 20th, 1937, page 1

78 Again, details vary slightly: Mosley & Keeley say one hundred and one went; Skidelsky [***Oswald Mosley, op. cit.***] says 110 ["from 140 to 30"]; and Cross says 113 ["from 143 to 30"]. He also says that this was half-expected:

"Rumours had circulated about Mosley's intentions but the truth was worse than most had feared. In curt sentences Mosley thanked them for their work ..."

The Fascists in Britain, op. cit.

Some effort was made to help those made redundant find other work:

"**DO YOU WANT A GOOD WORKER?**

A number of members of the British Union, who until recently were employed on the staff at National Headquarters and were affected by the recent economy staff cuts, have not yet been able to obtain other employment. As it is the natural desire of the Movement to assist these members in every way possible, I should be most grateful if readers of "The Blackshirt" who know of any vacancies in offices or trades, etc., would communicate with me, giving as many details as possible of the position available.

N. FRANCIS-HAWKINS,
Director-General,
British Union."

The Blackshirt, no. 207, April 10th, 1937, page 1

79 *Ibid.*

80 *My Life, op. cit.:*

> "Only four of the hundred-and-one dismissed turned against the party; the others remained entirely loyal. Those who stayed firm were headed by Raven Thomson ..."

This is also confirmed by a photograph [see page D], with a printed caption: "Discussing the Tour. From left to right, Raven Thomson, Clement Bruning, Wegg Prosser, Bill Risdon, and Mick Clarke." This was intended for publication in the Movement's newspapers, and the proof copy has a hand-written caption above; "COUNTRY-WIDE B.U. PLATFORM CAMPAIGN" and hand-written date at the bottom; June 1937; Raven Thomson also continued as editor of the ***British Union Quarterly.***

Print from private archive.

81 Beckett is understandably disenchanted, but the final assertion certainly would have applied to Wilfred; at the same time, it would have been both unreasonable and inaccurate to describe him as one of Mosley's "henchmen":

> "... in a cull of full-time staff, Mosley fired John [Beckett], William Joyce, and, according to John, 'every other man or woman on his staff who had ever reasoned with or contradicted him or his henchmen.'"

The Rebel who lost his Cause: etc., op. cit.

82 ***The Fascists in Britain, op. cit.:***

> "The purge included two men who, after Mosley, were the best-known personalities in the Movement - John Beckett, Director of Publications, and William Joyce, Director of Propaganda. Between them they had supervised the entire output of the Movement's printed and verbal propaganda, and their abrupt dismissal is inexplicable merely in terms of economy. The truth was that they had proved a pair of round pegs failing to fit in the square holes of the Francis-Hawkins hierarchy, and the purge provided a convenient opportunity to get rid of them."

This is a rather generalised assessment, ignoring as it does Wilfred's ongoing contribution to the Movement; especially given that Cross interviewed Wilfred personally for his book: however, Cross also asserts another, doctrinal reason to dispense with Joyce:

> "To the Francis-Hawkins group Joyce was a disturbing influence, a vain little man who had ideas at variance with those of the Leader and was using the Movement for his own ends. Out he had to go. The pretext seems to have been the private income which, it was argued, Joyce should hand to British Union funds. In a word, Beckett and Joyce were individualists and therefore bad Fascists."

Beckett's son does not report any remarks made by his father about his own dismissal, but as well as also implicating Wilfred somewhat in the rôle of an exception, he does confirm the Francis-Hawkins connection [Francis-Hawkins is honoured by the inclusion of a large head & shoulders portrait in Mosley's autobiography, when he comments very briefly on this episode]:

"An MI5 report said: 'The significant feature of this upheaval is the complete victory of the Francis-Hawkins "blackshirt" clique, which has practically eliminated those who were opposed to its conception of the BUF as a semi-military organisation rather than an orthodox political machine.'"

The Rebel who lost his Cause: etc., op. cit.

Cross has his own assessment of the inevitability of Beckett's fate:

"Self-confident of his own abilities, conscious of the special status he and Mosley shared as ex-MPs, Beckett had in the early days been a close colleague of Mosley, and very free with advice. By 1937 his status had declined and Mosley was less receptive to advice from Beckett than he was to advice from other quarters, notably from Francis-Hawkins. That he should cease giving advice would not occur to Beckett. Nor was he the kind of man to keep silent when he had a grievance. His witty but sardonic tongue became a major administrative inconvenience, a potential source of treason against the Leader."

The Fascists in Britain, op. cit.

Francis Beckett does detail his father's own loss of faith in Mosley:

"By 1936 John was certain that Mosley had finally lost all touch with reality. For the rest of his life he would tell the story of the moment he came to this conclusion. It happened during the new king, Edward VIII's abdication crisis. Both John and Mosley had met the king, as Prince of Wales, and taken to him … so John and Mosley threw themselves into a campaign to rally public opinion on the king's behalf … in John's words:

> 'When the crisis became front page news Mosley was in Liverpool, and had to stay overnight for a conference. He telephoned to London and asked Joyce and I [sic] to drive there and discuss the position with him. … Mosley was in a state of great excitement. He claimed to be in direct communication with the court. The king, he said, was strengthened by the knowledge of the support of him and his movement, and for this reason would accept Baldwin's resignation and call upon Mosley to form a government.
>
> Standing in the middle of the room, he detailed his plans for governing without parliament until the budget, pointing out that the financial estimates until then had already been passed, and he strode about the room in excitement as he explained that millions of pounds would be available to fight an election in such a cause, and that as Prime Minister he could broadcast as often as he wished. This, he was certain, could not fail to turn the electorate in his favour.
>
> At this point a telephone call came through from London. Explaining that this was an important call for which he had waited all day, he seized the instrument and began rapidly speaking in backslang. When he replaced the receiver he turned to us and explained that he had received most important news from court. He apologised for speaking in cipher, but said that he always used it because his calls were intercepted by the CID.
>
> I learned this simple method of talking at school, and Joyce said that he thought every London schoolboy understood it. … I am sure that Mosley really believed he was on the threshold of great power. The conversation confirmed my suspicion that he was deluded, and was dangerously near the borderline between genius and insanity. I knew the man to whom he had spoken. He was a dilettante society friend of Mosley's, who lived in as fictitious a world of grandeur as Mosley himself …
>
> We left Tom that night convinced that he already believed himself in charge of the nation's affairs, and agreed that his powers of self-delusion had finally

conquered his sanity. He could not realise that nobody except himself and the comical little group of ex-peddlers [sic] and humourless ex-officers with whom he was surrounded took him at all seriously.'"

The Rebel who lost his Cause: etc., op. cit.

83 Here, also, opinions vary, according to the source, as to the duration of this limbo; both Mosley [***My Life, op. cit.***] and Keeley [***BLACKSHIRTS TORN: etc., op. cit.***] maintain that it was after he was dismissed, although Mosley says that Joyce was expelled, whereas Keeley says that Joyce resigned [with Beckett]: Miles gives the impression that it must have been the same day, to all intents & purposes, unless he had an ulterior motive, which might only have occurred to him later. Notwithstanding his animosity towards Joyce, he "was informed by one of those present when Mosley dismissed over a hundred of his Headquarters staff" that Joyce

"took his dismissal with these words, - 'I am a Fascist first and a Mosleyite second. To Hell with you', and walked out of the headquarters."

The Streets are still: etc., op. cit.

84 Cross considered it unlikely:

"His lack of status outside Fascism made him cherish all the more the status he had won inside the Movement. Hard, dedicated, but sensitive to slights, Joyce had an ambition to become a great political teacher. Power in the conventional form of political authority interested him comparatively little. He had no ambition to replace Mosley as Leader of British Fascism. The power he wanted was over other men's minds, to teach them the ideas he had devised. He cherished the personal following he gained within the Movement and worked to extend it, an action which caused jealousies, especially when it became known that he had a private income subscribed by two or three of his wealthier admirers."

The Fascists in Britain, op. cit.

Farndale disagrees, however:

"After Cable Street, Joyce became disillusioned with Mosley, seeing him as a weak leader: he was mentally preparing himself to usurp Mosley. Knight in an MI5 report:

'Joyce is a greater force than Mosley himself. His personal vanity is great, and has incurred the hatred of many, but he never allows adulation to go to his head. He is highly suspicious and watchful. His brain is wonderful in its capacity for assimilation.' Joyce began to undermine Mosley: the joke was that the new police-style uniform seemed more like that of 'King Zog's Own Imperial Dismounted Hussars'."

Haw-Haw: etc., op. cit.

85 Apparently, Beckett and Joyce derogated British Union in the ***Morning Post***:

"**'Morning Post' And Dismissed Members**

The "Morning Post" was recently described by Mr. Beckett in the following terms in these columns: "Oil and Jewish insurance mix oddly with the picture that many people still cherish of the 'Morning Post'. It is natural that the outlook of this paper should be entirely reactionary and has no sympathy with the Fascist Movement, who sing in their marching song that they fight against 'Red Front and massed reaction'."

This was the paper which was naturally glad to accept an interview from Messrs. Joyce and Beckett containing a series of small and silly falsehoods against the organisation from which they had been dismissed.

The following statement has already been issued by the British Union, and we do not wish to waste further space on a subject which has already become insignificant. The facts are:

"These two men were dismissed from the staff some five weeks ago, and have since tried, without any effect, to make trouble for the British Union. Until the moment they were dismissed they loaded the Movement and the Leader with eulogy and voiced no complaint of any kind. Since their dismissal they have abused both Movement and Leader in a series of statements which are simply untrue.

There is no truth whatever in their claim to have split the ranks of the British Union. The measure of their claim to support may be judged by the fact that they name as a senior inspector of the British Union a man who has not been a member for a year past. Having failed to cause any dissension in the organisation which dismissed them, they started, nearly a month ago, a small society of their own in no way differing in policy from the British Union, and advancing no original idea, except the soul-stirring slogan: 'We have lost our salaries'.

There the interest of the British Union in these gentlemen ends, and, we believe, also the interest of anyone else."

The Press are never tired of telling us how lucky we are to have a free Press which will voice all shades of opinion.

It is interesting to see, therefore, that the "Morning Post", while printing the attack on the British Union very prominently, has, up to the moment of going to press, not printed the British Union's reply. That is "freedom of the Press", as understood by the organs of financial democracy."

The Blackshirt, no. 208, April 17th, 1937, page 5 [the identical article was printed in ***Action, no. 61, April 17, 1937, page 8***]

86 ***The Fascists in Britain, op. cit.:***

"He was the kind of man who needed a hero as a focus for his admiration - just one hero. Even the dreamy, humourless Joyce could see that in terms of practical politics Mosley was not a man of power and instead he turned all the fervour of his hero worship to Adolf Hitler. The transfer of allegiance was the easier for Joyce because of his awareness of his lack of British citizenship, although he kept it a secret."

Farndale has some more personal insights:

"Briefly Joyce grew a toothbrush moustache like Hitler's [and he had also taken to wearing a German style of leather overcoat, as indeed had Mosley] … he disliked jazz because the Nazis had deemed it decadent, so he would turn off the radio if it was on, wherever he was."

Haw-Haw: etc., op. cit.

87 ***The Fascists in Britain, op. cit.***

88 There is a slight discrepancy in dates between Dr. Wise's two documents below, and a factual inaccuracy [notwithstanding the understandable elevation in importance to the BUF of the locality]:

"By 1937 the BUF had been made illegal and Mosley, now unable to meet the mortgage and the salaries of the staff at Northumberland Street, closed his provincial centre and retreated to London."

The rise of independent orthodoxy in Anglo-Jewry: the history of the Machzikei Hadass communities, Manchester, ***unpublished Ph.D. thesis; Wise, Z, Y., University of Manchester, 2006***

"The principal financial backer of the strictly orthodox Jewish community, the Machzikei Hadass [those who firmly grasp the law], the furniture importer and wholesaler Abraham Jacob Pfeffer quickly stepped in to buy 17 Northumberland Street in 1937 [the above thesis is slightly at variance here, stating 'A J Pfeffer quickly stepped in to buy 17 Northumberland Street from the BUF's bank in the spring of 1938'] until the community, which had been founded in 1925 at the Polish Synagogue, 115a Bury New Road, could raise sufficient funds. It was rented to the Machzikei Hadass until a nominal purchase (Pfeffer donated most of the value to the community) was made two years later."

http://www.manchesterjewishstudies.org/fascism-in-manchester

89 *Oswald Mosley, op. cit.:*

"… after the war Mosley admitted that 'half the Movement was running to Headquarters every five minutes …'"

9: THE SLIPPERY SLOPE TO WAR

In the spring of 1937, if Mosley's assertion that "[o]nly four of the hundred-and-one dismissed turned against the party" [see note 80, Chapter 8] was correct, then the work of British Union at National Headquarters in Great Smith Street, Westminster, will have continued very much as it did before the large-scale cull of salaried staff, although the offices will very likely have been much quieter, given that those who were in a position to earn a living elsewhere were doing so, or endeavouring to find it: no doubt there were plenty who were unsuccessful. While acknowledging his current usefulness to the Movement, in his usual self-deprecating manner, Wilfred will nonetheless have considered himself quite lucky to have retained a salaried position within Mosley's financially straitened organisation. In one sense, Mosley's acceptance of the plainly obvious, in financial terms, that the Movement could no longer support such a large paid personnel, was an admission of failure, if one believed the official line that the organisation was predominantly financed by the membership, with their subscriptions, and thereafter by the sales of the two British Union weekly newspapers, ***Action*** and ***The Blackshirt***; there was also the ***British Union Quarterly***, but that was regularly advertised in the pages of the other two papers, so it more or less sold itself. Mosley had injected a great deal of his own money, and there had been some well-heeled sponsors along the way, but notwithstanding the virtually unavoidable fluctuations in member numbers, for a variety of reasons, there had been suspicions almost from the beginning, in October 1932, that the British Union [as it was now] was relying to a significant extent on one or more financial lifelines from abroad.

Mosley had always stressed categorically that, although his Movement was modelled to some extent on Italian Fascism and, indeed, inspired by it, it was one hundred percent British, and should not be compared with fascist movements in other countries, despite any similarities: it was a British Movement, set up to offer a specifically British solution to a British crisis. Nevertheless, and particularly in view of Mosley's acknowledged reluctance to divulge membership numbers, it was hardly surprising that many commentators [especially the hostile ones] should seek to besmirch his reputation by alleging foreign support. In a purely commercial peacetime trading environment, that could not easily be cast in a negative light, but political movements are highly emotive, and Fascism in particular, first in Italy, and then in Germany, had aroused very strong feelings, both support and opposition, from the very beginning, so Mosley must have been painfully aware of the danger of any provable association with a foreign Fascist Movement, both of which were perceived, rightly or wrongly, as having very poor 'human rights' [to use a more recent expression] records. He had been very careful to dissociate himself from the financial dealings of the organisation and had been perfectly willing to publicise that fact [see note 31, Chapter 8]; in itself, that was perfectly innocuous: very few managing directors would have day to day control of their company or corporation's finances, but to many people, Mosley **was** the Movement, so his assertion of detachment from, and consequent ignorance of the Movement's financial affairs sounded to them at best disingenuous, and at worst downright mendacious.

The subject of foreign financing, as a 'subset' of the general theme of foreign influence, was to constitute one of the main accusations, against Mosley and his Movement, by the Government in a few short years; in his autobiography, ***My Life***, to which many references are made in this work, as well as rationalising his attitude towards accepting financial contributions "from other Europeans" [**1**], he maintains that, as late as 1946, no evidence was forthcoming from the Government "to show that I had accepted funds from Italy on behalf of British Union in the years 1934 and 1935." [**2**] It is interesting that he should choose to be so specific about only these two years; Mosley was later accused of having been financed by Mussolini between 1933 and '37, but according to Skidelsky, MI5 was extremely protective of some of its source material at the time [with the effect of positively constraining the case against Mosley], and for many years subsequently: "Presumably, this [was] to protect sources. The chief source may have been a wealthy businessman, Bill Allen, a close friend of Mosley, who received the Mussolini payments on the BUF's behalf." [**3**] The contacts with the Italian *régime* were obviously common knowledge at NHQ, certainly among the executive officers [although wider dissemination of this information will undoubtedly have been discouraged]: Box was one who was openly "critical of Mosley's pro-Italian position, claiming that Rome was dictating BUF policy." [**4**], before he left in early 1936, and Wilfred, to whom the description of one "of Mosley's obsequious senior officers" [**5**] could only apply if used by someone particularly wanting to denigrate him, also had his doubts.

In 1940, at Wilfred's 18B Appeal tribunal [**Appendix D**], he related some details of his challenge to Mosley and Francis-Hawkins on the subject of Italian funding, although again, curiously, there is some confusion and consequent inaccuracy about the chronology of events which occurred, in reality, only three years previously: perhaps one should not judge this too harshly, in view of the inevitably frenetic activity of the intervening years, and the pressure surrounding the appeal hearings, for both sides with their individual and specific requirements [undoubtedly worse on the defendant's side: according to Skidelsky, "Detainees were not allowed the services of counsel" **6**]. Discrepancies of timing notwithstanding, Wilfred relates that he brought to the attention of Mosley and Francis-Hawkins a photostatic copy of a letter, allegedly written by the Director General "to a man … who had been working in Manchester". Wilfred's reason for doing this was that "a man by the name of Bethell of Sunderland wrote anonymous letters to me saying he was in possession of documents that showed [Italian funding] to be the case." This is curious in itself, because it begs the question [as he omits any details, for want of prompting] of how Wilfred knew the source of the letters if they were anonymous! Perhaps that became clear when he "followed that up" and "eventually managed" to obtain the photostat copy of the letter purporting to have been written [and signed] by Francis-Hawkins: "As soon as I got possession of the copy of that document I took it to Sir Oswald Mosley and the Director-General, and challenged them to say was this true or was it not. They both repudiated indignantly, and classified the document as a forgery."

Wilfred's suspicions were aroused when "they said there was not a shred of truth in the charge, and I then urged them to take proceedings in Court against Bethell for the dissemination of this report. They refused to do that, but what they did do very shortly afterwards was to publish a reproduction of the letter in the periodical ***Action*** and stigmatise it as a forgery and challenged any person to produce the original." [**7**] In fact, apart from an outright denial, no challenge was actually issued: perhaps such an intention was stated at the original meeting referred to by Wilfred, but between then and the committing to print of the denial this element appears to have been conveniently dropped. There is also no mention of any question of the authenticity of Francis-Hawkins's signature on the letter, "written on British Union official notepaper", which could have been a damning piece of evidence, and yet this was shown in the reproduction in ***Action***. The letter was referred to as "another forgery" because three weeks earlier, ***Action*** had printed a small boxed article entitled "'Ware Forgeries", explaining that the facsimile of an identity card shown, of a member of the "secret services department" of the British Union, was "a palpable fake", because no such department existed; not only that, the card was supposedly authenticated by what purported to be Mosley's signature, which was "a forgery" [**8**].

The card also carried an identification number, "59Z", which is very significant because it appears to confirm the existence of the shadowy "Z Intelligence Department", which naturally enough, British Union would be keen to deny and, indeed, not referred to by name in the article. This department was run by BU's 'in-house' MI5 mole, 'Major' P. G. Taylor, one of the several pseudonyms of a reclusive and camera-shy figure, whose real name was probably James McGuirk Hughes [**9**], or a variant thereof. As was alluded to in Chapter 4 [see particularly notes 21 & 39], the Propaganda Department, which was under Wilfred's overall control in June 1934, had a subsection that was called the Industrial Section, and it was this section which superseded the Fascist Union of British Workers [FUBW] when it was disbanded; this section was headed by Taylor, so Wilfred will have had plenty of opportunity to get to know him [as well as Taylor would have allowed, anyway] and, as will be enlarged upon in Chapter 12, this relationship would later prove to be significant for Wilfred when he was in some difficulty. However, it was the second "forgery" which was of more concern to Wilfred in late 1937. Following on quite soon after the fiasco of the Action Press Uniform, Wilfred's dismay at his Leader's attitude over the question of foreign funding [the Director General's was very much to be expected, no doubt] was the focus of a definite turning point in his faith in, and commitment to a Movement [and, indeed, an ideology] which had totally absorbed him for at least five years: "... I say frankly I was not satisfied with that step [Mosley's refutation], I should have preferred legal action being taken because then I should have felt that everything was all right. ... it was from that incident that my own confidence and faith were somewhat shaken, and it did mark a definite change in my attitude and outlook." [**Appendix D**]

The re-evaluation of his vocation was not in view, however, in the aftermath of the east London Municipal election, and this was in fact the beginning of a very busy and productive period for Wilfred, making him very visible, both to the members with his articles in both weekly periodicals, and with his public speaking. Understandably, elections and everything associated with them figured very highly in his writing: he introduced a 'question & answer' feature in ***The Blackshirt*** ["**THAT VOTING BUSINESS / QUERIES ANSWERED BY THE CHIEF AGENT" 10**], to supplement the 'bread and butter' articles and further engage the membership, but he also branched out into another subject with which he was familiar; Socialism, and what he perceived as its failure, with articles such as "How the Socialists Began" [which was graced with a large photograph of "The late Keir Hardie, who was one of the first two Socialists elected to Parliament" **11**], "Can a Marxist become a Fascist? / Socialism is torn by internal Dissension" [**12**], and "Is Russia copying Fascist Economics? / Nationalism is a more potent Force to-day than Internationalism" [**13**]. He followed these up with an interesting digression: "Yeomen of England / How they originated and what they can mean now" [**14**]; by now, page 11 in ***Action*** seems to have become a regular 'spot' for him. Coincidentally, in this same issue, Mosley also had a full-page article on the same theme: "The Yeoman and the Soil" [**15**].

This was a recurrent theme in British fascist ideology and it also had, with respect to its antiquity, a connection with Magna Carta [or Charta, as it was generally written] and common law, although this particular term tended not to be used; even though the Movement made no secret of the fact that it was authoritarian in principle, the issue of dictatorship was usually fudged: if there was to be a dictatorship, it was to be a 'dictatorship of the people', elected by the will and common consent of the people, as had happened in Germany. Freedom of speech had always been an issue for Mosley, hence his use of the Fascist Defence Force, to enable him to exercise his right to free speech [although it was acknowledged, after the imposition of the Public Order Act, that there was no substantive right to 'freedom of speech' in Great Britain]; the 'freedom' of Democracy, as trumpeted by the corrupt politicians in thrall to international finance, was risible, and before very long, one of the primary elements of Magna Carta, *Habeas Corpus*, would be suspended by an understandably nervous Government, in an ironic reversal of reasoning imposed by wartime 'necessity'. In the meantime, there was work to be done, and Wilfred was commendably, and visibly, very busy.

Mosley had no doubts that what he was doing was right, and that he had the only solution to what ailed his beloved country, and that of his fellow-travellers and acolytes; no doubt he had plenty of time later to regret his insistence on the emphasis of Fascism as his creed: Wilfred's ambivalence towards this has already been mentioned, but according to Skidelsky, Mosley did not see Fascism, *per se*, as the ultimate goal: "The Fascist Party [sic] was simply the instrument for bringing about the new civilisation." [**16**]. Despite the setbacks, there was also some cautious encouragement to be found: "One of the first reputable public-opinion polls organised by Dr. Gallup in 1937 asked: 'If you had to choose between Fascism and Communism, which would you choose?' 56% gave Fascism and 44% gave Communism. Seven out of ten respondents under 30 preferred Fascism …" [**17**] Clearly, a very limited range of options, but nonetheless relevant and significant in those easily and, in a way, necessarily polarised times. Wilfred was still trying to demonstrate a link between his background and the creed he now espoused, in public at least; he wrote a long [eight page] article in the third ***British Union Quarterly*** of 1937, entitled ***The Heritage of National Socialism***, which might have unconsciously served to convince himself, as well as his readers, of the progression achieved, and the legitimate connection of what he was championing now to his earlier 'left-wing' ideology; or perhaps it was, as Philip Coupland put it: "Rather than seek to distance itself from socialism, the BUF sought to present itself as the inheritor of a specifically British socialist tradition represented in fascist eyes by figures including William Morris and Robert Owen." [**18**]

Wilfred certainly wasn't confined to the office in 1937: as previously stated, he was again regularly speaking in public, and at the beginning of June, British Union, personified by its principal speakers, hit the campaign trail. Although it might have seemed a bit 'previous' to be campaigning for a general election which was probably still two years hence, Wilfred was absolutely convinced [and, no doubt, backed to the hilt on this issue, if not actually propelled, by Mosley] that it was never too early to be campaigning ceaselessly, canvassing, and building the electioneering machinery which was vital to an organisation such as theirs, with the publicly stated goal of achieving power by legitimate electoral methods. Both weekly periodicals carried virtually the same story: ***The Blackshirt*** informed readers that BU was

"Going to the Country" [**19**], and helpfully printed an intentionally candid shot of five of the speakers, albeit posed in a semi-circle, "[d]iscussing the Tour", now uniform-less in their workaday, slightly crumpled business suits. Wilfred, looking relaxed as ever, is surrounded by Raven Thomson, Clement Bruning, Wegg Prosser and Ernest ["Mick"] Clarke. These, and others, were described as "the Big Men" in the "Great British Union Platform Campaign", but in ***Action***, they were the big men of Fascism [**20**], and in ***The Blackshirt***, they were the big men of National Socialism: notwithstanding page layout considerations, perhaps the appellation 'Fascism' was considered more palatable, given its longer existence and consequent familiarity, to the general public readers of ***Action***, than was National Socialism, with its connotations of Nazism, regarded as acceptable to the mostly Blackshirt [now in name only] readers of ***The Blackshirt***? Even if he had not arrived at the definition himself, as the figurehead and public mouthpiece of the Movement, Mosley had cleverly sought to define the new name of British Union in a way that simple working people could easily understand: "If you love our country you are National; if you love our people you are Socialist". The campaign was due to run until Sunday, July 11th.

Wilfred's importance to the campaign was recognised, albeit relatively briefly, under the paragraph heading "Forceful Speakers", in the longer of the two articles: "He is the Chief Electoral Agent of the British Union, and to him falls the responsibility of preparing the technical details of the forthcoming electoral campaign when the British Union will seek the vote of the British people in their Parliamentary campaign. He is an old member of the Labour Party, in which he held various executive posts." [**21**] He was to open his contribution to the campaign on Saturday, June 5, at Grays, and he was scheduled to speak thereafter at Guildford, Worthing, Cardiff, Leicester, Huddersfield, Crewe, Chester, Bedford, and finally, conveniently, in London. The articles also gave details of speakers' schools, "primarily intended for speakers who are already qualified but need a refresher course", which were to be held in London, Birmingham, Leeds, Cardiff, Manchester, Edinburgh and Exeter, and given, "[i]n addition to their public-speaking activities" not only by Wilfred, one of the Movement's acknowledged authorities, but also by Raven Thomson, Clement Bruning [**22**], and Tommy Moran [**23**]. Only a week into the campaign, Wilfred published "Some Thoughts on Modern Election Methods", the main title of the article being "Joy in Contest"! The article informed its readers, as well as what they most probably already knew: "A Parliamentary General Election looms ahead."; that "Borough Council elections are coming along in November. … Once again I ask … 'Are you on?' It can be great fun, great effort, and excellent training for future VICTORY." [**24**]

Near the end of the summer speaking campaign, there was a march on Sunday July 4th; the route was from north London to Trafalgar Square: this was in order to prevent the march being banned by the Home Secretary, the previously planned march, originating in Limehouse, east London, "surrendering to violent threats" because "[t]he Reds threatened another riot" [**25**]. The event was to commence at 3 p.m. at Kentish town, with a speech by Mosley, then the march would proceed to Trafalgar Square, where the Leader would again speak, at 5 p.m. Apparently, "gangs of hooligans from all over England" were expected [**26**]; as it happened, Wilfred was watching the march [not being required, by virtue of his position, to participate] "at the foot of Charing Cross Road", near its destination, and this appears to be the one and only time that he mentions Nellie accompanying him: his report, a week later, is written in a humorous vein, and alternates between observation from his point of view and that of a non-member, adopting the commonly-used device of referring to protesters as "angry verkers" [**27**]. He doesn't mention any trouble occurring, although along the route, two potentially dangerous missiles were thrown at Mosley, and the Leader fended off a "Red [who] rushed at [him] with swinging fists … with a punch on the jaw, and the man went reeling back and was collected by the police." [**28**] Presumably, Mosley continued undaunted on his way!

The campaign was regarded as a success; in an article in ***Action*** entitled "Many Great Meetings / Trafalgar Square Rally Stimulates Interest!" [**29**], two of Wilfred's meetings were highlighted, and he was duly honoured with the inclusion of a half-length profile photograph. The speakers' schools also discovered "a number of promising new speakers" [which rather runs counter to the previously stipulated suggestion that they were primarily for existing speakers who wished to improve], and, either optimistically or naïvely, the article noted that "a great number of votes at the next General Election have been promised." Wilfred's articles continued thereafter with another Socialism/Fascism comparison, but this time using the device of winning over old friends from his Socialist days, which might or might not have been fiction, but it reads convincingly enough [**30**]; there are a few lines which, if honest [not just dutifully trotting out the expected doctrine] give some insight into his justification [or rationalisation] of his current attitude: "I am bound to say that the Socialist movement is not what it was. Changed it is, beyond recognition. … And what of myself. Have I changed? Of course I have. … Society itself has changed and developed in the past ten years, and people have changed correspondingly. … The Socialists have grown far away from the Socialism of those earlier days, and we who have learned National Socialism have grown just as far away in a different direction. … Hankering after the past would be both futile and undesirable. … This is the new spirit, evolved of the new creed – Fascism and National Socialism."

Wilfred also alludes to his attitude towards pacifism in this article ["although I hated war (as who would not after experiencing four years of it), nevertheless I was not prepared to say I would never fight again."], but a candid demonstration of his involvement in one of its antitheses was exemplified in a concurrent article by the soon-to-be appointed editor of ***The Blackshirt***, A. K. Chesterton, one of a series comprising a suitably laudatory appraisal of Mosley called "Portrait of a Leader" [in the previous article, he referred to Wilfred as "splendid" **31**], and he tells how Wilfred was one of five "headquarters officers, all in plain clothes" who intervened at a meeting in Newcastle to prevent a BUF speaker "from receiving terrible injuries" [**32**]. This does rather give the impression that it was all deadly serious business for Fascists [*aka* National Socialists], but they did 'let their hair down' [metaphorically speaking] occasionally: there had been summer camps for the Movement from the earliest days, and 1937 was no exception. On the weekend at the end of July, Mosley joined hundreds of members and cadets at Selsey for a camp which had been organised by one of Francis-Hawkins's deputies, Captain Bryan Donovan [**33**], who was Assistant Director General (Organisation), Southern Administration; notwithstanding that he was referred to, with no detectable irony [as the now more familiar connotations were still many years hence] as the Camp Commandant, the occasion was semi-relaxed, but the Fascist ethos was ever-present, and many members saluted when the Leader made his foray into the sea, to the bemusement of the "holiday-makers": "The next general assembly was the bathing parade (if the custodians of the Public Order Act will allow so martial an expression). Clustering around the Leader, chanting the songs of the National Socialist struggle, the whole twelve hundred left the Blackshirt camp and passed through the encampment of the general public in one huge procession." [**34**]

Wilfred was there [whether by accident on this particular weekend, or by design, is unknown], but no mention was made of Nellie, even though "well-known" women Blackshirts were present, albeit relegated to vital duties "sweltering all day getting [tea in the marquee] ready" [**35**]; as well as the presentation to Mosley of an MG sports car, "a result of the initiative of [National Inspector W. H. "Peter"] Symes … with a view to placing the Leader's Bentley on the superannuation list", which left him "very deeply touched" [**36**], there was a somewhat surprisingly frivolous diversion in "'Selsey Bilge', the Camp newspaper, a bright little publication in which almost every well-known member of the Movement finds his leg remorselessly pulled." [**37**] No prizes for guessing whose leg was not pulled, remorselessly or otherwise! Wilfred's was [perhaps only about his name], about which he would very probably have been quite pleased, to be considered 'one of the boys': the week after the camp, there is a photograph in ***The Blackshirt***, purporting to show him having "just discovered to his horror that he has been exposed in 'Selsey Bilge'. His usual sunny smile is missing!" [**38**] when in fact, he is grinning from ear to ear, standing between Bill Luckin, a Blackshirt speaker and reporter from south London, and Archibald Garrioch Findlay [**39**].

Co-synchronously with this, an article appeared in ***Action*** under the headline "Rights of Animals", and because it is unattributed, it is tempting to infer that it was written by Wilfred but, to be fair, animal welfare and humane consideration towards them was a fundamental part of the fascist ethos; however, the article included some interesting sentiments, within the rubric of the general contemporary understanding of fascist ideology: "We have reached a stage to-day when it is an accepted theory that all human beings have the right to be treated in a humane manner, regardless of class, sex or colour. … There is only one moral and just law, which is that to cause suffering to any living thing is wrong—a wrong that must be fought and abolished if we want to attain a better world." [**40**]. Notwithstanding Wilfred's possible authorship, the article also has a connection, in terms of treatment of human beings, with another matter in the news at the time, about which Wilfred definitely did write: the Palestine mandate. At the end of July, Michael Goulding had written in ***The Blackshirt*** in general terms about the currently 'hot topic', the Royal Commission on Palestine [**41**]; a month later, Wilfred took up the baton, and in the lead story on the front page [possibly the one and only time] of ***The Blackshirt***, complete with the same half-length profile picture that had been used with the report on the Trafalgar Square rally, he postulated a controversial theory [which could generally have been considered even more so, in light of subsequent events]: "Give Germans the Palestine Mandate". His reasoning was purely logical [and couched in his individual humour]: "… we have too many pre-occupations of our own to be able to give the problem that undivided attention which it deserves. After all, we *have* an Empire to look after …", and "Germany–now there's a possibility. A power of proven administrative capacity, deprived of her own colonies but hoping and deserving of eventually regaining them, but meantime out of practice. *What about handing over the mandate to Germany?* 'S-an-idea! Think of all the fascinating possibilities." [**42**] Unfortunately, this appears to have only been thrown in as a sort of 'catchpenny', without being developed fully as a hypothesis, subsequent events conspiring to thwart further discussion, and this will have undoubtedly remained very much a minority suggestion, unlikely to be even considered in official circles, despite its apparent practicability.

Throughout that autumn, Wilfred wrote non-stop, with articles appearing in one or both periodicals nearly every week, and several of the articles were substantial in length, occupying either the whole page, or the major part; this did not preclude alternative formats, however: at the end of the year, starting in December, a series of 'bite-size' articles entitled ***Elections are won on the Doorstep*** appeared in ***Action***, which cleverly combined the dual necessities of concentration on electioneering, and the propaganda work that was essential to facilitate it. In October, one of his major contributions to the canon of British Union literature was serialised over five weeks in ***Action***, before its publication in collected form as a pamphlet,

Strike Action or Power Action, in December, for the princely sum of one penny! This was one of the very few examples from his deluge of writing either on or for National Socialism with British Union which was available independently, and all of his reasoning, the culmination of many years of experience and observation, was presented in five and a half pages of tightly-packed type in a large paperback-size format; the cover was very striking [no pun intended], with a specially-commissioned [and very probably voluntarily contributed] monochrome ink or watercolour picture, depicting the apparently hopeless situation of an unemployed worker, lolling against his front door jamb, observing a strike meeting in progress, while in the house his wife sits disconsolately at the table, head in hands, with only a meagre piece of bread on the breadboard for sustenance [**43**]. Like earlier in the year, Wilfred was not confined to the office during this period, still speaking regularly, and deputising for the Leader on at least two occasions [**44**], following the serious head injury he received when giving an open-air speech at Liverpool [**45**].

The long-term goal was still the expected general election, and there were borough elections to look forward to in November, but looming over all of this like a storm cloud was the threat of international war. British Union applauded the British Government's decision not to become embroiled in the Spanish civil war, but it was highly critical of the support given by the Socialists and Communists to the republicans, including eliciting and receiving substantial financial contributions from hard-pressed working people, which all of the senior British Union commentators, including Wilfred, were at pains to disparage: this was money which could have been used more appropriately and effectively at home ["How much more to the point it would be if the ***Land Worker*** would run a campaign to obtain at least 10s. per week for every child of every farm worker in England, instead of making futile appeals to the most miserably paid section of Britain's wage-workers to contribute on this (comparatively) lavish scale to the upkeep of children brought into this country as a propaganda dodge by Spanish church-burners." **46**]. There was also concern that opposition to German policies, although not explicitly defined as such, could precipitate war; taking the lead, as ever, at the opening of "[t]he British Union's autumn campaign ... Mosley ... showed how all the political parties were bankrupt of any solution for the impending slump, apart from the solution of war. In particular, he denounced the Labour Party as the War Party, showing how completely it had run away from Socialism in Britain in order to ally itself with the Tories and High Finance and thus expedite a European War on behalf of the blood-stained Russian Soviet." [**47**]

One diversion for Wilfred from all this seriousness would have been the Labour Party conference at Bournemouth, and it is interesting to speculate whether he will have stayed at his older sister Jessie's modest detached house in Southbourne, to enable him to observe the event at close quarters; no doubt he wasn't able to visit as often as he would have liked, but there might occasionally have been a spare room after his father died in 1931, because it is known that Jessie took in lodgers to help make ends meet: perhaps Wilfred had been helping Jessie financially in the meantime, with a view to having a permanently available 'bolt-hole' should the necessity arise? [and it is altogether possible that he might have either bought the house for them or taken over payment of the mortgage, as soon as he was in a position to] His report on the conference in ***The Blackshirt*** ["Political Marionettes by the Sea / Labour at Bournemouth **48**] is full of his, by now, customary wry humour; Labour unity was very unlikely: "it was just the usual Labour Conference, everybody thoroughly hating everybody else". His erstwhile colleague and friend, Aneurin Bevan, was making waves [as usual], but Wilfred was restrained in his reporting: "High Light Number Two came when the Conference decided by nearly two millions of a majority in favour of a full defence and rearmament policy. This policy was opposed by Mr. Aneurin Bevan, of Ebbw Vale, on the grounds that it did not impose an obligation on the executive to secure a guarantee from the Government that these arms would be used only to fight Fascism.", although he did describe this indirectly as a "naïve opposition". Wilfred did manage to get in another dig at the Labour Party, on the back of "one other objection of Mr. Aneurin Bevan, who raised the plaint that the Labour Movement was 'handing itself over to the National Government WITHOUT EVEN HAVING ITS PRICE.'"

There appeared to be some confusion over whether British Union was putting up official candidates for the November borough council elections; many people obviously thought that this was the case, and this probably partly explains the decision of some candidates such as Bailey, who had been very much under the impression that official support would be forthcoming [a belief that was clearly substantiated by Wilfred's tacit support **49**], to withdraw; albeit some, such as Bailey, more precipitately than others [see note 41] but ***The Blackshirt*** offered a clarification at the end of September: "While certain districts in other parts of the country have decided to try out their electoral machines at the forthcoming local elections, such contests are no part of the general policy of the British Union." [**50**] Although it did not explicitly pre-empt or convey the message of official participation, Wilfred's article on contesting municipal elections in ***Action*** back in May was very informative, insisting that "[t]he time to start winning an election is as soon as the previous election is finished", and more specifically, "If Borough Council elections are the immediate objective you should start at the end of August or the beginning of September to overhaul your electoral machine and plan your campaign for the elections which will be held on the first of November." [**51**].

In another example which will undoubtedly run counter to the general preconception of Fascists/National Socialists as anti-democratic, thuggish automata, Wilfred wrote about "Intimidation of British Union Candidates", in the run-up to the borough council elections: "Our intervention in certain cases in Borough Council Elections has introduced our members all over the country to the full degree of political spite and terrorism which is being fomented by our opponents", and went on to quote five specific examples, as well as general problems; "On this occasion we are contesting only local government seats, and that in only sixteen different boroughs. If we take the present instances as a fair indication as to what is likely to happen in the future members will be able to realise what sort of situation will confront us in the next General Election when we intend to contest one hundred Parliamentary constituencies." They had been warned at the very outset of British Union not to expect an easy ride, but this was hardly the sort of treatment which should be expected in an allegedly civilised democratic country. If nothing else, it served to convince them that they were following the right path, and it stiffened their resolve: "The reign of the reactionaries is over, the future lies with the new forces so well represented in the ranks of the British Union." **[52]**

The elections were held on Monday, November 1st, and when the results were in, Wilfred was again very positive: in the London boroughs, he stated that "[w]e have every reason to congratulate ourselves on the results obtained", and elsewhere, "In all other cases throughout the country we were breaking entirely new ground, and the votes polled by our candidates showed a gratifyingly high standard of public support for British Union principles." It was certainly not a question of resting on any laurels, such as they were, thereafter; it was 'back to work', immediately: "My last word is addressed to our own members in all districts, to whom I offer a word of advice to the effect that elections are won in the periods between elections, and not during those hectic few days of the election period proper. Those who intend to engage in electoral activities in the future should start on the job here and now." **[53]** Even though it is more likely that the choice of wards to contest will have been made either by Mosley himself, or by Francis-Hawkins, and endorsed by Mosley, perhaps with some advisory input from Wilfred, the operation of the machinery to support the official candidates will have been indisputably Wilfred's responsibility, so he will no doubt have had cause for some private relief, in addition to the public cautious optimism about the potential for the future; however, if he was any sort of pragmatist, he must have realised how concerted the effort from there on would have to be, if the Movement was going to be able to extrapolate from these patchy results a momentum which they could parlay into a general election victory in two or three years' time.

As if the acquisition and dissemination of all that very specialised information was not enough, Wilfred also started reviewing books for ***Action***. He was known to have devoured a great many tomes on political and economic matters in the course of his self-education, but in those mostly pre-television days [**54**], reading was an extremely popular pastime and, conscious of its mission to provide a rounded and varied output, ***Action*** had been giving its readers book & film reviews consistently since its reappearance in February 1936, but it was only in autumn 1937 that Wilfred started to make his own contributions [or, at least, attributed to him: he might have made anonymous contributions previously]. One of the first books he reviewed, in reasonably glowing, but unsycophantic terms, was ***The Socialist Case***, by Douglas Jay, who was currently City Editor of the ***Daily Herald***, although it is likely that Wilfred's interpretation was probably not what Jay himself had in mind: "This is one of the most interesting publications which has come my way in recent months. … the reader will probably be able to follow my line of reasoning when I say that it is a departure from the old school of Socialist thought, which departure brings the writer more into line with National Socialism than with the old theories of Socialism hitherto advocated. This is a book which should be read by discriminating students of National Socialism." [**55**]

As the year drew to a close, foreign concerns such as Palestine, Spain and Russia, apparently despite British Union's best efforts, overshadowed the problems at home that the organisation wanted to overcome; notwithstanding the alleged Jewish connections, most, if not all, of the problems currently afflicting the world were attributable to finance, and all of the Movement's main correspondents, including Wilfred, made the connection between the seemingly inescapable, endlessly repeating cycles of 'boom' and consequent 'slump', and war, which was acknowledged, with varying degrees of reluctance, by the established politicians, as a solution, albeit a morally questionable one. In an editorial in ***Action***, the new editor, Geoffrey Dorman, wrote that "Financial Democracy the world over finds itself in a fatal dilemma. Either it must plunge into a depression even worse than the last, or it must seek an escape in another world war. [hence] Depression creates Fascism", and the thrust of the piece was that the benefits of Fascism in Britain, even after the inevitable precursor of "renewed depression", were by far preferable to "the unknown dangers of another war" [**56**]. This was followed by a double-page article by the aforementioned Michael Goulding entitled "Slump or War? Are Politicians Heading for War to Save Themselves?", which expanded on this question.

Nearly two years before this, Mosley had written in the very first edition of the relaunched ***Action*** about the political situation in Europe, under the banner headline "War or Peace?", with a graphic captioned "The Encirclement of Germany" [**57**], but at the end of 1937, the financial situation was seen as equally portentous as the political one, if not actually the demonstrable catalyst for the worsening political climate. Despite Germany's attitude of "sceptical hope" towards Lord Halifax's "private and unofficial" visit to Hitler at the end of 1937 [**58**], there were other worrying moves afoot, such as an Anglo-American trade pact; in a long and very detailed article in ***Action***, Robert Gordon-Canning asked, among other questions, "from the British point of view …: Is this pact to be used as a means of creating a 'democratic' front against 'dictator' countries?" [**59**] There was also "a plan to divide the world into two mutually hostile camps", put forward by the former Labour Solicitor General Sir Stafford Cripps: "No method of ensuring war could be devised more certain than this cool proposal to exclude Fascist States from all access to the sources of raw material." [**60**]

So the year ended, with a certain amount of determined 'business as usual', and a renewed attempt to break the BBC stranglehold that was preventing Mosley from putting his message across ["let Mosley Broadcast" **61**]; as yet, there was no activity occurring either at home or abroad which gave immediate cause for concern that Wilfred's hard work would not come to fruition in a year or two's time, when a general election should be called, but despite that, British Union must have been collectively steeling itself for another year to come of recurrent and increasing desperation from the Government in the face of a worsening economic situation, persistent apathy and outright hostility on the part of the electorate, and all this overlaid with the inexorably gathering clouds of war in Europe.

NOTES

1 ***My Life, by Sir Oswald Mosley:***

"… while our branches were self-supporting, a number of people were always busy collecting for our headquarters. Their guide lines were to receive subscriptions from any British people within the Empire, provided no strings were attached. It seemed a just principle that funds should be raised for a movement within the sphere in which it operates; our principal interest was then the British Empire. It is true that all my life—as my very early speeches show—I felt myself an European, and that as a movement we were greatly interested in keeping peace between Europeans and also in the gradual development of some common aims in European policies. It would therefore have been quite legitimate in my view to raise money, also on the condition that no strings were attached, from other Europeans; certainly the charge of the movement raising money in this way and on these conditions would not have worried me in the least. We should merely have been in the same position as so many members of the Second International, not to mention the Third."

2 ***Ibid.:***

"After the war the Home Secretary, Mr. Chuter Ede, prefaced a reference to me in the House of Commons on June 6, 1946, with the curious observation for a Minister in a supposedly judicial position: 'I can only hope this will be an instructive foreword to the book he proposes to publish'. … His allegation in effect was that letters had been found among Mussolini's papers which purported to show that I had accepted funds from Italy on behalf of British Union in the years 1934 and 1935. I challenged him next day to produce the evidence, adding that 'evidence on any subject could now be available at a penny a packet' in alleged archives. …

Leaders such as Mussolini would indeed have been starry-eyed philanthropists if they had held such sinister designs against the British Empire and yet financed the only movement in Britain which was standing for its rearmament, and agitating continuously, publicly and furiously to that end. … In reality, fascist and national socialist leaders everywhere were quite content to let us get on with our business, which was preserving and developing the British Empire, if we would let them get on with their business, which took them in a totally different direction to the British Empire and our vital interests."

3 ***Oswald Mosley, by Robert Skidelsky:***

"One of the crucial files HO 283/65 - containing MI5 letters to Birkett - remains closed [when this book was written in 1975]."

The book was reprinted in 1981, and a third edition printed in 1990:

"By far the most interesting study which has appeared since this book was published is Nicholas Mosley's 2-volume life of his father, ***Rules of the Game*** (1982) and ***Beyond the Pale*** (1983). … Mr. Mosley provides some interesting new political material about the BUF period. … Another interesting suggestion [as well as the Grandi information on Mussolini's support] is that Mosley's friend WED Allen, an ex-Conservative MP and Belfast businessman who received the Italian payments on Mosley's behalf, worked for the British security service. Through Allen, as well as other sources, the British Government must have known about most of what was going on in the BUF, as well as the Mosleys' contacts with Hitler, in the late 1930s, arising from Mosley's plan to set up a network of commercial radio stations."

This will be dealt with in more detail in a later chapter.

4 ***Special Branch Report, 24 October, 1935. PRO HO144/20145/12-17, cited in BLACKSHIRTS TORN: INSIDE THE BRITISH UNION OF FASCISTS, 1932-1940, by Thomas Norman Keeley, MA Degree submission, Simon Fraser University, Canada, 1998***

5 ***Ibid.***

6 ***Oswald Mosley, op. cit.***

7 Unfortunately, it has only been possible to view a very poorly scanned copy of this page, so some of it is indecipherable:

"**ANOTHER FORGERY**

The Assistant-Director-General of Organisation (A) [?Headquarters] Administration reports [?under] confidential cover that you have been secretly informing members that this movement is financially supported by Italian and German funds.

[?I] must remind you at the Leader's conference, at which [?his] statement to his inspectors was given in the strictest confidence and not before he had bound everyone to their word of honour [?regarding] the entire proceedings.

In view of [illegible] report, it will be necessary for you to attend at these headquarters at 10am on the [?13th] inst. [?that] the [?whole ?matters] will be investigated.

Kindly arrange your inspections etc. so that you may comply with these instructions.

[signed] N. Francis-Hawkins,

Director-General of Organisation

We print above, written on British Union official notepaper an impudent forgery, [?photographs] of which, we understand, are being circulated at the present time. It is unnecessary to state that the Director-General of the British Union never wrote any such letter, and that no such conference ever took place. Owing to elementary blunders on the part of the forgers, it is, happily, very easy to prove this letter a forgery.

If our enemies must introduce these tactics into British politics, they should employ more skilful instruments."

Action no. 94, December 2nd, 1937, page 3

THE SPACE BELOW IS LEFT INTENTIONALLY BLANK

8 *"'WARE FORGERIES*

This card has come into the hands of the British Union. It purports to be a card of identity of a secret service member of the British Union. It is a palpable fake and Mosley's signature is a forgery. No such cards have been issued, and there is no secret services department at the B.U. and no secret service members. The card has probably been issued either in an attempt to discredit the B.U. or is an attempt by Financial Democrats (including Communists) to pry into B.U. affairs. Anyone in possession of such a card should be handed over to the police."

TO ALL RANKS
This man is on
SPECIAL DUTY
of a confidential nature, and must be given every assistance by all ranks of the
British Union

No. 59Z
(London)

[signature purporting to be Mosley's]

Action no. 91, November 13th, 1937, page 14

9 Taylor will be dealt with in more depth in the next chapter, but according to Brian Simpson,

"The Special Branch had at least one informer in the party, P. G. Taylor, the industrial advisor; he was known to Mosley. ... He appears by profession to have been a private detective, but virtually nothing seems to be known about him."

In the highest Degree odious: Detention without Trial in Wartime Britain, by Alfred William Brian Simpson

He was also Alex Miles's superior; Miles recalls that:

"At the end of February, 1934, I was recalled to national Headquarters, by that time located in King's Road, Chelsea. ... At the same time and on the same or the following day, I was appointed Deputy-Director of the Industrial Section ..."

The Streets are still/Mosley in Motley, typescript memoir, undated [c.1937] by Alexander Miles, MSS 292/743.11/2, University of Warwick Modern Records Centre

Miles also appears to have sometimes referred to himself as "Assistant Director of Industrial Policy".

Private information, courtesy of Jeffrey Wallder

10 ***The Blackshirt no. 209, April 24th, 1937, page 5:***

"The Chief Agent receives many interesting questions on election law and procedure. A selection of these, with the answers, will be published each week. If you have a question coming under this heading, send it in and watch for the answer in future issues."

11 **Mosley Needs You:** ***Action, no. 58, March 27th, 1937, page 11:***

"The British Union, through its Leader, Sir Oswald Mosley, has announced its intention of contesting more than 100 Parliamentary seats in the forthcoming General Election. This is a new gesture in the realm of electoral endeavour. Never has such a colossal undertaking been tackled by a new movement in its first bid, and after only four years of preparation.

The Socialist movement had been in existence as an active propaganda force for fifty years before its first Parliamentary candidate was brought forward. As early as 1833 Robert Owen was advocating Socialism and had worked out the Socialist theory in some detail. Continuous Socialist propaganda brought into being the Social Democratic Federation (1881), who [sic], in 1884 – more than fifty years after the beginning of Owen's Socialist propaganda – decided to run Parliamentary candidates.

In November, 1885, the first three candidates were put up and polled, between them, 702 votes. Eventually, in 1900, the Labour Representation Committee was formed. This was the infant form of the Labour Party of to-day. Fifteen candidates were put up in that year, two of whom – James Keir Hardie and Richard Bell – were returned to the House. This was after eighty years of Socialist propaganda effort.

Audacity

The audacity of a movement four years old pledging itself to so many Parliamentary candidates can only be appreciated by such a comparison. Such an undertaking is staggering, and those who are with us must view with pride the rate and scope of our progress as compared with that of Socialism.

To obtain any measure of success that pride will have to be translated into active effort. Mosley needs you in the team of active workers who will have to put over his first hundred candidates.

There is a colossal amount of work to be put into the selected constituencies before the next General Election, and every member and sympathiser can help in his or her own way. Agents will have to be found and trained; canvassers will have to be mobilised and taught the finer points of canvassing; the forces in each constituency will have to be organised in their spheres of useful activity; canvass cards and election envelopes must be written up for the constituencies; marked registers must be built up; propaganda teams organised; election funds provided, and a thousand and one jobs attended to, which will be dealt with in detail in subsequent articles.

All Are Wanted

All this active effort will necessitate every available member and sympathiser getting into the team and pulling his or her weight.

This is a great adventure, and every one is able to help in some way. Those who are able to help openly and boldly can do much useful work in the field of propaganda, refuting the misrepresentations of Fascism, putting forward the constructive proposals of the British Union; canvassing on the streets and in the factories and workshops; distributing Action, Blackshirt, and other British Union publications; active at all times in the forefront of the fight to build up the body of popular support that will give us victory.

Those, on the other hand, who through fear of victimisation are unable to help us in a manner that will bring them into prominence can help very substantially in other ways. They can subscribe regularly (sums from one penny per week upwards) to the election funds; they can address envelopes and write up canvass cards at home; they can supply information as to people of Fascist sympathies with whom they come into contact; they can distribute our literature unobtrusively through the post or by leaving it in trains, trams, buses, reading rooms, etc. There is positively no limit to the help which may be given by ALL who desire to see the establishment of the Corporate State for Britain and the Empire at the earliest possible moment.

If any reader is in doubt as to the best way in which assistance may be given we shall welcome the opportunity to help if he or she will write for our advice. Such communications will, of course, be treated as confidential.

You need Mosley – Mosley needs you! Give your help, and victory is assured."

12 ***Action, no. 60, April 10th, 1937, page 11:***

"'How can a Marxist become a Fascist?' I was asked last week. I had spoken overnight at a meeting in the constituency where I had been Socialist candidate thirteen years ago, and the question was put to me by one of my supporters of those earlier days who had called to see me before my return to London.

He registered astonishment when I smilingly told him that Marxism had led me to Fascism before I knew it to be Fascism. Explanations were asked for, and I gave them as follows:

'Marxism teaches that civilisation develops in three phases; that those phases grow up, become decrepit, and finally pass away just as human beings do, or plants, or any other form of living organism; that out of the conditions of their final decay emerges the seed of the next phase of civilised society – correct?'

Economic Determinism

'Yes. That's right enough,' said my questioner, 'that's economic determinism.'

'Right', said I. 'Now let's have a look at Capitalist Society of to-day. It has grown up – more rapidly in some countries than in others – and is now reaching the stage of decrepitude.' So far we were agreed.

'Now,' I continued, 'I want you to take special notice of this fact. Socialism is a theory of an alternative form of society. The Socialist theory emerged during the infancy of Capitalism, developed and grew in direct ratio with the development and growth of Capitalism. The Great War, 1914 to 1918, marked a great forward spurt in Capitalist development and the post-war years, 1918 to 1928, witnessed the final stages of that development.'

Decrepitude and Decay

'From that stage onwards Capitalist society in Britain has shown greater and ever-increasing evidence of decrepitude and decay. Post-war problems have proved incapable of solution under Capitalism, and Capitalism is now in a state of disintegration. Not only is Capitalism disintegrating, however, but the Socialist movement which grew up within the Capitalist system is also on the downgrade, splitting up into conflicting sections, baffled just as badly as is Capitalism itself by the problems of modern society.

Post-war problems are not capable of solution by slogans, and that is all that the Socialist movement has yet produced. Nationalisation of the means of production, they say, will solve the problem. That is merely a slogan. What is their plan for nationalisation? There isn't one. There are dozens of half-baked and – mark this – conflicting plans for nationalisation.'

Divided Opinion

'One section wants to nationalise only the bankrupt or near-bankrupt undertakings such as mines, railways, land, etc. Another section wants to nationalise banking, transport, and the key industries. One section wants to confiscate. Another section wants to compensate. One section wants to nationalise in a hurry (twenty-five years), and call their policy '***Socialism In Our Time***'. Another section insists on the 'inevitability of gradualness', and are prepared to wait a hundred years or so for their plans to emerge and develop.

All this, to put it mildly, is not encouraging. Socialism, as a political force, torn and rent by internal dissension, is weaker to-day than ten years ago. In other words, it is declining, together with the system of Capitalism.

It is not an *alternative* to Capitalism, but merely a negative of Capitalism – the obverse of the same coin, so to speak. It is imperative, therefore, that we seek for the true alternative to the decaying Capitalist state.'

Prejudice Excluded

'We who set out to do this in the New Party in 1931 had to exclude from our minds all prejudices and start from the existing evil to find a remedy for that evil. We gradually built up an economic policy (and that policy incidentally has never yet been seriously criticised by any of our present-day economists) which fitted the needs of the moment.

In that policy we found three vital factors, all of which were essential to success, all of which constitutes fundamental differences from Socialism. We found that Nationalism was essential as opposed to Internationalism. We found that class collaboration was essential on a national basis, as opposed to class antagonism on an international basis. We found that the preservation of the rights of private property, carrying with it certain new obligations for the owners of private property, was essential, as opposed to the abolition of private property rights. (Please remember those three points – they will crop up again later.)'

As in the Human Body

'We also decided that the interests of the State as a whole comprised the interests of every section within the State. That just as in the human body every limb and every organ is attuned to serve the whole of the body, so in society every sectional interest must be subordinated to the general interest of the State as a whole. This is the corporate conception of society, and this was where we arrived definitely at what is called Fascism or National Socialism.

Next we turned, quite naturally, to a consideration of other Capitalist states in decline to see what was happening to them.

Italy and Germany both had reached the stage of Capitalist disintegration. In each of these countries the parties of Socialism had tried and failed to solve the problem of a disintegrating industrial system just as the parties of Socialism in France are at present trying and failing. In all these cases we find Fascist forces emerging from the joint collapse of Capitalism and Socialism; Fascism or National Socialism, springing in each case from the decay of the preceding system; in each case, success crowning its efforts where Socialism fails. What about it?'

What About Russia?

'Well,' said my erstwhile Socialist supporter, 'I didn't think there was that much of a case for Fascism, but, even so – what about Russia, its achievements, its five-year plan, and so forth? That's Socialism, and it has succeeded.'

To which I retorted that the only success attained in Russia had been gained by dropping some of the most cherished of Communist dogma and adopting quite a substantial slice of Fascism in method, although not in name. This, too, I was able to prove to him, but owing to limitation of space I shall have to ask my readers to wait for the details of that proof."

13 ***Action, no. 61, April 17th, 1937, page 11:***

"This is a question which is cropping up with ever-increasing frequency in the minds of students who are interested in post-War social experiments. Such a question would not, and could not, arise unless there had been considerable divergence from the fundamentals of Communism as originally conceived and practised in Russia.

The fundamental differences between Fascism and Communism are those of class antagonism versus class collaboration, internationalism versus nationalism, Collective State ownership versus private ownership of the means of production, distribution and exchange.

In the early days of the Communist experiment there was a great 'liquidation' of property owners, employers, technicians, and all others who could not be defined as of the proletariat. (It should perhaps be mentioned for the benefit of the uninitiated that the term "liquidation" meant precisely the same thing as the cruder Americanism, 'bumping off'.)

Their Own Rules

Having effectively disposed of all who held different views from themselves, the Soviet then proceeded to operate the social system according to their own rules. Much to their amazement, they found that even the proletarian peasant held hard and fast views re the importance of the profit motive, and that unless he could retail his produce 'at a profit' he was not prepared to bring these goods into the market.

Moreover, unless he could see a prospect of a future profit on his produce he wasn't prepared even to grow crops, and as a result of his obstinacy in these respects there was crop shortage and widespread hardship. As a result of widespread crop shortage, wheat was used to make bread which should have been the seed reserve for the following year. Livestock was killed for meat which should have been reserved for breeding purposes, and for a number of years there were appalling conditions of famine, which resulted in the 'liquidation' of the proletariat themselves.

In The Towns

This was what happened in the countryside. In the towns and the industrial areas conditions were equally disastrous. Owing to the lack technical direction (remember, the technicians had been 'liquidated') there was a terrific falling-off in production, and, as production is the only real wealth, there was consequent impoverishment for all concerned.

The Communist experiment was not delivering the goods. Consequently, Lenin – the realist – came forward with the New Economic Policy, which jettisoned quite a considerable slice of the sheer 'dogma' of Communist doctrine, and by the reintroduction of the 'profit motive' on a restricted scale, set out slowly and painfully to rectify his errors.

From that time onward there has been an ever-increasing tendency to move in the direction of Fascist method rather than Communist method.

The Five-Year Plan

If we take as an instance the 'The Five-Year Plan', which is by far the most outstanding achievement of Soviet Russia, we find that it was put through only by virtue of the fact that Communist shibboleths were entirely dropped and every other consideration subordinated to gaining the desired end.

Capital was raised on loan and *interest on that capital was guaranteed* by the State, although Communism has always taught that 'interest is robbery'.

German and American technicians were imported to supervise the various schemes of work involved in the plan, and were paid princely salaries for their services.

Concessions and leases were granted to foreign capitalists to develop certain mineral areas on the 'profit basis'.

All this was on the material side of the undertaking.

Propaganda

At the same time there was a use of the great propaganda machine directed toward the creation of a great volume of national patriotism. Pride of Soviet achievement was sedulously fostered, and the desire for Russian predominance was carefully inculcated in the masses of the Russian peoples. In this new constitution recently introduced this principle of nationalism has been carried forward yet a further stage. There are in the new constitution two chambers, one to represent the people of the Soviet Union and the other the Council of Nationalities. The Council for the Union is to be elected by the citizens of the U.S.S.R. on a population basis, while the Council of Nationalities will consist of representatives appointed by the supreme councils of the union and autonomous republics and soviets of workers' representatives in the autonomous provinces. In other words, the 'national' legislatures.

Liberal Comment

Ivor Jennings, commenting on this second chamber in the *Manchester Guardian* (8.12.36) quoted Stalin's speech in defence thereof, the reason for which he claimed was 'a little curious'. It was that: 'In addition to their common interests the nationalities of the U.S.S.R. have their own specific interests connected with their specific national features'. The commentary continues: '... The assumption is, then, that there may be a conflict of interests between the people of the Union as such and the peoples of the nationalities.'

Nationalism is a more potent force in Russia to-day than is internationalism.

The shibboleth of 'equality' has gone by the board. In an address to members of the '95 Club, at Manchester on November 25, 1936, Col. T.F. Tweed, who had just returned from a six weeks' tour of Russia, claimed that the Bolshevists who had destroyed, and believed they were right in destroying, all their middle-class and technicians were now working day and night and offering fabulous rewards to create it again.

Straws in the Wind

These are all straws in the wind of economic tendencies, and the obvious lesson is that if all the slaughter, torture, and destruction which accompanied the

Communist revolution merely created hindrances to progress, and the root ideas behind all the slaughter and destruction had to be dropped before any progress could be made, it will be much more expeditious for us to avoid a repetition of such errors, and to apply the Fascist technique knowingly and intelligently instead of being forced into the use of that technique as the only way to remedy the colossal evil and wastage accruing from Communist methods.

It is not claimed that Stalin and his co-directors of Communist experiment have knowingly turned their backs on Communism and accepted Fascism. If that had been the case they might have made a better job of it. Our claim is that the application of the Communist method has been a ghastly flop, and that, driven by economic necessity to find alternative methods of 'producing the goods'. Russia's leaders have had to adopt the Fascist technique without realising the significance of what was being done.

Towards Fascism

Each step away from Communist method has been a step in the direction of Fascist method. The steps are now beginning to develop into quick march. Just one snag remains. Although the march step is changing from Communist to Fascist, the band still plays the tune of Communism. Consequently, the march is somewhat crude and the pace leaves much to be desired.

Is it too much to hope that the Communist discord will be scrapped in favour of Fascist rhythm and that the Russian peoples will at last emerge into that state of ordered security which is long overdue? And if so, under whose leadership? Perhaps a Voroshilov, perhaps some figure not yet emerged from the dust and smoke of Communism's blundering. Only the future can tell, but we watch and wait with close interest."

14 ***Action, no. 62, April 24th, 1937, page 11:***

"What a phrase! What power to stir the pulses and quicken the spirit! What does it mean? Why does it stir the most sluggish pulse? Whence is its inspiration derived?

Nine out of ten people would fail to give a definition of the word 'yeomen', and the tenth would probably be hazy about it.

It is traditional, its origins reaching back to another era ante dating the present industrial system. An era in which mankind was in closer contact with the soil. A more natural period of time in a more leisurely age.

Free Farmers

The yeomen of England were free farmers as distinct from serfs. They represented the element of sturdy independence in a feudal system, and their tradition has long survived – as a tradition. The word itself is of the Middle English period (1200 to 1500).

These yeomen were qualified to serve on juries and vote for knights of shires.

At a later stage the name was used in a different sense when applied to the 'yeomanry', a mounted force of voluntary soldiers recruited largely from the ranks of farmers. They provided their own mounts, for which they were given forage allowances during their periods of training in camp.

Fine Tradition

The yeomen of England have left us a fine tradition which is inevitably bound up with the interests of agriculture and the soil. The conditions of agriculture to-day are not conducive to the maintenance of the sturdy independence of the yeoman spirit.

The yeomen of England have left us a fine tradition which is inevitably bound up with the interests of agriculture and the soil. The conditions of agriculture to-day are not conducive to the maintenance of the sturdy independence of the yeoman spirit. An industrial age has completely changed the conditions in which that spirit flourished. The depopulation of the countryside and the migration from country to town, from agriculture in industry, has turned over an intensely romantic page in our history.

Is it possible in modern society to reopen that page – or, alternatively, to open a new page based on similar fundamentals?

If it is possible to do so, would it be desirable?

The Future

The answer to the above questions may be of vital importance to us as a nation in the future. I do not profess to know the full answers to those questions, but, thus far, I am prepared to commit myself. If it is economically possible to re-establish on a wide scale homesteads of free farmers, to cultivate the millions of acres not under cultivation at the present time, to produce from our English soil food for England's millions of population, to replace in the countryside some of the teeming thousands who have been brought into the towns during the past century; if these things be proven economic possibilities, then I should say very definitely that these things are eminently desirable.

A Perilous Position

Industrialism, developed at the expense of agriculture, has placed us in a perilous position. It has reduced our physical fitness. It has left us dependent for our food supplies on sources which may be closed to us in a national emergency. It has inculcated a spirit of bitterness in our agricultural communities who feel themselves relegated to the role of 'Cinderella' in the industrial family.

These are evils of paramount importance, and those who are responsible for the future welfare of Britain *must* give due consideration to these problems if Britain is to survive."

15 ***Ibid., page 9***

16 ***Oswald Mosley, op. cit.:***

"Like Marx, Mosley believed that the solution of the economic problem would mean the end of politics. The basic idea of his utopia is not the one-party state, but the no-party state. 'In such a system', he wrote, 'there is no place for parties and for politicians. We shall ask the people for a mandate to bring to an end the Party system and the Parties. We invite them to enter a new civilisation. Parties and the Party game belong to the old civilisation, which has failed.' [***Oswald Mosley: Fascism; 100 questions asked & answered***]"

17 ***Ibid.***

18 **'Left-Wing Fascism' in theory and Practice: The Case of the British Union of Fascists*; Philip M. Coupland, Twentieth Century British History, Vol. 13, No. 1, 2002, pp 38-61***

Wilfred's article was given a glowing tribute in a review of ***British Union Quarterly***, which was otherwise somewhat ambivalent:

"It is with mixed feelings that the announcement to the effect that as from October next a Monthly will take the place of this highly successful and admirable publication is read in this issue of the "British Union Quarterly". If the proposed Monthly succeeds in maintaining the increasingly high standard that is being set by the "Quarterly" it will be well worth reading. … The most admirable article in this number has been contributed by W. Risdon and is a study of "The Heritage of National Socialism"; an examination of the parallel between the early Labour Movement of the nineteenth century and the present growing National Socialist Movement in this country."

The Blackshirt, no. 222, July 31st, 1937, page 5

Action also reviews it, and mentions the Owen connection:

"The July-September number of the ***British Union Quarterly*** is worthy of its predecessors.

W. Risdon, writing on "The Heritage of National Socialism", proves beyond doubt that the Mosley Movement is the true inheritor of early British Socialism, not the Socialist or Communist Parties. The parallel between Owen and Mosley is very cleverly drawn."

Action, no. 76, July 31st, 1937, page 16.

19 ***The Blackshirt, no. 214, June 5th, 1937, page 5.***

20 ***Action, no. 68, June 5th, 1937, page 3.***

21 ***Ibid.***

22 ***Ibid.:***

"Mr. Clement Bruning is in charge of District Propaganda. He is a young man, but in spite of that he has already had very considerable experience of public speaking. He has a pleasing manner on the platform, which often has the effect of gaining the support of a previously hostile audience."

Clement Bruning was also the prospective parliamentary candidate for Wood Green at the relatively tender age of 26, and he was:

"one of the young men who rallied round Oswald Mosley at the inception of the British Union, and has made a prominent place for himself by his considerable powers of oratory, hard work and loyalty to the principles of Fascism. A Catholic, educated at St. Benedict's Priory, Ealing, he was a commercial traveller by profession."

Action, no. 44, December 19th, 1936, page 7.

Clement had a brother, Guy, who was also in the Movement but, according to Simpson [***In the Highest etc., op. cit.***] "was a national speaker of no great prominence; in 1938 he … looked after printing. His brother Clement, who in 1936 was an Administrative Officer concerned with propaganda, [went] to Germany [presumably after 1939], and [was] employed in Goebbels's propaganda service. By 1940 Clement, for obscure reasons, had been sent to a concentration camp, where, apparently, he died." This was, according to Jeffrey Wallder, in Poland in 1942 and, no doubt with his tongue in his cheek, "which many would say was poetic justice". In March 1938, Clement opened a café in Green Street, Bethnal Green ["Opposite D.H.Q."], and it was advertised in ***Action*** as "The Café which caters for White Men"; for example:

Action, no. 109, March 19th, 1938, page 5;

and the following month a photograph could be seen of Bruning standing in the doorway of his premises, somewhat incongruously wearing a technician's white lab-coat!

The Blackshirt, no. 249, April, 1938, page 4

23 ***Action, no. 68, June 5th, 1937, page 3.:***

"Tommy Moran is the British Union Inspector in South Wales. Here, by sheer pluck and against enormous odds, he is already gaining a large following in what has been one of the strongest Communist areas.

It is now a matter of history how, at the famous Blackshirt Rally in Royal Mint-street [sic], on October 4, he was set on by a crowd of Reds when leaving Mark Lane Station. Most of the cinemas of England have seen and cheered how he felled nearly a dozen of his armed opponents with his bare fists.

He is one of our most popular speakers, with a glorious sense of humour, which seldom fails sooner or later to get the audience laughing with him, and many are the would-be hecklers who have retired from the fray, smarting from a direct hit with a barb from his tongue. He opens his campaign at Hull on Saturday, June 5, and will visit Newcastle, Middlesbrough, Cardiff, Rochester, Hitchin, Luton, Limehouse, Brighton, and Hastings."

24 Again, it has only been possible to view a poorly scanned copy:

"Are you, who read this, one of those people who view elections as a necessary evil, with accent on the 'evil'? Do you think that elections are of no moment to you, that they are occasions which impinge from time to time on the even tenour [sic] of life's ordinary occasions, upsetting things, and generally annoying people who would far rather go on in their own sweet way? There are many who take such a view, and they are, for the greater part, those who have never come into real contact with the 'business' end of electioneering.

I can quite well imagine any such person seizing on the last sentence of the above paragraph and snorting indignantly 'Business – that's what they make of politics', and with that phrase condemning the whole outfit out of hand. Why is it considered so heinous an offence to organise electioneering on business lines? The result of an election is virtually the same as the appointment of a board of directors to manage the affairs of the community, therefore it would appear that the matter should be tackled in a business-like manner.

For Five Years

A Parliamentary General Election takes place, and as a result of that election the Party with a majority in the House of Commons conducts the business affairs of the nation for a period of anything up to five years. The finances for the conduct of the business affairs of the nation are drawn from the British public in any way that seems fit and proper to the Government in power. Surely, then, there is ample justification for the claim that parliamentary elections should be run on more business-like lines than is at present the case.

The same is true of local government elections. The cash which is spent in local affairs is raised by rates levied on the local residents. Why not use business methods to decide who shall spend it and how?

Any movement which holds serious views as to the way in which public business should be conducted must, therefore, inter? in this business of electioneering.

New Methods

Is it necessary to follow the rule-of-thumb method of the 'old gang' politicians in such ?intervention? A new movement such as ours, virile and resurgent, finds the old methods irksome and would welcome a breakaway where such might be possible.

One thing must be remembered, namely – that the laws under which contests, both local and parliamentary, are conducted, are ?those for which the old gangs are ?responsible – some of them going ?back for an incredibly long time ?in history.

?I once compiled a list of them ?which ran into several hundreds, ?in spite of the fact that there was wholesale scrapping of redundant Acts when the Representation of the People Act was passed ?, there remain well over ? Acts of Parliament, ?going back to the time of William III, ?nearly 250 years ago, and many hundreds of Orders in Council, ? affecting the conduct of elections.

Increased Electors

?This naturally circumscribes ?someone's desire to express a new ? ?in electioneering to some extent, but there are many directions in which it is possible to introduce a new note in spite of all this. In the past 100 years many new factors have come into politics. When the Reform Act was passed in 1832 the electors of the United Kingdom were about one million. By 1935 the electors of the United Kingdom, exclusive of Southern Ireland, were thirty-one and a quarter millions.

This quantitative change has been accompanied by qualitative variations. Better education, greater mobility, tremendous increases of real wealth, Empire development, scientific and technical achievement, the emergence of women from the domestic into the wider spheres of life, and a hundred and one changes of equal significance have made their marks with no uncertain emphasis, and the net result of all this is that far more brains are needed to win elections nowadays than was the case in the 'good old days'.

More Picturesque

To meet such changes we have to use more imagination, introduce more colour, utilise more picturesque and up-to-date methods in appealing to the electorate.

The conduct of elections in the old days was a 'business' for lawyers only. The conduct of modern elections is far more a 'business' for highly efficient publicity experts.

The British Union is emerging at a time when 'change' is the one 'constant' factor, and is fortunate in its complete lack of past traditions to hamper it. To those of the 'old gangs' who wring futile hands and moan that 'Things aren't what they were', we can reply with cheerful detachment, 'No. But then they never were, you know.' We don't have to worry about things as 'they were', but as 'they are'.

Old Gangs Horrified

The 'old gang' representatives were horrified at our departures from hoary tradition in the recent contests in East London in connection with the L.C.C. elections. Crowds of young men and women thronging the streets wearing the bright coloured red, white, and blue paper hats and streamers, singing the Blackshirt marching song, yelling for Mosley, Clarke, Thomson, Prosser, Griggs, etc., and holding a jubilee for the sheer love of the fight and regardless of the figures of the result which had not yet been recorded, scandalised these good people. The joy of the struggle for its own sake as well as the struggle as a means to an end was something outside their comprehension. Hence they frowned, pursed their lips, and disapproved, but there was not a thing they could do about it.

Coming Elections

Borough Council elections are coming along in November. A Parliamentary General Election looms ahead. What are you going to do about it? Do you intend to gird up your loins for the contest, to prepare, gladly and joyfully, for the struggle to come? Let me assure you if you do you will enjoy it.

Those who have 'safe seats' will never know the thrill of adventure which will be yours in tackling these first fights, with little funds, new machinery of organisation, little or no past experience, but with stout hearts, the capacity to take a drubbing and come up again asking for more until victory is yours.

Once again I ask – 'What are *you* going to do about it?' November is not far away in any case, and Parliamentary General Election is in the offing. 'Are you on?' It can be great fun, great effort, and excellent training for future VICTORY."

***Action*, no. 69, June 12th, 1937, page 7.**

25 ***Action*, no. 72, July 3rd, 1937, page 1.**

26 ***Ibid.*, page 3:**

"At Hull on Sunday, after Mosley's great meeting there, the Reds were openly boasting that the Communist Party were going to send gangs of hooligans from all over England to riot in London on Sunday with the object of preventing the Blackshirt march.

On October 4 the Communists sent train-loads of hooligans from the North. These arrived at the London terminal and were drafted to the "Cable-street Front". After the riot they were returned back North again with all expenses paid.

Apparently it is the intention of the Communist Party to repeat this performance on Sunday."

27 **CLAQUE THAT DIDN'T CLICK: *Action*, no. 73, July 10th, 1937, page 12;**

"Standing in the midst of a close-packed section of the crowd at the foot of Charing Cross Road my wife and I were much amused by the efforts of a claque-leader to get his troops ready for a 'spontaneous' outburst.

'As soon as he is opposite us,' said this naive organiser of nit-wits, 'all together "Down with Fascism", and try to make it uniform.' With many similar exhortations he earnestly schooled them to their parts. Everything possible had been done to make sure that the contribution of his team would go off smoothly and they just waited as hopefully as possible for the psychological moment. They were all set.

THE BLACKSHIRTS' APPROACH

The throbbing of drums approached and then could be heard the undernote, the rhythm of marching feet. The great moment was drawing near and the face of our hero became set and purposeful. His hand shot up in the clenched fist salute. He drew a deep breath in readiness and then —

What's this? Two arms have shot up right bang in front of his nose in the Fascist salute. He is rattled. He forgets to lead his claque in the yell to down

Fascism. One of his followers, seeing what has put his leader off form, hurriedly decides that this is Fascist provocation and charges – from the rear – the nearest of the two Fascists who are daring to salute a patriotic movement.

The Fascist who was attacked turned in time to identify the aggressor, dived into the crowd after him, and after a brief scuffle resumes his place at the curb and again takes up the salute.

Tck tck! [sic] This cannot be allowed to go on. Something must be done about it.

Two stalwarts promptly approach, again from behind, and, seizing the upraised arm, seek by main force and sheer weight to drag it down.

Alas! He is a treacherous one, this Blackshirt. Just when the full weight of the drag falls on his upraised arm he yields to it instead of struggling against it. The arm sweeps down in a short arc, bending at the elbow in the process, said bent elbow connects disconcertingly with short ribs, a grunt, weight removed from arm, which again lifts proudly in salute and that was the end of the affair.

TOO BAD

It really is too bad that these Blackshirt people will not see reason. Only two of them, one man and one woman in the midst of a crowd of 'angry verkers', and in spite of all attempts to show them the wrongness of their attitude they have persisted in saluting the whole column.

This is bad, of course, but what is worse one of the by-standers has also followed suit and is giving a very creditable representation of same salute. He looks a trifle shamefaced about it, but mutters defiantly in self-justification: 'can't let this rabble of reds and yids get away with it.'

Across the road another little group gives the salute based on the age-old gesture of peace, hand open, palm outward, arm fully extended, which contrasts markedly with the bellicose gesture of the clenched fist favoured by the Red Front.

FORGOTTEN TO CHANT

It really was most annoying. The claque in its squeaking excitement had forgotten to chant its 'war-cry', several of the spectators had been so annoyed by the bullying and hectoring attitude of the front which by now was only pink that they would undoubtedly have taken sides with the 'detested' fascists had any further trouble developed and the whole of the carefully planned 'spontaneous' demonstration against Mosley and Fascism had been a 'flop' in that particular key position, and the 'comrades' at their next committee meeting will have lots of strictures to convey to the hapless claque-leader whose claque didn't click.

Really it was most annoying!"

28 ***Ibid., page 10:***

"Going down Great College Street an open knife was hurled at Mosley, but fortunately it missed its mark and was picked up by the police. In Crowndale road, a heavy file, ten inches long, an inch wide, and a quarter of an inch thick, was also thrown, but like most things of Red origin missed its mark."

29 ***Action, no. 74, July 17th, 1937, page 10:***

"**CHIEF AGENT**

Bill Risdon, Chief Election Agent of the British Union, had a fine meeting in the Market Place, at Bedford on Sunday. The police had arranged that the evening should be divided into two halves; the Labour Party was to use the Market Place from 8-9 and the British Union from 9-10. A large crowd gathered and listened to Mr. Risdon with great interest. It is not so long ago that the British Union found it impossible to hold a meeting in the Market Place owing to the hostile demonstrations by the Red Front; this, however, has now faded away.

On Monday, Mr. Risdon spoke at the Play Field, Bury St. Edmunds. The meeting was a great success in spite of threatening weather. …

This week sees the finish of the specially planned meetings of the summer campaign. This campaign has proved a big success, and almost everywhere our speakers have had good audiences. The result has been that a great number of new members have joined, and a great number of votes at the next General Election have been promised.

All speakers have enhanced their already great reputation, and as regards big names and fine speakers the British Union is now in a better position than it ever has been. What is still more satisfactory is that at the Speakers' Schools which have been held all over the country a number of promising new speakers have been discovered."

30 ***Action, no. 75, July 24th, 1937, page 15:***

"Strange Socialist Somersault

By W. RISDON

Occasionally, in the course of my wanderings throughout the country on propaganda tours, lecture tours, and the like, I encounter erstwhile friends with whom I worked side by side in the Socialist movement a decade ago.

Sometimes I have met them in debate, at other times I have recognised them as individuals in the audiences which I have addressed, again, at times I have met them in the street as casual passers-by. Such encounters, whatever the attendant circumstances may have been, invariably send my mind back along the paths of memory, seeking, comparing, and analysing.

Always there is an uncertainty as to my reception on these occasions. In some few cases I am greeted on the grounds of old friendship which is strong enough to triumph over a present difference of opinion.

ARMED NEUTRALITY

In most cases there is an atmosphere of 'armed neutrality'. In the majority of cases, however, the atmosphere is open and intense hostility. This makes me wonder. Is it that I have changed? Is it that 'they' have changed? I strive to treat the problem objectively.

I address a meeting and in the audience I recognise some of my earlier socialist friends. I read positive hate on the faces which previously registered respect and even admiration in the old days. My speech is punctuated by cries of 'traitor', and sometimes much worse epithets.

At question time I am subjected to questions of a personal character which seek to convey the idea that I left the Socialist Party for monetary considerations. I know the inference to be false, and so, in many cases, do my questioners, nevertheless they persist that such is the case with some show of artificial indignation.

I have to conclude that they have changed – for the worse. In the old days they would have been prepared, nay, anxious to argue on the details of an opposition case. Now, they will not argue a case but, instead, they indulge in personal abuse. Yes, they have definitely changed.

THE PACIFISTS

On another occasion I recognise in my audience certain well-known pacifists. They, in the old days, viewed me with a certain amount of suspicion because of the fact that although I hated war (as who would not after experiencing four years of it), nevertheless I was not prepared to say I would *never* fight again. They, who were pacifists claimed that only those who would give such a pledge could be viewed as above suspicion.

I argued that if my country were attacked it would be my inclination as well as my duty to defend my home, my family and my race, and that could be done only by bearing arms or by serving those who were bearing arms if I were no longer fit to do so. I was invariably told in reply that there is *no* consideration that can justify fighting and killing in war between peoples. *I* was *not* convinced but my critics *were* quite sure of their point.

NO AFFAIR OF OURS

On this occasion I am pleading that a war which is going on in a distant country is no affair of ours, and that we should keep out of it. I argue that it is not our business to fight Arabs for the purpose of making Palestine a land fit for Jews to live in; that it is none of our business to fight Italy so that slave-raiding might continue to be carried out by Ethiopians against the subjects of the British Empire in Kenya; that there is no justification for the loss of a single British life in a fight between Japan and the forces of the Soviet or in a fight to make Spain safe for church-burners and the murderers of nuns and priests. All of which seems to me to be eminently logical.

BITTEREST OPPOSITION

To my amazement, however, I find that the bitterest opposition to my point of view comes from my erstwhile socialist-cum-pacifist friends. Not only do they conceive it to be both justifiable and imperative that we should go to war in such cases where war has arisen for which we are not responsible, but they will go further and claim that we should plan a war of our own in addition to intervening in those already taking place.

Strange though it may seem they feel perfectly justified in attempting to arouse in this country hatred against the people of Germany – the sort of hatred which leads inevitably to war – and they will even justify such a war merely because they do not like the form of government for which the German people have voted. Surely these have changed.

NOT WHAT IT WAS

Yes, viewed objectively, I am bound to say that the Socialist movement is not what it was. Changed it is, beyond recognition. Fenner Brockway and the I.L.P. organising recruits for the Reds in Spain and sending British boys out to fight – to kill and be killed – is a picture which would have appeared fantastic in those earlier days.

And what of myself. Have I changed? Of course I have. I was reminded of the fact at a meeting in the South of England lately when a Socialist questioner asked, 'Was it not a fact that I once believed in Internationalism'? I could but admit that there had been such a time just as there had been a time when I believed that babies came from gooseberry bushes.

On both these questions my views have changed. Society itself has changed and developed in the past ten years, and people have changed correspondingly.

FAR AWAY

The Socialists have grown far away from the Socialism of those earlier days, and we who have learned National socialism have grown just as far away in a different direction.

To-day is the day of a new alignment of National forces. Hankering after the past would be both futile and undesirable.

Change is of the very essence of life, let us not, therefore, deplore the changes which we notice. But let us rather seek to understand and to rationalise those changes, bearing always in mind the fact that the greatest mission in life is to change conditions in an upward direction, building rather than destroying, creating the new rather than condoning the old, frankly admitting where we have been wrong in the past, so that we may be right in the future.

This is the new spirit, evolved of the new creed – Fascism and National Socialism."

31 ***Ibid., page 18:***

"... Thus came to be formed the British Union of Fascists, with headquarters still [as of the New Party] at Great George Street. The men who were still with Mosley had been, without exception, the only people on whom he had been able to place absolute reliance during the short, turbulent life of the New Party, and they were destined to do still finer work in the days ahead. Prominent among these were 'Bill' Risdon, now chief political agent, and R.A. Plathen, now chief organiser in Scotland – both splendid men. ..."

Interestingly, prior to joining the BUF late in 1933, Chesterton had married a Fabian Socialist and pacifist, to whom he stayed married for the rest of his life, so there must have been some interesting discussions at home! At the point when he was writing the above quote, Chesterton had not long returned from Germany:

"Chesterton's old demon of alcoholism, combined with overwork, led [in 1936] to a 'nervous breakdown'. Mosley recommended he consult a German neurologist, and for six winter months of 1936-1937 he lived in Germany. This stay provided him with ample opportunity to observe the Nazi regime and German society, ... Chesterton returned to Britain in the spring of 1937 and published a series of articles in the ***Blackshirt*** describing his impressions of the new Germany, which earned him appointment as editor of the ***Blackshirt***. This position provided what would become a convenient pulpit for his increasingly anti-Semitic rhetoric."

http://www.bpp.org.uk/chesterton.html

32 The speaker who was rescued was undoubtedly brave, but also foolhardy:

"... While there seemed a likelihood of these battles [at BUF meetings] ending in victory for the Reds, the old gang politicians of both Right and Left were well content not to intervene, but the moment it became clear that the disciplined force of British Fascism was overcoming the rabble, and allowing the one man in Britain whom they really feared to address great and increasingly enthusiastic audiences, they sent up a series of cries about 'Blackshirt brutality' and 'Blackshirt provocation', even though there was no single instance of a Blackshirt charged with disturbances at an opposition meeting, while scores of Reds had been convicted for violence at Fascist demonstrations, even though the Blackshirts, always heavily outnumbered, were manifestly concerned only to protect their own meetings; and even though many Conservative members had experienced, and usually succumbed to, the same kind of Red ruffianism. Noting the remarkable success of the Blackshirts they shrieked out that it was this factor which inflamed the good, honest, patriotic Red mobs against Fascism. One speaker very courageously volunteered to demonstrate the absurdity of this parrot-cry by speaking without the usual Blackshirt stewards at a huge gathering at Newcastle. Directly the speech began about a thousand roughs in front set up a roar in which nothing could be heard, and a rush was then made for the platform. Only the fortunate fact that Piercy [head of the Defence Force], Risdon, and three other headquarters officers, all in plain clothes, happened to be in the crowd watching the experiment, prevented the speaker from receiving terrible injuries. They came charging to his assistance and held the mob at bay until the police belatedly intervened. …"

Action, no. 76, July 31st, 1937, page 18

33 ***Action, no. 77, August 7th, 1937, page 11:***

"… the British Union has progressed to such an extent that this year the arrangements demanded something more than the rudimentary, happy-go-lucky organisation of previous times. Donovan himself took the job in hand, and the result is what one would have expected–everything thought out down to the smallest detail, excellent catering, abundant recreational facilities and that firm but friendly touch which ensures that everybody has the best possible time without losing contact with the requirements of National Socialist discipline."

34 ***Ibid.:***

"The holiday-makers tumbled out of their tents in amazement, and–apart from one or two offensive remarks by women spectators–stood watching the proceedings very quietly and with an air of puzzled interest, as though they were finding it difficult to reconcile what they had read about Mosley and his men with the spectacle of health and vigour and obviously decent manhood and womanhood which confronted them. Some followed the throng to the beach, anxious to take a snap of Mosley entering the water, and members managed to secure several friendly contacts while chatting on the shore."

35 ***Ibid.***

There were also separate women's camps; ***The Blackshirt*** informed its readers at the end of July [***no. 222, July 31st, 1937, page 5***] that "[t]he Camp at Selsey is reserved for women members from Sunday, August 29, to Sunday, September 5 inclusive." There was a subsequent report:

"WOMEN BACK FROM CAMP

Account Of Jolly Week

A whistle blows – tent flaps fly open – merry 'Good mornings' – splashing water – sounds of happy shouts under the cold shower – heavenly smell of bacon and eggs frying – eager feet trooping into the mess tent – hearty appetites and a spirited discussion of plans for the day.

After breakfast tents tidied – walls rolled ready for inspection. Then the solemn ceremony of the day. Our Women's Camp Commandant breaks the flag while the camp stands tensely at the salute.

Then off to various activities …"

The Blackshirt, no. 228, September 11th, 1937, page 7

36 ***Action, no. 77, August 7th, 1937, page 11***

37 ***Ibid.:***

"It is sometimes said that the Blackshirts are so deadly serious about their cause that they are never able to take themselves light-heartedly.

Disproof of this fact is to be found in "Selsey Bilge", the Camp newspaper, a bright little publication in which almost every well-known member of the Movement finds his leg remorselessly pulled.

Here, for instance, is a parody on the style of a writer whose articles often appear in these columns. No prize is offered for the solution of his identity.

"SPLURGE AND RAMPAGE"

'The glorious fields of this our irresistible England have been made putrescent by the foul streams of alien breath. Instead of our waving golden cornfields vile grey, green, blue, black stones have been laid by our decadent masters of moribund Financial Democracy. Where is the stolen creed of the iron age? Lost in an illimitable splurge of oriental rampage.

The stern staunch stench of an uplifted and resurgent aristocracy is swept away in a sea of green blood. The wheel of the wagon is broken.

… Carry on for yourself from there. I'm tired of it.'"

38 ***The Blackshirt, no. 223, August 7th, 1937, page 4:***

"Another photograph taken on the Great Day of the Blackshirt Camp at Selsey. 'Bill' Risdon has just discovered to his horror that he has been exposed in 'Selsey Bilge'. His usual sunny smile is missing! A.G. Findlay, on the left, appreciates the joke."

A more detailed assessment is provided by J. A. Booker:

"The Selsey Camp also produced a display of humour hitherto unseen in official Blackshirt literature. That serious-minded journal ***The Blackshirt*** had already commented that when the corpulent Editor of its rival ***Action***, Geoffrey Dorman, entered the water off the West Beach 'the tide came in at least another ten feet.' But there was worse to come. Anticipating the 1960s cult for cruel political satire by some 25 years, the normally stricter-than-strict BU Assistant Director General (A) Bryan Donovan brought out a special camp newspaper called '***Selsey Bilge*** - A Paper for Reading and other Homely Purposes'. In those pre-***Andrex*** days readers would be in no doubt as to what those 'homely purposes' were.

A review of ***Selsey Bilge*** in the August 7th issue of ***The Blackshirt*** suggested 'the facts given in it should make admirable reading for members of the British Union when they feel that the Headquarters Staff of their Movement have no sense of humour.' Indeed, all of this unique fascist paper's contents consisted of poking fun at the leading Blackshirt officials. 'Mac' McKechnie, the National Meetings Organiser, was lampooned for his obesity while the bureaucratic Colonel Sharpe, the Assistant Director General (G), was taken to task for his obsession of requiring everything in triplicate.

The highly idiosyncratic literary style of A. K. Chesterton, Director of Propaganda/Publications and cousin of the famous English author G. K.

Chesterton, was mercilessly parodied by ***Bilge***. Even the Christian names of top BU officials were considered enough to send the readers of ***Bilge*** into uncontrollable mirth. It was revealed that the well-known one-armed official in charge of the London Administration had been baptised 'Ughtred' (which rhymed with putrid) whilst other Fascist dignitaries had been given the almost equally outrageous names of 'Hector', 'Cedric' and 'Lanfear'. Next, the Assistant Director General (E), Bill Risdon, was exposed as a smirk-provoking 'Wilfred' rather than the more acceptable 'William'. However, no mention was made of 'Oswald'. Even ***Selsey Bilge*** knew where to draw the line.

Elsewhere the camp paper contained a spoof advertisement for GLUP: the new remedy for tired fascist feet that were always on the march. Although ***Selsey Bilge*** only ran to a single issue, its publication was not without significance. It at least showed that British Fascists were able to laugh at themselves without anyone taking offence: something inconceivable among German Nazis or the upper echelons of the Russian Soviet Politbureau."

Blackshirts-on-Sea, by J. A. Booker, Brockingday Publications

39 Findlay was the officer who either exclusively or mainly collected 'contributions' in mainland Europe from [**Appendix D**] "as he said, British sympathisers with the Movement who desired to remain anonymous and not to be known ..."; he was quite young [27 in 1936] with a very responsible position, Deputy Chief of Staff and in charge of the Leader's Department, which was effectively Mosley's *aide de camp*:

"His duties include responsibility for the Leader's personal arrangements and the handling of much important business, the passing of recommendations for promotions and appointments and the organisation of the 'Appeals Board'."

Action, no. 42, December 5th, 1936; page 8

There appears to have been a definite attempt, at Wilfred's 18B Appeal Hearing [**Appendix D**] to associate him with Findlay in particular, but this should probably be viewed more as an attempt to corroborate the suspicions about Findlay's possibly [although only tenuously so] treasonous money-gathering activities, rather than a specific element in the case against Wilfred, and he sidesteps this ploy very easily - it was perfectly normal for him to associate with other high-ranking executive officers, in the course of his work:

"Q. Headquarters officers or staff met to discuss things. You would usually attend those meetings, would you?

A. Yes, there were very few of those meetings held. They were held because of the unpleasant atmosphere created by the clash of personalities working one against the other.

Q. You formed a little group yourself with Gordon Canning and Archibald Garrioch Findlay rather opposed to Francis Hawkins?

A. As a matter of fact, I found myself associated with first one person and then another who appeared to be getting annoyed with the same things that I was. There was no ideas of forming a group to campaign or anything like that, but in putting up a point of view at a meeting of officers of that description certain people would have a similar point of view, one would find that there was a common outlook on problems and work with these people. Gordon Canning was certainly one with whom I worked a good deal like that, and he appeared just as annoyed as I was."

The National Archives, HO 45/23670

40 It was not uncommon for articles to be unattributed, especially as it became clear that war was inevitable.

"There are people who think it right to cause or, without protest, permit to be caused, pain and fear to animals, but who would raise an outcry if the same treatment were meted out to their fellow human beings. These people are apt to forget that in each fight for the emancipation of the oppressed sections of human beings down the ages, the reformers had a similar argument to contend with, such as:—

'They are ... only poor people ... only women ... only children ... only blacks ... they don't feel the same as we do, therefore it doesn't really matter what treatment they receive; in fact, they enjoy slavery, etc.'

We have reached a stage to-day when it is an accepted theory that all human beings have the right to be treated in a humane manner, regardless of class, sex or colour. What is this extraordinary conceit which accedes this right only to our own kind?

FEAR AND PAIN

Both animals and humans have been created with senses which feel acutely both mental fear and physical pain. If, in the Universe, there is a just law which works with cause and effect, surely it is common sense to assume that if animals are to be put outside the code of fair treatment and to suffer at our hands, chiefly for monetary gain, they would have been created without these acute senses. If, on the other hand, there is no ultimate justice, it is a complete waste of time to fight and work for any reform.

The whole question boils down to the fact that to cause or permit suffering is the greatest evil and reacts on those responsible by brutalising them. King Edward VIII recognised this truth and expressed his view that cruelty to any living thing hinders the progress and evolution of mankind, quite apart from the misery of the victim.

HUMANS AND ANIMALS

It is ridiculous to assume that to cause suffering to animals is right and to humans wrong, just as it would be ridiculous to assume that to cause suffering to one section of the human race is right and to another section wrong. There is only one moral and just law, which is that to cause suffering to any living thing is wrong—a wrong that must be fought and abolished if we want to attain a better world.

Christianity as opposed to Churchianity [sic] is founded on compassion which is the motive power in all reforms for the emancipation of the enslaved and oppressed. Animals are enslaved to-day. National Socialism is prepared to recognise their claim for emancipation and will not fail in this object as has Financial Democracy.

Both in Germany and Italy, under National Socialism and Fascism the rights of animals are recognised and laws for their welfare and protection from exploitation have been passed."

Action, no. 76, July 31st, 1937; page 9

41 At the end of 1937, because of the withdrawal of Jim ["Bill"] Bailey from his candidature for the municipal by-election at Shoreditch, ***Action*** printed a short biographical profile of Goulding. Bill Bailey was a very popular East End speaker, and the explanation for his withdrawal and subsequent expulsion is somewhat confusing; perhaps he was aggrieved at the lack of official support he received, after the hullabaloo surrounding the contest the previous March, with his respectable 14.8% poll alongside William Joyce:

"**Shoreditch And Mr. Bailey**

The British Union organisation has issued the following statement with reference to Mr. Bailey's withdrawal of his candidature from a Municipal By-Election in Shoreditch, and his subsequent attack in the *News Chronicle* and *Star* on the Leader and the Movement:

'Local elections are entirely a local matter for the District concerned. The primary cause of the trouble was that Mr. Bailey's candidature did not have the support of the local officials and members. Nevertheless, in view of the urgency of the by-election, local members, in loyalty to the Movement, were prepared to assist him. Mr. Bailey was nominated, but at the last moment he withdrew his candidature, thus making it impossible for the Movement to nominate a fresh candidate.

At a meeting of Shoreditch members, Mr. Bailey was permitted to state his case. The District Leader then stated that Mr. Bailey was out of the Movement, and invited any members who agreed with him, forthwith to follow him out. Not a single member took this action, and the entire membership remains loyal to the Leader and Movement.

Mr. Bailey's resignation, to avoid disciplinary action, was not accepted, and his membership has been terminated. The other candidate, Mr. Warnett, whose single candidature was rendered impossible by Mr. Bailey's action, remains loyal.'"

Action, no. 94, December 2nd, 1937, page 14

Bailey was also the official prospective parliamentary candidate for Shoreditch; ***Action, no. 69, June 12th, 1937, page 7: Warriors for the General Election***

Goulding had proved his loyalty by continuing voluntarily, undeterred by being included in the March 1937 cull:

"**THE MAN FOR SHOREDITCH**

Michael Goulding, well-known writer in *Action*, is the new prospective Parliamentary British Union candidate for Shoreditch.

'Mike' Goulding is one of the outstanding veterans of the British Union, joining in 1932, and taking a leading part in the earliest struggles. Trained as a speaker in Mosley's own speakers' class of those days, he soon became one of the finest orators holding open-air audiences by his own mixture of Celtic fire and downright good nature.

Always one of the most zealous of the younger revolutionaries, his only real fault has been excess of enthusiasm, and he has given the Movement most valuable services all over the country. His loyalty has come unchallenged through all trials, and he has given a great example by working voluntarily in

London during the past year when his service on the paid staff had to be terminated owing to economies last March.

Shoreditch is to be congratulated on obtaining such an excellent candidate, who is in every way suited to the task of turning local revolutionary fervour to a useful purpose. 'Mike' Goulding is representative of the youthful fervour which will carry the British Union to success against all the odds."

Action, no. 98, December 30th, 1937, page 7

Apart from one unrelated reference to Germany in his article, Goulding does not touch on the thrust of Wilfred's article:

"It is worthy of note that our 'National' Government has no hesitation in handing over some of its mandated territory to Jewry, even at the cost of jeopardising the peace of Europe and the Empire communications, yet refuse to contemplate the peace-making gesture of handing back any of the ex-German colonies to that nation."

The Blackshirt, no. 222, July 31st, 1937, page 5

42 The Palestine Mandate was undoubtedly problematic for Britain:

"Nobody is pleased about Palestine. Britain holds the mandate baby and finds it a particularly troublesome brat. Members of the Palestine police, who have from time to time had to nurse the baby, have a large amount of 'no enthusiasm' for it. Members of His Majesty's armed forces who have been called upon to risk (and in many cases to forfeit) their lives on its behalf are quite convinced that the loathsome monstrosity is not worth it. So much for the purely British point of view.

The League of Nations is responsible for the infant. The League 'passed the baby' to Britain to act as nurse-maid. The League, according to the findings of its commission, is not at all pleased with Britain as nurse-maid.

The Jews are not pleased. The Arabs are not pleased. Nobody is pleased.

The Jews, who are well known for their martial valour, have commented harshly on the lack of fighting quality of the British troops. They (the Jews), it must be assumed, could have done much better in this connection.

WHOSE PERFIDY?

The Arabs have commented with equal harshness on the perfidy of British politicians who promised Palestine to the Arabs and then promised it to the Jews and then tried to fulfil both promises (which obviously was ridiculous).

Now, with all this volume of no-enthusiasm in the air it would appear that (to quote J. H. Thomas of Ferring fame) 'fresh avenoos should be hexplored.' Something must be done about it.

One suggested remedy is that Jolly Judah should raise its own army of martial marauders and win by conquest the territory which it desires. The conquering lion of Judah heading the battalions of razor-slashers from all the ghettoes of Europe would surely inspire terror in the hearts of the Arabs and 'victory-in-advance' would, pro-tem, replace the Jewish racial slogan of 'payment-in-advance' – or would it? There are those who have 'every confidence in the Arabs'.

A NEW SOLUTION

I have a brand new solution to offer. I have 'hexplored hevery havenoo' and I have given the problem very weighty consideration. Perhaps the reason we have failed to satisfy either ourselves, the Arabs, the Jews, or the League of Nations, is because we have too many pre-occupations of our own to be able to give the problem that undivided attention which it deserves. After all, we *have* an Empire to look after, and Mr. Eden has all the troubles of Europe, Asia, Africa and the 'Half-League' to keep him busy. Horeb Elisha [sic] has the War Office to attend to, and even Winston Churchill has too much on his hands to be able to attend to Palestine. This is the penalty of far flung possessions.

Who, in the 'family of nations' (good League language that) can be found with (a) energy and (b) desire to do things but not too many preoccupations.

Stalin won't do. He's much too busy in the 'bump-off' business at home, besides which things are happening both in Spain and in the Far East on which he must keep a watchful eye and poke an occasional meddling finger, so to speak. He's out.

THEY'RE ALL TOO BUSY

Italy is too busy looking after her own home and Empire.

France it [sic] too busy laundering her own popular front to be able to play nurse-maid to the Jewish bib and tucker.

Germany–now there's a possibility. A power of proven administrative capacity, deprived of her own colonies but hoping and deserving of eventually regaining them, but meantime out of practice. *What about handing over the mandate to Germany?* 'S-an-idea! Think of all the fascinating possibilities."

The Blackshirt, no. 222, August 28th, 1937, page 1

43 ***Strike Action or Power Action, Abbey Supplies Ltd.***

This publication was considered sufficiently important for a whole page of the Christmas Eve edition of ***The Blackshirt*** to be devoted to the front cover, which was accompanied by supply details; this was mirrored on the facing page by an article by Wilfred, occupying two-thirds of the page, on a Coal Bill that was "now dragging its weary way through Parliament", and which amounted to a "Gross Betrayal of Brave Men". Please see **Appendix G** for a reproduction of the full ***Strike Action or Power Action*** pamphlet.

The Blackshirt, no. 243, December 24th, 1937, pages 8 & 9

44 The first was very soon after Mosley's injury:

"**LEGIONS ON THE MARCH**

The Midland area Speakers' School was held at Leicester and in the unavoidable absence of the Leader was conducted by Mr. W. Risdon, assisted by Mr. Barnett. Speakers from all round attended. 'A most enjoyable and interesting School', was the universal expression of all."

The Blackshirt, no. 235, October 30th, 1937, page 6

The second was a fortnight later:

"**BRITISH UNION SPEAKERS**

The high light of the coming week will be Mr. Risdon's meeting in the Ilford Town Hall, November 15, where, deputising for Mosley, he will introduce Miss King to the electors of Ilford as the British Union Parliamentary Candidate."

Action, no. 91, November 13th, 1937; page 14

45 Mosley gives his assessment of the cause of the trouble:

"The cause was simple and easily foreseeable. Our members surrounded the platform in the usual way at a meeting I was to address. The reds massed for a militant counter-demonstration, which our members could quickly have seen off as usual under the previous law. A large force of police was present to maintain order under the newly made law. They placed a strong force in a ring between our members and the reds, and pressed our people against the platform. The result was to bring the platform within easy range of red missiles, and to prevent our members moving among the reds to stop them being thrown.

On arrival, I was informed that the previous speaker had been knocked out by a brick, and a barrage of considerable variety was crashing on the platform with such profusion that it was clear no speaker could long survive. In fact, I was hit by a piece of metal on the left side of my forehead within two minutes of mounting the platform. The surgeon who operated in the Liverpool hospital informed me that an inch farther back it would have killed me."

My Life, op. cit., p.261

Nellie Driver, one of the Lancashire organisers, has a slightly different recollection:

"Mosley was reckless. He defied his opponents and was determined to speak, but his immunity from injury could not go on for ever. At Walton, Liverpool, whilst he was addressing a meeting from the top of a van, he was stoned, and he was knocked down by a stone on the head. As he was rising to his feet a huge stone struck him on the back of the head and he fell back unconscious. The St. John's ambulance men who went to his aid were subjected to a similar barrage. Strong men wept with rage as Mosley was carried to his car and his supporters pleaded with him to speak to them if he could - A faint smile went over his face and a hand was raised in salute. He was in hospital for weeks, and a youth was charged in court for throwing the stone. I cannot remember what sentence he got, but I do know that one dark night he was beaten up and given the hiding of his life by some of Sir Oswald's supporters. One can hardly blame them. They were thoroughly enraged by this cowardly attack, and by the long series of organised riots."

From the shadows of Exile: *Unpublished autobiography, by Nellie Driver, cited in BLACKSHIRTS TORN: etc.; op. cit.*

46 ***The Blackshirt, no. 228, September 11th, 1937, page 4: PINK NAUSEA***

47 ***The Blackshirt, no. 230, September 25th, 1937, page 1***

48 ***The Blackshirt, no. 233, October 16th, 1937, page 3***

49 ***Ibid., page 6:*** **LEGIONS ON THE MARCH:**

"**SHOREDITCH.** Risdon, Bailey, and Cox addressed a very large interested crowd at Harmon Street. 'Bill' Bailey received tremendous support when he announced that Blackshirts intend to fight the Borough Elections. New members enrolled immediately, and all papers sold out. Meeting closed with singing of "Marching Song" and National Anthem."

50 ***The Blackshirt, no. 230, September 25th, 1937, page 7:***

"**FIGHTING LOCAL ELECTIONS**

Leader's Policy Explained

The Leader was mis-represented by the Edinburgh pressmen in the interview last week, which received wide publicity. He did not say that the British Union would be contesting Municipal Elections all over the country.

What he said was that the Movement would probably be contesting one or two wards in Edinburgh against Councillors who had shown themselves anxious to deprive us of public meeting facilities in that city.

While certain districts in other parts of the country have decided to try out their electoral machines at the forthcoming local elections, such contests are no part of the general policy of the British Union."

This was reiterated at the end of October, when the full list of wards to be contested was known; Wilfred states [see note 52, below] that a total of 16 different boroughs was to be contested: if East & West Ham are counted as one borough [even though each has a separate ward] then that is correct. The full list was: Shoreditch [Whitmore, Hoxton, Kingsland & Haggerston], Stepney [Mile end Centre & South East & Limehouse North], Bethnal Green [north, south, east & west], East Ham, West Ham, Ilford, Liverpool [Wavertree West], St. Pancras, Northampton [Castle], Sheffield [Burngreave & Sharrow], Leeds [Burmantofts & Armley], Southampton [St. Mary's], Mitcham [north], Croydon [Addiscombe], Hackney [Chatham], Merthyr [Penydarren] and Edinburgh [St. Giles & Canongate].

The Blackshirt, no. 235, October 30th, 1937, page 4

51 ***Action, no. 66, May 22nd, 1937, page 11:***

"HOW TO FIGHT MUNICIPAL ELECTIONS

MAKE IT A REAL ISSUE

By W. RISDON *(Chief Election Agent of the British Union)*

The conduct of local elections is very similar to that of Parliamentary Elections. The organiser of local elections will, therefore, run his campaign on similar, but, of course, restricted, lines following the same general routine.

The effective period of public activity in these contests is from a week to ten days.

To arouse enthusiasm it is essential to fight on 'Party' lines. A challenging Fascist and National Socialist policy must be put forward by British Union candidates and a frontal attack made against the forces of reaction. …"

52 Wilfred was unequivocal about the dangers facing British Union candidates:

"DEMOCRACY'S ROTTEN SOUL REVEALED

Intimidation of British Union Candidates

by W. RISDON

Our intervention in certain cases in Borough Council Elections has introduced our members all over the country to the full degree of political spite and terrorism which is being fomented by our opponents, who see the red light warning them of their imminent replacement by a Movement which will know how to represent the interests of the British people more faithfully than they have ever been represented in the past.

Incidents have occurred all over the country showing us quite clearly the lengths to which the sub-men attached to other movements will be prepared to go in their attempts to thwart British Union Candidates.

THREAT AND INTIMIDATION

In one Northern town a chemist who had the courage to submit his name as a National Socialist candidate had his shop picketed and his customers threatened with all forms of physical violence if they dared to do business with a National Socialist. As a result of the picketing this candidate had to withdraw from the fight.

In East London another shopkeeper, whose name had gone forward as a candidate, experienced similar treatment, and he, too, had to withdraw from the fight.

In yet another East London constituency a casual labourer working as a docker was threatened with the loss of his livelihood and told, categorically, that he would be "passed over" if his nomination, which had already been accepted by the Returning Officer, were not withdrawn.

In Merthyr the one candidate fighting in the Socialist stronghold of Dowlais, has been handicapped by refusal of the courtesy issue of a free copy of the Register to candidates engaged in a municipal contest. The refusal in this instance has been backed up by the Home Office.

In another instance in East London a tradesman who had let a part of his premises to a National Socialist candidate for use as committee rooms, was threatened by representatives of a mob who indicated that, unless his tenancy was immediately terminated, they would wreck his premises. In this case, although the candidate in question could have fought the issue and insisted on a clear week's notice before vacating the premises, out of consideration for the landlord in question, who, although not a National Socialists, had been decent enough to afford accommodation in a district where he knew that his action would be unpopular, he withdrew voluntarily from the committee rooms rather than expose the landlord to the victimisation and terrorism which would have been used against him.

These are a few cases, selected at random from a list, which have come to my notice during the past three weeks.

THE CONTEST IS ON

On this occasion we are contesting only local government seats, and that in only sixteen different boroughs. If we take the present instances as a fair indication as to what is likely to happen in the future members will be able to realise what sort of situation will confront us in the next General Election when we intend to contest one hundred Parliamentary constituencies. It may be urged that in most of the instances above quoted these matters could have been dealt with by the police which, up to a point, is a perfectly correct comment, but how much satisfaction would a tradesman find in having his business premises picketed by police for the purpose of warding off the more sinister picketing by Reds and Yahoos?

Customers approaching such a shop are not likely to feel very much reassured if they find a policeman standing on either side of the entrance-door. Moreover, even police protection during a given period is not going to prevent the unruly actions of a mob of low mentality, inflamed to hatred of a creed which they do not understand and which has been so foully misrepresented to them that it would appear likely that some considerable time must elapse before our propaganda will eventually wear down the opposition which has been aroused and bring home to them the fact that future security in a well-ordered state will permit people to hold views which are not inimical to their own country without incurring the odium of the sweepings of the ghetto, who are prepared to hire the worst forms of humanity to carry out, on their behalf, the dirty work of terrorism and suppression of a faith newly emerging.

GREATER SUPPORT FORTHCOMING

We who have experienced so much of this form of opposition in the past need not be unduly concerned thereat. The decent elements of society will rally more and more to our aid and give us greater and greater support for every evidence which is shown to them of such foul and un-English tactics. What the sub-human opposition fails to appreciate is the fact that 'They can fool all of the people some of the time, they can fool some of the people all of the time, but they can't fool all of the people all of the time'.

The tactics which they are now adopting are precisely the tactics which will speed up our advent to power; the tactics which will attract to our ranks the type of real Britisher who glories in a tough job of work; the type who, throughout the ages, have refused to be browbeaten or intimidated; the type slow to anger but desperately dangerous to their opponents when their anger and righteous indignation is fully aroused. Many thousands of such are already in our ranks, the tactics of terrorism used against us will multiply every thousand into one hundred thousand, who will mobilise behind our colours a great mass movement of Britons who intend to keep their country clean and to ensure that their own territory shall be British territory for British people, or as we more briefly put it, 'Britain for the British'.

The old gangs of graft and corruption are aware of the fact that the hour of their final extinction is close at hand; they are fighting at the moment like cornered rats in their attempt to retain the old order, which has served their petty interests so effectively in the past. A measure of their consternation may be gauged by the hysterical methods which they are adopting.

The time is at hand for their passing, and for the triumph of a new order which will bring cleanliness in methods of administration, individual responsibility for every person who holds authority, the spirit of public service in place of the desire for private graft. The reign of the reactionaries is over, the future lies with the new forces so well represented in the ranks of the British Union."

The Blackshirt, no. 235, October 30th, 1937, page 5

53 The optimism was backed up with solid information:

"BLACKSHIRTS DISPLACING OLD GANGS

MOVE TO SECOND PLACE IN LONDON WARDS

by W. RISDON

In March of this year the British Union staged its first electoral contest. On that occasion we fought three constituencies in the LCC Election, and the results in these three cases were surprisingly good. With the advent of Borough Council Elections we found that many of our districts were straining at the leash and anxious to enter into this form of activity (a) for the purpose of getting acquainted with electoral methods, and (b) for the purpose of determining what measure of support could be relied upon in their localities.

The fight on this occasion has been on an infinitely wider front than our contest in March last. Then we had six candidates contesting three areas. On this occasion we had 68 candidates contesting twenty-nine wards in different parts of the country.

As was only natural, much of the interest has been concentrated on East London, and we may, with advantage, give a little consideration at this stage to a comparison between their results in March and the results on the present occasion. In Bethnal Green, Shoreditch, and Limehouse, we fought on the last occasion, and achieved a creditable result in displacing the Liberals at Bethnal Green, where we took second place, and the old-established Liberal Organisation had to content themselves with a position at the bottom of the poll. In both Shoreditch and Limehouse we ran the established opposition very close, and although we were at the bottom of the poll in those two districts, there was very little in it. On the present occasion we retained the second position in Bethnal Green, we moved up to the second position in two out of three wards contested by our Limehouse members in the Borough of Stepney, and we occupied second place in two and shared second place in a third Ward of Shoreditch. This represents an amazingly good result, especially when we remember that in the case of both Bethnal Green and Limehouse we had extended our front. In Bethnal Green we were contesting South and West, as well as North and East, the two which had previously been contested, and in the case of Stepney, we had made our first onslaught on Mile End Constituency, in addition to Limehouse. We have every reason to congratulate ourselves on the results obtained, namely, taking second place from Liberal-Tories in Bethnal Green, and from a coalition of both in Shoreditch and Stepney.

In all other cases throughout the country we were breaking entirely new ground, and the votes polled by our candidates showed a gratifyingly high standard of public support for British Union principles.

The experience which has been gained by our members all over the country, whilst engaged in these contests, will be invaluable to them in the future. All the theoretic instruction in advance is useful only insofar as it enables them to vizualise the outlines of electoral machinery; the details of that machinery can only be properly appreciated by people who, in addition to theoretic training, have had the experience of actually operating the machine. Our candidates have been subjected to different forms of victimisation and terrorism in different parts of the country. Their speakers have met the usual tactics of the howling front. In many cases they have been handicapped by petty-fogging restrictions and discrimination against them on the part of local officials of Borough Councils, who should have known better, but in spite of all these handicaps they have come through their contest with great credit. By comparison with these instances the few cases in which our candidates have been given a clear field and the co-operation of local authorities in their fight, have stood out like beacons, exemplifying the real traditions of that important department of the Civil Service, which is responsible for local government administration. To those who have complied with the tradition of their calling and have granted impartial treatment to all candidates alike, we extend our hearty congratulations. We do not offer them thanks because no thanks are due, but we do congratulate them on having lived up to the high standard, which should apply in all cases where Civil Servants have to hold an even balance between all contending candidates. To those who have not lived up to that standard, we here and now issue the warning that in the future they will be held responsible for the acts, some overt and some covert, by which they have sought to serve the interests of particular political groups in a manner which is not consistent with the terms of their employment.

My last word is addressed to our own members in all districts, to whom I offer a word of advice to the effect that elections are won in the periods between elections, and not during those hectic few days of the election period proper. Those who intend to engage in electoral activities in the future should start on the job here and now. There is much preparatory work which can be done immediately: the organisation of a constituency into wards or polling districts; the splitting up of those wards or polling districts into street blocks under the supervision of reliable members, who will get to work on them immediately and keep at them right up until the day of the next election, is in itself a very important undertaking, and one which, rightly carried through, will go far in the future to give us victory in the place of defeat. In addition to this, there is a vast amount of classified information to be prepared: lists of schools and halls for meetings; lists of workers for the different categories of jobs which have to be done during an election; getting to know the different printers and their capacities of output, so as to know just where to go with your orders during an election. There are a hundred and one jobs of this description which can be tackled immediately, and those districts who do tackle them now instead of waiting until an election is upon them, will most definitely be the districts that will yield the best results in the fight when ever it may come along."

The Blackshirt, no. 236, November 6th, 1937; page 4

54 Given the popularity of radio for 'ordinary people', there was already a "Radio Flashes" column in ***Action***, but television was now starting to be discussed as a viably possible competitor for radio; the commentator, *Bluebird*, asked "What future has television?": whilst conceding that "Anything novel always has an attraction for me", he divulged that a "television set" would cost "£50 odd", and "I agree that it will be a great advantage to invalids or people who are by force of circumstances isolated from their fellows … but even they, I believe will soon get heartily sick of the faces of the announcers and people who are much better heard and not seen."; not yet much choice, given that "the programmes … are confined to two hours per day", and the reception was also limited: "at present only 25 miles from the transmitting station (although it has been received 75 miles away)" so, on balance, "I very much doubt whether television will seriously rival sound broadcasting as a means of entertainment."!

RADIO FLASHES: *Action, no. 90, November 6th, 1937, page 4*

55 ***Ibid., page 14 :***

"'THE SOCIALIST CASE'

By Douglas Jay

(Faber & Faber, 12s. 6d.)

This is one of the most interesting publications which has come my way in recent months. It is an economic analysis of society for the express purpose of determining whether Socialism is an economic and political possibility. In reading it through the first time I received a general impression of a new angle of approach to Socialist propaganda. In reading it through the second time I was struck by the fact that this new angle of approach is very much akin to the National Socialist attitude on the relationship of economics and politics to society. A third reading confirmed my point of view.

I feel tempted to make an extensive quotation from the book, but the following limited quotation will perhaps suffice to explain the impression created. In the section dealing with Confiscation and Taxation, Chapter 22, the following may be found:—

'... it must not be supposed that Nationalisation or Socialisation is itself any solution to the problem ... if public ownership is secured by the purchase of the shares of a firm or industry at market value, no transfer of income from rich to poor will take place at all. For if new stock or cash equal to the market value of the shares is given to the shareholders in the industry to be nationalized they will still hold or be able to buy, claims to unearned income approximately equal to what they previously received ... Socialists have long tended and are still tending to evade this crucial dilemma ... Confiscation must, consequently, also be ruled out as a normal method of peaceful transition to Socialism. There is no escaping the fact that when an industry is nationalized in a democratic community either new government stock or terminable annuities equivalent in value to the market price of the existing shares – or, of course, cash – must be granted to the stockholder ... if confiscation is thus to be avoided, however, and if fixed-interest Government stock or annuities are to be given in exchange for industrial securities or land, how can any progress be made in abolishing unearned and inherited incomes? There remains in effect only one method, taxation, or (what amounts to the same thing), modification of the inheritance laws. For taxation is little more than confiscation so adjusted as to cause the minimum of inequity and the minimum of economic dislocation.'

From the above quotation the reader will probably be able to follow my line of reasoning when I say that it is a departure from the old school of Socialist thought, which departure brings the writer more into line with National Socialism than with the old theories of Socialism hitherto advocated.

This is a book which should be read by discriminating students of National Socialism. W.R."

56 ***Action, no. 96, December 16th, 1937, page 8***

57 ***Action, no. 1, February 21st, 1936, page 9***

58 The editorial was written by A. K. Chesterton, one of the Movement's more strident commentators:

"Britons, Beware!

Germany's attitude towards the Hitler-Halifax talks was described in a British newspaper as being one of 'sceptical hope'. That seems accurately to describe the situation, even if one is inclined to think that there is less justification for the hope than for the scepticism, especially upon reading the joint Anglo-French Communique issued in London.

This affirmed that the French Ministers 'were glad to recognise that while Lord Halifax's visit, being of a private and unofficial character, was not expected to lead to any immediate result, it had helped to remove causes of international misunderstanding and was well calculated to improve the atmosphere.'

Even the greatest dunderhead to-day recognises that assertions about removing the causes of international misunderstanding and improving the atmosphere are just so much sheer diplomatic jargon, meaning nothing at all where they do not mean exactly the opposite of what they state.

The operative phrase in the paragraph quoted is that Lord Halifax's visit 'was not expected to lead to any immediate result.'

That phrase throws a remorseless light upon the howling insincerity of the British approach to Germany, and indicates the frantic desire of the British Government to appease Paris and New York. If the Government wished to have friendship with Germany nothing could be easier, always providing that it was willing to face up to the hostility of the international financial racket.

Since courage of this kind is quite beyond the power of Democratic politicians to find, it follows that all discussions with Germany are but camouflage to give the appearance of seeking peace, while all the time rearmament is pushed ahead to be ready for the day when loan-capital decides that the time is ripe for a war in defence of the great financial interests, so grievously jeopardised by the totalitarian states, with their whimsical desire to be masters in their own homes instead of the playthings of Wall Street Jews. Britons, beware!"

The Blackshirt, no. 240, December 4th, 1937, page 4

59 ***Action, no. 93, November 25th, 1937, page 6***

60 ***Action, no. 96, December 16th, 1937, page 19***

Sir [Richard] Stafford Cripps, the barrister whose knighthood had been acquired by virtue of his appointment in 1931 as Solicitor General, with which the post was "customarily accompanied", was the product of mixed, albeit relatively illustrious parentage: his father was a Conservative MP [but later, as Lord Parmoor, converted to Labour]; his mother was the sister of Beatrice Webb [née Potter]. Cripps was quite far-left, in the conventionally understood sense, but in 1936, he caused some consternation in Labour circles with a speech, from which the National Executive Committee dissociated itself, in which he did not "believe it would be a bad thing for the British working class if Germany defeated us." He held his parliamentary seat for Bristol East until 1950 [the constituency having been restyled as Bristol South East] when he was succeeded by Anthony Wedgwood Benn.

The Impact of Hitler. British Politics and British Policies, 1933-1940, ***Maurice Cowling, Chicago University Press, 1977, cited in Stafford Cripps, Wikipedia;***

http://en.wikipedia.org/wiki/Stafford_Cripps

61 ***The Blackshirt, no. 241, December 11th, 1937, page 7, and Ibid., no. 242, December 18th, 1937, page 1***

10: REFUSING TO ACCEPT THE INEVITABLE

The relatively quiet start to 1938 was to be the proverbial 'calm before the storm', the latter of which could not be accurately predicted by anyone without paranormal prescience, although British Union was consistently vocal in its warnings of impending disaster, as a result of its reading of the signals inferred from world events. Wilfred Risdon was by no means [to paraphrase Colin Cross] dropping "into the background" [**1**] during this period; he was as busy as ever: British Union speakers embarked upon a "strenuous spring campaign", and Wilfred's first public speech of the year was at the Co-operative Hall, King's Lynn [**2**]. A few days after that, he gave one of the first lectures for the National Headquarters Study Group, which was to be "open to all interested in British Union policy", and there was "no doubt that the Group is destined to play an important part in the cultural life of the Movement." [**3**] Unsurprisingly, the first lecture was given by Mosley, on the subject of "The Philosophy of National Socialism"; inexplicably, this was not reported upon fully in either periodical, although there was an observation that "[t]he sheer brilliance of his talk left his hearers electrified" [**4**], but a "precis of the lecture delivered" by Wilfred the following week, on the subject of "Marxism and National Socialism", occupied half a page in ***The Blackshirt*** [**5**]. This considered the thesis of Capitalism, its antithesis of Communism, and the synthesis which was "that of the 'Corporate State', which views society as organic—each organ serving the wider interests of the whole body and deriving its health of condition from the health of the whole body which it serves and of which it is a part, one and indivisible."

This lecture followed hard on the heels of a searing indictment of "Communism in Theory and Practice", which quoted "ex-Communists whose bona-fides are well established" who had written "the fact that Communism as it has been applied in Russia is an abject failure when judged by the standards even of Capitalist civilisation", and ended by warning darkly: "Let the authors of Russian Sovietism beware. The people of Britain and the Empire will extract a terrible vengeance on any who would seek by intrigue and deception to add British possessions to a Soviet World Empire. British Union will form an impregnable bulwark against any attempt to impose Soviet slave-conditions on a people who still adhere to the ancient tradition that 'Britons never shall be slaves'." [**6**] There was also a new weekly column, "Industry", most likely written in collaboration with P. G. Taylor, who also wrote his own columns, in ***Action***, which was a clever way of combining real information of interest to workers in all sectors of British commerce, with propaganda about the whole *raison d'être* of the Movement; in the first column, Wilfred quotes the ***Annual Circular*** of the West Norfolk Farmers' Manure and Chemical Co-operative Company, Ltd., which asks: "… who is the politician or the political party that dare go to the voters in our great towns and tell them that it is their duty to support home agriculture in the interests of national security?" The answer comes back: "Mosley has done this at great meetings in the Albert Hall, London, the Free Trade Hall, Manchester, the Bingley Hall, Birmingham, and many other great meetings in industrial centres throughout Britain. Mosley, however, is not a politician, thank heaven, but merely a great Englishman, and the British Union, which he leads, is not merely a political party, but a great national movement of renaissance." [**7**]

Mosley had spent the three weeks after Christmas ["a characteristically busy time" **8**] completing his new 33,000 word book, ***Tomorrow We Live***, which, readers were informed, "bids fair to become a classic of the English language" [**9**], although Wilfred wasn't so sure. In his 18B Appeal Hearing [**Appendix D**], he admitted that he had "not so much regard for 'Tomorrow We Live' as [he] had for the original booklet, 'Greater Britain'". He is about to relate an incident which happened "when that book was published" when he is interrupted by his interlocutor, Mr. Norman Birkett KC, the chairman of the Advisory Committee, but after agreeing with the comment that "[w]ith an Independent Labour background I should have thought that kind of picture in 'Tomorrow We Live' would be rather repugnant", he goes on to say: "That is just one of the whole series of things which marked a change in my attitude since the period I first mentioned when I questioned the Italian origin of funds …". The predictably reverential review by Chesterton of Mosley's new book, and the excerpts printed in ***Action*** [**10**] are full of the usual metaphorical and even mythic aspirations, with the emphasis on the eternal struggle, but, regrettably, the reader is not offered any specific suggestions or directives to exemplify one of the watchwords of the Movement, action; perhaps it was this quality of the text which Wilfred found less attractive, given that he was a man used to dealing with specifics.

There was a specific requirement at this time, namely funds for a new and vitally important project, which had been laid out by Chesterton, the editor, on the front page of ***The Blackshirt*** late in January, on behalf of Francis-Hawkins; this was "one of the greatest propaganda campaigns in the political history of Britain, and by far the biggest drive ever conducted by the Movement", and the intention was, during the spring and summer of that year, "to place a copy of Mosley's famous ***Ten Points of British Policy*** in every single home throughout the land", and with total conviction, they believed that with this action "every voter in Britain will have had the opportunity to study a concise and comprehensive statement of the National Socialist case, which will result in a vast increase of active members, and a huge swing over to our side of public understanding and support." [**11**] Obviously, this would be expensive so, in addition to a general appeal for contributions from members, a reduction in frequency of ***The Blackshirt*** to monthly, commencing in March [facilitated by the "important contribution towards the project" by the directors of Sanctuary Press Ltd.] was announced; Mosley very generously arranged to give the whole of his income for that year to the Movement; also, rather more ominously, "National Headquarters has arranged a general reorganisation in order to release funds for the campaign", although no details were given, neither was a later paragraph any help: "The carrying out of the mighty propaganda drive necessarily means a certain amount of reorganisation and curtailment in other directions, and these things will imply a certain sacrifice, but the end in view is of such tremendous importance that the sacrifices will be made with readiness and goodwill." Wilfred had no need for concern, at least for the foreseeable future, but it is possible that this was one of the instances where his involvement, "as a politician and propagandist of some years' experience" was not called for by Francis-Hawkins, "a man who had been put into a high position without a real political background that would enable him to do justice in that position", and at various times, "we had the rather peculiar situation that while I was supposed to be handling propaganda there was also a Director General who had authority - that was another grievance I had - who could distribute stuff over my head that I knew nothing about." [**Appendix D**] As if to emphasise this, although it was not likely to have been any sort of overt protest by him, Wilfred's first article in the new monthly ***Blackshirt*** was called "Propaganda in Print" [**12**]. It would seem that, whatever his job title and primary function within the Movement might have been at different times, he never strayed very far from where he started, in one of his most influential spheres of activity, that of propaganda, by virtue of his experience and his seniority.

He was not tasked with spearheading the new "Great British Union Cotton Crusade", which was announced in February in ***Action*** [**13**], although he was publicised as one of the "National Speakers" who were charged with speaking at one or more of their 48 meetings during the fortnight of the campaign. This time, it appears to have been led, appropriately enough, by the Leader himself, and it was made clear that no financial help was to be forthcoming from national headquarters [**14**], which was reiterated in the next ***Blackshirt***, albeit retrospectively, when the "spirit and the enthusiasm" was applauded, because "[n]ever before by this or by any other movement or political party has a propaganda drive of such dimensions been held in Lancashire almost exclusively by volunteers." [**15**] No speeches by Wilfred are referred to in this report, so it is possible that his participation did not happen, for whatever reason; other speeches around this time were mentioned elsewhere: near the end of the campaign, he spoke at Cambridge, to the CUFA [although this acronym is not defined **16**], and in the weeks following, he spoke at East Sheen [**17**]; Leeds, where he spoke to a Business Men's Group on British Union foreign policy [**18**]; and he held "a very successful meeting in the Music Hall, Aberdeen." [**19**]

After the meeting, the "Reds … attempted to mob several members", including Wilfred [**20**], which was not the first time this had happened to him, but it could well have been the last.

There was also news [although of unproven reliability] back at the beginning of the year of a highly emotive call for funds from a group, albeit geographically separated from British Union, but with which British Union had plenty of cause for criticism in societal terms, "rich jews", who were allegedly meeting at some unspecified juncture in Switzerland "with the object of forming a £500,000,000 fighting fund for use in economic warfare against what are called 'persecuting states'. 'Persecuting states', of course, are the nations which prefer to control their own affairs instead of having their affairs obligingly controlled for them by jews." The ***Sunday Chronicle*** asserted that this fund was to be used for "Stock Exchange activities … international manipulation … in an attempt to smash the internal economy of countries such as Germany." To Chesterton, who wrote the article, this was tantamount to "open war" [**21**] and, as Chesterton carefully pointed out, "[i]f this information be correct", it is not hard to understand how Hitler could very easily have construed this as a hostile action, given that he had worked very hard, he considered, to rid his country of financial manipulators and establish an independent economy in Germany. Apparently, "a jewish-controlled New York daily paper … a day or two before Christmas urged precisely the same thing", and Chesterton was unequivocal that "jewish finance intends its economic war to be expanded into actual war between the nations" [**22**]. Whatever the truth of that statement, and even though there were plenty of other portents to be found contemporaneously, it was nonetheless accurate in its prediction of a likely dénouement.

That notwithstanding, Wilfred's responsibility toward a general election which was still confidently expected could not be ignored. In April, he was writing about the "street-block" system that he had worked out with Robert Forgan [see Chapter 5] in an article entitled "Organising for Elections" [**23**], and which formed a fundamental element of his concept of an efficient electoral machine. Somewhere along the line, he had acquired a colleague by the name of C. V. S. Hillman, who was presented in a front-page article [with accompanying photograph] in April's ***Blackshirt***, as being "Electoral Instructor to British Union", and proceeded to write about the street-block system with no reference whatsoever to Wilfred, who was also expounding upon its benefits a few pages further into the same issue! In addition to the regular overlap/sharing of doctrinal elements [or just outright plagiarism?] that was commonplace in British Union propaganda, for example with the "Power Action" meme, the reason for this could very possibly be that Wilfred was training a replacement, as he explained in his 18B Appeal Hearing [**Appendix D**], and by mid-1938 it sounds like he had already unequivocally decided that his future did not lie with British Union:

"I had come to the position where I had not sufficient faith in the *bona fides* of the Movement to continue as a speaker. I was still more or less under an obligation to serve them in the matter of building up election machinery, which I had undertaken to help to do. … I had that obligation to help establish a sound basis of electoral organisation, and train someone else to take my place, which I did." This begs the question of what else he actually did have in mind for employment; also, without any information as to Hillman's background, it is impossible to know whether he was junior to Wilfred, or equal in status: the old-style ranks were no longer used. The whereabouts of Wilfred's erstwhile subordinate, Erskine Atherley, who only a year previously [see Chapter 8, note 52] had been responsible for "Canvass organisation and training, the real foundation of election machinery", were not given.

In addition to Wilfred's vast reservoir of information on electoral matters being passed on directly to a successor, the book that was a compilation in print of his valuable knowledge, "A guide to Constituency Organisation", which had originally been available for one shilling, not a fortune even then for a proper book [around the price of a dozen eggs, but perhaps only worth spending to someone positively desirous of such specific technical information], was now to be sold "at the ridiculously low price of 2d to members of the British Union. This has been done so that you may be prepared for the big struggle." [**24**] If this was possible [assuming the presentation was identical] without incurring a financial loss, there must have been a reasonable profit in the previous edition? Wilfred's "Industry" columns in ***Action*** were still a weekly fixture, and covered a wide range of industry-related topics, usually comprising a set of responses to current newspaper stories, company results or union reports, all reiterating the British Union industrial policies as they related to the overall umbrella of the Corporate State; this did not preclude him from writing in separate articles on associated matters however. In April, he published a story about the AEU [Amalgamated Engineering Union] condemning, with no apparent irony, [and following a general theme] "the leaders of the A.E.U. [who] are making the mistake of utilising a given situation for political purposes to the ultimate detriment of their own industrial interests, … doing it in such fashion as to gain them the unqualified approval of those Communist interests which have sought so often in the past to destroy this great union." The executive of the union had issued a manifesto on the 8th of that month which "cuts across the very principles of democracy to which the Trade Union movement of Britain is pledged. It declares that the cause of the legally-elected government of Spain is the cause of the British workers, and calls for voluntary work by its members in aid of Spain, and then proceeds to ask its members in their leisure time to turn out material for the use of the 'Red' Government of Spain in the civil war." [**25**] This is undoubtedly symptomatic of the ambivalence that he felt about championing democracy in the trade union environment which he was convinced was crucial for British workers, within an anti-democratic [apolitical] administrative system for which British Union stood. The fact that he had been able to last so long, fighting for workers' democratic rights and yet ostensibly espousing authoritarian [or at the very least, syndicalist] government is a testament not only to his pragmatic ability to see the bigger picture in his career with British Union [for all that it entailed a rationalising of his convictions], but also to his loyalty.

The theme of workers' democratic rights was very much to the fore in what was intended to be a series of articles in ***The Blackshirt*** on the subject of the Tolpuddle Martyrs ["A Century of Struggle"], the first of which was published in the May edition [**26**], and it was subtitled, almost inevitably, "From Tolpuddle Martyrs to British Union". The second instalment, the following month [**27**], crystallised the message of the articles as "the early efforts of the Tolpuddle martyrs to bring Trade Unionism to this country"; even today, the transcript of the trial makes powerfully affecting reading, exemplifying and underlining [perhaps ironically, in the circumstances] the resolutely authoritarian attitude of the Bench: "The judge then told them that, '*Not for anything they had done, or, as he could prove, they intended to do, but for an example to others* he considered it his duty to pass sentence of seven years' penal transportation across His Majesty's high seas upon each and every one of them.'"; and the surprisingly eloquent words written by one of the defendants, George Loveless ["The acknowledged leader of the six"], hastily and spontaneously "jotted down" after hearing their sentence of transportation, cannot fail to stir the emotions:

God is our Guide! From field, from wave,
From plough, from anvil, and from loom,
We come our country's right to save,
And speak a tyrant faction's doom;
We raise the watchword – Liberty.
We will, we will, we will be free!
God is our guide! No swords we draw.
We kindle not war's battle fires,
By reason, union, justice, law,
We claim the birthright of our sires:
We raise the watchword – Liberty,
We will, we will, we will be free!

The concluding instalment was scheduled for July, when Wilfred would "draw a comparison between the struggles of the Tolpuddle martyrs and that of the New Movement" but there was no mention of a concluding article either in the July or the August edition so, assuming the article was actually written in the first place, it seems to have been a casualty of a combination of a common problem with newspapers, pressure on space for regular features caused by the need to react to circumstances [**28**], and a change in September to regional editions of the paper, of which there was notification in August [**29**]: this was not necessarily a direct result of yet another 'heavyweight' of the Movement, A. K. Chesterton, 'jumping ship' at the end of March [**30**], but that did remove a stalwart, albeit highly opinionated, from the editorial roster of British Union's publications.

It has to remain a matter for speculation whether Wilfred had a hand in organising a meeting [also referred to as a "Rally"] at which "Mosley has been invited by a group of London Trade Unionists to attend and speak to the assembled workers on the creed of the British Union", at the Denison Hall ["near Victoria Station"] on April 3rd, but ***The Blackshirt*** trumpeted it as "a landmark in the history of our Movement and is the first of its kind." [**31**] The meeting "was an unqualified success", and at the end, a resolution "to spread [British Union Industrial Policy] through the British Trade Union Movement ... with an amendment ... that a copy should be sent to the T.U.C. ... was passed unanimously." [**32**] Alongside the, by now, firmly established belief that electoral success was the way for his Movement to achieve power in Britain, Mosley knew that recognition by official workers' groups, and acknowledgement from them of his policies was crucial, in terms of sheer numbers, if he was to gain the support he would need to achieve that electoral victory. By October, in an unattributed article [but immediately adjacent an article by Wilfred, referred to as "British Union's Chief Electoral Advisor"] "the General Election [was] now forecast as taking place next spring", and the question was asked if it would "be fought with an entirely new line-up of political allegiances?" [**33**]

In the meantime, however, there were local elections to think about, and in August, members were informed [presumably by Hillman, as the article was unattributed] that "Municipal elections are the feature of November 1 in all municipal boroughs in England and Wales except the London Metropolitan boroughs", but also that "[i]f you seriously intend at a later date to contest Parliamentary elections there is no better training than that obtained in fighting local government elections and it doesn't cost much." [**34**] By October, Wilfred was weighing in to the campaign, and he particularly praised the contribution made by women members: "As in times of crisis, so in times of hum-drum, perseverance for the building of an electoral machine, our women are magnificent. Theirs is the quality of patience which strives day in and day out for the final establishment of the rule of 'People's Justice'." [**35**] The last paragraph of this article, which referred to "generations of Britons yet unborn" was pertinent, in view of world events which were currently unfolding, and this was underlined by a photograph that was incorporated into it with the caption "Women Demonstrators at Westminster", and the women were holding placards, the frontmost of which read "OUR CHILDREN WERE YOUNG IN 1914 / HAVE WE BROUGHT THEM UP FOR WAR".

Although an uninformed observer [the archetypal 'alien from another planet' perhaps, rather than the sort of alien who was the concern of British Union] would justifiably very quickly gain the impression that war was the predominant concern at this time, which it most certainly was, in truth, its proximity was all too clear and the concomitant threat had not lain very deep below the surface of the consciousness of the British people more or less since the end of the previous war; 'the war to end all wars' [in August, ***The Blackshirt*** reprinted an article "from the issue of September 16, 1933. It clearly shows B.U. consistency in affirming its desire to avoid war in a world seething with war-rumours during the war month of August. It is rightly desirable that it should once more be read."]: probably the Treaty of Versailles, metaphorically, but also ironically, for all its good intentions, fired the first shot in the race towards another war. International relations, which realistically could never have been said to have been regularly or consistently pacific since the earliest days of empire-building and mass colonisation, as a result of the covetousness and consequent militarism inspired by a lust for earning potential, now were increasingly poised on a knife-edge. Individual powers were still jockeying for position, if not actual supremacy, but alliances were also beginning to form again, after having been sundered by the previous conflagration, and that was a virtual guarantee that things would end badly. For the first half of the relatively short existence of British Union [or the British Union of Fascists, initially] to date, the only foreign power which had presented any sort of a threat to Britain and, by extension, to Mosley's organisation, had been Russia; this threat was still seen as ever-present, and all the more dangerous because of the already somewhat successful insinuation of its principles and its methodology into, and thereby contaminating, the minds of a significant section of the British workers, with their perfectly justifiable grievances; and the tangential Jewish support, allegedly, with their connections to International Finance, was seen as a menace about which the British public as a whole needed to be educated.

Italy was the first foreign power to present the possibility of war when it overwhelmed Abyssinia in 1935; to the credit of the Government of the day, this was avoided, even if that was more by accident than by design [see Chapter 8]; Spain was another internal quarrel we managed to stay out of, despite demands for material help and concerted agitation for our involvement from the 'left', which inspired many idealists to go to a futile death on a foreign field. Before long, however, Germany started becoming a force to be reckoned with; the reasons for, and the justification of its ascendance and the methods employed to achieve this have been argued and contested ever since, but it surely must be conceded that, even if it was only a fortuitous peripheral benefit, as a result of the restructuring that was regarded as an essential prerequisite, of an injection of revitalising finance into the previously stultified German economy, which was required to facilitate a bellicose expansion of the Third Reich's military capability, the bulk of the German people enjoyed greatly improved living conditions before the war economy took precedence over social necessities. No doubt it has been argued that Hitler was clever enough to structure his strategy in such a way that all of his tactics were executed in a timely fashion, so as not to give the impression of a headlong rush to war; this is very easy to assert with the benefit of hindsight; or else, the luck of the devil was with him until it ran out at Stalingrad: suffice to say that, at the beginning of 1938 anyway, the more immediate direct threat was seen, by British Union, as Japan.

Other than regularly dissecting Marxist doctrine and highlighting the unsuitability of its internationalism for British workers, Wilfred tended to leave the detailed reporting of foreign affairs and their potential repercussions to his apparently better-informed colleagues [although his knowledge was clearly very wide], but this did not preclude him from drawing comparisons between industrial matters in Britain and those in other countries, where they were relevant in his many columns on this subject [**36**]. One of those colleagues was Major-General Fuller [C.B., C.B.E., D.S.O.] and, whilst he was not universally well-liked, his knowledge of military matters both at home and abroad, was accepted, within British Union at least, as authoritative. At the end of January, he posed the question "On what should our foreign policy be based?" but then, of course, proceeded to answer it, in a wide-ranging, full page article in ***Action***. As ever, in Mosleyite thinking, the Empire was sacrosanct, but we were being faced by a whole parade of hostile nations; "we should not antagonise these Powers"; and "Baldwinism" was to blame: "Except for the U.S.A. and France, Baldwinism has violently annoyed them all; so much so that our Imperial backbone has been completely dislocated in its central section ... In fact, were we in another war to be faced by Germany, Italy, Japan and Spain, we should find our Empire as backboneless as a jelly-fish. No rearmament can solve this question, for its solution lies in the political field." [**37**] Notwithstanding the correctness, albeit admittedly not paranormally prescient, of the assessment of the threat, in 3 out of these 4 cases, the final sentence is particularly interesting, especially coming as it did from an ex-military man.

Fortunately, Japan's "amok-run ... in and around Shanghai" didn't result in war with Britain, at least not in 1938, although ***Reveille***'s attitude in ***Action*** was by no means conciliatory: "Whatever contingency arises, therefore, there will be nothing to do but send 'strongly worded' protests to Japan instead of the heavy boot which the situation may infallibly demand for the restoration of British prestige in the East." [**38**] This attitude was somewhat contradicted, only a fortnight later, in the same column, although it was used as an opportunity to condemn Labour for putting forward Japan's hegemony as a pretext for war with Germany, so that it could enjoy the fruits of "Financial Democracy" with its Jewish associations: "Labour has already tried to bring us into war on behalf of Abyssinia and Spain, not because of altruism, but because of a desperate attempt to destroy the modern movement in Europe before it spoils Labour's chance of entering fully into the heritage of Financial Democracy. Its leaders believe, moreover, that if Germany in particular can be reduced to ruins Mosley's rapidly advancing crusade in Britain will be discredited and brought to an end. … The latest attempt to force an attack on Germany by means of a Japanese war is a clear revelation of Ikey's hand." [**39**] The prospect of the former was presented as a distinct possibility in a banner headline just over a month later, when readers of ***Action*** were entreated to "STOP THIS WAR" [**40**].

In an article that looked almost like a Victorian playbill, with its wide variety of font-sizes crammed into a narrow column down the middle of the page, "Fellow-Britons" were entreated to "wake up", because "[t]he politicians are using every effort to send you into the slaughter-house of another European War". The response to the question of whose quarrel it was, turned out to be not the answer which might have been expected: "The quarrel of the politicians, backed by International Capitalism and International Socialism, marching hand in hand to attempt the destruction of Germany with precious British lives." This led immediately into the hot topic of the moment: "Not one British interest is involved in Austria. At this very hour millions of Austrians rejoice because Hitler has brought about their union in the new brotherhood of the German people." In many people's eyes, this was merely another stage in Hitler's devious plan [reoccupying the *Rheinland* in March 1936 being the first] to conquer mainland Europe [almost inevitably with a view to going further east], for which his concept of *Lebensraum* [living space] was a very poor, and easily demolished justification. The perceived [or imagined] pressure from Hitler on Austria to accept the *Anschluß* [meaning nothing more sinister than joining, or unification] indirectly brought about the resignation of Foreign Secretary Anthony Eden on the 20th of February, to be replaced by Lord Halifax. Prime Minister Neville Chamberlain wanted to isolate Germany by being as conciliatory as he could be toward Italy, to the extent of being prepared to recognise Italy's conquest of Abyssinia which, in tandem with Chamberlain's independence of action on foreign affairs, convinced Eden to resign. British Union saw this as a positive step, albeit narrowly; Chesterton, in one of his final articles for the Movement, detailed "[w]hy Britain should be relieved at his downfall" [**41**], and the front page article had Mosley explaining why this meant "Humiliation instead of World War … Eden's policy means war—Chamberlain's policy means humiliation. The lesson for Britain is never again to be placed in such a position." [**42**] The answer was to "Mind Britain's Business" and for "the people of Britain [to] demand the immediate rupture of the corrupt alliance with Soviet Russia which has divided the world into two armed camps." In one of his increasingly rare public meetings at this time, Wilfred "spoke at Leeds Business Men's Group lunch and dealt with the topical subject of British Union foreign policy in relation to the Eden exit. He outlined the British Union's pledge for peace and the Leader's assurance that no British soldier shall ever be called upon to fight for an alien financial interest." Evidently, this did not prove to be an unpopular theme as "[m]embers invited him to come again when the Group had expanded." [see note 18 above] Another piece of the jigsaw, which would subsequently prove to be pivotal, made its appearance in the public consciousness, although the problem had not only newly arisen in 1938; Czechoslovakia was not seen initially by British Union as a means by which Germany could increase its population, or its territory, or both: when it was mentioned early in 1938, it was within the rubric of the Treaty of Versailles, the context being that an ill-armed Germany, as a result of the duplicity of the signatories of the Treaty, who did not fulfil their side of the bargain by disarming to match Germany's reduced level, was surrounded by heavily-armed nations, one of which was Czechoslovakia, "fast becoming a vassal state of the Soviet" [**43**].

The first mention in 1938 of the problem with Czechoslovakia that would prove to be damning for Germany, although not the final straw, was early in March, when there was recognition that "[t]here is in Czechoslovakia a very large and disgracefully ill-treated German minority which looks to the Fatherland sooner or later for release from an intolerable position. In order to keep this minority in chains the Left Wings of the democracies are quite willing that millions of British lives should be sacrificed, and in so far as the Conservative Party backs French policy Chamberlain inevitably finds himself lined up on the side of the Left." [**44**] From then on, the cry was "Czechoslovakia not Britain's Business" [**45**], and Wilfred would have been expected to adhere to this line in public, although there do not appear to be any published articles on this particular subject; Germany would have been a subject for discussion in general since 1933, but it wasn't until 1938 that Wilfred started mentioning it in his ***Industry*** columns, in connection with current events, and even then, only occasionally. Apart from condemnation of Russia and the doctrine of Communism in general, he appeared to be consistent in concentrating on matters at home; this was very much the theme of a speech he gave [by his own recollection; see **Appendix D**] "at Buckhurst Hill in the Epping division, the Prime Minister's constituency, on the 4th May 1938, where there was persistent questioning from people who wanted to get my opinion about what had happened in Germany. That questioning was so persistent, it was maintained for nearly half an hour on that one point despite the fact that I said I knew nothing about the system in Germany, I cared less about what was happening in Germany, the only thing I did know was that I was advocating changes that I considered to be appropriate and useful in the system of Government in this country. … I quote that meeting in particular because a fairly full account was given in the Press that stressed in particular my attitude towards this question of the system of Government in Germany. I am not an admirer of German systems of Government, and never have been …"

Whilst not wanting to accuse him of disingenuousness, it is fair to say that Wilfred must have known, at the very least, a modicum about Germany, its government, and current events; notwithstanding all the news reporting with which everyone would have been bombarded at that time, all of which will, admittedly, have had a propaganda slant one way or another, ***Action*** regularly carried articles and editorials about Germany and they were generally positive about Hitler's policies [**46**], so it is much more likely that Wilfred will have wanted to steer clear of issues that were not specifically part of the British Union policy and keep minds focused on how much work needed to be done at home, especially in view of their desire to "Mind Britain's Business". Interestingly, a contemporary report on the meeting in a local paper [**47**] didn't mention any questions on Germany, but it did make an oblique reference to the subject: "In answer to further questions, he declared the Union had an unswerving loyalty to the Crown, which it recognised as the most vital link of the Empire. They were not out for international Fascism, but for Britain alone." The first matter mentioned in the questions, according to the article, concerned "the position between the British Union of Fascists and the Jewish race. He declared the movement was definitely anti-semitic, but it had not always been. For the first two years of its existence the members had refused to be drawn into any discussion on the subject. But it became quite obvious that the Jews were going to smash the movement if it was within their power, not because the Fascists had attacked them, but because their policy was detrimental to their world domination." In general, the article seems to be a surprisingly impartial reporting of the event; perhaps an inference can be drawn about the political affiliations of the area, given that the meeting was "remarkable for its quietness and the orderly behaviour of the fair-sized audience"?

He was still writing regularly, and he wrote another article, albeit shorter than its predecessor, "The Old Socialism and the New", in the first ***British Union Quarterly*** of 1938, but there doesn't appear to have been a review of this edition at all, for some reason. The party conferences still took place more or less as normal, despite all the nervousness about foreign situations [in fact, they gave the various parties ample opportunity for loaded rhetoric], and Wilfred made sure that his readers were apprised of the absurdities; he could not resist a gentle dig at his erstwhile hero, "Jimmy" Maxton: "we feel that Jimmy will continue president of the I.L.P. until one or the other dies." [**48**] It was also of vital significance to the Movement, in terms of how it was perceived by the public, and very much part of Wilfred's ethos, that everyday matters of importance to working people should not be neglected, so on the same page as the one referred to above, he detailed a case where a 'bus conductor maimed in the course of his work had failed to gain compensation because of "a legal anomaly. … This is a most vicious principle which must be fought tooth and nail." It did give him the opportunity, however, to 'take a poke' at domestic political leaders, and their misplaced loyalties: "What a chance for a Keir Hardie or an Arthur Cook! Unfortunately there are none such among present-day Labour leaders. If one half the energy and fighting spirit had been shown in this case as has been poured out in hatred of Franco, Hitler or Mussolini, things would begin to move in the right direction." [**49**]

Life at home was still just about normal enough for the municipal elections, publicised in August [see note 34] to take place, and in October, some of the candidates' details were published in ***The Blackshirt***, with the editorial telling its readers that "we may turn our attention again to domestic affairs", even though "[s]ince publication of the last issue of this paper the whole of Europe has experienced a dramatic convulsion that has left its mark in the minds of every man and woman." [**50**] In the event, the results were not inspiring; Cross describes them as "humiliating, the 22 candidates mustering a grand total of only 2,474 votes - an average of 112 each …" [**51**]; even though ***Action*** naturally put a brave face on the results ["Everywhere the British Union record of polling a far higher vote than the Labour Party at their first attempt was fully maintained." **52**], Wilfred will no doubt have found this particularly frustrating, in that the personal attention he would have been able to give to the fight was strictly limited, as it had been made clear that it was up to local districts to make their own individual arrangements: "This, despite the fact that British Union stands for the scrapping of the local government system, and that these fights are purely a local matter in which the British Union national machine is not engaged." There was one victory worth celebrating, however: "Particular congratulations are due to R. N. Creasy for winning a seat and defeating a sitting councillor at his first attempt in the rural area of Eye, Suffolk." [**53**] Only a year earlier, Wilfred had been telling his readers "How to fight municipal elections: make it a real issue" [see Chapter 9, note 51]. The "dramatic convulsion" referred to here was Munich, and some later observers, notably Colin Cross, are of the opinion that Mosley's front page article on the October 1 edition of ***Action*** "was prepared on the assumption that war had started." [and the article was actually written on Tuesday September 27th **54**] It is true that he commenced the article by saying "British Union has declared against this war.", but later on, he says "I say without hesitation that this plan can, even now, secure peace with honour. … In this eleventh hour this is a plan which will secure peace.", which sounds like there is significant room for doubt: being still on the brink is more plausible than having already fallen into the abyss. The Munich [*München*] meeting, at which the 'final' agreement was signed, was actually after the aforementioned article; it was Chamberlain's flight to Berchtesgaden that had prompted Mosley to use the expression "eleventh hour". Hitler had either initiated, or at the very least, acquiesced to false allegations of atrocities against the Sudeten Germans ["During August the German press was full of stories alleging Czech atrocities against Sudeten

Germans, with the intention of forcing the Western Powers into putting pressure on the Czech [sic] to make concessions." **55**], and the SdP [*Sudetendeutsche Partei*] used these as an excuse to break off further negotiations on behalf of its supporters. At a Nürnberg rally on September 12th, Hitler promised the Sudeten Germans they would not be left defenceless; the next day, Chamberlain requested a personal meeting with Hitler, which was granted on September 15th.

British Union was quick to praise this, in an article by Michael Goulding in ***Action*** with a sub-heading "Democracy Driven To Fascist Technique" [**56**], but apart from a general reference to the crisis in October's ***Southern Blackshirt*** [see note 35] Wilfred's only specific contribution on the circumstances surrounding Chamberlain's meeting of the 15th, without actually mentioning it, laid the blame firmly at France's door: "Shall British Youth be sacrificed to French War Party?" [**57**] It is most likely that the copy for this article, given that it was published on October 1st, will have been prepared in advance of the Munich Agreement; he indicated the likely military significance to France of Czechoslovakia, but reiterated that Britain's primary consideration, after Britain itself, of course, was our empire: "Is that Empire, which is our first responsibility, to be jeopardised for the sole purpose of ensuring to France a Czechoslovakia eternally hostile to Germany? We say no! a thousand times 'no!'." There was also another aspect to this situation which Wilfred was at pains to point out, since this was something of a 'hobbyhorse' for him: the potential involvement of Russia: "Russia could intervene at two vital points. … Well and good. That is the affair of France and explains her Russian alliance, but there is in it no vestige of a reason why Britain should join in such a 'line-up'. There is nothing in that war-plan which would benefit either Great Britain or the Empire. What insane folly it would be, therefore, for us to join in such a stupid quarrel. … France has chosen as her ally – Russia; as her policy – war (in the future); as her enemy – Germany, the three factors following automatically from the first factor. This I believe to be a stupid choice."

The Munich Agreement was ostensibly the result of Chamberlain's appeal to Hitler on September 28th; both the British and French governments had accepted Hitler's demand that Germany should assume control of the Sudetenland to put an end to the alleged slaughtering of the German population by the Czechs, but in the face of Czech government resistance, the two governments would only guarantee to Czechoslovakia a French commitment to support contingent upon Czech acceptance, which caused the Czech government to capitulate. The Czech army was willing to fight, and Russia was publicly willing to assist, but president Beneš refused to go to war without the support of the western powers. In an amazing snub, the Czech government was not invited to the September 29th conference: the resulting agreement was signed by representatives of Britain, Germany, Italy and France, and as a consequence, Czechoslovakia was informed that it could either resist Germany alone, or submit to the agreed annexations, which were the Sudetenland by the 10th of October, and very possibly the other disputed areas, subject to the findings of an international commission. The Czech government reluctantly agreed. In a very canny move before coming home, Chamberlain asked Hitler to sign a peace agreement between Britain and Germany, "which I had prepared beforehand" and that "he happily agreed" to do, once it had been translated for him: this was the "piece of paper with Herr Hitler's signature upon it" [**58**], waved jubilantly in the air by Chamberlain on his return to Heston Aerodrome, just outside London. Wilfred's only other direct comment on the tension attendant upon this situation followed immediately after his indictment of the French; there is only a very brief reference to Czechoslovakia: "Remember that once before peace seemed to be assured and then, owing to rapid moves taken (surely on outside advice), in Czechoslovakia, the clouds gathered even more ominously than before." Other than that, the article was devoted to an examination of "Backstairs intrigues to wreck peace" and, although there was only one specific reference to Jews ["Certain organs of the Jews in Britain add their quota of 'hate' to this insane chorus."], the implication would seem to be that theirs was the guiding hand in "the Dangerous Party": "There is a steadily mounting accumulation of evidence which goes to indicate that there is a 'party' in our midst which aims at imposing its will by the methods of underhanded intrigue in defiance of those who seek to establish peace in Europe." All was not lost quite yet though: "Do not be rattled whatever may happen in the future, but hold fast to the one demand for peace, peace in our time. For Britain, peace and people." [**59**] This was not automatically tacit approval for Chamberlain, but certainly approval of his belief in the sanctity of peace and his efforts to preserve it in the face of increasing pessimism.

This theme of the 'hidden hand', which was eerily premonitory [although probably not entirely unpredictable] of the 'fifth column' hypothesis employed as one of the justifications for wartime internment, that was only eighteen months in the future, was continued in one of the last of Wilfred's attributed ***Industry*** columns, which followed soon after: Colin Cross asserts [**60**] that this move to anonymous articles and editorials "was probably an attempt to disguise the accelerating leakage [of contributing members]". This was inevitably one of several factors, although realistically, there had always been a regular turnover of members at all levels, and for a variety of reasons, from the earliest days of Mosley's independent Movements, and it is unlikely that the impending catastrophe was close enough yet for this to be a major cause; it is also likely that, for all their undoubted and genuine bravery, the leading and most outspoken members must have been aware of the possibility of potentially fatal reprisals instigated by cretinous and official propaganda-led mob-mentality, and the likelihood [or even inevitability] of legal strictures, as 'national security' began to assume a much more prominent rôle in everyday life.

The story in the aforesaid column, published on the 22nd of October 1938, and quoting from the ***Evening Standard***, wrapped up several of Wilfred's favourite elements: trade unionism, democracy, and the perceived malign influence of the Jews. It concerned a Nevada county sheriff who had been empowered [using "250 regular and special deputies"] "to shoot trade union organisers who try to enter the State of Nevada from California. The order was 'shoot to kill if necessary'." Given that he had no reason to be supportive of America, Wilfred's response, demonstrating his literary knowledge, but in his usual wry style was:

> "And all this in the home and stronghold of Democracy – the Jewnited States.
>
> What a pity that neither Hitler, Stalin or Mussolini can be blamed for it. It would have been first-class anti-Fascist propaganda if only it had happened in one of the 'authoritarian' states, but that home of 'democratic liberty', the U.S.A., is another matter. It's a little way they've always had there as readers of Jack London, Upton Sinclair, and 'Big Bill Haywood' will know.
>
> Why not a 'war against Democracy and T.U. Oppression'? The boy-friends of the pink tie and the clenched paw might give it their consideration. Or they might not." [**61**]

Following the apparent success of Munich, the predominant focus of British Union was peace and its preservation, although the quotidian demands of the Movement's members and the remaining potential converts were not overlooked; hopes that the constitutionally mandatory general election would still take place the following year had not been officially renounced [see note 33 above], but persuading the British public of the folly of war was uppermost in their minds; how much of an effect and influence this could have been expected to have on those at the seat of power is another matter. In addition to the "energetic peace campaign, with propaganda marches [and] distribution of leaflets" was "the posting of chain letters" [**62**]; this appears to be the one & only time that this device was employed by the Movement, so the level of individual involvement necessary for it to succeed must have meant that it should only by considered in times of dire need, which of course these were. There was no attribution attached to the exhortation to "Copy out the following message on postcards and send them to at least ten other persons TO-NIGHT [sic].", published in the "Crisis Special edition" of ***Action*** [see note 54], so it is tempting to assume that the "Chain Peace Letter" was not Wilfred's initiative: it concluded with "Yours for peace,", but it is not clear whether that was how the insertion was supposed to end, or if this was a recommendation for the end of the peace message; in fairness, the piece might have been cobbled together under some pressure, but it does exemplify Wilfred's concern over the lack of an overall control in the area of propaganda [**63**]. One is also minded to wonder if it would not have been more efficient to print this as a sort of 'sacrificial piece' that could have been printed in a suitable place in the edition, with appropriate copy on the reverse, so that it could have just been popped into an envelope and, given the absence of modern photocopying technology, this might have encouraged increased sales of the paper [or a whole batch of them could have been printed on one page?]; the same convenience would have resulted if the idea had been to paste the copy onto a postcard to reduce the cost of postage. Perhaps Wilfred came up with suggestions such as these, only for them to be rejected?

Possibly the last matter for contention between Wilfred and Francis-Hawkins, the Director General of British Union, and perhaps even the source of Wilfred's decision to cut loose from his vocational, if not his spiritual home, for the preceding six years, was the issue of Danzig, which arose, at least in the form which was to prove terminal for the fragile peace that still existed in Europe, immediately after Munich, in October 1938; the semi-autonomous city-state of Danzig was another product of the Treaty of Versailles and, similarly to Czechoslovakia, it was in a somewhat iniquitous position, given that it was situated between two sections of the German Empire, with the "Polish Corridor" acting as a buffer to the west; consequently, it was always going to be a realistic target for Hitler. The City's government was taken over by the local NSDAP [Nazi Party] in June 1933, so the city-state will have been in contention from then on [although not for the first time, by any means], and this was brought to a head in October 1938, when German Foreign Affairs Minister, Joachim von Ribbentrop [German Ambassador to Great Britain from August 1936 to February 1938 **64**] demanded the incorporation of the Free City into the Reich [**65**], although this was only made public in March 1939, having previously been confined to private meetings between German and Polish officials [see note 64]. There does not appear to have been any article about Danzig, or any "pamphlet on Danzig" [as referred to in Wilfred's 18B Appeal Hearing, **Appendix D**] mentioned in either of the regular British Union publications before the end of the year, so if Danzig materialised as a potential problem before the beginning of 1939, it must have been decided to treat it as an internal matter; but whenever it arose, even though, according to Norman Birkett, "the Leader had given instructions that that particular pamphlet should be distributed to all districts", Mosley's instructions will inevitably have been issued to Francis-Hawkins in the first instance, so despite Wilfred "handling propaganda at that time ... there was also a Director General ... who could distribute stuff over my head that I knew nothing about."

He was obviously not ready to move on just yet, especially given the precarious political situation, but he must have seen out 1938 with a real dilemma: when to go, and what to do. He very probably looked upon the writing he did for the Movement, which was not directly propounding its guiding principles, as a welcome diversion [although, inevitably, the ethos of British Union was never far away whenever conclusions were drawn]; one of his last book reviews of 1938 concerned the world-view of Dean W. R. Inge [**66**], who was Dean of St. Paul's Cathedral, and not by any means averse to making his views known in public. Although some of Inge's ideas were obviously counter to the British Union doctrine; "The Roman Church is essentially a form of dictatorship, like Communism and Nazism.", Wilfred declined to condemn the book, describing the introduction as "the most interesting of all this book's sections", perhaps because Inge abhorred "the horrors of the Red revolution in Spain … for the British public have been shamefully deceived." Wilfred's final comment is non-committal, but brief to the point of dismissiveness: "Well, that is a selection. Make your own choice." [**67**] The other review, in the same issue, was of a book with an anodyne title by a currently little-known politician, but the title belied a serious attempt at a recommendation for a purposive change in British politics by an author who would become a household name in the late 1950s and early '60s, when he became Conservative prime minister [**68**]. The book was ***The Middle Way***, by Harold Macmillan, who was something of a radical in his early career, and it was "a book for the serious student of politics" so, in theory, the readers of ***Action*** were a good target audience. "The tragedy is that it will most probably be read by many who do not analyse and do not understand, hence they may follow the conclusions drawn by the author and fall into the trap of believing that there is a 'middle way' which is practicable between the opposites of Bolshevism and Corporativism." As with the previous review, he stops short of outright derogation, given that Macmillan succumbs to a "dropped brick" when he says that, in the area of industrial democracy [and which Wilfred capitalises without comment, so perhaps that was intentional] "too much democratic interference would militate against efficiency." In what seems to be a characteristic of his literary style, Wilfred leaves his readers, winking metaphorically, with what could well be a rhetorical question: "He advocates also an Economic Planning Authority comprising representatives of the Central Bank, the Investment Board, the Foreign Trade Organisation and the Industrial Advisory Council. This Authority would be known as the Economic Council and would meet under the chairmanship of a Minister of Economics. It would include also a representative from the Treasury, President of the Board of Trade, Minister of Agriculture and Minster of Labour. Imagine such a meeting. … who knows what problems they might solve?" [**69**]

The ***Industry*** columns continued into 1939, but without attribution; it is not possible to state categorically that these must have been by Wilfred, but the writing style seems consistent with that which was previously identified as his. There was the occasional reference to current events in Germany; commenting on a report in the ***Daily Express***, he said [with tongue firmly in cheek, as usual]: "Adolf Hitler is a most annoying person. He just won't play politics as they should be played according to the rules of Democratic party politics. He is actually carrying out his promises and fulfilling his pledges. The National part of his programme is already fulfilled. That is bad from a 'Democrat's' point of view, but now it is feared that he means to go further and implement the Socialist section of that programme – and there is no power that can stop him. Such an unfortunate example to set. With such an example before them people in this country might demand fulfilment of Party pledges and that would be 'Fascism'. Most disturbing!" [**70**] On *Kristallnacht*, however, he had nothing to say; a night of violence, for which Jewish-owned shops and synagogues were the target, had erupted on November 11th, 1938, in Germany, following the death of a secretary of the German legation in Paris, Ernst vom Rath; he had been shot by a Jewish German youth, Herschel Grynzpan, apparently without motive.

The Movement could hardly ignore the event, but it was seen in a wider context: under the banner headline "'Pogrom' in Germany; What Is The Truth?", the front page of ***Action*** said "British papers once more tell the story of the destruction of the synagogues and Jewish shops in Germany. This, according to our Press, has happened already on three previous occasions. The average man is finding it increasingly difficult to understand how it is possible even for the National Socialist regime to destroy that which it is alleged has already been destroyed before." [**71**] A full page article on page 3 contrasted what happened in Germany with "a time-honoured policy of Great Britain", in Palestine: "To-day in Palestine Arab communities are punished for individual Arab 'atrocities'. Villages are blown to smithereens, houses and crops are burnt. British Government counters terror with terror."; in Ireland: "So far the Press of this country, always wild and exaggerated in its stories of alleged repression in Germany, has only been able to find one instance of a Jew being killed in Germany, due to this new wave of anti-Semitism. Yet such, regrettably, is not the story of the British occupation in Ireland."; and the 'north west frontier': "A mad Fakir arms a few men, attacks British sovereignty, the British Air Force is immediately dispatched to blow the villages of these men to smithereens. Instance after instance has been quoted in the daily papers to prove that this bombing was indiscriminating." [**72**] Using information "From Our Berlin Correspondent", the paper set out to discover "What really happened in Germany":

> "Filled with anger at the death of Herr vom Rath, numbers of men went out and smashed the windows of Jewish shops. In most cases, nothing further occurred, but in a few instances some of the goods in the shops were damaged. There is no evidence to show that any Jews were attacked. Some (not all) the synagogues were set on fire, as being the places where the anti-German plots were believed to have been launched.

> Our special correspondent personally investigated literally hundreds of cases, and found the situations as described above. The fire brigade extinguished the fires in the Berlin synagogues. Our special correspondent saw them at work, as did, in fact, thousands of persons who collected to watch the operations.
>
> **We do not hold any brief for the men who laid fire to the synagogues or smashed windows. Nor do we agree with their action in any shape or form. But we do remark that during the great War, shops believed to be owned by Germans were demolished in numerous parts of the British Empire, especially in the East End of London and Manchester.**
>
> We suggest, therefore, more objectiveness in reporting. And those who are wildly against the action of the populace in Germany should not forget that lynching is still a regular occurrence in the United States, where democracy is praised. It is unfair to quote the one, but refuse to see the other." [**73**]

Even though the clouds of war must have been really looming large overhead as 1939 proceeded, Wilfred was still able to restate his vision for "Trade Unions in the New State", and in the process reversing the name of his essential pamphlet [which was now being advertised anonymously] to "Power Action not Strike Action" [**74**]; an assessment of a book on this subject appeared in his continuing series of book reviews, and very magnanimously, given his own not insignificant contribution to the Movement on this subject, he commented that "[t]his book will fill a long-felt need", but it was an 'in-house' publication, with a foreword by Mosley, who concludes by saying "The People's State awaits the building of the workers." [**75**] Wilfred's last two book reviews, printed together in the same issue of ***Action*** in mid-March, are of a factual book called ***The New Ireland***, by J. B. Morton, and a novella called ***Jubilee John***, by Alum Llewellyn. In the former, Wilfred demonstrates that his political knowledge was not confined to Britain: "How many know anything about the 1937 Irish Constitution? It is one of the most important documents of the twentieth century; and yet its passage is only *one* of the many achievements of Mr. de Valera and Fianna Fail." The latter, "a fast moving story of incredible adventure", is obviously an entertaining diversion, but it is, nonetheless, "[a] rollicking story, well told." [**76**]

Possibly Wilfred's very last public speech for British Union was reported in ***Action*** on the 18th of March, 1939; he was very much on 'home territory': "Speaking to a group of busmen-trade unionists – at Oddfellows Hall, Tottenham", he reiterated his arguments to what should have been a particularly receptive audience; "The people who accuse British Union of intending to smash trade unionism lie. … The Power Action of British Union is now the only hope of salvation for the Trade Unions and the rank and file members are rapidly awakening to its immense possibilities in spite of officially inspired misrepresentation." [**77**] Even at the end of March, when thoughts of leaving the Movement must have been occupying his mind more and more, in an after-dinner speech as the guest of Kingston upon Thames District [British Union], Wilfred was still able to commend Mosley for the foresight of his analysis: "Mosley alone, of contemporary politicians, clearly foresaw and warned the country about the economic blizzard which in July, 1931, struck us with its full force."; he also reminded his admittedly partisan audience of the need for British Union; "Capitalism – the thesis – is now working. Communism is the antithesis which grows up to oppose capitalism. Out of the conflict between them emerges a new school of thought which in this country is called British Union."; but it was also important to restate the importance of trade unions: "The 100 per cent. trade unionism of British Union will be a bigger, better, finer thing than the trade unionism of the present day, and its accession to power will be the finest thing for the workers in the community that could ever be conceived." [**78**]

Also present at that dinner was Wilfred's colleague on industrial matters, P. G. Taylor; this was not mentioned in the article, and it is only known because a photograph of the event exists, in which Taylor is seen [or not, to be accurate] characteristically avoiding the camera's gaze. He was notoriously camera-shy, which is understandable for someone such as he who was an MI5 'mole', but it does seem somewhat unnecessary, given that he wrote frequently under his own name or initials in the Movement's newspapers, and spoke publicly for it on a very regular basis, so it was not as if he couldn't be widely and very easily identified. In addition to the fears about impending war, there was renewed concern about the unemployment situation, although in March the organisation's two regular papers presented a somewhat contradictory picture: "207,000 more workless; Unemployment Register tops two million mark; worst figures for three years" [**79**], although this referred to "the enormous increase in workless which occurred between December 12 and January 17", which probably reflected the difficulty of trying to be current for ***The Blackshirt***, which was now monthly, whereas ***Action*** could present a more accurate picture, as it was still published weekly: "The large fall in unemployment will come as a welcome relief from the menace of two million workless last month … Unfortunately, there are a number of indications that the present spring recovery is being forced by the false stimulation of inflation, which is bound to prove fatal in the long run." [**80**]

However, peace, and its preservation, were still the overriding concern of British Union in the spring of 1939. Although Mosley and all his active speakers, including Wilfred, albeit sporadically by now, were spreading the message at public meetings far & wide, it had become increasingly difficult to book halls of any significant size, for a variety of reasons, but Mosley was keen to really ram the message home at a huge public rally, of the type it had been Wilfred's responsibility to organise in the early days of British Union. The previous November, Hector McKechnie, who was now in charge of national meetings, had spoken personally to the general manager of Earl's Court, which was owned by British Sports Arenas Limited; "apparently it may not be used for a meeting in support of a system to bring peace and prosperity to British people", but "[t]he hall has been let to the Left Book Club for a meeting in support of war with Germany and for a meeting by Harry Pollitt declaring solidarity with Russia." In his letter to the manager, Francis-Hawkins concluded "that you have no intention of letting the Empress Hall for a meeting to be addressed by Sir Oswald Mosley—in other words you propose to discriminate against British Union, the Movement of which he is leader." [**81**] By the beginning of June, ***Action*** was able to roar triumphantly on its front page "THE BAN BROKEN!", although why it was possible for British Union to book the Earls Court Exhibition Hall ["the World's Largest Hall"] when previously, "the hidden powers, which have been organising the ban" had prevented a booking of the Empress Hall at the same venue, was not explained [**82**]; presumably, British Union made sure the booking was confirmed before making this announcement!

It is altogether possible that Wilfred's unsettled state of mind in the spring of 1939 was not only the result of his realisation that electoral success for British Union was a virtual impossibility, even though a request for contributions to "the Director General's Appeal Fund", on the basis that it needed "to raise every possible penny for the forthcoming Election" [**83**], certainly gave the impression that there was no doubt that British Union would be contesting it; it was not Wilfred's way to be defeatist, but there had just been another round of necessary redundancies at national headquarters, so he was one of the "[t]hirty-six people [who] remain in the whole-time employ of British Union, which is now an adequate staff", but there was also great emphasis placed on "such a large number of devoted volunteers always ready to put their spare time at the disposal of the Movement" [**84**] so, in addition to the distinct feeling of disenchantment that had been germinating in Wilfred's mind since the Italian funding question [**Appendix D**], the writing was very much on the wall. A suggestion was made, very much *post facto*, that one of the reasons for Wilfred leaving was that he had been careless with his timekeeping [**85**] but there is no proof of this, and it would have been uncharacteristic.

Exactly when Wilfred made the irrevocable decision to leave British Union is unknown, and it certainly looks like he was continuing to write articles for ***Action*** until the middle of May [**86**]; in his own words in 1940, he tells the Appeals Committee that he 'left' the Movement, by the simple device of ceasing to pay his subscriptions, "and … just dropped out" at the beginning of July: "It was actually July when I left. I should have left a month earlier, but I was asked if I would stay on an additional month to help with the meeting at Earls Court." [**Appendix D**] This is confirmed by a Special Branch report [**87**], which also mentions the NHQ economies and the possible reasons therefor [**88**], as well as going into some detail about Earls Court. The report purports to throw some light on how the booking of the hall was secured, but in a way which betrays inside knowledge [although hardly surprising, in the circumstances], by mentioning a person whose contribution was not mentioned! Bryan Donovan was, according to Special Branch, the man in charge of the arrangements [although that is contradicted by an article in ***Action*** **89**], with a man who had been a colleague and friend of Wilfred for a number of years, Hector McKechnie "as assistant on the commercial side" [**90**], so no doubt he will not have been averse to receiving helpful advice from Wilfred in the run-up to the event.

It is conceivable that Wilfred might have acquired some intelligence, in advance of the aforementioned Special Branch report, and it is unknown how reliable this information can have been, that executive officers would be arrested in the event of war, although thinking that making a voluntary decision to leave the Movement when war was so obviously close would offer any sort of protection does seem rather naïve in retrospect, but it might also have been a deciding factor behind Wilfred's move. The report mentions a "Senior Officials' Week End School held at Manchester on 3rd/4th June" where this likelihood was laid out; although the School was "attended by 36 persons", other than Donovan the report does not detail attendees, so it is a matter for speculation whether Wilfred will have attended: although he was effectively 'serving his notice', he had not tendered it officially, and was still in receipt of his salary, so it might have been incumbent upon him to be there [**91**]. From the records of the now-defunct London & Provincial Anti-Vivisection Society [held by the NAVS] it appears that the possibility of his joining that organisation, very likely supported by its Secretary, who was known to Wilfred in his current employment, was being considered 'officially' early in July 1939 [**92**], presumably following earlier informal discussions. It seems that there was no ceremony in his leaving British Union: at a given point, apparently the last working day of June, he just stopped going to work at headquarters. Mosley did make an unsuccessful attempt to lure him back, but this will be explored in the next chapter; for Wilfred the crucial thing was that he had paid employment to go to, so his reliance upon Mosley for a source of income to support himself and his family was at an end, and he was effectively a Fascist and/or National Socialist no longer: how this affected him on a personal level is unknown, because he does not appear to have written specifically about politics ever again.

NOTES

1 ***The Fascists in Britain, by Colin Cross***

2 ***Action, no. 101, January 20th, 1938, page 5:***

"**Mosley At Bradford On Sunday**

During the coming week British Union speakers will begin on the first part of a strenuous spring campaign which has been prepared to inform the people of Britain of the dangers which confront them with the coming of the depression which will follow the present slump. The political forces of both Right and Left are doing their utmost either to disguise the slump or to bring it into a false perspective. It is left to the British Union to lay before the people of Britain the true state of affairs.

...

Other National Meetings of the British Union will be held as under:

...

Jan. 21 W. Risdon at the Co-Operative Hall, King's Lynn"

3 ***Ibid., page 2***

4 ***The Blackshirt no. 248, March, 1938, page 1***

There was a *précis* under the heading of "Per Ardua Ad Astra" in an editorial by Geoffrey Dorman, in ***Action***:

"Sir Oswald Mosley's recent lecture on the philosophy of the Modern Movement was a revelation to many of the depth of thought that underlies his oratorical brilliance and propaganda ability. Analysing the philosophical trends of the last century, and condemning the paralysing influence of materialism since the war, he laid the foundations of the Modern Movement in a revolt against the theories of pre-determination and a return to faith in the spirit of man.

Despite this vigour of outlook he gave full credit to Spengler for his monumental work as completely exploding the easy creed of progress held by the materialists, but denied his pessimistic conclusion that all civilisations are doomed. Certainly automatic 'progress' can only be another name for decadence and decline, but Mosley maintained that modern man, armed with the powers of science, can yet triumph over decadent materialism, and by a great effort of will escape his impending doom. It is to this hard upward path that Mosley calls the youth of Britain."

Action, no. 102, January 29th, 1938, page 8

5 ***The Blackshirt, no. 247, January 29th, 1938, page 7:***

"**MARXISM AND NATIONAL SOCIALISM**

By W. RISDON

(A precis of the lecture delivered to the B.U. Headquarters Study Group, Tues., Jan. 25)

Marxism in recent years has been translated in terms of the Russian experiment with which the world is but just becoming familiar. It is essentially a creed of class hatred, hence it is destructive. It is, moreover, essentially materialist, hence its hatred of all spiritual values, and especially the spiritual values of Christian religion.

One may reasonably ask why a creed of class hatred and materialism sponsored by a Jew should have made such an impression on the Western mind, as is evidenced by the growth of Marxist Communism in the post-war period. To answer that question it will be necessary to consider the nature of the Capitalist system which obtains in Europe and which provided the soil in which Communism has flourished.

Capitalism, right from its earliest days, has thrown up many glaring instances of abject poverty at one end of the social scale co-existent with glaring instances of wealth and luxury at the other extreme of the social scale. It was as a result of observation of these dizzy extremes that there emerged, in those early days of Capitalism over a century ago, the embryo Socialism which first concerned itself with an agitation against social injustice and a propaganda aiming at a more equitable adjustment of society calculated to give better conditions to the bitterly oppressed workers of that day.

This theory of Socialism passed through many vicissitudes in its development and was variously interpreted by people like Robert Owen, Kingsley, and other idealists on the one hand and by Labriola, Marx, Engels and other materialists in the alternative school.

Capitalism, as the established system, provided the thesis for the gamut of disputation which raged. Capitalism contained these social inequalities to which I have referred, hence it is not greatly to be wondered at that the chief motif in the antithesis which was developed was class hatred or, to put it more mildly, class antagonism. This was the factor which brought Marxism to the fore and kept it there for a very long time.

Thesis and antithesis then took the field in opposition one to the other, and that position was maintained from then on to 1917 when the revolution in Russia gave the opportunity for Communism to triumph, and, in passing, it is worthy of note that even up to that date it remained a fight between thesis and antithesis, no synthesis having yet clearly emerged. It should also be remembered, however, that Russia was a Feudal State rather than a Capitalist State, hence the conditions obtaining were more akin to those of the period of the French Revolution than to those of modern Capitalist States.

The first instance of rapid decline of a Capitalist State was that of Italy. Here the antithesis was applied but failed to establish itself and now, for the first time, there is a fairly clear emergence of the synthesis which successfully established itself in the form of Fascism when the antithesis in the form of Communism had failed.

The next Capitalist State to enter into a revolutionary period was Germany, which was even more typically representative of Capitalism than Italy. Here, moreover, was the source-country of Marxism. Communism was better organised as a political force in Germany than in any other Capitalist State in the world and yet here, once again, we get the synthesis, the comparatively infant National Socialism emerging triumphant from the acid test and the antithesis totally inadequate to meet the new situation.

Meantime, similar movements representative of the now clarified synthesis have sprung up in almost all the European states. In Britain, the British Union, in Spain National Syndicalism, in France several separate movements with similar tendencies, in Denmark, Holland, Belgium, even in

Russia, belatedly appearing is this new creed which represents the modern synthesis drawn from the conflicting thesis of Capitalism and antithesis of Communism. It emerges in different countries under different titles, thus giving point and emphasis to one of its salient features – Nationalism. Whatever the title, however, the fundamental characteristics by which it may be identified are evident. They are (1) Nationalism as distinct from the internationalism of the Communist-Jew-concept. (2) Class collaboration as distinct from the Communist-Marxist class antagonism. (3) Recognition of private property rights as distinct from the Communist denial of property rights.

It should be noted, however, in passing, that recognition of this right is conditioned by the application of responsibility in the exercise of the right.

The whole concept of the synthesis is that of the 'Corporate State', which views society as organic – each organ serving the wider interests of the whole body and deriving its health of condition from the health of the whole body which it serves and of which it is a part, one and indivisible.

This brief outline given in its present form may tend to support the theory that the new creed is an importation into Britain, copied from Italy and Germany. If that were so it would not necessarily be anything against the creed, but our opponents are not entitled to even that small grain of argumentative solace, for this creed is more essentially British and owes more to British thought than to that of any other nation, as I will show in a further article on the subject.

It is fitting to close the present article with an acknowledgement that if 'Socialism' be viewed as the attainment of the original objective of social equity, by eradicating the social injustices inherent in uncontrolled capitalism, it will be attained far more rapidly and infinitely more smoothly by the new creed than by any other conceivable means. If a rough epigram be permissible, we might claim that the modern movement seeks 'Nationalism without nationalisation and Socialism (in the above-quoted sense) without socialisation'."

6 ***The Blackshirt, no. 245, January 15th, 1938, page 4:***

"Communism in Theory & Practice

By W. RISDON

An epigrammatic politician once said 'That man who at the age of 21 is not a Socialist has something wrong with his heart; the same man who at the age of 40 remain a Socialist has something wrong with his head.' The above theory may give some degree of explanation to the fact that the one Socialist State which the world has ever known – (the U.S.S.R.) – is doing such extraordinary things at the present time.

Assuming the revolution to have been representative of the 21-year-olds of 1917 and that they – as the authors of the revolution – assumed control of the machinery of the new state, they would now, in the year 1938 be somewhat beyond the 40-year-old mark. Can it be that this is the reason why all semblance of Socialism has been dropped and a soulless bloody repression has taken its place in this alleged 'Paradise of the Workers'? Who knows?

THE DISILLUSIONED

Whatever may be the reason the facts remain, and those facts make it abundantly clear that Russia is not a pleasant country in which to live at the present time.

There is an ever-growing literature of anti-Sovietism – written by ex-Communists whose bona-fides are well established – which brings home with an ever increasing clarity the fact that Communism as it has been applied in Russia is an abject failure when judged by the standards even of Capitalist civilisation.

Eugene Lyons (U.S.A.), Andre Gide (France), John Brown (Britain), Andrew Smith (U.S.A.), Sir Walter Citrine (Britain), Kleber Legay (France), these are just a selection of names – all Socialist and Communist – of those who have recently written scathing indictments of the modern Russia.

They appear to have followed the promptings of their hearts in supporting Socialism in the first instance – the type of Socialism envisaged by Edward Bellamy in 'Looking Backward' or William Morris in 'News from Nowhere'. They have found the applied process to be so grotesque a caricature that it has revolted them and their reason has rejected that which is so opposite to what their emotions desired.

THE ACID TEST

The test of practice has been applied to the theories of Communism and the results have been surprising. That which was thought to be pure gold has emerged from the acid test as the sheerest dross. Under the working of the system 'class domination' has been replaced by the emergence of a new and less efficient 'class domination'. Even the 'liquidation' of the previously dominant class has proven an unmitigated evil, for the new dominant class – 'the bureaucracy' – is totally unfitted for the exercise of the power it has assumed.

'Imperialism' under the cloak of 'Internationalism' is a greater and an infinitely more real menace under the Soviets than was ever the case under the Tsars. The technique has been changed admittedly, but the evils are even greater. World domination is the end in view and the method is intrigue instead of conquest. Spies, propagandists and 'agents provocateurs' take the place of armies. Civil wars, fomented by these subsidised forces of evil, take the place of wars of aggression from without. The effect on the victims is, however, no whit more pleasant than the effects of the old wars of Imperialism.

Meanwhile, what is the fate of those who show any evidence of disapproval of the new orientation of 'Communist' development? Let us go further and enquire as to the fate of those who do not express disapproval but who, because they are presumed to know the difference between this shoddy presentation and the real thing might be assumed capable of disapproval.

'Liquidation' is the fate of all such. They are 'framed', arrested by the O.G.P.U., subjected to the travesty of a 'trial' ('confessions' are extorted from them by God alone knows what means), and butchered as 'enemies of the State'.

Great Heavens! What a consummation is this to be witnessed by the victims of a misplaced idealism. Is it to be wondered at that those who are able to escape the meshes of the Soviet net should pour out their souls in denunciation of so foul a system?

Let those of our easily fooled democratic politicians who have been bluffed into support of such a system beware. The British people in their wrath would destroy utterly any who might betray them into such bestial conditions.

Let the authors of Russian Sovietism beware. The people of Britain and the Empire will extract a terrible vengeance on any who would seek by intrigue and deception to add British possessions to a Soviet World Empire.

British Union will form an impregnable bulwark against any attempt to impose Soviet slave-conditions on a people who still adhere to the ancient tradition that 'Britons never shall be slaves'."

7 INDUSTRY: ***Action, no. 103, February 5th, 1938, page 13***

8 ***The Blackshirt no. 248, March, 1938, page 1***

9 ***Ibid.:***

"Every word was written in manuscript and the whole polishing up process was completed in a matter of days. It must be something of a record for a book of this nature, which bids fair to become a classic of the English language, to be produced in so short a time."

10 ***Action, no. 108, March 12th, 1938, page 9:***

"“TO-MORROW WE LIVE”

MOSLEY'S NEW BOOK REVIEWED

By A. K. CHESTERTON

"To-morrow We Live"* is a re-statement by Oswald Mosley of the National Socialist faith which he has proclaimed for the last five years and towards which he has advanced during the twenty years of his high political crusade.

It is a terrific document: in a sense, indeed, it is too terrific—it overwhelms the reader with its sheer fecundity of argument, which is another way of saying that it is the work of a great orator.

Here, as on the platform from which he sways great multitudes, Mosley's tireless intellect ranges over the widest possible field of community life collecting instances and arguments in support of his theme, while his dynamic eloquence feeds upon this wealth of material and gains from it such strength that the cumulative effect is tremendous and irresistible.

The orator's technique, however, cannot with complete success be employed, in the writing of a book, and in "To-morrow We Live" the author packs into 34,000 words such profusion of ideas and such profundity of thought, and at the same time carries them forward with such easy sweep of style, that the reader is apt to be convinced by the totality of effect instead of being persuaded step by step by the author's remorseless logic.

Because Mosley's logic is indeed irresistible: it has in it that mystic quality which transforms logic into truth—something which his opponents are impotent to answer, except by misrepresentation and abuse.

Henceforward, at all events, it will be an impertinence of the worst kind for any opponent to dare to attack Mosley and British Union without first possessing the data upon which to base his criticism; threepence is no ruinous sum to pay for letting light into the pitch darkness of the average anti-Fascist mind.

"To-morrow We Live" is more than a political document: it is the passport to a new concept of life, offering majestic opportunities to man, summed up in Mosley's unforgettable words:—

So man emerges for the final struggle of the ages the supreme and conscious master of his fate to surmount the destiny that has reduced former civilisations to oblivion even from the annals of time. He advances to the final ordeal armed with weapons of the modern mind that were lacking to the hand of any previous generation in the crisis of a civilisation.

The wonders of our new science afford him not only the means with which to conquer material environment in the ability to wrest wealth in abundance from nature, but, in the final unfolding of the scientific revelation, probably also the means of controlling even the physical rhythm of a civilisation. Man for the first time in human history carries to the crisis of his fate weapons with which he may conquer even destiny. But one compelling necessity remains that he shall win within himself the will to struggle and to conquer. Our creed and our Movement instil in man the heroic attitude to life because he needs heroism. Our new Britons require the virility of the Elizabethan combined with the intellect and method of the modern technician. The age demands the radiance of the dawn to infuse the wonder of maturity. We need heroism not just for war, which is a mere stupidity, but heroism to sustain us through man's sublime attempt to wrestle with nature and to strive with destiny. To this high purpose we summon from the void of present circumstance the vast spirit of man's heroism. For this shall be the epic generation whose struggle and whose sacrifice shall decide whether man again shall know the dust or whether man at last shall grasp the stars.

We know the answer for we have felt this thing within us. In divine purpose the spirit of man rises above and beyond the welter of chaos and materialism to the conquest of a civilisation that shall be the sum and the glory of the travail of the ages. In that high fate to-morrow we live.

**Published by Abbey Supplies, Ltd., Sanctuary Buildings, Great Smith St., S.W.1, at 3d.*"

Some longer extracts had been published in previous editions of ***Action***, but they didn't appear to be saying anything revolutionary [in the sense of being new and radical], although Mosley's inconsistency towards hereditary wealth and position were made apparent [given that he supported unswervingly a monarch who acquired the position by hereditary succession]:

"Above all they have created the fatal distinctions of social class which British Union is determined to remove for ever. Their class values are based on money value and on nothing else. The accident of birth and the mere fact of being their "father's son" is held by these miserable specimens of modern degeneracy to elevate them without effort of their own above their fellow men. Not only are they given opportunity by their forebears' exertion, but many of them neglect that opportunity for any other end than the idle pursuit of pleasure while they cumber the directorates of their hereditary businesses which underpaid technicians conduct. Here we see the apotheosis of of the parasite deriving his snobbery from his father's efforts and marking the value of the snob by the capacity to squander in face of the starving. The snob and the parasite shall go, with him shall go his values in the classless State which accords 'opportunity to all but privilege to none.'"

Action, no. 105, February 19th, 1938, page 20

"In practice, however, most ownership of urban land will pass to the State as that category of landlord is a great deal less likely than the leader of the countryside to justify his hereditary wealth by public service. It is unfair to discriminate between the land and any other form of hereditary wealth, but he who lives on the land without service to the nation will pass with other parasites."

Action, no. 106, February 26th, 1938, page 20

11 ***The Blackshirt, no. 246, January 22nd, 1938, page 1***

12 ***The Blackshirt no. 248, March, 1938, page 5:***

"**PROPAGANDA IN PRINT**

By W. RISDON

Printed propaganda, introduced into the houses of the people, has much to be said in its favour if the job is rightly carried out. To put one piece of printed matter into a house and leave it at that is, however, a waste of both time and money. Repetition is the factor which counts. Moreover, such repetition should be at such intervals as to make the effect cumulative rather than sporadic.

Let us consider our present propaganda drive in relation to the above statement. I have no hesitation in saying that the distribution of Ten Point leaflets, which is now being arranged, will be, to a very great extent, waste effort if it be viewed as an end in itself. To give real results it should be viewed as the initiation rather than the culmination of a printed-propaganda drive.

A glance at the heading of the ***Ten Points*** reveals that their appeal is general rather than specific, the intention being to cater for all interests in our briefly worded leaflet. When this leaflet has been received and read the next requirement is to relate the general interest which it was calculated to arouse, to the specific interests of the readers. The general appeal having been made the specialised appeal should follow. This specialised appeal requires a good deal of intelligent forethought if it is to be 'put over' successfully.

STRATIFICATION OF PROPAGANDA

For the want of a better term let us call this specialised appeal the 'stratification of propaganda' for that title conveys the correct impression. In human society there are sundry strata of interests which must be catered for. Such stratification may be found in the first instance in the predominant interests as they differ from each other in different localities. Let us call them 'predominant local interests'.

As classic instances of these 'predominant local interests' let us quote coal and cotton. In the Welsh valleys coal is of paramount importance. The industrial interests of those valleys is coal-mining. The bulk of the people living in them draw their wages and salaries (their purchasing power) from the mines. The traders and shop-keepers sell to those whose purchasing power is derived from coal. The local authorities levy their rates on wages and salaries drawn from coal. If the mining industry suffers a reverse the shop-keepers feel it, the social services feel it, the railway services, builders and contractors, all the trades and occupations who have been accustomed to cater for the one predominant interest feel it, in addition to the miners themselves.

Coal is indeed the very life-blood of the communities of the valleys. Just as this is true of coal in relation to the Welsh valleys and other great coal-producing areas, so it is also and equally true of cotton in relation to the cotton-belt of Lancashire. One could go on selecting such predominating interests as they apply geographically, Iron and steel, shipbuilding, agriculture, wool, shipping, and many other like cases could be quoted.

SELECTION OF PROPAGANDA MATTER

In the chain of follow-up propaganda the first thing to do is to relate general policy to the requirements of these 'predominant local interests' of cotton in Lancashire; Wool in Yorkshire, West Riding; Coal in South Wales, parts of Durham, Yorkshire, Lancs, Derbyshire, etc.; Agriculture in East Anglia, etc., etc. There is a specific policy, sponsored by the British Union, applicable to all these 'predominant local interests', and that policy should 'go over' on a scale just as wide-reaching as the original distribution of ***Ten Point*** leaflets.

The next selection of propaganda matter, however, calls for more detailed 'stratification'. It is concerned with the differentiation between the various interests contained within the main 'predominant local interests'.

Here we find special shopkeepers' interests, employees' interests, employers' interests, trade union interests, co-operative interests, ex-service men's interests, educational interests, and a host of other interests of a more or less technical aspect which we will call 'detailed interests'.

CATERING FOR "DETAILED INTERESTS"

A good deal of close thought and planning will be required in dealing with these 'detailed interests'. The simplest interest will be the individually owned shopkeeper [sic]. These shopkeepers can be located at their shops and supplied with suitable literature, either free leaflets such as ***Big Fish and Little Fish*** or sold pamphlets such as ***'Gainst Trust and Monopoly***.

Trade unionists can be located either 'on the job' or in their homes. They can be supplied with free leaflets such as ***British Union stands for Trade Unionism*** or purchase pamphlets such as ***Strike Action or Power Action***. This process may be carried a stage further by preparing and issuing special leaflets and literature dealing with the problems of particular trade unions such as railwaymen, transport workers, dockers, miners, etc.

All other detailed interests in any given locality can be specially catered for along these lines, but the successful accomplishment of the job presupposes a high efficiency organisation of the district. Propaganda must be well organised if it is to be efficient.

The best form of organisation for such propaganda efforts is, undoubtedly, the 'street block' system, which is now being generally developed for electoral purposes. Here your street workers will be able to classify the 'detailed interests' of their own 'street blocks' and will also be able to distribute the appropriate literature to the right houses.

COMPOSITION OF THE CHAIN

Let us now pass in brief review the chain of propaganda which we have in mind. First, we have the links of general appeal, such as ***Ten Point*** leaflets (there are several other general appeal leaflets besides the 'ten pointer'). These can go to every house in the district.

Next we have the links of 'Predominant Local Interests' such as ***Lancashire Betrayed***, etc. In the case quoted these also would go to every house in the district, on the assumption that even those not directly engaged in the predominant industry are yet dependent on its prosperity for the maintenance of their particular trade. In some cases, however, it might be found that some sections of the populace are entirely divorced from the 'predominant local interest' and in such cases discretion would be used.

Then we have the 'detailed interests' with specially selected literature for groups within the populace, the literature in each case made appropriate to the views and requirements of the particular group. This is the really difficult section, but, on the other hand, it is the section that will yield the best results.

In many cases districts will find it possible to produce their own leaflets for local distribution covering such subjects as will be more familiar to local than to national writers.

There is ample scope for the exercise of local literary gifts in this connection, but the principle should always be borne in mind that brevity is the essence of a good leaflet.

Short paragraphs, well spaced and carrying a verbal punch in every sentence are the ingredients of a good leaflet: Sloganised propaganda in fact.

In some cases it may be thought worth while to use the method of 'trick' propaganda aimed at inducing opponents to read it not knowing its source of origin. A typical instance of this came my way recently in the form of a neatly printed folder inviting the reader to *Visit the U.S.S.R.* On opening it to read the inside one found a series of short paragraphs condemnatory of Sovietism, each paragraph illustrated by a photographic reproduction of suffering under the soviets. Then right at the end came the imprint of the association responsible for its production, 'The Anti-Communist International'.

This form of propaganda should not be overdone, but, used occasionally in very exceptional cases, it is capable of giving excellent results."

13 ***Action, no. 103, February 5th, 1938, page 17:***

"**ON THE BRITISH UNION FRONT**

Big
Push In
Lancashire

February 7 to 20 is the period arranged for the Cotton Campaign to bring the message of British Union into the homes of Lancashire people, and expose the menace of International Finance to their great industry.

Including 48 meetings by National Speakers, there will be a total of 250 meetings held during the fortnight of the campaign. The Leader will himself speak at Platting next Sunday, and at Burnley on Sunday, February 13.

The campaign includes the distribution of copies of the new Cotton Policy pamphlet, and also special hand-bills. For the purpose of the campaign Lancashire has been divided into three parts, but the campaign only affects the actual cotton districts."

14 ***Ibid:***

"No help (apart from speakers) is being given in any way from National Headquarters, and success depends entirely upon the efficiency and effort of local organisation in Lancashire."

15 ***The Blackshirt, no. 248, March 1938, page 1***

16 ***Action, no. 106, February 26th, 1938, page 17:***

"**C.U.F.A. MEETING**

A successful meeting of the British Union was held at Cambridge on February 17.

Mr. Risdon, in a very clear and interesting speech, outlined the failure of successive governments to solve the nation's difficulties since the war, or to carry out the things they promised to do at elections.

He then gave the constructive policy of the British Union for solving these problems. That a deep impression was made was evident by the number of questions asked at the end."

17 ***The Blackshirt, no. 248, March 1938, page 6:***

"**LEGIONS ON THE MARCH**

RICHMOND An interested audience assembled at the Vernon Hall, East Sheen, to listen to the policy of the British Union explained by Risdon. Several contacts were made by the Richmond District. A sub-District has now been formed in this part of the Richmond Constituency and an active Unit is working there. A good collection was taken for District Funds, and many literature sales were made, proving beyond doubt that there are a good many people in Sheen who are already keen on British Union."

18 *The Blackshirt, no. 249, April 1938, page 6:*

"LEGIONS ON THE MARCH

LEEDS W. Risdon spoke at Leeds Business Men's Group lunch and dealt with the topical subject of British Union foreign policy in relation to the Eden exit. He outlined the British Union's pledge for peace and the Leader's assurance that no British soldier shall ever be called upon to fight for an alien financial interest. Members invited him to come again when the Group had expanded. Good meeting held at South End Mount, March 7."

19 This is from an article in the Friends of Oswald Mosley ***Comrade*** archive:

"1938-1940 Aberdeen Takes The Lead

March saw Wilfred Risdon, Chief Agent for British Union hold a very successful meeting in the Music Hall, Aberdeen. To a packed audience he described in great detail the Movement's policies and the far reaching strategy for putting Britain 'back on its feet' (see Mosley's ***Ten Points***). Outside the 'usual suspects' were lying in wait to attack any lone Blackshirts or small party of supporters that they could lay their hands on. As the senior officers, 'Bill' Risdon, Dick Plathen, Chambers-Hunter and Mrs. Botha left the hall and walked towards their waiting car, the mob charged forward throwing a series of kicks and punches. As usual the communists paid particular attention to Chambers-Hunter and Mrs. Botha. For weeks previous they had been subjected to constant abuse and physical violence for their high profile support for British Union. Mrs. Botha had had her arm slashed with a bottle while Chambers-Hunter had received a server [sic] gash to head from a brick thrown at him when he addressed a meeting at Torry."

Bravehearts in Blackshirts by John Anderson; Comrade, May 2005, p11; http://www.oswaldmosley.com/comrade/index.html?pageNumber=455

20 *The Blackshirt, no. 249, April 1938, page 7:*

"**ABERDEEN** Reds in this district are resorting to hooligan violence in an effort to stop the progress of National Socialism. Following a meeting in the Music Hall they attempted to mob several members, including W. Risdon, the Chief Agent, N/I Plathen, D/I Chambers Hunter and W/D/L Mrs. Botha. The culminating incident of this long series of attacks, however, took place last Sunday, when a crowd of Reds attacked Mrs. Botha and Mr. Chambers Hunter while they were on "Action" sales in Union Street. The situation became so serious that traffic was blocked and the police were obliged to stop all paper sales in the street. This led to more disorderly scenes, and necessitated our members being escorted to Diamond Street police station. During this time the police station was besieged by the mob, which was ultimately dispersed only with great difficulty."

21 *The Blackshirt, no. 244, January 8th, 1938, page 1:*

"If this information be correct, it can mean only one thing; open war declared by the small but enormously powerful gangs of parasites, who corner commodities without producing them, against scores of millions of honest workers by hand and brain in order to deprive them of the raw materials without which they cannot live."

22 *Ibid.:*

"Evidence of this conspiracy, indeed, may be found in the editorial columns of a jewish-controlled New York daily paper, which a day or two before Christmas urged precisely the same thing—the "peaceful" withholding of raw materials vital to the existence of the authoritarian states. That word "peaceful" was an insult to Gentile intelligence, since great nations reawakened into manhood are not at any price prepared to suffer starvation and ruin at the hands of jewish moneylenders who wish to exert a dictatorship over the world.

Clearly enough, therefore, jewish finance intends its economic war to be expanded into actual war between the nations—a war in which men of finer clay must die to keep the world fit for financial anarchists and sharks to inhabit."

23 *Blackshirt British Union News, no. 249, April 1938, page 4:*

"ORGANISING FOR ELECTIONS

By W. RISDON

Most districts are now manifesting a keen interest in the 'Street-block' system of organisation. This is all to the good, for the system is, without doubt, a winning system.

In view of the fact that National Headquarters are already providing lectures for all districts on this subject I do not propose to deal with it in detail here, but I do propose to deal with the query which has been raised in some quarters as to the reconciliation of this method of organising with the procedure for contesting Parliamentary elections.

Members who are undergoing training as Agents are wondering what differences will be made by this method to what they are learning in the Correspondence Course. The answer is – very little, and that little only in method. Most electoral conditions are established by law, and, of course, our methods must comply with that law.

LEGAL REQUIREMENTS

The appointment of an Agent remains a necessary requirement of the law. His power to appoint sub-agents is based on legal provisions (but applies only in the case of Parliamentary counties, not Boroughs). The same applies in the case of appointments of clerks, messengers and polling or personation agents. In fact all that is contained in part 1 of the course remains entirely unaffected. So also does Part 2 of the course, which deals with pre-election activities. All the activities indicated can be well carried out by the street block workers. Part 3 deals with the duties of an Agent in the early stages of the election and remains unaffected.

In reading Part 4 it will be necessary only to remember that 'canvassers' are members of the ward teams who are responsible for 'street-blocks', and that for the period of the election their work may be directed by the ward leader working from ward committee rooms if such have been provided. The ward leader in that case becomes the committee room clerk, and is appointed to that office by the Agent.

The detailed instructions to committee room clerks will still be applicable with 'a few minor alterations' as originally indicated.

SLIGHT ADJUSTMENT

On page 11 of Part 5 a slight adjustment becomes necessary in view of the fact that the members responsible for given blocks of streets will already know what district they are working, hence it will not be necessary to allot districts, but instead it will be necessary for such workers to inform the Agent of the amount of progress already registered and to apply for additional assistance in any case where it may be necessary.

In Part 6 there is more scope for adaptation. For instance, much of the work attributed to the clerical department will be done by members in charge of street blocks. Writing up polling cards and envelopes for their own blocks, filling and delivering, and also the obtaining of signatures for nomination papers may to a great extent be done in the wards by street block workers working in and on their own sections, but if this is done some satisfactory method of supervision will have to be operated, preferably through the ward leader. The remainder of Part 6 is not affected.

In Part 7 checkers at polling stations and messengers to collect from checkers may be dispensed with **if the street block system is working smoothly enough for each elector to be individually attended by the person in charge of the block.**

Cards 'A' and 'B' and form 'C' will also be used through the 'Street Block' machinery.

HOURLY RETURNS

Hourly returns of the progress recorded in polling promised votes will be passed from 'Street Blocks' to ward leaders, who in turn will make hourly aggregate returns to the Agent.

No other part of the course of instruction is materially affected, hence a generalisation may be made to the effect that embryo electoral machinery will be permanently in existence in the district, and that machinery will be placed under control of the Agent during the period of the election for the purposes of the election.

The Agent will be able to operate the machinery forthwith instead of wasting time in the improvisation of the necessary machinery before doing the thousand and one things that fall to him to do during an election. That is, of course, assuming that the 'street-block' system is already functioning.

In the case of County Divisions the term 'polling-district' should take the place of 'ward' in all except urban areas where wards exist."

24 *Action, no. 108, March 12th, 1938, page 4*

25 *Action, no. 113, April 16th, 1938, page 13:*

"METHODS OF A.E.U. LEADERS

GOVERNMENT BY MINORITIES

By W. RISDON

We have been told in days gone by that democracy means government by consent of the majority and that elections are the means whereby the majority express their desires in relation to government.

If the above statement be true the present government, elected by ballot, is the governing power by virtue of the vote of the people. In making that statement it must be borne in mind that all of the people are responsible for the government, elected by their votes, and that any attempt on the part of any organised minority to dictate policy to the elected government, is a negation of the principles of democracy.

The manifesto issued by the executive of the A.E.U. on April 8 cuts across the very principles of democracy to which the Trade Union movement of Britain is pledged. It declares that the cause of the legally-elected government of Spain is the cause of the British workers, and calls for voluntary work by its members in aid of Spain, and then proceeds to ask its members in their leisure time to turn out material for the use of the 'Red' Government of Spain in the civil war.

WHO IS TO GOVERN

The policy of the Government is 'non-intervention', but this minority calls for intervention, regardless of the fact that such intervention, if sanctioned by the Government would, almost certainly, bring about a general European conflagration which would result in the final extinction of modern civilisation.

Once again the leaders of the A.E.U. are making the mistake of utilising a given situation for political purposes to the ultimate detriment of their own industrial interests, are doing it in such fashion as to gain them the unqualified approval of those Communist interests which have sought so often in the past to destroy this great union.

The ***Daily Worker*** of April 6 gloated as follows:–

> 'The leaders of the amalgamated Engineering Union have spoken in plain terms to Sir Thomas Inskip.
>
> They have declared they have no confidence in the policy behind the Government's rearmament.
>
> They have demanded the right of Spain to arms, if arms are to be produced for the defence of democracy.
>
> They have refused any assurance of support or co-operation to this Government of friends of Fascism.
>
> That is the way to speak to this Government. It is for the engineering workers now to see that this stand is maintained, and that it is carried forward to a positive fight for their concrete demands.'

Remember that when the Communist Party talks about a 'positive fight' they mean literally what they say and would be glad to create in Britain the same conditions which they created in Spain and which led up to the present bloody business in that unhappy country.

GET THE FACTS RIGHT

If the A.E.U. think so much of the rights of a "legally elected government" it behoves them to remember, before it is too late, that ours, too, is a legally elected government, and if they defy their own government they at once destroy that part of their argument.

Mr. J. C. Little, the president of the A.E.U., was reported in the ***Manchester Guardian*** to have said: 'No speed-up of British or French re-armament is needed to guard against a danger that democratic Spain would become an ally of the dictators.'

Does Mr. Little really believe that? If the Red forces had triumphed in Spain nothing is more certain than that Red Spain would have become a puppet state of the U.S.S.R. under Stalin, the bloodiest dictatorship this world has ever conceived. It was part of the Soviet plan and was openly announced by them.

Mr. Jack Tanner, a member of the Executive Committee of the A.E.U., speaking in London on April 7, is reported in the ***Daily Herald*** as having said: '... Once the Spanish (Red) Government was allowed to buy arms the engineers could guarantee that British rearmament would not be allowed to suffer because more arms were required for Spain.'

POLITICAL PRESSURE

In that statement is to be found a classic instance of impertinent attempted political pressure. Interpreted, it means just this: 'You, the Government, are in a jam. You want material urgently for re-armament. We will not work to produce arms for our own country until we have provided arms for Red Spain. Therefore, if you intend to carry out your re-armament programme you must first repudiate the policy of non-intervention and give material aid to the Soviet forces in Spain before you can have any material for home use.'

That is the attitude which is being adopted by the political bosses at the head of the A.E.U.

Meanwhile, what of the rank and file?

I, for one, refuse to believe that this is a faithful reflection of the views of the men at the benches and in the workshops. It is true that in recent years there has been a terrific attempt by the 'Reds' in this country to subvert the rank and file in the engineering industry, but in spite of all the subtle propaganda to which they have been subjected, they are still British, and I am convinced that a direct appeal to them on this issue would prove satisfactory.

GO TO THE RANK AND FILE

If the Government go to the rank and file with a clear issue they can beat the 'political bosses'.

What is the issue? The issue is a speed-up in production in connection with re-armament.

With very lively memories of the results of a previous speed-up of this description during the World War the engineers are suspicious, and justifiably so. It is this justifiable suspicion which is being exploited by leaders of the left.

The only way to overcome these suspicions is to put all the cards on the table and guarantee continuity of employment to all concerned after the re-armament is completed. Men who have served many years acquiring skill in an industry do not want to introduce dilution into their ranks which might mean unemployment for themselves as soon as the job is over. Hence they should have advance guarantees that their jobs will be guaranteed to them by the Government.

Where over-time is to be worked it should be guaranteed the recognised trade-union rates."

26 *The Blackshirt, May 1938, page 5:*

"**A CENTURY OF STRUGGLE**

FROM TOLPUDDLE MARTYRS
TO BRITISH UNION

By W. Risdon

At the Dorchester Assizes on March 15 in the year 1834 six Dorset labourers were brought to trial – a trial which was destined to make history. They were: George Loveless, James Loveless, James Hammett, James Brine, Thomas Standfield and John Standfield, and to-day their names stand in the scroll of fame as the 'Tolpuddle Martyrs'. They received the savage sentence of seven years' penal transportation, and on May 25, 1834, they left Portsmouth on the 'William Metcalfe' for Botany Bay.

Let us briefly consider the 'crime' for which these men were sentenced, and let us consider, too, what manner of men were they.

First, the men in the case. The acknowledged leader of the six was George Loveless. He, like his five colleagues, was an agricultural labourer. He was also, incidentally, a Wesleyan Methodist local preacher, a man of considerable intelligence and no small literary ability. His memory has been kept fresh in his native village to the present day, and his name connotes to this generation the qualities of integrity, piety and absolute trustworthiness.

With the single exception of James Brine, all were associated intimately with the same Wesleyan Methodist chapel, three of them being local preachers. This brief sketch will suffice to introduce the characters, now for the details of the 'crime'.

FREEDOM AND BREAD

The early 1830s were marked by a general movement of the working classes for better wages and improved conditions. Robert Owen's 'Grand National Consolidated Trades Union' was establishing itself, and about the end of October, 1833, two delegates from that organisation visited Dorset and a 'friendly society' was formed among the labourers of Tolpuddle. In his account of the formation of this 'friendly society' Loveless writes: "Having sufficiently learned that it would be vain to seek redress of employers, magistrates or parsons," he consented to form a friendly society.

What prompted the bitter comment above-quoted? Let us draw from the pages of George Loveless's diary. First it must be stated that the labouring men of Tolpuddle had received from their masters a promise that they should receive the same scale of remuneration as was general in the district.

> Loveless affirms that that promise was not kept. He says, "Shortly after we learnt that in almost every place around us the masters were giving their men money, or money's worth to the amount of ten shillings per week. We expected to be entitled to so much, but no, nine shillings must be our portion. After some months we were reduced to eight shillings per week."
>
> This caused great dissatisfaction, and all the labouring men in the village, with the exception of two or three invalids, made application to a neighbouring magistrate, namely, William Morton Pitt, Esq., of Kingston House, and asked his advice. He told us that if the labourers would appoint two or three and come to the County Hall the following Saturday, he would apprise the chief magistrate, James Frampton, Esq., (whose name I shall not soon forget), and at the same time our employers should be sent for to settle the subject. I was nominated to appear, and when there, we were told that we must work for what our employers thought fit to give us, as there was no law to compel masters to give ANY FIXED MONEY to their servants. In vain we remonstrated that an agreement was made, and that the minister of the parish (Dr. Warren) was witness between the masters and the men: for this hireling parson – who at the time said of his own accord, "I am witness between you men and your masters, that if you will go quietly to your work, you shall receive for your labour as much as any men in the district: and if your masters should attempt to run from their agreement, I will undertake to see you

righted, so help me, God." So soon as reference was made to him, he denied having a knowledge of any such thing. From this time we were reduced to seven shillings per week, and shortly after our employers told us that they must lower us to six shillings a week.'

The union was duly launched and the farmers took alarm. They saw that such a movement, if it grew to any great extent, would seriously challenge their right to impose their will in the matter of wages, conditions of labour, etc., and eventually, on February 21, 1834, they induced the local magistrates to issue placards warning the labourers that anyone joining the union would be sentenced to seven years' transportation. We must realise that the labourers knew full well that this was no idle threat. They knew sufficient of their times to understand that as surely as the night follows the day so surely would their action involve them in the fulfilment of the threat. Despite this, they continued their fight and three days after the publication of the warning, George Loveless and his five colleagues were arrested and lodged in Dorchester Gaol.

CORRUPT COURT

On March 15 the Dorchester Assizes opened, and the six men were taken to the County Hall to stand their trial for having dared to assert the right of human beings to live. The trial throughout was a farce, a mere caricature of the administration of the law, and as for justice, it was never presumed that that would be accorded to these six men, who had opposed themselves to the claims and privileges of 'vested interests'. The most unfair and unjust means were openly resorted to in order to frame an indictment. The characters of the six men were investigated from infancy, inquiries were made of their employers to know whether they frequented public-houses, if they were not idlers, or, in fact, anything which might be in any way used against them at the trial. The Grand Jury appeared, as George Loveless said, 'to ransack heaven and earth to get some clue against us', but in vain. Even their employers, much as they were opposed to them, 'had common honesty enough to declare them good labouring servants, and to state that they never heard of any complaint against them'. When nothing whatever could be found against them Judge Williams, who must always be remembered as one of the most cruel, unjust, and infamous controverters of justice, ordered them to be tried for Mutiny and Conspiracy under an Act dating back to George III, for the suppression of mutiny amongst the marines and seamen at the Nore. The charge preferred was that of the administering of an oath by an unlawful society."

27 ***The Blackshirt, June 1938, page 2:***

"**From**

Tolpuddle to British Union

In the previous article W. Risdon described the early efforts of the Tolpuddle martyrs to bring Trade Unionism to this country. He continues in this issue with a description of their trial and sentence. The series will be concluded in July, when the writer will draw a comparison between the struggles of the Tolpuddle martyrs and that of the New Movement.

Before he was committed for trial George Loveless had been interviewed by his solicitor, who held out to him as an inducement a promise of instant release if he would but give evidence against the other labourers who were members of the Union. The reply to this base insinuation was typical of the integrity of the man concerned. 'What!' said he, 'Do you mean to say I am to betray my companions? No, I would rather undergo ANY punishment than do so base a thing.' Again, later, whilst in gaol awaiting trial they were visited by the Chaplain of the Prison who also tried hard to influence them in like manner. Loveless says of him that he – 'poured a volley of instruction into our ears, but as it was mixed in the cup of abuse, it did not exactly relish with me.' He then taunted the prisoners with being idle and discontented, and asked finally if they could point out anything more that might be done to increase the comfort of the labourer. Loveless took instant advantage of this question, to the great discomfiture of the Chaplain. 'Yes.' said he, 'I would suggest that the farmer and the squire instead of spending their money wastefully on fox hunting, should devote it to increasing the labourer's wage, and the gentlemen wearing clerical livery like yourself, might do with a little less salary, and that would also assist the rest.'

The address of the Judge, to the jury, in summing up the evidence is particularly worthy of note. After giving in round terms his opinion of those accused he continued that 'if such societies were allowed to exist it would ruin masters, cause stagnation in trade, destroy property and that IF THEY SHOULD NOT FIND THE ACCUSED GUILTY HE WAS QUITE CERTAIN THAT THEY WOULD FORFEIT THE OPINION OF THE GRAND JURY.'

Loveless in commenting upon this said, 'I thought to myself, there is no danger but we shall be found guilty, as we have a special jury for the purpose, selected from among those who are most unfriendly towards us; the Grand Jury, landowners; the Petty Jury, land-renters.' The Judge then asked them if they had anything to say. Loveless forwarded to him the following defence in writing:

MY LORD, IF WE HAVE VIOLATED ANY LAW, IT WAS NOT DONE INTENTIONALLY. WE HAVE INJURED NO MAN'S REPUTATION, CHARACTER, PERSON OR PROPERTY; WE WERE UNITING TOGETHER TO PRESERVE OURSELVES, OUR WIVES AND OUR CHILDREN FROM UTTER DEGRADATION AND STARVATION. WE CHALLENGE ANY MAN, OR NUMBER OF MEN, TO PROVE THAT WE HAVE ACTED, OR INTENDED TO ACT, DIFFERENT FROM THE ABOVE STATEMENT.

The judge asked Loveless if he wished that to be read in court, and he replied 'Yes.' The statement, says Loveless, was then mumbled over to a part of the jury in such an inaudible manner that, although I knew what was there I could not comprehend it.'

At this point one of the counsel prevented sentence being passed by declaring that 'not one charge brought against any of the prisoners at the bar was proved, and that if they were found guilty a great number of persons would be dissatisfied. He 'should,' he added, 'for one.'

It was two days later that they again stood at the bar for sentence to be passed. The judge then told them that, 'Not for anything they had done, or, as he could prove, they intended to do, but for an example to others he considered it his duty to pass sentence of seven years' penal transportation across His Majesty's high seas upon each and every one of them.' As soon as sentence was passed Loveless obtained a pencil and a scrap of paper, on which he jotted down as they occurred to his mind the following lines:

God is our Guide! From field, from wave,
From plough, from anvil, and from loom,
We come our country's right to save,
And speak a tyrant faction's doom;
We raise the watchword – Liberty.
We will, we will, we will be free!
God is our guide! No swords we draw.
We kindle not war's battle fires,
By reason, union, justice, law,
We claim the birthright of our sires:
We raise the watchword – Liberty,
We will, we will, we will be free!

These lines he carried, screwed up in his hand whilst being marched back to prison. The six were marched back locked one to the other by the wrists, and on the way Loveless managed to toss the lines to some people whom they passed. The guard however got hold of them and they were carried back to the judge. The writing and attempted passing on of these lines was viewed by some as being a crime of no less magnitude than 'High Treason'. To those who understand the circumstances under which they were written those few lines, hurriedly scribbled at such a time, and in response to the promptings of such an unconquerable 'Will to freedom' will represent perhaps the most inspiring of all those hymns which throughout the years have been used as a call to rally men and women together in the sacred cause of Liberty."

28 ***Blackshirt British Union News, July 1938, page 8:***

"Owing to extra space being devoted in this issue to London Regional Marches and Meetings, one or two of the regular features have had to be held over. These, however, will be continued in the next issue – Ed."

29 ***Blackshirt British Union News, August 1938, page 1:***

"THE NEW BLACKSHIRT

PROGRESS
DEMANDS
CHANGE

THREE EDITIONS

The great progressive strides the movement has recently made warrant British Union undertaking a new venture. And on September 16, "Blackshirt" will be transformed into a penny monthly propaganda paper.

As this change is primarily being made due to the enormous demand for local propaganda, it has been decided to grant to certain areas a local edition of "Blackshirt".

In these local editions the four outer pages will be entirely devoted to local affairs and problems, and the four inner pages will deal with problems of national importance."

30 ***Action, no. 110, March 26th, 1938, page 17:***

The very small box which was allotted for the purpose of announcing his resignation on Chesterton's behalf was perhaps indicative of a slightly condescending acknowledgment of an obligation by those left behind; his decision was obviously not precipitate, but it certainly wasn't a fond farewell:

"**RESIGNATION**

A. K. Chesterton wishes to announce that with the publication of this issue he resigns from the editorship of "Action" and from active membership of the British Union."

However, he was allowed to 'sign off', as it were, in his last ***Reveille*** column:

"Oswald Mosley proclaims the old truths—the old ascertained verities of our British soil and our British soul: he proclaims as well the new truths, the verities of the modern age which are no less lightly to be ignored.

May the creed advanced by this intrepid man win through to save our land, and may the policy he upholds with such skill and passion soon scatter the policies of darkness and treachery which now imperil the British race—that, readers of "Action", is not only my valedictory message: it is, and shall remain, my prayer."

Ibid., page 2

According to his Wikipedia page, Chesterton was "disillusioned" when he left British Union, and later the same year, he published an explanation in ***Why I Left Mosley***, sneeringly referring to him as "Oswald in Blunderland":

"He asserted that the party was rife with incompetents, and accused Mosley of being closely associated with the intrigues within the movement - of conspiring with his favourites at private party conferences against their opponents. Chesterton criticized Mosley for avoiding the truth about the plight of his party, asserting that the leader would go to great lengths to protect those members who eagerly indulged his delusional enthusiasms ..."

Why I Left Mosley, ***by A.K. Chesterton, National Socialist League, 1938, cited in BLACKSHIRTS TORN: INSIDE THE BRITISH UNION OF FASCISTS, 1932-1940, by Thomas Norman Keeley, MA Degree submission, Simon Fraser University, Canada, 1998***

Ten years later, "he distanced himself from this form of prejudice" in ***The Tragedy of Anti-Semitism***, but it didn't prevent him from engaging with so-called right-wing movements, one of which was the British People's Party.

http://en.wikipedia.org/wiki/A._K._Chesterton

The potted biography served up by the British People's Party website is, as could be expected, partisan, although it is correct about the date of his departure from British Union, on which it offers some insight:

"the close rapport between Chesterton and Mosley was short-lived, due in part to the latter's preoccupation with electioneering strategy on the local and national level. Chesterton was far more interested in the purity of BUF ideology, and he decided to resign from the organization in March 1938, to write more freely on his pet themes of anti-Semitism, Nazi greatness, and democratic failure."

http://www.bpp.org.uk/chesterton.html

31 ***The Blackshirt, no. 249, April 1938, page 1:***

"MOSLEY AND TRADE UNIONISTS

FIRST RALLY ON APRIL 3

The activities of Trade Union members will have an important culmination in the meeting to be held on April 3. This meeting is a landmark in the history of our Movement and is the first of its kind. Mosley has been invited by a group of London Trade Unionists to attend and speak to the assembled workers on the creed of the British Union. This will be the beginning of a drive within and without the Trade Unions, a drive which we hope will bring before every worker the creed for which we all work, and which will bring the long awaited dawn of security to the workers.

T.U. members should make a point of being at this meeting and to bring along with them some non-member to hear our Leader lay down the industrial programme of our Movement.

National Headquarters has had some tickets placed at its disposal by the T.U. organisers of the meeting and they are priced at 1s. and 6d. There are also a limited number of free seats.

If those of us who are interested in industrial propaganda, and who are interested in Trade Union questions want to hear Mosley, they must make immediate application, as the stock of tickets is dwindling every day. London members, and those of the Home Counties must make a note of this date—Sunday next, april 3, at 6.45, at the Denison Hall, Vauxhall Bridge Road, S.W.1 (near Victoria Station).

Let the slogan for this day be 'Rally to Mosley and Peace!'"

32 ***The Blackshirt, no. 250, May 1938, page 5:***

"... The chairman, an old member of the Amalgamated Engineering Union and a former industrial leader of the Communist movement, said quite frankly that he had consented to take the chair not because he had any love for National Socialism (I must emphasise that he was not a member of the British Union) but that after nineteen years' membership and work for the Trade Union movement he felt that the workers were not getting full worth from the present leadership and he was interested to hear what Sir Oswald Mosley had to offer the British worker instead of the present-day international clap trap of the so-called leadership in power.

Mosley dealt fully with British Union and Trade Unionism and in dealing with the oft-repeated lie that the Blackshirts are against Trade Union [sic] said:

'Those who say we wish to smash the Trade Union lie. If that were true we should be lunatics for by smashing Trade Union we should be smashing ourselves. Our whole system depends on the principle of Trade Unionism: without those principles our system cannot work.'

RESOLUTION

For over an hour the Leader answered questions, and then from the body of the hall a representative of the National Union of Textile Workers put a resolution to the effect:

That this meeting of Representative London and Provincial Trade Unionists welcomes this exposition of British Union Industrial Policy from Sir Oswald Mosley and affirms its determination to spread this policy through the British Trade Union Movement.

This was seconded by a delegate of the Railway Clerks' Association who very briefly stated the railway grievances and how they were persistently neglected by the lords of the political bench. …

Members of the Public Employees Union, the Transport Workers, the Electrical Trade Union, the National Union of Railwaymen and the National Union of Clerks spoke in support of the resolution and an amendment was put and agreed to that a copy should be sent to the T.U.C.

The resolution was passed unanimously."

33 ***Southern Blackshirt, no. 255, October 1938, page 4:***

"Will a 'Popular Front' Party emerge out of the present squabbling in the 'Old Gangs'?

Will there be a coalition between the many conservatives who have voiced disapproval of the Government's foreign policy and the members of the Parliamentary Attlee brigade?"

34 ***Blackshirt British Union News, no. 253, August 1938, page 1***

35 ***Southern Blackshirt, no. 255, October 1937, page 4:***

"***BACK TO WORK!***

"Speed The Dawn of British Union."

By W. Risdon.

The past fortnight has been a hectic period of activity to defeat the warmongers. Our forces have emerged strengthened and tempered as a result of their period of trial and stress.

Many cases of real heroism have come to our notice during this period. From one 'red' town came the story of a speaker who, in a time when feeling was running high, challenged the Communist speaker, who was clamouring for war. The name of our speaker shall remain unmentioned, but his pluck is duly recorded.

Rushed by the red elements in the crowd, thrown to the ground and in imminent danger, his voice was still uplifted for Mosley and a policy of peace.

Eventually he got back to his feet, and by sheer physical pluck triumphing over terrorism attained his objective and stated the case in favour of keeping out of a war which was not Britain's business.

WOMEN WERE MAGNIFICENT.

Throughout this period our women members have been magnificent. In poster parades, in sales drives and in door-to-door work they have manifested a quiet courage, which has been a potent stimulus to we mere men.

They have faced coolly and bravely, threats, physical violence, ostracism and curses, secure in the knowledge that they were fighting for peace, the ideal nearest to the heart of every true woman.

As in times of crisis, so in times of hum-drum, perseverance for the building of an electoral machine, our women are magnificent. Theirs is the quality of patience which strives day in and day out for the final establishment of the rule of 'People's Justice'.

AFTER THE CRISIS – WHAT?

The immediate crisis is over. Peace is assured. What now is the next job? The first responsibility is to safeguard the peace which has been so narrowly won.

There are many small-minded people whose spleen is insatiable, and who will start a new crusade for war. This crusade must and shall be defeated.

It must be defeated, so that our campaign for work and wages may go forward. So that our fight for a Britain reborn to strength and greatness of attainment may be successfully waged. So that the at present unwanted millions (unwanted only under financial democracy), the unemployed, may be given back their sense of self-respect and, in work for the nation assured, that they are truly valued and justly appreciated.

It **shall** be defeated, because our ranks have been cleansed and purified in the fires of tribulation, and our members have the indomitable will to success.

ELEMENTS OF SUCCESS

In our great movement we have all the elements for a great success. We have a leader second to none. We have a policy which defies criticism. We have a membership which has proved its devotion to policy and leader alike.

Now to work again! The doorstep drive must be in full swing, so that our policy shall get into every home in the country.

Every previous effort should now be redoubled. Men and women marching together in British Union are assured of success BY THEIR OWN EFFORTS. Use those efforts NOW, unsparingly.

Speed the dawn of British Union in Britain, thus ensuring a glorious heritage to generations of Britons yet unborn."

36 For example, from the aforesaid ***Annual Circular*** issued by the West Norfolk Farmers' Manure and Chemical Co-operative Company, Ltd. [note 7]:

> "'... Mr. Eden, while admitting that protection would do away with the need for subsidies and other devices, invites farmers to rejoice in the restrictions placed on agricultural production in this country in the interests of international trade, and offers to purchase their acquiescence in this state of affairs by allowing them to share in some of the profits of the overseas trade which is ruining their own industry ... Mr. Eden pictures agriculture as the poor man sitting under the rich man's table and accepting, with gratitude, such crumbs as may be thrown to him.'

This surely is of a piece with Mr. Eden's view of Britain as a whole. Does not he expect us as a nation to adopt the same position of 'poor man, etc.–' at every meeting of the 'League of "Notions"'?

> 'There is probably nothing that gives a competent foreign observer a more unfavourable view of British farming than the vast acreage of land we have down under what is dignified with the name of grass. This is simply the result of the derelict condition into which British farming has been allowed to fall by the action, or lack of action, of one government after another. Whilst German farmers have by far the greater proportion of their farm area under the plough, the exact reverse is the position in this country ... whilst the best British farmer is at least the equal of the best German farmer; the average German farmer feeds about 80 persons on each 100 acres of farmland, whilst the British farmer feeds only about half that quantity ...'

The difference is, of course, that British politicians still have the international outlook of their financier lords and masters, whilst Germany has the national outlook of the well-being of German people."

Action, no. 103, February 5th, 1938, page 13: INDUSTRY

37 *Action, no. 102, January 29th, 1938, page 7*

38 *Action, no. 100, January 13th, 1938, page 2*

39 *Action, no. 102, January 29th, 1938, page 2*

40 *Action, no. 109, March 19th, 1938, page 1*

41 *Action, no. 106, February 26th, 1938; page 9*

42 *Ibid., page 1*

43 *Action, no. 99, January 6th, 1938, page 6*

44 *Action, no. 107, March 5th, 1938, page 3*

45 *Action, no. 108, March 12th, 1938, page 4:*

"NOT ONE DROP OF BRITISH BLOOD

CZECHO-SLOVAKIA NOT BRITAIN'S BUSINESS

By R. GORDON-CANNING

That evil spawn of the Treaty of Versailles, Czecho-Slovakia, whose existence is one long-standing accusation of either imbecility or incompetence against the framers of this Treaty—for even our world-notorious Lloyd George has written in 1928 'that the documents and evidence provided by certain Allies during the negotiations of peace were lies and fraud, and the decisions taken were based on false premises'—comes once more into the foreground of world politics.

'To be or not to be?' If the peace of Europe is desired then the liquidation of Czecho-Slovakia is essential and long overdue.

Of what does this artificial state consist?

14,730,000 persons (1931) made up
of 7,447,000 Czechs
3,218,000 Germans
2,309,000 Slovaks
720,000 Magyars
569,000 Ruthenes
100,000 Poles"

46 For example, this editorial from Raven Thomson:

"HITLER TRIUMPHANT

Hitler's success is not to be measured in the votes of the delighted German people alone, but in his complete success in crushing the financial bogey that terrifies the Democrats. The significant point in all his recent speeches has been his insistence upon a commodity basis of German currency which, he says, is backed not by gold but by the productive capacity of the nation. This statement by a great responsible political leader is of tremendous significance, as it proclaims to the world the adoption of a sane monetary reform by Germany and the complete overthrow of the golden calf

in that country. All monetary reformers, the enemies of finance, in this country should read these passages carefully, and realise the absurdity of the myth that Hitler is a tool of international finance.

It is in their difference of attitude to the financial question that France and Germany differ so completely. In France, finance can still make or break governments; in Germany, the Government has complete control over finance, and can break any financial interest that dares to set itself up against the national will.

We do not ask Britain merely to learn a lesson from this, we ask the people to realise that they have ten times the resources of the Germans, and once in British Union with the will to use these resources they can produce ten times the result."

Action, no. 113, April 16th, 1938, page 10

47 If there were any questions on Germany as Wilfred asserted, it is likely that he will have adhered to the line set out by Mosley after the second war, in his autobiography:

"Hitler had said again and again that he wanted the union of the Germans and living room in the east, not the take over of crowded areas in the west. The idea of conducting our large multi-racial Empire was also entirely contrary to national socialist ideas for the proper employment of German energy. To attempt any of these things would have been to stand Nazi doctrines on their heads. It is true that all this was exactly the opposite of our British ideas, derived from the long Imperial experience, and it was precisely this difference which gave us the best chance of peace; the Germans wanted something quite different."

My Life, by Oswald Mosley

The Woodford Times, Friday, May 6, 1938:

"BUCKHURST HILL FASCISTS' MEETING

Speaker Outlines Policy

A meeting of the British Union of Fascists, remarkable for its quietness and the orderly behaviour of the fair-sized audience, was held at the Buckhurst Hill Hall on Wednesday.

The speaker was Mr W Risdon, from the Union headquarters, who outlined the policy of the British Fascists [sic], led by Sir Oswald Mosley, dealing at length with their economic plans.

A national department of industry would be set up to deal with working conditions and standardisations of high wages, and when it had achieved a sufficiently high level in these respects would work for a gradual reduction in working hours. At the same time the people would be educated to use their leisure profitably, having sufficient means wherewith they could enjoy leisure.

He went on to declare that protection was vital to economic security. The Union did not confine itself to hatred of any particular countries, but they would keep out goods that were manufactured abroad at a low standard of wages when they were being produced at home at high rates.

WAGE CUTS

At the present time a decent employer who wanted to pay high wages was unable to do so, as another employer in the same industry would make wage cuts and be at an unfair advantage.

The Union recognised the need for Trade Unions in industry, but they should have one hundred per cent membership, and not the present twenty per cent, Mr Risdon continued. Only two out of every ten trade unionists struggled to bring up the strength of their unions, but all members took the benefits.

Dealing with class distinctions, he saw many big heads of industry, such as Lord Nuffield, had justified their ownership. But they would be against gamblers in business, who impoverished the community.

Mr Risdon declared the House of Lords, formerly a valuable part of the Government, was now full of profiteers – people with 'big noses and small consciences', who bought honours from corrupt governments with money corruptly gained.

The Union would replace this with a second chamber of people who had made great contributions in art or industry.

FASCISM AND JEWS

It was only in answer to questions that the speaker dealt with the position between the British Union of Fascists and the Jewish race.

He declared the movement was definitely anti-semitic, but it had not always been. For the first two years of its existence the members had refused to be drawn into any discussion on the subject.

But it became quite obvious that the Jews were going to smash the movement if it was within their power, not because the Fascists had attacked them, but because their policy was detrimental to their world domination.

In answer to further questions, he declared the Union had an unswerving loyalty to the Crown, which it recognised as the most vital link of the Empire. They were not out for international Fascism, but for Britain alone.

The meeting concluded with the singing of the National Anthem."

Courtesy of Lynn Haseldine-Jones & the staff at Loughton Library

48 ***Action, no. 114, April 23rd, 1938, page 15***

"CONFERENCE COLLYWOBBLES

Easter, as usual, has produced its crop of conferences, and from these conferences, the usual crop of contradictions.

The big guns go off with a great sound and fury. Some people there are who still attach a good deal of importance to utterances made on these occasions; however, I must frankly admit that after many years of experience of these emanations I find it extremely difficult to take any of them seriously.

Here are a few for your consideration from this year's Easter conferences:–

CO-OPERATIVE PARTY
CONFERENCE AT BRIGHTON

Mr. Alfred Barnes, M.P., Chairman of the Conference, advocating the Popular Front:—

'I believe that if anything is certain in this uncertain situation, it is that the way to avert universal disaster is to make the League of Nations immediately effective against aggression.

The Trade unions, the Co-operative Party and the Labour Party believe that.

The Liberal Party believes it.

The majority of religious leaders in this country believe it.

A good section of the Conservative Party believe it.

If you think this issue at the moment transcends all else, it is the overriding responsibility of the leaders of parties and movements believing in the League to let that belief find political expression.'

He advocated a peace alliance which would aim at reaching a basis of agreement between all parties and groups who desire 'to make the League of Nations immediately effective against aggression.'

Mr. George Dallas, Chairman of the Labour Party, damning the Popular Front:—

Mr. Dallas made an indirect reference to the question of Popular Front movements.

'We have in our Movement', he said, 'a trinity that is a real unity – Labour, Trade Unionism, and Co-operation.

I believe it will solve this country's problems and ultimately those of the whole world.

Keir Hardie raised the banner of liberty for the Labour Movement, from the political Parties both of the Right and the Left, and we of the Labour Party will never surrender that freedom to anybody.'

From Popular Front the conference proceeded to discussions on Franco Spain and Japan (not particularly well-informed discussions, let it be noted), then on to old-age pensions of £1 a week at 60. This was much better informed, as was also the discussion on rising prices, and, at a later stage, the 'holidays with pay' discussion.

I.L.P. CONFERENCE AT MANCHESTER

Jimmy Maxton, M.P., in his presidential address (we feel that Jimmy will continue president of the I.L.P. until one or the other dies) made it clear that he does not want a 'Popular Front'.

'I see', said Mr. Maxton, 'the Labour Party Executive has been condemning certain of these Popular Front activities, and I support that condemnation. But it is no good the Labour Party condemning such activities and itself carrying on a Popular Front policy.'

Conferences continued in sundry places over Easter. The Teachers (N.U.T.) conferred at Margate, the National Union of Journalists at Brighton, the Young Communist League at Glasgow, Commercial Travellers in London, etc., etc.

They all talked quite a lot, mostly about other countries.

All their talk will quickly be forgotten, however, and the procedure will be repeated once again next Easter.

The wiser people are those who have spent Easter in their gardens, I think."

49 *Ibid.*

"<u>TRADE UNION NOTES</u>

LAW IS NOT ALWAYS JUSTICE

New Snags In Workmen's Compensation

By W. RISDON

A new point arose recently in connection with workmen's compensation which brings home in a striking manner the need for a drastic reform in legislation bearing on this subject.

The case in question was that of Frederick Henry Metcalfe, a Chingford 'bus conductor who was crippled for life as a result of an accident which occurred during his hours of employment.

His 'bus and a tramcar were in collision and owing to injuries sustained Metcalfe lost his left leg.

This serious injury means that Metcalfe is now completely incapacitated from following his occupation, and a judge of the King's Bench ruled that fair compensation for such loss in this specific case would be £3,715.

LEGAL ANOMALY

The same judge, however, was bound to dismiss the action for damages on account of a legal anomaly. The defence used was that of 'Common Employment' under which a servant 'undertakes as between himself and his master to run the ordinary risks of his service, including the risk of negligence on the part of a fellow servant.'

Under this doctrine it was claimed that all the servants of a road transport company must be in common employment, whether they were engaged on the company's premises or on the public roads.

NEW CONDITIONS

Here is the important point which now arises for consideration. Had the accident occurred a few years ago when trams and 'buses were operated by different companies, Metcalfe's claim would have been valid.

Meantime, however, the forced combination of all these services in the London Passenger Transport Board renders the claim invalid. The bigger the combine the greater the risk borne by the individual employees; and conversely the greater the immunity enjoyed by the employers.

This is a most vicious principle which must be fought tooth and nail.

The real point for consideration is whether the employee in question was

(a) Incapacitated while in the execution of his duty.

(b) So incapacitated through no fault of his own.

The above points, if established, should constitute a claim for compensation in full, regardless of common employment or any other considerations.

BRITONS OR BASQUES

In the above there is material in abundance for a real fight in which all the forces of Labour could be usefully engaged.

What a chance for a Keir Hardie or an Arthur Cook! Unfortunately there are none such among present-day Labour Leaders.

If one half the energy and fighting spirit had been shown in this case as has been poured out in hatred of Franco, Hitler or Mussolini, things would begin to move in the right direction.

Day after day in Parliament there are pages of Hansard filled with questions from the Labour Party opposition on conditions in Spain, in China, in Germany, in Italy, and anywhere else in the wide world except Great Britain.

Great demonstrations are arranged in Hyde Park and in all the great provincial centres to protest against injustices, real or imaginary, in foreign countries, and Trade Union leaders vie with Labour Party members of Parliament as to who can say the most scathing things about conditions in some foreign country.

IN OUR MIDST

Meanwhile, in our own midst we see cases such as I have quoted above. Cases affecting the conditions and the very lives of workers in our own country. These are entirely neglected in most cases, and in the exceptional cases one parliamentary question is asked and nothing further is done. No nation-wide campaign for British workers' interests. No fight in Parliament on these issues.

And, remember, mergers resulting in greater and yet greater combinations are becoming more and more the order of the day with modern capitalism.

The 'common employment' danger is steadily increasing with every new merger which is effected.

PAST FIGHTERS AND THEIR MODERN SUCCESSORS

It is to be wondered at that one should sigh for the Cooks, the Keir Hardies and the other great fighters of the past when confronted by a generation of the Labour movement, both political and industrial, who are so blinded by hate of other countries that they neglect the very real injustices which are so abundant at home and which, moreover, are their first responsibility.

The early fighters in the cause of Labour did not seek foreign issues to fight, they concentrated on the fight against injustice at home and therein lies the reason for their success. The present generation of Labour are squandering that success which others built up, and the only movement to-day which concerns itself with the fight on the home front against social injustice is British Union. We have inherited the historic role, once filled by the Labour Party, of champions of the British worker in his struggle for human conditions.

Mosley to-day is carrying on the fight which in earlier days was conducted by Keir Hardie. Mosley's followers are to-day giving the kind of service, selfless and devoted, which built up a great Labour movement in the past. Service which in the brief period of five years has built up miracles of achievement.

The past has been betrayed by political place-seekers – yet the future is secure because of this new movement of National Socialism which sweeps forward with ever-accelerating momentum to the goal of final justice for the workers of Britain."

50 ***Southern Blackshirt, no. 255, October, 1938, page 2***

51 ***The Fascists in Britain, by Colin Cross***

52 ***Action, no. 143, November 12th, 1938, page 1***

53 ***Ibid.***

54 *Action, no. 137, October 1st, 1938, page 1*

Unsurprisingly, the ***Blackshirt*** seized upon the opportunity to trumpet both Mosley's clarity of thought, in his analysis of the situation and the requisite solution, and his prescience in timing:

> **"On Wednesday, September 28, British Union members distributed thousands of copies of an "Action" Crisis Special edition, carrying a detailed plan formulated by Mosley as a means of solving the Czechoslovakian problem and ensuring world peace.**
>
> **That plan was basically the same as the one finally agreed upon by the Munich four-power conference. Mosley suggested the only sane solution three days ahead of anyone else."**

Southern Blackshirt, no. 255, October, 1938, page 5

55 A very full, and apparently reliable account is given at http://en.wikipedia.org/wiki/Munich_Agreement

56 *Action, no. 136, September 24th, 1938, page 7*

57 *Action, no. 137, October 1st, 1938, page 4:*

"SHALL BRITISH YOUTH

BE SACRIFICED TO FRENCH WAR PARTY?

By W. RISDON

Henri de Kerillis, a well-known French journalist, writing in the Paris *L'Epoque*, on Monday, September 12, was reported by the Newcastle Evening Chronicle to have given reasons as under why France would not 'desert' Czechoslovakia.

One of the chief reasons, said M. de Kerillis, was because Czechoslovakia's aerodromes, which could be used by French and Russian planes in time of war, are within striking distance of Berlin.

M. De [sic] Kerillis often gives prominence to views which are known to be those of France's military chiefs, says British United Press.

To-day, he says, the French General Staff has warned the French Government against any proposals for the neutralisation of Czechoslovakia.

He suggests that neutralisation would dislocate the entire French military system in Europe, deprive France of aerodromes on the Bohemian plains, and open to Germany supply regions which she cannot now reach.

Note well the implications of the above. A neutral Czechoslovakia would be of no use to France's General Staff – they require nothing less than a Czechoslovakia hostile to its near-neighbour Germany. Anything less 'would dislocate the entire French military system in Europe'. To maintain a base for French and Russian 'planes, within effective striking distance of Berlin, these 'mad-dogs of war' would be prepared to plunge Europe – and perhaps the world – into the blood-bath of war.

Here, at last, is the grim truth emerging from one who speaks the mind of militarist France. The attitude of France in this matter need no longer puzzle the minds of those who have been concerned as to her attitude in this crisis. We now know her motives, but what of Britain?

SHALL BRITAIN BLINDLY FOLLOW?

There is, in Britain, an ever-growing body of opinion which has felt and expressed grave doubts as to the wisdom of a policy of being dragged at the chariot wheels of France. This country of ours has its own grave responsibilities to face. Responsibilities for an Empire scattered across the entire face of the globe. An Empire, as yet, developed only to an infinitesimal degree of its full potentialities and with resources not yet recovered from the devastation of the last world war. Is that Empire, which is our first responsibility, to be jeopardised for the sole purpose of ensuring to France a Czechoslovakia eternally hostile to Germany? We say no! a thousand times 'no!'.

Czechoslovakia may be of use to France's military plans. Henri de Kerillis says it is, and gives details as follows:–

> 'Although Paris and the great French industrial cities are within immediate reach of German 'planes, Berlin and the great German industrial cities are not within the reach of French 'planes because of their distance.
>
> In a war there would be an unfavourable balance if we could not count on the support of the incomparable aerodromes on the plains of Bohemia, only a few minutes from Berlin, from Silesia, and from Vienna.
>
> Russia could intervene at two vital points. First in the Baltic, where her submarines and 'planes could cut the German communication lines with the Scandinavian countries, which unfortunately remained open during the whole of the last war, and secondly, her 'planes would form a reinforcement of untold value to France and Czechoslovakia if the latter were able to establish lines of resistance in the advance regions of the Bohemian plains.'

Well and good. That is the affair of France and explains her Russian alliance, but there is in it no vestige of a reason why Britain should join in such a 'line-up'. There is nothing in that war-plan which would benefit either Great Britain or the Empire.

What insane folly it would be, therefore, for us to join in such a stupid quarrel.

WHICH PATH FOR PEACE

France has chosen as her ally – Russia; as her policy – war (in the future); as her enemy – Germany, the three factors following automatically from the first factor. This I believe to be a stupid choice. She could just as easily have chosen as her policy – peace; as her allies for peace – those European countries, including Britain, who experienced the horrors of the last war; as her mission, jointly with those allies – the rehabilitation of a modern Europe whose people should seek prosperity for themselves and peace with the rest of the world – such peace being an essential pre-requisite to the desired prosperity of the peoples.

The peaceful development of the Empires held by the European nations prior to the last great war would have been a magnificent undertaking. It is not yet too late to adopt such a policy but, if France will have none of that policy let us cut adrift from France and work with those who are willing to follow such a policy of realism. The future of the British Empire at least, and perhaps of the whole world, is in the balance. May our great country do the right thing at this juncture and thus help to secure the future of world peace."

58 Apparently, Hitler "felt as though he had been forced into acting like a

bourgeois politician by his diplomats and generals", and that, as well as being his first international conference, this would also be his last; he obviously also felt, rather petulantly, that he had been somehow inveigled by Chamberlain, referring to him as "that silly old man" and "an impertinent busybody … with his umbrella".

http://en.wikipedia.org/wiki/Munich_Agreement

Mosley and Wilfred's erstwhile colleague, Harold Nicolson, had his own 'take' on this document, which he incorporated in his openly propagandist polemic published a year later, specifically intended to inform and convert any sections of the British public not yet convinced of the necessity for another war:

> "Some of the more virulent of Mr. Chamberlain's critics have advanced the theory that when he spoke of "Peace in our Time" and "Peace with Honour" he was practising a deliberate deception upon both the German and British peoples. Their argument is that in that autumn of 1938, the state of our defences was not such as to allow us to enter a major war; that any frank discussion or disclosure of our unpreparedness would not only encourage our enemies but do much damage to the Conservative party; and that therefore Mr. Chamberlain tried to "get away with it" by making a great virtue out of an unpleasant necessity. In other words, he was merely "playing for time."
>
> I regard this criticism as ungenerous and untrue. Neither Mr. Chamberlain nor Sir Horace Wilson had experience of foreign politics, and their misconception of Herr Hitler's aims and character was absolutely sincere. I am convinced that the Prime Minister, on his return from Munich, really did believe that he had not only averted war but laid the foundations of peace. It may seem to some that a peace founded upon the betrayal and final coercion of a small country cannot accurately be described as "honourable." The point is whether the Prime Minister was justified at the time in regarding it as stable. According to the text of the agreements signed, and the assurances exchanged, he had some justification for this belief. Those of us who disagreed with his interpretation of the value of the Munich agreement were not basing our judgment upon the documents; we based it upon our knowledge of Herr Hitler's character. We felt certain that he would tear up the Munich agreement the moment that he found himself in the position to make a further attack.
>
> The documents themselves, therefore, do not appear to me to be of primary importance, but they must be mentioned. I have already summarised the agreements regarding Czechoslovakia and it remains to indicate the nature of the piece of paper which Mr. Chamberlain had waved above his head when he arrived at Heston aerodrome. That document, which was signed by the Prime Minister and Herr Hitler, contained three clauses. Under the first clause they agreed "that the question of Anglo-German relations is of the first importance for the two countries and for Europe." Nobody would question the truth of this assertion. The second clause stated that "we regard the agreement signed last night and the Anglo-German Naval Convention as symbolic of the desire of our two peoples never to go to war with one another again." And the third clause ran as follows: "We are resolved that the method

of consultation shall be the method adopted to deal with any other questions that may concern our two countries, and we are determined to continue our efforts to remove possible sources of differences and thus to contribute to assure the peace of Europe."

This somewhat illiterate document did not constitute a Treaty; it was little more than an expression of joint opinion coupled with assurances of joint regard. Its value depended entirely upon the spirit in which it would be interpreted by Herr Hitler. In the very next speech which the Führer made, he rendered it abundantly clear that he himself did not attach any importance to this sheet of paper. Mr. Chamberlain, on the other hand, continued until March 15th, 1939, to regard it as the very charter of appeasement. To a critic who suggested that Herr Hitler has made many other promises in the past, he replied: "Yes, but on this occasion he has made them to me!""

Why Britain is at War, by Harold Nicolson

59 These days, this sort of thinking would be regarded as 'conspiracy theory':

"THE DANGEROUS PARTY

WHO ARE THEY ?

Backstair Intrigues To Wreck Peace

By W. RISDON

There is a steadily mounting accumulation of evidence which goes to indicate that there is a "party" in our midst which aims at imposing its will by the methods of underhanded intrigue in defiance of those who seek to establish peace in Europe.

The reprint from the "American Hebrew" which appeared in "Action" a short time ago indicates that war is desired by a section in the United States.

A study of the Labour Party and Communist propaganda organs in this country makes it abundantly clear that these interests too are actively engaged in the promotion of hatreds which must, if persisted with, eventually lead to war.

Certain organs of the Jews in Britain add their quota of 'hate' to this insane chorus.

All this has been painfully apparent for a long time past, but, beyond these open advocates of hate there is a subterranean movement which has permeated throughout all walks of life with a skilfully designed line of propaganda.

HOW IT WORKS

Throughout the recent period of crisis this hidden hand of propaganda has been skilfully at work. Its activities have never abated.

In 'respectable' circles – i.e., in hotels, clubs, restaurants, business houses, etc., there has been the constant whispering campaign of those who 'have it on reliable authority – that this, that, or the other section are truckling to Hitler'.

'They have heard it from someone in the know' that there is unrest in Germany and if Germany is tackled now Hitler could be got rid of, etc., etc.

In purely working class circles the propaganda has been more blatant. Those who have stood for peace – and no organisation other than the British Union has maintained that stand – have been represented as pro-German and anti-British, a foul lie calculated to inflame the passions of the people against British Union and to remove by terrorism the one solid barrier which had been created against war.

STRANGE LINKS

Throughout all these intrigues names have been carefully canvassed of those who would take more effective action if allowed to do so. In some circles it has been a case of Hore-Belisha, Eden and Churchill. In others, Attlee, Morrison and Elvin, and these three in yet other circles have been linked with Pollitt, Blum and Stalin, and so the dirty game has been carried on.

Beyond shadow of doubt these moves have made it clear that there are forces in our midst constantly working for war. Working in all circles from that represented by readers of ***The Times*** – where Gollancz bought space to show Communist propaganda, right through to that section representative of readers of the ***Mirror*** and the ***Daily Worker***.

WATCH FOR THEM

At the moment the forces of peace appear to have won, but it is yet too soon to take respite from your labours in this great cause.

Keep constantly on the alert for the hate-mongers. Their efforts brought us perilously near the brink and what they failed to do on one occasion they will try again to do on a future occasion – perhaps soon.

Remember that once before peace seemed to be assured and then, owing to rapid moves taken (surely on outside advice), in Czechoslovakia, the clouds gathered even more ominously than before. Do not be rattled whatever may happen in the future, but hold fast to the one demand for peace, peace in our time. For Britain, peace and people."

Action, no. 138, October 8th, 1938, page 3

60 ***The Fascists in Britain, op. cit.***

61 ***Action, no. 140, October 22nd, 1938, page 15***

62 ***The Fascists in Britain, op. cit.***

63 ***Action, no. 137, October 1st, 1938, page 12:***

"**Chain Peace Letter**

Copy out the following message on postcards and send them to at least ten other persons TO-NIGHT.

Dear Sir (or Madam),

In this time of great emergency I beg of you to stand firm for peace, and resist every endeavour to involve this country in a foreign war.

Twenty years ago ten million people lost their lives in a war to end war. This folly must not be repeated!

It is agreed that the Sudetenland shall pass to Germany. It would be insane to sacrifice British youth over the method of this transfer.

Mosley says, 'Britons fight for Britain only.'

Do your bit for peace by copying out this message and sending it on to ten other persons AT ONCE. time is drawing short.

Yours for peace,"

64 http://en.wikipedia.org/wiki/Joachim_von_Ribbentrop#Ambassador_to_Britain

65 http://en.wikipedia.org/wiki/Free_City_of_Danzig

66 According to his Wikipedia profile, William Ralph Inge, who was born at Crayke, north Yorkshire, and lived from 1860 to 1954, was an author, Anglican priest, professor of divinity at Cambridge, and Dean of St. Paul's Cathedral, whence his appellation Dean Inge; his nickname, referenced by Wilfred, was entirely the result of his written output for a newspaper:

> "Inge was a prolific author. In addition to scores of articles, lectures and sermons, he also wrote over 35 books. He is best known for his works on Plotinus and neoplatonic philosophy, and on Christian mysticism. He was a strong proponent of a spiritual type of religion—'that autonomous faith which rests upon experience and individual inspiration'—as opposed to one of coercive authority; so he was outspoken in his criticisms of the Roman Catholic Church. His thought, on the whole, represents a blending of traditional Christian theology with elements of Platonic philosophy. He shares this much with one of his favourite writers, Benjamin Whichcote, the first of the Cambridge Platonists. In addition to this he was also a eugenicist and wrote considerably on the subject. In his book ***Outspoken Essays*** he devotes an entire chapter to this subject.
>
> He was nicknamed *The Gloomy Dean* because of his pessimistic views in his ***Evening Standard*** articles and he is remembered as a supporter of animal rights."

http://en.wikipedia.org/wiki/William_Inge_(priest)

On the basis of the above, Wilfred will have shared some [although maybe not much] common cause with Inge, but whether this will have extended to eugenics is unknown; the latter subject brought Inge to the attention of the arguably better known uncle of one of Wilfred's erstwhile colleagues, A. K. Chesterton:

> "There is increasing recognition that G. K. Chesterton was one of the greatest Christian apologists of the twentieth century. He was probably exceeded in this regard only by C. S. Lewis who was, of course, greatly influenced by the older man. Nevertheless, Chesterton, unlike Lewis, was busily engaged in political debate and public action for most of his life. It is here that his contribution has been almost forgotten, and yet – a typical paradox – it was in this area that his achievements were of the greatest public importance. This is true of Chesterton's writings and campaigning for a sane economics under the banner of 'Distributism,' but it is perhaps most true of his fight against eugenics."

The author of this piece explodes the myth that it was only the so-called 'right-wing' who propounded eugenics, but neither was Inge of the "radical Left":

> "Yet it was not just the radical Left which promoted eugenics. One of its most vocal advocates in Britain was the Dean of St. Paul's Cathedral from 1911-1934, Dr. William Inge. *Ex Officio* one of the most senior members of the Church of England, he was known as the 'Gloomy Dean' for his warnings about overpopulation. In an essay published in 1917 called simply ***Eugenics***, he pointed out that all the males in his family had won scholarships at Eton,

Oxford and Cambridge, but that: 'Unfortunately the birth-rate of the feeble-minded is quite 50% higher than that of normal persons.' The answer was eugenics, beginning with 'the compulsory segregation of mental defectives.'

Any regular reader of Chesterton's essays will have come across the name of Dean Inge, so it may be appropriate here to explain who he was, and what he represented. Chesterton never had any enemies, but if he ever had a regular opponent, that man was Dean Inge. Inge seemed to have little interest in the traditional doctrines of Christianity, calling himself 'a modern churchman.' He was however a convinced Erastian, that is, dedicated to maintaining the 'established' position of the Church of England as a pillar of the British State. In a late essay called ***The Erastian on the Establishment*** (1934), Chesterton wrote: 'A bitter and cynical man said, "The Church of England is our last bulwark against Christianity." This is quite unjust as a description of the Church of England. But it is not altogether unjust as a description of Dean Inge.' Inge was known as the 'Gloomy Dean' for his Malthusian worries about the poor overbreeding. He also proclaimed, in thoroughly modern terms, that global competition meant that the British workers simply had to accept lower wages and poor working conditions, although somehow this never applied to the members of the Establishment itself. In ***The New Theologian*** (published in ***A Miscellany of Men***, 1912) Chesterton takes him apart with wit and precision: 'When next you hear the "liberal" Christian say we should take what is best in Oriental faiths, make quite sure what are the things that people like Dr. Inge call best. . . . You will find the levelling of creeds quite unexpectedly close to the lowering of wages.'"

"RUSSELL SPARKES is the Editor of ***Prophet of Orthodoxy***, a compilation of Chesterton's religious writings, with a critical introduction, published by Harper Collins, and Chief Consultant on the ***Sane Economy Project*** of the Chesterton Institute. The present article [***The Enemy of Eugenics***] was published in ***The Chesterton Review*** for February-May 1999."

http://www.secondspring.co.uk/articles/sparkes.htm

67 ***Action, no. 148, December 17th, 1938, page 18:***

"ESSAYS OF INGE

This book is composed of a selection of the articles which have attached a certain fame to the name of the 'gloomy Dean'.

The articles (or chapters) are – as is to be expected – provocative, but none the less interesting.

Many people omit to read 'Introductions'. Such as are guilty of this omission will miss what I find to be the most interesting of all this book's sections. It runs in this case to 32 pages mostly devoted to the subject (Spain), of which the author writes – 'My editors have been most kind in giving me a free hand. There was only one subject on which I could hardly let myself go – the horrors of the Red revolution in Spain. On this I shall say something in this introduction, for the British public have been shamefully deceived.'

Also included in this introduction is the comment which will arouse some controversy:

'The Roman Church is essentially a form of dictatorship, like Communism and Nazism.'

The essays are conveniently arranged in sections under the headings: – International Affairs, England, Religion, Social Problems, History, Education, Science, Miscellaneous.

The whole book is conservative in tone and shows a complete distaste for all modern forms of government.

'The idea of attacking Germany, with such allies as we should have, just because we are afraid that their people are becoming too powerful, is to my mind utterly abominable … Most of us do not like their system of government. NO more do I. But after a revolution, some years of rule by a strong hand is necessary. It has always been so. Let us cease to scream "Fascism" … and consider instead that across the North Sea an extraordinarily interesting experiment is being tried, which may show us the way to end industrial strife.'

One gathers also that W.R. Inge has a certain regard for Jews. He contrasts them with Scots to the disadvantage of the latter:

'A friend of mine tried to find out whether there is anything at all like a Jewish stranglehold on the City of London. The result of his enquiries was that there is none, but there is a Scottish stranglehold!'

Well, that is a selection. Make your own choice. W.R.

'Our Present Discontents' by W.R. Inge (Putnam, 7/6)."

68 There was some overlap between Macmillan's and Mosley's economic politics:

"Maurice Harold Macmillan, 1st Earl of Stockton, OM, PC, FRS (10 February 1894 – 29 December 1986) was Conservative Prime Minister of the United Kingdom from 10 January 1957 to 18 October 1963.

Nicknamed 'Supermac' and known for his pragmatism, wit and unflappability, Macmillan achieved notoriety before the Second World War as a Tory radical and critic of appeasement. Rising to high office as a *protégé* of wartime Prime Minister Winston Churchill, he believed in the post-war settlement and the necessity of a mixed economy, and in his premiership pursued corporatist policies to develop the domestic market as the engine of growth. During his time as prime minister, average living standards steadily rose while numerous social reforms were carried out such as the 1956 ***Clean Air Act***, the 1957 ***Housing Act***, the 1960 ***Offices Act***, the 1960 ***Noise Abatement Act***, the ***Factories Act*** 1961, and the introduction of a graduated pension scheme to provide an additional income to retirees.

As a One Nation Tory of the Disraelian tradition, haunted by memories of the Great Depression, he championed a Keynesian strategy of public investment to maintain demand, winning a second term in 1959 with an increased majority on an electioneering budget. Benefiting from favourable international conditions, he presided over an age of affluence, marked by low unemployment and high if uneven growth. In his Bedford speech of July 1957 he told the nation they had 'never had it so good', but warned of the dangers of inflation, summing up the fragile prosperity of the 1950s."

http://en.wikipedia.org/wiki/Harold_Macmillan

69 ***Action, no. 148, December 17th, 1938, page 19:***

"For The Serious Student Of Politics

'The Middle Way' by Harold Macmillan, M.P. (Macmillan, 5/-).

This is a book for the serious student of politics. It should be read analytically and understandingly. The tragedy is that it will most probably be read by many who do not analyse and do not understand, hence they may follow the conclusions drawn by the author and fall into the trap of believing that there is a 'middle way' which is practicable between the opposites of Bolshevism and Corporativism.

The research work which has gone to the making of this book is of a very high order. Facts have been gathered from many sources and presented with so great a degree of lucidity that one can be wonder [sic] at the conclusions drawn from such useful statistics.

One of the author's fallacies has already come into the limelight in the 'Milk Muddle Legislation' which has just aroused the ire of the public and accordingly been dropped.

His main remedies fall into three main categories which may be cited as:

(a) Wage rates based on 'the minimum supply of necessities essential to physical welfare'.

(b) Standardisation and bulk handling in distribution.

(c) Full employment of capital resources.

The author is concerned with the part to be played in national planning 'by the millions of human beings who spend the greater part of their daily lives in the industries and services to be planned', but he goes on to say –

'There are obvious difficulties in the way of too wide an extension of industrial Democracy in regard to the managerial functions to be performed: FOR TOO MUCH DEMOCRATIC INTERFERENCE WOULD MILITATE AGAINST EFFICIENCY.'

As an offset to this 'dropped brick', he places emphasis on 'the right of the worker to withdraw or withhold his labour'.

Harold Macmillan is a great believer in the efficacy of (permissive) Enabling Acts with the State filling the role of 'vigilant neutral'. He advocates also an Economic Planning Authority comprising representatives of the Central Bank, the Investment Board, the Foreign Trade Organisation and the Industrial Advisory Council. This Authority would be known as the Economic Council and would meet under the chairmanship of a Minister of Economics. It would include also a representative from the Treasury, President of the Board of Trade, Minister of Agriculture, and Minister of Labour.

Imagine such a meeting. There would be, shall we say, Montagu Norman to represent the Central Bank, Hatry to represent the Investment Board, R.S. Hudson for Foreign Trade with Billmier [sic] as a possible alternative, reinforced by Capt. Euan Wallace for the Treasury (unless Montagu Norman could represent both Treasury and Central Bank), Oliver Stanley for the Board of Trade, W. S. Morrison for Agriculture and Ernest Brown for Ministry of Labour. With a potential Horatio Bottomley as Minister of Economics to preside over their sittings, who knows what problems they might solve? W.R."

Coincidentally, in view of the Inge book review and the Chesterton connection, there was also, on the same page as the above review, although not by Wilfred in this case, a review of "G.K.C.'s LAST BOOK" [he died in 1936], and it is effusive in its praise:

"'The Coloured Lands' is a Chesterton grand variety: a collection under one cover of a number of sketches, drawings, essays, articles, poems, and ballades. None have been published previously and they are representative of every period of his life. … The galaxy of illustrations recalls to mind that G.K.C. was an artist before he was an author. … G.K.C. appears in person in several sketches. He never tired of making jokes at his own expense. … The really sad thing is that this is most likely the last book of Chesterton's we shall see. Perhaps it is fitting that this book, containing as it does the last of his works to be published, should from the point of view of get-up, be the best."

70 The excerpt from the original article read thus:

"Hitler, having purged his army, diplomatic service and financial leaders of Conservative and orthodox non-Nazi elements, is now expected to swing towards the Left and start realising the Socialist section of his National Socialist Party programme drawn up in 1920. *Daily Express*"

Action, no. 153, January 28th, 1939, page 16

71 ***Action, no. 144, November 19th, 1938, page 1***

72 ***Ibid., page 3***

73 ***Ibid., page 10***

74 ***Southern Blackshirt, no. 257, January, 1939, page 6***

75 This book was another essential educative tool for British workers:

"**BOOK REVIEW**

For Trade Unionists

**'Towards Freedom', by H.W. Kenyon. (Greater Britain Publications, 6d.)*

This is a book* at a price within the reach of all, dealing briefly but informatively with the history and functions of trade unions in Britain. It is dedicated to '… the workers who fight for Freedom and to the Leader through whom this freedom can be attained.'

Sir Oswald Mosley in a short foreword writes:

Kenyon, in this short book, discovers a great truth. As a trade unionist, with a life-long struggle to his credit in the workers' cause, he discovers that their struggle today can only be carried through to victory by British Union. He tells his fellow trade unionists the further truth, which many have found already for themselves, that this is no new struggle, but the same struggle for which they have suffered so much.

He tells the old and heroic story of the workers' fight for freedom, for the right to organise and to win their own salvation. He recognises the early betrayals leading to disillusion and disappointment, which seem inevitable in the early history of all human struggle that leads to later achievement.

He learns, from these lessons and reverses, how, with new method, and with reliable and tested instruments, that same struggle of the workers can be carried through to triumph. The victories of the workers have come from their own spirit. Their defeats have come from men and methods whom they have trusted, but have failed them. So they learn to judge systems only by the results that they bring.

We know now that from our own land and our own people alone will come salvation. The Union of the British will realise the dreams of the worker martyrs, and in that day it shall be said they did not die in vain. Their old enemy, the corrupt power of financial capitalism, is shaken at last on its golden throne. The People's State awaits the building of the workers.

Here is an idea of the contents of this book from its chapter headings:

(1) The Legal Protection of the Workers.
(2) The Legal Persecution of the Workers.
(3) Attack and Counter-Attack.
(4) The Introduction of Marxism.
(5) Towards Political Control.
(6) The Betrayal of the Workers.
(7) The Policy of Internationalism.
(8) The Policy of the Future.

A novel feature is found in the last page where there is a full copy (words and music) of Edward Carpenter's famous song, 'England, Arise'.

This book will fill a long-felt need. Every reader of this paper, who wants to gain a better understanding of the Trade Union Movement and its place in the scheme of things should buy it and read it.

It should be introduced to every member of the Trade Union Movement as an explanation of the relations between British Union and the Trade Unions.

The price is sixpence only. W.R."

Action, no. 158, March 4th, 1939, page 15

76 Moral tales were acceptable in addition to self-education:

"***'THE NEW IRELAND', by J.B. Morton.**

(The Paladin Press, 3s. 6d.)

Until the partition question is finally settled, there is not much possibility of Anglo-Irish relations resting on a firm basis. It is about time that we realised that events of great significance have been occurring in Ireland in the last few years. Mr. Morton's little book* tells us something of them, and it is clearly and concisely written.

How many know anything about the 1937 Irish Constitution? It is one of the most important documents of the twentieth century; and yet its passage is only one of the many achievements of Mr. de Valera and Fianna Fail.

This, the Conditions of Labour Act, and the gradual change, now being effected, in agriculture from ranching in the direction of small holdings, are but a few of the many indications of the appreciation there of the union which must exist between politics and morals, and economics and morals. If anyone ever says: 'Is there such a thing as a Christian country in the world?' the answer should be unhesitatingly: 'Yes, there is – Ireland.'

'JUBILEE JOHN', by Alum Llewellyn.

(Arthur Barker, Ltd., 7s. 6d.).

This is a fast moving story of incredible adventure. A Welshman accompanied a party from his native Llanbryn on a day-trip to London. He has a yearning to see the 'Lights of London', and when the rest of the party returns to Wales he absents himself to get his glimpse of London by night.

The story of his adventures is hilariously told, and character after character is brought into the fabric of the story. Bright Young Things make way for crooks, who in turn make way for a rollicking gang of furniture removers.

John John, the central figure, is ancient but knowledgeable, and plots his course through unusual surroundings with considerable guile.

He out-confidence-tricks professional confidence tricksters, and out of the 'wad' thus acquired gives a £100 bounty to one of the gang who wanted to quit crime for the quieter life of keeping hens.

A rollicking story, well told. W.R."

Action, no. 159, March 11th, 1939, page 14; Two Books To Read:

77 ***Action, no. 160, March 18th, 1939, page 17:***

"The New Power Of Trade Unions

Speaking to a group of busmen-trade unionists – at **Oddfellows Hall, Tottenham**, on Thursday last, **W. Risdon** said:

'The people who accuse British Union of intending to smash trade unionism lie. In some cases the lie is deliberate and calculated, in which case the liars are knaves and rogues. In other cases the lie is unconscious, in which case the liars are just too stupid to have learnt the truth about us.

British Union will, in fact, give to trade unions a status infinitely greater than they now possess, by giving them the power to legislate their own working conditions. Instead of being treated as inferiors in industry they will have a controlling power in industry equal to that of employers. Instead of a strike weapon as a last desperate weapon for gaining their legitimate demands, they will have statutory power to legislate on such questions as hours, wages, and general working conditions.

Strike action has failed. Political action has merely created new careers (at £600 a year) for those who have failed to justify themselves in the Trade Union world. The Power Action of British Union is now the only hope of salvation for the Trade Unions and the rank and file members are rapidly awakening to its immense possibilities in spite of officially inspired misrepresentation.'"

78 ***Action, no. 162, April 1st, 1939, page 17:***

"*Spirit Of Britain*

Bill Risdon, speaking at **Kingston District Dinner**, said:–

'Mosley alone, of contemporary politicians, clearly foresaw and warned the country about the economic blizzard which in July, 1931, struck us with its full force. As a result of this blizzard the Labour Party were driven out of office … Thomas, Snowden and the rest went over and formed the so-called 'National' Government. Mosley left the Labour Party and formed the New Party.

Mosley realised that the spirit that would build the Britain of the future had to be found in the hearts of the back streets and slums of our industrial centres. That is where he found it and that is where they rallied to the cause. In October, 1932, was formed the British Union – a group of people who realised that the interest of the State as a whole came before the interest of any particular interest within the State … British Union is the finest spirit of a united nation working for its salvation.'

'What', asked Risdon, 'is this new creed? Capitalism – the thesis – is now working. Communism is the antithesis which grows up to oppose capitalism.

Out of the conflict between them emerges a new school of thought which in this country is called British Union. This movement has grown in the face of hostility and Press misrepresentation; we wanted to put over an idea, not to fight, but we had to face physical violence, organised by and given the blessing of Labour leaders.

We did not run to the police for protection, as the Labour Party do, but kept order at our own meetings and re-established the right of free speech. We emerged from this with a great Leader and the spirit of our members hardened by struggle and oblivious of any physical injury. Next the British Union lived through a period of Press lies, slanders and misrepresentations. This was followed by a conspiracy of silence, the refusal of halls to British Union speakers, the refusal to allow Mosley to broadcast. This forced us on to the street corner, and developed the beginning of our 'door-step' work. Every effort made by the Press and the Old Gangs to check-mate us has been too late. …

Out of the situation of coming crisis we shall gather the Trade Unions, and for this reason Trade Union officials are bitterly against us. The principle of British Union is: Give a man a job to do and let him get on with it. If he fails, sack him. If he makes a success, give him honour. The new movement will not leave the workers to go cap in hand to the employer, but will arm them with an equal power to legislate their hours and working conditions in the Trade Unions. The 100 per cent. trade unionism of British Union will be a bigger, better, finer thing than the trade unionism of the present day, and its accession to power will be the finest thing for the workers in the community that could ever be conceived.

We will attain the ideal of the early Socialists who were not concerned with internationalism … Our job is to free the people of Britain, not the people of other countries; to set an example for other countries to follow in our footsteps. They will do it for themselves if once we show the way.'"

79 ***Southern Blackshirt, no. 259, March, 1939, page 1***

80 ***Action, no. 159, March 11th, 1939, page 10***

81 ***Action, no. 144, November 19th, 1938, page 5***

82 ***Action, no. 171, June 3rd, 1939, page 1***

83 ***Ibid., page 3***

84 ***Ibid.:***

"**ECONOMY AND ELECTIONS**

The Need for Support

ECONOMIES HAVE RECENTLY BEEN EFFECTED BOTH IN BRITISH UNION HEADQUARTERS AND, ACCORDING TO THE 'EVENING STANDARD' OF MAY 27 LAST, ALSO AT TRANSPORT HOUSE, THE HEADQUARTERS OF THE LABOUR PARTY. THOSE AFFECTED ON BRITISH UNION STAFF WERE GIVEN A MONTH'S NOTICE, BUT, ACCORDING TO THE 'EVENING STANDARD', THOSE AFFECTED AT TRANSPORT HOUSE WERE ONLY GIVEN A WEEK'S NOTICE. YET THERE IS NO DOUBT THAT THE LABOUR PARTY IS A VERY MUCH RICHER ORGANISATION THAN BRITISH UNION.

Thirty-six people remain in the whole-time employ of British Union, which is now an adequate staff in view of the devolution of so many functions and duties on to voluntary area leadership which has taken place during the last two years.

British Union is in a far stronger position to economise on Headquarters Staff than any other movement because it has such a large number of devoted volunteers always ready to put their spare time at the disposal of the Movement. In the course of our struggle such tried and tested area and local leadership has been discovered, that it has been possible to hand over to them most of the functions and duties which originally had to be performed by Headquarters.

As a result, in relation to the duties which it has to perform, the present Headquarters Staff of thirty-six is more adequate than the larger staff which had to be employed in the early days of organisation.

The consequent economy of funds to a poor and revolutionary movement is of the greatest possible benefit. Headquarters thereby is able to set an example to the Movement for the effort it asks to raise every possible penny for the coming Election.

DO YOUR BIT, AND SEND A CONTRIBUTION TO THE DIRECTOR GENERAL'S APPEAL FUND."

According to Special Branch:

"On the evening of 30th May a conference of District officers in the London Administration - described in the convening letter as 'special and urgent, taking priority over all other activities' - was held at headquarters.

Sir Oswald MOSLEY presided over the gathering. He reviewed the position of the movement and put forward as proof of its 'fortunate position' that it should be able, in troubled times like the present, to effect economies in headquarters staff without detriment to the smooth working of the organisation. This step was only rendered possible by the voluntary efforts of many of the officers. Of course, there would inevitably be some hostile elements who would seek to convey the impression that such economies indicated the movement was on the down grade, but those present would know how little reliance could be placed upon such despicable defeatist propaganda. (As those at the conference were all voluntary officials and none of the paid staff was present, they had no objection to raise against the dismissals (details of which have already been reported) of certain of the salaried officials.)"

TNA [PRO], HO 144/21281, Report 12/06/39

85 Private correspondence with the author; two different sources mention a letter written literally the day before he died in 1999 by a member, Robert Row, who joined the Lancaster branch of British Union in 1934 at the age of 17, but does not appear to have worked at NHQ before the war. He evidently had minimal contact with Wilfred after the war, but it is unlikely to have been sufficient for the reasons for Wilfred's departure from British Union to have been discussed, so his assertion is probably the result of hearsay of dubious provenance, or perhaps a simple mistake.

86 The final ***Industry*** column was published in mid-May, but it had been unattributed for some time, so it is impossible to say with any degree of certainty that these had been compiled by Wilfred; on the same page of issue no. 168 of ***Action***, May 13th 1939, there is also an article about a trade union dispute, but Wilfred was by no means the only member who wrote about those matters, so the same circumspection must apply.

87 ***TNA [PRO], HO 144/21281, op. cit.:***

"W. RISDON is remaining at headquarters until after the Earl's Court rally, working in a voluntary capacity. Capt. U. A. HICK and Lt.-Col. C. S. SHARPE have also provisionally agreed to carry on there as volunteers (expenses incurred by them being reimbursed)."

88 ***Ibid.:***

"It seems certain that the sudden decision to effect economies by reducing the number of paid officials must have resulted from some unexpected stoppage of a source of revenue, or the failure to materialise of a definite promise of funds, as up to a day or so before that, expenditure was being incurred in painting and furnishing a new office for DONOVAN, in a part of the building which is now to be sublet, whilst a full-time Contacts Officer was on the point of being engaged."

89 ***Action, no. 172, June 10th, 1939, page 3:***

"The meeting organiser, Mr. H. G. McKecknie [sic], is very busy – there can be no doubt about that. I found him surrounded by the piles of correspondence that have come to him since the announcement of the Earls Court Exhibition Hall meeting appeared in print – only four days previously.

...

First of all I wanted to know just how the responsibility for this vast undertaking was being apportioned. Mr. McKecknie explained that the Director General of British Union, Mr. N. Francis-Hawkins, is personally supervising all arrangements, with Mr. B. D. E. Donovan, assisted by Capt. U. A. Hick, in charge of all stewarding and ceremonial procedure and matters closely affecting the Movement itself. To Mr. McKecknie falls the 'business' organisation, publicity and ticket sales, and a hundred and one minor but important matters that are so necessary in the arrangement of so colossal a venture.

COMPLETE CONFIDENCE

To the man who was responsible for similar work in connection with Mosley's great Albert Hall meeting in 1936, even the enormous project now before him presents no serious misgivings. When I ventured to suggest a doubt that the hall would be filled to capacity he pooh-poohed my fears by saying, 'I am confident that the hall will be packed on the day of the meeting. On that score you may be positive.'"

90 ***TNA [PRO], HO 144/21281, op. cit.:***

"Mosley next turned to the subject of the 'biggest indoor political meeting in the world', namely, that which is to be held by the movement at the Earl's Court Exhibition Hall on Sunday 16th July next. He dilated upon the magnitude of the project, the shock it would give to the 'democratic and economist parties', and the effect it would have on national (and, inferentially, international) politics. It was anticipated that 3,000 stewards would be needed, complete with first aid detachments and kit. The hiring of special trains to convey Provincial supporters to London for the rally and of buses to bring East London supporters to the hall was under consideration.

B. D. E. DONOVAN was stated to be in complete charge of the arrangements, with H. G. McKECHNIE as assistant on the commercial side. Praise was given to N. L. N. FRANCIS-HAWKINS for having secured the hall in the face of considerable difficulty. The person who first mooted the idea and performed some of the essential spadework, an employee of Earl's Court Exhibition, who is a member of the movement, was not mentioned"

91 *Ibid.:*

"At a confidential session of the Senior Officials' Week End School held at Manchester on 3rd/4th June, and attended by 36 persons, DONOVAN stated the leaders were aware that in the event of war the Government would close down the movement's headquarters, arrest the higher officials and attempt to seize the funds. Arrangements were being made whereby one key man would have charge of each area and would be responsible for transmitting messages to all under him. The funds would be scattered, so that the authorities could not obtain possession of them."

92 Minutes of Executive Committee Meeting held on Tuesday July 4th 1939 at 3.30 p.m.:

"Political Activity. It was agreed that an extra man be found if possible to try out a political activity campaign in certain districts."

London & Provincial Anti-Vivisection Society archive, courtesy of the NAVS.

11: WAR

Leaving behind a group of people, many of whom were genuine friends who shared a common struggle and highly commendable cause, in an organisation which had sustained him both materially, in terms of the financial reward, and intellectually, through a pivotal period of the twentieth century, must have been quite a wrench for Wilfred Risdon in July 1939, but, notwithstanding the impending cataclysm that his group had been demonstrably unable to prevent, and the understandably distressing associated internecine bickering and personal denigration that incorporated [and the distinct possibility of legal ramifications, which will be detailed below, when they materialise], he obviously felt that his energies and talents could be put to better use in an alternative environment with, ideally, a more uniform and consistent ethos. He was clearly a man who relished the challenge of a crusade, probably both despite and because of the religious connotations, not for its own sake in this case, or any consequent implications of any righteous hubris, but because he genuinely felt impelled to be a force for positive change in the world, and to work towards it in whatever way possible. Human beings had proved to be, as had been recognised and acknowledged by innumerable sages and commentators down through the ages, an intractable and virtually [inevitably, the pessimist would say] 'un-unifiable' species, dogmatically and infuriatingly so; in which case, so-called 'dumb' animals would seem to offer the alternative Wilfred needed, notwithstanding the humanitarian element of the work.

Whether his move into animal welfare, in the short hiatus before normal life ceased for a period of six years, was a conscious and deliberate choice, or merely a serendipitous opportunity which he gratefully seized without a backward glance, can only be guessed at: in common with many of his friends and colleagues, he was known to have a love of, and respect for animals in general, which appears to have been an integral part of the ethos of British Union; this could have had a solid base in the Christian faith of the majority of members but also, several of them were farmers, and [without wishing to ascribe a purely cynical motive to the observation, given that animals were regarded as business assets in that context] the mixture of traditional class segments within farming meant that they comprised a potentially highly influential group. Wilfred does not appear to have written about animals, if at all, in the specific context of medical research during his time with Mosley; generally speaking, given Mosley's technocratic preferences, and notwithstanding previous observations about the all-pervasive status of propaganda within his organisation [and, undoubtedly, all other political or quasi-political organisations], specific areas of interest to both existing and potential members were handled by acknowledged 'experts' in their respective fields, where a demonstrable grasp of the extent of available detail was called for, rather than just the inevitably somewhat superficial level of knowledge required by the foot-soldiers, the street-corner speakers, which would enable them to deal effectively with the anticipated range of questions from predominantly uninformed listeners.

How much Wilfred's prior knowledge of, and regular association with, one of the members of British Union who eventually came to be trusted by Mosley enough to handle BU funds, influenced his choice of alternate career, can only be speculated about, given the lack of any documentary corroboration. Norah Elam, also known as Mrs. [or occasionally 'Lady'] Dacre-Fox, who was Irish by birth, née Doherty [**1**], was a controversial figure who had been politically very active well before she joined British Union, so she was very useful to Mosley, not least because of her gender, given that Mosley was very keen to demonstrate the gender equality of British Union, with its consequent equality of potential for meritocratic career advancement. In 1912, only 3 years after her marriage to Charles Richard Dacre Fox [**2**], she had joined the Women's Social and Political Union [WSPU], a militant women's suffrage campaign group, which was formed in 1903 by Emmeline Pankhurst and her daughters Christabel, Sylvia and Adela [**3**], and "her remarkable rhetorical skill" was such that she was able "to rise quickly through the WSPU ranks to become, by March 1913, its General Secretary" [**4**]. Despite having been imprisoned several times for her militant campaigning, when war broke out in August 1914, Norah was in total agreement with the leadership of the WSPU, which was unanimous in its support for the Government, causing some dissent in the ranks [**5**]; at the end of the war, after standing unsuccessfully as an Independent in the Surrey constituency of Richmond, with two other women she formed the Women's Guild of Empire, "a right wing league opposed to communism." [**6**]

Although Norah's new romantic partner [having separated from her husband], Edward Descou Dudley Vallance Elam, was married, she moved in with him at his home at Northchapel, near Chichester [West Sussex], changed her name by deed poll to Elam, and had a son by him in 1922: "as a feminist she had chosen not to marry her partner to save her fortune being transferred to her husband" [although he was independently wealthy **7**]. Dudley [as he was generally known], who was six years older than Norah, had first studied to become an Anglican priest, gaining both a BA and MA and, although he worked at several churches, it is not clear if he was ever ordained; later in life he is described as a civil servant at the Ministry of Health; however, they were both moderately active in the local Conservative Party for a while until they became aware of the fledgling British Union of Fascists, joining early in 1934 ["almost at its inception", according to ***Action*** **8**]. Her 'husband' was initially a Sub-Branch Officer for Worthing, but after he retired and they had both moved back to London in 1938, he became an unpaid receptionist at NHQ. Norah shared a platform with her local Area

Administrative Officer, William Joyce [whom she very quickly came to dislike intensely] at Chichester in April 1934, and by August, she had been appointed Women's County Organiser for Sussex & Hampshire [**9**]; in November 1936, she was selected as the prospective parliamentary candidate for Northampton. However, notwithstanding her political views of a 'right wing' nature, the predilection which would have been of most interest to Wilfred, certainly in 1939 [although he must surely have known about it much earlier] was her concern for animal welfare.

According to her Wikipedia profile [known to not always be 100% reliable, of course; see note 11], "Norah Elam claimed to be a founding member of the London and Provincial Anti-Vivisection Society (LPAVS). Documentary evidence of this has not been found, but it is known that she was a member from about the time of its inception circa 1900. In the 1930s she had published under the auspices of the LPAVS two pamphlets: ***The MRC: What it is and How it Works*** and ***The Vitamin Survey***. The pamphlets were widely distributed throughout the UK, including public libraries." [**10**] Another, although closely related source, the Wikipedia page for the National Anti-Vivisection Society, doesn't clarify this confusion a great deal: "An active member of the LPAVS was Norah Elam who had been a member (possibly even founding member) from its very beginnings around 1900."; but it does throw light on how she had inside knowledge of the Medical Research Council [MRC], which enabled her to publish the two condemnatory papers, containing language strangely similar to that in current anti-corporate arguments, in 1934 and '35 [**11**]. There is also a biography, written by a granddaughter and great granddaughter, which obviously concentrates predominantly on family matters, but provides some useful supplementary information. A paucity of knowledge, probably a direct result of the chronological separation from the events concerned, creates an understandable confusion surrounding the three primary animal welfare groups that existed at this time and which are of interest to us here, and conflation thereof, partly due to a possible sharing of premises and facilities by two of them; Dr. Hilda Kean, that assiduous researcher on two subjects which are often associated, for fairly obvious reasons, women's democratic rights and animal rights, wrote: "While anti-vivisectionists were united in their opposition to the experimentation of the physiologists, there was little else in their views to suggest a political homogeneity. ... This plethora of groups gives some idea of the problems associated with campaigning against vivisection, for opposition was not united by religious, political or philosophical agreement." [**12**]

Very briefly: before the 1870s, vivisection was relatively uncommon in Great Britain and was generally regarded as a "continental practice", but "by the 1870s a small number of British physiologists were actively promoting continental experimental methods at home" [**13**], much to the horror of those, predominantly with a Christian outlook, who considered such ideas an anathema. A First Royal Commission on Vivisection was instigated in July 1875, in response to public opposition, but the resulting Cruelty to Animals Act of the following year was regarded by the 'antis' as an unacceptable dispensation for the medical fraternity to continue as before. In the meantime, seeing the Royal Commission as an opportunity to improve decisively on the work of the pre-existing Royal Society for the Prevention of Cruelty to Animals [RSPCA] and campaign vociferously, the Society for the Protection of Animals Liable to Vivisection was founded by the philanthropist and campaigner of Irish birth, Frances Power Cobbe, in December 1875, and "a humanitarian who published many leaflets and articles opposing animal experiments", Toni Doran [**14**], but it was renamed the Victoria Street Society relatively quickly because of its location at 20, Victoria Street, London, its sole purpose being to campaign for a significant restriction of vivisection, in the face of strong opposition from medical practitioners and researchers, who resisted any attempt at, or even suggestion of such restriction.

In response to the farrago of the 1876 Act, and in recognition both of the intransigence of the medical fraternity and the unreliability of politicians, the Society voted in November 1876 to move from a policy of restriction to one of total abolition; in 1884, Cobbe retired as Hon. Sec., but this was reconsidered in February 1898, when the Society, now known as the National Anti-Vivisection Society [effected October 1897], led by Stephen Coleridge [the poet's great grandson] passed a resolution that the Society was prepared to accept "lesser measures" in its quest, rather than insist unequivocally on abolition: Cobbe and some of the older members were incensed, and resigned their membership, and later that year Cobbe founded the British Union for the Abolition of Vivisection, originally known as the British Union, or simply the Union, with its first headquarters in Bristol, the place of its origin. As its name suggests, "[t]he British Union ... was to be a union of anti-vivisection societies. Some existing anti-vivisection societies converted to become branches of the Union, while others remained independent but became part of the federation. New branches were also established." This being the case, it is hardly surprising that it is difficult to establish with absolute clarity which individual societies were truly independent, or were branches of the Union, although "LAVS [see below] had been founded in 1876 on the principle of total abolition and had agreed to be 'in alliance' with the British Union" [**15**].

The London Anti-Vivisection Society [LAVS] was founded on the 10th of June, 1876 at its first address of 180, Brompton Road, London S.W., [**16**], so it actually preceded the Victoria Street Society's vote to campaign for total abolition by a few months; during the 1880s, the Society published pamphlets and articles in newspapers and periodicals of the day [**17**]; in 1907, the Society decided to widen its perceived geographical reach from the seemingly parochial catchment area of only 'London' by the addition of "and Provincial" to its name [although it never acquired any branches], and probably then removed to 22a, Regent Street, before moving to its final address of 76, Victoria Street, London S.W.1 [**18**] and constituted itself as a non-charitable unincorporated society, the significance of which will be explained later [**19**]. This move seems slightly odd, given that the NAVS was initially located at number 20, Victoria Street: it is possible that both these organisations maintained separate premises while so closely situated, but [to jump forward somewhat] in 1957 the LPAVS was wound up and became part of the NAVS [**20**] which, by then, was headquartered at a different address on the same street, number 92, so it would seem logical to suppose that they might have shared some office facilities somewhat earlier? There is some confusion as to the connection, if any, between the LPAVS, BUAV and British Union which the foregoing [note 15] should help to clarify: there might have been some overlap and informal sharing of information, and there certainly were some high-level supporters and/or members of the BUAV in the ranks of British Union.

As stated at the end of the previous chapter, in July 1939, Wilfred started work for the London & Provincial Anti-Vivisection Society at 76, Victoria Street, initially at the invitation of, and under the tutelage of Norah Elam, who also edited the Society's publication ***The Anti-Vivisection Journal***, but she was by no means 'in charge', so the reference to an "extra man … to try out a political activity campaign in certain districts" in the Society's official records might have been a good way for Wilfred to slip in 'under the radar', given his very recent associations and the LPAVS Executive Committee's politically mixed membership; although the NAVS archive contains some biographical information about LPAVS Committee members, Wilfred himself is a very good [and, one would also hope, reliable] independent source of information, to be found in his 1940 18B Appeal Hearing testimony [**Appendix D**]. Wilfred tells us that, although Norah Elam was the General Secretary, and he agrees when asked: "She was very active for the Committee?", she did not "run" the LPAVS; he points out that "the Committee was a very mixed committee … Some of them, people like Dr. Allinson, opposed the British Union very vigorously." Although probably very easily dismissed as an eccentric, the good Dr. Allinson was very much an activist in his own way [**21**], and he & Wilfred had the RAMC in common, although it is not known if their service paths crossed. However, this does give some indication of the diplomacy that Wilfred will have been required to exercise when he was in a more organisational rôle, but as yet, he was ostensibly 'only' employed in a technical capacity [although see note 22, for details of another aspect of his work at the LPAVS, tutoring Alwyn Armstrong], using his patently obvious analytical skills: "They wanted to get a detailed analysis of what support there was for their cause amongst the public, and I organised a canvass for them, which is more along the lines of a political canvass, and a petition formed for people to sign saying they wanted to get Vivisection abolished. It was a technical job, an organiser's job, not so much propaganda as organising an analysis of the support available for the Movement."

It is interesting that Wilfred should refer to propaganda, in view of his work with Armstrong, although as with many other statements in his 18B testimony, there is a certain ambiguity of meaning, in the view of this author: was he implying that propaganda was not a regular element of the operation of the LPAVS, notwithstanding the plethora of interpretations of the term; or was he trying to convey the impression that, contrary to his previous occupation in a now-discredited organisation with its ever-present propaganda element, he had commenced in a position in which his activity was entirely above board and transparent? The former meaning, although perhaps slightly tendentious as an interpretation, would be unquestionably disingenuous, [so it is to be hoped, therefore, that it is incorrect] because the LPAVS did, in fact, have a Propaganda Officer. Without wanting to be repetitious, this is not so difficult to accept, because it must have been possible to use the term, even at a time of such disconcerting international tension, without the spectre of the virtually inescapable, invariably negative, connotation it has today. The Head of Propaganda [which implies that there might have been subordinates?] was Alwyn Armstrong, a British Union member since 1934, Propaganda Organiser for South-East London, who joined the LPAVS in 1936 and lectured for them, and wrote pamphlets & news-sheets; he was even planning to put up candidates in elections on an anti-vivisection platform, something of a stunt perhaps, but this was thwarted by the war: without wishing to suggest that Armstrong couldn't have achieved this without Wilfred's help, his knowledge and expertise in this field would have proved invaluable. Armstrong married a 24-year old typist at the LPAVS in October 1938, and Sylvia Armstrong also joined British Union, albeit only temporarily, which undoubtedly ensured her internment at the same time as her husband, and even though she was not the author, it almost resulted in a criminal prosecution for producing [at the behest of Norah Elam] a leaflet satirising Winston Churchill. It is clear from their combined Home Office file [although each had individual documents assigned to them] that Wilfred would not have had any difficulty working very closely with Alwyn before his arrest: he was described by Special Branch as "a well educated, studious type of person, and there is no doubt that in view of the position he held and his proposed promotion to District Inspector, that he was a valued member of the B.U.F."; and both of the Armstrongs appear to have become as anti-fascist as Wilfred professed to be, once the war had begun, which was emphasised in their 18B Advisory Committee Appeal Hearings [**22**].

Another member of the Committee who was also a member of British Union, albeit a clandestine one, for reasons explained below, was Commandant Mary Allen; according to Robert Edwards: "Mary Allen was known mostly for her part in the creation of a women's police force in Britain and then to champion the cause of women police officers, campaigning for their greater role in police work. Their virtual equality with male police officers today is a direct result of the earlier efforts of this great woman. It is said that the reason for her secret membership of Mosley's British Union of Fascists was to avoid jeopardising her pioneering work on behalf of women police officers. … As a member of the Council of the London and Provincial Anti-Vivisection Society (LPAVS), Mary understood perfectly that experiments on animals were not just cruel but pointless because the results of these experiments were both unreliable and often detrimental to the humans that were supposed to benefit from them. The breeding of certain species purely for the purpose of inflicting terrible pain in vivisection was something that shocked Mary Allen and her enthusiasm for the anti-vivisection cause was no less than her support for Sir Oswald Mosley and his fight for a greater and better Britain." [**23**] This might appear to give some credence to the impression reported by one Special Branch agent that Mrs. Elam "only employs rabid fascists there" [see note 22, and note 52 for a possible source for this assertion], but, for a start, committee members were not employees, and Dr. Kean is convinced that this is a rather lazy assumption, because it was a fact that many Fascists were also genuinely concerned for the welfare of animals, but that while they were employed [whether gainfully or voluntarily] in the business of animal welfare, Fascism was a secondary consideration; it was also well known that members of the security services could be 'creative' in their reporting, to enable them to justify their continued employment, as well as facilitating wider strategic considerations.

Wilfred's prowess as an organiser was immediately put to good use and the success of his canvassing activities was recognised by the Committee; whatever his feelings towards British Union generally and Mosley specifically, he was surrounded by like-minded people, so he must have felt comfortable, and the more focused attitude of his co-workers, and the calmer atmosphere that would have engendered, must have helped to compensate for any sense of failure he might have felt after at least fifteen years working as a political organiser and, in material terms, a reduction in salary [**24**]. Although the exact timing is not clear from his 18B Appeal Hearing testimony [**Appendix D**], he did request and receive a reference concerning his work for British Union from Mosley, and it is possibly this which prompted Mosley to write to Wilfred "through the Director General asking me to go and see him, which I did. … I went to see him and he told me then they were preparing to engage in by-elections, and he asked me would I take a re-appointment on the staff to conduct those by-elections, but that offer I declined. Although I was not earning big money by the work, I was at least having peace of mind, and I did not want to get back again." However, he had only just 'got his feet under the table', as it were, when everything changed irrevocably: only two months into his new post, the war that British Union had tried so hard to convince the British people could be prevented, began when the Government's patience passed its limit.

According to Wilfred's stepson, Brian: "When the War ... started, Bill was one of the first to volunteer, but he was turned down." [**25**] This would certainly be in character, but probably impossible to corroborate; it is also somewhat contradicted by Wilfred's own words, again from that treasure-trove of personal recollections, his 18B Appeal Hearing testimony [**Appendix D**], when he responds to the hypothetical question of what he would propose to do if he were released, by saying: "As a matter of fact, my wife, who is a pacifist, was rather concerned because at the time of the invasion of Norway and Denmark I had wanted to go and enlist as a volunteer, but she did not like the idea. She is the sort of wife who would have let me have my way, but while I was discussing this point with her and trying to get an understanding this other affair came up." It must be presumed that, by "this other affair", he means his arrest, so it seems hardly likely that he would have considered enlisting if he had already been previously turned down. Either way, he was obviously ready & willing to do what he considered his patriotic duty, but this avenue was not to be open to him. The invasion of Norway and Denmark was in early April 1940, so that begs the question of why he didn't try to volunteer in September 1939, as believed by his stepson: the likeliest answer is that he was very well aware of the low regard in which British Fascists were held at that time, and any hint of his previous occupation would have immediately disqualified him [as well as leaving him vulnerable to the inevitable obloquy], whereas eight months later, with a well established alternative employment, he would have stood a much better chance, even though he seems to have been nearly two months in the process of trying to win Nellie round to his point of view!

The first months of the war were referred to as the 'phoney war', so called because not much happened 'on the home front', but it was not exactly 'business as usual' [the term originated in America as early as September 1939, so it was initially more a comment on its causes than a description of its lack of action]; many changes to normal everyday life were either introduced by the government, or occurred as a response to the prevailing circumstances, which was to be expected, but was predominantly unwelcome nonetheless: the pound dropped dramatically in value [**26**] and, not unsurprisingly, food prices very quickly rose [**27**]; overt press censorship [albeit "voluntary"] was imposed [**28**]; large public gatherings were banned "on the grounds of air raid danger if large crowds assemble" [**29**]; and petrol rationing was introduced almost immediately, to name but a few: this last measure might not have affected Wilfred unduly, as it is highly likely that he will have commuted into work on the tube. One social repercussion that tends to be overlooked is how children's education suffered, almost from the very beginning of the war; in what seems like something of an overreaction [and an abandonment of hope in any successful conclusion to ongoing negotiations; or a predetermined acceptance of the necessity of war as the only 'beneficial' course of action, depending upon one's viewpoint] the plans for evacuation of the capital were activated on September 1st, before the war had actually started, and the plan which dealt specifically with the evacuation of children was called *Operation Pied Piper*.

Although evacuation was not compulsory, 1.9 million children were evacuated from the six cities designated as being vulnerable to German bombing, and there were 1,589 assembly points in London alone [**30**]. London schools were closed on the expectation of a lack of pupils, but in addition to the patchy takeup of the scheme, a significant number of children also returned fairly quickly, for a variety of reasons, which meant that there were large numbers of children at a loose end in the capital, which did not bode well [**31**]; unfortunately, the effect this had on Brian Risdon, the younger of Wilfred's two stepchildren, who would have been 14 years of age in 1939, if their local school was among those which closed, is unknown. At this time, Wilfred and his family were living in Ruislip Manor, north-west London, a semi-rural area [but with a tube connection to town, as mentioned above], so some sort of home schooling might have been a possibility [**32**], although this might not have fallen to Nellie, whether she felt able or not, given that she very probably worked full-time; and it would have been a pretty safe area for outdoor recreation: it is highly unlikely that Wilfred would have seen taking one or both of his stepchildren to work with him on any sort of regular basis as a practical option, other than perhaps the occasional, probably weekend day, to give them a chance to 'help out'.

The first Christmas of the war would have been relatively normal, although despite perhaps seeing the spending of money as a way of alleviating the psychological gloom, many people would very probably have been reticent to overspend, preferring to hang on to as much money as possible as a hedge against an uncertain future, and some sort of reservoir which could be tapped if the morally dubious 'black market' needed to be taken advantage of; also, the gloom was palpable, because blackout regulations had been imposed with almost undue haste, at sunset on September the first, again before the war had actually commenced [**33**]. These regulations also applied to motor vehicles of course, so what with that and the petrol rationing, Wilfred was probably in no particular hurry to use a car, assuming he possessed one, although it is more than likely, unless it was an absolute necessity. Any lightening of the national mood would have been very quickly dispelled after Christmas, with the imposition of food rationing on January 8th, 1940; this did not apply right 'across the board' [**34**], but it was enough to bring home the reality of the situation, if this was not already the case, before the first bomb had dropped [**35**]. Air raid precautions, usually known by the acronym ARP, were also very important in this initial 'phoney war' period, despite the relative calm, albeit unsettling in its portent. The system was, in fact, already very well established, even if its application could be inconsistent and was, inevitably, treated as a marketing opportunity by enterprising businesses [**36**].

ARP, with an administrative Committee, had been set up in 1924, well after the end of the previous war, although directly in response to it, albeit somewhat delayed, and with an [undoubtedly jaundiced] eye towards the next conflict which many felt was inevitable [**37**]; for all that Wilfred might have felt he could have helped, if a traditional service rôle was to be denied to him, his previous career would undoubtedly have cast him in the rôle of a potential 'fifth columnist' here as well, although as the war ground on, the authorities might have been forced to reconsider their doubts as a matter of necessity. The whole theme of the perceived 'fifth column' threat was, inevitably, subject extensively to the whims & vagaries of official policy, as much as it was to such mob-mentality and rabble-rousing as might have been induced by gutter-press journalism [although there were some real concerns for the Security Service, as will be detailed below]. As soon as war had been declared, any Germans or Austrians, including ostensible refugees from Hitler's *régime*, were immediately considered 'enemy aliens', all those over 16 were called before tribunals, and nearly 600 were immediately interned [**38**]; more worrying than this, however, for Wilfred, was the potential for arrest of anyone who was considered a threat to national security, and as previously stated, he cannot have been so naïve as to believe that his leaving British Union so close to the commencement of hostilities [of which he could not be aware prior to the event, of course] would provide him with immunity.

Wilfred must, in recognition of the necessity for caution and circumspection in public, have discouraged any discussion of a contentious nature in his office; notwithstanding his ostensibly 'lowly' status within his new employer's organisation, he had, according to his own testimony [**Appendix D**] "rebuked the girls in the office for getting into political argument about the war", which on the surface might seem somewhat high-handed, but realistically, he was no mere office clerk: his former colleagues would have been only too well aware of his previous status, and would have treated him with the appropriate respect. Despite that, his worries about a threat to his liberty from the authorities cannot have been other than exacerbated by the news which, if not common knowledge from the mainstream press media of the day, would undoubtedly have filtered through to him via the inevitable office gossip, or even direct contact with current Fascists and/or peace campaigners, that a British Union member and prospective parliamentary candidate was arrested before the war had 'officially' begun, on September 1st, under the Emergency Powers (Defence) Order in Council, amending the Defence Regulations, 1939, Section 18B, and held in detention without trial for nearly two months: Mosley himself justifiably fulminated about the case in a full-page article in ***Action***, deploring the un-British suspension of due process, under the headline of "I Expose and Accuse" [**39**]. This appears to have been part of a pattern, if not an overt policy, of intimidating observation and harassment by the security services, on behalf of the Government, of paid-up British Union members; the former no doubt were convinced that this was entirely justified. In the meantime, Wilfred had to try and concentrate on his task in hand to the best of his abilities; although Britain was traditionally considered, justifiably or not, a nation of animal lovers, the welfare of animals that were used in experiments which were not open to public scrutiny cannot have been uppermost in the minds of the majority of Britons as the significance of the war began to sink in, making Wilfred's task all the harder; domestic pets were a different matter, however. In times of peace, pets were seen to have many advantages, but in times of war, they would no doubt be seen by many as a liability. Food would have been one of the immediate problems, given that special pet food was still relatively uncommon, so in the towns & cities, rationing would have drastically reduced the supply of food scraps with which cats and dogs could be fed [although, according to Dr. Kean, the contemporary version of food for pets was not rationed **40**]; also, although most people's understandably emotional bond with their pets would have convinced them to keep their animals as long as practicably possible, it could easily be envisaged, in advance of the actual occurrence, how problematic it would be having large numbers of pets, predominantly cats & dogs, running around loose and very likely quickly turning feral, as a result of German bombing.

Unfortunately, this was an area in which LPAVS had very little direct influence and, however strong the aforementioned emotional bond might have been, many people could be distressingly cavalier when facing up to the practicality of the situation, albeit as yet only anticipated, so in only four days in September 1939, over 400,000 cats and dogs were killed in London alone, a level of destruction which is almost impossible to comprehend; in fairness, it should be pointed out that this was not the result of a Government edict - it was a unilateral decision by individual owners [**41**], although it seems hard to conceive how such a widespread wave of destruction can have been unleashed without some common trigger, such as a newspaper article, or a radio feature. This circumstance must have had a profound effect upon the participants of the LPAVS, not least upon Wilfred himself, and his practical response to it will be described later. His concern about possible apprehension by the authorities because of his previous, and still very recent, association with an organisation so readily connected in the easily-influenced public mind with the allegedly brutal dictatorships in Germany and, albeit to a lesser extent, Italy, cannot have been assuaged when high profile LPAVS Committee member Mary Allen, now Commandant, Women's Auxiliary Service [**42**], published an article in ***Action*** in early November 1939, entitled "A Lead for Peace", in which, after making it abundantly clear that "though I am in no way connected with your movement" she states that "the stand which you have taken with regard to the war has been one with which I heartily agree." [**43**] The credibility of that ostensive lack of a connection was stretched more than somewhat when ***Action*** announced that she, "who has had considerable experience in dealing with the vice racket", had "agreed to write a series of articles ... on the amazing development of this social evil of recent years under the influence of refugees from the Continent." [**44**] She was writing in her capacity as Commandant ["head"] of the WAS and, interestingly, her address was given as 68, Victoria Street, London S.W.1, which was not exactly the same as that of the LPAVS (76), but so close for a suggestion that both organisations shared facilities to be not inconceivable. A later article was credited to Mary S. Allen, O.B.E. [**45**] This was around the time that the 'fifth column' hysteria was being widely promulgated in the national press and although, as described above, it had first been directed towards refugees and possibly 'suspect aliens', it was an entirely logical progression that it should also include 'home-grown' Fascists and 'Nazi sympathisers' [**46**], so Wilfred must not have been under any illusions that they would also very soon be targeted.

Mosley's desire to prevent war was totally genuine [notwithstanding the obvious consequent loss of earnings for him and British Union with the failure of the German radio project], and he was able to campaign openly through the medium of British Union, but there was also collaboration between disparate personalities who shared Mosley's goal, albeit for a variety of reasons, and this collaboration had to be conducted in secret, because of the obvious national security implications. The informal group encompassed anti-war campaigners like Mosley, but also known 'anti-Semites' and fervent pro-Nazis and, even though Wilfred would not have been in the Victoria Street offices all the time, it is nevertheless hard to believe that he was totally unaware, especially when leading lights of the LPAVS such as Norah Elam and Mary Allen, and members such as Captain Sir George Drummond [**47**], were involved, and the LPAVS offices were used for some of the secret meetings, which understandably gave rise to the suspicions of the Security Service that the LPAVS was a 'front' for subversive activities [**48**]: it is almost comical to envisage, even if the premises had a secluded entrance, such well known public figures coming and going in a clandestine manner, perhaps even in disguise! Unfortunately, it is not now possible to come to a realistic visualisation of this scenario, because large swathes of that side of Victoria Street have recently undergone large-scale redevelopment.

There were at least two such meetings before the end of 1939, although it is not clear if these were at the LPAVS offices [**49**], and it was undoubtedly as a consequence of these that Norah Elam's London home address and the LPAVS offices were raided by the police on December 18th, either under the instructions of the Security Service, or conducted by actual Security Service officers. Assuming that he was working on that day, there is no suggestion or indication that Wilfred was in any way implicated or included in the police investigations, which produced "papers relating to Mosley's contingency plans" [**50**], including a list of eight names that effectively represented a council to choose Mosley's successor in the event of his death [**51**], and a letter from Mosley, apparently granting Norah permission to manage funds on British Union's behalf [**52**]. It is quite possible that these details might not have been broadcast in the offices at the time, although Wilfred would have been only too well aware of their import. To seasoned political campaigners like Norah and Wilfred, this incident might not have caused them too much concern, but they probably took the pragmatic view that this was not the end of the matter, and this was vindicated just over a month later, when Norah was arrested on January the 23rd. During her interrogation [of unknown duration] she was questioned about the British Union money and the suspected Italian connection and, as well as the theory that she was using the LPAVS as a "front", the implication, if it was not stated explicitly, was very much that: "Along with her dubious marital status and her past history of militancy, she began to fit a criminal bill." [**53**] The next development illustrated, in retrospect, the capricious nature of such circumstances: very soon after Norah explained her plight to Mosley in person, Special Branch arrived to speak to him about a more serious matter, but Mosley immediately assumed that the British Union finances were the pretext, so he obligingly furnished the officers with more information than they had bargained for! [**54**] Actually, MI5 wanted to question Mosley about Peter Whinfield, "a suspected German spy. The raid on Norah's flat and offices had in fact been in connection with Whinfield and the finds they made about BUF finances were opportunistic." Whinfield had had contact in Austria, during the *Anschluß* in 1938, with "Peter and Lisa Kruger, known spies. Mosley had also met Peter Kruger at the Elam's [sic] flat"; MI5's suspicion had been aroused by Norah posting letters to Peter Kruger on behalf of his mother. [**55**]

At one of the secret meetings referred to above, on February the 7th 1940, that was "convened by Mosley", he had ensured that "[t]he chief decision taken … was to fight Silvertown and Leeds North-East by-elections." This rather begs the question of why a secret meeting was required for this presumably uncontroversial decision, but the answer must surely lie in the identity of the participants [**56**]; also, there could have been other matters of a more sensitive nature discussed. In addition, it vindicates Wilfred's decision to reject the offer from Mosley, notwithstanding the apparent hiatus of around six months from when Wilfred left British Union [so perhaps Mosley's offer did not actually follow hard on the heels of Wilfred's request for a reference?], in view of the personalities who would have been associated with it, even if only indirectly: it would not be unreasonable to infer from this that Wilfred might have had advance or 'inside' knowledge of the offer? Around this time, in recognition of the worsening political and military picture, which appeared to herald the end of the period of relative calm, the so-called 'phoney war', during which people of many different persuasions nevertheless hoped for a peaceful outcome, prompting the aforementioned meetings, the Government decided to assess the state of public confidence in its prosecution of the war.

It was very much to be expected that the Government would create a Ministry of Information [MOI] at the beginning of the war, and it was based at the Senate Building at the University of London. The first two ministers had very short incumbencies [**57**]; Lord Hugh Macmillan was there from the outbreak of the war until January the 5th 1940; his successor, Sir John Reith, in a sense ideally qualified, only lasted a similarly short length of time, until the change of prime minister, when Churchill replaced him on the 12th of May with "his friend and political ally Duff Cooper" [**58**]. The first quasi-official assessment of the 'phoney war' period, called ***War Begins at Home***, was published in March 1940 by Mass Observation [MO], and its unequivocal message was that [surprise, surprise!]: "A gulf of mutual incomprehension separated the politicians and the civil servants in Whitehall from the broad mass of the British people." [**59**] Apparently, prior to this there was "much argument within the MOI [before] it was decided to establish a Home Intelligence department" and, although it might have raised a few eyebrows to learn that the Director, Mary Adams, wife of Conservative MP Vyvyan Adams, was "a fervent atheist and advocate of humanism", it would not, consequently, have been unduly surprising that she was also "a socialist, a romantic communist", which must have made for some interesting discussions at home! [**60**] Taking a technocratic approach [almost 'fascist'?], given that she was an admirer of MO, she commissioned "the social anthropologist Tom Harrisson ... who was now in sole charge of the organisation ... to undertake studies of morale for her department. ... The initial plan was for Home Intelligence to compile a monthly report on the state of morale, but following the collapse of Norway, Belgium and Holland, and the German invasion of France, there was an immediate demand within the MOI for day-to-day information about the state of public opinion. Adams's department was thus instructed 'to report daily on people's reactions throughout the country, with special reference to morale, rumours, and the reception of ministerial broadcasts and pronouncements'." [**61**]

The reports, which were more comprehensive for the London region, as a result of the "special arrangements [which] were put in place", commenced on the 18th of May, 1940, and although "Home Intelligence reports were often impressionistic and never more so than at this early stage, ... The first of the daily Home Intelligence reports reflected the shock and confusion caused by a fast-moving sequence of military disasters." [**62**] This was very quickly followed by the 'fifth column' hysteria, which also encompassed conscientious objectors [**63**], so the Government decided to act, although Thurlow believes that, prior to this, with reference to the secret meetings, Defence Regulation 18B was amended on the 23rd of November 1939 as "a result of back bench pressure", and that "it is clear that the Security Service had the home front well under control and that growing dissatisfaction with the infringement of civil liberties during the phoney war period was justified." [**64**] Be that as it may, the new Regulation stipulated, in concise terms "that the authorities must have reasonable cause to believe the hostile origins or association of individuals or that internees must have been recently concerned in actions which had compromised national security" [**65**], but the full text is rather more comprehensive than this [**66**]. Churchill wanted "a very large round-up of enemy aliens and suspect persons in Britain" [he is reputed to have said "Collar the lot!"], but Home Secretary, Sir John Anderson, twice argued against this: he "pointed out to the Cabinet that the police would be overtaxed just processing the aliens, and as there had been no evidence of fifth column activities by either fascists or communists he would not proceed to move against either of these groups at present." [**67**]

Anderson's hand was forced by the Tyler Kent affair and, again, the secret meetings did play a part in the overwhelming weight of evidence, but the allegedly unpatriotic or counterproductive clandestine machination of the anti-war faction had to be the public justification for the suspension of the right of individuals to the protection of the ancient law of *habeas corpus* [although it was not an absolute guarantee of liberty **68**]; what the country was not told was that Chamberlain's Government could have collapsed if the Kent revelations had been made public, which was quite possible. It was believed by the Government's Code and Cipher School's intercept system that the German ambassador in Rome, Hans Mackensen, had been looking at Churchill's correspondence with Roosevelt, of which the War Cabinet was unaware; although Roosevelt was supporting American isolationism in public, behind the scenes he was working to increase aid to the beleaguered British. The connection with Rome was a link between a cipher clerk at the American Embassy in London, Tyler Kent, and the Italian Embassy, and MI5 agents in Maule Ramsay's Right Club discovered that Kent and a Right Club member, Anna Wolkoff, "had shown crucial intercepted documents between 'Naval Person' (Churchill) and President Roosevelt to Maule Ramsay": all it needed was for Kent to publish what he knew in an American pro-interventionist publication, or Ramsay to ask a question in the House of Commons, and it would be 'game over'. The Cabinet enacted the Emergency Powers for three reasons: "Tyler Kent was caught red-handed on 20 May 1940, not only with a girl friend in bed but also with copies of 1,500 secret documents, including the Roosevelt-Churchill correspondence, and the 'red book', the list of members of the Right Club";

according to "supposedly reliable information ... Maule Ramsay and Mosley were 'in relations'"; and "that attempts were being made to unify fascist, anti-Semitic and peace groups" [**69**].

The Defence Regulations, which had existed, and been constantly revised, in draft form throughout the inter-war period, were implemented with the passing of the Emergency Powers (Defence) Act on the 24th of August, 1939, when Parliament had been recalled from its summer recess because of the tensions over Poland; it had been decided early in 1939 that, since a war might break out without warning or time to pass an Act of Parliament to bring in emergency regulations, the Regulations should be split into two codes. Code A would be needed immediately if war broke out and could be passed in peacetime, while Code B, that contained the more severe restrictions on civil liberties, would be brought in later. Code A was simply numbered consecutively, so as not to alert the public to the existence of Code B; Defence Regulation 18 concerned restrictions on movement of aircraft. It was originally intended that Code B would be imposed by an Order in Council [**70**], with retrospective indemnity being granted by an Act of Parliament should anyone dispute the actions of the authorities. Code A was brought into effect first, in August, and Code B followed on 1st September [see note 38]. Foreigners (enemy aliens) were detained using powers under the Royal Prerogative while 18B was used mainly for British nationals [**71**]. Before widespread internment of alleged Nazi sympathisers could begin, however, Regulation 18B required an amendment, 1A, and this was secured on the evening of May the 22nd, 1940 [**72**].

Mosley was later very much of the opinion that, in addition to the Tyler Kent affair, the subterfuge surrounding it and the potential repercussions therefrom, the wholesale arrests under Regulation 18B (1A) were a direct result of an ultimatum from "some Labour leaders [who] had made the arrest and imprisonment of Mosley a condition of their entering the Government." [**73**] Thurlow corroborates this, and also gives some insight into the internal tensions in the Security Services, before "the triumph of the hawks" [**74**]. Considering the expedition with which the arrests in the first 'wave' were carried out, the organisation of manpower in the police force, both Special Branch and ordinary officers, must have been well worked out in advance, and at least one civil service 'mandarin' might have had to 'burn the midnight oil' to prepare the relevant paperwork, so that there could be no accusation of flouting of correct procedures, even with the aid of retrospective legislation: the Under Secretary of State for the Home Department, Sir Alexander Maxwell, signed Wilfred's Order for Detention at some time on the same day that Regulation 18B was amended, the 22nd of May. Wilfred would, no doubt, have had plenty of reason to dispute the legitimacy of his inclusion in the first wave of arrests, along with Sir Oswald Mosley and the other 'dangerous' Fascists, and although they were to be given the opportunity to appeal against their detention in due course, initially, they had to accept, however unwillingly, that they were now part of a process whose progress could not be interrupted.

It is difficult to be precise about the exact number of arrests on the first day, but around 80 men & women were detained on Thursday, May the 23rd; Wilfred might not have been amused to be included in the list printed in ***Action*** the following week, with no indication as to who were not actually current members of British Union [**75**]. Mosley maintains that he was arrested in the afternoon of the 23rd [**76**], although another source puts it "in the early morning of 23 May" [**77**]; Mosley's own version seems to be corroborated by the events of Wilfred's own arrest. Although there is no indication that he was on the receiving end of any 'persuasion', from either the police or the military, it would appear that the Government was taking no chances: "Since the fascists were thought dangerous there was a show of military force; C. F. ('Charlie') Watts, one of those detained, saw four tanks in Albemarle Street where he worked." [**78**] Albemarle Street is approximately one mile north, 'as the crow flies', from Victoria Street, so it is more than possible that Wilfred will have seen tanks on the move [not unusual in wartime, but generally not on the streets], even if they were not intended to intimidate him and his colleagues. For some odd reason, the police officers who were detailed to arrest him went first ["proceeded", in archetypal 'police-ese'] to British Union national headquarters, Sanctuary Buildings, S.W.1. There could be a variety of reasons for this: Special Branch was definitely aware, just under a year previously, that Wilfred was no longer a paid official, given that he was working in a voluntary capacity; however, it was obviously assumed, erroneously, that he was still involved with the organisation on a day-to-day basis, which does beg the question of whether he somehow managed to avoid observation at the LPAVS offices during the period of the secret meetings or, if he was observed, that perhaps his presence was not considered significant by the officer/s concerned?

There is another possibility: it transpired from the transcript of the arresting officer, Inspector Charles Allen [Special Branch, New Scotland Yard], that when Wilfred commenced his employment with the LPAVS, "[a] temporary office was obtained in the locality which the Society intends to canvass for signatures to petitions etc., and at the present time a room is rented at 279 Goldhawk Road, W.", which is somewhat ambiguous, giving rise to the inference that the Goldhawk Road office was not the first one? This address is roughly four miles from Victoria Street, but even allowing for a telephone connection [which was not guaranteed if it was only a temporary arrangement], it is not stretching credibility unduly to suppose that Wilfred will have called in to the Victoria Street 'head office' from time to time; he could also have been given advance warning of the secret meetings however, and advised not to visit at these times. This information about the address is given at the end of Inspector Allen's report, so it is more than likely that it was the result of some sort of questioning on the day, clearly without the benefit of legal representation. Wilfred's case cannot have been enhanced greatly by the revelation that the address was "the residence of Mrs Allport, age about 60, a friend of Mrs Elam and a member of the B.U." [**79**] Perhaps it was simply the easiest option to look for Wilfred first at BU NHQ, as officers were going there anyway; it must surely have been unlikely that they were expecting violent resistance from Wilfred, but perhaps they were under orders to take no chances. Because of the conciseness of the detail, notwithstanding the police-speak, it is worth transcribing the report in full:

> "In company with other officers I proceeded to Sanctuary Buildings, S.W.1, (headquarters of the British Union) with a view to arresting Wilfred RISDON (not RISDEN) under Regulation 18B of the Defence (General) Regulations, 1939. He was not there and Francis-Hawkins, director-general of the organisation, stated that Risdon was no longer an official and had left the movement about a year ago. In company with P.S. Ewing I proceeded to Risdon's address, 70 Torrington Road, Ruislip Manor. He was not there and I was informed by his wife that he was employed by the London Provincial Anti-Vivisection [Scy] 76 Victoria Street, S.W., as a canvasser in the Hammersmith district where he had an office.
>
> Risdon was arrested at 3.0.p.m., today when he was about to officiate at the Annual General meeting of the Anti-Vivisection Society, at 76 Victoria Street, S.W. He was served with a copy of the Detention Order, informed that he would be given an opportunity of making any representations he wished to the Secretary of State and that he had a right to make objections to an advisory committee against his detention. He replied that he had ceased to be an official of the British Union since June, 1939, had not paid any subscriptions or dues since that date and maintained [?] he was not a member. He admitted, however, that he had not officially resigned.
>
> At 6.0.p.,[sic] today Risdon was handed over to the Governor of Brixton Prison together with a copy of the Order, his National Registration Card, and gas mask. On his person was found a note book containing a number of addresses also visiting cards (submitted) which he said referred to his friends, the majority [?] having now left the British Union.
>
> A search of his house carried out in accordance with Chief Constable's authority granted under the [?] Defence Regulations 88a(2) revealed a large quantity of British Union documents and propaganda. Practically all this matter was about a year old and contained nothing of importance and of little interest at the present time. The following documents were taken possession of and herewith submitted:
>
> (1) British Union warrant card dated 26th July 1939 wherein he is described as Chief Agent and Propaganda Administrator. He stated that he has never been asked to return the card.
>
> (2) Copies of correspondence between R.A. Plathen former member of the British Union, and Sir. O. Mosley concerning the former's reasons for resign- [sic] from the movement.
>
> (3) A letter from the British Union dated 25/1/40, asking Risdon to attend the B.U., headquarters with a view to seeing the "Leader". Risdon states that he was invited by Sir O. Mosley to again take up Parliamentary election work, but he refused to do so.
>
> (4) A pamphlet by Risdon entitled "Strike Action or Power Action". This he states was written by him about three years ago.

(5) Three sketch maps by Risdon of the area in which he lives. In one Northolt Aerodrome is clearly marked. The maps, he states, were used for canvassing new B.U. members.

(6) An undated letter, postmarked Bexley Heath, 10th January, 1940, addressed to Mrs Lloyd, 25 Linden Avenue, Ruislip manor, from her son Gunner J. Lloyd, serving with the 9/13 Bty, Royal Artillery, B.E.F. The letter was brought from France to this country by Lloyd's friend and posted here. Lloyd speaks bitterly of conditions in France, remarks that things there are definitely Fascist, and alleges that the men would return home if there was a man strong enough to lead them. Risdon states that the letter was given to him by Mrs. Lloyd to read some months ago. He forgot to return it, and they are not now on very good terms because she is a member of the B.U., and he has left it.

(7) In a draw [sic] of his bureau was found a box containing 25 rounds of 6.35m.m., pistol ammunition. When Risdon was asked if he had a firearm certificate, he replied "No, the ammunition is mine, but I have'nt [sic] a firearm". I cautioned him, and he made the follow- [sic] statement, "I found the ammunition together with an automatic pistol and a small plated revolver at the headquarters of the British Union in Preston when I took over that area in 1936. I took the lot to the B.U. office at Northumberland Street, Salford, intending to get them destroyed. I forgot to do so and shortly afterwards the office was closed down. Somebody must have taken the weapons away as I could not find them and never heard of them again. The ammunition got packed in with my things and has been overlooked". Risdon was informed that the matter would be reported for further consideration. I am retaining the ammunition pending instructions as to its disposal, but respectfully suggest that it be handed to Mr. Coleman, ?B.1. (Firearms).

When Risdon left the British Union Mrs. Elam, secretary of the London Provincial Anti-Vivisection Society, found him employment as canvasser to the Society. A temporary office was obtained in the locality which the Society intends to canvass for signatures to petitions etc., and at the present time a room is rented at 279 Goldhawk Road, W, the residence of Mrs Allport, age about 60, a friend of Mrs Elam and a member of the B.U. Risdon is in charge of this office and at his invitation it was searched but nothing of interest was found.

The original Detention Order together with Chief Constable's search warrant, duly endorsed, is submitted herewith."

As is often the case, Wilfred's family name had been incorrectly spelled 'Risden' at an early stage of the operation, understandable enough if the name is communicated verbally; it was probably corrected by Francis-Hawkins, when shown a list of intended victims. At his "address", the Special Branch officers were lucky to find Nellie at home; it is unknown whether she was in remunerative employment at this time, but the fact that she was at home around lunchtime on a Thursday would not automatically indicate that she wasn't; although she would, no doubt, have been primed that a visit from the authorities was on the cards, the arrival of two men who would have been easily identifiable as police officers, plain clothes or not, must have been perturbing for Nellie, especially if the children were at home, and any neighbours happened to be watching, as they inevitably do, when one doesn't want them to! She might already have had some experience of dealing with police officers from her involvement with British Union, such as it was [although very little is known], but Wilfred is most likely to have advised her to be courteous and helpful, to minimise the possibility of aggression on the part of the police; consequently, she told the officers that Wilfred was at work, although the police report gives the impression that Nellie told them Wilfred would be at his Hammersmith office, and yet they went straight to Victoria Street [unless the report conveniently omitted that they had gone to Goldhawk Road first].

Once again, Wilfred's arrest cannot have been totally unexpected but, whether by accident or by design, the police could not have come at a more embarrassing time, "when he was about to officiate at the Annual General meeting of the Anti-Vivisection Society" [**80**], given that at least one member of the Committee, Dr. Allinson, "opposed the British Union very vigorously" [**Appendix D**]. This does raise one minor inconsistency though: officiating "at the Annual General meeting of the Anti-Vivisection Society" would not be something normally associated with, or entrusted to a mere canvasser, so it seems more than likely that his initial post was seen as a non-threatening way of easing him into the organisation, in which he could 'learn the ropes' with a view to assuming control at some point in the future, rather than imposing him on a committee, some of whom might be alarmed by such a move. For some inexplicable reason, given that they were already under surveillance, the Armstrongs were not arrested at the same time as Wilfred and the Elams, so Alwyn Armstrong was able to deputise for them during their detention [although Norah Elam's was much longer than Wilfred's: indeed, she appears not to have returned to the LPAVS on her release **81**], and Sylvia Armstrong was promoted to Assistant Secretary [the post Wilfred filled when he was accepted back], after being "examined by the officers of the Society" [**82**]. Wilfred's absence during the search of their house must have been a real trial for Nellie; the minutiae of the search will be considered in the next chapter, but at 6 p.m. on Thursday, May 23rd, 1940, Wilfred found himself at the forbidding pile of Brixton Prison, in company with many of his erstwhile colleagues, although he would not have known that straightaway, and they were all, for the foreseeable and unknowable future, to be unwilling guests of His Majesty the King, as a result of actions which were considered to have been a threat to the security of his country at a time of war [even if those actions had been carried out before the war started].

NOTES

1 http://www.spartacus.schoolnet.co.uk/Wdacrefox.htm

2 *Ibid.*

3 http://www.spartacus.schoolnet.co.uk/Wwspu.htm:

"Emmeline Pankhurst was a member of the Manchester Society for Women's Suffrage but became frustrated at the NUWSS [National Union of Women's Suffrage Societies] lack of success. With the help of her three daughters, Christabel Pankhurst, Sylvia Pankhurst and Adela Pankhurst, on 10th October 1903, she formed the Women's Social and Political Union (WSPU). The main objective was to gain, not universal suffrage, the vote for all women and men over a certain age, but votes for women, 'on the same basis as men.' This meant winning the vote not for all women but for only the small stratum of women who could meet the property qualification. As one critic pointed out, it was 'not votes for women', but 'votes for ladies.'"

4 http://www.spartacus.schoolnet.co.uk/Wdacrefox.htm

5 *Ibid.:*

"A former member of the WSPU, Jessie Stephen, who resigned over the issue of the First World War, argued that 'Dacre Fox and the Pankhursts' were members of a 'close cadre of middle and upper class conservative women leading the WSPU' after the outbreak of war."

6 *Ibid.*

7 Susan McPherson:

"… my mum's family was somehow connected to Bernadotte, Napoleon's General; there was some family silver that had gone missing; my mum's father [Norah Elam's son, Tony] was a tyrant and a bully."

Mosley's Old Suffragette: A Biography of Norah Dacre Fox, by Susan McPherson and Angela McPherson;

http://www.oldsuffragette.co.uk/6.html

8 ***Action no. 40, November 21st, 1936, page 7***

Dudley, with the incorrect initial 'L', was awarded the Bronze Distinction in 1937, at the same time [and the same award] as Ralph Jebb and Robert Saunders of Dorchester:

"**Birthday Honours For Distinguished Service**

We have very much pleasure in announcing, on this Fifth Birthday Anniversary, the names of members whose magnificent services to the Movement have led to the bestowal upon them of the higher British Union honours. These will be presented to them by the Leader at the forthcoming area conferences.

It should be noted that the list is not complete, owing to the late arrival of recommendations from many districts."

The Blackshirt no. 231, October 2nd, 1937, page 7

9 ***The Blackshirt no. 69, August 17th, 1934, page 9:***

"**SUCCESSFUL MEETING AT LITTLEHAMPTON**

Mrs Dudley Elam, Area W.O. [Women's Organiser] for Sussex and Hampshire held a very successful meeting at Littlehampton, addressing a crowd of over 100 people. She spoke for about an hour and gave a clear and lucid exposition of Fascist policy notwithstanding a certain amount of heckling from the Communist element in the audience."

10 http://en.wikipedia.org/wiki/Norah_Elam

11 London and Provincial Anti-Vivisection Society:

"An active member of the LPAVS was Norah Elam who had been a member (possibly even founding member) from its very beginnings around 1900. Elam was a prominent suffragette who was part of the Pankhurst inner circle from late 1912 to 1917 (under the name Dacre Fox).

During 1916/1917 Elam obtained work as supervisor of a typewriting pool at the Medical Research Council (MRC), gaining a wealth of information she was to use later in articles published under the auspices of the LPAVS during 1934 and 1935. In March 1921 Elam advertised in The Times and chaired a public meeting of LPAVS to discuss 'The Dog's [sic] Bill' (Bill to prohibit the vivisection of Dogs) that was being debated in Parliament at that time. The meeting was held at Aeolian Hall in London and as Chair, Elam read out 20 letters from Members of Parliament in support of the bill, and stated that, 'A large majority of the public were strongly in favour of the measure, and she felt sure that victory would be theirs if a determined effort were made, especially if women made proper use of their new political power'.

In 1932 the MRC had produced a paper called ***Vitamins, A Survey of Present Knowledge***. Elam's 1934 response was entitled ***The Vitamin Survey, A Reply*** and was a critical appraisal of that survey and its results. This was followed in 1935 by ***The Medical Research Council, What it is and how it works***. The second paper was based on the same arguments about MRC research practices and remits as the first paper, but distilled and argued more cogently on a broader front. Elam's argument was that 'powerful vested interests' had managed to 'entrench' themselves behind 'State-aided research', and had managed to make themselves unaccountable; the public were unable to influence the decisions about what research should be undertaken, and it operated like a closed shop, only answerable to itself. Elam also argued that the research involved the cruel and inhumane use of animals, and that any thinking person had to question how and why research and results based on animal models could safely be extrapolated to humans. Finally, she complained that animal experimentation was doubly cruel because of the unnecessary repetition of experiments to replicate or prove the same point, which in many cases she argued could have been arrived at by simple, common sense. These papers were widely distributed and copies could be found in libraries throughout the UK."

Mosley's Old Suffragette, op. cit., cited in National Anti-Vivisection Society;
http://en.wikipedia.org/wiki/National_Anti-Vivisection_Society

There appears to be some unresolved dispute about the information on this page, but unfortunately it is not clarified by following the link [see below] from here:

"The neutrality of this article is disputed. Please see the discussion on the talk page. Please do not remove this message until the dispute is resolved. *(December 2010)*" http://en.wikipedia.org/wiki/Talk:National_Anti-Vivisection_Society

12 ***Animal Rights: Political & Social Change in Britain since 1800, by Hilda Kean***

13 ***Campaigning Against Cruelty: the hundred year history of the British Union for the Abolition of Vivisection, by Emma Hopley***

14 http://en.wikipedia.org/wiki/National_Anti-Vivisection_Society

15 ***Campaigning Against Cruelty etc., op. cit.:***

> "The British Union also had a practice of not establishing branches where one already existed for the London Anti-Vivisection Society as long as this society continued to adhere to abolition principles."

16 This is confirmed by a document detailing the history of "the troublesome antivivisectionist [sic] movement" in Britain, prepared in 1962 to support passage of two supposedly 'animal welfare' bills through the American Congress, to which Hearing Wilfred supplied a statement on behalf of the NAVS, which will be covered in Chapter 14. The ***Dictionary of Victorian London*** has an entry for the Society, although the entry is incorrect, because the Society did not acquire the "and Provincial" addition until 1907, possibly coinciding with the move to the Regent Street address [see note 17 below]; this is probably because the guide was compiled ten years later, and it must have been assumed that the full name of the Society had applied from the time of its foundation:

> "Anti-Vivisection Society, The London and Provincial; 1876; 22A Regent Street, London, S.W.; The legal prohibition of vivisection."

There was also, somewhat surprisingly, an anti-vivisection hospital:

> "Anti-Vivisection Hospital, Battersea General Hospital (Incorporated); 1899, opened June 1902; Prince of Wales Road, Battersea Park, London, S.W.; For the relief of human suffering by physicians and surgeons who are opposed to vivisection. General Hospital for the needy and deserving. Free admission and attendance by Governor's letter."

Herbert Fry's Royal Guide to the London Charities, edited by John Lane, 1917;

http://www.victorianlondon.org/charities/charities.htm

The Secretary of the London Anti-Vivisection Society in 1899 was Sidney G. Trist, erstwhile Editor of the ***Animals' Friend*** Magazine, and American author, Mark Twain [real name Samuel Langhorne Clemens, 1835-1910] is known to have written to him, in support of its work, as detailed by the synopsis below; the Animal Rights History website, from which this synopsis is copied, has the complete text:

> "[1900] Mark Twain, letter to the editor, 'Mark Twain on Scientific Research,' ***Animals' Friend*** [London:1894-?] 6 (1900 Apr): 99-100; Online at ***Animal Rights History, 2003***; [Letter to Sidney G. Trist (Editor of the ***Animals' Friend*** Magazine), in his capacity as Secretary of the London Anti-Vivisection Society; Also published in pamphlet form as ***Pains of Lowly Life*** (London: Anti-Vivisection Society, 1900)]."

http://www.animalrightshistory.org/1837-1901-animal-rights/victorian-t/twa-mark-twain/1900-scientific-research.htm

By 1896, the LAVS was based at number 32, Sackville Street, Piccadilly, London W. [now W1].

LAVS Minute Book January 1896 to December 1898, courtesy of the NAVS

17 Prior to Sydney Trist, the Secretary appears to have been one R. Sydney Glover, and the publications were such as the ***Morning Post*** and ***The Spectator***; Courtesy of Dr. Richard Ford:

"**Extracts from two Letters from Dr. George Hoggan, on Vivisection.**
(/catalogue/8880)
Author:
Dr. George Hoggan (1837-1891) [London Anti-Vivisection Society, R. Sydney Glover, Secretary]
Publication details:
Undated [1880s?]. 'London Anti-Vivisection Society, 180, Brompton Road, S.W.'
12mo, 4 pp. Unbound bifolium pamphlet. Text clear and complete. Fair, on aged paper. Divided into two sections: 'Experimental Physiology' ('From the ***Morning Post***') and 'Anaesthetics and the Lower Animals' ('From ***The Spectator***'). Note at end of pamphlet reads 'London Anti-Vivisection Society, 180, Brompton Road, S.W. Price 1/2d., per post 1d., 12 copies 5d.; 1/6 for 50; 2/6 per 100 post free; to be had of Mr. R. SYDNEY GLOVER, Secretary, of whom also may be had (free) a Form of Petition to Parliament against Vivisection.'"

http://www.richardfordmanuscripts.co.uk/keywords/anti-vivisection

18 This is clear from the details given on the head of a letter, written on official stationery, by Wilfred in 1943 to the BBC, by which time he was already Secretary: "London & Provincial Anti-Vivisection Society / Known from its foundation in 1876 until 1907 as / The London Anti-Vivisection Society. ... 76 Victoria Street, London, S.W.1."

Courtesy of Dr. Hilda Kean

The information about the absence of branches was volunteered at the 1956 Annual Meeting of the Council of the NAVS:

"MRS BEDDOW BAYLY: I think it is true to say that the London & Provincial Anti-Vivisection Society have no branches and never had any branches.

THE CHAIRMAN: That is so.

MRS BEDDOW BAYLY: They deal direct with their members.

THE CHAIRMAN: That is right...."

Minutes of Proceedings of the Annual Council Meetings and Annual General Meetings of the National Anti-Vivisection Society, 1940-1956, courtesy of the NAVS

19 http://en.wikipedia.org/wiki/Re_Recher's_Will_Trusts

20 ***Ibid.***

The NAVS moved to the address of no. 92 Victoria Street some time after 1901. A pamphlet published by the NAVS at this address with the text of a sermon by "the late Bishop Westcottt", who died in 1901, is reproduced on this website:

http://animalsmattertogod.wordpress.com/tag/anti-vivisection/

21 The Dr. Allinson referred to here was Dr. Bertrand P. Allinson M.R.C.S., L.R.C.P, and he was the son of Dr. T. R. Allinson [1858-1918], who was a food reformer and dietetic expert:

> "The wholemeal bread advocate, Dr Allinson, reported how his rheumatism had declined with vegetarianism; and he drew upon Darwin's work

to highlight the fact that the nearest relative of man, the monkey, was a simple fruit-eating animal. At the end of the nineteenth century widespread food contamination was still rife. … Bread too was adulterated. … Dr Allinson, the food reformer, developed and marketed wholemeal flour; a branded loaf using such flour still sports his name. "

Animal Rights, etc., op. cit.

The son would have been brought up in a vegetarian household, where the ethos of the healthy lifestyle was all-important:

"In 1885 the Vegetarian Society merged with the London Food Reform Society. The LFRS had been formed in 1877, with baker Thomas Allinson (you can still buy his bread in the UK today) one of its founding members. He advocated the vegetarian diet due not only to its health benefits, but also because, as a lifestyle, it was cheaper than eating meat."

http://thevictorianist.blogspot.co.uk/2011/06/abuse-of-our-powers-over-animals-or.html

Allinson senior was also an early anti-vaccinationist:

"Instruct the people by means of public lectures and meetings. Show them as plainly as you can the uselessness and dangers of vaccination. Teach them that they must not go to the medical profession for counsel on the matter. If cases of small-pox were isolated and the clothes of the sufferers disinfected, the disease would not spread. If you wish to avoid smallpox, you must live pure and simple lives."

Medical Men and Vaccination, by Dr Allinson [from Vaccination Inquirer, 1883];

http://www.whale.to/vaccines/smallpox20.html

It is hardly surprising that the son was no less of an activist than his father, and adopted the healthy lifestyle:

". . . the London Vegetarian Society has had the outstanding services as President, from 1922 to the present time [sic] of Dr. Bertrand P. Allinson, a son of Dr. T. R. Allinson, one of the earliest members of the L.V.S., known everywhere for his courageous and successful advocacy of vegetarianism. Dr. Bertrand is not one whit behind his father as a well-known medical man - fearless in his advocacy of natural methods of healing. For a medical practitioner to take a prominent part in the practice and advocacy of unorthodox methods of treatment calls for courage, and testifies to the strength of his convictions. The devoted services of so many gifted and generous men have played a great part in gaining the favourable opinion of the general public and advancing the Progress of the vegetarian movement."

From a lecture on the vegetarian movement, presented in 1955;

http://www.ivu.org/members/council/b-p-allinson.html

Bertrand gained his qualification at University College Medical School, and as well as being President of the LVS and Vice-President of the NAVS, he was active at the Nature Cure Clinic, which was founded in 1928, and tried to help people of limited means. As well as writing regularly for vegetarian journals such as the ***Vegetarian Messenger***, he also wrote for ***Health and Efficiency***, which was created in 1902, to champion a physical culture ethos of social progressivism, and the naturist aspect with the tantalising photographs of naked sun-worshippers didn't appear until the early 1930s. The magazine was originally called ***Vim: An Illustrated Monthly Devoted to Promoting Health & Vigour in Body & Mind***! He died in 1975, but during his life, he criticised the tendency of the medical professional to carry out unnecessary and non-beneficial operations, and idealistically foresaw the demise of vivisection:

"... Orthodox medicine condones ill-conduct and seeks to restore health without rectifying it. True health cannot be attained in this manner. Vivisection has no philosophy, no ethics, and no width of vision. It will, therefore, disappear in the course of time." *[no date]*

1000 DOCTORS (AND MANY MORE) AGAINST VIVISECTION, by Bertrand P. Allinson, M.R.C.S., L.R.C.P.: Edited by Hans Ruesch; First published 1989 Ó Hans Ruesch Foundation;

http://www.hansruesch.net/articoli/1000_Docs_4.htm

Bertrand was present at a meeting of the LVS in 1931 that was addressed not only by the writer and "controversialist" Henry S. Salt, but also by Gandhi [not the BUF member for whom this was an ironic nickname], with whom British Union had much cause for argument, given his promotion of the cause of Indian independence:

"The autumnal social meeting of London Vegetarian Society at Chelsea Town Hall on November 20th was eagerly anticipated as a most notable occasion, mainly on account of the presence, on the same platform, of Mr. Gandhi and Mr. Henry S. Salt. The full significance of the event will be apparent from the quotation from Mr. Gandhi's autobiography. ... Following upon Mr. Gandhi's speech and upon his answer to a question put to him from the audience by Mr. Edwin S. More, came the rare privilege of listening to Mr. Henry S. Salt, whose name and fame as writer and a controversialist – gracefully touched upon by the Chairman in introducing him – need no recommendation to vegetarians and more especially to readers of ***The Vegetarian News***. ... Both Mr. Gandhi and Mr. Salt were accorded what can only be described as an ovation on leaving the platform, the audience thereafter, for a further hour and a half, betaking themselves to refreshments, conversation and the enjoyment of a programme of music and recitation, in the midst of which the President of the Society, Dr. Bertrand Allinson, was prevailed upon to interpose with an address in which he emphasised the welcome offered by the Society to the visitors present amongst the audience and made appeal for new members."

The Vegetarian News, Vol. 11 No. 132 , December 1931; Henry Salt and Gandhi: A Notable Occasion, by E.J. T.;

http://www.henrysalt.co.uk/studies/essays/henry-salt-and-gandhi

22 The Armstrongs' Home Office file was only released early in 2013 [although originally classified as closed until 2017; the redacted documents are now classified as "Closed until 2026"!] as a result of a Freedom of Information request by this author, which was a legitimate avenue made available by the National Archive; given that it took almost nine months for the file to be examined, to enable any potentially sensitive material to be 'weeded', before a redacted version was made available, it begs the question of how much actually has been removed: the amount of redaction on the remaining documentation is minimal.

It is interesting that Alwyn Armstrong first joined British Union in 1934 at Worthing, where Dudley Elam was Sub-Branch Officer for a while, and Norah Elam was probably a member [although this is difficult to corroborate: within a matter of months, she was appointed Women's County Organiser for Sussex & Hampshire; see note 9]. Armstrong would also have come into contact with Wilfred's nemesis, William Joyce, down there; Armstrong's reason for being in Worthing, when he originated in the Southall area of London, is plausibly explained, albeit somewhat condescendingly, in the transcript of his Appeal Hearing in the file:

> "The Objector [sic] was born 29.1.1910 at Southall, and after leaving school in 1925 he was employed in various jobs of little importance, by Thomas Cooks [sic], Peter Jones and Singer Sewing Machines at Worthing."
>
> ***HO 45/23763; A.44; Report of Advisory Committee Appeal Hearing 22/11/40***

Any association between Armstrong and Joyce, after the likely initial contact at West Sussex, appears to have been missed by the Security Services in their monitoring of Norah Elam, who was more interesting to them:

> "Norah would later claim that she had visited Germany to meet Hitler with Unity [Mitford] along with a group of four or five other British women, but on the day it had rained and they had gone back to their hotel to change their clothes. When they returned, Hitler had been and gone. If this story is true it would have happened between 1934 and 1938 before MI5 began recording Norah's activities, since there appears to be no record of Norah's visit in the MI5 files currently available which record many of her activities from 1938 onwards."
>
> ***Mosley's Old Suffragette: etc., op. cit.***

The connection between Armstrong and Elam was definitely not missed, however:

> "In 1936 he joined the staff of the London and Provincial Anti-Vivisection Society (and this was because in his British Union activities, which had begun in 1934, he had run across Mrs. Elam)."
>
> ***HO 45/23763; 860984: A.44; Report etc., op. cit.***

The leaflet satirising Winston Churchill was actually instigated by Norah Elam, but the incident almost resulted in a prosecution for libel against Sylvia Armstrong, who had typed it, and made the copies, at Elam's instruction:

> "(5) There was another political activity, if the obedience of a typist who types something that she is told by her employer to type is rightly described as an activity. One day in the office Mrs. Elam told her to make a stencil and 300 copies of a pamphlet - very short - only one page of quarto paper. That she recognised under its description in the statement of case as "a vile and criminal libel on the Prime Minister when he held office as First Lord of the Admiralty", when the point was put to her by the Committee. Of that pamphlet a copy will be found in H.O. 860985, and it will be noticed, as the Objector told the Committee in answer to a question, that there is no mention of British Union. The Objector made the 300 copies from the stencil and gave them to Mrs. Elam. What became of them she does not know, but she did get frightened at having done them, and asked Mrs. Elam twice whether she might go and tell the police about the pamphlet. Mrs. Elam would not let her do so."

The leaflet mercilessly lampoons the man regarded as Britain's saviour:

"
W A N T E D .

ON CHARGES OF MURDER, PERJURY, SEDUCTION, CONSPIRACY WITH HIS MAJESTY'S ENEMIES THE JEWS TO CREATE WAR TO THE MANIFEST DISCOMFORT AND DANGER OF HIS MAJESTY'S LIEGE LANDS AND SUBJECTS, CRIMINAL MISMANAGEMENT OF PUBLIC RESOURCES WHILE HOLDING HIGH OFFICE RESULTING IN THE MURDER OF THOUSANDS OF BRITONS IN THE DARDANELLES, TREASON, and CREATING A PUBLIC MISCHIEF IN THAT HE DID FELONIOUSLY MISLEAD AND BETRAY HIS MAJESTY'S SUBJECTS AS TO THE FACTORS GOVERNING THE INTERNATIONAL SITUATION.
Winston Leonard Spencer CHURCHILL.

Age: 65. Height about six feet. Hair partly grey, eyes green, complexion: Yellow.

APPEARANCE: Fat, Gross and ungainly, Overfed and bilious, four chins and pop-eyed. Fatbin stomach, walks with clumsy clubmans gait. Usually smoking cigar, wears excellent suits and double Albert across waistcoat.

HABITS: Heavy smoker of fat and expensive cigars. Frequents expensive restaurants and juicy chorus girls. Fond of young men and of Jewish company in general. Glib of tongue, known in underworld as "Winston of Master Touch".

ALIASES: Is also known as Winnie the Pooh, Winnie the Bad Smell, and the Yellow Scourge.

WAS LAST SEEN FURTIVELY ENTERING THE SIDE DOOR OF THE ADMIRALTY. May be found in the House of Commons or other bright spots of London's Underworld.

REWARD: For his apprehension and Delivery to the Underground, Dead or Alive, preferably the former, the Gratitude of all true Britons, Peace to Mankind and Blessing of all Christians.

Given under our Hand this second Thor's Day in the month of September in Year of Our Lord 1939, in His Majesty's City of Westminster.

The Council of British Liberators.

GOD SAVE OUR PEOPLE."

HO 45/23763

Churchill decided not to press charges, although his reasons are unknown:

"With reference to Chief Inspector's minute on marginally quoted correspondence:-

...

... it is definitely known that ARMSTRONG knew that his wife Sylvia - in the offices of the Society - typed a document which constituted a vile and criminal libel on the Prime Minister when he held Office as First Lord of the Admiralty. A successful prosecution would have been possible but Mr. Winston Churchill did not think it worth while. Copies of the offending leaflet are submitted."

HO 45/23763; A.44; letter from Inspector J. Bridges, 11/07/40

Inevitably, this leaflet came to the attention of some or all of the Executive Committee, and although it took a year to be acted upon, the Committee felt it necessary to voice its disapproval of the situation:

"... the following resolution proposed by Mr V. Rienaecker, seconded by Dr. Allinson was passed unanimously:-

'That Mrs. Dacre Fox be requested to apologise for the use of the Society's stencil cutting machine for political purposes.'"

Minutes of LPAVS Executive Committee Meeting 06/05/41, courtesy of NAVS

It is curious that, although Sylvia Marchant married Alwyn Armstrong in October 1938, she is referred to throughout by her maiden name in the LPAVS Executive Committee minutes: it is hard to believe that the Committee would not have been aware of her change of status, but it is possible, of course. Armstrong wrote a letter, dated 6th December 1940, to the Chairman of the Appeal Committee, from the internment camp at Ascot, after his hearing on November the 22nd [almost a full four months after his arrest: surely an indication of the strain under which the system was labouring], endeavouring to clarify some issues that he evidently felt had been dealt with inconclusively on the day: "… perhaps matters could be facilitated by a short analysis of facts concerning my case." In this letter, he also provided evidence that Wilfred was not actually working at the LPAVS only in a relatively junior capacity, although he was very careful not to suggest any involvement with propaganda on Wilfred's part:

> "From July 1939 to May 1940 I worked for the Society under the personal supervision of Mr. W. Risdon who has very definite anti-Fascist views and who has been released from detention by the Home Secretary."

HO 45/23763; letter from 90537, Room A, P.O.W. Camp 7, Ascot, 06/12/40

This was a confirmation, albeit more specific, of what he had said during the Appeal Hearing, corroborating Wilfred's *volte face* on the subject of British Union, and elucidating the consternation caused at the LPAVS by the arrest of Wilfred and the Elams [although no opprobrium seems to have attached to Wilfred thereby]:

> "(6) The Objector had stated in a petition which he sent on 30.9.40 to the Secretary of State that he had suspected that a reason for his detention might be because he was employed by the Anti-vivisection Society, whose former secretary, Mrs. Elam, was at present detained. He had said in the petition, and he told the Committee, that he did not associate himself with Mrs. Elam's views, that at the time of her detention the new officials of the society had caused a thorough investigation to be made in the political proclivities of the society's staff, that they were thoroughly satisfied regarding his anti-Fascist views and that otherwise he would not have been allowed to go on in the employment of the society (they had, on account of Mrs. Elam's detention, called upon her to resign). One of his colleagues in the Anti-Vivisection work was Risden [sic], who was a member of British Union but had himself become unfavourable to its policy, and whose influence was one of the factors which induced the Objector to go into opposition to British Union.
>
> …
>
> (10) The Objector flatly denied the suggestion in the statement of case made by a "most reliable informant during the early stages of enquiries into Mrs. Elam's activities that she believed that ARMSTRONG had only left the British Union as a blind, and that it was positively known that he used his employment with the Society as a cover for his Fascist activities. For example, it was known that on certain days he used to distribute Fascist literature when he should have been working for the Society". He said that there was no truth whatever in this. It is possible that the mistake of the informant arose from the fact that for the period just before his detention the Objector's job was, with Risden, the arranging for the Anti-Vivisection Society some sort of Parliamentary Electoral registration or something of that sort."

HO 45/23763; A.44, Report of Advisory Committee Appeal Hearing, op. cit.

23 *WHEN BRITISH UNION CARED FOR ANIMALS, by Robert Edwards; European Action No 10;*

http://www.oswaldmosley.net/animal-rights.php

24 Initially, Wilfred was only paid a peppercorn amount, probably as a retaining fee, if the LPAVS Accounts are a true reflection of every payment he received: the first payment, for September 1939, is shown on the October account sheet, showing that he was paid three guineas [£3.3s.], but his skill was immediately evident, and a more appropriate recompense was recommended [although the desired meeting noted below appears not to have taken place, as there is no record in the succeeding Minutes:

"Canvassing Campaign: Secretary made full report on the new political canvass which is being carried out in the constituency of South Paddington and the great success of this work ever since the war started. Secretary reported that this was being organised by Mr. Risdon who was working all lecturers as a team. Committee expressed great satisfaction over this matter and expressed a wish to meet Mr. Risdon at next Committee. Mr. Elam proposed that Mr. Risdon be paid £4- a week. This was seconded by Mrs. Pearce and carried unanimously."

Just by way of comparison, Norah Elam's salary as Secretary and Editor of the LPAVS ***Anti-Vivisection Journal*** at this time was £50 per month, excluding any additional fees for "literary work" and/or articles published therein!

Minutes of LPAVS Executive Committee Meeting 03/10/39, courtesy of NAVS

25 Letter to the author from Brian Risdon, February 9th, 1998

26 ***Action*** couldn't resist an 'I told you so' response:

"“Action” Foretold Collapse of the Pound

For two years now we have predicted that it would be impossible to maintain the pound sterling beyond September, 1939. We have now seen this date anticipated by a few weeks because of the crisis. …

FUND EXHAUSTED?

It is estimated that no less than £332,000,000 have left this country for America and Canada since March, when the last accounts of the Exchange Equalisation Fund were published. This would mean the virtual exhaustion of the fund, so that the present move was inevitable even without any crisis. We drew attention to this danger only a few weeks ago.

As is pointed out by our City correspondent, **in 1914 the pound appreciated to $7 on August 4**, showing that crisis actually improves the position of a powerful financial centre. It is a measure of the relative decline of London and the rise of Wall Street that the exchange should move the other way in 1939. …

A weak sterling makes all these foreign purchases so much more expensive at a time when the nation can least afford to pay, and the pound looks like falling below $4."

Action, no. 184, September 2nd, 1939, page 3

27 ***Action, no. 191, October 26th, 1939, page 1:***

"After one month of war the Ministry of Labour have to record that their general index has risen by 10 points and their index of food prices alone by 12 points. These are the most rapid increases in a single month for over nineteen years since the post-war "boom" of 1920.

Statistics such as these may not mean much to many people, but the following increases in prices have hit every housewife in the land.

Butter (lb.)	**.........**	**1/3 to 1/7**
Eggs (doz.)	**.........**	**2/4 to 2/9**
Bacon (lb.)	**.........**	**1/5 to 1/9**
Sugar (lb.)	**.........**	**2d. to 4½d.**
Steak (foreign)	**...**	**1/6 to 2/-**
Plaice (lb.)	**.........**	**10½d. to 1/6**
Cod (lb.)	**.........**	**6d. to 1/2"**

28 ***Action, no. 185, September 16th, 1939, page 1:***

"“ACTION” AND CENSORSHIP

We owe an explanation to *Action* readers for the non-appearance of this paper last week.

The facts are as follows: On Wednesday last we were informed by the printers that they would not print the paper unless it was submitted to the censorship of a Government Department. We were informed that this censorship was voluntary, but, at the same time, we were unable last week to secure the printing of the paper without submission to the censorship.

Action was in the hands of the censor from 4.50 p.m. on Wednesday last until mid-day on Saturday. It was, therefore, impossible to produce the paper in time for distribution.

Arrangements have now been made for *Action* to be published regularly each week."

29 ***Action, no. 185, September 16th, 1939, page 8***

30 ***Children and World War Two;*** http://www.historylearningsite.co.uk/children_and_world_war_two.htm

31 ***Action, no. 191, October 26th, 1939, page 4:***

"HALF LONDON'S CHILDREN STILL AT HOME

At a recent meeting of the L.C.C., Mr. Herbert Morrison revealed that the percentage of schoolchildren evacuated from London under the government scheme was only 49, while it was known that seven per cent. had since returned and there might be more.

So over half London's schoolchildren are still at home and yet London schools remain closed. What is to be done about the education of these hundreds of thousands of children who are at present on a permanent holiday?"

32 ***Children and World War Two, op. cit.:***

"What impact this had on the children involved was never overly studied at the time as the government simply wanted to herald evacuation as an overwhelming success. That some children continued their education in pubs, church halls or anywhere else there was the space to accommodate them was seen as the accepted face of a requirement that had been foist [sic] on the government."

33 From an article published in ***The Telegraph*** on September 2nd, 1939:

"An official notice from the Lord Privy Seal's office stated: 'A lighting order has been made under Defence Regulation no. 24 and comes into operation at sunset tonight as a further measure of precaution.

The effect of the order is that every night from sunset to sunrise all lights inside the buildings must be extinguished, subject to certain exceptions in the case of external lighting where it is essential for the conduct of work of vital national importance. Such lights must be adequately shaded.'"

http://www.telegraph.co.uk/history/world-war-two/6082126/World-War-2-Blackout-in-force-for-all-of-Britain.html

34 As ever, Wikipedia seems like a clear source of information:

"After World War II started in September 1939 the first commodity to be controlled was petrol, but food rationing was introduced quite soon. On 8 January 1940, bacon, butter and sugar were rationed. This was followed by meat, tea, jam, biscuits, breakfast cereals, cheese, eggs, lard, milk and canned fruit. Strict rationing inevitably created a black market. This was illegal, and buyers could be tricked with cheaper substitutes such as horsemeat instead of beef.

Almost all controlled items were rationed by weight, but meat, exceptionally, was rationed by price. (All prices need to be considered in the values of the time: the buying power of one shilling was much more than its equivalent (5p) in modern British currency.)

Some types of fruit which had been imported all but disappeared. Lemons and bananas became virtually unobtainable for most of the war; oranges continued to be sold but greengrocers customarily reserved them for children and pregnant women, who could prove their status by producing their distinctive ration books. Other fruit such as apples still appeared from time to time, but again the sellers imposed their own restrictions so that customers were often not allowed to buy, for example, more than one apple each.

One of the few foods not rationed was fish. The price of fish increased considerably as the war progressed, but the government allowed this, since it realised that fishermen would need to be able to collect a premium for their catch if they were to be persuaded to put to sea in the face of enemy submarines. However, like other non-rationed items fish was rarely freely available, and long queues built up at fishmongers and at fish and chip shops. The quality of wartime chips was often felt to be below standard, because of the low-quality fat available to fish friers."

http://en.wikipedia.org/wiki/Rationing_in_the_United_Kingdom#World_War_II

35 Tom Driberg [*alias* William Hickey], whom British Union erroneously accused of being Jewish [but for which factual inaccuracy it graciously apologised], described in the ***Daily Express***, as observed by ***Action***, an air raid false alarm at the very beginning of the war:

"There were about a hundred people in the church. No doubt many had stayed at home to listen in. Hardly had the service begun when we heard the sirens. I confess without shame that it was for me a bloodcurdling, spine-shivering sound."

Action, no. 185, September 16th, 1939, page 2

36 ***Action*** was very quick to seize upon the social injustices of the situation though, perhaps unusually, without pointing the finger at Jewish perpetrators:

"All sales to-day are A.R.P. bargains. So does commerce exploit even the horror of war. Disinfectants, factory alarms, tinned foods, patent extinguishers—they all put forward their claims as part of A.R.P.

Country houses unsaleable a few months ago now command gigantic prices, as the rich escape in luxury the ordeal the poor must face in the crowded cities."

Action, no. 185, September 16th, 1939, page 2

37 Here, again, Wikipedia is an excellent source:

"The 1924 ARP Committee produced figures estimating that in London there would be 9,000 casualties in the first two days and then a continuing rate of 17,500 casualties a week. These rates were thought conservative.

It was believed that there would be 'total chaos and panic' and hysterical neurosis as the people of London would try to flee the city. To control the population harsh measures were proposed—bringing London under almost military control; physically cordoning London with 120,000 troops to force people back to work. A different government department proposed setting up camps for refugees for a few days before sending them back to London.

These schemes remained on paper only and while estimates of potential damage remained high, the Air Raids Commandant (Major General H. Pritchard of the Royal Engineers) favoured a more reasoned solution. He discerned that panic and flight were basically problems of morale, if the people could be organised, trained and provided with protection then they would not panic. As part of this scheme the country was divided into regions each having its own command and control structure, *in potentia* at least."

http://en.wikipedia.org/wiki/Air_Raid_Precautions

38 The suspect aliens were divided into three groups:

'A' - high security risks, numbering just under 600, who were immediately interned;

'B' - 'doubtful cases', numbering around 6,500, who were supervised and subject to restrictions;

'C' - 'no security risk', numbering around 64,000, who were left at liberty. More than 55,000 of category 'C' were recognised as refugees from Nazi oppression. The vast majority of these were Jewish.

Fact File: Civilian Internment 1939-1945; WW2 People's War, Timeline - 1939~1945;

http://www.bbc.co.uk/history/ww2peopleswar/timeline/factfiles/nonflash/a6651858.shtml

39 ***Action, no. 194, November 16th, 1939, page 3:***

"Unless Mr. Thomas's facts can be shaken in public cross-examination he presents a very grave indictment of a Government which postures before the country as a defender of liberty. He and those whom he accuses should both be subject to cross-examination in the full light of day. ... On these two established facts alone I denounce this outrage on British liberty and demand a Public Enquiry."

A fortnight later, ***Action*** could not resist the opportunity for a tongue-in-cheek swipe at the Government about the significance of Magna Carta:

"It is announced that the copy of Magna Carta, which was lent by this country to the United States for exhibition at the World's fair, is not to be returned immediately. It is to be lodged for safe keeping in the library of Congress at Washington. —*Daily Telegraph*, November 20

We presume this is because the government has no further use for the document."

Action, no. 196, November 30th, 1939, page 2

40 In March, 1941, the LPAVS gave this advice to pet owners:

"FEEDING YOUR PETS.

In the present state of rationing many people experience difficulty in feeding their pets. Some are even considering having their pets destroyed, but so far we are not by any means convinced that this is necessary or even desirable. If you cannot give them the food they have been accustomed to there are alternatives on which they may be fed. [details followed]"

The London & Provincial Anti-Vivisection Society News-Sheet, 09/03/41, courtesy of the NAVS

41 Dr. Kean regards this as "a forgotten part of Londoners' history":

"Today people do not know about this massacre, although the killing was never 'covered up': daily newspapers and animal charities reported it. However, in our 'nation of animal lovers', many people romanticise the Home Front and do not know about this event. This forgotten moment in Britain's history makes us re-think the way we 'remember' the War and also shows the ways in which animal and human histories are inextricably linked."

The Great British Cat and Dog Massacre of World War Two; illustrated lecture by Dr. Hilda Kean, at the University of Greenwich, May 5th, 2010;

http://www2.gre.ac.uk/about/news/articles/2010/a1821

42 The official status of the WAS was ambiguous; the Women Police Volunteers, set up in 1914 and renamed the Women Police Service in 1915, was never sanctioned by the Government, but it was tolerated, for the most part, and Allen was awarded the OBE for services during the war. After the war, the Metropolitan Police set up its own women's division, and expected the WPS to disband; Allen was arrested in 1921 for impersonating a police officer but, amazingly, she was allowed to continue her activities; even after appointing a Committee, chaired by Baird, to investigate the organisation, now known as the WAS, she was invited by the Government to advise on the policing of the British Army of the Rhine, thereby affording her tacit recognition, allowing her to be welcomed as an official representative in many foreign countries. The Home Office started taking an interest in her in 1927. In 1933, she was involved in the formation of the Women's Reserve, "which was intended to serve the country in the event of subversive forces taking over". When war started in 1939, she joined the Women's Voluntary Service and spoke regularly at British Union peace rallies. Despite her connection with Mosley and Admiral Barry Domvile, Special Branch regarded her as a "crank … trailing around in a ridiculous uniform" and, instead of recommending internment under Defence Regulation 18B (1A), agreed to a very liberal interpretation of house arrest. Her private life was similarly unconventional; like some of the friends & colleagues who shared her moral & ethical convictions, she was a lesbian, "known as 'Robert' by her close circle of female friends, and she was called 'Sir' by her officers."

Hurrah for the Blackshirts: Fascists and Fascism in Britain Between the Wars, Martin Pugh, cited in

http://en.wikipedia.org/wiki/Mary_Sophia_Allen

43 Curiously, an alternative spelling of her surname is used here; nearly all other sources use the spelling Allen. Notwithstanding the collusion with

Mosley to conceal her link with British Union, whether actual membership or not, the tenor of her article didn't leave much doubt about her affiliations, and the editorial postscript was appropriately laudatory:

> **"I venture to hope that you will publish this letter for, though I am in no way connected with your movement, I read your literature not only with great interest but with an open mind. For many weeks the stand which you have taken with regard to the war has been one with which I heartily agree. There are thousands of men and women entirely outside any political organisation or pacifist group who view with abhorrence the present trend of events, but who, owing to the very real menace of misrepresentation, feel unable to voice an opinion.**
>
> **No one can, by any stretch of the imagination, accuse me of being unpatriotic for my public record is known to be the reverse. I have been and still am, engaged in dealing with women of all types and ages and encouraging them to become efficient in suitable forms of service, and to enrol in any government department in which their services are required. ...**
>
> **I am no defeatist and I consider that what we as a nation put our hand to we shall carry out. But I cannot believe that, even at this late hour, we could not thresh [sic] out with perfect goodwill a method which would ensure security for our Empire without sacrificing its whole resources, together with the youth of both sexes. There are, as many realise already, far more deadly perils threatened by this war, if it continues, than any we have yet considered.**
>
> **These problems can only be grappled with if we have a united and virile population. The superficial content of those who so confidently assert that the present conflict will settle anything, will have a rude awakening. Since all countries to-day have to face the unparalleled horrors of modern warfare and its consequences, it is surely not too much to demand that a solution be found by one or by a group of nations to end the imminent destruction and slaughter.**
>
> **MARY S. ALLAN,**
>
> **Commandant, Women's Auxiliary Service.**
>
> *Commandant Allan organised the first Women's Police Force during the last war, and has been prominent in the organisation of women for civil duties in this country. She has an extremely fine record of public service. —Editor.*"
>
> ***Action, no. 192, November 2nd, 1939; page 7***

Richard Thurlow was of the opinion that Mosley used this arrangement in a calculated way, although hardly surprising for such a politically 'savvy' operator:

> "There were other signs that Mosley was very conscious of the activities of the Security Service. In the late 1930s he kept the membership of Commandant Mary Allen in the BUF secret in the hope that her unofficial women's police force could provide advance intelligence if the authorities were about to move against the organization."

This was a period of intense, but highly secret, work by Mosley and several others in the so-called 'right-wing' pro-peace fraternity; the secrecy did not prevent information reaching the Security Service, of course, although the interpretation of the information was often approached subjectively, according to the agenda of the operative; there were even attempts by the Security Service to convince the War Cabinet of the possibility of a "major right-wing coup"; the Elams were implicated, and Mary Allen was obviously involved at the highest level:

> "A close survey of the first three releases of Home Office papers on British fascism does produce one document which throws some light on this matter.

This is a Special Branch report of 25 June 1940, in the Commandant Mary Allen file. It states that when Aubrey Lees was detained on 20 June 1940 under DR 18b he was found to be in possession of two typewritten letters, unheaded and unsigned, concerning meetings at 48 Ladbroke Grove, W11, in March, April and May 1940. Lees refused to discuss the object of these meetings but said they were secret affairs and stated that amongst the people attending were Sir Oswald Mosley and Commandant Mary Allen. What was described as 'a very reliable informant' reported that these meetings were convened by Mosley and Ramsay and attended by leading members of the various pro-nazi and anti-semitic organizations in Britain. The object was to secure the greatest possible collaboration between them and make preparations for a coup d'état. [*ref. PRO HO 144/21933/330*] On her Advisory Committee appeal Commandant Allen denied having attended such meetings but thought the address was the home of Mrs. Dacre-Fox who ran [sic] an anti-vivisection society. This was a known fascist front organization [sic] and 'Professor Dacre-Fox' was later interned (pseudonyms for Dudley and Norah Elam)."

Fascism in Britain: From Oswald Mosley's Blackshirts to the National Front by Richard C. Thurlow

The latter reference to Norah Elam's home address was almost certainly disingenuous on Mary Allen's part, most likely an attempt at dissimulation, as she must have known that they now resided at 5, Logan Place, London SW:

"[Norah's son, Tony] moved to London [in 1940] and stayed in his parent's [sic] flat at 5 Logan Place where he remained until the end of the war."

Mosley's Old Suffragette, op. cit.

44 Her moral indignation was, apparently, very popular:

"Commandant Allen informs us she has had a very large number of letters congratulating her on her protest, and will deal with the points raised in her series of articles."

Action, no. 215, April 18th, 1940, page 2

45 ***Action, no. 216, April 25th, 1940, page 2***

46 Richard Thurlow encapsulates the background well:

"The decision to terminate the activities of British fascism and to intern the leading members of the various organizations represented the conjunction of several influences. The collapse of the dominoes in western Europe before the nazi blitzkrieg in April and May 1940, with the fall of Norway, Denmark, Holland and Belgium and the failure to stop the attack on France, brought to an end the complacency of the phoney war period. This was succeeded by a 'fifth column' scare, manufactured by credulous diplomats in Holland and reinforced by a hysterical Rothermere press, which threw suspicion on all aliens, fascists and fellow travellers as potential traitors. The same spy fantasies which had been projected by popular novelists like William Le Queux and E. Phillips Oppenheim before 1914 suddenly seemed much more plausible in 1940. [*ref. Andrew, Secret Service, pp34-5*] Fascism was now seen as a potential nazi Trojan horse within Britain. Given what had happened in Norway, the public leaped to the conclusion that Mosley was a prime candidate for a potential British quisling [sic], and overnight indifference to his person turned into outright hostility as signified by the physical assault on him at the Middleton and Prestwich by-election in May 1940."

Fascism in Britain: etc, op. cit.

47 Sir George Drummond appears to have been a member of both the BUAV and the LPAVS, which could be one explanation for a conflation of both organisations, in some people's minds:

"Mention should be made of Sir George Drummond, a major donor to the BUAV as well as a NHQ member of the British Union of Fascists. He was active as a speaker for the BUAV and wrote articles for its journal 'The Abolitionist'. Chairman of Drummonds Bank, High Sheriff of Northamptonshire, President of the Northampton branch of the Link, host to Joachim von Ribbentrop at his country home at Pitsford Hall, he used his influence in trying to avoid another world war. In 1940, he went into voluntary exile on the Isle of Man for the duration of that unnecessary war."

WHEN BRITISH UNION CARED FOR ANIMALS, op. cit.

Sir George, who also appears to have had a military career, was very well connected, and his membership of the LPAVS might go some way towards explaining Norah Elam's somewhat unexpected prospective constituency when her candidature was decided, although it was by no means unusual for prospective parliamentary candidates to be assigned constituencies unconnected with their 'home' areas:

"Norah was described by a local Northampton newspaper as a strange candidature, occasioning 'initial surprise'. The choice may also have been strange for Norah who had no obvious connections to the area, although she was probably familiar with Captain George Drummond, a friend of the Duke of Windsor, who was also a member of the London & Provincial Anti-Vivisection Society and a local Northamptonian who has latterly been identified as having supported the BUF."

Northampton and County Independent, 27/11/36: Norah Elam; Why I am contesting Northampton; and

The Blackshirts in Northampton, 1933-1940: a postscript; Philip Coupland, cited in Mosley's Old Suffragette, op. cit.

48 The Elams were generally present at these meetings, if only as facilitators:

"Norah and Dudley also regularly attended secret meetings to help organize collaboration between other 'patriotic societies'. These included The Link, The Nordic League, and The Right Club. The Right Club was a secret society that had been formed by Archibald Ramsay in 1939 to try to get unity among the different right-wing groups in Britain including the BUF. Ramsay was virulently anti-Semitic and pro-Nazi, and The Right Club included among its members William Joyce who had split with Mosley in 1937.

Many of the secret meetings, including meetings between Mosley and Ramsey [sic], were held at the premises of LPAVS. The LPAVS had played a large part in Norah's adult life long before she had joined the BUF and the LPAVS continued to work for animal rights into the 1960s [sic]. However, MI5 and Special Branch came to suspect that it was a conduit for secret Fascist activities because of the number of leading members of the LPAVS who were also active BUF members (including Mary Allen and Sylvia Armstrong). Contrary to MI5 theories, their concern for animal welfare was completely genuine, but Norah's unconventional accounting methods may have muddied the water and attracted suspicion."

Mosley's Old Suffragette, op. cit.

In the next chapter, this assertion that Sylvia Armstrong was an "active" BUF member will be shown to be erroneous. It is interesting to speculate whether Mosley and Joyce attended one or more meetings together, given their recent antipathy. Captain Archibald Henry Maule Ramsay achieved the singular distinction of being the only serving member of Parliament to be incarcerated under Defence Regulation 18B (1A).

http://en.wikipedia.org/wiki/Archibald_Maule_Ramsay

On the subject of the LPAVS being a 'front', Hilda Kean, among many others, is convinced that this was a lazy and incorrect association [as a result of a specious syllogism: many Fascists were against vivisection; Norah Elam was a committed anti-vivisectionist with fascist connections; therefore any anti-vivisectionist who worked with Norah Elam must be a Fascist], and that

"Thurlow is wrong in defining the group merely as a front organization. The ***Newssheet*** for members indicates clearly that whatever positions members may have had on Fascism or Socialism they were totally committed to anti-vivisection."

Fascism in Britain. A History 1918-1985, by Richard Thurlow; LAPAVS Newssheet, vol. II, no. 2 , February 1942; cited in Animal Rights: etc., op. cit.

However, this did not prevent the actual 'question in the House'; after the raid on the LPAVS offices on the 23rd of May 1940, Mr. Graham White asked the Home Secretary in a debate on 'Subversive Activities' on the 30th of May:

"42. *Mr. Graham White* asked the Home Secretary whether he has yet received the report on the police raid on the London office of the National and Provincial Anti-Vivisection Society; and, if so, what action he has taken on it?

Sir J. Anderson Yes, Sir. One of the people connected with this Anti-Vivisection Society was an adherent of the British Union of Fascists and was using the office of the society for British Union business. The searching of this office was one of a number of steps taken for the purpose of investigating the activities of the British Union."

Yet again, the Society's name is given incorrectly; also, it is interesting that Anderson only makes reference in the past tense to "one of the people", when it must have been common knowledge that more than one person had current or previous links with British Union, notwithstanding Dr. Kean's assertion above, so he could have been referring to either of the Elams, Armstrongs or Wilfred.

SUBVERSIVE ACTIVITIES: ***HC Deb 30 May 1940 vol 361 cc652-4; cited in In the Highest Degree Odious: Detention without Trial in Wartime Britain, by Alfred William Brian Simpson;***

http://hansard.millbanksystems.com/commons/1940/may/30/subversive-activities

Graham White's full name was Henry Graham White [which is presumably why there isn't a 'live' link to him within the Hansard site in this excerpt] and his background doesn't lead one to suppose that he would be a 'natural' anti-Fascist: he was a Liberal, representing Birkenhead East for the whole of his parliamentary career, and according to his own records which were deposited in the House of Lords record office, the papers included memoranda on topics such as unemployment benefit and old age pensions, but perhaps what spurred his interest in the LPAVS was his campaign on behalf of German internees during the current war; presumably a humanitarian concern without necessitating any fascist leanings.

http://en.wikipedia.org/wiki/Henry_Graham_White

Graham White was a member of a delegation from Parliament to Buchenwald, "less than three weeks after the allies had liberated that camp." Another member was Ness Edwards, who was very possibly one of Wilfred's colleagues from his Welsh mining days, and potentially another of his rivals for a SWMF scholarship place with Aneurin Bevan:

> "Ness Edwards: SWMF scholarship student 1919-21. Prior to his entering Parliament, he was, apart from his trade union activities, organising and teaching Labour College classes in the mining valleys. Also provided the miners with the printed word: ***Industrial Revolution in South Wales, Frost & the Chartist Movement,*** and ***History of the SWMF.*** Ness took his seat in the House of Commons in 1939 as the Labour Member for the Caerphilly Division of Glamorgan, which he … continued to represent until [1964]."

The Central Labour College, 1909-29 by W.W.Craik

The reference to Ness Edwards, which also mentioned Graham White, was made by his daughter, Llin Golding, member for Newcastle under Lyme, in a parliamentary debate on war crimes on the 12th of December, 1989.

HC Deb 12 December 1989 vol 163 cc868-910; WAR CRIMES;

http://hansard.millbanksystems.com/commons/1989/dec/12/war-crimes#S6CV0163P0_19891212_HOC_311

49 These were on the 8th of November, and the 6th of December, and at the first meeting

> "Mosley read out a long statement relating to a BUF internee named Thomas and that the meeting was about the preservation of civil liberties."

Fascism in Britain: etc, op. cit.

50 ***Mosley's Old Suffragette, op. cit.***

51 Brian Simpson provides the details here:

> "Amongst papers belonging to Norah Elam was found a suspicious list of eight names (HO 283/48). British Union did not have a governing body; policy was the will of the Leader. But the constitution did provide for the succession if the Leader died without having nominated his successor. A council would choose, its members being nominated by Mosley in a document held by his solicitors (normally Messrs. Randolph & Dean or Iliffe Sweet & Co.). I [Simpson] suspect the eight merely constituted this council; they were McKechnie, Donovan, Francis-Hawkins, E. Dudley Elam, J. H. Hone,

Commander C.E. Hudson, K.E. Marsden and R. Temple-Cotton. These could not conceivably have been leaders of an underground organization; their association with British Union was public knowledge. MI5 must have accepted this; otherwise all would have been long-term 'leader' detainees, but only Donovan, McKechnie and Francis-Hawkins were so categorized."

In the Highest Degree Odious: etc., op. cit.

52 Once again, Mary Allen is shown to be heavily involved:

"The list of eight names was found, incriminating Dudley. Norah was also incriminated in a letter on BUF notepaper thought to be referring to BUF funds in which Mosley had written that 'Mrs. Elam had his full confidence, and was entitled to do what she thought fit in the interests of the Movement on her own responsibility'. Strangely, the letter had been found inside an envelope marked 'Private and Personal Mrs Dacre Fox', perhaps because within the LPAVS Norah used her former name for authorship, administrative and accounting purposes, or perhaps because as Mary Allen later revealed under questioning, 'Professor Dacre Fox' was used as a pseudonym for the Elams in the organization of secret meetings."

Letter from Mosley passing authority, PRO HO 283/48; and Microform Academic Publishers, Sir Oswald Mosley, KV2/884, cited in Mosley's Old Suffragette, op. cit.:

53 ***Ibid.:***

"The interrogation aimed to establish whether her handling of BUF funds had been illegal or improper. There had been some suspicion that Mosley had been receiving funds from Mussolini, and MI5 developed a theory that Norah was using the LPAVS front as a conduit for these Italian gifts. MI5 investigations had by this time uncovered her former bankruptcy, which would have made Norah an even greater object of suspicion as she would have been presumed to have experience in moving funds and hiding assets from bankruptcy administrators. ... Her interrogators noted that 'Having regard to Mrs. Elam's past experience in connection with 'Funds' I think it reasonable to suppose that she herself suggested it would be advisable for BUF money to be withdrawn from the trust account. Mrs. Elam said that Mosley trusted her completely and she was proud of it.' The obvious implication is that MI5 considered it foolish of Mosley to trust a former bankrupt with party funds."

54 Mosley's explanation was perfectly plausible:

"I know, he said, why you have come here today. Poor Mrs. Elam has been round to see me and has told me of the trouble she has been in. If you had only come and asked us we could have explained it all to you so easily. I simply cannot understand why you should go to all this trouble in connection with BUF finances. Our position is perfectly clear ... As regards the money paid to Mrs. Elam we have nothing to be ashamed of and nothing to conceal. When war became imminent we had to be prepared for any eventuality. There might have been an air raid, our Headquarters might have been smashed by a mob, I myself ... was expecting to be assassinated. I may tell you quite frankly that I took certain precautions. It was necessary then for us to disperse the funds in case anything should happen to Headquarters or the leaders. Mrs. Elam therefore took charge of part of our funds for a short period before and after the declaration of war. There was nothing illegal or improper about this."

KV2/884, pp. 1-4, Visit to British Union Headquarters in Gt. Smith Street, 24/01/40; Microform Academic Publishers, cited in ibid.

55 Mosley appeared unconcerned about Special Branch's suspicions:

"Peter Whinfield and his parents, Lieutenant-Colonel HC & Mrs Muriel Whinfield, were regular visitors and close friends of the Elams. Norah had met Muriel in her West Sussex days, when Muriel had also defected from the Conservative Party, and they had shared a platform at Alton when they were heckled and shouted down by 'Reds'. Mosley had met the Whinfields at the Elams [sic]. ... Mosley had also met Peter Kruger at the Elam's [sic] flat, and described him to the Special Branch Officers as someone who had 'written a book about the Jews, a work of scholarship' and who impressed him as 'being a serious research worker and not at all the kind of person who would act as an agent'."

Votes for Women, the Story of a Struggle, by Roger Fulford; and KV2/884, pp. 1-4, op. cit., cited in Ibid.

56 Thurlow gives very useful information on the personalities involved:

"One other released Special Branch report refers to a secret meeting between prominent fascists and anti-semites on 7 February 1940. This was convened by Mosley and amongst those who attended were Francis Hawkins, Domvile, Lane Fox Pitt-Rivers, Aubrey Lees, the Earl of Mar and Norman Hay. This was similar to a previous meeting held on 9 November 1939. The chief decision taken at the 7 February meeting was to fight Silvertown and Leeds North-East by-elections. [***ref. PRO HO 45/24895/16***] The important thing about this report is that its reliability with regard to who attended the 7 February meeting can be confirmed from an independent source, the diary of Admiral Sir Barry Domvile. The entry for 7 February 1940 states that Domvile attended a Mosley meeting and that amongst others attending were Lane Fox Pitt-Rivers, Francis Hawkins and Aubrey Lees. [***ref. Dom. 56, 7 Feb. 1940***] Domvile also attended another Mosley meeting on 8 November (the discrepancy of one day was probably accounted for by the fact that Special Branch reports were sometimes written the day after events took place). The most interesting fact about this meeting was that Mosley and Ramsay were the main speakers.

The evidence in Domvile's diary suggests that he was one of the motivating forces behind the initiative to gain a greater degree of unity amongst the fascist and anti-semitic movements. Indeed, his organization the Link [sic] was aptly named. Not only did it provide a channel for Ribbentrop and Goebbels to influence British public opinion, [***ref. S. Wiggins, The Link, MA diss., University of St. Andrews, 1985, p6***] but Domvile saw his role as the key link man between the various groups. He wrote for the BUF newspaper under the pseudonym 'Canute' or 'Naval Expert', he spoke for the BPP candidate in the Hythe by-election, he was on friendly terms with Ramsay, Norman Hay, Lane Fox Pitt-Rivers and Tavistock, as well as founding the Link. As a retired admiral, an ex-assistant secretary to the Committee of Imperial Defence 1927-30, and president of the Royal Navy College at Greenwich 1932-4, his patriotism and the accuracy of his diary seem beyond reproach. His daily addiction to the writing of his diary spanned his long active life from the 1890s to the early 1970s; it can now be consulted at the National Maritime Museum at Greenwich. What information can be gleaned from the Home Office Papers confirms much of the detail of Domvile's account, as do the internment files on Aubrey Lees and Neil Francis Hawkins.

Domvile's diary for the phoney war period is a significant document because it lists many of the people who attended the meetings he was at, as well as some cryptic references to the discussion. The general picture which emerges from the diary is that there were loose connections between fascists, anti-semites and peace movements from before the war."

Fascism in Britain: etc., op. cit.

57 http://en.wikipedia.org/wiki/Ministry_of_Information_(United_Kingdom)

58 Addison & Crang's study is very comprehensive; one interesting snippet of information which can be found is that Wilfred's future inquisitor, Norman Birkett KC, broadcast to the nation under the pseudonym of ***Onlooker.***

LISTENING TO BRITAIN: Home Intelligence reports on Britain's Finest Hour—May to September 1940; Edited by Paul Addison & Jeremy A. Crang, Centre for the Study of the Two World Wars, School of History, Classics and Archaeology, University of Edinburgh

59 ***Ibid.:***

"Founded in 1937 by the social anthropologist Tom Harrisson, the poet Charles Madge and the documentary film-maker Humphrey Jennings, M-O employed a range of experimental and unorthodox techniques for assessing popular attitudes. Whereas conventional surveys reported the opinions expressed by members of the public to investigators, 'Mass-Observers' eavesdropped on conversations and reported on behaviour as well as opinion. Many of its early reports had focused on working-class life in the Lancashire town of Bolton ('Worktown' in M-O publications), but with the outbreak of war Harrisson, who was now in sole charge of the organisation, turned the spotlight on the problems of the home front. The message of ***War Begins at Home***, M-O's account of the phoney-war period published in March 1940, was unequivocal. A gulf of mutual incomprehension separated the politicians and the civil servants in Whitehall from the broad mass of the British people. Neither the press nor the House of Commons could bridge the gulf: Mass-Observation could."

60 ***Ibid.***

61 ***Ibid.:***

"Secret sources were drawn upon too. Postal censors provided analyses of letters, Special Branch reports were made available, and RIOs [Regional Information Officers] were in touch with Chief Constables. At the same time, special arrangements were put in place to cover the London region."

62 ***Ibid.:***

"On 9 April Hitler's forces had invaded and occupied Denmark and Norway. The political crisis precipitated by the defeat of the British expeditionary force to Norway had compelled Neville Chamberlain to step down as Prime Minister on 10 May. His successor, at the head of a new all-party Coalition government, was Winston Churchill. At dawn on 10 May Hitler's armies launched an invasion of Belgium and Holland, accompanied by a drive through the Ardennes into northern France. Within a few days the Allied armies were in retreat. On 15 May the Dutch High Command capitulated. By 18 May the German armies were advancing rapidly towards the Channel coast and threatening to encircle the British Expeditionary Force (BEF), along with the French First Army and the Belgian Army."

63 ***Ibid.:***

"As Home Intelligence commented, the rumours were mainly home-grown but often attributed, by those who passed them on, to 'Lord Haw-Haw', the nickname for the Nazi propagandist William Joyce who broadcast regularly from Hamburg. Press reports alleged that in Belgium and Holland German parachutists had disguised themselves as peasants or clergymen and been assisted by a 'Fifth Column' of enemy sympathisers among the local population. Home Intelligence noted many rumours of parachutists landing in Britain disguised (for reasons best known to the enemy) as nuns. Rumour also pointed the finger of suspicion at enemy aliens, most of whom were of course refugees from Nazi persecution, and there were signs of growing intolerance towards conscientious objectors."

64 ***Fascism in Britain: etc., op. cit.:***

"As a result of back bench pressure the government was forced to amend DR 18b on 23 November 1939 to the effect that the authorities must have reasonable cause to believe the hostile origins or association of individuals or that internees must have been recently concerned in actions which had compromised national security. This change was to cause problems when the grave military situation in May 1940 led the new government to a drastic alteration in security policy and the decision to intern not only most aliens but British fascists as well."

65 ***Ibid.***

66 It can be found here:
http://en.wikipedia.org/wiki/Defence_Regulation_18B

67 ***Fascism in Britain: etc., op. cit.:***

"This was a view he maintained at both the Cabinet meetings of 15 and 18 May when the issue was discussed. [***ref. PRO Cab. 65/7 WM 128 (40), p177***]"

68 There are "certain limitations:

It is technically only a procedural remedy; it is a guarantee against any detention that is forbidden by law, but it does not necessarily protect other rights, such as the entitlement to a fair trial. So if an imposition such as internment without trial is permitted by the law then *habeas corpus* may not be a useful remedy. Furthermore, in many countries, the process may be suspended due to a national emergency."
http://en.wikipedia.org/wiki/Habeas_corpus

69 Somewhat predictably, there was also a party political element involved:

"The Security Service had claimed that Maule Ramsay was organizing meetings of the pro-nazi and anti-semitic groups with Mosley, and Anderson later confirmed that one of the main reasons why the fascists had been interned and the communists left free was because of the secrecy surrounding the former's activities and the open manner of the latter. During the phoney war the BUF and the communist party both opposed the war. The authorities, not noted for their belief before June 1941 that communists were fine upstanding patriotic gentlemen who eschewed secretive subversive activity, undoubtedly had other motives. The decision to intern fascists and to leave communists free reflected the rise of the Labour party to share power in a coalition government. Whereas Labour was militantly anti-fascist, the left wing of the party had been co-operating with communist popular front policies since 1935."

PRO Cab. 65/13 WM 133 (40), 22 May 1940, cited in Fascism in Britain: etc., op. cit.

70 Although these instruments might initially be drafted by the Government, they effectively bypass the procedural authority of Parliament:

"In the United Kingdom this legislation is formally made in the name of the Queen by the Privy Council (Queen-in-Council), but in other countries the terminology may vary. ... Although the Orders are nominally made by the Queen, in practice, royal assent is a formality only. What actually happens is that a representative of the government (generally a cabinet minister or the Lord President of the Council) reads out batches of Orders in Council drafted by the government in front of the Queen, who, after every couple of orders, says 'Approved'. They then pass into law, and come into effect. However several instances have been recorded where a governor has questioned the technical basis of a proposed regulation, refused assent, and the order has been returned to the relevant department for revision."

http://en.wikipedia.org/wiki/Order_in_Council

71 The complete technical reference name for this rule was ***Regulation 18B of the Defence (General) Regulations 1939.***

http://en.wikipedia.org/wiki/Defence_Regulation_18B

72 ***Hansard, 23/05/40, cited in My Life, by Oswald Mosley***

73 ***Ibid.:***

"Why then were the Labour Party so strongly in favour of silencing me in the Second World War with a special regulation to permit imprisonment without trial? A prominent member of the party supplied some answer. Hugh Ross-Williamson, the author and playwright, wrote: 'At the Bournemouth Conference of the Labour Party in 1940 one of the main subjects of conversation which I heard at "unofficial" talks was whether or not some Labour leaders had made the arrest and imprisonment of Mosley a condition of their entering the Government. The general feeling was that they had (or, at least, that they ought to) and, though the matter is, obviously, incapable of proof, it is still accepted by many of us as the real reason for 18B.' A week later he wrote: '... May I be permitted to make an addendum to last week's letter on a matter of fact. At the time of writing I had not, unfortunately, access to ***Hansard***, and was loth to trust my memory in the matter of dates. The Amendment to Regulation 18B which made possible the arrest of Mosley was made on the evening of May 22nd, 1940 (***Hansard, May 23, 1940***). This was the second sitting-day after Labour joined the Government, and four days after the close of the Bournemouth Conference of the Labour Party.' Would we have been imprisoned if some Labour leaders had not made it a condition of entering the government? Would we have been released, when all the facts had been examined if political pressure had not been exercised?"

74 ***Fascism in Britain: etc., op. cit.:***

"The decision to intern represented the triumph of the hawks in the Joint Intelligence Committee, MI5, War Office and the War Cabinet and the defeat of the policy of Anderson and Vernon Kell, the head of the Security Service, who until the Tyler Kent affair considered with some justification that Britain's security defences had not been breached. Kell, who was in poor health, was to be the main victim of the security crisis and was to be sacked by Churchill."

75 ***Action*** printed the "Truth About Police Raid" the following week:

"ON THURSDAY LAST, PLAIN CLOTHES POLICEMEN, ACTING ON INSTRUCTIONS FROM THE HOME SECRETARY, CARRIED OUT A RAID ON BRITISH UNION NATIONAL HEADQUARTERS AT SANCTUARY BUILDINGS, WESTMINSTER.

EVERY PERSON ENTERING THE BUILDING WAS REQUIRED TO PRODUCE PROOF OF IDENTITY AND SUBMIT TO QUESTIONING AND SUBSEQUENTLY SEVERAL OFFICIALS OF BRITISH UNION WERE TAKEN INTO CUSTODY.

During Thursday, Friday and Saturday, the police conducted an examination of papers and documents in British Union offices. After Saturday the building returned to normal.

It was afterwards learned that the raid had covered a wider field. According to the Press, some 70 or 80 persons have been detained."

On page four [the last page of the understandably reduced size, penultimate edition; the final one appeared on June the 6th] there was also a short biographical review, including Wilfred's military service, among those of "the men named below [who] each have a record of service to the country" so, consequently, Wilfred's was above that of Francis Hawkins who, notwithstanding that he was "[a]mong the younger men detained", had not:

"W. RISDON, served in His Majesty's forces throughout the last War, 1914-1918, was wounded and now suffers from heart trouble through shell shock. He was only 17 years of age when he enlisted to fight for his country."

Action, no. 221, May 30th, 1940, pages 1 & 4

76 Mosley appeared unruffled by the whole affair:

"I was arrested on May 23, 1940, together with all the leading men of our movement, and Diana was arrested some six weeks later on June 29. … We had spent the evening of May 22 in my house at Denham, and left the children there on the afternoon of the 23rd to motor the twenty-odd miles to our flat in Dolphin Square. I was surprised to see obvious plain-clothes police outside the front door; ingenuously, it had not occurred to me that I might be arrested. Getting out of the car, I recognised among them detectives whom I knew because it was their job to attend meetings where there was any chance of disorder. They informed me I was to be arrested and I accompanied them to the flat which was swarming with police. They were all most courteous throughout, and after collecting a few things I parted from Diana and went with some of them in a car to Brixton. There I found a large number of our people had already been imprisoned."

My Life, op. cit.

77 http://en.wikipedia.org/wiki/Defence_Regulation_18B

78 ***In the Highest Degree Odious: etc, op. cit.***

79 ***Superintendent's Report by Inspector Charles Allen, Special Branch, New Scotland Yard, 23/05/40, Subject: Wilfred RISDON; TNA, HO 45/23670, R5***

80 Both Norah and Dudley Elam were also arrested at the same time at Victoria Street; Norah in her capacity as Secretary [although she was always referred to by her actual married name of Dacre-Fox, and at this time the Secretary's name was routinely not stated in the Minutes], and Dudley was an Executive Committee member, so barring extenuating circumstances, both would have been at the meeting which Wilfred was going to chair. Unsurprisingly, the meeting was abandoned; the earliest opportunity to convene again was on the following Tuesday, when an Emergency Meeting was held:

"Mrs. Dacre-Fox: Dr. Allinson proposed that Mrs. Dacre Fox be offered a retaining fee of £150 per annum payable monthly in consideration of her agreeing to resume her duties with the society at the earliest possible moment if called upon to do so. She to make up the proposed monthly News Sheet and to act generally in a non-consultative capacity without further remuneration this engagement to be subject to review by the Society. Mr. Geoffrey B. Gush was instructed to inform to [sic] Mrs. Dacre [sic] to that effect.

Outdoor Lecturers: With reference to the four outdoor lecturers the Committee came to the conclusion that for reasons of economy it was impossible to employ all of them and it was decided to keep only Mr. Armstrong and Mr. Large. Letter from Mr. large was read and Mr. Gush was instructed to answer it. The men given notice to receive one month's money in lieu of notice. Query, is this to apply to Mr. Risdon.

Office Staff: It was decided that Miss Marchant carry on with management of office at her present salary. It was decided to dispense with the services of Miss Knight and that she be given a month's money in lieu of notice."

Minutes of Emergency LPAVS Committee Meeting held on May 28, 1940, courtesy of the NAVS

The question of Wilfred's status, following his arrest, was not resolved at this meeting; the Committee was obviously very keen to keep Norah 'on board', not knowing that she had no intention of appealing her detention, but they must have been prepared to accept the absence of a monthly publication, even if only for a short period. Norah was taken to Holloway prison in due course; the tone of Inspector Allen's report allows for the inference that Wilfred's was the only case with which they were dealing on that particular day, but it quite possible that Norah had her own 'case officers'.

81 After her release from Holloway "by at least February 1942" [Dudley having been "released fairly early on in the war … probably … late in 1940"], Norah saw her enthusiastic fund-raising for Mosley's "18B Detainees (British Aid Fund) and the 18B Publicity Council, that were registered as a war charity under the War Charities Act in 1940" as a good way of continuing to ingratiate herself with him; however, the snap election called for only two months after the end of the war in May, 1945, caused Mosley to reassess his plans for a comeback so, notwithstanding the following tendentious assumption:

> "Mosley's withdrawal from politics and the closing of the 18B Detainees Fund (which was effectively the former BUF), meant that Norah had no political home. Dudley was now 73 years old and had been in poor health for some years. Norah was also in her 60s. Dudley and Norah moved out of central London to live at Gothic Cottage in Twickenham."

Mosley's Old suffragette, op. cit.

82 ***HO 45/23764; A.47, Report of Advisory Committee Appeal Hearing, op. cit.:***

> "On the detention of Mrs. Elam, who has been detained and has not objected to the Order, she was appointed by the Committee of the Society to be Acting Secretary. … On Mrs. Elam's detention she was examined by the officers of the Society, particularly with regard to her political proclivities and activities, and as they were satisfied that she had no connection with British Union she got the appointment."

12: PRISONER NUMBER 2205

At six o'clock in the evening of May the 23rd, 1940, Wilfred Risdon must have arrived at Brixton Prison, south London, with a whole range of conflicting emotions all jostling for supremacy in his mind; irritation at the interruption of his work, especially when he was, by invitation [and in recognition of his obvious abilities] exceeding his original brief; perhaps even anger, especially in view of the obvious association with his former career and erstwhile colleagues, if this was not already known to such members of the organising Committee of his employer, who might be hostile to this, but also for the exposure of Nellie and their children to this association in the minds of friends & neighbours; trepidation, not for himself particularly, given that conditions of physical hardship and even assault on his person were not unknown to him, but for the safety of his family; frustration at the knowledge of how slow and intractable the system by which he could appeal his incarceration would be; but also, by way of compensatory balance, perhaps amusement [in the sense of ironically appropriate gallows humour] that many of his former associates and acquaintances who might well have considered themselves virtually 'untouchable' would also find themselves in the same socially levelling situation. Prior to this, the process of Wilfred's transition from a 'free' man [always a relative term] to a captive had begun with the serving of the Detention Order, signed by Under Secretary of State for the Home Department, Sir Alexander Maxwell, which detailed the reasons for his arrest [**1**].

After a full transcript of the relevant section of Regulation 18B of the Defence (General) Regulations, 1939, paragraph (1A), which had been inserted after paragraph (1), under which the Secretary of State [Home Secretary, Sir John Anderson] "in pursuance of the powers conferred on him by the above mentioned Regulation" made an order directing that Wilfred should be detained, he was informed that, in addition to having the right to make his objections to an advisory committee appointed by the Secretary of State, he would have "an opportunity" of making any representations he wished to the Secretary of State [although it is not specified whether this would be directly or indirectly], and that this would not have any bearing upon the former right: it would appear that he did not avail himself of the latter. Assuming that Wilfred was, indeed, blameless in his current activities [although the doubts of the Security Service about this will be detailed below], the only part of the Detention Order about which he can have had any worries was the retrospective scope of the Regulations which specified that "the persons in control of the organisation have or *have had* associations with persons concerned in the government of, or sympathies with the system of government of, *any power* with which His Majesty is at war" [my emphasis], hence his immediate statement to the arresting officers that he was no longer a member of British Union.

The Inspector's report of the arrest and its associated circumstances is somewhat out of sequence: it begins by detailing how Wilfred was arrested at the third attempt, after the officers had twice gone to the wrong address; it then describes how he was handed over to the Governor of Brixton Prison [in effect 'into the jurisdiction of', rather than in person] with the personal effects he had with him at the time, none of which appeared suspect although, again, it is most likely that this 'frisking' will have been done almost immediately by the arresting officers, rather than on handover, as the prison authorities must surely have carried out their own personal search procedures. The report then goes on to itemise the search of Wilfred's house "in accordance with Chief Constable's authority granted under the Defence Regulations 88a(2)" [presumably a blanket authorisation] and Wilfred's response to nearly every item, so even though he was not present for the search, it meant another chance for the neighbours to gawp and gossip. His British Union warrant card was dated 26th July 1939 [a Wednesday], which seems a rather odd date, given that he claimed to have "paid subscriptions right up to July, but since then I have paid no subscriptions" [**Appendix D**]; but if members paid in advance, immaterial whether weekly or monthly, then surely the date should have been either the 30th of July [the last Sunday of the month] or the 31st? Also, it would seem odd for a warrant card to be updated on such a regular basis, but it is plausible at least.

The sketch maps, especially the one on which "Northolt Aerodrome is clearly marked", could very easily have been regarded as suspicious, but again, Wilfred's explanation, that they "were used for canvassing new B.U. members", is plausible, notwithstanding a natural curiosity as to why someone who claimed to have severed his links with this organisation nearly a year ago would have bothered to keep impedimenta such as these, and an observation that it was very selfless on his part to involve himself in activities that were more suited to local rank & file members [assuming that such were available] rather than an executive officer such as he with national responsibilities. The letter from the serving soldier in the British Expeditionary Force [BEF], who "speaks bitterly of conditions in France, remarks that things there are definitely Fascist, and alleges that the men would return home if there was a man strong enough to lead them", would probably have been more of a problem for the Artilleryman author than it might have been for Wilfred. The discovery which was evidently to cause Wilfred most concern, if the transcript of his Appeal Hearing [**Appendix D**] is anything to go by, was "a box containing 25 rounds of 6.35m.m. pistol ammunition", for which he had no "firearm [sic] certificate", whereupon he was cautioned, but he obviously felt it was in his interest to be candid about its origin, even to the extent of disclosing that in his possession at the Manchester headquarters in Northumberland Street he had also had, four years previously, two handguns which had been discovered at the British

Union headquarters in Preston, but they had gone missing, a matter that he appears not to have pursued; there is no mention of a question from Inspector Allen as to why this should have been, but he did inform Wilfred "that the matter would be reported for further consideration [and that he was] retaining the ammunition pending instructions as to its disposal".

The Inspector's report concludes with a synopsis of Wilfred's current employment status, including the location of his own office, "and at his invitation it was searched but nothing of interest was found", so it is hardly surprising that it was three hours from when he was initially apprehended until he was deposited at Brixton Prison. His loss of individual liberty would have been impressed upon him very quickly by the assignment of a number, 2205, no doubt less intellectually demanding for the prison bureaucracy although, in fairness, many administrative systems that handle large numbers of individuals, such as the military, also use this system; following this homogenisation, prior to being assigned a 'living' cell, as it were, he would have been put in a holding cell, but the latter was preceded by a humiliating forced bath, as described by one of his former colleagues [**2**]. Another ex-colleague, Hector McKechnie, was assigned number 2170, which implies that he was processed some while before Wilfred. They were housed [if that is not an overstatement] in F wing, although it is not clear where that was in relation to the overall plan of the gaol [**3**], but it made sense, from an operational point of view, to keep all the category 18B prisoners, including the 'enemy aliens', predominantly German and Italian, in the same wing. Unfortunately, overcrowding appears to have been a perennial problem at the gaol [see note 3] and, according to Mosley, who "was put in No. 1 cell" [**4**], F wing had, prior to its latest function, been condemned as unfit for use, although the Governor, Captain Clayton, didn't think to mention that in his autobiography [**5**]. Mosley's recollection is that he "was surrounded by familiar faces and the most variegated collection of bed-bugs I had ever encountered since the First War." [**6**]

Wilfred will also have been surrounded by many familiar faces, perhaps not immediately adjacent, depending upon the location of his cell [despite the overcrowding, there is nothing to suggest that inmates had to share cells] and, whilst it might have boosted his morale to some degree by having to share again a common experience, he might also have felt that fate was condemning him to prolong his association with people in an organisation from which he had only just managed to move away. According to Mosley, "Nearly all the men in our wing were members of our movement, except for some Germans and Italians who had been naturalised British, and a few members of the 'Right Club', to which Ramsay belonged." [**7**] Clayton also remarked upon the curious mixture of internees, of types which a member of the establishment might not otherwise expect [**8**]. No less than most, if not all of Wilfred's fellow detainees, he would have wanted to find the quickest way out of prison, so his first priority was to set in motion the appeal process, to which he was entitled. The very next day after his arrest, he wrote a note which covered nearly a full page of the regulation issue embossed and lined prison paper [although the prison name was printed with a rubber stamp]; subsequent to this, the note was transcribed by typewriter for his Home Office file. It is slightly curious that the note does not specifically request an appeal hearing [**9**], although perhaps that was a matter of pride. The note is courteous and informative:

Reg. No.: *2205* Name: *W. Risdon* Prison: BRIXTON

Having been detained under Regulation 18B of the Defence (General) Regulations I beg to submit the following relevant facts to the Secretary of State:–

(1) I am not now a member of any political organisation whatsoever. My membership of British Union has been lapsed since July 1939 and I have joined no other organisation.

(2) I solemnly declare that I have no desire to engage in any act prejudicial to the Public Safety, the defence of the Realm, the maintenance of public order, the efficient prosecution of any war in which His Majesty may be engaged, or the maintenance of supplies or services essential to the life of the community.

(3) In guarantee of the above statements I place myself unreserevedly at the disposal of the Secretary of State to serve in any capacity considered to be beneficial to any of the above items detailed in para (2) above.

[signed] *Wilfred Risdon*

This is clearly the language of a man who knows how to deal with officialdom: his refutation quotes the exact terminology of the Detention Order, after his statement that he is neither a current member of British Union, nor “any political organisation whatsoever”, and he makes it abundantly clear that he wants to make himself available for useful service, something that not all of his compatriots would have done; although, to be fair, many of his former colleagues did manage to join the fighting services either at or before the beginning of the war, only to suffer the indignity of being arrested in uniform. It would have been perfectly natural for Wilfred to enquire of the Governor, or the highest available functionary in the administrative chain at the prison, as to how soon he might be able to expect a response to his statement but, whether he did or not, he must have been pragmatic enough to know that it would be a laboriously slow process, notwithstanding the status of the 18B detainees within the judgmental hierarchy of the prison population, so his best option would be to accept the privations he and his fellows would have to endure and accommodate them with the best possible grace. Officially, according to special instructions issued by Sir John Anderson, the '18Bs' were to be regarded not as convicted prisoners [with no apparent irony, given that they weren't!] "but as if they were on trial and remand. They were also to have certain additional privileges. These were:

1. That parcels of food and drink might be sent in to them.
2. That they might be visited once a week by friends and daily by their solicitors.
3. That they might be allowed to write and receive an unlimited number of letters, subject to censorship.
4. That they were to be permitted to associate at meals, labour and recreation.
5. That provision was to be made for their outdoor exercise at which games might be played.
6. That they could apply for special rooms and furniture and have their cells cleaned for them." [**10**]

The final one of these seems so unbelievable as to be laughable; it will, no doubt, come as no surprise that they did not materialise in totality, and the primary ground for this, according to Clayton, was shortage of staff [**11**]. Mosley, who assumed, in continuance of his now only notional position of Leader, the rôle of negotiator on behalf of his acolytes [**12**], was prepared to be magnanimous towards the Governor in this regard [**13**], although whether this was his contemporaneous attitude, or one that was the result of subsequent reflection, and whether he would have included ex-members such as Wilfred in this noblesse can only be speculated upon. Notwithstanding the Governor's egalitarian approach [see note 12], Mosley seemed to be thinking ahead at this time, at least in the early stages of the war, beyond the resolution of the current conflict, and a fellow inmate, another high-profile previous member, John Beckett, [who "was horrified to be thrust back amidst the 'miniature followers' of the 'Mosley circus'" **14**] was to receive an invitation via "Mosley's emissary", Hector McKechnie, to join Mosley in a "government-in-exile"; Beckett gave this very short shrift, and sent McKechnie packing [**15**]: there is no record of Mosley having approached Wilfred in the same manner.

In the first days of his confinement, while he was waiting as patiently as it might be possible to, in the circumstances, for a response to his statement, Wilfred will have perhaps enjoyed, as did Mosley, one of the pleasures which can be indulged in a solitary manner, that of reading, assuming that Nellie will have been able to accommodate him at the earliest possible opportunity, given that cell doors were only unlocked for three hours a day; Mosley also later maintained that he was instrumental in overturning this stricture "against my interests … My request was eventually granted, and the cell doors were opened; all hell then broke loose." [**16**] There was another possible reason for this initial draconian treatment: the suggestion of the possibility of an attempt to free Mosley by force [**17**] and Mosley observed in his autobiography "[i]t was rumoured that at first the prison was surrounded by troops at night; I do not know if this was true." [**18**] As a result of a lack of personal observations, it is impossible to be sure how the experience of prison affected Wilfred at any stage of his incarceration, but while he was in Brixton Mosley, at least, appears to have been able to maintain a cheerful demeanour [if for no other reason than "*pour encourager les autres*"] and even relaxed his personal grooming regime, according to his son Nicholas, although the "something like a boiler suit" [**19**], which might have been initial prison-issue, was to be fairly quickly superseded by his own clothes [leading to the inevitable press speculation and sheer invention, in view of Mosley's reputation **20**] and this will, presumably, have also made Wilfred feel marginally more comfortable. It is difficult to imagine Wilfred, in view of his generally cooperative nature and his immediate conciliatory offer to the Home Secretary, raising his voice against the less than satisfactory conditions in Brixton, or actually participating in any acts of disobedience by way of wanton sabotage; Mosley's contention that: "In pursuance of our principle to do nothing to impede the war effort of the nation, I at once instructed our members to behave with complete propriety, which they did." [**21**] is undoubtedly true, but the Governor's recollection was also that "certain [unidentified] malcontents" were disruptive [**22**].

In Wilfred's Home Office file [***TNA HO 45/23670***], there is an entry on one of the minutes sheets which is so brief as to be beyond cryptic: "Appeal" against the date of "28.5.40"; on the same line, it notes "Sent copies to M.I.5 & H.O. 29/5". However many copies of this appeal might have been made originally, regrettably there is none in the folder now [unless the note detailed above constituted an appeal: see note 9], so its content must remain unknown. As related by Bellamy [see note 9], it is unlikely that Wilfred would have been permitted to avail himself of the services of a solicitor at this juncture, although it is also quite possible that he would previously, as an element of his preparation for almost inevitable arrest at some point, have considered an approach to employ at an appeal, perhaps briefed by a colleague with what might be regarded as 'inside knowledge' [perhaps Mr. Gush], which will be enlarged upon below. June must have been a month of almost interminable *longueur* for Wilfred, as there is no entry [that can be deciphered, anyway] on either of the minute sheets in his file with this date at all, although that does not automatically imply that his case was not receiving attention: during this month, the wife of one of Wilfred's erstwhile colleagues, Archibald Garrioch Findlay [who was to receive special attention from the Appeal Committee, because of the interest of the Security Service, on behalf of the Government, on the subject of the question of Italian funding for British Union, and who would be mentioned in this context in Wilfred's Appeal Hearing] wrote to her MP, Colonel Llewellyn [although this appears to have been a misspelling], requesting that he could take up, on her behalf, the matter of making enquiries at the Home Office as to the nature of the charges against her husband. For no apparent reason other than that Wilfred, as "another constituent of yours, is in a similar position to my husband. I should therefore be very grateful if you would include him in any action you take on behalf of my husband."

The letter is dated June 17th, but the item in Wilfred's file is a copy, thus marked, so perhaps its inclusion implies nothing more sinister than the fact that Wilfred was mentioned, so a copy for completeness should have been included in his file, but it does seem something of a coincidence, given the specificity of Wilfred's questioning by the Appeal Committee on the subject of the Italian funds and Archibald Findlay's alleged involvement. In a parallel with Wilfred's situation, Mrs. Findlay tells Colonel Llewellin that her husband's [unnamed] employers, "knowing the situation, are keeping his job open for him, but of course they are not in a position to do this indefinitely." Realistically, this was probably a very common situation, but Colonel Llewellin [assuming he was prepared to treat the request with genuine concern] might have seen that as an incentive on the part of the Home Office to treat Findlay's case with some expedition, especially if his employment was any sort of war work. Unfortunately, however, this was a faint hope; Colonel Llewellin's letter from the Ministry of Aircraft Production, Millbank, S.W.1. [Tel: Victoria 4411], dated 19th June, to "My dear Osbert" [Peake, MP] at the Home Office [Whitehall, S.W.1.] was cordially deferential: "I do not, of course, wish to influence you in any way, but it would be helpful if you could let me have a reply that I can pass on to my constituent."; Peake's letter, minus introductory salutation, dated 2 days later, from roughly half a mile away on the same road [Millbank leads into Whitehall on the north/west side of the Thames], was polite but uncompromising: "It is open to these men to make representations - which I expect they have already done - but we cannot undertake to deal with appeals otherwise than in their turn. I will let you know the final decisions in these cases." There the matter had to rest for just over a week.

On the 2nd of July, E. B. Stamp [**23**] of MI5 [Box No. 500, Parliament Street, S.W.1.; between Millbank & Whitehall], sent the "statements of cases and reasons for Order against WILFRED RISDON and GEORGE J. SUTTON" to "Dear Churchill", the Secretary of the Advisory

Committee [**24**], but no address was shown on the small letter. There is probably no inference to be drawn from the combination of Wilfred and George Sutton, Mosley's longtime private secretary and ardent Fascist; it is most likely the result of their alphabetical proximity. The Statement of Case, which follows below, signed by Stamp and also dated July 2nd, was significantly different from the Reasons for Order: the latter was, rather confusingly, a statement of the Government's position using its assumed jurisdiction of Defence Regulation 18B (1A), although it is fairly comprehensive and somewhat tendentious; the former was a collection of allegations, in the guise of general information about the accused, some of which was also decidedly tendentious, and some of which was factually incorrect, but it is more than possible that this did not cause Wilfred undue concern. It is worth quoting the entire document, as it is directly related to Wilfred's appeal:

STATEMENT OF CASE AGAINST

WILFRED RISDON

This man was, until shortly prior to the outbreak of war, an Assistant Director General of the B.U. attached to the Headquarters staff and responsible for the election of B.U. nominees both to local councils and Parliament. He was at the time of the 1937 autumn municipal elections one of the leaders of the "Press Propaganda Group".

He was among the Headquarters officers present at the more important gathering of the B.U. He, together with CAPTAIN GORDON CANNING and A.G. FINDLAY, formed a group opposed to FRANCIS-HAWKINS. He was the writer of pamphlets, among others "Power Action", "Gainst Trust and Monopoly", and "Women and Fascism".

In November, 1938, he was noted as propaganda administrator and the author of a circular consisting of notes on distributing propaganda.

He left Headquarters in August, 1939, and claims then to have ceased to be a member of the B.U. He admitted, however, at the time of his detention that he had not formally resigned, and the very fact that he ostensibly severed his connection with the B.U. may be highly significant in the following circumstances. About the same time that he left Headquarters he joined the staff of the ANTI-VIVISECTIONIST SOCIETY, and from thenceforth he worked under MRS. ELAM,(known also as MRS. DACRE FOX) a former suffragette and active worker in the B.U. at the offices of the ANTI-VIVISECTIONIST SOCIETY, who was using those offices as a cover for B.U. activities and was also holding funds on behalf of the B.U. RISDON, moreover, is known to have continued to communicate with B.U. Headquarters.

In the drawer of his bureau was found an automatic pistol and a small plated revolver, together with ammunition for which he had no certificate.

[signed] *E.B.Stamp*

It is not necessary to dissect this tract item by item, because a reading of Wilfred's Appeal Hearing testimony [**Appendix D**] should suffice, but it is worth highlighting a couple of points: Wilfred was not the author of the latter two named pamphlets in paragraph two [although it is entirely possible that he might have had some contributory input], only the first; he is again linked with Findlay in the same paragraph; and it is difficult to understand why the allegation about the weapons, in the final paragraph, which could be, and indeed was, so easily refuted, was made, but perhaps one should not look any further than the simplest explanation of human shortcomings: ineptitude and/or poor communication on the part of Special Branch. The other document that was required to stand against Wilfred, in the matter of '*Rex vs.* Risdon', as it were, was the Reasons for Order; there are two copies in Wilfred's file: one is undated, whereas the other was dated 4th July, which postdates Peake's letter to Churchill, so perhaps this was a later copy for some reason, and it was the undated original of the copy in the file which was sent by Peake. Again, if for no other reason than that of completeness of information, it is worth reproducing the Reasons for Order in full here:

4th July, 1940.

REASONS FOR ORDER MADE UNDER DEFENCE REGULATION 18B IN THE CASE OF WILFRED RISDON

The Order under Defence Regulation 18B was made against you, Wilfred RISDON, for the following reasons:-

1. The Secretary of State has reasonable cause to believe that you have been a member of the organisation now known as "British Union"; and to have been active in the furtherance of its objects; and that it is necessary to exercise control over you.

Particulars.

You, Wilfred RISDON, have been a member of the said organisation since some years and have been active in the furtherance of its objects in performing the functions of an Assistant Director-General of the said organisation, and as one of the leaders of the Press propaganda group.

2. The organisation known as "British Union" is subject to foreign influence and/or control.

Particulars.

(a) The constitution of the organisation is influenced by Italian or German political and/or national organisations.

(b) The constitution of the organisation has been and is subject to Italian or German influences in the original name of the organisation, "The British Union of Fascists"; its later name, "The British Union of Fascists and National Socialists"; its emblems, its uniforms, its procedure, its form of public meetings and similar matters.

(c) The policy of the organisation has been and is subject to Italian or German influence; e.g. the anti-semitic campaign of British Union.

(d) There is reasonable cause to believe that between the years 1932 and 1937 the organisation has been in receipt of monies from Italy.

3. That Oswald Ernald MOSLEY, as one of the persons in control of the organisation, has or has had associations with persons concerned in the Government of Germany, a power with which His Majesty is at war. [page break]

<u>Particulars.</u>

(a) In or about the months of June or July 1938, the said Oswald Ernald MOSLEY entered into close association with persons concerned with the Government of Germany in connection with the erection of a wireless broadcasting station in Germany, to be used by an English company in which he was closely interested.

(b) German propaganda literature has been regularly received by the organisation for the purpose of distribution by arrangement between the organisation and persons concerned in the Government of Germany.

(c) That the said Oswald Ernald MOSLEY has paid visits to Germany and has been received with every sign of honour from Herr Hitler. His reception by Herr Hitler was in consequence of the affinity existing between his organisation in Great Britain and the Party organisation in Germany.

(d) That many members of British Union have been encouraged by the said Oswald Ernald MOSLEY, as leader, to visit Germany to consider and study the organisations existing in that country, for the purpose of strengthening the British Union.

4. That the said Oswald Ernald MOSLEY, as one of the persons in control of British Union, and other persons in such control, have sympathies with the system of Government in Germany, a power with which His Majesty is at war.

<u>Particulars.</u>

(a) In public speeches and writings, the said Oswald Ernald MOSLEY and other persons in control of the British Union have extolled the system of Government existing in Germany and condemned the democratic system of Government existing in Great Britain.

(b) That one of the objects of British Union is to replace the present system of Government in Great Britain by the system of Government now obtaining in Germany with appropriate modifications.

5. There is danger of the utilisation of the organisation known as British Union for purposes prejudicial to the public safety, the defence of the realm, the maintenance of public order, the efficient prosecution of the war in which His Majesty is engaged, or the maintenance of supplies or services essential to the life of the community.

This was, effectively, a much expanded version of the Detention Order that was served on Wilfred when he was arrested [see note 1], so he might have had chance to discuss it at an early stage with his solicitor [although that is by no means guaranteed] and consider its ramifications in the meantime, but it would have been only when he first had sight of the latter document above that he would have been able to formulate and itemise the defence that he would be using at his Appeal Hearing, whenever that might be. The letter from MI5, enclosing the Reasons for Order and the Statement of Case, was received by the Chairman of the Advisory Committee, Mr. Norman Birkett KC, on the 4th of July; he approved them, and determined to proceed with the action, and the file was annotated to that effect with a date stamp of the same date; also on this date, the Reasons for Order only, not the Statement of Case, was sent to the prison, but it is not specified whether this means by normal post or some sort of courier service, so it might well not have arrived until the next day. This was standard practice, but it meant that the detainee was not in possession of all the allegations against him or her before the appeal hearing, which could very easily wrong-foot a nervous or unprepared applicant [as they were officially classified]. Wilfred had less than a full week to absorb the case against him and formulate his defence [and much as expected, there is no mention anywhere in his file of a solicitor] although, to be fair, he must have had a reasonable idea of what to expect before the specific details arrived.

His appeal was heard on Thursday, July the 11th at number one Court, 6 Burlington Gardens, W1, the base of the Advisory Committee [adjacent the Royal Academy] that was used by the Home Office for this purpose in the early days of the war [**25**]; this is about six miles from Brixton Prison via a dense network of interconnecting and circuitous roads so, even given the reduced level of traffic consequent upon the war, the journey will have taken anything up to an hour, but even if Wilfred's case was heard in the morning [and judging by the length of the testimony, it is possible that two such appeals could have been heard in one day], the early start [to facilitate necessities such as 'slopping out' and breakfast] of the prison regime will undoubtedly have enabled him to be ready in plenty of time to be prepared for when he would be collected for delivery to his appointment. Although the appeal was notionally heard in a court, it was essentially an informal hearing; however, the transcript of the appeal, noted, somewhat curiously, by Treasury Reporters, would undoubtedly have had a 'legal' status. The Advisory Committee, whose makeup could vary from time to time [possibly according to availability] consisted, on this particular day, of four members: Chairman [**26**] Norman Birkett KC; the Rt. Hon. Sir George Clerk, GCMG, CB [**27**]; Sir Arthur Hazlerigg, Bt. [**28**]; and Secretary Mr. G. P. Churchill.

Although Wilfred can have been in no doubt as to the gravity of the situation, it is clear from the transcript of the meeting [as it is described in the official record, **Appendix D**] that his interlocutors, predominant of whom was the Chairman, had no intention of subjecting him to a 'third degree' style of cross-examination, but it is also clear that Birkett was not just asking general questions about Wilfred's loyalties: the Reasons for Order was the script, and the Statement of Case was MI5's ammunition. Unfortunately, as intimated above, the latter frequently contained errors, and these arose for a variety of reasons, primary of which was laxity and inefficiency in MI5 procedures [**29**]; the view could also have been taken, of course, that 'if enough mud is thrown, some of it is bound to stick'. Wilfred's was dated July 2nd; Mosley's first Advisory Committee Hearing was on this date, and he was questioned by Birkett, but briefed by Aikin Sneath, about leading members and officials of British Union, a list that included Wilfred, so on that score, as in the cases of Chesterton ["Mosley typically claimed he had been expelled"] and Geoffrey Dorman ["who had resigned well before the war and was in the RAF"] it "was quite out of date" [**30**]. In Wilfred's case, Mosley refers to having to release him from the salaried staff in July 1939 "as an economy measure" [**31**]; if any reference was made to this [assuming it could have been transcribed quickly enough] in preparing Wilfred's Statement of Case, Mosley's date of July was clearly not used.

From the very beginning, the tenor of the conversation appears to be relaxed and courteous; Wilfred is asked if he would like to "make a statement now or at the conclusion", rather than for them "to ask questions to bring the matters out"; he opts to make a statement although, inevitably, it is punctuated by associated questions. The first matter on which he dwells at any length is the question of foreign influence in British Union, and he is very quick to register his dislike of the name "Fascist", and the Action Press uniform, to which he "strenuously" objected. There was no Italian or German influence on British Union policy, specifically "the anti-Semitism campaign … as well as I remember"; rather it was "a fight, as it was expressed to me, that was forced on us by Jewish interests in this country." He then goes on to detail his suspicions, and his attempts to get to the bottom of "really the worst one": that "moneys from Italy" had been received by British Union between 1932 and 1937. He had not been satisfied with Francis Hawkins and Mosley's resolution of his concerns and that "it did mark a definite change in my attitude and outlook." He "certainly did not" know about the "secret account with the Westminster Bank dealing with the British Union of Fascist [sic] Funds", but Birkett was prepared to accept this "because this finance business seems to have been done cloaked with the greatest mystery and secrecy that [he had] ever discovered in any concern or organisation." Findlay is mentioned here, in connection with the funds, given that "he was supposed to deal with the finance", but Wilfred is not specifically asked if he knew of Findlay's activities, neither is his wife's entreaty on Wilfred's behalf mentioned.

Wilfred is quite ready to confirm that "Mosley himself, as one of the persons in control of the organisation, has or has had associations with persons concerned in the government of Germany"; he is unequivocal: "That I believe to be perfectly true", but also "that in addition to that of course he had similar associations with Mussolini". Birkett very quickly observed that this was not automatically damning: "That word 'associations' may mean very much or very little." Wilfred recounts that he "could see very little inducement" to be a member of the British Union group visiting Italy, presumably for the last time, and that, although there was no official report of the visit, there was a meeting "held at the Dennison Hall shortly afterwards at which Sir Oswald Mosley and one or two others spoke about their experiences on that visit." Unfortunately, the occasion was soured by a *contretemps* when "the spirit of discipline of one of the famous Italian regiments" was attacked, to which the wife of an officer serving in that regiment, who happened to be in the audience, took great exception. This gave Birkett the opportunity to seek confirmation that "Sir Oswald Mosley, so to speak, kept a good many matters to himself?" Birkett almost falls over himself in his willingness to absolve Wilfred of any knowledge of Mosley's Italian associations: "… if, for example - I do not say it is so for a moment - he had any understanding with Mussolini about assistance or help, that might quite conceivably be one of the things he would keep to himself?" Answer: "Yes." Similarly, on the subject of the radio station project, "you need not trouble your head about that because in any event it had nothing to do with you".

The next matter was potentially dangerous: that of German propaganda literature. Wilfred gave this very short shrift: any propaganda material, "both German and Italian literature … just remained in the office and naturally [was] carried out again as waste paper … the reason, quite frankly, why I never used it is because I do not consider it to be good propaganda. I do not think foreigners ever understand the British …" He was pressed as to the source of the material, and although he did concede that "official German propaganda I suppose we can call it" [Birkett's term] did reach him, yet he did not use it; he thought "it would be sent through people here in England" and "as the person who had to make the decision on that … I just treated it as junk that was not wanted." He is asked about "one particular matter … a pamphlet on Danzig, presenting the German case, and we rather gathered the leader had given instructions that that pamphlet should be distributed to all districts." but he deflects that [either serendipitously by accident, or cleverly by design] by complaining about "a Director General who had authority … who could distribute stuff over my head that I knew nothing about. … to my knowledge - and I speak in all sincerity - I never allowed any foreign literature to pass out from the British Union during the period I had any control over that department." Another mention of visits to Germany gives him the opportunity to restate his attitude: "people who are working for an improvement in the social system in England could learn far more about what they wanted to do by visiting the slums of England than by going to Nuremberg or any of those other gatherings."

For some reason, initially, Birkett inclines to the belief that Wilfred's background is as a member of the Society of Friends, not the ILP, but he is pleased to discover that Wilfred had some association with an educational establishment for working men, Fircroft College, that was run by a Quaker, George Cadbury Junior, so they have a mutual interest, although Birkett's connection predated Wilfred's by around fifteen years. Wilfred then takes the opportunity to restate his opposition to "some members of the British Union [who] have taken a line in propaganda of attempting to justify what happens in Germany rather than concentrating on what is our problem in this country. … I believe you to be right in forming [that] conclusion", and he goes on to mention the Buckhurst Hill meeting in 1938, at which he was persistently questioned about his opinion of what had happened in Germany, about which he "knew nothing [and] cared less". The end of his propaganda activities led him into the remaining obligation to build up election machinery within the Movement, giving him an opportunity to mention "[t]he street blocks system … that I first worked out with an old colleague, Dr. Robert Forgan who left the Movement many years ago"; Birkett seems unaware that Wilfred had been in the New Party with Forgan. Wilfred is then able to lead on from that into an explanation of how and exactly when he left British Union, although he does mention, no doubt prudently, the meeting with Mosley about the proposed by-election participation, and his decision to demur.

This gives Birkett the opportunity to quiz Wilfred on how much he knew about his new employer's activities; the fact that she "was really an active [sic] in the B.U." was merely coincidental: "I have a wife and two youngsters to support and that was the first thing I could get." He did not believe that Norah Elam had been using the LPAVS offices as a cover for British Union activities, and he "would not know" that she had accepted £4,000 of British Union funds for safe keeping "because it was thought that the funds of the B.U. would be seized by the Government. This is since the outbreak of war." Birkett persists that the officers who brought Wilfred in had "information which … would indicate to them, I think properly, that whatever Mrs. Elam was doing she was indeed actively working for the British Union in that kind of way." Wilfred is adamant that the LPAVS committee would have opposed that: "That she must have been doing quite personally and individually. I do not think the Committee would have known anything of that." After briefly describing his function at the LPAVS, Wilfred mentions, also briefly [although probably very significantly] his only other contact with British Union, apart from Mosley, since he left: "a colleague with whom I had worked when I was there, … who went by the name of P. G. Taylor." Wilfred admits that he knows Taylor's "true name": "J. M. Hughes", but he puts that down to having "business interests outside and he did not want to appear under his own name in British Union." Wilfred is not questioned further when he reveals that "I have theories about him, but I do not know whether they are correct and so I would prefer not to mention them."

The apparently unconnected question which follows this, as to whether Wilfred had "any interest in … the pugnacious side … the militant side of the British Union", allows Birkett to quiz Wilfred about the weapons which were supposedly found at his home, and the ammunition which actually was. Wilfred is careful not to accuse the officers who brought him in of any impropriety; on the contrary, he is confident that they would confirm his testimony, but Birkett does not seem unduly concerned: "It is a small matter and would not weigh greatly, but I imagine the Committee would like to know how things got into this form." He appears to be happy to accept that Wilfred freely volunteered the information about the missing handguns, which somehow [courtesy of Aikin Sneath of MI5, perhaps?] were reported as being present with the ammunition. The "last one in the order", as far as Birkett was concerned, was that "British Union, since the war broke out … were using the organisation for purposes prejudicial to the efficient prosecution of the war". Wilfred does not argue: "It would appear so." He dismisses British Union's performance during the war until its very recent proscription as "a case of dancing on two stools with the danger of falling between them." Birkett has another question not directly related to the Reasons for Order script: "With your background, your training and upbringing with the I.L.P., it was a curious body to be in, this British Union, was it not?" This enables Wilfred to enlarge on his background, and his gradual disenchantment with British Union.

Birkett seeks more information about the internecine antagonisms within the Movement: "You formed a little group yourself with Gordon Canning and Archibald Garrioch Findlay rather opposed to Francis Hawkins?" Wilfred denies that, preferring to say that he was concerned about issues, not personalities: "There was no idea of forming a group to campaign or anything like that … Gordon Canning was certainly one with whom I worked a good deal like that, and he appeared to be just as annoyed as I was." Gordon-Canning left British Union in 1938, breaking with Mosley apparently on personal grounds [**32**]. After another negative observation about Francis-Hawkins, and how he was instrumental in pushing out members such as Chesterton, the discussion comes back to the weapons, and it transpires that Wilfred did not actually see the officers look in his bureau drawer, and neither was he told where they had found the ammunition, but freely volunteered the information about the handguns, for which he was thanked by the officer: "As a matter of fact, he said 'Thank you for telling me about that. I appreciate your straightforwardness in this matter', and that is all that was said about it." By now, Birkett has pretty much run out of official questions, so Clerk and Hazlerigg start asking their own questions. Hazlerigg seems surprised that Wilfred is in favour of doing away with parliamentary government ["as we know it now, yes"], but he supports his viewpoint by emphasising his belief that "[t]he Trade Union machinery would be responsible for a very big section of the machinery of

Government, and I had always a rather Syndicalist point of view in the Socialist Movement, the sort of Guild Socialism as opposed to the other form of Socialism."

Clerk is curious as to why Wilfred kept in touch with "one Taylor alias Hughes … I do not want to probe into your personal affairs; but why did you keep particularly in touch with him?" Wilfred says that "He was a personal friend as well as being a colleague. … I sympathised with his failure to do the things he wanted to do in the British Union." He also reveals that he knows where Taylor lived [Sloane Street], although it is curious as to why the past tense was used. This evident level of personal knowledge of a known MI5 informant must have been highly significant, and this will be expanded on below. Birkett returns to clarify Wilfred's written statement, made on his first full day in Brixton, asks him about his experience with the Army of Occupation in Germany, and that it would not be "contrary to any of your principles" to now "be of help in the prosecution of the war to this country at this time", which was probably one of the most crucial questions he was asked. When given a final "opportunity of saying anything at all you wish", Wilfred pushed for "the matter of the automatic pistol to be satisfactorily cleared up … I should be much happier if you could get a statement from the officers concerned". Somewhat presumptuous perhaps, but Birkett was unruffled: "I have no doubt that your statement will be shown to be perfectly accurate - not that I think that the mere position [sic] of an old revolver which one has had for many years is very strong evidence of one's subversive tendencies, but it is a small point we want to clear up." It is very likely that such a reasonable attitude would not have been taken with another member or ex-member who was considered to have "subversive tendencies"!

Hazlerigg asked Wilfred if his job would still be available to him if he were to be released, and he tells them that Nellie has been told by "the Chairman of the Committee [that] if I were out from here they would be only too pleased to have me back." [**33**] Birkett then makes a statement that appears to exonerate Wilfred completely: "What is clear about that is that whatever the activities of Mrs. Elam or Dacre Fox may have been, and whatever use she may have made of those offices, you never had any knowledge it was a kind of cover or cloak for the British Union." Despite the fact that it was not a question, Wilfred is quick to confirm it: "None at all. As a matter of fact, I have on occasion rebuked the girls in the office for getting into political argument about the war." Lastly, Birkett asks Wilfred if he has already been questioned by "any officer of M.I.5 or anybody since the officers detained you?" Wilfred says not, but that he is perfectly willing to "deal with them … Just as I have with you. I have nothing to hide." Birkett wraps up the meeting with an admission of the limit of the Committee's remit, but that they will attempt to move things forward: "We will deal with this matter as quickly as we can. There have been a good many delays which have not been the fault of this Committee but which are almost inevitable in this kind of thing, and it may take a day or two but we will try and deal with it as quickly as we can and make our recommendation as soon as we can." Naturally, Wilfred thanks them.

The way Birkett phrased his statement about Norah Elam could simply have been a product of his juristic circumspection, but it could also have been partly the result of a lack of details acquired 'from the horse's mouth', as it were: although most detainees did avail themselves of the opportunity to appeal their detention [and a few unsuccessfully mounted legal challenges on the basis of wrongful arrest] and, in the process, furnish the authorities with additional information, Mrs. Elam chose to be her own version of a martyr, and refused to do so; when Diana Mosley joined the other women detainees in Holloway prison four weeks after the initial wave of arrests, inevitably Norah made it her business to fraternise with Diana Mosley [**34**], and she was sufficiently impressed by Norah's stand but also sympathetic to her situation to ask her solicitor the following year if it should be possible for him to do something to help Norah and Dudley, who had apparently already been moved "and had a very bad time at Stafford and some other prison [**35**], although in Dudley's case, it was probably Brixton.

Birkett's final statement could also have been influenced by Wilfred's reference to P. G. Taylor, which appears to have been a very clever move on Wilfred's part. He had, by his own admission, kept in touch with Taylor since leaving British Union, although it is not known when the most recent meeting prior to Wilfred's arrest had been, but it is entirely plausible that Taylor might have 'coached' Wilfred on the approach he should adopt, if he should happen to be arrested. On the basis that Wilfred was an honourable man [possible knowledge of 'secret meetings' notwithstanding], and within the rubric of Wilfred's evidently genuine disenchantment with his latterday experience of British Union and willingness to be as open and honest as possible in his dealings with the authorities, and his readiness to aid the war effort in whatever way was open to him, Taylor might well have recommended that Wilfred should mention him to the authorities, but in a casual, totally believable way, and even confess to some uncertainty about Taylor's status, without having to actually declare that he thought Taylor was an informer for the Security Service [which, although most likely known to Wilfred, was unquestionably known to Mosley]. This assessment of Wilfred's integrity is certainly borne out by his subsequent activities, which will be detailed in the final chapters, but is also fair and, indeed, necessary to state that Wilfred's assertion that he liked Taylor as an individual is unlikely to have been anything other than the absolute truth. Wilfred knew him, in addition to his status as a fellow-traveller with common ideals within Mosley's Movement and an evidently successful, if not automatically accomplished public speaker, as an industrial advisor, with a history of [albeit not always honourable] trade union activity, so he and

Wilfred would have had plenty of shared experience.

Taylor was unusual within the British Union organisation, apart from his duplicity [although neither was he unique in that], in one very obvious respect: he eschewed any rank or elevated status, which does seem odd, despite his aforementioned aversion to being photographed, given that he was a public figure, so lack of rank or status in British Union would certainly not have afforded him any measure of anonymity. Birkett asks Wilfred if Taylor was "an office-holder of any sort?", and Wilfred's answer has a sardonic edge to it: "No, I do not think he could be described as an office-holder: he was an industrial advisor [the past tense alluding to British Union's current proscription], and that is such a nebulous title when you realise that he was dealing with folk who nine times out of ten would not take advice: the title "Industrial Advisor" then does not mean much." How much Wilfred knew of Taylor's actual background and ongoing covert activity can only be guessed at; what is clear from the minimal but greatly informative biographical information that is available is that his political beliefs seem to have obviated the necessity for any equivocation within Mosley's Movement. Thurlow does give some details, particularly in connection with one of Mosley's more mercurial converts, John Beckett [**36**], but the most complete picture is that presented by John Hope, in his comprehensive & fascinating article [originally published in the journal ***Lobster***, November 1991] ***Fascism, the Security Service and the Curious Careers of Maxwell Knight and James McGuirk Hughes***. Of course, there could also be others, unknown to this author, but what these two sources posit is very much an unorthodox and minority viewpoint and, given the perceived all-pervading power and influence of the Security Service, they are to be applauded for their courage in presenting the other side of the accepted wisdom, if for no other reason than that of balance.

Hope asserts that, contrary to the general argument that "MI5 … viewed fascism as a potential danger to state and national security against which it acted once that potential became actual … there is evidence that collusion did indeed take place, much of it to be found in the careers and activities of two of the more prominent MI5 officers involved in the surveillance of inter-war fascism, Charles Henry Maxwell Knight and James McGuirk Hughes." Knight was first recruited to the Security Service by its contemporary head, Sir Vernon Kell, in 1925, and within a few years headed section B5b, "which conducted the day-to-day monitoring of both left- and right-wing subversion. It was Knight and his agents who were primarily responsible for the surveillance of Britain's fascists and other 'fellow-travellers of the right', and for engaging in whatever counter-espionage against them was deemed necessary." As detailed in Chapter 11 [and note 44 below], it was Knight's section which uncovered Tyler Kent's apparently pro-Nazi activities: "This earned Knight the reputation of being as staunchly anti-fascist as he was anti-communist." However, from 1924 to 1927,

Knight served as Director of Intelligence with "Britain's first fascist movement of any significance, the British Fascists (BF)", and evidence to confirm this "is available from a number of sources", not the least of which is the Advisory Committee testimony of Neil Francis-Hawkins [**37**], "one of the more influential members of the BF before joining the BUF". Among his many duties as DofI with the BF, Knight's responsibilities included "establishing and supervising the fascist cells it set up and operated in the trade unions and factories". Interestingly, one of the instigators of the "Clear Out the Reds Campaign", launched not long after Knight left the BF, to which Knight offered his assistance in support of the campaign, was Winston Churchill [**38**].

Apparently, "Knight's ... sympathies for fascism only began to wane in 1935 when he and his colleagues became increasingly concerned about the British Union of Fascists' growing Italian fascist and German nazi links." [**39**] Before then, however, he had cultivated links with at least one member of the BUF [and former BF member], William Joyce [**40**], and he is widely accepted as being the source of the tip-off which enabled Joyce to evade capture by slipping out of the country to Germany only days before the beginning of the war, and then working for Goebbels in his Propaganda Ministry as a radio broadcaster in English, popularly known as 'Lord Haw Haw'. "Like Knight, McGuirk Hughes had first served an apprenticeship with the British Empire Union's private intelligence and counter-espionage network, which he combined with his position as secretary of the BEU's Liverpool branch." Although it is not clear exactly when the BEU was first formed, "[t]he involvement of the Security Service in the intelligence activities of the BEU began during the First World War." On the surface, Hughes's background would not seem compatible with Wilfred's ideals, certainly in his pre-British Union career: "the sole purpose of this [BEU] section was to infiltrate and sabotage trade unions and left-wing groups. For five years Hughes and his agents broke into premises, stole and forged documents, and behaved as agents provocateurs. For Liverpool employers Hughes provided the names of the most active trade unionists in the area, along with their plans and preparations for strike activity." [**41**]

Hughes's involvement with the BEU ended in July 1925, and his career between then and 1932 "remains unknown, but by the time he joined Mosley's movement he was an established MI5 agent and identified himself as such on many occasions." Among his many duties with BU was "[a]n ambitious scheme to establish [secret cells, modelled on those of the German Nazi party and the Italian *Fascisti*] in the Civil Service, the Armed Forces, key manufacturing and commercial enterprises, and the trade union movement, [which] was launched at the beginning of 1933. Of particular importance was the setting up of secret cells in the trade unions and in factories, considered vital if the BUF was to rival and successfully combat the Communist Party on its own ground." [**42**] Apart from the duplicity in its relations with the trades unions, a programme of positive action to counter the insidious influence of the Communist Party was undoubtedly something Wilfred would have been able to get along with, and Hughes's "enthusiasm for and commitment to the BUF appears to have been quite genuine". Although Wilfred thought of himself, latterly, as an electoral expert, he never lost his enthusiasm for trade unions, if they could only be encouraged to embrace the philosophy of corporate government, and industrial affairs, Hughes's ostensible area of expertise, were inextricably connected with trades unions, as evidenced by Wilfred's many ***Industry*** columns for British Union in ***Action***; hence it was entirely plausible that the two men would have worked very closely together in British Union and, whilst it is reasonable to suppose that Hughes would not have divulged details of all of his activities [and background] to Wilfred, they would have been able to compare notes on the vast majority of their workaday affairs, nevertheless. "As for Hughes, his service to the fascist cause appears to outweigh the information he relayed back to the Security Service." [note 36]

Unsurprisingly, Hughes was not caught in the '18B net'; one of the websites dedicated to the memory of Oswald Mosley provides some biographical information additional to that in the above article: he died in 1983, outliving Wilfred by nearly twenty years, and among his many aliases was John Vidor, under which he wrote a novel in 1929, ***Spying in Russia*** [**43**], but the last time he and Wilfred attended a public meeting together [albeit that attendance was by invitation only] was at the end of March, 1939, when Wilfred was guest speaker at the annual dinner of the Kingston upon Thames District of British Union [see Chapter 10, note 78]. There is no record that Hughes/Taylor spoke on this occasion, so it is interesting to speculate as to why he should have been there, but there are many possible reasons. Nothing appears to be known of Hughes's activity after the mass arrests and British Union was closed down; it is possible that, despite his obviously high-level protection, there might have been a real danger of an attempt on his life by murderously aggrieved Fascists who regarded Hughes as a betrayer, so perhaps he went into hiding for a while, or moved to an alternative theatre of operations for a period of time. Wilfred was certainly not the only 18B detainee in whose Advisory Committee appeal hearing the name of Hughes came up [**44**], so the non-committal demeanour of Wilfred's three interlocutors was not necessarily an indication of professional detachment at the reception of new information: rather an unwillingness to reveal a prior knowledge. There is also no record, known to this author, at any rate, of any meetings between Wilfred and Hughes/Taylor in his post-18B activities. How helpful it proved to be for Wilfred to mention his close association with Hughes can only be guessed at: it is possible he 'sailed very close to the wind', but contrary to the experience of some of his erstwhile colleagues, it proved to be no detriment in Wilfred's case.

Exactly one week after Wilfred's hearing, an R. Llewellyn Davies [who appears to have been a different individual from the Colonel J. Llewellin who wrote to Osbert Peake at the Home Office on behalf of his two constituents, Wilfred and Archibald Findlay] wrote from the same office at the Ministry of Aircraft Production to an Ian Roy, who was a Private Secretary at the Home Office:

> Dear Roy,
>
> Mr. Peake wrote to my Minister on the 21st June and promised to let him know when a final decision was reached in the case of Mr. A. G. Findlay and Mr. W. Risdon, who had been detained under the Defence Regulation 18B.
>
> Are you in a position to let us have a reply yet?

Presumably, Findlay's Advisory Committee hearing must have preceded Wilfred's, because there is a handwritten note pencilled at the bottom: "Findlay already dealt with by P.P.S." but unfortunately, the initials are indecipherable. Roy replied two days later that "I understand that these cases have now been heard by the Advisory Committee and that we may expect a report very shortly. Consideration will be given to this report with the least possible delay in the Home Office and Mr. Peake will not fail to let Colonel Llewellin know the result as soon as it is available." Unfortunately, in between these two, on the 19th, Aikin Sneath of MI5 had written to Birkett, expressing doubts about releasing Wilfred; shorthand notes, a verbatim record of the Appeal proceedings, were entered into the file on the 13th of July, but that was a Saturday [even in wartime, top civil servants probably only worked Monday to Friday] so, presumably, these must have been transcribed for Aikin Sneath's usage the next day after the hearing, to enable him to write to Birkett, but this document is no longer in the file. Aikin Sneath's reasons [or motives?] for taking this line are unknown but, aside from some obscure agenda [a concern that Wilfred might investigate his concerns about Hughes perhaps, although Wilfred would surely have known how risky a strategy that would be?], perhaps he was just being understandably cautious, in the circumstances? He mentions a meeting with Birkett, probably a regular occurrence, on the Wednesday two days prior to his letter, so it looks quite likely that Birkett will have mulled over Wilfred's case during the weekend after the hearing, before discussing it with Aikin Sneath:

> 19th July 1940
>
> P.F.50258/B.7
>
> Dear Brikett, [sic]
>
> At our meeting last Wednesday you mentioned to me the case of Wilfred RISDEN. You will remember that RISDEN claimed before the Advisory Committee that he had nothing to do with the B.U.F. since July 1939. I have taken a good

> deal of trouble to check up RISDEN's statement, and have even gone so far as to interview the officer at Special Branch who was in touch with the person who had special knowledge of RISDEN's B.U. activities. This person, whose reliability is beyond question, states that RISDEN was a frequent visitor at B.U. headquarters right up to the time of the police raid. He was giving advice on questions connected with parliamentary elections. He also used his position as canvasser for the London and Provincial Anti-Vivisection Society to disseminate Fascist propaganda. The Special Branch informant did, however, state that RISDEN had never expressed to him any pro-German sentiments. It seems in fact that RISDEN is at bottom not at all a bad character and is in a sense not unpatriotic, but his statement to you that he had had nothing to do with the B.U. since the outbreak of war was quite definitely not true. I am afraid he must be counted under the category of those who were active B.U. members up to the time of their arrest, and as such it is difficult to see how he can be released.

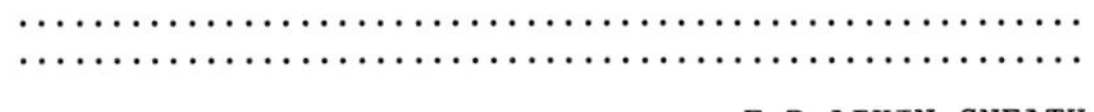

F.B.AIKIN SNEATH

It is interesting that the letter in Wilfred's file is a copy, on plain foolscap, and yet it only deals with his case, so there is no obvious duality of purpose. The most likely candidate for the "Special branch informant … whose reliability is beyond question" is Wilfred's erstwhile "personal friend as well as being a colleague", P. G. Taylor *alias* Hughes, but some doubt must remain, given that Wilfred is accused of lying to the Committee about his involvement with British Union subsequent to his departure in July 1939, which could have effectively scuppered his chances of release, despite the positive and conciliatory observations near the end of the letter. It is always possible that this was Hughes 'earning his money' for MI5, with little obvious regard for Wilfred's welfare [although to demonstrate that could have been awkward for Hughes], and Aikin Sneath tends toward the view that Wilfred was still active for British Union up to the time of this arrest, although if there was any evidence that he "also used his position as canvasser for the London and Provincial Anti-Vivisection Society to disseminate Fascist propaganda", Aikin Sneath is not forthcoming, so it is effectively only hearsay, albeit apparently reliable. Aikin Sneath's doubts notwithstanding, on the Monday of the following week, the 22nd of July, possibly after a weekend consultation with the other members of the Committee, but principally the chairman, Birkett, Sir George Clerk, the ex-diplomat and probable former Security Service operative, dictated the

Advisory Committee's report in Wilfred's case, and it was filed the following day, with handwritten margin notes, including the single word "Release", initialled by Churchill, the Committee Secretary.

However, a copy had to be sent to Aikin Sneath for his official perusal, and this was done by Churchill on the 24th: "Please let me know as soon as possible whether you have any further observations to offer on this case before the recommendation for release is sent in." Aikin Sneath shunted this [apparently one of several] across to the lawyer, Stamp, who replied to Churchill two days later that "we have no further observations to offer on this case", but that "Aiken-Sneath [sic] has in fact spoken to Mr. Birkett", so it would appear that Birkett had been able to allay Aikin Sneath's concerns verbally, during that week. The final report, recommending release, dated the 27th of July and bearing Churchill's name and position by rubber-stamp, was submitted to the Home Secretary's subordinate, Sir Alexander Maxwell. The 27th was a Saturday, nine weeks since Wilfred's arrest and incarceration; assuming that release might have been possible at the weekend, Wilfred would no doubt have been delighted to be released so soon, but the bureaucratic system didn't work that quickly. One of the minutes sheets in Wilfred's file has an entry dated the 30th of July, with some [occasionally indecipherable] notes about the case, headed "Advisory Committee report within":

> *Risdon was a long standing and important member of the B. U. but fell out with Mosley when he suspected that the B. U. was receiving a subvention from Italy. He resigned last July & Mrs. Elam gave him a job with the L.&.P. Anti Vivisection Society. It is a matter of surmise whether he thereupon abandoned his B. U. activities & became a good anti-vivisectionist & Insp. Bridges, N.S.Y. is inclined to think he did not. Mr. Aikin Sneath, MI.5, discussed the case with Mr. Birkett & the facts about the Anti-V Society.* [page break] *were before the [?] Cttee. MI.5 were not able to prove any active B. U. sympathies on the part of Risdon after he resigned & having no strong feelings on the matter have agreed that he should be released. His resumption of his former duties with the Anti-V.Society pre-supposes that they were innocuous & neither MI.5 nor N.S.Y. have any*

information to suggest that the Society is not now an innocent body.

Revocation order for signature herewith if approved.

So it would seem that Aikin Sneath's concerns were overruled, without any tangible evidence to corroborate them, and the "the officer at Special Branch who was in touch with the person who had special knowledge of RISDEN's [sic] B.U. activities" is named here as Inspector Bridges, of New Scotland Yard. The recommendation for release appears to have been approved on the 31st of July [which is somewhat ironic, given that this was the day the Armstrongs were arrested], but the addition of four more sets of initials was necessary [another on the 31st; and one each on the 1st, 3rd and 5th of August] before the official Revocation Order was signed by the Home Secretary, Sir John Anderson, on Tuesday August the 6th; one of the minutes sheets in Wilfred's file shows an entry "Extract of letter from Mr. Aiken-Sneath [sic]" against the date of August the first, but this is not to be found in the file, so perhaps it has been 'weeded' because it mentioned something sensitive? On the same day that the Revocation Order was signed, Wilfred's release was arranged, somewhat unusually perhaps, by telephone, but it is not clear how soon that would actually take effect: there are two other letters in the file, both dated August the 9th; one is to the Commissioner of Police of the Metropolis, but there is no name or signature appended: "Sir, I am directed by the Secretary of State to inform you that he has unconditionally revoked the order made under Defence Regulation 18B for the detention of Wilfred RISDON. I am, Sir, Your obedient Servant,"; the other, to S. O. King, Esq., whose function is unknown, reads: "Dear King, In confirmation of my telephone message I now enclose a copy of an order revoking the detention order made under Defence Regulation 18B, in respect of Wilfred RISDON. Yours sincerely,"

Perhaps the latter letter was confirming the verbal instruction for Wilfred's release from Brixton, made by some anonymous Home Office functionary, and King could be the Assistant Governor. Irrespective, Wilfred was released from Brixton some time during the week in which August the 9th was a Friday. He might not have been aware of Doreen Findlay's efforts on his behalf; come to that, neither might Archibald Findlay, for his own sake; but if Wilfred was aware, no doubt he will have apprised Doreen of what he knew at the earliest possible opportunity. That first weekend out of prison will have been a sweet release for Wilfred, and Nellie & the two children [although by now well into their teenage years] were undoubtedly mightily relieved to have him home. There was only one immediate 'fly in the ointment': Wilfred was now effectively unemployed. On the Wednesday following his release, the 14th, he wrote to G. P. Churchill, restating his offer to make himself available for war service:

70 Torrington Road,
Ruislip,
Middlesex.

14th. August, 1940.

G.P.Churchill Esq. C.B.E.
Advisory Committee to consider
Appeals against Orders of Internment,
Home Office,
6, Burlington Gardens, W.

Sir,

I am pleased to inform you of the fact that the result of my appeal to the Advisory Committee has been my release from detention.

In my appeal I stated my willingness to place my services at the disposal of the country in any capacity in which I might be of greatest service. The Chairman of the Advisory Committee especially referred to that pledge when I appeared for my examination, and at the same time asked me if I would be willing to submit to an interrogation by M.I.5. I said I would be perfectly willing to do so. I am writing you, therefore, to renew my undertaking on both those points and holding myself at the disposal of the Committee in respect of same. I am completely free for the time being, as my previous employers have filled my place and I have not yet found any alternative employment.

I have the honour to be, Sir,

Yours Faithfully,

W Risdon

W.Risdon.

This letter was written the very day after a "Special Executive Committee Meeting" of the LPAVS, held on Tuesday, August the 13th. Dudley Elam was back on the Committee, and it was carried unanimously that he "'be appointed provisionally from August 14th.1940 as Acting Secretary and as Editor of the News Sheet, and to deal generally with the business of the Society.' Mr. Elam is to be paid a salary of £25 per month and to be at liberty to contract articles for the News Sheet such articles to be paid for by the Society". Wilfred had obviously already written to the Committee, formally requesting reinstatement, but "Mr. W. Risden's [sic] letter was read. The Committee regretted that it was impossible to engage him at present for full time, but will welcome an article by him in the News Sheet and if satisfactory, would wish him to continue to do this until further notice." As a reflection of his status as a relative newcomer to the organisation, notwithstanding the Committee's previous expression of satisfaction in his work, prior to his arrest, Sylvia Armstrong's value was expressed, by way of a contrast: "A letter was read from Miss Marchant and it was decided, in the special circumstances and taking into account her length of service that she be granted an honorarium of £3 per week until her appeal to the Advisory Committee is adjudicated upon, or for 12 weeks from the 14th.August 1940 which ever event happens first. This was proposed by Mr. Rienaecker and seconded by Countess de Fleury". It would seem that, as is often the case, tawdry financial considerations were the deciding factor. It took nearly a week for a reply to Wilfred's appeal to Churchill to be written although, from the point of view of fairness to those detainees who were still fighting to gain their 'freedom', this was a less serious matter comparatively, for the Advisory Committee. A Secretary, whose initials do not resemble GPC, politely stated the Committee's refusal to help: "Sir, I am advised by this Advisory Committee to acknowledge the receipt of your letter of the 14th instant, and to say that the matter referred to is outside the competence of this Committee. I am, Sir, Your obedient Servant. [?] Secretary". There the matter had to rest; it should have been obvious, to a man of Wilfred's intelligence, that the Committee would be unlikely to help, but perhaps he felt that, having opened a civil, and apparently honest and genuine line of communication with 'the Government', someone amongst all the hierarchies in the interconnected and often overlapping echelons of administrative bureaucracy would respond to a request for help in the country's time of need. However, it was not to be, and the door was politely but firmly slammed in his face. Notwithstanding the possibility of a legitimate accusation of moral relativism [or possibly even hypocrisy] on the part of Committee members such as Drs. Fergie Woods and Allinson, the latter of whose own lifestyle was not what would likely be categorised by the general populace as 'normal' or 'conventional', the Committee was determined to distance itself from any unpatriotic taint, and continue with business as usual; the first wartime edition of the new ***News-Sheet*** published a definitive statement:

> "A DISCLAIMER.
>
> In order to prevent any possible misunderstanding, the Executive Committee of the London and Provincial Anti-vivisection Society thinks it right to state that no member of the present Committee is or has been a member of any suspect organisation.
>
> It is quite obvious that in the past it would have given offence to question either the members of the Society or the staff as to their private political leanings, so long as politics were not introduced in the Society.
>
> At no time has the London and Provincial Anti-Vivisection Society taken any part in any political movement.".

This is surely rather stretching credibility, in the case of Dudley Elam; it could even be considered distinctly disingenuous although, to be fair, he had tendered his resignation from the Executive Committee some time after his arrest [this was accepted at the July Executive Committee Meeting], so strictly speaking, it is correct; also, Alwyn Armstrong had a final article ["FUTILE THE TORTURES!"] printed in the August ***News-***

Sheet, just before his arrest under Regulation 18B. As for Wilfred's desire for employment, inevitably, there was some degree of urgency, not merely activity for its own sake, notwithstanding the impetus to be of assistance to 'the war effort'; Nellie might have been working at the time, but with another mouth to feed and all the associated household expenses, one income would have been barely enough: without it, the situation would have been dire indeed. Wilfred would have shared the plight of the majority of the 18B detainees, that of a suspension or termination of income while they were 'inside': only a few relatively lucky individuals, those British Union officers who had remained on the salaried staff at the time of their arrest, continued to be paid, after a struggle [whose irony was undoubtedly lost on the 'victims'] with the Home Office [**45**]. Even for a man of Wilfred's obvious, and proven abilities, finding paid employment in that period of upheaval would have been a daunting prospect, and being categorised in gullible public minds, into which category many potential employers would undoubtedly have fallen, as a 'fifth columnist', an 'enemy of the state', would have made Wilfred's employability very poor. There had been a very positive response from the country as a whole at the news of the mass arrests of Fascists, and the Home Intelligence report for the day following the initial onslaught presented an almost jubilant picture, although when the information about the Emergency Powers Bill [sic] trickled out, there were some stirrings of discontent about the implications for civil liberties [**46**].

Following the incarcerations, the mood of the country had fluctuated to quite a high degree, but the British stoicism and black humour usually managed to prevail, albeit leavened with a certain amount of pragmatism [usually denigrated as 'defeatism'] and safety of the nation's children continued to be an understandable concern [**47**]. The employment picture was dire [**48**], and suspicion that Fascists were being treated with undue leniency cannot have helped to foster understanding while Wilfred was detained [**49**], but 'democratic totalitarianism' would not be readily accommodated [**50**]. The week of Wilfred's release was perhaps serendipitous, because it followed a Bank Holiday weekend [although it would have been much more attractive to Wilfred at home than 'inside'], and this, combined with the sense of relief generated by the realisation that an invasion was now not imminent, might have enabled him to re-integrate into his local community relatively unscathed, but there was also a growing interest in the overall aims of the war, beyond mere defence, and the hitherto heretical idea of "a compromise peace" was being considered [**51**] albeit, perhaps, only at a local level. Unfortunately, however, Wilfred's release also coincided with "a ratcheting up of the German air assault with a day-long sequence of massed attacks on targets in the south-east of England" [**52**]: the "Battle of Britain" was about to begin.

Wilfred's best hope for employment would seem to lie back with the London & Provincial Anti-Vivisection Society: as detailed in Chapter 11, note 22, after the 23 May 1940 arrests, "the new officials of the Society had caused a thorough investigation to be made in the political proclivities of the Society's staff"; Hilda Kean tells us [**53**] that: "The committee of the LAPAVS [sic] was subsequently reorganized and new members included Lady Tenterden [**54**], a former supporter of the BUAV and a manager of the Battersea Anti-Vivisection Hospital." Notwithstanding G. P. Churchill's non-committal reply to Wilfred's request for help, the now reconstituted LPAVS Committee was prepared to accept a written submission, entitled "Try it out on the Dog?" [referring ironically to the continuing propensity of the medical research fraternity for animal testing] from him for inclusion in the September ***News-Sheet***, but in a [no doubt deliberately] risibly transparent attempt at an assignation of a *nom de plume*, the article was by-lined "W. Arr"; this was particularly apt, given Wilfred's West Country roots, although his natural brogue had very probably become somewhat moderated as a result of his many itinerant years hitherto. He would continue to write thus for many years to come, as well as under his own name. It seems unlikely that the earlier canvass would have been considered relevant while the country was at war [and voter registration was not considered to be necessary during wartime **55**]: presumably the Committee accepted the impracticability of 'political' canvassing at that time, but the necessity of trying to convince people of the awful nature of vivisection should continue, and they must have recognised Wilfred's usefulness anyway, wanting to keep him 'on board' regardless, as there might be a chance he wouldn't be available when better times came along. As a result of Alwyn Armstrong's arrest on the last day of July, the opportunity to put Wilfred's status with the LPAVS on a firmer footing presented itself, and he was paid retrospectively for the work he had done in the interim, including cataloguing "all the Society's books", but the Committee was not yet ready to see him as a replacement for Armstrong [**56**]. By the time of the August "Special Executive Committee Meeting", Dudley Elam had also been released, and although as mentioned above, his resignation from the Executive Committee had only been accepted a month earlier, he was provisionally appointed Acting Secretary and Editor of the ***News-Sheet*** "and to deal generally with the business of the Society. Mr. Elam is to be paid a salary of £25 per month and to be at liberty to contract articles for the News Sheet such articles to be paid for by the Society."

Presumably, this turn of events interested the Security Service which, unsurprisingly, had been keeping an eye on the Society since the arrests in May and July; although this isn't reflected in the Society's official record, on the 10th of February, Special Branch describes Wilfred as Assistant Secretary, answering to Dudley Elam, who is still Acting Secretary, so Wilfred's position now seemed more secure; at the end of October, he had written to the Committee requesting a pay-rise, which was granted [ten shillings per week], and was given, along with other members of staff, a

Christmas present: in his case, £3. However, the Committee was still keen to have back Sylvia Armstrong, whose salary continued to be paid ["It was resolved to continue Miss Marchant's salary until the next Committee Meeting Jan 7th 1941 or until her release whichever happens first."; ECM, 03/12/40], so at their behest, Elam wrote to the Home Secretary in January to ascertain the current position and "the probability of [her] early release". Although the receipt of a reply is noted in the Minutes of the February ECM, its content, presumably non-committal if not actually negative, is not disclosed.

It is scarcely credible that Wilfred could have been unaware that his public utterances at this time would inevitably be passed on to the Security Service, which gives rise to the inference that if a Special Branch report of early February, 1941, could observe the following, Wilfred's actions must have been calculated and deliberate: "Risdon, according to information which has reached the police, was recently heard to say he was sure Mrs. Elam would, when released, return to her former post with the Society, because she and Gush were on the closest terms. Gush, Risdon said, was as much mixed up with the Society's fascist activities as was Mrs. Elam." Geoffrey Gush was the Society's solicitor, so if this was an unguarded or unplanned observation, it seems to be a very indiscreet assessment of a man who could have made Wilfred's life very difficult if he so chose; to have expressed publicly his dislike for his former affiliation was less problematic [in fact, quite the reverse], but for its disloyalty still feels uncharacteristic, especially given Dudley Elam's continued presence within the organisation, unless it was made with the acquiescence of the other parties [**57**]. As mentioned above, Wilfred's first written submission to the ***News-Sheet*** was printed in September 1940, and he was already putting the finishing touches to a very detailed and well thought-out major contribution that concerned one issue above all others which had been galvanising his interest: protecting domestic pets during air raids.

Pets were banned from public air raid shelters [**58**], but Wilfred, like his fellow animal protectors at the LPAVS, abhorred the idea of wantonly and heartlessly destroying pets because of fear of the damage that might be caused by air raids, or the horrific injuries and death that might, and did, result from them [**59**], so he designed a practical solution: an air raid shelter for pets, which was, in fact, actually a side-extension for an Anderson-type shelter [although the extra space needed appears to be minimal, perhaps 2 or 3 feet {60-90cm}, so only likely to be a problem for the tightest of gardens]. The 4th of October, 1940, edition of the London and Provincial Anti-Vivisection Society ***News-Sheet*** includes a set of drawings under the caption "An Air-Raid Shelter for Your Pets. By W. RISDON", and there are four separate drawings: a front elevation of the visible [i.e., above-ground] section of an Anderson shelter [with dotted lines to show concealed sections]; and three details drawings, two of which are dimensioned [the square section from which the entrance is constructed is shown as 17" {43cm} in size]. As observed by Dr. Kean, the "illustrations [were] complete with instructions" [**60**], so the partly schematic nature of the drawings should not have presented many problems for moderately capable craftsmen to interpret. It is difficult to know if many of these shelter extensions were constructed; Hilda Kean describes his design as "[p]erhaps his most important contribution to the publicity work of the LAPAVS during the war" [**61**] but, unfortunately, the responsibility for, and care of domestic pets during wartime was something of a 'grey area'.

Just before the war began, an organisation called the National Air Raid Precautions Animals Committee [NARPAC] was formed to advise the government on "all problems affecting animals in wartime". NARPAC included representatives of the veterinary profession, government departments and the police. It also included animal welfare organisations such as the Battersea Dogs Home, PDSA, National Canine Defence League, Our Dumb Friends League/Blue Cross, RSPCA and the Home of Rest for Horses; NARPAC did popular work in cities reuniting animals and humans, but there were tensions between the charities and the vets [**62**]. As far as dealing with pets was concerned, as long as people did not try to take them into public shelters, the attitude was pretty much '*laissez faire*'. Most people seem to have taken their pets into their garden shelters with them, but this was obviously not ideal as, aside from the 'natural functions' of animals, they could not always be reasoned with, and sometimes their urge for freedom or fresh air could prove fatal [**63**]; some people also had Anderson shelters inside their houses, into which they took their pets [**64**]. NARPAC ran a registration scheme, and supplied free celluloid identity discs, but of course, not everybody bothered to register their pets, which made clearing up after air raids much more difficult [**65**].

Wilfred's home area of Uxbridge had its own NARPAC "Guard" [**66**], so it is altogether possible that he might have liaised with this lady about his idea; there were alternative ideas for self-contained animal protection containers around at this time [**67**], but they were bulky [and probably expensive] and not the same thing as having one's pet conveniently close and relatively well protected, but also hygienically separated! Later in the war, at least one dedicated communal Air-Raid Shelter for Dogs was built "near London" [**68**], the vagueness of location probably a censorship necessity, but it will have been the exception to the rule; it is to be hoped that at least an appreciable number of people had access to Wilfred's design [which was made available as a supplement: see note 60], and took the necessary action. Other than this contribution to the 'war effort', because he was not considered suitable for official war work [see Chapter 11] Wilfred's activities for the rest of the war consisted essentially of consolidating his position and level of influence within the sphere of animal welfare, and contributing many well-researched entreaties to the world at large via his Society's ***News-Sheet*** to reconsider entrenched preconceptions about the value of animals. There was the occasional brief respite, such as when he was visited “in his office in Victoria Street” by a nephew who was in the Royal Navy [**69**]; he did not know it then of course, but Wilfred had now entered the final phase of his working life.

NOTES

1 The Detention Order was typed out on two sheets of foolscap paper, both of which had a plain embossed crest of the Home Secretary's department:

"Regulation 18B of the Defence (General) Regulations, 1939, having been amended by the insertion after paragraph (1) of the following paragraph:

"(1A) If the Secretary of State has reasonable cause to believe any person to have been or to be a member of, or to have been or to be active in the furtherance of the objects of, any such organisation as is hereinafter mentioned and that it is necessary to exercise control over him, he may make an order against that person directing that he be detained.

The organisations hereinbefore referred to are any organisation as respects which the Secretary of State is satisfied that either -

(a) the organisation is subject to foreign influence or control or

(b) the persons in control of the organisation have or have had associations with persons concerned in the government of, or sympathies with the system of government of, any power with which His Majesty is at war,

and in either case that there is danger of the utilisation of the organisation for purposes prejudicial to the public safety, the defence of the realm, the maintenance of public order, the efficient prosecution of any war in which His Majesty may be engaged, or the maintenance of supplies or services essential to the life of the community":

The Secretary of State in pursuance of the powers conferred on him by the above mentioned Regulation has made [page break] an Order directing that you Wilfred RISDEN, of 70, Torrington Road, Ruislip Manor, be detained.

You will have an opportunity of making any representations you wish to the Secretary of State; and you have a right, whether or not you make such representations, to make your objections to an advisory committee appointed by the Secretary of State.

A Maxwell,
Under Secretary of State
for the Home Department.

HOME OFFICE,
WHITEHALL.
22nd May, 1940.

A copy of this Order was served by me, in company with P.S. Ewing, on Wilfred RISDON (not RISDEN) and he was informed of his right to make representations against the Order to the Secretary of State. RISDON was detained at 3.0.p.m., 23rd May, 1940, and later handed over to the Governor of Brixton Prison. together with a copy of this Order.

Charles Allen

```
Inspector.
Special Branch,
New Scotland Yard."
```

TNA, HO 45/23670, R5

2 Mosley's prison number was 2202, as revealed by Skidelsky in his biography; assuming that detainees were processed sequentially, it is very possible that he and Wilfred were present together in the same holding area, waiting to be processed; no doubt under guard and probably prevented from conferring. There is a mocked up 'mug-shot' photograph, front & side view, to be found in an internet search for images associated with Brixton Prison which depicts the fictitious character Norman Stanley Fletcher, from the British television comedy series ***Porridge***, and he is shown with his prisoner number 2215, quite similar to Wilfred's, when he was 'on remand' at Brixton; presumably, prisoner numbers are 'recycled', but it would be interesting to know if the writers researched actual holders of this number.

Whereas Wilfred had been British Union's first Director of Propaganda, Richard Reynell Bellamy was its last; in his recently published "Authorised History of The British Union of Fascists", ***We Marched With Mosley***, he gives a wealth of grim detail about the shared experience of Brixton Prison. His description of the registration process is illuminating:

> "The newcomers were locked into reception cells, each about the size of a telephone kiosk, but even less interesting as they were without windows and were entirely closed in. Here they were left to ruminate for hours. For anyone who suffered from claustrophobia, hours of gazing at a blank wall within inches of one's nose, must have been a distressing experience. One 18B prisoner, an ex-Serviceman who had been buried alive by an exploding shell, found the hours of solitude confined in a tiny space without outlook, nerve-wracking in the extreme.
>
> …
>
> At last, and one by one, they were let out of their hutches, and were conducted each in turn to a bath, and there bidden to wash thoroughly, with particular attention to their scalps. Which exhortation Watts, for one, considered superfluous; when he came to record his memories of his first days in Brixton, he wrote:* "… as I found, there were already so many bugs … that a few more would have made no difference."
>
> This compulsory bath for the destruction of vermin, followed by a medical check that was in fact a degrading inspection of the prisoner's person, were humiliating formalities which however necessary in the case of low criminals of the Bill Sykes species, and of gutter-type hooligans, were not really essential for the reception into a verminous and filthy prison of loyal and honourable gentlemen, many of whom had held His Majesty's Commission, and had been decorated for their gallantry, and against whom no charge had been made, or was ever to be preferred.
>
> …
>
> After the de-lousing process and medical check, there was an impounding of personal possessions, and an issue of bed linen. Carrying their coarse oatmeal-

hued sheets, the prisoners were escorted one at a time across an inner courtyard to a four-storeyed block of two hundred cells, 'F' Hall. Everywhere iron-covered doors had to be unlocked to let them through, and were secured again behind them. Watts followed a blue-uniformed warder up a flight of iron stairs to No. 2 landing; the door of cell No. 38, officially "F2/38", was unlocked, revealing a bare, bleak little room about eleven feet by seven, containing a bed board and lumpy mattress, a chair and a tiny table. In a corner was a wash-stand with a chipped and scarred enamel basin and jug; beneath the wash-stand was a battered and most unpleasant looking chamber-pot. In a heap on the bed were three soiled blankets.

The cell window, composed of twenty panes, one of which was hinged to allow some direct contact with the four winds of heaven, was set so high that it called for a balancing act, with the heaped up furniture, to look out. The view however was not encouraging, as it afforded no more than a view of a small exercise yard."

It Has Happened Here, *C.F. Watts (unpublished/MS), cited in We Marched With Mosley, by Richard Reynell Bellamy

The humiliation for some started before being incarcerated:

"As we took our seats on the Liverpool express at Euston Station, we were aware of a stir and commotion on the platform. People were stopping and staring; then they stood back to make way for a line of men handcuffed together. The prisoners were not manacled in pairs in the usual manner, but in single file, each man shackled by his right wrist to the left wrist of the fellow in front, and by his own left wrist to the right of the man next in line behind. They were hustled along by a strong guard of police.

...

Later, I learned too that these men had been thus marched through the streets of Horsham, and instead of being conveyed across London from one main line station to the other in chartered buses or army lorries, had been taken on the Underground shackled together exactly as I had seen them. Hundreds of persons must have viewed them thus, and either gaped in amazement or glared in aversion.

It has been suggested that this public parading of political prisoners was done purposely to raise morale on the Home Front, and to show that despite the defeats suffered on the Continent the Government of Great Britain was still able to wield a big stick at home."

Ibid.

3 It is difficult to make an accurate comparison between the ground plan and layout of the prison of today, understandably as a result of security considerations, and the original buildings of 1820. The Wikipedia page does give a reasonable history, but there is precious little for the period when it accommodated Wilfred. The original angular D-shape connected arrangement of the wings has now been replaced by a more rectangular layout of separate buildings with much less open space surrounding them than previously; virtually the only remnant of the original Surrey House of Correction design is the central Octagon, an almost folly-like eccentric building designed by Thomas Chawner, with a small clock tower on its narrow three-storey core. There was a plan to demolish it "to facilitate traffic flow", but consent was refused:

http://www.georgiangroup.org.uk/docs/cases/index.php?id=3:13:0:27
http://en.wikipedia.org/wiki/Brixton_(HM_Prison)

4 Mosley suspected devious intent in the selection of his neighbour:

"I was put in No. 1 cell and found to my mild surprise that my next-door cell companion was a Negro. Some whimsical jackass in office probably thought it would annoy me, but on the contrary I found him a charming and cultured man. I understood that he was alleged to have played in the Berlin Philharmonic Orchestra before the war and was arrested on account of the peculiarity of this occupation at that time for a coloured man; the facts of his case were never fully revealed to me, but he certainly knew a lot about music and I enjoyed his company and this mutual interest."

My Life, by Oswald Mosley

5 ***The Wall is Strong: The Life of a Prison Governor, by Captain Gerold Fancourt Clayton***

6 One of Mosley's erstwhile colleagues, a fellow anti-war activist, concurred:

"Captain Ramsay, the Conservative M.P. for Peebles, was in the same wing. An ex-Guards officer, he also had a considerable experience of that war, and agreed that the bugs were more plentiful than in any billet we had ever enjoyed, except in some deep dug-outs at one place just behind the front line, where both we and the Guards had been on different occasions; I think it was called Vermelles. The old familiar tramping of the massed battalions began directly we lay down to sleep."

My Life, op. cit.

Direct action could sometimes achieve results:

"Complaints were made daily to the Governor and to the Medical Officer. Cells were inspected, and some of them temporarily closed. New bed boards and other furniture were supplied to others, but the bugs were never cleared out.

One chap caught some, put them in a match-box, applied next morning to see the Governor, and then emptied the contents on the Governor's table. It caused quite a sensation ..."

We Marched With Mosley, op. cit.

Nicholas Mosley relates that "An ex-BUF inmate wrote:

'One of the chief afflictions was that of bed-bugs. ... We used to have bug-hunts every night. They would lodge in the cracks in the bed-boards and tables. Night after night one could hear hammering from cells all over the hall. This was caused by the bed-boards being knocked against the floor to dislodge the inhabitants, which could then be dealt with.'

This inmate had a memory of Mosley:

'I went into OM's cell one morning just after he had finished washing. I happened to catch sight of his arms as he was in the act of rolling up his sleeves. His arms were covered in bites, by far the worst I had seen. I asked him if he had made any complaint about it. Not he! He would have let himself get eaten alive before complaining. "If the boys can take it so can I" was his answer.'"

Beyond the Pale: Sir Oswald Mosley and Family, 1933-1980, by Nicholas Mosley

7 ***Ibid.***

8 ***The Wall is Strong: etc., op. cit.:***

"It is not often that a governor finds himself in charge, in one prison, of a baronet, a full admiral, a retired officer of the Grenadier Guards, an ex-Mayor of a London borough and a Justice of the Peace, not to mention a former MP who had once removed the mace from the House of Commons [not strictly accurate]. These were among the 18b detainees who were in Brixton in the early days of the war. … The admiral I have mentioned was always patient and courteous, and faced his uncomfortable existence in a way which, having regard to his very distinguished career, earned my deep respect. John Beckett, of course, was the former MP who took the mace from the Commons. [sic]"

9 One of the folders within Wilfred's Home Office file has a printed front sheet, which allows for handwritten progress notes, and on this is written "Appeal lodged. Copy inside", but there is no document inside specifically requesting an appeal, so one has to assume that this note constituted Wilfred's appeal. Unfortunately, the cursive script is often almost indecipherable.

Bellamy, again, provides some detail:

"Within a day or two of arrival the detainees were interviewed by the Prison Governor, who as a matter of form checked their names and other particulars, read out a list of each prisoner's personal possessions that had been impounded, and promised to provide facilities for writing an appeal to the Advisory Committee then in process of being set up by the Home Secretary.

Everyone, almost without exception, took advantage of this opportunity to write indignant protests against their arrest and imprisonment, and to express the fury and deep injustice that they felt at the slanders on their characters, and baseless imputations against their loyalty to their King and Country.

In the majority of cases the victim was prohibited communication with his solicitor; where a lawyer was employed by the detainee's relatives and friends to set legal machinery in motion on his behalf, he was generally refused access to the prisoner, and was met by governmental obstruction and stone-walling. Those few lawyers who were able to make personal contact with their clients were horrified not only by the terms under which Regulation 18B operated, but by the physical conditions which imposed on its victims. Actually it proved a waste of time and money to employ solicitors, as the new Regulation deprived them of all power to help.

…

Legal help being forbidden, their written appeals to the Home Secretary's Advisory Committee were the only outlets allowed the captives who, according to their disposition, couched their protests in terms of pain, bewilderment, rage or abuse."

We Marched With Mosley, op. cit.

10 ***The Wall is Strong: etc., op. cit.***

11 ***Ibid.:***

"With a staff depleted by the call-up of reservists, I found it impossible to carry out these instructions to the letter and, on my return from sick leave–I had gone into a nursing home with internal trouble–I reported this to the Prison Commissioners."

12 ***Ibid.:***

"Sir Oswald Mosley, during the first days of his internment, was inclined to constitute himself the spokesman for all the Fascists until I pointed out to him that I was prepared only to hear applications on his own behalf but not on behalf of other people. I found him cooperative and, in his own peculiar way, a patriot."

13 ***My Life, op. cit.:***

"The prison staff on the whole were a fine lot, mostly ex-servicemen; one warder had been a sergeant in my regiment. The prison governor, Captain Clayton, a much-wounded soldier of the first war, was a fair and honourable man, and so was the chief warder, Watson. Our particularly disagreeable jail experiences were in no way due to them. They had nowhere else to put us, except the condemned wing, and orders had been given from above that this was to be our accommodation. We were there under war conditions with a shortage of staff, and at first there appeared to be a lively apprehension concerning the possible conduct of this considerable company of men, who were accustomed to act together in a disciplined movement."

Interestingly, Clayton, who was subject to both physical & mental illness during his service [he had to take 6 months' sick leave during 1938, mainly as a result of mental turmoil following the savage assault of a "very young but very smart and promising officer" when he was Governor at Wandsworth, prior to his tenure at Brixton], was not above his own anti-Semitism, although it is very unlikely that he would have breached professional etiquette and discussed this with Mosley:

"When I went to see the men in the punishment cells I noticed that the first man had bruises on his face, and I asked him how he got them. He replied that he had fallen from the boundary wall on his face on to a heap of stones. I then passed to the other, the nastiest type of Jew and a well-known mischief maker. However, at the time he made no reference to what had happened although he was marked."

The Wall is Strong: etc., op. cit.

14 ***Very Deeply Dyed in Black: Sir Oswald Mosley and the Resurrection of British Fascism after 1945 by Graham Macklin***

15 ***Ibid.:***

"The rift [between Beckett & Mosley] was to be cemented shortly after Beckett's imprisonment, when he was approached by Mosley's emissary, Hector McKechnie, and told: 'The Leader says that in this hard time for our country we must all sink old past differences and he is prepared to offer you a place in the government-in-exile.' Beckett sent McKechnie packing, telling him exactly what he thought about Mosley's government-in-exile. McKechnie returned only moments later and indignantly retorted:

'The Leader says, if that's your attitude you shan't be in the government at all.'"

McKechnie was a fairly unsurprising choice for go-between [although very probably not the only candidate], given his almost fanatical devotion to Mosley; it is possible that an ill-advised assertion at his 18B Appeal Hearing

[*TNA HO 283/48*] was made on the spur of the moment, but he cannot have been unaware that this attitude would damage his prospects of an early release [which proved to be the case]:

"Hector McKechnie, one of his leading lieutenants … at his Advisory Committee hearing - in a moment of candid genuflection, and with a nod towards Mosley's own papal infallibility - stated that 'I accept Sir Oswald Mosley in the same way as the average Catholic accepts to [sic] Pope.'"

Ibid.

16 ***My Life, op. cit.:***

"Official instructions were given in the early days that for security or other reasons we were to be locked in our cells twenty-one hours out of the twenty-four, and only let out for one hour's exercise in the morning and afternoon and other necessary routines. This suited me reasonably well, for we were allowed books and I spent the whole time reading. There was complete silence and the considerable number of our people who also enjoyed reading found this monastic existence relatively tolerable. Paradoxically, the trouble began when the cell doors were unlocked, and my readers would have some difficulty in guessing what it was. When conditions were relaxed the curse of prison was noise.

I had to take action altogether against my interests, for I heard that a number of people were being very adversely affected by this seclusion. The Italians were particularly stricken, for they are a happy people who like a gregarious life and a merry din. It was clearly in the interests of the many to press for the doors of cells to be opened except at night, and to give every assurance of orderly conduct in this event. My request was eventually granted, and the cell doors were opened; all hell then broke loose. Imagine trying to read amid a genial babble of Mediterranean voices in an enormous room which echoes exactly like a swimming bath; it needed some concentration, to put it mildly. The final nightmare was permission to bring in a ping-pong table, when the echoing seashell of the building resounded with the music of ping and pong and Latin laughter. The subsequent discomfort of being locked in cells while bombs were falling round the prison was nothing to it."

17 ***The Wall is Strong: etc., op. cit.:***

"… as soon as Mosley and his Fascists arrived, I was warned that there might be an attempt to rescue him from outside and, whilst this scare was on, I paid much more attention to security than to privileges."

18 ***My Life, op. cit.***

19 Nicholas Mosley reports on one visit with his sister Vivien to Brixton:

"When he bounded in he was, as he always was, full of energy and ebullience and light. He wore something like a boiler suit and had grown a reddish beard."

Beyond the Pale: etc., op. cit.

20 Robert Skidelsky throws some light on the clothing situation:

"In the early days, privileges were largely on paper: the authorities made little effort to live up to them, and it was not till Mosley and others threatened to prosecute the prison governor for breach of statutory regulations that freedom of association was permitted: Mosley recalled spending his first months locked up in his cell for 21 hours out of 24 … As for his clothes (contrary to popular press reports) there is an actual request scribbled by Mosley to his solicitors on the 12th of July 1940: "Please send corduroy trousers, thick blue polo neck sweater, two sets of winter underclothes, oldest country coat. Fetch washing and send no more clean clothes unless asked for."

Oswald Mosley, by Robert Skidelsky

21 ***My Life, op. cit.***

22 ***The Wall is Strong: etc., op. cit.:***

"[the impossibility of carrying out the Home Secretary's instructions to the letter] led to discontent which was ably fanned by certain malcontents who continually threw spoons, tins, brushes and clothes down the drains. This, of course, resulted in the overflowing of lavatories and sinks and made things most unpleasant for officers and prisoners alike. These men were a tricky bunch to handle, and the varying grades of society from which they came did not make the problem any easier."

23 E. Blanshard Stamp was a lawyer working for MI5:

"MI5 used some of its lawyers, not its investigative officers [such as Aikin Sneath] to prepare both documents [the Reasons for Order and the Statement of Case]; they relied on MI5's personal files. Gonne St. Clair Pilcher* appears to have been in charge. Birkett, or Churchill on his behalf, formally approved the Reasons for Order. Birkett's MI5 information was normally confined to the Statement of Case unless, as in Mosley's case in 1940, MI5 was more forthcoming. The Home Office would also pass on relevant letters.

*Footnote: Pilcher [1890-1966] became a judge in 1942 and in ***Who's Who*** recorded his war service as 'Attached War Officer War Office Sept. 1939-Oct. 1942'. Ironically his father, Maj.-Gen. T. D. Pilcher, had been a member of the British Fascisti Ltd., back in 1924 [ref. ***The Fascists in Britain, by Colin Cross***]. The others were A. A. Gordon-Clark [Cyril Hare, the novelist], James ['Jim'] L. S. Hale, Sydney H. Noakes, E. Blanshard Stamp, John P. L. Redfern and Thomas M. Shelford."

In the Highest Degree Odious: Detention without Trial in Wartime Britain, by Alfred William Brian Simpson

24 ***Ibid.:***

"George P. Churchill [Secretary to the Committee] 1877-1973; retired in 1937; his last recorded appointment was Consul-General in Algiers until 1927. The last 10 years of his service may have been with MI6. Peter Morland Churchill [1909-1972, G. P. Churchill's assistant], not his son, was the well-known agent in France."

25 This situation changed not long after Wilfred's Appeal, probably because of safety concerns:

"Early in the war interaction between the Home Office, the Committee, and MI5 were easier than it later became, since all were based in London. But by late 1940 the Committee was at Ascot, MI5 at Blenheim Palace near Oxford, and the relevant department of the Home Office seems to have remained in London.

Footnote: Some administration concerned with 18B was, however, conducted from Bournemouth."

Ibid.

26 Birkett was originally one of two Chairmen, the other being Walter T. Monckton, who was appointed "by warrant" on the 13th of October 1939, but never presided over a hearing. Birkett began his work on Monday, the 16th of October 1939.

Ibid.

27 Clerk was a fairly traditional career diplomat, with pretty obvious connections to the Security Service, which undoubtedly continued after he 'retired' in 1937. Some of his placements had a direct bearing on Wilfred's politics:

> "Clerk was appointed a clerk in the Foreign Office in 1899, and in 1901 was appointed an acting Third Secretary as Secretary to a Special Mission to the courts of Europe to announce the accession of King Edward VII. He went to Addis Ababa in 1903 as Assistant in HM Agency, where he became Acting Agent and Consul-General from 1903–04 and Chargé d'Affaires at the British Legation in Abyssinia, 1906–07. While in Abyssinia, Clerk worked to curb the excesses of the slave trade in the border regions of Sudan and Uganda and gained the nickname of 'the Buffalo'. In 1907 he was recalled to London as an Assistant Clerk in the Foreign Office, and in 1910 went to Constantinople as First Secretary in HM Embassy to the Ottoman Empire, becoming Senior Clerk in 1913 and Acting Counsellor in 1917, when he was knighted.
>
> In the aftermath of the First World War, Clerk was very sympathetic to the cause of the national minorities of the former Austria–Hungary and to the liberal ideals associated with the journal ***The New Europe***. In 1919 he was appointed as Private Secretary to the Acting Secretary of State for Foreign Affairs, giving him an opportunity to influence the face of the new Europe when they embarked on a mission to Hungary. Later in 1919 he was sent as First Minister to Czechoslovakia, serving also as Consul-General there from 1921 to 1926. As British minister in Prague, Clerk pursued his ambition to support the Czechs and make Prague a centre of British influence. Although his policy ended in failure, Clerk had a greater sympathy for the Czechs and Slovaks than any of his successors. …
>
> At the time of the Italian invasion of Abyssinia of October 1935 to May 1936, Clerk had only limited success in urging Pierre Laval, the French Foreign Minister, away from a policy of benevolent neutrality, and was disappointed by French expressions of sympathy for Italy.
>
> In August 1936, Clerk warned Yvon Delbos of the dangers of French intervention in the Spanish Civil War.
>
> In 1937, Clerk finally retired from the Diplomatic Service."

http://en.wikipedia.org/wiki/George_Clerk_(diplomat)

28 Hazlerigg came from an old aristocratic family, and served as Lord Lieutenant of Leicestershire from 1925 to 1949, but it is not obvious that he had connections to the Security Service: perhaps he was just regarded as a well educated, dispassionate witness-cum-arbitrator, whose loyalties would no doubt lie with what is generally termed 'the establishment'.

http://en.wikipedia.org/wiki/Arthur_Hazlerigg,_1st_Baron_Hazlerigg

29 The Security Service was undoubtedly under pressure at the beginning of the war:

"The foundation of the Home Defence (Security) Executive (HD(S)E) [the object of which was 'principally to consider questions relating to defence against the 5th Column and to ensure action'] coincided with the circulation of Lord Hankey's report on MI5, which urged that 'the fullest possible weight' be given to MI5's recommendation to counter subversion. MI5, however, was ill prepared for the task in hand. At the end of 1938 it had 30 officers and 103 administrative and registry staff, all of whom laboured under an intense workload, vetting personnel and chasing the largely chimerical 'fifth column'. Its surveillance section had a mere 6 men. Maxwell Knight's MS Section was similarly restricted, with only 14 agents operating within 'subversive' organisations in 1939; while as late as July 1939 Special Branch had a fleet of only 4 cars with which to cover the entire Metropolitan Police district - and one of these, a Hillman Minx, was being rented from a private car hire firm. These were hardly ideal circumstances as British Intelligence struggled to cope with not only an impending world war, but also with a sudden flurry of IRA activity across the capital."

British Intelligence: Secrets, Spies and Sources, by Stephen Twigge, Edward Hampshire & Graham Macklin

Thurlow also gives some useful background here, and alludes to an officer who was also involved in Wilfred's case, F. B. Aikin Sneath:

"With hindsight it is clear that the Security Service surveillance of British fascism was a model of restraint and sophisticated analysis of the various intelligence sources by F. B. Aikin-Sneath [sic], the officer in charge of assessing fascist activities in F division, and the case officers in B5b, until the autumn of 1939. Then the unorthodox behaviour of Maxwell Knight, the head of the agent running activities of B5b, in not informing the American Ambassador that Tyler Kent was a security risk, signalled a change to a less charitable view of the activities of British fascists. The failure fully to penetrate the BUF, Mosley's counter-intelligence precautions, obsessive secrecy and other protective measures to shield his activities from the Security Service, were seen in a different light from the misguided patriot view of the old professionals by the new intake following the rapid expansion of MI5 in 1939. The clear indication that the fascist fringe were secretly collaborating with each other was not interpreted in a similar manner in the hysterical atmosphere of spring 1940, and Churchill's order to 'collar the lot' was to be almost as relevant for British fascists as for aliens. This change in the general viewpoint of MI5 derived mainly from the cloak and dagger activities of Maxwell Knight's agents and an increasingly suspicious view of the gaps in that intelligence."

Fascism in Britain: From Oswald Mosley's Blackshirts to the National Front by Richard C. Thurlow

30 ***In the Highest Degree Odious: etc.; op. cit.***

31 ***TNA PRO HO 283/13***

32 Canning's Home Office file was released in November 2002:

"Canning, a captain in the Royal Hussars during World War I, was the great grand-son of the poet Lord Byron. In 1934 Canning joined the British Union of Fascists (BUF), became a close associate of Mosley and met senior Nazi officials. In 1938 he broke with Mosley on personal grounds, becoming the treasurer of the anti-war group, the British Council for Christian Settlement. He was detained under 18b of the Defence Regulations until 1943. These two files have been reconstituted from the original microfilm."

25 November 2002 Releases: Right-Wing Extremists; Captain Robert Cecil Gordon Canning; File ref KV 2/877-878;

https://www.mi5.gov.uk/output/25-november-2002-releases-right-wing-extremists.html

33 That might have been the chairman's private sentiments, but as ever, for the sake of legal correctness, this was a matter to be decided by the organisation's Committee; Nellie must have written to the Committee within days of Wilfred's arrest, because the matter is dealt with at the very next meeting [unfortunately, neither the actual letter, nor its content has been preserved]:

"Mr. Risdon: Mrs. Risdon's letter considered. Mrs. King proposed that Mr. Gush be instructed to reply that Committee would like to have the call on Mr. Risdon's services when free and that all speakers whose employment has been terminated be granted one month's salary in lieu of notice."

London & Provincial Anti-Vivisection Society Executive Committee Meeting 04/06/40, courtesy of the NAVS

34 This was communicated to the Governor of Brixton, Captain Clayton, in a letter during June of 1940.

KV2/884, Microform Academic Publishers, cited in Mosley's Od Suffragette: A Biography of Norah Dacre Fox, by Susan & Angela McPherson

35 Information supplied by a Holloway Prison guard.

"Then there is Mrs. Elam known as Dacre-Fox her first husband's name – she has an old husband who is not very strong, has been interned and had a very bad time at Stafford and some other prison - she is worried to death about him and also that she may have to go to the Isle of Man it would be so dreadful for her as she can see him now and he is such a dear [sic]."

Solicitor visit to Diana Mosley, 1941, KV/1364, p.78, Microform Academic Publishers cited in ibid.

By that time, Dudley Elam had already been released, which is not obvious from the above quote. Prison visits were routinely & openly monitored, including those by solicitors, as confirmed by both Clayton and Thurlow:

"Scotland Yard entirely objected to the solicitors of these men being allowed to interview them out of hearing of an officer, which is the practice for ordinary trial and remand prisoners."

The Wall is Strong: etc., op. cit.

"Prison warders were present at all visits to internees and reported on conversations."

Fascism in Britain: etc., op. cit.

36 Taylor was, apparently, regarded as a "very reliable source" by the Security Service, although the conclusion of this piece is somewhat ambiguous:

"Beckett, whose collaboration with William Joyce in the National Socialist League in 1937-8 meant he was regarded with deep suspicion by both MI5 and the general public, and whose quarrel with Mosley in 1937 led him to be viewed with equal hostility by the BUF, singled out an '*agent provocateur*' called P. C. Taylor (sic) whom he regarded as responsible for many of the allegations in his case. Anne Beckett, his wife, wrote to Birkett claiming that at a meeting at their flat early in 1940 between Mr Taylor, Beckett and herself propaganda alleged to have been made by her husband was in fact made by Taylor in an apparent attempt to elicit information. The Committee decided that they were unable to deny or confirm MI5 allegations but in general were impressed with Beckett's case."

PRO HO 45/25698, MI5 report on John Beckett; Advisory Committee Report on John Beckett, 10 July 1940; HO 283/26, Anne Beckett to Norman Birkett, 14 July 1940, cited in ibid.

37 ***PRO HO 283/40/22, cited in Fascism, the Security Service and the Curious Careers of Maxwell Knight and James McGuirk Hughes, by John Hope***

38 ***Ibid.***

39 ***Typescript of the Tyler Kent case pp. 94-5, in Tyler Kent Papers, Princeton University; cited in ibid.***

40 See also Chapter 8 and notes *passim.*

Haw-Haw: The Tragedy of William and Margaret Joyce, by Nigel Farndale

41 ***Ron Bean and Cunard papers, Liverpool University, D. 42/C2/108, cited in Fascism, the Security Service, etc., op. cit.***

42 ***Mosley versus Marchbank Papers, statements made by Mr C.M. Dolan at conference at Unity House on 2 November 1934, MSS 127/NW/GS/3/5A; PRO HO 144/20144/126; HO 45/25385/28; and PRO HO 144/143-144, cited in ibid.***

43 ***Major P G Taylor - Agent Provocateur, by Bryan Clough; Author of State Secrets: The Kent-Wolkoff Affair:***

"P G Taylor's role in the BUF was first revealed to a wider public by Alex Miles, a 'sometime Director of Industrial Propaganda' of the BUF. Miles had decided to go public after resigning his job in 1936.

Miles ... reported that 'Taylor ... lived at Sloane Street, Chelsea where he had three separate telephone lines ... each listed under a different name, none of which is Taylor ... [He] openly boasts that he was expelled from Soviet Russia for espionage and of his membership of the CPGB (Communist Party of Great Britain) for the same purpose'. Taylor lived in a flat at 144 Sloane Street from 1935 to 1960. (MI5's Maxwell Knight had a flat at number 38 for a couple of years in the thirties.)

The late Mrs Margaret Bowie who had worked at National Headquarters during the Thirties, also remembered him. 'He was then in his mid-thirties ... and always smartly dressed'. She has also confirmed that Taylor's affiliation to the Home Office was general knowledge and that, when he was in the office, he gave a ready grin whenever he was asked 'if he had caught anyone today'.

Mrs Bowie also recalled seeing Taylor on one occasion when he was leaving a local Catholic church with a woman and a teenage girl whom she assumed to be his wife and daughter. On that occasion, Taylor cut her dead. 'It was as though he didn't want to mix family with business'.

James McGuirk Hughes - the man who posed as P G Taylor - was born in Toxteth Park, Liverpool on 18 June 1897. His father, Arthur Hughes, was a tram owner and his mother was the former Katherine McGuirk.

Hughes married Valerie Julia Taylor Tahan at a Catholic church in Fulham on 19 June 1920. He gave his occupation as 'Political Organiser'. Valerie's father, Zachary, was described as an Oriental Merchant. When their daughter Patricia Valerie Catherine arrived on 29 March 1923, Hughes had become James Patrick McGuirk-Hughes but Valerie had dropped 'Taylor' perhaps coincident with the creation of Hughes' best known alias.

Over the years, Hughes continually rang the changes on his real name: sometimes, it was hyphenated; at other times, it was double barrelled but un-hyphenated but, in 1940 when Captain Ramsay listed him as a member of the Right Club, he was entered as Captain J Hughes.

Hughes' military background is not supported by the Army Lists or the War Office records but he does appear on the MI5 Staff List as a Lance-Corporal in the Military Foot Police from 18 February 1916 to 6 August 1919."

http://www.oswaldmosley.com/p-g-taylor.htm

44 Two known Fascists, one a British Union member, and the other who was not, both mentioned Hughes in connection with MI5 in their Advisory Committee appeal hearings. The BU member was John Preen, who also appears to have been granted some access to Hughes's carefully compartmentalised personal life, had been one of the four who were arrested for a break-in at the home of Major Vernon, a technical officer at the Royal Aircraft Establishment at Farnham, who was later proved to be a Russian spy:

"In 1937, Taylor persuaded four BUF members to burgle the home of Major Vernon, a technical officer at the Royal Aircraft Establishment at Farnham and, on this occasion, he claimed to have been working for MI5. Vernon was away on holiday at the time but, unfortunately for the burglars, a neighbour reported the break-in and their car number to the police who caught them while making their getaway. At their trial, the four burglars were found guilty of larceny and bound over for 12 months. However, some of the papers that they had stolen from Vernon were deemed sensitive and Vernon was prosecuted under the Official Secrets Act. He was found guilty, fined £30, and lost his job. One of the burglars, John Preen, who was later interned under Defence Regulation 18B then used the work he had done for Taylor in a plea to secure his release.

Q: There was Major Vernon and P G Taylor?

A: Yes. Taylor led me to believe that he was connected with MI5.

Q: Do you mean that he was connected with MI5?

A: ... I was given the idea he was; and I played darts with him and I have been to his flat once or twice.

Unfortunately for Preen, the 'brownie points' that he may have earned from his efforts on behalf of national security were not recognised by the Advisory Committee.

Thanks to Nigel West, we now have confirmation that Major Vernon was, indeed, a spy employed by the GRU (Soviet Military Intelligence) in a cell run by Ernest D Weiss, a concert pianist. This revelation is in West's book Venona (1999), even though it wasn't culled from any of the Venona material (collection didn't start until February 1943). Thanks to Frank Johnson (The Spectator), we also know that Vernon resurfaced after the war as the Labour MP for Dulwich division of Camberwell (1945-1951). Naturally, it was the late John Warburton who pulled these strands together."

TNA PRO HO45/25115 & Major P G Taylor, etc., op. cit.

The other person to mention Hughes was Aubrey Lees:

"One man, Aubrey Lees (not to be confused with Arnold Leese, the leading light of the Imperial Fascist League) had particular cause for grievance because he was arrested and interned on 20 June 1940, even though he had never been a member of the BUF.

Lees, who was vehemently anti-Jewish, had attended meetings of The Link and the Nordic League, both of which closed down on the outbreak of war. Later, when Lees was interviewed by the 18B Advisory Committee, he told them that he had come across a man whom he considered to have been an *agent provocateur*.

Q: Was the man's name Hughes?

A: No, Sir.

Q: Taylor?

A: No, Sir, but I am coming to him.

The man whom Lees fingered was E G Mandeville Roe, formerly a senior member of the British Fascists who had joined the BUF at the same time as Neil Francis Hawkins. In 1937, Mandeville Roe had been named as the prospective British Union candidate for Balham and Tooting.

It is extraordinary that the Committee should have prompted Lees in this manner but Lees then went on to tell the committee that he knew 'this fellow Hughes' and that he also knew him to be an agent of the Home Office. He said that they had become 'quite friendly' and that, on one occasion, he had asked him: 'By the way, aren't you a Home Office agent, or expert, or something?' Hughes replied, 'I was'."

Ibid.

Hughes was also instrumental in the Tyler Kent affair, and his action which helped to trigger it, came not very long before Wilfred was arrested; there is also the question of whether Wilfred knew of Hughes's presence at the 'secret meetings':

"On 9 April 1940, P G Taylor - or rather his alter ego James Hughes - played the most important role of his career when, after being introduced to Anna Wolkoff, he asked her if she could send a communication to William Joyce who was then in Germany broadcasting Nazi propaganda. Wolkoff's family had been dispossessed by the Russian revolution and she was vehemently anti-Jewish. When Hughes told her that the letter contained some 'good anti-Jewish material' that Joyce could use in his broadcasts, Wolkoff said that she would see what she could do.

It was her lucky day – or so she thought – because later that evening Hélène de Munck visited the Russian Tea Rooms that were run by Anna's parents and she casually mentioned to Admiral Wolkoff, Anna's father, that she had a friend at the Rumanian [sic] Legation who was leaving for the Continent the next day. It was a good card to play because de Munck had some Rumanian blood in her.

The old Admiral trotted off to share the news with Anna who swallowed the bait by rushing across to de Munck and demanding if it were true. On receiving de Munck's confirmation, she demanded 'Why didn't you tell me this before?' She then handed the letter to de Munck.

Of course, de Munck was an MI5 undercover agent and, at her trial, Wolkoff's indiscretion would be sufficient for her to be categorised as 'an enemy agent' under the Official Secrets Acts. This then ensured that Tyler Kent could similarly be brought within the ambit of the Official Secrets Acts. More immediately, it also resulted in the internment of Captain Ramsay and for the allegation to be made that Mosley and Ramsay were 'in relations' presumably on the strength of a few meetings that they had both attended at which Taylor had also been present."

Ibid.

45 ***TNA PRO HO 45/24891, among others, refers.***

46 The report for the 23rd of May does not include any information on the mass arrests, although the civil liberties aspect is explored, but ironically, there is the mention of the Fascist candidate, losing his deposit at the Middleton by-election, during the campaign for which Mosley was physically assaulted [the textual emphasis is that used in the reports]:

"**THURSDAY 23 MAY 1940**

In general there is a noticeable increase in cheerfulness and general calm, a distinct decrease in pessimism and nervousness. The intense gloom which affected London particularly yesterday is not conspicuous today.

However, there is little over-optimism.

Today's reports suggest that there is a growing basis for a more durable morale. People are rallied not simply by what appears to be better news, but also, though to a lesser extent, by facing up to the facts and by feeling that they are now taking a more active part in the war.

There is an increased tendency to say that there has been disgraceful neglecting the past [sic], that something must have been badly wrong at the top. With this goes a new feeling that a big effort is going to be required and that the new government is tackling the problem realistically. Verbatims reflect this:

'Well, everyone's in it now.'

'I'm prepared to do anything.'

'It looks as if we're going to do something really big now.'

Many of these reactions came from the emergency Powers Bill, which has had an excellent reception, particularly from men and from working-class people. In certain districts there is criticism e.g. 'We're imitating the Nazis now it comes to the point'

The importance of the new Bill is that it has made people more conscious of their part in the war and of the seriousness of the situation. It is a nail in the coffin of wishful thinking. In the minds of many the Bill means compulsion, and there is a growing tendency for compulsory powers to be welcomed. The Bill provides an important background for action (the kind of background which has been lacking so far). It is important that the Bill should constantly be interpreted, explained, and followed up by suitable propaganda. As far as one can judge people feel the Bill makes for national unity, and for that reason it has been welcomed.

London morale still lags behind that of provincial towns and of the countryside. In London some social workers express doubt about the effect of air raids upon the working-class population.

54% of the electorate voted in the Midddleton by-election. A notable increase over recent by-elections. Fascist candidate lost deposit.

Rumours

There are generally speaking fewer reports of rumours today, and there are none that would appear to be of major importance. … A large number of those which are brought to our notice are still reported as having their origin from the German wireless. One in particular which seems to be causing some alarm to the inhabitants of Twickenham is to the effect that Kneller Hall, the Military School situated in the district, would be one of the first places to be bombed. It may be worth noting in this connection that there is said to be a considerable amount of Fascist feeling in this area."

The assessment of the response to the arrests, although concise, is unequivocal:

"**FRIDAY 24 MAY 1940**

… The arrest of Mosley and other Fascists has overwhelming approval. Our observers report that they have seldom found such a high degree of approval for any Government action. The most frequent comment is that it should have been done long ago.

Points from Regions

1. Great satisfaction at arrest of Fascists.

…

There is a growing local feeling against the Cotswold Bruderhof. If parachutists landed locally Bruderhof might be lynched. [the Cotswold Bruderhof was a German Hutterite community founded in 1936 at Ashton Keynes in Wiltshire]"

LISTENING TO BRITAIN: Home Intelligence reports on Britain's Finest Hour—May to September 1940; Edited by Paul Addison & Jeremy A. Crang, Centre for the Study of the Two World Wars, School of History, Classics and Archaeology, University of Edinburgh

The August edition of the LPAVS ***News-Sheet*** also carried a small item, presumably written by Dudley Elam, which included a 'fifth column' reference, and it is hard not to see a 'tongue in cheek' element to this:

"LESSON FROM THE ISRAELITES

We are surprised to see in the ***Medical World***, July 5th, the following statement:

"We want to see anti-typhoid inoculation made as compulsory for the ordinary citizen as for the serving soldier."

Especially as ***The Lancet***, June 15th, said in an editorial:

"In considering safety we must remember the tribe whom the Israelites persuaded to be circumcised and on the third day when they were too sore to resist they were smitten down. T.A.B. inoculation, as practised in this country, is not devoid of reaction, which may be severe enough to cause several days' invalidity."

In other words, such inoculation could be as dangerous as any "fifth column" activities."

LPAVS News-Sheet, No. 2, August 1940, page 1; courtesy of the NAVS

47 There were calls for an extension of the evacuation scheme, and one of Mosley's earlier expressions, "the old gang", had become common currency, although the meaning had changed somewhat from Mosley's:

"**MONDAY 17 JUNE TO SATURDAY 22 JUNE 1940**

In a Sunday evening 'Postscript' on 16 June, J. B. Priestley expressed the wish that all children of Britain could be sent across the seas to the Dominions, leaving the adults to fight back against the Nazis with easier minds. Home Intelligence recorded strong popular support for the idea and the announcement on 20 June of a voluntary, state-assisted scheme prompted a rush for places, with 210,000 requests over the next fortnight. Since air raids were already frequent, and the threat of invasion was looming, fears for the safety of children were inevitable but not necessarily a sign of low morale. *From the Midland region there were 'many reports of talk among working and lower middle classes that "they would be just as well off under Hitler"* [my emphasis], but such expressions of defeatism were outweighed by the strength and frequency of demands for the more effective prosecution of the war. …

The most unpopular feature of the government was the continuing presence in high office of 'the old gang': Neville Chamberlain and his closest political allies. Chamberlain, who was a member of Churchill's War Cabinet, had become the scapegoat for military defeat after Dunkirk, and his pre-war record as an appeaser of Nazi Germany gave rise to the suspicion that he was still in favour of peace at any price or even perhaps a potential traitor."

Ibid.

48 *Ibid.:*

"With 650,000 men and women still unemployed the government was under attack for failing to use its powers to mobilise and arm every able-bodied citizen. As one critic put it: 'The Jerries will arrive to find many still in the streets with their hands in their pockets.'"

49 *Ibid.:*

"**WEDNESDAY 10 JULY [Points from Regions]**

LONDON Some expression of suspicion in Chelsea that Sir John Anderson has Fascist sympathies and is protecting or releasing Fascists who have been detained."

50 *Ibid.:*

"**TUESDAY 23 JULY 1940 [Points from Regions]**

WALES (Cardiff) … Although most people are willing to accept totalitarian methods to combat Hitler, proposed censorship and prosecutions have created feeling that complete totalitarianism is neither desirable nor necessary.

…

SOUTH-EASTERN (Tunbridge Wells) Pointed out that case of man fined for saying 'this is a capitalist war in defence of dividends' contrasts with freedom of *Daily Worker*."

51 In the meantime, there had been something of a backlash when the existence and implications of the Home Intelligence surveys had been discovered:

"**MONDAY 5 AUGUST TO SATURDAY 10 AUGUST 1940**

'At the moment the war is somewhat in the background', observed Home Intelligence on 7 August. After the seismic events of May and June, and the blood-curdling threats which had accompanied Hitler's 'peace offer', no invasion had taken place and there was something of a lull in hostilities. There was still some scepticism about the official figures for British and German losses in the air, which always seemed to show that Fighter Command was victorious, but popular confidence in the defensive capacities of the RAF was growing. Far away in the Horn of Africa Italian troops were invading British Somaliland, an event that Home Intelligence reported as briefly causing some unease: 'people everywhere want to hear that we are taking the initiative, but instead we are once more on the defensive, this time against the despised Italians.' In Chelsea, it was reported the following day, 'the intelligentsia' were 'almost defeatist in consequence'.

On 2 August German aircraft had dropped leaflets containing an English translation of Hitler's Reichstag speech over the south of England. 'There is evidence', Home Intelligence recorded, 'that the public is dissatisfied at the actions of the police (and wardens) in collecting the German leaflets ... these would be valued as souvenirs and many people declare that they would like to read with their own eyes what was written in the leaflets.' There was also 'some interest', the Cambridge regional office noted, in the plea for a compromise peace made by Richard Stokes, the Labour MP for Ipswich. Hitler had declared that Germany was fighting to create a New European Order. This raised the question of what the British were fighting for, a topic of some significance for the propaganda war in which the Ministry of Information itself was engaged. The regional office in Reading reported a 'growing local demand that Government should formulate a peace aims programme for Europe. Even unimaginative Slough Information Committee has voiced this.'

August the 3rd marked the beginning of the Bank Holiday weekend, and Home Intelligence remarked on the large holiday crowds, but on Bank Holiday Monday itself most factories and offices worked a normal day. So did Home Intelligence, which reported with an almost audible sigh of relief that the press campaign against 'Cooper's Snoopers' had made scarcely any impression on the public. On the home front more generally there were problems: 'The Prime Minister's leadership is unchallenged but evidence suggests that there is no such close identification between the people and the government as a whole.'"

Ibid.

52 There was also a growing scepticism, surprising perhaps, about the reliability of the mainstream news media:

"MONDAY 12 AUGUST TO SATURDAY 17 AUGUST 1940

Home Intelligence returned, at the start of the week, to the theme of popular mistrust of the news media. Following the great air battle over the Channel on 8 August, a photograph in the press had appeared to show five enemy aircraft shot down in flames and plunging headlong towards the sea. The Air Ministry, however, subsequently put out a statement explaining that it was not an official photograph, and that no such incident had been reported by RAF pilots. The photo, in other words, was a fake, or as one anonymous member of the public was quoted as saying: 'There's some dirty work going on somewhere.' ...

After the military disasters of May and June the daily reports were beginning to reflect a more optimistic view of the progress of the war. The news from Somaliland, where the Italians continued to advance, was eclipsed by the 'Battle for Britain', as Home Intelligence called it: the Churchillian phrase 'Battle of Britain' had yet to catch on. August the 13th, to which the Luftwaffe gave the code-name *Adlertag*, or 'Eagle Day', marked a ratcheting up of the German air assault with a day-long sequence of massed attacks on targets in the south-east of England. An even larger air battle, in which the Luftwaffe mounted simultaneous attacks on Tyneside and the south of England, was fought two days later. 'Confidence and cheerfulness prevail', ran the report for 16 August. 'Intensified raids are everywhere received with calmness, the results with jubilation.' Almost every account Home Intelligence received of the public's response to air raids suggested that morale was holding up strongly. …

There was, however no shortage of minor complaints and anxieties. From Driffield in Yorkshire resentment was reported at the burial with full military honours of a Nazi airman. Eggs were in short supply in the South East and many women living in hotels in Kensington were said to be prone to depression. But Home Intelligence no longer warned of pockets of defeatism. 'Streamers already being made privately in East end to celebrate victory', it was noted on 14 August, 'and remarks made that "it will only be a matter now of a few months".'"

Ibid.

53 ***Animal Rights: Political & Social Change in Britain since 1800, by Hilda Kean***

54 Luckily, a potted biography of all the new Committee members, including Lady Tenterden, is to be found in the LPAVS ***News-Sheet***:

"In the hope of future achievement, changes have recently taken place on the Committee of the society. It is thought that members might like to hear of those newly elected to the management.

…

Mention may, however, be made of MR. VICTOR RIENAECKER for, not only is he a fairly new recruit to the Committee, of which he has missed no single meeting, but it is owing to his initiative, determination and hard work that changes have been brought about. Formerly Assistant Keeper of the Ashmolean Museum at Oxford, he is widely known for his artistic and philosophic interests. It is a matter of congratulation that now to these is added his advocacy of Anti-Vivisection.

MRS. AYLMER HORT, young, business-like, active and a doctor's wife, is another whose services should be valuable. She has already proved them so by giving most practical and efficient voluntary help in the office of the society.

MISS NINA M. HOSALI, M.Sc., is famed for the great part she played with her mother in improving the conditions of animals in North Africa. …

MISS MARGARET BRADISH'S name will always be associated with her magnificent help in bringing about legislation against the caging of British wild birds. …

LADY TENTERDEN was brought up in opposition to medical cruelties by her father, the late General Sir Alfred Turner, a notable anti-vivisectionist. She also sat for several years on the committee of the British Union for the Abolition of Vivisection, of which the late Lord Tenterden was for some time the Chairman. He was afterwards Chairman of the Board of the Battersea Hospital in the days when it lived up to the tenets in which it was founded, and was the first Anti-Vivisection Hospital. Lady Tenterden has thus always been allied with the Anti-Vivisectionist Cause.

MRS. HEDLEY THOMSON, as Miss Hume, was another recruit to the movement through one of the Animal Protection Congresses of 1909. Until 1913, she sat on the Committee of the British Union for the Abolition of Vivisection. After her marriage, she sat for several years on the Board of the

Battersea Hospital, and has also been connected with R.S.P.C.A. work and the work of the Animal Defence Society, as well as the World League against Vivisection. At one time she took a strenuous part in both indoor and outdoor lecturing and opposition to the vivisectionist enemy. By use of different methods she has made her way into a number of research laboratories. She writes under her maiden name, E. Douglas Hume, and, in her own opinion, her chief use to the Cause is her book *Béchamp or Pasteur?* now nearing the end of its second large edition. Her last book, *The Mind Changers*, which oddly enough, found its way on board the *Graf Spee*, tells the history of the Animal Protection Movement and mentions the founding of the London and Provincial Anti-Vivisection Society.

This new Committee now greatly hopes for the help and support, financial or otherwise, of its general members in struggling to gain for sub-human creatures those rights that are the boasted human aims and objects for which we are warring in the present terrible world conflict."

LPAVS News-Sheet No. 16, 16/10/41, p.1; courtesy of the NAVS

Lady Tenterden was probably the relict of the fourth Baron Tenterden, Charles Stuart Henry Abbott, [1865-1939]: on his death, the title became extinct;

http://en.wikipedia.org/wiki/Baron_Tenterden

55 The legitimacy of such polls as did take place must have been suspect:

"Registers … have been compiled annually since 1832, except 1916-17 and 1940-44 inclusive (when the most recent register or the National Register of 1939 was taken as the basis for the electorate) …"

Electoral Registers Since 1832 & Burgess Rolls, by J. W. Gibson and Colin Rogers, Federation of Family History Societies

56 Wilfred was still only being paid a pittance, compared to earlier years, but he was undoubtedly grateful for an income, and he would certainly have been aware of the potential in the position, as reflected by these Minutes:

```
"Staff:   The following alteration and appointment to staff were made:-
          Miss Hill to be given a week's notice on September 6th.
          Mr. Risdon's salary for three weeks ending September 7th., at
          £2 per week was granted, also Mr. Risdon's appointment in
          place of Mr. Armstrong, at £3.10.0. per week was approved,
          this appointment to continue until the return of Mr.
          Armstrong, when Mr. Risdon's position will be again
          considered.
          Mr. Armstrong to be paid one month's salary, £14 (fourteen
          pounds) in lieu of notice, the same as the other speakers
          were granted.
          Mr. Large to be instructed to take at least two outdoor
          meetings per week, in addition to all indoor meetings which
          may be arranged for him by the Secretary.
...
Books     It was decided that Mr. Risdon be instructed to catalogue all
and       the Society's books and that all superfluous books be
Pictures: dispensed with; and that Mr. Rienaecker and Mr. Elam shall
          inspect all pictures and reject those not suitable for
          retaining."
```

LPAVS Executive Committee Meeting, 03/09/40; courtesy of the NAVS

57 Dudley Elam wrote to the Home Office on Sylvia Armstrong's behalf, and no doubt the basis of the request was more about securing the release of Sylvia Armstrong than it was a comment on Wilfred's capabilities:

"Sir,

My Committee has instructed me to respectfully enquire as to the probability of the early release of Mrs. Sylvia Armstrong, who is at present detained at H.M.Prison, Holloway, under Defence Regulation 18.b.

The reason for this enquiry is that she has been for several years employed by this Society and and is the only one competent to efficiently compile the Annual Report, which has to be got out for presentation to the Annual Meeting in May next. This work entails a great deal of research work and collation of accounts and should be in draft not later than March.

Any information that can be vouchsafed on this subject will be greatly appreciated.

I am, Sir,
Your obedient servant,
[signed] E. Dudley Elam
Secretary."

HO 45/23764; letter to H.M. Secretary of State, The Home Office, Whitehall, S.W. 1., 9th January, 1941

The Home Secretary must have continued to have doubts about the LPAVS, and MI5 was the conduit for this to be resolved:

"In view of the Secretary of State's question about the Anti-Vivisection Society, I have consulted Scotland Yard. They inform me that the Society is still functioning at the old premises, 76, Victoria Street, where it keeps an office open for enquiries. A temporary staff is employed, and in charge of it is Dudley Elam, a former *détenu*, who has gone there since his release.

When I asked the Special Branch for a candid opinion they said that they suspect that the Anti-Vivisection Society will take as much rope as is afforded them; and Special Branch feel that they have to be watched carefully. They remind us that Elam assisted to distribute the libellous pamphlets about the present Prime Minister.

Please see in this connection the letter dated 9th January from the Society, which has since come in. If anything it tends to strengthen one's suspicion.

[signed: illegible]
16.1.41

15.2.41 Comm [sic] of Police, N.S.Y, return C'ttee [sic] reports with obsns [sic].

It appears that the Anti-Vivisection Society included on its staff two fascists - Elam and Risdon - who were detained and afterwards released; the office is frequently visited by Elam's son, an ardent Fascist, who distributed the pamphlet about Mr. Churchill; and the solr. [sic] to the Society, who is also on the executive cttee is Mrs. Elam's solr., and is said by Risdon to be as much mixed up with the Society's Fascist activities as she was.

There is nothing to indicate that these people are engaged in objectionable activities but there is a little nest of them which the police think might carry on any political activity that suits their purposes."

HO 45/23764; file notes

The Special Branch report is also in the Armstrongs' file, and it does go into rather more detail; MI5 seemed happy to exonerate the Society, but Special Branch preferred to speculate, as above:

"10th day of February, 1941

With reference to Home Office letter 860984/5 of 18th January, 1941 asking whether there was still reason to suspect the London and Provincial Anti-Vivisection Society of objectionable activities and to the reports of the Advisory Committee on the cases of Mr. and Mrs. Armstrong:-

The facts about the fascist activity which was formerly carried on at the Society's offices at 76, Victoria Street under the direction of Mrs. Dudley ELAM alias Mrs. DACRE-FOX are well known to the Home Secretary, and Mrs. ARMSTRONG's part in the production of the pamphlet which was a criminal libel on Mr. Winston Churchill, then first Lord of the Admiralty, has also been reported. It may be well, however, in view of the reports of the Advisory Committee, to say that when the police raided 76, Victoria Street on 16th December, 1939, Armstrong still had in his personal possession fascist booklets and notes of various kinds, including a speaker's warrant and a copy of 'Action' of 14th December, 1939 - this although he has made great play of resigning in November, 1939. Moreover, when the flat occupied by the Armstrongs was searched as late as July, 1940, the police found a quantity a [sic] fascist literature and uniforms.

At the time of the raid, the following were the leading officials of the London and Provincial Anti-Vivisection Society.

President:- [the rest of the page is redacted] [page break]

None of the committee has come under adverse notice of Special Branch. Gush, however, is the solicitor for the society and also for Mrs. Dudley Elam. He practises at 86, Rochester Row, S.W.1, and although he is not known to have taken any part in British Union activities, it is significant that during the war he has twice defended members of the organisation who have been prosecuted for contravening the Defence Regulations.

Dr. H. Fergie Woods wrote to the Commissioner on 7th May, 1940, and said:- "I am President of the London and Provincial Anti-Vivisection society, whose offices were raided by Police last December. Information which has recently come to me causes me not to be satisfied with the explanation of the search that I had been given. I am naturally anxious, as President, to know whether any evidence was found at the offices of my Society being used for purposes subversive to the interests of the country. If this should be so, I should like to know if there is any way in which I could help to counteract such activities.". M.I.5, who had collaborated with the police in the extensive enquiries about the Society, were asked for their observations, and replied thus:- "Would you kindly inform Dr. Fergis [sic] Woods that the offices were searched by Police on account of the political activities of Mrs. Elam alias Dacre-Fox and that no suspicion attaches to the London and Provincial Anti-Vivisection Society as a whole.".

It is known that Mrs. Elam had told Dr. Woods that the offices had been searched because of the Government's opposition to the general work of anti-vivisection organisations. It is hardly conceivable that the Doctor accepted this explanation, but it appears that he only heard later of the fascist tendencies of the staff.

Despite the President's apparent anxiety to ensure that no subversive activity was carried within [sic] his Society, it is a fact that two well known fascists are still working there. They are E. Dudley ELAM and Wilfred RISDON: the former is secretary and the latter assistant secretary. These two were interned on 23rd May, 1940 (when a general round-up of fascists was made), but have since been released. Risdon, according to information which has reached the police, was recently heard to say he was sure Mrs. Elam would, when released, return to her former post with the Society, because she and Gush were on the closest terms. Gush, Risdon said, was as much mixed up with the Society's fascist activities as was Mrs. Elam.

Dudley Elam has recently said Mrs. Armstrong would certainly be re-employed if she were released. Her former wage of £3 per week has been paid regularly to her mother since her internment. Armstrong, Elam said, was almost certain to get work with the Society again if released, although he had not been paid directly or indirectly during his internment.

Whether or not the committee of the London and Provincial Anti-Vivisection [sic] were aware of the fascist tendencies of members of the staff prior to the arrest of some of them must be a matter for conjecture. If not, they must certainly have known of them following the police raid, the extensive enquiries, and the subsequent internments, and one can only assume that in so much as two former fascists are already employed and two more will be re-employed if released the more active members of the committee do not condemn these political activities.

One cannot fairly say that the Society as a whole is engaged on objectionable activities, but should the Armstrongs return, the former principals of the staff, with the exception of Mrs. Elam, will be engaged at 76, Victoria Street. In addition, [redacted] E[redacted] who is known to have distributed the offending pamphlet about Mr. Churchill, and to have been an ardent fascist, frequently visits the offices. Altogether, it is difficult to avoid the conclusion that this group of people would carry on any political activity which might suit their purpose."

HO 45/23764, Special Branch report dated 10th February, 1941

58 ***Animal Rights: etc., op. cit.***

59 The LPAVS suffered some air-raid damage early in September 1940, which was noted in the Minutes of the October ECM with admirable restraint:

"The Secretary reported that he filled in a form for compensation for Air Raid Damage to the premises on Saturday September 7th., and that the Government representative called to inspect on September 20th, stating that no payment would be made until after the war, but instructing him to get on with the work of repair."

LPAVS Executive Committee Meeting, 01/10/40, courtesy of the NAVS

The scale of the pre-emptive destruction of pets is quite staggering:

"Within the first four days of declaration of war in 1939, 400,000 pet cats and dogs were destroyed by their owners fearful of imminent invasion and gas attacks, despite protestations of the Battersea Dogs' Home, anti-vivisectionists and the NCDL [National Canine Defence League], which deplored the massacre as the 'September Holocaust'. The National Anti-Vivisection Society was horrified to report that outside the Wood Green animal shelter in north London, an area marked for evacuation, people stood in a queue half a mile long waiting to have their pets destroyed. Bombardments of

British cities, bringing the war directly home to people and animals alike, killed thousands of domestic animals, particularly in London. Petrified animals were rescued by animal charities from bombed houses, often being the only member to survive, and the Home Office issued guidelines for the return of animals to their owners. Fears also grew that stray cats and dogs were being trapped by vivisectors …"

Animal Rights: etc., op. cit.; see also Chapter 11, notes 39 & 40.

60 ***Ibid.***

Funds were short, but the LPAVS endeavoured to publicise Wilfred's work:

"**NOTICE**

The supplement to this month's News-Sheet, An Air-Raid Shelter For Your Pets, has been printed in sufficient quantity to supply additional copies to give to your friends. They will be supplied free of charge on receipt of a stamped addressed envelope."

LPAVS News-Sheet No. 4, October 1940; courtesy of the NAVS

61 ***Ibid.***

62 From a blog posting by Hilda Kean, 8th of May 2012:

"As the president of the National Veterinary Medical Association at the time, Harry Steele Bodger, put it, 'Born in faith, nurtured with hope, died through charities. Thus sums up the National ARP Animals Committee but it is not the whole story. I feel that the villain of the piece is that fairy godmother the Ministry of Home Security which was present at the birth, gave it its blessing, and proceeded to starve it to death.'"

The Times and The Great Escape, by Hilda Kean;
http://hildakean.com/?p=969

63 ***My father's Anderson air Raid shelter:***

"saved my mother and father when their home in London received a direct hit during the war. … My mother and father survived in this air raid shelter. Their pet dog did not. 'Montmarency Fits Boodle' had his nose up against the air vent to get fresh air. The bomb blast travelling down the vent burst his lungs."

http://www.flickr.com/photos/doublejeopardy/4509937943/

64 From the BBC public history archive:

"At home father was out most evenings on "Home Guard" duty somewhere in Hove/Portslade and I can recall being very impressed with his uniform, gun and ammunition. Meanwhile, whenever danger loomed, my mother and I (and latterly my baby sister) together with the pet dog, Dutchy, 2 cats, Danny and Micky, budgies and a parrot would squeeze ourselves into the Anderson air raid shelter which seemed to take up most of the space in our dining room."

My thoughts from Hangelton;
http://www.bbc.co.uk/history/ww2peopleswar/stories/99/a4394199.shtml

"One night a landmine (much bigger than the usual bombs, and suspended from a parachute), came floating down our road. It was about 3:35am on 16th November 1940. The landmine was a tiny bit too high to hit our house, and the houses of our friends, but it hit the school just around the corner, where the French soldiers had stayed, with an almighty bang. … Some people dug air raid shelters in the garden, but after the landmine we had a corrugated iron shelter called an Anderson put in our front room. It was like an up-side-down U and it was packed around with sandbags, and the windows in the room had yellow sticky mesh put on them, and there were orange and apple boxes filled with sand and stacked against the outside of the walls. There were four bunks, one on top of the other on each side of the Anderson where we children slept, and our parents slept on the floor below. I remember it as being quite a big shelter, but I have seen one over from the war recently and it's really very small. I can't think how we all managed to squash into it."

Bournemouth, Bombs, and My Two Brothers;

http://www.bbc.co.uk/history/ww2peopleswar/stories/35/a3526535.shtml

65 Volunteers often helped the Civil Defence forces:

"Originally a volunteer branch of Worthing Animals Dispensary, the Animals ARP Volunteer Corps later became part of the town's ARP system as a whole. After successful appeals for volunteers, the local service established a dozen first aid and reporting centres in and beyond Worthing, rendering assistance to animals injured, frightened or lost in air raids. The ***Herald*** of 27 September 1940 reported the rescue of 27 cats, 14 dogs and 6 cages of budgerigars and canaries. Mr Crouch pleaded that their work in reuniting rescued animals with their owners would be made significantly easier if owners fitted their pets with identity discs, supplied free by the National ARP for Animals Committee, to which the local scheme was affiliated."

The Worthing Animal Clinic; 1930-1939: The Burgeoning Years;

http://www.worthinganimal.co.uk

66 There is a Registration Book in the Museum of London:

"This National Air Raid Precautions Animals Committee Registration Book was issued to Mrs E Reeves, a National Animal Guard in the Uxbridge area, during the Second World War. The committee was a voluntary service run by guards who would patrol local areas and help any animals injured in air raids. The registration book was used to take the name and address of all animals reported lost or missing during air raids. The book has been partly used and lists cats and dogs that had gone astray in the Uxbridge area. The wartime animal registration scheme was open to all horses, ponies and donkeys, and pets 'to which the registration disc can be attached'."

http://www.museumoflondon.org.uk/Collections-Research/Collections-online/object.aspx?objectID=object-517064&start=0&rows=1

67 Some of them were claimed to be gas-proof:

"Volunteers were given a course of anti-gas lectures, and the general public as a whole were asked to visit the Dispensary, where a gas proof kennel was on view. In an emergency, a dog could be hermetically sealed in and would have breathed through a filter, similar to a gas mask."

The Worthing Animal Clinic; op. cit.

The effects of gas, although different for animals, were taken seriously:

"*S. Evelyn Thomas's Handy War-Time Guide* said:

> It is not only on humane grounds that we should protect animals from the dangers and horrors of an air raid; it is also in the general interest of the community for, apart from their value to us, there is the danger that if we do not give them protection, frenzied and terror-stricken animals may well add to the confusion and perils of a raid. Although animals are immune from the effects of tear gases, and almost immune from the effects of nose gases, they are affected in the same way as human beings by the more deadly lung and blister gases.
>
> Moreover, animals contaminated by liquid blister gases, besides suffering themselves, would be a source of danger to persons coming into contact with them …

No satisfactory animal gas mask has yet been devised.

The National Canine Defence League designed a special kennel to protect small animals against gas, splinters and blast. It was a steel cylinder, closed at one end. A gas-proof cover with a glass window would be fitted at the other end once the dog was inside."

Animals on the Home Front;

http://www.livingarchive.org.uk/includes/external/nvq/tracey/animals_dog.html

68 There is a delightfully quaint clip in the British Pathé archive:

http://www.britishpathe.com/video/dog-shelter-aka-animal-shelter-issue-title-is-quie

69 Wilfred was clearly very much his own boss by this time:

"During the war whilst I was in the R.N. I visited London. I was a Sick Bayman [sic] and as Uncle Bill had been in the R.A.M.C. during the First World War I visited him in his office in Victoria Street. I found that he had never lost his interest in Medical matters and we therefore spent a few hours of interesting conversation."

In the same letter, Len offers a very personal insight into Wilfred's assessment of one of his notorious British Union colleagues:

"During his days in the B.U.F. he moved to Manchester which I believe was Mosley's H.Q. I think it would have been about 1934 [more likely 1935] my father took us to Manchester to visit him. He had then married Auntie Margaret, who had also been involved in the B.U.F. and I suppose how he met her [sic]. Whilst we were there he took us to visit his office and in the same building the B.U.F. had a licensed club. We went into the Club where there were a number of people all of whom were wearing the party uniform. I remember he introduced us to a rather unpleasant looking man who had a nasty scar running from his left ear to the corner of his mouth. I learned that I had shaken hands with the notorious William JOYCE, later to become known as 'Lord HAW HAW'. I remember afterwards Uncle Bill said to me, "You have just met a very unpleasant and dangerous man." He was of course also a member of the B.U.F."

Letter to the author from Leonard Risdon, 28th November 1996

13: ANIMALS

In general terms, Wilfred's war was very quiet; luckily [for him; not for the unfortunate victims] 'The Blitz' started on a Saturday, September 7th 1940, so it is probable that he will have been at home, and the damage was concentrated on the central part of the capital [**1**]. Although Victoria Street was at the heart of the city, it appears to have escaped virtually unscathed [**2**]; one minor incident was noted in the LPAVS Executive Committee Meetings Minutes for October 1940, early in this period of bombardment [see Chapter 12, note 59] but otherwise, Wilfred's work appears to have continued uninterrupted during the war. 'Outer London' also 'copped it' subsequently, but there is no evidence that Wilfred and Nellie's home in Ruislip Manor suffered any damage [although see below, with reference to the nearby Northolt Aerodrome]; however, for the total period of the war, nearly 30,000 civilians [which included Civil Defence workers] were killed by enemy action in the London Civil Defence region, against 60,595 who were killed over the same period in Great Britain, including Northern Ireland, overall [**3**]. There is no obvious or automatic correlation in these figures with the number of people made homeless, however [see note 2]. The implications for domestic pets, notwithstanding the 'September Holocaust' [see also Chapter 12, note 59] and, indeed, animals of all sizes, which were liable to vivisection, can only be guessed at, but the LPAVS, personified by Wilfred Risdon and his colleagues, continued with its admirable work, despite the war which will, understandably as well as inevitably, have been a totally absorbing matter for most people, into which such relatively insignificant topics as vivisection will not readily have intruded.

As detailed at the end of Chapter 12, by early in 1941, if a Special Branch report is to be believed, Wilfred was Assistant Secretary at the LPAVS. The news that "Mr. Armstrong had got a very good job which he was starting on March 5th" [**4**], as reported by the Secretary at the March ECM, must have come as something of a relief for Wilfred; not only would he have been pleased for his erstwhile colleague and partner in adversity, but it meant that there was no longer a question mark hanging over his position on the staff of the LPAVS. He was already having articles that had been written by his alter ego of W. Arr printed on a regular monthly basis, sometimes more than one per issue, which will have boosted his income modestly. In May that year, he represented the Society at a "successful" debate "where a vote of 13 to 5 was registered 'That Vivisection should be abolished'." although unfortunately, details of the debate and its venue were reported neither in the ECM Minutes nor the Society's ***News-Sheet***.

A serious matter arose in August 1941 that called into question the integrity of his titular superior Dudley Elam, and the validity of his continuance as Acting Secretary of the Society: when Norah Elam was arrested the previous year, on the same day as Wilfred, it had been assumed by the remaining Executive Committee members that she would return to her duties when released; sooner rather than later, all being well; consequently, the Committee had agreed to pay her an annual retaining fee of £150, payable monthly, "in consideration of her agreeing to resume her duties with the society at the earliest possible moment if called upon to do so". Curiously [and, arguably, displaying a distinct lack of fairly common knowledge] it was assumed that she would be able to continue her editorial work while incarcerated: "She to make up the proposed monthly News Sheet and to act generally in a non-consultative capacity without further remuneration this engagement to be subject to review by the Society." The Society's solicitor, Geoffrey Gush, over whom there was also a question mark, was instructed to inform Mrs. Dacre Fox [by which name the Committee referred to her] accordingly [**5**]. At the ECM of the 2nd of July, 1940, the question of her resignation was raised by the President, Dr. Fergie Woods [**6**], but a decision was deferred until the next meeting, when the matter was settled by the appointment of her 'husband' provisionally "as Acting Secretary and as Editor of the News Sheet, and to deal generally with the business of the Society". After this, the Society's affairs continued smoothly for just over a year, but in August 1941, precipitate resignations were tendered by Gush, as Chairman and Trustee, and another Executive Committee member, Mrs. King, from the Committee and also as a Trustee. Dudley Elam held onto these letters for over a week, and when he was asked why he had not seen fit to inform either the President or the Treasurer, he "replied that as the letter had been addressed to him as Secretary he did not consider it necessary to inform anyone else." In itself, this was probably not more than a minor procedural error, but it was indicative of a somewhat high-handed attitude; another very influential Executive Committee member was having misgivings about the continuing rôle of Norah Elam, however, because a letter [again, content unknown] from Dr. Allinson was read at the 2nd of September ECM. Dudley Elam responded by informing the Committee that his 'wife' had had a five-year contract with the Society since early January, 1938, and that he held a copy on her behalf: "the other copy held by Mr Gush on behalf of the Society. Mr Rienaecker asked why no reference was made to this contract at the time when it was agreed to pay a retaining fee to Mrs Dacre Fox. No satisfactory reply was forthcoming."

This explained Geoffrey Gush's resignation, but it also put the Society in an awkward position: they needed to see the contract, to ascertain what its stipulations were but, probably because of the somewhat convoluted status of the Elams in relation to the Society, they chose not to demand that Dudley Elam should surrender his copy; instead, for the official record, they instructed the office-holder of Secretary, currently Dudley Elam, "to take immediate steps for the recovery of the copy held on behalf of the Society so that legal advice may be sought thereon." Understandably, this rendered Dudley Elam's position untenable, so he was asked "to withdraw while the whole matter was discussed." This he did, and in the ensuing discussion it was agreed that he should be removed from office forthwith, paid two months' salary in lieu [£50], plus £5 "Payment for Literary work for September News Sheet"; Norah Elam's salary of £12.10s. for the month of September was also paid, and it was agreed that the retaining fee paid hitherto should be discontinued, "to-day's payment to be the last." It was carried unanimously that Wilfred should be appointed forthwith as Acting Secretary, "on the same terms as Mr. Elam". It is unlikely that Wilfred will have seen this as any sort of achievement on his part, unless he had any reason to be less than enamoured of the Elams, which is always possible. That was not quite the end of the matter however: for some reason, Dudley Elam took with him an item of some value [and it is unclear whether this value was monetary, or intrinsic, if it was a reference manuscript], and although Norah Elam did write a letter of resignation from her position as Secretary, she did not mention the link to the post of Editor. Wilfred was instructed to present the facts on the former matter to the Society's new solicitor, a Mr. Green, and to write to Norah Elam on the latter matter, "linking up the post of Editor (to which there was no reference in Mrs Dacre Fox's letter) with that of Secretary to make it quite clear that she had no further connection with either of these two posts." [**7**] The business with Dudley Elam rumbled on for a couple of months, but the item ["the Spurrier M.s.s."] was eventually returned; of Norah Elam, *aka* Mrs. Dacre Fox, no more was heard, by the LPAVS, at any rate.

While she was in Holloway Prison, she totally ignored the LPAVS, and concentrated on ingratiating herself with Diana Mosley [**8**], seeing that as a way to getting her husband's attention, and thereby manoeuvring herself into the core of what she expected to be an influential post-war group whose natural leader would, again, be Oswald Mosley; she continued this after her release which, despite her refusal to appeal [or perhaps because of it, given her propensity for intransigence] was early in 1942, and she was able to speak to Sir Oswald in person, during her visits to Holloway, after he had been allowed to join his wife there, but he was less enthusiastic: although his solicitor thought that she was "not of the same class as the others" who would constitute a Committee "to work on informing MPs of the facts about detention under 18B with a view to 'aid justice' for the detainees", he did however "seem to think Norah could be useful for fundraising though" [**9**]. Some saw the 18B Detainees Fund as having "had a dual purpose which was to act as a cover for BUF activity and to prepare for Mosley's return to politics after the war", but while the latter might have some credence, the former is highly debatable, and for want of credible sources of information, is more likely to depend upon one's view of Mosley's honesty [**10**]. If Norah Elam thought that her involvement with fund-raising on Mosley's behalf was any sort of passport to permanent acceptance by him, his precipitate decision not to contest the 1945 election left her out in the cold [**11**]; thereafter, her life seemed to go gradually downhill. She and Dudley moved from their Logan Place flat to Gothic Cottage in Twickenham, and associated very closely with the extreme anti-Semite Arnold Leese [whose concerns for animal welfare, especially that of those he considered as his speciality, camels, were probably more of a coincidence than an incentive], which would certainly not have endeared her to the Mosleys, and from then on until her death on March 2, 1961, she gave a very good impression of "losing the plot" [**12**].

Only a matter of months after the departure of the Elams from the LPAVS, in January 1942, the confirmation of Wilfred's permanent appointment as Secretary was announced; in an echo of his experience during the latter couple of years with British Union, the following month he either wrote or edited a notice in the ***News-Sheet*** informing members of a reduction in permanent staff at the LPAVS [**13**], but it did not appear to be a suggestion of the organisation's possible demise, or any threat to his position, and he did not hesitate to use, or endorse the use of the word 'propaganda'; also, he was now compiling, again under his pseudonym, a regular column like he did for British Union; the name of the column and often controversial theme of the content varied over time, but the first one was called ***From the Torture Chamber***. Later, this emotive location was moderated slightly to 'Laboratory'. Another of the organisation's *bêtes noires* was immunisation, and the war gave the allopathic fraternity the opportunity to subject the populace to a mass programme with the intention of avoiding the outbreak of diphtheria, using the enforced congregation of large numbers of people sheltering from air attacks as justification; this was co-ordinated by the Ministry of Health [**14**]. A public meeting was held in June, 1942 at the Caxton Hall which, very conveniently, was in Victoria Street; the subject was: "What Diphtheria Immunisation REALLY Means". The LPAVS was one of "The following Societies ... co-operating in the organisation of this meeting of protest against the mass immunisation now being conducted throughout the country by the Ministry of Health", and, by virtue of Lady Tenterden being the Honorary Treasurer for the protest group, the LPAVS offices were used as a central location, and Wilfred co-ordinated the work of the Joint Organising Secretaries [**15**], something he would increasingly become accustomed to as time went on. This was obviously a subject of some import and, as is generally the case when the Government of the day wants to persuade a credulous populace of the advantages of a particular policy, in addition to ensuring that the mainstream media all stick to the same script, it significantly restricts the opportunity for contrary opinions to be heard; consequently, the LPAVS was concerned that the situation with the diphtheria immunisation programme, essential though it was to arrive at an equitable solution, was being presented in a very one-sided way, so it was keen to redress the balance, and in September 1943 Wilfred wrote, on behalf of the Committee, to "The Director of Talks, B.B.C., Broadcasting House, W.1." [**16**]. Notwithstanding the gravity of the matter, he could not resist the opportunity to make a sardonic political observation, but in a way that was not obviously attributable to his former affiliations:

14th September, 1943.

Dear Sir,

For some time past talks have been sponsored by the B.B.C. concerning the advantages of diphtheria immunisation. So far so good, but these talks have presented only one side of the case although it is very evident that there is a considerable minority opinion which is opposed to the practice of so-called immunisation.

My Executive Committee have asked me to write pointing out that the persistent presentation of one side of an argument without affording any facility for the presentation of an opposition point of view is contrary to the basic principles of democracy which we are all so keen to maintain. Would it, therefore, be possible to arrange for some future talk on this subject to take both sides of the case under consideration in the one discussion, placing any well-known advocate of the principles of immunisation in opposition to a qualified medical practitioner who is opposed to the practice, and allowing a full discussion of both pros and cons instead of merely presenting the one point of view?

If you could see your way to arranging such a discussion we should have very great pleasure in submitting a list of names of qualified medical practitioners, any one of whom would be willing to take the opposition point of view.

I am, Sir,

Yours faithfully,

[signed] W. Risdon
Secretary.

Within three days, a politely dismissive reply came back: "Your suggestion will be given careful consideration, and if we are able to act upon it, we shall get in touch with you again." [**17**] Wilfred must have been aware of how difficult a task it was to try and make people understand how carefully controlled was their world-view, as presented by the mass media, and his many years of political experience will have told him how reluctant people are to relinquish their established perceptions, perhaps as a result of an undefined [yet inherent] fear of cognitive dissonance, especially as this might not be understood or recognised; no doubt the BBC also was not in a hurry to acknowledge an unbalanced presentation of technical matters such as this, which would have much wider implications for the population of the country. Realistically, Wilfred must have known that the work he was doing was going to consist of continually pushing to change beliefs and attitudes, which would inevitably annoy or upset people, or both, so although the object of the work was honourable, in a way it was a continuation of what he had been doing previously, but on a different battleground; at least there was less likelihood of physical attack, compared to previously [although evidently, the debates could be distinctly acrimonious here as well; see note 6]. Given the contemporary popularity of radio, it was surely only a matter of time before there was a controversy over the promotion of 'established' and widely accepted medical views, to the exclusion of the alternative viewpoint, and it would appear that in 1943, Wilfred was picking up on work that had been done by either the LPAVS before he joined, or one of the other major 'players' in the anti-vivisection arena, like the BUAV or the NAVS, all of which shared an ethos of collaborating wherever possible. This had achieved a limited measure of success in March 1933, when pressure for a debate on vivisection paid off, but the debate seems to achieved little in the way of tangible progress, and for the rest of that decade, the subject "returned to the 'black-list' at Broadcasting House and it could not be referred to, either directly or indirectly, without first gaining special permission." Amazingly, according to the Director of Talks in 1932, who might or might not have been the same one to whom Wilfred wrote thirteen years later, nobody had the 'right' to express his opinions through the BBC! [**18**] It took until 1961 for Wilfred to be able to participate in a radio debate on the subject of vivisection himself, on the BBC Home Service; it is not known if this was a result of his lobbying, or if he was invited, in his capacity as a well-known campaigner on the subject: unfortunately, the archive material at the BBC is confined to a transcript of the debate itself. Although mentioning it in the narrative at this point is jumping ahead somewhat, this debate deserves to be reproduced in full, so as a recognition of its importance, please see **Appendix F** for the transcript.

An interesting situation arose quite early in Wilfred's tenure at the LPAVS, concerning his former employer: although it is unlikely that he would have intervened, in view of the nature of the case, of which he cannot have failed to be aware, given the high profile nature of the defendant, it would be interesting to know Wilfred's response to the charge of cruelty to the pigs on his Wiltshire farm, which had been levelled at Mosley in 1945, quite soon after his release from Holloway Prison; the action was thrown out because the evidence for the prosecution's case was so thin, but that did not inhibit Mosley from reportedly flying "into a rage" when his level of care towards his animals was criticised, and thereafter "he fired off letters to the Home Office and the lord chancellor", to no avail [**19**]. Other than the animals under his own care, Mosley does not appear to have involved himself with the fight to guarantee the welfare of animals in general. The strictures on everyday activities during the war do not seem to have curtailed the activities of the vivisectors, even though that might have been an understandable expectation: by 1943, over one million medical experiments involving animals were being carried out every year [**20**]. The

Government was keen to keep these statistics secret however: the Home Secretary announced in Parliament that the annual returns of experiments on living animals would not be published for the duration of the war [**21**].

This admission of secrecy was only the tip of the iceberg of course; the security surrounding the experiments conducted at the Porton Down site in Wiltshire must have been extremely tight: it is hard to understand how rational human beings could accommodate the idea of innocent animals being forcibly subjected to all the atrocities presented by contemporary weaponry, including gases and chemicals, which could somehow provide psychological comfort if medical care for the human cannon-fodder or accidental casualties was thereby improved [**22**]. On the plus side, building on the ethos alluded to above, co-operation between the various disparate anti-vivisection and animal welfare societies, or at the very least, "greater ideas of co-operation" [**23**] were fostered during the war: six months after the aforementioned anti-immunisation event, the Conference of Anti-Vivisection Societies first met on the 20th of November 1942, again at the Caxton Hall, Westminster [with no apparent irony in the use of a phrase that Hitler had used, and would be used regularly in the future to signify authoritarian oppression] "for the purpose of discussing and making plans for a joint intensive campaign, after the war, to claim the total abolition of vivisection as a necessary step toward securing for animals their rightful place in the new world order, which is generally believed will follow the peace." [**24**] This joint effort proceeded steadily over the next few years, and as soon as possible after the war had ended, attempts were made to convene a World Congress on anti-vivisection, as Wilfred was able to report in 1950, in an article entitled "CONFERENCES AND CONVENTIONS": "In the post-war world there is evidence of a feeling of the need for closer collaboration and more frequent consultation between the various organisations engaged in activities for the promotion of better treatment of animals by human beings." [**25**] It is clear that Wilfred and the LPAVS were at the forefront of this collaboration between the various Societies, providing co-ordinating support, and it is surely a tribute to Wilfred's hard work that the impression was created that the LPAVS was a much bigger Society, not the relatively small organisation with no branches that it actually was.

All this could have been interpreted as encouraging, and there were several known anti-vivisectionists in the new Labour Government after the landslide victory in the election of 1945: Peter Newman, Secretary of the Welsh Theosophical Society and a vegetarian; George Mathers, President of the National Temperance Federation; and Ernest Thurtle, George Lansbury's son-in-law [**26**]; unfortunately however, these few individuals were not able to create enough momentum to bring about a reversal of the trend of an increase in the number of animal experiments, as alluded to above, and during a Parliamentary debate on the 30th of October 1946, the Home Secretary, Chuter Ede, displayed a boorish combination of uninformed condescension, punctilious obstinacy and breathtaking callousness, when he refused to withdraw the licence of a vivisectionist at Oxford University, Professor Dr. E. G. T. Liddell, who had been convicted of causing unnecessary suffering to cats in the course of his experiments at the University [**27**]. Anti-vivisectionists obviously needed as much help as they could get, and for all that might be achieved by Wilfred and his associates in the various organisations at that time with letters, petitions and the like, the best chance they stood of achieving change was by using the parliamentary system, despite its known flaws, and to do this, they needed a very well-placed and committed supporter.

It would have been around this time when Wilfred became acquainted with Hugh Dowding, who by 1943, a year after his retirement from the RAF, was now known as Baron Dowding of Bentley Priory [**28**]. Wilfred almost certainly knew of Dowding through Mosley, as their career progressions had been quite similar, albeit that Dowding was fourteen years older than Mosley; both had attended Winchester College, and Mosley had arrived at Sandhurst at the beginning of 1914 [**Appendix A**, note 12], only two years after Dowding had attended the Army Staff College, Camberley [just over the border from Sandhurst **29**; previously he had attended the Royal Military College, Woolwich, after Winchester]. At the end of 1913, Dowding gained his Aviator's Certificate [no. 711], then shortly afterwards, his wings; Mosley learned to fly in 1915, gaining his pilot's certificate from the flying school at Shoreham, but a leg injury prevented him from progressing any further: he would undoubtedly have heard of, and possibly discussed Dowding's exploits during his time on active service in France, when Dowding was Commander of no. 16 Squadron. Mosley was certainly in favour of a well-equipped military, including a modern and up-to-date air force [which he did not see in any way as incompatible with his desire to prevent another war], so he would naturally have followed Dowding's career with interest, becoming promoted to full Air Marshal in 1933 and Air Chief Marshal in 1937. Although in the normal course of events he should have retired in June 1939, he is generally credited with being the most significant factor in our victory in the Battle of Britain, but in the way that most people are a combination of outwardly conflicting characteristics, he "was known for his humility and intense sincerity" [**30**], and he was also outspoken; his opponents and detractors finally succeeded in manoeuvring him into relinquishing command in November 1940, and after a [for the two governments] somewhat uncomfortable stint for the Ministry of Aircraft Production [**31**] in the USA, and heading a study of economies of RAF manpower, he accepted the inevitability of retirement in July 1942.

Dowding was obviously a thoughtful and contemplative man, so it should come as no great surprise that when he retired, he became actively involved in spiritualism, as well as espousing the cause of animal welfare; it has to remain a matter for speculation what Wilfred's attitude towards the former would have been, given that he was probably a traditionalist Anglican Christian, but it is unlikely to have been entirely out of place within the mindset of the Committee of the LPAVS. As for the latter, Dowding made it part of his life as soon as he was a civilian again, and his first speech on the issue in the House of Lords was on the 18th of March, 1948, the subject being the pain and distress suffered by animals during slaughter because of the inconsistency in the methods used: he wanted to "obviate all cruelty in the process of slaughter" [**32**]. The speech was comprehensive but, in addition, he encompassed a matter which would have been regarded as particularly sensitive, given that the stated aims for the defeat of Hitler would still have been relatively fresh in the memory: the ritual slaughter methods employed by Jews and Moslems. He did not mince his words when he referred to "the religious ceremonial of the strangers within our gates" [**33**]. After calling for a clear indication of the Government's intentions: "In the interests of decency and humanity this question ought to be answered, so that plans may be considered and may be ready for implementation when the national situation allows this blot to be removed from the national conscience"; he admitted that although he had "lived on this planet for sixty-five years … this is the first time that I have raised my voice in the interests of the animals", and "I am not one of those who believe in the literal truth of every word of the first chapter of Genesis … Man, through his association with animals, is responsible to God for their evolution. Man can take, but he cannot destroy life. If in his greed and blindness he sends his charges across the border, crazed with terror and agony, he sets in motion a cause which by immutable law will be followed by its inevitable effect."

If at this juncture Wilfred was not already aware of Dowding's feelings on the subject, this speech will undoubtedly have marked Dowding out as a potential ally, and Wilfred made it his business to establish [or re-establish] contact with him. Dowding would have been a very busy man; he evidently did not see retirement as an excuse for idleness, joining the Theosophical Society and writing five books in quick succession, the first of which, ***Twelve Legions of Angels***, was actually written in the year preceding his retirement, although it was suppressed by the government until 1946, on the grounds that it contained information that "might be of use to the Germans" [**34**]. His next four books were all on themes associated with Theosophy's quest for "some universal truth supposed to be common to all religions" [**35**], spiritualism and reincarnation: ***Many Mansions*** (1943), ***Lychgate*** (1945), ***God's Magic*** (1946) and ***The Dark Star*** (1951). If he had only been occasionally or intermittently engaged by animal welfare concerns hitherto, it was his marriage to his second wife Muriel [née Albino] in September 1951 that created the circumstances in which they could both 'step up a gear' in their animal welfare and anti-vivisection activities. Lady Dowding had contacted the former Air Chief Marshal after her then husband, Jack Maxwell (Max) Whiting, a bomber pilot, had been reported missing during a mission over Norway in May 1944, and their shared interests had culminated in marriage after her husband's death had been confirmed [**36**]. She converted him to vegetarianism, he gave up shooting animals, "and they lived contentedly at her home, 1 Calverley Park, Tunbridge Wells" [**37**].

Now that he was comfortably settled into his position 'at the helm' of the LPAVS, as it were, Wilfred gave every indication of not wanting to 'let the grass grow under his feet'; by 1955, there was a veritable plethora of joint organisations [leading to understandable fears that this could be counter-productive], one of which was the Standing Co-ordinating Committee of Anti-Vivisection Societies, with an address of 76, Victoria Street, and Wilfred had become the Secretary of this august body, which is confirmed by a letter he wrote to the ***Manchester Guardian***, printed on the 22nd of November, 1955 [**38**]:

EXPERIMENTS ON ANIMALS

To the Editor of the Manchester Guardian

Sir.–Sir Henry Dale is reported to have said in his lecture to the Research Defence Society (November 16) that medical and veterinary research involving the use of animals is "essentially humane" and that the opponents of this form of research conduct a "cruel and cowardly campaign of misrepresentation" against it.

The official publications of the anti-vivisection societies, far from using the methods of misrepresentation, rely entirely on quotations from the reports of vivisectors themselves to show that many of the experiments conducted upon living animals must cause excruciating agony and long-drawn-out suffering quite irreconcilable with the term "humane", which we understand to mean kind, tender, or merciful.

Furthermore these publications rely on quotations from orthodox medical periodicals to show that the products of such forms of research are quite often misleading to the medical profession and dangerous—sometimes fatally so—to the patient. These are the essential facts and they make it clear that the terms "cruel and cowardly" rest far more naturally on those who inflict pain and suffering on inoffensive animals in the vain hope of avoiding suffering themselves than they do on those who seek the abandonment of this particular form of research in favour of the more rewarding bedside study of the human patient and his ailments.—

Yours &c.,

W. RISDON, Secretary
Standing Co-ordinating
Committee of Anti-
Vivisection Societies.
76 Victoria Street, London, S.W.1.

By now, he is clearly accustomed to acting at his own instigation, as he does not mention being asked by "his Executive committee" to pursue this matter. The ominous-sounding Research Defence Society [RDS] had been set up in 1908 by Stephen Paget, the son of an eminent surgeon, and for the previous twelve years, he had been Secretary of the forerunner of the RDS, the Association for the Advancement of Medicine by Research [AAMR], which had been established in 1882 to 'educate' the public about the value of experimental medicine. The object of the RDS was to "make generally known as to experiments on animals in this country and the regulations under which they are conducted, the immense importance of such experiments to the welfare of mankind, and the great saving of human and animal life and health which is already due to them." [**39**] Needless to say, to Wilfred and his associates, notwithstanding the stated fallacious nature of the experiments, the ends most certainly did not justify the means, and he was determined to do everything within a lawful ambit to change government policy and public attitudes.

As mentioned briefly at the end of Chapter 6 [and note 20 for the background], in 1936 Wilfred had bought a house in the Ruislip area of north west London, when it became necessary [or expedient?] to relinquish his position in Manchester [and note 68 in Chapter 7 refers to his final address in Manchester] and return to work at British Union national headquarters, and the house would need to be large enough for his family. It is a decent size semi-detached property in a leafy suburb, and it is far enough out of central London to be away from the hectic and urgent atmosphere, but not so far as to be beyond good transport connections: Ruislip Gardens tube station is only a comfortable ten-minute stroll away. The proximity of the house [about a mile away] to Northolt Aerodrome [**40**] might have been a total coincidence; very possibly there weren't many developments of new housing of this type to choose from at this time, and if a new house with all 'mod. cons.', which Wilfred could clearly afford, was preferred, then the fact that this development was widely advertised might have made it an easy choice; also, the potential for recruitment among local patriotic service personnel and their family might have been purely serendipitous; however, this was a potentially damning aspect of the evidence against him when he was arrested in May 1940 which seems to have been treated surprisingly casually, given the possible national security considerations. He might have had cause for concern about his choice however, when the aerodrome became a target for German bombing in August 1940; in any event, the house remained habitable until at least the end of 1943, despite the fact that the bombing threat did not recede completely after the Battle of Britain had been won.

The house is large enough to have at least three, and possibly four bedrooms; at the beginning of the war, when Brian and Sheila were 14 and 16 respectively, at least three bedrooms would have been necessary, but by late 1943, after he had turned 18 in September, Brian had either been called up or volunteered to join the Mercantile Marine [**41**], so it is most likely that he would have left home to engage in the necessary training, and there could have been at least one spare room in Wilfred's house: unfortunately, Sheila's whereabouts at this time are not known. This change in domestic circumstances might help to explain another interesting development: at some stage before November 1943, Wilfred acquired a lodger, a Polish RAF pilot by the name of Jan Falkowski [**42**] who, at that time, was a Flight Lieutenant. It is entirely possible that Wilfred might have seen the proximity of his house to the airfield, in view of the prevention of his direct involvement by enlisting, as an opportunity to help with the war effort and make a room available as a temporary billet for a pilot; he might not have had a specific preference for a pilot of Polish nationality, especially given the resistance of his former colleagues to the validity of the British Government's justification for the war, with which he must have had at least some sympathy in the early stages, but for whatever reason, the lucky candidate for Wilfred's help was Polish. The arguably most successful Polish Air Force squadron, no. 303 [**43**], had been at Northolt intermittently since August 1940 [it was formed on the 2nd, and became operational on the 31st], but other Polish squadrons were also based there: Falkowski first arrived at Northolt at the end of July 1941 to join the Polish 315 squadron [**44**], after being assigned for about a year to number 32 squadron [**45**].

Another possibility, which also fits the facts, is that Wilfred had decided, for whatever reason, to sell this house after only a relatively short period of time, and as the prospective purchaser, Falkowski was keen to move in as quickly as possible, especially as he might not have had a permanent billet at the time, and Wilfred was prepared to accommodate him; a trawl through the National Archives' online resource has, regrettably, failed to locate any official memo or ruling with regard to billeting arrangements for service personnel generally in this area, and Air Force personnel specifically, so it has to be assumed that Wilfred's arrangement was a private one, but it is intriguing to speculate as to how it was engineered. The logic behind the assumption that Flt. Lt. Falkowski was a lodger is that his address is the same as that for Wilfred on the transfer deed for the house, dated the 2nd of November 1943 [**46**]; the deed also confirms the name of the owner of the house prior to Wilfred, George Ball (Ruislip) Ltd., the builder. Without the address given on Brian's Registration Card [see note 41], it could have been tricky to ascertain Wilfred's whereabouts for the next few years, at least until the end of the war, given that there were no parliamentary general elections during wartime, obviating the necessity for new voters' registration lists, but we now know that Wilfred and Nellie moved to 38 Wood Lane, which was still in Ruislip. The land on which this property stands was registered at the Land Registry on the 18th of December, 1943, but there is no conveyance registered in Wilfred's name, so it must be assumed that it was the owner who registered it, having decided to let the property to Wilfred [**47**]. Flt. Lt. Falkowski did not remain very long at Torrington Road himself: in 1947, he sold the house and emigrated to

Canada [which must be a definite clue with regard to Brian Risdon's decision to emigrate: see **Appendix E**] and possibly a local passenger aeroplane crash in December 1946 [**48**] made up his mind for him, notwithstanding the obviously better career opportunities that then existed in Canada; anecdotal evidence from Canadian pilots would have helped here as well.

Four years after the end of the war, possibly in the April of that year, Wilfred's home circumstances changed again to a degree, because his eldest sister Jessie came to live with him and Nellie; this might have been an acceptable, or even pleasurable development, given that Jessie had been a surrogate mother to him after their mother died in 1911, at the relatively early age of 60, when Wilfred was only 14 or 15 years old but, notwithstanding the possibility of contributing to a somewhat crowded atmosphere in the house, the 'baggage' which accompanied Jessie might well not have been particularly welcome. When the war ended, Jessie, who was then entering her 70s, and was still living in the house [**49**] in Bournemouth where she had cared for her father, Edward George Fouracres Risdon, who had died in 1931, probably quite sensibly decided that it was time to relinquish the potentially onerous responsibilities of a houseowner. She cast around the family for possible patrons, and if the second-hand account of one relative is anything to go by, Wilfred was not the first choice, but after the relative's father refused, Wilfred agreed to take her in. The problem was, she had a 'gentleman friend' in tow [the aforementioned 'baggage']; he was John Allen, a rather eccentric and dogmatically religious individual [although the latter characteristic, and perhaps also the former, also applied to Jessie, it has to be said] who did not go out of his way to be amenable, so the fact that he was part of the deal, as it were, meant that, as a couple, the two of them were much less attractive, even to a family member [**50**]. Allen might have been married before Jessie came on the scene [although there is room for doubt about this], and even though he and Jessie never married, they obviously had some sort of relationship, within the confines of the morals of their early adulthood in the Edwardian period, and their religious beliefs, which were distinctly puritan, so they would have required separate rooms: there is definite scope for hypocrisy here [**51**]. Even Wilfred's patience was sorely tested, and the arrangement did not last long, although it is difficult to be precise about this [**52**]. However, Jessie must have had some interest in Wilfred's current work, because at the end of 1946, she contributed a gift of some description to an Animals' Fair, which was an annual event at that time; unfortunately, the LPAVS ***News-Sheet*** [**53**] omits to give a location for it [for that particular occurrence, at any rate], but it is most likely to have taken place in London. Jessie died in 1964, and by all accounts, Wilfred acted as the executor for her estate, such as it was.

There are no records of any purposive and/or regular contact after the war between Wilfred and his former colleagues, including P. G. Taylor, which would support the contention that Wilfred distanced himself completely from active involvement in politics, other than those directly associated with his anti-vivisection work, although there is an anecdotal account of a chance meeting which occurred in London, some time after the war. A very junior member of British Union before the war, Robert Row [**54**], who gravitated into the postwar Union Movement [**55**], recalled how he had been with one of Mosley's then most ardent supporters, Jeffrey Hamm [**56**] and Hector McKechnie one day, on their way back from "a midday repast at some Pimlico joint" when they bumped into Wilfred, and he was "obviously well pleased with the publicity" he had gained "in [the] national press over a case where a dog … had been roughed up and shot at and pictures of Risdon and animal appeared in most papers." It is likely to have been after 1955, as that was when Row took over as editor of Union Movement's periodical, ***Union***, on the death of its first incumbent, Raven Thomson [see note **56**], prior to which he would only have visited NHQ occasionally; Hamm had moved back to London from Manchester at the end of 1952 however [**57**].

McKechnie, generally known as 'Mac', would certainly have been pleased to encounter Wilfred, a response which seems to have been reciprocated, and this chance meeting did give rise to the not entirely implausible idea that Wilfred could be recruited into Mosley's latest vehicle, but Mac did not have an official position at UM, given that he was working there voluntarily in retirement, so it was Hamm who approached Wilfred on the subject of joining UM; "they met but Hamm got nothing out of him regarding interest in any political activity." [**58**] This is unlikely to have been because it was Hamm who approached Wilfred, instead of Mac: had Wilfred been interested, knowing that it was Mosley's organisation, the other personalities involved would have been irrelevant; John Warburton didn't find it difficult to understand that Wilfred would adopt a pragmatic approach, whatever his current political viewpoint might have been [**59**]. No doubt on that first occasion, Mac might have regretted missing the opportunity to have a drink together [**60**], but John Warburton alludes to "the conversation which I would guess, with much mirth etc was devoted to 'old times'." [**61**] An unfortunate consequence of this [according to Row] was that "[Wilfred] made a great fuss of Mac, obviously well remembered from pre-war NHQ days but Hamm and I were ignored, obviously, he did not know us." [**62**] This is perhaps a little harsh, although it supports John Warburton's observation that "[t]hey have felt a little 'peeved' at being somewhat left out of the conversation", and he vindicated Mac by noting: "He was popular with those who knew him. He most certainly would have properly introduced the two to Bill." [**63**]; this rather contradicts Row's assertion that they were ignored. In view of how closely situated were Wilfred's office in Victoria Street, and the UM NHQ at number 208 Vauxhall Bridge Road, Victoria [**64**], it is perhaps surprising that this encounter, or one similar, did not occur before or again [although this might just be the result of a lack of other references].

Publicity has always been essential to campaigning organisations, of which Wilfred had been only too well aware from his earliest days in politics, so he was determined to use his experience to its best advantage from the very start of his tenure with the LPAVS. The same ***News-Sheet*** that had published Wilfred's plan for an air-raid shelter for pets in 1940 described how fears were growing that stray cats & dogs were being trapped by vivisectors or cat skinners, since one of the ostensibly positive vicissitudes of the war was that there were import restrictions on furs, but as ever, human vanity created a 'necessity' for circumvention of this measure; this had also been picked up by the national press. Unfortunately the Board of Trade refused to prohibit cat skins for manufacture or export [**65**], although the Home Secretary, Herbert Morrison, denied that the Metropolitan Police was aware of any cases of illegal trapping [**66**]. There were plenty of other instances of animal cruelty that could be highlighted with a view to shaming the perpetrators, if not preventing them altogether; as news of experimentation upon concentration camp inmates started to become public knowledge, but before the tragedy of Bergen-Belsen was revealed on April 15th 1945, the LPAVS was fearless [and shameless] in pointing out the links and the similarities between human and animal experimentation, which would have driven home the highly emotive message in a way that would have been hard to ignore. This built on work done by the Humanitarian League "so many years before"; the nub of the message was this: "Those who have been prepared to condone the application of such diabolical tortures to animals should now take pause and consider this, the logical outcome of what they have condoned." [**67**]. The LPAVS was also one of "all the anti-vivisectionist groups" that protested against the use of animals in the atom bomb tests carried by the USA in the Pacific, "in which 4,000 animals placed in boats in the explosion area died. … cruel, unnecessary and likely to be misleading if the results were applied to human beings. Far from leading to peace, as the tests were alleged to do, they increased insecurity and fear." [**68**]

One aspect of British life that has always been highly contentious is hunting; whereas with vivisection, the main problem faced by organisations such as Wilfred's was public ignorance [coupled with an unhelpful level of inertia where altruism towards animals was concerned], which was actively encouraged by the vivisectors by means of widespread secrecy with government connivance, the problem associated with hunting was general public acceptance, not because a large proportion of the country participated, but because those who didn't, and who didn't bother to speak out against it, tended to support it out of some spurious notion of 'heritage' [or even 'conservation', ironically]. Notwithstanding the support for the monarchy by Mosley, among British Fascists there was less of a consensus with regard to the aristocracy, who were the most regular and vociferous supporters of blood sports, mainly because they had a surfeit of leisure and funds to support this activity; however, many Fascists were also animal lovers, and there was an obvious correlation between anti-vivisection and hunting. Unfortunately, the medium of film was never used to its maximum potential by British Union, but as the weary and troubled decade of the 1940s became the slightly less austere and more hopeful 1950s, film remained ever-popular with the British public, and the LPAVS committee was graced by the membership of the distinguished actress Sybil Thorndike, with whom Wilfred must have had some stimulating conversations. It is undoubtedly stretching credibility to speculate that Wilfred might have brought any influence to bear upon Ms. Thorndike to participate in a 1950 film critical of hunting, but he will definitely have been gratified to learn of her participation, nonetheless, and no doubt helped to publicise it [**69**].

A major blow which Wilfred "and all anti-vivisection societies suffered" [**70**] in 1947 was a change to their charitable status, although the process had actually started in 1943. In a move that can only be construed as being a product of a Government desperate for funds to sustain a war which was proving to be ruinously expensive [although what other kind is there? It could almost be described as vindictive; certainly not charitable - no pun intended] the Inland Revenue challenged the charitable status of what, by now, Wilfred very probably regarded as his 'parent' organisation, the NAVS. Hitherto, "The legal status of anti-vivisection societies as charities had been established by a legal ruling back in 1895 and had been recognised ever since." [**71**] At this time, the LPAVS [and, quite likely, all of the others, with the possible exception of the BUAV **72**] was constituted as a non-charitable unincorporated society [**73**], which does rather contradict the previous statement, but the law in most countries, not least of which is England, is a veritable minefield of legal definitions, and judgements arising therefrom. The legal standing of such an Association was somewhat precarious, which does seem rather surprising, but the primary deterrent to incorporation was probably cost, and in view of the above statement about charitable status, this aspect was probably not considered significant. The rules for these associations were quite clear, but also quite restrictive:

- They should be governed by a constitution;
- they should have a management committee;
- they were not recognised in law as a legal entity;
- the liability of members and the governing body was unlimited;
- they could not own property in their own right; and
- they could not enter into contracts: e.g., rental agreements [**74**]

The Inland Revenue decided to make this a test case by demanding Income Tax from the NAVS for the year ending April the 5th 1943. Aside from the tawdry financial aspect of the case, it is difficult to accommodate the

the fact that at no stage did the welfare of the animals concerned appear to enter into consideration [other than by default, by virtue of the organisation's area of activity]: it hinged on the "many valuable cures for and preventives of disease" that had been allegedly discovered from vivisection. "Special Commissioners concluded that a large amount of present-day knowledge was due to experiments on living animals … [and they] decided that these arguments far outweighed the advancements of morals and education that would be brought about by the abolition of vivisection as had been argued in 1895. The advantage of the continuation of vivisection therefore outweighed its abolition; an anti-vivisection stance was deemed to be against public interest, and therefore not charitable." [**75**]

A definition of charity dictated by Mammon, indeed. It took four years for the case to work its way up to the highest level of appeal, the House of Lords, but when it was heard on July the 2nd, 1947, it was dismissed with costs, which must have been devastating [although luckily not terminal] for the NAVS, so Wilfred can only have thought himself lucky, on behalf of the LPAVS, that his organisation was not chosen to be the victim of the Inland Revenue, although he would have taken no great comfort from that. Needless to say, Wilfred made it his business to explain the judgment to his members and subscribers, but in this particular case, he predominantly confined himself to the facts, probably not wanting to rush into an assessment without due time to weigh the implications, notwithstanding the danger of unguarded comments on legal procedures [**76**]. The loss of tax benefits would have left a distinct chasm in their finances, which would have required Wilfred to work harder still [if such was possible] to fill this with increased subscriptions and donations, notwithstanding the potential loss of prestige, as there was always a certain cachet about 'giving to charity'. One might have expected that the position regarding charitable status would be re-examined in the light of this ruling, but it was certainly not done during the following ten years, and in 2013, the NAVS is a non-governmental organisation [NGO **77**] in a group of four under the same 'umbrella', rather than a charity [**78**]. As the 1950s progressed however, there was plenty to keep Wilfred and his fellow anti-vivisectors busy, but co-operation between the groups became ever more important, and another major move, that would take Wilfred to the very top of his proverbial tree, lay ahead for him.

NOTES

1 Details of the Blitz were meticulously recorded by London Fire Brigade, and ***The Guardian*** newspaper printed an 'anniversary' report marking 70 years since the event [albeit a day early], with the details of the damage caused on the first night of this ghastly event; the damage appears to have been confined to 'inner London', and it is tabulated, area by area [although Rotherhithe suffered quite extensively, Risdon Street, SE16, seems to have escaped without damage, on that particular night anyway]:

> "At 5.30pm, some 348 German bombers escorted by 617 fighters pounded London until 6.00pm. Guided by the flames, a second group attacked with more incendiary bombs two hours later, lasting into the next day."

London Blitz 1940: the first day's bomb attacks listed in full; http://www.guardian.co.uk/news/datablog/2010/sep/06/london-blitz-bomb-map-september-7-1940

2 At the end of the war, the London County Council [LCC] surveyors produced a series of maps detailing the bomb damage suffered during the war, and these are held at the London Metropolitan Archives; they have also been compiled in book form.

The London County Council Bomb Damage Maps, 1939-45; http://www.locallocalhistory.co.uk/studies/bombingmap/index.htm

3 Interestingly [but only in a macabre way] the deaths for the whole country were almost equally split between men & women; 26,923 men against 25,399 women; the other constituents were 7,736 children and 537 who were classified as 'Unidentified'. An amateur researcher, Peter Risbey, who was a teacher, compiled these statistics unofficially as part of a teaching programme, but became enthralled in the subject of how the war affected ordinary people. The statistics were compiled by the Ministry of Home Security sources [police & medical reports] and from the Civil Defence Department of the Home Office.

> "The above tables include Civil defence workers on duty (the General Services and the Regular and Auxiliary Police and Fire Services) who suffered 6 838 casualties (**2 379** killed and 4 459 seriously injured). Of these 6 220 were men, and 618 women.
>
> The above tables do not include the Home Guard (**1 206** of whom died of wounds, injury or illness due to their service), nor merchant seaman dying in Britain as a result of enemy action of any kind, nor civilians killed by the enemy at sea (about another **663** in total)."

Deaths and injuries 1939-45; http://myweb.tiscali.co.uk/homefront/arp/arp4a.html

4 It is most likely that this "very good job" would have been as a 'Progress Chaser', which was the position he held when he died, tragically only two years later and, ironically, it was not as a direct result of enemy action, but from an illness: the death certificate states that he died from pneumococcal meningitis, on April the 6th, 1943, at Hillingdon County Hospital; See Chapter 11, note 22

5 ***Minutes of Emergency LPAVS Committee Meeting held on May 28th, 1940; courtesy of the NAVS***

6 It is difficult to discover any biographical information about H. Fergie Woods Esq., MD (Brux.), MRCS, LRCP. This gentleman does not have a Wikipedia page, but he was evidently an ardent anti-vivisectionist [unfortunately, this quote is neither dated nor referenced]:

> "I have studied the question of vivisection for thirty-five years and am convinced that experiments on living animals are leading medicine further and further from the real cure of the patient. I know of no instance of animal experiment that has been necessary for the advance of medical science, still less do I know of any animal experiment that could conceivably be necessary to save human life."

1000 DOCTORS (AND MANY MORE) AGAINST VIVISECTION, ***by H. Fergie Woods Esq., MD (Brux.), MRCS, LRCP: Edited by Hans Ruesch; First published 1989 Ó Hans Ruesch Foundation***

http://www.hansruesch.net/articoli/1000_Docs_4.htm

In common with most, if not all, anti-vivisectionists, he also opposed the widely accepted practice of vaccination, and was a member of the board of the National Anti-Vaccination League [which also had premises in Victoria Street], from at least 1929 until 1952, according to the website, which alludes to inevitable opposition from the conventional medical fraternity, including implied vindictive deletion of sources and information by "Allopathic editors":

> "See the Wikipedia page where it was put up for deletion (ref), and all links to their books on whale.to have been deleted by Allopathic editors (ref). Notice how the books of the Society for the Abolition of Compulsory Vaccination have vanished. Now all links to whale.to are banned. See: Wikipedia. …
>
> The organised campaign against compulsory vaccination may be said to have commenced in 1866, when Mr. R. B. Gibbs formed the first Anti-Compulsory Vaccination League in this country. After his death in 1871 the League underwent various changes until 1876 when it was revived under the presidency of the Rev. W. Hume-Rothery.
>
> In 1880 the movement was enlarged and reorganised by the formation of The London Society for the Abolition of Compulsory Vaccination, an office was opened in Victoria Street, Westminster, with Mr. William Young as secretary, and ***The Vaccination Inquirer***, established by Mr. William Tebb in 1879, was adopted as the organ of the Society.
>
> A series of ***Vaccination Tracts***, fourteen in number, was commenced by Young in 1877 and completed by Dr. Garth Wilkinson in 1879.
>
> The movement grew, and as the influence of the London Society soon became national in its character it was decided in February 1896 to re-form the Society as The National Anti-Vaccination League. Its objectives were also then defined as follows:—
>
> *'The entire repeal of the Vaccination Acts; the disestablishment and disendowment of the practice of vaccination; and the abolition of all regulations in regard to vaccination as conditions, of employment in State Departments, or of admission to Educational, or other Institutions.'*

In 1921 the following clause was added:— *'and vindication of the legitimate freedom of the subject in matters of medical treatment.'"*

The National & International Anti-Vaccination League;
http://www.whale.to/a/navl.html

A blatantly propagandistic dismissal of the credibility of the whale.to site has been presented by the mainstream scientific community [although its remit is very wide, so it is not hard to understand why it is considered risible]:

"Some of you may have heard of John Scudamore's Whale.to site. I've referred to it in the past as a repository of some of the wildest and most bizarre 'alternative' medicine claims out there. However, I will admit that I've only ever scratched the surface of the insanity that is Whale.to.

Kathleen Seidel has dug deeply into the madness.

It goes far beyond what even I had thought. She found parts of the website that I had never known to exist. For example, the complete text of the ***Protocols of the Elders of Zion*** is there. There's also the complete text of ***Maniacal World Control Thru The Jesuit Order: Well-Hidden Soldiers Of Satan***. At one time, the site hosted ***The Illuminati Formula Used to Create an Undetectable Total Mind Controlled Slave***, although it's no longer there. Maybe even Whale.to can be embarrassed, but I doubt it, given that it still hosts the ***Protocols***. I mean, come on! What's next? ***Mein Kampf***? After all, Nazis were into 'alternative' medicine big-time, especially naturopathy, because they viewed it as more '*volkish*.' [sic] It was even referred to as *Neue Deutsche Heilkunde* (the New German Science of Healing). Read Robert N. Proctor's ***The Nazi War On Cancer*** and ***Racial Hygiene: Medicine Under the Nazis*** for a lot more. …

Finally, whenever anyone tries to cite Whale.to as 'evidence' for anything, remember a newly formulated law of Internet debates (similar to Godwin's law). This law is Scopie's law:

In any discussion involving science or medicine, citing Whale.to as a credible source loses you the argument immediately..and gets you laughed out of the room.

This cannot stand. Scopie's law deserves to be enshrined in Wikipedia every bit as much as Godwin's Law! For that purpose, I urge all fellow bloggers and you, my readers, to use the term 'Scopie's law' at every opportunity. Eventually, it will come into such common usage that even the woo-friendly Wiki-saboteurs who try every chance they get to purge from Wikipedia anything that might be construed as disparaging to alternative medicine (in other words, anything based on scientific evidence) will no longer be able to stand against the adage!"

Respectful Insolence; The nuttiness that is Whale.to: Save Scopie's Law!
http://scienceblogs.com/insolence/2008/06/14/the-nuttiness-that-is-whaleto/

7 ***Minutes of LPAVS Executive Committee Meeting, 02/09/41; courtesy of NAVS***

8 As well as her recent work for Mosley, she also had her suffragette past to recount to a captive audience:

"While in Holloway, Norah spent much time with Diana in her cell regaling the young women fascists with stories of her heroic times as a suffragette. One detainee Louise Irving wrote:

I met Mrs Elam when I was in F Wing in Holloway. I was a little in awe of her – she was of course a much older woman, and highly intelligent and erudite. Lady Mosley sometimes invited me to her cell with a few others for a small friendly get-together. All sorts of topics – art, music, literature etc were discussed, and Mrs Elam was invariably there … I was never close enough to her to hear about her suffragette experiences, but she was certainly a staunch member of BUF."

A Suffrage Reader, *by Eustance, C., Ryan, J., and Ugolini, L.: cited in: Mosley's Old Suffragette: A Biography of Norah Dacre Fox, by Susan McPherson and Angela McPherson*

It is possible that her ingratiation did achieve at least one positive result:

"They were never sent to the Isle of Man indicating that they were assessed as low risk to national security, perhaps owing to Dudley's age and ill-health, or perhaps owing to successful lobbying by Diana [Mosley] and her lawyers."

Ibid.

9 Mosley was transferred to Holloway after eighteen months in Brixton, but he already had his doubts about Norah:

"Although Diana was clearly fond of Norah, and in spite of Norah's efforts to portray herself as belonging to the same class as the Mosleys, her disguise was not entirely successful, and Oswald Mosley clearly began to tire of her now there was little use she could be for him. His attitude seems to have begun to change while he was in Brixton."

Ibid.

The Elams even went to the extent of accommodating Diana Mosley's critically ill sister, Unity Mitford [who had survived a suicide attempt in Germany on hearing of the outbreak of war], albeit on a strictly temporary basis, at their Logan Place flat, so that she could visit Diana in Holloway on March 18th, 1943, and this meant that they could accompany Unity, but Sir Oswald was not best pleased, as the prison Governor's report reveals:

"*Sir Oswald asked them not to say they had seen him as he could not possibly see all who wised to see him and he therefore made it a rule only to see relatives and business callers. He thought it was Lady Redesdale as she had written she was coming that was why he had come along.*

Mr Elam brought Lady Mosley a slab of chocolate.

Governor and Medical Officer 25.3.1943

This report reveals that Mosley never gave Norah and Dudley permission to see him, and he had accompanied Diana to see her visitors because he mistakenly thought it was his mother-in-law accompanying Unity. Norah, ever the opportunist, had used her relationship with Diana Mosley and Lady Redesdale, to get a visit for herself and Dudley to see 'The Leader', and had looked after a very ill young lady in her home to secure the visit. Mosley's response must have been a disappointment to her. Norah had been keen to impress Oswald and Diana about the 18B Detainees fundraising work she had been doing, but she seems to have been brushed aside and made to feel her visit was unwelcome."

The Governor, Holloway Prison. "Sir Oswald & Lady Mosley 18Bs", 18/3/1943, KV/887 & H45/24891/342: p. 84, Microform Academic Publishers, cited in ibid.

Mosley's concern for the 18B detainees extended beyond his own situation:

"Mosley worked with his solicitor Mr. Swan to set up a committee to work on informing MPs of the facts about detention under 18B with a view to 'aid justice' for the detainees. Mrs. Dacre Fox was among the names Mosley proposed to form the committee but Mr. Swan advised him that '… he did not think Mrs. Dacre Fox would fit in with the other people [as] she was very domineering and not of the same class as the others so Sir Oswald agreed to cross her off the list.' Mr. Swan did seem to think Norah could be useful for fundraising though, and he informed Mosley in October 1942 that '… a committee had been formed to get in money for the case (appeals to Advisory Committee) and that Mr. & Mrs. Elam and Miss Marsden formed the committee and he felt it was in good hands.'

These initial plans made by Mosley and Swan eventually led to the formation of 18B Detainees (British Aid Fund) and the 18B Publicity Council, that were registered as a war charity under the War Charities Act in 1940. A number of those Mosley had hoped to engage such as Henry Williamson and Hugh Ross Williamson declined to be involved with the work and in spite of Swan's reservations about Norah, she remained an enthusiastic and willing worker such that Mosley may have had less choice in the Council's membership than he hoped. George Dunlop ran the charity from its inception in September 1942 and Dr. Margaret Vivian [another ardent anti-vivisectionist], Norah Elam, and Viscountess Downe were all involved in fund raising. In the course of this work Norah was described as 're-apply[ing] the tactics she had used during suffragette days when she had agitated for the release of other fellow dissidents. …'

Blackshirt: Sir Oswald Mosley and British Fascism, by Stephen Dorril, cited in ibid.

10 The Fund appears to have been instigated by some former Blackshirts, so it is hardly surprising that some commentators, such as Stephen Dorrill above, see a direct correlation with Mosley's postwar political activity:

"The initial efforts of William 'Bill' Luckin to raise a financial fund to alleviate the plight of the detainees crystallised in late 1941, when several sympathisers visited Mosley in Brixton seeking his blessing for the formation of an official 18B organisation. Fearful of the effect it might have on his chances for release, Mosley insisted that the organisation was nominally, at least, non-political. [***TNA HO 45/24891/403-4***] In early 1942 the 18B Detainees (British) Aid Fund was founded & registered under the 1940 War Charities Act, giving its appeal for financial supplications greater respectability. [***The Times 12/02/42***] The Fund dispensed financial sustenance, legal and medical advice, helping former internees find employment and, most importantly, nurturing a sense of social cohesion through gatherings like that held in Lysbeth Hall in March 1945, which was attended by 400 Fascists. Many were convinced, however, that the fund was being 'played' by the authorities and kept away from its functions.

[Footnote: During the course of its lifetime the fund raised an estimated £6,000, which it dispersed to 140 families, with a further 350 receiving temporary assistance. 180 Fascists also received 'token' monthly sums for periods

periods ranging from 3 months to 4 years. The fund did indeed serve a useful purpose for MI5, which noted that 'not much money had been forthcoming but that the names & addresses of those who were still active supporters of the movement were being brought to light.' See ***Nigel West [ed] The Guy Liddell Diaries vol 1: 1939-42, Routlege, London, 2004, p241***]"

Very Deeply Dyed in Black: Sir Oswald Mosley and the Resurgence of British Fascism after 1945, by Graham Macklin

Mosley does not offer any hints in his autobiography about his expectations of post-war political activity, while he was incarcerated, merely saying that he read psychology and resumed a political career once released:

"Directly the war was over and I was free to move anywhere in Britain I began the organisation of a political movement. The first action after resuming contact with my friends was the organisation of book clubs, which was followed by the issue of a newsletter in November 1946."

My Life, by Oswald Mosley

11 It is hardly surprising that Mosley was cautious in his choice of associates at this time, but Norah Elam's descendants are happy to endorse Stephen Dorrill's emphatic view that Mosley was being disingenuous:

"The Mosleys were released from Holloway in November 1943 and were kept under house arrest. The 18B Detainees Fund had had a dual purpose which was to act as a cover for BUF activity and to prepare for Mosley's return to politics after the war, since the BUF had officially been banned. Mosley's right hand man at this time was George Dunlop who ran the 'Fund'. With Dunlop's help he had made detailed plans for a post-war election campaign, including names of candidates who would not be readily associated in the public mind with the former discredited BUF. Mosley clearly realized that his former BUF leaders were too notorious to help him be successful and he wanted new blood to help see him into power.

The war ended in May 1945 and an election was called for July. Mosley suddenly changed his mind about taking part in the election. He held a meeting of the 18B committee on 14 June 1945 at his London flat and announced that

'recent events had … rendered obsolete much of the painstaking work which had been prepared.' The sudden general election had 'placed them at a great disadvantage and now they must wait.' He intended to retire to the country and for twelve months would 'write books and breed cattle', but would be back 'at the appropriate time.'

Mosley's explanation for his withdrawal was general and contextual, yet George Dunlop waited until Mosley had left the room to accuse the Committee itself of being responsible for Mosley's retreat:

It was 'thanks to some of you fellows' that the project was 'indefinitely suspended'. He had had to tolerate Flockhart, Franklin, Spicer, who all 'worked against me. The movement was killed by publicity and innuendo, and by your blah-blah's [sic] and petty jealousies, before it had a chance of survival.'

Whether or not Norah was present at this meeting, and whether any specific allegations were made about her by Mosley or Dunlop, we do not know. But Mosley's withdrawal from politics and the closing of the 18B Detainees Fund (which was effectively the former BUF), meant that Norah had no political home."

Blackshirt: Sir Oswald Mosley and British Fascism, by Stephen Dorril, cited in Mosley's Old Suffragette: etc., op. cit.

12 Leese was certainly not the sort of person with whom Wilfred would have wanted to associate, if he had any intention, as it would seem, of distancing himself from his previous political affiliations:

"His writings and activities were such that they earned him several prison terms. In 1936 he was jailed for two articles published in the July issue of ***The Fascist*** and later was arrested under the 18B regulations. On this occasion he remained interned until December 1943, when he was released for health reasons, but later in 1947 served another six months in prison for his part in aiding members of the *Waffen SS* to escape.

Although heavily involved in right wing anti-Semitic movements because of the extremist nature of his beliefs, Leese was a fringe figure. After the curt and brutal dismissal of the 18B Detainees Fund activists in June of 1945, Norah would have wanted new political friends. Leese shared her main lifelong concern, love of animals, also sharing her extremist right wing beliefs. It is quite possible, therefore, that she and Dudley found themselves in sympathy with Leese, and that they gravitated towards each other, finding solace in their shared experiences of now being on the fringe of fascist right wing politics. If Norah was only 'moderately' anti-Semitic during her membership of the BUF, Leese would no doubt have encouraged the deepening of this ideology during the post-war period.

The secret services had been monitoring Leese and received information that Norah had broken from Mosley:

'Source SR72' - Leese (PF52953) alleged that Mrs. Elam had broken away from Mosley; it was a surprise as she was a supporter of very long standing. Her reasons for doing so, according to Leese were Mosley's proposed conversion to Roman Catholicism and a rumour that 'Mosley will join up with Churchill in one National anti-Russian Front.'

There is no evidence at all to back up either of these suggestions about the reason for Norah breaking with Mosley, and so it can be assumed that either Leese or Norah were losing the plot or that Leese knew that his listener 'SR72' was an agent and was deliberately giving misleading information. Yet the essential fact that Norah was now distanced from Mosley seemed to have some truth in it. While Norah may have lost touch with the Mosleys after their move to Ireland and then France, she seemed to have remained fond of them, particularly Diana. Norah kept a signed photograph of Diana Mosley in an esteemed place in her bedroom until she died. Of her other fascist friends, Commander [sic] Mary Allen and Arnold Leese were among the few that she kept after the war, and they are both remembered as visitors to Gothic Cottage between 1954-8. The Mosleys never visited."

Memories of Norah Elam by her Daughter-in-law, by Olive James; and Section B1C: "Extract - Mosley", 1945, KV/890: Microform Academic Publishers, cited in ibid.

13 The notice was brief, because wartime paper restrictions limited the ***News-Sheet*** to four pages, but it was 'upbeat' and optimistic:

"FOR YOUR INFORMATION.

Our permanent staff is now reduced to two. In pre-war days we had nine permanent employees on our salary list. In spite of this very considerable reduction of staff we pride ourselves on the fact that there has been practically no diminution in any of our essential activities–in fact, it is true to say that a certain amount of new work has been undertaken which is additional to our pre-war work. The energetic Executive Committee plays a great part in all these activities and a loyal membership throughout the country give us most valued help in keeping up the high standard of efficiency in our propaganda which has always been our aim. We are facing the year just commencing with confidence in the justice of our cause and the active assistance of our supporters to bring that cause to a successful issue."

LPAVS News-Sheet Vol. II, No. 2, February 1941; courtesy of the NAVS

14 Unsurprisingly, a search engine enquiry brings up proponents of the widely accepted view first, and in great variety; it is not quite so easy to find the historical context in such detail:

"Mass immunisation trials in the 1930s led to a significant reduction in the death rate in Canada and America. Diphtheria continued to account for a third of all childhood deaths in Britain because there was no co-ordination of local councils to tackle immunisation. World War Two gave the opportunity for a successful national immunisation programme prompted by fears that close contact in communal air raid shelters would spread disease. War made health a priority and diphtheria was eradicated within a decade"

http://www.bbc.co.uk/learningzone/clips/why-didn-t-diphtheria-immunisation-begin-in-britain-until-the-1940s/14342.html

"Allopathic Medicine" is a term used only by opponents of mainstream medicine:

"Allopathic medicine is an expression commonly used by homeopaths and proponents of other forms of alternative medicine to refer to mainstream medical use of pharmacologically active agents or physical interventions to treat or suppress symptoms or pathophysiologic processes of diseases or conditions. The expression was coined in 1810 by the creator of homeopathy, Samuel Hahnemann (1755–1843). Never accepted as a mainstream scientific term, it was adopted by alternative medicine advocates to refer pejoratively to mainstream medicine. In such circles, the expression "allopathic medicine" is still used to refer to "the broad category of medical practice that is sometimes called Western medicine, biomedicine, evidence-based medicine, or modern medicine"."

http://en.wikipedia.org/wiki/Allopathic_medicine

15 The other participating Societies were:

"THE NATIONAL ANTI-VIVISECTION SOCIETY,
92, Victoria Street, London, S.W.1.

THE BRITISH UNION FOR THE ABOLITION OF VIVISECTION,
138, Widemarsh Street, Hereford.

WORLD LEAGUE AGAINST VIVISECTION (English Branch)
42, Aberdeen Road, Highbury, London, N.5.

THE NATIONAL ANTI-VACCINATION LEAGUE,
25, Denison House, 296, Vauxhall Bridge Road, London, S.W.1.

THE CHURCH ANTI-VIVISECTION LEAGUE,
Hon, Director., The Revd. R DAUNTON-FEAR, B.D.,
The Rectory, Street, Somerset."

LPAVS News-Sheet Vol II, No. 5, May 1942; courtesy of the NAVS

16 ***My thanks to Dr. Hilda Kean for finding this letter***

17 ***Courtesy of Louise North at the BBC Written Archives Centre***

18 The Director of Talks at the BBC in 1932 was a Mr. Siepmann:

"... but he did accept that significant issues had been raised and the [BUAV] deputation felt assured that the issue would receive consideration. ... In January 1933 a definite promise was made for a debate to be held on vivisection and the British Union expressed appreciation at what had been a major concession by the BBC.

The debate took place on 25 March 1933 and was part of a series called *Should They Be Scrapped?* Reverend Walter Long of the British Union's Executive committee spoke in favour of the abolition of vivisection while the opposing view was put by Professor AV Hill of University College, London. The Radio Times reported that the protagonists would be in separate studios, although whether this was for technical reasons or because of fears that they might 'set about each other' was not explained. The debate was anticipated to be one of the most controversial yet broadcast.

The debate however passed off without incident and a verbatim report was printed in the May edition of ***The Abolitionist***.

The debate turned out to be a one-off broadcast. ... Throughout the rest of the decade the BBC would hold no further debate on vivisection and the British Union began to look for a radio station overseas to publicise its cause. The Union eventually had to concede that radio as a means of promoting the cause 'is completely debarred to us' after refusals came from both Radio Luxembourg and Radio Normandy."

Campaigning against Cruelty: The Hundred Year History of the British Union for the Abolition of Vivisection, by Emma Hopley

There were at least two radio programmes which dealt with the subject of vivisection subsequent to Wilfred's letter to the BBC in 1943, but they were both only heard regionally, as there was not yet a true national network; the first was in 1949:

"On Thursday, March 3rd, there was a debate on vivisection, over the Midland Regional Programme. It was a four-cornered talk in which a vivisector, two doctors and a spokesman of the Universities' Federation for Animal Welfare took part. One of the doctors was in favour of vivisection and one was against–Dr. Pro., and Dr. Con., respectively. Dr. Con., made the point that he had been in practice for a good many years and had never needed to use the products of vivisectional research in the treatment of his patients. He had successfully treated diabetes without insulin, and he claimed that it was quite unnecessary to torture animals to find remedies for human ailments.

...

We sincerely hope that this is not to be viewed as an isolated instance of discussing this question on the air, but that there will be further discussion in an atmosphere of calm reasoning between those who believe in and those who are opposed to this deplorable practice. We should particularly welcome a straight debate on the question between a vivisector and a qualified spokesman of the antivivisection school of thought."

LPAVS News-Sheet, Vol. IX, No. 4, April 1949, p. 13; courtesy of the NAVS

The previous month, before the broadcast, Wilfred had urged the members to take positive action to make their voices heard:

"Members are strongly urged to listen to this broadcast and to write to the B.B.C. immediately after hearing it to say what they think about it. It is a happy augury that the virtual ban which has existed for so many years should now have been lifted and it would be a nice gesture on the part of our members to let the sponsors of the programme know that the opportunity to state the case against vivisection has been appreciated. Although only one out of the four speakers will put the "anti" point of view, this is at least a beginning, and if evidence is forthcoming that it has been appreciated it may lead to more."

LPAVS News-Sheet, Vol. IX, No. 3, March 1949, p. 9; courtesy of the NAVS

The second programme was seven years later, and is clear evidence of the lack of rivalry between the leading anti-vivisection societies:

"We offer our congratulations to Peter Turner, of the B.U.A.V. on the high standard of his performance when, in the "Challenge" series, a controversial programme feature of the Northern Region of the B.B.C., he took on the formidable task of arguing our case against two medically qualified supporters of vivisectional experiments.

The programme does not come through very clearly in the London area, but from what we were able to hear we feel that he did a very fine job of work, deserving of our best thanks. More such occasions would be welcomed, but perhaps this is too much to expect, in view of the fact that the cause against animal experimentation seems to have had the better of the argument."

LPAVS Anti-Vivisection Journal, Vol. XVII, No. 3, March 1956, p. 17; courtesy of the NAVS

19 ***"Fascist chief incensed by pig cruelty claim":***

"He had no qualms at being called a fascist or an anti-semite. But so incensed was Sir Oswald Mosley by suggestions that he mistreated animals, he appealed to the Home Office to try to clear his name. …

The former leader of the British Union of Fascists had already spent three years interned as a threat to national security when in 1945 he was charged with over-crowding and under-feeding his pigs.

The evidence was so thin that Kingsclere magistrates court threw out the case without hearing Mosley's defence. He had been anxious to prove his pigs suffered from a worms infestation which gave them their emaciated appearance, and had expert witnesses to support him.

Mosley flew into a rage when the chairman told him: 'The bench do not consider the prosecution has proved its case. We do, however, consider you should have been fully aware of the state in which the pigs were, and should have taken earlier steps to see they were properly cared for and better housed.'

The ***Daily Herald*** described the reaction: 'Striding towards the bespectacled, elderly Colonel Kingsmill, the former fascist leader shouted: "Am

I to be subject to stricture because of your observations, against which I have no right of appeal?"' ..."

Martin Hodgson, The Guardian, Monday 2 April 2007

In his autobiography, Mosley could be sanguine about the event with the benefit of retrospect, although he admits that, at the time, "I was incensed":

"I spent the whole morning cross-examining the official evidence on pigs' stomachs without disclosing an inkling of the defence. To my consternation, just before lunch, the magistrates unanimously and heartily dismissed the case. I was a free man; great was my indignation. Vehemently I protested that I wanted the case to continue so that I could call my evidence; I wanted to make the other side look a proper Charlie. The magistrates, however, decided they had heard more than enough, and apparently some hilarity still prevails in legal circles at the tale of the defendant who so vigorously resisted his own acquittal."

My Life, op. cit.

20 ***Campaigning against Cruelty: etc., op. cit.***

21 ***Ibid.:***

"This was yet another hindrance as the statistics gave valuable information about the number and types of experiments being carried out, where and by whom."

22 ***Ibid.:***

"In Britain, warfare experiments were conducted at Porton Down in Wiltshire, first established as the War Department Experimental Ground during the First World War in 1916. Experiments conducted were even more secretive than usual as the results were regarded as matters of national security. Here, animals of all species were used in experiments to observe the effects of poisonous gases and chemicals, and in wounding experiments where animals were shot to see the resultant blast injuries. Other animals were burnt, irradiated, infected with gangrene and exposed to other forms of traumatic shock.

In 1942 Porton scientists were responsible for supervising experiments to test anthrax bombs. This involved shipping about 30 sheep to Gruinard, a remote Scottish island, and exploding an anthrax bomb. All the sheep died within a week. The island was only decontaminated in 1986, over 40 years after exposure to this lethal gas."

23 ***Paragon Review; One Hundred Years of the BUAV; Brynmor Jones Library;*** http://www.hull.ac.uk/oldlib/archives/paragon/1998/buav.html

24 ***Campaigning against Cruelty: etc.; op. cit.***

25 After the defeat of ideological motives widely held to be objectionable, and despite the widely shared humanitarian principles, it was the strictures of the hard-fought 'freedom' of financial democracy which proved to be the initial stumbling block inhibiting global collaboration:

"Here, in our own country, this need for closer collaboration was made manifest some years ago and resulted in the periodical meetings of Animal Welfare societies, first sponsored by the National Council for Animals' Welfare and which has grown into a Conference of Animal Welfare Societies which meets once a quarter at the offices of some one or other of the individual societies attending its meetings. A little later the various Anti-Vivisection Societies also felt the need for closer collaboration and there came into being the Quarterly Conference of Anti-Vivisection Societies. At these quarterly conferences ideas are exchanged, projected work is discussed, and sometimes, co-operative propaganda efforts are undertaken. It is of interest to note in passing that this latter development took place during the war years, in spite of all the difficulties existing in such conditions, and has been found, in practice, to be so well worth while that we doubt if any of could now view with equanimity a return to the old conditions of seclusion and isolation which previously existed.

With the ending of hostilities at the close of World War II came the realisation of a need for the re-introduction of the International Conferences of Animal Welfare Societies which had often been successfully organised in pre-war days, but, at first, difficulties arising from currency control regulations in most of the countries affected, and from other similar causes, seemed to rule out all possibility of satisfactorily arranging and convening such a conference. These conditions persisted until 1949/50 but then, with some return towards normality, slight though the indications were, attempts were made to get International Conferences under way. As early as January of 1947 the Conference of Anti-Vivisection Societies, meeting at 76 Victoria Street, London, agreed to invite Anti-Vivisection Societies from all over the World to a World Congress on their particular question, to meet in London in 1948. As events transpired this attempt failed, for the reasons above mentioned, but although the attempt was premature, the seed had been sown."

LPAVS News-Sheet, Vol, X, No. 10, October 1950, p. 42; courtesy of the NAVS

26 These three were members of a group of "nearly twenty supporters of the BUAV", but it is very likely that these and others, if not actually paid-up members of one particular Society, supported anti-vivisectionist aims overall.

Animal Rights: Political & Social Change in Britain since 1800, by Hilda Kean

27 James Chuter Ede's background as a Labour politician was pretty average, but he was no pacifist, as his biography [link below] illustrates, having served in the army during the 1914-18 war, reaching the rank of acting RSM with the Royal Engineers, and his professed concern for animal welfare was obviously only superficial:

"*Mrs. Manning* asked the Secretary of State for the Home Department whether his attention has been called to the dismissal of the appeal by a professor of physiology, Dr. E. G. T. Liddell, against his conviction for causing unnecessary suffering to cats at Oxford University; and whether he will consider withdrawing his certificate to experiment.

Mr. Ede Dr. Liddell has not been guilty of any offence or irregularity in the performance of experiments, and after reviewing all the circumstances I have come to the conclusion that I should not be justified in withdrawing his licence. It is, however, essential that proper care shall be taken of animals kept on laboratory premises, and I am taking up with the appropriate authorities the question of improved arrangements for supervising the care of animals at the laboratory in question."

HC Deb 30 October 1946 vol 428 cc117-8W: ANIMAL EXPERIMENTS

(CONVICTION); as quoted in LPAVS News-Sheet vol. VI, no. 12, December 1946, p45, cited in Animal Rights: etc., op. cit.

http://hansard.millbanksystems.com/written_answers/1946/oct/30/animal-experiments-conviction

http://en.wikipedia.org/wiki/Chuter_Ede

28 http://en.wikipedia.org/wiki/Lord_Dowding

29 The setup of the Royal Military College is quite complicated, as its roots lie in three separate institutions, but two Wikipedia pages explain the details.

http://en.wikipedia.org/wiki/Royal_Military_Academy_Sandhurst

http://en.wikipedia.org/wiki/Staff_College,_Camberley

30 ***Fighting the Blue; Yesterday [TV channel], airdate [UK] 25/06/2011, cited in Hugh Dowding, 1st Baron Dowding, Wikipedia, op. cit.***

31 This was a very interesting coincidence, and could consequently have been a useful point of mutual interest between Wilfred and Dowding, because Wilfred's MP, Colonel J. Llewllin, who interceded [albeit somewhat perfunctorily] on Wilfred's behalf, at the instigation of Archibald Findlay's wife, to try and ascertain the position of his two constituents in the early stages of their 18B incarceration, worked at the Ministry of Aircraft Production; see Chapter 12 & **Appendix D**.

32 The noble Lord set out his intentions very succinctly:

"LORD DOWDING had the following Notice on the Order Paper: To ask His Majesty's Government, whether they will (a) forthwith extend to other domestic animals the provisions applicable to cattle and calves in licensed slaughterhouses, (b) forthwith prohibit the slaughter by knife of domestic animals in full consciousness, in any circumstances, and (c) at the first opportunity legislate for the improvement of existing slaughterhouses, both in design and in capacity, so as to obviate all cruelty in the process of slaughter; and to move for Papers. The noble Lord said: 'My Lords, it is with some diffidence that I have taken it upon myself to raise this question in your Lordships' House. There are many noble Lords who are more qualified by experience to deal with the question, and many perhaps who know more about the facts; but I yield to nobody in the depth and sincerity of my feeling on this subject, and this must be my excuse for rushing in where angels, for one reason or another, have not recently trod. For convenience in handling, I have divided my subject into three parts. The first part deals with the killing of animals in licensed slaughter-houses; the second part aims mainly at practices obtaining outside licensed slaughter-houses, and the third part deals with the adequacy both in capacity and design of the slaughter-houses themselves.'"

http://hansard.millbanksystems.com/lords/1948/mar/18/slaughter-of-animals#S5LV0154P0_19480318_HOL_192

33 Dowding was clearly very moved by the animals' suffering:

"I come to an aspect of the question which I had hoped to avoid. I refer to ritual laughter by Jews and Moslems for their requirements. I had hoped to make plain that it is quite unreasonable that we should be hampered in the process of setting our own house in order in this matter, which affects the national conscience, by the religious ceremonial of the strangers within our gates:

I still maintain that view very strongly. At the same time, it is unfortunate that the specific immunity granted under subsection (1) (b) of the first section of the Act should undermine the law in all slaughter-houses where the two methods are practised concurrently. If a complaint is made that the law is being broken, it is only necessary to plead that the infractions are due to the requirements of the Jewish population and the issue is hopelessly clouded. The members of the Animal Defence Society subscribed to build a model abattoir at Letchworth. They leased this out to a private tenant under the most rigid guarantees that only humane methods of killing would be used. The Government stepped in and took over the abattoir: and then what happened to all the guarantees!

Two other points in connection with this immunity are that it is granted specifically as regards animal slaughter without 'unnecessary suffering' and for the food of Jews and Moslems. This latter proviso is openly flouted. Many more beasts are killed by the Jewish method than are required by the Jews. The balance are sold to Christians. As regards the former proviso, that animals shall be slaughtered without 'unnecessary suffering,' I do not know what was in the minds of those who drafted the Act when they spoke of 'unnecessary suffering.' What suffering do they consider to be necessary? A noble lady, noble in every sense of the word, the Duchess of Hamilton, has told me that she was present at a demonstration of the Jewish method of slaughter and she timed the proceedings by stop watch: it was seven minutes before unconsciousness released the poor victim from its pain. Seven minutes, my Lords! Think of the two minutes silence which we used to observe between the wars on Armistice Day. Think how long that seemed. Take three of these periods; add another half for good measure—and then talk about necessary suffering."

Ibid.; HL Deb 18 March 1948 vol 154 cc989-1009

34 The book was an 80-page essay, subtitled "***An Essay in Straight Thinking***", and it was a detailed account of the Battle of Britain that he began in June 1941, on his return to Britain from America, and it was completed that October. However, on the not unreasonable grounds of national security, Churchill barred publication [although chapter 7 might have been more than a little controversial!], and it was not available to the public until 1946, although as author, his full military title was also used, as well as his aristocratic title, even though he was, by then, retired. The list of chapters was:

The things which are Cæsar's: Introductory;
Bombers;
Fighters;
Other types;
Defensive fighting;
Working with the army;
Why are senior officers so stupid?;
Winning the war;
Winning the peace (Cæsar's method);
The things that are God's: Speaking of God;
The morality of governments;

Wessex and Mercia;
Twelve legions of angels.

http://www.oxforddnb.com/view/article/32884

http://www.worldcat.org/title/twelve-legions-of-angels/oclc/3679308

35 Dowding's ***Oxford Dictionary of National Biography*** entry is very comprehensive, and thereby very useful here;

Dowding, Hugh Caswall Tremenheere, first Baron Dowding (1882–1970), by Vincent Orange; Oxford Dictionary of National Biography, Oxford University Press;

http://www.oxforddnb.com/view/article/32884

In common with the experiential viewpoint of many aviators, he also believed in the existence of UFOs [a belief shared, apparently, by the Duke of Edinburgh and the late Lord Louis Mountbatten, his uncle], and wrote "a long statement on [the subject]" in the ***Sunday Dispatch***, "[w]hen the flying saucer wave hit Europe in 1954":

> "More than 10,000 sightings have been reported, the majority of which cannot be accounted for by any 'scientific' explanation, e.g. that they are hallucinations, the effects of light refraction, meteors, wheels falling from aeroplanes, and the like.... They have been tracked on radar screens...and the observed speeds have been as great as 9,000 miles an hour.... I am convinced that these objects do exist and that they are not manufactured by any nation on earth. I can therefore see no alternative to accepting the theory that they come from some extraterrestrial source.... I think that we must resist the tendency to assume that they all come from the same planet, or that they are actuated by similar motives. It might be that the visitors from one planet wished to help us in our evolution from the basis of a higher level to which they had attained."

Sunday Desputch, 11/07/54, cited in Royals & UFOs – Lord Dowding, the spiritualist general (Pt.2)

http://www.openminds.tv/royals-ufos-pt-2-680/

Apparently, 1954 was a peak year for UFO 'events':

> "It is true that most of what we know about the 1954 UFO wave is based upon press reports, but while there certainly were scattered hoaxes, one gains the overall impression that the tone of the stories appeared to be have been matter of fact reporting of eyewitness accounts."

The Worldwide UFO Wave of 1954, By Donald Johnson; National Investigations Committee on Aerial Phenomena

http://www.nicap.org/reports/waveof1954.htm

In common with another author, Sir Arthur Conan Doyle [although writing was his primary source of income], Dowding also believed in fairies and ghosts:

> "Dowding was a member of the Fairy Investigation Society and of the Ghost Club. Although he knew that people considered him a crank for his belief in fairies, Dowding believed that fairies 'are essential to the growth of plants and the welfare of the vegetable kingdom'."

Dowding of Fighter Command: Victor of the Battle of Britain, by Vincent Orange, cited in Hugh Dowding, 1st Baron Dowding, Wikipedia, op. cit.

36 Hilda Kean is very active in promoting the work of women in many & various fields of campaign, and has written this comprehensive DNB entry.

Dowding, Muriel, Lady Dowding (1908–1993), by Hilda Kean; Oxford Dictionary of National Biography, Oxford University Press

http://www.oxforddnb.com/view/article/51842

37 ***Dowding, Hugh Caswall Tremenheere, etc.; op. cit.***

38 ***Manchester Guardian, 22/11/55, page 6: Letters to the Editor***

39 The vivisectors very quickly learned to be secretive about their activities:

> "As well as forming organisations to protect their interests, vivisectors in Britain also learnt quickly to adopt a cautious style in the presentation of their work. This was because anti-vivisectors were constantly monitoring the scientific press for exposure of cruelty inadvertently admitted when scientists wrote up their experiments. This self-preservation, alluded to as a 'cloak of caution', contrasted greatly with the 'engaged frankness' of the continental vivisectors of the late 19th century. Vivisectors in Britain were exposed to 'a much more active and highly organised criticism than exists on the continent' and they therefore learnt quickly the art of concealment and would take precautions when writing accounts of their work for a British scientific journal."

A Century of Vivisection and Anti-vivisection: A Study of Their Effect upon Science, Medicine and Human Life during the Past Hundred Years, by E. Westacott; and The Abolitionist, 15/01/1907, p90, cited in Campaigning against Cruelty: etc.; op. cit.

Unfortunately, few biographical details about the above author are available, other than [barring coincidences] that the forenames are Evalyn Dingwall [although the latter might be a 'former' name], she was born in 1888 and the book was published in 1949; an edition of one of her books, ***Roger Bacon in Life and Legend***, was published as late as 1974, but this could have been a posthumous new edition. There is a Wikipedia page for the RDS, but it is minimal, because since 2008, when it merged with the anodyne and worthy-sounding Coalition for Medical Progress, the slightly more descriptive [but nonetheless rather condescending] Understanding Animal Research was formed. The UAR site is replete with soft-focus photographs of latex-gloved hands tenderly cradling small furry animals, and apparently ill children, for whose possible salvation these production-line creatures are to be sacrificed.

http://en.wikipedia.org/wiki/Research_Defence_Society

40 The aerodrome predated the housing estate by fifteen years, opening in May 1915; the land, allegedly on the 'wrong' side of the railway line, was requisitioned by the government to be used by the Royal Flying Corps. It wasn't until 1939 that the airfield acquired a concrete runway, and Polish pilots were based there almost from the beginning of the war; they were taught English at the nearby RAF Uxbridge, which was a mile or so to the south west; this station grew out of a private estate which was bought by the government at the same time as Northolt, and the two worked in tandem until Uxbridge closed in 2010.

The airfield was bombed in August 1940 as part of a concentrated effort against the airfields and sector stations of no. 11 group, RAF:

> "A total of 4,000 bombs were recorded as falling within two miles (3 km) of the airfield over a fifteen-month period, although only two were recorded as hitting the airfield itself. Under the leadership of the Station Commander, Group Captain Stanley Vincent, the airfield was camouflaged to resemble civil housing. Vincent had been concerned that camouflaging the airfield as open land would look too suspicious from the air; Northolt was surrounded by housing and so a large open area would draw attention. A fake stream was painted across the main runway while the hangars were decorated to look like houses and gardens. The result was so effective that pilots flying to Northolt from other airfields often struggled to find the airfield."

During the war, Churchill's personal aircraft, a modified Douglas C-54 Skymaster, which was used to fly him to meetings with other Allied leaders, was housed at Northolt, but there seems to be some discrepancy in the public domain sources as to whether the timescale of this could or could not have enabled it to be used as a factor to support Wilfred's interment: the Wikipedia page states that it was from June 1944, but a recent Department of Culture, Media and Sport web page states that "a C-type hangar … was used throughout WWII to house Churchill's personal aircraft …". The hangar is one of three buildings which were "listed … at Grade II by Tourism and Heritage Minister John Penrose" in 2010; either way, there was no mention of any potential security threat in this direction from Wilfred in his 18B Appeal Hearing [**Appendix D**]. Coincidentally, there was a connection with Dowding at this aerodrome, because another one of the now-listed buildings, the former 'Z' sector Operations Block "was the prototype of the 'Dowding System', a method of communication allowing the command chain to communicate to intercept enemy aircraft, the first such system in the world."

http://en.wikipedia.org/wiki/Northolt_Aerodrome
http://en.wikipedia.org/wiki/RAF_Uxbridge
http://www.culture.gov.uk/news/news_stories/7521.aspx

41 The Mercantile Marine is more commonly known as the Merchant Navy; both terms are equally acceptable; although Merchant Marine is also used, it tends to be used more commonly in the United States. Brian Risdon's Seaman's Pouch is available at the National Archive, and although it only contains two separate items, the larger of the two [by virtue of being fully opened out], his British Seaman's Identity Card, displays a great deal of very useful information; the other item, a small brown double-sided tag with the code C.R.1., shows what appears to be the earliest date, 31 Mar[ch] 1944, so that was probably the date when he officially entered service, given that there is a "Declaration to be made if occasion arises": on the reverse:

> "I hereby certify that I am not now in possession of an unfilled Continuous Certificate of Discharge (U.K., Eire, or Canadian) for the following reason:-"

under which was the date stamp, and Brian's signature, but no reason that the statement required. His identity card, C.R.S. 53, "... issued to British seamen of the Merchant Navy in lieu of a National Registration Identity Card", was signed by the "Supt. of Mercantile Marine Office" on "5-4-44", and as well as a 'mugshot' style photograph of a serious looking but slightly chubby young man, holding his registration number [R312625] in front of him, it lists his identifying features: colour of eyes, grey; hair, fair; complexion, fresh; and height, 5 ft. 10½ ins. He held an E.D.H. certificate [the initials presumably standing for Enlisted Deck Hand], but his rank was Cadet. Although latterly, the term National Service is understood to mean compulsory military service outside war in the commonly accepted sense, during world war two National Service meant any military service, so Brian also had a National Service Registration Number. He appears to have served until June 1947, when his "M.6.560525 [was] surrendered containing 15 Comfort [sic] Coupons"; very soon after this, he emigrated to Canada, which will be covered in more detail in note 1 of **Appendix E.** The other vitally important information imparted by Brian's Identity Card is his mother's address, which must also have been, officially at least, his own home address, in view of the fact that no address is shown under the question "Address of holder (if different from above)".

TNA BT 372/0742

42 Jan Falkowski is a sufficiently interesting figure, both generally, but also by virtue of his specific connection with this biography, to warrant an appendix, so please see **Appendix E.**

43 It is not clear how the squadron acquired its number; very possibly there was no significance to it, and it was merely happenstance. It did have a name, however: ***Kościuszko***, after the Polish and American Revolution hero General Tadeusz Kościuszko; it was formed in Britain as part of an agreement between the Polish Government in Exile and the United Kingdom. It had a distinguished combat record: it was the highest scoring RAF squadron of the Battle of Britain; and was disbanded in December 1946.

http://en.wikipedia.org/wiki/No._303_Polish_Fighter_Squadron

44 315 Squadron was formed in January 1941 at RAF Acklington [Northumberland: part of No. 13 Group], under British command; in March that year, it moved to RAF Speke [Liverpool; previously Liverpool (Speke) Airport, later just Liverpool Airport, and now Liverpool John Lennon Airport] as part of No. 9 Group; in July, it moved to Northolt and came under Polish command.

http://en.wikipedia.org/wiki/No._315_Polish_Fighter_Squadron

45 No. 32 Squadron was formed as early as January 1916 as part of the Royal Flying Corps, but by May 1940, it was based at RAF Biggin Hill, using Hawker Hurricanes.

http://en.wikipedia.org/wiki/No._32_Squadron_RAF

46 ***Courtesy of Graham Cole at the Land Registry, Durham:***

"In consideration of ONE THOUSAND TWO HUNDRED POUNDS (£1200.) (the receipt whereof is hereby acknowledged) I, WILFRED RISDON formerly of 31 Howe Street, Higher Broughton, Salford, Lancashire, Political Organiser, now of 70 Torrington Road, Ruislip, Middlesex, as Beneficial Owner hereby transfer to JAN FALKOWSKI of 70, Torrington Road Ruislip, Middlesex, a Flight Lieutenant in the Royal Air Force the land comprised in the Title above mentioned AND I JAN FALKOWSKI with the object of affording to the said WILFRED RISDON a full and sufficient indemnity but not further or otherwise hereby covenant with the said Wilfred Risdon that I the said Jan Falkowski and my successors in title will at all times hereafter observe and perform the covenant restrictions and stipulations contained in an instrument of transfer dated the 28th day of February 1936 from George Ball (Ruislip) Ltd. to the said Wilfred Risdon and will indemnify and keep indemnified the said Wilfred Risdon and his estate and effects from and against all actions proceedings costs damages expenses claims and demands arising thereout or in respect thereof And I hereby apply to the Registrar that notice of this covenant be entered in the Register of the title above referred to."

http://en.wikipedia.org/wiki/Northolt_Aerodrome

47 The legal obligation to register land was effectively introduced in 1925, which was actually the year when this property was first sold, but the land had been sold by "The Provost and Scholars of the Kings College of Our Lady and St Nicholas in Cambridge" in May, 1921 to the developer, Ruislip Manor Limited; the 1925 Land Registration Act was intended to enforce registration:

"The Land Registration Act 1925 (LRA) was an act of Parliament in the United Kingdom that codified and extended the system of land registration in England and Wales. ... After the Land Registry Act 1862 and further attempts in 1875 and 1897 failed, as they either tried to register everything or largely relied on voluntary registration, the 1925 Act was drafted to ensure a more complete, but progressive system. ... The basic premise of the Act was that interests in registered land had to be registered in order to bind future purchasers of the property."

"Land Registration Act 1925";

http://www.legislation.gov.uk/ukpga/Geo5/15-16/21/contents

cited in Land Registration Act 1925;

http://en.wikipedia.org/wiki/Land_Registration_Act_1925

However, registration was not enforced nationally from the outset:

"Over time various areas of the country were designated areas of compulsory registration by order so in different parts of the country compulsory registration has been around longer than in others."

http://en.wikipedia.org/wiki/Land_registration#United_Kingdom

so it's quite possible that there was no legal obligation to register the property before 1943, even though the 1925 Act had been amended in 1936, albeit only relatively superficially; also, registration might have been seen as an additional safeguard to cover the owner against any counter-claim by a tenant. There were "restrictive covenants" attached to "such lands forming the remainder of the said Kingsend Estate as then belonged to the College", that might seem strict, but which were designed to ensure a pastoral appearance:

> "No original building should be erected unless and until the plans drawings and elevations thereof should have been previously submitted to and approved of in writing by the owner or the surveyor for the time being of the owner who should only be entitled to require such modifications or alterations in any plan drawing or elevation submitted as might in the opinion of such owner or surveyor be reasonably required for the due and consistent development of the said lands together with the rest of the estate of the College on the lines of a Garden Suburb. A reasonable fee not exceeding £1.11.6 in respect of each house might on such occasions be charged by such surveyor for his trouble and the approval might be withheld till payment of the fee."

Land Registry; Register MX394853

48 http://en.wikipedia.org/wiki/Northolt_Aerodrome

49 The house, which was a modest three bedroomed detached, originally had the name of *Aroosva*; the provenance of this word is obscure: separated into *aroos va*, it appears to be of Farsi origin, in connection with weddings. It was probably built just before the first world war, so perhaps the original owner had served with the military in the Middle East previously? This could perhaps have been a Mr. Mark Sellick, who owned the house until 1922. The date of construction is a presumption based on the date when an almost identical house, in which the author of this work lived as a child, only about five miles away, was built. On the basis of entries in the ***Kelly's*** Directories for Bath and Bournemouth, EGF Risdon moved to the house when he was in his late 60s and happily into an active retirement; Jessie, who had been in domestic service in Bristol with a well-to-do family at the turn of the century, gave up her work with the death of her mother in 1911, and returned home to look after her father and the children who were still at home, including Wilfred. Why Edward should have chosen Bournemouth [if, indeed, the decision was his] is unclear; at the time, there were no known connections with the town, but perhaps the sea air, combined with the balmy scent of the ubiquitous pine trees and mild climate provided sufficient incentive? Perhaps Jessie was the one who decided the issue, and Edward was happy to go along with it; perhaps Jessie already knew John Allen somehow, which could also have been a determining factor? [see note 51 below]

A couple of years into the new century [and millenium] the house had been divided into two flats "a number of years ago", and the first floor flat, with one bedroom of roughly 3.5m [11'6"] square was going for the princely sum of £44,950 on a leasehold basis, with 88 years of a 99 year lease remaining, so it was probably converted some time around 1990.

Information gathered personally by, and on behalf of, the author; my thanks to Peter Risdon for the translation into English.

50 Leonard Risdon relates that Jessie approached his parents before Wilfred; unfortunately, his recollection of the ownership of the house is incorrect [see note 51 below]:

"The house at Bournemouth was of course Grand Dad [sic] RISDON's which went to JESS upon his death. She stayed in Bournemouth until after the war, she then sold up and went to live with Uncle Bill in Hillingdon, taking John ALLEN with her. I believe Uncle Bill handled her financial affairs. She had asked if she could come and live with Dad and Mum, but there was no way my Dad would have John Allen to live with him!"

Letter to the author 28th November 1996

Desmond Risdon, the author's uncle, provides personal experience:

"Yes, I believe Aunt Jess was born 1875 and that her mother's name was Harris. And I seem to recall hearing that she lived with her father and fellow Plymouth Brethren devotee until his death. ... I believe you are right that Wilfred looked after Jess's estate and so was probably the designated executor. My brother Bill talked at length about Wilfred and told me that W. had made the arrangements for Jess to leave Castlemain Avenue (probably following the death of John Allen) ... Your dad and I stayed with Jess and JA shortly after mother's flight. We stayed 7 days and I do think they were the most miserable days of my whole life. Prayers twice a day; no music or 'entertainment' allowed; forced attendance to the Plymouth Brethren 'meeting hall' and their austere form of god worship; radio only on for 15 minutes for the 6 pm news. It was misery. I think that Dad (Charlie) subsequently insisted that we visit Jess and JA on a couple of occasions (I am certain that we didn't volunteer) and the first words we heard were 'have you seen the light, yet?' spoken in an accusative tone."

Email to the author, 24th July 2011

51 The ***Kelly's*** Directory entry for 66, Castlemain Avenue, Southbourne, Bournemouth, 1922, gives a hint, because there is only a Mrs. Allen listed; a year later, it has changed drastically:

"Castlemain Avenue:

66 Allen, John
66 Risdon, Miss Jessie, apart[ment]s.
66 Risdon, Edward, boot ma[ker]"

So it would seem that Jessie has taken on the rôle of landlady; by 1924 [listed in the 1925 directory] there is also a Murray Richard Osmond Wilson MRCS Eng, LRCP Lond, Physician & Surgeon (Surgery) listed, so perhaps he had a consulting room at this address? It is interesting to speculate whether Wilfred was ever able to discuss vivisection and/or vaccination with him? In the 1931 directory, there is no John Allen listed, although Jessie & Edward are both still there [Edward is still listed as a boot maker, at the ripe old age of 75], but according to the deeds for the house, John Allen was still alive in 1949, so Desmond Risdon's suggestion that Allen died before Jessie sold the house appears to be incorrect, but to be fair, he was not in any hurry to visit at all regularly, at the time [see his next recollection below]. The 1931 Directory is the last in which Edward is listed.

The information gleaned from the Land Registry has a curious detail: as mentioned in note 49 above, the house was owned in 1922 by a Mark Sellick [so when the ***Kelly's*** entry shown above was compiled, one can only assume that the sale of the house was already proceeding, subject to contract, and he had already moved out, or he was not on the relevant list, such as a voters list, from which the directory was compiled]; on the 26th of January of that year, the sale of the house was registered, to a John Allen, whose name remained on the deed as the owner until 1936, when the conveyance of the property was registered on the first of April [no joke!] by Mr John Allen to a Miss J. E. Risdon and Mr John Allen! There has only ever been one John Allen listed at this address, so it seems improbable that this was a father [John Allen senior] selling or transferring ownership of the house to a namesake son and his 'partner', but this seems like an odd way to add Jessie's name to the title deed; this does not explain the Mrs. Allen mentioned above as listed at the address in 1921/2 however: it seems unlikely that this would have been Jessie pretending to be Allen's wife, only to revert to her real name once he moved in?

In 1949 [date of conveyance May the fifth] John Allen and "another" [who is very sensibly assumed by the Land Registry to be J. E. Risdon, "as there are no intervening deeds"] sold the property, so this has to be the time when Jessie and John Allen moved in with Wilfred and Nellie, albeit temporarily.

Kelly's Directories, various; courtesy of Emma Sturdy at the Land Registry

Desmond's experience that would support the hypocrisy theory is thus:

"I first became aware of Jess when she stormed into our Kingswell Road kitchen and confronted mother May about May's relationship with Ted. I had no idea who she was, Jess was livid about May 'corrupting my Nephew' and mother responded by telling her in no uncertain terms to 'mind your own damn business'. Let's see. I was 9 at this time, didn't know who the elderly lady was or what she was talking about. I have no further memory of that event but it must have occurred shortly before mother absconded with Ted and that was April 1st 1940."

Email to the author, 24th July 2011, op. cit.

52 Leonard Risdon gives some detail, without a specific timescale though:

"I felt sure that the arrangement would not last and they eventually went to live in a house in Bristol which had been left to Jess by one of her wealthy old Lady friends. I never went there but I believe it was in the Horfield area, the rear of which overlooked the Bristol Rugby ground."

Could the Bristol connection have been a remnant of Jessie's time in domestic service with a wealthy family, as mentioned in note 49 above? That was 1901 [but the census entry cannot give any indication of her period of service], which was a considerable length of time before she moved back, so the link could be only very tenuous. Bristol RFC ground was then situated about two miles north of the city centre.

Letter to the author 28th November 1996, op. cit.

53 Despite sounding like a charmingly amateur affair, it was evidently a success:

"The Animals' Fair was held this year on Friday and Saturday, November 29th and 30th, and we had a stall as usual. We met many old friends there and made quite a number of new friends who show a keen interest in our particular branch of activities.

Financially, we had the best year yet, and our grateful thanks are due to all who helped us to attain this fine result. We would specially like to thank Mrs. A.C. Hudson, Mrs. Doris Norman, Miss A. Lawrie, Miss E. Masham, Miss C. Wright, Mrs. Taylor, Miss V. Fauré, Miss G. East, Miss M.E. Rutledge, Miss Young, Miss L. Teed, Miss J. Risdon and Mrs. Hort, for their gifts which contributed so much towards this success, and to Miss Caffyn, Mrs. Hort, and Mrs. Hedley Thomson, for their valuable help at the stall.

Next year we would like to have more helpers at the stall and shall be very grateful for offers from sympathisers who can spare a few hours for this purpose."

LPAVS News-Sheet, Vol. VII, No. 1, January 1947, p. 1; courtesy of the NAVS

54 Robert ['Bob'] Row was imprisoned under Defence Regulation 18B (1A) in 1940, after joining British Union at the age of 17, in 1934, in his native Lancaster, but he "would certainly not have known Bill [sic], even if he was aware of his existence as one of the 'hierarchy'." [***courtesy of the late John Warburton***]. When he was released, he joined the army, serving in Palestine, where our troops were targeted by those the recent war had been fought to save, so they were led to believe. After demobilisation, he worked on a farm "down Guildford way" [***courtesy of Jeffrey Wallder***] and started contributing articles for Union Movement's first periodical, ***Union***, which later became ***Action***. The first editor of ***Union***, Raven Thomson, asked Row to be his deputy, and on Raven's death in 1955, Row took over, which was when he would have started working in London, so it would have been around this time that the meeting with Wilfred took place. Row died in 1999, aged 83, and in his later years, he "built and operated an extensive research and reference archive which was used by many groups apart from Union Movement."

http://www.oswaldmosley.com/robert row/

55 It would be negligent to give too brief a summary here of Union Movement, because although there is no evidence that it had any connection with Wilfred's postwar activities, there is a certain 'what if?' element to this incident, and its revelation does have a direct bearing on the impetus for the biography. The incident was related in a letter to another Mosley supporter, erstwhile ***Friends of Oswald Mosley*** archivist, latter-day British Union member and ever-gracious correspondent with the present author, the late John Warburton, written by Robert Row, sadly the day before he died in October 1999. As alluded to in notes 9, 10 & 11 above, at the end of the war, Mosley had declared that he had no intention of returning to active involvement in politics, and his prison reading had caused a re-evaluation of his ideas:

> "he saw that the struggle [between fascism and democracy] had been waged on too narrow a front. Old national antagonisms reinforced by new ideological hostilities had driven the European nations into disaster. A new healing synthesis was required, drawn from the whole panorama of European culture and experience. Mosley set himself the task of learning to think and feel as a European ...'"

Oswald Mosley, by Robert Skidelsky

Near the end of 1945, at a 'reunion' dance, Mosley thanked those who had worked to raise funds for the 18B detainees, although there seems to be some disagreement about the aims of the organisation that achieved this, and the personalities involved: the McPhersons [***Mosley's Old Suffragette etc., op. cit.***] say that the 18B Detainees (British Aid) Fund and the 18B Publicity Council were the direct result of initial plans by Mosley and his solicitor, Mr. Swan, and that the charity thus constituted was run by George Dunlop; note 9 above has the details. However, Macklin [not a 'fan' of Mosley] throws two other names from the recent past into the mix:

> "Conscious of [the] fact [that the majority of Fascists continued to revere him], Joyce's devoted younger brother Quentin was assigned a minder when he attended the "Reunion Dance", to stop him soliciting support from Mosley's followers for a petition for clemency being organised by the British People's Party, led by Joyce's erstwhile colleague John Beckett, with which any association would be damaging for Mosley."

Very Deeply Dyed in Black: Sir Oswald Mosley and the Resurgence of British Fascism after 1945, by Graham Macklin

Whatever the truth of this matter, Mosley made it clear he was being careful:

> "On the 15th of November, 1945 a most peculiar gathering took place in the hall of the Royal Hotel, London. That evening, between 800 and 1,000 expectant Mosleyite Fascists immersed themselves in what the Stalinist ***Daily Worker*** described as a scene 'of the wildest hysteria.' On this occasion the Home Office overcame its natural antipathy to anything printed in the ***Daily Worker,*** acknowledging that this description was no exaggeration. …
>
> Addressing the adulatory throng, Mosley announced that not only had his ideas been strengthened by his internment but that - for the moment - he was not prepared to give the Government an excuse to re-intern him. Thus, temporarily at least, Mosley proposed to confine himself to literary endeavours. …"

Ibid.

Skidelsky fills in the gaps:

> "With his old supporters, Mosley kept in touch by means of a monthly newsletter commenting on current affairs (1946-7). He also addressed private meetings of his supporters organised into Book and Thought clubs. Even these limited activities were not carried out without difficulty. Printing unions made trouble about the printing of the newsletter; attempts to revive a newspaper were foiled by the simple expedient of refusing a paper quota. Irate proprietors of halls cancelled meetings of the 'Modern Thought' groups when they learned the identity of their guest speaker. In October 1947 came ***The Alternative***, the statement of the postwar faith which, like ***The Greater Britain***, was clearly intended to relaunch the political movement. To a conference of Mosleyite book clubs on the 15th of November 1947 at the Memorial Hall, Farringdon Street - site of the New Party's first meeting 16 years before - Mosley explained the new idea: 'If they linked the Union of Europe with the development of Africa in a new system of 2 continents, they would build a civilization which surpassed, and a force which equalled, any

power in the world ... From that union would be born a civilization of continuing creation and ever unfolding beauty that would withstand the test of time.' On the 8th of February 1948, the decisive step was taken: Mosley returned to active politics as leader of the Union Movement, campaigning for 'Europe a Nation'. In this concept he found a final faith which reconciled the 2 powerful urges of his life: to build his 'land fit for heroes' and to heal the wounds of the First World War. ...

...the prevalence of the 'old guard' soon gave it a depressingly familiar look. Like the Bourbons, the fascists seemed to have learnt nothing and forgotten nothing. ... Naturally, the revival of the fascists reactivated a violent opposition from Communists and Jews (Jewish bodies such as the 43 Group and the Association of Jewish Ex-Servicemen taking the lead) and this in turn revived the 'quarrel with the Jews' though on a much narrower front. Officially, the Jewish question no longer existed. Prewar policy proposals were dropped. Jews were even welcome to join Union Movement; but the consistent fights with Jews at meetings and processions in Hackney and elsewhere brought back much of the old anti-Semitic truculence.... Nevertheless, it would be wrong to imply that Union Movement was simply the postwar version of the old British Union. By adopting the European cause, Mosley renounced the old nationalist support which had sustained the prewar Movement: much of this now went to the late A K Chesterton's League of Empire Loyalists (1954). The fact that Mosley encouraged his movement's anti-Semitism to die away by refusing to recognise a Jewish question meant that anti-Semites sought other pastures....In other words, Mosley deliberately renounced much of his old chauvinist, racialist following and tried to win new converts, and a new type of convert, to new ideas. In particular he was much more chary than of old in getting involved with cranks & extremists who would discredit him...

Although at the time the period 1947-50 looked like a simple revival of fascism, [Skidelsky in 1975 could] see it as a process of extrication from the dead hand of prewar fascism and a rededication to a new, and more moderate, crusade. In other ways too, Union Movement was different from British Union. Although both idea and movement were projected against an anticipated background of capitalist disintegration and struggle against Communism, the atmosphere was much less military than before the war. It was never an ex-serviceman's movement as the prewar one had been: the Second World War was not Mosley's war. There was much less centralisation. Above all, Mosley was only intermittently active. Union Movement was never the centre of his life as the British Union had been. From 1946-50 he farmed in Wiltshire; after 1950 he was in England only for relatively short periods...."

Oswald Mosley, op. cit.

56 Jeffrey Hamm was also relatively inactive for British Union before the war, joining in March 1935; he was originally from Bevan country, Ebbw Vale. In 1940, when the mass arrests took place, he was working in the Falkland Islands in his profession as a teacher; he was surprised to be arrested on the 3rd of June, and after a few months in a local prison, was transferred to South Africa, where he shared accommodation with 'the enemy', against whom he had no animosity about events. By June 1941, he was back in England and, despite being registered as a subversive, he joined the Royal Armoured Corps; however, he was obviously regarded as something of an embarrassment, and by 1944 he had been peremptorily discharged. He formed the British League of Ex-Servicemen and Women with several other ex-BUF members, and this group was one of several disparate groups which accepted Mosley's leadership in 1948, when Union Movement was launched on February the 7th. Initially, "he was incorporated into the NHQ Staff", according to the late John Warburton, but "June 1949 saw him move to Manchester as the local Union Movement organiser." [FOM, source below] By 1958, he was living in Holland Park, West London, although he had arrived back in London before this. John Warburton told me that he "ultimately became Secretary" of UM [actually from January 1957, ref. ***Action Replay*** below], and he remained so until his death from Parkinson's Disease in 1994, as well as being Mosley's Personal Secretary, helping with the compilation of his memoirs, published in 1968 as ***My Life***. In 1976, when he was interviewed for BBC Television, asked if he ever felt he was wasting his time in politics, he said:

"Yes … friends often say that to me, but what are they really asking me to do? To give up what I believe in, because it is difficult, and to take up something I know to be wrong, because it is easier. That seems to be so absurd that I must reject it out of hand."

He published two books; ***The Evil Good Men Do***, in 1988, and his autobiography, ***Action Replay***, in 1983:

"As yet I have no grey hairs, but I have passed the fifty mark, and so must start on the same journey myself. But why, it may be asked, should I want to write an autobiography at all? To this I answer that, in my opinion, every human life ought to hold enough of interest to merit some record, if only as a contribution to family history. But because the greater part of my life has been spent in the service of the political movements founded and led by Sir Oswald Mosley, both before and after the war of 1939—1945, and because for several years I was closely associated with Sir Oswald as his private secretary, up to his death in December 1980, I believe that the story of my life has a wider interest, and that I write as a witness of events of more than passing significance."

Action Replay, by Jeffrey Hamm
http://en.wikipedia.org/wiki/Jeffrey_Hamm
http://www.oswaldmosley.com/jeffrey-hamm-2/
Letter to the author from John Warburton, 28 April 2000

57 ***Action Replay, op. cit.***

58 ***Courtesy of John Warburton***

John Warburton [1919-2004] was the epitome of gracious encouragement and a great help to me, with no hidden agenda or preconditions, from the earliest days of this project. He was Assistant District Leader (Sales) for the Clapham branch of British Union, and served on several Union Movement committees after the war. The Friends of Mosley [FOM] was formed in 1982:

"to provide comradeship for veteran members of British Union and Union Movement. This included an annual dinner and buffet each year in central London regularly attended by up to 200 friends and comrades. In 1986 FOM began to publish 'Comrade', a journal that used original research to counter misinformation about the character of Mosley and his followers that was in danger of passing as accepted 'fact'. ... John Warburton [was] Founding Editor of 'Comrade' ... [and] later became the Senior Council Member for the FOM."

http://www.oswaldmosley.com/john-warburton/

59 John Warburton was of the opinion "that Bill and 'Mac' were overjoyed at meeting again after some 15 years ... [but it] was also probably clear that Bill was no longer interested in political activity. Why should he be? He, like others in British Union had paid heavily in the war for their beliefs, and he, no longer a young man and seemed at last to have a good and steady job. He had 'done his bit'. Hamm and Row would have surely welcomed someone like Bill, with his experience, to have joined them in the new 'struggle', and the writer [JW] if he had been present might have felt the same. Only in retrospect, with some wisdom of age, I hope!, can one appreciate that situation."

Letter to the author from John Warburton, 28 April 2000, op. cit.

This pragmatism seems to have been very much bound up with and, in a sense, a direct result of the release of 18B detainees from their captivity, which might seem counter-intuitive, but it exemplified the attitude of many of the ex-Fascists:

"I am leaving prison for a bigger one - Britain under Democracy."

In the Highest Degree Odious: Detention without Trial in Wartime Britain, by Alfred William Brian Simpson, cited in Very Deeply Dyed in Black: etc., op. cit.

Although Macklin, as a source, needs to be used with caution, given his propensity for showing British Fascism in a negative light, he does go into some detail about the rationale of the released Fascists:

"Others agreed. 'I am not overjoyed at being out in this cold world;', remarked another, 'behind the wire at least we could enjoy ourselves!' [***'Scotty' to Robert Saunders in C10 Saunders papers, 15/12/43***] Those whose ardour remained undiminished experienced a peculiar state of limbo, demanding a large degree of self-censorship and circumspection, encapsulated by one as 'the strangeness of being physically free and mentally imprisoned instead of mentally free and physically imprisoned.' [***RS to 'Jeffrey' in C15 RS papers, 09/11/41***] Such feelings were exacerbated by the realisation that, once freed, the comradeship and communion gained in the camps soon dissipated.

In many ways, this withdrawal [from a society from which they felt alienated] was a consequence of a certain domestic Realpolitik. While detainees suffered the travails of arbitrary detention, their families were frequently 'treated like lepers' and, on occasion, 'subjected to actual bodily harm.' [***R.R. Bellamy, We Marched with Mosley, p1000***] This set a limit to the level of political activity which many detainees were willing to commit to once released. [***Ralph Jebb to RS, C10 Saunders papers, 18/07/43***]

As a result, many Fascists 'reformed politically'. [***Joan Griffin to RS, C10 Saunders papers, 01/11/44***] … While the maintenance of domestic harmony was one reason for inactivity, another was fear. Many were terrified that any revival would be 'broken up or boycotted' or worse, that it would endanger Mosley's recently found liberty, not to mention their own. [***JG to RS, 14/10/43 & RJ to RS 04/01/46 in C10 Saunders papers***]

Others deliberately hid their 'negative qualifications' from employers or simply refused to jeopardise an already precarious position. [***'Keith' to FC Wiseman in Frederick Wiseman papers, IWM 86/1/1, 08/02/42***] Rebuffing an invitation to rejoin the struggle, another former Fascist explained:

'You see I hope one day to join my father in the dairy business, that being the only profession left to me after having internment stop me from going to university, and should there be any hostile publicity in the Jewish press mentioning names - and there may well be - it would hardly do business any good. My politics are half forgotten in this neighbourhood now and I want things to stay like that.' [***Jack Forward to RS, 21/11/46 in C10 Saunders papers***]

Another put it more starkly: 'Everything that I hold dear would collapse at my feet if I associated myself with the movement's activities however they may be camouflaged.' [***Vincent Swindon to RS, 17/07/46 in C10 Saunders papers***]"

Very Deeply Dyed in Black: etc., op. cit.

60 John Warburton gives an insight into Mac's favourite tipple:

"I am unaware of Bill's likings in the way of liquid refreshment but I do know that 'Mac', surviving to the good age of 85, 'struggled' through his last years on a bottle of Scotch a day!"

Letter to the author from John Warburton, 28 April 2000, op. cit.

Jeffrey Hamm corroborates this with an anecdote about Mac's funeral:

"I attended his funeral at Frinton, with our mutual old friends 'Inky' and Louise Irvine. We made the occasion one of jollity rather than solemnity, because we knew that was the spirit of the real 'Mac' we knew and loved, beneath his somewhat haughty exterior. So we were pleased when by happy coincidence the cortege passed his favourite pub, where he so much enjoyed his whisky: neat.

It was the haughty Mac who once waved aside a waiter who was trying to pour water into his glass of whisky. 'Water?' asked Mac. 'That's for washing in.' So when the priest at the graveside sprinkled Mac's coffin with holy water one of us irreverently muttered that Mac had never seen so much of that element in his lifetime."

Action Replay, op. cit.

61 ***Letter to the author from John Warburton, 28 April 2000, op. cit.***

62 ***Courtesy of John Warburton***

63 ***Letter to the author from John Warburton, 28 April 2000, op. cit.***

64 The two streets intersect by Victoria Station, and number 208 Vauxhall Bridge Road is only about a quarter of a mile [approx. 600m] from 76 Victoria Street, but in such a populous metropolis as London, even in 1955, it would be very easy to miss someone on a regular basis.

Courtesy of Jeffrey Wallder.

65 ***Daily Sketch, 02/04/1941, as quoted in LPAVS News-Sheet, no.11, May 1941; vol. III, no. 6, June 1943, cited in Animal Rights: Political & Social Change in Britain since 1800, by Hilda Kean***

66 ***Hansard, HC Deb 08 January 1942 vol 377 c69W; CATS (TRAPPING):, cited in ibid.:***

> "*Lieut.-Commander Tufnell* asked the Home Secretary to what extent the information of the Metropolitan police shows that there has been illegal trapping of cats in the London area for the sake of their skins which, owing to the restriction of imports, are much in demand by furriers?
>
> *Mr. H. Morrison* I am informed that no such case has come to the notice of the Metropolitan police during the past six months."

http://hansard.millbanksystems.com/written_answers/1942/jan/08/cats-trapping.

67 ***LPAVS News-Sheet, vol. IV, no.2, February 1944, p. 5; vol. V, no. 8, August 1945, p. 29, cited in Animal Rights: etc., op. cit.***

The argument of humanitarians such as Wilfred was that the capacity of the majority of the medical fraternity to differentiate between cruelty to 'the lower orders' of creatures, and to human beings, was inevitably [even if only gradually, but nevertheless irrevocably] eroded by the acceptance of the principle of good coming from evil [i.e.: a tangible benefit to the human population as a result of 'necessary' experiments upon animals, however painful], which found its realisation in the abhorrent experiments upon concentration camp inmates, and Wilfred was keen to elucidate the debate that found a home in the respected medical journal, ***The Lancet***:

> "*The Lancet* (30/11/46) in a deeply thoughtful annotation under the heading of *A Moral Problem* raised the whole issue of the permissibility of publication of the results of human vivisection alleged to have been conducted in the concentration camps of Germany during the war.
>
> Both sides of the question are posed. We are told that those who would refuse publication argue that a crime has been committed and that we should make ourselves accessories if we were to profit by it in any way. To do so would make it somewhat easier for someone in the future to justify another crime of the same kind; and, the argument continues,
>
> "… the value of medical progress is as nothing weighed against the harm done to human values by promoting tolerance to systematic murder."
>
> Here, on the other hand, is the line of argument of those who would seek to justify utilisation of the results of these crimes. Be it noted, in passing, that it is the German's [sic] own justification which is quoted, and it is put forward in these terms:
>
> "Having accepted the Nazi view that extermination of Jews and other enemies was necessary and legitimate, a number of doctors in concentration camps assisted in destroying those lives. From this it was but a step to persuade ourselves that the men and women doomed to death should previously be employed as experimental material; if they were killed under controlled conditions–for example, by measured exposure to cold–data could be obtained which might later save the life of a good German soldier. Why should not science, and German arms, make use of this unusual opportunity?"

In this annotation the question was put but not answered. It was left to readers to continue the discussion, and the first to enter the lists in correspondence was Kenneth Mellanby. In the following week's issue of *The Lancet* he wrote:

"*At times I have felt a good deal of sympathy for some of those who were responsible for carrying out the experiments*. Accounts of the trials leave little doubt that many of the so-called scientists were men of no academic standing, with no idea how to carry out an experiment, and some were no more than irresponsible sadists; all these deserve the appropriate treatment at the hands of the courts. But others were serious research workers. *If one were given the chance of using prisoners for experiments which one believed to be of great importance and value to mankind, what would one do, particularly if government propaganda had convinced one that the victims were dangerous criminals, who were anyhow condemned to death, and likely to die in some particularly abominable manner?* … I believe that while capital punishment is retained, condemned murderers should be given the opportunity of volunteering to serve as subjects for experiments. The question is rather different when the victims are innocent prisoners, *though to a keen research-worker with little contact with the world outside his laboratory and who believes what the government tells him the answer may be simpler* …"

The italics are ours in the above quotations. Mr. Mellanby argues that the information should be published, the only stipulations being that Sensationalism must be avoided and that it might perhaps be well to grade the publications as "confidential" and make them available only to bona-fide investigators.

Here we have, from his own words, the point of view of an eminent vivisector. Not one of those brutal foreigners, but one of the British School. Not only does he think that a serious effort should be made to collect together the results of all the experiments carried out on prisoners in German camps, and that anything of value will be published … : but he goes on to express *a good deal of sympathy* for some of those responsible for carrying out the experiments. Is any further argument required to justify our oft-repeated argument that one of the evil results of the practice of vivisection is the harm that it does to the personality of those who engage in it?

Vivisection of trusting animals, dogs, cats, rabbits, guineapigs, hamsters, etc., who have done no harm to any living person, is perhaps an even more cold-blooded crime than the vivisection of human beings whom one has been falsely taught to view as enemies of human progress, so why should one expect squeamishness from those who have been engaged for a lifetime in such business. To those who have not had their sensibilities blunted by such an occupation, however, there can be no doubt that the whole business is repugnant and loathsome. Such as these will, undoubtedly, agree with the expression used in the original annotation and which we here repeat:

> "The value of medical progress is as nothing weighed against the harm done to human values by promoting tolerance to systematic murder" (whether it be murder of human beings or of the so-called lower animals)."

LPAVS News-Sheet, vol. VII, no. 1, January 1947, p. 3; courtesy of the NAVS

68 ***BUAV Annual Report, 1946; LPAVS News-Sheet, vol. VI, no.7, July 1946; Smith, The Blue Cross at War, p. 67, cited in Animal Rights: etc., op. cit.***

69 Sybil Thorndike was ennobled in 1931 despite being a pacifist, with strong left-wing views, supporting the General Strike in 1926, and being a member of the Labour Party, the Peace Pledge Union, for whose benefit she gave speeches, and the League Against Cruel Sports.

http://en.wikipedia.org/wiki/Sybil_Thorndyke

The film was made in 1950, by two giants of contemporary film, Powell and Pressburger, and it was called ***Gone to Earth***, based on Mary Webb's novel of the same name. Another more widely known and loved film which, in addition to opposing hunting, also "emphasized the corrupting influence of humans on animals and the deceit they practised towards them": this was ***Bambi***, released in 1942, and it was based on a book, ***Bambi, a Life in the Woods***, by the Austrian author Felix Salten. When an English edition of the book was published in 1928, the foreword was written by John Galsworthy, who especially commended it to sportsmen!

Michael Powell, A Life in Movies (London, 1986), p.684; LAPAVS Newssheet, VI, no.6, June 1946, cited in Animal Rights: etc., op. cit.

70 ***Campaigning against Cruelty: etc., op. cit.***

71 ***Ibid.***

72 The information available from The National Archive website detailing the information held on the BUAV, situated at the Hull History Centre (Hull University Archives) appears to tell a slightly different story from the one in the 'official' history of the organisation [***Campaigning against Cruelty: etc., passim***; see text and note 54 above] about the organisational setup, because the book gives the impression that the NAVS and, by association and implication, the BUAV, was not liable for any income tax until after the ruling of the Special Commissioners, but the BUAV archive tells us:

> "The 1930s was a decade of change. This was immediately preceded in 1929 by the society's changing status to that of a corporation under the Companies Act of 1929. Its Articles of Association are dated 22 November 1929. This effectively meant that BUAV was now a limited company, governed by company rules, and liable to taxation"

Records of the British Union for the Abolition of Vivisection (Buav); http://www.nationalarchives.gov.uk/a2a/records.aspx?cat=050-dbv&cid=0#0

To be fair, the book does mention the incorporation in a short paragraph, but not specifically the tax situation:

> "When the Companies Act was passed in 1929, the British Union became incorporated as a company. This gave it a number of legal advantages, in particular about receiving legacies from abroad and by removing individual committee members from liability, for example in the case of a libel trial. The Union was incorporated in November 1929 and the necessary Memorandum and Articles of Association were published."

Campaigning against Cruelty: etc., op. cit.

73 This definition is taken from a site giving examples of cases which set a legal precedent, and the case of the LPAVS is very significant, but it will be dealt with in the next chapter. Below is a synopsis of what the site offers:

"Wills and Probate. Includes Inheritance Provision cases. See also Inheritance Tax, Equity and Trusts Law.

The case shown here are derived from the lawindexpro case law database. lawindexpro is a low cost case law database, with over 260,000 case listings, and over 200,000 links to full text judgments. The free service below shows the core information on the case, but is restricted in several ways. A small proportion of cases do allow access to the full lawindexpro information. These cases are selected at random, and may be different on your next visit. The active links through to lawindexpro are extremely powerful allowing full access to all linked cases.

This page lists 32 cases, and was prepared on 13 May 2012."

Wills and Probate - 1970-1979; Re Recher's Will Trusts [1972] Ch 529

http://www.swarb.co.uk/lisc/WilPr19701979.php

74 Although this information is taken from a relatively recent site, the general organisational requirements do not appear to have changed since the time of this particular case.

http://www.transitionnetwork.org/organisational-forms-initiatives

75 ***Campaigning against Cruelty: etc., op. cit.***

76 "EDITORIAL: THE INCOME TAX JUDGMENT

Much interest has been aroused by the recent judgment of the House of Lords, ruling that the National Anti-Vivisection Society should not be exempted from payment of income-tax on its investment income.

This, in effect, is a ruling that such a Society is not a Charity within the legal definition of the word, and this conclusion was reached on the evidence before the Noble Lords who considered the case.

Previous procedure had been by way of appeal to the Special Commissioners against the refusal of the Commissioners of Inland Revenue to allow the exemption. The Special Commissioners found in favour of the Society. Their Decision [sic] was subsequently reversed by Mr. Justice Macnaghten, who disallowed the claim for exemption, and Mr. Justice Macnaghten's decision was affirmed by a majority of the Court of Appeal, Lord Justice Mackinnon, and Lord Justice Tucker, The Master of the Rolls dissenting.

The grounds on which the judgment was reached were two-fold; first, that the objects of the Society were partly political in that they sought the abolition of vivisection by legislation, and secondly that, on the evidence submitted, such legislation would not be for the public good.

...

Our supreme task is to educate the public mind to an appreciation of the fact that human ailments are the result of wrong living in one form or another. It may be wrong food, or right food grown by wrong methods, or wrong habits, or wrong environment, or a combination of all or several of these. There is infinite scope for research but there is no justification for limiting such research to the exploitation of defenceless living creatures."

LPAVS News-Sheet, Vol. VII, No. 8. August 1947, p. 30; courtesy of the NAVS

77 An NGO is a rather nebulous concept which dates from 1945; it appears that any group or association can nominate itself an NGO, within certain preset parameters, with all the perceived kudos and official recognition that accrues therefrom, but unless it is specifically a charity, there are ostensibly no dispensations with regard to tax, and Wikipedia concedes that:

"NGOs are difficult to define and classify, and the term 'NGO' is not used consistently. As a result, there are many different classifications in use. The most common use a framework that includes orientation and level of operation. An NGO's orientation refers to the type of activities it takes on. These activities might include human rights, environmental, or development work. …

One of the earliest mentions of the acronym 'NGO' was in 1945, when the UN was created. The UN, which is an inter-governmental organization, made it possible for certain approved specialized international non-state agencies - or non-governmental organisations - to be awarded observer status at its assemblies and some of its meetings. Later the term became used more widely. Today, according to the UN, <u>any kind of private organization that is independent from government control can be termed an 'NGO'</u>, provided it is not-profit, non-criminal and not simply an opposition political party.

Professor Peter Willetts, from the University of London, argues the definition of NGOs can be interpreted differently by various organizations and depending on a situation's context. He defines an NGO as 'an independent voluntary association of people acting together on a continuous basis for some common purpose other than achieving government office, making money or illegal activities.' In this view, two main types of NGOs are recognized according to the activities they pursue: operational NGOs that deliver services and campaigning NGOs. Although Willetts proposes the operational and campaigning NGOs as a tool to differentiate the main activities of these organizations, he also explains that a single NGO may often be engaged in both activities. Many NGOs also see them as mutually reinforcing." [my emphasis]

What is a Non-Governmental Organization, by Peter Willetts, cited in

http://en.wikipedia.org/wiki/Non-governmental_organization#Campaigning

http://www.ihrnetwork.org/files/3.%20What%20is%20an%20NGO.PDF

78 This is taken from the NAVS website [***About Us*** page]:

"The NAVS group is comprised of [sic] four NGOs (non-governmental organisations) working to end the suffering of animals: the National Anti-Vivisection Society; Animal Defenders International; the Lord Dowding Fund for Humane Research; and the Animal+World Show."

http://www.navs.org.uk/about_us/26/0/0/

This change of status possibly happened in 1986:

"After a hard fought campaign for improved legislation, the Animals (Scientific Procedures) Act received Royal Assent on 20 May 1986. … Branded at the time as a 'Vivisectors' Charter', over a decade in operation has seen the dreadful failings of the 1986 Animals (Scientific Procedures) Act cruelly exposed.

The setback of the 1986 Act led to a major rethink at the NAVS and a drive to become a stronger voice for animals. It was also time to take vivisectionists on head-on, on the issue of the use of animals in medical research. A revitalised NAVS, with new Director Jan Creamer would in the coming years pull together many of the Society's historic strengths: producing detailed scientific reports highlighting the futility of vivisection; lobbying in Parliament; organising the biggest rallies against vivisection the world has ever seen; developing the Lord Dowding Fund and even adding two new bodies to the group - the Animal Defenders and Animal+World Show; putting NAVS Field Officers undercover inside the animal laboratories."

http://www.navs.org.uk/about_us/24/0/299/

14: INTO ENEMY TERRITORY

At the end of 1956, The London & Provincial Anti-Vivisection Society was wound up, and closed its offices at 76 Victoria Street, and on the first of January 1957, it merged with the National Anti-Vivisection Society, which was literally only 'a few doors down' Victoria Street, at number 92. Wilfred took over as the Secretary of the new, enlarged NAVS, and the business of the retitled National Anti-Vivisection Society (incorporating the London & Provincial Anti-Vivisection Society) continued with barely a ripple in the waters of its work. This was not by any means a hasty or ill-considered development: quite the opposite; it had been mooted in the spring of 1956 [very possibly not for the first time], and no doubt Wilfred was an advocate of amalgamation, the benefit of which would have been obvious to him as a result of his wide experience of collaboration with the other national Societies. The records of both the LPAVS and the NAVS make it abundantly clear that they were very conscious of their responsibilities to adhere to the legal requirements of this type of organisation, and leave a concise and easily-understood ledger of their activities, so the official process of moving toward amalgamation was made by an approach from the Chairman of the LPAVS by letter to the Chairman of the NAVS, which he could submit to his Executive Committee for consideration, before a proposal could be drawn up for a vote by the members at the Annual General meeting. This was in June, 1956, so the preliminary informal discussions could have started weeks, or even months, before this. The LPAVS Annual Meeting [**1**] preceded that of the NAVS [**2**], which was appropriate, because if there had been significant objections from the members at that stage, it would have been pointless for it to be considered by the NAVS members. Given the size of the NAVS membership, it is perhaps slightly surprising that not one dissenting voice was heard, but it was only natural that members would want to know more about the anticipated benefits of amalgamation, as well as whether a wider merger, taking in the BUAV, could be a possibility; there is also a subtle hint from the Chairman which suggests that Wilfred's future position, although not a foregone conclusion, had definitely been considered [**3**].

Although the resolution was agreed at the members' meeting, it could not be enacted immediately: there would have to be an Extraordinary General Meeting of the Council "probably at the end of September, in order to put the finishing touches on this amalgamation", because "It really is extremely important. The future of a large section of the movement depends upon what happens at that Meeting." Curiously, at the public meeting that followed the members' meeting, nothing was said about the proposed merger, but Wilfred was present, and answered a question, albeit on a very minor issue [flag days] on behalf of the NAVS, without actually identifying himself in any specific capacity [**4**]. The operational technicalities of the merger were considered at the subsequent regular monthly Council meetings, and despite no specific reference being made to the future of the current NAVS Secretary, a Mr. G. H. Bowker, the fact that he is prepared to work so closely with Wilfred during the transition period means that it is most likely that he intended to retire as soon as the merger was complete, which is confirmed in the Minutes for the October Meeting of the Central Executive Committee, under the anodyne [and unceremonious] marginal heading of "Staff" [**5**]. Once again, the wheels of progress, moving through the legally circumscribed procedures of company regulations, ground seemingly snail's-pace slowly, so although the Committee agreed in July to offer Wilfred the post of Secretary of the amalgamated Society "if Mr. Risdon is prepared to accept", it was not until the eleventh hour, December 1956, that he confirmed "his acceptance of the appointment of Secretary according to the terms agreed by the Executive Committee" [**6**]. At the Special Meeting of the Central Executive Committee on the 27th of November 1956, it was agreed that Wilfred should be the Editor of the new journal of the amalgamated Society, ***The Animals' Defender & Anti-Vivisection News***, which "should consist of 12 quarto pages, the heading to be similar in lay-out to that of the present 'Anti-Vivisection News'", and although his official commencement date as the Secretary of the NAVS was not specified, this was implicit at the Central Executive Committee Meeting of December the 19th, in the motion that was "carried unanimously that the appointed day for the amalgamation with the London & Provincial Anti-Vivisection Society shall be the 1st January 1957." [**7**].

As explained at the end of Chapter 13, the NAVS is now a multifaceted organisation, so it is understandable that the merger of a small Society, working in parallel with it, would not rate very highly in the story of its development: the 'official' history, on the NAVS website, does not even mention the merger; there is also a Wikipedia page for the NAVS, which does include a section on the LPAVS, but the merger is dismissed in a single line: "In 1957 the London and Provincial Anti-Vivisection Society (LPAVS) became part of the NAVS." The following three paragraphs, the entirety of the section, are devoted to Norah Elam, and her involvement with the Society [see Chapter 11], so it is interesting to speculate as to the source of this information; unfortunately, neither site mentions Wilfred, which is probably more the result of a lack of relevant information, rather than any comment on his abilities, or his significance: there can be no doubting his abilities, as these had undoubtedly been adequately [and, arguably, admirably] demonstrated in the preceding fifteen years that he had been steering the LPAVS safely through the choppy waters of public indifference and hostility from the scientific community [**8**]. Before the merger was a serious consideration, however, there was still plenty of important work that the LPAVS could do; in addition to his regular and erudite writing, Wilfred was continuing to develop his involvement with international anti-vivisection organisations: in May, 1954, "the World Congress [of Animal Welfare Societies] met in London, 117 societies from 26 countries being represented" and, as well as seconding a proposal by Peter Turner of the BUAV, demanding "the total prohibition of all experiments calculated to cause pain", Wilfred also took the Chair on two occasions "in the absence of Lord Burden, whose Parliamentary duties made it impossible for him to attend" [**9**]. At the National Convention of Animal Protection Societies, in 1951, Wilfred spoke at some length, and in response to UFAW's Dr. Jean Vinter's "resume of the work of the Universities' Federation for Animal Welfare, in the course of which she stressed that whatever may happen in the future the fact is that at present animal experimentation is a recognised form of research and animals used for such experiments must be considered in the light of existing circumstances"; because "The Convention was restive throughout the period of Dr. Vinter's address", he "was called on to reply, two minutes being allowed for that purpose", and "in the time allowed he felt he could best deal with the matter by the use of a homely little parable ... From the sustained applause which followed, the point appeared to have been well taken." [**10**] He also [not for the first time] demonstrated that his concerns were not only limited to the subject of animal welfare, when he spoke at a public meeting at Caxton Hall in October 1950, to discuss "The Dangers of 'Preventive' Inoculations and particularly their connection with Infantile Paralysis (Poliomyelitis)" [**11**].

Despite not having a direct connection with the British parliamentary system [apart from a few well-placed MPs and the occasional peer, such as Lord Dowding], Wilfred was acutely aware of how important it could be to use that system to the LPAVS's advantage, so he used his previous electioneering experience wherever possible, and this included encouraging members to engage with the electoral process when opportunities arose: in 1950, the LPAVS ***News-Sheet*** published a list of present MPs who were "sympathetic, in greater or lesser degree, to our aims", urging members to write and ask their parliamentary candidates if he or she supported those aims [**12**]; and five years later, the tone was somewhat more strident: "Badger your candidates ... mobilise your friends and relatives to write on this issue NOW." [**13**]. All this contributed to a very well informed, and potentially politically aware membership becoming part of the much larger NAVS and, in fact, several LPAVS Executive Committee Members were co-opted onto the NAVS Executive Committee, "for the remainder of the present Society's year", following a Resolution in July 1956, although it was hedged with the reservation "on condition that if the amalgamation does not take place their co-option becomes void" [**14**]. The amalgamation did take place, however, thanks to concerted, and evidently harmonious work by the two Secretaries, during the intervening period; Mr. Bowker was even concerned that if he took his usual three week summer holiday, it "might cause delay in getting the amalgamation through", but it was not seen as problematic taking "a few odd days if this could be managed … the Secretary was advised to take a fortnight if possible." Readers of the LPAVS periodical, currently ***The Anti-Vivisection News*** [after having been a rather clumsy hybrid, The ***Anti-Vivisection Journal News-Sheet*** following the war, and then, in a reversion to the prewar name, ***The Anti-Vivisection Journal***], who were unlikely to have been unaware of the impending merger, described as "a marriage rather than a birth", were bidden farewell with a moderate flourish at the end of the year, and an apology: "it will be impossible for us, this year to send our usual cards of Christmas Greetings." [**15**].

However good the previous Secretary, Mr. Bowker, might have been, the Executive Committee and all the patrons and supporters of the NAVS must have been delighted to gain an asset such as Wilfred who, as well as his proven administrative abilities, was no stranger to public speaking, in his capacity as Secretary, who could be just as much the public face of the Society as a better-known, 'celebrity' President, and he could be relied upon to perform flawlessly in the public forum, such as when he spoke in Glasgow, not long after his elevation, in May 1958, at a meeting of the Scottish Anti-Vivisection Society [**16**]. His voice was even heard [or his words read, to be more accurate] as far away as Oxnard, California [**17**], courtesy of the UPI news agency, when the NAVS plan [although incorrectly categorised by this particular newspaper, the ***Press-Courier***, as "Britain's Anti-Vivisection Society"] "for a five-acre dog cemetery" was reported in April, 1962 [**18**]. The potentially controversial aspect of this was that "the cemetery would accommodate dog victims of vivisection, as well as those which die of natural causes." This was probably something of an exception: most of Wilfred's press appearances were made in Great Britain, although there was another high-profile matter, coincidentally the same year as the foregoing, which would have been widely reported in the American Press, and this will be detailed later in this chapter. On June the 20th, 1961, the NAVS annual report covering the previous year was published, and at the meeting where this took place, Wilfred made a speech as Secretary, and this was quoted in the ***Guardian*** of the following day [**19**]. The report referred to "[p]laces in England where there is a 'flourishing traffic in unwanted pets, principally cats and dogs, which are sold to research laboratories' … We have made a beginning at Doncaster, which is one of the worst centres of this inhuman trade". In fact, Doncaster had been known about in this context for at least ten years [**20**], but it had obviously proved extremely difficult to limit this ghastly trade, one of the main problems being [as ever] apathy and/or incredulity on the part of the general public.

A very interesting situation occurred in 1972, which had a profound effect on English case law, but also had a direct connection back to Wilfred's change of circumstances explained at the beginning of this chapter. A lady by the name of Recher made a will dated the 23rd of May 1957 [**21**], in which she indicated that a share of the residue of her estate should be given to "The Anti-Vivisection Society, 76 Victoria Street, London SW1"; unfortunately, she omitted to notice [or if she did, she omitted to make the requisite amendment] that the Society which had previously existed at that address was no longer extant, at that or any other address. The irony of this situation, given the outcome as described below, is that since early 1947, Wilfred had gone to some trouble to try and prevent this precise result occurring, inserting specific details for potential legators in nearly every issue of the Society's periodicals [**22**]. Mrs. Recher died in 1962, and her husband in 1968; it is not known whether it was a disgruntled relative [and potentially aspirant beneficiary] who initiated the court action or if it was merely a procedural result of the probate process, after the death of the husband, but in 1968 the matter of the destination for the gift had to be decided [**23**].

In 1972, the case came before Judge Brightman, in the High Court, Chancery Division [literally: a court of equity **24**], and the question that was being considered, aside from the specific matter of the legacy, was "the beneficiary principle, and unincorporated associations" [**25**]. The judgement was very detailed, and several sources quote it either in full or virtually so; the difficulty arose in that the gift was intended for a specific donee [but not the donee's purpose], namely the Society that had existed at 76 Victoria Street, the inaccuracy in its designation notwithstanding, not the larger combined Society: "It was not to be construed as a gift in trust for the purposes of the Society. It could have taken effect as a legacy to the members of the society beneficially, as an accretion to the funds which constituted the subject matter of the contract by which the members had bound themselves *inter se* [**26**]. But since the Society had been dissolved, the gift could not be construed as a gift to the members of a different association and they [sic] therefore failed. A trust for non-charitable purposes, as distinct from a trust for individuals, was clearly void because there is no beneficiary." [**27**] The tragedy is that it was only the dissolution of the LPAVS that caused the gift to fail:

> "… In the absence of words which purport to impose a trust, the legacy is a gift to the members beneficially, not as joint tenants or as tenants in common so as to entitle each member to an immediate distributive share, but as an accretion to the funds which are the subject-matter of the contract which the members have made *inter se*.
>
> In my judgment the legacy in the present case to the London and Provincial society ought to be construed as a legacy of that type, that is to say, a legacy to the members beneficially as an accretion to the funds subject to the contract which they have made *inter se*. Of course, the testatrix did not intend the members of the society to divide her bounty between themselves, and doubtless she was ignorant of that remote but theoretical possibility. Her

> knowledge or absence of knowledge of the true legal analysis of the gift is irrelevant. The legacy is accordingly in my view valid, subject only to the effect of the events of January 1, 1957.
>
> A strong argument has been presented to me against this conclusion … If the argument were correct it would be difficult, if not impossible, for a person to make a straightforward donation, whether *inter vivos* [**28**] or by will, to a club or other non-charitable association which the donor desires to benefit. This conclusion seems to me contrary to common sense …" [**29**]

Of course, Wilfred was not to know about this happenstance when the amalgamation was being planned, given that the *dénouement* was fifteen years in the future but, had he somehow been given foreknowledge of it, the legacy would have had to be a very significant one to provide sufficient incentive to delay the changeover [and at the time, the delay would, barring any malice aforethought, have been indeterminate]; unfortunately, in none of the sources found for this event is the amount of the legacy given [neither is the eventual beneficiary, which could have been the Government] and, realistically, notwithstanding that this was very possibly only one legacy among several, there were sufficiently compelling reasons for the changeover to be made in any case. In 1963 the Society was incorporated, and henceforth was known as the National Anti-Vivisection Society Limited; in legal terminology, the assets of the Society were vested in it, but it was still not a charity, presumably because the loss of tax benefits mentioned at the end of Chapter 13 was still applicable. The Minutes of Meetings of the Council give the impression that there was a possibility of Wilfred having intimated that he was considering moving on: either to a different position, or perhaps retiring, because at the first Meeting of the Council after the incorporation had become effective, "Lady Dowding reminded the Council of their wish some months ago to make Mr. Risdon a Director, and that the reason for such an appointment was that the then Committee wished to acknowledge what Mr. Risdon has done and to keep him with us. This now seemed an appropriate time to make the change." However, the Articles of Association did not allow for that, so it was agreed to make Wilfred the Secretary of the incorporated Society, but also to make him a Member of the Council [which was not normal for a Secretary] so that he could have a vote. The registered office was also changed to 27, Palace Street, London SW1 [**30**].

As detailed at the beginning of this chapter, at around the time of the merger of the LPAVS & NAVS, the possibility of an amalgamation with the BUAV had also been considered, but the stumbling block always seemed to be the BUAV's insistence upon an outright ban on vivisection [see note 3]; according to the official history of the BUAV, "[it] even considered a proposed merger with NAVS", which leaves open the source of the proposal but nonetheless, by August 1959, the idea was scrapped because of at least one [fairly obvious] "substantial obstacle", although in an ample demonstration of the willingness of the Secretaries of both organisations to work as closely as possible together, "the first meeting of the Joint Consultative Council took place on 20 November 1959." [**31**] Otherwise, in addition to continuing co-operation between the various animal welfare and anti-vivisection societies, it was 'business as usual' for the NAVS. One device that was very common for campaigning organisations was the petition, and although in practice, in general, their efficacy was not guaranteed in terms of effecting change, they usually did achieve a fairly high level of public recognition and involvement, which was half the battle. In 1957, the NAVS emulated the Humanitarian League's efforts of the 1890s and initiated a petition intended to highlight cruelty to animals which was not seen by the public, namely the export of live animals for slaughter abroad, something it quite rightly considered should be stopped [**32**], although the efforts were unsuccessful as sadly, it still goes on in the twenty-first century, despite persistent appeals.

Another petition with which Wilfred definitely had an involvement, with its drafting as well as its delivery, followed the publication of one of the tragic milestones in the shameful history of government intransigence and callous [if not actually venal] support for the 'medical research' fraternity, the Littlewood report. It was widely recognised, within the animal welfare community, that the 1876 Cruelty to Animals Act, which at the time was regarded "as no more than a charter for vivisectionists" [**33**], nearly one hundred years later was being criticised "for allowing almost unlimited and uncontrollable experiments on animals, and ... for not being administered properly." [**34**] Clearly, something had to be done; even "the RSPCA adopted a more radical tone in its campaign against vivisection and ... undertook a 'forthright' advertising campaign which criticised the 1876 Act" [**35**]; in 1961, the Home Secretary, R. A. Butler, did little or nothing, but the next year, in November, the new Home Secretary, Henry Brooke, conforming to the snail's-pace administrative procedures of Parliament, announced that he was setting up a Departmental Committee to examine the workings of the 1876 Act: it took six months just for the Committee to be selected.

The Chairman of the Committee, which had fourteen members, was a lawyer, Sir Sydney Littlewood; unfortunately, the possible effectiveness of the Committee was hobbled from the start, given that its terms of reference were to "consider the present control over experiments on living animals, and to consider whether, and if so what, changes are desirable in the law or its administration." Apparently, neither the morality nor the "utility" of vivisection were to be considered: "These questions, according to the government, had been addressed by the first two Royal Commissions and it saw no point in returning to them. Vivisection, it seemed, was set to continue no matter what." Wilfred's views were requested on this subject by ***The Daily Express*** twice [**36**] while the Committee was deliberating [very slowly]; also, the various anti-vivisection organisations met at various times to consider a possible response, obviously without wanting to pre-empt the Committee's decisions; inevitably, the old divisions were present, so as a member of the British Council of Anti-Vivisection Societies [BCAVS], Wilfred's real negotiating skills, honed over many years in political debate, would have been called upon many times to try and convince the BUAV that it was worth while engaging in the process, given that its policy was one of total abolition, whereas the NAVS had always embraced an arguably less implacable, but probably more realistic, gradualist approach. The BUAV did attempt to introduce some concessions to its policy, but it took until 1966, after the publication of the Littlewood report, for these to be passed, and this led to internal strife and resignations.

The report of the Littlewood Committee was finally published on the 29th of April, 1965, only one month short of two years since its membership was announced. During the preceding months, a petition to protest both the Act, and the expected findings of the Committee, was put together, and by the time of publication, over 300,000 signatures were collected. Naturally, all the participating organisations of the BCAVS saw the benefit of making a public event of the handing in of the petition, so the BUAV hosted the last-minute preparations in the committee room of its premises at 47, Whitehall, and a tired-looking but distinguished 69-year old Wilfred is seen in a photograph in a rank of five senior gentlemen who are standing behind a long, narrow table, at which at least seven gentlemen are seated, and on which is placed the petition, bundled up neatly in brown paper packages tied up with string. Wilfred is also seen in a group of six venerable gentlemen outside the Houses of Parliament, part of a deputation from the BCAVS to present the petition on May the 5th 1965, with the petition on the ground at their feet; in this photograph, he is smiling, looking more relaxed [**37**]. No doubt Wilfred would have been pragmatic enough to know that the Littlewood Committee was very unlikely to bring about any positive change, but even on that basis, the Committee was, as is generally the case, a costly waste of time: although "[i]n general, the recommendations would have increased the level of control over vivisection in Britain … the report was never fully debated in Parliament." [**38**]

Although deputations were useful for making contact with governmental bodies, they were generally less useful as far as the public profile of groups such as the NAVS was concerned, so this was probably a rare occurrence for Wilfred; where the presence of a legitimate medical authority was required, this often fell to Dr. Maurice Beddow Bayly; although he is generally described primarily as a member of the Animal Defence and Anti-Vivisection Society, he was definitely also a 'paid-up' member of the NAVS; his views were perfectly in tune with theirs, and there was a very close connection, because articles & books written by him had been published under the auspices of the LPAVS, before the amalgamation in 1957, as they also were after it [**39**]. In January 1958, Dr. Beddow Bayly was one of a deputation of three from the Conference of Anti-Vivisection Societies, which was received at the Soviet Embassy to protest the use of a stray dog, named Laika for the event, in a 'space-shot' whose object was to test the effect of space flight on her vital organs, with a misguided notion that these results could be extrapolated for a human situation; almost inevitably [but no more acceptable for that] she did not survive the experience [**40**]. Although the Russians had announced their plan well in advance of the blast-off on the 3rd of November 1957, and the Conference had written to the Soviet Embassy straight away, the deputation was not received until two months later. The other two members of this deputation were Wilfred Tyldesley, Wilfred's 'opposite number', as it were, in the BUAV, and Miss Louise Lind af Hageby [**41**], both of whom were also prominent figures in the field of anti-vivisection.

Apart from the Annual General Meeting, and other regular NAVS meetings as & when they arose, Wilfred did not speak in public as often as he had for British Union, but the impression that comes across is that for him, speaking was a part of his job that he took in his stride, and quite possibly still enjoyed, rather than an end in itself. Although he did not speak on this particular occasion [which might have been possible however, if there had been sufficient advance warning] he did submit a statement to the American Government in 1962 [**42**], for a committee that had been set up to examine the implications of two very similar Bills, H.R. 1937, whose author was "the Congresswoman from Michigan, the Honorable [sic] Martha W. Griffiths", and H.R. 3556, whose author was "The Honorable Morgan M. Moulder, a Representative in congress from the State of Missouri"; the wording of both was identical, except for the substitution of "tests" in the first by "research" in the second: "A Bill to provide for the humane treatment of animals used in experiments and tests by recipients of grants from the United States and by agencies and instrumentalities of the U.S. Government, and for other purposes". The licence implied in the description of these bills by the final two words, "other purposes" is obvious: 'anything else we've forgotten, or not thought of, or which might occur to us at any time in the future'. There was also another significant difference between the bills that was not evident from their wording: Moulder's bill specified that administration of the proposed law would be under a presidentially appointed commissioner; for the other bill, the responsibility would lie with the Welfare Secretary. The hearings were before a subcommittee on Health and Safety of the Committee on Interstate and Foreign Commerce, House of Representatives, during the second session of the eighty-seventh Congress, and they were held on September the 28th and 29th, 1962, in room 1334 of the New House Office Building in Washington, DC.

Initially, it might seem incongruous for this matter to be dealt with by the part of the American Government that had responsibility for commerce, but commerciality is a central theme of the government of that country, given that it was essentially a commercial venture from the very beginning [with a subtext of religious 'freedom'], and Fred Myers, Executive Director of The Humane Society of the United States, told the Hearing that "We are … talking about something which is a major part of interstate commerce of the United States. … We are talking about a problem that involves the use of 300 million animals a year. … by 1970 the value of the animals to be used annually in research and allied pursuits would equal the monetary value of all the livestock produced by all of America's farms and ranches, and this is not a fantastic statement." The financial implications of the perceived strictures that would be imposed by these regulations, over & above the proclaimed worthy [but fundamentally blinkered] objects, were always a primary concern. The report on these sessions, which included graphic details of the suffering inflicted on animals in the course of 'research', makes for disturbing reading, as indeed it should. It was published with commendable openness by the U.S. Government Printing Office, was scrupulously comprehensive, running to 382 pages and, given that it was acknowledged that the American policy was based to a very large extent on the British Cruelty to Animals Act of 1876, it was considered to be appropriate to include a summation of that legislation, which was submitted for consideration by one of the co-sponsors of H.R. 1937, "the Honorable Maurine B. Neuberger, Senator for Oregon", and her reasoning [resort to a categorisation of irony being, again, unavoidable] included this gem: "I urge the favorable [sic] consideration by your committee of legislation, which will assure American citizens that institutions or researchers aided by tax revenues give proper care and treatment to animals used to unlock the riddles of human illness. A civilized society can do no less for creatures of a lower order." She was, in addition, respectful of the experience that was being drawn on from Britain: "When I found that a bill on which this is modeled [sic] has been in effect, or legislation on which this is modeled has been in effect in Great Britain for 80 years, I thought what better laboratory do we have than to look to their experience with this sort of legislation. On reading it, I was very proud to add my name as a sponsor."

Unfortunately, the 1876 Act was explained in a leaflet that had been compiled by the Research Defence Society, possibly because no such official publication by the British Government existed [in the pre-Freedom of Information era], but the only reasonable conclusion that could be drawn from this was that the British Government condoned, or actively supported research using live animals. There appeared to be no valid reason to exclude the "… application form for membership of the Research Defence Society [which] will be found at the end of this pamphlet" in the submission. Life membership of this august body was five guineas [over £90 at 2012 value]. Opposition to the proposed legislation was generally from the point of view of cost, from the increased administration that would be necessary, but also the time it was expected would be wasted in extra administrative burdens, that "could make it difficult, if not impossible, to recruit and retain talented young men in scientific research. This, in turn, could jeopardize the Government's medical research program [sic]." [quote from Cyrus R. Vance, Secretary of the Army] In a reflection of the modernity of the times, NASA was also included in the Committee's deliberations, and this agency was concerned with the continuation of "the policy of using animal experiments to determine the effects of spaceflight.", no doubt with the 'Space Race' against the Soviet Union in mind.

The question, which obviously concerned Wilfred and all his anti-vivisection colleagues, of whether living animals of any description should be used in tests and/or research at all, was not being considered; the only possibility for debate on this issue, which the 'cons' would argue to the utmost of their abilities, was in the declaration of policy of the United States "that living vertebrate animals used for scientific experiments and tests … shall be used only when no other feasible and satisfactory methods can be used to ascertain biological and scientific information for the cure of disease, alleviation of suffering, prolongation of life, the advancement of physiological knowledge, or for military requirements"; it is another testament to the American openness, which can be construed either as naïveté or unconcerned matter-of-factness, that the final reason, "military requirements", is stated here, and this candour has traditionally been conspicuous by its absence in similar British pronouncements. The bottom line, and irony [very probably generally unperceived] of these bills was that the Americans were concerned that these animals should be given the best possible treatment, to ensure that they were not uncomfortable or stressed, before they were tortured and subjected to excruciating pain, and then killed, to put them out of their totally unsolicited misery: a strange comparative rationalisation. Mrs. Griffiths described it thus: "The bill is modeled upon the British act of 1876 and *it is not intended in any way to impede or limit* genuine scientific research involving *experimentation upon living creatures.* It is designed simply to prevent wanton, needless, or sadistic torture of animals; it calls for elementary decency in the treatment of animals before experimentation; and it calls for care consistent with the experiment in *putting them out of their misery* when the experiment is over." [my emphasis] Moulder's reasoning was more forthright: "I think that it ought to be noted that all of the so-called antivivisection organizations of the United States have registered violent opposition to my bill. They oppose the bill because it would not interfere with any *necessary* use of animals in research. So I hope that your committee and the Congress, Mr. Chairman, will not permit a confusion of the issues before you. Whether animals are to be used in research is not at issue. *My bill contemplates that animals will be used in research of all kinds*. The issue before you is solely whether, when animals are used, their suffering shall be reduced to the minimum possible." [ditto]

It is possible that Wilfred might have researched the progress of this issue in the American media in the minimal time that was available to him before his submission, but whether he did or not, he must have been aware of how forlorn would be his hopes and those of his compatriots of changing the entrenched attitudes of the Americans: "Animal experimentation has done much and will do more to help in the advance of medicine and surgery in this country. I should be completely opposed to anything which would interfere with *bona fide* use of experimental animals by competent personnel. I have great respect for and love of dogs. For all that experimental animals do in their own way to help in medicine and surgery they should be treated and cared for in as an [sic] humane way as possible. Mrs. Griffiths' [sic] bill would provide for such." [Paul C. Kiernan, M.D., consultant in surgery at the Washington Clinic, Washington, D.C.] Wilfred's statement, which was one of five submitted for filing before the Committee broke for lunch on the first day of the hearing, was relatively modest in length by comparison with the voluminous statement from Dr. Beddow Bayley which preceded it; Wilfred's, ambiguously listed as representing "the National Anti-Vivisection Society of Great Britain", was followed in the record by the statement from Harvey Metcalfe, on behalf of the Scottish Society for the Prevention of Vivisection [SSPV]. All of the submitted statements in this batch were from anti-vivisectionists, the first two being written by Owen B. Hunt, President of the American Anti-Vivisection Society of Philadelphia, Pennsylvania, who was actually present at the hearing, but filed his statements, possibly to save the Committee's time [and this action follows a remark to that effect by a Mr. Stevens, although it is not clear if this is a mistake, referring to Mrs. Stevens, President of the Animal Welfare Institute of New York, New York, or if it is a different person, whose affiliation is not specified], but his reason is not actually given. [see note 42]

Wilfred's statement is entitled "Vivisection is fundamentally evil", which was guaranteed [no doubt intentionally] to raise the hackles of the medical and scientific community; however, he does use a device that he had employed previously in his contributions to the British Union papers, that of giving an example of an Americanism which has found its way into the English language [in this case, "ballyhoo"] and although the point for which it is used draws on his propaganda experience, it is not written in such a way as to appear patronising. He then laments the credulity "in this country" of "people who believe that something controlled by act of Parliament cannot be completely cruel", which is countered by the advice that, as is often the case, the legislators have vested interests: "the people who determine the degree of protection for the animals are the very people who are themselves indulging in the practice of vivisection which causes the suffering to the animals". After questioning the morality of thinking of animals as "the lower creation", he continues the theme with another example the Americans would understand, that of slavery, and a hint of the old socialism creeps in: "We were told that slavery was necessary for the preservation of the plantations in the South: no other labor [sic] could do the same work that the slave labor could, and therefore the slaves must not be emancipated. But eventually they were emancipated, and the plantations all continued and thrived and flourished pretty successfully, as one can see when one considers the millionaire fortunes of our tobacco kings." After comments on vivisection for the sake of medicine: "this vicious practice, which so often proves to be misleading", he finishes with a defiant definition of his organisation's position: "There is our case and there are our lines of territory. And all these arguments for the old vicious system to go on because it is necessary and because it is harmless as long as it is controlled are fallacious, misleading, and can lead only to damnation." [**43**]

The afternoon session commenced with testimony from two British contributors who could be there in person, and somewhat unsurprisingly, they were pro-vivisection; the first was Professor A. N. [Alistair] Worden, Director of the Huntingdon Research Centre [**44**], and the second was Major C. W. Hume, Secretary General of the Universities Federation for Animal Welfare, whose headquarters were in London [**45**]; neither of these gentlemen was discouraged from presenting compendious statements, and Major Hume was also able to read out a large number of letters from supporters, all of whom appeared to be distinguished in their respective fields of expertise, so on balance, it seems quite clear that both of these contributors must have had sufficient warning to prepare their submissions and to ensure that they would be available, whereas Wilfred did not and could not, always assuming that he would have been able to justify the cost of a transatlantic return flight, and possibly short-term accommodation, to his committee, especially given the low degree of likelihood that his personal testimony would contribute to a prohibition of vivisection in the United States; however, the NAVS was not pledged unequivocally to abolish vivisection, as was the BUAV, so had Wilfred made a case for a personal appearance, it could have been argued that he was exceeding his brief somewhat.

As far as the American situation was concerned, notwithstanding the unity of purpose of the anti-vivisectionists [with allowances for slight differences in ultimate objects, as mentioned], they were rather 'out in the cold', because the so-called 'animal welfare' representatives were working very much hand in glove with the vivisectors; while the anti-vivisectors generally knew each other and collaborated [Harvey Metcalfe of the SSPV had addressed the NAVS AGM "[n]ot so very long ago"], the vivisectors and their apologists also, understandably, all compared notes and contributed to research papers, and there had been significant co-operation prior to these American hearings, notwithstanding the precipitate nature of the eventual scheduling: Worden & Hume obviously knew each other quite well, and had worked together in the past [**46**]. They were introduced by Mrs. Stevens [see note 29], the president of the New York Animal Welfare Institute and a co-sponsor of one or both of the bills, so it is very likely that she arranged for them to appear together, on the basis of their prior collaboration, Worden's expertise 'at the sharp end' and Hume's 'animal welfare' beliefs; their greeting from the Chairman was also a warm one [**47**]. Realistically, in the time that was allowed for this Hearing, which amounted to only slightly more than one day [the actual business on the second day, Saturday September the 29th, lasted precisely one hour and 25 minutes], there was no way that the subject could be given anything like the attention it deserved, especially in view of the number of written submissions which were put forward, so the question is whether the subcommittee scrutinised all these documents to any extent, if at all, after the Hearing; it was declared that the record would be left open "for 10 legislative days" thereafter, for the tendering of further submissions, an opportunity of which Hume took advantage on the 29th, writing from "London, England … comments on the testimonies of two witnesses." [**48**]

Perhaps unsurprisingly, it appears that it took another four years for the legislation proposed by these two bills to become enacted, as Public Law 89-544 Act of August the 24th, 1966, and was commonly referred to as The Animal Welfare Act, "although that title is not mentioned within the law" [**49**]; during the intervening period, the provisions of the legislation had broadened out to encompass three main areas of concern:

1. To protect the owners of pet dogs and cats from the theft of their pets;
2. To prevent the use or sale of stolen dogs or cats for purposes of research or experimentation; and
3. To establish humane standards for the treatment of dogs, cats, and certain other animals by animal dealers and research facilities. [**50**]

The concomitant licensing of animal dealers and promulgation of the associated regulations would be undertaken by the Secretary of Agriculture, not either of the options suggested in the foregoing bills as described above; as is customary within the realm of legislation, it was amended and extended in the succeeding years, but it is unlikely that Wilfred had any hand in that. Although he would not have viewed the legislation as any sort of victory, neither was it a failure in the sense that, notwithstanding the pain that many of the animals would inevitably suffer during the operative or test procedures, at least they would be humanely treated prior to that, assuming that the legislation was observed and enforced.

By 1963, Wilfred had realised that, for all the success the NAVS might be able to achieve with legitimate lawful protest, using methods like petitions and campaigns enlisting the help of high-profile 'celebrities', it was always likely to be limited, and even such illustrious supporters as Lord Dowding, who became the president of the NAVS after the second world war, could only hope to influence the legislative programme to a minimal extent, given the paucity of support in both Houses, and painfully slowly at that; what was needed was a sensational public relations coup so, building on the success [with an associated financial stability?] of the incorporation of the Society [see note 30], the NAVS started looking for suitable new premises, and Wilfred drew on his propaganda experience to support the most audacious slap in the face of the opposition of which he could conceive: moving the whole of the head office organisation into the very heart of the medical establishment - Harley Street. This London street has become synonymous almost everywhere in the world with generally top-class medical care and surgery, and consequently, if not the most expensive in the world, undoubtedly a strong contender for the title. Harley Street, if not unique in London, is certainly unusual in that the whole street is privately owned, by the de Walden family, and it is managed by the de Walden Estate [**51**]; although "an eclectic collection of residents have inhabited this exclusive area of Marylebone, including writers, musicians, politicians, soldiers and scientists", over the years, "[t]he Estate has always been particular about the type of people allowed to practice [sic] from Harley Street" so, given that "Harley Street enjoys a long-standing reputation as a centre of private medical excellence and the district around Harley Street is more often referred to as *Medical London* because it has several private hospitals within the vicinity and the largest concentration of medical proficiency in the world" [**52**], it is perhaps somewhat surprising, in view of the aforementioned particularity of the Estate with regard to the business of its tenants, that Wilfred managed to pull off this cheeky stunt: perhaps there had been a certain relaxation of expectations following the "real catalyst for change" of the second world war [**53**], or perhaps there was a sympathiser or two on the board of management for the estate?

In the year of the change of premises, 1964, there was yet another anti-vivisection organisation in existence, of which Wilfred was also Secretary, although it had not been founded specifically to fight for the abolition of vivisection, but to sponsor the search for alternative methods that could be used in medical research; it was the Lawson Tait Memorial Trust, [LTMT] and it was this organisation [or The Trustees of the Trust, to be strictly accurate **54**] that leased the premises which became the new headquarters of the National Anti-Vivisection Society. It was unlikely that any substantial building in Harley Street would be unimpressive or unsuitable for an organisation such as the one Wilfred administered, but the building that was selected, number 51, certainly exudes the appropriate gravitas, externally at least, which would have conveyed the all-important first impression; it is a beautiful six-storey red-brick corner building in a Tudor revival style [**55**] with projecting bays and mullioned stone windows, and with its two-storey arris bay it is quirkily attractive. This might have seemed like an odd move, administratively speaking, given that the NAVS was the better-known organisation, by the public at least, but to all intents & purposes, the NAVS was the occupant of the building, using the basement and ground floor [**56**]; also, there was sound financial reasoning behind this administrative structure, in view of the fact that the LTMT was a charity, in addition to being a trust, which has certain distinct financial advantages where tax is concerned, and Wilfred will have been acting on the best available advice. The LTMT occupied the first & second floors, a sizeable area [although realistically, there might have been some sharing of facilities and storage area] and Wilfred was given the use of the top two floors as his own private apartment, so he and Nellie were able to move out of their current, presumably rented flat, and occupy this as their main residence [**57**].

The LTMT had already been in existence for three years when it took on the lease of 51 Harley Street, so it is more than likely that this was not a prime consideration in the formation of the Trust, but it nevertheless served a very useful purpose. Wilfred's latter-day *magnum opus*, a ***Biographical Study*** of Robert Lawson Tait [**58**], "Surgeon and Controversialist" [the sub-title of the book] was published in 1967, and the final chapter is an explanation of how the Trust came into being, but unfortunately, although there is a fair amount of detail, it does not throw much light upon how he had originally become aware of Tait and his work, one very important [and, for Wilfred, very relevant] aspect of which was his opposition to testing of surgical theories and methods on animals. The most likely explanation is that Tait made it very clear, as soon as he was in a position to have his views listened to, that he saw no value in vivisection: "The position of vivisection as a method of scientific research stands alone amongst the infinite variety of roads for the discovery of Nature's secrets as being open to strong *prima facie* objection. … for the physiologist, working upon a living animal, there are two strong objections: that he is violating a strong and widespread public sentiment, and that he tabulates results of the most uncertain and often quite contradictory kind." [**59**]; and, although he would not necessarily have considered himself a campaigner, he made it his business to associate with like-minded people, hence his connection with the anti-vivisection movement from its earliest origins [**60**].

The fact that Tait had been 'adopted' by Birmingham, despite hailing from Edinburgh, and had attained a fair degree of celebrity there as a result, might have meant that Wilfred encountered him, by repute, when he was living and working in that city, especially as a large proportion of Tait's work was concerned with the problems associated with pregnancy and gynaecology, and as was detailed in Chapter 6 of this work, Wilfred's wife Nellie, whom he had met in Birmingham, was a trained and qualified Midwife; however, it could also be a complete coincidence. The first official moves in the campaign to commemorate the man and his work in a more permanent manner, further to the celebration of his centenary [see note 60] came during 1959; the matter was raised at the first meeting of the Joint Consultative Council in November that year, and the wording of the Minute item makes it clear that the subject was already under discussion, but the form or content of these discussions was not specified [**61**]. Wilfred enlarges on the public aspect of the planning in his book and, curiously, the chapter on the subject is written in the third person, but there is no indication that it was written by anyone other than Wilfred himself, as he is the accredited author of the work; also, the writing style is somewhat anodyne, not displaying any of the characteristic humour or wordplay in which Wilfred liked to indulge in his earlier incarnation as a National Socialist: perhaps this was just his manifestation of the style that he thought was necessary for this type of written work. He knew very well the public relations value of involving the media, in an age before the advent of global communications, in a project such as this, and the original meeting was described thus:

> "On the first of December, 1959, four men sat around a table, in a room on the second floor of a business house in London; on the wall at the head of the table hung a portrait of Robert Lawson Tait. They comprised one journalist, (at that time London Editor for Empire News an influential Sunday newspaper, since defunct, based on Manchester); one public relations executive; one advertising specialist and the convenor of the gathering, Mr. Wilfred Risdon—at that time the Secretary of the oldest-established and one of the most respected Anti-vivisection Societies in the world, the National Anti-vivisection Society of Great Britain. The subject was 'Animal Experimentation, What is Wrong, and What Changes, if any, Are Desirable?'"

Late in his life, Wilfred seems to have experienced some sort of change of attitude in his approach towards animal testing: an epiphany perhaps, or possibly just pragmatism, but he obviously realised that there had to be a more practical solution that lay somewhere between the absolutism of the BUAV and the Fabianesque gradualism practised by his own organisation, and that was that it was all very well stating their opposition to animal testing in varying degrees of stridency, but unless they could actually offer the medical profession a practicable alternative to it, the medical profession would continue using it, and the standoff between the opposing sides would continue indefinitely:

> "Mr. Risdon was asked to open the discussion and he said that for a very long time he had held the view that anti-vivisection societies should not accept the responsibility for finding methods alternative to animal experimentation; the onus was on those who do that sort of work, for, if the use of animals in this connection was forbidden by law they would find alternatives—necessity being the mother of invention.
>
> Although he still thinks that to be true in the main, he does not now think it to be the whole truth. He now feels that a stage has been reached where something more than denunciation is required from opponents of animal experimentation and that they must be prepared to give some indication of positive and creative activities.
>
> In the field of positive alternatives there are some already in existence, although not developed to anything like their full potential; instances are: clinical observation and investigation, substitution of tissue cultures for living animals, use of three-dimensional photography and plastic models in teaching

> anatomy and physiology, use of computers utilising results of case records in pathology, and many other such means. All these could be speeded up and given greater emphasis, not only without detriment to medical progress but actually to its advantage."

What is interesting here is that, despite his relatively advanced age [at the tail end of an era when the age-related categories into which life had traditionally been divided were still generally evident] Wilfred was obviously very well informed about the latest technology, that would nowadays be described as 'cutting-edge' [no pun intended], such as three-dimensional photography, and computers, which at the end of the 1950s would have been laughably primitive compared to even the humblest mobile 'phone of the twenty-first century. It was vitally important that something constructive should be done as quickly as possible, "because of the fantastic increase in the numbers of animals used annually in the laboratories of this country during the post-war period": in 1958, the figure was "3,245,990 in this country alone", and by 1964, that figure had increased by 37% to 4,494,931. There seemed to be two alternatives for action, related though capable of existing independently: lobbying central Government for a grant to support research using methods which did not involve animal testing; and the offer of "a substantial award" to teams of researchers who published results that would do away with the 'necessity' "so often quoted by the apologists in the past as a 'regrettable necessity'" for the use of living animals in their own line of research. The former idea, although practicable, within the traditional, established structure whereby the Government of the day was lobbied for grant money, was discounted because "their response in a matter of this description must be pious and might not necessarily be more than pious." The subject was actually broached ten days after this meeting, when the Member for Heston and Isleworth, Richard Harris [**62**], asked if the Government would make a grant for "research to be made into alternative methods of discovering remedies for illnesses which do not involve the necessity for experiments on living animals" in a House of Commons session of written answers, but the answer, from the Minister of Health, Derek Walker-Smith, was indeed pious, and could also be construed as disingenuous when he said that "Much research sponsored by the Medical Research Council is already devoted to this purpose", when in fact, the BUAV estimated that only 5% of the MRC's grant from public funds was devoted to non-vivisectional research [**63**].

The latter suggestion, the offer of "a substantial award", was discussed at the "business house" in terms of a "memorial" award, perhaps along the lines of the Nobel Prizes, although "on a more modest scale", and they could be named after "some famous opponent of animal experiments"; this gave Wilfred the opportunity he had been waiting for, to expound on the significance of Lawson Tait, and the validity of association of his name with such an award. One of the group at the aforementioned meeting appeared to be sceptical initially, but he was convinced by Wilfred's well-honed rhetoric: "The journalist in the party then said he would have been inclined to frown on the idea of any particular 'memorial' prize until Mr. Risdon 'so brilliantly described the work of Lawson Tait'", and he was canny enough to see how all the different elements of the strategy would "put us on a winner": associating Tait's work with motherhood and babies [even though that had not been a conscious and deliberate 'tactic' of Tait's work]; "adopting a modern concept and devising a policy not so much a line of expediency but based upon the virtue of experience and knowledge"; but finally and most crucially [with a sort of tawdry inevitability] there was the financial aspect "which struck him forcibly as a Scotsman", in that because Tait had worked predominantly in Birmingham "which is also a very wealthy city", they could hope for "an appreciable amount of help from industrial organisations there, many of which donate considerable sums of money to what they call charitable objects and which they are allowed to do by the income tax authorities."

No doubt building on his regular research and familiarisation with technical developments in the field, to ensure that he was sufficiently well-informed beforehand, Wilfred had also been conscious of the need to avoid any accusations of exclusivity: the contact with at least one of the other significant anti-vivisection and/or animal welfare groups prior to these informal discussions was alluded to, although in recognition of the "Private and Confidential" nature thereof, not with any specific reference [**64**], but he did seem to be hedging his bets somewhat, because "Mr. Risdon stressed the fact that other societies had shown interest in the 'prize' part of the scheme and the additions thereto would be submitted to them so they might have the option of supporting it. He was convinced that his own society would back the scheme to the limit—even if they had to go it alone. In fact, he felt that this latter course might have advantages if such a course became necessary." Wilfred was not necessarily the first to suggest the use of alternatives [**65**], but it certainly looks like his initiative to offer a financial incentive was a groundbreaking step; at the end of the decade in which the LTMT was formalised, the BUAV emulated Wilfred's pioneering work when it announced plans to set up a humane research institute in honour of one of their medical experts, Dr. Hadwen, although it appears that the project never came to fruition, at least in the form it was originally intended to take, despite "[d]iscussions about the institute and fundraising for alternative research methods [that] started in 1970, and led to many important debates on the subject." [**66**]

Whatever or wherever might have been the source of the original idea, it seems fairly obvious that Wilfred initiated the public discussions [which probably took place at the NAVS's premises in Victoria Street, even though it is not actually specified in his book] with a pretty clear idea of the agenda, and was able to steer the progress in the direction he wanted; a tribute to his skills as a negotiator, gained from years of experience working with intransigent groups with widely differing viewpoints, no doubt. He confirms that the other interested Societies did, indeed "support the scheme with its additional details … after much preliminary work such as taking Counsel's opinion on how best to secure the purposes of the Trust and to give it legal and charitable status, under the insignia of the late Robert Lawson Tait, Father and Perfector of Abdominal Surgery … The Trust was approved as a charity and started functioning on November 16th, 1961." [**67**] Although Wilfred omits the details in his book of how much each interested Society had contributed, the JCC Minutes note the "desire" of the Scottish Society for the Prevention of Vivisection [SSPV] "to be associated with the scheme and had subscribed £2,000 towards its finances." [**68**] Each subscribing body appointed [although the BUAV calls it "elected" **69**] a Trustee. The first three were the Rt. Hon. Lady Dowding, Mrs. Nora C. Turnbull, and Mr. Arthur Charles Tawse Nisbet; Wilfred "agreed to act as Hon. Secretary until a formal appointment could be made", but either nobody suitable could be found, or Wilfred was too good at the job, because he remained in this position for the rest of his life.

With the move of headquarters as yet some time in the future, it was decided to use the Society's bank in Victoria Street as a contact address for the new Trust, and its creation was announced publicly before the event, in two long-established and well-respected 'broadsheet' newspapers, ***The Times*** and ***The Observer***, as well as a large number of medical publications [**70**], presumably to allow any or all interested parties to formulate an approach, if they wanted to consider participating; the same year, "Lord Dowding announced at the annual meeting that an annual award would be given to a medical researcher who makes the greatest contribution to medical science without using experiments on animals." although he didn't specify to the assembled paragons of the NAVS in 1961 that this was to be the Lawson Tait Memorial Trust prize award. Wilfred had already introduced the award scheme at a local meeting in Birmingham eight months prior to this [**71**]. On at least one occasion around the time that his book was being written, Wilfred did publicise the amounts that each of the initiating Societies had contributed as 'seed-money'; perhaps he considered it a betrayal of trust or business confidentiality to include it in his book, but there must have been some sort of public debate about it early in 1967, including letters to ***The Observer***, because on Sunday, March the 5th that year, a letter from Wilfred, signing himself "Secretary, Lawson Tait Memorial Trust", was published in which he corrected a Mr. Slatter from the previous Sunday, by announcing that the SSPV gave £2,000, and the BUAV & NAVS each gave £1,500 [**72**]. To be fair, there was no excuse for confusion on this issue, because the magnitude of the initial prize fund, "a New Nobel type fund with an initial foundation of £5,000", had been clearly stated in the public announcements [see note 70].

By February 1966, when it was well established in its salubrious new headquarters, the work of the LTMT had become sufficiently well known for the suggestion of Government funding to be raised again in the House [see notes 62 & 83]: a Mr. Hobden [**73**] asked the Secretary of State for Education and Science, "in view of the value of the work being done by the Lawson Tait Memorial Trust on the curing of human disease, if he will give financial assistance to this organisation"; although he was neither the portfolio holder [Anthony Crosland **74**] nor the Under-Secretary [Denis Howell **75**], the answer was given by Reg Prentice, who was just coming to the end of his stint as Minister of State at Education and Science in Harold Wilson's first Government [**76**]; nevertheless, his answer, although perhaps surprisingly honest, commencing with a direct negative, was not unduly inspiring, revealing the regular bias towards animal-based research: "No. The Medical Research Council, which is the main Government agency for the promotion of medical research, gives financial support to approved projects; but neither the Government nor the Council contributes to voluntary fund-raising organisations as such. The Council is always ready to consider on merits any application for grant-support for a specific project, whether with the backing of the Lawson Tait Memorial Trust or otherwise." [**77**]

The first award by the Trust for non animal-based research was actually made before the Trust took up residence in Harley Street, to a surgeon working at Whipps Cross University Hospital in Waltham Forest, London [**78**]; again, Wilfred is somewhat parsimonious with the specifics in his book, apart from giving the amount of the award, £1,000, although there is plenty of background detail. Very wisely, it was decided to engage the services of a panel of medical advisors to 'vet' the proposals submitted, "thus enabling the Trustees to deal with them on their merits"; it would appear, at least in the beginning, that these experts were almost exclusively male [**79**]. Over fifty projects were submitted for consideration for the first award, from which a shortlist of three was selected; one of these three was almost certainly 'nobbled' when his hospital "denied the facilities … for continuing his researches there", so he had to withdraw his application. The winner's project was actually ongoing work, "only partially completed", hence the scale of the award ["The Trustees are authorised, as finances permit, to award prizes at their own discretion (up to £3,000—outright for completed work) or grants in aid of partially completed work which is still continuing, on projects with approved aims, conducted by approved methods."] but "[t]he work which was finally selected as fit to receive the first Prize Award was the outcome of more than twenty years of research carried out by an eminent surgeon working at one of the great hospitals in the London area, following up a conception of phylogenetic aspects of cancer causation." [**80**]

Ever conscious of the public relations value of such events, Wilfred laid on "a luncheon arranged for the occasion and the presentation was made on the Trust's behalf by the Vice-President of the British Medical Association, in the presence of a distinguished gathering which included such names as Air Chief Marshal Lord Dowding, Mrs. E. ["Bessie"] Braddock, MP, and several well-known doctors and medical journalists. Lady Dowding presided." [there is a photograph in Wilfred's book of Lady Muriel Dowding giving her speech, looking the epitome of 1960s elegance in a probably hideously expensive skimpy confection of a hat, and wearing the oval-framed spectacles of the style favoured by middle-aged ladies of the period; Lord Dowding, impassive and studiously avoiding the camera, is seated one person away from her] Bessie Braddock, described by Pamela Brown in her history of the Humane Research Trust, ***Animal research: the progressing change in attitude*** [**81**] as "the formidable Bessie Braddock" [**82**], tried to elicit financial help from the Government for the LTMT [**83**], regrettably without success, but her zeal in the face of obfuscation helped to propagate the conciliatory atmosphere of willingness to acknowledge and accommodate alternative methods of research, embraced by Wilfred, which is still in existence, even if a permanent end to animal testing is not on the horizon. Wilfred was keen to point out in his book that the Trust's reach was global, not parochially restricted to Great Britain: "It should be noted that awards are not limited to people resident or working in Great Britain. Any research worker in any part of the world whose work comes within the limits laid down by the Trust may be eligible."

In the first year of the Trust's existence, there were enquiries about its formation "from Australia, Canada and USA", with a view to either forming their own "similar trusts or, failing that, to establish branches of this Trust in their own territories. So far one result has come to our knowledge—in Canada a branch of the Lawson Tait Memorial Trust has been established [in Toronto]". If nothing else [although that is clearly not the case], the LTMT provided the impetus and the vehicle by which Wilfred could establish the NAVS in a location worthy of its mission and, although in 1964 he would not have thought of it in these terms, given that he surely thought that he had many years of life in front of him, in which he might hope to see a satisfactory [and spiritually rewarding] solution to his quest for reduction of animal testing to an absolute minimum if total prohibition was not to be achieved, the facilitating of a constructive [and, arguably, productive] dialogue with the traditional 'enemy' would prove to be the crowning achievement of his career. However, in 1964, he had every reason, and justification, to think that 'the world was his oyster'; as Secretary of possibly the best known and, in its own way, the most prestigious anti-vivisection society in Great Britain, he would have been a very busy man, but as his earlier career amply demonstrated, he did not shirk from work: he "represented the Society in public, he liaised with governments and MPs and other officials. He also managed all of the Society's affairs." [**84**]

At various times, Wilfred also still engaged in one of the pleasures of his life for which he might have considered that he did not have sufficient opportunity: writing; while he was employed by the NAVS [although he must surely have thought of it in terms of a vocational employment] he appears to have written easily as frequently, and a similar volume as he did when he was working for Mosley, given that an aptitude for communication was essential to his efficacy in that situation, and the many titles of articles either written by or attributable to him in the NAVS archives are clear evidence of the passion he had for this mission. Apart from what was probably his final written work of any magnitude, his ***Biographical Study*** of Lawson Tait, the subject matter suggested by the titles, although obviously related, is not mono-thematic: ***An Accused Instrument; Animal Experiments on Live Animals - are they necessary?***; ***In Memoriam - Maurice Beddow Bayly 1887-1961***; ***Side by Side - some facts about cancer***. Around the time of the relocation to Harley Street, he wrote an article, ***Why this needless Cruelty***, for the NAVS magazine, ***Animals' Defender***, lambasting the absurdity of, after wittingly allowing two cows to graze on reportedly contaminated land, subjecting a large numbers of dogs - "(some accounts refer to a 'lorry-load of dogs')" - as well as guinea pigs to large doses of rat poison to substantiate the contamination of the land in question. Once the events highlighted in the article became known, "a strong protest" was sent to the Ministry of Agriculture by the Emergency Committee of the British Council of Anti-Vivisection Societies, of which the NAVS was a member [**85**]. The article is slightly unusual, in that it includes a photograph [page **G**] of Wilfred leaning comfortably, on the edge of the footpath, with his left leg crossed behind him, against the limousine belonging to NAVS Council member Miss Diana Hamilton-Andrews, who is holding the lead of her corgi [Topaz Regina of Teifi (popularly "Dum Dum")], whose head is turned towards the camera [probably in response to a call]; Miss Hamilton-Andrews's Chauffeur is also watching the dog with a respectfully amused expression on his face. The photograph was very possibly taken in Harley Street [although it is difficult to be certain] and Wilfred is not looking at anything in particular, but smiling broadly nevertheless [**86**]. Some of Wilfred's longer articles, written under his initially expedient wartime pseudonym [but evidently retained for consistency] of *W. Arr*, were published by the LPAVS as pamphlets, and retained by the NAVS in their archive: one such title, ***What Goes On***, published in 1954, is available at the British Library; some of his regular 'round-up' articles were also published as collections, and some, such as ***This Brave New World***, were updated as appropriate [**87**].

The beginning of 1967 was very busy for Wilfred; on the personal side, he was finalising his biography of Lawson Tait. Although the finished product, a neat, slim volume of 98 pages, excluding the usual peripheral pages of dedication, foreword, preface, contents and index, appears to be complete, it is impossible to know if there was the intention to extend it in any way [but the preface suggests a supplemental work was being considered:

the tenth and final chapter, ***DELAYED RECOGNITION***, which contains information on the formation of the LTMT quoted above, suggests not. The two-page foreword was written by Wilfred's by now long-time vocational colleague, and very probably personal friend, Lord Dowding GCB, GCVO, CMG [as per the book]:

> This book is a history and appreciation of the life work of the most eminent surgeon of this age if not of all time. I refer to Robert Lawson Tait whose life work was spent between Edinburgh and Birmingham, but latterly and principally in Birmingham.
>
> From the point of view of those anti-vivisectionists concerned in the foundation and carrying on of the Lawson Tait Memorial Trust, his fight against vivisection, even if it cannot be claimed to be the most important part of the work, is the most important from the point of view of Lady Dowding and the other Founders of the Trust which was formed in his name, because it gave the Society the most important Ally which they have ever had.
>
> The majority of the medical profession is still deeply committed to the support of vivisection as a central assistance to the progress of human surgery whereas Lawson Tait and those who follow his line of thought are convinced that the contrary is the case and that in fact this has misled the medical profession on many aspects of human physiology.
>
> It even appears to me that Lawson Tait's claim to be absolutely the leading surgeon of his day has been damaged by his opposition to the common view of the medical profession on this subject.
>
> From this point of view a careful study of Mr. Risdon's remarkable book is important as it shows in how many aspects of surgery Lawson Tait's work has led the surgical profession and to what extent it has caused surgeons to change their minds on many important matters. An instance of this latter state of affairs is supplied by the change of instructed views towards aseptic versus antiseptic surgery where Lawson Tait's thinking and teaching post dated those of Lister.
>
> It was in 1867, when Tait was twenty-two years old, that Lister published his first work on the antiseptic principle in surgery (Lancet, 1867, Vol. 1, pages 326-29, 357-59, 387-89, and 507-09). It was nearly four years later that Tait challenged the soundness of the Listerian method and backed his criticism with the records of 6 cases. His own method from then on was scrupulous cleanliness and occlusion of wounds.
>
> I think that any dispassionate reader of the book will come to the conclusion that Lawson Tait deserves not only the appreciation but the affection of the public at large not only for his forceful and original mind but also for his many loveable traits.

The foreword was not dated, but it can be assumed fairly safely that it was written late enough for Lord Dowding to have read a draft of Wilfred's book that was, if not the finished version, certainly essentially complete; the final paragraph, indeed the very last words, of Dowding's foreword is interesting where he mentions Tait's "loveable traits": not what one with a superficial knowledge of the airman who effectively ensured that the Battle of Britain was won might normally expect from him, but as detailed elsewhere in this book, Dowding was known to have a warm heart beneath his gruff exterior, and this is warm praise indeed. Wilfred's preface shows the date of December 1966, so it was very likely the last part of the book he wrote, apart from possible minor corrections and/or additions, and his time between then and when the book was finally published was probably spent either organising or finalising printing arrangements [the printer's address was shown as south west London]; it was published by the NAVS, so there must presumably have been some notion about distribution, not only to propagate its message, but also to at least cover the production costs, if not to actually accrue some funds for the Society. In the preface, he gives a very brief synopsis of Tait's career [and thereby perhaps a suggestion of Wilfred's identification with Tait as something of a rebel and iconoclast], as well as referencing earlier biographies:

> Why was this book written when there were already in existence two biographies of this truculent but highly successful nineteenth century surgeon.
>
> Firstly, it is true to say that anyone who studied the life and career of Lawson Tait must have been impressed that here was a character larger than life-size. He was outstanding in a period when men (and women) were setting new standards in the fields of science, of letters, of drama, of industrial progress and of exploration and discovery in many new directions.
>
> Secondly, it became apparent that because of his precociousness he had incurred the odium of many of his elders who attempted in their several ways, but without marked success, to put this young upstart in his place. This atmosphere brought out the fighting spirit which lies close beneath the surface of any true Scot and which becomes apparent when challenged. Here was a man who disdained to "pull his punches" when engaged in a fight and his strong reactions did not further endear him to those whose malice and/or envy he aroused.
>
> Thirdly, there were aspects of his work which, because of his own forthrightness and of the smugness of the age in which he lived and worked, appear to have been suppressed in his own times and overlooked by following generations. This, perhaps, accounts for the fact that there is a firmly established and highly influential Lister Foundation to commemorate the life and works of one of his outstanding contemporaries, but as was lamented by one of his admirers on the occasion of the centenary of Lawson Tait's birth, his "original mind and services to surgery deserved to be commemorated in a statue in his adopted city. If Birmingham delayed, perhaps Edinburgh might claim the privilege."
>
> So commenced a search of the records of his time which brought out ever more clearly the stature of this half-forgotten surgeon to whom thousands of women who might have died owe their lives.
>
> The search also brought to light the fact that Tait was almost a collector of lost and/or unpopular causes; item: he opposed animal experimentation because it had been responsible for delaying the development of an operation to deal with the tragedy of ectopic pregnancies for some fifty years; item: as early as 1874 he became associated with the campaign for women to be admitted to the medical

profession on equal terms with me and in 1887, in his presidential address to the British Gynaecological Society he reiterated with force this plea for equality of status; item: Lister's advocacy of the antiseptic principle in surgery had been enthusiastically accepted by the profession but Tait challenged it on the strength of his own experience and so attracted to himself the hostility of all those who had so readily accepted the popular fashion of anti-sepsis, carbolic spray etc., while he had decided to follow the lead of men like Oliver Wendell Holmes and Ignaz Semmelweis with whom he shared the honour of establishing the aseptic school of surgery which today holds the field. The one thing quite certain about this is that his records, using the methods of his choice, compared more than favourably with those of his antiseptic opponents, but this merely added to his unpopularity.

These facts, emerging from a study of his writings and lectures seemed to afford good grounds for a re-appraisal of this outstanding character in the light of modern knowledge and practice, so the book has been produced with the intent to highlight these facets of his personality which deserve to be pinpointed for what they are worth. Not all of them can be produced in a "paper-back" publication of these dimensions but a further (limited) edition with added documentation from official medical sources as appendices to the various aspects of his life and works is planned:

I would like to acknowledge the help which I have derived from such publications as Harvey Flack's *Lawson Tait* 1845-1899; *Lawson Tait, His Life and Work, with Personal Reminiscences* by Christopher Martin; *History of the Royal College of Surgeons of England* by Sir Zachary Cope; *The Early History of Surgery* by W. J. Bishop; *The Surgeon's Tale* by Robert G. Richardson; *The Triumph of Surgery* by Jurgen Thorwald and sundry articles by Tait himself in such publications as *The Lancet, British Medical Journal, Animals' Friend, Birmingham Post*, etc.

If it should be noted that the most important of all sources on Tait—John Stewart McKay, Tait's biographer—does not figure in the above list it is merely because the present writer has been unable to secure a copy of that study and so has been unable to quote directly from it. Quite recently the writer's hopes of securing a copy seemed about to be realised when it appeared in a Dawson's catalogue as available. A telephone call was met with the assurance that it was still available and would be set aside for confirmation in writing which was promptly sent off, only to receive the disappointing reply that it had been purchased by a caller at the Pall Mall premises while these details were under negotiation. If any reader can find a copy available, in whatever condition, it would be greatly appreciated.

It is with deep regret that we record the recent death of Harvey Flack, whose Thomas Vicary Lecture to the Worshipful Company of Barbers in 1947 formed the basis of his study of Lawson Tait, published by William Heinemann Medical Books Ltd., in 1949. He was a great help to the present writer.

There are several unfortunate, or positively sad, aspects about the foregoing: the fact that Wilfred was apparently planning some sort of new work about Tait, either an extended version of this book, or a supplemental book that contained some of the biographical information but with more documentary references; the *chagrin* of being 'pipped at the post' with his intended purchase of an essential reference work; and the presaging of his own death in the final paragraph. There are ten chapters in the book; the first chapter, appropriately, deals with the man and his origins although, inevitably, it includes details of his work and, ever aware of the validity of including modern technology and culture in his written work, Wilfred mentions a television programme shown by the BBC on the 22nd of February 1961, ***Your Life in Their Hands***, which had demonstrated a gall bladder operation called a chole-cystotomy, first performed by Lawson Tait in 1879. The second chapter, unsurprisingly in view of Wilfred's concept of the *raison d'être* for his book, is the longest, for it deals with ***LAWSON TAIT ON VIVISECTION***. In actual fact, after a brief introductory paragraph, the whole chapter is a verbatim reproduction of Tait's address to the Birmingham Philosophical Society, of which he was "an influential member", on the 20th of April, 1882, in which he read a paper with the title of ***On the Uselessness of Vivisection upon Animals as a Method of Scientific Research***; from its length, it can be appreciated that it was extremely detailed [see notes 59 & 60 for excerpts].

Chapters three to nine all concern different aspects of Tait's work, apart from chapter seven, which is entitled ***LAWSON TAIT AS SEEN BY A CONTEMPORARY (ALEX BOWIE, M.D., C.M., ETC)***. This was also a transcription *in toto* of an article by a man who was evidently a fellow animal lover; it was entitled ***Appreciation***, and it was published in ***The Animals' Friend*** in August 1896: Bowie was editor of ***Harvey on the Circulation of the Blood***, some-time Physician and Lecturer on Dermatology, St. John's Hospital for Diseases of the Skin, Fellow of the British Gynaecological Society, and holder of a number of other distinctions. At the end of his article, he describes how Tait came to champion anti-vivisection:

> He has told the story of his conversion to the principles of anti-vivisection elsewhere, and how he found the results of experiments upon animals totally misleading when applied to the human subject … A lover of animals, sentiment played no part in his conversion. He attacked that subject as he has approached all the others mentioned, by examining their claims in the light of history and practice, and with a mind free from bias. The method must be accepted by opponents and advocates alike as eminently just and scientific. In reading either ***The Uselessness of Vivisection*** before-mentioned, or his later ***A Wrong Method*** it seems impossible to avoid the conclusion that sentiment is, after all, most practical, and science, true and holy science, most spirituelle. [sic] The results to men and women from the labours of this man, true and great as the present and future must proclaim him, are quite incalculable. …

Bowie also recounts how Tait refused ennoblement:

> … In 1886 he was approached on behalf of the government of the day as to whether the honour of knighthood would be acceptable. With rare consistency he declined to have his name submitted, and again in 1892, when a baronetcy was in the same way proferred [sic]. While admiring his adherence to his professions in regard to titles, it cannot but be a source of regret to his

> numerous friends and admirers that his views did not permit his accepting either honour.

The final chapter, as described above, is entitled ***DELAYED RECOGNITION***, and deals almost exclusively with the formation of the LTMT, which Wilfred saw as the embodiment of that recognition, for which opportunities had previously been overlooked:

> It may be recalled (see reference on page 9) that Professor Eardley Holland—now Sir Eardley Holland—was mentioned, in ***The Lancet***, July 14, 1945, as having suggested at the Celebration of the Centenary of Lawson Tait's birth, that the great surgeon's "original mind and services to surgery deserved to be commemorated in a statue in his adopted city. If Birmingham delayed, perhaps Edinburgh might claim the privilege …"
>
> Twenty years have passed since the above statement was made and, in that time, no statue has been erected to Lawson Tait's memory either in Edinburgh or Birmingham, but a more permanent, and to him we feel a more pleasing memorial now exists in the form of a research Trust bearing his name, which has carried that name into the University of Edinburgh, where a Lawson Tait Memorial Trust Research Fellowship was established and to which Dr. J. N. Harcourt-Webster was formally seconded on April 1st, 1965, for the twelve months ending March 31st, 1966, investigating enzymes in surgically removed thyroid glands in an attempt to determine the place of such studies in diagnosis of malignant and pre-malignant diseases.

The book carried a dedication on one of the front fly-leaves to "The memory of Maurice Beddow Bayly, MRCS, LRCP, a Colleague whose help and encouragement, so freely given on all occasions, is remembered with affection; and to the service of all who follow the path on which he led"; Bayly died in 1961, but his friendship and his contribution to the anti-vivisection movement had had a profound effect on Wilfred. The book was produced with a cloth cover in an eye-catching cardinal red with gold-blocked lettering in a utilitarian sans-serif font similar to the latterly ever-present Helvetica [**88**], although it was still very new in 1967, so it could have been an individual variant used by the printer or binder; the overall effect of this presentation was quite sober, nonetheless, so it is unlikely that the book was released into the world with any fanfare. No doubt Wilfred had every justification feeling well pleased with the finished product, but if his previous energy, enthusiasm and commitment to his vocation are anything to go by, it is very unlikely that he would have considered 'resting on his laurels' at this point in his career. Indeed, the other very important matter that would have occupied his mind at this time, was that reunification with BUAV was 'back on the table'. As detailed above, there had been several attempts made to bring the two Societies back together under a combined administration [see note 31], which obviously had certain advantages logistically, but the biggest obstacle that had to be overcome was ideological; it is clear from the foregoing that Wilfred had been aware of, and evidently accommodated, a necessity to adopt a gradualist approach to reduction of vivisection, ideally with the ultimate aim of dispensing with it altogether of course, and if his political experience had taught him nothing else, he had learned that there is normally only one way that rapid and radical change is achieved in any field of human endeavour, and that is by revolution, which is almost inevitably violent; hence his embracing of the principle of finding and encouraging practicable alternatives to vivisection, rather than doggedly [and dogmatically] persisting in accepting nothing less than total abolition. This being the case, it is hard to see how he could have been optimistic about the prospects for an understanding being reached by the two Societies, in view of the BUAV's traditionally 'hard-line' approach, but nevertheless, it appears to have been the wish of the Committee of the NAVS at this time to at least consider the mechanics of a possible merger. According to the BUAV, "negotiations with NAVS about a possible merger" were re-opened following the 1966 BUAV AGM when Jon Evans had been voted in as the new President [**89**].

The background to this final development, where Wilfred was concerned anyway, was the Littlewood Report, as described above. Because the remit of the Littlewood Committee was so restricted, from the point of view of anti-vivisectionists, especially the abolitionists, the BUAV "should have boycotted the Littlewood inquiry, as it had the second Royal Commission, because it knew that abolition was not on the agenda." However, the BUAV did realise that this was an opportunity that should not be missed, because "it could be many years before such an opportunity came up again." The BUAV's Executive Committee considered the matter, and eventually a Memorandum of Evidence was submitted to the Littlewood Inquiry [**90**]. It was only at the third attempt, at the 1966 AGM, that an amendment to Article 47 of the BUAV's Constitution, that "was intended to release the Executive committee from its obligation to 'oppose' any measures of partial reform", was passed, which resulted in the appointment of a new President, Jon Evans, who was presumably 'pro-merger' [**91**]. Unfortunately, it is difficult to be precise about the timetable of these events, but what can be said with absolute certainty is that Wilfred did not live to see their conclusion; however, it is perhaps a tendentious assumption to make that their failure was directly attributable to this fact, given the number of individuals involved, and the obvious strength of feelings expressed on both sides. It has to be presumed that Wilfred would have been broadly, if not enthusiastically, in favour of the merger, but the BUAV history makes no mention whatsoever of any involvement by Wilfred in this endeavour [although, to be fair, he does not rate a mention anywhere at all in the book, curiously]. The effective 'death sentence' for the proposed merger, which had been given the green light "after well over two hours of 'solid wrangling'" at the BUAV AGM, was passed "within just four months … [when] amalgamation talks had broken down. At the Executive Committee meeting of 16 November 1967 a resolution was 'reluctantly' passed confirming that amalgamation negotiations had been discontinued." All this was academic for Wilfred, however, and it is not clear what his function within the hoped-for new "large and powerful force" [**92**] would have been if he had wanted to continue such a demanding occupation: perhaps he would have seen it as his signal for retirement, the successful culmination of a life's work. It was not to be, of course: on the 11th of March, 1967, he suffered a fatal heart attack at Harley Street, and although it is difficult to avoid the irony of such a situation, he could not be saved, and a life of work devoted to various humanitarian causes over a period of more than fifty years [including his medical work during the first world war] came to a sudden end. This is reflected in the text on a narrow paper sleeve which was produced for slipping over the outside of his remaining Lawson Tait biographies:

LAWSON TAIT - Surgeon and Controversialist

Wilfred Risdon, the author of this outstanding Biographical Study of Lawson Tait, died suddenly on March 11th 1967. This book is the last published work of a man who, devoted to the encouragement of humane methods of medical research, was mainly responsible for the foundation of the LAWSON TAIT MEMORIAL TRUST.

"A REMARKABLE BOOK" — Lord Dowding, G.C.B., G.C.V.O., C.M.G.

It is also not unreasonable to speculate that the stress of the negotiations aimed at facilitating the possible merger of the two societies might have been Wilfred's own 'death sentence'. There were two obituaries [**93**] in the regular 'first port of call', ***The Telegraph***; the first was two days later, and was minimal, what is now generally referred to as a 'lineage' entry:

RISDON.—On March 11, suddenly at his home, 51 Harley Street, W.1. WILFRED (Bill), most dearly loved husband of MARGARET RISDON.

This was clearly Nellie's own personal notification, and it is interesting for two reasons: the first, that she used Wilfred's commonly-known nickname, albeit in parenthesis, as well as his given name by which he would invariably be known through his work; and secondly, that she used her 'official', given name instead of her own commonly-used nickname [although perhaps only by Wilfred]. The second, more detailed entry [although not anywhere near as comprehensive as most obituaries of public figures these days], which was most probably inserted by the NAVS or LTMT, was on the 15th:

Wilfred Risdon. In London, General secretary National Anti-Vivisection Society; secretary Lawson Tait Memorial Trust, founded to promote medical research without using live animals.

There does not appear to be any sort of memorial to Wilfred's work for animal welfare other than this: there is no mention of him in current NAVS publicity material on its website; he was mentioned in glowing terms in the Minutes of the Council Meeting immediately following his death, however, and his part in the moribund merger negotiations was also highlighted [**94**]; there was also a brief mention in the April edition of the NAVS magazine, ***Animals' Defender***, of the memorial service that had been held for him on the morning of the Council Meeting [**95**]. He had had an unspecified illness three years earlier, which "occasioned a short spell in hospital for him" in October 1964, so it is possible that this was some sort of collapse, brought on by the work [and possibly stress] involved in the move into Harley Street; in the "Apologies for Absence" at the 20th of October Council Meeting, it was noted that he was returning "next week", hence the commendable gesture "agreed unanimously that flowers be sent from the Council to Mr. Risdon with their best wishes, to reach his flat when he returns"; however, his recovery must have taken longer than anticipated, because the November edition of ***Animals' Defender*** noted that he was "making an excellent recovery and is now recuperating in the country, and hopes to return to the office in the near future." [**96**] For whatever reason, he must have thought that the time was not yet right for retirement, so he threw himself back into the demanding schedule of his work when he did return, and he only just made it into his seventies. Somewhat surprisingly, he had not made a will when he died, so it took just over a whole year for the estate to be cleared through Probate and assigned to his wife [or more correctly now, his widow and relict], who was named formally as Margaret Helen Risdon on the certificate which states that "Letters of Administration of all the Estate which by law devolves to and vests in the personal representative of the said intestate [Wilfred] were granted by the High Court of Justice at the Principal Probate Registry thereof to [her] of 51 Harley Street"; she was the "only person now entitled to the estate of the said intestate." It is not known if any or all of his living expenses, including rent for the two-floor apartment, were paid by the LTMT or NAVS, as part of his 'package' as Secretary: in the early stages of the merger between the LPAVS and NAVS, it was carried unanimously that the Committee was in favour of accepting him as Secretary "at a salary of not less than £1,000 per annum, plus increments" [**97**]; however, by the time of the Special Meeting of the Central Executive Committee, on Tuesday 27th November 1956, there was no mention of increments, when the Resolution was "passed confirming the salary of the appointment of Secretary on amalgamation to be £1,000 per annum".

The question of the minimal size of Wilfred's estate is raised by the wording of the following section of the Probate certificate: "And it is hereby certified that an Inland Revenue affidavit has been delivered wherein it is shown that the gross value of the said estate in Great Britain (exclusive of what the said deceased may have been possessed of or entitled to as a trustee and not beneficially) amounts to £1983 - 15 - 0 and that the net value of the estate amounts to £1882 - 8 - 0". As a simple 'off the top' reduction, this amounts to approximately 5%, which seems very modest; at 2012 values, this means that the estate lost around £1,450, leaving a net amount of £26,937: although that is not 'chickenfeed', it is not as much as one might expect if Wilfred and Nellie had been living rent- or mortgage-free in their Harley Street apartment for three years, given that they had sold the last house they had actually owned [presumably the one in Torrington Road, Ruislip], before they took up residence in Harley Street? Wilfred was paid £1,200 for the house in Torrington Road in 1943; at 2012 values, that is about £44,437, which seems ridiculously cheap for a house in London, albeit some distance from 'town', but it must have been the going price; if he put that straight back into another house of a similar price [or even less] and then sold in 1964 when he moved into Harley Street, he might easily have increased his equity by a very large factor. Given that no mortgage was mentioned on the 1943 transfer deed, it is possible that this was a 'cash' transaction, which would also have applied to his next purchase, with no call on the proceeds from that eventual sale; according to the website on which the above calculations are based [**98**], general inflation between 1943 and 1964 was just under 125% [there are separate figures for house price and mortgage inflation, but only between 1999 & 2009: 123% & 107% respectively; by way of comparison, average salary grew by only 13.6%] so if we use that ratio on Wilfred's £1,200, in 1964 that would have been worth £2,700 [2012 = £44,550]. If he had banked that [not allowing for a larger inflation ratio, or investing the money], it could mean that in the three years or so since moving into Harley Street, his capital [**99**] had reduced by £716 [£10,246] or approximately £240 [£3,400] per year; it is difficult to even speculate upon what he might have spent his money, if his living expenses were found as part of his salary [which might have been minimal, to limit the liability for income tax] he would only have had to spend any amount of money on 'luxury' items: it is more than likely that he did not own a car, by then, living in central London.

In 1960, a packet of 20 cigarettes cost 4s/- [20p] so if he was still a smoker, he might have spent around £100 [£1,500] over 3 years, on the basis of smoking 20 a day and allowing for 10% price inflation per year in the budget, so this is plausible. What it does mean is that, although he was not a rich man when he died, he was certainly not poor, and both he and Nellie must have enjoyed a reasonable standard of living for the latter part of their time together. Without access to Wilfred's contract of employment, it is impossible to know if any clauses were specifically written into it with regard to Nellie, if he should predecease her: for example, if there would be any continuing responsibility for the LTMT/NAVS to provide her with living accommodation until she was in a position to organise that for herself.

As the Probate certificate quoted above indicates, her address a full year after Wilfred's death was still 51 Harley Street but, assuming that the existing arrangement for the Secretary's accommodation was considered appropriate for an incoming incumbent, she would have had to vacate the Harley Street apartments before too long. At the first Council Meeting after Wilfred's death, the finance Sub-Committee very generously approved a pension of £500 per annum, to take effect immediately, "a lump sum of £750 immediately to help her at the present time", and "Lady Dowding referred to the sub-committee's suggestion that we pay Mrs. Risdon £250 for furnishings in the flat when she moves and this was agreed." [**100**].

As mentioned in Chapter 6, at some stage after this, Nellie moved to the Reading area [**101**] and worked in a book shop there for a while, probably just as much for mental stimulation and social interaction as it would have been a possible source of 'pin money'; her children had long ago both made lives of their own, although it is very possible that she and Sheila had reciprocal visits, but at some stage before Nellie's death, Sheila moved to Oklahoma City in the USA; later, according to her brother, she returned to live in or near Southampton, which although it was too late for Nellie, is approximately only an hour's drive from Reading. Nellie died in 1981, coincidentally the same month as Wilfred, March, albeit a week or so later; when she died, she was living in a Sue Ryder hospice in a lovely location at Nettlebed, which is not far from Reading. She must have been diagnosed as terminally ill by then, because the cause of death is given [in layman's terms] as pancreatic cancer. It is not known if Nellie ever visited her son Brian in Toronto, but he returned to England for a visit at least once, according to his son Gary, who came along for the trip with his siblings [**102**]. The work Wilfred had started continued after his death, but whether it was in a form of which he would have approved, can only be guessed at; animal experiments are still carried out, even if overall numbers have been reduced, but alternative methods, which he helped to champion, are now a reality, albeit nowhere near as prolific as Wilfred would have liked: the 'industry' of vivisection is still thriving. As described in note 81, the Humane Research Trust, which superseded the LTMT, continues its work, in a relatively low-profile way [notwithstanding the celebrity endorsements on its website], and is based in Manchester [**103**].

On the basis of the foregoing which is, necessarily [and regrettably] an incomplete account of Wilfred Risdon's life and career, it seems surprising [to this author, anyway] if not incomprehensible, that there is no permanent memorial of any sort, however minimal or trivial, to him, although this will be examined in more depth in the concluding chapter, before the appendices; one plausible explanation for this has to be a significant degree of embarrassment caused by the opprobrium with which the environment of his former political career is generally assessed, as a result of [it has to be said] very successful reinforcement of negative analysis of political activism for social change during that period of history, by the "Establishment", which is fickle at the best of times: it is surely not stretching credibility to see this, in addition to a resolutely entrenched [and symbiotically connected] element of financial enslavement, and the populist distractions such as sport and 'entertainment', as a very effective weapon in its armoury, to enable it to maintain the *status quo*, thereby keeping a potentially volatile populace in check, with ever-increasing levels of 'necessary' surveillance, and the occasional 'war' to boost patriotism, thrown in for good measure.

NOTES

1 The news might have come as a surprise to some, but no doubt word had already got around:

> "Will this year's Annual Meeting be viewed in later years as having been especially significant? It may be so—and it may prove to be the line of demarcation between two phases of development in this struggle against the evil of vivisection.
>
> The routine business of an Annual Meeting was dealt with as usual. The Minutes were read and accepted as a correct record. The Annual Report and Balance Sheet was presented by our Treasurer, Dr. Allinson, seconded by Mr. Rienaecker, discussed with special reference to the beneficial results of the advice of our stockbroker, Mr. Pritchett, who was present, and in due course were approved and passed.
>
> The retiring members of the Executive Committee—Lady Tenterden, Mrs. Hort and Mr. Rienaecker—were re-elected en bloc to serve for a further year on a motion from the Chair, the Chairman having paid due tribute to the gratitude which their past services merited. Our auditors, Messrs. Oakley Wederell & Co., were also re-elected to serve for a further year. So far, all had been as usual, but now came the special business which may make this a memorable occasion.
>
> Dr. Allinson, our Treasurer, was called upon to move the adoption of a Special Report which had been circulated to all members and, if the report found acceptance, to move a resolution that:
>
> > "the steps taken by the Executive Committee as detailed in the Special Report … be approved and that the Executive Committee be authorised to complete the amalgamation along the lines indicated in that report."
>
> The Special Report above mentioned was a two-page document outlining changed conditions which had led to an approach being made to the National Anti-Vivisection Society with a view to an exploration of the possibilities of amalgamation of the two Societies with a consequent reduction of overheads and hopes of increased efficiency if such an amalgamation should be found possible.
>
> The last paragraph of the Special Report reads thus:
>
> > "If these preliminary approaches are approved and if the principle of amalgamation be found acceptable, you are asked to vote accordingly in support of the resolution to be moved at the Annual Meeting and to authorise your Executive Committee to proceed to a conclusion of the amalgamation if all outstanding details can be settled to their satisfaction."
>
> The notion that the special report be received and approved was carried unanimously and the Resolution was then moved by Dr. Allinson, seconded by Mr. Rienaecker and carried unanimously after a short discussion of some of its implications.
>
> The Chairman thanked all those who were present for their attendance and placed on record his appreciation of the help and support which he had received throughout the past year from members of the Executive Committee, members and supporters throughout the country and from the staff.
>
> Dr. Allinson, on behalf of all present thanked the Chairman for his services

through the year and for presiding over the meeting then drawing to a close.

Thus concluded a meeting which, if the amalgamation can be carried to a successful conclusion may well come to be recognised as one of the more important milestones on the road to achievement of the emancipation of all animals from the régime under which they are viewed as living material for "experiments calculated to inflict pain"."

LPAVS Anti-Vivisection Journal, Vol. XVII, No. 6, June 1956, p. 42; courtesy of the NAVS

2 The NAVS was different from the LPAVS in that it had two annual meetings: one for the members, and one for the general public; given the smaller size of the LPAVS, there would not have been a need for this. The NAVS Chairman, Colonel G. T. Wards, CMG, OBE, explained the proposed merger at the members' meeting:

"THE CHAIRMAN: Item number 3 is the Resolution from the Executive Committee. I will read the Resolution to you: "That, subject to a mutually satisfactory arrangement being agreed by the respective Executive Committees of the National Anti-Vivisection Society and the London & Provincial Anti-Vivisection Society, the two said Societies shall amalgamate under the title of 'The National Anti-Vivisection Society (incorporating the London & Provincial Anti-Vivisection Society).'" This suggestion of an amalgamation came originally from the Chairman of the London and Provincial Anti-Vivisection Society in a letter which he addressed to me, as Chairman of our society, saying that he thought it would be a very good thing from the point of view of both Societies if we amalgamated. That letter, of course, I put before my own Executive Committee and we gave it very careful consideration. Having given it very careful consideration we came to the view that we would have a great deal to gain by amalgamation and that we would have very little, if anything, to lose. I feel that all of you probably will agree with that. Surely at the present moment there has never been a time when the anti-vivisection societies are more necessary than now and surely, therefore, the stronger we can be the more we will be able to carry on the fight, and I do feel that by amalgamation we shall be stronger. We shall first of all be stronger financially because we shall gain a good deal by cutting down our overhead expenses in rent, office staff, postage, and so on; secondly we will have in the combined organisation naturally more members than each of us has singly. Therefore, taking all those factors into consideration, the Committee have unanimously agreed that amalgamation would be a good thing and they put this resolution before you."

Minutes of Proceedings of the Annual Meeting of the Council of the National Anti-Vivisection Society: 26/06/56; courtesy of the NAVS

3 Understandably, the likely financial benefits were very important:

"THE CHAIRMAN: I do not know whether anybody would like to say anything about it. If so, now is the time.

MRS. I. M. PAGE: Could we hear a little more about the benefits? I think we would be in a much stronger position if we amalgamated. I have always felt it such a pity that more societies, for instance the British Union, do not amalgamate; but I would like to know for my own personal interest how we would benefit besides from a financial angle.

THE CHAIRMAN: Well, the benefits that accrue would be as the result of having more money. If we have more money we can have a bigger staff and we can have more vans on the road. We can have more district lecturers and we can be more active in many ways if we have more money. Another point over which we gain is this. It is becoming more and more difficult to find suitable full time employees for head-quarters staff. If you want to fill a certain appointment in anti-vivisection head-quarters you have to have a very unique person. First of all you have to have a person who is interested in our cause. If you want a man, for example, who is going to write your monthly bulletins you have to look round for a man who is a good writer. You might get twenty people coming along but not one of them in fact might be interested in anti-vivisection and, of course, they are not suitable. It is getting more and more difficult to find suitable qualified people and also, of course, more and more difficult to give those people a salary which to-day is adequate. In actual fact until quite recently in some societies some of these people have been battling on with pitiable salaries. They are very very low indeed. You cannot expect them to go on like that much longer.

Another point is that there are is a criticism very often that there are too many anti-vivisection societies. When I go round the towns and cities talking about anti-vivisection I am asked, "Why have you got so many societies?" - it is like religion. "Why have you got so many religions?" - and people ask, "Why cannot you get together because the ultimate object is the same." I went, for example, to a certain town in the North of England not long ago and by a stroke of good fortune I got a new Branch Secretary. When that lady got going and found her way around one of the first thing [sic] that lady said to me was, "You know, there is already a society here".

MR BELLIS: Are there many members of this London & Provincial Anti-Vivisection Society?

THE CHAIRMAN: Very few. They call themselves the London & Provincial Anti-Vivisection Society but I do not know how many members they have. It is probably something like 1,500 which is about 1,000 less than we have.

MRS BEDDOW BAYLY: I think it is true to say that the London & Provincial Anti-Vivisection Society have no branches and never had any branches.

THE CHAIRMAN: That is so.

MRS BEDDOW BAYLY: They deal direct with their members.

THE CHAIRMAN: That is right. This is only a provisional resolution. It is subject to a mutually satisfactory arrangement being agreed. We have not yet come to a satisfactory arrangement because we have not had the time for it. The matter arose only some 3 or 4 months ago and for the last 2 months at any rate it has been in the hands of the legal people.

MR BELLIS: I am all for amalgamation really.

MRS SHARLAND: Might it be possible to add this to what has been said. I personally would hope that might be a lead and that eventually all the societies would amalgamate into one large one. That would be very much more effective than a whole lot of small ones. That is another advantage.

THE CHAIRMAN: I think there is a desire to amalgamate so far as is constitutionally possible. The British Union cannot amalgamate with any other society unless they have as their basic charter the total abolition and nothing less, of vivisection. According to our rules and charter our ultimate object is the total abolition of vivisection but we are not precluded from taking part in other measures which, although not going to total abolition, will benefit our friend the animal. The British Union say they could not amalgamate but others, perhaps smaller ones, could.

MR BOWKER: ... supplements this saying that it had been our experience in the NAVS office during the last few weeks - and the London & Provincial Anti-Vivisection Society said they had precisely the same experience - that scores of letters of approval of the idea of amalgamation had come in as well as many verbal messages to the same effect, and not a single person has been opposed to it."

Ibid.

4 When Wilfred refers to "us", it is not clear which Society he means:

"A QUESTIONNER [sic]: Have you a flag day?

THE CHAIRMAN: There is not an anti-vivisection flag day.

MR RISDEN [sic]: There is an animal flag day, but not an anti-vivisection flag day. The Metropolitan Police are the people who lay down the conditions in regard to flag days and there is a committee that allows them. One of the causes which have been ruled out is anti-vivisection. For the same reason they ruled us out as a charity.

THE CHAIRMAN: Ladies and gentlemen, I am told tea is ready. I will now close the meeting and ask you to have tea."

Ibid.

5 The confirmation of Mr. Bowker's retirement was not so brief as to be peremptory, but there was no purple prose in evidence:

"It was unanimously agreed that a pension of £400 *per annum* be granted to Mr. Bowker on his retirement from the Society, and that a letter be sent to him recording the appreciation of the Executive Committee for the work he had done over a long period for the Society."

Minutes of NAVS Central Executive Committee Meeting, 17/10/56; courtesy of the NAVS

6 The need to formalise Wilfred's position was recognised in July, as soon as the NAVS officially received notification of the acceptance by the LPAVS of the necessity to cease operations:

"The Secretary informed the Committee that the London & Provincial Society had agreed that their organization should be formally dissolved and merged in the N.A.V.S. He had accordingly drawn up a set of Rules as so far agreed, and these would be submitted to our Solicitors in the course of a few days with a request that they proceed with the amalgamation scheme at their earliest convenience. Proposed by Mrs. Beddow Bayly, seconded by Dr. Young and carried unanimously, that a Resolution be sent to our legal advisors that the amalgamation of the two Societies shall be carried forth as quickly as possible.

The Secretary pointed out that Mr. Risdon's position at present was somewhat anomalous, as he had never been formally asked to become Secretary of the Amalgamated Society nor had any indication been given him as to the salary it was proposed to offer.

It was agreed that the actual engagement could not be made until after the amalgamation, but the following Resolution was passed and the Secretary was instructed to communicate its terms to Mr. Risdon:–

Proposed by Mrs. Beddow Bayly, seconded by Mrs. Gott and carried unanimously, that if Mr. Risdon is prepared to accept the Secretaryship of the amalgamated society, this committee is in favour of accepting him as Secretary at a salary of not less than £1.000 per annum, plus increments."

Minutes of NAVS Central Executive Committee Meeting, 19/09/56; courtesy of the NAVS

7 ***Minutes of Special Meeting of NAVS Central Executive Committee, 27/11/56; Minutes of NAVS Central Executive Committee Meeting, 19/12/56; courtesy of the NAVS***

8 http://en.wikipedia.org/wiki/National_Anti-Vivisection_Society
http://www.navs.org.uk/about_us/24/0/299/

9 Another substitute Chairman was Dr. Hugenholtz, President of the World Federation for the Protection of Animals:

"WORLD CONGRESS OF ANIMAL WELFARE SOCIETIES

On May 17th, 18th and 19th the World Congress met in London, 117 societies from 26 countries being represented.

The Congress opened on Monday, May 17th, with an address of welcome from the Chairman, The Right Hon. The Lord Burden, C.B.E., followed by speeches on various aspects of animal welfare …

The afternoon session was presided over by Dr. Hugenholtz, President of the World Federation for the Protection of Animals in the absence of Lord Burden, whose Parliamentary duties made it impossible for him to attend.

…

On Tuesday, May 18th, the whole of the morning session was devoted to the papers and discussion on Anti-Vivisection following the proposal by Peter Turner, British Union for the Abolition of Vivisection, of a motion seconded by Wilfred Risdon (London and Provincial Anti-Vivisection Society), in the following terms:

"This World Congress of Animal Welfare Societies declares that it is wrong to inflict suffering on any animal except for the individual good of the animal concerned; that the practice of vivisection is immoral; and that no plea of utility, either to man or to other animals, can justify animal experimentation of a kind that results in pain or suffering. It therefore demands the total prohibition of all experiments calculated to cause pain."

…

The Chairman announced that once again he would be unable to preside over the afternoon session and that Mr. Risdon would take the Chair in his stead.

…

On Wednesday, May 19th, Lord Burden again took the Chair at the morning session …

…

For the afternoon session, Mr. Risdon again took the Chair in place of Lord Burden ..."

The LPAVS Anti-Vivisection Journal News-Sheet, Vol. XV, No. 6, June 1954, p. 43; courtesy of the NAVS

10 "At the Convention of Animal Protection Societies held in London on April 23rd, 24th and 25th 1951, the whole of the last morning was devoted to a discussion on vivisection. A Resolution was submitted in the following terms:

"WHEREAS the practice of experimentation on living animals is morally unjustifiable, and

WHEREAS animal experiments yield misleading results when applied to treatment of human disease, and

WHEREAS alternative therapeutic measures can be and have been developed apart from animal experimentation with its attendant suffering,

THIS CONVENTION THEREFORE AFFIRMS that the practice of animal experimentation (generally known as vivisection) stands condemned and should be prohibited by law."

...

Mr. W. RISDON, of the London and Provincial Anti-Vivisection Society, said:

The plausible case put up by the other side on the scientific value of treatments resulting from animal experimentation made anti-vivisectionists sometimes wonder whether they were indeed the "cranks". So many imponderables were involved in animal experiments he claimed, that science had nothing to do with such matters. Scientific knowledge should be precise knowledge, but there was no precision in a system so full of "ifs" and "buts" as vivisection. Was it of scientific value to deliberately create diseases in animals and apply the results of study of such artificially induced diseases to the treatment of disease occurring spontaneously in human beings?

He quoted Lord Moynihan's observations as reported in *The Lancet* of 11th October 1930:

"The material of the human body is neither the same, nor subject to the same influences, as that of animals nearest to man; similar functions are not wholly discharged by precisely similar mechanism; the pressure of environment is not comparable in the two cases; and above all the mind of man is infinitely complex in comparison with that of the mot intelligent of animals. Other reservations are also necessary in respect of the validity of animal experiment. The changes produced in experiments upon normal animals are relatively gross; the change produced by disease in man, in the stages which should arouse our chief interest, are minimal, and of so fine a texture that we cannot properly compare them with these coarser induced conditions."

It was not only the anti-vivisectionist who stopped to think about such things, but eminent men in the medical profession had, from time to time stated that such experiments were misleading and they involved varying degrees of suffering to millions of animals. There was no cessation in the flow of animals into the laboratories year by year. Anti-vivisectionists must stop that flow of animals.

Vivisectors claimed that the "wonder drug", Penicillin, was the result of animal experimentation, and if there were no vivisection the drug would never have been discovered. This was quite untrue. The discovery of the drug was purely accidental, the result of a contaminated culture plate. The discovery of the drug came first then animal experimentation, which was really quite unnecessary followed. Furthermore, animal experiments seldom revealed toxic effects which only became manifest when the final experiment was made–on the human being.

Experiments on animals were increasing. Last year, in this country alone, more than 1,700,000 such experiments took place. There was no clear evidence to show that vivisection was truly scientific or that it had brought beneficial results to human beings which could not have been achieved by other means. A vast amount of time and money was spent on something which was sending the medical profession into "blind alleys" and producing nothing appreciable in return. Beneficial results could have been produced by other methods if vivisection had been closed to medical research.

...

During the afternoon session Dr. JEAN VINTER gave a resume of the work of the Universities' Federation for Animal Welfare, in the course of which she stressed that whatever may happen in the future the fact is that at present animal experimentation is a recognised form of research and animals used for such experiments must be considered in the light of existing circumstances. U.F.A.W. concentrated its efforts on mitigating the conditions of these animals and, for that purpose, maintaining friendly relations with the research workers in the laboratories throughout the country, many of whom were humane people who wished to do all in their power to alleviate unnecessary suffering to the animals which they used.

The Convention was restive throughout the period of Dr. Vinter's address and at its close the Anti-Vivisection Societies asked permission of the Chairman to make a brief reply to some of the points which had caused this restiveness. Permission being granted, Mr. Risdon, of the London and Provincial Anti-Vivisection Society was called on to reply, two minutes being allowed for that purpose.

Mr. RISDON said that in the time allowed he felt he could best deal with the matter by the use of a homely little parable along these lines:– Assume that there is a dangerous cliff-path where accidents are of frequent occurrence. Walkers using the path frequently miss their footing and fall to the bottom of the cliff, some being killed, some being crippled and some escaping with less serious injury. Recognising the dangers of the situation, one well-intentioned body of persons set out to deal with it by organising a well-equipped ambulance service at the foot of the cliff, ready to give first-aid to victims of such accidents and to make them as comfortable as human ingenuity combined with modern scientific methods could contrive. Another well-intentioned body of persons approached the problem from another angle. They too, recognised the danger and the suffering which fell upon the victims, but their remedy was to go to the *top* of the cliff, where they built a good stout fence, thus preventing the accidents and rendering unnecessary the ambulance service which would have dealt with the casualties. He went on to pay a very warm tribute to Dr. Vinter for her personal work of which he knew a great deal from association with her in various conferences of Animal Welfare Societies, but, he said, he felt that the work of U.F.A.W. was essentially ambulance work in this matter of laboratory animals, whereas the work of the Anti-Vivisection Societies was the work of erecting a barrier which would save such animals from the need for ambulance services of this description. Only by stopping at its source the practice of using living animals for experimental research could their sufferings be eliminated.

From the sustained applause which followed, the point appeared to have been well taken."

LPAVS News-Sheet, Vol. XI, No. 7, July/August 1951, p. 36; courtesy of the NAVS

11 ***LPAVS News-Sheet, Vol. X, No. 10, October 1950, p. 39; courtesy of the NAVS***

12 The whole process was very polite:

"THE GENERAL ELECTION

Before you receive the next issue of the News-Sheet the elections will have come and gone, and the composition of a new Parliament will be established.

Here, alphabetically arranged, is a list of members of the present Parliament who are sympathetic, in greater or lesser degree, to our aims:

[32 MPs listed]

All members should make a point of asking their candidates whether, if returned, they will help to protect and support legislation for the prohibition of experiments on living animals. The best way to seek this information is by writing, enclosing a stamped addressed envelope for a reply. This should be done whether the candidate appears in the above list or not, and we should be grateful to members for any information received in reply."

LPAVS News-Sheet, Vol. X, No. 2, February 1950, p. 5; courtesy of the NAVS

13 ***LPAVS Anti-Vivisection Journal, Vol. XVI, No. 5, May 1955, p. 40; courtesy of the NAVS***

14 It was

"Proposed by Mrs. Sharland, seconded by Mr. Harrold and carried unanimously that the following members of the present L&P Executive Committee be co-opted as members of the Executive Committee of the N.A.V.S. for the remainder of the present Society's year:-

Dr. Allinson, Mme de Chrapowicki, Dr. Dole, Mrs. Hort, Mr. Rienaecker, and Lady Tenterden."

Meeting of the NAVS Central Executive Committee, 17/10/56; courtesy of the NAVS

It took three months for the names to be put forward, by which time, the LPAVS had only just over two months of existence left, if everything went according to plan; given that the annual meetings of both Societies were in July, it seems slightly illogical that January should have been chosen as the start date for the new, amalgamated Society [and April has traditionally been the transition month for tax purposes in England], but the calendar year is universally recognised, in England at any rate, so this choice of date for the changeover is not entirely surprising. It was acknowledged at the July Meeting that there was no immediate urgency for the co-options to be decided, hence the lack of names being put forward:

"Proposed by Mrs. Beddow Bayly, seconded by Miss Stevens and carried unanimously, that this Committee hereby co-opts and [sic] six present members of the London and Provincial Committee to this Executive Committee on condition that if the amalgamation does not take place their co-option becomes void and that their first attendance is to be at a proposed Extraordinary General Meeting of the Council of the National Anti-Vivisection Society, to be called to settle the amalgamation."

Meeting of the NAVS Central Executive Committee, 18/07/56; courtesy of the NAVS

15 Readers were assured that their subscriptions were safe:

"PLEASE NOTE

Readers of the "Anti-Vivisection News" are asked to note that this will be the last issue to appear under that title. In the New Year, owing to the forthcoming amalgamation of the National Anti-Vivisection Society with the London & Provincial Anti-Vivisection Society, it has been decided to streamline the monthly publications of both organisations into one paper bearing the title "ANIMALS' DEFENDER & ANTI-VIVISECTION NEWS". All present subscribers to either of the existing papers will receive copies of the new publication for the whole of the unexpired portion of their subscriptions and we trust that it will meet with their approbation. It will be published from the office of the National Anti-Vivisection Society, 92 Victoria Street, London, S.W.1, to which address all future communications for the paper should be addressed.

We take this opportunity of thanking our very substantial list of subscribers for the loyal support which they have given in the past, without which the paper would not have been able to exist, and to plead for a continuance of such support for the new publication, which will be "new" in the sense of representing a marriage rather than a birth, for it will bring together two papers which have appeared side by side for a number of years.

In preparing for the amalgamation above-mentioned our staff have been working under great pressure and it will be impossible for us, this year to send our usual cards of Christmas Greetings. May we, therefore, through this message, wish all our members and readers—

A PEACEFUL CHRISTMAS AND A PROSPEROUS NEW YEAR"

LPAVS Anti-Vivisection News, Vol. XVII, No. 12, December 1956, p. 85; courtesy of the NAVS

16 Calls for Government action were always a preferred course of action:

"Nearly 3,000,000 experiments were carried out on living animals in this country alone each year, Mr. Wilfred Risdon, secretary of the National Anti-Vivisection Society, said last night in Glasgow at a meeting of the Scottish Anti-Vivisection Society.

The meeting passed a resolution to be sent to the Prime Minister, the Minster of Health, and the Secretary of State for Scotland calling on the Government to afford facilities for discussion in Parliament of ways and means to abolish vivisection."

The Glasgow Herald, Tuesday May 6, 1958, page 2

17 Oxnard is situated in Ventura County, Southern California, almost due west of Los Angeles, just inland from the Pacific coast, and is the 19th most populous city in California [motto: "The City that Cares"!].

http://en.wikipedia.org/wiki/Oxnard,_California

18 Unfortunately, no location was given for the development:

"**RESEARCH DOG CEMETERY**

LONDON (UPI) — Britain's Anti-Vivisection Society today went ahead with plans for a five-acre dog cemetery. Wilfred Risdon, 65, said the cemetery would accommodate dog victims of vivisection, as well as those which die of natural causes. But "fancy" burials for dogs are out, Mr. Risdon said. The cemetery will have simple metal plaques above the graves."

The Press-Courier, Friday, April 27, 1962, page 2

19 By 1961, the number of experiments had increased by around 15% in only 3 years, from the 3 million quoted in note 4 above:

"**UNWANTED PETS TRAFFIC**

"Ghastly trade"

Places in England where there is a 'flourishing traffic in unwanted pets, principally cats and dogs, which are sold to research laboratories', are referred to in the annual report of the National Anti-Vivisection Society which was published yesterday. Mr. W. Risdon, secretary, said the society had started a campaign to stop the traffic.

'We have made a beginning at Doncaster, which is one of the worst centres of this inhuman trade', he added. 'Voluntary helpers have been intercepting dogs on their way to Doncaster market to be sold to dealers who trade on the resale of healthy pets to laboratories where they undergo experiments carried out in the name of scientific progress ...

Upward of 3.5 million animals are being used for research experiments each year, so we decided to take action to try to check this ghastly trade in pets. After Doncaster we shall be moving to other trouble spots where this lucrative trade in animals is carried on. These include March in Cambridgeshire, Aldershot and district, and certain London districts.'"

Guardian, Wednesday, June 21, 1961, page 2

20 The BUAV had highlighted this problem in 1950:

"Doncaster was also a hot centre for the trade in dogs and volunteer workers kept a continuous watch for activity. As the trade was not illegal, it was important to educate the public about what might happen if they sold their dog to a stranger. A shop was offered rent-free for BUAV to run a campaign, and the Doncaster branch staged a demonstration at Doncaster central station on 10 May 1950 where a consignment of dogs awaited despatch to London. BUAV later hired a stall at Doncaster market which was used for distributing propaganda against the trade in dogs, together with general enlightenment on vivisection issues."

Campaigning against Cruelty: The Hundred Year History of the British Union for the Abolition of Vivisection, by Emma Hopley

21 ***Trusts Law: Text and Materials, by Graham Moffat, pp.859-861; Re Recher's Will Trusts [1972] Ch 529***

22 The wording very sensibly appears to anticipate a possible change of address, but not name:

"LEGACIES

To those of our readers who intend to benefit this Society under their wills we would respectfully urge the necessity of accurately describing the Society by its full title. The following form of wording is suggested:

I bequeath unto the Society called THE LONDON AND PROVINCIAL ANTI-VIVISECTION SOCIETY, *which has or had offices at 76 Victoria Street, London, S.W.1, the sum of .... free of Legacy Duty and I direct the same shall be paid to the Treasurer for the time being of such last mentioned Society."*

LPAVS News-Sheet, Vol. VII, No. 2, February 1947, p. 8; courtesy of the NAVS

23 ***swarb.co.uk; Wills and Probate - 1970-1979; Re Recher's Will Trusts [1972] Ch 529;***

http://www.swarb.co.uk/lisc/WilPr19701979.php

24 The Chancery division is a part of the High Court of Justice. The areas of work that it deals with include trust claims.

http://www.justice.gov.uk/courts/rcj-rolls-building/chancery-division

25 http://en.wikipedia.org/wiki/Re_Recher's_Will_Trusts

26 This legal term simply means among themselves:

"**inter se**

(in-tur say) prep. Latin for "among themselves," meaning that, for instance, certain corporate rights are limited only to the shareholders or only to the trustees as a group."

http://dictionary.law.com/Default.aspx?selected=1007

27 ***swarb.co.uk; Wills and Probate, etc., op. cit.***

28 Literally; among the living:

"**inter vivos**

(in-tur veye-vohs) adj. Latin for "among the living," usually referring to the transfer of property by agreement between living persons and not by a gift through a will. It can also refer to a trust (inter vivos trust) which commences during the lifetime of the person (trustor or settlor) creating the trust as distinguished from a trust created by a will (testamentary trust), which comes into existence upon the death of the writer of the will."

http://dictionary.law.com/Default.aspx?selected=1012

29 ***Trusts Law: etc., op. cit.***

30 ***swarb.co.uk; Wills and Probate; op. cit.***

At this first meeting, Wilfred was described as the General Secretary:

"MINUTES OF THE FIRST MEETING OF THE COUNCIL

Held at 7 Montagu Mansions, W.1.; on Tuesday, 16th July, 1963; Time 1.45pm

PRESENT: The Lady Dowding (Chairman), Mrs. Brash, Miss D. Hamilton-Andrews, Mrs. J. LeFevre, Mr. Rienaecker, Mrs. Sharland, Miss Stevens, Mrs. Stevenson-Howell, Mrs. Williams, Mr. Spens (Fladgate & Co.), Mr. W. Risdon (General Secretary), Mrs. Joynson and Mr. Colin Smith in attendance.

The Chairman opened the meeting by remarking that we were very delighted to have Mr. Spens with us at the first Meeting of the Council.

...

MATTERS ARISING: Incorporation. (Mr. Spens was present to assist in this connection).

(a) The Members of the Council appointed by the subscribers formally took their seats.

(b) The Certificate of Incorporation was produced and handed over to the General Secretary.

(c) Election of Chairman. It was moved by Mrs. Sharland, seconded by Mrs. Stevenson-Howell and agreed unanimously that Lady Dowding be elected as Chairman for the ensuing year.

(d) Mr. Spens produced the seal, which was adopted as the Seal of the Society, and it was agreed that an imprint of it should be made in the Minute Book as a formal record.

(e) Appointment of:-

(i) Secretary. Lady Dowding reminded the Council of their wish some months ago to make Mr. Risdon a Director, and that the reason for such an appointment was that the then Committee wished to acknowledge what Mr. Risdon has done and to keep him with us. This now seemed an appropriate time to make the change.

Mr. Spens pointed out that the Articles of Association, as at present constituted, did not provide for a Director but that the Council could make Mr. Risdon a Member of the Council if they so desired. He would then have a vote and could serve in this capacity as well as Secretary.

It was proposed by Lady Dowding and carried unanimously that Mr. Risdon should be appointed as Secretary and as a Member of the Council. It was further agreed that Mrs. Joynson should be appointed as Deputy Secretary, and Mr. Colin Smith as Assistant Secretary.

...

(f) It was resolved that the registered office be 27 Palace Street, London, S.W.1.

(g) The Agreement between the Trustees of the unincorporated Society and the Society in the form approved at the Council Meeting of the unincorporated Society held on June 18th 1963, was duly signed and handed to Mr. Spens to have it stamped.

(h) It was unanimously resolved that the Incorporation be reported to members of the unincorporated Society and that their signatures should be obtained to written forms of Consent to becoming members of the Society."

Minutes of Meetings of the NAVS Council; courtesy of the NAVS

No explanation is given for this, and subsequent meetings being held at Montagu Mansions, but it must be assumed that the lease for the property was owned by the Society, because at the Council Meeting in March, 1964

"It was proposed by Mrs. Williams, seconded by Dr. Allinson and carried unanimously, that the Secretary be empowered to go ahead and either try to find a buyer for the lease of 7 Montagu Mansions or to sub-let."

Minutes of the NAVS Council Meeting, 17/03/64; courtesy of the NAVS

31 As ever, these proposals for a merger were a long time in the gestation and, in this case, still-born:

"At the AGM in 1958 a resolution was passed requesting the Executive Committee to explore the possibility of a fusion with NAVS. BUAV approached NAVS and it was agreed to hold a joint conference with four committee members from each society. The first meeting was held on 30 January 1959 at which two main points were considered: firstly, whether fusion between the two societies was possible; and secondly, if it was possible, then how could this best be achieved.

The whole matter proved to be a great deal more complicated than had been anticipated. The financial aspect of the proposal in particular proved to be a 'substantial obstacle'. Eventually, at a further joint conference on 8 August 1959, it was decided to recommend that the idea of fusion should be dropped. Instead it was agreed that the two societies should find a way of working together more closely through a Joint Consultative Council. These recommendations were adopted by the committees of both societies and the first meeting of the Joint Consultative Council took place on 20 November 1959."

Campaigning against Cruelty: etc., op. cit.

Wilfred appears to have had a very cordial relationship with his namesake Wilfred Tyldesley, Secretary of the BUAV; at the first meeting, several points were covered, including the somewhat sensitive issue of earlier expulsions of several members, now influential members of the NAVS, from the BUAV; also, a scheme was mooted which will be dealt with in more depth later in this chapter:

"Private & confidential

JOINT CONSULTATIVE COUNCIL
of the B.U.A.V. and N.A.V.S.

FIRST MEETING
20th November 1959

PRESENT: Dr. M. Beddow Bayly, Mrs. Beddow Bayly, Dr. Belden, Mrs. Lief, Mr. Risdon, Mr. Rushbrooke, Mr. Tyldesley.

…

CHAIRMAN: Dr. Belden was elected to the Chair for the present meeting. Dr. Beddow Bayly was elected permanent Chairman for future meetings and Dr. Belden was elected Vice-Chairman.

INAUGURATION: The Chairman moved, and it was unanimously agreed, that the meeting constitute itself the Joint Consultative Council of the British Union for the Abolition of Vivisection and the National Anti-Vivisection society.

EXPULSIONS: Mrs. Beddow Bayly referred to the expulsion from the B.U.A.V., many years ago, of Dr. Beddow Bayly, Dr. Fergie Woods and others. It was generally felt that something ought to be done to make amends for this, and the Chairman said he would bring the matter to the attention of the B.U.A.V. Executive Committee.

FINANCING OF BURSARIES: The question of financing bursaries for individuals to be trained as anti-vivisection doctors and scientists was discussed, but in view of obvious difficulties was deferred.

DEPARTMENTALISATION OF ACTIVITIES: The question of organising the work of the two Societies in such as way as to avoid duplication and competition was considered at length, and it was agreed to do everything possible in this direction. N.A.V.S. delegates drew attention to the work of their new Research Bureau and Library, and the B.U.A.V. delegates agreed to recommend to their Executive that the B.U.A.V. should finance a further full-time worker at the Bureau by taking a suitable person on their staff and seconding him/her to the Bureau.

PRIZE FOR HUMANE RESEARCH: There was further discussion of the proposal to offer prizes for research leading to the discovery of a technique which would render obsolete the use of experimental animals in any particular branch of research. Other interesting suggestions which could be related to this approach were discussed and approved in principle. The whole scheme will be reported upon in detail at a later stage. … "

Minutes of the Joint Consultative Council of the BUAV and NAVS; courtesy of the NAVS

32 ***The Animals' Defender and Anti-Vivisection News, vol.1, no.9, September 1957, cited in Animal Rights: Political & Social Change in Britain since 1800, by Hilda Kean***

33 ***Campaigning against Cruelty: etc., op. cit.***

34 Although Lord Shaftesbury, the first President of the ancestor of the NAVS, the Society for the Protection of Animals Liable to Vivisection, had urged his fellow campaigners "to accept it as a framework on which subsequent amendments could be made … when the Act was eventually superseded 110 years later by the Animals (Scientific Procedures) Act of 1986 it had not been amended once."

Ibid.

35 ***Ibid.***

36 ***Ibid.***

This caused two interruptions to a significant Council Meeting:

> "REPORT OF ANIMAL RESCUE AND ORGANISING SUB-COMMITTEE: Reports had been submitted and discussed at the morning's meeting, and it had been agreed to re-order 'Bic' pens.
>
> …
>
> During this discussion Mr. Risdon was twice called to the telephone to make a statement to the 'Daily Express' with regard to the forthcoming Home Office Departmental Committee of Inquiry. They claimed to have received information that the Inquiry is not prepared to accept evidence on questions previously reviewed by two Royal Commissions to show whether experiments on animals are justified or if they have any useful results.
>
> The question was raised whether, in view of this new information, we should refuse to have anything to do with the Inquiry. The answer to this question was that if the facts were as stated we should want to have even more to do with the Inquiry to ensure compliance with the original terms of reference."

Minutes of the First Meeting of the NAVS Council, 16/07/63; courtesy of the NAVS

37 ***Ibid., page 72***

38 ***Ibid.***

39 Dr. Maurice Beddow Bayly, MRCS, LRCP, 1887-1961, was also a Theosophist, and a member of the National Anti-Vaccination League; many of his publications were on the subject of vaccination, whose efficacy [and necessity] he refuted, and one of these was called ***The Schick Inoculation Against Diphtheria***, so it is most likely that Wilfred will have been collaborating with him during his dealings with the BBC on the subject of Diphtheria, and in his own output on the subject. Four months before his death in June 1961, Bayly was admitted a Chevalier of the Order of the Lion and the Black Cross, which seems curious for a member of the Theosophical Society, with its generally ecumenical remit, but he had received the minor orders in the Catholic Church earlier in life; he had eschewed the life of a priest as he knew that he would not be in a position to carry out the regular duties required. He wrote on vaccination in 1944, and these views are still finding a resonance in the twenty-first century:

> "Perhaps the greatest evil of immunization lies in its diversion of public attention from true methods of disease prevention. It encourages public authorities to permit all kinds of sanitary defects and social problems to remain unaddressed, particularly in schools. It ignores the part played by food and

sunlight and many other factors in the maintenance of health. It exaggerates the risk of diphtheria and works upon the fear of parents. The more it is supported by public authorities, the more will its dangers and disadvantages be concealed or denied."

http://san-luigi.org/2012/08/15/members-of-the-san-luigi-orders-maurice-beddow-bayly/

http://en.wikipedia.org/wiki/Maurice_Beddow_Bayly

40 The Russians did not reveal the true cause of the death of Laika, which translates literally as 'Barker', until 2002; initially, they claimed that she was euthanised prior to oxygen depletion. It is likely that she died within hours of the launch, possibly caused by a failure of the central R-7 sustainer to separate from the payload, so her death appears to have achieved virtually nothing.

http://en.wikipedia.org/wiki/Laika

41 Louise [generally known as Lizzy] Lind af Hageby was Swedish by birth, but became a British citizen in 1912. She was very active in animal welfare and protection, and with Nina Douglas-Hamilton, wife of the 13th Duke of Hamilton, co-founded the Animal Defence and Anti-Vivisection Society, and ran a 237-acre animal sanctuary with her at her home, Ferne House near Shaftesbury in Dorset. She was a skilled orator, either waging or contesting at least two libel suits, defending herself in one, although the praise she received for her advocacy was inevitably, in the male-dominated manner of the time, very condescending.

http://en.wikipedia.org/wiki/Louise_Lind-af-Hageby

http://en.wikipedia.org/wiki/Animal_Defence_and_Anti-Vivisection_Society

42 The details of the Hearings are given in the text, but there is distinct ambiguity about whether Wilfred could have appeared in person or not, had the circumstances been different. The first morning had been occupied by 'learned' testimony from pro-vivisectionists who were nonetheless professing their aspirations for 'humane' treatment of research animals; Mrs. Christine Stevens, President of the Animal Welfare Institute of New York, New York, had read out her own voluminous testimony and given the Committee "a few large pieces of literature, which you might wish to examine." The length of time this took caused the Chairman of the Subcommittee on Health and Safety, Mr. Roberts [Kenneth A. Roberts, Alabama] to consider winding up the morning session:

"I see that we are running pretty close to the noon hour. I would like to see if I can make some arrangements to proceed with the two witnesses from Great Britain after we resume the hearing this afternoon, which will be at 2 o'clock, and, before we recess, I would like to talk to Dr. Jones to see if we can make some arrangements to cover the witnesses who are in opposition to the bill. I want to hear from all sides and all segments of this problem. I am going to try to be as fair as I can with the distribution of time. ... We do have a large number of witnesses, and the Chair would appreciate any consideration which any witness may give to the committee. Are there any witnesses who plan to leave the city this afternoon and who might like to file their statements for the record? If you will hold up your hands, I will be glad to allow you that privilege."

A Mrs. Henry Gardner, president of the Montgomery County [Maryland] Humane Society, offered to file her statement, even though [as the record shows immediately thereafter] it was only three paragraphs long. Mr. Stevens, who was not identified by his affiliation, asked leave to "file also a number of statements given to me by people who are not going to appear, knowing the time is short"; presumably this did not include Owen B. Hunt, president of The American Anti-Vivisection Society, Philadelphia, Pennsylvania, who followed immediately thereafter, because although he filed his submission, he was there in person, and could therefore speak for himself. His submission actually consisted of two separate articles: ***Vivisection versus Regulation***, and ***Can Vivisection be regulated? England's Experience says "no"***, but before that, he bemoaned the lack of notice he had been given:

"We learned of this public hearing on the two bills now being considered by this committee only Tuesday, September 23, and we therefore are unable to present to you at this hearing the witnesses and their testimony as to why, in our opinion, this is bad legislation."

The Chairman of the Subcommittee, the Hon, Kenneth A. Roberts, had clarified the situation regarding the scheduling of these Hearings straight away:

"These bills attracted a great deal of interest throughout the country. For some time we have been trying to work out a schedule for hearings on these bills but, as it is well known, the Committee on Interstate and Foreign Commerce has been very busy this session with legislation on transportation, communications, health, war claims, drugs, and other subjects. We have just now had an opportunity to hold hearings on these bills."

However, one of Hunt's colleagues, the branch director from Washington, D.C., echoed Hunt's criticism of the precipitate scheduling of the Hearings:

"Mr. Chairman, the National Anti-Vivisection Society wanted very much to present testimony to this committee when hearings were scheduled on these measures now before you, and we have diligently made this known. As recently as July 28, 1962, the Honorable [sic] Oren Harris, chairman of the full committee, assured us by telegram that we would be given ample notice when hearings would be scheduled.

The notice we received on Tuesday of this week did not give us that ample time to prepare the material we regard as vital for the committee's consideration of such an important, but complex problem, involving not only uncounted millions of animals, but every man, woman, and child in America, nor to bring to Washington experts in this field who could give testimony invaluable to this committee for its careful consideration."

Hunt's second, and much shorter statement, is concluded by the following, which precedes the statements of the three British experts:

"Let us heed rather the experience of those, who have seen the actual results of such alleged regulation over a long period of years. This experience has amply demonstrated that abolition, not regulation, is the only answer."

After these submissions, at 12:20 p.m., the Hearing was adjourned for lunch, so Dr. Jones was not able to give his testimony until well into the afternoon session.

Hearings before a Subcommittee of the Committee on Interstate and Foreign Commerce, House of Representatives, Eighty-Seventh Congress, Second Session, on H.R. 1937 & H.R. 3556, 28 & 29 September, 1962;
http://www.nal.usda.gov/awic/pubs/AWA2007/hr19621937.pdf

43 Presumably Wilfred's statement was read out and transcribed contemporaneously, because of the Americanisation of the spelling, which is evident in all of the British statements:

"VIVISECTION IS FUNDAMENTALLY EVIL

(By Wilfred Risdon, Secretary of the National Anti-Vivisection Society of Great Britain)

It is a fundamental fact that if a thing is evil it does not become beautiful by putting a new frock on it or by wrapping it up in pretty wrapping paper. It is evil, it is fundamentally evil, and the thing to do with something that is fundamentally evil is to fight it uncompromisingly until you have strangled it out of existence. That is our attitude to vivisection. We view it as an evil, an evil which must be fought and which must be driven out of existence.

Now, we have from time to time had the English language enriched by words added to it from across the Atlantic, and there is one which comes to my mind at the present moment which seems to sum up this American bill very effectively— "ballyhoo". And it does, indeed, sum up the whole intent, as I see it, of the American bill. It is ballyhoo; it is to bamboozle the public and to kid them into believing that something effective is now being done to harness an evil and to make for humane treatment of animals.

We have our own problems in this country and I am firmly convinced that many of our problems have been made more difficult owing to the number of people who believe that something controlled by act of Parliament cannot be completely cruel—a misguided belief on their part, but a sincerely held belief. We come up against it all the time with well-intentioned people who say "We think you must be exaggerating because, after all, vivisection in this country is controlled by act of Parliament and therefore there should be no cruelty." We have then to point out to them that the people who determine the degree of protection for the animals are the very people who are themselves indulging in the practice of vivisection which causes the suffering to the animals; and to be judge and jury in one's own cause and to give oneself acquittal is not consistent with English standards of justice, at least.

SPECIOUS ARGUMENTS

Now, we have had similar cases in the past: specious arguments, the old selfish arguments, come up from time to time—that this is necessary for human welfare. We learn so much for human medicine by these practices; and that seems to give them sanction for all these atrocities which they perpetrate on our fellow creatures, which are often referred to as "the lower creation". Heaven help us if we consider ourselves to be the higher creation, so long as we can do such things. We have had, in the past, the same arguments applied to slavery. We were told that slavery was necessary for the plantations in the South: no other labor [sic] could do the same work that the slave labor could, and therefore the slaves must not be emancipated. But eventually they were emancipated, and the plantations all continued, and thrived and flourished pretty successfully, as one can see when one considers the millionaire fortunes of our tobacco kings.

We in this country had the same argument applied to child labor and slave labor and, owing to the activities of such pioneers as Lord Shaftesbury, also a pioneer in the fight against vivisection, child labor in the factories and mines was abolished in this country, and the factories did not go bankrupt, and the mines did not go out of existence because they could not get child labor. They just went on flourishing.

And the same is true of medicine. If we can abolish this vicious practice, which so often proves to be misleading, I am sure that we shall get more accurate information about the treatment of human diseases and human ailments than ever we can get in this way. Let us develop the infinitely great lines of research that are concerned with clinical investigation, investigation of what happens to human beings who are suffering from disease, and learn from them, from the accumulation of knowledge of successful treatment as compared with unsuccessful treatment. There you have the sort of remedy that can make for human health, together with a better way of living that avoids the causes of illness. There is our case and there are our lines of territory. And all these arguments for the old vicious system to go on because it is necessary and because it is harmless as long as it is controlled are fallacious, misleading, and can lead only to damnation."

Ibid.

44 In 1973, HRC was describing itself as "the largest independent laboratory in the Medical and Biological Sciences in Europe and due to a new phase in our extension coupled with unprecedented increase [sic] in related research work" was advertising six categories of vacancy, some of which required multiple incumbents, in the ***Glasgow Herald***:

"All of the vacancies advertised are located in modern laboratories just north of the London commuter belt, where excellent career opportunities exist [sic]. The Company offers excellent working conditions with progressive general benefits and a competitive salary. The usual pension, canteen, sports and social facilities, etc., exist and removal expenses will be paid if appropriate."

Glasgow Herald, Monday 26/02/73, page 2

Very little biographical information seems to be available about Professor [or more usually, Dr.] Worden, other than that he was the Director [later Chairman] of HRC and a member of the Society of Toxicology. He appears to have had long-standing associations with the USA, as he submitted a discussion paper, ***Handbook on Laboratory Animals***, to the American journal ***Science***, in June 1944. In 1982, he was Professor of Toxicology at Bath University.

http://www.nzavs.org.nz/mobilise/10/10.html

http://www.sciencemag.org/content/100/2587.toc.pdf

Only eight months after his submission to the Congressional Hearing, he cast doubt, no doubt unintentionally, upon the validity of his own methods, when he gave a report on the problem with the drug Thalidomide, rather curiously in the closing session of the American Industrial Hygiene Conference:

> "One reason Thalidomide was unsuspected so long in birth defects was that laboratory animals seem less sensitive to it than humans, according to a British researcher. Dr. Alastair Worden said … his studies at Huntingdon Research Center [sic], Huntingdon, England, indicated rabbits, rats and mice required five or six times the comparable human dose of thalidomide to produce similar deformities. He said many defects were minor and may have been missed by research teams, and not all could be blamed on the drug."

Hamilton, Ohio, Journal and The Daily News, Tuesday 14/05/62, page 11

Late in his life, he seems to have had an attack of conscience, or something approaching it:

> "Scientists who experiment on living animals agreed this week that they could halve the number of animals they use immediately—if ministers co-operate. The scientists from firms like Shell and Pfizer, and the Porton Down and Huntingdon research stations, joined with University academics to compile a report for the Fund for the Replacement of Animals in Medical Experiments (FRAME). … Professor Alistair Worden, the group's scientific secretary and the professor of toxicology at the University of Bath, told *New Scientist* that a combination of 'bad science and bad legislation' has led to the present state of affairs, where four million experiments are conducted on animals in Britain each year. … A mindless insistence on crude body counts—such as the LD50 test, which determines how much of a chemical will be required to kill half the treated animals—is largely to blame for today's impasse, they argue. 'Governments like LD50 because it is a number, like a traffic speed limit', Worden said. … The civil servants who regulate the marketing of new drugs often know little about toxicology. They 'ask rather foolish questions and demand another test', says [Dr. Vernon] Brown [of Shell's toxicology laboratory]. That way they are covered 'in case a drug turns out to be another Thalidomide', says Worden. … The group does not report any startling new alternatives to animal tests. … The group does urge more detailed research in humans, however. 'There is no substitute for human use', says Worden."

newscientist, vol. 96, no. 1330, 4 November 1982, page 275

45 The Universities Federation for Animal Welfare [UFAW, founded 1926], "is an internationally recognised, independent, scientific and educational animal welfare charity concerned with improving knowledge and understanding of animals' needs in order to promote high standards of welfare for farm, companion, laboratory, captive wild animals and those with which we interact in the wild". It is interesting [and informative] that none of the recognised anti-vivisection societies has a link from this site, although plenty of so-called "welfare" and "prevention of cruelty" sites, and those dealing with alternatives to animal testing do.

http://www.ufaw.org.uk/index.php

For want of a unified source of biographical information [such as

Wikipedia], it is necessary to assemble a partial biography from disparate sources. Hume was one of those people with an odd, incongruous combination of character traits: a devoutly religious military man:

"Charles Westley Hume also known as Major C. W. Hume was an important figure in British twentieth century thought about animal welfare. He was also a professing [sic] Christian in the Anglican Church, and wrote works on animals and Christian thought (***The Status of Animals in the Christian Religion*** [1956], ***Man and Beast*** [1962]), and also argued in other books the case for the humane use of animals in scientific experiments. Richard Haynes remarks about Hume's influence that (page 7):

Major C. W. Hume should be credited as the father of the animal welfare movement. He was instrumental in founding the University of London Animal Welfare Society (ULAWS) in 1926, which subsequently became the Universities Federation of Animal Welfare (UFAW)"

Animal Welfare: Competing Conceptions and Their Ethical Implications, Richard P. Haynes, cited in Animals Matter to God blog, 09/05/2012;

http://animalsmattertogod.wordpress.com/2012/05/

The "father of the animal welfare movement" quote above is risible, for obvious reasons, which is not to diminish Hume's work, of course, but especially because in another blog post on the same site only a month later, a reference by Hume to an illustrious precursor [by around a century] is mentioned:

"Major C. W. Hume's (1957:1) study ***The Status of Animals in the Christian Religion*** was not intended to be a work of history. Nevertheless, C. W. Hume did look back at aspects of the Christian tradition noting which theologians contributed helpful and unhelpful understandings about the status of animals. At the start of his book C. W. Hume mentions Broome …:

The founder and first secretary of the R.S.P.C.A. was an Anglican priest, the Rev. Arthur Broome, who gave up his living in order to reform the treatment of animals. Owing to the apathy of the public he was soon in prison for the Society's debts, from which discouraging situation he was rescued by the generosity of a Jew and of a jovial Irish duellist and humanitarian, Richard Martin."

Ibid., 16/06/2012;

http://animalsmattertogod.wordpress.com/tag/major-c-w-hume/

During his life and military career, Hume acquired the appellations of O.B.E. [awarded in 1961 'for his services to animal welfare'], M.C., B.Sc., M.I. Biol., and he was later appointed Director-General of UFAW. He was also a founder and member of the Society for Freedom and Science. In 1940, prior to his later promotion, he was known as Captain Hume, of the Royal Corps of Signals:

"CAPTAIN C. W. HUME resigned from the editorship of the ***Proceedings of the Physical Society*** on January 1, after having been responsible for that journal for a period of twenty years. A member of the reserve of Army officers, he rejoined his unit some time previously, and continued his editorial work until impending changes made it no longer possible. During his tenure of the office, he had seldom missed a Council meeting, and was usually present at science meetings, to obtain a record of the discussion on papers at first hand. He took great pains with the preparation of the ***Proceedings*** to ensure that papers should be free from ambiguity and obscurity, and printed in uniform style. His other interests were many. He founded the University of London Animal Welfare Society and the Universities Federation for Animal Welfare, and had also taken an active part at one time in the Association of Scientific Workers and the Parliamentary Science Committee, as it then was."

Nature 145, 180-180 (03 February 1940) | doi:10.1038/145180b0; News; http://www.nature.com/nature/journal/v145/n3666/abs/145180b0.html

46 In the eight years before these Hearings, Worden had contributed to a research project with which Hume and his organisation was involved:

"In 1954, the Universities Federation for Animal Welfare decided to sponsor a systematic research on the progress of humane technique in the laboratory, and in October of that year we began work on the project. ... In 1956, we prepared a general report to the Federation's committees, and this report formed the nucleus of the present book, which was completed at the beginning of 1958. ... Throughout our work, we have received constant help of many kinds from the staff and committees of the Federation, and over much of the period we worked with a special Consultative Committee, with Professor P.B. Medawar, C.B.E., F.R.S., in the Chair. We have also received valuable assistance from the Animal Welfare Institute of the U.S.A., which also contributed financially to the UFAW research.

A large number of individuals, inside and outside UFAW, have contributed helpful information. Without attempting an exhaustive list, we may mention M.R.A. Chance, Phyllis G. Croft, D.G. Davey, P.S.B. Digby, T.G. Field-Fisher, Professor H. Heller, **Major C.W. Hume**, M.C., W. Lane-Petter, F.K. Sanders, Christine Stevens, F. Jean Vinter and **Professor A.N. Worden**. Chance, Croft, **Major Hume** and Lane-Petter read drafts of the whole text and provided further helpful comments."

The Principles of Humane Experimental Technique, by W.M.S. Russell and R.L. Burch;

http://altweb.jhsph.edu/pubs/books/humane_exp/preface

The American ***Science*** magazine had discussed a precursor of these bills, Senator Cooper's S.3570 [which was also mentioned in the Hearings], and how the negative image of scientists observed among young people was not helping their cause:

"When Mead and Metraux asked high school students to describe a scientist, the composite image turned out to be that of a pretty unpleasant sort of fellow: 'He may wear a beard, may be unshaven and unkempt ....' His laboratory is identified by 'the bubbling of liquids in test tubes and flasks, the squeaks and squeals of laboratory animals, the muttering voice of the scientist . . . . He experiments with plants and animals, cutting them apart, injecting serum into animals' [***Science 126, 384 (1957)***].

This unpleasant, even sinister, image seems to have influenced the 13 senatorial sponsors of a bill (S. 3570) aimed at curbing scientists' presumably inhumane treatment of their animal subjects [***Science 131, 1658 (1960)***]. The sponsors agree that animal experimentation is essential. They agree that experimental animals should be treated humanely. With these premises scientists would also agree. But few will agree with the implicit assumption that cruelty to animals is a common occurrence in research laboratories or with the proposed means of preventing it. …

It would be silly to deny that there may be occasional violations of good practice, but passage of this bill would punish the many in the hope of preventing lapses by the few. It would hamper the work of many laboratories and especially those that observed its requirements most meticulously.

The bill will not be acted upon this year; but it may be introduced again. … The supporters of S. 3570 seem to have taken their cue from the high school students' image of a scientist instead of from the behavior [sic] and principles of scientists themselves."

Humane Treatment of Animals, by Dael Wolfe; Science, v. 132, no. 3418, 01/07/60;

http://www.sciencemag.org/content/132/3418/7/full.pdf

The discussion was also aired in Britain the following year, mainly at the instigation of Hume's UFAW, in an article entitled ***Biologists back British vivisection practice***:

"Three blunt questions about British law and practice in respect of experiments on animals have been put to 88 research workers, most of them biological Fellows of the Royal Society, by the Universities Federation for Animal Welfare. The questions are, first, whether it is true that, in consequence of the Home Office system of licensing and inspection, medical research of the highest quality cannot be carried out in Britain. The second is whether they would prefer Home Office control to be abolished so that persons without scientific training would be permitted to experiment on animals without supervision: and the third is whether, in their experience, they have found that the British system seriously frustrates legitimate research. The almost overwhelming response in favour of the British system (only one unnamed scientist out of the 88 approached felt that he was frustrated by Home Office control) may do much towards influencing opinion on the subject in the USA where experiments are virtually uncontrolled. The views of the the British scientists have now been sent by UFAW to the Animal Welfare Institute in New York.

UFAW is an organisation with a reputation for handling exceptionally delicate matters in an exceptionally delicate manner. What persuaded it to intervene in an apparently national issue was a sharp attack on British medical science, a side-effect of the stormy passage of the so-called Cooper Bill in the United States. This was legislation introduced into both houses of Congress last year by a distinguished group of thirteen senators including Cooper, Mansfield, Kefauver and Morse.

The bill 'to provide for humane treatment of animals used in experiment' was based, essentially, on British practice and contains a clause to the effect that no grant from Federal funds will be given to any person experimenting on animals unless he gets a 'certificate of compliance' with the act from the Minister of Health, Education and Welfare. The bill lapsed for reasons of time but has now been re-introduced into the current session by Representative the Hon. Martha Griffiths. Curiously enough, it has been attacked, violently, by the anti-vivisectionists on one side and the National Society for Medical Research on the other.

The NSMR has taken the line that medical research in Britain is backward and it is so because of the frustrating effects of Home Office control. The opinion of Major C. W. Hume, the Secretary-general of UFAW, is that although certain minor amendment of our law and practice, not involving questions of principle and not relevant to the Cooper Bill, might be desirable, there can be no doubt, from answers to the questionnaire, that Home Office control is a great success. Of the scientists approached, 21 simply answered 'No' to each question put to them, and 66 answered 'No' and added comments, most of which strongly reinforced their support for the British system, though there were a few minor criticisms on matters of detail. The one who felt frustrated by Home Office control wanted to carry out certain experiments on the brain and considered that the pursuit of knowledge in this field was impeded by the 'Pain Rule'."

New Scientist, no. 220, 2 February 1961, pp. 257-8; Notes and Comments

47 No praise was spared for these speakers:

"Mrs. STEVENS. Professor Worden, as you have stated, is the director of the Huntingdon Research Center [sic]. He is a biochemist and a veterinarian and a pharmacologist. He is coeditor of the ***'Handbook on the Care and Management of Laboratory Animals'***, which I submitted to the Committee this morning, which is the well-known text, the very best one on this subject.

Professor Worden is also the editor in chief of the scientific journal, ***Animal Behaviour***, which is Anglo-American; it operates on both sides of the Atlantic. …

Mr. ROBERTS. … We will have the pleasure now of hearing from Prof. A. N. Worden.

The Chair would like to say that we are very grateful to you for coming. We know that you have traveled [sic] many miles, and probably in some bad weather, too, to be here, and we are certainly appreciative of your fine work in your own country. And we appreciate the efforts you have made to be here and give us the benefit of your testimony. We are very grateful to you.

…

Mrs. STEVENS. Major Hume is the founder of the Universities Federation for Animal Welfare, which is a unique animal protective society in that all of its members are either students or graduates of universities, and there are many, many biological members; for example, Professor Medawar, the Nobel Prize Medal winner in 1960 in biology and medicine was the Chairman of their scientific sub-committee.

And many of the most distinguished scientists assist in the work of the Universities Federation.

Major Hume was also a founder and member of the Society for Freedom and Science and has all his life been a scientist, a physicist, and devoted his efforts for the past 25 years to animal welfare. Last year he received the Order of the British Empire for his services to animal welfare.

Mr. ROBERTS. Thank you very much.

Major, it is a pleasure to have you. And we appreciate the effort you have made to be our guest, our witness. And we will certainly be delighted to hear from you."

Hearings before a Subcommittee; etc., op. cit.

48 As previously noted, virtually all the spelling in British documents has been Americanised. Hume is quite caustic:

"Hearings on H.R. 1937.

To the Honorable KENNETH ROBERTS.

DEAR CONGRESSMAN ROBERTS: May I add to the record the following comments on the testimonies of two witnesses?

Dr. Helen Taussig's fanciful account of the hindrances to which Dr. Blalock's work would have been exposed is sufficiently refuted by the letter from Sir Russell Brock, which is included in my testimony. Brock originated some well-known improvements in the blue-baby operation and his letter shows that Dr. Taussig's statements are pure inventions without any foundation of fact.

Dr. Pfeiffer raised a valid objection to the Moulder bill, but did so in a manner which calls for comment. His sneer about two worms on a hook prompts me to compare Charles Darwin, who always killed his worms before using them for fishing, with Dr. Pfeiffer who set a boy of 17 to poison mice with the venom of the black-widow spider and to watch them die the excessively painful death which resulted. However, although the inclusion of invertebrates in the ambit of the bill is logical enough, it simply is not practical politics. If British experience is any guide, the line must be drawn between vertebrates and invertebrates, if there is to be any hope of eventually rallying enlightened scientific opinion behind the desired reforms. In this matter we have to be guided not by rigorous logic but by what is practicable of the existing level of ethics.

Believe me, with repeated thanks for the honor of testifying to your Committee,

Yours sincerely,

C. W. HUME."

Ibid.

49 ***Public Law 89-544 Act of August 24, 1966:***

"***Summary***: Enacted August 24, 1966, Public Law 89-544 is what commonly is referred to as The Animal Welfare Act although that title is not mentioned within the law. It authorizes the Secretary of Agriculture to regulate transport, sale, and handling of dogs, cats, nonhuman primates, guinea pigs, hamsters, and rabbits intended to be used in research or 'for other purposes.' It requires licensing and inspection of dog and cat dealers and humane handling at auction sales. The complete amended act can be found in United States Code, Title 7, Sections 2131-2156.

89th Congress, H. R. 13881
August 24, 1966
An Act"

http://awic.nal.usda.gov/public-law-89-544-act-august-24-1966

50 ***Animal Welfare Act - Senate Report 1281 on 1966 Animal Welfare Act:***

"In order to accomplish these goals, the law directed the U.S. Secretary of Agriculture to set up a regulatory program to license all dealers in dogs and cats, to register all animal research facilities, and to provide humane care provisions, enforceable through inspections. To help eliminate the black market in pets, research facilities were required to purchase dogs and cats from licensed dealers. To help track down stolen pets, a system of record keeping was required for all animal dealers and animals research facilities. To assure the humane treatments of animals, the Secretary of Agriculture was authorized to establish an inspection program and adopt the necessary regulations. One of the more curious aspects of the 1966 Act was the limited list of animals which came under it: dogs; cats; primates; guinea pigs; hamsters; and rabbits.

Material in Full:

The Committee on Commerce, to which was referred the bill (H.R. 13881) to authorize the Secretary of Agriculture to regulate the transportation, sale, and handling of dogs and cats intended to be used for purposes of research or experimentation, and for other purposes having considered the same, reports favorably [sic] thereon with amendments and recommends that the bill as amended do pass."

http://www.animallaw.info/administrative/adussrep1281_1966.htm

51 Harley Street has not always been owned by the de Walden family:

"In 1711 the grid of streets around Harley Street, known as The Estate, was passed to Henrietta Cavendish Holles (the Duke of Newcastle's daughter) who married Edward Harley (the 2nd Earl of Oxford). Between 1715 and 1720, Edward, with the assistance of architect John Prince, decided to develop the streets around Cavendish Square for residential purposes naming many of the streets after members of the family. When Edward died the Estate passed to his daughter, Margaret Cavendish Harley who married the second Duke of Portland, and the area became known as The Portland Estate.

The Dukes of Portland had ownership for five generations until the fifth Duke died without issue in 1879 and the land passed to Lucy Joan Bentinck, widow of the 6th Baron Howard de Walden and thus it became the Howard de Walden Estate."

History of Harley Street;

http://www.harleystreetguide.co.uk/about/History/

"Today, Harley Street is owned by the de Walden family and the Howard de Walden Estate has been managing almost all of the 92 acres of real estate from Marylebone High Street, Portland Place and from Wigmore Street to Marylebone Road for the past 300 years. The Estate was responsible for the redevelopment of many of the houses in 1900, which followed strict guidelines to maintain the original Georgian style architecture."

About Harley Street, London; http://www.harleystreetguide.co.uk/about/

52 Harley Street is very much marketed as a commodity, hence the website:

"All the latest technology and cutting edge medical expertise has been moved into the area, and not surprisingly Harley Street is a highly desirable location from which to practice. [sic] The area attracts a large ever growing, number of top medical practitioners, dentists, psychiatrists and plastic surgeons providing first class care, each of whom require [sic] a licence from the Estate in order to practice. ... Today, there are some 1,500 professional medical practitioners in and around the Harley Street area, offering a broad range of services from complementary medicine to cosmetic surgery and the range and quality of services available continues to expand as new treatments and new diagnostic techniques emerge. ***The Harley Street Clinic*** receives patients from all over the world and has established a ground breaking cancer centre, which is affiliated to the ***London Cancer Group*** and contains the latest oncology technology and expert care for cancer patients. Harley Street is at the forefront in medical science and technology advancements and firmly on the map for medical excellence."

Ibid.

53 ***Ibid.:***

"The Estate has always been particular about the type of people allowed to practice [sic] from Harley Street, and between the two world wars for example an application from a resident to let out a room to a dancing teacher was strongly rejected. Until after the Second World War, which was a real catalyst for change, masseurs and psychologists were treated with suspicion."

54 ***Courtesy of the Howard de Walden Estate Ltd.***

55 This architectural genre "first manifested itself in domestic architecture beginning in the United Kingdom in the mid to late 19th century based on a revival of aspects of Tudor style."

http://en.wikipedia.org/wiki/Tudor_Revival_architecture

Number 51 Harley Street was rebuilt in 1894, to the designs of the architect F. M. Elgood, who did a great deal of similar work for the Estate; on the site before that, there had been a public house called *The Turk's Head*, and that was built in 1758. Up until 1755, there had only been four houses built in Harley Street, even though John Prince's plan for the Estate had appeared in 1719, mainly as a result of delays in the development process and the notorious 'South Sea Bubble' affair.

Courtesy of the Howard de Walden Estate Ltd.

56 *Ibid.*

57 It wasn't until two months before the NAVS & LTMT moved into 51, Harley Street, at the end of June 1964, that any mention of Wilfred [and Nellie, although this is not explicit] occupying the residential section of the building was made in the Minutes of the Council. Of course, it is attractive to speculate that this might have been a special consideration, or reward, for Wilfred in recognition of all his hard & dedicated work, and it was most definitely appreciated: at the March Council Meeting, "Mrs. Sharland said she would like to congratulate our Secretary on all he had done in connection with 51 Harley Street because it was his brilliant, quite extraordinary letter, that pulled it off. All present endorsed this view."; but it is more likely that the apartment was seen as a 'perk' for the Secretary, taking on the additional responsibility of caretaker, while living on site. It is interesting that a residential usage of the premises, even if only partial, was allowed, because they had previously been classified as residential, but it had been deemed necessary to change this for the new lessees:

> "New Premises. The Secretary reported that everything is going through satisfactorily. Planing permission to change from "residential" to "business user" is now with the L.C.C. If they satisfy themselves, they refer the matter to the Marylebone Council. If there are no objections, we can then go ahead with preparation and signing of the Lease. … "

Minutes of the NAVS Council Meeting, 15/10/63; courtesy of the NAVS

There is no reason to suppose that Wilfred's offer to cover the renovation cost was anything other than genuine:

> "Premises. The Secretary reported that everything seems to be moving forward now. The builders are working at 51 Harley Street at present and it was hoped it would be possible to move in on the week-end following Whitsun. It now remained for the Lawson Tait Memorial Trust to decide how to arrange the first and second floors. The flat was going ahead and Mr. Risdon said he would bear the expenses of the renovations to the flat himself.
>
> …
>
> Mrs. Harrison referred to the remark made by Mr. Risdon that he would bear the expense of making the flat habitable himself. She said that surely except for the fact that we have taken the lease on 51 Harley Street he would not be moving from his present flat, and therefore should not the Society see that the flat is habitable for whoever is going to occupy it.
>
> This proposal was seconded by Mrs. Brash and it was unanimously agreed that a recommendation to this effect be made to the Lawson Tait Memorial Trust."

Minutes of the NAVS Council Meeting, 21/04/64; courtesy of the NAVS

58 Tait's career, despite his relatively short life, is too comprehensive to be able to do it justice in a few lines or paragraphs, but there are several biographies to be had, not all of which are still in print; this author understands that the NAVS should still have some copies of Wilfred's excellent biography, which should be available on request, and some of the internet book resellers seem to have copies also. A synopsis from Tait's

Wikipedia page [which references Wilfred's biography] is a useful supplement to the information in the chapter above:

> "**Lawson Tait**, born **Robert Lawson Tait** (May 1, 1845 – June 13, 1899) in Edinburgh, Scotland, became a pioneer in pelvic and abdominal surgery and developed new techniques and procedures. He emphasized asepsis and reduced surgical mortality significantly. He is well known for introducing salpingectomy in 1883 as the treatment for ectopic pregnancy, a procedure that has saved countless lives since then. Tait and J. Marion Sims are considered the fathers of gynecology. [sic] … he was instrumental in the opening of the Birmingham Hospital for Women where he worked for 20 years. …
>
> Tait was a strong opponent to animal experimentation. His comment: ' ... after we have found out what (experimental drugs) do in one animal we find that in another the results are wholly different and the process of investigation has to be repeated in man.'
>
> Tait was well recognized during his time, a founder and member of professional societies, and published extensively. He died of kidney failure.
>
> The Lawson Tait Society, an undergraduate history of medicine society at the University of Birmingham Medical School, is named in honour of Tait. They have embarked upon a project of digitising Tait's work and resources related to Tait."
>
> http://en.wikipedia.org/wiki/Lawson_Tait

Note: since the above page was compiled, the Lawson Tait Society has become dormant, "as no students have stepped forward to organise their programme for [the] last two years" hence the lack of a link; courtesy of the Director of the History of Medicine Unit at the University of Birmingham, Jonathan Reinarz.

Email to the author from Jonathan Reinarz, 3 September 2012

59 This quote is taken from Wilfred's 1967 biography of Tait and, although there is no specific date given for any sort of 'Damascene conversion', nor any obvious assertion that this viewpoint was congenital, so to speak, it can be extrapolated from the following additional extract from the paper called *On the Uselessness of Vivisection upon Animals as a Method of Scientific Research*, that he read before the Birmingham Philosophical Society, of which he "was an influential member" [ref. WR], on April 20th 1882, that his viewpoint was formed in the early 1860s, when he was at Edinburgh University [entering at the age of 15], if not earlier:

> "I dismiss at once the employment of experiments on living animals for the purpose of mere instruction as absolutely unnecessary, and to be put an end to by legislation without any kind of reserve whatever. In my own education I went through the most complete course of instruction in the University of Edinburgh without ever witnessing a single experiment on a living animal.
>
> It has been my duty as a teacher to keep myself closely observant with the process of physiology until at within the last four years, and up to that date I remained perfectly ignorant of any necessity for vivisection as a means of instructing pupils, and I can find no reason whatever for its introduction into English schools, save a desire for imitating what has been witnessed on the Continent by some of our most recent additions to physiological teaching.

In Trinity College, Dublin, the practice has been wholly prevented and, on a recent visit to that institution, I could not find, after much careful inquiry, the slightest reason to believe that any detriment was being inflicted upon the teaching or upon those taught."

Robert Lawson Tait, 1882, quoted in Lawson Tait, A Biographical Study, by Wilfred Risdon

60 The connection with the NAVS went back to 1897, if not before:

"Also read communications, as follow:–

...

note and telegrams of Nov. 1st and 2nd, from Mr. Lawson Tait, asking for copies of the "Hecatorish" [difficult to discern from handwriting] to go to the Midland Medical Society and reported that these had been sent;"

Minutes of the NAVS Central Executive Committee, 03/11/1897; courtesy of the NAVS

Although no specific references to Tait's association with the LPAVS are to be seen, its predecessor was formed in 1876, and would have been just as much a part of the London anti-vivisection movement as was the NAVS, to which Tait wrote:

"On a certain afternoon in June, 1876, an Anti-Vivisection meeting was held at the house in Prince's Gate, the London home of Mrs. Madden Gordon. On that occasion, Miss Marston founded, on a basis of total abolition, the Association now known as the London and Provincial Anti-Vivisection Society. ..."

LPAVS News-Sheet, No. 16, October 1941, p. 1; courtesy of the NAVS

Either Wilfred found some documentary evidence of Tait's association with the LPAVS when he joined, or he was already aware of it from discussion with like-minded colleagues, but that notwithstanding, in 1945 he published a short piece on Tait's centenary, and it included a reference to Tait's 1882 lecture quoted in note 59 above, so perhaps this was where the seeds of the idea for the biography were sown?

"On May 1st, 1845, Robert Lawson Tait was born in Edinburgh. He was destined to become one of the most outstanding figures of modern times in the realm of surgery. In commemoration of the anniversary, the Midland Medical Society, the University of Birmingham and the Women's Hospital will organise a joint Lawson Tait Celebration ceremony at Nuffield House, Queen Elizabeth Hospital, on June 20th, and an oration in his honour will be delivered by emeritus Professor Leonard Gamgee. Is it, we wonder, merely coincidence that the name of the chosen orator is the same as that of one of Lawson Tait's most bitter opponents during his lifetime–Mr. Samson [sic] Gamgee. Lawson Tait was wholeheartedly opposed to vivisection and Samson Gamgee was all for it. Will Professor Gamgee give credit to Lawson Tait for the great stand that he made against the antiseptic technique of Listerism, which was based upon animal experiments, and his own successful use of the aseptic technique. One quotation of Lawson Tait's which is well worth remembering at this time is that which he made on the occasion of the paper read before the Birmingham Philosophical Society in 1882, on the "Uselessness of Vivisection as a Method of Scientific Research", in the course of which he said:

'I am inclined to make the claim for physiology, pathology, and the practice of medicine and surgery that the very retention of this cruel method of research is hindering real progress, that if utterly stopped the result would certainly be the search for, and the finding of far better and more certain means of discovery ... If the method of obtaining evidence by torture was occasionally successful, there can be little doubt that as a rule it failed and led the inquiries astray. So I say it has been with vivisection as a method of research, it has constantly led those who have employed it into altogether erroneous conclusions, and the records teem with instances in which not only have animals been fruitlessly sacrificed, but human lives have been added to the list of victims by reason of its false light.'"

LPAVS News-Sheet Vol. 5, No. 6, June 1945, p. 23; courtesy of the NAVS

61 It is obvious from the Minutes of the Meetings of the JCC that the BUAV was included in the planning for a suitable vehicle for a memorial to Lawson Tait at the earliest possible stage; in fact, it was an integral part:

"PRIZE FOR HUMANE RESEARCH: There was further discussion of the proposal to offer prizes for research leading to the discovery of a technique which would render obsolete the use of experimental animals in any particular branch of research. Other interesting suggestions which could be related to this approach were discussed and approved in principle. The whole scheme will be reported upon in detail at a later stage."

Minutes of the Meetings of the Joint Consultative Council of the BUAV and NAVS: first meeting 20th November 1959; courtesy of the NAVS

62 Richard Reader Harris represented Heston and Isleworth for the Conservatives from 1950 until the 1970 general election on June the 18th, when he was replaced by 'Barney' Hayhoe; the reason for this supplanting was that there was an ongoing trial because he had been charged the previous year with "carrying on company business with intent to defraud the company's creditors, falsifying the balance sheet, and deceiving investors as to the company's financial state." That company was Rolls Razor Ltd., of which he was the Chairman, and it acquired some notoriety in the 1960s, going bankrupt in 1964, but the opprobrium was more generally associated with the company's owner, John Bloom, who came in for heavy criticism regarding his direct sales business methods. It is difficult to discern from Harris's obituary, in 2009 [in the accompanying photograph, he looks for all the world like a passable *Doppelgänger* for Ronnie Barker, with his thick-framed spectacles] what his interest in animal testing might have been; other than being a member of the Church of England's House of Laity, his business practices sailed very close to the wind, and the only obvious association with animals seems to have been when he

"was a director of Livestock Marketing, an armchair pig farming scheme which crashed, after he left, with losses of £1 million. Its promoter, Norman Mascall, was jailed for fraud; Board of Trade inspectors would say it was 'difficult to understand or accept' Reader Harris's answers to their questions, and while he had done the work he had been paid for, he clearly knew nothing about pig breeding."

http://www.telegraph.co.uk/news/obituaries/politics-obituaries/5780068/Richard-Reader-Harris.html

http://en.wikipedia.org/wiki/Richard_Reader_Harris_(politician)

The occasion when Harris asked about animal testing seems to be the only one when this subject was raised by him:

> "*Mr. R. Harris* asked the Minister of Health, as representing the Minister for Science, if Her Majesty's Government will make a grant for research to be made into alternative methods of discovering remedies for illnesses which do not involve the necessity for experiments on living animals.
>
> *Mr. Walker-Smith* Much research sponsored by the Medical Research Council is already devoted to this purpose and my noble Friend is satisfied that as and when further research on these lines offers a reasonable prospect of results, the Medical Research Council will undertake it."

HC Deb 11 December 1959 vol 615 c83W; Illnesses (Remedies);

http://hansard.millbanksystems.com/written_answers/1959/dec/11/illnesses-remedies#S5CV0615P0_19591211_CWA_14

63 ***Campaigning against Cruelty: etc., op. cit.***

64 The official BUAV history reflects the fact that it, the NAVS, and most, if not all, of the other anti-vivisection & animal welfare organisations were thinking along very much the same lines at that time, even down to the form of words here:

> "Increasingly, BUAV began to see promotion of alternatives as a more realistic way to end vivisection, rather than through an Act of Parliament on which it had pinned its hopes for so many years. It was estimated that by using techniques such as tissue culture and computer models over 90 per cent of all current animal experiments could become obsolete. However there was an increasing realisation from the anti-vivisection movement that it would have to take the initiative itself, as successive governments failed to allocate funds specifically for non-vivisectional medical research. The Lawson Tait Memorial Trust was founded jointly by BUAV, NAVS and the Scottish Society for the Prevention of Vivisection in 1961."

Ibid.

65 As ever in these situations, there is a sequential, and necessarily derivative, progression of ideas, so it is difficult to pinpoint where the suggestion of viable alternatives to animal testing originated; it seems odd that such an obvious strategy was not the cornerstone of animal welfare organisations before the 1950s but perhaps, as stated in the body of the text before this reference, the two camps were diametrically opposed before this, and perhaps they squandered energy in this opposition rather than investigating possibilities of reaching an accommodation. In 1955, a three-year project that considered alternatives to animal testing was initiated by UFAW: although the UFAW website is not specific about the original brief for the study, one of the available documents which elucidate this study [and there are several] describes what can probably safely be assumed as a rationale:

"Supporting key research initiatives has proved a very effective strategy for bringing about major changes of attitude and improved animal welfare on a large scale. For example, during the 1950s, a UFAW project undertaken by William Russell and Rex Burch resulted in the development of the principles of the Three Rs as set out in their influential book: ***The Principles of Humane Experimental Technique***. The Three Rs have been adopted around the world as the key guiding principles for the welfare of animals in research and this has resulted in, and continues to drive, huge welfare improvements."

http://www.ufaw.org.uk/ufaw-sawi.php

The "Three Rs" are to be found in a different document:

"UFAW supports the principle of the 'Three R's' in the use of animals in scientific procedures:

- Replacement - the use of non-animal subjects wherever possible, and the research, development and validation of new non-animal research and testing models;
- Reduction - where replacement is not currently possible, the minimising of the number of animals used by, for example, better research design, appropriate statistical methods and use of information databases;
- Refinement - improvement of experimental procedures and aspects of housing and husbandry so as to minimise risks to welfare."

http://www.ufaw.org.uk/animal-welfare.php

A modicum of clarification of the timescale is to be found in the above document:

"2005 marks the 50th anniversary of the initiation of the UFAW project by William Russell and Rex Burch which led to the publication in 1959 of The Principles of Humane Experimental Technique (reprinted in 1992). This introduced the Three Rs concept of Replacement, Reduction and Refinement which has been adopted as a guiding principle for the welfare of research animals worldwide"

Unfortunately, even this description of the timescale of the project is not complete, so a supplement has to be found in yet another document:

"The principles of the Three Rs - Replacement, Reduction and Refinement were developed by the UFAW Scholars, Professor William MS Russell and Rex Burch. The Three Rs have had a huge impact in improving the welfare of animals in research and are now used and accepted World-Wide. The Three Rs were first presented at a UFAW symposium in 1957 entitled ***Humane Techniques in the Laboratory***. ***The Principles of Humane Experimental Technique*** was published in 1959."

http://www.ufaw.org.uk/highlights.php

66 The BUAV's plans for premises went one step further than the LTMT's:

"In 1969 BUAV announced its own plans for a humane research institute which was to be set up in honour of the man who was the 'backbone' of the society for 28 years, Dr. Hadwen. This would be a centre where scientists could use non-vivisectional techniques to carry out research into human diseases and to train other scientists in these methods. The proposal was the 'brainchild' of General Secretary, Sidney Hicks. The proposed name of the institute was The Walter Hadwen Foundation and the initial target was to raise £100,000 over a five-year period which would be put into a separate account to establish a charity. Discussions about the institute and fundraising for alternative research methods started in 1970, and led to many important debates on the subject. …

The Dr Hadwen Trust for Humane Research was registered as a charity in 1970 to raise funds for building the institute and in order to develop as an independent organisation. In the meantime the Trust offered sponsorship to postgraduate students who were training in non-animal research techniques. By 1973 however plans to build a research institute were put on hold, partly

> because of the huge amount of money needed, but also because it appeared that scientists preferred to work in existing, established laboratories. The trustees therefore decided to concentrate on raising funds to combat three major diseases: arthritis, cancer and diabetes. The money raised was used to make grants to scientists working on non-vivisectional techniques to research into these diseases, and to buy essential equipment for their research work."

The BUAV does allow a small amount of space to explain the LTMT in its printed history, but their medical expert Dr. Hadwen is also credited with realising the importance of Lawson Tait early in the anti-vivisection campaign:

> "The object of the Trust was to make grants and award prizes for original work of outstanding value to medicine, conducted without the use of live animals and of such a nature that research with living animals in a particular field would be shown to be inexcusable. The founding of the Trust brought widespread publicity and the Trust hoped to set an example for the government to follow.
>
> The Trust was named after a famous 19th century Scottish surgeon, Robert Lawson Tait. Tait had been an anti-vivisectionist and when Dr Hadwen wrote to him for his views on the subject he replied that 'vivisection has done nothing for surgery but lead to horrible bungling', a quote which Hadwen used many times in his debates on the anti-vivisection platform. The Trust was to be an autonomous body, entirely independent from any of the societies which had established it.
>
> ... on 25 September 1964, the official headquarters of the Trust opened in Harley Street, London ..."
>
> ***Campaigning against Cruelty: etc., op. cit.***

67 At the final minuted JCC Meeting on the 7th of April, 1961 [there was a note at the end, to the effect that "the next meeting [would] be convened on a suitable date following the preparation of the Lawson Tait Trust Deed.", but this appears not to have taken place, or it was minuted elsewhere], the Lawson Tait Memorial "was discussed at some length and the following points were agreed:

> "1. The need to appoint Trustees as soon as possible after the terms of the Trust Deed have been finalised. Also, to treat as a matter of urgency the invitations to suitable people to act as "monitors" for the project. (In this connection a suggestion of Mr. Risdon's that Major Hume might be invited to act as one of these was approved).
>
> 2. That as soon as the Trust Deed has been approved it should be submitted to the Charity Commissioners for recognition as a Charity.
>
> 3. That we synchronise the various elements which we have in mind so as to yield the maximum impact, these being (A) The presentation of the petition with approximately 100,000 signatures; (B) The release of review copies of the new publication "Clinical Medical Discoveries"; (C) The Question in The House asking for allocation of funds for non-animal research; (D) Press Conference to bring these matters together in one parcel for the information of the general public.
>
> 4. After discussion it was agreed that there should be no attempt to provide for "grants in aid" from the fund. It was thought that this would introduce too great a risk of biased claims on the fund and awards might lead to charges of discrimination in favour

of specialised forms of treatment. It would be much more satisfactory to urge the allocation of a certain proportion of public funds to research free from animal experimentation and to give from the fund awards for results rather than grants for actual projects to be undertaken.

5. Again it was stressed that once the Trust was established it should be the aim of its sponsors to interest other individuals or companies who had philanthropic intentions to subscribe to the continuance and extension of its work with the possibility in view of the endowment of chairs in the teaching of medicine and surgery by means other than experiments on living animals, and that this aspect should be made known to the press, at the press conference."

Minutes of the Meetings of the Joint Consultative Council of the BUAV and NAVS: seventh meeting 7th April 1961; courtesy of the NAVS

68 Once again, the progress was the result of the close co-operation between the Secretaries of the two JCC Societies; also, as seen in note 67 above, the need for action at parliamentary level was recognised:

"Correspondence which had passed between the two secretaries and correspondence with the solicitors was discussed. It was also reported that the Scottish Society for Prevention of Vivisection had expressed a desire to be associated with the scheme and had subscribed £2,000 towards its finances. This sum had been placed in a separate deposit account earmarked for this purpose.

It was left to the Secretaries to get agreement on the instructions to Counsel and to try to synchronise the publicity for the launching of the scheme with the presentation of the next batch of signatures to the parliamentary petition."

Minutes of the Meetings of the Joint Consultative Council of the BUAV and NAVS: sixth meeting 25th November 1960; courtesy of the NAVS

69 ***Campaigning against Cruelty: etc., op. cit.***

70 These were: ***British Medical Journal, The Lancet, British Journal of Clinical Practice, British Journal of Experimental Pathology, British Journal of Pharmacology, British Journal of Surgery, Journal of Clinical Pathology, The Practitioner, Cambridge University Medical Society Magazine, Oxford Medical School Gazette, Kings College Hospital Magazine, University College Hospital Magazine, Queens Medical Magazine, Midland Medical Review, Quarterly Journal of Experimental Physiology, Veterinary Record, and The New Scientist.***

Some of the notices took the form of adverts, and included either a photograph of Lawson Tait seated at his desk, as in the case of an advert placed on the first of September 1962; there is an example of a proof, or what could actually have been used as a handbill, which is large enough for that purpose, at 210 x 275 mm, containing a large amount of information, on sale on a "History through Advertising" website; it was placed, appropriately enough, given Lawson Tait's Scottish heritage, in a publication called ***Braemar Gathering***, that was issued as a book supporting the Braemar Highland Games, which were held in September 1962. The book is published each year to provide information on past & present Games. Courtesy of Richard Roberts at Blue Angel;

http://www.blueangel.org.uk/product.asp?session=20090006A2WKXO6TX9B7MMQ0Z9VROKL5PWXTUTSZ4VKOZ9XFMV&product=51602

while other notices were somewhat more minimal, such as the one placed in the ***New Scientist***, on the 10th of May, 1962, which featured a photogravure reproduction of Tait's head only, above the text:

"BIG PRIZES
are offered for original
MEDICAL RESEARCH

by a New Nobel type fund with an initial
foundation of £5,000 which we hope will
be increased by Public Subscription

Further information from
Secretary to the Trustees
LAWSON TAIT MEMORIAL TRUST
c/o Midland Bank Limited
22 Victoria Street
London, S W 1"

New Scientist (No. 286), 10 May 1962, page 290

71 UNWANTED PETS TRAFFIC: ***The Guardian, 21st June, 1961, page 2:***

"**"Ghastly trade"**

Places in England where there is a "flourishing traffic in unwanted pets, principally cats and dogs, which are sold to research laboratories", are referred to in the annual report of the National Anti-Vivisection Society which was published yesterday. Mr W. Risdon, secretary, said the society had started a campaign to stop the traffic. ..."

It appears that the earlier meeting was not called for the specific purpose of 'unveiling' the scheme, but it was seen as an appropriate opportunity, albeit local:

"Lawson Tait Memorial. It was agreed that the meeting of Birmingham Rotary Club, which Mr. Risdon had been invited to address on 17th would be a suitable occasion for the introduction of the scheme in that area."

Minutes of the Meetings of the Joint Consultative Council of the BUAV and NAVS: fifth meeting 23rd September 1960; courtesy of the NAVS

72 LETTERS TO THE EDITOR : ***The Observer, Sunday, 5th March, 1967, page 12:***

"Animal experiments

Sir,—As Mr Slatter says in his last Sunday's letter, the Lawson Tait Memorial Trust was started with donations from three societies (not one, as stated by Mr Blue the week before), but his remark that each society gave £3,000 is incorrect. The Scottish Society for the Prevention of Vivisection gave £2,000; the British Union for the Abolition of Vivisection and the National Anti-Vivisection Society gave £1,500 each.

Because of its original foundation there appears to be a growing misconception that this is 'another anti-vivisection society'. In fact, the Trust is a medical research society formed to encourage the search for alternative methods of medical research which would not depend on the use, or misuse, of living animals. The Trust has received support from a very wide section of the community, including doctors and scientists who wish to see greater use made of such modern techniques as computers and of other promising but hitherto neglected methods of investigation and treatment. The Trust is willing and anxious to co-operate with others working in the same way.

W. Risdon,
Secretary, Lawson Tait
Memorial Trust
51 Harley Street, W1."

The letter from Mr. Blue was also referred to in the same edition by the founder of FRAME who, notwithstanding her ignorance on the subject of "a fund to assist research work" was keen to point out the difference between the LTMT and her precursor organisation:

"Sir,—Mr M. A. Blue suggests (19 February) that Dr Foister, whose letter about the Promoters of Animal Welfare you printed recently, should have mentioned the Lawson Tait Memorial Trust as a body active in seeking improved alternatives to the use of animals in medical research. May I say that while this body is concerned with long-term studies, the Promoters of Animal Welfare believe that the use of tissue culture methods should be widely adopted straight away.

We know that scientists who use these new techniques say they are scientifically, economically and ethically superior substitutes for animals and we think there should be a fund to assist research work in developing these techniques to an even greater extent.

(Mrs) Dorothy Hegarty,
Organiser,
The Promoters of Animal
SW10. Welfare."

Ibid.

73 Hobden's Wikipedia page is minimal and, apart from disclosing a prior career as "a postal and telegraph worker who became an officer in the Union of Post Office Workers", after which he was elected MP for Brighton Kemptown in 1964, thereby becoming the first Labour MP for a Sussex constituency, there is no indication of an obvious interest in animal welfare.

http://en.wikipedia.org/wiki/Dennis_Hobden

74 Crosland was appointed Secretary of State for Education and Science in 1965 under Harold Wilson's premiership; prior to that, just after the war, he had tutored the likes of Tony Benn [previously Sir Anthony Wedgwood Benn] and the McWhirter brothers in Economics at Oxford. He had a coincidental, albeit tangential, connection with Wilfred, in that his parents were members of the Exclusive Raven Taylor Plymouth Brethren.

http://en.wikipedia.org/wiki/Anthony_Crosland
http://hansard.millbanksystems.com/people/mr-anthony-crosland

75 Denis Howell was Under-Secretary from 1964 to 1969, after which he was twice Minister of State, from 1969 to 1970 (Housing and Local Government), and 1974 to 1979 (the Environment). He was also Minister for Sport from 1964 to 1970, and for Sport and Recreation from 1974 to 1979. His stint at Environment attracted some ridicule when he was made Minister for Drought in 1976 [but nicknamed Minister for Rain], but after heavy rain at the end of the driest summer in 200 years caused widespread flooding, he was made Minister for Floods! This associative procedure was continued during the harsh winter of 1978-9 when he was appointed Minister for Snow.

http://en.wikipedia.org/wiki/Denis_Howell,_Baron_Howell

http://hansard.millbanksystems.com/people/mr-denis-howell

Minister of State can mean different things in different countries, but in the United Kingdom, this is a relatively new position, only existing since 1945, and it is an extra level of administration, being 'shoehorned' in between the top post which is Secretary of State, and the Under-Secretary:

> "A Minister of State is a member of Her Majesty's Government, junior only to a Secretary of State but senior to a Parliamentary Under-Secretary of State and Parliamentary Private Secretaries (PPSs). Ministers of State are responsible to their Secretaries of State. This position has only existed since 1945 - previously, each parliamentary under-secretary was directly beneath a secretary of state. There can be more than one Minister of State at any government Department. Ministers of State may have departmental PPSs, or a PPS might be assigned to them. Of a similar standing to Ministers of State are positions such as the Solicitor General, the Deputy Leader of the House of Commons, Treasurer of HM Household, Captain of the Yeomen of the Guard, Paymaster General, Financial Secretary to the Treasury and Economic Secretary to the Treasury. Ministers of State are bound by the Ministerial Code of conduct."

http://en.wikipedia.org/wiki/Minister_of_State#British_diplomacy

76 On the 6th of April that year, he took over as Minister of State for Public Buildings and Works, for just over a year, and took over at Education and Science in March 1974, although he was only in office there for fifteen months.

http://en.wikipedia.org/wiki/Reg_Prentice

77 ***HC Deb 17 February 1966 vol 724 c287W; Lawson Tait Memorial Trust;***

http://hansard.millbanksystems.com/written_answers/1966/feb/17/lawson-tait-memorial-trust

78 ***Campaigning against Cruelty: etc., op. cit.***

The original infirmary on the site was completed in 1903, and the hospital housed London's first hyperbaric unit:

> "The hospital is geographically close to the site of the 2012 Olympics, has one of the largest and busiest A&E departments in the UK and serves a diverse community from Chigwell to Leyton. The hospital also has the lowest MRSA rates in London for three years running as of 2008."

http://en.wikipedia.org/wiki/Whipps_Cross_University_Hospital

79 There is room for some doubt about the exclusivity, although the Council Minutes are slightly ambiguous:

> "51 Harley Street. The recommendation from the sub-committee that a meeting of doctors be held as soon as practical was approved and it was agreed to recommend to the Lawson Tait Memorial Trust that invitations to the meeting be extended to: The Lawson Tait Memorial Trust panel of doctors; Drs. Latto; Dr. Jordan; Dr. Allinson; Dr. Stoddard; Mr. Lang Stevenson; Mr. A.M.A. Moore; Dr. Geoffrey Knight; Dr. George Miller; Dr. Frank Wokes."

Minutes of the NAVS Council Meeting, 21/04/64; courtesy of the NAVS

80 With reference to paragraph 4 of note 67 above, this seems to be something of a *volte face*, as previously, grants in aid were thought to be open to claims of bias:

> "4. After discussion it was agreed that there should be no attempt to provide for "grants in aid" from the fund. It was thought that this would introduce too great a risk of biased claims on the fund and awards might lead to charges of discrimination in favour of specialised forms of treatment. It would be much more satisfactory to urge the allocation of a certain proportion of public funds to research free from animal experimentation and to give from the fund awards for results rather than grants for actual projects to be undertaken."

Minutes of the Seventh Meeting of the Joint Consultative Council of the BUAV and the NAVS , 07/04/61; courtesy of the NAVS

81 The Humane Research Trust [HRT] was formed in 1974 by the Trustees of the LTMT "[w]ith the help of the Commissioner of Charity … to give the wider scope that was needed while retaining the original aims." This would no doubt have been seen by the absolutists [such as the BUAV] as yet another dilution of the necessity for abolition and a concession to the vivisectionists, but it is a testament to Wilfred's pragmatism that the trend of numbers in animal testing is definitely downwards, and even the late Chairman of the Research Defence Society, Professor D. H. Smyth, was moved to write a book called ***Alternatives to Animal Experiments*** after visiting HRT headquarters in 1976. It is not entirely clear why the LTMT could not have embodied this more realistic approach, but perhaps it was felt by the Trustees that, in the public mind, it was too closely associated with the anti-vivisectionism from which it emerged, so a new identity would not be tainted in the same manner:

> "Gradually the new Trust became known, and grants were applied for. There was a wariness on both sides. Although the Trust sought advice from scientists about the quality of programmes seeking grants there was some hesitancy on the part of the scientific world to align itself with this new, unknown body with its 'dubious background'. But techniques were being developed that would eventually reduce enormously the number of animals used in research. …
>
> Then problems of a more fundamental nature showed the great gulf between the anti-vivisectionist and the forward-thinking scientist. When the Trust was formed it seemed that the obvious approach was to support only those scientists who did not hold a Home Office Licence (such a licence enables researchers to use animals in research). This proved a restriction since many scientists still holding licences (at least for the moment) wished to work towards looking for new non-animal methods.
>
> There appeared to be an impasse, since the Deeds of the Lawson Tait [sic] could not knowingly be broken. Diehard anti-vivisectionists were unable to bring themselves to agree to a Trust that would do business with any scientist involved in any way with animal research; yet these were the very people whose methods they wanted to change, and many of whom were eager

to initiate and try out new non-animal methods.

With the help of the Commissioner of Charity, the Trustees of the Lawson Tait formed the Humane Research Trust in 1974 to give the wider scope that was needed while retaining the original aims. This was very much welcomed by many far-sighted supporters of The Lawson Tait and has encouraged many lay people, not necessarily involved in the anti-vivisection scene, to applaud and support the HRT.

In the early days there was a wary attitude among scientists. Of course if money was forthcoming they were not likely to be backward in applying for it. On the other hand they kept their distance, certainly wondering what sort of people were running such a Trust. "

Humane Research; Animal research: the progressing change in attitude, by Pamela Brown; Project Appraisal, volume 5, number 3, September 1990, pp. 189-192

82 Elizabeth Margaret Braddock, generally known as Bessie, was also known as "Battling Bessie", thanks to her reputation as a fiery campaigner. She left the CPGB "reportedly because of its lack of commitment to democracy", and her special interests, according to her Wikipedia profile, which does not include any mention of animal welfare, "included maternity, child welfare and youth crime"; she is also "often erroneously associated with a celebrated exchange of insults with Winston Churchill, also ascribed to Nancy Astor", almost qualifying it for apocryphal status:

"**Braddock**: 'Winston, you are drunk, and what's more you are disgustingly drunk.'

Churchill: 'Bessie, my dear, you are ugly, and what's more, you are disgustingly ugly. But tomorrow I shall be sober and you will still be disgustingly ugly.'"

http://en.wikipedia.org/wiki/Bessie_Braddock

83 Pamela Brown says that Braddock became interested in the LTMT and its work in the first year, which is true in the sense that "The Trust was approved as a charity and started functioning on November 16th, 1961", according to Wilfred [although one charity listing website* shows the registration date as the 22nd of December, 1961], but Battling Bessie did not waste any time; on the 5th of December of that year, she asked a question about funding for the LTMT in the House, which was answered with the Parliamentary Secretary addressing her somewhat flippantly as "sir":

"Mrs. Braddock asked the Parliamentary Secretary for Science if he is aware that a fund to be known as the Lawson Tait Memorial Fund has been established and registered as a trust to find alternatives to the use of living animals in medical investigations; and, in view of the importance of research in this matter, if he will consider making a grant to this fund to assist its work.

Mr. Denzil Freeth The reply to the first part of the Question is yes sir. As to the second part, the Medical Research Council would consider on its scientific merits any detailed research programme which might be submitted to them.

Mrs. Braddock Is the Parliamentary Secretary aware that there is so much resentment about the rise to 3,750,000 in experiments on living animals that any opportunity or attempt to find alternatives ought to have the fullest financial support of the Government? Would the hon. Gentleman be prepared to meet a deputation in order to discuss ways and means to deal with this situation from a financial point of view?

Mr. Freeth I should certainly be most happy to receive any deputation which the hon. Lady cared to bring to me. But I think that she must remember that the Medical Research Council exists to give grants for specific research and not to give grants to bodies which themselves make grants to other people."

HC Deb 05 December 1961 vol 650 cc1114-5; Medical Research (Animals);

http://hansard.millbanksystems.com/commons/1961/dec/05/medical-research-animals#S5CV0650P0_19611205_HOC_37

*http://opencharities.org/charities/201245

The final sentence, after the positive response from Denzil Freeth about meeting a deputation, is very much 'on script' for the Government. Freeth's relatively short parliamentary career, distinguished only by a three-year stint as a Parliamentary Private Secretary [PPS] from 1956-59 and a one-year appointment as Parliamentary Secretary, in which position he answered Mrs. Braddock in lieu of the Secretary of State for Education and Science, was cut short in 1964 when he was caught in the fallout from the Profumo affair, being asked to stand down as an MP after his homosexuality was discovered by Lord Denning. Freeth, "for nearly 20 years … a Churchwarden of the leading London Anglo-Catholic Church, All Saints, Margaret Street … then worked as a stockbroker."

http://en.wikipedia.org/wiki/Denzil_Freeth

http://hansard.millbanksystems.com/people/mr-denzil-freeth

Bessie Braddock's initial approach to the government appears to have been successful, according to Pamela Brown, because she

"arranged a meeting at The House of Commons with the Parliamentary Secretary to the Minister of Science and a representative from the Medical Research Council (MRC). Even this meeting was a big step forward. However, although the aims of the new Trust were applauded, no financial help was offered. The suggestion was turned down that, from the immense sum allocated to research, a tiny fraction should be set aside explicitly for the development of alternative systems."

Humane Research; etc., op. cit.

84 ***Courtesy of the former Head of Research at the NAVS, Christine Brock***

85 In this article, Wilfred employed a well-honed technique of referencing national newspapers [in one of which he had himself made an appearance] to demonstrate the relevance of the subject matter in a public forum, and he appears to have collaborated with his opposite number from the BUAV:

"On Sunday, January 5th, an account appeared in the ***Sunday Telegraph***, under the heading 'Lorry-load of dogs died in drug test' which aroused the wrath of many of its readers and was followed by an article the following day in the ***Daily Mirror*** quoting the views obtained by them from the present writer and from colleague Wilfred Tyldesley. Several other dailies carried details of this affair on the same date, from which it appeared that a farmer at Smarden, Kent, believing that his land was contaminated by the chemical fluoroacetamide seeping into his field from a nearby factory making rat poison, had sought the aid of the Ministry of Agriculture.

The facts, briefly stated, seem to be that as long ago as last July the trouble started and the farms affected reported the loss of some 30 dairy cattle and a number of sheep.

Now it should be quite possible to determine by analysis of specimens from the dead animals whether the drug fluoroacetamide was present in quantities sufficient to be significant and if so to take whatever steps seemed appropriate to deal with the danger but, we learn, the Ministry of Agriculture sent two cows to the farm to graze on the suspect land! The ***Daily Herald*** account refers to these two as 'Gert and Daisy' (which should make the members of the original Gert and Daisy family really wrathful) and they say that 'Gert' died after a few weeks. That was followed by experiments on large numbers of dogs (some accounts refer to a 'lorry-load' of dogs) and on guinea-pigs.

The dogs would appear from the reports to have been given the poison in doses which caused death within ninety minutes, but what must those ninety minutes have meant to the poisoned animals in terms of suffering? And the guinea-pigs? The ***Sunday Telegraph*** report stated that guinea-pigs dosed with the drug 'became so sick they had to be destroyed' but did not state how long it was after administration before the victims were destroyed.

Although the report on which these details were based has only just come to light the events which it records may have taken place long ago—even as far back as last July, but if they have occurred recently they are quite stupid as well as sickeningly cruel for it was already known from experience in Merthyr Tydfil last September that more than one hundred dogs had been killed by eating meat from the carcase of a horse killed by the same drug so it was known to be a killer without trying it on any living animal. ..."

WHY THIS NEEDLESS CRUELTY, by WILFRED RISDON; ANIMALS' DEFENDER, February, 1964, pp. 18/19, courtesy of Hilda Kean

86 There was potential for some controversy in October, 1963, had Miss Greener chosen to contest the matter [assuming she was apprised of all the facts] prior to the move into the new premises at Harley Street, and it is hard not to see some irony in the following; without wishing to be unduly cynical, and with no aspersion upon the lady's capabilities intended, perhaps Miss Hamilton-Andrews or her family [or both] were wealthy patrons of the Society:

"There followed a discussion on planning and organisation in connection with staffing at 51 Harley Street-

1. The Secretary reported that we could not fit in Miss Greener under the new set-up as there would not be enough for her to do. Mrs. Hort's report on her work was read. It was agreed that Miss Greener would be asked to look out for alternative employment.

2. It was felt that all staff should be available in one pool and not departmentalised, as at present.

3. The Secretary reported on the fact that Miss Hamilton-Andrews had discussed with him the possibility of her employment with the Society when she returns early in the New Year, and it had

been agreed that she would admirably fill the gap left by Mr. Wye [he resigned, effective at the beginning of 1964 with 3 months' notice]. A salary of £850 per annum was agreed.

4. In general, it was agreed that efficiency should be increased without increasing costs; and that further cuts in staff should be made at a later date.

5. It was stressed that due to increased expenditure, we cannot envisage any extension of our work for at least a year."

Minutes of the NAVS Council Meeting, 15/10/63; courtesy of the NAVS

87 Although ***What Goes On?*** is only a relatively short work, 11 pages, in octavo format, as a pamphlet it is relatively large, and it was extracted from the LPAVS periodical, ***Anti-Vivisection News***. The first of Wilfred's publications listed below was originally written in 1946, and "reprinted with additional details by request" in January 1955:

"**GOOD PUBLICITY VALUE**

Among recent issues of leaflets and pamphlets of proved propaganda value the following have already established themselves as publications of outstanding merit:

By Dr. H. Fergie Woods:

Modern Medicine–Its Cause and Cure ... ... ½d.
Medicine–Present and Future ... ... ½d.
A Short Anti-Vivisection Catechism ... ... ½d.

By E. Douglas Hume, Author of "Béchamp or Pasteur", "The Mindchangers", etc.

Christianity and Animal Sacrifice ... ... ½d.
The Indwelling Intelligences ... ... 1d.

By Victor Rienaecker:

The Knowledge of Good and Evil ... ...½d.
Science or Morality ... ... 1d.

By W. Arr, Editor of The News Sheet:

This Brave New World ... ... ½d.
Wonder Drugs ... ... ½d.
Vivisection–Where Does it Lead? ... ... 1d."

LPAVS News-Sheet Vol. VII, No. 1, January 1947; courtesy of the NAVS

88 http://en.wikipedia.org/wiki/Helvetica

89 ***Campaigning against Cruelty: etc., op. cit.***

90 ***Ibid.:***

"The matter was given 'long and careful consideration' by the Executive Committee. The Littlewood Committee was approached and eventually a way was negotiated for BUAV to contribute evidence without infringing the society's fundamental rule. A comprehensive 7,000-word memorandum of Evidence was prepared. Although this made the policy of the society crystal clear, the Memorandum concentrated on showing that the act had totally failed to prevent the suffering of laboratory animals, or even to mitigate suffering to any great extent. This submission was later supplemented by oral evidence."

91 ***Ibid.:***

"This led to the resignation of some Committee Members, and the President, Mr Gerald Curtler, in protest at what they saw as a departure from the total abolition policy. Mr Jon Evans was elected President in Curtler's place."

92 Initially, there was "a spirit of optimism" about the venture, but the cracks soon started to appear:

> "The advantages of amalgamation were clear: better and more economic use of all resources (ending the vast amount of duplication of work by the two societies), the ability to operate on a larger scale, and the presentation of a more effective and united front to both supporters and adversaries. These aims were all 'absolutely desirable' in the best interests of laboratory animals and 'the cause is greater than any one society'. The hope was that working together would bring a speedier end to vivisection. The time was seen as ripe for this amalgamation; it was thought that many people were probably already members of both societies.
>
> The new society was to have a completely new name and a new Memorandum and Articles of Association. A joint statement from NAVS and BUAV was published with the nominations for the holders of office in the new society. Lady Dowding was to be President with Mr John Lefevre as Honorary Treasurer. A Board of Managers of nine was to be chaired by Jon Evans. Plans were taking a very definite shape and the 'deafening' silence from the BUAV membership was taken by its leaders to be a voice of consent.
>
> Ultimately, though, amalgamation was a matter for the members and, at the 'historic' 1967 AGM, BUAV members were asked to vote on the principle of merging with NAVS. However the AGM was to prove that BUAV members had many great concerns over the proposed plans and there was 'considerable apprehension'. There were many objections. In particular there was concern about the way in which members of the new Board of Managers had been selected as it was felt that this was a matter on which the membership should have a say. However after well over two hours of 'solid wrangling' the resolution giving the green light to the proposed merger with NAVS was carried.
>
> Many concerns were raised after the AGM about the actual process of amalgamation. Many thought that a Board of Managers of just nine members would be far too small. The appointment of staff to various posts was the cause of much uneasiness. There were also considerable misgivings over the proposed branch structure and, perhaps most crucially, over the question of the policy of the new society. Whereas NAVS wanted the new society to be committed to a step-by-step approach towards the eventual abolition of vivisection, BUAV still adhered to a policy of abolition without compromise of any kind."
>
> ***Ibid.***

93 ***Courtesy of R. A. S. Gray at The Telegraph, fax to the author 25/07/95***

94 The Chairman, Lady Dowding, contributed a Spiritualist perspective, but there still seemed hope of the merger negotiations succeeding:

> "In opening the meeting the Chairman said that she felt sure those of us nearest to Mr. Risdon in his work would like to have a few minutes' silence to remember him. Although many of us had attended the funeral and Memorial Service they were for everyone. The Chairman said she knew that we all felt that we had lost a very wise and very kind friend. She did not think we had lost him because she was quite convinced that he will continue to help us in the work that we are doing and perhaps if this Council shows particular wisdom it will be him behind us.

Those present then sat in silence for a few minutes as a tribute to Mr. Risdon's memory.

The Chairman referred to the beautiful Memorial Service which had taken place earlier in the day. Mr. Ian Johnson had been responsible for arranging the Service and it was agreed unanimously that a letter be sent to Mr. Johnson from the Council expressing appreciation of the beautiful Service and thanking him for all the work he did in connection with it.

...

MATTERS ARISING: Amalgamation. The Chairman reported fully on the last meeting of the negotiating sub-committee at which difficulties arose concerning the position of the Animal Defence and Anti-Vivisection Society. Lady Dowding said she personally felt that these difficulties could be overcome and there was to be a meeting of the Council of the Animal Defence Society before the next meeting of the negotiating sub-committee.

Miss Wilson said that now Mr. Risdon has gone and as his wisdom was very great in this amalgamation, she had certain fears, which are probably groundless, but she wondered if there will be any attempt by the B.U.A.V. for a take-over. She said she was sorry to be suspicious but she had known it happen in so many cases.

Lady Dowding said she did not think so because the way in which the two Societies work are completely complementary to each other.

Miss Wilson asked about the B.U.A.V.'s policy and was concerned that our step by step approach would be safeguarded.

Lady dowding replied that the final Constitution, acceptable to both Societies, had been agreed.

Lady Dowding said that after consulting members of the Council she had written to the B.U.A.V. and the Animal Defence Society saying it would be helpful to know their intentions. A reply had been received from the B.U.A.V. and this was read. Their Committee said that they did not think anything could be gained by calling an Extraordinary General Meeting immediately which, in any case, could not be held before May, and therefore they would bring the matter of the amalgamation before their Annual General meeting in July, as originally planned. The B.U.A.V. Council affirmed that they were committed to the principle of amalgamation."

Minutes of the NAVS Council Meeting, 21/03/67; courtesy of the NAVS

95 The entry was quite brief:

"OBITUARY WILFRED RISDON

A Service of Memorial to Mr. Risdon was held on Tuesday, March 21st, at All Souls Church, Langham Place, The Rev. Stott, Vicar of All Souls conducted the Service and Canon Pearce Higgins gave the Address. A.M.A. Moore Esq., read the Lesson."

Animals' Defender, Vol. XI, April 1967; courtesy of the NAVS

96 While he was away, two people shared Wilfred's work:

"GENERAL BUSINESS: It was agreed that reference should be made in Animals' Defender to Mr. Risdon's illness. The Council expressed appreciation of the work done by Mr. Smith and Mrs. Joynson and all the staff in Mr. Risdon's absence and it was agreed that mention should be made in "Animals' Defender" of the Council's vote of thanks."

Minutes of the NAVS Council Meeting, 20/10/64; courtesy of the NAVS

"EDITORIAL NOTES

Our readers will be sorry to learn of the recent illness of our Secretary and Editor, Mr. Wilfred Risdon, which has occasioned a short spell in hospital for him.

We are glad to report, however, that Mr. Risdon is making an excellent recovery and is now recuperating in the country, and hopes to return to the office in the near future.

In his absence the work of the Society has been carried on by the Deputy Secretary, Mrs. J. Joynson and the Assistant secretary, Mr. C. Smith. At their recent Meeting the Council passed a vote of thanks to Mrs. Joynson and Mr. Smith and to all Headquarters Staff for their help during this period, and instructed that this be recorded in the "Animals' Defender"."

Animals' Defender, Vol. 8, No. 11, November 1964; courtesy of the NAVS

97 ***Meeting of the Central Executive Committee, 18/07/56; courtesy of the NAVS***

98 http://www.thisismoney.co.uk/money/bills/article-1633409/Historic-inflation-calculator-value-money-changed-1900.html

99 This is assuming, of course, that his estate consists entirely of cash, which is extremely unlikely, but it will have to serve as a rough guide, for want of more accurate information, which is most probably irretrievable. If his estate had comprised possessions/effects as well as cash, he would have had proportionately less money per year to spend.

100 The Council was obviously willing to be very sensitive to Nellie's needs:

"It was agreed unanimously that a letter be sent to Mrs. Risdon expressing the council's sympathy in her grievous loss and also conveying the Council's great appreciation of her husband's work for the Society and cause. It was agreed that this letter should also inform Mrs. Risdon of the Council's decision concerning pension and financial help."

Minutes of the NAVS Council Meeting, 21/03/67: Report of Finance Sub-Committee; courtesy of the NAVS

101 From a general overview of the area [and without any specific information from the local authority] her final address prior to her death [which was not automatically her first address in the area, of course] at Inglewood Court, Liebenrood Road, Reading, appears to have been a "warden controlled" area for senior citizens, rather than exclusively privately-owned dwellings.

102 Specific information is scarce, but presumably Gary's two older siblings, Catherine and Alison, accompanied Brian and his first wife, Mary, on this visit which must have been some time between 1964 and 1967; Gary would have been about ten years old; there were also two younger brothers, Colin and Terry, who very probably were also present. Gary's recollection is touchingly personal:

"I remember Wilfred being a very quiet person. On our arrival in the UK and upon our arrival at Harley St. Wilfred had a small luncheon/party ready for us. He had a reel-to-reel tape recorder going and was taping the festive atmosphere conversation. Yes, the flats were on floors 5, and 6. The 4th floor was storage. There was a postage stamp outdoor area at the rear. Mostly, as very young persons we were enthralled with the cage-type elevator and its workings."

Email to the author from Gary Risdon, 20/01/2013

103 http://www.humaneresearch.org.uk/

CONCLUSION

How to sum up the life and work of a man like Wilfred Risdon? Not a quick or easy task, and one that will, inevitably, be fraught with subjective interpretation, but that is the lot, while also the privilege, of the biographer. It is at the same time a blessing and a curse for this biographer: not to have met my subject, which would have allowed me the benefit of such personal reminiscences as the occurrences provided, against the objectivity [although incorporating an inherent necessity for the subjective interpretation] resulting from second- or third-hand acquaintance. The title of the book required a good deal of introspection, and many alternatives were considered, but the one chosen was suggested by a very experienced friend, and after some consideration, it was selected; although a subtitle was considered appropriate, the main title incorporates references, which serve to entice potential readers, to the two most public phases of Wilfred's life. They are well-known symbols, of course, hopefully not clichés, but there was more to the life of this as yet virtually unknown person, which this book sets out to redress. One alternative title that was discarded positioned Wilfred as a lifelong activist: notwithstanding that his activism, such as it was, does not set him apart from a great many other people before or since, there is also the danger that a categorisation as an activist can cast him in the mould of being belligerently anti-social or anti-establishment, which he was not, as such, but as always, the definition of terms is crucial and, of course, open to subjective interpretation. Even though it is improbable that he would have set out to be, and it is interesting to speculate as to whether he might have acknowledged it in reflective moments late in life, in his own way he was a lifelong activist, first as a young person, for Jesus, next for his fellow man using the associated [but popularly believed to be polar opposites] vehicles of first Socialism then National Socialism, and finally he was a committed and dedicated activist for animals. His political stance after he severed his connection with such an overtly political movement as was Mosley's is unknown; the only hint I have at my disposal is that from Len Risdon, his nephew, who told me that he did become "more conservative" as he got older, but while undoubtedly correct, that is not unusual or entirely unexpected: it only serves to emphasise the irrelevance [if not actual speciousness] of labels where politics are concerned, because his later work for animals had an inherent humanism, which is normally seen in certain circles as evidence of 'left-leaning' politics [although, to be fair, throughout the whole of his time with Mosley, his political convictions were always described as 'socialist', as opposed to Socialist].

To return to the beginning, his religious zeal as a child was by no means unusual even in someone so relatively young and, while acknowledging what is undoubtedly a truism [but also not overlooking his possession of free will], that he could not be anything but a product of the age into which he was born, the moulding and directing influence of his Plymouth Brethren father must have been a very significant factor. Without wishing to embark upon a discussion of the potential for good or 'evil' bound up in the morality of this particular manifestation of the Christian faith, the self-confidence that the impulse for proselytising gave him, in no small part encouraged by his father no doubt, set him almost inevitably upon a path of activism, whereby being a passive commentator, no matter how well-informed or vociferous, was not an option. One possible version of his life could have seen him as a preacher, probably itinerant, but he seems to have had a need, if not an actual hunger, for action, of the type that would have been seen as incompatible with the rôle of a preacher. His home area with its coal mining gave him the opportunity to find the next stage of his activism but, again, the tide of the time he was living in sent him to South Wales, where the industry's trade union was well supported, while at the same time riven with internal strife, something apparently inescapable where desperate social conditions give rise to many competing [and often conflicting] possible solutions. Although this was a relatively brief stage, it was a very influential one, including the association with several personalities whose thinking was to have powerful repercussions in the years to come, not the least of whom was Aneurin Bevan.

Unfortunately, very little that can be corroborated is known about the service Wilfred gave for that first disastrous [and arguably unnecessary] conflagration of the twentieth century, between 1914 and 1919, other than that the majority of his service was spent in France providing medical support and care as a non-combatant with the Royal Army Medical Corps, but it was very possibly the most formative interlude of his life, as it was for many other survivors [not all of whom would have considered themselves lucky], some of whom became his close friends & colleagues before very long, in a shared crusade which followed on inevitably, when humanity was beginning to comprehend the depth of the abyss into which it had stared and only narrowly avoided falling into [while also beginning to question the rationale that had instigated it], and the creation of a brave new world was seen as a real possibility, one to be striven and, if necessary, fought for with all the urgency and strength at their disposal, in the face of sluggard and persistently patrician governments evidently wanting only to pander to the Establishment by reinstating the previous very satisfactory [for a privileged minority] *status quo*. If a political mantle free of the taint of commercialism [of which Liberalism clearly was not] was thought preferable, the only possible avenue in the 1920s open to activists such as Wilfred was Socialism.

Again, the necessity for speculation here cannot be avoided, but it is interesting to ponder whether Wilfred would have become disillusioned with the international character of Socialism at all, or so quickly at any rate, as indeed he did, had it not been for his encountering of Oswald Mosley, who was an indisputably magnetic personality as well as possessing what many considered a ferocious intellect, while still being unashamedly human, incorporating all the flaws & foibles we have such difficulties with. Mosley attracts reverence and odium in almost equal measure, although the latter probably predominates thanks to the pernicious effect of the purposive shaping of history, using the powerful media of popular culture and official propaganda; this is increasingly being questioned and countered, which can only be positive, but the vested interests have very powerful weapons with which to fight their rearguard actions. Mosley has been accused of many things, not the least of which was that he was a political gadfly, but his argument seemed to be that one had to adapt to the prevailing circumstances, while at the same time not losing sight of the ultimate goal, so a change of political mantle, regardless of the labels that might have been attached to it, was not only unavoidable but essential, and he very quickly came to realise that party affiliations were a distraction from the issues which he saw as his *modus vivendi*; also, he was canny enough to know that it is a given in politics that you cannot please everybody, so that was the surface coating which enabled his armour to repel all the criticism.

One thing which is very clear from the different strands of Wilfred's life is that he saw education as being crucial to his mission, however he might have defined it; and of course, this mission will have changed in character on several occasions during his life. The proselytising of Christianity embodied an educative element [albeit often unsolicited]; Socialism acknowledged from the very beginning the fundamental necessity of education for working people, to give them the knowledge with which to strive for better working conditions by joining trade unions and supporting Socialist politicians, as well as enriching their own lives by broadening their mental horizons, hence Wilfred's association with Fircroft College in Birmingham; Fascism and National Socialism similarly saw education as a vehicle to inform all strata of British society, but not the least of which, in terms of membership numbers and potential votes, were the manual and semi-skilled workers, of how they were being duped and exploited by the vested interests of the money-power of 'Financial Democracy'; and finally, anti-vivisection had a hugely important educative rôle, given the ignorance or blithe acquiescence on the part of the British public with regard to the fallacious nature of the promised benefits supposed to accrue from animal testing, and that was notwithstanding the cruelty involved, for all the lengths to which the perpetrators were prepared to go, to conceal or dissemble it. The inherent didacticism embodied in the education that Wilfred conveyed meant that he was naturally qualified as a speaker, and as well as having no obvious inhibitions when it came to public speaking, he also saw it as his duty to pass this faculty on to others, on the basis that, although natural talent was an asset, a proficiency could be taught and developed.

This leads on to the question of what might have been the fundamental impetus of the man: what drove Wilfred Risdon to do the things he did? Again, each of the distinct phases of his life will have provided this impetus, although it was not always identical. Presumably, in the youthful Christian phase, it will have been the joy of sharing the knowledge [and, ideally, the experience] of the Holy Spirit; this was not always welcome within the house of Socialism, notwithstanding the 'Labour church', which was essentially secular, although in South Wales, Chapel and Socialism seemed to be able to peacefully co-exist; so the Christian zeal was often transmuted, and in Wilfred's case into a less obviously denominational desire to help his fellow man, especially those who found it almost impossible to raise themselves out of the poverty trap into which their circumstances [mere birth generally being sufficient] had cast them. War and its concomitant shared experience of suffering and injustice inevitably created a need and a palpable will for change: perhaps this was in part a result of the heightening of the senses which was imbued by the [to those lucky enough to avoid them] unimaginable horrors of brutal and senseless slaughter? The need for action of men such as Mosley and T E Lawrence was ascribed to this by Colin Wilson, although he describes it as a contraction: "This is the state of insight, when all the faculties seem to be speeded up. It explains why men become racing drivers and mountain climbers, or go into the desert like T. E. Lawrence: because they want to face an emergency that forces them to 'contract' to this new level of control." [**1**].

This could also manifest itself in an assertion of individuality, as was plainly manifest in Lawrence, and Mosley was clearly not afraid to go his own way, although his movements for social change were predicated to some extent upon a relinquishing of individualism, for which their recent armed forces discipline was a prerequisite, so it was virtually inevitable that Wilfred's natural individualism would get him into trouble at some stage, for all that he was a loyal National Socialist, and to a lesser extent [albeit not entirely willing] a Fascist; by way of contrast with this homogenisation, Wilson goes so far as to say that "without individuality, life would not build up the same desperate force. The man of the crowd is a weakling; people who need people are the stupidest people in the world." [**2**]. Mosley's single-minded pursuit of his own path toward social regeneration within the political arena was reminiscent of that of an English commentator and agitator just over a hundred years earlier, William Cobbett: "I am resolved to walk in the trammels of nobody" [**3**]. As for Wilfred's embracing of the ethos of Fascism in its British manifestation, whatever reservations he might have had at the time, it is impossible with our access to the kaleidoscopic nature of the many strands of history thereafter, with the multitude of slanted observations, and the subjective hindsight to which they give access, to have any chance of viewing it objectively, so to that extent, it is probably fair to say that as a political ethos, Fascism is irrevocably tainted: to describe someone as a Fascist nowadays can be nothing other than derogatory and pejorative. Many people have written on the subject at great length, from the very beginning of the concept, and their interpretation will inevitably depend upon their political outlook [always assuming that they are able to form their own opinions, independent of mainstream media propaganda], no matter how well they think they understand the subject, which can often be not very well. Detractors are legion, but impartial observers [who inevitably run the gauntlet of guilt by association: 'closet Nazis' all!] are few: surely it cannot be a difficult concept to grasp, that no society of human organisation can ever be perfect, and no matter what labels might be hung upon a political ethos [however well deserved or otherwise], any group of like-minded people must have something among its many layers of reasoning to offer the world, in a spirit of respectful co-operation, if the most equitable & enjoyable life for the maximum number of creatures upon this earth is the ultimate goal, so as a matter of academic evaluation, this must of necessity also apply to 1930s British Fascism, if the elements of it beneficial to human- and animal-kind could be extracted and assimilated with those of other philosophies, however much more 'socially acceptable' they might be, which is always a relative term?

The outcome of the second world war has ensured that any suggestion that Germany's apparent motives for fomenting it were other than those repeatedly confirmed by the victorious nations, or that the involvement of any sections of German society who held financial and culturally persuasive power [the scapegoats for which are commonly understood as being the Jewish community] was contrary to the interests of the German people as a whole, has come to be regarded as a heresy, and the character of anybody propagating those views to be regarded with particular suspicion; Mosley's prewar movements are an unfortunate victim of guilt by association, even though the events which shaped the postwar version of history were still then playing out, and subject to interpretation and repackaging, with the appropriate emphasis, by the various organs of propaganda of all the interested parties. Viewed in this light, Wilfred was quite fortunate to escape without greater censure, although his timely 'Damascene conversion', genuine or otherwise, no doubt played a very significant part in his virtually flawless rehabilitation, which he must have been only too well aware was his only viable course of action.

The interests of the German people were seen by the National Socialist Government from an authoritarian perspective, in which individual liberties were seen as subservient to the interest of the nation as a corporate whole [in the sense of a body comprising many individual, but essential components], which does rather beg the question of why such an extensive and effective security organisation would need to be in place, if the population was so willingly participating in the grand project; history shows, of course, that populations are generally very slow to realise and accept when a government's actions are for the good of the nation [or the wider global populace], assuming they are, which is very often debatable, depending upon which self-interest group one happens to belong to. Whether Mosley's version of authoritative government, to which Wilfred subscribed, at least until about 1938, would have been applied with the same degree of paranoia and suppression of minorities as Hitler's was, has to remain a matter for conjecture; Mosley always stressed the uniqueness of his British Union movement, its quintessential Britishness setting it apart from the often underhand tactics of its Italian progenitor and its German associate and, in terms of the thuggery surrounding his movement, claimed with significant and legitimate justification that those of his members who were involved were more sinned against than sinning, their involvement involuntary.

Despite the Italian origins of the original Fascism, Wilfred embraced the concept of the Corporate State, in its entirely British implementation as envisaged by Mosley [what Robert Edwards has described as "the ideal of the all-embracing Organic Nation" **4**] because for Wilfred, with his belief in the necessity for the Syndicalist approach to governance, an expectation by the State of "service and duty" [**5**] from its citizens was perfectly acceptable, notwithstanding his recent military service, and he must have believed that sufficient reciprocal trust between a majority of British citizens and a Fascist/National Socialist Government would exist to enable it to function effectively, once they understood the benefits. That reciprocal trust is clearly non-existent in modern times, and it is probably true to say that it has never existed at any time, of recorded history in the British Isles at any rate, so what was it about Mosley's unique reasoning which made him and his many followers, including the subject of this biography, think that this could be achieved? It is surely not a truism to say that people respond better to respectful and humane treatment than they do to abuse and contempt, so Mosley obviously thought that if people's natural self-interest [regarding reasonable necessities, as opposed to unjustifiable luxuries] was serviced, they would be prepared to place their trust in him and give the "service and duty" that was required as a *quid pro quo* but, unfortunately, events [at human instigation] conspired to prevent him being able to 'come up with the goods', so his Movement never achieved a critical mass, to the obvious relief of the vested interests of Financial Democracy [**6**]. Another aspect of Mosley's ethos, with which Wilfred was entirely comfortable, due in no small part to his recent experience with Socialism, was nationalism, which was also very closely linked with patriotism, both of which are very persuasive sentiments, but which lead inevitably to a narrowing of mental horizons, because they are judgmental of different races and creeds as a result of the inherent categorisation. The observation that this was very much a mental attitude of the time in which they lived is necessary here as well, although it was by no means a prerequisite.

It is understandable that in early history, small tribal communities developed organically into larger communities and the demands of greater numbers of inhabitants living in a static geographical area meant that, unless it was possible for 'breakaway' communities to establish themselves independent of the progenitors and their resources [as seems to have been the case with 'native' or 'first nation' Americans] some sort of advanced form of resource management had to be arrived at, if these larger numbers were all to survive; unfortunately, instead of what is now accepted by enlightened individuals as being a use of resources that was not guaranteed to lead to conflict and violence; that is, sharing, gifting, and co-operation, conservation and re-use, the notion of 'trade' was born [and its pernicious subsequent concomitant, currency], so the idea that land and the resources it provided had a 'value' and must be protected very quickly took hold, leading inevitably to nationalism to protect notional borders, and this was taken to its logical conclusion in the British Empire, another *shibboleth* to which Wilfred and Mosley's movement clung as devoutly as they did the British religion and the British monarchy, both symbols and indivisible elements of the Empire. This generalised tendency towards nationalism is illustrated very interestingly in a biography of Nelson Mandela, where the situation is the paradoxical combination of a tribal society surrounded by, but also oppressed by, a modern 'civilised' society, and the way that the tribal society organises its forward development [probably because of the outside influence, rather than despite it] tends to give rise to nationalism **[7]** again, presumably, because of the perceived need for protection of resources [although culture would also be an important consideration]. Religion was also a prominent factor in Wilfred's life, and that had an association with the nationalism which was one of the main planks on which the middle period of his life were built, and one very obviously negative aspect of that was the inherent racism.

The cause of this racism, the main focus of which was Jews, as was speculated upon in Chapter 1, was the particular brand of Christianity that was inculcated into Wilfred at an early age, although notwithstanding his own capability to think independently, had he so chosen, there was also a ubiquitous, often only barely submerged anti-Jewish sentiment prevalent in all strata of British society. The generic term 'anti-Semitism' is used to cover this, and any challenging of accepted terminology is never easy, but it is surely misleading, because while ethnic Jews are acknowledged Semites, not all Semites are Jews, so a more accurate name for this sentiment should surely be 'anti-Jew'? This is my own personal interpretation, which I will not labour because of my lack of specialised knowledge of the subject, on which there is, however, no lack of commentators, from a diverse selection of backgrounds and levels of knowledge and experience. On the subject of the nomenclature, one of Wilfred's contemporaries [although not likely to have been a friend or even an associate], Captain Archibald Maule Ramsay, no doubt frequently referred to as 'a rabid anti-Semite' [whose opinion is therefore consequently of no value to most] quotes in a book called ***The Nameless War*** a Mr. Douglas Reed who described the term anti-Semitism as "meaningless rubbish" [**8**], but he also considered the term 'anti-Jew' inaccurate, because "a fair proportion of Jews are not engaged in this conspiracy"; he was also likely to have been in a minority: most people were probably quite happy to use the common term, even if they were conscious of the lack of clarity in the meaning.

Another member of this minority was T E Lawrence, yet another personality who seemed to attract admirers and detractors in equal measure, and who considered that he served his country well in a military capacity at the same time, although not in the same 'theatre', as when Wilfred's political thinking was being forged. Lawrence's experience in the Middle East, which thereby qualified him as a commentator, was generally respected, even if his views weren't popular; he also made no secret among his Arab associates of his Christian faith, while being ever conscious of the danger of flaunting it. His observation of the multifarious tribes in the region gave him the credibility to comment on the relevance [or otherwise] of the term 'Semitic': "Before the Moslem conquest, these areas were inhabited by diverse peoples, speaking languages of the Arabic family. We called them Semitic, but (as with most scientific terms) incorrectly." [**9**]. He also commented anodynely on the diversity of Jews in the region, including a foreshadowing of future conflict with "the sullen Palestine peasants" [**10**], a subject on which Wilfred evidently only commented once [see Chapter 9, note 42], publicly at any rate. Lawrence also comments subjectively on a personal experience which put his Christianity into perspective in the area he generally referred to as "Syria", and refers to Jews without the conventionally Christian slant that Wilfred appeared to have: "Galilee was Syria's non-Semitic province, contact with which was almost uncleanness for the perfect Jew." [**11**]. Whatever Wilfred's feelings about a "conspiracy" as envisaged by Ramsay might have been, his sentiments towards Jews appear to have been more generalised. The historical Christian source of this is referred to by Geoffrey Hindley, in his excellent examination of the Magna Carta: "The official stance of both Church and state [in the Middle Ages] to Jews was bound to be ambivalent." [**12**].

It is difficult to locate an obvious causal link between Wilfred's early Plymouth Brethren indoctrination and his later denominational dislike of Jews so, as is often the case, and assuming that he absorbed or possibly developed it from his father, it is probably a matter of personal interpretation. There do not appear to be any direct references to Jews in the doctrines of the group [or groups, to be more accurate], but the figure of Jesus Christ as an embodiment of God seems to be very prominent, and although they could not claim any proprietorial exclusivity, "they hold the Bible as their sole authority in regard to matters of doctrine and practice." [**13**]. A respected British authority on the subject of 'anti-Semitism', in its specifically British manifestation, is Professor Colin Holmes. In his 1979 work ***Anti-Semitism in British Society*** 1876-1939, "with reference to mediæval society" he points to "two conspicuous developments" that were pointers along the way to the association of "the charge of ritual murder" with Jews [**14**], at a time of virtually inescapable observance of Christian worship. Although it might seem rather obvious [under the premise that British Jews later defined themselves as much by their Judaism as by their heredity], in the 18th and 19th centuries, "Jews were denied social rights because they could not subscribe to an oath supporting the Church of England" [**15**], another anticipated 'bone of contention' for Wilfred. Two other aspects of the British assessment of Jews, that were very probably influential in his osmotic education, were their perceived "low moral character" and "their concentration upon financial gain" [**16**]; these would also play a part in Wilfred's later, adult opinion of them. As early as 1875, an expression that was to resonate during Wilfred's National Socialist career began to gain currency: "Britain for the British" [**17**], so the ground for the society into which Wilfred was born in 1896 was well & truly laid. It is impossible to speculate with any degree of certainty whether Wilfred's evident dislike of Jews was on the grounds of ethnicity as well as the choice of religion, for the reasons given above, which could be a concomitant of ethnicity [albeit at some remove], but not necessarily so. With regard to his service for Mosley's Movement, there is no reason to suppose that Wilfred's doctrinal policy was any different from Mosley's, that of only opposing Jews who made trouble for his Movement [given that they were reportedly on the receiving end of allegedly Jewish-instigated violence on occasion], and criticising as a group those involved in international finance, whose principles ran counter to those of humane economic management, some of whom appeared to be Jews. Wilfred's public expressions of his personal views were certainly not strident or sociopathically oriented in the same way that some of his colleagues' were.

The middle section of his life, from 1924 to 1939, was the one when he was arguably most versatile, although he was to use most, if not all, of his talents similarly from 1940 until his death, albeit at a less frenetic pace, when his attention was focused almost entirely on animals, rather than only human beings. Given the inherently fractious nature of Mosley's Movement for social change, after the false start in 1931, it is unlikely that Wilfred would ever have been regarded as anything more than a trusted lieutenant, even though he did attain the rank of Assistant Director General (Electoral); the only colleague who was deemed to be Mosley's second-in-command for any length of time was Neil Francis-Hawkins, who was an obsequious martinet; the only people classed as social equals were to be found outside the Movement, probably intentionally so. Having said that, by all accounts Wilfred did have a cordial relationship with Mosley, who respected ability in his officers, probably significantly better than a 'master-servant' arrangement, at least until 1937 or '38 [after the minor *contretemps* in Manchester] but it probably never extended to actual 'friendship'. Despite

Mosley's aristocratic heredity, his concern for his fellow countrymen [in a generic sense] seemed entirely genuine, more than in a merely patrician way, and this is undoubtedly what drew Wilfred to him, especially as Mosley's wealth and the dynamism, that was a consequence of the supreme self-confidence bestowed upon him by his social standing, meant that he stood a very good chance of actually achieving his stated goals. If Wilfred is to be believed, from his own testimony, this cordial relationship suffered a setback whose effect appeared to be cumulative and probably irrevocable, when Mosley declined to investigate the allegation of Italian funding for the Movement in its early years, which clearly offended Wilfred's principles, however simplistic or naïve that might have been interpreted as, by such a canny political animal as Mosley [the opinion of the toady Francis-Hawkins having little value]; if Wilfred was in fact dissembling, he was either very well informed, or a consummate actor, or both, given the level of intellect present in the interlocutors who had the power to determine his freedom or continued captivity in 1940. Perhaps he saw his success in this arena as a signal that he should thereafter relinquish overt involvement in politics, and only comment obliquely [but nonetheless in a way that would be understood by those 'on the same wavelength'] in the course of his animal protection activism.

The determining characteristic of the latter period of his life [which is not to say that it was absent in the earlier phases, of course, but perhaps not predominating] was compassion, on behalf of creatures who were not able to defend themselves against cruel or inhumane treatment, and it must have been a constant source of frustration [not to say annoyance, on occasion] to him that this was not common to more of his fellow human beings than it appeared to be. Another characteristic he obviously possessed was determination, one he evidently put to good use in working to abolish the evil of vivisection, not only with outright opposition, but also with an intelligent application of a tried & tested aspect of human nature: give someone an acceptable [and, in this case, practicable] alternative, and he will be prepared to relinquish a long-accepted practice or belief. He must have been an idealist to some extent at least, to want to change society to the extent that he did, but he appears to have been a pragmatic one as well, if that is not a contradiction in terms. Whether he would have summed up his life as a whole as a success or failure is moot: notwithstanding the evidence that he was planning to retire very possibly quite soon when he died, it is quite possible that he saw his life as a sequential development, rather than a series of separate, and only tangentially connected phases, so despite the fact that his personal quest did not succeed in removing the blight of vivisection from British society, I feel that he must have taken some satisfaction in the raising of the level of awareness that the didactic nature of his work would have achieved, in the knowledge that social activism movements tend to have their own momentum which is entirely independent of the participants, but that the contribution he made was an integral and invaluable part, however small he felt it might have been. His political work, when seen in this context, was an essential preparatory stage, so it should not be assessed in terms of success or failure, notwithstanding any potentially less desirable character traits that might have been displayed therein.

It seems virtually impossible to be able to credit his work with any sort of legitimate legacy, other than keeping the organisations to which he gave the majority of his working life moving forward in the right direction, using his acknowledged and indisputable talents as an efficient administrator, often in difficult, and occasionally trying circumstances, but with implacable good humour. In 1973, the work of the Lawson Tait Memorial Trust, which became the Lawson Tait Medical and Scientific Research Trust after Wilfred's death, was supplemented by the creation of the Lord Dowding Fund for Humane Research, still based at Harley Street [**18**]; at around the same time, in a move reminiscent of the original schism in the NAVS which created the offshoot BUAV, to cater for those anti-vivisectionists who wanted to support the work of scientists holding Home Office licences, who also did want to work towards "new non-animal methods", which ran counter to the ethos of many LTMT members, "[d]iehard anti-vivisectionists [who] were unable to bring themselves to agree to a Trust that would do business with any scientist involved in any way with animal research … [w]ith the help of the Commissioner of Charity, the Trustees of the Lawson Tait [sic] formed the Humane Research Trust in 1974 to give the wider scope that was needed while retaining the original aims. This was very much welcomed by many far-sighted supporters of the Lawson Tait and has encouraged many lay people, not necessarily involved in the anti-vivisection scene, to applaud and support the HRT." [**19**] Thus was the LTMT subsumed into the HRT, and thereafter ceased to exist, which might explain the foundation of the Lord Dowding Fund; although it was not necessarily a deliberate strategy, from which conspiratorial inferences could be drawn, nowhere in all of this has Wilfred's name been mentioned once. "In 1990, the fast-expanding [NAVS] had long outgrown its premises in Harley Street, and so moved to larger premises in Goldhawk Road, London, and in 2006 NAVS moved to Millbank Tower, London, where it remains today." [**20**] The Government eventually made a somewhat grudging acknowledgment of the potential for non-animal research with a pitifully small contribution: "The government made its first financial support to the development of alternatives in 1984 when it awarded grants to FRAME, the Fund for the Replacement of Animals in Medical Experiments (£185,000), and to the Universities Fund [sic] for Animal Welfare (£30,000)." [**21**]

This brings me to the final assessment of the book: would I have liked Wilfred as a person? Perhaps this is an abuse of the professional detachment that a biographer is supposed to exercise, but given that he was a direct relative, and a contemporary [albeit with only a small amount of overlap] I do feel it is justified. My perception of the span of Wilfred's life is barely relevant: I was in my formative years when he died, which means that it is impossible for me to have any concept, no matter how much I might internalise or meditate upon it, what it felt like to be alive in those turbulent, and often frightening, early years of the twentieth century; colour film of the period, of which there is, thankfully, no shortage and, to a lesser extent, the now well-used vehicle of dramatised reconstructions, can only begin to convey the effect upon a person, born into the 'last hurrah' of the Victorian age, being alive then would have, especially from the perspective of the technologically obsessed and increasingly impersonal and paranoid twenty-first century. People were not necessarily less sophisticated then, but their priorities, and the means at their disposal, by which they hoped to achieve them, were indeed different. This can't excuse the character flaw of racism, as detailed above, but it is specious to highlight that in isolation because, unacceptable though it is to any right-thinking person in what we like to believe [notwithstanding the above pessimistic assessment] are somewhat more enlightened times, all human beings, without exception, embody a mix of ridiculous contradictions, when analysed rationally, but these are probably the result of the confusion that is caused by the instilling of supposedly 'adult' values onto the infant *tabula rasa*, and it can take a lifetime of introspection [or, in some cases, therapy] to see them for what they are and make the appropriate adjustments, and that is always assuming that the will to achieve this exists in the first place: often, the risk of cognitive dissonance, whether consciously recognised or not, militates against this.

The conclusion to be drawn from this, by me, at any rate [and, hopefully, by at least some of the readers of this work] is that it is all too easy to dismiss or denigrate a person with whom we are not personally acquainted purely on the basis of an inherently less than comprehensive assessment of the totality of his character, especially by taking one negative trait in isolation [and this regrettable consequence is becoming all too common in social networking, an indisputably twenty-first century phenomenon, whereby it is widely regarded as being acceptable to express disrespectful or downright abusive comments to another person when no physical recourse appears to be possible]: how many of us could examine the character of our friends [whom we believe, rightly or wrongly, we have the prerogative to choose] or family [whom it is generally believed we don't] and say in complete honesty that that person's character embodies not one single negative trait? More to the point, how many of us could examine our own character, and say the same thing? How we interact with other human beings probably operates as much at a non-verbal level as it does a verbal level, and the metaphysical 'chemistry' of our relationships can't be underestimated, so my ultimate assessment is that I would have liked Wilfred, not least for his compassion and his principles, but also for his sense of humour and obvious warmth, and I hope I would have had the moral courage to engage him on the subject of his most evident negative character trait, in the appropriate situation; notwithstanding the subjunctive nature of that observation, that is always assuming that I could have engaged with him as the person I am today, whereas I would be less than honest if I were to maintain that I have always been the person I am today, which I could not, because I am not. So on balance, I have no reservation in endorsing Wilfred Risdon's life, and I feel that, taken overall, his work stands as a testament to that life, which was lived as an embodiment of his principles: not perfect, but human. To the extent that he was self-motivated, he was most definitely an unconventional campaigner, and he was, without a shadow of a doubt, a man of principle.

NOTES

1 Wilson calls this "feeling of inner contraction" Faculty X:

"It is the first step towards what Shaw calls 'the seventh degree of concentration'. This is what Proust experienced when he tasted the madeleine dipped in tea and suddenly ceased to feel 'mediocre, accidental, mortal'. The feeling was not an illusion. He had accidentally stumbled upon a perfectly normal power of the human soul: Faculty X. We are not 'mediocre, accidental, mortal', even though most of the time we feel we are. I have pointed out that there is an impressive mass of evidence for the existence of the astral body. But for present purposes, it makes no difference whether it really exists, or whether it is regarded as a figure of speech. To verify the reality of the 'inner contraction', you only have to take the trouble to observe yourself next time you experience sudden intense delight. Once this is recognised, the analysis may be carried further. It will be seen that a certain degree of 'contraction' produces the sense of poetry, Shelley's spirit of beauty, the 'peak experience'. A further contraction produces a sense of 'being', of being able to act, that Priestley calls the third dimension of time. This is the state of insight, when all the faculties seem to be speeded up. It explains why men become racing drivers and mountain climbers, or go into the desert like T. E. Lawrence: because they want to face an emergency that forces them to 'contract' to this new level of control."

The Occult, by Colin Wilson

2 Wilson believes that Man can break out of this mindset:

"The great unsolved mystery is that of individuality. If life is somehow a unity, how is it that each of its units feels so separate and unique? Chesterton expressed it in the magnificent last chapter of *The Man Who Was Thursday*: "Why does each thing on the earth war against each other thing? Why does each small thing in the world have to fight against the world itself? Why does a fly have to fight the whole universe?" Not only why, but *how*? Perhaps there are creatures in the world, as Sir Alister Hardy suggests, who possess a 'communal consciousness'. Perhaps there are gnats, hovering in a cloud, who are as aware of one another's existence as of their own. But we cannot even conceive of this. A crowd of pot-smokers practising 'togetherness' are deceiving themselves, as a child might deceive herself that her doll was alive. Human individuality is so absolute that we can no more imagine ourselves without it than we can imagine one and one making three.

The 'how' is unanswerable; we can only assume that the force of life began its conquest of matter by somehow splitting itself into units, each of which felt 'separate' from the rest of the universe. Chesterton answers the 'why': "So that each thing that obeys the law may have the glory and isolation of the anarchist. So that each man fighting for order may be as brave and good a man as the dynamiter." Which means simply that without individuality, life would not build up the same desperate force. The man of the crowd is a weakling; people who need people are the stupidest people in the world. And so the basic paradox of human nature seems to be inherent in the force of life itself: without challenge or crisis, it takes things easy, and collapses into mediocrity. So far, all life on earth has had to be driven forward, as slaves once had to be whipped into battle. It has never possessed positive purpose - only the negative one of staying alive and avoiding pain. 'Evil is physical pain', said Leonardo, going to the heart of the matter. The old theological question 'Why evil?' is answered by the recognition that without evil, there would be universal mediocrity, terminating in death. It is only at this point in the earth's history that this has ceased to be wholly true. Without the development of art, science, philosophy, man has acquired the possibility of a *positive purpose, a purpose towards which he can drive forward, instead of being driven from behind.* (It is true that religion has always been an expression of that purpose; but religion was content with paradox: the assertion that 'the world' must somehow be denied by 'the spirit', without trying to understand why this should be necessary.) *If* positive force could be established as the human driving force, it would be a turning point in evolution, for it is many times stronger than the negative purpose of avoiding pain. A man can do things out of love or enthusiasm that would be impossible out of fear. His chief problem at the moment is to escape the narrowness of everyday triviality and grasp the nature of his goal; this, in turn, will require the development of what Blake called 'imagination', but which it would be more accurate to call Faculty X."

Ibid.

3 Cobbett appeared to be similarly fearless:

"Poised between the radicals and the Whigs, with few political allies let alone a party, Cobbett more than ever resembled a one-man band. It was not a situation that he resented. On his return from America in 1819 he had written: 'I shall pursue my own cause singly. My banishment was productive of this advantage, among others, that it taught me to *depend on myself.* I am resolved to walk in the trammels of nobody; and to have no intimate connection, as to public matters, with any man.' It was an appropriate manifesto for Cobbett the rural rider, one man going forward alone on his horse."

The Life and Adventures of William Cobbett, by Richard Ingrams

4 Mosley's Corporate State was not the commercial behemoth envisaged now:

"The Corporate State was an attempt to unite the many factions within society for the purpose of realising the ideal of the all-embracing Organic Nation. It brought an end to sectionalism by emphasising the role of individuals and organisations within the new state machinery. The Corporate State was the catalyst for all the elements within the nation, the ultimate reconciliation of warring factions, for the worthy task of construction and the achievement of ever higher ideals. Far from being an oppression, this central theme of the fascist faith envisaged that only when the nation was free from the internecine struggle of its various elements, class against class and capitalist against worker, could there be true freedom for all. A nation that was not free could not give freedom to the people."

Understanding Fascism, ***by Robert Edwards (published in League Review under the pen-name of Robert Brady, 1979);***

http://www.europeanaction.com/id19.html

5 Wilfred's war service inevitably coloured his thinking:

"Fascists, like soldiers, do not permit their minds to crystallise around any formulas but simply use them as working hypotheses which, in the event that they become detrimental, are easily discarded. This dynamic pragmatism was fascism's hallmark and genius. With this philosophy fascism protested a revolt against all forms of phrase worship and useless sentimentality which are all inhibitive. The theoretical abstractions of social democracy, "liberty", "equality" and "inalienable rights", were attacked by fascism simply because they were abstractions. They are words without any concrete importance meaning nought. They are used as objects of worship and, therefore, prevent objectivity and creative thought. Within the fascist context the concept of "rights" had meaning only when connected with service and duty, and so fascism emerged as a revolt against the cult of unrealities to become the force for pragmatic realism consistent with the new age of science."

Ibid.

6 Edwards accepts that Fascism should be superseded by a new ethos:

"The tragedy of fascism was that it was not given a chance to blossom. A second disastrous war with all the hysteria and propaganda blurred a lot of the truth. Fascism should be remembered for its dynamism, its heroism and its vision during a time when something new was desperately needed to save man from self destruction. Fascism faced the facts of the pre-war world; and now we face the facts of a world which has changed so rapidly. What new force for the future can inspire hope in the same way that Fascism did so many years ago?"

Ibid.

7 There is a distinct parallel with Mosley's movement:

"[pp. 32-3] From 1943, Mandela's university classes brought him into contact with a number of other communists among the white and Indian student community. ... Important as these new friendships were— ... at this early stage the main contribution to his political formation was from people closer to home, especially among the group whom he encountered in his visits to the Sisulu household. In particular there were Anton Lembede and Oliver Tambo. Lembede was born in 1914, the son of a Free State farm labourer, educated at Catholic mission schools, and training as a teacher at Adams College in natal; he first worked as a teacher in the Free State where he was impressed by the organised gathering strength of Afrikaner nationalism evident in the small country towns where he lived. He took three correspondence degrees including an MA in philosophy as well as an LLB before serving articles in Johannesburg between 1943 and 1946 with Pixley ke Seme, one of the very few black South African legal partnerships in Johannesburg. By the time of his meeting with Mandela, in 1943, Lembede had already worked out a philosophical base for a new creed of racially assertive African nationalism.

Lembede's ideas were based on his conviction that each nation had its own peculiar character and that national communities were subject to Darwin's eternal law of variations. In such a social universe, no nation could find common philosophical ground with another. Africans, continentally, formed a single nation, reflecting a uniform cultural predisposition derived from a spirit of the environment—in other words, a social consciousness formed by adaptation to the geography of a particular region. Such adaptations, in the case of the coloured races, endowed their members with physical superiority. Africans on the whole shared a view of the universe:

> ... as one composite whole; as an organic entity, progressively driving towards greater harmony and unity whose individual parts exist merely as interdependent aspects of one while realizing their fullest life in the corporate life where communal contentment is the absolute measure of values. His philosophy of life strives towards unity and aggregation; towards greater social responsibility.

For Lembede one of the implications of this viewpoint was that black South Africans were participants in an anti-colonial national struggle that was indivisible from other struggles on the continent, despite South Africa not being, in the strictest sense, a colony. Accordingly, they should avoid engagement with 'foreign ideologies' such as communism and they should acknowledge the political imperatives of racial solidarity as opposed to those arising from class oppression.

[p. 39] … Within the ANC in the 1940s, a leadership discourse that employed metaphors of virile masculinity to project a programme of national revival accorded a privileged status to young men who were no longer expected to defer to the authority of elders. Mandela was a particular beneficiary of a quite startling reversal of generational authority, perhaps especially amenable to assuming a 'youth' cohort identity because of his rural upbringing as a member of a privileged age set."

There is also a very interesting parallel with Wilfred's and Robert Forgan's 'street block' system of electioneering put to good use:

"p. 57 … Mandela is generally perceived to have been the architect of the ANC's new organisational scheme, in which the base units of the ANC would be 'cells', one for every township street, themselves divided into 'blocks' of seven households each. Seven cells would constitute a zone, four zones would embody a ward headed by 'prime stewards', who when they met together would embody a branch secretariat. Although the ANC announced these plans publicly, Mandela and other leaders understood this structure as more suited to the 'new methods in our struggle' which he described to a Soweto audience that included plain clothes policemen on 13 December 1953—methods that would require activity 'done behind the scenes, even underground', a phrase that has suggested to some commentators that he and other ANC leaders were anticipating the organisation's legal suppression. The new structure would enable the ANC, as Mandela noted in his presidential address to the Transvaal provincial congress that year, to undertake activities that would 'find expression in wide-scale work among the masses, work that will enable them to make the greatest possible contact with working people' From now on, he urged, 'the activity of the Congresses must not be confined to speeches and resolutions'."

Mandela: A Critical Life, by Tom Lodge

8 Ramsay was one of the more strident commentators:

"Ever since the fall of Mr. Chamberlain's Government, the interests of the Jewish Empire have been advanced as prodigiously as those of Britain and her Empire have been eclipsed.

Stranger than all this -- should any dare to state the truth in plain terms - the only response is an accusation of anti-Semitism. As Mr. Douglas Reed has clearly shown, the term "anti-Semitism" is meaningless rubbish -- and as he suggests it might as well be called "anti-Semolina."

The Arabs are Semites, and no so-called "anti-Semite" is anti-Arab.

It is not even correct to say that he is anti-Jew. On the contrary, he knows better than the uninformed that a fair proportion of Jews are not engaged in this conspiracy.

The only correct term for the mis-called "anti-Semitic" is "Jew-wise". It is indeed the only fair and honest term.

The phrase "anti-Semite" is merely a propaganda word used to stampede an unthinking public into dismissing the whole subject from their minds without examination: so long as that is tolerated these evils will not only continue, but grow worse."

The Nameless War, by Captain Archibald Maule Ramsay

9 Lawrence was originally an academic, albeit a dynamic one; a sort of 'proto-Indiana Jones':

"Thomas Edward Lawrence was born in Wales in 1888 and educated at Oxford High School and at Jesus and Magdalen Colleges, Oxford. He was later made a research fellow of All Souls College, Oxford. From 1910 to 1914 he was an assistant in the British Museum's excavation of Carchemish on the Euphrates. He was commissioned on the outbreak of the First World War and in 1917 he was officially attached to the staff of the Hejaz Expeditionary Force, under General Wingate. In 1918 he was transferred to General Allenby's staff. He attended the Peace Conference in 1919 as one of the British Delegation, and in 1921 and 1922 was Adviser on Arab Affairs in the Middle Eastern Division of the Colonial Office."

He was well qualified to observe the geography as well as the people:

"p. 31 A first difficulty of the Arab movement was to say who the Arabs were. Being a manufactured people, their name had been changing in sense slowly year by year. Once it meant an Arabian. There was a country called Arabia; but this was nothing to the point. There was a language called Arabic; and in it lay the test. It was the current tongue of Syria and Palestine, of Mesopotamia, and of the great peninsula called Arabia on the map. Before the Moslem conquest, these areas were inhabited by diverse peoples, speaking languages of the Arabic family. We called them Semitic, but (as with most scientific terms) incorrectly. However, Arabic, Assyrian, Babylonian, Phoenician, Hebrew, Aramaic and Syriac were related tongues; and indications of common influences in the past, or even of a common origin, were strengthened by our knowledge that the appearances and customs of the present Arabic-speaking peoples of Asia, while as varied as a field-full of poppies, had an equal and essential likeness. We might with perfect propriety call them cousins — and cousins certainly, if sadly, aware of their own relationship.

The Arabic-speaking areas of Asia in this sense were a rough parallelogram. The northern side ran from Alexandretta, on the Mediterranean, across Mesopotamia eastward to the Tigris. The south side was the edge of the Indian Ocean, from Aden to Muscat. On the west it was bounded by the Mediterranean, the Suez Canal, and the Red Sea to Aden. On the east by the Tigris, and the Persian Gulf to Muscat. This square of land, as large as India, formed the homeland of our Semites, in which no foreign race had kept a permanent footing, though Egyptians, Hittites, Philistines, Persians, Greeks, Romans, Turks and Franks had variously tried. All had in the end been broken, and their scattered elements drowned in the strong characteristics of the Semitic race. Semites had sometimes pushed outside this area, and themselves been drowned in the outer world. Egypt, Algiers, Morocco, Malta, Sicily, Spain, Cilicia and France absorbed and obliterated Semitic colonies. Only in Tripoli of Africa, and in the everlasting miracle of Jewry, had distant Semites kept some of their identity and force. The origin of these peoples was an academic question; but for the understanding of their revolt their present [sic] social and political differences were important, and could only be grasped by looking at their geography. This continent of theirs fell into certain great regions, whose gross physical diversities imposed varying habits on the dwellers in them.

...

p. 34-5 For the people of the desert were as little static as the people of the hills. ... the inexorable trend northward continued. The tribes found themselves driven to the very edge of cultivation in Syria or Mesopotamia. Opportunity and their bellies persuaded them of the advantages of possessing goats, and then of possessing sheep; and lastly they began to sow, if only a little barley for their animals. They were now no longer Bedouin, and began to suffer like the villagers from the ravages of the nomads behind. Insensibly, they made common cause with the peasants already on the soil, and found out that they, too, were peasantry. So we see clans, born in the highlands of Yemen, thrust by stronger clans into the desert, where, unwillingly, they became nomad to keep themselves alive. We see them wandering, every year moving a little further north or a little further east as chance has sent them down one or other of the well-roads of the wilderness, till finally this pressure drives them from the desert again into the sown [sic], with the like unwillingness of their first shrinking experiment in nomad life. This was the circulation which kept vigour in the Semitic body. There were few, if indeed there was a single northern Semite, whose ancestors had not at some dark age passed through the desert. The mark of nomadism, that most deep and biting social discipline, was on each and every one of them in his degree."

Seven Pillars of Wisdom [A Triumph], by T. E. Lawrence

10 It seems the 'incomers' were the main cause of suspicion in the region:

"p. 337 Nature had so divided the country into zones. Men, elaborating nature, had given to her compartments an additional complexity. Each of these main north-and-south strip divisions was crossed and walled off artificially into communities at odds. We had to gather them into our hands for offensive action against the Turks. Feisal's opportunities and difficulties lay in these political complications of Syria which we mentally arranged in order, like a social map.

...

... On the banks of the Jordan valley lived bitterly-suspicious colonies of Algerian refugees, facing villages of Jews. The Jews were of varied sorts. Some, Hebrew scholars of the traditionalist pattern, had developed a standard and style of living befitting the country: while the later comers, many of whom were German-inspired, had introduced strange manners, and strange crops, and European houses (erected out of charitable funds) into this land of Palestine, which seemed too small and too poor to repay in kind their efforts: but the land tolerated them. Galilee did not show the deep-seated antipathy to its Jewish colonists which was an unlovely feature of the neighbouring Judea.

...

A fifth section in the latitude of Jerusalem would have begun with Germans and with German Jews, speaking German or German-Yiddish, more intractable even than the Jews of the Roman era, unable to endure contact with others not of their race, some of them farmers, most of them shopkeepers, the most foreign, uncharitable part of the whole population of Syria. Around them glowered their enemies, the sullen Palestine peasants, more stupid than the yeomen of North Syria, material as the Egyptians, and bankrupt.

East of them lay the Jordan depth, inhabited by charred serfs; and across it group upon group of self-respecting village Christians who were, after their agricultural co-religionists of the Orontes valley, the lest timid examples of our original faith in the country. Among them and east of them were tens of thousands of semi-nomad Arabs, holding the creed of the desert, living on the fear and bounty of their Christian neighbours. Down this debatable land the Ottoman Government had planted a line of Circassian immigrants from the Russian Caucasus. These held their ground only by the sword and the favour of the Turks, to whom they were, of necessity, devoted."

Ibid.

11 Lawrence's account is both sensual and spiritual:

"p. 364 I lay there quietly, letting the clear, dark red water run over me in a ribbly stream, and rub the travel-dirt away. While I was so happy, a grey-bearded, ragged man, with a hewn face of great power and weariness, came slowly along the path till opposite the spring; and there he let himself down with a sigh upon my clothes spread out over a rock beside the path, for the sun-heat to chase out their thronging vermin.

He heard me and leaned forward, peering with rheumy eyes at this white thing splashing in the hollow beyond the veil of sun-mist. After a long stare he seemed content, and closed his eyes, groaning, 'The love is from God; and of God; and towards God.'

His low-spoken words were caught by some trick distinctly in my water pool. They stopped me suddenly. I had believed Semites unable to use love as a link between themselves and God, indeed, unable to conceive of such a relation except with the intellectuality of Spinoza, who loved so rationally and sexlessly, and transcendently that he did not seek, or rather had not permitted, a return. Christianity had seemed to me the first creed to proclaim love in this upper world, from which the desert and the Semite (from Moses to Zeno) had shut it out: and Christianity was a hybrid, except in its first root not essentially Semitic.

Its birth in Galilee had saved it from being just one more of the innumerable revelations of the Semite. Galilee was Syria's non-Semitic province, contact with which was almost uncleanness for the perfect Jew. Like Whitechapel to London, it lay alien to Jerusalem. Christ by choice passed his ministry in its intellectual freedom; not among the mud-huts of a Syrian village, but in polished streets among fora and pillared houses and rococo baths, products of an intense if very exotic provincial and corrupt Greek civilization."

Ibid.

12 The ascription of Jewish 'guilt' was obviously not the whole story:

"The official stance of both Church and state [in the Middle Ages] to Jews was bound to be ambivalent. Following the Gospel account of the crucifixion, which attributes the blame for the death of Jesus Christ to the Jerusalem mob primed by the chief priests, Church teaching held all Jews guilty – had not that mob shouted, 'his blood be upon us and on our children'? Equally, the Church did not, nor did it wish to, deny the origins of Christianity in Judaism. Christ and his disciples were Jews, as was St. Paul, originator of much Christian doctrine. The books of the Jewish scriptures, the 'Old' Testament, were almost as important in the theology of the Church as the New Testament of Christ and his teaching. King David's Psalms, in their Latin Vulgate version, constituted one of the most beloved treasures of medieval churchmen.

A common image of 'Synagogue', the emblem for Judaism, was depicted as a beautiful woman blindfolded, so as to symbolise a tradition rich in the beauty of Truth which had wilfully closed its eyes to the fulfilment of that Truth in the coming of Jesus. For the state the position was simple. To most kings the enemies of Christ were no more and no less than a necessary part of the economic management of the state. But there could be ambivalent attitudes in the upper reaches of educated society. People recognised that Jewish culture represented by the city of Jerusalem was ancient. An early tradition concerning the Roman persecution of the Christians in Britain gives one of the most revered martyrs, a native of Carlisle, the name of Aaron – a classic 'Jewish' name during the Middle Ages. The city itself, according to Geoffrey of Monmouth, was built by King Leil at the same time as Solomon was beginning to build the kingdom of Jerusalem, and the Queen of Sheba came to listen to his wisdom. Such ideas seem to make some attempt to accommodate the enemies of Christ into the world of Christendom."

A Brief History of the Magna Carta: The Story of the Origins of Liberty, by Geoffrey Hindley

13 The British manifestation in Plymouth, hence the name, started in 1831, so it is even possible that Wilfred's grandmother could have become a member, following her husband's suicide in 1862, as related in Chapter 1:

"The first meeting in England was held in December 1831 in Plymouth. It was organised primarily by George Wigram, Benjamin Wills Newton and John Nelson Darby. The movement soon spread throughout the UK. By 1845, the assembly in Plymouth had over 1,000 people in fellowship. They became known as "the brethren from Plymouth" and were soon simply called "Plymouth Brethren". The term "Darbyites" is also used, especially when describing the "Exclusive" branch where the influence of John Nelson Darby is more pronounced. Many within the movement refuse to accept any name other than "Christian".

...

Not surprisingly, given such a divisive principle, the Exclusive Brethren have suffered many subsequent splits. McDowell records at least 6. Even the Open Brethren suffered one split, which occurred at different times in different parts of the world. But both sides continued to expand their congregations, with the opens, with their emphasis on faith missions, expanding more rapidly than the exclusives.

...

Essentially, therefore, the Brethren have no central hierarchy to dictate a statement of faith, and even local assemblies tend not to give tacit adherence to any of the historic "Creeds" and "Confessions of Faith" such as are found in many Protestant denominations. This is not because they are opposed to the central sentiments and doctrines expressed in such formulations but rather because they hold the Bible as their sole authority in regard to matters of doctrine and practice. Like many non-conformist churches, Brethren observe only the two ordinances of Baptism and Communion.

...

The term "Elder" is based on the same Scriptures that are used to identify "Bishops" and "Overseers" in other Christian circles, and some claim that the system of recognition of elders by the assembly means that the Plymouth Brethren as a movement cannot claim full adherence to the doctrine of the priesthood of all believers. However, this reveals a mistaken understanding of the priesthood of all believers which in the Assemblies has to do with the ability to directly offer worship, whether silently or audibly, to God and His Christ, at the Lord's Supper without any human mediator being necessary – which is in accordance with 1Tim 2:5 where it is stated that Christ Jesus Himself is the sole Mediator between God and men ("men", being used here generically of mankind, and not referring simply and solely to "males")."

http://en.wikipedia.org/wiki/Plymouth_Brethren#.22Open.22_and_.22Exclusive.22_Brethren

14 Suspicion and superstition were clearly prevalent in mediæval England:

"... with reference to mediæval society, there were 2 conspicuous developments. It was in England that the charge of ritual murder was raised in Norwich in 1144 when the body of a young skinner's apprentice was discovered. It was rumoured that he was killed by Jews "who had enticed him away from his family and crucified him after synagogue service on the 2nd day of Passover, in mockery of the passion of Jesus". This was, in fact, "the first recorded instance in the mediæval world of the infamous ritual murder accusation, which subsequently caused the jews throughout Europe untold misery." A later accusation came at Lincoln in 1255 in the case of "Little" St Hugh of Lincoln, a legend which was recounted by the Prioress in Chaucer's *Canterbury Tales*, and which became firmly embedded in English folklore. These accusations do not stand alone as evidence in England of mediæval opposition to Jews as Jews. In 1290 ... Jews were expelled from the country and although such an act was difficult to enforce in an absolute sense, it provided an example which was to be emulated elsewhere."

Anti-Semitism in British Society 1876-1939, by Colin Holmes

15 This attitude was well-established by the time Wilfred was born:

"... it was not until the 17th century that Jews were officially readmitted to England and, although at first the law ignored them, they soon found themselves touched by its provisions. The country was still Christian and legal restrictions were placed upon those who did not share this faith and, indeed, for some time even upon those Christians who were not communicants of the Church of England. The major instances of opposition to Jews in the 18th & 19th centuries developed out of this kind of situation and, in the sense that Jews were denied social rights because they could not subscribe to an oath supporting the Church of England rather than being singled out as Jews for discrimination, the principle behind the hostility cannot be regarded as specifically anti-Semitic in intention, although in practice it might assume that form. It should also be realised that whatever reasoning lay behind the restriction it succeeded in creating and sustaining an image of Jews as a problem."

Ibid.

16 In the 19th century, British Jews still lacked 'emancipation':

"In the course of the prolonged discussion [about emancipation, the Jews] were charged with foreignness and divided loyalties and also with possessing a low moral character as evidenced by their concentration upon financial gain. Both sets of charges provide a significant link with later expressions of anti-Semitic hostility. ... What can be said with certainty however, is that opposition had been manifested towards Jews from mediæval times onwards. In particular, it is not without significance for later expressions of hostility that for much of the 19th century Jews in Britain were treated as a difficult case, a social group whose emancipation was achieved only after a prolonged debate, which in itself was likely to induce an impression that Jews must be a special minority, an awkward element in society. By 1876 therefore, it was not only religious images of Jews which gave rise to antagonism. The social structure of the Jewish community - in particular the concentration of Jews in business, especially as middlemen - and the sojourning image which attached to a minority scattered over the earth whose history had been one of migration, exposed it, or sections of it, to charges of an undue concentration upon material gain and a shaky allegiance to British society. It is clear, in fact, that the conflicts after 1876 were influenced by these prior images of Jews which were [already] present in British society."

Ibid.

17 This concept, to combat the 'Nation within a Nation', is regarded as elusive:

"Shortly after James Picciotto had written about the secure position of English Jewry in 1875, the first instances of an anti-Semitism which was to recur at frequent intervals down to the First World War began to manifest itself in British society [*Sketches of Anglo Jewish History, London 1875*]. In surveying these attitudes an initial emphasis is placed upon these expressions of hostility which revealed an underlying concern with "Britain for the British", which stressed that the scarce resources of British society should reside in those who might be labelled 'British', and that there was a British culture and way of life which was worth preserving. The elusive nature of such concepts did not deter those who took up the battle on their behalf."

Ibid.

18 This has succeeded in saving "Tens of thousands" of animals:

"In 1973, the NAVS, now based in Harley Street, London, sought a new strategy and founded the Lord Dowding Fund for Humane Research. The Fund was named after Lord Dowding, the Air Chief Marshal who played a such a vital role during the Battle of Britain. After the war, Lord Dowding became President of the NAVS and in the House of Lords made many impassioned speeches on animal experiments. His wife Lady Dowding was also an NAVS Council member (later becoming President after her husband's death).

This new strategy was to make positive steps to replace the use of animals in research, and to show that animal research is not necessary for medical and scientific progress. Another aim would be to encourage, by publicity and publications, research without the use of animals. The Lord Dowding Fund has gone from strength to strength and continues today, to be responsible for ground breaking medical and scientific research that does not involve animals. Tens of thousands of animals have been saved, through the introduction of techniques and technology funded by the Lord Dowding Fund."

The history of the NAVS; http://www.navs.org.uk/about_us/24/0/299/

19 It seems pragmatism was again the way forward:

"... problems of a more fundamental nature showed the great gulf between the anti-vivisectionist and the forward-thinking scientist. ... There appeared to be an impasse, since the Deeds of the Lawson Tait could not knowingly be broken."

Animal research: the progressing change in attitude, by Pamela Brown; http://www.tandfonline.com/doi/pdf/10.1080/02688867.1990.9726771

20 ***The history of the NAVS, op. cit.***

21 ***Campaigning Against Cruelty: The hundred year history of the British Union for the Abolition of Vivisection, by Emma Hopley***

APPENDIX A

Although Sir Oswald Mosley, as he became in 1928, acquiring the hereditary baronetcy on the death of his father [also Sir Oswald], is not the subject of this biography, he was, arguably, the most significant and influential of the associates with whom Wilfred had any dealings during his life, so it would be negligent to omit at least a synopsis of Mosley's life up until his 'conversion' to the cause of Labour, taking him into 1924 when, it is generally reckoned, Wilfred first came into contact with him, and very quickly established a relatively close working relationship. Given the nature of the shared experiences over the course of the subsequent fifteen years, Mosley will be mentioned frequently as an active participant [and, inevitably, instigator] in most of the events in which Wilfred was involved during this period. The primary source of objective biographical information on Mosley is generally reckoned to be Robert Skidelsky, from which many of the references in this work will be drawn, although there are many others; Mosley's son, Nicholas, wrote two very useful companion biographies, ***Rules of the Game: Sir Oswald Mosley 1898-1932*** and ***Beyond the Pale: Sir Oswald Mosley 1933-1980***, which, although sometimes adversely critical of his father, still display some familial influence and filial subjectivity. Mosley's autobiography, ***My Life***, is also very useful, and is used here to a significant extent, even though it does not, regrettably, mention Wilfred by name; although that, given the many hundreds of people with whom Mosley must have come into contact during his life, is not unduly surprising in retrospect.

Mosley is probably mostly associated, if anywhere specifically, with London, given that it was where his operational base was located, for obvious reasons, while he was in Parliament, and Birmingham was his administrative centre for the second half of the 'twenties, while he was building up a political power-base, but Manchester was the source of his ancestors' wealth [**1**], which transferred to Staffordshire, the earliest origins of the family, as late as 1845 [**2**]. Mosley's family background was, somewhat unusually, a broken home, and he spent most of his childhood, apart from his school years, in Staffordshire [**3**]; his grandfather, the 4th Baronet, Sir Oswald Mosley, for whom he had a reciprocated fondness, was reckoned to be a kindly man, but mainly due to his somewhat squat and rotund stature, was nicknamed "Baronet John Bull", because of his resemblance to the fictional national personification of Great Britain [**4**].

Mosley's father, the 5th Baronet, was a proverbial latter-day 'black sheep of the family'; a spendthrift and a lothario, who was not above attempting to besmirch his own son's reputation, when he became a Socialist, making a brazen attack of unintentional irony in an interview for the national Press during the 1924 Ladywood election campaign, when he accused his son of being "born with a golden spoon in his mouth, and never having worked a day in his life"! Suffice to say, it was a matter of no great regret when his father died in 1928, and Oswald became Sir Oswald, which was no less divisive for his supporters than any other aspect of Mosley's character. Schooldays were not particularly inspiring; "School to me was not a happy interlude before facing the harsh responsibilities of adult life. It was a necessary but tedious progress through which we had to pass before the wide life of opportunity, adventure and great experience could begin." [**5**] His first school, where he arrived "just after my ninth birthday … after the home tuition of the excellent Miss Gandy, an intelligent woman and kindly guide", was West Downs, Winchester, which had "an enlightened headmaster, Lionel Herbert, who had given up being a clerk in the House of Lords, to found a small boys' school." [**6**] After only one year there, he progressed to the public school, Winchester, "just from a sense of urgency"; "one of the errors of my perpetual sense of haste." [**7**] At West Downs, boxing had been his "first love", when "in my opening fight I experienced for the first time incredulity that I could be winning", but "I only turned to fencing, in which my main successes were won, when competition boxing was forbidden to me. The headmaster of Winchester tolerated the sport within the school but would not allow any of us to go to the public schools competition, on which I had set my heart with some assurance of success from my instructor." [**8**] Skidelsky picks up on an aspect of Mosley's school life, whose inclusion could arguably be construed as sensationalist, but Mosley is not shy about an honest declaration: "Apart from games, the dreary waste of public school existence was only relieved by learning and homosexuality; at that time I had no capacity for the former and I never had any taste for the latter." [**9**] However, Mosley is at pains to point out a surprisingly liberal attitude on this subject: "My attitude to homosexuality was then much less tolerant than now, because I have long taken the view on basic ground of liberty that adults should be free to do what they wished in private, provided they do not interfere with others." [**10**] After convincing his mother to allow him to leave school early [again!] to pursue fencing "in a wider sphere … based on the general ground that I was wasting my time by staying any longer", his plans were thwarted by a combination of his mother's concerns that the European tour might be "a little gay", and the removal of the "means of financing the venture with ease" because of his father's temporary reconciliation with his grandfather [**11**].

After a "rather dull interval" which did, however, include six weeks which he considered "well spent" in the late summer of 1913 learning French at Brest, he arrived at Sandhurst in the beginning of 1914 [**12**]. Once again, he displayed precocious ability, entering at "just seventeen, an earlier age than was usual." [**13**] He unashamedly admits that "We broke every rule, and off parade had not the least regard for discipline.", but the apparently hardwired sense of duty asserted itself soon enough: "Few changes could have been more dramatic than the complete reversal in our attitude at the outbreak of war, when the playboys of the summer became overnight completely serious and dedicated young soldiers." [**14**] Again, Skidelsky picks up on a somewhat dubious escapade during this period, when Mosley acquires the first of his leg injuries which were later to present a somewhat less than perfect physical appearance, which was self-evident in person, but not generally remarked upon in reports, probably for very obvious reasons. The details are not particularly noteworthy, but the event resulted in a broken right ankle, which did not prevent his being passed A1 for service. Initial enthusiasm on being posted to France gave way to frustration at being held in reserve, so he applied to transfer to the Royal Flying Corps [RFC] which was taking on untrained men as observers. A short spell of duty, including a couple of minor injuries [one of which was a damaged knee, which was remedied by "a visit to a skilful bone-setter in London", did not deter him from taking up an opportunity to be trained as a pilot, which was being offered to "observers with some experience" [**15**]. He attained his flying certificate, after a necessarily short period of training, but he did not engage in active flying service thereafter, notwithstanding a serious leg injury [**16**], because his old regiment, the 16th Lancers, needed officers to replace recent losses. The medical board did not detect the injury, and he shortly found himself at the Front [**17**], where holes in the trench duck-boarding frequently caught him out in the dark, and he had to rely on the integrity of "the men" to keep his secret [**18**]. Before long, the condition of his leg deteriorated, and he was invalided out, and the result of the necessary treatment, although he did not lose the leg, as was a distinct possibility, was a pronounced limp [**19**]. He was now "fit for office work only." [**20**]

Until the end of the war, the 'duty' side of Mosley's life consisted of "administrative experience in the Ministry of Munitions and then in the Foreign Office", attained by shameless use of the "old boy … network [which] was working quite well even in those days, and I used it realistically and relentlessly"; relaxation was not overlooked, however [**21**]. It was via the social scene that Mosley received his *entrée* into politics [**22**] and, although he would have been adopted without opposition at Stone, in his native Staffordshire, he opted for the more difficult, given that he was an unknown, but also more practicable, given its proximity to London, constituency of Harrow, and after something of a 'baptism of fire' as a speaker, he was adopted as the Conservative candidate for the 1918 election [**23**]. A slogan used by Mosley during this election, which foreshadowed his later much-maligned ethos, was "socialistic imperialism", and "Even in the tranquil air of Harrow the sober burgesses were able to support such novel thinking in the flash of post-war enthusiasm to meet the problems of peace." [**24**] Perhaps a combination of the passing of the Edwardian era and the awareness, if not actual experience of, the maelstrom of the war just concluded meant that the Harrow voters were able to ignore the argument of Mosley's Independent Conservative opponent that he was too young, and elect him with a large majority. Outside Parliament, the other significant event in Mosley's life was his marriage in 1920 to the daughter of Lord Curzon, Cynthia ["Cimmie"] Curzon, whom he had met just after the war, and she remained a dutiful wife & mother, despite Mosley's philandering, as well as an independently-minded politician, until her death from peritonitis, in 1933.

The 'Irish Question', which precipitated Mosley's "crossing the floor", is summarised quite well by Skidelsky, but can be further summarised: Ireland in 1918 was in a state of separation from the United Kingdom, by a combination of the declaration of a Republic by the 73 Sinn Féin MPs elected to Westminster in 1918, and the resolution of the IRA, headed by Michael Collins, to gain independence by force of arms. The origin of the decision of Lloyd George, in the spring of 1920, to reconquer Ireland with force by countering "terror with terror" has since been endlessly debated, but "The likely answer is that the Government condoned rather than sanctioned the actions taken in its name." **[25]** The catalyst for Mosley's action was reprisals against the rebels, about which Mosley [among others, it should be noted] had been haranguing the Irish Chief Secretary, Sir Hamar Greenwood, born in Canada, who had previously been a Temperance lecturer; Mosley, and one of his close associates, Lord Henry Cavendish Bentinck, "crossed the floor" of the House, on the grounds that "he preferred to face his critics and interrupters rather than remain amongst them." **[26]** This was early November 1920 and, according to Skidelsky, Mosley's principled stand opened the 'liberal' phase of his career; he worked closely with the Liberals, but he never took their whip [although he did have access to notices sent out from the Whips' office, courtesy of a close friend]; he also started speaking out publicly on the economy, although Skidelsky calls his explanation of the economic crisis which had thrown two million people out of work [something of an overstatement, perhaps] in the winter of 1920-'21, "highly orthodox" **[27]**. Mosley was not so closely tied to the Liberals that he couldn't criticise Lloyd George's Middle East "imbroglios", citing policy which is depressingly familiar today, and which also brought home to him the potent source of conflict of "the unchecked operations of international finance" **[28]**. His status in Parliament was now Independent, and at the election in 1922 he was returned for Harrow with a large majority, beating the 'official' Conservative candidate almost two to one, in a reversal of the situation at the previous election.

Mosley politely rebuffed an invitation [via his good friend Lord Robert Cecil] to join Bonar Law's Conservative administration, feeling that "the rift between me and Conservatism had then grown too wide, and that my sense of purpose led me toward far more positive action than it then presented." **[29]** The next election came within a year, and the economy with its wider implications was the point of contention; Mosley stood on the platform of free trade, and he saw his approach as "purely pragmatic" [**30**]. He was returned, but with a reduced majority; his speech in the House thereafter, during the hiatus caused by the indecisive result [the Conservatives were in a minority, with the Liberals under Asquith holding the balance between them and Labour] was savagely critical of the previous Government, but also proposing a radically new approach to politics, with what could arguably be described as a Hitlerian reforming zeal [**31**], and the consequent ostracism, whether expressed or implied, could only have one outcome: "My path now led inevitably to the Labour Party." [**32**]

NOTES

1 Mosley was the 6th Baronet of Ancoats:

"Sir Oswald Mosley, the leader of the Blackshirts in Britain in the 1930s was from the Staffordshire and Lancashire Mosley family. This family tree is taken from two sources. Croston giving a more traditional family tree while Baines and Harland focus on the tortuous descent of the manor of Manchester until its sale to the City in 1845.

The family has its origins in Staffordshire. Near Wolverhampton lies the village of Mosley where there was a half timbered hall. Charles II is reputed to have taken temporary shelter there after the battle of Worcester. Ernold de Moseley lived in the reign of King John and from his second son, Oswald, the Lancashire branch descended. This branch is first mentioned in the reign of Edward IV with Jenkin Moseley in 1465. In 1473 a Robert Moseley is mentioned with a tenement believed to be near Deansgate and Victoria Street. He had a coat of arms quartered with that of his wife, which was eventually allowed by the Visitation of the Heralds in 1613 (Richard St. George).

The family tree is very complicated because of the failure of male lines and the transfer of property to cousins. In generation 4 … Nicholas and Anthony became wealthy cloth merchants with Nicholas handling trade in London. Anthony was the eventual ancestor of the Moseley families of Ancoats and Hulme; the latter became extinct in the early 18th century."

http://www.thornber.net/cheshire/htmlfiles/mosley.html

2 ***Ibid.:***

"In 1579, Nicholas Moseley, with a friend John Layce, advanced £3,000 on the security of the manor, lordship and seignoury of Manchester to Sir William West. When Sir William failed to comply with the conditions for redemption he lost these assets. Lacye [sic] was Lord of the Manor from 1582 to 1596 but then Nicholas Moseley bought him out for a further £3,500. The Moseleys then held the manor until they sold it to the Manchester Corporation in 1845 for £200,000."

3 http://en.wikipedia.org/wiki/Oswald_Mosley:

"Mosley was born at Rolleston Hall, near Burton-on-Trent on November 16, 1896. When his parents separated he was brought up by his mother, who initially went to live at Betton Hall near Market Drayton, and his paternal grandfather, Sir Oswald Mosley, 4th Baronet. … He lived for many years at Apedale Hall near Newcastle-under-Lyme."

4 http://en.wikipedia.org/wiki/Sir_Oswald_Mosley,_4th_Baronet

5 ***My Life, by Oswald Mosley***

6 ***Ibid.***

7 ***Ibid.***

8 ***Ibid.***

9 ***Ibid.***

10 ***Ibid.***

11 ***Ibid.***

12 ***Ibid.***

13 ***Ibid.***

14 ***Ibid.***

15 ***Ibid.***

16 This was, in Mosley's recollection anyway, the result of "some mild exhibition within the narrow limits of my knowledge and capacity as pilot", somewhat less self-critical than the 'showing off' to his mother, as some commentators have it: it was also "striking proof of a capacity to make mistakes". He failed to notice, due to the use of a rather primitive indicating device, "a wood and canvas frame pivoted on the ground in the shape of a T with the cross-piece facing the wind", a change of wind direction while he was flying, so his first attempt at a landing damaged the undercarriage, and although his "pancake" landing was good enough to avoid fatality, as was the result with many of this type, it was sufficiently heavy to injure his right leg severely, and which was beyond the skill of his London bone-setter to rectify.

Ibid.

17 Interestingly, his first posting in the trenches was with a Welsh battalion, composed largely of ex-miners; this would surely have warranted a mention in connection with Wilfred's association with Mosley if they had met here for the first time, so it must be assumed that they did not, because Wilfred was already serving with the RAMC.

Ibid.

18 ***Ibid.***

19 ***Ibid.***

"News of my condition eventually got around, and reached the ears of Colonel Eccles. There was a strong degree of paternalism in the colonels of these great regiments, which were conducted very like a large family. He sent for me and put me through some simple tests. I did not see him again until my wedding day in 1920, for the following morning I was on my way home by his arrangement and pursuant to his orders. A great surgeon, Sir Watson Cheyne, was on the point of retirement, but fortunately his son was a 16th Lancer and he took a special interest in my case. He warned me that only a fifty-fifty chance of saving the leg existed, which was in a sorry state after long neglect. He operated, and his skill saved the leg, though after a second operation towards the end of 1916 it was an inch and a half shorter."

20 ***Ibid.***

21 ***Ibid.:***

"Otherwise my time until the end of the war was occupied by a plunge into social life, which began on crutches in London and was pursued with zest through the ample opportunities then provided; followed by a return in happy circumstances to the Curragh, a period as instructor to wounded officers at Eastbourne which gave me more opportunity for reading, relieved again by some London life, … All contributed to my political education, not least the social life, whose value in some stages of experience should by no means be dismissed or even underrated."

22 ***Ibid.:***

"Another visitor from politics was Freddie Guest, a chief whip of the Lloyd George Liberals, an energetic and enterprising man who combined politics and air-racing until he reached quite an advanced age. He suggested that I should enter Parliament under their banner at the post-war election, but I already had some engagement to that other formidable Whip, Sir George Younger, the chief organiser of the Conservative party."

Mosley's early public speaking experience was for a contact made at the Foreign Office, who inevitably moved within Mosley's social *milieu*:

"Aubrey Herbert drifted in one day with his subtle blend of charm and vagueness in manner which covered a very acute intelligence. If I remember rightly, he had just escaped from a German prison camp and was seeking Foreign Office advice in certain difficulties. He was a brother of Lord Carnarvon and very English, but became so involved in the affairs of the Balkans that he was offered the crown of Albania. After the war, during week-ends in his beautiful Adam house at Pixton, I used to combine shooting with speaking for him in his constituency at the neighbouring town of Yeovil."

23 ***Ibid.:***

"I decided to write out my fifteen-minute speech and learn it by heart. It was quite a good speech but shockingly bad in delivery. As one of the old politicians present said afterwards, good stuff, but badly chanted. I was far from having acquired the range of voice and variation in rhythm and tempo in which I later attained some competence. I did not even realise the necessity. To stand up and say something sensible seemed to me adequate. The speech consequently fell flat, though they applauded politely, possibly in sympathy with a very young man in uniform. Then came questions, and in that hour I was launched into politics. They were good, pointed, often expert questions, for Harrow was a dormitory of London where men and women lived who worked in the city and were versed in every intricate question of Britain and the Empire. I had by then read enormously and was vastly interested in politics; the fascination of the argument brought me alive and evoked some latent power of exposition. Questions ended in a scene of considerable enthusiasm. I was adopted as prospective candidate by over ninety per cent of the votes of those present."

24 ***Ibid.:***

"It was an ugly phrase, but it was pregnant with the future. Let no one ever say that the combination of the socialist and nationalist ideas was a foreign invention copied by me."

25 ***Oswald Mosley, by Robert Skidelsky***

26 ***Ibid.***

27 ***Ibid.:***

"What made him liberal was his preoccupation with preserving peace. ... Thus we find Mosley giving a highly orthodox explanation of the economic crisis which in the winter of 1920-1 had thrown 2m people in England out of work:

'What is the cause of the trouble today? The cause is that half the world has been ruined. Half the world is not working. Half the world is unable to buy the goods which this country is in a position to offer. This is the first, the primary, the fundamental cause of unemployment today.'

The remedy followed logically: 'to set to work at once upon the business of European reconstruction ... good Christianity ... is good business'"

28 ***Ibid.:***

"The Conservative Party's break with the Coalition [at the 1922 election] had left it free to criticise Lloyd George's policy. Even before the Carlton Club meeting [where the vote for the break away had occurred] Bonar Law had repudiated Lloyd George's Middle East imbroglios with the words 'We cannot act alone as the policeman of the world' - a sentiment which was in complete harmony with the thrust of Mosley's own criticism. ... Not that Mosley thought Britain was in Iraq for purely altruistic, law-keeping reasons. Behind the rhetoric of bringing good government to primitive peoples he discerned the sinister scramble for oil. 'If we go to war in the Near East [sic],' he warned, 'it is a commercial war and nothing else ... the world will again be plunged back into an immense catastrophe for commercial, money-collecting reasons.' Already he was beginning to see the unchecked operations of international finance as a potent source of conflict."

29 ***My Life, op. cit.***

30 ***Ibid.:***

"The question of free trade or protection was in those days to many people almost a religious issue. My approach to it was purely pragmatic. Whether you had one system or the other was a question of circumstance. If it was raining, you needed an umbrella, if the sun was shining, you did not. The wider considerations presented to me by certain subsequent experiences had not then occurred to me, but even at that early date my ideas were remote from the old-fashioned concept of Conservative tariffs. At the 1923 election I accepted the classic free trade argument, with an important addition or variation derived from the contemporary situation and extending to the present day, which I believe I was the first to note in debate. My novel argument was that fluctuations in the exchange rate of foreign countries made nonsense of any tariff barrier, and they were then continually occurring. Mr. Baldwin did not appear to understand these rather complicated arguments, though perhaps he was only 'playing stupid', at which he was as apt as some of our ambassadors."

31 ***Ibid.:***

"Let us substitute another policy which does not wait in sycophantic adulation, punctuated by snarls, upon any individual or upon any country, but which defines a policy of our own, pro-British, pro-European, and pro-humanity. Let us be the enemies of no country, but the friends of all peoples, the unflinching opponents of any policy that is the enemy of mankind. . . . In all lands there is a revival of the progressive spirit today. In every country the forces of progress are looking to our land to give a lead. We shall achieve this not by quarrelling with any country, but by rallying those forces ... in all the lands to the banner of progress, and that banner must be raised by some country and some people. There is the opportunity lying in the hands of this Parliament, in the overwhelming majority of this Parliament, of one of the greatest missions which historic destiny has ever imposed on the people of this country ... of placing itself at the head of the peoples of Europe and leading them on the great march back from those dark lands of suffering and sorrow in which we have sojourned so long ... to lead the peoples of the world in re-establishing a system of justice, of reconciliation, of peace upon earth."

32 ***Ibid.***

APPENDIX B

This is a transcription of any references to Wilfred Risdon, and any other significant details, in the minutes of the meetings of the West Bromwich branch of the Independent Labour Party [ILP] from 1929 to 1931; taken from ***Archives of the Independent Labour Party, series 2: minutes and related records, part 2: branch minutes and related records 1892 - 1950***; microform, courtesy of The British Library DSC Microform Research Collections. It is worth mentioning that, understandably enough, the minute books were, to the best of my knowledge, always handwritten, and therefore subject to 'individual' spelling manifestations and sometimes virtually indecipherable script, so apologies are in order if any entries have been incorrectly transcribed. Original capitalisation and spelling has been preserved for authenticity; original line breaks have not been preserved, however. Punctuation was not always clear, so I have used my own judgement. The original page numbers are shown for reference; I have not used a font in a 'handwriting' style for the sake of legibility.

---

155 Minutes of E.C. Meeting Held June 28th [1929]
Com. J. Holland presided

...

3 Letter read from Mr. W. Risdon the new organising Secretary for M.D.C. asking for a date in which to visit the Branch. Sec. reported that he had fixed up July 3rd for his visit.

Circular read from M.D.C. calling our attend-tion to the new resolutions drawn up by that [?] body. The chairman read each clause seperate and it was decided to recommend the question of Subs be brought forward to the General meeting.

---

156 Minutes of General Meeting July 3rd
Com. J. Holland Presided.

...

Risdon 3 The Chairman then welcomed Mr. W. Risdon the organising secretary to the Branch.

Mr. Risdon in the cause of his few remarks out lined the policy of the I.L.P. and its relationship to the Labour Party and also hoped that each member would take his or her part in the work of the Branch and not leave it to the few.

Question were asked Mr. Risdon in which he able answered.

---

177 Minutes of General Meeting held Nov 6th/29
Com. J. Holland presided

Secy read letter from H.O. also letter from W. Risdon Re. Stamfords expences which amounted to £1 - 10 - 0 this matter to be brought up at the next Fed. Meeting.

---

184 Minutes of General meeting held on January 8th [1930] Com T. Worker presided:–

Minutes of last meeting read & confirmed. Com [illegible] requesting that notice be taken of the roundabout way in which correspondence referring to Traders Council business was received. Comrade Cook moved that we send one delegate to Midlands divisional Conference at Leicester on Jan 25th & 26th. Comrade Pugh's nomination for same was carried unanimously & Conference resolutions. It was decided to give the delegate discretionary powers on all resolutions except No. 2 on Final Agenda which reads "That the Labour Party having now become in theory & in practice both Capitalist & Imperialist it is now necessary for the Independent Labour Party to cease affiliation to it." The delegate was given instructions to vote in favour of this resolution. …

---

185 Minutes of special General Meeting held on Jan 15th 1930.
Comrade J. Holland presided. Brockhouse Memorial Meeting. Comrade Pugh reported that after trying to get national speaker himself & failing he solicited the help of W. Risdon, Divisional Organiser, who fixed us up with J.J. McShane, for Feb 9th. It was felt by some members that McShane would be unable to fill the Town Hall & that the best plan would be to have the meeting in the Labour Church.* After a lengthy discussion it was moved by Comrade Mynett that we have the meeting in the Town Hall, with Roberts M.P. as second speaker or put the meeting to a later date, & get a more popular speaker. This was carried. …

---

189 Minutes of Branch meeting; date unknown [probably early February 1930]
…

The following programme was drawn up for the Brockhouse Memorial Meeting.

Organ recital 6- to 6-30
1st Song "Lift up the peoples' Banner"
Chairman's Remarks
Solo by com. Welch
J.J. Mc Shane — Collection
W. Risdon — Guild Speaker
Solo Announcements
F.O. Roberts — "Red Flag"

This concluded the business

---

213 **Minutes of Branch meeting**; date unknown [probably early part of 1930]

...

Sec instructed to write Sec of Trades Council urging them to press for direct labour schemes to be undertaken by Town Council. Letter from H.O. asking for nomination for N.A.C. in place of our late comrade John Wheatley. M.D.C. report. Circular from Risdon recommending nomination of Alan Young for N.A.C. ...

---

214 **Minutes of Gen Meeting held Aug 13th 1930**

...

Correspondence ...

Letter from Comrade Maxton saying he could not attend Brockhouse Memorial.

...

Circular from M.D.C. re nomination of Alan Young. Decided to nominate Alan Young, but to protest to Risdon against methods used.

...

---

221 **Adjourned Gen. Meeting held Sept 21/30** Com. Worker in the chair.

...

Letter from Fenner Brockway saying he would be in the Midlands from Feb. 6-8 Sec. instructed to get in touch with Risdon, it was also decided to write to Kirkwood thanking him for speaking date and asking him to accept Feb. 8th 31

...

Cir. re. M.D.C. conference it was decided to send one delegate, Com Mrs. Pugh was chosen and given discretionary powers. ...

---

222 **Minutes of E.C. held on Monday, Sept 29th 1930.** Com. Worker in the chair

...

Brockhouse Meeting.It was decided to recommend to General Meeting that they make a choice of the following choice of speakers. Comrades F. Brockway, Jennie Lee, E.F. Wise, Dr. Forgan, & J. Beckett & to rescind previous minute re. Kirkwood. This after Secretary had reported, an interview with W. Risdon who had stated that those Comrades would be in Birmingham the week-end

...

---

224 **Minutes of General Meeting held on Wednesday evening Oct 1st 30** Comrade Merther in the chair. Minutes of previous meeting read and confirmed. Matters arising.

Resolution re David Kirkwood rescinded it was decided to get in touch with Risdon with a view to getting Fenner Brockway and Jennie Lee.

...

Rec.

...

The rec re disaffiliation rejected and it was moved that instruct our delegates to vote against disaffiliation the voting was even and the chairman gave his casting vote in favour of disaffiliation

...

---

231 Minutes of General meeting held on Sunday morning Nov 16th
Comrade Merther in the chair
Minutes of previous meeting read and accepted.
Correspondence Circular from Risdon re propaganda meeting for Feb 8th. J. Beckett [re?]allocated to West Bromwich. Sec instructed to write re possibility of exchanging Maxton & Beckett for a short time. Advertising of meeting to be got in hand by advertising sheets. Com Groom put in charge of same. Committee to get adverts. Meeting to open at 7-0pm Financial Sec to book Town Hall & make deposit. Not to engage organ. It was moved that we call the meeting the "Harry Brockhouse memorial Lecture."

...

Circular from N.A.C. re Labour Party Conference. The following resolution was carried for the Midlands Divisional Conference. That the West Bromwich Branch of the I.L.P. calls on this Conference to disaffiliate ...

---

236 Minutes of Branch meeting; date unknown [probably late 1930]

...

Conference Resolutions

...

Res. No. 1 "Governmental managed paper currency" instead of "managed paper currency"
Res. No. 5 addendum "and all persons whose income does not exceed £8 per week shall be compulsory insured"
Res. No. 16 addendum "and to this end we oppose the proposals embodied in the Mosley Memorandum"
Amend "abolition of Capitalist exploitation" instead of "Extermination of the Capitalist exploiting class"

---

236 Minutes of E.C. meeting held Sunday 11th Jan 30 [should be 31]
Com Worker in the chair

Minutes of previous meeting read and accepted
Advertising Sheets, decided to call the G.M. attention to the need for speedy action in this matter. Write Risdon for block of speakers and to see if it was possible to exchange speakers. It was decided to have a silver collection in the Gallery at the Town Hall.

---

241 Minutes of G.M. held Sunday Jan 17/31 Com Merther in the chair
Minutes of previous meeting read and accepted
Letter from Risdon re cancellment of Dates by Beckett and Maxton
The following arrangements were made for the Brockhouse Meeting:- I .
Bowen to speak ? Strachey is able to be present …
…
Correspondence
Letter from Prime Minister acknowledging resolution …

---

246 Special E.C. held Feb 6/31 Com Merther in the chair

The meeting was called because a telegram had come from Paton asking us if we desired Kirkwood to speak at the Town Hall, the Sec had replied in the affirmative, another telegram from Paton informed us that we were too late Kirkwood had gone to Scotland.

It was therefore decided to send an express letter to Kirkwood's home address asking him to break his journey to the House and speak for us.

Letter from Risdon making special appeal for delegates to conference. Two or three members decided to go on their own.

…

NOTE*

The Labour Churches were an interesting hybrid, a practical, utilitarian solution to the very real problem of the difficulty of spreading the socialist message to a large potential audience, whose only day of freedom from the constraints of sheer economic survival was Sunday, and they were also sometimes formed in response to church ministers supporting Liberal and Conservative candidates in parliamentary elections. According to Wikipedia [**1**]:

> "The Labour Church was an organization intended to give expression to the religion of the labour movement. This religion is not theological but leaves the theological for the individual to consider and contemplate."

According to Henry Pelling, in his 1954 reference work ***The Origins of the Labour Party*** [**2**], the ethos being preached was "vague and materialistic" and, although the movement originated in Manchester, founded by a Unitarian minister, John Trevor, in October 1891, it was particularly strong in Birmingham, and is mentioned frequently in the above Branch minutes. In his contemporary review [**3**] of Pelling's work, Philip Poirier tells us:

> "Pelling's most important contribution is a chapter on the Labour Churches, those peculiar institutions which thrived in the pioneering period of the nineties and died out when the movement entered a more opportunistic and administrative phase. Untheological in teaching, largely nonconformist in spiritual ancestry, vague and materialistic in its creed, the Labour Church in some cities such as Birmingham became the center of socialist activities. It was usually strong where the Independent Labour Party (the I.L.P.) was strong, especially in Yorkshire, and it enabled socialist propagandists to preach on Sunday to thousands whom otherwise they might never have reached."

Both ***Wikipedia***, and one of its specified sources, ***Spartacus Education*** [**4**], assert that the Labour Church had ceased to exist by 1914, having suffered a decline with the resignation, for unspecified reasons, of its founder in 1900, but this is clearly not the case; perhaps one of the possibly many reasons for its survival in Birmingham was the evident strength of Christian Socialism in that city? George Barnsby, another very useful source on West Midland history, confirms the existence of the West Bromwich Labour Church up to 1940 , and illustrates the Brockhouse connection [**5**], a name mentioned in the above Branch minute book:

> "The next and most celebrated of the Black Country Labour Churches was West Bromwich, the Victoria County History quoting D.F. Summers's unpublished Edinburgh PhD thesis of 1958, states that there was a meeting … in 1899 of the Church at Groves Assembly Rooms with Henry Brockhouse [joint secretary] in the chair. By 1901 it was established in its own premises, the People's Hall, which had been 'built' by the local ILP. From this time the Church existed continuously, not only to 1914 but up to 1940.

> The People's Hall was a corrugated iron building on a site between Shaftesbury Street and Temple Street, between the old Hippodrome and a row of shops. It held nearly 200 people, and club and committee rooms were attached. It was lighted by electricity installed by members. Its most important feature was the decoration which was supervised by Walter Crane, the celebrated artist of the Labour movement. The cost was £700, of which £400 had been raised. The opening ceremony was on Sunday 10th November 1901. The building was still the property of the ILP in 1970."

No reference has been found, so far, of Wilfred's attitude towards, or involvement in, the Labour Church.

REFERENCES

1 http://en.wikipedia.org/wiki/Labour_Church

2 ***The Origins of the Labour Party, by Henry Pelling***

3 ***The Journal of Politics, Vol. 17, No. 3 (Aug., 1955), pp. 464-466; published by Cambridge University Press on behalf of the Southern Political Science Association;***
http://www.jstor.org/stable/2127022

4 http://www.spartacus.schoolnet.co.uk/RElabour.htm

5 ***Socialism in Birmingham and the Black Country, 1850-1939, by George J. Barnsby***

ABBREVIATIONS

Cir	Circular
Com	Comrade
E.C.	Executive Council
Fed	Federation
H.O.	Head Office
M.D.C.	Midlands Divisional Council
N.A.C.	National Administrative Council [governing body of the ILP]
Rec	Recommendation
Sec	Secretary
Secy	Secretary
Subs	Subscriptions [i.e., to qualify for continued membership]

APPENDIX C

INDEPENDENT
LABOUR PARTY
EASTER
CONFERENCE
1930
BIRMINGHAM
SOUVENIR
1930

[Note: this flyleaf page was left blank in the original; only the most relevant pages have been reproduced here, hence the gaps in the pagination - the left & right orientation of the original pages has been retained]

Independent Labour Party

SOUVENIR

of the

38th Annual Conference

to be held at
BIRMINGHAM
EASTER – 1930

3

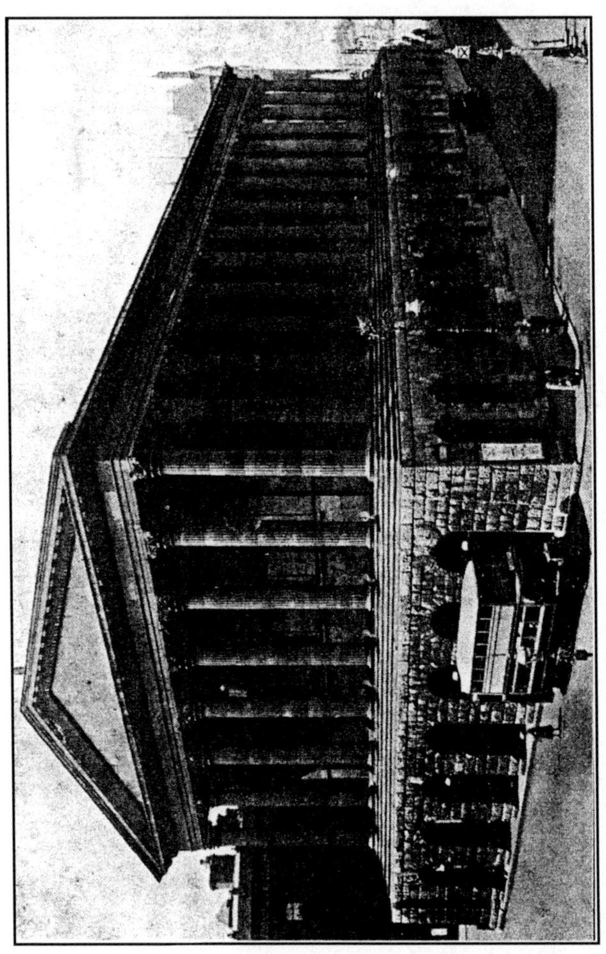

THE TOWN HALL, BIRMINGHAM.

4

CONTENTS

❦

5

ACKNOWLEDGMENTS

ACKNOWLEDGMENTS FOR ASSISTANCE GIVEN IN THE COMPILATION OF THE CONFERENCE SOUVENIR.

❦

I WOULD like to take this opportunity to place on record the appreciation of the Conference Arrangements Committee in general, and my own gratitude in particular, to all those who by their generous assistance have helped to make this year's Conference Souvenir something worthy of the I.L.P.

First, a word of thanks to Mr. Faulkner, of the Town Clerk's Department of the City of Birmingham, for the loan of the blocks which illustrate various aspects of Birmingham's municipal life, and to the various committees who, as owners of those blocks, gave permission for their use in the Conference Souvenir. Also to the Librarian at the Birmingham Lending Library for the facilities given to photograph the splendid engraving of the "Gathering of the Unions," which is reproduced in this booklet. This illustrative matter adds very considerably to the value of the Souvenir and our best thanks are tendered to all those concerned.

We are grateful, too, to those contributors who have written up the various subjects covered in the publication. George Butler, for his very excellent contribution on the History of Birmingham; W.J. Chamberlain for his notes "From Chartism to Socialism" ; W. H. Milner for the article on "Municipal Enterprise in Birmingham"; and

7

H. W. Whatley for the article on "Birmingham and Co-operation." The provision of matter for the booklet has been truly Socialist in its method, representing the work of no single individual but the joint effort of a number of specialists who have given of their best.

The printing of this Souvenir has been carried out in the works of The Blackfriars Press, Ltd., at Leicester, and it would not be fitting to close without expressing my own thanks for the very great assistance rendered by the staff of the Blackfriars Press in advising as to the "lay-out" so as to get the best possible results.

The ready assistance of all those mentioned above has made my own undertaking as the editor of the booklet a comparatively simple matter, and that duty, which I undertook with some degree of trepidation because of my inexperience, has proved to be much more simple than I had anticipated.

Last, but by no means least, we owe a debt of gratitude to our comrade Joseph Southall, for preparing the very effective cover design. This very distinctive finishing touch enables us to place this Conference Souvenir in your hands with pride in the knowledge that it is worthy of the traditions of a great movement.

W. RISDON.

8

Conference Programme

(Subject to alteration)

FRIDAY, APRIL 18TH.

10-30 a.m.	Meeting of the National Administrative Council.
8 p.m.	Divisional Representatives' Conference at The Shakespeare Rooms (Dickens Room), Edmund Street, Birmingham. (Open only to accredited representatives.)

SATURDAY, APRIL 19TH.

2-30 p.m.	Annual Conference opens at the Town Hall.
to	Chairman's Address : James Maxton, M.P.
5 p.m.	Fraternal Delegates.
8 p.m.	Reception to Delegates at the Town Hall.

SUNDAY MORNING, APRIL 20TH.

9-30 a.m.	Annual Report of N.A.C.
to 1 p.m.	Voting for N.A.C.

SUNDAY AFTERNOON, APRIL 20TH.

2 p.m.	Conference photograph.
2-30 p.m.	*Conference goes into Committee.
to 5 p.m.	

SUNDAY EVENING, APRIL 20TH.

8 p.m.	Conference Demonstration, the Town Hall, Birmingham. Chairman : E. F. Wise, C.B., M.P. Speakers : James Maxton, M.P., D. Kirkwood, M.P., Kate Spurrell, John Nixon (Guild of Youth).
	Other Demonstrations at various centres.

11

BOOKS TO GET AT THE CONFERENCE BOOKSTALL

J. KEIR HARDIE

A Biography by
WILLIAM STEWART
With an Introduction by the
Rt. Hon. J. RAMSAY MACDONALD, M.P.

INDEPENDENT LABOUR PARTY
PUBLICATION DEPARTMENT
14 GREAT GEORGE STREET, LONDON

THE MEANING OF SOCIALISM
By J. BRUCE GLASIER
Introduction by J. A. HOBSON, M.A.

INDEPENDENT LABOUR PARTY
14, GREAT GEORGE ST., WESTMINSTER

THE CASE FOR SOCIALISM

BY
FRED HENDERSON

I.L.P. PUBLICATION DEPARTMENT
14 GREAT GEORGE STREET, LONDON

Socialism for To-Day

by
HENRY NOEL BRAILSFORD.

INDEPENDENT LABOUR PARTY
14 Great George St., Westminster, London, S.W.1.

16

GREETINGS FROM M.D.C.

TO the Delegates attending the 1930 Conference at Birmingham the Midlands Divisional Council extends fraternal greetings.

We venture to express the hope that this year's Conference will be, in the truest sense of the word, historic. The indications contained in the formidable list of resolutions, are that the Conference will at least prove to be both interesting and useful.

The last occasion on which the annual Conference was held in the Midlands was 1926, when we met at Leicester. Then we were living in the shadow of a crushing Tory majority in the House of Commons, which has, fortunately, been swept away in the meantime. This year we meet in the knowledge that Labour is the largest Party in

GEORGE BUTLER,
(*Chairman of Mid. Div. Council.*)

the House, and in the confident anticipation that the next election, come when it may, will see Labour outnumbering the forces of both the other Parties combined.

On another page will be found a reproduction of a photograph taken at one of the earliest of the I.L.P. Conferences, the Nottingham Conference of 1896. Some, at least, of the delegates who were at that Conference, will also be at this one but many have passed from the scene in the years which have intervened, having added their quota

18

to the work of building up the movement which has enabled Labour to gain for the second time the reins of Government in this country. To those of us who remain associated with the work of the I.L.P. remains the perhaps more difficult task of seeing that the machine which has been created shall function definitely in the interests of Socialism and not merely as an organisation for the patching up of Capitalism.

WILFRID RISDON,
(*Midlands Organiser*.)

We trust that every delegate and every visitor attending this year's Conference will return to their respective branches with energy renewed and faith revived to conduct on an ever-increasing scale the fight for "Socialism and nothing less than Socialism." In the light of present-day happenings the outline of I.L.P. policy which Keir Hardie wrote for the "New Review" in March of 1893 assumes an almost prophetic significance. "The aim of the I.L.P." he wrote, "is to create a genuinely Independent Party in politics to take charge of the revolution which economic conditions are leading us toward ; and its object is to build up an industrial commonwealth in which none will suffer want because of the over-abundance of others." This indicates something of the magnitude of the job which we have not yet accomplished. We are hopeful that the 1930 Conference will give a lead which will mean renewed vigour applied to the attainment of the Socialist objective, and to the abolition of want from our midst.

19

APPENDIX D

Chronological sequence of events preceding the detention under Defence Regulation 18B (1A) in May, 1940, of Wilfred Risdon; During the transition from British Union to the LPAVS:

12/06/39 Special Branch report [via PGT?]: HQ meeting ["a conference of District officers in the London Administration"], 30/05/39, at which OM put forward that "it should be able, in troubled times like the present, to effect economies in headquarters staff without detriment to the smooth working of the organisation"; "none of the paid staff was present". ... "MOSLEY next turned to the subject of the 'biggest indoor political meeting in the world', namely, that which is to be held by the movement at the Earl's Court Exhibition Hall on Sunday 16th July next." ...

"At a confidential session of the Senior Officials' Week End School held at Manchester on 3rd/4th June, and attended by 35 persons, DONOVAN stated the leaders were aware that in the event of war the Government would close down the movement's headquarters, arrest the higher officials and attempt to seize the funds. Arrangements were being made whereby one key man would have charge of each area and would be responsible for transmitting messages to all under him. The funds would be scattered, so that the authorities could not obtain possession of them."

"W. RISDON is remaining at headquarters until after the Earl's Court rally, working in a voluntary capacity."

Working for the LPAVS:

22/05/40 Order for detention, signed by Alexander Maxwell, Under Secretary of State for the Home Department.

23/05/40 Served by Inspector Charles Allen, Special Branch, and P.S. Ewing at 3.00 p.m., and "later handed over to the Governor of Brixton Prison, together with a copy of this Order."

23/05/40 Report by Inspector Allen detailing the detention and search of home.

24/05/40 Statement by WR from Brixton; taken to be request for appeal? No other request in file.

28/05/40 Letter from Assistant Commissioner [on behalf of] Metropolitan Police, Special Branch, to USoS, Home Office, enclosing detention report, together with original Order [for detention], "duly endorsed".

17/06/40 Letter from Mrs. Findlay to her MP, Colonel Llewellyn [sic], enquiring as to the situation of her husband, A.G. Findlay, and WR, "another constituent of yours".

19/06/40 Letter from J. Llewellin at the Ministry of Aircraft Production to Osbert Peake, MP, at the Home Office, enquiring about Findlay & WR; "I do not, of course, wish to influence you in any way, but it would be helpful if you could let me have a reply that I can pass on to my constituent."

21/06/40 Letter from Peake promising to let Llewellin know the final decision "in these cases": "It is open to these men to make representations - which I expect they have already done - but we cannot undertake to deal with appeals otherwise than in their turn."

02/07/40 Letter from E.B. Stamp at the Home Office [MI5] to G.P. Churchill [Secretary of the Advisory Committee], enclosing Statement of Case & Reasons for Order against WR [and George Sutton, OM's personal secretary].

HOME OFFICE
ADVISORY COMMITTEE TO CONSIDER APPEALS AGAINST ORDERS OF INTERNMENT.

Notes of a meeting held at 6 Burlington Gardens on Thursday, **11th July, 1940**.

PRESENT: Mr. Norman Birkett, K.C. (Chairman)
The Rt. Hon. Sir G.R. Clerk, G.C.M.G., C.B.
Sir Arthur Hazlerigg, Bt.
Mr. G.P. Churchill, C.B.E. (Secretary)

NAME OF APPLICANT: WILFRED RISDON.
Note taken by Treasury Reporters.

CHAIRMAN: You have had the reasons for the Order that has been served upon you, I suppose?
A. Yes.
Q. It begins "We have reasonable cause to believe" and so on. What will be the most convenient method to deal with it? Would you like us to ask questions to bring the matters out, or would you rather make a statement now or at the conclusion?
A. (**MR. RISDON**) It may help you if I make a statement to start with.
Q. Certainly do that.
A. In the personal particulars, in paragraph one, it is quoted that I have been a member of the "said organisation since some years and have been active in the furtherance of its objects......Assistant Director-General of the said organisation". That is quite true, I was until last July in that capacity, but the term "Assistant Director-General" is not really correct, it is a misnomer,

it is one I always objected to because a Director-Generalship without any authority is not a Director-Generalship. The only thing I did was to act as the Chief Agent in the political sense, training people to build up constituency organisation. That was my function. I am an election agent, and that was my function as an alleged Assistant Director-General. I think it well to make that point clear. The next point is that "as one of the leaders of the Press Propaganda Group", I have never occupied that position at all. I was known as Propaganda Administrator, but that did not cover any press work at all. That was for the purpose of taking speaker schools and training speakers.

Q. Was there a Press Propaganda Group?

A. I believe there was at one time.

Q. Perhaps that was for a specified thing, was it? We are told that was the 1937 Autumn Municipal Election, and there was a press propaganda group for that specific purpose of which you were one of the leaders. I think that is what that refers to.

A. I was not at any time nominated as that.

Q. Very well.

A. The next point, "The organisation known as British Union is subject to foreign influence and/or control".

Q. You realise that is taken from the regulations under which the detention orders are made. You have probably seen that?

A. Yes. The next goes on, "The constitution of the organisation is influenced by Italian or German political and/or national organisations". That is not so, to my knowledge. As a matter of fact, there have been occasions - and this covers part of the next section as well - there have been occasions when I bitterly opposed anything approaching any copying of foreign methods. If I may take the next sub-section of that paragraph, "The constitution of the organisation has been and is subject to Italian or German influences in the original name of the organisation, the British Union of Fascists. It is later named the British Union of Fascists and National Socialists. Its emblems, its uniforms, its procedure, its form of public meetings and similar matters". In the period I was with the British Union I occupied many positions. I was with them of course from the inception. I expect you know I left the Labour Party with Sir Oswald Mosley and remained with him throughout until July last year. The British Union of Fascists was the first name of the organisation after the New Party ceased to function as such, and I did not like the name "Fascist" because it represented not only a foreign name but it represented a name which I with my background had some cause to dislike. My individual opposition perhaps was not too much use at that time, but it is interesting to note that the title "British Union" which is now the title of the Movement was the one I suggested as a better title at that time.

Q. I see, from the copy of the constitution that I have, which was published in

1936, "The Movement should be called the British Union of Fascists and National Socialists......the first two words of this title, "British Union", should be used for purposes of abbreviation."
A. Yes, that is the title I liked. The symbol of the fasces was another thing I did not like, although I had not so rooted an objection to that because it was pointed out to me the fasces were used not only as a political symbol but in most of the civil institutions in the country, so I did not maintain the opposition to that so much. As to the uniforms, there were two sets of uniform used in the British Union, the first was the plain fencing jacket with ordinary flannel trousers, and I had never any objection whatsoever to that. I want to make that quite clear. That was a uniform I thought to be something fit for a political uniform, but when the later uniform was adopted, which was known as the "Action Press" uniform, with jackboots and peaked caps and so on, I did strenuously object, and I refused ever to wear it because that struck me as being the introduction of militarism at least in form.
Q. With the armlet?
A. Yes. I never wore that uniform, I refused ever to don it. "The policy of the organisation has been and is subject to Italian and German influence", instancing the anti-Semitism campaign of British Union. That campaign, as well as I remember, was not influenced in any way by Italian or German influence, but was rather a fight, as it was expressed to me, that was forced on us by Jewish interests in this country. I had some evidence to believe that was true, because I had seen well organised Jewish opposition to the Movement, which did at least give colour to that statement and made it appear feasible. The next one is really the worst one, "There is reasonable cause to believe that between the years 1932 and 1937 the organisation had been in receipt of moneys from Italy". I had some suggestion of that brought to my notice some, it would be, three years ago at least, I think, when a man by the name of Bethell of Sunderland wrote anonymous letters to me saying he was in possession of documents that showed that to be the case.
Q. That showed that to be the case? That is to say, Italian moneys were......
A. Yes. I followed that up and eventually managed to obtain a photostatic copy of a letter which was alleged to have been written by the then Director-General of the organisation, Mr. Francis Hawkins, to a man by the name of Armstrong, something Wiley Armstrong, who had been working in Manchester, in which some conference was referred to at which there had been statements made to the Inspectors present that information given them about this must be treated as confidential. As soon as I got possession of the copy of that document I took it to Sir Oswald Mosley and the Director-General, and challenged them to say was this true or was it not. They both repudiated indignantly, and classified the document as a forgery.
Q. Do you remember what year that was - about?

A. I think I could work it back. You may be able to help me by telling me when Beckett left the British Union.
Q. I think that was 1936, was it not?
A. Early 1936. It was later in that same year, anyway. Armstrong was one of the men who went at the same time, and he was the person referred to in this correspondence.
Q. They both repudiated?
A. Yes, they said there was not a shred of truth in the charge, and I then urged them to take proceedings in Court against Bethell for the dissemination of this report. They refused to do that, but what they did do very shortly afterwards was to publish a reproduction of the letter in the periodical "Action" and stigmatise it as a forgery and challenged any person to produce the original.
Q. Do you remember whether that would be about the end of 1936 in "Action"?
A. Yes, later in 1936. It could be looked up. That was the only step that was taken on it, and I say frankly I was not satisfied with that step, I should have preferred legal action being taken because then I should have felt everything was all right.
Q. That is what you wanted to say on that?
A. As a particular item, yes: but I did want to comment in passing that it was from that incident that my own confidence and faith were somewhat shaken, and it did mark a definite change in my attitude and outlook.
Q. We have in the few days we have been dealing with this matter tried to get at the truth of that matter. We find it very difficult. Did you know there was a secret account with the Westminster Bank dealing with the British Union of Fascist Funds?
A. I certainly did not.
Q. That was opened in 1933 and operated until May, 1937?
A. No, I did not.
Q. For example, just to take one year, the year 1935, £86,000 was paid into the account.
A. I had not the least knowledge of that. If there were anything I knew that I could help you with, I should be only too pleased to do so, I assure you of that.
Q. I am merely indicating that we have a lot of detail about it. I am not saying the £86,000 is Italian money at all, or any of it, but it seems a very large sum to come into a secret account.
A. It does.
Q. I took the peak year 1935. In 1936 it was £43,000 and in 1937 £7,000.
A. I only know that during most of these years I was on a salary, nothing like the salary I was on in the Labour Party, and the reason given for that was that the Movement was too hard up to pay me any more.
Q. That is the figure which was paid in there. It was paid in in foreign currencies, in dollars and Reichsmarks and French and Swiss francs, and so

on. But you knew nothing of that?
A. I assure you I had no knowledge of that whatever.
Q. I accept what you say, because this finance business seems to have been done cloaked with the greatest mystery and secrecy that I have ever discovered in any concern or organisation.
A. I assure you I knew nothing at all about it.
Q. No. I am only trying to deal with you quite frankly, because you have told us what you know about it. We had one of your members here the other day, Archibald Garrioch Findlay: he was supposed to deal with the finance, and had been out to Geneva, he told us, to collect money for the British Union from, as he said, British sympathisers with the Movement who desired to remain anonymous and not to be known, and that was the purpose of the visit: but how much he got, or how he got it, or what he did with it, or where it came from, these things he professed to have completely forgotten or not to have known about them, and he said that if he went into the books it would not be possible to trace them, and all that kind of thing. So the thing is unsatisfactory in the sense that it is cloaked with mystery which, in spite of all our best endeavours, we cannot probe: and when we find that an immense sum like this is paid into a secret account in foreign currencies for the most part, the suspicion does arise that it is all an elaborate cloak to hide the allegation that there is reasonable cause to believe it came from Italy. You follow me?
A. I do.
Q. But speaking from your own personal knowledge……
A. Speaking from my own personal knowledge, the only doubt I ever had was the occasion I have just described to you.
Q. Thank you.
A. I did say in passing that that did mark a definite mile stone, as it were, in my association with the British Union. I felt from that period right up to the present there was never any real clearing up of that position: it looked as if the issue had been burked, and thinking it over more recently it seems to me reasonable to assume the reason why there was the refusal to take the matter into Court was that possibly close investigation would have been instituted, which was not welcome. I only give that as a suggestion. I do not know that it was so, but I certainly had that uncomfortable feeling in my mind ever since.
Q. Certainly if it had gone into Court there would have been a complete investigation.
A. Yes. That is the reason why I have never felt so happy about things since that occasion. The next is that "Mosley himself, as one of the persons in control of the organisation, has or has had associations with persons concerned in the government of Germany". That I believe to be perfectly true.
Q. You believe that?

A. I believe that to be true: and I also believe, and know it to be true, that in addition to that of course he had similar associations with Mussolini, the occasions that were blazoned in the Press at the time - again things I was not altogether enthusiastic about: I had never much opinion of the Italians as Italians during the war.
Q. That word "associations" may mean very much or very little. The whole world knew through the blazoning in the Press, as you say, the visits to Rome and Germany, because there were pictures of Sir Oswald Mosley being received with honour.
A. Yes. As a matter of fact, I was given the opportunity to go on that visit to Rome myself, but I just did not take advantage of it.
Q. What was the purpose of the visit? Was it to show the affinity between your Movement and Mussolini, or what?
A. It was because I could never find any satisfactory reason for going that I did not go with that party. A party of about a dozen went on that occasion to Rome from the British Union. They were just ordinary members and one or two higher officers went with them. But, quite frankly, I could see very little inducement to go with them. Naturally one likes to travel……
Q. Was an official report, so to speak, made to your body of the visit or of the contacts made?
A. A meeting was held at the Dennison Hall shortly afterwards at which Sir Oswald Mosley and one or two others spoke about their experiences on that visit. I remember that occasion particularly because one of the speakers made a very tactless remark dealing with the visit, in which he attacked the spirit of discipline of one of the famous Italian regiments - I do not remember which it was: he said what a sloppy lot they were, and there happened to be a lady in the audience whose husband was an officer serving in that regiment, and she got very excited: but that was the only reference that was ever made to the visit publicly.
Q. But so far as you can tell, the leader, Sir Oswald Mosley, so to speak, kept a good many matters to himself? He had of course under the constitution almost autocratic and dictatorial powers.
A. That constitution, incidentally, has been varied from time to time: there have been several constitutions.
Q. Yes, but the dictatorial position of the leader has never been really varied at all?
A. No. That has been practically unqualified throughout.
Q. I suppose he was entitled under the constitution to keep all sorts of matters to himself if he wished.
A. Yes.
Q. And if, for example, - I do not say it is so for a moment - he had any understanding with Mussolini about assistance or help, that might quite conceivably be one of the things he would keep to himself?
A. Yes.

Q. About the broadcasting station, you knew nothing whatever about that?
A. Nothing whatever, I can assure you.
Q. It is only fair to say we have investigated a good deal of that, and as far as we can tell it has nothing to do with the British Union as such, that it was a private venture in which Sir Oswald Mosley was concerned with other persons commercially for the erection of a broadcasting station for the dissemination of advertising propaganda, like Radio Luxemburg [sic] or one of those stations, so that you need not trouble your head about that because in any event it had nothing to do with you and nothing to do, as far as we can see at the moment, with the activities of the British Union as such: so do not trouble about that insofar as you are concerned.
A. That is a help anyway.
Q. I put it in that way lest you should have any misunderstanding in your mind about it. When those particulars were put there I understand it was not known the purpose of the broadcasting station in Germany, and what use was to be made of it, and all the rest of it, but it would appear, from such evidence as we have at the moment, that in any event it would not affect a man in your position because you are not supposed to know anything about it: and without saying anything final about it it would not appear to affect the British Union as such. Whatever other indications there may be, you do not get a wireless broadcasting station erected with German money unless you are friendly with German people and so on: but that does not affect you or at the moment the British Union, so do not trouble further about it.
A. Then the reference to German propaganda literature. That is something that should have come to my notice if it had been a regular practice, because at different times I have been interested in propaganda. In the very early days of the British Union of Fascists, as it was then called, I was in charge of meetings and propaganda, and organised the earliest meetings, at the Free Trade Hall meetings at Manchester, the Albert Hall meeting, and the Olympia meeting. They were all meetings for which I was responsible, and I was responsible for a good deal of the propaganda literature that has been published from time to time: but I have never received any considerable quantities of literature that emanated from any foreign source. There have been occasions when parcels of literature have been passed into the organisation, both German and Italian literature, and whenever that has happened, such parcels have arrived in any period when I was dealing with propaganda, it has just remained in the office and naturally been carried out again as waste paper, because I always think we can produce propaganda to suit our taste in Britain far better than anybody else can produce it for us.
SIR ARTHUR HAZLERIGG: Was this propaganda printed in English?
A. Yes, propaganda in English but produced in foreign countries. The reason, quite frankly, why I have never used it is because I do not consider it

to be good propaganda. I do not think foreigners ever understand the British……
CHAIRMAN: Did it come by arrangement? Would the Germans say "The British Union is a good distributing centre"?
A. I cannot say, because literature would be brought in a parcel and left at our stores: and the storeman would ask me what was to happen, and as to its disposal.
Q. The position is that German propaganda, official German propaganda I suppose we can call it, did reach you, but you did not use it?
A. That is right. I have had sundry packets brought in at different times, but I have never used it because I did not think it good propaganda.
Q. Do you remember how it came to you? Did it come through a neutral country?
A. I should think it would be sent through people here in England. They were quite small parcels.
Q. Someone in England would bring them to the British Union headquarters for distribution?
A. Yes: and as the person who had to make the decision on that I did not use [sic] to use it.
Q. Did you refer to this matter to anybody, or discuss it?
A. No, I just treated it as junk that was not wanted.
Q. There was one particular matter. There was a pamphlet on Danzig, presenting the German case, and we rather gathered the leader had given instructions that that particular pamphlet should be distributed to all districts. Do you know anything about that?
A. I should do because I was handling propaganda at that time: but again we had the rather peculiar situation that while I was supposed to be handling propaganda there was also a Director General who had authority - that was another grievance that I had - who could distribute stuff over my head that I knew nothing about. That has been done to my knowledge and I cannot quote any particular literature, but I could find specimens of literature to show where stuff had been issued that I knew nothing about, although I was supposed to be in charge of literature. I remember one classic instance that I kicked about. A leaflet was published. It had been devised by the Director General, and the message that it contained in bold type with small type interspersed, but the lay-out made it read, "Mosley right: Eden wrong. Sack them both". That was a leaflet that I, as a politician and a propagandist of some years experience, should never have put out. It was distributed and I found it had been printed and distributed on the direct instructions of the Director General who himself had prepared it. The wrong type was accentuated, it was a very bad lay-out, and it made a mess of the propaganda matter that was supposed to be contained in it. That was something, I believe, referring to the Abyssinian dispute of some years ago. I merely mention it as one instance of literature passed without the

knowledge of the person responsible, to show that although one may be nominally in charge of propaganda it was possible for something to be distributed without that person knowing it: but to my knowledge - and I speak in all sincerity - I never allowed any foreign literature to pass out from the British Union during the period I had any control over that department.

Q. The next, (c), visits to Germany, you have really dealt with?

A. Yes. With reference to encouraging other members to visit Germany I do not know if that was done to anybody, but I do know that my own reaction to that has always been to say that people who are working for an improvement in the social system in England could learn far more about what they wanted to do by visiting the slums of England than by going to Nuremberg or any of these other gatherings.

Q. What was your history? You are not a member of the Society of Friends?

A. No, but many of my friends are.

Q. I seemed to recall the name?

A. I was for some years the I.L.P. organiser for the Midlands division, and did a lot of work in connection with Fircroft and institutions like that.

Q. What years were those? I used to know Fircroft many years ago?

A. My years in the Midlands were 1928 and 1929, but I used to go there a lot when I was organising the South West counties of England.

Q. There was a time - 1911 - when I did quite a lot of work for Fircroft College.

A. That was rather before my time.

Q. That was a residential College for working men?

A. Yes.

Q. It was really run by George Cadbury, Junior, at that time?

A. I think it still is: and a number of my friends were there, people like Reuben Farrow.

Q. You had really got an Independent Labour Party history background?

A. Yes.

Q. Very well.

A. As I say, I never encouraged people to go to Germany. I was only once in my life in Germany and that was when I was with the Army of Occupation after the last war, and that is all I need say about that, I need not labour that point. As for sympathy with any system in another country, dealing with these particulars I believe you to be right in forming the conclusion that some members of the British Union have taken a line in propaganda of attempting to justify what happens in Germany rather than concentrating on what is our problem in this country. Again, I have always bitterly opposed that, and there was a meeting - I can only quote this from memory, but I think I have the details right because I have been able to check them since I have been in here with someone from the particular district - I remember a meeting I addressed at Buckhurst Hill in the Epping division, the Prime Minister's constituency, on the 4th May 1938, where there was persistent questioning from people who wanted to get my opinion

opinion about what had happened in Germany. That questioning was so persistent, it was maintained for nearly half an hour on that one point despite the fact that I said I knew nothing about the system in Germany, I cared less about what was happening in Germany, the only thing I did know was that I was advocating changes that I considered to be appropriate and useful in the system of Government in this country. It is true that in so doing I have condemned the system of Government that exists in this country, but I believe that most people with a political career have done the same. It is not only in recent years that I have done that, I did it in my I.L.P. days: I was an advocate of the Committee system of Government, and ideas sponsored by Fred Jowett, and I have always felt and still feel today there is much wrong in our system of Government because it does not allow changes to be made with sufficient rapidity. I quote that meeting in particular because a fairly full account was given in the Press that stressed in particular my attitude towards this question of the system of Government in Germany. I am not an admirer of German systems of Government, and never have been: I do believe that a system of Government, to be effective, must be native to the people where that system of Government is applied. As a life-long Trade Unionist, too, I have always insisted that Trade Unions as such, as an organised force, should be a responsible section of the Government of a country. That still is my attitude, and that was my attitude in that particular meeting in answering the persistent questioners. I refused at all times to discuss a system of Government in another country: I believe that the only thing which concerns us is what is happening in our country. As for my position in the British Union, I told you gentlemen that from the time I took up that question of Italian money I was not so happy as I had been. I have just quoted a meeting held in 1938. Until then I did a very considerable amount of propaganda for the British Union of Fascists, and I believe not unsuccessful propaganda. I brought hundreds of people into the Movement. But that represented practically the end of my propaganda activities: I had come to the position where I had not sufficient faith in the bona fides of the Movement to continue as a speaker. I was still more or less under an obligation to serve them in the matter of building up electoral machinery, which I had undertaken to help to do. The street blocks system was the idea that I first worked out with an old colleague, Dr. Robert Fordham [sic: Forgan] who left the Movement many years ago.

Q. He was a member of the New Party, was he?

A. Yes.

Q. Were you in the New Party?

A. Yes. We worked that system out between us, and I had that obligation to help establish a sound basis of electoral organisation, and train someone else to take my place, which I did. I then left the staff of the Movement in July 1939.

Q. I have it as August, but it was July?

A. It was actually July when I left. I should have left a month earlier, but I was asked if I would stay on an additional month to help with the meeting at Earls Court. I paid subscriptions right up to July, but since then I have paid no subscriptions and have taken no part in the activities of the Movement, because I felt I had done all I had any obligation to do for them.
Q. Did you make a formal resignation in writing?
A. No. I just left. I paid no more subscriptions, and I just dropped out.
Q. After all your long connection with them I should have thought you might have made a formal break and given the reason.
A. To be quite honest, I had seen so many people make formal breaks and immediately go into a splash of vilification and scurrilous attacks.
Q. By the people who were left?
A. No, on their own part, people like Joyce and Beckett and others who had left in unhappy circumstances and immediately launched a scurrilous campaign and so on. I just felt I did not want any of that dirty water, I was glad to be clear of it and just dropped out in a quiet way without causing any fuss.
Q. You did not send a letter, not to be published or anything of that kind, in some such terms as "Dear Sir Oswald, I find I can no longer support the British Union, and therefore after our many years association it is with the more regret that I feel I must resign, and I do so in July 1939. Yours sincerely"? You did not write anything like that?
A. I did not bother even to do that. I just got a reference from Sir Oswald Mosley as to the work I had put in for him, and after that he wrote to me through the Director General asking me to go and see him, which I did.
Q. You did?
A. Yes, I went to see him and he told me then they were proposing to engage in by-elections, and he asked me would I take a re-appointment on the staff to conduct those by-elections, but that offer I declined. Although I was not earning big money by the work, I was at least having peace of mind, and I did not want to get back again.
SIR GEORGE CLERK: Were you drawing a salary until you left?
A. Yes, I was drawing a salary until I left in July 1939.
CHAIRMAN: What did you do when you left?
A. I took a job with the anti-Vivisection Society, the London and Provincial Anti-Vivisection Society.
Q. Was that run by the lady we know as Mrs. Dacre Fox or Mrs. Elam?
A. It was not run by her. She was the General Secretary. There was a Committee who actually were responsible for the running of that organisation.
Q. She was very active for the Committee?
A. Yes.
Q. It was rather a curious change, to leave the B.U. and go to someone who was really an active [sic] in the B.U.?

A. I had to get another job of some sort, because I have a wife and two youngsters to support and that was the first thing I could get. She offered me the job, and I took it.
Q. What we are told is that she was using those offices just as a cover for British Union activities.
A. I do not believe that to be true, although the two police inspectors who came to bring me in here assure me that was so.
Q. For example, did you know she was in receipt of very large sums of money belonging to the British Union for safe custody?
A. No.
Q. Thousands of pounds.
A. No.
Q. You may take it that is an admitted fact.
A. To be used through the anti-Vivisection Society.
Q. No, do not misunderstand me - that a sum of £4,000 was paid to Mrs. Elam by Archibald Garrioch Findlay who paid her £4,000 to the British Union funds, because it was thought that the funds of the B.U. would be seized by the Government. This is since the outbreak of war.
A. I would not know that, of course.
Q. And she kept that money for a certain time, and when things seemed quieter it was repaid to the funds of the British Union. You may take that as an accepted and admitted fact.
A. I do take that.
Q. That kind of activity you would know nothing about?
A. No, I would not know that.
Q. There is no doubt what the officers that you referred to were speaking of.
A. They told me they had information.
Q. That and other information which they had would indicate to them, I think properly, that whatever Mrs. Elam was doing she was indeed actively working for the British Union in that kind of way.
A. That she must have been doing quite personally and individually. I do not think the Committee would have known anything of that.
Q. The Committee of the Anti-Vivi section [sic] Society?
A. No. I can hardly imagine they would be, because the Committee was a very mixed committee, and I do not think they would have countenanced anything like that for a moment. Some of them, people like Dr. Allinson, opposed the British Union very vigorously.
Q. What was the capacity in which you were engaged there?
A. They wanted to get a detailed analysis of what support there was for their cause amongst the public, and I organised a canvass for them, which is more along the lines of a political canvass, and a petition formed for people to sign saying they wanted to get Vivisection abolished. It was a technical job, an organiser's job, not so much propaganda as organising an analysis of the support available for the Movement.

Q. Apart from that visit to Sir Oswald Mosley at his request which you told us about, did you have any other contact with the Headquarters of the British Union?
A. No, the only person I had anything like regular contact with in the British Union was a colleague with whom I had worked when I was there, who was interested in the industrial propaganda of the Movement, the Trade Union Organisation side, who went by the name of P. G. Taylor.
Q. What was his true name?
A. J. M. Hughes.
Q. Why did he go in the name of P. G. Taylor?
A. I think because he had business interests outside and he did not want to appear under his own name in British Union. As a matter of fact, I have theories about him, but I do not know whether they are correct and so I would prefer not to mention them; but he was concerned on that side which was the particular side in which I was interested, and I met him fairly regularly at intervals as much as once a week. I used to go and have a glass of beer with him at a 'pub' round the corner.
Q. Had you any interest in what I would call the pugnacious side of the British Union, the militant side of the British Union?
A. As a propagandist, I suppose I should have to say I was fairly militant.
Q. You had an automatic pistol at your house, had not you?
A. No, I had not an automatic pistol. What I did have was some old ammunition, and the officers who found that asked me what it was, and I told them that some years ago I had collected that, together with an automatic pistol, but I did not know what had happened to the automatic pistol.
Q. What about a small plated revolver?
A. Yes.
Q. Had you one?
A. No. I was not able to find either of those for him, although I told him I had them at one time.
Q. That is where the information came from?
A. Yes.
Q. You told him?
A. I told him I got the box of ammunition from an old place I was clearing out in Preston, and at the same time those other two things had been picked up.
Q. I will tell you what I have heard. It is a small matter and would not weigh greatly, but I imagine the Committee would like to know how things got into this form. We have it that "In a drawer in his bureau was found an automatic pistol and a small plated revolver together with ammunition for which he had no certificate".
A. I am sure that is not true. The two police officers who were there will tell you that.
Q. I put it quite bluntly and starkly like that, because I daresay the Committee

would accept from you......
A. They would never have known I had had such a thing in my hands unless I had told them.
Q. In that event this is a clear mistake - "In the drawer of my bureau was found", and your explanation is......
A. 25 rounds of ammunition.
Q. Some ammunition was found?
A. Which at one time had evidently been tried and found to be "dud".
Q. You said that ammunition you have explained by this, that "at one time I had an automatic pistol for which this ammunition was suitable, but where that pistol is now I do not know" - something like that?
A. That is right. I told them I had cleared out some old premises at Preston and had found the ammunition and an automatic pistol and a small plated revolver, but had never been able to find the plated revolver or the automatic pistol from that time although I had remembered them and searched for them, but the ammunition had been with me ever since. They would not have known about the pistol and revolver if I had not told them.
Q. Were they special officers?
A. Ordinary officers. I do not remember their names, but it should be easy to find them.
Q. That runs through these things except the last one in the order, which is, "There is danger of the utilisation of the organisation - (this really applies to the organisation, as indeed most of the particulars do apart from paragraph 1) - known as British Union......Community". That is taken directly from the regulations, of course. That is true in the ordinary sense, is it not? British Union, since the war broke out - take these words, "The efficient prosecution of the war", they were using the organisation for purposes prejudicial to the efficient prosecution of the war?
A. It would appear so.
Q. Their pamphlets?
A. They have been so vague since the outbreak of war that it has been difficult to determine. A reader of "Action" would read one week a diatribe condemning the war and everything about it, and next week there would be an article saying how the war could be more efficiently conducted - which appeared to me to be a case of dancing on two stools with the danger of falling between them.
Q. I have been putting that to a good many members because it is a thing I cannot see. I can understand a situation in which a man says, "I am honestly opposed to this war and propose to oppose it as long as I can, and to say I shall not support and shall ask other people not to support it", but I cannot understand a man who does that at the same time saying, "I shall really fight for the efficient prosecution of the war which I oppose". I cannot understand that.
A. I cannot, either.

Q. I can understand this, rather cleverly used, "We oppose this war and the Government that started this war, and just look at what a Government you have got, they do not even know how to run a war which they have started". I can understand that, which is part of one thing, "We are opposed to the war and our propaganda is directed to the people supposed to be running it", and pointing out that their muddling and inefficiency, which is all part of the one point, and that is I think rather what the activities of the British Union were directed to, to saying "We are opposed to this war. Join our Union. Make peace. Mosley will lead you to peace; and if you are wanting further arguments look at the muddling gang running this war, Churchill and so on", as part of the same propaganda. There are large numbers of pamphlets issued by the British Union addressed to the women, addressed to other people, and then the articles in "Action" and so on; but that would be right, would it not, the Union itself was being used for purposes prejudicial to the efficient prosecution of the war?

A. I should certainly think so. That is the opinion I should form.

Q. The other thing I wanted to ask you was this. With your background, your training and upbringing with the I.L.P., it was a curious body to be in, this British Union, was it not?

A. Well, you may be familiar with the history throughout. We went from the I.L.P. to the New Party. The New Party was a movement that was created at a time when there was urgent need to awaken the country to the real danger of a financial collapse, and I think that 1931 showed we were right in that assumption. From the New Party it became obvious there must be something more than merely a call to arouse the people of the country if we were to build up any real body of opinion, and it was from that point we went on to formulate an economic policy that would impress a wider Britain than merely the financial collapse aspect, and it was in the formulation of that policy that many of the "snags" cropped up that led in the direction of what has since become known as authoritarian methods of Government; but I can say quite honestly that as all those "snags" were met and a suitable policy built to deal with them, speaking for myself at least there was no idea of copying any other country whatever, it was merely a method of finding a machinery that would work in England to deal with something we knew in England.

Q. You have read "Tomorrow We live", no doubt?

A. Yes. I have not so much regard for "Tomorrow We Live" as I had for the original booklet, "Greater Britain". As a matter of fact, when that book was published, which was at a time subsequent to the incident I told you of which did mark a real changing in my attitude towards the British Union......

Q. With an Independent Labour background I should have thought that kind of picture in "Tomorrow We Live" would be rather repugnant.

A. It was, very.
Q. Because there is the German, Italian, military…
A. You are quite right, that was repugnant. That is just one of the whole series of things which marked a change in my attitude since the period I first mentioned when I questioned the Italian origin of funds up to the time when I eventually dropped out altogether.
Q. But you had been associated with the Movement since its inception right down practically to the outbreak of war?
A. Yes, I had. The latter two years were much less happy than the others.
Q. From what you have been telling us of your background and history and outlook, I should think myself you would have been most unhappy inside such a Movement.
A. The last three years practically that I was there were more and more unhappy.
Q. We do not know a great deal about it, but we hear a great deal which leads us to suppose that inside this Union there was a great deal of intrigue and plotting for place.
A. There was that from the very beginning.
Q. Trying to turn other people out, and this man plotting against the other man.
A. Yes, there was.
Q. The other thing, too, is this. There were meetings, I will not call them secret meetings, but there were occasional meetings where the heads of departments met either for lunch or talks or something of that sort, were not there?
A. Yes.
Q. Headquarters officers or staff met to discuss things. You would usually attend those meetings, would you?
A. Yes, there were very few of those meetings held. They were held because of the unpleasant atmosphere created by the clash of personalities working one against the other.
Q. You formed a little group yourself with Gordon Canning and Archibald Garrioch Findlay rather opposed to Francis Hawkins?
A. As a matter of fact, I found myself associated with first one person and then another who appeared to be getting annoyed with the same things that I was. There was no idea of forming a group to campaign or anything like that, but in putting up a point of view at a meeting of officers of that description certain people would have a similar point of view, one would find that there was a common outlook on problems and work with these people. Gordon Canning was certainly one with whom I worked a good deal like that, and he appeared to be just as annoyed as I was.
Q. What were the kind of things that annoyed you with regard to Francis Hawkins and the Movement?
A. Just the fact that he had no political knowledge whatever. He was a man who had been put into a high position without a real political background that would enable him to do justice in that position, and the fact that one after the other people whom I believed to be decent clean and

loyal were pushed out of their positions and eventually out of the Movement.

SIR ARTHUR HAZLERIGG: Such as whom?

A. It is rather invidious to quote cases, but there was a man like Chesterton, for instance.

CHAIRMAN: A. K.?

A. Yes. He was a man with a brilliant background and had a really good Army record, but he was always in trouble because these people did not just like him. He had a weakness upon which they played. He was a vain man, but one would expect vanity in a member of the Chesterton family: but he was a brilliant and honest man.

Q. There was a great deal of vanity in the Union?

A. Yes. I think that uniform catered for that vanity.

Q. Did you go to the Olympia meeting?

A. Yes.

Q. When the leader stands on a platform in a spotlight, and there is this "Hail Mosley" and the hands, there is a good deal of vanity there, is not there?

A. Yes, I think it was possibly for that reason I ceased just after that meeting to be active in propaganda, because the people who arranged the spotlight were people who did so contrary to my advice, and because I was opposed to that sort of thing I was given a different job.

SIR GEORGE CLERK: What relation was this Chesterton to G. K.?

A. A nephew.

CHAIRMAN: Those are the questions which I myself wanted to ask you.

SIR ARTHUR HAZLERIGG: About the ammunition and revolver you actually saw them look in the drawer?

A. No, I did not: I was not at home at the time.

Q. You were not at home?

A. No.

Q. Can you say in your own words what happened when you were detained?

A. Yes. The two officers who detained me detained me at my place of employment at the office in Victoria Street.

Q. At the anti-Vivisection Society?

A. Yes. When they read the order for my detention they said, "We have been to your home and we want you to give an explanation of some ammunition we found there". I said, "Oh yes, I can do that". It was some ammunition I collected from a place in Preston that I was clearing up, and at the same time I collected that I collected an automatic pistol and a small plated revolver". And one officer asked me then, "Where were they?". I said, "I am sorry I do not know. I have never been able to find them since. I merely mention it as part of what I collected, and it may have been very careless, I ought to know what happened to them, but I have always suspected that someone to whom

they had belonged previously had seen me collecting them."
CHAIRMAN: The officers did not say where they found them?
A. No. As a matter of fact, he said "Thank you for telling me about that. I appreciate your straightforwardness in this matter", and that is all that was said about it.
SIR ARTHUR HAZLERIGG: The other point is, I understand that the Fascist Movement, if they came into power, would really, after the first Parliament, when I suppose they would have to rely on the vote of the people, would do away with Parliamentary Government altogether in the ordinary sense?
A. With Parliamentary Government as we know it now, yes.
Q. I should have thought that one with your views would rather have objected to that?
A. No, because in doing away with that form of Government it did do the thing I had always hoped to be an essential part of Government, it did bring the Trade Unions in as a real factor of Government, and they received authority to govern industrially, a point……
Q. By occupational franchise?
A. Yes. The Trade Union machinery would be responsible for a very big section of the machinery of Government, and I had always a rather Syndicalist point of view in the Socialist Movement, the sort of Guild Socialism as opposed to the other form of Socialism.
SIR GEORGE CLERK: If I understood rightly, you said that after you dissociated yourself from the British Union, you did keep in touch with one Taylor alias Hughes, are [sic] Hughes alias Taylor?
A. Yes.
Q. He was still in?
A. He was still there, yes.
Q. As far as you know he still is?
A. Yes.
Q. Was he what I might call an office-holder of any sort?
A. No, I do not think he could be described as an office-holder: he was an industrial advisor, and that is such a nebulous title when you realise that he was dealing with folk who nine times out of ten would not take advice: the title "Industrial Advisor" then does not mean much.
Q. I do not want to probe into your personal affairs; but why did you keep particularly in touch with him?
A. I liked him as an individual.
Q. As a friend?
A. Yes. He was a personal friend as well as being a colleague.
Q. It would be fair to say you had naturally a general interest in the British Union, although you left it, and that he kept you more or less au courant with what was happening?
A. I should almost say it would be rather a case of sympathy than interest. I

sympathised with his failure to do the things he wanted to do in the British Union.

SIR ARTHUR HAZLERIGG: Do you know where he lived?

A. Sloane Street.

CHAIRMAN: We have your statement, of course, that you are not a member and resigned in July, which you have told us, then your second paragraph, that you declare you had no desire to engage in any act prejudicial to the public safety, following that last paragraph, and that in guarantee you place yourself unreservedly, and so on, the items detailed in paragraph 2, that is to say defence of the realm, maintenance of public order, prosecution of the war.

A. Yes.

Q. That represents your attitude?

A. Yes.

Q. You referred to being a member of the Army of Occupation in Germany. Did you serve in the Army then?

A. Yes. I joined in August 1914 and had to put my age on.

Q. What age were you in fact?

A. I was actually just short of my seventeenth birthday and the age limit was nineteen. I saw my next birthday in France, I joined in August and was overseas in November: I served with the Army in France and Belgium throughout the war, and went through with the Army of Occupation in Germany and stayed there until my Division, the First Division, came back to England in cadre strength, and later I was demobilised.

Q. In what capacity?

A. I was in the R.A.M.C. with No. 1 Field Ambulance, and spent a good deal of the war as a stretcher bearer attached to the First Black Watch.

Q. Your rank being?

A. I left the Army with the permanent rank of Sergeant.

Q. Supposing the Home Secretary were to decide that you may be released - which is a matter for him, of course, we are only an Advisory Committee, but supposing he released you, what would you propose to do?

A. I should be prepared to do anything as long as the war is on to help. As a matter of fact, my wife, who is a pacifist, was rather concerned because at the time of the invasion of Norway and Denmark I had wanted to go and enlist as a volunteer, but she did not like the idea. She is the sort of wife who would have let me have my way, but while I was discussing this point with her and trying to get an understanding this other affair came up.

Q. What age are you now?

A. I am actually 43, in my 44th year now.

Q. So that as things stand at present it would be a matter of volunteering for any service of that kind?

A. Yes.

Q. Did I understand you to say from that paragraph that your attitude, in a

sentence, is that if you can be of help in the prosecution of the war to this country at this time you would be glad to do so?
A. I would be perfectly ready to do so, and to give my very best service.
Q. It has not been contrary to any of your principles?
A. No.
Q. I think that is all we would like to ask, and in view of the fact that you made your statement at the beginning perhaps you may think that everything is covered, but I want you to feel that you have the opportunity of saying anything at all you wish, on anything that we have asked you about or anything which we have not asked you about. If you would like to add anything to your statement, do so, but if you feel it is all there......
A. Yes, I do feel it is all there.
Q. We will give this matter our earnest consideration, and try to deal with the matter as quickly as we can.
A. I would like the matter of the automatic pistol to be satisfactorily cleared up.
Q. Speaking merely for myself, I hope that through the years I have gained some experience in these things, and for myself I am perfectly ready to accept your explanation, but I thought it right in fairness to put the matter to you. I thought that some mistake might have crept in, as they do into these cases.
A. I should be much happier if you could get a statement from the officers concerned.
Q. The reason I did it in that form was I made a mental note "We will clear this up", and I have no doubt that your statement will be shown to be perfectly accurate - not I think that the mere position of an old revolver which one has had for many years is very strong evidence of one's subversive tendencies, but it is a small point which in your interest we want to clear up.
SIR ARTHUR HAZLERIGG: Can you get back to your job if you are released? Have you a job open to you?
A. I have been told that my wife has seen the Chairman of the Committee recently, and he has told her that if I were out from here and wanted a job they would be only too pleased to have me back.
Q. Thank you.
A. The Committee have apparently considered that.
CHAIRMAN: What is clear about that is that whatever the activities of Mrs. Elam or Dacre Fox may have been, and whatever use she may have made of those offices, you never had any knowledge it was a kind of cover or cloak for the British Union.
A. None at all. As a matter of fact, I have on occasion rebuked the girls in the office for getting into political argument about the war.
Q. One other question which may or may not be important in view of your frank statement. Have you been questioned by any officer of M.I.5 or anybody

since the officers detained you?
A. No.
Q. Supposing they said, "In view of Mr. Risdon's evidence we would like just to satisfy ourselves by asking him a few questions", you would have no objection?
A. None at all.
Q. And you would deal with them?
A. Just as I have with you. I have nothing to hide.
Q. We will deal with this matter as quickly as we can. There have been a good many delays which have not been the fault of this Committee but which are almost inevitable in this kind of thing, and it may take a day or two but we will try and deal with it as quickly as we can and make our recommendation as soon as we can.
A. Thank you.

Sequence of events subsequent to the Appeal hearing:

18/07/40 Letter from R. Llewellyn Davies [sic] at the Min of AP to I. Roy at the Home Office, referring to Peake's letter to RLD's Minister of 21/06/40, requesting advice about a final decision.

19/07/40 Letter from Aikin Sneath [MI5] to Birkett expressing doubts about releasing WR.

20/07/40 Reply from Ian Roy, Private Secretary, Home Office, to RLD's letter of 18/07, that "we may expect a report [from the Advisory Committee] very shortly".

24/07/40 Letter from GP Churchill to Aikin Sneath c/w copy of the AC's recommendation re. WR, requesting "whether you have any further observations to offer on this case before the recommendation for release is sent in".

26/07/40 Letter from Stamp, HO [MI5?], on behalf of AS, to Churchill: "In the case of WILFRED RISDON, Aiken-Sneath has in fact spoken to Mr. Birkett, and we have no further observations to offer on this case."

27/07/40 Official report from the AC re. WR, to USoS, HO, recommending release.

06/08/40 Revocation Order signed by John Anderson, "One of His Majesty's Principal Secretaries of State".

09/08/40 Letter from undisclosed sender to S.O. King [?] enclosing copy of Revocation Order.

09/08/40 Letter from undisclosed sender to "The Commissioner of Police of the Metropolis" confirming unconditional revocation of Detention Order.

14/08/08 Letter from WR [home] to Churchill restating willingness to serve and to submit to MI5 interrogation, mentioning that his "previous employers" have filled his place & he is "completely free" "for the time being".

20/08/40 Letter from Churchill to WR "to say that the matter referred to is outside the competence of this Committee."

APPENDIX E

Given the amount of material it has been possible to find about Flight Lieutenant Jan Falkowski, it seemed sensible to collect it in an appendix, rather than making the chapter notes even more copious than they already are! It is true that he is, in Britain, a relatively unknown figure, and his association with Wilfred was relatively brief, but it must have been cordial, at the very least, and it does seem plausible that he might have had some influence over Wilfred's stepson Brian's decision to emigrate to Canada [**1**]; it is tantalising to speculate about the political discussions Falkowski and Wilfred might have had. Falkowski does have a Wikipedia page, including a reasonable description of his background, before coming to England, but it is in his native language, Polish [**2**]. He was an agricultural student until 1934, when he graduated from the Faculty of Agriculture at the Stefan Batory University in Vilnius.

Perhaps because of the political situation in Poland at the time, or just because he had a desire to become a pilot, after leaving University he immediately enrolled at the Dęblin Aviation Cadet School [between Warsaw & Lublin] and graduated as a Second Lieutenant in October 1936; he was assigned to a unit at Torun, but within 2 years, he was back at the Dęblin school as an instructor, so his prowess as a pilot was evident very early on. When the war began, he was one of a group of pilots evacuated to France via Romania [probably just as much to save the aircraft as the pilots], but they had only got as far as Lublin when they were attacked by a couple of German aircraft; on the Wikipedia page for the PWS-26 ["a Polish advanced training aircraft"] Falkowski's exploit is quoted, whereby he contrived by his flying skill that one of the German pursuers crashed into the ground, and the other one had to return to base, most likely because of fuel shortage [**3**]. He was an instructor again in France thereafter, but was put in command of a unit at the end of May 1940; only a month later, he came to England when the Germans invaded France. His first posting, after a short induction course in the English language and RAF procedures, was delivering new and refurbished aircraft around the country; quite soon, he was assigned to 32 Squadron which was, at that time, based in "northern England" [**4**], flying Hawker Hurricanes, and in the dogfight on January the 16th 1941, during which he downed his first Heinkel 111, his own 'plane was badly damaged, so he had to bail out, but he broke his leg on landing.

It was the end of July that year before he was operational again, and he was sent to join the Polish 315 Squadron [nicknamed the City of Dęblin Polish Fighter Squadron **5**] at Northolt, so this would have been the earliest opportunity for Wilfred to encounter him; by September the 22nd, his performance had been sufficiently impressive [possibly in combination with command losses] for him to become the commander of Squadron A. At some stage before June 1943, he was transferred to no. 316 Polish Fighter Squadron ["City of Warsaw" **6**], in which he took part in several operations over France: from December 1941 until April 1942, it was based at Northolt, so the encounter might have been during this period; at the end of June 1943, he was transferred to no. 303 Squadron, which had recently returned to Northolt, and was now flying the new Supermarine Spitfire Mk IX. He was now a Squadron Leader when he took over the leadership of 303 in July; most of 303's work was escorting USAF heavy bombers, but there was still the occasional dogfight. The date [2nd of November 1943] on the transfer deed for Wilfred's house was probably quite significant, because on the 12th of that month, 303 was posted to RAF Ballyhalbert in Northern Ireland; it will probably be impossible to ascertain for sure if Falkowski was with 303 when it moved - there is some doubt, because "soon after S/L Koc assumed command" [**7**] - but it certainly would have provided a real incentive for him to finalise the deal before he left. Unfortunately, his own Wikipedia page is not much help here, because the next we hear of him is January the 30th 1945, when he was appointed commander of the 3rd Fighter Wing [**8**] "and returned to the missions", meaning, presumably, active service.

On the 9th of March 1945, he had to bail out of his aircraft because of some unspecified "failure" and was wounded in the leg by a German bullet, then he was captured after landing; luckily, this captivity did not last long, because exactly two months later, he returned to England [although a Canadian newspaper story from 1952 states that he escaped within five days: see note 12]. Unfortunately, there is another gap until "demobilisation in 1947 [when] he moved to Canada, where he had a farm 20 miles away from Toronto." In so doing, he returned to his 'roots', occupationally speaking, but it appears that Brian Risdon did not demonstrate any inclination to join him in this occupation or, at least, if he did, it would not be a permanent choice. Here the admirably comprehensive Canadian newspaper digitisation programme comes into play, although the Wikipedia page does have one final entry, cataloguing an event in the 1960s which will figure in the main local newspaper, ***The Stouffville Sun-Tribune***, and will be alluded to below [see notes 12 & 26]. Within two years of arriving in Canada, farming [of an unspecified nature] at Gormley, 25 km north east of Toronto, had ceased to be sufficient for him, and he was again a flying instructor [**9**] at Buttonville, 10 km to the south of Gormley. In a 'local interest' section of the 'paper, which might seem more than a little intrusive to our 21st century sensibilities, but was probably accepted in a quaint, 'howdy neighbour' sense back then, the local populace was informed that, in 1950 "Mr. and Mrs. Jan Falkowski are the first ones in our community to enjoy television in their home." [**10**] This is the first mention of his wife, of whom more below, but it is not known if she was acquired in England or

Canada; the probability is the latter.

At the end of 1950, Falkowski was already moving on, 10 km eastwards from Gormley to Whitchurch Township, just north of Ringwood [a preponderance of instantly recognisable English place-names in this area], but again to a farm [**11**]; perhaps there were tax advantages? In 1952, he celebrated "his 20th anniversary as an aeroplane pilot" [**12**], and as well as a special "Jan Day" at the "Buttonville flying field", the newspaper article also gave the first mention of his recently completed autobiography, ***With the Wind in My Face***. The next seven years seem to have been sufficiently quiet to not warrant any mentions in the local 'rag', but in 1959, in a development for which the "promoter" was very possibly a fellow expatriate Pole, "Mr. Joseph P. Koblensky of Markham" [which is adjacent Buttonville], 250 acres of cattle-grazing land way out in the country to the north east "on conc. [concession] 3, Uxbridge Township" was ploughed up for "a modern private airfield" [**13**], but in the wide-open spaces of rural Canada, it was probably nowhere near enough for anybody to get excited about. Falkowski had evidently left his previous position of instructor at Buttonville to move to this new airfield, but the story did not mention if he had also moved house. By April 1960, the "Airport" was "literally 'humming' with activity" and 60 students had enrolled on the training course; we also get to see our first photograph of Jan Falkowski [**14**]. At the beginning of the following year, he accepted the position of "the Commanding Officer of the new Stouffville District Air Cadet Squadron", [**15**] no doubt willing to work within a quasi-military system as well as the civil aviation sphere, although the position seems to have been honorary, notwithstanding his obvious practical experience, rather than one which involved actual flying instruction.

In August 1961, Falkowski took over "the complete flying program at the local Port", with "plans to promote flights to the United States" [**16**], so it would appear that farming had become a secondary activity. Exactly a year later, he was obviously flying a lot further afield, because his aircraft went missing during a flight from Calgary to Vancouver, and in the newspaper report, we learn the name of his wife [Alma] and that he has a step-son by the name of Tommy [**17**]. Within a week, the same local 'paper was reporting that all four people on the flight had been found safe, but that the 'plane had had to be left after an emergency landing, although it appeared possible that it could be recovered in the near future [**18**]; it also becomes clear that Jan was not Alma's first husband or, at the very least, he was not Tommy's father, because Tommy's surname is Tanski. In October that year, Falkowski moved to another airport at Peterborough, to take over the training school there; this was in the order of 100 km in a straight line from his previous area, so although it seems almost futuristic by contemporary British standards, he might have commuted by 'plane, because the newspaper report stated that he would continue to reside in the area [of Goodwood]; there was also the hint of a dispute between Falkowski and the airport, but this was played down by "a spokesman for the firm." [**19**] Apparently, Alma had an artistic side, because she won 3rd prize in a local photographic competition, entering a colour slide in the category "Something of Interest in Stouffville"! [**20**] Rather quaintly, she was listed as "Mrs. Jan Falkowski", but that could have been a genuine mistake, as she is the sole exception to the regular practice on the list.

The aircraft which Falkowski had skilfully piloted to a safe crash-landing the previous year [note 18] had now acquired the sobriquet '"jinx" aircraft', because it stalled on takeoff from Saskatoon [having been flown there from Calgary, after being repaired] and "was badly damaged ... [but t]he deep snow cushioned the shock"; the report also contains at least 2 mistakes [over-valuing the aircraft at $23,000, and referring to Tanski as Falkowski's son-in-law!] and, bizarrely, quotes Falkowski as saying that he wanted to "fly 'door-to-door' as a salesman for a stainless steel cookware firm."! [**21**] He was enough of a public figure to help officiate at a "safety awards" ceremony at a local school [**22**], although the category or type of safety was not actually specified in the report. The change of career mooted looks like it could have been a joke, because by the middle of 1963, Falkowski had taken up yet another flying instructor post, this time at what was described as "The Markham - Toronto Airport at Locust Hill", but which is likely to be Buttonville [which is adjacent Markham; there is no airfield shown currently at Locust Hill, about 15 km away: if it was "presently a grass airstrip" at Locust Hill, it would seem somewhat grandiose to describe it as "Markham-Toronto"] so that would actually be a return for him although this is not mentioned in the article; the scenario also seems somewhat reminiscent of an earlier episode, given the expansion plans, and the fact that the developer could have been another fellow expatriate Pole [**23**]. A frothy editorial a month or so later sang the praises of Falkowski and his flying skill, but the author seemed genuinely bemused that entry to a flying display Falkowski put on was free [**24**].

By early 1965, Falkowski appears to have taken the initiative and developed his own airfield west of Uxbridge, with the eponymous name of Janalma, but it is not clear if this was his main activity, or whether he still worked at one of the other airfields from his recent past [**25**]; this wasn't mentioned in the review of his autobiography, which he finally got around to publishing a couple of months later, citing the reason for the twelve year hiatus as: "At that time, the book market was flooded with war stories and he felt that his would only run with the rising tide." [**26**] It is possible that this release was timed, somewhat opportunistically [but understandably so] to coincide with his prospective visit to England and Poland in September that year, as mentioned in this article [only the former], for the 25th anniversary of the Battle of Britain, although it took another 15 years for it to be published in Poland, for reasons which are not given on his Wikipedia page [see note 2 for the link]; he & his wife spent "21 days in England and the Continent, … arriving back in Uxbridge on Oct. 5th." [**27**] By February 1966, the book had been published, and the local newspaper was promoting it with an advert which included a large picture of the front cover design, but there was also a coupon to clip and send to Falkowski for a CoD order [for an "Autographed Limited Edition"], so it was probably a paid advert [**28**]. In early April, Falkowski "appeared on the Elwood Glover television program, channel 6" [**29**], although the small gossip piece doesn't say if that was a local or national channel, or if he was promoting the book, although it must be assumed that he was. The same week, he very public-spiritedly presented a copy of the book to the local High School [**30**]. Nothing more is heard of him, as far as the local press is concerned, for the next five years, but his book was still figuring in the public consciousness, because in June 1971, a painting by "well-known artist, Arnold Hodgkins", based on the book and entitled "Falkowski-Portrait of Poland", was exhibited at an annual showing of Hodgkins's works at a gallery 6 miles north of Uxbridge [**31**]; no dimensions are given for the painting, but if the head-and-torso representation of Falkowski is anything like life-size, it will be quite large: Falkowski is pictured holding a ceremonial dagger, blade down, by the blade, staring melancholically out, in front of a *mélange* of images of war. No selling price was specified. The latest news we have for Falkowski is in July that year, that he was still working as a flying instructor, aged 59, this time at an airport about 40 km south east of Uxbridge, for another expatriate Pole, albeit this time himself a pilot with a similar career, Jan Lewandowski [**32**]. According to Falkowski's Wikipedia biography, he died on the 27th of July 2001, at the age of 89, in Peterborough, Ontario, so it must be presumed that he moved there from Uxbridge, about 100 km away, some time after 1971, but for reasons which are not stated. It is not known if he kept in contact with Wilfred after he moved to Canada, but on the basis that Falkowski was very probably instrumental in Brian Risdon's decision to emigrate eventually to the same area, it is more than possible that he did; either way, he led an eventful life, most of the time doing what he loved doing: flying.

NOTES

1 Fortunately, it has been possible to establish contact with Brian Risdon's son, Gary, who lives in Toronto, and he has been able to impart some useful information about his father, in addition to what Brian told me himself in a letter in 1998. Brian first went to Corner Brook, on the western seaboard of Newfoundland island, for unknown reasons, but perhaps there was a connection with his recent seagoing experience, during which he presumably also learned the plumbing skills that he later put to good use in Toronto; evidently, it proved difficult to carve out a career there, as his son explains below, together with some fascinating insights into Wilfred and Nellie's lives, as well, including a touching mention of Wilfred's generosity, although I think the date of 1962 for a stay at Harley Street is incorrect [an understandable mistake], because the tenancy undertaken by the LTMT did not commence until 1964 [see Chapter 14, and note 41]; the original spelling in the email has been left uncorrected:

> "Brian came to Canada in 1947, I believe … . He originally settled / spent some time in Cornerbrook, Newfoundland. Newfoundland has always been a poor, harsh province and like many others Brian headed west to Toronto 1949/50. Brian married Mary in 1951. Brian and Mary separated in 1965 and divorced. … Brian was a great father. As a household we had the first color TV in the neighbourhood; the first convertible top car; etc. We would go to fun holiday spots. He loved to go fishing at Lake Temagami [about 300 km north of Toronto]. He coached all our sports teams. I can really only remember good times. I can remember meeting Wilfred in 1962 on family holiday to London. We stayed at Harley Street. Brian Rowley [Sheila's husband], my father, and myself drove across to Cornwall with the remainder going by train, including Wilfred and Margaret. We had a wonderful time.
>
> I also remember two specific things about Wilfred. Brian and Mary purchased a house in 1952 outside of Toronto. I'm sure it took all they had. I remember not so many presents under the tree. But early in January there would always arrive a large package with a large construction toy within. The family was always awaiting its arrival. Also, we always had 2 of Wilfred's pencil etchings of cathedrals on the walls of our living room so I think he must have been wonderful at drawing, among other things. …
>
> Brian had a great personality. He was always in good humour and had good humour. He loved a prank. He loved cloths, cars, reading, gardening and the horseraces. Believe it or not we had a golf green that was the front lawn to our home. On one ocassion in winter of 1974 [Gary's wife] Ann had her rent stolen - we went to the race track and Brian won it back for her. 20 years later we would go to the races and he would buy a $1 winning ticket on every horse in the field. He would always give the winner to [Gary's daughter] Jordan who was thrilled, of course.
>
> Brian was a plumber by trade. He took a position with the City of Toronto as a plumbing inspector and eventually became Chief Plumbing Inspector. … I am a Chartered Accountant by profession and Brian worked for

> us for 25 years from about 1986/87 to 2011. In his own words, he was our "office boy". I was very lucky to see my father every working day for most of my life. Everyday Jordan would come to the office from primary school. There would be a game of hangman and a $1 coin was hidden somewhere in the office. Something of Jordan's would be hidden from here. After about a year something of Brian's would be hidden from him.
>
> Brian remarried to Anne (also British) in 1984. … Sometime around 2011 Brian lost the family home was separated from Anne. However as my father became unwell she certainly stood up. Sometime during 2008 [sic] Brian was diagnosed with prostrate cancer that eventually mutated to bone cancer and was the cause of his death. I only remember good things."

Email to the author from Gary Risdon, 13/01/2013

In a different email, Gary tells me in response to my question: "I have no recall of Falkowski ever being mentioned" although, to be fair, Falkowski did have a somewhat peripatetic lifestyle! Brian Risdon died on the 13th of January, 2003.

2 I am indebted to David Coleman for the translation, which is a big improvement on the online translation!

http://pl.wikipedia.org/wiki/Jan_Falkowski_(pilot)

3 http://en.wikipedia.org/wiki/PWS-26

4 http://en.wikipedia.org/wiki/No._32_Squadron_RAF

5 http://en.wikipedia.org/wiki/No._315_Polish_Fighter_Squadron

6 http://en.wikipedia.org/wiki/No._316_Polish_Fighter_Squadron

On a Polish web page about this Squadron [part of a comprehensive website about the Polish Air Force] is to be found the information that on the 11th of June 1943, he appears to have had a minor 'prang', when his Spitfire crash-landed, but the website on which the photograph appears does not give any information regarding the airfield or the circumstances which led to the crash; the caption under the small photograph is minimal:

"Spitfire IX SZ-G (BS433) after the accident, Captain Jan Falkowski June 11, 1943"

http://www.polishairforce.pl/dyw316zdj.html

7 http://en.wikipedia.org/wiki/No._303_Polish_Fighter_Squadron

8 The 'wing' nomenclature is somewhat confusing, especially where the Polish squadrons are concerned, because the constituents changed fairly regularly, making the status of each one rather nebulous.

http://en.wikipedia.org/wiki/3rd_Polish_Fighter_Wing

9 ***The Stouffville Sun-Tribune, 24/03/49, p. 7*** fills in some gaps from his Wikipedia page:

> "Farmer from Gormley teaching others to fly – Wing Commander Jan Falkowski began flying with a University Flying Club at Wilno, Poland in the year 1931 and flew with this club until he completed his studies of agricultural subjects. In 1933 he joined the Polish Air Force and went to Officers' School from

1934 until the middle of 1936. He was promoted in 1936 to Pilot Officer and sent to the Fighters' Regiment. He flew all types of fighter aircraft in Poland. Towards the end of 1938 he was transferred to the Officers' School as an instructor of aerobatics and fighter tactics. The Wing Commander is now teaching others to fly at the Gillies Flying School, Buttonville."

10 ***The Stouffville Sun-Tribune, 16/03/50, p. 7:***

"We understand Mr. Metro Sudeyko is interested in selling these sets in this district."

11 ***The Stouffville Sun-Tribune, 30/11/50, p. 1:***

"The sale was negotiated this week by Ken Campbell, representative of W. J. Warren real estate, of the Bruce Johnson farm just north of Ringwood in Whitchurch Township. The new owner is Jan Falkowski of Gormley who recently disposed of a farm at the rear of the A. S. Farmer property.

The farm of approximately 90 acres was the original Johnson place, and the solid brick dwelling was erected by Mr. Johnson's grandfather. The house has modern conveniences. there is a stream on the property and two flowing wells. Mr. Johnson is giving up farming for health reasons and will locate in the United States.

Mr. Falkowski was a member of the Polish airforce during the last war."

12 ***The Stouffville Sun-Tribune, 26/06/52, p. 1:***

"Jan Falkowski, instructor at the Buttonville Gillies Flying Club is this month marking his 20th anniversary as an aeroplane pilot. He has given one thousand hours instruction at this township flying club in the last four years. He resided for a time at Gormley and is now just north of Ringwood.

Jan began flying in 1932. When the war started, he took part in the battle of Poland, afterwards he fought in France and then as a member of the R.A.F. he was in the Battle of Britain. He has to his credit, 12 enemy planes shot down. Jan was wounded twice during the war and his last exciting experience was when as a Wing Commander based in England, he was shot down over enemy occupied territory and was captured by the Germans. However, within five days he escaped from prison and returned to England. He is one of the few living Polish fighter aces and among his many decorations he won the British Distinguished Flying Cross.

He has recently completed his biography and hopes to publish it this next winter. the title of the book will be "With the Wind in My Face".

Sunday, July 6th, is being observed at the Buttonville flying field as "Jan Day". There will be a special exhibition of flying and aerial acrobatics beginning at 2 o'clock."

13 ***The Stouffville Sun-Tribune, 04/06/59, p. 1:***

"The once-peaceful countryside on conc. 3, Uxbridge Township, three miles north of Goodwood, is currently the scene of a large-scale earth moving project. Two farms, previously owned by Morgan Degeer and Jack McGillivray, will be the site of a modern private airfield. The promoter is Mr. Joseph P. Koblensky of Markham. Although the first plane is expected to touch down on the new air strip next month, the entire project will not be totally completed for five years.

Where cattle once grazed quietly over 250 acres of hills and valleys, giant tractors and bulldozers now bounce and bob over the slopes like over-sized, yellow kangaroos. The equipment, six earthmovers and three bulldozers, is the property of Mohawk Construction co., Toronto. All gravel needed for the construction of the two runways is available on the site. None has to be trucked in from private pits. The builder has received tentative approval from the Department of Transport.

Only light aircraft will be accommodated on the field. A large workshop hangar will be constructed and a similar clubhouse will be erected at a later date. Night flying will be permissible. No complaints have been received from neighbouring farm residents.

Mr. Jan Falkowski, a Polish World War II ace, will be chief Instructor. He was a former Instructor at Gillies Flying Club in Buttonville, Markham Twp. …

Mr. Koblensky informed the Tribune that he has been planning such a project in the immediate area for the past five years. He said that he particularly was interested in hilly terrain in order to obtain a "built-in" gravel pit for runway construction. The scheme has been approved by the Uxbridge Twp. Council."

14 The "promoter" obviously had grand plans for the airport:

"At the present time, the Goodwood port has four planes and another will be added shortly. Two new hangars will be constructed in the near future and a 5,000-foot paved runway will be laid. The existing strips will be lengthened and gas lighting will be installed. The Management is hopeful that some day, the Goodwood port may be an auxiliary landing field to Toronto and will accommodate larger aircraft, including D.C.3's and Viscounts.

In spite of the activity, the noise of the planes has presented no problem for adjacent residents. The airfield is set well back off the concession road. "It's been terrific", commented Mr. Falkowski."

The Stouffville Sun-Tribune, 21/04/60, p. 1

15 ***The Stouffville Sun-Tribune, 05/01/61, p. 1:***

"Mr. Jan Falkowski, former World War ace and now the Chief Flying Instructor at Goodwood Airways Ltd., has been named the new Commanding Officer of the new Stouffville District Air Cadet Squadron, No. 94. His assistants will be — Messrs. Fred White, Wm. Kingston, Dr. Donald Smith and Harry Heatherington. Dr. Smith will be the squadron's honorary medical officer and will hold the rank of Flying Officer.

The cadet squadron will include membership from the Markham, Gormley, Claremont, Uxbridge and Stouffville areas. The civilian committee will include the Chairman, Mr. Joseph Koblensky of Markham; Vice Chairman, Reg. Button of Stouffville; Treasurer, Lachlan Cattanach, Markham; members — Fred Kelland, Uxbridge and Dr. Donald H. Smith, Stouffville.

The initial membership will include boys ranging in age from 14 to 16 years. The Legion Hall has been acquired and meetings will be held weekly, commencing on Tuesday, Jan. 10th at 7 p.m. The project has received the verbal approval of both Stouffville Public School and High School Boards. The boys will be completely outfitted with uniforms, including shoes, socks, shirts, and ties. The unit will line up for their first inspection in May, 1961. In the summer, twelve members will be selected to attend a two-week camp at the R.C.A.F. base at Trenton. The four year course is designed to promote good citizenship and will include first aid, meteorological training, physical fitness, etc. The first year's program will centre mainly around drill and discipline. Transportation will be provided, where required.

Enrollment will be conducted on Tuesday evening. Parents are invited to attend. A film, entitled "The Air Cadet Story" will be shown. The squadron will retain its original number (94). Mr. H. R. Button was an officer in the unit at that time, some ten years ago. The Legion members have worked in co-operation with the squadron promoters and have offered their Hall as a weekly meeting place at a nominal fee."

16 ***The Stouffville Sun-Tribune, 17/08/61, p. 1:***

"Mr. Jan Falkowski, Chief Flying Instructor at Goodwood Airways Ltd., has taken over the complete flying program at the local Port. This division will be known as the Goodwood Aviation Company. There is no change in the direct ownership of the firm. the policy change was effective as of Aug. 1st.

Mr. Falkowski plans to promote flights to the United States. Four persons can travel from Goodwood to Florida in nine hours. Eight fly-in breakfast flights have been planned for the months of August and September. They will include flights to Barrie, Hamilton, St. Catharines, Muskoka, Oshawa, Brampton, Wiarton and Picton. The first of these was held on Sunday. The above mentioned Ports will return the favour to Goodwood. A paving program is planned for the runways in an effort to alleviate the dust nuisance.

The Goodwood Port will mark its second anniversary of operation in September. During this time, more than 75 pilots have received their licences. Thirty-one of this number have gone to residents of Stouffville and Uxbridge district.

A display of aerobatics and parachute jumps has also been planned for this summer. Mr. Falkowski was a member of an aerobatic team with the Polish Airforce prior to World War II. He displayed his skill at the recent opening of Goodwood Kartways on Sunday, July 30th."

17 ***The Stouffville Sun-Tribune, 16/08/62, p. 1:***

"Mr. Jan Falkowski, Chief Flying Instructor at Goodwood Airways Ltd. and a distinguished World War II air ace is missing on a flight between Calgary and Vancouver. He is accompanied by his wife, Alma, a step-son, Tommy and a friend, Grant McGregor of Oshawa. A search was started on Tuesday in hopes of locating the single-engined aircraft."

18 ***The Stouffville Sun-Tribune, 23/08/62, p. 1:***

"Mr. Jan Falkowski, Chief Flying Instructor at the Goodwood airport has left his $15,000 single-engined, four-seater aircraft in the wilds of a British Columbia muskeg swamp, following a miraculous rescue last week, about 300 miles north of Vancouver.

'If anyone can get a plane over the mountains, Jan can", said a spokesman at the Goodwood Port following the report on Tuesday that Mr. Falkowski, his wife, Alma, his step-son, Tom Tanski and a student flyer, Grant McGregor of Oshawa were long over-due on a flight from Calgary to Vancouver.

An American pilot, flying north in search of Caribou, spotted the downed plane, late Tuesday afternoon. The discovery has been termed as a "one in a million chance." Mrs. Falkowski summed up the whole dramatic story in a few words—"flying skill and an awful lot of luck. Only a great pilot could have landed the plane safely in that muskeg and only a miracle could have made that American pilot spot us there", she said. Mr. Falkowski plans to leave the craft in the bog until freeze-up time when he hopes to get it out. One wing tip suffered slight damage.

Not A Scratch

When the foursome left Calgary, the weather was perfect. On the last lap of the flight, they ran into thick fog. Mr. Falkowski headed north, hoping that the mist might clear. When unsuccessful and with their fuel almost gone, he turned back. "We knew all we could do was find a good spot and try to set the plane down." He picked out a clearing between two 13,000 foot mountain peaks and glided in for a landing. The craft made a "belly landing" in the swamp and settled down only six inches below the surface. "A less experienced pilot would have had us in up to the cabin windows", said his step-son Tom. Not one person received as much as a single scratch.

Drank Swamp Water

With thirty-nine toffee candies, four bottles of pop and two half-packages of cigarettes, the party was prepared to hold out as long as possible. "We all pitched in to make the best of the situation", said Mrs. Falkowski.

The men walked two miles to a swamp pond for water which the four drank, diluted with ginger ale. Mrs. Falkowski made pillows and mattresses out of plastic bags filled with crumpled newspapers and maps. Calls were sent out over the plane's radio every hour of the day. They lit a fire in an effort to attract attention but nothing would burn. They spent much of their time in the cabin of the aircraft as shelter from below-freezing temperatures at night and the mosquitoes during the daytime. Near sun-down on Tuesday, they heard the faint hum of an airplane motor. They waved and shouted frantically and were spotted. The pilot said he was attracted to the scene by a red sweater that Mrs. Falkowski held in her hands. He could not land in the rugged terrain but shouted to the party to hold on until he could find help. The next morning, a rescue helicopter picked up the group and took them to a nearby hunting camp. They were later flown to Vancouver and on Thursday returned by bus to Calgary.

Always Had Hope

"We never gave up hope", said Mrs. Falkowski. She said that the party planned to set out on foot. They later learned that a village, located forty miles away was vacant and a forest ranger station, not too far away was unattended. Mr. and Mrs. Falkowski returned home on Sunday. The couple still plans to fly over the Rockies, possibly in a year or two.

"We'll make it next time", he said."

19 ***The Stouffville Sun-Tribune, 04/10/62, p. 1:***

"Although the flying program at Goodwood Airways Ltd. will cease to function as of Oct. 15th, the port will continue its year-round operation, according to Mr. Ron Owens, a spokesman for the firm.

Mr. Owens discounted a report that the company would close down. He said, in fact, that the air-training program might be resumed at a later date.

Chief Flying Instructor, Mr. Jan Falkowski will take over the training school at Peterboro [sic] but wil [sic] continue to reside in the area."

20 ***The Stouffville Sun-Tribune, 15/11/62, p. 1***

21 ***The Stouffville Sun-Tribune, 21/03/63, p. 1:***

"A $23,000 "jinx" aircraft, owned by air ace, Jan Falkowski, of Uxbridge was badly damaged on take-off from Saskatoon last week only a few days after it was repaired and flown out of a swamp area in the mountainous regions of British Columbia. The plane had soared to about 150 feet before it plummeted into deep snow at the edge of the landing strip. Neither the pilot, Alfred Casson, 29, of Toronto, nor his passenger, Tim Wees, 18 of conc. 2, Uxbridge was injured.

Last fall the owner, Mr. Falkowski, his wife, son-in-law and Grant McGregor, 20, of Oshawa were rescued after he guided his 4-seater, Mooney Mark 20 in for a perfect crash landing in a B.C. bog. This winter it was repaired and flown to Calgary and then to Saskatoon.

Mr. Falkowski credited the pilot with preventing a tragedy through his adept handling of the plane when it stalled on take-off. The deep snow cushioned the shock.

"I'm fed up with commercial flying", said the owner, in conversation with the Tribune. He plans to purchase a small Super Cub craft and fly "door-to-door" as a salesman for a stainless steel cookware firm."

22 ***The Stouffville Sun-Tribune, 04/04/63, p. 1:***

"Seventy-five boys and girls at the Summitview Public School in Stouffville were the recipients of individual safety awards on Monday morning. The membership cards and lapel pins were earned by the students last summer as part of a campaign among pupils at both schools. A similar presentation program will be conducted at Orchard Park next week.

Mr. Harry Heatherington, former officer with the Stouffville Police Department and chief organizer of the safety program, made the presentations assisted by Mr. Jan Falkowski of Uxbridge. A special student assembly was held at Summitview and the winners' names were announced."

23 ***The Stouffville Sun-Tribune, 30/05/63, p. 1:***

"The Markham - Toronto Airport at Locust Hill, closed down during the past few months, will re-open shortly under new management. Mr. Adam Letki of Agincourt, an electrical engineer has acquired the business. Mr. Letki, a veteran pilot with many hours flying time, served overseas during World War II.

Mr. Jan Falkowski has been appointed Chief Flying Instructor for the airport. He had formerly held similar posts at Goodwood and Peterboro.

A flying school and a charter flying service will be opened up in the field. The aircraft to be used for these operations will include two Aeronca Champions, a PA-12, a Cessna 120 and a Cessna 182.

Markham-Toronto Airport is presently a grass airstrip but the new management plans to pave the main runway and extend it to 4,000 feet.

It is expected that operations should resume in about two weeks."

24 ***The Stouffville Sun-Tribune, 11/07/63, p. 2:***

"When it comes to wizardry in the air, it is unlikely that any pilot in this area or in all Canada for that matter can match the skill of one, Jan Falkowski. It was this same Mr. Falkowski that stole the show on Sunday afternoon at Locust Hill when thousands of spectators arrived from all directions to see him perform.

This terminal that, during the past few months, has been deader than a fried fish, was transformed into a seething mass of humanity. The entire program was free, although the reason behind this move is still not entirely clear. We feel sure that no one would have resented a minimum admission fee and the entertainment provided was well worth some charge.

The name Jan Falkowski has become synonymous with aeroplanes. He is more at home in the cockpit than in a living room chesterfield. He appears to be able to do anything and everything with an aircraft and makes the business look as simple as riding an elevator in a department store.

The entire show was well-organized and even the withdrawal of the parachute jumps due to wind conditions failed to lower the spirits of those in attendance.

We feel that the combination of new owner Adam Letki and instructor Jan Falkowski may be just the pill the Locust Hill port has needed to put it on its feet. If Sunday's program is any indication, it's certain to be a sure-fire success."

25 ***The Stouffville Sun-Tribune, 29/04/65, p. 8:***

"JANALMA Airfield, west of the town of Uxbridge, will be the scene of a big airshow on Sunday, May 23rd, beginning at 2 o'clock and running through to 4:30 p.m.

The entire afternoon's program is being promoted by Mr. Jan Falkowski, well-known World War II air ace and now a flying instructor.

One may reach the new airfield site by driving north from Hwy. 47 up the 5th concession of Uxbridge or proceed into the Town of Uxbridge and go west about one mile.

One of the features of the air show on May 23rd will be a display of aerobatics by Mr. Falkowski. There will also be exhibitions of parachute jumping.

On May 1st, Mr. Falkowski opens courses in advanced training and precision flying for private pilots. The course includes 11 hours of aerobatics and 4 hours of formation flying. For this program, a new Champion Citabria is used."

26 ***The Stouffville Sun-Tribune, 10/06/65, p. 2:***

"A book, entitled "With the Wind in My Face" is soon to be published. The author is Mr. Jan Falkowski of Uxbridge, a renowned fighter pilot with the Polish Airforce during World War II. His many exciting experiences are contained within the book's 250 pages and we would recommend it as a prize possession for any home or public library. Mr. Falkowski is, in fact, such an amazing man, that no descriptive portion of his life-story could surpass reality. He began his memoirs twelve years ago and, when nearly completed, he laid it aside. At that time, the book market was flooded with war stories and he felt that his would only run with the rising tide. Following a crash-landing in a B.C. muskeg when both he and his wife were all but given up for dead, he decided to return to his task. It is now ready to go to press, possibly next week. The front cover presents a scene so exiting [sic] in itself that one is forced to delve into the facts contained within. It shows the writer plunging earthward as his disabled Hurricane goes down in flames. Following the invasion of his country by Germany in 1939, Mr. Falkowski escaped by plane, truck and train to France. When France was over-run by the Germans, he joined the R.A.F. in England and later was made Commanding Officer of Polish Squadron 303. Six times he was decorated for bravery including the Vir Tuti Mili Tari, a medal equal to the Victoria Cross. He received the Distinguished Flying Cross from the King and the Polish Distinguished Service

Order on four occasions. He was twice shot down in action, twice wounded and twice captured by the enemy. He escaped both times. In 1941 while in combat action over England, he destroyed a German bomber. Before it went down, however, his Hurricane was badly riddled by bullets and he had to bale out. In attempting to jump clear of the craft, his one leg [sic] was broken when hit by the tail. His squadron claimed a total of 204 enemy aircraft. Jan personally shot down 10 and teamed up with another pilot to gain half credits on another. Out of the 3,000 pilots who took part in the historic Battle of Britain, less than 1,000 are still alive. A gala reunion will be held in England on Sept. 15th to mark the occasion of that defensive miracle. Mr. and Mrs. Falkowski plan to attend. In reference to the book, solicitor Paul Mingay of Markham paid the writer this tribute in a personal letter — "I read every word in two sessions because I couldn't put it down." We could describe it in no better way. We hope to be one of the first to own a finished copy."

27 ***The Stouffville Sun-Tribune, 28/10/65, p. 1:***

"UXBRIDGE — World War II pilot, Jan Falkowski, was accorded a hero's welcome recently, when he returned 'home' to Poland, his native country. It was his first trip back since the early days of the German invasion in 1939.

Mr. and Mrs. Falkowski visited Warsaw after attending the 25th anniversary of the Battle of Britain, a reunion with airmen from all over the world. Only 1,000 of the original 3,000 pilots remain.

Part of the program included a banquet in the Guild Hall, London, as guest of the Lord Mayor. On September 19th, a Memorial Celebration was held in Westminster Abbey with the Queen in attendance. It was at that time, that a plaque was unveiled in honour of the late Prime Minister, Sir Winston Churchill. Mr. Falkowski received an autograph from Prime Minister Harold Wilson, the Lord Mayor of London and Sir Sidney Camm, the designer of the famous Hurricane fighter plane. Sixteen members of his Polish squadron that performed over the skies of Britain, were also reunited.

In Warsaw 9 Days

Mr. and Mrs. Falkowski spent nine days in Warsaw. He was given an audience with the Bishop of Poland and laid a wreath at the tomb of the Unknown Soldier. On his recommendation, a monument to Poland's pilot heros [sic] of World War I will be re-built. He has been invited to return and unveil it in a few years' time. Few battle scars of the war days are visible in the capital city, according to Mr. Falkowski. "They have done a tremendous job", he said.

After 21 days in England and the Continent, the couple returned home, arriving back in Uxbridge on Oct. 5th."

28 ***The Stouffville Sun-Tribune, 03/02/66, p. 9***

29 ***The Stouffville Sun-Tribune, 07/04/66, p. 4:***

"Mr. Jan Falkowski of Uxbridge, author of the book 'With the Wind in My Face', appeared on the Elwood Glover television program, channel 6, on Wednesday."

30 ***The Stouffville Sun-Tribune, 14/04/66, p. 4:***

"A complimentary copy of the book 'With The Wind In My Face' was presented to the Stouffville District High School by the author, Mr. Jan Falkowski of Uxbridge. Mr. Falkowski (right) is shown here with high school principal Wm. E. Duxbury and vice principal Ronald E. Mercer."

31 ***The Stouffville Sun-Tribune, 24/06/71, p. 12:***

"This year's annual showing of paintings by well-known local artist, Arnold Hodgkins, opens at Deerfoot Gallery, Leaskdale, with receptions, Saturday and Sunday. A highlight is the work entitled 'Falkowski-Portrait of Poland', based on Jan Falkowski's book, 'With the Wind in my Face'. It touches on events related to the famed Polish flying ace, from 1919 to 1945. Mr. and Mrs. Falkowski now reside in Uxbridge. The Deerfoot Gallery is open from 2 to 5 and 7 to 9 p.m. The location is 6 miles north of Uxbridge Town."

32 ***The Stouffville Sun-Tribune, 24/06/71, p. 12:***

"[photo caption]: The Toronto-Markham Airport, Hwy. 48, near Dickson's Hill, is a busy site. The owner and operator is Jan Lewandowski. Airborn [sic] here is chief flying instructor, Jan Falkowski of Uxbridge.

...

DICKSON'S HILL - It's a long way from Pomerania to Ontario - even by air.

For Jan Lewandowski, manager of the Toronto Markham Airpark on Highway 48, the trip was not a direct one. After the fall of Poland in 1939 Mr. Lewandowski, already a qualified pilot, made his way to England and joined the Royal Air Force. He flew Spitfires with the RAF during the war.

This may help to explain why the Toronto-Markham Airpark is the only flying school in Canada approved to teach aerobatics, and why Mr. Lewandowski owns the only Cessna 150 Aerobat in this country. But if flick rolls and Immelmanns aren't quite your thing, the school also teaches flying for normal private and commercial licences.

Besides the Aerobat, you can learn on a normal Cessna 150 or 172, a Cherokee Arrow, or a Twin Apache.

The airpark itself has a wide variety of planes, ranging from sleek Commanches to a Harvard trainer. The park normally holds about 75 aircraft. At peak periods, the runway handles landings and takeoffs at the rate of one every 25 seconds. The hangar holds about 6 aircraft and basic repairs can be done by the staff of two engineers.

An Air Show is scheduled at the field, Sept. 11. Twenty-six entrants are expected to take part in stunting, formation flying, and aerobatic competition. There may also be a team of skydivers. One entry, by Professor Bob Lyjak, will be interesting to antique buffs: Lyjak will fly a restored Waco Taperwing biplane. A similar event last year attracted an overflow audience.

The airpark also rents aircraft for sightseeing trips, pilot supplied if you aren't qualified yourself. But be warned: flying with Jan Lewandowski in his Aerobat is not for the faint-hearted."

APPENDIX F

This is a close approximation of the dialogue during the course of a broadcast on the BBC Home Service, which went out live, on June 30th, 1961, at 19:30, as part of an ongoing series called ***What's the Idea?***; Wilfred Risdon was questioned on the subject of anti-vivisection by Dr. W. Lane-Petter, Honorary Secretary of the Research Defence Society [see Chapter 13, notes 31 & 32 for more details; he is also mentioned in note 33 of Chapter 14], and Dr. H. O. J. Collier, "a Director of Pharmacological Research", which appears to be [2012] "a rapid exchange medium for specialists within the discipline of pharmacology. The journal publishes papers on basic and applied pharmacological research and is proud of its rapid publication of accepted papers." Volume 65 was current in 2012, so assuming that they have been published sequentially prior to this, the journal must have been in existence since 1947 [**1**]. Both of Wilfred's interlocutors could be legitimately said to have had a vested interest in the continuation of research using live animals.

"

VOICE: This is the B.B.C. Home Service. In tonight's ***What's the Idea?*** Wilfred Risdon of The National Anti-Vivisection Society is questioned by Dr. W. Lane-Petter (Honorary Secretary of the Research Defence Society) and Dr. H. O. J. Collier (a Director of Pharmacological Research). Dr. Lane-Petter speaks first.

LANE-PETTER: Mr. Risdon: an anti-vivisectionist Minister of religion once wrote that animal experiments were and I quote: "bankrupt of any decent result." He then went on to say, rather surprisingly, and I quote again "You and I are filching our health from the hideous fate of these creatures." Would you like to clarify your position?

RISDON: Yes, I wouldn't go all the way with that statement; it doesn't define my position. My position is this: that I consider it to be morally reprehensible to take a healthy sound animal, to maim it or to deliberately inflict disease on it so that one can study something which may not be apposite in the treatment of human patients in any case, although it may act in the knowledge of the individual who does the experiments.

COLLIER: But Mr. Risdon, do you not think this addition to knowledge ultimately is to the benefit of human patients? Let me take an example: the drugs called 'sulphonas' have ... were tested in guinea pigs, infected with tuberculosis and found to be active, and they were therefore tried in man. They were found not very effective in tuberculosis. You'd agree with me there?

RISDON: Yes. I would agree, Dr. Collier.

COLLIER: But they were then tried in man in the related disease of leprosy and they were found extraordinarily valuable and they have completely revolutionised the outlook of the leper throughout the world.

RISDON: But isn't that rather making my point? An accidental discovery as a result of a failure of animal experimentation in one case, an accidental discovery of its efficacy in another case, without being first tried on animals, [interjection: NO] would surely make my point.

COLLIER: It doesn't make your point, because the ... the disease of leprosy ha ... bears a relationship to that of tuberculosis; it is impossible to test sulphones of leprosy in animals, or it was at that time, but it was possible to test it on tuberculosis and the essential implication was that it might be useful in leading towards a useful result.

RISDON: You want to come in Dr. Lane-Petter.

LANE-PETTER: And of course, by the animal experiments that have been done in the early days of sulphone experimentation it was found that sel ... sulphones were a drug, not too toxic, that had some use in the treatment of disease.

CHORUS: I …

LANE-PETTER: I know that without animal experiments.

RISDON: I ... I have it also in mind that a lot of these animal experiments in the sulphonamides, for instance, were tested on many animals and given a clean bill of health; they were non-toxic; they had no side-effects; they were safe to use on the human patient. But the human patients were killed by them in a number of cases through a deposit of crystals in the kidney.

LANE-PETTER: No, your facts are not quite ...

RISDON: Isn't that true?

LANE-PETTER: Your facts are not quite right there ... The sulphonamides were indeed shown to be relatively non-toxic but there were certain dangers in them. And if they are used unwisely in man, or I might say in animals, they do produce in a comparatively small number of cases a bad side effect. We know a great deal about that partly from animal experiments and partly from practice in human medicine.

COLLIER: These animal experiments do not show that the drugs are without toxicity but they do show probably the safest way to use them in man. So that by animal experiments do you not think that we would be protecting man and saving human life by this toxicological study?

RISDON: I wonder if you would allow me to quote here certain authority: "There was held a symposium in London in 1958 on Quantitative Methods in Human Pharmacology and Therapeutics."

COLLIER: I attended that symposium.

RISDON: Do you remember Dr. A. C. Dawnhurst of St. Thomas?

COLLIER; I do.

RISDON: And did he or did he not say, I quote: "The majority of the drug responses can be quantitatively studied in man, the main advantages of course, relevance. Species differences are essentially unpredictable and sometimes, as mentioned earlier by Professor Gadum, may be seriously misleading."?

COLLIER: Species differences are misleading but they're not nearly so misleading as not doing experiments in animals. Take penicillin; if that had been taken straight from the test tube we … against … where it was tested against bacteria in glass cultures to man; had such a dangerous thing been done undoubtedly very many people would have suffered. It was put through animals and in animals it was learnt the particular way the drug was absorbed and distributed, the particular dangers to beware of, and the particular way in which it would be best given to man. The result was that it could be given successfully to man as it was from the very first.

RISDON: I wonder what you would call successfully, Dr. Collier. There's a point here that I would like to make. I've just been reading a book on toxic side effects and in it is the definite statement that up to the end of 1957, 1,000 deaths had occurred as the result of the administration of penicillin in the United States alone.

LANE-PETTER: 1,000 deaths out of how many millions of people who have received penicillin and owe their lives to it?

RISDON: But that doesn't affect the point, does it, Dr. Lane-Petter? That those 1,000 deaths were attributed to penicillin.

LANE-PETTER I'd like to know on what basis they were attributed to penicillin. But still there have been millions, tens of millions of people, who have been treated with penicillin and very many of them owe the ... owe their lives to the treatment. But there's a point I want to follow on from what Dr. Collier said a moment ago. Of course animals do not behave exactly in the same way men behave, or as other species of animals behave, but we know a great deal about the differences between the species and the resemblances. Through experiments on animals we can get a very good and an intelligent lead on what is likely to happen when we do the first experiment with a new drug on man. We go very carefully indeed. We look very carefully for side-effects. But we save ourselves perhaps from trying dangerous drugs on man by previous animal experiments. No investigator would dare to try out a new and powerful drug if he hadn't tested its toxicity on animals first.

COLLIER: I agree with that but there were drugs introduced before the modern days to which chloroform is an example; I believe that was not tested on animals first. Would you agree with that, Mr. Risdon?

RISDON: Yes, I would.

COLLIER: Well now, chloroform is a very dangerous drug, an anaesthetic, and has been largely abandoned. Had it been tested on animals first it might never have been introduced and safer anaesthetics might have been used.

RISDON: What would you call safer anaesthetics?

COLLIER: Well…

(Two voices here) Nitrous oxide.

RISDON: But nitrous oxide was already in use with chloroform wasn't it, before chloroform?

COLLIER: Many anaesthetics, modern anaesthetics, derived through animal experiments, (interruption from Risdon) barbiturates given intravenously and new gaseous anaesthetics which are undoubtedly safer than chloroform. And the whole technique of anaesthesia now is based also on drugs like Curare and Saxaninecoline, and these of course, again, were studied in animal experiments. In fact the … they were subject of many early experiments and of course these drugs have been the subject of much discussion and propaganda.

RISDON: I wonder if I might be allowed to make another quotation? I ... I'm ... I don't want to weary you with quotations but there's a very good one from the same symposium that we referred to before by Mr. A. L. Bacchera who said; I'm quoting, I think you'll be able to correct me if my quotation is wrong: "How are we to know, if ever, that when a drug has been tried on fifteen different species of animals, including primates, and shown to be harmless it will be found harmless to man, and harmless to all men. And how are we to be sure that a drug shown to be toxic to fifteen different species of animals will in fact also be toxic to man?"

COLLIER: We cannot be sure, Mr. Risdon, but we can say the probability is far higher if in fifteen species the drug is non-toxic. But the word non-toxic is not a reality; what we mean is: if we have measured the toxicity in fifteen species we know what the risks are.

LANE-PETTER: Mr. Risdon, I would like to take you up on a remark you made earlier implying that the experiments in which we cause diseases or abnormal conditions in mice are necessarily cruel or give a lot of suffering to the animals. In fact, I would make the point very strongly that the great majority of experiments, so called, which … in which animals are involved in this country, produce virtually no pain. When I say virtually: no more pain than a domestic animal suffers from the course of his ordinary day: he can't get out. Nor can the mouse get out of its cage. A great majority of experiments cause little or no pain. I want to correct the impression that all animal experiments are hideously painful. They are not.

RISDON: Well, I'll agree with you there, Dr. Lane-Petter. I'll agree that not all of them are painful and not all of them are hideously painful. But the very fact that a proportion are, even if … even if they're a very small proportion, when you're dealing with numbers like 3½ millions animals in one year, a very small proportion of those inflicting pain and suffering means quite a big toll, doesn't it?

LANE-PETTER: Oh I quite agree with you and I wouldn't like to give the impression I that am indifferent to the sufferings of even the small proportion that are painful. But we have in this country a system of controlling animal experimentations; there is a law that governs it, and a very strictly applied law. It was a law that was introduced with the goodwill and, to a large extent, on the initiative of British scientists, and it has been made to work very well; far better than in any other in the world. Now you mentioned the figure of 3½ million experiments. I've no doubt you would like to say something also about the way that the law is enforced to see that even that small proportion of painful experiments are not unjustifiably prolonged, or painful.

COLLIER: I would like to take you up there Mr. Risdon.

RISDON: Yes.

COLLIER: We (clearing his throat here) workers in (clearing throat again) experimental biology and medicine do in fact attempt to reduce the number of experiments on animals. We, for example we devise where possible techniques in glass-ware: the virologists use tissue-cultures: the pharmacologists use isolated tissues in glass-ware in order to avoid the necessity for animal experiments and to do more precise more economical and completely and ... experiments to which people like yourselves would have your ... yourself, would have no objection. So we do not wish this number to increase; we work in the opposite direction if we can.

RISDON: But it is true isn't it, Dr. Collier, that the number does increase in spite of that?

COLLIER: That is true.

RISDON: And we ... we consider that to be a deplorable thing which is almost - I have crossed swords on previous occasions with people who defend vivisection on this and liken this to almost drug addiction; a bad habit which exists: because the method is there, it's part of the training; it's been trained into the student during his student days; all the the present generation of teachers have been brought up with the method of animal experimentation; it's in all the text-books. I know the difficulty of doing away with it because it's just the accepted thing of the day. But it's still wrong.

COLLIER: Now Mr. Risdon, that's a fairy story that won't wash, you know. Animal experimentation is a ... is an expensive occupation, and no research laboratory has any money to throw away. It goes on growing because it produces such useful and beneficial results. If it was an unsatisfactory method it would have died out long ago. It goes on growing steadily each year because of the tremendous results it produces. In the last hundred years - which is the time when animal experimentation has grown from very little to a considerable volume of work today - those last hundred years have seen fantastic advances in medicine. You suggested that the law in this country was a white-wash. This means to say that the Home Office which administers the law is colluding in white-washing vivisectors. And yet, you know, that law has been going since 1876. A Royal Commission took evidence for 2½ years between 1906 and 1909. They examined the working of the law. It has been examined on a number of occasions since, even since the second world war. And the evidence of these impartial bodies completely refutes your suggestion that the law is a white-wash.

RISDON: But the facts do not refute my suggestion that the law is a white-wash.

COLLIER: What are these ... facts?

RISDON: In fact the facts are that a number of atrociously cruel experiments to the eye of the lie ... layman who reads about them and sees them in the Medical Journals, in the Scientific Journals. They're so atrociously cruel that they would revolt most people. And they still go on under the law; the law permits them. (I) If the law permits that sort of thing and then you're allowed to come to the public and say "you can be quite sure that this is not cruelty because the law is a very strict law and is strictly enforced." How can it be strictly enforced with a miserable five inspectors to study 3½ million experiments? They don't inspect the experiments; they merely see that the law is complied with; the law that permits those experiments to be carried out. And what use is that: it doesn't save the animals in the least.

COLLIER: The law has very much more to say, in my opinion, than you suggest; it does ... it is in fact customary to ... to prevent experiments which are considered cruel, and the experimenter is under an obligation to destroy an animal that he considers, and anyone else who visits the lab - and the inspector is entitled to visit any time, and he often does - considers to be suffering.

VOICE: Yes.

(TWO VOICES TOGETHER HERE)

RISDON: May I take that point ...

VOICE: Yes.

RISDON: Dr. Collier's point. What do we have there. The vivisector himself must destroy the animal if the animal is suffering severe pain which it's likely to endure. Now who's to define those terms? And I challenge you as a scientist: if you're engrossed in an experiment which you are making, aren't you liable to make the facts fit your own feelings, because you want to carry it to a successful conclusion?

COLLIER: Certainly not.

RISDON: Ah well, maybe you're an exception, but I think that the average scientific mind is so keen on getting the answer that your own conscience would be satisfied a little more easily than mine would be if I were looking on and you were doing this.

(TWO VOICES HERE)

COLLIER: I don't think we would get an answer in those circumstances.

LANE-PETTER: Mr. Risdon scientists work in groups and if that ever did happen to one scientist, I think his colleagues would very soon stand on him because we, no more than you, like cruelty to animals. We differ in what we mean by cruelty to animals perhaps, but we do not ... we do not like it. In 1948 I think it was, your society that sent a deputation to see the Home Secretary, and in the evidence presented to the Home Secretary there were a number of allegations of cruel experiments such as you've just referred to. They were presumably the worst that you could produce; the worst allegations of cruelty that could produce ... that you could produce of experiments done in this country under our law.

RISDON: No, I'll correct that. They were a selection of different classes of experiments showing that cruelty occurred in all those classes. They weren't the cruelest that could be produced; they were one each from several classes of experiments to show that it isn't just in one isolated department of experimentation, but that suffering and cruelty permeates this whole practice right through all its departments.

LANE-PETTER: Yes, you produced this evidence and it was examined by the Home Secretary at that time, and he found that there was no substance in your allegations. Is that right?

RISDON: No, it isn't. On the contrary, what he did find was that his advisers told him that there was no grounds in those ... in the data presented which would justify the appointment of a new Royal Commission, or of any other commission of enquiry that ...

LANE-PETTER: Aren't you rather quibbling?

RISDON: Oh no!

LANE-PETTER: He had to rely on his advisers ....

RISDON: But he didn't tell us there was no substance in the claims that had been made. They were substantiated. What he did say was that those claims did not, in the opinion of his advisers, justify the appointment of another commission.

LANE-PETTER: I happen to remember one or two of those cases that you cited on that occasion. And one of them which sounded if there were very severe experiments on cats. When one came to look them up one discovered that they were done on cats as described, but all the time under anaesthesia from which the animal never recovered. Now this strikes me as rather sharp practice; to quote as a horror story experiments which were done in conditions to which the animal could not possibly have suffered at all.

RISDON: I'm very dubious whether that was the case but ... (interruption here) or if so it certainly was not conveyed to us in that way; we were never given that information.

LANE-PETTER: If you'd read the original paper Mr. Risdon, you would have seen that was so.

RISDON: I have read all the papers for everything that my society quotes. Incidentally that deputation represented several different societies. The Duchess of Hamilton was one member of it; of one society.

VOICE: She quoted this experiment …

RISDON: And our doctor ... our Dr. Beddow Bailey was another. But I do know this: we have a very extensive literature of detailed experiments. I helped to compile them. And sometimes the business that I had to read to compile them gives me sleepless nights. And I can assure you that the things that I have seen and read do mean atrocious suffering to animals. The eye experiments for instance where two eyes of a given animal are taken and damaged, and one of them treated and the other left untreated as a control. And not only for hours but for days, for weeks, that wretched animal has to suffer that until one of the eyes just becomes a suppurating mass of sore. Is that cruel or is it not?

LANE-PETTER: I think that I have seen very many more animal experiments in this country - and I do stress in this country because I'm ... I'm only prepared to defend this situation under the law which you have attacked.

I have seen very many animal experiments, in a large number of laboratories in this country, and the sort of picture that you've painted of animals suffering intolerable pain for days and weeks and months on end just doesn't exist, because we have an inspection system and it is rigidly enforced. There (interruption here) are five inspectors who la ... in 1959 ...

RISDON: Most of whose time is taken up with paperwork.

LANE-PETTER: No sir. No, Mr. Risdon. In 1959 five inspectors made 1550 to 535 registered places [sic]; about three visits to each place in the course of the year. Now cer ... many of those places will have been hospital laboratories with a few guinea pigs in which undergo experiments which are virtually painless because they're killed before the disease develops. So that the places where severe experiments may have been carried out were visited more frequently than three times in the year. Now the inspector's job is not to inspect every experiment any more than it is the customs man job ....customs man's job to open every piece of baggage that comes into the country. What he is doing in fact is to inspect the places to see if they're suitable for animal experiments and to get to know the people ... the scientific competence, and, I would say, their reliability to be trusted with a licence. And I would have thought that three or four times a year was an adequate number of inspections to make, bearing in mind they are nearly always without notice.

RISDON: I'll agree with you that it's an adequate number of inspections to make to see that the law is complied with; the law as it exists. But the law, as it exists, allows the infliction of suffering; it ... it actually states that it deals with experiments calculated to cause pain.

COLLIER: But it does restrict that ...

RISDON: Yes.

COLLIER: ... that infliction that is also in the law and also

RISDON: And it also gives exemption ...

COLLIER: and enforces ...

RISDON: ... in cases where exemptions are asked for. Doesn't it Dr. Collier? You can get your different certificates to waive almost every condition that ever was made ... (interruption from Collier)

LANE-PETTER: But that is not so. The conditions under which you can do experiments on conscious animals are very strictly controlled. You've already quoted part of the condition controlling them; "That the animal must be killed if it is suffering from severe pain likely to endure." How do you define that? Well if you're dealing with animals as much as I, for example have to deal with animals (and my interest as you know is in the care of ... and proper management of laboratory animals), you get to know your animals very very quickly indeed. And moreover an animal in pain is a bad piece of scientific material.

RISDON: Yes, but your ...

LANE-PETTER: Of no use to us.

RISDON: Your ... your standards of pain may be different to mine.

I'm a mere layman. But you're accustomed to experiments that inflict pain. And I venture to challenge that people who do that as a business do become callous; they become hardened. They must do by very virtue of the things they do. I don't say that you're a cruel man intentionally, but I do say that that's something that just happens in the course of events.

LANE-PETTER: Mr. Risdon. Animal experiments are, in the opinion of the great majority of doctors and medical scientists, productive of great advances in medicine. They have resulted in the saving of much suffering, human suffering, and the prolonging of human lives. Diabetics, severe diabetics, who, before the days of insulin, could expect to live not more than about five years can now live an almost normal life and marry and have children. Poliomyelitis, which is a killer - and remember it is more of a killer the better the conditions of general sanitation - can now be not entirely eliminated, but very many people can be protected quite efficiently against poliomyelitis. Are you really going to try and eliminate animal experiments as they are decently conducted in this country, and so sacrifice your own fellow human beings and the benefit they get from modern medicine?

RISDON: No, I wouldn't ask for them to be done away with overnight in that way. But I would ask for a change of attitude towards them. I would ask that the public should be allowed to see that there's a possibility of developing some other methods that would not be open to the stigma of causing suffering to animals. And to get towards that I would like to ask that the government would definitely ear-mark a small proportion of its annual research grant to be devoted to the purpose of finding methods, or alternatives, to animal experimentation in the study of disease and pathology.

COLLIER: Many methods without animal experimentation are already in use and they are extending all the time. You quote the enlargement of experiments on animals - most of which of course are very mild experiments - but the ... the enlargement of work in glass-ware and so on without animals is really great, or greater. This is going on all the time. But do you not think, Mr. Risdon, if suffering is, on occasion, involved that it's more humane to protect men rather than animals. In other words that if an an ... an experiment must be done, which will essentially protect men that that should not be done? For example: with polio vaccine, unless that is tested in animals there may be many dangers with it, it may carry a dangerous virus of another type that could kill people. That surely should be prevented by administering it to animals. Probably very very few would develop this disease because the polio virus would be clear of it ... the polio vaccine would be clear of this virus. But one might ... but surely it would be better that, say, one monkey developed this virus that [sic] the child developed it. This is the sort of situation in which I would like to know whether you think an experiment on an animal is justified? There is no other way of testing this.

RISDON: That is where I would like to come in on this. And I would like to say that my attitude is not - once again I repeat - to say that this should be stopped overnight. It's going on. I deplore the fact that it's going on. But in addition to asking the government to do something positive about it - you see you've mentioned that already certain things have been done in this direction but they've happened fortuitously. Eh ...

VOICE: No opportunity.

RISDON: ... in an everyday job. The government tells us when we question them about this that vivisection is a regrettable necessity. Alright, if it's regrettable as a necessity, let them show their regret by doing what I've just asked them: asking for a very small, even if it's only a half of 1% of the annual allocation for research to be devoted especially, positively, to finding alternatives to animal experimentation. If they'll do that we, for our part, as anti-vivisection societies, are willing to encourage that by putting up a substantial prize to any team that comes forward with positive results along those lines.

COLLIER: I'm sure more than that amount of money is being spent already on these ... this very aim.

RISDON: No ... no ... no ... not ...

COLLIER: The aim of the ...

RISDON: Not ... not ... on this aim.

COLLIER: The aim of many bioassayists [sic] that is to do away with their jobs.

LANE-PETTER: Mr. Risdon may I ask you one last question? You ... I understand that you take the view that vivisection is morally wrong even if it produces useful results. Now others like myself take the view that it would be more morally wrong to refuse to do animal experiments which we know from experience produce useful and valuable results for human kind. Now if you claim a ... a ... that it's right to hold your point of view are you going to stand up for me when I claim it's right to hold my point of view from (no) your standpoint?

RISDON: No I'm not. You have to satisfy your conscience. I have to satisfy my conscience. The thing that satisfies my conscience is not necessarily the same thing that will satisfy your conscience. I'm prepared to accept that position. But I'll still go on fighting to the bitter end to get the point of view that I represent because ....

VOICE: And there we must leave it. Wilfred Risdon of the National Anti-Vivisection Society was questioned by Dr. W. Lane-Petter and Dr. H. O. J. Collier. ”

NOTE

1 Unfortunately, this has to be surmise, because there appears to be no way on the website of confirming this; neither is there any mention of animal experiments on this page:

http://www.journals.elsevier.com/pharmacological-research/

APPENDIX G

Strike Action Political Action or Power Action— *WHICH ?*

From the earliest beginnings of Fascism and National Socialism in this country our opponents have sought to discredit us in the eyes of organised workers by persistently repeating the lie that we–the British Union–are out to smash the Trade Union movement. This pamphlet is the reply to all such lying statements. We seek to strengthen, not to smash, the Trade Union movement, and a study of this pamphlet will, I am sure, prove to the real trade unionist that we make no idle boast when we say that industrial organisation has more to gain from National Socialism than from any other conception of civilisation.

Far from desiring to smash trade unions, we take pride in the past history of the unions; we appreciate the difficulties under which they operate; we intend to strengthen the unions (by legislation not by pious wishes and resolutions); we intend the unions, strengthened to 100 per cent. membership and built up to full industrial status, to play an important part in the government of the State.

Thus, you will see that we take a vital interest in the past, present and future of the trade unions in this country.

The rôle which the unions will fulfil under National Socialism in Britain is one for which they will be endowed with full statutory powers, hence we describe the exercise of these powers as "Power Action" in contradistinction to the "Strike Action" and "Political Action" which has previously marked the limits of trade union activity.

In the following pages we give our criticism of both strike action and political action. We then set forth the details of our new "Power Action," which we are convinced will meet with the approval of every sound trade unionist. Will you consider these proposals before you allow anybody to bluff you into the belief that the British Union is anti-trade union?

THE MISSION OF TRADE UNIONS.

The early Trade Unions were formed in the teeth of an opposition as bitter and as vindictive as that which is brought to bear against National Socialism to-day. Its active spirits were victimised, imprisoned and persecuted. After a stern and bitter struggle, the Unions were given legal recognition. It was their mission to represent the collective interest of wage-earners in the newly industrialised state, a state in which inhuman conditions were the rule rather than the exception.

STRIKE ACTION.

The only weapon possessed by the workers in the early stages of their fight was the strike weapon – the ability to effect a bargain with their employers by withholding their labour. This was, at best, a poor weapon because it injured the workers themselves and meant starvation for them and their families. Moreover, whenever organised workers withheld their labour, blackleg labour was brought in to take the place of the workers on strike, leading to rioting and the use of troops to defeat the Unions in their fight. Many a page of English history was written in the blood of those early pioneers of the trade union movement with singularly little to show on the credit side of the workers against the price which they were called upon to pay for their right to organise and combine.

Although the methods of fighting have somewhat changed, the strike weapon, after a century of effort to improve its efficacy is still a poor weapon which can be justified only by the assumption that there is nothing better to take its place.

It is my contention to-day, as it always has been my contention, that strikes are futile. The only time when a strike could be successful would be during a "boom" period when markets are rising. At such a time concessions are granted at the *threat* of a strike without the threat being carried into effect.

In modern times, however, the great majority of trade disputes are fights in defence of existing standards when, during periods of depression, those standards are threatened with reduction. In such conditions the strike is able to achieve little or nothing which will be of benefit to the workers concerned.

NO REAL BENEFITS.

At the worst a strike or lock-out in such circumstances benefits the employers by allowing them a period of time in which accumulated stocks may be cleared, during which period they are relieved from the necessity of paying wages and the workers are starved into submission. The miners' lock-out of 1926 is a classic instance of this process.

At the best the workers concerned win a partial victory amounting to a fraction of a penny per hour after forfeiting many weeks' wages whilst on strike and their losses are seldom completely recovered.

POLITICAL ACTION–ITS TEST AND FAILURE.

In consequence of a realisation of the inherent weakness of strike action, Keir Hardie and others associated with him set out at the latter end of the nineteenth century to forge the alternative weapon of political action for inclusion in the armoury of the Trade Unions. In 1900 the T.U.C. combined with the I.L.P., the Fabian Society and some smaller associations to form the Labour Party. In 1906 twenty-nine Labour M.P.s were returned and the second weapon became available.

SWING OF THE PENDULUM

From that time onward there has been a constant swinging of the Trade Union pendulum from Strike Action to Political Action, and from Political Action back to Strike Action.

In the thirty years which have intervened there have been two Labour Governments, but the problems of adjustment between employers and employed have not been solved.

That whole period has been marked by alternating disillusionment. Strikes have been tried and they have failed. After every such failure has come a phase of political action which in turn has failed. Then has followed another phase of industrial action, and so the game has gone on. Small gains have been registered in each sphere, but the sum total of all the gains has not been commensurate with the progress of industrialism as a whole.

TOO MANY IRONS IN THE FIRE

Political Labour (the Labour Party) has had too many irons in the fire to be able to look after the particular iron which it was their duty to forge.

As politicians they have ceased to represent the interests of Labour in the factories and workshops. Dabbling in Internationalism (the affairs of other nations) has occupied far more of their time than attention to Nationalism (the affairs of our own nation).

When these political leaders are sent to Parliament they are set in a new atmosphere entirely divorced from the atmosphere of the worker in the pit, the factory, the farm or the workshop. They join "the best Club in London" and behave as "club-men" rather than as workers. The problems which are of life-and-death seriousness to you become merely interesting subjects of debate for them. They feel no economic pressure. Their salaries are secure and adequate. By comparison with your wages, even their old salary of £400 per year was adequate, but they have been able to secure a £200-per-year increase in their own rate of remuneration by political action without a strike. How happy you would be if they would so well represent your interests as to obtain £200-per-year increase on your income of much less than £400 per year for *you* through political action which *you* have built up.

Your political leaders have graduated from the workshop to the talkshop. *You* are still living far below the conditions which should be available from the resources of modern technique in industry, although *you* have generously placed them in a position where they receive a standard of living which is the workers' just due. What are you going to do about it?

SACK THEM, AND THEN WHAT?

Of course, if you do what you should in your own interests, you will sack them for abusing your trust, but even then your problem remains. How are *you* to improve *your* conditions until they approximate to what they should be?

Sacking one set of leaders and replacing them by another set will not solve your problem if you leave undisturbed the conditions which have led to your betrayal. Your problem is not solved until you can devise machinery which you can operate for the solution of your problem.

Let me state your problem briefly. *You* know full well that of the wealth which you produce you do not receive your full share. *You* know, moreover, that you *could* produce far more wealth (that is to say "goods") than you do produce. You know that if you *were allowed* to produce all the wealth which you *could* produce and to receive your fair share of that wealth the menacing features would be forever removed from your life. Poverty, unemployment and insecurity would no longer have the power to haunt your waking hours and make nightmares of the hours which should be spent in sleep. The problem is twofold in nature. It is to (a) produce more, and (b) receive more of what you *do* produce.

WORKERS' CONTROL IN INDUSTRY.

We National Socialists contend that a measure of workers' control in industry is essential to the solution of that twofold problem. Workers' control can be exercised only through workers' organisation, therefore, it is frankly ridiculous to suggest that we desire to smash the unions. On the contrary we want to improve the unions to make them fitting instruments of control and then to invest them with the statutory authority which will enable them to exercise that control.

Let us consider in order of importance the improvements we have in mind. First of these is 100 per cent. Trade Unionism. At the present time, out of 18,873,000 insured workers, a little over 4,000,000 are members of Trade Unions, less than one-quarter of the total. Thus, in spite of all the best efforts of the Unions, for every worker who is a trade unionist there are three non-unionists.

HOW TO GET 100 PER CENT. TRADE UNIONISM.

There is only one satisfactory method of securing 100 per cent. Trade Unionism – that is, by State legislation. Every worker will be compelled by the law of the land to become a member of the trade or industrial union appropriate to his trade, profession or calling just as at present he is compelled by the law of the land to insure against sickness and unemployment. The compulsion in one case is no more an encroachment on the liberty of the individual than is the compulsion in the other case quoted. It follows quite naturally that if workers are to be compelled to join their appropriate unions, these unions must be National not sectional, industrial not political, in character.

The concern of the unions under National Socialism would be with industrial rather than Party political affairs. It would be obviously unfair with unions on their present basis to compel workers who are fundamentally opposed to the politics of the Labour Party to join a trade union which is controlled and used to the Party advantage of the Labour Party.

INDUSTRIAL CONCERNS OF THE TRADE UNIONS.

The industrial questions with which trade unions will be concerned will be those connected with and arising from their own industry, not the affairs and conditions of other industries. The scope of their considerations will be much wider than is at present the case and will cover not only wages and hours of employment, but every phase which may re-act on the wellbeing of the industry in which they, as workers, have invested their most valued possession—life itself.

These workers' organisations will be concerned with planning for the equitable distribution of the present product of industry with full authority to assert just claims, but, in addition, they will also have the authority to take their own decisions for increasing the total output of their industry and the equitable distribution of the increased output.

LEADERSHIP OF THE UNIONS.

The leadership of the unions would, of course, be based on the same industrial considerations, and party politics would play no part in their selection, They would be selected as leaders because of their knowledge of affairs and service in their own industry, The members of the union who elect them will elect them to attend to the affairs of their own, not some other industry, and the members will hold such leaders *personally* responsible for satisfactory progress and good conditions in their own industry.

CONTROL OF THE CORPORATIONS.

Under National Socialism every great industry will be controlled by a corporation, conferring upon that industry powers of economic self-government. In that corporation will be represented employees, employers, and consumers. Each group possesses equal power, and in the event of a deadlock between employees and employers, the Government will secure a fair deal for the workers by direct intervention.

The employees' representatives will be elected by all the workers engaged in the industry (exclusive of managers and high executives). These employees' representatives would be the "leaders" of the Unions and would be dependent on the vote of the employees concerned for their continued leadership.

POWER ACTION.

It is now made clear that the "Power Action" of National Socialism is something to be applied by the workers themselves through the Corporate Machinery of the organised state. They will not have to plead a case to the employers of their own industry, asking for charitable consideration which they know in advance will not be forthcoming. Neither will they have to "lobby" corrupt politicians who know little and care less about the problems of workers in this, that, or the other industry. They, as the workers in their own industry, will be given statutory powers of control, equal to those of the employers, which they can use to determine the conditions which shall obtain in their own industry.

They will be an integral part of the corporate machinery governing their own industry, and as such have "power" in their own hands which they can bring into action to secure for themselves progressively increasing standards of living and the general improvement in conditions which they require and which they know to be practicable.

THE SUPREMACY OF POWER ACTION.

This Power Action is constructive. It gives to those concerned in industry the power to increase the yield of wealth from their own industry; Power to direct the flow of this increased yield into the homes where it is needed; Power to overcome the technical difficulties at present standing in the way; Power to defeat the machinations of the vested interests of International Finance which, at present, bar the way to prosperity; Power, through the direct vote upon which the Government will depend, to change that Government if at any time it fails to carry out its duties effectively.

Compare the above with the futility of strikes or lock-outs and all the unnecessary suffering which they involve (strikes and lock-outs which are mutually destructive for employees, employers, and the whole community). Compare it, too, with the farce of present-day political action with glib-tongued politicians, Labour leaders in the political field roaring like lions when in opposition and braying like asses or bleating like sheep when power is placed in their hands.

YOU GET THE POWER.

They promise you the millenium when seeking office and give you the "bird" when they get there.

We offer you the "power" to do for yourselves the things you want done.

You, as the people vitally concerned in your industry, will have the power, through your industrial corporation to *legislate* conditions for that industry. *You* will no longer be compelled to await legislation from a Parliament which does not understand the requirements of your industry. You are the people who understand the needs of your industry – miners for mining, engineers for engineering, farmers and farm-workers for agriculture, spinners and weavers for the textile industries, etc. Why should you wait on the will of lawyers, financiers, and racketeers in Parliament for the essential requirements of *your* industry ?

National Socialism will give to *you* and *your* industrial corporation the power to legislate your own industrial conditions.

The principles of organisation of the Trade Unions functioning within the corporate state of National Socialism may be briefly summarised as under:—

1. The respective unions must be on a basis of "one big union" for each industry.

2. Each union must comprise within its ranks 100 per cent. of the workers engaged in the particular industry.

3. Octopus unions which have sought to merge under one control members of different clearly defined industries must hand back to the union from which they have been "pirated" those sections of workers engaged in such industries.

4. Where members of a craft union are employed in a separate industry they must function as members of the industrial union concerned, but without prejudice to their right to membership of their craft union.

5. Reorganisation, where necessary, to meet these requirements, must be carried out from within the unions.

6. Where one industrial union comprises clearly defined groupings of workers engaged in widely different categories it should be organised on a basis of category unions within the industrial union.

7. The funds of each union will be reserved for the benefit of contributors.

8. The rights and responsibilities of the unions will be incorporated in a "Charter of Labour" drawn up by the unions and approved by the Government.

Now let us consider the National Socialist attitude to existing trade unions.

We view it as an obligation on all our members working in occupations covered by trade union organisation to join and to serve their appropriate unions.

They will work loyally within those unions for the attainment of our ideals. They will not "scab" or "blackleg" in the event of a dispute. We have a "fighting" reputation. That reputation will be fully justified by our members in any dispute. They are not "quitters" and you will find them standing loyally with you shoulder to shoulder in closed ranks in any dispute affecting their own industry and willing to give financial support to workers of any other British industry who may need such support to help them through a dispute.

They will not, however, advocate or accept any responsibility for a strike which has a political significance (i.e., any general strike which seeks the overthrow of an elected Government). There is, and can be, no justification for an effort on the part of any section of the people (however well organised such section may be) to seek to reverse a majority decision, recorded by ballot, of the whole of the people.

Further Copies of this Pamphlet obtainable at 9d. doz., 6/- 100, £3 1,000.

MOSLEY WILL WIN!

If you love our Country you are National
If you love our People you are Socialist.

The members of British Union are National Socialists because they love their country and are determined to build in it a civilisation worthy of that love, and because they love their people and are determined to release them from the cruel dictatorship of international finance.

The Conservatives and Liberals say Britain for the financiers, the Labour Party and Socialists say Britain for Moscow.

MOSLEY SAYS
BRITAIN FOR THE BRITISH PEOPLE

The National Socialist State can be won by hard work and organisation. You have the power to contribute to the new civilisation. If you have the WILL then

Join British Union and march with your fellow countrymen to the National Socialist State

....

COMPLETE THIS FORM AND FORWARD TO

BRITISH UNION

NATIONAL HEADQUARTERS:
Sanctuary Buildings, Great Smith Street, Westminster.

I wish to become An Active / A Non-Active Member of British Union.

Please forward the necessary forms, etc.

Name ....

Address ....

....

Printed by Illustrated Periodicals, Ltd. (T.U., all depts.), for Greater Britain Publications (Abbey Supplies, Ltd.), Great Smith Street, Westminster.

BIBLIOGRAPHY

Books [including pamphlets and unpublished MSS editions]

Addison, Paul and Crang, Jeremy A. (Eds); ***LISTENING TO BRITAIN: Home Intelligence Reports on Britain's Finest Hour—May to September 1940***

Barnsby, George J.; ***Socialism in Birmingham and the Black Country 1850-1939***

Beckett, Clare & Francis; ***Bevan***

Beckett, Francis; ***The Rebel who lost his Cause: the Tragedy of John Beckett, MP***

Bellamy, Richard Reynell; ***We Marched With Mosley: The Authorised History of the British Union of Fascists***

Brereton, Bt.Lt.-Col. F.S.; ***The Great War and the Royal Army Medical Corps***

Brewer, John D.; ***Mosley's Men: The British Union of Fascists in the West Midlands***

Briggs, Asa; ***History of Birmingham vol. II: Borough & City 1865-1938***

Brome, Vincent; ***Aneurin Bevan***

Booker, J.A.; ***Blackshirts on Sea***

Carpenter, Humphrey; ***Spike Milligan; The Biography***

Carsten, F.L.; ***The Rise of Fascism***

Clayton, G.F.; ***The Wall is Strong: The Life of a Prison Governor***

Charnley, John; ***Blackshirts and Roses***

Cole, G.D.H.; ***Socialism & Fascism, 1931-1939***

Craig, F.W.S.; ***British Parliamentary Election Results 1918-1949***

Craik, W.W.; ***The Central Labour College 1909-1929***

Crick, Bernard; ***George Orwell: A Life***

Cross, Colin; ***The Fascists in Britain***

Davies, Paul; ***A.J. Cook***

Dietzgen, Joseph; ***The Nature of Human Brainwork***

Dorril, Stephen, Blackshirt; ***Sir Oswald Mosley and British Fascism***

Edwards, Ness; ***History of the South Wales Miners' Federation, vol. 1***

Edwards, Robert, ***Sir Oswald Mosley & The British Union of Fascists: a pictorial history***

Farndale, Nigel; ***Haw-Haw: The Tragedy of William and Margaret Joyce***

Fieldhouse, Roger & Associates; ***A History of Modern British Adult Education***

Foot, Michael; ***Aneurin Bevan, I, 1897-1945***

Francis, Hywel; ***Miners Against Fascism: Wales and the Civil War***

Goldberg, Jonah; ***Liberal Fascism: The Secret History of the Left from Mussolini to the Politics of Meaning***

Gray, Todd; ***Blackshirts in Devon***

Gregory, Roy; ***The Miners & British Politics 1906-1914***

Hamm, Jeffrey; ***Action Replay***

Hampshire, Edward; Macklin, Graham and Twigge, Stephen; ***British Intelligence: Secrets, Spies & Sources***

Hastings, R.P.; ***The Birmingham Labour Movement, 1918-1945***

Hauser, Kitty; ***Bloody Old Britain: O.G.S. Crawford and the Archaeology of Modern Life***

Hindley, Geoffrey; ***A Brief History of the Magna Carta: The Story of the Origins of Liberty***
Holmes, Colin; ***Anti-Semitism in British Society, 1876-1939***
Hopley, Emma; ***Campaigning Against Cruelty: The Hundred Year History of the British Union for the Abolition of Vivisection***
Ingrams, Richard; ***the Life and Adventures of WILLIAM COBBETT***
Kenny, Mary; ***Germany Calling: A personal Biography of William Joyce - 'Lord Haw-Haw'***
Kean, Hilda; ***Animal Rights: Political and Social Change in Britain since 1800***
Laski, Harold J.; ***Democracy in Crisis***
Lawrence, T. E.; ***Seven Pillars of Wisdon***
Llewellyn, David; ***Nye, The Beloved Patrician***
Lodge, Tom; ***Mandela: A Critical Life***
Macklin, Graham; ***British Intelligence: secrets, spies & sources***
Macklin, Graham; ***Very Deeply Dyed in Black: Sir Oswald Mosley and the Resurrection of British Fascism after 1945***
McPherson, Susan & Angela; ***Mosley's Old Suffragette: A Biography of Norah Dacre Fox***
Miles, Alexander; ***The Streets are Still: Mosley in Motley***
Miller, Russell; ***Codename Tricycle***
Mosley, Nicholas; ***Rules of the Game: Sir Oswald & Lady Cynthia Mosley 1896-1933***
Mosley, Nicholas; ***Beyond the Pale: Sir Oswald Mosley & Family, 1933-1980***
Mosley, Oswald; ***My Life***
Mowat, Charles Loch; ***Britain Between the Wars, 1918-1940***
Nelson, Craig; ***Thomas Paine: His Life, His Time and The Birth of Modern Nations***
Nicolson, Harold; ***Why Britain is at War***
Pelling, Henry; ***The Origins of the Labour Party***
Risdon, Wilfred; ***A Guide to Constituency Organisation***
Risdon, Wilfred; ***Lawson Tait: A Biographical Study***
Risdon, Wilfred; ***Strike Action or Power Action***
Robbins, Keith; ***The Abolition of War: The Peace Movement in Britain, 1914-1919***
Rose, Norman; ***Harold Nicolson***
Shaw, George Bernard; ***The Intelligent Woman's Guide to Socialism & Capitalism***
Simmons, Jim; ***Soap-box Evangelist***
Simpson, A.W.B.; ***In the Highest Degree Odious: Detention without Trial in Wartime Britain***
Smith, John T.; ***Tracing a Soldier in the RAMC - Notes for the talk; Milton Keynes Branch, Western Front Association, 11/12/09***
Thurlow, Richard C.; ***Fascism in Britain: From Oswald Mosley's Blackshirts to the National Front***
Skidelsky, Robert; ***Oswald Mosley***
Wearmouth, Robert F.; ***Methodism & the Struggle of the Working Classes 1850-1900***
West, Nigel; ***MI5: British Intelligence***
Wood, H.G. & Ball, Arthur E.; ***Tom Bryan, First Warden of Fircroft***

Worley, Matthew [ed.]; ***Labour's Grass Roots: Essays on the Activities of Local Labour Parties and Members, 1918-45***
Worley, Matthew; ***Labour Inside the Gate: a History of the British Labour Party Between the Wars***
Worley, Matthew; ***Oswald Mosley and the New Party***
Young, Allan; ***The Political Problem of Transition***

Academic theses/dissertations

Morgan, Craig; ***The British Union of Fascists in the Midlands, 1932-1940; University of Wolverhampton, PhD, 2008***
Keeley, Thomas Norman; ***Blackshirts Torn: Inside the British Union of Fascists, 1932-1940; Simon Fraser University, Canada; Department of History, MA, 1998***
Smith, Cairns King; ***A Comparison of the Philosophy & Tactics of the Independent Labour Party with Those of the Labour Party of England, 1924-1931; Chicago, PhD, 1936***
Twigg, Julia; ***The Vegetarian Movement in England, 1847-1981: A Study in the Structure of its Ideology; LSE, London, PhD, Autumn 1981***

Online articles/sources

By their very nature, websites & online articles are subject to frequent change and updating, so specific sources for references in the notes have been given where appropriate, but it seemed supernumerary to repeat them.

Magazines/newspapers/periodicals

Action; February 1936-June 1940
Blackshirt; February 1933-May 1939
British Medical Journal
Comrade, various; Newsletter of The Friends of Oswald Mosley [FOM]
Dorset Daily Echo and Weymouth Dispatch [thanks to Maureen Attwool]
Fascist Week; November 1933-May 1934
Guardian
Glasgow Herald
Independent on Sunday
New Scientist
Southern Times and Dorset County Herald [thanks to Maureen Attwool]
Various LPAVS & NAVS periodicals [as per individual notes]
Woodford Times [thanks to Lynn Haseldine-Jones]

Magazine/periodical articles

Coupland, Philip M.; ***'Left-Wing Fascism' in Theory and Practice: The Case of The British Union of Fascists;*** Twentieth Century British History; ***vol. 13, no. 1, 2002, pp. 38-61; Oxford University Press***

Dowse, Robert E.; ***The Independent Labour Party and Foreign Politics 1918-1923;*** Bulletin of the Institute of Historical Research; ***1962, pp. 33-36; British Library***

Johnson, J.; ***Birmingham Labour and the New Party;*** The Labour Magazine; ***vol/part no. 9, 1931, pp. 534-6; Brotherton Library, University of Leeds***

Mandle, W.F.; ***The Leadership of The British Union of Fascists;*** The Australian Journal of Politics and History; ***December, 1996, pp. 360-383; University of Queensland Press, Brisbane***

Marwick, Arthur; ***The Independent Labour Party in the Nineteen-Twenties;*** Bulletin of the Institute of Historical Research; ***vol xxxv, 1962, pp. 62-74; British Library***

Thomas, Brinley; ***The Migration of Labour into the Glamorganshire Coalfield 1861-1911;*** Economica, ***vol. 10, October 1930, pp. 275-294; London School of Economics***

Archive sources

Archives of the Independent Labour Party, Series 2: Minutes & Related Records, Part 2: branch Minutes & Related Records, 1892-1950; microfiche; Document Supply Shelfmark MFE 894; Harvester; The British Library DSC Microform Research Collections

BBC Written Archives Centre, Caversham Park, Reading, RG4 8TZ

Bodleian Library, Department of Special Collections & Western Manuscripts; Conservative Party Archive; Oxford; thanks to Jeremy McIlwaine

General Register Office; regional offices

HM Land Registry; online Customer Contact Centre and regional offices; Durham

National Archives; DocumentsOnline and personal visits, sincere thanks to Phil Tomaselli and Jeffrey Wallder

National Anti-Vivisection Society, Millbank Tower, London SW1P 4QP

Science Museum, London, thanks to John Liffen

Special Collections & Archives, The University Library, The University of Sheffield; thanks to Lawrence Aspden, past Curator of Special Collections & Library Archives

INDEX

LATE PRE-PRESS INFORMATION

On the 12th of October 2013, a story appeared on the BBC ***News Magazine*** website, which threw new light on the 'September Holocaust' referred to in Chapter 12 [see notes 58-68 inclusive]; my initial information was that "Within the first four days of declaration of war in 1939, 400,000 pet cats and dogs were destroyed by their owners fearful of imminent invasion and gas attacks …", whereas it now appears, from "a new book" by Clare Campbell [with Christy Campbell], called ***Bonzo's War: Animals Under Fire 1939 -1945***, that the actual figure for this "little-discussed moment of panic" was much larger: "[a]s many as 750,000 British pets were killed in just one week." During my original research, I had not been able to find an obvious 'trigger' for this action, but this new book has revealed that the Government was primarily responsible:

> **"At the beginning of World War II, a government pamphlet led to a massive cull of British pets. ...**
>
> The cull came as the result of a public information campaign that caused an extraordinary reaction among anxious Britons. In the summer of 1939 just before the outbreak of war, the National Air Raid Precautions Animals Committee (NARPAC) was formed. They drafted a notice - **Advice to Animal Owners**. The pamphlet said:
>
> > "If at all possible, send or take your household animals into the country in advance of an emergency."
> >
> > It concluded:
> >
> > "If you cannot place them in the care of neighbours, it really is kindest to have them destroyed."
>
> The advice was printed in almost every newspaper and announced on the BBC. It was "a national tragedy in the making", says Clare Campbell, author of new book **Bonzo's War: Animals Under Fire 1939 -1945**. Campbell recalls a story about her uncle.:
>
> > "Shortly after the invasion of Poland it was announced on the radio that there might be a shortage of food. My uncle announced that the family pet Paddy would have to be destroyed the next day."
>
> After war was declared on 3 September 1939, pet owners thronged to vets surgeries and animal homes. "Animal charities, the PDSA, the RSPCA and vets were all opposed to the killing of pets and very concerned about people just dumping animals on their doorsteps at the start of the war," says historian Hilda Kean. Battersea Dogs and Cats Home opened its doors in 1860 and survived both wars. "Many people contacted us after the outbreak of war to ask us to euthanise their pets - either because they were going off to war, they were bombed, or they could no longer afford to keep them during to rationing," a spokesman says. "Battersea actually advised against taking such drastic measures and our then manager Edward Healey-Tutt wrote to people asking them not to be too hasty." But Campbell cites an Arthur Banks of the RSPCA who, "gloomily pronounced that the primary task for them all would be the destruction of animals".
>
> In the first few days of war, PDSA hospitals and dispensaries were overwhelmed by owners bringing their pets for destruction. PDSA founder Maria Dickin reported: "Our technical officers called upon to perform this unhappy duty will never forget the tragedy of those days." ...The first bombing of London in September 1940 prompted more pet owners to rush to have their pets destroyed. Many people panicked, but others tried to restore calm. "Putting your pets to sleep is a very tragic decision. Do not take it before it is absolutely necessary," urged Susan Day in the **Daily Mirror**. But the government pamphlet had sowed a powerful seed. "People were basically told to kill their pets and they did. They killed 750,000 of them in the space of a week - it was a real tragedy, a complete disaster," says Christie Campbell, who helped write **Bonzo's War**.

Historian Hilda Kean says that it was just another way of signifying that war had begun. "It was one of things people had to do when the news came - evacuate the children, put up the blackout curtains, kill the cat." It was the lack of food, not bombs, that posed the biggest threat to wartime pets. There was no food ration for cats and dogs. But many owners were able to make do. Pauline Cotton was just five years old at the time and lived in Dagenham. She remembers "queuing up with the family at Blacks Market in Barking to buy horsemeat to feed the family cat". And even though there was just four staff at Battersea, the home managed to feed and care for 145,000 dogs during the course of the war.

In the middle of the pet-culling mayhem, some people tried desperately to intervene. The Duchess of Hamilton - both wealthy and a cat lover - rushed from Scotland to London with her own statement to be broadcast on the BBC.:

"Homes in the country urgently required for those dogs and cats which must otherwise be left behind to starve to death or be shot."

"Being a duchess she had a bit of money and established an animal sanctuary," says historian Kean. The "sanctuary" was a heated aerodrome in Ferne. The duchess sent her staff out to rescue pets from the East End of London. Hundreds and hundreds of animals were taken back initially to her home in St John's Wood. She apologised to the neighbours who complained about the barking. But at a time of such uncertainty, many pet owners were swayed by the worst-case scenario. "People were worried about the threat of bombing and food shortages, and felt it inappropriate to have the 'luxury' of a pet during wartime," explains Pip Dodd, senior curator at the National Army Museum. "The Royal Army Veterinary Corps and the RSPCA tried to stop this, particularly as dogs were needed for the war effort."

Ultimately, given the unimaginable human suffering that followed over the six years of the war, it is perhaps understandable that the extraordinary cull of pets is not better known. But the episode brought another sadness to people panicked and fearful at the start of hostilities. The story is not more widely known because it was a difficult story to tell, says Kean. "It isn't well known that so many pets were killed because it isn't a nice story, it doesn't fit with this notion of us as a nation of animal lovers. People don't like to remember that at the first sign of war we went out to kill the pussycat," she says."

http://www.bbc.co.uk/news/magazine-24478532?ocid=socialflow_facebook_bbcnews

The astute observer will have noticed that nowhere in the foregoing are Wilfred Risdon or his admirable design for an air raid shelter for pets to be seen: not entirely surprising perhaps, so although it was not possible to comment directly on the BBC website, in a spirit of didactic altruism, I pointed this out in the ***Facebook*** posting from which this link was taken, and very helpfully drew people's attention to my forthcoming book, so that those people who do have an interest in relatively recent history, and the place of domestic animals in it, can avail themselves of an aspect of the story which deserves to be much better known.